CARL NIELSEN
A Cultural Biography

Michael Fjeldsøe, Katarina Smitt Engberg, Bjarke Moe

CARL NIELSEN
A Cultural Biography

Aarhus University Press

Carl Nielsen. A Cultural Biography
© The Authors and Aarhus University Press 2025
Translated from the Danish edition *Carl Nielsen. En kulturhistorisk biografi*
(Aarhus: Aarhus University Press, 2024) by Peter Hauge
Cover: Camilla Jørgensen, Trefold
Cover illustration: Detail of portrait photo, 1891, © Carl Nielsen Museet
Layout and typesetting: Hans Mathiasen
Publishing editor: Henrik Jensen
This book is typeset in Minion Pro and DINPro
and printed on 100 g Munken Premium Cream 13
Printed by Narayana Press, Denmark

Printed in Denmark 2025
First edition, first impression

ISBN 978 87 7597 332 3 (printed book)
ISBN 978 87 7597 701 7 (e-pdf)
ISBN 978 87 7597 702 4 (epub)

Aarhus University Press
Helsingforsgade 25, DK-8200 Aarhus N
unipress@unipress.au.dk
aarhusuniversitypress.dk

Published with the financial support of:
Carl Nielsen and Anne Marie Carl-Nielsen's Foundation

All rights reserved. Except for the quotation of short passages for the purpose of criticism and review, no part of this publication may be reproduced, stored in a retrieval system, or transmitted, in any form or by any means, without the prior permission of the publisher.

Every effort has been made to trace all copyright holders, but if any have been inadvertently overlooked the publisher will honour valid claims as if clearance had been obtained beforehand. Reuse of any third-party material requires permission directly from the copyright owner.

The carbon emission of this book is calculated to be 2,47 kg according to ClimateCalc.eu. Cert.no. CC-000159/DK

CONTENTS

9	**Foreword**
11	**Introduction**
	People and Culture · The European and the National · Modernism and the Modern · Literature and Sources · The Structure of the Book

I EXPANDING HORIZONS

21	**Chapter 1 – A PLACE IN THE WORLD**
	The Place · The Three Childhood Homes · Family Background and Its Significance · Niels and Maren Kirstine · Klaus Berntsen as a Role Model · Musical Background and Education
48	**Chapter 2 – SYMPHONIES ARE FICTION**
	The Conflict · The Narrative
52	**Chapter 3 – MUSICIAN IN ODENSE**
	A Provincial and Garrison Town · Nielsen's Odense · Regimental Bandsman · Apprenticeship · Access to Music · Participating in the Town's Musical Life
78	**Chapter 4 – DEPARTURE**
	A Detective Story
84	**Chapter 5 – NIELSEN'S COPENHAGEN**
	The City of the Newcomer · The Cultural Centre · Two Artist Residences
106	**Chapter 6 – THE ACADEMY OF MUSIC**
	The Tuition · The Violin · Music Theory and Harmony · Counterpoint · The Path to Musical Life
128	**Chapter 7 – MUSICIAN IN COPENHAGEN**
	Concert Venues in Copenhagen · Life as a Musician · A Foothold
142	**Chapter 8 – FROM MUSICIAN TO COMPOSER**
	A Threshold · Among Friends · Under Rosenhoff's Tutelage · *Suite for String Orchestra* · Mastering the String Quartet Genre · The First Symphony
169	**Chapter 9 – THE RADICAL AND INTELLECTUAL ENVIRONMENT**
	Radical Copenhagen · Georg Brandes and His Associates · Emil Sachs · Victor Bendix · Rudolph Bergh · Freethinking in the 1880s · Holger Drachmann's *Snefrid* · The Great World

II THE TURN-OF-THE-CENTURY CULTURE

197 **Chapter 10 – TURN-OF-THE-CENTURY CULTURE**

200 **Chapter 11 – A MUSICAL TURNING POINT**
The Young and the New · Symphonia · The Music Society of 14 March 1896 ·
Danish Concert Society · Radicalism and Modernity

219 **Chapter 12 – ON THE THRESHOLD OF THE MUSICAL MODERN**
Travel Plans · Dresden · Berlin · Leipzig · Epilogue 1894

240 **Chapter 13 – MEETING *FIN-DE-SIÈCLE* PARIS**
The Scandinavian Colony · Musical Life in Paris · A Crucial Encounter

257 **Chapter 14 – ANNE MARIE**
Family Background and Upbringing · Arts Education · Stormy Years ·
Sharing the Art

277 **Chapter 15 – ROYAL MUSICIAN**
The Experience · The Repertoire · The Resignation

287 **Chapter 16 – MUSIC FOR EVENTS**
The Inauguration of the Student Society Building · The Sound of Youth
and Progress · Ambitious Cantatas · A Wide Range of Assignments

308 **Chapter 17 – THE LIED COMPOSER**
Nielsen's Lied Production · Lied Studies · Content-Saturated Composition ·
Lieder in Public · The Art of Simplicity

329 **Chapter 18 – THE SYMBOLIST**
Mood · Stylisation and Archaisation · Mystery and Inspired Nature ·
Poems and Dreams · The Literary Shift

348 **Chapter 19 – WRITING OPERA AROUND 1900**
Dramatic Music · *Saul and David* · The Way out of the Thorn Bushes ·
Maskarade

373 **Chapter 20 – PROGRAMME MUSIC**
The Four Temperaments · *Helios* · Music and Words

III CLASSICITY AND LIFE

389 **Chapter 21 – CLASSICITY AS A SOURCE OF INNOVATION**
The Mozart Anniversary, 1906 · Mozart as a Paragon · Nielsen, Mozart and
the Future · Choral Music as a Description of the Universally Human ·
Hymnus Amoris · De-Romanticisation · A Kindred Spirit

411 **Chapter 22** – TIME

419 **Chapter 23** – THE VITALIST
Nature and Vitality · Positive and Life-Affirming Vitalism · *Sinfonia espansiva*

432 **Chapter 24** – THE COLLABORATION WITH LAUB
The Ballads · Nielsen and Laub · From Ballads to Popular Songs

447 **Chapter 25** – THE THEATRE COMPOSER
Music's Role in the Theatre · The Literary Stage · *An Evening at Giske* ·
The Fights in Stefan Borg's House · *Tove* · The Large Productions ·
Sir Oluf He Rides – · *Aladdin or The Wonderful Lamp* · The Open-Air
Theatre · *Hagbarth and Signe*

471 **Chapter 26** – COMPOSER OF HYMNS
Grundtvigian Hymn Singing · Disputes over Hymn Singing · New Tunes ·
To Compose Hymns … · … and Spiritual Songs

484 **Chapter 27** – THE AESTHETIC-SENSORY

487 **Chapter 28** – 'MUSIC *IS* LIFE'
The Inextinguishable

IV MODERNITY AND POPULARITY

503 **Chapter 29** – THE POPULAR AND THE MODERN

505 **Chapter 30** – THE GREAT REFORM PROJECT
The Prelude · Borup's Songbook · Tunes of Daily Life ·
The Folk High School Melody Book

524 **Chapter 31** – MODERNISM AND MODERNITY
Symphony No. 5 · Form and Narrative · The Music-Historical Context ·
Away from the Keys? · The Technique of Avoiding · Free Modulations and
Counterpoint · Freedom and Tonality

546 **Chapter 32** – THE KAPELLMEISTER
Royal Kapellmeister · Conductor of Musikforeningen ·
Gothenburg Orchestral Society

565 **Chapter 33** – MUSICAL PROBLEMS
A Unique Work

571 **Chapter 34** – THE CREATIVE PROCESS
Creativity · Resistance

577 Chapter 35 – **THE TEACHER**
Private Pupils · The Academy of Music · Pedagogical Commitment

595 Chapter 36 – **THE LEGACY OF PALESTRINA**
'Power and Simplicity' · The Culture of the Line · *Three Motets*

612 Chapter 37 – **MECHANICAL MUSIC**

618 Chapter 38 – **ORGAN MUSIC**
The Organ Revival Movement · *Commotio*

626 Chapter 39 – **A SERIOUS GAME**
'Music is Sound' · *Sinfonia semplice* · Order or Chaos · Narratives

V LEGACY

651 Chapter 40 – **REPUTATION**

654 Chapter 41 – **NIELSEN BECOMES THE NATIONAL COMPOSER**
The Canonisation of Nielsen · A National Composer? · Spectacular Performances · Popularity and Danish Nature · Legends · The Outcome · Publishing · Presence · A Man of Power · When the Bill is Settled

680 Chapter 42 – **CURATING THE LEGACY**
Nielsen's Birthday in 1925 · *Living Music* · Self-Curating · *My Childhood* · The Nielsen Myth

694 Chapter 43 – **INQUISITIVENESS AND TENACITY**

VI NOTES AND INDEXES

703 Notes

753 Bibliography

776 Index of Names

786 Index of Works

793 Illustrations

FOREWORD

This book is the result of 'Carl Nielsen – A European Composer', a research project initiated in 2018. Its aim was to provide a comprehensive account of Nielsen's music and his significance as a musician, composer and cultural figure. A monograph on Nielsen had long been in demand and, with the completion of the collected editions of his musical works, his letters, his published texts and the comprehensive catalogue of his musical oeuvre that brings it all together, the time was ripe.[1]

The task was to write a book that would cover all of Nielsen's lifelong activities, for he was much more than a composer. The important cultural and musical environments in which he was involved gave him experiences that he carried with him, not only in terms of music, but also in terms of fundamental views and ways of working. He also influenced a wide range of people through his activities. One aim is to show how the professionalism and the profound immersion in a European musical culture that formed Nielsen the composer was rooted in his musical training and in the general education he received in the social-liberal (then known as the Radical) and intellectual environment of Copenhagen in his youth and on his travels in Europe.

The purpose was not to write a traditional biography. Rather, the book uses Nielsen to provide an insight into the cultural and musical environment of his time and to examine what it meant to him. This approach is reflected in the book's subtitle: 'a cultural biography'.

The organisation into five main sections with individual chapters – each telling its own story – reflects the authors' ambition to write a book that can be read by both professionals and the general public. The book is widely readable without compromising the academic standard. All quotations are translated into English, using *Carl Nielsen. Selected Letters and Diaries* (CNL) for letters and diary notes whenever possible. The same applies to quotations from *My Childhood*. In the music examples, the technical terms are often placed in the text accompanying the example, while the main text refers to the example in a more general way.

The project also organised two international conferences on Nielsen: one in Newcastle in collaboration with Newcastle University (2021) and one at the University of Copenhagen (2022). During the project, the research team was expanded to include Peter Hauge in order to fulfil the task of preparing the content for the new Carl Nielsen Museum in Odense, which opened in June 2023. As an integral part of the project, Hauge was also responsible for the English translation of this book, which is published in parallel in Danish as *Carl Nielsen. En kulturhistorisk biografi* by the same publisher.

As part of the project, the online *Catalogue of Carl Nielsen's Works* (CNW) has also been updated with data on the performances of his works up to 1931. Readers wishing to continue their study of Nielsen and his music are encouraged to use the CNW as a starting point. Further information about free access to the electronic editions of his music and letters can be found in the 'Standard Works' section of the bibliography.

Another result is *Carl Nielsen og århundredeskiftekulturen i København* (Carl Nielsen and the Turn-of-the-Century Culture in Copenhagen), a doctoral dissertation by Katarina Smitt Engberg, accepted by the University of Copenhagen in 2022. The dissertation was written with the overall research project in mind, and extensive parts of the dissertation are included in this book in an edited form.

Carl Nielsen. A Cultural Biography is the result of a collaboration between three authors. All chapters have been discussed and revised in joint meetings, and each author has expanded on texts initiated by the other two. This also applies to the parts that are based on the dissertation, and thus Katarina Smitt Engberg has also made a substantial contribution to the book as a whole.

Although the research project is based on the major editions of Nielsen's musical works, letters and writings, it also makes extensive use of alternative sources. The cultural-historical perspective has necessitated a deeper and broader approach to the sources than is often the case in composer biographies. The literature on Nielsen is vast, and the intention has been to consult the primary sources as much as possible without ignoring the existing literature. However, references have only been included where the existing literature has been of immediate use. The bibliography covers only the literature consulted. Endnotes have been used and generally do not contain detailed elaborations.

The authors would like to thank the members of the research project's advisory board, who acted as consultants and sparring partners throughout the project: Niels Krabbe, Bertel Krarup, Peter Hauge and Daniel M. Grimley. The authors have also received invaluable help from the project's three student assistants, Lærke Lundskov Eriksen, Kasper Ravnsgaard Jensen and Nanna Staugaard Villagomez.

Finally, the authors wish to express their gratitude to Carl Nielsen and Anne Marie Carl-Nielsen's Foundation for generously funding the research project, including the publication of the book. Without their unconditional support, a research project of this magnitude would not have been possible.

Michael Fjeldsøe, Katarina Smitt Engberg and Bjarke Moe

INTRODUCTION

The fascinating thing about Carl Nielsen is that he was never satisfied with what he had achieved. Throughout his life he was constantly developing, looking for new directions and trying out new ideas. He never settled into a particular style or followed a particular path. It is unusual for a composer approaching sixty to still be more interested in experimenting than in adhering to the style that made him famous.

It is also fascinating that his output spanned so many different genres and with such different expressions. The fact that he looked at each task individually and found a solution that suited the task at hand is a common thread running through all of his music. What binds it all together is not a personal style, but an approach to composing music that suits the purpose. The greatest beauty, he says, comes when the object is completely suited to its function.[1]

The approach of this book is to try to understand Carl Nielsen as a whole. This involves exploring Nielsen's significance as a musician, composer and cultural figure in the context of the society and time in which he lived. The book offers a picture of what he meant in and for his time and what it meant to him. The point of departure is to examine all the activities in which he was involved. Thus, the book considers all genres and areas of working as valuable and relevant to the experience he brought to his work.

The book is a gateway to learning more about Nielsen and his music, which is still of great importance in the musical culture of today. Many know, hear or sing his music and it matters to them. Yet it is also a book that, by studying Nielsen, allows us to look at the cultural and social life of the time and makes us all more aware of the roots of the musical culture we know today.

People and Culture

This book is a cultural biography in that it describes a specific person, Carl Nielsen, but it is equally an introduction to the European musical culture of which Nielsen was a part and in which he was an active participant. A subject cannot be understood without its context.

Since the subject is Nielsen and his music, we define 'life and work' as an entity that needs to be understood in its cultural context. Context, though, is not just what surrounds us; it is not a passive term for the environment in which a person has been raised. A person is not only *part of* an environment, but also an individual *who actively participates* in it: he or she acts and so does everyone else in the environment. Thus a cultural environment is a group of social actors who act and react to each other in the creation, maintenance and development of the culture of which they are a part.

Employing this concept of culture as a basis, the relationship between individuals and the culture in which they operate becomes dynamic. We do not believe that individuals simply reflect or are the result of the culture around them. Nor do we believe that history, or the history of music, comes from the creative power of a single individual – even a particularly gifted one. Nielsen does not change music and music culture, but he contributes to their transformation and changes with them.

The central question, then, is how Nielsen is embedded in the surrounding musical culture and how he leaves his mark in terms of the means by which he approaches the tasks he is given or chooses to solve. In other words, it is the musical culture that offers the composer and the musician assignments to fulfil, not necessarily in the form of a specific commission for a musical work intended for a given purpose. It can also take the form of an existing need, such as the renewal of the lieder repertoire. The musical world has needs that a composer can help to meet. On the other hand, by solving the task in a certain way, composers are able to leave their mark on the development. The new solutions contribute to musical culture and, if successful, can steer it in a certain direction.

So our strategy is often to pose the question: how did he approach the task? Composing an opera, a hymn or a piano piece was not just a matter of conceiving an idea, a text or a theme. It was a piece of musical craftsmanship that had to be executed, and functioned in dialogue with the expectations of those who would hear, sing or play the music.

Viewed in that light, the sharp distinction between functional music or commissioned works on the one hand, and free creative expression on the other, vanishes. There is a need in the world of music for the occasional new symphony that can encourage a renewal of concert life and perhaps change the perception of what a symphony can be. Similarly, short piano pieces that become popular in piano tuition can change children's understanding of what music is. New songs can change the way we sing and the way we understand the communal aspect of singing. And when Nielsen provides music for an important event, a large group of people will have the same sonic reference that they associate with what the event represents. A composer can, for instance, modify the sound of modernity or the sound of what is perceived as Danish.

Our cultural-historical approach meant that it was important to collect and process a large amount of material that, at first sight, has no direct connection with

Nielsen. Instead, it has been possible to reconstruct some of the musical, social and cultural environments that were important to him. And it was crucial that the cultural-historical material should not be seen merely as background or as a way of understanding Nielsen: what did it mean to him? Nielsen also serves as a prism through which the reader can gain insight into the cultural history of a time that we no longer have direct experience of. Even if we knew the world and culture in which Nielsen lived, not many of us today have lived in Nielsen's time, from 1865 to 1931.

This book is also about music history. Much of the knowledge presented here tells us details about Nielsen's contemporary colleagues at home and abroad, and about the music-historical reality he encountered in the form of traditions and discussions in musical life. Much of the exchange of ideas about the direction in which music should develop draws its arguments from different parts of the musical past. Similarly, many of the traditions of musical craftsmanship central to the professional composer are based on historical models. The history of music presents composers and musicians with choices to which they are bound to relate.

The European and the National

Culture exists at many levels. To grow up in Denmark, or with Danish culture, is to grow up as part of a Danish 'we'. This 'we' is created by the notion that there is a Danish national culture and that those who live in it share it and are part of it. At the same time, people who have been born and raised elsewhere or in other cultures have been brought up to look at this 'we' from the outside. In both cases, the assumption is that the national culture is the interpretive framework that is applied almost naturally to a subject such as 'Nielsen and his music'. It is a framework of understanding that became widespread in the 1830s and 1840s and has been maintained, furthered and changed in several waves of historical development. The very fact that it has evolved historically shows that it is not eternal and unchanging.

Our approach is different. We see Nielsen as a European composer who lived and worked in a highly integrated northern European musical culture, which was a cultural reality during Nielsen's lifetime. Repertoires, musical education, musical cultural norms and forms were widely shared across national borders, despite local variations. To interpret Nielsen and his music solely on the basis of national frameworks would be far too narrow and, like all national histories, would overemphasise differences at the expense of commonalities. The way that much music history traditionally has been written, pretending that Danish composers learned most things from other Danish composers, is essentially a distortion of history.

This is not to say that Nielsen was not a Danish composer. He was, but it is important to recognise that he was not born a Danish national composer. He became one around the time of the First World War, when reviews and music literature began to attribute national characteristics to his music. Another point is that Denmark and Europe should not be seen as opposites. Europe is not abroad. If we see Nielsen as a European composer, it is because we see Danish culture as part of a wider European culture. In other words, Nielsen does not have to travel to Germany or France to be in Europe – he is already there. Therefore, it is not recognition abroad that determines whether he can be considered a European composer. He already is.

By placing Nielsen in a wider context, the present book seeks to counterbalance the national perspective that has characterised some Danish scholarship on the subject. At the same time, it provides a vantage point from which to analyse and relate how Nielsen's status as a great Danish composer is established and evolves over time. Nielsen's path to becoming a national composer is thus one of the themes of the book.

Our aim is to present a nuanced picture of Nielsen, so that we can gain a deeper understanding of the prerequisites for the culture of our own time. Precisely because Nielsen and his music have become part of the Danish cultural heritage, an understanding of Nielsen is also highly relevant to how we understand ourselves as part of that culture. The same is true when we look at the culture as outsiders.

That our approach to Nielsen's status as a national composer is analytical rather than normative stems from our interpretation that he became a national composer as the result of a collective social process in which he was given an increasingly high status by society. We interpret this process as a reception-historical reality that combines a gradual canonisation of his oeuvre with an identification of his music as Danish. This does not mean that we accept the premise that he should therefore be interpreted from a national perspective – nor does it mean that we see it as the purpose of the book to confirm that he should have this status. The book is not a hagiographic portrayal of Nielsen.

However, this should not prevent us from highlighting the qualities of Nielsen's music and the specific features of his abilities as a composer. To do otherwise would be to leave the readers to their own devices. Rather, we would like to invite the reader to experience the qualities we have identified, while maintaining a critical and analytical perspective.

Modernism and the Modern

Concepts of modernism and the modern play an important role in this book, and were hotly debated in Nielsen's time. Readers should bear in mind that these are also concepts that change over time. In the book we distinguish between turn-of-the-century modern music, which is the music that was considered modern in the

1890s and around 1900, and the music that was labelled modernism after the First World War. Nielsen undoubtedly belongs to the turn-of-the-century modern, and he is part of a group of younger composers who, in their own way, are identified with innovation, modernity and youth. At the time, modernism was stylistically open, and Nielsen shared the view that the moderns were those who had left Wagner and Brahms behind.

Around 1900, the movement that followed in Wagner's footsteps was labelled modern. Nielsen now distanced himself from the term, positioning himself as someone who wanted renewal based on classical ideals. After the First World War there was another shift, as younger, radical composers such as Schoenberg and Stravinsky took over the position as the most modern and were labelled modernists. Again, Nielsen does not identify with the word modern, but he shares the efforts of the time to create 'new music', even in radical ways.

Literature and Sources

This book is part of a new tendency that has dominated international Nielsen research since the 1990s. It includes the Danish contributions that view Nielsen as a European composer among other European composers, each participating in their own way in European musical culture. This literature discusses the composer's relationship to the national as part of the research field, but does not assume that the national is the obvious framework of understanding.

Indeed, one of the first books to deal in depth with Nielsen as a participant in European cultural currents was Jørgen I. Jensen's book, *Carl Nielsen. Danskeren* (The Dane). Jensen takes the culture of Symbolism as the starting point for his interpretation and treats it as a European phenomenon. More recent Anglo-American scholarship has also taken it for granted that Nielsen must be seen in a European context. Scholars such as Anne-Marie Reynolds and Daniel M. Grimley, as well as the many contributions to the journal *Carl Nielsen Studies*, have made the European framework a common approach.

During the same period, research on Nielsen has progressed with a number of major publications and research projects. The *Carl Nielsen Edition* (CNU) has published all of Nielsen's works in scholarly, critical editions. The *Catalogue of Carl Nielsen's Works* (CNW) has gathered all works in a systematic list with unique work numbers and extensive references to sources and literature. The electronic, updated and freely accessible online edition is an invaluable tool. All of Nielsen's published texts and interviews are collected in *Carl Nielsen til sin samtid* (Nielsen to his Contemporaries; abbr. Samtid), and 5,960 letters and 1,912 diary entries have been published in *Carl Nielsen Brevudgaven* (CNB), which is also available as a searchable e-book. A selection of the letters has been translated into English in *Carl Nielsen. Selected Letters and Diaries* (CNL), and projects are in progress to translate the entire *Samtid* and CNB into English. In addition, a large body of secondary literature has been published, which we have, of course, drawn upon, even when we make extensive use of primary sources.

It has been a great advantage in studying Nielsen that virtually all the primary sources are now available in reliable and scholarly editions, and that they are largely searchable and linked through the CNW catalogue. At the same time, it would be a mistake to think that it is possible to arrange the sources in a sequence and then write a book on the subject. As well as reading the sources critically, it is important to recognise that published (that is, edited) sources do not tell the whole story. The editions of the works naturally focus on Nielsen's compositions, and thus also narrowly on his role as a composer. Nielsen was more than that: he was also a musician, cultural personality, child, opinion leader, etc. In addition, it often appears that Nielsen wrote letters when he was not composing. There are periods when he is concentrating on writing music, when he is travelling, when he is too young, or simply when no immediate sources have survived. Finally, it is important to distinguish between what he says and what he does: his music is a form of expression, and what he says in words is not necessarily consistent – and may indeed not even be true. And then there are all the other things he just does without saying anything about it. In fact, some of the most surprising insights have emerged where there were no obvious sources directly linked to Nielsen, so the authors had to find other and new ways of unravelling what had happened in certain environments or situations.

The Structure of the Book

The book is in five parts. The first four form a chronological framework of periods in Nielsen's life, each covering about fifteen years of musical activity. The first part describes an extensive formative process leading up to his emergence as an independent composer in the early 1890s. The second part examines Nielsen as a member of the group of young composers who shaped musical life as part of the culture at the turn of the century. The third part of the book deals with the period when his ideas about life as a vital force really came to fruition in his music, and the fourth part deals with the 1920s, when the urge for constant renewal combined with his great efforts to raise the level of general musical education. In addition, some of the chapters summarising a particular activity cut across the chronological structure. In the fifth part of the book, the perspective shifts to show how Nielsen became the figure that has been handed down to posterity, and how he himself contributed to this process. Occasionally, the reader will come across short, reflective chapters dealing with a specific theme or principle that is not tied to a specific point in time.

The focus of the book is on Nielsen as a professional. It is therefore natural that the emphasis shifts from the biographical to the musical as his work as a composer becomes more and more central. The biographical still plays a role, and some of the chapters that cover a long period also provide a framework for understanding the later years of his life. At the same time, as the book progresses, it becomes increasingly important to answer questions about his compositional processes.

In addition to the general chronology, there are a number of thematic threads running through the book. One is his musicianship, which was crucial to his approach to music, from his childhood experiences playing with his father, through his training as a military band musician and as a professionally trained violinist, to his work as a chamber musician, a Royal Musician, Kapellmeister and conductor. A second thread is Nielsen's work as a composer, covering a wide range of areas, all interesting: music for events, symphonic music, chamber music, incidental music, lieder, songs and hymns, as well as music for specific instruments.

A third thread is the cultural and musical milieux of which Nielsen was a part, in Odense, Copenhagen, Leipzig, Berlin and Paris, and the trends in which he was involved, from the freethinkers in the Copenhagen of the Modern Breakthrough to Symbolism, Vitalism and the cultivation of modern currents seeking innovation from a fundamental level. A fourth thread is his lifelong interest in pedagogical projects, from his own teaching career to the great popular education projects with the renewal of Danish song culture and his contribution to new and contemporary educational music. Finally, the book is concerned with his work as a cultural figure of his time. Nielsen was a person with whom even people outside the circle of professional musicians could identify.

Each chapter is structured around a specific period, activity or theme, which is presented in a comprehensive form, inviting the reader to explore the chapters individually and not necessarily in the order in which they appear. Similarly, because of the chronology and the integrated threads, there are of course stories that are pursued across the chapters. Taken as a whole, the forty-three chapters form a jigsaw puzzle that eventually reveals a picture of the whole Nielsen: the musician, the composer and the cultural personality. We have tried to do justice to what Nielsen does in music: to create good stories.

I

EXPANDING HORIZONS

ILL. 1. Nielsen was born in Sortelung, outside the village Nr. Lyndelse. This map, published in 1886, shows the location shortly after the time when Nielsen lived there. The house in which he was born was situated in the field to the south of the Frydenlund farm. A few hundred metres east of the house was the brickworks where he worked as a child, and behind it was the clay pit where the small lake is today, just below the place name Sortelung. To the right of the lake was Arvensminde, where the family moved in 1873 when Nielsen's birthplace was demolished. The third childhood cottage, Petersborg, which is now a museum, was on the main road south of Nr. Lyndelse.[1]

Chapter 1

A PLACE IN THE WORLD

On the island of Fyn, Nielsen grew up in a family of many children near the village of Nr. Lyndelse, which lies south of Odense. In his memoirs, *My Childhood*, he describes his upbringing largely from a child's perspective. It is a story of a world that expands both geographically and spiritually. It is from the child's immediate surroundings that he absorbs and expands his horizons. But we also need to understand what he was surrounded by. It is a specific place where he takes part in the social life that unfolds around him. The country life of 150 years ago seems familiar to us, but it is also a time and a society that no longer exists. This is where he spent his first fourteen years. Having had such a childhood, what do you take away with you?

Taking *My Childhood* as a starting point, which is a nostalgic review from a sixty-year-old's perspective and world of experience, it is largely a 'whole world' that is portrayed. It is complete in the sense that it forms a coherent world view, and in the sense that it is a representation without major fractures or conflicts. It is a manageable world on a small geographical scale, where a traditional but socially well-defined life is pursued. The perspective he takes in the memoirs could be described as a modern retrospective on a pre-modern way of life.[2]

But this is not the whole picture. It is also a world in the process of becoming modern, where the old village communities are being replaced by democratically elected parish councils, where tenant farmers are disappearing, where the public administration is monitoring the citizens, where all children attend school and where the manors and towns establish industries. It is a world in which German-born farm bailiffs and German migrant workers are among the closest neighbours and an immediate part of everyday life.

Musically, it is a world in which traditional dance music plays a central role. Nielsen had direct access to it through his father, Niels Jørgensen, who was a musician. But it is also a place where the trade in music publications and the knowledge of a common European musical culture are part of the music and repertoire, in terms of both new dance melodies and the music played by the local orchestra, Braga. Fyn was an integral part of Europe.

It is a well-organised world, but at the same time there is an undercurrent of social dynamism. There is a clear social stratification, which seems to be a natural part of the world, but also a hierarchy, a power relationship. In Nielsen's memoirs there is no resentment of social differences and poverty, but rather an acceptance of them as a condition. He also reflects the fundamental view that people's nature, their 'value', is independent of their social status. It is the adult Nielsen who speaks here. The qualities of the poor and the rich are presented in terms of their human nature, and Nielsen shows a receptiveness that recognises good qualities even in the very poorest. This reflects a self-esteem he has gained from his relatively poor upbringing. As a result, he has an ability to relate to both high and low. There are stories that he would rather talk to the coachman than to members of high society, yet there is also a photograph showing that during his holiday in Skagen, Nielsen went over to greet the King, who was staying at the royal summer residence, Klitgaarden.

The 'new' is in the making. It is a time when there is a clear sense that opportunities exist if you have the will and the ability. But the upbringing also provides a profound experience that progress does not come of itself. On the one hand, Nielsen sees his parents' generation, made up of common people who remain in the region and social conditions in which they were born. On the other hand, his mother represents a conscious social distancing from the miserable environment in which she grew up. And with the future prime minister Klaus Berntsen as a local role model, Nielsen is able to see how, through hard work, something new can be created, as is the case with the so-called high school and the private independent school movements.

Social mobility presupposed physical mobility. If you stayed in your home region, you ended up like your relatives as a smallholder, a small skilled workman or a farm labourer. If you left the region, you might be able to fulfil your dreams. It is no coincidence that of the twelve siblings in Nr. Lyndelse, one died as an infant, the eldest brother Peter emigrated to Australia, and Sophus, Anders, Albert, Julie and Lovise to the United States.[3] Two of Carl's sisters died young of tuberculosis and a third did not live long either. In addition to Carl, his brother Valdemar remained in Denmark. Valdemar was admitted to a teacher's college and then became a teacher in West Jutland and a member of parliament for the Social Liberal Party (Det Radikale Venstre). If you believe in fairy tales, it seems natural to set out in search of happiness and a better life. For Nielsen, this happened several times. Odense was the first step on the way.

The Place

Nielsen experienced the place where he grew up as a slowly expanding world. As he describes in *My Childhood*, his world at first constituted the most immediate boundaries: the fields, the brickworks, the stream, the neighbour, his siblings, his parents. As he grew older, it included Nr. Lyndelse, the neighbouring farms such as Frydenlund and the manor of Bramstrup. Later it included the 'region' where his family originated, but it was still a rather limited area that included the nearest villages in

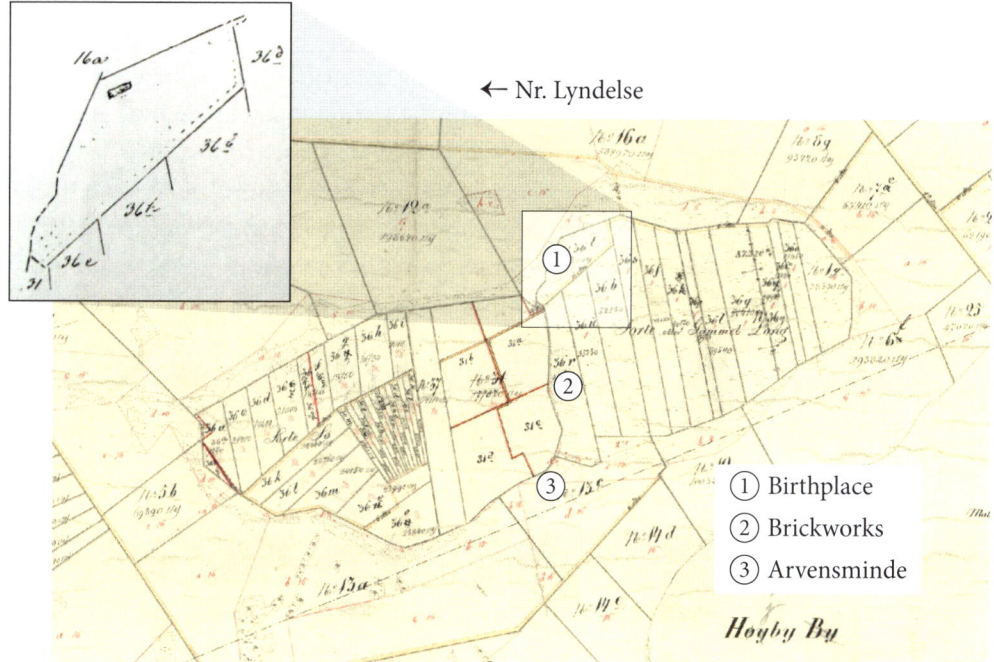

ILL. 2. Sortelung. The map used from 1859 to 1895 shows the area as it was when Nielsen lived there. North is to the right. Sortelung itself is an elongated area, about 1,300 metres long and 400 metres wide. To get to Nr. Lyndelse you have to follow the road that leads straight to the village, about a kilometre and a half south-west. Nielsen's birthplace was on cadastral plot 36t. A surveyor's drawing from 1857 shows the exact location of the cottage in the field where Carl Nielsen lived. The brickworks were on 36r and Arvensminde, his next home, was on plot 13c.[4]

both directions. To the south, on the other side of Nr. Søby, the village of Heden is the furthest outpost, the 'region' ending just before the manors of Brahetrolleborg and Egeskov. To the west were the neighbouring villages of Fangel, Bellinge and his father's hometown of Brylle. To the north, Odense was only just included, but it was already a place worth visiting. To the east it covered the area around Højby. The 'region' was oriented towards Odense, and neither Faaborg nor Svendborg were perceived as towns with which the locals had any connection.

Nielsen was born in the summer, on 9 June 1865. He grew up in a small cottage in the area of Sortelung, between the villages Nr. Lyndelse, Højby and Lumby. On old maps the area is called 'Sorte' or 'Gammel Long' at the northern end and 'Sorte Sø' (black lake) at the southern end.[5] The lake was drained around 1800, although it was still a marshy area, with a peat bog in the middle of the old 'Sorte Sø'. In the northern part, 'Sorte Lung', clay was dug for the brickworks, which was moved to different places over the years. Both 'Long' and 'Lung' are the old forms of the name of the plant heather – that is, it was a low-lying area covered with heather, a moor. Nielsen's

A PLACE IN THE WORLD 23

home was on the western edge of the bog, in a field by the road that runs through the area. Today there is a small memorial stone, an information board and a few tables where you can sit and have a cup of coffee.

The cottage was isolated, although it was by no means an uninhabited area. In 1870 there were twenty-two dwellings on Sortelung, eight of which housed two families. A total of 121 people lived there of which about half were children; half of the men were day labourers or labourers, three were farmers and some were skilled craftsmen; virtually all of the wives listed their occupation as farm wife. As well as being housewives, the women also did occasional work on the farms – as did Nielsen's mother, Maren Kirstine Johansen. The two that stand out are a millwright and a musician, Nielsen's father.[6]

> My birthplace stood in the middle of a field. It was an old grass field that was rarely ploughed up, and then only to be laid down as grass again. No road led to the cottage, but there were two footpaths, one of which went east across 'the sluice' [Dømmesrenden], where there was a bridge and a road leading to a brickyard a few hundred yards away. The other path went to Frydendal Farm, which belonged to Bramstrup Manor estate. Frydenlund was only a few minutes' walk from our cottage, and Bramstrup about half a mile farther west on the Odense-Faaborg road. These four places – our home, the brickyard, Frydenlund, and Bramstrup – were the four corners of the world in which my brothers and sisters and I grew up.[7]

In his memoirs, *My Childhood*, written in the spring or summer of 1927,[8] Nielsen pays little attention to the other inhabitants of the area. The memoirs must be read as the elder Nielsen's selective presentation of what he considers important to preserve for posterity. In this way he prepares the story for later generations to tell who Nielsen was. The impressions he wants to convey are his experiences of nature or particular people, often with a strong sensuous touch. Children were often left alone at home while their parents worked. Nielsen describes such a situation, when the mother comes home at lunchtime, as a momentous experience:

> Four of us small brothers and sisters were lying one day on the grass; the sun was strong and we were both hungry and thirsty, as my mother was haymaking at Bramstrup Manor in the neighbourhood. She came home in the dinner-hour, but as we were all lying on our backs and, I suppose, dozing, we were not aware of it until she stood over us, stooped down between us with a big smile under her white haymaking hat and said, 'Just look what I've got for you!' She had brought from the manor some warm apple fritters dipped in caster-sugar and a bottle of something to drink, whether beer or milk I cannot remember. Sufficient to say

that the way my mother's image, the sun, the sky, the grass, and the food flowed together in sheer bliss – this can never be forgotten. Then off she went, brisk and cheerful, saying, 'Now be good little boys and girls and I'll be back before dark.'[9]

What is unusual is not that the children are alone at home, but that there is good food and sunshine. This is contrasted with an episode he recounts when his father was away for a week or so playing music, and his mother had nothing in the house but a jar of yellowish horse fat, which they spread on bread and seasoned with salt.[10]

There was a waterhole near the cottage, known as the Well, where Nielsen almost drowned as a child. They played and fetched water, and the children explored the stream Dømmesrenden, which in the summer consisted only of puddles; here they also found snail shells and sticklebacks, and tumbled up and down the slope. The stream follows the road to Sortelung. There was a bank around the garden and some cherry trees. The plot where the cottage stood was quite large, about a hectare of land, but as they only rented the house, it was not their pasture that surrounded the dwelling. They kept chickens and a pig, and at Arvensminde, his next childhood home, they also had some goats.[11]

The brickworks played an important role in Nielsen's childhood. Not only was it an exciting place to explore on Sundays when there was no work to be done, but it was also a place where he was involved in brick cutting from an early age. The task involved using an iron tool with handles at either end to cut off the rough edges of the air-dried raw bricks before they were placed in the kiln. It was considered a real job for which the boys were paid; they were given a canvas apron, tools and a small three-legged sloping table on which to work. It was an outdoor job and they worked their way through stacks of ten bricks so that they were easy to count when the foreman checked the day's output in the evening. Carl's description suggests that he saw it as a kind of game, trying to keep up with his brother Albert, who was two years older and both more skilled and faster. They were allowed to keep some of the money to save for toys, wooden shoes or a new cap. It was not only Carl and Albert who did this kind of work, but also his other brothers and a number of boys from Sortelung. It is not entirely clear how old they were, but they were probably around 8–10 years old, and when they were not at school they worked in the brickworks.[12]

But the brickworks are also important in another way, for it was here that the wider world was already present as part of the microcosm of childhood. Every year a group of German workers would arrive from the county of Lippe-Detmold, a small principality to the south-west of Hanover, which had a strong brickworks tradition. Three of them can be named: Conrad Stuckenbrock, Conrad Siekmann and Wilhelm Grotegut. In the years between 1854 and 1868, each of them took over the position of master of the brickworks, leading a team of seven or eight workers.[13]

ILL. 3. A brick stamped with Bramstrup brickworks, where Nielsen worked as a boy.

The workers were accommodated in one of Bramstrup's houses, so it was not just when they arrived each year that they passed the Nielsen family's cottage. It was a special experience for Nielsen when they arrived; however, they were also part of everyday life:

> As spring came round a gang of workmen would arrive, knapsacks and tools on their backs. They would be covered in dust and dirt and look as if they had come from the world's end … they were German workmen from Lippe-Detmold, and the name sounded so foreign that I felt it must be a tremendous way off. When, back from their journeys, they passed our cottage there was a youngish man with a thin beard who always gave me a particularly friendly nod, and once or twice a copper that was very warm and rather moist and sticky from chewing-tobacco. I was loath to touch the coin, but Ferdinand and I were good friends for all that … We often talked together, without my understanding a word of what he said.[14]

The brickworks belonged to Frydenlund, which in turn belonged to Bramstrup. The manager at Frydenlund was also German and a natural part of the local environment: 'The farm was managed by an old bailiff from Holstein, called Schmidt; he was a bachelor and a fine type of the old school.'[15] Jep Jepsen Schmidt, who was not from Holstein but from the Duchy of Schleswig, lived at Frydenlund with a number of farmhands and maids. Nielsen portrays Schmidt as a popular and respected man of few words. Schmidt was a man of great importance, for it was he who recommended that Nielsen work as a goose-boy at Bramstrup during the summer months for a few years, when he was, as he remembers, eight or nine years old.[16] It was a job he did during the school holidays until the beginning of autumn, where he was responsible from early morning until evening for a large flock of geese that had to be driven into the meadows. He was sent out without any help or training, and it is clear that, in retrospect, he sees this as a huge responsibility that he fears he will not be able to live up to. The situations he describes are about the danger of not being up to the task and the many long hours alone in the field. He had a ring sundial, small and portable, to keep track of time.

The work with the geese was based at Bramstrup Manor. It gave him a glimpse of life on a manor with managers, farmhands and maids, day labourers and their wives. It was also an important social experience. It is clear that he knew the brickworkers, the farmhands and the manager, but he only knew the landlord, Niels Langkilde, to whom it all belonged, from a distance. The social gap was too wide. Nielsen was submissive to the landowner: 'the estate-owner and his family … were so high up in my visions that I hardly dared look at them, but snatched off my cap at meeting them and was delighted when they gave me a friendly nod.'[17] He worked for Langkilde and portrays him sympathetically, but he was never in the manor house. In Nielsen's memoirs, Langkilde appears in only one anecdote from when he was five or six years old. It is the oft-told episode of Carl playing tunes on the stack of logs with one of his brothers when Langkilde passed by.[18] This story is widely interpreted as the first proof that we are looking at the future great composer, although they could not know it at the time.

The Three Childhood Homes

Nielsen's early experiences came from his childhood homes. The house that is now known as his childhood home and serves as a museum was the third place he lived. The one the family lived in when Nielsen was born was called Uglehuset (the Owl House), and Nielsen's father, Niels Jørgensen, moved there with his family in 1861. About two years earlier, the fire brigade had classified the building as unsafe, prompting it to be renovated as well as extended from eight to ten bays. It was a half-timbered cottage with a clay-lined framework, a mud floor and a thatched roof, and the size of the dwelling can be estimated at around sixty-one square metres. It was one of the cottages in Sortelung that was occupied by two families. His parents moved in with five children and had another six, including Carl, while they lived there.[19]

It was Nielsen's first childhood home and is described in his memoirs as the place with the strongest childhood memories, although many of the stories associated with growing up took place after he moved to Arvensminde on the other side of Sortelung. Mentally, Uglehuset seems to be the place where the sensuous memories of the childhood environment left their longest-lasting marks.

According to the census of 1870, Nielsen's family lived at one end of Uglehuset, consisting of Niels Jørgensen, his wife Maren Kirstine Johansen and their eight chil-

ILL. 4. The picture, painted from memory by Nielsen's brother Albert in 1931, shows Uglehuset (the Owl House), undoubtedly beautified. The cottage was built in 1837 and belonged to the landlord Langkilde of Bramstrup, who acquired it and the plot of land in 1858. Niels Jørgensen was given a lease on 11 June 1861 and paid 12 Rigsdaler a year in rent. In comparison, he received 2–3 Rigsdaler for playing at balls and up to 9 Rigsdaler for a wedding.[20]

dren, all with the surname 'Nielsen': Sophie, Karen Marie, Peter, Sophus, Albert, Carl, Anders and Lovise. The eldest sister, Caroline, had already left home. At the other end lived the family Nielsen refers to as 'Store Hans Jensen and Store-Marie' (big Hans Jensen and big-Marie) and their five children.[21] All in all, seventeen individuals in a tenement with three window bays in each half of the cottage.

But even in such a dwelling there were marked social differences. In *My Childhood*, the other family is described as a working-class family, a term Nielsen never uses for his own family.[22] Nor does he give the impression that the two families had anything more to do with each other than what came out of ordinary neighbourliness. The working-class family is not only portrayed as (even) poorer; in his account it functions as a counterpart against which he describes his own family: it was 'as different from us as chalk from cheese', the cleanliness was moderate, the parents are portrayed as simple, 'rough in thought and feeling', and the man could be drunk and violent. They were 'good-natured and inoffensive', Nielsen recalls, and the 'few ideas' that Hans Jensen had seemed 'always right if extremely simple'. But, he points out, 'we kept pretty well to ourselves'.[23] Nielsen thus gives the impression that his own family

ILL. 5. Arvensminde, painting by Herman Madsen, who also wrote about it in the book *Carl Nielsens Fyn*. According to Madsen, Nielsen lived in the wing facing the clay pit, behind the two small windows in the middle of the picture. Another local story places the dwelling at the end of the farmhouse facing the road, that is, the windows in the gable that can be seen on the left side of the painting.[24]

were not simple people, even though they were quite ordinary and only marginally better off than their neighbours.

In 1873, when Nielsen turned eight, the family moved, and at the end of the year Uglehuset was demolished. But they did not move far, just across the brickworks to a property called Arvensminde. Here they rented dwellings in one of the wings from the smallholder, Johan Jensen, who lived in the farmhouse. The following year Jensen sold the smallholding to Langkilde, but stayed on as tenant of the house and garden, while the Nielsen family remained as Jensen's tenants.[25]

The family, including eight children, had moved to Arvensminde under very austere conditions. Caroline, Sophie and Karen Marie had left but Peter still lived at home. It was here that the twelfth child, Anna Dusine, was born and died shortly afterwards in the spring of 1875.[26] Yet, the dignity of the home does not seem to have

A PLACE IN THE WORLD   29

come about by chance. Kirstine Godske, who went to school with Nielsen and was a year younger than him, remembers the home as 'poor, very, very poor', but says of his mother: 'She could make something out of nothing, that woman, and she looked so decent. She seemed fit and was always so clean, which was also the case at home.'[27]

This was Nielsen's second childhood home, where he lived for five years until the spring of 1878. It was during his time at Arvensminde that his childhood memories of being in service during the summer must have been formed. In addition, most of his schooling took place while he lived here. It was thus a formative period in his life, from the age of eight until around his thirteenth birthday. It is remarkable that nowhere in *My Childhood* does he mention the family with whom they lived, nor does he give a more detailed description of the house or the place.[28]

If Nielsen remembers correctly, he got his first job as a herder of geese in the summer when they moved to Arvensminde or perhaps the following year. He also worked in the brickworks at that time. It is portrayed as natural for children to work, and Nielsen does not question this. But work is not only a duty or a necessity, it is also something that gives status: it is something you are allowed to do and want to do, because it also brings recognition. You show that you know something. This is evident, for example, when Nielsen talks about his father's work in grating the colours he used for paint:

> In the spring or early summer Father would often be busy grinding and mixing colours and we boys sometimes had to help him. It was very exciting work. We had a big, polished, rectangular stone slab and on top of that another stone, smaller and half-spherical, with which we mixed the colour and oil in a circular, rubbing movement. ... It was very interesting ... and one could get into quite a dreamlike state when the whole slab gleamed yellow, red, blue, or other colours, each of them seeming to have its own mood.[29]

Here it is clear that being allowed to participate in the work, a fascination with the work itself and the aesthetic impression of the result are all important.

It is also a clear indication of a key aspect when Nielsen, speaking of his first workplace where he did not live at home, emphasises the concept of being useful: 'I had now grown old enough – ten or eleven – to begin to "make myself useful" in the summer ...'.[30] That summer he herded cattle in Nr. Lyndelse, and later on he also tended cattle on a farm.[31] In one instance he describes his father helping with the harvest on one of the neighbouring farms, and 'it was after just such a long and regular day's work that he ... felt best'.[32] These two themes – the homage to solid, regular work and the desire to be useful – were to play an important role as cornerstones of Nielsen's attitude to the world.

Nielsen attended the village school, Nr. Lyndelse Skole. He had seven years of formal education, from the time he started as a seven-year-old in 1872 until he was confirmed in the spring of 1879. The family's move to Arvensminde coincided with Nielsen's second year at school. The teacher at Nr. Lyndelse, Emil Petersen, was the son of a teacher and church singer, that is, of a church clerk's family. He had attended the teacher's college in Skaarup and was therefore part of a new generation of teachers who had received a proper teacher training when he was employed in Nr. Lyndelse in 1873. He stayed at the same school until he retired in 1920.[33] Although he was only an assistant teacher in the early days, he became very important to Carl. There is no doubt that Nielsen had a good relationship with Petersen, who also gave him violin lessons from the age of eight or nine. He points out that Petersen was a gifted teacher whom he remembers with gratitude. They kept in touch until late in life.[34]

Nielsen's final year at school was at Nr. Søby Skole, the family having moved to the third childhood home in 1878. He recalls that he was 'not very good at book studies, neither … one of the worst',[35] and his classmate Kirstine Godske spontaneously answered the question of whether he was a diligent pupil with 'well, no, far from it'.[36] But this is apparently not entirely true, for a surviving page of the school's examination book from the autumn of 1878 shows quite good grades. His score in religion, Bible history and written work is '5', in reading and arithmetic '4x', which on the six-point scale are 'mg' (very good) and 'g+' (good+) respectively. He is number six in the class of twenty-four boys, and the general level of the class as a whole is also praised.[37]

Similarly, when he was confirmed in Heden Kirke on 20 April the following year, Pastor Briand wrote in the church records: 'very good knowledge and very good behaviour'.[38] In other words, the boy had potential. The teacher at Nr. Søby, on the other hand, is not praised in *My Childhood*; he is described as skilful, but out of touch with the children and the community, and completely unmusical.[39] This is probably an exaggeration, however, as the examination book, which also indirectly assesses the teacher's instruction, says of the class as a whole: 'singing skills excellent as usual'.[40] The teaching could not have been completely off the mark.

In the spring of 1878, when Nielsen turned thirteen, his parents bought the third childhood home on the road between Nr. Lyndelse and Nr. Søby, just across the parish boundary to Nr. Søby. In many ways, this marked the beginning of the next phase of Nielsen's life, the transition to adulthood. It was his last year at school, he was confirmed, and he was apprenticed to a shopkeeper before coming to Odense to join as a military band musician in the autumn of 1879.

The new house was a big step forward for the family. It was of considerable size and very good quality compared to what they had lived in before. In 1855–56 it had been altered from a clay-floored half-timbered house to a stone house with a foundation wall, thus effectively building a new one, and it was extended in 1874 by three bays. The house cost 1,700 Kroner with a down payment of 200 Kroner.[41] By comparison, Niels Jørgensen had earned around 450 Kroner the previous year from playing music.[42]

It is the only surviving childhood home and Nielsen did not live there for long. The deed of sale was signed on 23 March 1878 and states that the buyer was to take possession of the property immediately, which suggests that they moved in shortly afterwards. After his confirmation the following year, Nielsen was apprenticed to the shopkeeper in Ellinge and moved there which lies about 17 km from Nr. Lyndelse.[43] It is unclear exactly how long he was there, but soon the shopkeeper fell ill and Carl came home for a time while he prepared for the entrance examination as a military musician in Odense. He was accepted and was employed from 1 November 1879.

In all, he lived in the third childhood home for a year. It is during this time that he remembers his eldest brother, Peter, emigrating to Australia. A significant part of his memoirs about playing with his father must relate to this time, although he continued to do so while living in Odense.[44]

Family Background and Its Significance

That Nielsen's mother was 'quite proud' of the fact that the windowpanes in the two bays in their part of the house on Sortelung were larger might sound like a slight ambition to be better than others. But Nielsen tells the story to show the dignity and decency with which his mother ran the household. Although the place was very modest, she put flowers in the windows, made sure it was clean and tidy, and that the children had decent clothes and were raised properly.[45] They were taught not to be inferior to others, which also gave them the perspective that you are not destined to live the same way all your life if you use your abilities to the full.

Nielsen's mother was a strong woman who managed to keep a large family together and who was determined to provide her children with a good start in life. But it was not always easy, and there is much to suggest that it was an active and conscious choice on her part to rise above the lower social strata that she knew from her childhood in Odense. The story that her mother, Helene Andersdatter, came from a wealthy family of skippers in Seden, north of Odense, turns out on closer inspection to be a tale that covers a somewhat less glorious lineage. It is a story that has been retold many times, and one that Nielsen seems to have bought into.[46]

In order to see how it really was with Nielsen's mother's background, it is necessary to unravel the somewhat complicated family relationships. Her family can be traced back to the beginning of the eighteenth century, when Nielsen's great-great-great-great-grandfather settled in Odense. His son-in-law, who came to Odense as a Swedish-born Danish soldier, eventually became a schoolmaster in Stige, a village north of Odense. Until the opening of the Odense Canal in 1804, the boats of the Odense skippers moored there. One of his daughters became Nielsen's great-great-grandmother. She married a tailor from Stige, whose father had also ended up in Odense after serving in the Danish army.[47]

Thus Nielsen's mother did not come from a wealthy family of sailors, but rather from a family of soldiers, tailors and a single schoolmaster. The family probably came from Stige, where Odense originally had its harbour, but settled in Odense in precarious circumstances.

Now we come to Helene Andersdatter, whose mother, Mariana, was born in 1766. She married a farmer's son who supported himself as a farmhand, but ended up as a day labourer living on the outskirts of Odense. They had four children, the youngest of whom was Nielsen's grandmother, Helene, born around the turn of the year 1803–4. After 1813 the family lived in a small house in Kræmmergyden, which stretched from Skibhusgade to Nørregade. The alley was just north of today's railway station, where the main post office is located. The house consisted of a single storey with a kitchen, a bedchamber and a living room. In 1827 Helene's father was placed under the care of the welfare system, and when he died in 1833 the house was sold at auction. Six years later her mother died as a pauper.[48]

Yet, Helene got a decent education as a pupil at Lahns Stiftelse (Lahn's Foundation) in Odense, which was a school for poor children and which was a well-regulated institution with detailed rules for education. However, her life was not shaped according to the framework of the pious foundation. In 1823, at the age of nineteen, she had a child born out of wedlock, who died shortly after birth. Two years later, she gave birth to a daughter who was delivered at Den kongelige Fødselsstiftelse (the Royal Maternity Hospital) in Copenhagen. Someone apparently had the means to organise and pay for the stay. In 1828 she had a son, whose father, Andreas Larsen, was a journeyman hatter from Odense. Two years later, he was registered as the father of another son, but this time listed as being absent. In 1833 she had a daughter with another journeyman hatter, Johan Larsen. The daughter was Maren Kirstine Johansen, Nielsen's mother.

The following year, Helene gave birth to another child with Johan Larsen, who is now also reportedly absent. The child died soon after. Then in 1837 she had twins with the first journeyman hatter, Andreas Larsen. One of the twins, Niels, died in 1840, and the other, Hans, who was almost blind, was later to play a role in Nielsen's musical education, as Hans became an organist. It was at his home that Carl first saw a piano.

In 1840 Helene lived with her children in a property near the cemetery. In the same house lived a tailor, Jens Rasmussen Brylle, who became the father of her youngest child. Rasmussen Brylle and Helene married in 1843, the latter having been receiving poor relief since 1830, which continued into the marriage. Her husband must have been an alcoholic, for in 1853 he was admitted to the poorhouse with delirium tremens, where he probably died some years later. In 1860 she moved in with her former neighbour, the clogmaker Johan Christopher Holm. Two years later he had left, and where exactly she lived after that is uncertain. In the last year before her death, she lived with her son Hans.[49]

Helene Andersdatter gave birth to nine children in all, probably with five different men, of whom she was married to one who was an alcoholic and lived with at least one other man, while the rest seem to have been looser relationships. At the same time, for twenty-five years – in addition to the three years she received child benefit from the maternity foundation – she had been a regular recipient of poor relief. She died in the workhouse hospital on 17 March 1874 and was buried as a destitute by the Poor Law authorities.[50]

For Nielsen, however, Helene was an almost mythical figure, and his description recalls one of Agnes Slott-Møller's stylised paintings of a chatelaine:

> When my mother's mother, Helene, came to see us, we children would stop chattering. She would walk proud and erect into the room, looking strict, and with her smooth hair and white cap she was like a queen as she sat down in our one and only armchair. She was a skipper's wife from Seden on the Odense Fjord and is said to have been a very handsome woman, a reputation borne out by a photograph of her in late life that is still in my possession. At Seden they called her 'Belle Helene'. The nickname was familiar in our district as well, but one day when one of the neighbours tried to flatter her by using it, she got very annoyed. I forget her curt reply, but I still remember the way her eyes flashed and her nostrils dilated.[51]

As his grandmother died in the spring of 1874, Nielsen could not have been more than eight at the time of this anecdote. But his sensual portrayal matches the experiences with animals and people that he reproduces elsewhere with great precision, giving the story credibility. It is clear that there was an aura of respect and aloofness around her, but it is also clear that Nielsen instinctively realised that this was not something to ask about. A connection with the shipping environment in Odense's original harbour, combined with the fact that she was already a widow, leads Nielsen to conclude from his childhood experiences that she must have been a skipper's widow. How this was 'in reality' was not articulated. Her nickname, 'the beautiful Helene', may well have been one she acquired in an environment where it was not unusual to have relationships and children without being married – but it was apparently not to be used in other contexts.

The crucial question is what effect growing up in this environment had on Nielsen's mother, Maren Kirstine. Born on 9 April 1833, she spent her first year as the

ILL. 6. In his memoirs, Nielsen refers to a surviving photograph of his maternal grandmother, Helene Andersdatter. He associates the picture with the story that she came from a wealthy family. The photograph is clearly a studio shot taken by a photographer.

youngest of four children with her mother in Kræmmergyden. Together with several siblings and her stepfather, Jens Rasmussen Brylle, she grew up in a property by Assistens Cemetery. When the family moved to another house near the cemetery, she still lived at home. These houses were tenements.[52] Immediately after her confirmation in 1847, she went to work as a maid in the more respectable households: first in Odense at a grocer's in Skt. Knudsstræde, then with a widow, Mrs Salomon, in Vestergade, then with a plumber in Overgade and finally with a jeweller in the same street. These were middle-class families in the better parts of central Odense. Then she went into service at Reverend Briand's house in Nr. Søby, where she stayed for two years from November 1852.[53]

It looks like a deliberate strategy to get away from the environment she grew up in and gain experience of how to live and behave in middle-class circles. She acquired a role model for the norms and standards she sought to set for her children's upbringing. In order to provide a safe environment for her offspring, she did not tell them the whole truth about her own background, but instead created a family life in which her perseverance and honesty, despite her poverty, served as a role model. Her own upbringing also explains her great fear that Carl would fall into bad company when he moved to Odense and later to Copenhagen.[54] In this sense, it is not surprising that she let her children live under the illusion that she came from a more respectable background than she actually did. Her strategy was indeed an escape, but also the realisation that it is possible to succeed if the effort is made and the desire is strong enough. Carl inherited this mindset.

A PLACE IN THE WORLD

Niels and Maren Kirstine

Similarly, the family of Nielsen's father can be traced back to around 1800. Looking into the background of his father's family reveals that they were only minor workmen, homesteaders and day labourers living on the outskirts of Odense.

His grandfather, Jørgen Nielsen, was the son of a day labourer in Lille Ubberud, west of Odense. He started working at an early age and at the age of twenty-two was apprenticed to a clogmaker in Tommerup. From there he went to Bellinge to work for another clogmaker. He then became a miller at the nearby Borreby Mølle, where he met Nielsen's grandmother, the maid Karen Christensdatter, whom he married in 1831. Shortly before the wedding, they had bought a small property east of Brylle, consisting of a farmhouse and outbuildings with just over a hectare of land. The house was called Abildkroghuset. They had two children, Anne, born in 1831, and Nielsen's father, Niels, born on 22 January 1835.[55] A few months later Jørgen Nielsen died, and in February of the following year Karen remarried, this time to Peder Andersen, who was a farmhand on a nearby farm.

Peder Andersen, the stepfather, was the only father Niels Jørgensen knew. Andersen was the son of poor smallholders from Brylle. The new family consisted of six additional children, who were Niels Jørgensen's half-siblings and therefore Carl Nielsen's uncles and aunts.[56]

Abildkroghuset, where Niels Jørgensen's parents lived, later became important to Maren Kirstine. While working as a maid for Rev. Briand, she met Niels Jørgensen and became pregnant. Obviously she did not want to return to her mother and Odense, and when her employment ended at an advanced stage of her pregnancy, she moved in with her future parents-in-law. She stayed there for half a year until she went to work for Rev. Brummer, in the parish of Tarup-Pårup near Odense.[57]

She must have had a good reputation, as she was allowed to stay with Rev. Briand until shortly before she gave birth, and was quickly given a new job in another vicarage. Briand also wrote in her conduct book: 'Maren Kirstine Johansen has served me for two years as a maid, and in this service she has shown a rare availability, fidelity and honesty.'[58] She maintained a good relationship with the Briand family, and he became their pastor again when they bought the house in Nr. Søby.[59] The next pastor was perhaps not so understanding, for when she became pregnant again, she left her position and travelled to Odense.[60]

So Maren Kirstine met Niels Jørgensen at the beginning of 1854 at the latest, as their first child, Caroline, was born in November of that year. We do not know how they met, but perhaps Niels Jørgensen played music at a party or had a job as a painter, for Nr. Søby was not far from the neighbouring village of Fangel, where he had lived since the beginning of 1850. In Fangel he worked for his uncle and trained as a painter and fiddler.[61]

In May 1854, Niels Jørgensen moved in with a carpenter on the road between Nr. Lyndelse and Nr. Søby and was thus even closer. Perhaps this was a way of getting a job, as a carpenter might often need a painter, and there were already at least two in Fangel – that is, two of his relatives. The house was on the west side of the road, a few hundred metres from the parish boundary with Nr. Søby.[62] When Maren Kirstine's employment as a maid ended on 1 November, she moved in with her future in-laws at Abildkroghuset, as mentioned above. Six months later, when she got a job at the vicarage in Pårup, a few kilometres north-west of Odense, they must have kept in touch, since Maren Kirstine became pregnant again.

ILL. 7. Maren Kirstine, Carl Nielsen's mother, photographed as a young woman in Odense.

Now Maren Kirstine was at a crossroads. When she left the vicarage, she had an almost one-year-old baby, she was unmarried, she was pregnant again with a painter's journeyman and fiddler with whom she did not live, and she moved to Odense, where she had come from. It is not known for certain where she lived, but it seems likely that it was with her mother. Would she end up like her mother, who had raised a group of children in Odense alone, with changing partners, in a miserable environment? Or would she break out of that environment and create a better life for herself and her children?

She made a major decision: when she moved to Odense in October 1855, the first thing she did was to get married. The wedding to Niels Jørgensen took place in the cathedral Skt. Knuds Kirke on 29 November 1855. One of the best men was Christian Larsen, an instrument maker, and the other one was Johan Christopher Holm, the clogmaker, with whom her mother later lived.[63]

Half a year later, on 5 June 1856, Maren Kirstine moved in with Niels Jørgensen, who had settled in the carpenter's small house on the opposite side of the road between Nr. Lyndelse and Nr. Søby. Here their second child, Mathilde Sophie, was born on 12 June, and in October of the following year Maren Kirstine gave birth to their third child, Karen Marie.[64] In 1858 they moved again, first to Nr. Søby and shortly afterwards to a third dwelling on the road between the two villages.[65] Here Peter was born in October 1859 and Sophus in January 1861. Later that year the family moved to Uglehuset.

In general, it appears that the entire Nielsen family on both sides, far back and through its many branches, came from the area north, west and south of Odense or

A PLACE IN THE WORLD

from the city itself, but not much further than 15–20 km. It was this limited area within the old county of Odense that constituted the family's home territory; in the countryside, people married in the immediate vicinity, and in Odense there were visiting soldiers and journeymen who settled down or became fathers of children in the family.

Klaus Berntsen as a Role Model

However, it was not only through his family and neighbours that Nielsen acquired his values and worldview. It was also by experiencing the social and political conditions of the time and the strategies used to change or preserve them. Nielsen's upbringing took place in a period that can be seen as a long process of democratisation and liberation: from the political struggles of the 1840s to the adoption of the constitution in 1849 and the revision of the constitution in 1915, which gave (almost) free and equal suffrage, including women as well as servants. Many saw this as the fulfilment of the promises of the original constitution.

In this context, Klaus Berntsen, the advocate of private independent schools known as 'friskoler', played a real and important role. Only twenty-one years older than Nielsen, and a teacher at a 'friskole' in the neighbouring village of Højby, he eventually became prime minister in the government that prepared the provisions for the constitutional reform in 1910–13. In both word and deed, he showed that it was possible to achieve success despite a humble background and, not least, how to do it. In many ways, he was a role model for Nielsen. Unlike Hans Christian Andersen and the linguist Rasmus Rask, who were also boys from Fyn and who achieved a great deal in life, Berntsen was a contemporary of Nielsen. Throughout his career, he embodied the movement that, through long-term political and organisational work, established an alternative to the prevailing conditions: politically through the Liberal Party, Venstre, intellectually in the private independent schools and the so-called 'high school movement', and spiritually in Grundtvigianism.

Nielsen had known Klaus Berntsen since childhood and maintained a close relationship with him throughout his life. In *My Childhood*, Nielsen notes the results of Berntsen's lectures:

> Before Johannes Clausen [came to] Nr. Lyndelse [as pastor in 1877], the spiritual life of a large area was at a low ebb. At Højby, however, Klaus Berntsen was a free-school teacher, and occasionally we would all go and hear him speak in the parish hall. He had a most extraordinary gift of infusing warmth and feeling into people's minds … by [his] popular yet distinguished appeal. … Klaus Berntsen treated people like neglected plants that have had neither water nor light, and my brothers and sisters would be quite transformed when they came home from one of his lectures.[66]

Enlightenment is the key word. In general terms, Nielsen grew up in an area where the ideals and practices of the Enlightenment had become widely accepted. The area around Odense was well-ordered and well-structured, and if we exclude Altona in the Duchies of Schleswig-Holstein, Odense was the second largest and most modern city in the realm until the middle of the nineteenth century. Agricultural, educational and administrative reforms had modernised society and most things were essentially in order. Everything was documented and conducted according to transparent rules: poverty relief, military service, real estate, debt repayment, inheritance, relocation, births, baptisms, confirmations and funerals. Power was exercised according to rules, not arbitrarily, and education was established and functioning.

Enlightenment, however, is more than rational administration and modernisation. It is also the education of the people. The school reform of 1814 was a direct result of the Age of Enlightenment, when a school commission set up in 1789 had completed its legislative work and introduced seven years of compulsory education for all. The awareness that things had been different was still alive: Berntsen recounts in his memoirs that his father never went to school, but instead had to serve eight years in the army and only learned what his mother could teach him.[67] Nielsen's father could read, write and do sums easily. The progress made in educating the population was thus experienced in a vivid and concrete way.

At the same time, the nineteenth century saw the emergence of spiritual revival movements that demanded a more personal relationship with faith. Ecclesiastically, both Grundtvigianism and the Evangelist movement of the Danish Lutheran Church arose from a rebellion against a Church that was perceived as both conservative and rationalist. It was as much a continuation of the Enlightenment as it was a reaction to it. On Fyn, Grundtvigianism was represented by people such as Rev. Birkedal in Ryslinge and Christen Kold, who started his first 'friskole' in Dalby near Kerteminde.[68]

The Grundtvigian movement was also in favour of parochial autonomy. They wanted to be able to choose their own pastor, which could be done either by forming an independent or an electorate congregation or by freeing themselves from parochial ties. Similarly, the basis for private independent schools was that they would enable people to break free from the public school system, in which the pastor was the supervisor, and allow them to choose their own teachers and teaching methods. The legal basis for this was established in 1855.[69] These congregations were strong on Fyn, and the independent schools in particular established a stronghold here that still exists today. Almost all the smaller towns on Fyn still have a 'friskole'.

At its heart, the movement also represents a profound process of democratisation and self-organisation. The breadth of the movement is demonstrated by the fact that it included not only independent schools and high schools, but also lecture and reading societies, shooting clubs, village halls and, as in Højby, an evening school for the local population. The schools, congregations and societies were built from the ground up and supported by people who shared the same views. Similarly, the co-operative movement with local dairies, slaughterhouses and co-operative societies is based on self-organisation, on the democratic idea of 'one man, one vote' as opposed to the preferred organisation of capital in limited companies. The co-operative movement is the economic companion to the liberation and love of independence that could be achieved by organised communities.

Courses at the evening school in Højby were held during the winter season and consisted partly of lectures and partly of readings of Danish and Norwegian literature.[70] The way in which Nielsen describes his meeting with Berntsen shows that it was not a question of faith or schooling, but rather a broad, enlightening revival of the spiritual life of the region. People were encouraged. Continuing Kold's and Grundtvig's emphasis on the personal narrative, the living word was the cornerstone of all teaching. Berntsen's audiences left with the experience of having been lifted out of their everyday lives and opened to new thoughts.

It may be difficult to imagine how Berntsen achieved this effect. But we have a first-hand account of how he – through sincerity, recitation and communal singing – created a strong sense of community among those who attended. One of the locals, Mads Bødker, wrote in a letter to Berntsen:

> Oh, how vivid it is to me, the first time I was with you and the little flock you had gathered in the little classroom. I was somewhat anxious because I was then mostly reckoned as one of the bullies. I stayed as close to the door as possible; what you read that evening I don't remember and of the songs that were sung I only remember the last one, it was 'Dejlig er Jorden'. Yes, when it was sung I felt that now I had come to the flock I desired …[71]

Berntsen was also responsible for a number of other activities in Højby: one evening a week he would gather the elderly for Bible reading, and he led a choral society. He was also chairman of Højby Shooting Club, and describes how they occasionally organised evening entertainments 'with singing, music and fencing. "Niels Maler", father of the composer Carl Nielsen, and "Blinde-Anders" [Jacobsen] played duets; the latter also recited various poems and sang to his own accompaniment'.[72] Berntsen also remembers that as a boy Nielsen played with his father at balls and meetings at the shooting club.[73]

It was Nielsen's father who first had a connection with Berntsen. When Højby Shooting Club wanted to have a march, they asked Niels Jørgensen to compose it. Niels Jørgensen recorded in his notebook that he played at a so-called 'Fanefest', a festival at the shooting club. The event took place at the shooting club in Højby on

9 September 1866, and it was undoubtedly for this occasion that he wrote the *Højby Skyttemarch*. Much later, Nielsen arranged for the march to be played for Berntsen by a military band in Copenhagen when Berntsen was Minister of Defence.[74] The close relationship of trust between Berntsen and Nielsen's father is also reflected in the fact that Niels Jørgensen, who was otherwise very reluctant to ask anyone for anything, later suggested that Nielsen speak to Berntsen about the old-age pension, as 'we could probably also apply for it … without it harming our reputation'.[75]

Apparently there was never any talk of Nielsen attending a 'friskole', despite the family's connection with Berntsen, who, in addition to leading the 'friskole' in Højby, was also involved in founding the one in Nr. Lyndelse in 1873.[76] It is clear that they could not afford it. Carl's two youngest siblings, Julie and Valdemar, attended the 'friskole' in Nr. Lyndelse, as by then most of the children had left home and the family's finances had improved.

Nevertheless, the connection with Berntsen remained important to Nielsen throughout his life. On a personal level, this was particularly evident on two occasions. The first was Nielsen's admission to the Academy of Music in Copenhagen, for which Berntsen played a role by using his connections with Niels W. Gade and by helping to secure Nielsen's livelihood – and probably also by encouraging him to apply. The other occasion was much later and was in connection with Nielsen's negotiations with The Royal Theatre around 1905 and 1908, when Berntsen, as an influential member of parliament, pulled the strings behind the scenes.[77]

But another, equally important, aspect is the broad cultural influence that Nielsen received from Berntsen. The Grundtvigian-Koldian school and the Enlightenment movement, which Berntsen represented, had a lasting influence on the intellectual life of Nielsen's home region and thus on the basic views on life that he carried with him from his youth. Nielsen also emphasises this: 'And as for me, I loved and admired this man who in my youth stirred my mental life, not only by what he said … but by his whole personality'.[78] Berntsen was a real role model for Nielsen, and the inner thoughts of Grundtvig and Kold worked primarily through the power of example. It seems that Nielsen found a kindred spirit in Kold late in life. When he read Berntsen's memoirs in 1922, he remarked: 'I would like to know more about Kold; he must have been quite interesting.'[79]

What was special about Berntsen was that he took on important positions at an unusually young age, helping to build a movement from scratch. In 1862, Kold had personally asked the very young Berntsen to lead the almost newly established 'friskole' in Højby. At that time there were only ten pupils and the teacher took it in turns to live with the farmers associated with the school. During the first few years the school met with massive resistance, and it was only when the parish bailiff sent his child there that the mood changed. In 1869 Berntsen was able to inaugurate a new school building, and when he left the village in 1882 to establish a high school in Særslev on North Fyn, the 'friskole' had eighty pupils, while the municipal school had only ten.[80]

At the same time, Berntsen began a very early career as a member of the Liberal Party, Venstre. In 1867 the Parish Municipalities Act came into force, and democratically elected parish councils became the basis for local self-government. After the election, Berntsen was asked to take up the post of secretary to the parish council, a post usually held by the pastor, the parish clerk or a representative of the local conservative elite. Two years later he was elected to the Højby parish council and became its chairman at the age of twenty-six. In 1873 he was elected to Parliament and served, with a short interruption, until 1926. He still holds the record of having been the longest serving member of the Danish Parliament, Folketinget.[81]

Nielsen's political views could be explained by his upbringing in a region where there was a strong social movement rooted in the population. This can be seen in the strong network of societies, independent schools, Grundtvigian congregations and high schools, and politically through Venstre, the Liberal Party. Not unlike the labour movement, Venstre was a tight-knit movement with a high degree of unity, created by consciously breaking out of a traditional pattern and becoming an opposition movement that was built from the ground up. Venstre was an opposition party that, despite many splits and internal conflicts, consisted of a pragmatic wing, to which Berntsen belonged, and a more radical, European-oriented wing led by the brothers Georg and Edvard Brandes. The latter wing finally established itself in 1905 as the independent Social Liberal Party, Det Radikale Venstre.

Nielsen grew up in Berntsen's circle and later, in Copenhagen, he entered radical and intellectual circles without distancing himself from his background. His brother Valdemar was a co-founder of Det Radikale Venstre and a member of parliament for eight years. Once, Carl and Valdemar spent a whole night in the parliament at Christiansborg while crucial political negotiations were taking place.[82] Although Nielsen had a strong social commitment, he was never part of the labour movement, nor did he speak as a social democrat. His descriptions of rural life show that it was not the social conditions that were most important to him, but the people. Conditions needed to be improved, but they were not the reason why people were as they were.

Musical Background and Education

In order to understand Nielsen's musical background, it is important to take a closer look at the musical craft he learned in his childhood. His father was a workman, that is, a painter and fiddler, which required professional knowledge and skill. In the same way that the children could take part in painting, and Albert eventually trained as a painter like his father, Carl and his brothers learned to play music. When their father needed, they assisted him on his music jobs, and in Carl's case this continued after he moved to Odense.[83] When he reflected on his childhood in 1905, it was clear that playing the violin was a central part of his early identity:

> at that time [i.e. when Nielsen was *c.* thirteen years old] I was really good on the violin, and that made me friends everywhere. In these years and until my 18th year I was very often with my father all over Fyn playing for parties, feasts and the like.[84]

His brother Sophus, four years his senior, also played the violin, and sometimes the two of them would be sent out to play alone when their father was otherwise occupied. Albert also played the violin and the cello when needed.[85] The youngest brother, Valdemar, mentioned how his father passed on his love of music to his children by playing the violin, and how Valdemar also went out to play music.[86] In *My Childhood*, Nielsen reflects on the fact that all his siblings were musical, and that it may not have been Carl himself who was the most talented.[87]

At the same time, it is important not to reproduce the naive image that Nielsen was trained as a rural musician in the sense that popular music was an ancient, shared, pristine rural musical tradition. Firstly, it is clear that his father and his musicians provided music that was needed in different social contexts in the area. It was mainly music for dancing, but also for other social occasions, such as weddings. On Fyn it was customary to march to church with the music leading the procession,[88] and here Niels Jørgensen played the cornet, but for dance music he usually played the violin; only when there were many musicians did he take the cornet. When it is said that he was a skilled and favoured dance musician who 'played with the measured beat of pistons in a steam-engine,'[89] it is the rhythmic life and precision of the dance musician that is meant. This is what makes the dance work and keeps it going, just as a good DJ does today.

Secondly, the many fiddlers' music books that have survived show that this was notated music and that the musicians were able to read and write music, even if they played many of the pieces by heart.[90] There are parts of this music, such as the lower violin parts, that were improvised according to a rehearsed and familiar practice, yet it is basically not improvised music. These are known pieces played according to accepted rules. Music notation in manuscript was both a tool for expanding the repertoire by notating new tunes and for preserving the familiar. The melodies in the manuscript music books differed from region to region, or even from musician to musician, but this was not so important when it came to performing the music. In those days, people would just adapt to one another.

The music was not only put down on paper, but was often composed by a particular musician. One example is the piece *Højby Skyttemarch*, composed by Nielsen's father, or some dances by Jørgen Felding, another local musician mentioned in

Nielsen's *My Childhood* as 'Jørgen Fællig'; in addition to composing music, Fællig or Felding was known for his ability to notate music by ear:

> When his competitors had procured the score of some new dance-music from Copenhagen or Germany and were playing it for the first time at feasts, he would ensconce himself in the ditch outside the farm with a sheet of music paper and write it down. A few days later he and his troupe would be heard playing it …[91]

The story tells us not only that this was a highly valued talent, but also that it was common in the region to import new dance music from music dealers in Copenhagen and Germany. New music was in great demand and also available from the several music dealers in Odense.

Nielsen mentions several times that he was first allowed to try his hand at the violin when he was about six years old.[92] He received basic instruction from his father, but from the age of eight or nine he also received lessons from Emil Petersen, the teacher in Nr. Lyndelse, 'properly and by reading music'.[93] This suggests that his father's teaching was in the nature of peer training, showing him how to play the violin. Petersen had a more systematic approach to teaching. This was not just because he had seen the boy's great musical talent. According to the Education Act of the time, one of the teacher's duties was to reward musically diligent children by giving them lessons on an instrument.[94] In his last year at school, when Nielsen had moved to Nr. Søby, he received no musical education. He mentions several times that he took the violin with him to school or practised on the instrument in the fields while herding cattle in the summer.[95] There is no doubt that the violin was his main instrument as a child.

Niels Jørgensen's career as a musician was at its height during the period from the 1860s to the 1880s. It is no coincidence that he is registered as a professional musician in the census of 1870, even though he is always listed as a painter in other official documents.[96] During the last years in Nr. Søby, that is until Maren Kirstine and he decided to join the children in the United States in 1891, he had a hard time managing music jobs.[97]

Jørgensen kept accounts of his income as a country-town musician during several periods. They reveal that he was a much sought-after musician. The accounts also provide us with an idea of the musical demands of the region. Over the course of a year from May 1865, he played at twenty-four weddings, eight so-called maternity parties and fifteen other celebrations in the area, typically seasonal events such as shrovetide parties, harvest festivals, Michaelmas and Christmas celebrations. In addition, he played at eighteen 'woodland balls' as well as balls at inns. He calculated that his total income was 242 Rigsdaler, twenty times the rent they paid. Some weeks there were weddings on Friday and Saturday, and in one particularly busy week in March 1866 he provided music for a ball at Fangel Inn on Friday, weddings on Satur-

ILL. 8. Højby Shooting Club parading through the village, led by Niels Jørgensen and Blind Anders. Frieze by Frands Johan Ring, *c.* 1941, in Højby Forsamlingshus.[98]

day and maternity celebrations on Sunday and Monday. It was quite normal for him to be away for several days at a time.[99] Being a musician was sometimes a hard life.

Jørgensen's regular fellow musicians formed the backbone of the group, but the size and composition of the ensemble varied according to the circumstances. Jørgensen often played in Fangel, where he had received his own musical training from his grandfather and other local musicians. The area he covered as a musician was mostly the villages south of Odense up to 10–15 kilometres from his home.

'Blind Anders', mentioned by Berntsen as one of the musicians Jørgensen worked with, was a central figure in the region's musical life. Anders Jacobsen, as he was baptised, was four years older than Nielsen's father. Blind from childhood, he was born to poor parents in Højby, but a schoolteacher and the local pastor took action and arranged for Anders to attend the Institute for the Blind in Copenhagen as a teenager, where he learned to play music. After finishing his education at the institute, he returned to Højby. He played the clarinet, but also the violin, flute, horn, tuba and ocarina. He was known both as an accomplished musician and as a lively storyteller who entertained at the feasts.[100] Occasionally he even arranged concerts or evening entertainments. He was a member of Højby Shooting Club and provided the music for the society's events;[101] later a mural frieze was painted in Højby's village hall showing Blind Anders and Jørgensen leading the marksmen.

The fifteen-years-younger Christian Larsen Bellinge, named after his home village, was another of Jørgensen's regular fellow musicians. As a young man, he had spent half a year in Copenhagen taking violin lessons from Valdemar Tofte, who would later become Nielsen's teacher at the Academy of Music.[102] Larsen was the youngest, but he carried on the tradition, and it was he who was later remembered in the region as one of those responsible for the dance music. Because of his training, he was able to play solo pieces and was highly respected for this. In the intervals between the dances, he would take his violin and play a solo, and everyone would fall silent.[103] There was indeed both an interest in and an awareness of the 'more serious music' among the ordinary people of the region.

A PLACE IN THE WORLD

Mads Pedersen, who lived in Nr. Søby, was also one of the local musicians with whom Jørgensen played.[104] Like Nielsen's father, Pedersen mastered both the violin and the cornet and also gave lessons. He had fought in the Second Schleswig War in 1864 and knew the bugle signals. It is told that Carl was sent by his father to Pedersen to practise bugle signals when he was preparing for the entrance examination as a military band musician.[105]

Playing in his father's ensemble, Nielsen was introduced to the musicians and their style of playing at an early age. At the same time, he learned what could be called practical musicianship. Whether he was playing with experienced musicians or with one of his brothers, he had to work within that specific context. It was through this experience that he acquired some of the norms, hierarchies and unwritten codes of musicianship.

From an early age, however, he was also aware that there was something beyond this tradition-bound music. Larsen's solos were one thing, but through his father's and mother's families he came into contact with the musical community in Odense. Once, when he and his mother went to collect his father's violin from the instrument maker Larsen in Odense, they were buttonholed by a distinguished looking gentleman who mocked Carl for carrying a finely decorated violin case with inlaid mother-of-pearl. His mother told Carl that the old man was the gunsmith Wittrup, who himself gave violin lessons.[106]

A more direct connection was his uncle mentioned above, the nearly blind Hans Andersen, who was organist at Dalum Kirke in Odense. Carl and his mother visited him in Odense and the uncle also called on them in Nr. Lyndelse. He died when Carl was fifteen years old. It was at his uncle's house that Nielsen saw a real piano for the first time, and of course he had to try it out. He remembers it as a great experience. He may even have listened to his uncle play.[107] Another early musical experience was with the amateur orchestra Braga. This was a group of local farmers, teachers and musicians, some of whom also played dance music. In the literature on Nielsen, Braga is often described as playing music by Mozart, Haydn and Beethoven, although this was in fact an absolute exception. They did play 'higher' music, but certainly not the more extensive works; rather, it was orchestral music similar to the lighter genres played by Odense's musical directors in the city's entertainment life. The repertoire of the surviving orchestral material includes marches, waltzes, polkas and other dances by Hans Christian Lumbye, Johann Strauss and others, especially Austrian composers. Overtures and excerpts from popular operas were also performed. Concerts of this kind were common in Odense, although in the countryside a society like Braga's was a rare sight.[108]

Sometimes he would come along when Braga was playing at a venue further away, and he remembers being allowed to play the triangle in Lumbye's *Dagmar Polka* at one of the orchestra's concerts. He describes it as his debut, which in this context suggests that he considered it to be the first time he had played in a real concert.

ILL. 9. Braga was founded at the latest in 1873, and the first documented concert took place at the Verninge Inn on 4 January the following year. The concerts were held in the local inns and were always advertised as concerts followed by a few hours of dancing. Braga consisted of up to fourteen musicians. In a photograph from around 1877, the musicians are Christian Larsen Bellinge with a violin, Niels Jørgensen with a trumpet, Mads Pedersen with a cornet and Carl's older brother Albert with a cello. Before Nielsen moved to Odense, a concert was held at Nørre Lyndelse Inn at least once a year, which he probably attended.[109]

According to Nielsen, 'they were some of the finest hours of my life and I was delighted and happy the whole of that night'.[110] Even though they were not playing Mozart, it was important for him to attend the concerts. It was an entry into a part of the musical world to which he had previously had no direct access.

In the beginning, the arrow did not point in this direction. The old inn in Ellinge, one of the places where Braga performed, had a small grocery shop at one end of the building. It was here that Nielsen's father apprenticed Albert and then Carl to the shopkeeper. After two or three months the shopkeeper, who was suffering from tuberculosis, went bankrupt and Carl was left without an apprenticeship.[111] Exactly how he heard about the vacancy in the military band is somewhat unclear, as no one has been able to find an announcement or date for the entrance examination. Nielsen's version is probably correct: 'my father [had] heard there was a vacancy for a regimental bugler in the 16th Battalion at Odense'.[112] The network of musicians worked.

Chapter 2

SYMPHONIES ARE FICTION

When writing or reading a book about Nielsen, it is worth considering how the role of the composer should be understood: what is he or she doing when composing? A very common view, stemming from nineteenth-century popular aesthetics, is that composers express their inner selves. According to this view, musical works – at least those that are not composed with a particular practical purpose in mind – are to be understood as autobiographical fragments.[1] Composers express *themselves*, it is said.

However, studying a composer in this way is also an approach that has some obvious limitations. One would soon come up short if one thought of a composer solely as a medium or channel through which inspiration flows. Yet the composer must be understood as a professional, creative person. There is no reason to believe that they are any less conscious of their means of expression than a novelist for instance.

There are indeed statements by Nielsen that seem to support the view that the act of composing is a partly unconscious process. While working on his opera *Maskarade*, he wrote:

> Sometimes I have the feeling that I'm not myself at all – Carl August Nielsen – but only like an open pipe through which a stream of music flows, moved by gentle yet strong forces in a kind of blissful oscillation. At such times it's bliss to be a musician, believe me.[2]

He used the same image in 1922 when he sent three newly composed songs to the folk high school principal, Harald Balslev:

> I feel so strongly about the popular song that when I write such a melody it's as if it's not me composing, but friends, relatives and the people of the country who want it thus, and it comes of its own accord and I'm only the channel through which the stream flows.[3]

Such descriptions imply in part that he was in a state of what would today be called flow, and in part that in such situations he felt connected to something greater than himself. There are many instances where Nielsen refers to music in this way, as if it were an independent force or an undercurrent that one might come into contact with and express. In other situations, when he feels that he has achieved the popular tone, he describes it as if he is in touch with some kind of 'soul of the people', which then manifests itself in his songs. But what he really experiences is being in touch with his own creative powers. He composes unhindered, completely focused on the task at hand, forgetting the world around him.

It is obvious that Nielsen consciously uses specific musical means in many of the genres in which he composes. Thus, when writing music for a play, he has to tailor a particular character or mood that will work in that particular place in the play. When composing a song, Nielsen works on finding the musical clothing or staging that he feels will best highlight and interpret the lyrics. Similarly, when working on an opera, he will have certain characters in mind and create connections, contrasts and variety that will shape the theatrical experience as he imagines it. Even when writing a simple popular song, he will choose certain musical means and deliberately ignore others. He certainly knows what he is doing.

What happens then, when composing in those genres in which there is no tangible effect or mood to be achieved? How should we understand the work of the composer when he can compose freely, so to speak?

The Conflict

In this case, one possible approach would be to consider symphonies, and instrumental music in general, on a par with fiction. This involves viewing the composer as someone who does not express him or herself more or less unconsciously; rather, the composer is a creator who, similar to the author of a novel, consciously frames a course, a text, a narrative – but how?[4]

Nielsen grew up at a time and in a musical culture in which the nineteenth-century concept of form was a common framework for all musicians. The understanding that instrumental music consists of form and content, and that the latter is shaped by themes and their development, pervades the academic as well as the more popular music literature of the time. Both musicians and audiences were therefore educated to be able to identify the themes of a piece of music. Contemporary concert guides and programmes used this perception of listening to music to describe and introduce a symphony. Nielsen also used this approach when introducing his own works.[5]

An integral part of this approach to listening was the attribution of qualities to themes, almost invariably explained by the inclusion of a characteristic descriptive adjective. In simple movements a single theme would suffice, but in larger movements several subject themes are most often employed to provide contrast and variety. This can be seen most clearly in the sonata form, which usually constitutes the framework for the first movement of a sonata or symphony. The form was developed to include two subject themes that were not only in different keys, but also had their own individual character. As a standard, first subject themes were described as vigorous and second subject themes as lyrical – these characteristics were associated with masculine and feminine qualities.[6]

Sonata form was considered the most developed form according to the perception of the time and the music literature. It is suitable for a progression of some length because it has a built-in flexibility in which the individual parts can be expanded or modified. The listener is able to follow, because differences are based on well-known basic premises and models.

This is not to say that Nielsen assumed a schematic understanding of form and composed according to textbook models. Far from it. In the second half of the nineteenth century, a composer who adopted a schematic approach was regarded as scholastic or pedantic and was therefore seldom held in high esteem. It cannot be ignored, however, that Nielsen adopts and internalises the underlying principles, which in a more abstract sense might be termed 'sonata form thinking'. The principles that govern the form work at a deeper level. Throughout his career, he applies these basic ways of thinking and constructing form, and in order to explain the line of reasoning, it is necessary to cut to the chase and describe some fundamental features. Reality, of course, is more refined.

The principles of the sonata form were formulated in the mid-nineteenth century according to an aesthetic ideal inspired by Viennese Classical music. The Viennese Classical period, and Beethoven's music in particular, became the preferred object of study from which principles were derived and exemplified in textbooks.[7] A fundamental premise of Classical-oriented aesthetics is the pursuit of 'balance' and 'unity'. At the same time, however, there are always built-in conflicts, such as the contrast between the first and second subject themes. To achieve balance and unity, the conflicts have to be resolved, and this is done at the end of the movement, where the themes are usually in the same key. This kind of abstract conflict management is absolutely fundamental to the sonata form way of thinking. You introduce a conflict and you resolve it.

Once the norm of conflict and resolution has been established, it is possible to challenge it. This opens up the possibility that conflicts may not be resolved, or only partially resolved. Because both audiences and composers knew the norm, composers of Nielsen's generation and later were given some latitude to articulate that the modern world is not harmonious and conflict-free. The way is thus paved for the musical expression of 'imbalance' and 'fragmentation' – qualities that correspond to an aesthetic that seeks to bring the conditions of modernity into view. It offers musical and formal possibilities that have been exploited in the production of symphonies in both the Romantic and modern periods.

The Narrative

However, this is only one side of the issue. Another parallel with fiction is the nature of the narrative. The starting point is that music consists of recognisable themes, so that the listener can hear when they appear and follow what happens to them along the way. Themes must therefore be concise enough for the listener to discover and remember them immediately. It is an approach that characterises the composer's and the listener's way of experiencing music.

In such an understanding of narrative, themes function in a similar way to 'characters' in a play or novel.[8] These characters can be experienced as fictional persons – that is, as performing and acting and undergoing transformation. Once this function of the theme as a 'musical individual' is established in the listener's consciousness, the composer can begin to play with it. It becomes a basic model on a par with the principle of conflicts that are resolved (or not).

Because of the concise and recognisable themes, it is possible to experience an orchestral movement as a narrative process – as a story. When there are two themes, they work not only as contrasts or conflicting material, but also as elements in a temporal progression. The experience of form becomes a process. Similar to a stage play, the musical themes interact with each other just like characters in a play. The interactions between them become part of the listening experience.

As a composer, Nielsen takes his point of departure from these conventions. His themes are presented and staged in such a way that they are easily recognisable: here comes a theme. However, when he sometimes does not do this, but lets a theme appear gradually, he does so in the knowledge that the audience expects one to appear. First subject themes usually have a strong character and often an open ending, so they prepare the ground for development. When it comes to second subject themes, he tends to work with those that are more singable, coherent and stable than first subject themes, but that nevertheless have an immediately recognisable character for Nielsen's contemporaries: ah, a second subject theme. There is also a tendency for Nielsen's second subject themes to become absolutely pivotal, often providing the power necessary to make a symphony work.

It is in dealing with these two elements – the subject of conflict and the narrative – that the composer, like the novelist, emerges as an autonomous creator of musical artefacts comparable to fiction. He creates narratives in music of which he himself is a master. And Nielsen is an outstanding narrator.

Chapter 3

MUSICIAN IN ODENSE

Nielsen's time in Odense was to influence the formative years of his youth, between the ages of fourteen and eighteen. The mere fact that he was living in a city opened up new possibilities. 'It was new for me, who came from a small village, to be in a city as big as Odense,' he would later say.[1] There is no doubt that it was a turning point for Nielsen when he passed the audition for the army bugler in the summer of 1879.[2] It had become a family matter to get the future on track. When his father heard of the vacancy, 'we agreed that I should practise the trumpet diligently and register for the competition,' Nielsen recalled.[3] As a member of the military music band, he lived the life of a professional musician in an environment with experienced colleagues, including several Germans who had arrived in Odense when their military units were transferred from Holstein. They formed the nucleus of the city's musical life, of which Nielsen became a part.

A Provincial and Garrison Town

What kind of city did Nielsen move to? Odense was not just the nearest market town to where he grew up. When he moved there in 1879, Odense was the third largest city in the country, with around 20,000 inhabitants. Although it had been overtaken by Aarhus in terms of population by 1870, Odense was the province's most important cultural centre and the country's second largest industrial city.[4]

In the period up to 1848, successive crown princes held the title of Governor of Fyn and Langeland and used Odense Slot as their residence. The unique title of governor was created in 1814 and was not used anywhere else in the country. In this way, Odense was closely linked to the capital. It was not without reason that the city on Fyn was nicknamed 'Little Copenhagen'.

Odense was largely a garrison town. When Nielsen arrived, it was home to three infantry battalions, the Fifth, Sixteenth and Twenty-sixth, the first two of which had a music band. Nielsen was enlisted on 1 November 1879 as 'Musician V' in the Third Company of the Sixteenth Battalion on probation. In addition to the infantry, there was also a dragoon regiment, and in total almost a thousand of the townspeople were connected with the armed forces.[5] The number of craftsmen and day labourers exceeded this figure, but the military as a whole was the city's largest employer. In

ILL. 1. The members of the battalion's music band were divided into five ranks, and on 1 November 1879 Nielsen was placed at the bottom of the hierarchy as 'Musician V', corresponding to the rank of lance corporal. On 1 November 1883 he was promoted to 'Musician IV' (equivalent to corporal) and two months later, on 31 December 1883, he was relieved of his duties.

1878 a barracks was built for the dragoon regiment, but there were no barracks for the infantry. The private soldiers therefore billeted in the homes of local townspeople and were part of the daily life of the city. The infantry's military activities took place at between ten and fifteen different locations, including the drill house in Nørregade and its grounds on Sdr. Boulevard.[6]

For centuries Odense had been the trading centre of the region, and in the second half of the nineteenth century the city's industry grew. From the 1870s, Odense had four large iron foundries that produced agricultural machinery, for example. A number of specialised factories were established during this period, such as that of the pioneer Hans Demant, who started producing sewing machines in the 1860s. His family would turn out to be of great importance to Nielsen. The city's textile industry was also considerable and, in 1869, Morten Kisbye Brandt founded his clothing factory, which today houses the Brandt Art Museum.[7]

The industrial boom was supported by the city's infrastructure. The construction of the Odense Canal in 1804 made it possible for ships to enter the city, and in the second half of the nineteenth century the port played an important role in the export of grain, butter and pork. The construction of the railway through Odense in 1868 also had a major impact on the city's external relations.[8] Its status as the region's capital and centre of innovation and trade was celebrated in 1885 with Den Fynske Industri- og Landbrugsudstilling (Fyn's Industrial and Agricultural Exhibition), which attracted more than 1,100 exhibitors.[9] Odense was an important city.

It was, furthermore, a town with close relations in Europe. Fyn was a neighbour of the Duchies of Schleswig and Holstein, and at a time when shipping was the main means of transport, there were close links between these parts of the country. Since the Middle Ages, the cattle trade had created a key route from the duchies via Assens to Odense.[10] In the 1870s, seven annual livestock markets were held in the town.[11] Odense's position meant that it was steeped in traditions, including contacts with the south, and consequently the townspeople had a vision that was shaped by a European perspective.

In the second half of the nineteenth century, foreign goods were in demand and the city's connections enabled merchants to emulate fashion trends in European metropolises. In Odense, specialised boutiques with all kinds of wares increasingly dominated the townscape. Most of the boutiques were located on the city's main streets, Albani Torv, Klingenberg, Klaregade and Kongensgade.[12] When Hans Christian Andersen was made an honorary citizen of Odense in December 1867, he visited what he himself described as 'the most elegant grocer in town … whose boutique has one large window pane just like those in Paris'.[13] In 1866 and the following year, he had been in the French capital and was therefore able to recognise the message the Odense grocer was trying to convey.[14]

The townscape was also influenced by French architecture. In 1873–74, a large modern emporium was built on Flakhaven, opposite the town hall. Just in front of the

ILL. 2. Flakhaven, Odense. Lendorf's emporium was built in 1873–74 in the centre of the town square, Flakhaven. It was designed by the architect Carl Lendorf in the French Renaissance style. The design, which later dominated the Magasin du Nord on Kongens Nytorv in Copenhagen, was inspired by stylistic elements from the revival of the historical trend called 'Europeanism'.[16] Flakhaven's emporium included a bookshop, a chemist's, a café, a restaurant, a photographic studio and a shoe shop.

emporium, Nielsen had stood with the regimental corps and played music in front of Colonel Zahlmann's residence.[15] The area around Flakhaven was not only one of the city's central trading places; it was also where the soldiers carried out their daily duties. The infantrymen were stationed at the town hall, where they had their main guard. It also housed the local court and the prison. A reveille was sounded every morning and a retreat every evening in front of the main guard, and in the same square the corps gave public concerts for the benefit of passers-by. At certain times of the week, it became a place where the townspeople could listen to music, whether they were actively listening or just passing by on an errand. The square became a musical venue.

Nielsen's Odense

When Nielsen moved to Odense, the soldiers were quartered in the town. As a musician, he was employed with the rank of lance-corporal, and like privates they were, in principle, allocated accommodation in the private homes of the townspeople. It is not entirely clear whether this was the case in practice. There is much evidence to suggest that the young musicians in the corps received special attention. It is clear, however, that in 1880 his commanding officer, Colonel Zahlmann, personally requested that Carl and two other musicians be given accommodation. A practical reason for the colonel's intervention may have been that the musicians needed to live in a place where they could play.[17]

Nielsen's first accommodation, where he only stayed for a few months, seems to have been arranged by his parents, for according to Nielsen he stayed with a family

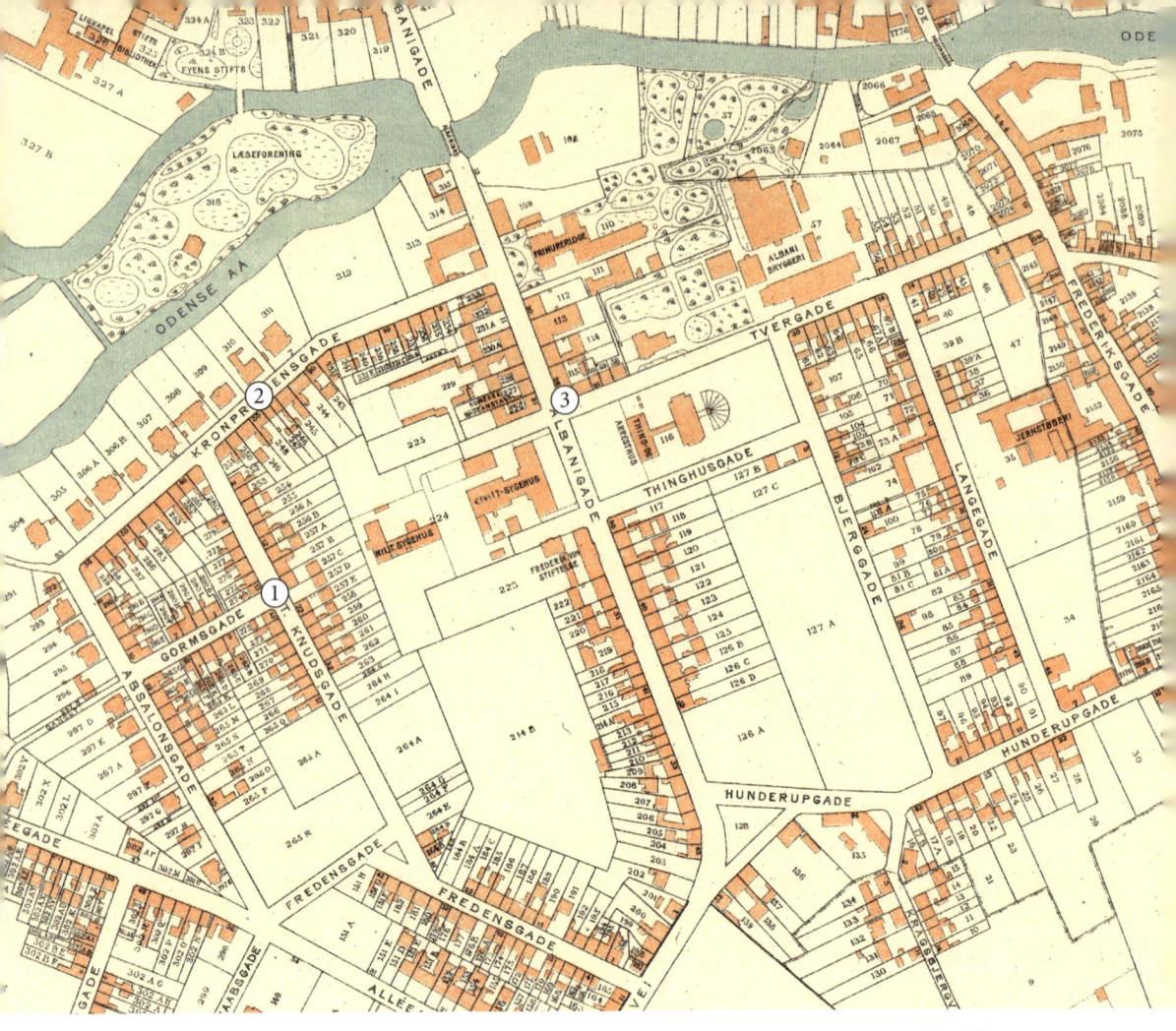

ILL. 3. Nielsen lived most of his time in Odense in the neighbourhoods south of the river. Until the summer of 1880 he lived in ① 13 Skt. Knudsgade; ② then a couple of months in 28 (now 30) Kronprinsensgade; and ③ from November 1880 in 18 Albanigade, which later became no. 26.[18]

of glaziers they knew.[19] After Christmas he was given a room at 13 Skt. Knuds Gade, which he shared with another band musician who was unclean and played out of tune, so it was not a success. Nielsen had to use the regimental rooms to practise his music.[20] He stayed at Skt. Knuds Gade until he had to take part in the field exercise at Hald near Viborg in mid-June 1880.[21] When he returned from Hald at the end of July, the colonel arranged for Nielsen to be accommodated in the house on Kronprinsensgade that is now no. 30. He was pleased with the quarters, as they were clean and tidy and provided good opportunities to play both the violin and the trombone.[22]

During the first year he lived in three different places, but from November 1880 he had more permanent lodgings, which he shared with his brother Albert. The house where they rented two rooms was in Albanigade, on the corner of Tværgade.

This time he was apparently allowed to choose where he wanted to live, and he stayed at this address until he moved to Copenhagen.[23] Significantly, all the places he lived were south of the river in Odense, an area that was in the process of being parcelled out and developed. This meant that Nielsen lived in newly built houses and not in the old part of Odense where his mother had grown up.[24]

The Sixteenth Battalion, of which Nielsen was a member, consisted of four companies, each with two 'fiddlers' – as army musicians were called referring instrumentalists in general – and one, two or three substitutes. In all, the battalion had eight musicians and up to seven substitutes, a corps size prescribed by the Army Act of 1867. The Act also stipulated that battalions should be deployed in pairs.

During the First Schleswig War in 1848–50, the Danish army found that a large number of German soldiers in Schleswig and Holstein had joined the rebel army. It was therefore decided to move these troops out of the duchies, and the Fifth Battalion moved from Rendsburg to Odense in 1859. The Sixteenth Battalion also left Rendsburg and spent some time in Copenhagen before moving to Odense, where it remained with the Fifth Battalion as a result of the aforementioned Army Act. Thus the music bands of the two battalions could play together when needed.[25]

The North German musicians who moved to Odense with the battalions in 1859 and 1867 continued to form the backbone of military music in the city when Nielsen began his daily routine there. Among the musicians in the Sixteenth Battalion were two from Holstein, Johannes Schreiber and Johannes Abel, who had been with the battalion in Copenhagen from 1859 to 1867. When they arrived in Odense, they were reunited with Johannes Simon, Friedrich Gundlach, Johan Lantow, Johan Schwartz and Georg Sass, with whom they had played together in Rendsburg.

Although they were often referred to collectively as 'Holsteiners', they came from the vast area surrounding the important garrison town of Rendsburg, which lay on the border between the Duchies of Schleswig and Holstein. Gundlach, Lantow and Schwartz came from the Duchy of Mecklenburg to the east of Holstein and had chosen to follow the army and their pro-Danish colleagues to Odense, where they settled with their families and became part of the musical life of the market town.[26] In addition to his military service, Schreiber earned his living as a party musician and as the leader of the orchestra at the restaurant Carlshaab.[27] Simon was also an active figure in musical life, for example as music director at Odense Theatre for several periods.[28] He was even in charge of the so-called 'Koncert a la Boulevard' at Hotel Skt. Knud, a type of musical entertainment that became very popular in large European cities from the mid-nineteenth century, inspired by the Parisian 'cafés chantants'.[29]

The surrounding area also benefited from the 'Holsteiners'. Gundlach offered his services as a piano tuner, assuring customers that the service could be carried out 'both in town and in the country'. He also arranged music and was the music director of the Kerteminde Theatre, as well as being a guitar and singing teacher.[30] If rural musicians needed suitable music, Gundlach offered to arrange 'new dances … in any instrumentation'.[31] Under the heading 'Music for Rural Musicians', Gundlach advertised that he would accept commissions and arrange dances, marches and arias from Offenbach's *La belle Hélène*.[32]

The musicians from Holstein became role models for Nielsen. These somewhat older musicians struck him as experienced and respectable, and he felt honoured when they took the time to talk to him.[33] He received one-to-one tuition from Schreiber, who instilled in the boy a fear of not being able to live up to expectations in terms of musical ability, as well as a fear of getting his fingers slapped.[34] The lessons lasted three months, starting every morning at nine. Schreiber then reports to the battalion commander that 'Musician V., Nielsen, has made good progress in both signal-blowing and music in the short time he has been in service; it is therefore believed that he can be accepted as a permanent "fiddler"'.[35] The fear of inadequacy was thus unfounded.

Military band musicians also had to learn military skills. After a three-month probationary period, Nielsen applied to the company commander to begin military service immediately if he was hired on a permanent basis.[36] His request was granted, and during the following period he had to attend a basic military course with the regular conscripts.

Nielsen was in a special situation, however, since he was also employed on a permanent basis, which was not the case for privates. In 1880, and for the next two years, Nielsen attended the lance-corporal school, which was not part of the conscription process, but a further training course for permanent employees. At the school he received instruction in drill, field service, weapons training and other military disciplines. However, the school was also designed to improve the soldiers' literacy skills, with four hours a week devoted to reading and four to arithmetic.[37] In addition to his schooling, Nielsen continued to receive music lessons from Schreiber.[38]

When the new Army Act of 1880 was introduced, battalions were reorganised and merged into regiments. As a result, Nielsen was transferred to the staff of the new Sixth Regiment on 1 November 1880. This meant that the number of military music bands – and hence band musicians – across the country was reduced. Although this also led to cutbacks in Odense, it had a different effect on Nielsen. Until then he had been used to playing in the battalion's large orchestra of eight musicians and occasionally with the Fifth Battalion. Now that the two battalions had been merged, the regiment formed a military band consisting of nineteen musicians and a bandmaster as leader.

Nielsen's first performance with the regimental orchestra was an experience he later described as powerful and sensuous:

> … when the conductor, Mr. Simon, gave the sign and the whole orchestra came in with a *fortissimo*, I nearly sank to my knees at the dreadful din made by all the

brasses and drums. It was like being thrown into a raging sea inhabited by all sorts of monsters that were dashing the spray over one another, crying and screaming, pushing and buffeting and pulling one another's tails in one mighty uproar. At the end of the first item – a military march – I was sweating like a galley-slave …[39]

It seems that Nielsen was not yet accustomed to the nineteen-member orchestra, nor to the sound of the brass, nor to the ensemble playing. This was probably due to the fact that the rehearsals took place in a room that, according to Nielsen, was not very large. Brass instruments are ideal for playing outdoors, but indoors in enclosed spaces they can have a piercing and – to Nielsen's ear – overpowering sound. The composition of the music band could vary, and Nielsen recalls that there were piccolo cornets, cornets, trumpets, alto trombones, tenor trombones, tuba, bass and side drums, and a triangle.[40] This is confirmed by a study of the regiment's surviving music, which also shows that the number of instruments could vary.[41] Most arrangements include two trumpets, while the number of cornets varies from two to three, depending on whether there are one or two piccolos. The number of trombones and tubas could also vary. Thus, musicians were used to switching from one instrument to another.

Regimental Bandsman

As a bugler, Nielsen was trained to blow signals. The purpose of the loud bugle was to convey important information over long distances, whether to wake soldiers in the morning or to give orders in the field. The instrument was first and foremost a means of communication.

There is no doubt that blowing signals was demanding, but not so much because of the musical content of the signals: the melodies were often short and simple in structure. Moreover, they consisted entirely of natural tones, that is, the notes that a bugle without valves could produce when the musician varied the airflow and the position of the lips. The actual execution of the signals was apparently no problem either. More importantly, Nielsen recalled that 'the one thing I found difficult was to remember what the various signals meant'.[42] This is hardly surprising. The army used up to ninety different signals, and it must have been difficult to distinguish between them and get them in the right order. To help memorise the signals and their meaning, Nielsen and his colleagues added lyrics to some of the tunes.[43]

The reveille sounded by the main guard in the mornings was easy to remember and recognise, even for civilians who passed by the main square in the early mornings. The tune was embedded in the memory through the many weekly repetitions.

Field signals, on the other hand, varied according to the nature of the command. Each had its own meaning and was used to communicate over long distances and

ILL. 4. Signals identifying the four companies, with additional text to help remember their meaning. The signals are from *My Childhood*, in which Nielsen notated the distinctive signals for the four companies.

to command the troops. An order might consist of a 'signature tune', unique to each brigade, regiment, battalion or company, which identified the recipient of the order. This was followed by the 'execution signal', which told the unit what to do.

During the field exercise at Hald in 1880, Nielsen, who was accompanying the general, was ordered to sound the signal for the command 'Twenty-Sixth Battalion to the Right'.[44] An ingenious little music book, printed in oblong format, contained all the most important signals to be memorised, and when used it was positioned so that the spine was up and horizontal, making it easier to turn the pages with one hand. Yet it took time to find the right pages in the book, and Nielsen was embarrassed when the general had to wait for him. Nielsen recalls that it was the only time during the Hald exercise that he had to flip through the music book to find the right signal. By this time he had been in the battalion for well over half a year, but it was perhaps the first time he had played the combination of these two signals.[45]

ILL. 5. During Nielsen's time as bugler in Odense, numerous small books of signals were published. The illustration shows the two signals he was asked to sound by the general during the exercise at Hald.[46]

Playing the horn is a lonely job. You are the one everyone is listening to. The bugler must act with confidence and be able to transmit the message clearly and unmistakably. It requires a mixture of musical ability and strong mental resources, which must have shaped the fourteen-year-old Nielsen and given him valuable experience. As he describes it, it was with a sense of courage that he played the morning reveille.[47] Only two trumpeters could sound the signal satisfactorily, giving the impression that his pride in the honourable duty overcame his nervousness at having to play for the whole town. It was important for Nielsen to be able to give a satisfactory performance.

In his eagerness to fulfil the expectations, he sometimes made mistakes that left a lasting impression on his memory. Even many years later Nielsen recounted that while playing a solo passage in Ferdinand Hérold's overture to the opera *Zampa*: 'I was so nearly bursting with self-importance I tooted it out so lustily that the trombone note cracked twice'.[48] On another occasion, when he arrived late to sound the reveille and was prevented from playing it, he took his dereliction of duty so seriously that he could neither eat nor sleep.[49]

Music was an important part of the soldiers' daily lives. After a long and exhausting day of field exercises in the terrain around Odense, the tired soldiers would get the necessary energy to return to the centre of the town when the military band came to greet them. One of the band's duties was to accompany the battalions as they marched home along the country roads.[50] Playing a regular duple time, the purpose of the band was to get the marching soldiers to keep the pace and their spirits up.

The corps also had to line up for parades in the town and for events in which the regiment took part and act as a sound image. Joseph Roth's novel *The Radetzky March*, the title of which refers to the famous march by Johann Strauss the Elder, describes life in a garrison town in Austria-Hungary. Carl Joseph, the son of the local prefect, hears the military band playing outside the family home:

> Every Sunday at noon-time it played outside the official residence of the district captain, who, in this little town, represented no lesser personage than His Majesty the Emperor. Carl Joseph, concealed behind the dense foliage of the vines on the balcony, received the playing of the military band as a tribute. He felt slightly related to the Hapsburgs, whose might his father represented and defended here and for whom he himself would some day go off to war and death.[51]

In Odense, too, regimental music represented the army and the state. The situation described from the perspective of an Austro-Hungarian provincial town also shows that military music was part of a common European culture. Throughout Europe it was a matter of course for military bands to play in public, and this was one of Nielsen's tasks.

The garrison commander in Odense made it a priority that the corps should have this kind of public activity. In May 1879, shortly before Nielsen joined the corps, Colonel Hammer announced a new plan for military music in Odense. The corps was now to play four times a week in public places around the city, in line with European

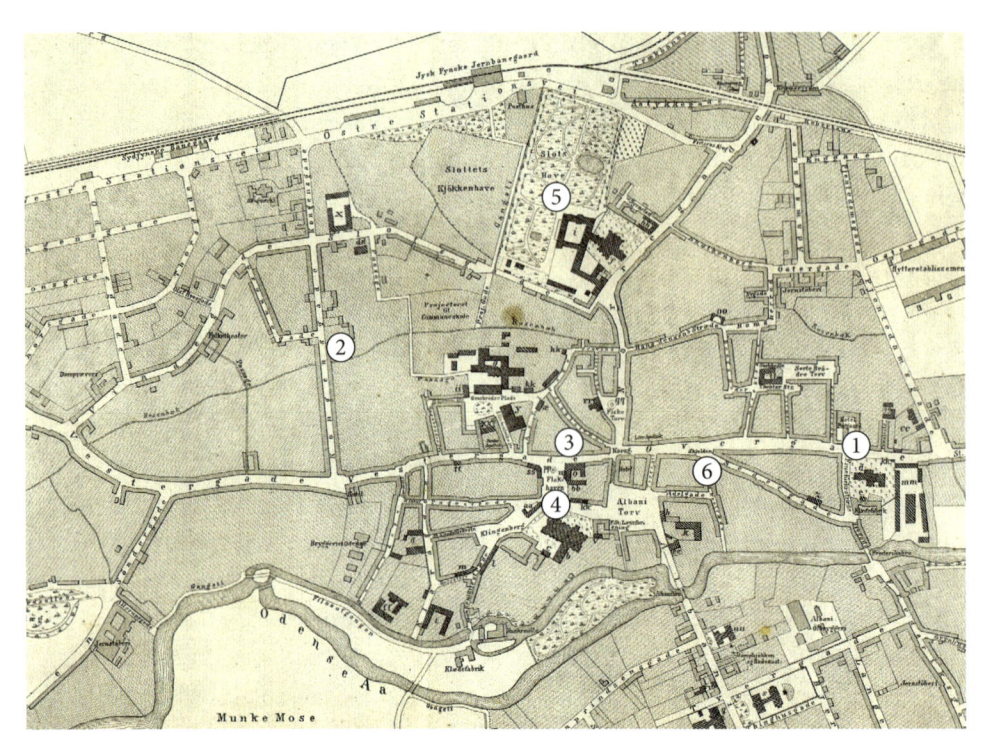

ILL. 6. Extract from a map of the centre of Odense, 1877. From 1879 the regimental music was played four times a week. On Tuesday afternoons, music was to be played in front of Colonel Hammer's residence at ① 58 Overgade, while on Fridays at the same hour, music was to be played alternately at Colonel Klüwer's residence at ② 25 Kongensgade and Colonel Zahlmann's at ③ 9 Vestergade. Overgade and Vestergade are the city's main east-west streets, running through the city centre and passing the large town hall square, ④ Flakhaven, in the middle. At the western end of Vestergade is Kongensgade and at the other end is the residence of Colonel Hammer. On Thursday evening at six the corps was to play alternately in the park, ⑤ Kongens Have, and on ⑥ Skjolden, the small square where Overgade and Nedergade meet. The traditional tattoo, originally used to call the soldiers home from the pubs, were to be played on Wednesday evening from half past eight as they marched through the streets of the city.[52]

trends. Most of the venues were in the city centre, but the corps' performance in the park, Kongens Have, meant that the northern part of the city could also enjoy the music. In all, there were four hours of music each week. Thanks to Hammer's plan, central locations in Odense were repeatedly enveloped in the military music of the nineteen-member band.[53]

Previously, the corps had played on Flakhaven on Sundays, next to the military main guard. These performances apparently attracted 'many appreciative listeners', partly because 'quite a number of visitors come to town on Sundays'.[54] One gets the

ILL. 7. The military main guard in front of the Town Hall on Flakhaven, *c.* 1875. The old town hall was demolished and replaced in 1881–83 by the new monumental building designed by the architects Lendorf and Herholdt.[55]

impression that the public performances helped to form Odense's identity in a larger context. However, the Sunday music had been banned a couple of years earlier by the chief constable, who believed that the performances violated the Holiday Act's restriction on 'public amusements or noisy exercises or enterprises of any kind'.[56] This led to a debate in the local newspaper *Fyens Stiftstidende* about whether the military music could be described as noisy, but the chief constable stood by his decision.[57]

The Sunday concerts at the town square were not resumed until October 1883, when the new town hall on Flakhaven had been opened in the spring of that year. The large open space in front of the building was once again occupied by the regimental music under the direction of Bandmaster Simon, and from then on the music on Flakhaven became a regular event in the years to come. An Odense resident recalls the Sundays around the turn of the century as follows:

> On Flakhaven the military band played every Sunday morning. The townspeople would wander around a bit to see if anyone they knew was there, or just stand in the sun and enjoy the music. It was the same musicians who played in the evening in the woods, so they had plenty to do.[58]

One can imagine the people of Odense idling away, listening to music, in the Parisian fashion. And at the end of the day they might take a boat trip up the river Odense Å to the woods at Fruens Bøge, where the same musicians were at work again, albeit in their leisure time. On the way, they might sing the song that Emilius Wilhelmi had composed for a summer revue in Odense in 1895 with this particular sailing trip in mind: 'Sejle op ad Aaen' (Sailing up the river) – today a popular party song.[59]

The military band musicians played on Flakhaven every Sunday from 12.30 p.m., performing seven pieces that always followed the same outline. The day before the event, the programme was advertised in *Fyens Stiftstidende* suggesting that it was indeed considered a real concert, as it was deemed appropriate to announce the concert programme in advance. Thus, the open-air concerts became events that involved the townspeople. The band had an extensive repertoire and took pride in putting together a new programme for each concert. Much of Nielsen's time as a band musician was spent rehearsing the repertoire for public performances. Only exceptionally did they play the same piece of music twice in a season.[60]

The band's repertoire was not specific to Odense. Both the extensive repertoire performed at the concerts and the way it was organised indicate that it was part of a common European musical culture. Again, the Holstein musicians were important because they brought their repertoire from Rendsburg in the form of manuscript music partbooks from which they played. These books were intended for practical use and, unlike a score, contained only the part that the individual musician would play. It was Nielsen's colleague Gundlach who added some of the music pieces in the surviving partbooks.[61]

When the band was to perform, each musician would take a partbook from one of the fifteen or so sets that the regiment had during Nielsen's time. Each set contained between fifty and a hundred pieces, and there was usually some overlap, so that the same work could appear in several different sets.[62] It was not considered a waste of time to copy the same works several times; it was a pragmatic way of organising the repertoire so that each musician could stick to one partbook when the band had to play.

The repertoire of marches, dances, overtures and excerpts from popular operas was not very different from that heard at other concerts. On the contrary, it was deeply rooted in contemporary European concert culture. At orchestral concerts in cities such as Paris, London, Vienna and Leipzig, excerpts were performed in the same way, and all-night programmes typically alternated between vocal and instrumental works. It was a principle of the concert organisers of the time that programmes

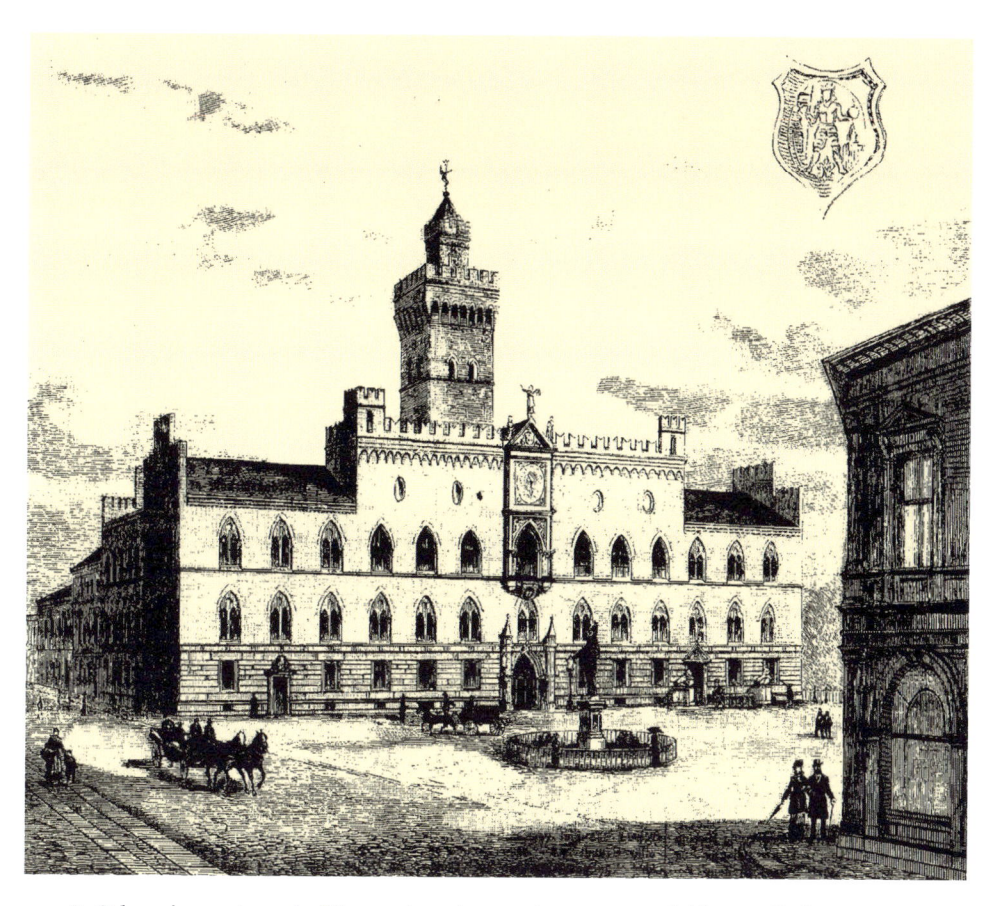

ILL. 8. Odense's new town hall located on the spacious square Flakhaven.[63] The concerts performed by the military band on Flakhaven consisted of seven pieces chosen according to a carefully planned pattern. Each concert began with a march, followed by an instrumental arrangement of a song, which could be a national anthem, an opera aria or a romance. This was followed by an opera overture, preferably from one of the popular French operas by Auber or Ferdinand Hérold, but composers from German-speaking Europe were also considered: Franz von Suppé and Béla Kéler. The fourth piece on the concert programme was always a dance: a waltz, a polka or a quadrille. For variety's sake, the fifth piece was an arrangement of a vocal work – such as excerpts from an opera, but it could also be a *Fantasi over Kuhlauske Sange* (*Fantasia on Songs by Kuhlau*). The penultimate item on the programme does not seem to be of a particular genre or type. It could be a dance, a potpourri or an arrangement of a song. The closing piece was always a galop.

should be varied in style and genre and include both new and old works.[64] Moreover, the repertoire in Odense was comparable to the promenade concerts that had become popular in London, and from the middle of the century they became a cos-

ILL. 9. The band of the Sixth Regiment, around 1890. In the centre, holding a sword, is Nielsen's teacher, the bandmaster Schreiber, who had been appointed as Simon's successor in 1889.[65]

mopolitan phenomenon in Paris, Vienna, Berlin and – with H. C. Lumbye's concerts in the Tivoli Gardens – also in Copenhagen.[66] For the musicians of the 1880s, works by composers such as Auber, Fahrbach, Gung'l and Boieldieu, who are little known today, were part of the standard repertoire. Their music was played in theatres, music societies and concert halls across the Continent.

To modern eyes, the members of the military band were musicians rather than soldiers. Yet even during the Second Schleswig War in 1864, music was part of the full field pack. The Fifth Battalion was stationed with the rest of the Danish army in the southern part of the Duchy of Schleswig. On the first day of the war, one of the musicians copied the overture to Wagner's *Tannhäuser*.[67] The corps retreated to the north and, after the defeats of the summer of 1864, retreated to Odense in the autumn. It is clear that during the military campaign the band members added music to their partbooks with confident and experienced hands, and arranged the music with care and great musical skill.[68]

Thus it was normal for the musicians in the band to copy and arrange music. Nor was it unusual for them to contribute new pieces when needed. Nielsen was therefore part of an environment in which it was common to arrange or produce music for practical purposes. On his arrival he became a colleague of the 32-year-old 'Musician III', William Willumsen, who was active as a composer, and his *Minerva Marsch* and

Aurora Polka became part of the military band's extensive repertoire.[69] Gundlach, Lantow and Simon also composed music for the regiment. Often the works were closely linked to the activities of the corps: Simon's *Sixth Regiment's March* was a signature march for the corps, just as Willumsen's *Greetings to the Fifth Battalion March* was performed as a musical welcome.[70]

The band received no formal training in such matters, although composing this kind of music was not much different from arranging an existing work for a different ensemble. Nielsen remembers that it was his slightly older colleague Jens Søby who encouraged him to compose some pieces for brass ensemble.[71] Søby also wrote music, including works such as *Hill dig vor Fane* (*Hail Our Standard*) and *Favorite de ma femme Mazurka*.[72] It was therefore natural for Nielsen to take up the challenge, but as the works do not appear to have survived, there is no way of knowing how he approached the task. However, he does recall the particular challenge of notating the music for the transposed instruments, which meant that the parts had to be notated in different keys. In the beginning it took him a lot of 'effort … to get the chords right'.[73] It was indeed a rewarding experience to realise that it was important to be able to notate transposing instruments. He knew the orchestra inside out, and if he wanted to convey his compositional ideas to the musicians, he had to be able to write down what they were supposed to play. His first attempts at composition thus grew out of his own experience as a musician.

Apprenticeship

The four years in the military band undoubtedly laid a solid foundation for Nielsen's understanding of what it meant to be a musician. He had to rehearse day after day, play concerts week after week and perform in front of a crowd of ambitious colleagues. He had to be able to learn new pieces quickly and still perform with confidence. He also gained an insight into the practicalities of a musician's life. Instruments had to be kept in good condition, and music had to be purchased, arranged and copied. At the same time, he was exposed to a varied repertoire which, consciously or unconsciously, left its mark on his musical understanding.

Nielsen was fourteen when he joined the military band, and although this may seem an early age, it was far from unusual. Søby also joined on his fourteenth birthday.[74] Musical training in the army can be compared to an apprenticeship as a craftsman, and military music education was indeed a gateway to a professional career as a musician – yet only a few of the many musicians of the time went on to study at music academies. But what did he really learn and what was the quality of the teaching?

From the army's point of view, the quality of the tuition was indeed central, as the training of new buglers was paramount to a well-functioning military band. In

1832, King Frederik VI encouraged the band musician Franz Keyper to publish the treatise *Militair Musik-Skole* (Army Music Manual), and decided that it should be used to teach musicians in the army. As well as being a band musician, Keyper was also a bassoonist in The Royal Orchestra and a church organist at Helligåndskirken in Copenhagen. The manual provided a basic introduction to music notation, major and minor keys, rhythm and beat, and how to play melodies. It also gave a detailed description of each brass instrument, its tuning and use.[75]

Keyper recommended that students should start at the age of twelve or thirteen with the bugle and only later move on to valve instruments such as the trumpet or trombone.[76] Nielsen had a little more experience of brass instruments than the beginners Keyper had in mind for his treatise. Prior to the competition for the vacant position of band musician, Nielsen practised diligently on the trumpet and cornet, and was soon assigned the bugle and trombone as well. At first he received daily lessons, and even before his first lesson he was equipped with a bugle – a brass instrument without valves whose conical tube produced a raw metallic sound. This type of instrument had been widespread in Prussia since the eighteenth century.[77] It was not to be his only instrument, however, and for his first lesson with Schreiber Nielsen was given an alto trombone. It was the type with valves that had been common in Prussian bands since the 1830s and had gradually been introduced into the Danish army.[78] Nielsen was used to valve instruments, so although the alto trombone was new to him, the fingerings were familiar – they reminded him of those of the cornet, he recounts.[79]

Nielsen's ability to play brass instruments was quite good. At least he says so: 'My lips were firm and not too thick, my tooth formation admirably suited to the bugle *embouchure*; and I could hold the top notes for nearly a minute.'[80] Schreiber's choice of instrument for Nielsen also seems to confirm this. Not every band musician could play the trombone satisfactorily. Keyper believed that 'the devotee of so large an instrument must be carefully acquainted with all the elements of the art of music.'[81] The alto trombone most often played the middle part of a music piece, and the part should therefore not stand out in the overall sound, except when playing solo passages. An alto trombonist thus had to be able to integrate the sound or sonority of the part into a unified whole. According to Keyper, the alto trombone was the most difficult of the three trombones (alto, tenor and bass).[82] Schreiber must have realised early on that Nielsen would be able to meet these demands. Indeed, another explanation for the choice of instrument could be that the size of the instrument suited the fourteen-year-old boy. It would not have been obvious for the young Nielsen to play the tuba or the helicon – the large brass bass instrument carried over the shoulder.

During his time in Odense, Nielsen also learned to play other instruments that were not part of his work in the corps. Over a period of time, he saved up to buy a piano. The quality of the instrument was secondary, as long as it worked. He apparently remembers having an old piano from a watchmaker in Overgade, and recalls: 'from then on I spent all my spare time at the piano'.[83] Nielsen received piano lessons from the pianist Jacob Kristian Outzen, who played in a restaurant in Vestergade. Outzen had studied in Leipzig, and Nielsen played chamber music for piano and violin with him.[84] It is difficult to ascertain how extensive the piano lessons were. It seems that the chamber music with Nielsen playing the violin made the greatest impression on him. Moreover, according to himself, Nielsen was not a very good keyboard player.[85] After acquiring the first volume of J. S. Bach's *Das Wohltemperierte Klavier*, he began to practise, although Outzen felt that Nielsen should wait with this repertoire as his basic skills were not yet developed enough to play the music at a reasonable pace.

ILL. 10. The well-known photograph of the fourteen- or fifteen-year-old Nielsen with the bugle in his right hand and the alto trombone in his left.

Piano music was completely new to Nielsen. It must be remembered that as an army musician he was used to playing one part and reading music written on a single stave. Piano music is polyphonic and notated on two staves. As well as being a different instrument, it required a new way of understanding the music. 'I started with the slow Preludes, which I played note by note at a snail's pace.' The approach brought results, and after playing Bach's E flat minor prelude about fifty times, 'I suddenly caught fire', he says, 'now the door was open, and now I could go exploring in an entirely new and strange world.' Nielsen noticed, for example, the 'clash of a couple of notes which moved me quite differently from any other music I knew'.[86] He is probably alluding to the dissonances that Bach used differently from the styles to which he was accustomed. He also wondered whether the music was devoid of melodic character, and noted that certain musical figures kept returning.

MUSICIAN IN ODENSE

ILL. 11. Prelude in E flat minor from Bach's *Das Wohltemperierte Klavier*, vol. 1. The ascending broken triads in bars 1 and 2 may correspond to the repetitions of figures noticed by Nielsen. They can be seen in the downward motion in bars 4, 6 and 8. Bach's collection of preludes and fugues was published several times in the second half of the nineteenth century; it is not possible to determine which edition Nielsen used. The illustration is from Czerny's edition (Leipzig: C. F. Peters, 1863).

This observation that music is made up of different components and structures testifies to a musician who is inquisitive about something other than simply perfecting the performance of the work. The purpose of playing the piano was obviously not to practise technique or to rehearse a concert repertoire. Nielsen played the piano to know the music and to study its content. This agrees with what his colleague in the regiment, Marius Hansen Hegeland, wrote about Nielsen in his memoirs in 1905: 'when he had eventually saved enough to rent himself a piano, it became his favourite occupation to sit and experiment with various chords, as well as studying music theoretically.'[87]

While living at home in Nr. Lyndelse, Nielsen had learned to play the violin. During his time in Odense, he continued to play the instrument, now with Outzen, although in retrospect he admitted that his technique was not fully developed at the time.[88] Nielsen's view of the violin developed during his time with Outzen, when he received coaching and played chamber music, and he realised that there was much more to learn.

After the summer of 1880, he began to receive violin lessons from Carl Larsen, who was a prominent figure in Odense's musical life. He was a bell-ringer and clerk at Vor Frue Kirke, which meant that he was responsible for the church's musical activities.[89] He had studied at the teacher's college in Jelling, received violin lessons from the Royal Musician Christian Schiørring and music theory lessons from, among others, the composer A. P. Berggreen in Copenhagen. From 1871 he was conductor

ILL. 12. Chamber musicians in Odense. Sitting from the left: counsellor Carl Larsen, tobacco manufacturer Ferdinand Jensen and parish clerk Axel Nielsen; standing from the left: the instrument makers, the brothers Christian and Vilhelm Larsen.

of Odense Workmen's Singing Society Choir, and in 1874 he was in charge of the choir of the Music Society in Odense.[90]

The lessons with Larsen were private and were arranged with the help of people such as the future prime minister, Klaus Berntsen.[91] Nielsen's skills gradually progressed to the point where he was able to join a string quartet with some of his colleagues. Larsen was also an active chamber musician, so Nielsen probably had the opportunity to listen to or participate in chamber music. In this respect, too, Odense provided him with important musical experiences.

Access to Music

Odense was a prosperous trading town, and printed music was an important commodity. If the music was not affordable, there were plenty of opportunities to rent it at a reasonable price.

The same was true in most of Europe. The Austrian music critic Eduard Hanslick thus wrote in 1853: 'Music rental libraries are undoubtedly one of the most influential and beneficial means of spreading musical education'.[92] He recommended that professionals and amateurs alike explore the music rental libraries, which consisted of collections of music on hire from their owners, such as booksellers or private individuals. In a later publication, Hanslick recalls his own musical upbringing in Prague in the 1840s. As a subscriber to one of the city's music rental libraries, he would choose his 'musical diet' almost daily, and then sit tirelessly at the piano and familiarise himself with new music.[93]

Before the establishment of public libraries, rental libraries were common, both for books and music. In Odense there was The Reading Society, where members could borrow books from the society's collection. In 1880 they had about 1,000 members and in 1884 it had a collection of about 20,000 volumes.[94] Even in a town like Nyborg, the collection of the rental library, the Nyborg Club, had reached 4,649 volumes by 1894.[95] Similar societies existed throughout the German-speaking world, where there were an estimated 2,000 literary rental libraries in the 1880s.[96] The importance of these libraries was such that book production was based on the number of copies required by the libraries.[97] The number of music rental libraries in the German-speaking world peaked at almost 400 in 1890. Since 1840, the number had increased tenfold.[98] Descriptions of nineteenth-century German music circles tell us that there was no need to buy music if one wanted to become acquainted with the latest music. Review copies were available in the rental libraries.[99]

The music trade in Odense was strongly influenced by international connections, which benefited both aspiring and professional musicians. The Braunstein brothers give a good impression of the music trade. They were of German origin and belonged to a family of army and court musicians.[100] From 1871, Christian Emil Braunstein ran a music shop in Odense, selling both instruments and music. Seven years later he became church organist at Vor Frue Kirke, and his brother Matthäus Wilhelm Braunstein, who ran a music shop with a rental library in Flensburg, moved to Odense and took over his brother's business.[101] Christian Emil's library already contained a well-assorted collection of foreign music publications, and with the addition of his brother's library the number of items increased considerably. Judging by the surviving catalogues of their music rental libraries, they must have had well over 10,000 volumes of music in total.[102]

The merger of the two brothers' businesses proves that there was a market in Odense that included an international repertoire. It also shows that a music business in Flensburg was not much different from one in Odense in terms of organisation and customer base. One of the reasons for this was probably that the operation of the Danish rental libraries followed German practice. It was based on an organised music business, which had essentially been established in Leipzig. A systematic handbook of printed music had been published there since 1817, and this provided a model for

3275.	*Arditi.*	Il Baccio	»	84
3276.	*Auber.*	La Muette, Cavatine	»	36
3277.	—	— Barcarole.........	»	24
3278.	—	— Arie	»	48
3279.	—	Fra Diavolo. *Romance: Paa Bjerget, dybt i Skoven ..	»	36
3280.	—	» — *Barcarole: Bag Gittrets tætte Gjemme..	»	24
3281.	—	Muurmesteren. Romance: Irma snart er her	»	24

ILL. 13. The catalogue of Braunstein's music rental library lists all available music in numerical order. In the category 'Romances and Songs for a Single Voice with Pianoforte' we find no. 3,276, Auber's *Die Stumme von Portici*, a translation of the French title *La muette de Portici*. It was an extremely popular work that was in many ways part of the musical life of Odense. The publication includes a piano arrangement of the cavatina and was printed in Hamburg by Böhme's publishing house. The present copy, with Braunstein's worn blue ownership label, is preserved in The Royal Danish Library, Dan Fogs Samling 50.

the way in which music retailers organised their assortment. The handbook became known as the 'bible' of the music dealers.[103] From 1829, a monthly or bi-monthly survey of new music publications in Germany was published. The reports also included information on music publications from most European countries, the United States, South Africa, Russia, India and Mexico.[104] Music shop owners used the lists to expand their range of stock. The same was true of rental library owners.

MUSICIAN IN ODENSE

During the years Nielsen lived in Odense, it was possible to visit Braunstein's music rental library on weekdays between 9 a.m. and 7 p.m. You could study the printed catalogue at home and decide which music you wanted to rent, or you could visit the shop and browse through the handwritten supplementary catalogue. Each music publication had a serial number, which was listed in the catalogue and also found on the printed music. It was not possible to examine the actual music in the shop. The borrower had to hand in a slip of paper with the exact serial numbers and wait for the staff to fetch them from the closed stacks. If the borrower was unhappy with the result, he or she had to return to the shop the following day, as music could only be exchanged once a day.[105]

Another music dealer in Odense was Thorvald Gundestrup, who from 1862 to 1894 owned a bookshop that included a music rental library.[106] At first he specialised in works for piano as well as for violin with piano accompaniment; later, however, he also included vocal music with piano accompaniment.[107] The repertoire immediately appealed to private individuals who played music at home.

It is not hard to imagine that Nielsen, like Hanslick during his studies in Prague, sat tirelessly at the piano, playing score after score borrowed from rental libraries. Once he had acquired a piano, Nielsen 'bought some cheap tutors and second-hand music, which included a sonata in C major by Mozart and the first part of Johann Sebastian Bach's *Das Wohltemperierte Klavier*'.[108] Although we do not know who sold him the music, he certainly knew how to obtain it.

Participating in the Town's Musical Life

As a musician, Nielsen was not restricted to military circles; he also played in civilian contexts. In this he followed his colleagues in the regiment who had musical careers in addition to their military service. Later in life he did not talk much about these activities, probably because they were a natural part of his everyday musical routine in Odense. However, it is clear from *My Childhood* that he also played for dances and concerts as an orchestral musician. In a lengthy passage recounting how his colleagues teased him with his little compositions, he writes:

> It was at a carnival where some of the bandsmen were playing for the dancing. During an interval in the early hours of the morning I was sitting with a comrade in a corner, drinking coffee. ... [A little later] we were at our music desks again, and the dancing went on for another hour.[109]

There is no doubt that Nielsen was a musician in the orchestra at this event, and from the way he describes the situation it seems that it was neither the first nor the last time he played in such contexts. One of the activities of the associations in Odense was the organisation of masked balls in February and March, and the events occupied many of the city's community halls. The venues were shrouded in a festive carnival atmosphere, with dancing and communal dinners, all accompanied by orchestras consisting of the city's musicians.[110]

The musicians who played in the military band were the backbone of the entire musical life of the city, including the musical activities at the Odense Theatre, whose orchestra was permanent and dependent on the regimental musicians. The core members of the theatre orchestra were Nielsen's colleagues Gundlach (double bass), Lantow (clarinet), Sass (percussion and flute), Christensen (violin), Simon (flute) and Willumsen (French horn and trumpet), who played together for decades. Jens Søby also played the violin in the orchestra. Visiting theatre ensembles were allowed to bring their own conductor, and if they did not have one, Simon would take on the role as leader of the theatre orchestra – at least during the period when Nielsen lived in the city.[111] However, the documentation is sparse, especially for the 1880s.

In general, it seems very likely that Nielsen was a member of the theatre orchestra, just as his colleagues were. Another explanation that links him to the theatre is that he was apparently in love with Gerda, the theatre painter's daughter, although this seems less credible. Gerda Poulsen's father was a painter who lived on Theaterstræde, but the work at the theatre was done by Aagaard, who was the permanent theatre painter. Apart from occasional work as a building painter, Gerda's father had no connection with the theatre.[112] It is thus more likely that it was his work as a military band musician that linked Nielsen to the theatre orchestra. This may also explain why Nielsen learned to play the flute in addition to the violin and piano – an instrument he was not required to play as an army musician.[113]

It seems plausible that Nielsen's first experience of music for the theatre was in Odense. If he was indeed a member of the theatre orchestra, this would suggest a very different view of Nielsen's development as a theatre musician and composer. Much of his life as a professional musician was to be spent at The Royal Theatre, first as a violinist and later as a conductor. As a composer, he was also interested in music for the theatre. His early compositions include works for plays staged in the theatres of Copenhagen, which would eventually lead to Nielsen writing incidental music for various contexts for the rest of his life.

Odense Theatre was thus an important place as one of the city's major musical scenes, for not only were plays performed there, but the theatre as a whole functioned as a place where it was attractive to come and listen to music. Just as the theatre buildings would be hired by travelling companies, so would the orchestra, which was of a high standard and the most expensive in the province. In Nielsen's time the orchestra cost 40 Kroner per performance, while the rent for the theatre was 50 Kroner. The performance material reveals details of the orchestra's constitution, as it comprises sets of 17–20 instrumental parts, including a full string section, 3–6 woodwinds, 2 French horns, 2 trumpets, trombone and percussion.[114]

As a theatre musician in Odense, Nielsen may have learned how music formed part of stage performances, and he may have experienced how orchestral music could be used to convey different moods. He must also have experienced how the pieces he knew from the military band could be used in plays. One example is the overture to Auber's *La muette de Portici*, which was performed nine times at the theatre in the 1878–79 season and at Fruens Bøge on 30 May 1880 and 8 July 1883. Not only was there a considerable overlap between army and theatre musicians, but the repertoire performed on the theatre stage was quite similar to that of the military band.

In the theatre, music was used to enhance the narrative of plays. On the one hand, there was the music that was invariably included in the plays. Some performances in the theatre consisted of music-dramatic works, such as operas and operettas, in which music was of course a primary element. Most evenings, however, were devoted to plays, often two or three a night in the high season. In these cases the orchestra drew on its extensive music archives, which included overtures and music for entr'actes and individual plays. For an all-night performance lasting three hours, between three and five instrumental works were usually performed as entr'actes.[115]

The way in which all-night performances were organised also reveals how the music director used the orchestra to create new contexts for a theatrical performance. In the 1878–79 season, Simon's predecessor, Emilius Wilhelmi, was music director. By using Mozart's overture to *Le nozze di Figaro* as an introduction to Molbech's play *Ambrosius*, Wilhelmi indirectly drew attention to the similarities between the two works: the social inequality between high and low in an aristocratic setting – and not least the wedding theme. All eleven performances began with Mozart's overture. The programme shows that the music director was more concerned with the impact and external circumstances of the staging than with the original purpose of the works. This focus meant that the audience was presented with a wide repertoire of music over the course of a season, during which ninety-eight different instrumental works were performed as entr'acte. This made Odense Theatre an important and attractive stage for high-quality musical performances.

As mentioned above, Simon was also the leader of the orchestra that gave concerts in the society known as Fruens Bøge – that is, named after the privately owned woods south of the town. The merchant Albert Sachs, who was among those who financially supported Nielsen's education, had raised money in 1880 to hold concerts in the woods during the summer. The concerts were so successful that in 1882 the town council subsidised the construction of a pavilion and a dance floor.[116]

As with the concerts at Flakhaven, those at Fruens Bøge were advertised in the newspaper *Fyens Stiftstidende*, with information about which specific pieces would be played. The repertoire was similar, but there was rarely any overlap. A musician who played in both orchestras had a busy season: at Flakhaven and Fruens Bøge alone, thirty concerts with over two hundred different works by nearly one hundred composers were performed from the beginning of June and throughout the year. It seems likely that Nielsen was occasionally involved when they played in the woods.

Thus, Odense was not a provincial backwater when it came to providing access to music. Odense was a city of music that reflected European trends. The theatre staged plays that had recently appeared on the scenes in Germany, Austria and France. There was access to extensive music collections and professional music teaching. And the city's orchestras gave priority to an international repertoire. Nielsen was well prepared.

Chapter 4

DEPARTURE

Sometime in 1883, Nielsen made the decision to apply to the Academy of Music in Copenhagen. However, there are several different versions as to how this happened. Not all of them can be correct and perhaps none of them is. The different stories may not fit together, although each story may be coherent in itself. It is therefore important to conduct an enquiry that pays attention to who is saying what, and to look for new evidence in the case. A lot of detective work is required to solve the puzzle of what really happened.

A Detective Story

Nielsen was ambitious and hoped for a musical career beyond Odense. It was in a local pub in the city that he met Olfert Jespersen, who would later become director of the orchestra at Copenhagen Zoo. Nielsen emphasises that it was the meeting with Jespersen that made him want to go to Copenhagen.[1] However, according to Nielsen's violin teacher, Carl Larsen, it was he who saw Nielsen's abilities and recommended that he apply to the Academy of Music, thus encouraging him to set his sights on the capital.[2]

At the centre of Larsen's story is Christian Schiørring, his former violin teacher and now a member of The Royal Orchestra, who was to ensure that Nielsen's admission to the Academy was a success. Twenty years later, Larsen recalled how he had written a recommendation for his young pupil to use when he approached Schiørring. Larsen was later told in passing that Schiørring was immediately interested in Nielsen, although Larsen does not give us any further information.[3] In *My Childhood*, Nielsen makes no mention of having visited Schiørring, but he does refer to Valdemar Tofte, the violin teacher at the Academy, with whom Schiørring shared a desk in The Royal Orchestra.[4]

The two stories are of course not mutually exclusive. Nielsen may well have visited both, but how the contact with Tofte was established is not known. It is possible that it was Schiørring who sent Nielsen to Tofte. Other sources show that Schiørring visited Odense and gave a concert at the Music Society on 6 October 1883.[5] In the same autumn, Nielsen was trying to establish contacts in the musical circles of Copenhagen. Perhaps it was in this connection that Larsen introduced his pupil to

Schiørring. In that case, it was a detail that Larsen forgot when he had to retell the story twenty years later. Or it was not important for the story he wanted to tell.

A crucial second-hand witness is Klaus Berntsen. In his autobiography he wrote that the initiative to send Nielsen to the Academy came from Larsen.[6] But unlike Larsen, Berntsen would have realised that the safe route to the Academy was through Niels W. Gade, the most influential of the institution's three founders. According to his own account, Berntsen sought out Gade and warned him that the young man from Fyn would be visiting. Armed with a letter from Berntsen, Nielsen is said to have approached Gade to plead his case. Nielsen confirms the story in *My Childhood*, where he writes that his visits, first to Tofte and then to Gade, gave him the firm feeling that he would be admitted to the Academy, although he writes that a place was not yet certain until he had passed an entrance test.[7]

Berntsen and Larsen each emphasise their influence on Nielsen's career. Their stories are told from their own perspectives and show only fragments of the course of events. There is good reason, therefore, to dwell a little on where their stories come from, as it may help us to understand why they describe the process differently. Above all, it may give us a clue as to what actually happened.

Larsen wrote his story in a letter to Knud Harder, who in 1905 was gathering information about Nielsen's musical background for an article in the German periodical *Die Musik*.[8] Harder had approached Nielsen and his teachers Carl Larsen and Orla Rosenhoff, the latter of whom had taught Nielsen at the Academy.[9] It is not surprising that Larsen emphasised to Harder his own involvement in the events and completely omitted Berntsen and Gade. Firstly, he probably had no idea how others had helped the young man. Secondly, it was Schiørring who made a difference to Larsen. The story thus became a purely personal view of the events, based on the information that Larsen knew. In his article, Harder included the information that Larsen had encouraged Nielsen to apply for admission to the Academy, but he left out Schiørring as an intermediary.[10]

At the same time in 1905, Klaus Berntsen collected biographical information about Nielsen for an article in *Søndagsbladet*, 'a weekly magazine for country and city'.[11] In the article, Berntsen said that he himself had sought out Gade prior to the entrance exam. Later, in his 1923 autobiography *Erindringer fra Manddommens Aar* (Recollections from Adult Years), Berntsen changed the story: now it seems that Berntsen had already sought out Gade prior to Nielsen's first visit. This discrepancy in the accounts raises questions about the reliability of the autobiography. As a publication by an influential political figure, the autobiography must be seen as a strategic presentation in which Berntsen could shape his legacy. It is therefore understandable that Berntsen should assign himself a leading role in Nielsen's career path. The story was designed to highlight Berntsen's role in facilitating Nielsen's meeting with Gade.

For readers in 1923, Berntsen's contribution would appear as a significant precursor to the great composer's ascension. However, when reading Nielsen's own account of the visit, it seems clear that he arrived unannounced to Gade. Yet, he also writes that he brought a letter from Berntsen.[12]

Berntsen's account in his autobiography also contains elements of exaggeration. According to Berntsen, Gade was so enthusiastic about Nielsen's visit that he wanted to give the young musician a scholarship: again, a timely underlining of Berntsen's strategic sense. Compared to Nielsen's own account in *My Childhood*, Berntsen's version casts him in a rosy light. According to Nielsen, Gade was somewhat reluctant and told the young applicant that he would have to audition first to be sure of a place.[13] In other words, Berntsen paints a picture in which it was his approach to Gade that determined the course of events.

Nielsen's retelling of the events at the end of *My Childhood* is also influenced by his desire to tell a good story. The narrative makes use of literary devices, and he does not seem to be concerned with recounting the actual course of events. He writes about the episode of his return from his first visit to Copenhagen. Back home on Fyn, he was determined to tell his parents that he was planning to move to the capital.[14] There was a forest fête near Havndrup on Fyn where Berntsen was to give a speech. Niels Maler, Carl's father, was to play at the event, and Carl went along. The reader thus knows that Berntsen was involved in Carl's plans for the Music Academy, and that Nielsen had to tell his father before Berntsen could inform his old friend. Nielsen now describes how he mentally prepared himself for the serious conversation:

> The woods and fields were in the full splendour of summer, and on reaching a narrow path through a rye-field I was overwhelmed by something I cannot explain; perhaps it was the fear of opposing my father and the delight at the beautiful surroundings which provoked this strange conflict in my mind.[15]

Nielsen needed a good hand to convince his father of the wisdom of giving up his job in the military band to pursue a career as a musician in the capital. To help the reader identify with the conflicting emotions in the young man's mind, the narrative is set against a familiar natural backdrop with a wealth of sensory impressions. It was probably an outdoor event, so it seems most likely that it took place in summer. But was it a real event, or is it rather a narrative technique used by Nielsen?

In *My Childhood*, the recollection of the episode appears to the reader as Nielsen's real-time experience, but the chronology of the narrative is not consistent with the course of events as they appear in other sources. He mentions two trips to Copenhagen, the first in May when he met Gade and the second in December when he attended an audition. He adds a vivid description of how he experienced the ambience of the capital when the Russian Tsar Alexander III and his entourage marched through the city.[16] One wonders if this is also a storytelling technique. It probably is, for the emperor visited Denmark from 30 August to 11 October – in other words, in neither May nor December.[17]

How do we separate fact from fiction? One way is to consult the army archives. As a military band musician, Nielsen was obliged to perform his duties in the corps, and any absence had to be agreed with his superiors. Captain Jacobsen of the Sixth Regiment was, by all accounts, one of the few people Nielsen was required to inform of his travel plans.[18] The regimental records show that he was granted leave once in 1883 – from 20 November to 23 December – to travel to Copenhagen.[19] This new information causes the chronology of *My Childhood* to collapse further and calls into question whether Nielsen really visited Copenhagen twice in 1883.

The highly sensuous descriptions in *My Childhood* may have determined the chronology on which Nielsen's stories are built. He had to travel to Copenhagen in the late spring so that he could return home to the summer blossoming fields and have a serious talk with his father. And to describe his first visit to the capital, he used the story of the royal visit to illustrate how the city was buzzing with excitement. Nielsen may well have seen Tsar Alexander III in Copenhagen on another occasion, but it seems highly unlikely that he saw the emperor on his visit in 1883.

There is another way to solve the mystery. The archives of the Academy contain administrative documents from its foundation in 1867 onwards: class schedules, lists of students, statements about students and information about entrance examinations. It was important for the institution to be able to document who had been examined and who had been admitted. Fortunately, the material from 1883–84 is held by the National Archives. The records show that entrance examinations were held on 2 December 1883, when twenty-five young and aspiring musicians auditioned. Nielsen's name does not appear on this list.[20] On 2 January 1884, however, it does, along with eighteen others.[21] Of these forty-four, twenty-two were accepted. Nine of them auditioned in January, just before the start of the school year.

Now that we know that there were two auditions a month apart, it seems reasonable to assume that the first day was fully booked when Nielsen reported to Gade. He probably took leave from November to be ready for the first test. Perhaps he was told instead that he could come back a month later. That was certainly not the message he had come to Copenhagen to hear.

An important source has been under our noses all along. It has received little attention and has been overshadowed by the narrative of *My Childhood*. In 1895, Nielsen wrote an extensive autobiographical sketch for the music critic William Behrend. The sketch was probably intended as a preliminary draft for an article that Behrend could then publish in Germany, a plan that was later abandoned.[22] In his sketch, Nielsen explains for the first time what happened around the turn of the year 1883–84, and although not all the details are given, the description seems to support a new sequence of events:

> During that time a well-to-do uncle had taken an interest in me, and he and a few other relatives started to talk about sending me to the Copenhagen Music Conservatoire, whose director was N. W. Gade. But it was no more than talk, because no-one was sure that I had any talent. I therefore took a desperate decision. Without letting anyone know, I travelled to Copenhagen, went straight to see Gade himself, and showed him the score of a string quartet that I had composed. He announced that I had talent, even praised the Andante, and said that if I was just remotely decent on the violin, I could be sure of being accepted on a scholarship at the Conservatoire. With this news I returned home and shortly thereafter took leave of the military, passed an audition at the Conservatoire, and soon became a student there.[23]

Nielsen apparently took a huge risk at the end of 1883, describing it in his own words as a decision made in desperation. He was probably in disarray because plans for the future were out of his hands. He was dependent on the goodwill of others, and even his talent could not guarantee success. The visit to Gade was not decisive, for Gade only said that if Nielsen could play the violin reasonably well, he would be sure to be accepted. An audition was therefore inevitable. In the following passage, Nielsen writes that on his return to Odense he took his leave from the army and shortly afterwards took the entrance examination at the Academy. At this point in the text, the story does indeed correspond to both the army's and the Academy's records. And now it becomes clear why he seized this opportunity. When he returned to Odense after his leave in December, he announced his future plans to his family, and on the last day of the year he was 'discharged from any remaining duty' in the regiment.[24] The problem was that he had not yet been accepted at the Academy.

Although he told parts of the story to Behrend in 1895, he kept the facts of his departure a secret for the rest of his life. Returning to *My Childhood*, it is surprising how the story takes a new turn, for Nielsen writes that 'in December that year [1883] I passed the entrance test to the Conservatoire, and was enrolled from 1st of January, 1884'.[25] Never before had he explained in such detail when the audition took place, and it is surprising that he should reverse the events. Was it a shift in memory forty-four years later, or an attempt to adapt reality to the story he had told his acquaintances?

There is no doubt that Nielsen did not want to disappoint his family with his bold decision to pursue a career as a musician in Copenhagen. Although he stood by his decision on that summer day in the country (or whenever it was), his father took comfort in the fact that his son still had a permanent position in the army, so it could not have been good news when Carl came home at Christmas and revealed his plans. Or he told a white lie, saying that he had been accepted to the Academy so that he could resign from his post with conviction in his voice. The white lie must not see the light of day, and in *My Childhood* the great reflections are woven into exciting events that leave the reader with the impression that the support of family and friends secured him a musical future.

He could not let his friends down either. The former shopkeeper Jens Georg Nielsen, the businessman Albert Sachs, the manufacturer Hans Demant and others supported him financially so that he could study.[26] While Nielsen was still living in Odense, they had made it a condition of their support that he 'succeeded in passing an examination in Copenhagen or securing a statement from the authorities there'.[27] In order to take the plunge, he had to convince them that everything was timed and organised, and forty-four years later he could not change the story.

Imagine dismantling and packing up your equipment and moving your belongings to help you settle into a new city – with no guarantee that it will work out the way you hope.

Chapter 5

NIELSEN'S COPENHAGEN

Nielsen became a Copenhagener. He was one of the many Danes who moved to the capital at the end of the nineteenth century, contributing to the rapid population growth that characterised the city at that time. In 1880 Copenhagen had a population of 261,000. By 1911 it had more than doubled to 559,000.[1] The figures partly reflect general growth in Denmark, but the proportion of the population living in Copenhagen also increased significantly during these decades.[2]

An important prerequisite for accommodating the many new citizens was the demolition of the city ramparts in the 1870s and 1880s, which allowed the capital to expand. The same trend was seen in a number of other European cities in the second half of the nineteenth century – including Paris, Vienna, Barcelona, Kraków and Riga.[3] In Paris, the old fortifications were demolished to make way for the modern boulevards that became an important symbol of Parisian urban life at the turn of the century. A similar trend was seen in Vienna, where the old ramparts were replaced by the Ringstrasse, a circle of wide boulevards with parkland in the middle, which became home to a series of magnificent public buildings.

It was these international trends that inspired the new use of Copenhagen's rampart terrain. Nørre Voldgade, known as the Boulevard, was established as part of the innermost of the three new ring roads around the centre of Copenhagen. This was followed by Farimagsgade and, at the far end, Gaden langs Søerne (now Søgade).[4] Four new public parks were laid out between the streets, almost creating a series of parks around the city centre from Kastellet to Tivoli Gardens. The new area succeeded in creating a Copenhagen cityscape reminiscent of the European models described in Nielsen's travel diary from Austria in 1894: 'Vienna reminds me more than a little of Paris, and its boulevards of those in Copenhagen.'[5]

In the old city centre, new buildings also helped to transform the Danish capital from a market town into a modern metropolis. Around Kongens Nytorv in the early 1870s, Hotel d'Angleterre was converted into a modern hotel of European standard, and The Royal Theatre received its new impressive building with 1,400 seats. In 1893, the Hotel du Nord and the adjacent building were demolished and replaced by the new Magasin du Nord, which, with its French-inspired architecture and fashionable range of wares, became Copenhagen's counterpart to the Magasin du Louvre in Paris.[6]

At the other end of Strøget, around the present City Hall Square, major changes also took place during this period. After the demolition of the ramparts on this site in 1885–87, work began on a large hall to house the Nordic Industrial, Agricultural and Art Exhibition in 1888. There had been two previous industrial exhibitions in Denmark, but this one was considerably larger and the closest the country had come to a real world exposition.[7] When it was over and the hall was demolished, work began on the construction of Copenhagen's new City Hall on the same site. The building combined a number of historical styles and reflected the taste for decoration of the 1890s with a wealth of adornments and monuments telling the story of Denmark and Copenhagen.[8] The new City Hall was completed in 1905, and prompted the shift of Copenhagen's centre from Kongens Nytorv to the City Hall Square after the turn of the century.[9]

However, the greatest urban changes took place outside the old city walls – that is, beyond the lakes, in the working-class districts, and in the suburbs further out. Much of the housing was for the many newcomers who moved to the city to work in the capital's growing industrial and commercial sectors.[10] As an account of Greater Copenhagen from 1907 explains, it was this enormous urban expansion that seriously changed the character of the capital as a city in the last decades of the nineteenth century:

> Since the city burst its narrow shell and the old ramparts disappeared, it has stretched and stretched, further and further out, spreading to all sides where space could be found. It is no longer a fortified city with suburbs outside its walls, but a single body, an organism that will and must grow.[11]

Like most newcomers, Nielsen began his life in Copenhagen in the new districts; however, after the European tour of 1890–91, when he married the sculptor Anne Marie Brodersen, he moved to the city centre. In the years that followed, the couple lived in various inner-city lodgings until they had achieved sufficient income and status to move into prestigious artists' residences: first a villa in Frederiksberg and later the honorary residence on Frederiksholm Kanal, which was to be their last home.

By following Nielsen's addresses in Copenhagen, it is possible to draw a picture of how his position as a citizen and cultural figure in the capital developed over time. At the same time, it becomes clear that he was not a rural figure, but rather an urban one, living most of his life in a burgeoning metropolis with an international outlook.

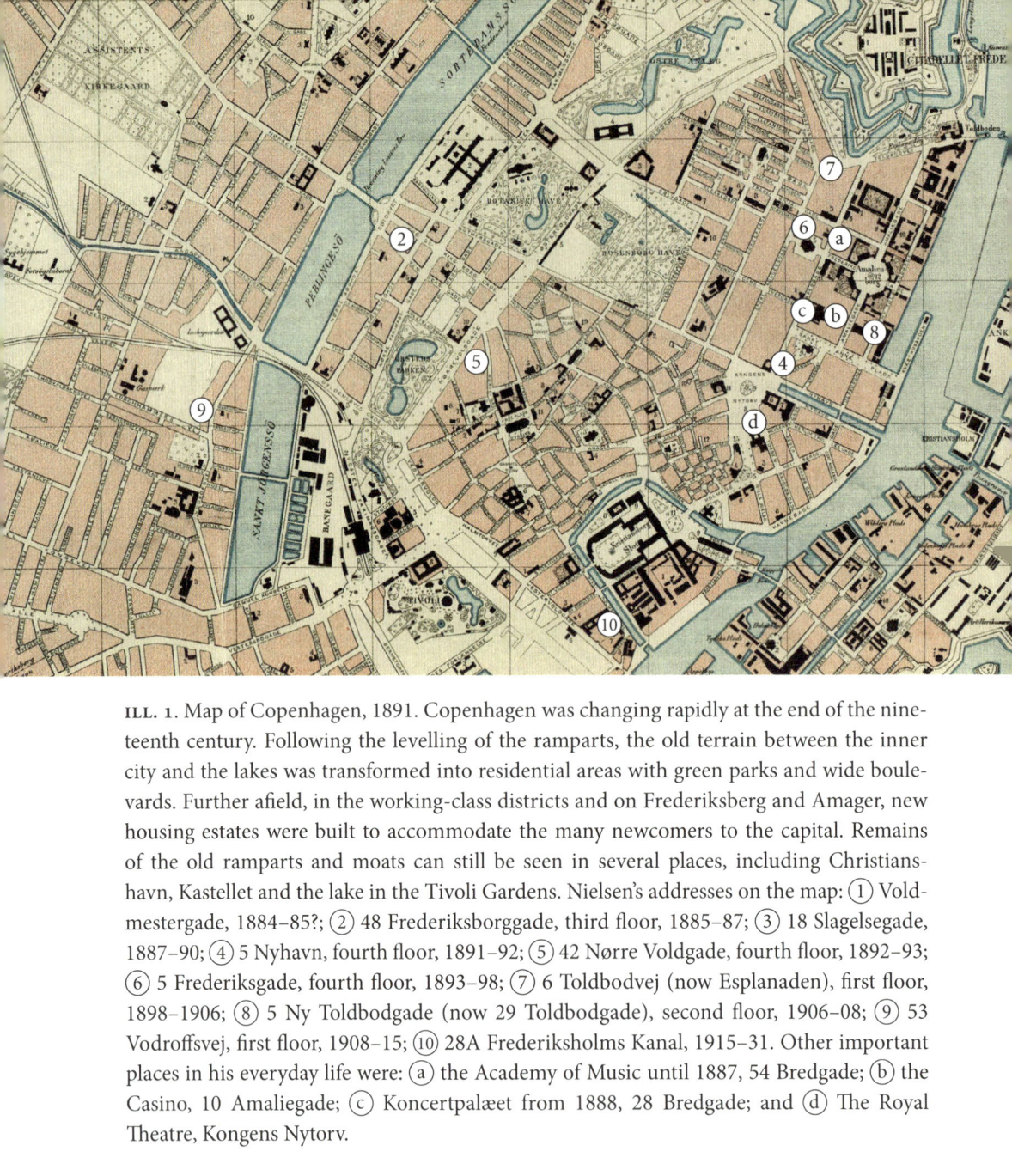

ILL. 1. Map of Copenhagen, 1891. Copenhagen was changing rapidly at the end of the nineteenth century. Following the levelling of the ramparts, the old terrain between the inner city and the lakes was transformed into residential areas with green parks and wide boulevards. Further afield, in the working-class districts and on Frederiksberg and Amager, new housing estates were built to accommodate the many newcomers to the capital. Remains of the old ramparts and moats can still be seen in several places, including Christianshavn, Kastellet and the lake in the Tivoli Gardens. Nielsen's addresses on the map: ① Voldmestergade, 1884–85?; ② 48 Frederiksborggade, third floor, 1885–87; ③ 18 Slagelsegade, 1887–90; ④ 5 Nyhavn, fourth floor, 1891–92; ⑤ 42 Nørre Voldgade, fourth floor, 1892–93; ⑥ 5 Frederiksgade, fourth floor, 1893–98; ⑦ 6 Toldbodvej (now Esplanaden), first floor, 1898–1906; ⑧ 5 Ny Toldbodgade (now 29 Toldbodgade), second floor, 1906–08; ⑨ 53 Vodroffsvej, first floor, 1908–15; ⑩ 28A Frederiksholms Kanal, 1915–31. Other important places in his everyday life were: ⓐ the Academy of Music until 1887, 54 Bredgade; ⓑ the Casino, 10 Amaliegade; ⓒ Koncertpalæet from 1888, 28 Bredgade; and ⓓ The Royal Theatre, Kongens Nytorv.

The City of the Newcomer

The neighbourhoods that emerged on the outskirts of Copenhagen were very different when the ramparts were removed. In the ramparts district, the architects' ideals of more light and air were evident; it had 'wide and metropolitan streets', green parks and, as home to the Municipal Hospital and the National Museum of Art, it also became the 'district of monumental buildings'.[12] Moving further out to the new working-class districts of the city, however, the impression was very different. In this area, urban planning was driven by the pursuit of profit, and Vesterbrogade and Nørrebrogade were the main streets in Copenhagen's new working-class districts, where tall blocks of flats shot up one after the other. In the early 1890s, the writer Johannes Jørgensen wrote of Nørrebro: 'The streets are short, narrow, dirty – and they wind into each other, as if the whole suburb were just one big, dirty backyard with lots of intermediate and rear premises.'[13] What the neighbourhoods around and outside the old ramparts had in common, however, was that they represented the new Copenhagen – and thus the change in mentality that was taking place at a time when city dwellers were becoming metropolitans.[14]

During his first few years in the city, Nielsen had the opportunity to settle in the new, expanding Copenhagen – more specifically, in Østerbro and on the rampart area by the lakes. Information about his early lodgings in Copenhagen is scarce, but it seems that during his time at the Academy he lived in a kind of building society house in Voldmestergade. Here he rented a furnished room on the first floor, where he had a piano and could study music and literature.[15] This accommodation is also mentioned in the memoirs of Emilie Demant Hatt, his teenage girlfriend, who mentions that Nielsen spent his first winter in Copenhagen in an attic room in Voldmestergade.[16] When he accompanied Emilie home to her front door at 21 Voldmestergade one evening many years later, he pointed out the room that was diagonally opposite her house.[17]

Voldmestergade is part of the Østerbro district known as Kartoffelrækkerne, which was built between 1873 and 1889. The streets were built on the land in front of the old ramparts between Farimagsgade and Søerne (the lakes), which had previously been largely undeveloped due to the demarcation clauses. The new terraced houses were intended for working-class families, but they differed in several respects from the other working-class housing of the time built outside the ramparts. They were built by the Workers' Building Society, founded in 1865 and inspired by similar societies in England. The idea was that workers could achieve better conditions by working together to provide their own housing.[18]

It was financed by each member paying 33 Øre a week to the Society. When a house became available, a lottery was held among the members to decide who should buy it. Members who had not become homeowners after ten years could get their money back with interest, and the Society therefore also functioned as a savings bank. The houses consisted of two flats – one on the ground floor and one on the first floor. The owner of the house could rent out the second flat in the house to another member of the Society for a fixed payment. Each flat consisted of a kitchen, living room and bedroom and there was a communal toilet in the yard. Newspaper advertisements from the time show that it was common practice to let rooms in the houses to young single people like Nielsen.[19] A closer look at who lived in the houses reveals that they were not the poorest of the poor, as was the case in many parts of Nørrebro and Vesterbro. In 1884–85, the houses in Voldmestergade were occupied by a university graduate, a carpenter, a teacher, a bookkeeper – and also by two musicians and a music director.[20]

So how did Nielsen experience the new Copenhagen of the mid-1880s, and how did he make use of the city? There are few sources to answer these questions, but one can imagine that it must have been overwhelming to witness the hustle and bustle of construction. Herman Bang's Copenhagen novel *Stuk* (1887) describes the 'activities of pounding, hammering and planing; the clattering of trowels and hammers in a tangle of scaffolding, beams and ladders, below and above …'.[21] Nielsen must have experienced this in his daily life *en route* between his room in Voldmestergade and the Academy of Music in Bredgade. The most obvious way would have been to walk down Øster Farimagsgade to Sølvtorvet, along the southern part of the Voldmester quarter, which was being built up at the time. From Sølvtorvet he had to enter the city via Sølvgade, which had not yet been extended beyond the city ramparts. He therefore walked along a simple footpath with the Botanical Gardens on one side and Østre Anlæg on the other. After crossing the newly created Øster Voldgade, he would enter the inner city and could follow the old part of Sølvgade along the park, Rosenborg Have (now Kongens Have), and then down the northern parallel street Fredericiagade into the Bredgade quarter, a stroll of just under half an hour that led to a very distinct part of Copenhagen.

When he arrived in Bredgade, where the Academy was situated from 1872 to 1887, he found himself in one of the city's most prestigious streets.[22] During Nielsen's time at the Academy, the street was home to three churches, the Supreme Court, the temporary Parliament building, several grand mansions and a number of expensive shops and restaurants.[23] Jørgensen has given a vivid account of how he experienced the area at the time:

> To the east of Kongens Nytorv lies Copenhagen's Faubourg Saint-Germain. … On festive days the flags of foreign nations wave from the envoys' hotels, and every day the King's Music can be heard from the nearby Amalienborg when the Guard pulls up at noon. Bredgade is the street of the men of power.[24]

In other words, it was a stronghold of the rich and powerful, and the vast majority of those who lived or visited the area belonged to a higher social class than Nielsen. As home to the Academy of Music, the Casino, Musikforeningen (The Music Society), Koncertforeningen (The Concert Society) and, from 1888, Koncertpalæet, the Bredgade area must have been one of the places in the city where Nielsen spent most of his time when he was away from home. But by this time, in the mid-1880s, he may well have felt that he was visiting a part of the city where he did not quite belong.

In the late summer of 1885, Nielsen moved into a room on the third floor of 48 Frederiksborggade. The arrangement was made in connection with a private concert that Nielsen had given in Odense during his summer holidays. Among those present was Waldemar Sempill Bauditz, a customs officer, who must have been enthusiastic about the young musician. In any case, he offered Nielsen the opportunity to move into his house in Frederiksborggade when the holiday was over. The agreement was that Nielsen could rent a room with board and laundry for only 19 Kroner a month, on condition that he taught Bauditz's ten-year-old daughter Agnes to play the piano.[25]

The premises where the family lived were part of the new extension of Frederiksborggade, which was laid out after the demolition of the ramparts. Like the houses in Voldmestergade, it was situated between Farimagsgade and the lake, Sortedams Sø, and had been built a few years before Nielsen lived there. But apart from that, the two neighbourhoods had little in common. The town planning of Søtorvet and, since 1872, the surrounding streets had been carried out by the Copenhagen Building Society, headed by Ferdinand Meldahl. The vision was a new, magnificent northern gateway to the centre of Copenhagen, modelled on the major European cities. The Søtorv complex itself was built between 1873 and 1876, while the extension of Frederiksborggade took place in the second half of the 1870s. 48 Frederiksborggade was occupied from 1880, and the Bauditz family lived on the third floor from 1883.[26]

A newspaper advertisement gives the impression that it was one of the finer flats in the building: '48 Frederiksborggade. An elegant flat on the third floor with five rooms, three of which face the street, as well as several good three-room flats facing the backyard are for rent.'[27] Nielsen's room faced the backyard, but he was allowed to move around the whole flat together with the host family.[28] This also applied when his musician friends Julius Borup, the brothers Wilhelm and Aage Matthison-Hansen and Frederik Schnedler-Petersen visited him.[29] The other flats were occupied by merchants and clerks, but also by a number of people who played a part in the cultural life of the city. A literary man and a ballet dancer lived in the same building, as did the sculptor Frederik Hammeleff. The organist and music teacher Georg Bohlmann lived in the neighbouring building, and from 1887 he was the music director at Dagmarteatret.[30]

During the two years that Nielsen had a room in Frederiksborggade, the last important part of Meldahl's plan for Søtorvet was realised: the construction of the

ILL. 2. Dronning Louises Bro. The bridge under construction as seen from Nørrebro towards Søtorvet and Frederiksborggade, 1886.

bridge, Dronning Louises Bro. It was moved a little further south than its predecessor, Peblingebro, so that it was on an axis with the two very different streets it connected: Nørrebrogade and Frederiksborggade. The new bridge was designed by Vilhelm Dahlerup, the architect who also designed The Royal Theatre and The Pantomime Theatre. With its four large flagpoles and beautifully curved benches, it became an important part of the new monumental entrance to the city centre. But the bridge also became a link in the other direction: from European-oriented, upmarket Copenhagen to the poor, working-class neighbourhoods of Nørrebro and the suburbs beyond.

It was characteristic of several areas outside the old ramparts that great urban contrasts could be experienced within a few hundred metres. This was also true of the area around Nielsen's last accommodation in the 1880s: 18 Slagelsegade in Østerbro. This part of Østerbro, around Rosenvængets Allé, had been a rural residential area until a few years earlier. In the second half of the nineteenth century, it was mainly artists who settled in the area, including the painters P. C. Skovgaard and Wilhelm Marstrand, the actress Johanne Luise Heiberg and the composer J. P. E. Hartmann.[31] In the mid-1880s, Anne Marie Brodersen also lived in the neighbourhood, in the same building as her teacher, the sculptor August Saabye.[32] In 1884 the villa known as Rosendal, just south of Rosenvængets Allé, was sold and demolished, and in its place Slagelsegade was established with blocks of flats on the former Rosendalsvej. Unsurprisingly, this development met with resistance from many who wanted to preserve Østerbro's residential idyll, and Jørgensen's introduction to the district reveals a certain disdain for the changes: 'Østerbro begins at Kastellet – the Østerbro that will soon no longer exist. Not the new Østerbro of Kasernegaderne, the poor districts of Slagelsegade and Viborggade – but the Østerbro of the big villas and the old gardens, the Østerbro of Rosenvænget.'[33]

In the early summer of 1887, Nielsen moved into a flat at 18 Slagelsegade with Marie and Jens Georg Nielsen, who had previously lived in Odense, where they had met Nielsen a few years earlier when he was a military musician. Jens Georg Nielsen had been a regular at the band's concerts and had apparently noticed Nielsen when he joined the corps in 1879.[34] Together with a number of other townspeople, he had supported Nielsen financially so that his wish to study at the Academy in Copenhagen could be fulfilled. Jens Georg Nielsen owned a grocery shop in Nørregade in Odense, which he had taken over from his father, but he decided to sell it in 1882 and lived the rest of his life on the money he had earned. His wife Marie was the aunt of Emilie Demant Hansen, whom Nielsen first met in the summer of 1887, when he was on holiday with Jens and Marie at Emilie's parents' home in the north-west Jutland village of Selde. Emilie, then fourteen, and the twenty-two-year-old Carl began a relationship that lasted until the end of 1889. Emilie visited Copenhagen during the summer of 1888 and described the building in Slagelsegade as 'a corner house – dull and dreary like the whole neighbourhood.'[35]

ILL. 3. Emilie Demant Hatt, née Hansen, and Nielsen at the photographer's in Copenhagen in summer 1888. Emilie described their relationship in her memoirs, *Foraarsbølger*, which, along with Nielsen's letters, are virtually the only surviving first-hand sources of information about his life in the 1880s. She met Nielsen in the summer of 1887 at her parents' merchant house in the village of Selde by Limfjorden. In the following years they spent summers together and kept in touch through letters. The relationship ended in the autumn of 1889, and Nielsen was so unhappy that he considered taking his own life. Emilie recounts a dramatic incident in which Nielsen bought a revolver and sent her a farewell letter. Many years later, they resumed contact and met for bridge evenings at Nielsen's place on Frederiksholm Kanal in Copenhagen.

Nielsen lived in Slagelsegade until September 1890, when he began his long and formative journey through Europe. It was during these years – the late 1880s – that he established himself as a musician in Copenhagen; in the early years as a freelance chamber musician and in various orchestras, and from the summer of 1889 as second violinist in The Royal Orchestra at Kongens Nytorv, which became his permanent workplace for many years. Both during his time at the Academy and in the following years as a musician, he had a strong connection with the cultural life of inner Copenhagen. At the same time, however, the fact that he came from the provinces and rented rooms in newly built premises outside the city centre means that he must have had an identity as a newcomer in the 1880s.

The Cultural Centre

When Nielsen returned to Copenhagen in the early summer of 1891 after his long European tour, he had to find new accommodation. He had married the sculptor Anne Marie Brodersen in Paris, and they were now expecting their first child, Irmelin, so it was imperative to find premises with enough space for a whole family. They moved several times during the 1890s and early 1900s as more children were born and their financial situation improved. What all these houses had in common, however, was that, contrary to Nielsen's various accommodations in the 1880s, they were all within the old ramparts.

The centre of Copenhagen also underwent urban change during this period, but probably not to the same extent as the rampart terrain and the suburbs. On the other hand, the old city provided a framework for a different kind of change.[36] It was here that writers, artists, students and 'flâneurs' lived and enjoyed modern city life. They strolled up and down Strøget and the Boulevard (that is, Nørre Voldgade) and discussed art and politics in the city's cafés. A particularly famous meeting place was the Bernina café in Vimmelskaftet, 'where an open-minded and radical youth often met with "Bohemians" from Norway, for whom the Bernina life, with its absinthes and "pjolter" [a Norwegian drink consisting of fizzy water with whisky or cognac], was the flower of Copenhagen'.[37] Moreover, the most important cultural institutions were located in the old part of the capital: The Royal Theatre, Charlottenborg, Koncertpalæet and the Casino were in the area around Kongens Nytorv, while the Tivoli Gardens, Dagmarteatret and Den Frie Udstilling (The Free Exhibition) were in the area that became known as the City Hall Square after the turn of the century. The centre of Copenhagen was the heart of cultural life, so it made sense for an artist and a musician to settle there.

The Nielsens' first home was a flat on the fourth floor of 5 Nyhavn. Newspaper advertisements show that it was offered for rent from October 1891 and consisted of 'four rooms with kitchen, maid's room and lumber-room etc.' It also had an 'excellent view of Kongens Nytorv'.[38] The building faced the sunny side of Nyhavn, and from the flat Nielsen could see his workplace, The Royal Theatre. The row of houses on this side was built between 1673 and 1700, but almost all of them were extended by one or more storeys in the eighteenth and nineteenth centuries. This includes 5 Nyhavn, which was one of the tallest buildings in the street.[39] Today it is the premises of Nyhavns Færgekro.

Nyhavn was the base for Nielsen's cultural activities in the city. He offered violin and ensemble lessons from his home and played in the theatre in the evenings, which was only a few minutes' walk from their home.[40] He also lived close to the fashionable Bredgade district, where there were also opportunities to attend concerts and the theatre. In Nyhavn itself, however, the atmosphere must have been very different from the surrounding streets:

> Full of masts and rigging, Nyhavn's narrow canal winds its way up to Kongens Nytorv between a double row of old houses, all smelling of the sea. … Here, sailors in black, soft felt hats and blue coats drift to and fro – now stopping at a shop where a hanging garment tempts, now at a tavern where a smiling girl in the window promises good accommodation.[41]

Like many of the houses in Nyhavn, no. 5 had a tavern in the basement.[42] Whether the Nielsens were bothered by this lively environment is impossible to say, but the following year they decided to look for a new home. It was probably the desire for more space that prompted the move, as they were expecting their second child, Anne Marie. The tenancy was advertised in the newspaper on 10 September 1892 with the following note: 'In 5 Nyhavn, on account of the tenant's changed circumstances, a cosy attic flat on the fourth floor is available immediately or in October.'[43]

During the weeks when they were looking for a new home, Anne Marie Carl-Nielsen stayed at her parents' farm south of Kolding, where the family had been spending their summer holidays, while Nielsen returned to Copenhagen alone. Reading their correspondence gives us an impression of the Copenhagen housing market and the couple's experience of the city in the 1890s. On 31 August 1892 Carl wrote to Anne Marie:

> … if we want to think about moving, there is no time to lose. Everyone says that the flats we are talking about have been rented long ago – unless we want to go all the way to the bridges, and we do not want to do that. The Borups has rented for a long time, as has Møllers. They say that the flats that are still available have some kind of problem. Either smoke or steam or hm, hm, hm! Joking aside … It would be bad if we stayed here … I'll start looking for a flat today![44]

Nielsen was reluctant to live in the working-class districts, so he confined his house hunting to the inner city. From his letters to Anne Marie in the following days, it appears that he found suitable accommodation on Hauser Plads, but for some unknown reason it failed. In Laxegade he looked at 'five good rooms for 460 Kroner', but added that it was 'a bad neighbourhood'.[45] Laxegade was a parallel street to Dybensgade, also known as the brothel street.[46] Finally, on 18 October, the family moved into an attic flat at 42 Nørre Voldgade.

ILL. 4. Nørre Voldgade, also known as the Boulevard, *c*. 1890. Nielsen and Anne Marie Carl-Nielsen lived at no. 42 from October 1892 to October 1893. The premises are one of the rear houses on the right-hand side of the street.

Nørre Voldgade was, as mentioned, part of the innermost of the three ring roads that were built around Copenhagen after the ramparts were demolished. No. 42 was on the old side of Nørre Voldgade, which used to be right up against the inner side of the ramparts. When the ramparts were demolished, the old houses suddenly had to be lined with facades as part of a more fashionable boulevard project, which was not entirely in keeping with their restrained expression.[47] During the bombardment of Copenhagen in 1807, the building was hit by English fire rockets, but it was rebuilt and in 1843 the height of the building was increased. The family in the flat on the fourth floor could therefore enjoy a fine view of Ørstedsparken.[48]

The following year the family moved again – this time to 5 Frederiksgade in the Bredgade area with a view of Marmorkirken; here they lived from 1893 to 1898. It was also here that their last child, their son Hans Børge, was born. Like Marmorkirken opposite, the luxury flat on the fourth floor was relatively new. Both were included in Frederik V's original plans for Frederiksstaden, drawn up in 1749. However, the subsequent king, Christian VII, was not particularly interested in the project which therefore came to a standstill in 1770.[49] The foundations of the church lay in ruins for many years, and despite various attempts to resume construction, no real progress was made until the 1870s. The entrepreneur C. F. Tietgen bought the site in 1874 and subsequently commissioned Ferdinand Meldahl to build the church. He financed the project by using the surrounding area in Frederiksgade to build modern apartments for the affluent class. It was to one of these new apartments that Nielsen and his family moved in the summer of 1883. The following summer the church was consecrated.[50] In her childhood memoirs, their daughter Anne Marie writes about this time:

> Now my father's composition concerts also began. Oh, how we often sat together in the Hotel Phønix, just opposite Koncertpalæet, and eagerly counted every ticket buyer, 'and there were really no more than there could be in a charabanc', as the doctor and composer Rudolph Bergh put it.[51]

Hotel Phønix and Koncertpalæet stood on either side of Bredgade, a few hundred metres from the family home. A little further down, Bredgade opened onto Kongens Nytorv by The Royal Theatre. Many of Nielsen's activities as a composer and musician thus took place close to home. He was no longer a visitor to the area.

Koncertpalæet, which opened in 1888 in conjunction with the Great Nordic Exhibition, contained both a large and a small concert auditorium. The large one was used when international celebrities performed in the city and for performances of orchestral and choral music. It was here that Nielsen's First Symphony (1894) and his choral work *Hymnus Amoris* (1897) were premiered. The small auditorium, which was used for most concerts by Danish artists and for chamber music, was the venue for composition evenings organised by Nielsen himself in 1892 and 1898.[52] Jørgensen's description of the atmosphere outside Koncertpalæet suggests that the performances were not only an opportunity for the public to enjoy music, but also a social ritual that was part of modern urban life for the city's wealthy residents:

> … Bredgade is worth seeing on a mild and wet winter's evening when music is played in Koncertpalæet. The electric balloons are lit in the courtyard of the mansion. Coach after coach and carriage after carriage enters through one of the gates, stops in front of the platform and then leaves through the other gate. … On this electric, silver-glittering rainy evening in front of the old, illuminated mansion, Copenhagen feels like both a metropolis and a modern city.[53]

The family's next home was a flat at 6 Toldbodvej (now Esplanaden), to which they moved in October 1898. The five-storey brick house was built in 1785 and was close to Kastellet and Langelinie, only a few hundred metres from their previous home in Frederiksgade. Yet the place must have had a very different character. The old Hussar barracks was opposite the building, and in 1899 the First Company of the

ILL. 5. The family in their home in 6 Toldbodvej, where a large part of the children's upbringing took place.

Twenty-first Battalion lodged a complaint about the heavy invasion of 'loose women' who visited the soldiers, especially on Sundays.[54] The street was also known for its taverns, and both neighbouring houses on either side of no. 6 had drinking establishments on the ground floor.[55]

The home on Toldbodvej is described in great detail in Nielsen's daughter's memoirs:

> It was a tall, red building. A mighty arched gate led in. … Then you came to a flight of broad, sand-strewn stairs … A beautiful, worn iron banister, which we used to slide down, led up to where we lived on the first floor. When you rang the doorbell, you almost immediately entered a large hall with old panelling and doors. This was the living room. It was divided by an old eighteenth-century goblin … My father's study was a little out of the way, with its own entrance and facing the courtyard, which was to the south, towards the first courtyard. For there were three courtyards in succession. In the second courtyard, a blacksmith worked in

ILL. 6. Toldbodvej, *c.* 1895. On the left are the long yellow wings that belonged to the old Hussar barracks. To the right are the houses nos. 4, 6, 8 etc. In no. 6 (the tall building) Nielsen and his family lived on the first floor with the balcony over the gate from 1898 to 1906. At that time, the distiller Peter Høeberg owned the neighbouring premises at no. 4, where Toldbod Bodega is located today. His son, Georg Høeberg, who later became the Royal Kapellmeister, played in The Royal Orchestra alongside Nielsen from 1897 to 1901. He also lived in Toldbodvej until 1901.[56]

> his forge from early in the morning, and you could hear his regular hammering. From the innermost courtyard came the sound of wailing cows, for they were still being kept. They belonged to Kapellmeister Høeberg's father, who had a parlour at no. 4 and used the milk to make toddies. All these noises amused my father. There was a lot of sunshine in his room, fiery red cactus flowers in the windows, and there was always someone playing the grand piano.[57]

We get an impression not only of the home, but also of the surrounding city life, which formed the soundscape when Nielsen sat in his study. Copenhagen was an industrial city with lots of machines and animals, and you could hear – and smell – it.

The home on Toldbodvej was also a place where prominent artists and musicians met and discussed the issues of the day. Nielsen's daughter mentions Joakim and Niels Skovgaard, Thomas Laub and Edvard Grieg among the family's guests.[58]

In April 1906 the family moved to 5 Ny Toldbodgade (now 29 Toldbodgade), close to Amalienborg Palace.[59] The house was built in the 1890s and the flat on the second floor was modern with a bathroom, toilet and electric light.[60] During the time after the move, Nielsen was busy rehearsing his opera, *Maskarade*, which premiered at The Royal Theatre on 11 November 1906. The rehearsals were demanding, and Nielsen had to make corrections and abridgements up to the last moment in order to make the opera work.[61] It was convenient that the new home was just around the corner from librettist Vilhelm Andersen's house on Skt. Annæ Plads, and only six or seven minutes' walk from the theatre.[62] However, it was Anne Marie who benefited most from the move, as she was able to use the atelier in the attic on Ny Toldbodgade. Previously she had used a workroom on Langelinie, which she had acquired when they lived in Frederiksgade.

Two Artist Residences

The desire to have an atelier in the home was also crucial for the Nielsen family's last two homes. These also suggest that Nielsen and Anne Marie Carl-Nielsen had become better off and had achieved a higher status in cultural life. In the early years of their marriage they had struggled to make ends meet, and Anne Marie's father had supported them with 400 Kroner a year.[63] Nielsen's income as a member of The Royal Orchestra was then 1,200 Kroner, and after a few years it rose to just over 1,400. Furthermore, they both had income from their work, and Nielsen from teaching a few pupils on the side. Nevertheless, they had to live frugally.[64]

When Nielsen was sent back to his second violin desk in March 1905 after serving as deputy Kapellmeister in 1904, he decided to resign.[65] Although he had other sources of income, the following period must have been more financially uncertain. This changed in the spring of 1908 when he signed a contract with The Royal Theatre to take up the position of Kapellmeister on 1 July. On that date he was paid half of his annual salary of 4,500 Kroner.[66]

It was also a significant financial improvement for the family when Nielsen was included in the Finance Act for 1901–2 and began to receive state support for his work as a composer. He was initially given a three-year grant, after which he received a permanent one. At first the grant was 800 Kroner a year, but it gradually increased to 1,200 in 1906–7, 2,000 in 1918–19 and 3,600 in 1921–22. Nielsen was given special status in the Finance Act for 1926–27, and the grant was increased to 7,500 Kroner, which he received annually until his death in 1931.[67] The increasing amounts reflect, of course, Nielsen's growing recognition as a composer in the years around and after the First World War, but also the fact that this was a period of historically high inflation.[68]

Anne Marie had also increased her income after the turn of the century. She earned well from private commissions, and in 1904 she had received a fee of 2,480 Kroner for her work in designing bronze doors for the cathedral in Ribe.[69] In the following years she made a serious breakthrough internationally, selling many of her works on the German art market.[70] Finally, in March 1908 – a few months before Nielsen signed a contract with the Theatre – she was named the winner of the prestigious competition to create an equestrian statue of Christian IX for the Riding Ground at Christiansborg Palace.[71]

The couple's success meant that they could demand more from a future home. They began their search in the summer of 1908, but as Anne Marie was in Germany at the time, Nielsen had to lead the project. As mentioned above, Anne Marie's dream of having her own atelier was a priority, but it also meant that they had to move out of the centre of Copenhagen, where all their shared homes had been until then. By the end of June, Nielsen had found some suitable accommodation, which he wrote to Anne Marie about:

> My darling! I would very much like to hear your opinion on this. We can buy it in two ways, both for the purpose of financial speculation; but in both cases we will be moving in six years' time. There is probably money to be made, but what do you think? I looked at another one for 25,000 Kroner on Rosenvænget yesterday, but it did not work out. Now I'm going to look at something on Vodrofsvej. Would you stay there?[72]

The property Nielsen refers to in the first line was a larger building on the corner of Rosenvængets Tværvej in Østerbro. He had enclosed a detailed description of the property with the letter, including the terms of purchase.[73] The location must have appealed to them, but the disadvantage was that they had to move out after six years. Rosenvænget was, as mentioned, a well-known artists' quarter, and it was here that Anne Marie had lived and studied in her early years in Copenhagen, and Carl knew the area from his time in Slagelsegade.

They were probably more hesitant about the prime location at 53 Vodroffsvej. In this part of Frederiksberg there was neither urban life nor a romantic artist's idyll. Rather, Vodroffsvej had the character of a country road where large loads of hay were transported and cows were driven to the abattoir at Kvægtorvet in the city.[74] The villa that Nielsen was to visit was built in 1882 and stood at the northern end of the road. At the end of Vodroffsvej, in what is now Rosenørns Allé, ran the railway, which the train passed on its way in and out of the city centre. However, the villa had the ad-

ILL. 7. The family in Anne Marie Carl-Nielsen's atelier in the basement of 53 Vodroffsvej.

vantage of a large atelier in the basement. The property was owned by the artist Axel Helsted, who died in 1907, and the first floor with his atelier was therefore empty. The annual rent was 1,600 Kroner, twice as much as the family had paid to live on Toldbodvej ten years earlier.[75]

Anne Marie liked the villa flat and the family moved in in October 1908. Shortly afterwards, her good friends Axel and Sofie Olrik moved in on the ground floor.[76] The composer Fini Henriques lived just around the corner at 2 Forchhammersvej. Nielsen and Henriques had previously been colleagues in The Royal Orchestra, and the two families enjoyed each other's company, according to Nielsen's daughter:

> The Henriques family lived nearby. He was so lively and interested in everything my father composed. He used to come over and when the last Sonata for Piano and Violin in G minor was being composed, he took my father's violin and played it quite fluently from the score. He was a perfect musical genius. They laughed and had a great time together.[77]

Although the neighbourhood may have seemed rural compared to where they had lived before, they did have other artists nearby. This must have been a key factor in their feeling at home in the area.

ILL. 8. Carl and Anne Marie in the large garden at 53 Vodroffsvej.

The director N. H. Rasmussen, who lived in the house next door, had founded a gymnastics institute in Copenhagen in 1887, based on the Swedish, so-called Lingian gymnastics. In 1898 he could afford to build his own sports hall at 51 Vodroffsvej. The house was designed by his fellow student at the Polytechnic, the architect P. V. Jensen-Klint. Rasmussen's daughter, Helle Gotved, later took over the management of the school, which is now called Gotvedinstituttet.

Nielsen's family soon developed a close relationship with their new neighbours; the children went to the house for gymnastics and the families spent time together in private.[78] Nielsen also established a professional relationship with his neighbour when, in 1909, he wrote a melody for J. C. Hostrup's *De unges Sang* (*Song of the Young*) to celebrate the twenty-fifth anniversary of the Gymnastics Institute. He dedicated the tune to Rasmussen and it was later included in *The Folk High School Melody Book*.

The neighbourhood on Vodroffsvej also had an impact on the family's lifestyle. As well as keeping up with the latest trends in gymnastics through their neighbour, Nielsen was also inspired to purchase a horse, which was kept further down the road.[79] He often rode to Dyrehaven, where from 1910 he was involved in the activities of the new Open-Air Theatre. However, the horse was hardly a suitable means

ILL. 9. 28 Frederiksholms Kanal, as the property was then in 1913. To the right of the gate was Anne Marie Carl-Nielsen's honorary residence, and to the far right on the ground floor was a large sculpture studio.

of transport when he needed to get to the centre of Copenhagen, in which case he walked or took the tram.[80]

After the family had lived on Vodroffsvej for six years, Anne Marie was offered a very special residence in Copenhagen: 28A Frederiksholms Kanal. The yellow building was built in 1771 and was originally a sculptor's atelier.[81] The large open courtyard behind the house was used for storing building materials. Among the former residents of the house was the sculptor H. E. Freund, who had the rooms decorated in the early nineteenth century, inspired by wall motifs from Pompeii and Herculaneum.[82] Freund was succeeded by H. W. Bissen, who, while living in the house, created the statue of Frederik VI for Frederiksberg Have at Frederiksberg Palace. His son Vilhelm Bissen later took over the house, where he lived and worked until his death in 1913.

When the Nielsen family moved in in April 1915, Anne Marie was still working on the equestrian statue of Christian IX. The artist's residence provided a good environment for this type of work, and Nielsen was able to have his own music room. He had set it up in the rearmost back of the three rooms in the house, all of which had windows overlooking the canal. The kitchen, the couple's two bedrooms and two large ateliers faced the small south-west courtyard. The house also had a cellar, and on the first floor there were rooms for their daughters and Maren, the maid, as well as several ateliers.

ILL. 10. Carl Nielsen and Anne Marie Carl-Nielsen in one of the rooms at 28A Frederiksholms Kanal.

Here they were able to combine their working needs with a home in the centre of Copenhagen. However, they now found themselves in a different part of the centre from what they were used to, in the western part close to Christiansborg Palace. Their daughter describes the special atmosphere and location of the house:

> The dining room was large and spacious, with two large windows overlooking the canal. In one of the windows was a 1.5 metre high plaster figure, an archaic cast of Diana, walking calmly forward with a small bow on her back. Behind her, you could see the great ships silently moving along the bulwarks, and on the other side, the huge auburn roof of the Arsenal Museum. Everything in this old house was beautiful, doors, panelling, small inlaid Pompeian compositions, the door frames to the large drawing room were beautifully decorated with ivy leaves …[83]

The Arsenal Museum, Tøjhuset, which the family could see from their windows, was built in the early seventeenth century. The museum's collection of weapons had been open to the public since 1857, and in 1928 the whole building was converted into a museum. A little further on was Christiansborg Palace, rebuilt after the fire of 1884. By the time the equestrian statue of Anne Marie was unveiled on the Christiansborg

Riding Ground in November 1927, the palace was almost complete. Proceeding in the opposite direction from the palace, one reached the area around the new City Hall and Vestre Boulevard (now H. C. Andersen's Boulevard). Here were important cultural institutions such as the National Museum, Glyptoteket, Tivoli Gardens and the Academy of Music in its new building from 1905. Further along were the blocks of the working-class district and the entertainment venues of Vesterbro.

The period around the move to Frederiksholms Kanal was one of great upheaval for the family. In the spring of 1914, Nielsen resigned as conductor and thus terminated his long association with The Royal Theatre. On the other hand, he was soon offered new posts at the Academy of Music and Musikforeningen, which must have been well paid. In 1916 his income was 12,000 Kroner, which may have included Anne Marie's earnings, but it was still a high income. The family also gained more financial breathing space by moving into an honorary residence, where they only had to pay 600 Kroner in rent. They could therefore afford to keep the atelier on Vodroffsvej, which Anne Marie continued to use for several years after the move.

Anne Marie's preference for working away from home was probably due to the marriage crisis that had arisen in the early summer of 1914. Anne Marie had discovered that Carl had been unfaithful to her for a long time while she was away on business. The crisis led to a separation in 1919–22, during which Nielsen led a rather nomadic existence. He substituted on several occasions as conductor in Gothenburg and spent long periods with friends at Damgaard near Fredericia and at Tibberup in northern Zealand. In 1918 he bought a summer cottage in Skagen, a town that had long been the home of Scandinavian artists. From the autumn of 1920 he lived with his daughter Irmelin and her family at 20 Nørrebrogade, near Dronning Louises Bro. Irmelin's husband, Eggert Møller, was a medical doctor and his mother owned Nørrebro Pharmacy in the neighbouring building. Nielsen remained in close contact with Anne Marie, however, and in the summer of 1922 they resumed their relationship. He returned to the artist's residence by the canal, which became the couple's last home.

The homes of Nielsen and Anne Marie Carl-Nielsen not only provided a setting for private life, but also for meetings between musicians and artists who played a role in Copenhagen's cultural life. In her memoirs, the youngest daughter recalls how friends often visited the family in the evening: 'They were immediately invited to the table with country hospitality, where many heated and lively discussions about artistic problems developed.'[84] In essence, the home must have functioned as a cultural meeting place, an exciting place to visit precisely because of the exchange of ideas and knowledge across the arts. It is therefore worthwhile looking at how Nielsen became part of the city's professional musical milieu, and how he and Anne Marie became part of Copenhagen's artistic and intellectual circles. The capital became the base from which Nielsen developed his work as a musician, composer and cultural figure over almost five decades.

Chapter 6

THE ACADEMY OF MUSIC

Nielsen's three years of study at the Academy of Music, Kjøbenhavns Musikconservatorium, from the beginning of 1884 to the end of 1886 became the basis for his life as a professional musician. Through a variety of different courses, he was trained to a high level in technical skills and thus in mastering the craft of playing music. It was at the Academy that he had his daily interactions with teachers and fellow students. For Nielsen, it was an unfamiliar world that introduced him to new ways of understanding music.

Choosing the Academy was by no means a foregone conclusion if one wanted to train as a musician, as it was far from the only option in the capital. Individuals could apprentice themselves to a professional musician and improve their skills by taking private lessons, or they could take lessons at one of the capital's other music colleges. No formal training was required to work as a professional musician, and competition for the coveted positions was a free-for-all. Studying at the Academy would indeed give the graduate certain advantages, as the students had at least undergone a comprehensive training programme with some of the best music professors in the country.

A musical institution such as The Royal Theatre originally had a well-established educational system to supply the institution with qualified musicians. In 1773 the Theatre founded a singing school and in 1790 a violin school to train the new generation of violinists. In 1834, at the age of seventeen, Niels W. Gade entered the violin school. As part of his training, he played for free in The Royal Orchestra for the next ten years, gaining valuable experience as an orchestral musician.[1] Several private initiatives in the nineteenth century led to the establishment of music schools to train professional musicians.[2] Giuseppe Siboni, a singing master at The Royal Theatre, founded his Academy of Music in 1827, which was associated with the Theatre, although it was an entirely private enterprise.[3] It was founded on the same principles as the Italian conservatoires – that is, to be a kind of educational institution for children who could make music their livelihood after completing their education.[4]

Kjøbenhavns Musikconservatorium was founded in 1867, and from 1872 it was housed in an imposing mansion in Bredgade. It was here that the teaching and musical activities took place, preparing the students for their future lives as professional musicians. The property was owned by the company Hornung & Møller,

ILL. 1. The Academy was housed on the ground floor of Dehn's mansion in Bredgade, built by Privy Councillor Friedrich Ludwig von Dehn in the 1750s. When Nielsen attended the Academy, the building was also home to Hornung & Møller's piano factory.

who had their piano factory in the building. They were the country's largest piano manufacturer and in 1872 they had furnished the spacious mansion to accommodate production, storage, exhibition and administration.[5] The Academy rented the ground floor and used the rooms for teaching. Eventually the space became too small, and when the lease expired in 1887, the Academy moved to a newly built residence at 9–11 Vester Voldgade that had been started in the summer of 1886, during Nielsen's final year.[6]

The students at the Academy in Bredgade immediately became part of the musical life of the city. On the first floor of the building was a concert hall named Hornung & Møller's Hall, where the Academy could hold recitals. The hall, which could seat an audience of 165, was also used for public concerts.[7] The Academy also benefited from the fact that the piano factory supplied instruments for use in the classroom.[8] It was also important for Hornung & Møller to establish a good relationship with potential customers.

ILL. 2. In connection with the production of the 10,000th instrument at Hornung & Møller's piano factory in Bredgade, *Illustreret Tidende* published this jubilee illustration depicting the various stages of production and their location in the building.[9]

Financially, the Academy was established on the basis of a bequest from the goldsmith and jeweller Peter Wilhelm Moldenhauer. The Academy's first board of directors consisted of the conductor of Musikforeningen (The Music Society), who was Niels W. Gade, the organist and lawyer J. P. E. Hartmann, and the Royal Kapellmeister Simon Holger Paulli. All three had teaching experience and held important positions in Copenhagen's musical life. Paulli, who like Gade had attended the theatre's violin school and was now director of The Royal Orchestra, had published textbooks on violin playing.[10] Hartmann had taught theory at Siboni's Academy, and when Siboni died in 1839, Hartmann took over as director of the institution until it closed three years later. It was Gade, however, who was responsible for preparing the curricula before the new Academy opened. Like many other European academies, it was modelled on the Leipzig Academy of Music, where Gade had taught harmony, instrumentation and composition between 1845–48. The Copenhagen counterpart adopted key elements of the Leipzig model, which emphasised the integration of a practical and academic approach to music. The Leipzig Academy was an important educational link to the famous Gewandhaus Orchestra, and in a similar way the new academy in Bredgade was intended to benefit musical life in Copenhagen.[11]

The new academy did not eliminate the need for other educational institutions in the city, and the board had to fight for its survival. The fact that C. H. Glass founded a piano academy in 1877 and C. F. E. Horneman his music institute in 1880 shows that Kjøbenhavns Musikkonservatorium by no means had a monopoly on training musicians in the capital.[12] During the first few decades, however, the Academy became a much sought-after institution, with applicants from all over the country competing for places. Twenty-eight students were accepted in the first year, but due to cancellations a further nine were admitted the following year. The total number of places was limited, but remained stable at between forty and fifty for the first few decades. Each student had to pay an annual fee of one hundred Rigsdaler. From 1875, when the new coinage law converted one Rigsdaler into two Kroner, the annual amount was adjusted to 224 Kroner. This covered only half of the institution's costs per pupil. Moldenhauer's bequest made this model possible. The Academy also had endowments which enabled it to waive tuition fees for particularly talented applicants without financial means.[13]

In November 1882, the Academy applied to the government for a grant to increase the number of free places. The reason for this was that the institution accepted students from all over the country and the board felt that the government should support the education. This was to encourage the admission of talented applicants who would otherwise not have had the means to pay for their education. As a result, the government granted an annual subsidy of 10,000 Kroner, of which 6,000 was to be spent on twenty-seven free places. Thus, when Nielsen was admitted in 1884, more than half of the fifty places were paid for by public endowments, including Nielsen's.[14]

The Tuition

Tuition at the Academy was organised to support the wide range of skills expected of a musician. Nielsen was admitted as a violin student. To become a good musician, however, he had to acquire skills not only in playing his instrument, but also in playing other instruments and in understanding what music is and can be. As well as practising technique, the aim of the tuition was to help the students to understand music: to increase their insight and understanding of music in all its aspects.

According to the syllabus, the subjects were spread over all three years. The Academy offered piano lessons, solo and choral singing, violin, ensemble and organ playing. In addition, music theory was taught alongside the practical subjects. Students at the Academy were entitled to study all subjects, although some were optional. However, they were required to take piano, choral singing and music theory.[15] Piano lessons were thus compulsory for all students.

Choral singing was also compulsory, probably due to the fact that the subject had elements of ensemble performance, and it was expected that musicians should be able to use their voice as an instrument. The teaching was not so much concerned with bel canto singing, for 'all pupils should, as far as possible, … take part in singing lessons, whether they had any particular aptitude or lacked vocal ability'.[16] As a potential music teacher or conductor, it was important to be able to demonstrate musical delivery, phrasing or expression vocally. As a pianist accompanying a singer or choir, it was also important to have some experience with one's own voice. Previously, Nielsen had mainly played instrumental music, but the Academy's comprehensive teaching programme showed him that vocal music should also be recognised. At first, Carl Helsted and Margrethe Bang were responsible for the vocal training. However, when the number of students at the Academy was increased in 1883 with the new government endowment, Viggo Bielefeldt was commissioned by Gade to 'establish a choral singing class'.[17] Bielefeldt was among the Academy's first graduates and was a popular tenor soloist. From 1880 he was cantor at Trinitatis Kirke in Copenhagen and thus had experience as a choirmaster.[18] Although Nielsen left no comments about his choral training, he must have attended lessons with Bielefeldt as his teacher.

The syllabuses drawn up in the early years after the Academy's foundation in 1867 were largely adhered to in the decades that followed.[19] It was originally intended that the students would be taught orchestral playing and conducting. This was not to be, however, and Paulli was instead given responsibility for the ensemble course, in which the students would play chamber music. From the first year it was a priority that the students in these classes should also play mainly piano arrangements of orchestral works for four or eight hands. Apart from the social aspects that the teachers at the Academy emphasised, the aim of the ensemble playing was to introduce the students to the current orchestral repertoire of the time.[20]

This was a common way of working with new music, as it was not practical to wait for the orchestras to schedule the music for performance, and although it was possible to study the score, it was the piano arrangements of the works that provided an excellent opportunity to hear the melodic and harmonic content of the music. Music publishers supported this practice by providing piano arrangements of popular orchestral works. After graduating from the Academy, Nielsen stayed in Berlin and heard Wagner's *Lohengrin* for the first time. He wrote home to his former theory teacher, Orla Rosenhoff, and remarked: 'Well, I like *Lohengrin*, and anyway I already knew most of it from the vocal score.'[21] While a piano score of an opera or other vocal work served the practical purpose of allowing singers to rehearse the music, it could also be used for study purposes. For Nielsen, four-hand piano playing became a way of practising music that he cultivated in the following years with the pianist Henrik Knudsen.[22] Later, when he was a teacher, he would gather his students together to play Mahler's symphonies, for example.[23] As a pedagogical tool, the piano excerpts were useful, and Nielsen emphasised 'the enormous cultural importance that the piano excerpts make possible for the individual'.[24] Moreover, the piano arrangements were readily available from music dealers.

The violin was Nielsen's main instrument, but all students had to take mandatory piano lessons. This reflects the idea that it was essential for students to be able to use a piano – not as a concert instrument per se, but rather to be able to use the instrument as an aid in teaching situations and to be familiar with a wide range of repertoire. Nielsen's abilities on the piano are described by Knudsen as 'hopeless, most of the time it sounded humiliating … apart from all musical and artistic grand intentions'.[25] This statement should be seen in the light of the fact that, for Nielsen, the piano was a utility instrument.

Nielsen's piano teacher at the Academy was Gottfried Matthison-Hansen, who was also organist at Trinitatis Kirke during this period. For the annual piano examinations, Nielsen played Beethoven's piano sonatas and works by Mendelssohn and Edmund Neupert.[26] These were not demanding works once the basic technique had been mastered. During his studies, Nielsen was 'very diligent' and 'very good' at the keyboard, although he often missed lessons.[27] In a 1931 interview, Nielsen recalled his final piano examination, when he nervously played 'a relatively easy Beethoven sonata'.[28] The mark was 'very good, second grade', a good result considering the piano was not his primary instrument.[29]

The Violin

Studying with Valdemar Tofte laid the foundation for Nielsen's professional career as a violinist. Through Tofte, Nielsen became associated with European musical traditions and a virtuoso culture strongly rooted in the German musical environment. Tofte was highly regarded and respected for his pedagogy and was able to pass on his wealth of experience of concert life at the highest level. It is not surprising, therefore, that he was appointed violin teacher at the Academy when it was founded. Tofte had studied for three years in Germany with Joseph Joachim, who was considered one of the best violinists of his time. Joachim was a much sought-after concert violinist and professor, and it is said that people would stop in the street outside his house to listen through the window as he played a quartet with, among others, Tofte.[30]

Tofte, who had excellent technical skills, sought to carry on the traditions he had acquired during his stays abroad. He was particularly interested in violin bowing technique, which he had learned from Joachim. Although Tofte left no written evidence of his teaching, his daughter Clara Tofte, whom he taught, summarised her knowledge of her father's methods in the manuscript *The Simple Outline of Joachim's Bowing Style*.[31] In addition, Clara meticulously collected her famous father's letters, and in 1915 she took the initiative of gathering written testimonies about her father from students and colleagues.[32] Nielsen did not contribute to Clara's initiative, but a newspaper review of one of Nielsen's performances as a violin soloist, after he had left the Academy, highlighted his beautiful bowing.[33]

Tofte based his teaching on his German models, but he was also tolerant of other styles of playing. Johannes Schiørring, a student of Tofte's at the Academy at the same time as Nielsen, explains:

> Tofte possessed the most outstanding qualities as a teacher, and his fidelity to the traditions of Spohr and especially Joseph Joachim was extraordinary, as was his memory of how these masters had conceived and performed the various masterpieces of the classical violin literature. Tofte rightly always informed his students of these great models, but at the same time he had an open ear for his students' personal perceptions and usually approved them if they were based on a solid musical foundation.[34]

The student's performance could reveal new insights – as Frederik Schnedler-Petersen, who attended the Academy in 1885–87, explained when he returned from studying with Joachim in Berlin in 1890 and paid Tofte a visit. On the occasion of the visit, Tofte played a piece for Schnedler-Petersen and asked him to correct it to see if 'there was anything that Joachim was doing differently *now*'.[35] Tofte was constantly concerned about whether he remembered the phrasing correctly or whether Joachim had changed his interpretation since Tofte had last heard him.

In his eagerness to perform a work in the style of his models, Tofte relied not only on his memory. On his travels abroad, where he met the greatest violin virtuosos of the day, he made sure to transcribe their fingerings and phrasing into his own copies of the music. These personal notes proved invaluable in his later teaching. Indeed, he thought they might be valuable to others, and he bequeathed his music collection to the Academy so that students could study his notes on the performance aspects of the music.[36]

Tofte had between two and three pupils a day, each of whom received tuition twice a week.[37] After six months of study, Nielsen auditioned on the violin in the summer of 1884, playing an etude by Federigo Fiorillo. After the examination, Gade remarked that Nielsen had a 'good arm', probably referring to his bowing technique. The comment that Nielsen was 'well trained' also suggests that the teachers considered him a diligent pupil.[38] Tofte, however, was less positive, noting that Nielsen 'must practise' in order to improve, although he also saw a positive development, adding that 'he is doing well now'. As a second-year student, he was required to take an examination twice a year. Nielsen's two examinations in 1885 show 'good progress all in all'.[39] His final examination in violin at the end of 1886 was also positive. Gade noticed his musical talent.[40]

Nielsen held Tofte in high esteem, both personally and for his teaching. When Tofte turned seventy in 1902, Nielsen congratulated him and called him 'our first and greatest violin teacher'.[41] He sent the telegram on his own behalf, so when he wrote 'our teacher' it must have been an expression of the recognition Tofte enjoyed in the musical establishment.

The Academy also served as a window to the European musical world. Naturally, Nielsen visited Joseph Joachim during his stay in Berlin in 1890 and was able to present the letter of recommendation he had received from Gade in Copenhagen.[42] Nielsen had been told that 'with Gade's recommendation in your pocket, all doors will spring open for you'.[43] Gade's recommendation enabled Nielsen to attend Joachim's rehearsals and concerts during his stay and to attend lessons at the Berlin Academy of Music, Hochschule für Musik, as often as he wished.[44] Together with some friends, he played his newly composed string quartet for Joachim.[45] When he left Joachim before Christmas 1890, Nielsen wrote in his diary: 'The impression I have of Joachim as an artistic personality is a harmonious one. Honesty, seriousness and rigour as an artist. Gentleness and kindness as a human being.'[46]

Music Theory and Harmony

Knowledge of music theory was an essential part of training as a musician, and the theory courses at the Academy had a great impact on Nielsen's understanding of music: an approach to evaluating the structural qualities of music and its potential was established. The music theory classes not only included genuine exercises to familiarise the student with musical styles, but were also an intimate setting in which possibilities were explored and tested in a reflective dialogue between teacher and student. Nielsen's teacher was Orla Rosenhoff. Shortly before Rosenhoff's death in 1905, Nielsen pointed out that Rosenhoff was the teacher to whom he owed the most.[47] Judging by the many assignments Nielsen completed during his studies at the Academy, he was extremely productive when it came to theory lessons.[48]

Since the founding of the Academy, the teaching of music theory had been divided into three courses. In the early years, Johann Christian Gebauer taught basic music theory and harmony. Those who had completed the basic theory course were then transferred to Hartmann, who taught them counterpoint. Gade ran the third course, which covered musical form and structure as well as instrumentation and music history.[49] This arrangement changed when Rosenhoff was appointed as the theory teacher in 1881. He had taught piano from the Academy's foundation until October 1869, and from 1881 he took over the first two courses in music theory. Thus Nielsen had Rosenhoff for all three years. In the third year, Rosenhoff's lectures were supplemented by Gade, whose lessons Nielsen later recalled as strangely incoherent, almost like a ramble through European cultural history.[50]

When Rosenhoff was recruited to teach music theory, he persuaded Gade and the rest of the board to combine the weekly seminars into a single day of one and a half hours. He also reduced class sizes from six to four, so that Nielsen's class included three others, one of whom was Daniel Hannemann, who later became a violist in The Royal Orchestra and an active member of the Chamber Music Society.[51] According to Rosenhoff, neither of the other two were at Nielsen's or Hannemann's level. This suggests that the students may have attended the theory classes for different reasons, some being interested in the subject, others simply to pass the compulsory course. Rosenhoff wrote in retrospect:

> Carl Nielsen was around 17 [*recte* 18 and a half] when he entered the Conservatoire, and he immediately became my student. But the class he was in didn't suit him at all, in that two of the students were pure nonentities and very inferior, and the third (the late Daniel Hannemann) was several years older and had learned so much that I let him work on his own. C.N. was quiet and occasionally looked into my eyes with that remarkable expression he still has. But he didn't particularly stand out.

> Occasionally he and I would walk together from the Conservatoire to my home, and then I several times had occasion to observe that he thought more deeply and more subtly than the other young men I was accustomed to working with. But then he became my pupil alone, and I soon felt that this was someone worth watching.[52]

When Rosenhoff reminisced in 1905, he recalled that Nielsen had been a quiet student and had not made much of an impression. However, was this in comparison with Nielsen's classmates – or was it in view of Nielsen's development into the up-and-coming composer that Rosenhoff was talking about at the turn of the century? It seems most likely that it was the latter reason, for already at the annual examination in the summer of 1884, when Rosenhoff had been teaching him for six months, he noted in the pupil register under Nielsen's name: 'Good. Diligent. Very good.'[53] Not many students achieved a top grade after only six months, so Rosenhoff must have noticed Nielsen's ability in music theory.

It is not entirely clear what Rosenhoff means when he writes that Nielsen became his private student. At some point he seems to have given Nielsen private lessons in music theory. The unfortunate combination of classmates thus worked in Nielsen's favour.

Nielsen learned elementary music theory based on Gebauer's *Exempelbog til Harmonilæren* (Book of Examples for the Teaching of Harmony, *c*. 1870). Just like other students, he copied scales and intervals to practise the many combinations of the tonal system.[54] The textbook was prepared for teaching at the Academy and reflected the examples that Gebauer, and later Rosenhoff, used in the classroom.[55] The treatise itself was not necessarily very informative, for there were no descriptions of the various concepts. If one did not know about augmented or diminished intervals, the circle of fifths or chord positions, the student was at a disadvantage. The textbook was thus an integral part of the Academy's teaching. The teacher gave the explanations in class and the student now had the textbook, which was a collection of the most important examples. The treatise was revised and reissued several times up to around 1910, indicating that Gebauer's collection of examples was the point of departure for the elementary teaching of music theory for generations.[56]

The Academy also followed German models in music theory. The Leipzig Academy of Music was an influential centre for music theory, particularly through Ernst Friedrich Richter, who was appointed as a teacher when it was founded in 1843. He taught music theory and produced textbooks that grew out of his pedagogical work on harmony, counterpoint, musical form and structure, and analysis.[57] These subjects also became a regular part of the Academy's courses in Copenhagen. In 1871 Gebauer translated Richter's primer on harmony, *Lehrbuch der Harmonie*. While preparing the second edition of the Danish translation, which was published in 1882,

Gebauer was assisted by his pupil Jørgen Ditleff Bondesen in revising the translation to adapt it to the teaching methods of the Academy. According to Bondesen, the revisions were made in the chapters dealing with intervals and in a subsection on chordal theory. In addition, the examples were now all in G and F clefs, rather than in C clefs as Richter had done.[58]

Rosenhoff continued Gebauer's pedagogical approach and published six textbooks during his time as teacher, including *450 firstemmige Opgaver til Brug ved den musikteoretiske Undervisning* (450 Simple Exercises for Use in Music Theory Teaching).[59] The books contain only short descriptions, similar to collections of examples, structured according to the progression of the course. Accordingly, the student solved the exercises as the lesson progressed, but was dependent on the teacher's instructions. In 1909, Carl Cohn published *Nøgle til Løsning af Orla Rosenhoffs firstemmige Opgaver* (A Key to Orla Rosenhoff's Four-Part Exercises), which explains in detail how the textbooks should be used.[60] Nielsen reviewed and welcomed Cohn's book. Rosenhoff's exercises had developed in such a close connection with his teaching that 'the understanding of the progress in solving the exercises depended on the author-teacher's personal instruction and oral reasoning'.[61] The books were difficult to use unassisted. The first four textbooks were published while Nielsen was still a student at the Academy. However, he also worked on the exercises in the final book, which was published in 1889 – that is, after Nielsen had graduated from the Academy.[62] This suggests that Rosenhoff had prepared the collection long before and used it in his teaching prior to its publication.[63] The collection provides a unique insight into the instruction Nielsen received.

The textbooks were based on Richter's theory of harmony, which required the student to write a four-part setting from a figured bass line. The important point was not to work out the order of the chords, but to decipher the harmony from the figures written over the bass line. Then the task was to determine the voice leading in each of the three upper parts, thereby implementing a regular dissonance treatment. Richter's exercises were a new way of learning harmony. They differed from traditional exercises in which the outer parts were given in advance and only the middle parts had to be added. Rosenhoff found Richter's exercises suitable because they emphasised 'the important relationship between melody and bass'.[64] The student had to strive to create an independent melody which, as the upper part of the setting, would become distinctive to the whole exercise.

Rosenhoff, however, took the exercises to a whole new level. He made 'an even more far-reaching attempt to bring harmonic analysis closer to modern music'.[65] At the end of each of the three collections of examples, he therefore added exercises that were more elaborate, with distinctly independent parts and often in complex rhythmic sequences. They also contained modulations that were 'more frequent and varied than in other similar collections of exercises'.[66] Rosenhoff found them more

ILL. 3. Rosenhoff's *450 firstemmige Opgaver*, textbook vol. 1, no. 2, exercise nos. 7, 8 and 9.

akin to modern music because, in his view, they reflected music in a tonal style that made use of extended triads, four-part harmonies and modulations to distantly related keys. If the pupil solved the exercises correctly – indeed, there was only one correct answer – small independent compositions with expressive melodies would emerge. This was training in deciphering analytical symbols, but it was also an explanation of the building blocks of prevailing musical styles.

The figured bass part has its roots in what is known as basso continuo notation, which has been used since the seventeenth century to notate chords as performance instructions for musicians. The practice continued into the nineteenth century as an analytical tool and was also used by composers as a means of notating their works.[67] Students at the Academy were taught the method and practised their skills by analysing C. E. F. Weyse's four-part chorales from his *Choral-Melodier* of 1839.[68] As a collection of melodies for church musicians, it had been replaced by Berggreen's chorale books of the 1850s, but as it was out of print, Gebauer arranged for a new edition to be issued in 1877, arguing that it had been lacking in the Academy's teaching.[69] Students were expected to have their own copy of the chorale book, and Nielsen's future colleague in The Royal Orchestra, Axel Gade, who had studied at the Academy from 1879

ILL. 4. An exercise in 'Theme with Variations' by Nielsen. A characteristic feature of the approach of composing a theme and a set of variations was that it was based on a simple framework. In principle, the same structure could be used several times, thus practising the skill of embellishing the same musical material in different ways from one version to another. By using the carefully prepared setting, written in long note values, the student was confident that the basic voice-leading was correctly arranged. The student would continue by applying the basic principles of music theory, gradually adding more and more elements to the structure until it became a complete composition. To ensure that the students got the most out of the exercises, they then had to analyse their own pieces. Signs such as crosses and small letters were used to mark dissonances and to show that the student could explain how the setting was constructed. This was directly modelled on the treatises of Richter and Gebauer.[72] At the top is the theme of a four-part arrangement in long note values. Below is the first variation, which makes use of chromatic passing notes (marked 'g'), anticipations (marked 'x') and échappées (marked 'v'). Rosenhoff marked the problem in blue pencil and suggested alternative solutions. Nevertheless, it was marked 'very good'.

to 1881, kept his chorale book from his student days, in which he had meticulously added his analyses of the first half of the chorales in pencil.[70] Nielsen did not keep his analyses, but it is clear that he used the method in his modulation exercises, where the harmonic analysis had to show the transition of the modulation from one key to another.[71] Solving the exercises thus went hand in hand with analysis and music theory.

On the other hand, Nielsen saved many of his harmony exercises, the purpose of which was to give the student an awareness of the musical means that could be used. His pencil sketches show that he based his four-part settings on figured bass lines, just as Richter's and Rosenhoff's exercises require. The purpose of the assignments varied, for some were in simple homophonic style, that is, with the parts in chordal progression forward and in the same rhythm, while in other assignments the parts were freer, with passing and alternating notes allowed. Still others focused on modulation. Sometimes the exercise consisted of treating a simple homophonic movement by adding passing notes, échappées, anticipations and other dissonances in more rapid note values. It is likely that one day the pupils themselves would be giving lessons, so pedagogical awareness was essential.

The primary purpose of teaching music theory was to provide students with an understanding of the elements and structures of music in order to strengthen their abilities as musicians. The exercises were intended to train them in basic musical craftsmanship and were designed with intrinsic possibilities for progression so that they could learn to understand the elements of music. This is reflected in Rosenhoff's approach to marking the exercises. He did not reward ingenuity or inventive solutions. Instead, he gave credit if the student explored and tried out the possibilities within the given rules. The theory lessons were not about learning to compose; rather, theory was an indispensable subject that had to be mastered if one was to compose.

Counterpoint

Nielsen put by far the most effort into working out counterpoint assignments. This is evidenced by the hundreds of exercises he kept from his time at the Academy. The study of polyphony left a lasting impression on his musical perception, and he often returned to the exercises after graduation. Skills in counterpoint became an essential part of Nielsen's approach to composition, although it was perhaps only gradually that he realised the importance of mastering the subject as a composer. In a 1920 letter to the Swedish music critic Julius Rabe, Nielsen reflected on his studies of counterpoint with Rosenhoff. Like many before him, Rosenhoff taught according to the principles developed by Joseph Fux in his textbook *Gradus ad Parnassum*, first published in Vienna in 1725:

> When as a boy I moved from the theory of harmony to counterpoint, I always had a flat taste in my mouth with his two-voiced lines (first species), and I couldn't understand what the many empty octaves and fifths were supposed to mean; I felt as though they were empty and childish. Eventually I realised that it was the voice-leading in *both* parts that was the most important thing, and then I understood everything. The octaves, fifths and unisons no longer seemed to me flat and childish, because my attention was now directed to the movement of the lines and not towards a harmonic clump or vertical chords.[73]

Nielsen hardly read Fux's work, which was originally written in Latin, but the treatise was so influential in Western European music theory that working with counterpoint became closely associated with Fux's name. Nielsen probably knew Fux from more recent books on counterpoint theory such as Heinrich Bellermann's *Der Contrapunkt* or Richter's *Lehrbuch des einfachen und doppelten Contrapunkts*, both of which acknowledged Fux's approach.[74] However, while Richter developed his own method, Bellermann adopted Fux's basic pedagogical approach.[75] Nielsen also possessed a small manuscript collecting the basic rules of counterpoint. He may have received it from Rosenhoff. It contains extracts from Bellermann's book and model examples by Fux and Cherubini.[76] Nielsen copied some of the examples himself and in this way learned about the subject – a subject so important to him that in 1905, when he had to recommend a textbook to his pupil Knud Harder, he chose Bellermann's book.[77] He gave the small manuscript to his student Judith Ahrendtsen in 1930.[78]

The teaching of counterpoint at the Copenhagen Academy followed the method of Fux and Bellermann. The student first composes a contrapuntal part on a set theme, a so-called cantus firmus (fixed song) consisting entirely of semibreves. The progression of the exercises is divided into five 'counterpoint species': in the first, the counterpoint consists only of semibreves; in the second, of minims; in the third, of crotchets. The fourth type includes syncopations, that is, tied minims starting on a weak beat, while the fifth species is a free mixture of the previous four. The five species are repeated in three-part structures and then in four-part structures.

Nielsen composed assignments in all five species in accordance with Fux, often naming them according to the species. There is no doubt that students needed to be made aware of the specific pedagogical approach on which Fux's treatise was based. Furthermore, Fux's influence was felt in other ways in the exercises that Nielsen worked with. Throughout his treatise, Fux used the same six cantus firmus melodies to demonstrate the various principles of the art of counterpoint. The melodies were defined as standard themes and included in many textbooks on counterpoint. Three of these themes appear in Nielsen's exercises.[79]

Indeed, it was in keeping with contrapuntal teaching that students should reuse the same cantus firmus in several exercises. As well as creating a familiarity with a theme, it trained the student to observe the infinite possibilities that lay in composing countermelodies to short themes. When marking Nielsen's exercises, Rosenhoff would refer to Fux.[80] It therefore seems quite natural that Nielsen should mention Fux so unequivocally in his letter to Rabe as the originator of counterpoint theory. However, a new trend at the time was to add new cantus firmus themes to the teaching material. Rosenhoff too resorted to this method, and Nielsen solved counterpoint exercises based on an estimated twenty-five different themes.

By far the greatest number of Nielsen's surviving exercises are those that belong to the first counterpoint species – that is, with long even notes – which explains why his work with 'the numerous empty octaves and fifths' left its mark on him for many years. The tasks may seem simple, and judging from his 1920 recollection, this was certainly his initial reaction. The work on the rhythmically simple themes was intended to sharpen the student's understanding of harmony on the one hand and melodic line on the other. The rules were clear: only consonant harmonies were allowed, and the arrangement of the voice-leading aspects of counterpoint should be formed in a balanced motion. Stepwise motion and some leaps were therefore acceptable, although the difficulty was to compose the progression in such a way as to strike a balance between the static and the unrestrained. The counterpoint, by its very nature, should not be a bland reflection of the cantus firmus, but should have its own character, a contrast to the theme. The work of composing two-part settings in long note values took the focus away from the rhythmic element and drew attention to the simple effects produced by the melodic intervals in the voice-leading layout of the countermelody.

In 1907, Nielsen explained to his student Knud Harder his idea of what such melodic effects were:

> Try for once to compose quite simple tonal melodies without any harmony (monophonic); imagine that you don't dare to move outside the eight notes of the scale, and that every note is a sanctuary that you shouldn't dare to touch ineffectively – on pain of death. Then within this cell and its associated prison-diet, set yourself the goal of writing as originally and uninhibitedly as possible. You'll see what a wonderful reward will some day come tumbling into your turban. You've achieved greater fluency, and so far as that goes it's very good; but I advise you over and over again, dear Mr Harder: *Tonality, Clarity* and *Power*.[81]

Although this was not about writing counterpoint exercises, but free composition, it describes an essence that has significant similarities with the melodic aesthetics of counterpoint theory. All melodic movements have an effect, even the most apparently simple ones. Only by being able to handle the details of a limited tonal material would it be possible to realise the range of melodic effects. The countless exercises based on Fux's principles gave Nielsen a sense that every movement in a melodic line has a consequence. This also explains how linearity became a fundamental part of his understanding of music.

The Fux exercises and those on imitation, in which two parts imitate each other, familiarised the student with basic contrapuntal techniques. But Rosenhoff's lessons went a step further, and Nielsen was given the task of composing fugues in the style of Bach. These assignments trained the student's stylistic knowledge and practised creating coherent settings from several different themes. Nielsen considered the Bach fugue exercises to be the culmination of his counterpoint lessons, for unlike the Fux exercises, which he sketched out in a hurry with a pencil, the fugues were rather complete compositions that had been reworked several times. The surviving

ILL. 4. Using only one cantus firmus theme ('C.F.'), Nielsen invented nine different contrapuntal melodies, which trained him to see the potential of the theme and to experiment with the many possibilities of composing a contrapuntal part. The exercises are in two-part counterpoint and, to save paper, are notated above and below the theme, which appears twice. It should therefore not be read as a score. Rosenhoff marked the assignments in red and blue crayon and added the comment 'good'. Two of the counterpoint parts have 'only three [different] notes', probably referring to the somewhat stilted melody. Nielsen must have corrected the countermelodies so that each now has four different notes. The theme occurs more than thirty times in his surviving manuscripts, making it one of the most common of Nielsen's contrapuntal exercises.

sketches show that the fugues were not simply self-contained works produced from one lesson to the next. They were rather corrected and adapted, refined and regarded as a kind of craftsmanship that could achieve the status of perfection. Once the ideal design was achieved, Nielsen copied them in ink, suggesting indeed that he regarded them almost as complete musical artefacts.[82]

The procedure is consistent with what appears to have been the compositional process in Nielsen's movement for string quartet, written while he was a student at the Academy or possibly immediately after his graduation. He used the first movement of Beethoven's String Quartet Op. 18, No. 1, as a template, copying its thematic and formal structure but filling it in with new material.[83] Nielsen later explained to Bror Beckman that such exercises were useful for aspiring composers:

> Do a lot of practice in counterpoint and modulation. That will purify, mature and solidify your talent. And then tackle the larger forms, because then you will find it easier with the smaller ones. For example, write a study for a quartet just like the Allegro first movement of Beethoven's Op. 18 No. 1. The same number of bars, the same modulations and the same working-out all through. You'll see that it's worth it. Or a fugue by Bach![84]

The theory classes at the Academy became an important foundation for Nielsen's way of thinking about composition, but the compositional process itself was something he had to work out for himself during his time at the Academy.

The Path to Musical Life

The Academy of Music was also a direct gateway to the musical life of Copenhagen. It was a meeting place for young musicians and experienced teachers, where personal relationships and in some cases friendships developed. During Nielsen's time at the Academy, around a hundred other students spent their days in the building on Bredgade. Some of them attended the same classes as Nielsen, others he might have met in the corridors, while others remained unknown to him. The music critic Gustav Hetsch, who published a book about the institution on the occasion of its fiftieth anniversary, summarises it as follows: 'The relationship between pupils and teachers was characterised by a mutual sympathy which not only made personal cooperation in the classes pleasant but also made the teaching more fruitful.' Hetsch never attended the Academy, and his testimony must therefore be seen as that of an outsider observing the social conventions of the institution. What he did see clearly was that 'the interest of the teachers in their pupils often lasted well beyond their time at the Academy. Many of the teachers followed the fate and development of their pupils with touching attention, and continued to assist them with advice and counsel even after their time at the Academy.'[85]

Nielsen's relationship with his teachers continued after his studies. As conductor of Musikforeningen and an internationally renowned composer, Niels W. Gade was an important figure with whom to keep in close contact. In a letter to the concert organiser Jean Louis Nicodé in 1896, Nielsen mentioned that he continued to take composition lessons from Gade after leaving the Academy; however, this was something he invented to impress Nicodé.[86] He never developed a particularly close relationship with Gade, but was nevertheless encouraged by him whenever Nielsen approached him, including when Nielsen was planning his trip to Germany in

1890.[87] Nielsen, on the other hand, maintained a close and trusting relationship with Rosenhoff, which was particularly important for his first period as a composer after graduating from the Academy.[88]

The new personal acquaintances that Nielsen made during his first years in Copenhagen also expanded his activities as a musician. He was surrounded by colleagues of his own age and found a community in which he could practise ensemble playing; among these colleagues were Julius Borup, Holger Møller, Frederik Schnedler-Petersen and Kristian Sandby. For a time, Nielsen also formed a string quartet with Valdemar Bloch and Robert and Edmond Henriques, which met regularly.[89]

Contacts at the Academy opened doors to the Copenhagen music scene. During the final year of his studies, Nielsen was accepted into the Chamber Music Society, a private society of musicians and music lovers that usually held weekly recitals during the winter season.[90] Some of the city's most renowned musicians played at these events, including Franz Neruda, Axel Gade and Anton Svendsen, as well as representatives of the younger generation such as Kristian Sandby, Julius Borup and Daniel Hannemann. Nielsen did not appear as a musician in the society until several years after he had joined it, so membership must initially have been a matter of wanting to become part of Copenhagen's musical life outside the walls of the Academy.[91]

There is no doubt that the transition from student to professional could be hard and needed to be prepared for. As a rule, students at the Academy were not allowed to play in public until they had passed their exams, and then only with special permission. This rule was intended to prevent students from stealing the thunder from their professional colleagues and to ensure that they were fully prepared before performing in public.[92] It could be detrimental to the Academy if a student without sufficient skills were to meet the critical press. However, this rule was not enforced outside Copenhagen, and Nielsen took advantage of this when he went to Odense in the summers of 1885 and 1886 to play concerts including the music he had studied with Tofte. Nielsen was in the fortunate position of having a musical network outside the capital and made no secret of his connection with the Academy. On the contrary, he signed himself 'student of the Academy of Music in Copenhagen' in concert advertisements issued in Odense. The Academy's summer holidays lasted from mid-July to the end of August,[93] and although activities at the Academy did not cease completely during the summer, Nielsen made it a priority to visit his family and use the holidays to play music.

His life as a military band musician in Odense had indeed left its mark, and when he visited Odense during the summer holidays of 1885, he sought out his musical acquaintances from the past. He must have contacted Simon, the bandmaster who was in charge of the open-air concerts in Fruens Bøge, and presented him with the idea of a concert in the music pavilion in the woods. Nielsen organised the event himself, and in the days leading up to 23 August 1885 he placed advertisements for

> **Koncert.**
>
> Søndagen den 23de August, Kl. 7½ Aften, agter Undertegnede at afholde en Koncert i Pavillonen „Fruens Bøge" med følgende Program:
> 1. LÉONARD H.: Solo pour Violin, Op. 41.
> 2. VIOTTI J. B.: Adagio af den 22de Koncert.
> 3. HAUSER M.: Wiegenlied, Op. 11.
> 4. BÉRIOT Ch. de: Air varié, Op. 1.
>
> **Carl Nielsen,**
> Elev af Musikkonservatoriet i Kjøbenhavn.
> Billetter faaes ved Indgangen à 50 Øre.

ILL. 6. Nielsen's concert at Fruens Bøge, outside Odense, in the summer of 1885 opened with a piece by violin professor Hubert Léonard, *Six solos faciles*, Op. 41. Since Léonard had composed the solos for his students, the pieces were based on the students' abilities: the title indicates the degree of difficulty ('six easy solos'). Although they are violin solos, they were composed with piano accompaniment. While Miska Hauser's *Wiegenlied* for piano and violin reflects a beginner's level, Charles-Auguste de Bériot's *Air varié*, Op. 1 offers a much greater opportunity to excel on the violin. These two pieces were also composed for violin and piano, while the Adagio from Viotti's Violin Concerto No. 22 was originally written for orchestra.[94]

the concert in the local newspaper, *Fyens Stiftstidende*, announcing the four pieces he intended to play.[95] It was a mixed programme, with both educational works for beginners and bravura pieces to impress the audience.

In the summer of 1886, Nielsen again visited the largest town on Fyn and gave a concert in the banqueting hall of the Odense Club. In advance of the concert, he placed advertisements in the daily press announcing free admission.[96] Located in the town centre at 10 Overgade, the banqueting hall was easier to get to than the music pavilion at Fruens Bøge, but judging by the review that *Fyens Stiftstidende* published the day after the concert, the attendance was not impressive.[97]

The programme included works that would demonstrate Nielsen's virtuosity and technical ability to an even greater extent than the year before. These included Louis Spohr's technically demanding Violin Concerto No. 11, which had been published in an arrangement for violin and piano.[98] The publication was made around 1880 by Spohr's pupil Ferdinand David, and it is clear that Nielsen had studied this piece with Tofte, who had himself studied with Spohr in the 1850s.

In the year that had passed between the two concerts in Odense, Nielsen must have made a great leap forward in his technical abilities on the violin. This is certainly the impression one gets when looking at the repertoire. Moreover, one reviewer pointed out that Nielsen had 'a real talent' and that he had 'developed it to a very high degree' since the previous concert.[99]

In the autumn of 1886, when he returned to Copenhagen after the summer holidays, Nielsen was to finish his studies at the Academy. This meant that he had to consider how to present himself as a violinist to audiences in the capital. He joined forces with experienced musicians who were used to organising concerts, and this gave him the opportunity to present himself as a professional violinist, with the express permission of the Academy.

On 11 October 1886, the banqueting hall in Nørre Voldgade, where the Workers' Association of 1860 had its monumental headquarters, opened its doors for a concert. On the ground floor were shops with windows facing the cobbled street, and on the first floor they had a banqueting hall with seating for around 1,000 people.[100] The concert was organised by the tenor Laurits Tørsleff, who was the centre of attention at the event, but Nielsen also attracted interest.[101] Although the Academy did not organise debut concerts in those days, the press knew that this was his first official performance.

Tørsleff, a former manufacturer in Flensburg, had trained as a singer with the help of Johanne Luise Heiberg and Gade. After studying in Italy, he made his debut at The Royal Theatre in March 1885 and performed there until the following summer.[102] He then toured as a concert singer.

At the concert, Tørsleff sang lieder by Mendelssohn, Schumann and Johan Bartholdy, as well as a duet from Verdi's opera *Aida* with his colleague, the alto Fanny Gætje. The enthusiastic audience, crammed into the banqueting hall, applauded throughout the concert – so much so that Tørsleff had to give encores. A vocal quartet from the Student Choral Society also took part, and their performance 'was greeted with rapturous applause, as was that of a very young violinist making his debut, Mr Carl Nielsen.' He played two movements from Bériot's Sixth Violin Concerto and music by Spohr. The reviewer at *Nationaltidende* commented that his performance 'seems to herald a truly artistic future'.[103]

The Workers' Association of 1860, whose aim was to support enlightenment and public educational initiatives, was an important concert venue in Copenhagen. They, too, organised public concerts, for which ticket prices were kept low and musical pieces or movements with foreign titles were translated into Danish in the pre-concert advertising. On one of these occasions the following year, Nielsen appeared again as a soloist playing the violin. The Workers' Association of 1860 was affiliated to the political right until the 1880s, when it became a non-political association.[104]

The collaboration with Tørsleff continued for the next six months after Nielsen's debut, and thus became his extended baptism of fire. Tørsleff was an experienced concert singer who performed all over the country. When Nielsen graduated in December 1886 and went on Christmas holiday, he and Tørsleff gave a concert in the banqueting hall of the Odense Klub on 27 December 1886, accompanied by Minna Hohn, who had lived in Odense before enrolling at the Academy the year after Nielsen.[105] The townspeople of Odense knew Tørsleff from the local newspaper reviews of his performances at The Royal Theatre. But it was Nielsen whom one reviewer remembered from his earlier concerts in the city. Their performance at the Odense Klub was well received and the concert was 'in all respects extremely successful'.[106] Nielsen repeated the two movements from Bériot's Violin Concerto and also played a violin romance by Beethoven and the movement from Mendelssohn's Violin Concerto that he had played for his final examination.[107] Back in Copenhagen, they resumed their concert activities and in the spring of 1887 they performed twice at Larsens Hall on Skt. Annæ Plads, another of the city's attractive concert venues with room for 800 listeners.[108]

As a graduate, Nielsen now had to find his feet as a performer. He already had experience as a musician who could work with professional colleagues. In a short space of time, he had experienced how, as a violinist, he could perform concert pieces that could be combined with other pieces and integrated into different concert contexts. Above all, the three years of study at the Academy had given him a basic musical understanding rooted in European trends, repertoires and performance traditions. At the Academy, he had made new musical contacts with fellow students and teachers who could follow their students' development with interest. And it was a place that, through its links with the musical life of the rest of the city, had gradually prepared the students for a life outside the institution in Bredgade. After three years at the Academy, Nielsen was ready to begin his career as a professional musician in the capital.

Chapter 7

MUSICIAN IN COPENHAGEN

On a misty day in May in 1888, a resplendent Copenhagen welcomed the Nordic Industrial, Agricultural and Art Exhibition. The square, Halmtorvet (later renamed City Hall Square), and the Tivoli Gardens had been transformed into a vast exhibition area displaying the technology of the future. Together with the Tivoli Gardens, a newly built hall formed the area where exhibitors from all over Europe could display their products. The exhibition marked the beginning of a new era for Copenhagen.

Expectations for the event were high. In the weeks leading up to the event, the exhibition commission published a comprehensive guide to the event, the nearly 6,000 exhibitors and the stalls that visitors should visit.[1] This included not only the exhibition area around Halmtorvet and Tivoli Gardens, but also historical sites in Copenhagen and environs. Also parts of the wider province and even Sweden were recommended. The guide was aimed at foreign visitors, providing detailed directions for those arriving from the south, by train from Hamburg or by ship from Kiel, Antwerp or London. The book contained numerous advertisements for local and foreign businesses.

Prior to the summer's events, the journalist Adolf Bauer gave an account of Danish and international exhibitions throughout the nineteenth century and described the benefits that Danish industry in particular – but also the country as a whole – had gained from organising and participating in the exhibitions. It was therefore not without reason that Bauer dared to express the wish that the 1888 exhibition 'might give new reality to Copenhagen's faded dreams of being a world city and restore to its life some of the splendour it has lost.'[2]

The grand event was designed to turn Copenhagen into Europe's biggest advertising pillar, with the idea of drawing all eyes – and ears – to the Nordic countries. At the same time as the exhibition, Copenhagen's music scene was stepping up its activities. The Royal Theatre extended its season, and the city's music societies joined forces to provide the city with a new, modern concert hall, Koncertpalæet, where the Nordic Music Festival could be held. It was indeed a busy summer for Nielsen.

ILL. 1. Paul Fischer, *Ved Glassalen* (1890), shows the crowds outside Tivoli's first concert hall.

Concert Venues in Copenhagen

If you wanted to make a career as a musician in Copenhagen, it was important to be where the action was. The city's concert venues were very distinct. To get a sense of Nielsen's early days as a musician in the city, it is therefore crucial to consider how the venues differed from each other and how a young musician could use them to further his career.

In the 1880s Copenhagen had several concert halls. Among the most important venues for orchestral music were the Tivoli Gardens and the Casino, as well as Koncertpalæet, which was inaugurated during the exhibition year of 1888. The city's theatres were also used for musical performances, and it was common for private associations, such as the Workers' Association or the Industrialists' Association, to hold concerts in their banqueting halls; even the function rooms of hoteliers or restaurateurs could be used. After graduating from the Academy, Nielsen sought out these venues in an attempt to make a living as a musician, and his career as a violinist in the city's orchestras grew, especially during the year of the exhibition. His efforts to earn a living as a musician would culminate in his appointment as second violinist in The Royal Orchestra from September 1889.

Judging by the number of musical performances, the Tivoli Gardens was the city's most important music venue during the summer season. Georg Carstensen's Tivoli, then known as Tivoli & Vauxhall, was a meeting place for the citizens of Copenhagen from its inception in 1843. The original name suggests that Carstensen was inspired by European amusement parks such as those in Paris and London. In Tivoli, built on the ramparts and embankments, the inhabitants sought to escape the dense city centre and found an entirely different world in the twilight and the glow of artificial lighting. Music and theatre, together with oriental scenery, created an atmosphere that gave visitors the illusion of being in a whole new world, far away from the capital. A Swedish visitor described the experience: 'The simple wooden houses are then transformed into oriental palaces, the small shrubberies into paradise gardens, the muddy waters of the moat into a swan lake'.[3]

The Tivoli Gardens must have been a bombardment of sensory impressions for the people of Copenhagen. Herman Bang's novel *Stuk*, in which the main characters Berg and Lange visit the Gardens, gives an impression of this. Bang succeeds in creating an atmosphere that he himself might have experienced in the Tivoli Gardens in the late 1880s:

> They turned and walked down to the bazaar, which lay before them as in a bright cloud; the gas domes made dull arabesques through the damp grass, and the artificial beds stood out in dewy splendour under the glare of the lamps. All around the edge of the trees the coloured balloons hung like glowing giants.
>
> They walked forward. Berg paused: in the midst of the music-filled air, the bazaar silently lifted its radiant arches. Everything shone, domes and minarets. Now and then a gust of wind drove the waving flames together, as if they were quivering lightning from the tops of the minarets; and above the slender turrets lay the starry dark blue of the late summer sky.[4]

He describes the area around the main building of the Tivoli Gardens, the Bazaar, a three-storey wooden structure with dragon carvings and covered arcades where guests could buy all kinds of merchandise. A restaurant in the middle section offered first-class food and drink.[5] The building was demolished in 1908 to make way for the new Copenhagen Central Station. The following year, Hotel Nimb opened in a Moorish-inspired palace next to the new western entrance to the gardens.

Since the first season of the Tivoli Gardens in the summer of 1843, music has been an important part of its identity. At the centre of the gardens was the great concert

ILL. 2. The original concert hall of the Tivoli Gardens, Glassalen, was renovated in 1885-86 and given a distinctive dome-shaped roof.

hall, which was located where today's Glass Hall was erected in 1946. The first concert building was a square pavilion with glass walls, and in 1863 it was rebuilt in the Moorish style with a characteristic octagonal floor plan. The hall itself was circular and designed as an amphitheatre. Above the main entrance was a balcony that could accommodate an orchestra, and at the opposite end of the room was a restaurant.[6]

In the novel, as the protagonists Berg and Lange continue their evening promenade in Tivoli, Bang describes the concert hall as a central place where the aural boundaries did not cease at the building's façade: 'It was as if they had entered the swirling hubbub of voices and sounds of a dance hall down at the Concert Hall.'[7] The open doors of the hall turned the building into a giant loudspeaker, feeding music to the garden's guests, whether they chose to sit inside and listen or dine outside in one of the surrounding cafés.

The concert hall was not only a central place for Tivoli. It was the city's main concert venue during the summer season. An account from 1888 describes the concert hall as the place where 'all Copenhagen' met between 9 p.m. and midnight, 'where one strolls up and down in the time-honoured slow tempo, takes in the music coming through the large windows and lets the pious, who crave it all, sit inside'.[8] The exaggeration that the entire population of Copenhagen gathered at Tivoli has a ring of reality to it. In July 1887 alone – when the city's population was around 300,000 – more than 150,000 visited the Gardens, and the season as a whole attracted more than half a million visitors.[9]

The Tivoli Gardens employed a large number of musicians. Throughout the summer there were two orchestras that played alternately during the day. From 1873 Balduin Dahl was the conductor of the large orchestra, which consisted of forty-six musicians. They played in the concert hall, while the Tivoli Gardens wind band, led by Carl Christian Møller and Georg Lumbye, played in an outdoor pavilion.[10] Together with the live music in the restaurants, the total number of musicians in the gardens was over one hundred.[11]

On a typical summer evening, music was played every half or full hour from 6 p.m. to midnight. The repertoire consisted of dance music and orchestral music that was easily accessible to a wide audience. From 1848 there was a major concert every Saturday, with one section reserved for a symphony and the other two sections for guest performances by international soloists or conductors.[12] On Saturdays, the concert hall was thus the venue for a type of musical performance that was intended to be more than just entertainment. This change was reflected in the behaviour of the patrons, and a description from 1888 states:

> Between 8.30 and 10 p.m., the concert gloves are put on, the section's high-quality music or the prepared song is listened to in silence, and the march is suspended outside. The audience occupies all the benches and tables in the hall, where Dahl stands on the tiny elevation, extremely well groomed, elegant in posture while his head is silently following the beat.[13]

Judging by the audience behaviour at the Saturday concerts, Tivoli Gardens was more than just an amusement park.

When Nielsen moved to Copenhagen, the concert halls in the Tivoli Gardens and the Casino in Amaliegade were the most popular venues for symphonic orchestral music. While the concert hall in Tivoli was closely associated with the other entertainment activities in the Gardens, the Casino was more broadly associated with the city's clubs and societies. It was originally established by Tivoli's founder, Georg Carstensen, as a winter entertainment venue. It opened in 1847 and was named Casino, the Italian word for a small house, which was then used for clubs and social societies. Carstensen's basic idea was that it should cater for 'the ever-growing musical sense and the interests connected with it'.[14]

As Tivoli was outside Copenhagen's ramparts, Carstensen wanted to set up the Casino in the city itself. Although he saw his idea as a 'necessity for such a populous and music-loving capital', he soon realised that a 'winter Tivoli' was not economically

ILL. 3. Concerts in the Casino were held regularly throughout the winter season. On weekday evenings, theatre performances were held in the large hall, while the small hall was used for concerts; at weekends, concerts were held in both halls. For example, on Friday, 19 March 1886, Musikforeningen held its fourth subscription concert in the Casino's small hall; on Saturday, The Concert Society used the large hall; and on Monday, the singer Marie Høst-Schottlænder gave a recital in the small hall.[15]

viable.[16] He resigned from the enterprise as early as 1848. The private limited company that had financed the construction of the building subsequently had the Casino converted into Copenhagen's first private theatre with the status of a second-tier theatre, which was thus allowed to break the monopoly of The Royal Theatre. However, in order to avoid competition with the national theatre – that is, The Royal Theatre – the Casino was only allowed to stage comedies, melodramas and vaudevilles.[17] Yet it became an important theatre, also staging modern plays that The Royal Theatre would not, such as August Strindberg's naturalistic play *The Father* in 1887.

Until 1937, the Casino was a home for the performing arts and music. It was also a kind of meeting place, with an ideal layout and beautiful decorations that provided an inviting setting for masked balls and political meetings alike. It was in this setting that important events in the musical life of the capital took place.

ILL. 4. Artists' carnival in the Casino's winter pergola on 7 March 1867, reproduced on an engraving in *Illustreret Tidende*.[18]

The Casino, with its two concert halls, was Copenhagen's main concert venue during the winter season. Musikforeningen and Koncertforeningen (The Concert Society) held most of their concerts in the large hall, and local soloists were happy to use the small hall for chamber music recitals.[19] The Casino was also used when international virtuosos were in town, as it provided the ideal setting for visiting artists to introduce themselves to Copenhagen audiences.

As in Tivoli, the design of the Casino was spectacular. Let us go through the doors and try to experience the atmosphere where thirty-five of Nielsen's works were performed during his lifetime alone.[20] The audience could enter the large building complex from both Amaliegade and Ny Toldbodgade.[21] Ticket booths and cloakrooms were located at both ends of the building. The central part of the ground floor was an important place for the audience before and after the concerts, with rooms for serving food and refreshments, a reading room and a billiard room. A staircase near the entrance from Amaliegade led to the second floor, where the theatre and concert halls were situated. The landing led to a resting place called the Winter Pergola, with exotic plants surrounded by carved railings and high wooden columns. From there you could enter the two halls. The main hall was used for theatrical performances and the audience area occupied most of the floor space; there was also seating in boxes on platforms along the walls and on balconies along the sides and at the rear of the hall. The total seating capacity was nearly 1,500, making it the largest concert hall in the city.[22] The musicians stayed at the far end of the hall, where the stage and orchestra pit were placed. The Casino's small hall was opposite the foyer on Amaliegade. It could seat about 500 guests.[23] Here the musicians were placed on a semi-circular structure at one end of the hall.

The construction of the Casino did not, however, mean that the city's need for concert venues was satisfied. In 1865, H. C. Lumbye proposed the building of a new large concert hall on Gammelholm, in the neighbourhood behind The Royal Theatre. The project failed, but the need for a new venue remained. In 1874, Dahl tried his hand at plans for a concert hall to be used during the winter season when he did not have Tivoli at his disposal. A site in Lille Kongensgade had already been purchased, although Dahl also had to abandon his idea.[24]

Concert-Palæet Ltd was founded in 1884 with the aim of raising funds to build a concert hall in the garden behind the Schimmelmanske Palæ in Bredgade. The initiative was led by Gade and several of the city's music societies, including The Concert Society with its chairman Jacob Fabricius.[25] Renovation of the mansion began in 1885.[26]

In the same year, the idea of organising a Scandinavian music festival was born in the music society known as Fermaten. A proposal to link the festival to Musikforeningen's fiftieth anniversary in 1886 fell through, and in early 1887 Fermaten began work on establishing a music festival in conjunction with the forthcoming Nordic Industrial, Agricultural and Art Exhibition.[27] It was a goal that the entire musical community could support. Using the momentum created by the planning of the Nordic Exhibition, the construction of Koncertpalæet was completed, and with the prospect of a new concert venue in the city, the various interested parties in the music community joined forces to plan six major concerts. The festival committee, led by composers J. P. E. Hartmann and N. W. Gade, invited choral societies from other Nordic countries to participate.[28] It is clear that they felt it was important to have a Nordic representation of music to match the exhibition.[29]

The building of Koncertpalæet was a bigger task than anticipated. The Nordic Music Festival was held in Copenhagen from 4 to 9 June 1888, and the opening concert was also the inauguration of the new hall, although the building was not yet finished. The 2,000 listeners had to put up with the temporary surroundings, including rough stone walls and a roof covered only by a canvas. From the audience's and critics' point of view, the event was a success, and Koncertpalæet was one of the main factors that proved the need for a new concert hall.[30] It was a sign of an expanding music scene, which was obviously good news for musicians looking for work.

Life as a Musician

There was plenty going on musically during the exhibition year of 1888 – more than usual according to the press reports:

> The orchestra musicians play their fingers off and blow their lips to bleed. The singers wear out their throats such that we, and they, are glad if there is anything left of them. And the audience – well, they have heard so much and for so long that you think it all sounds very much the same.[31]

Thus wrote music critic Charles Kjerulf in the magazine *Illustreret Tidende* when the festival was over. Twenty-nine years later, in his memoirs, he recalled the exhibition year with greater satisfaction, explaining that 'even music was plentiful that summer … We could not complain.'[32] Other critics had also commented on the sheer volume of music during the exhibition year, probably because such a tour-de-force of six major concerts in six days was, after all, unfamiliar to Copenhagen audiences and music critics.[33]

For a young musician like Nielsen, it was a chance to show off and get a foothold in the various orchestras. It was also a challenge to keep track of all the fees, so he started keeping records of the jobs he did and the fees he received. Nielsen used a small notebook to record the events in which he played. It reveals that he played thirty-nine concerts between May and September 1888, and thirty in the first eight weeks of the exhibition alone.[34] There are no notebooks by Nielsen from the period before this, so it is safe to assume that his work as an orchestral musician intensified from May 1888.

Even for those musicians on permanent contracts in the city's orchestras, life was marked by changing employers and working hours, and seasonal work meant that a musician's income was unevenly distributed throughout the year. The concert season in Tivoli began in mid-May and ended four months later at the end of September. During this period, the orchestra musicians in Copenhagen were busy with daily performances. During the rest of the year, however, many of the same musicians played in The Royal Orchestra or in the city's concert societies, which held their concerts during the winter season when Tivoli was closed.

Prospective musicians had to accept these conditions if they dreamed of a career in music. To be offered a permanent contract with an orchestra was indeed a stroke of luck. The Tivoli Gardens offered good opportunities, and it is no coincidence that Nielsen had his first experiences as an orchestra musician there. Until 1920, the conductor of the Tivoli Orchestra was responsible for hiring and paying the musicians.[35] From 1873 to 1891, Dahl was in charge of the music, and it was essentially Dahl's

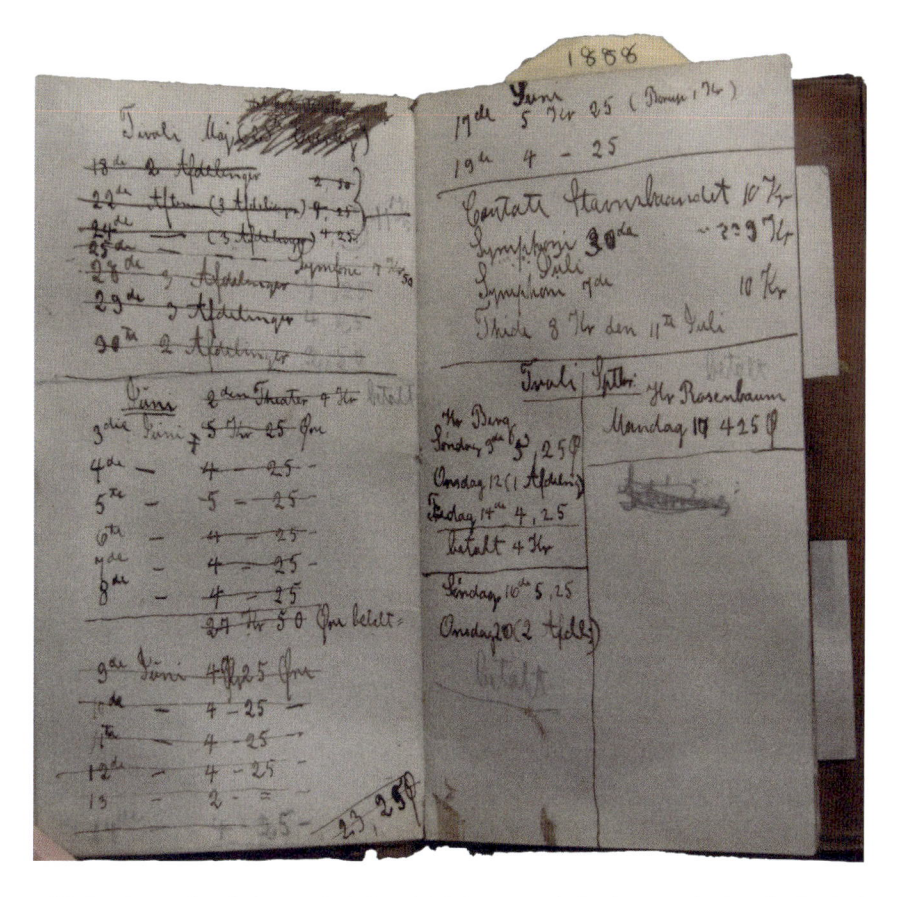

ILL. 5. Nielsen's notebook from 1888, in which he recorded where and when he had played, in cramped handwriting and with private remarks. The amount of the agreed fee is also noted, and he would cross out the amount when he had received payment. At the top of the left-hand page begins a section entitled 'Tivoli'. He played in the Gardens on 18, 22, 24, 25, 28, 29 and 30 May. For his participation in the symphony concert on Saturday 25 May he received 7.50 Kroner, while for the weekday concerts with two or three sections he received 2.50 and 4.25 Kroner respectively. On the right-hand side, Nielsen noted his work as a substitute for the Royal Musicians, 'Mr Berg' and 'Mr Rosenbaum', presumably when they had to play at The Royal Theatre and therefore did not have time to perform at Tivoli Gardens.

orchestra that played, not Tivoli's. When the season ended, he used the orchestra to organise his own concert evenings at venues around the city. In addition, Dahl ran a kind of impresario business, hiring out the orchestra, and so members of Dahl's Tivoli ensemble were chartered by Musikforeningen and formed the backbone of the society's concerts during the winter season.[36] From 1875 until his death in 1891,

Dahl had a contractual arrangement with The Royal Orchestra and was responsible for recruiting substitutes for performances at The Royal Theatre.[37] Dahl was indeed an important man to know.

But it was by no means a matter of course that musicians in Dahl's orchestra, for instance, enjoyed decent conditions in the 1880s. Since the 1860s, musicians had increasingly sought to organise themselves into professional associations through which they could maintain their influence.[38] One of the first was The Musicians' Association, founded in 1865. Its main aim was to strengthen the social contacts between its members, rather than to alleviate their concerns about poor employment conditions.[39] In 1867, The Violinists' Association was established to try to ensure that members were paid for their work.[40] As its name suggests, it could not admit all musicians, but its efforts became the model for the founding of the Copenhagen Orchestra Association in 1874. It was founded when the Musicians' Association of 1865 held an extraordinary general assembly to set up a committee to prepare a proposal for 'Laws and Tariffs for the Musicians of Copenhagen'.[41] The rules of the association included a kind of musketeer's oath, which required members to be 'mutually honour bound' and to play according to the tariffs in force. They were further obliged to play exclusively in orchestras formed by members of the association.[42] With this early example of basic trade union activity, the musicians in Copenhagen developed their self-image from an awareness of their social position to one of social-democratic organised solidarity. However, a member's initiative to transform the association into a social democratic union in the first decade of the twentieth century met with resistance, and the association maintained an outwardly apolitical stance.[43]

In the 1860s it was common for young aspiring musicians to play in the Tivoli Gardens for free, but a few decades later the Copenhagen Orchestra Association was strong enough to secure payment for them.[44] C. C. Møller made plans to hire an orchestra to play on the new frigate St George on the lake in Tivoli Gardens in the summer of 1888. When the Orchestra Association discovered that the musicians' fees were not being paid at the agreed rate, they effectively put a stop to Møller's plans.[45] Thus the conditions had become more or less decent, and a young musician like Nielsen could earn a reasonable income, especially in the year of the exhibition, when music was in great demand. As the notebook shows, he was usually paid four Kroner and twenty-five Øre to play at a concert.

ILL. 6. Photo collage of the Tivoli Orchestra in 1888. Nielsen was a substitute in the orchestra and is therefore not included. His fellow students Kristian Pedersen Sandby (third row from the top, second from the right) and Louis Glass (fourth row from the top, third from the right) were contemporaries of Nielsen. According to his notebook, Nielsen substituted for violist Bernhard Rosenbaum (bottom row, far left) and violinist Julius Ferdinand Berg (second row, far right). In the centre of the bottom row is the orchestra's leader Balduin Dahl.[46]

A Foothold

In the years immediately following his graduation from the Academy, Nielsen's primary ambition was to establish himself as an orchestra musician. As already mentioned, Dahl was a central figure in this context: it was important to know Dahl and to have a professional relationship with him. Not only was the Tivoli Orchestra the nucleus of Musikforeningen's orchestra, but there was also considerable overlap with The Royal Orchestra, to which an estimated dozen members of the Tivoli Orchestra belonged in 1888. Furthermore, an even larger number would later take up permanent positions there.[47] In other words, the Tivoli Orchestra was a step towards a career in The Royal Orchestra.

Dahl paved the way for Nielsen to join the city's orchestras. As early as the summer of 1887, he played in the Tivoli Gardens under Dahl's baton.[48] In interviews,

Nielsen later recounted how, as violinist in the orchestra, he presented one of his own compositions to Dahl the following year.[49] For other young musicians, too, Dahl's orchestra was a natural gateway into the world of music. Nielsen's fellow student Frederik Schnedler-Petersen, who entered the Academy of Music the year after Nielsen, was a substitute in Dahl's orchestra during his first year, while another fellow student, Kristian Sandby, and Nielsen's contemporary Louis Glass played regularly in the Tivoli Gardens.[50] Nielsen's notebook shows that he played at Tivoli, The Royal Theatre and the Nordic Music Festival in 1888. The book thus documents Nielsen's intentions to be widely involved in musical life. It also shows that, as a Copenhagen musician, he was naturally a member of several different orchestras at the same time. In Tivoli he substituted as both viola player and violinist, emphasising that his musical versatility was in demand, something that had also been a natural requirement for him as a military musician in Odense.[51]

Nielsen also gained a foothold in Musikforeningen. Under Gade's direction, he played with many of the musicians he knew from The Royal Orchestra and Tivoli. Musikforeningen's orchestra is a good example of the interwoven relationships that characterised the city's musical life. The Casino's musical director Carl Gottschalksen, who also played in the orchestra, remembers that before Koncertpalæet was inaugurated, rehearsals were held in the Casino's small hall, while concerts were held in the large one. The rehearsals could only start at 1 p.m. because the musicians of the Royal Guards had to be at the noon parade at Amalienborg.[52] This shows the complexity of the orchestra and the need to take into account the fact that the musicians had their main duties elsewhere.

The orchestra of Musikforeningen usually played four subscription concerts per winter season. Unlike the Tivoli Orchestra, the musicians under Gade's direction met at irregular intervals, which seems to have been reflected in the dynamic that developed between conductor and musicians during rehearsals, where the authoritative Gade would often express his opinion on the music, not only in terms of its performance but also how it should be interpreted.[53] Nielsen noted that Gade used the rehearsals to demonstrate his position in musical life, and on one occasion Nielsen was particularly struck by some condescending comments Gade made about Brahms.[54] According to Nielsen's recollection, it was also during an orchestra rehearsal that Gade suddenly rejected Nielsen for the scholarship known as Det Anckerske Legat.[55]

Although his contact with Dahl provided Nielsen with jobs, he found it a challenge to gain a foothold in the city's musical life. In a conversation with the Royal Musician Anton Svendsen in early 1888, Nielsen raised the idea of leaving Copenhagen, perhaps to seek better opportunities elsewhere. Svendsen advised Nielsen not to leave the city 'now that there seems to be such a good wind in the sails for your development as a composer and musician'.[56]

It was in instances such as these that the special conditions of the exhibition year revealed their great importance. They meant that The Royal Theatre extended its season by a month, to the end of June, in order to satisfy the many visitors to the capital. The Royal Orchestra was also involved in the Nordic Music Festival,[57] and the increased demand for orchestra musicians allowed for temporary jobs: those who played at the Theatre and in the Tivoli Gardens could certainly not do both. During the months of the exhibition, Nielsen played in six performances at the Theatre, including *Elverhøj*, Drachmann and Lange-Müller's *Der var engang–* and Bournonville's ballet *Toreadoren* with music by Edvard Helsted.[58] Nielsen's association with the Theatre continued into the 1888–89 winter season. In a letter to his girlfriend Emilie, Nielsen describes how busy he was at the theatre around New Year. He also relates that when he first met the orchestra's conductor, Johan Svendsen, at a private party on New Year's Eve 1888, Svendsen recognised him from the orchestra pit, although Nielsen remarks that Svendsen 'didn't know that I was the one who had written the Suite [for String Orchestra] and was called Carl Nielsen.'[59] Although he had no personal relationship with Svendsen as an ordinary substitute in the orchestra, he was far from a stranger when he applied for a permanent position in The Royal Orchestra in August 1889. He gained the ultimate foothold as a musician in Copenhagen when he was offered a permanent position as a Royal Musician from 1 September.

Chapter 8

FROM MUSICIAN TO COMPOSER

Nielsen's development from primarily a musician to mainly a composer was a long process that began in Odense and was not completed until the early 1890s. The decisive change took place in the years following his graduation from the Academy of Music, when he developed his skills as a composer, especially with the help of Orla Rosenhoff, and heard his works performed. This is particularly true of the years 1887–89, when he gained experience under Rosenhoff's private tutelage. Indeed, Nielsen's *Suite for String Orchestra*, Op. 1, reveals a working process in which he needed the help and participation of others to bring the composition to its final form, after which he took responsibility for it. The String Quartet in F minor, Op. 5, and the Symphony No. 1, Op. 7, mark the transition to Nielsen standing on his own two feet. These two works, composed in the two most prestigious genres of instrumental music, can be seen as his final assignments, completing his apprenticeship as a composer.

When it comes to his very early compositions – those composed before he enrolled at the Academy and during his years of study – it is often difficult to make sense of the chronology. These pieces are rarely dated, and when an early composition is mentioned in a source, it can be difficult to determine the exact composition. Information about the early works is therefore often conjectural. A considerable number of sketches and incomplete drafts of movements have survived, showing that Nielsen was prolific and tried out many ideas. That he composed is beyond doubt.[1] Furthermore, there are certainly compositions that have been lost or are incomplete, suggesting that it was not a priority for Nielsen to have all of his early works preserved for posterity. Thus, only a small number of works survive from this period that can be considered complete compositions.[2]

In the years following his graduation from the Academy, a number of characteristic circumstances become apparent. Firstly, many of the works are composed for a context in which Nielsen has a direct connection with the musicians who are to perform them. In this respect, Nielsen becomes part of the professional musician's environment in Copenhagen. Secondly, Rosenhoff plays a crucial role, first as a teacher and later as a mentor. Thirdly, several of his pieces are performed several times, allowing Nielsen to hear the effect of the music he composes – and the changes he makes along the way. And finally, he meets a music publisher who enables him to get his compositions into print.

With the String Quartet in F minor and his First Symphony, he gained access to the highest levels of musical life – and not only in Copenhagen. The String Quartet was rehearsed in Berlin for Joseph Joachim, one of the world's leading violinists. The symphony was premiered by The Royal Orchestra and the following performance took place in Dresden. With such performances, Nielsen could indeed call himself a composer.

A Threshold

On Christmas Day 1887, Nielsen refers to himself as a composer for the first time. He spends the holidays with his parents on Fyn and writes to his girlfriend Emilie Demant Hansen:

> I imagine you longing to hear from your composer. That sounds a bit strange, doesn't it, that I use the word 'composer' myself? But listen, there's something that gives me a right to use this title, which mustn't be taken as vanity. Shortly before travelling home [to Fyn] I was over at the house of my former theory and composition teacher from the Conservatoire, and I showed him a string quartet I had recently completed. He is a severe critic and gives his opinion point-blank.[3]

The piece is probably the partially extant String Quartet in F major (CNW 50 and 51), and the teacher mentioned in the letter is Rosenhoff.[4] In his student days, the relationship between teacher and pupil was not as close and confidential as it would become later. Rosenhoff thought that Nielsen moved in somewhat suspicious circles and therefore kept a certain distance.[5] But later Rosenhoff became Nielsen's most important and perhaps only real teacher of composition – if by that term is meant a person who gives critical feedback on the student's work. And that was precisely what happened on that day just before Christmas in 1887.

Rosenhoff had played through the quartet on his piano, muttering little positive comments, half to himself. Nielsen was tense and anxious. When Rosenhoff had finished, he turned around and praised the music for its warmth and speed, adding:

> 'will you promise to restrain yourself?' 'Yes, but what do you mean?' I asked. 'I mean that you should promise me not to have it performed anywhere; because I'm in the process of founding an association that's going to be called "The Composers' Society" … and I think that your quartet should have its first performance there.'[6]

Then they went through the composition again, and the result, according to Nielsen, was that it 'underwent some little alterations here and there, which could be made by a stroke of the pen.'[7] Nielsen accepted good suggestions because they were Rosenhoff's.

Reading the letter to Emilie, it is clear that calling himself a composer was not something Nielsen took lightly. Rosenhoff's reaction and his promise to perform the work in a newly established society gave Nielsen the confidence to call himself a composer. It was a barrier to be crossed. Rosenhoff's invitation was like an award, but it was also a challenge, an unfulfilled ambition.

At the same time, Nielsen's reaction shows that he already harboured the desire to take the plunge and call himself a composer. The letter is evidence of an inner process in which he changes his self-image. The fact that he was publicly announced as a composer at concerts also marks an incipient shift in his appearance in the city's musical environment. The mere fact of having his compositions performed in public was important to Nielsen, but not enough per se. It was Rosenhoff's recognition that was decisive. Now he dared to say it out loud.

However, the music society mentioned by Rosenhoff was not founded, and instead the 'String Quartet in F (new)' was performed at the Private Chamber Music Society on 25 January 1888.[8] Everything seems to indicate that this is the same quartet that Rosenhoff reviewed, otherwise it would imply that Nielsen had several new quartets ready at the same time just before Christmas. The Private Chamber Music Society was an organisation in which Nielsen himself played an active role. It had been founded the previous year by Anton Bloch, who, together with Nielsen, Julius Borup and Frederik Schnedler-Petersen, also performed the new quartet.[9] Nielsen thus acted as both musician and composer, a circumstance that applied to several of the early performances of his works. Twenty-five years later, Nielsen regarded this concert as his debut as a composer.[10]

For a concert to be recognised as a debut, it must be public, but it is difficult to make a sharp distinction between public and private concerts in the late nineteenth century, as much of concert life was organised within music societies. The boundaries between public and private musical events were fluid. In Tivoli, they were definitely public: anyone could buy a ticket, and the major concerts were announced and reported on in the newspapers, so there was public scrutiny and appreciation of the music being performed. To attend musical events at Musikforeningen, the city's most prestigious concert institution, however, required membership of the society, whose concerts were also advertised in the newspapers. In its heyday, although there were no specific requirements for membership, the society had a long waiting list, which in effect favoured the old bourgeoisie's access to the concerts.

As far as chamber music was concerned, public recitals were a relatively new phenomenon. It was not until the 1870s that it became common to perform chamber music in actual recitals, and the oldest society, The Chamber Music Society, founded in 1868, did not allow reviews of its musical events, and admission was conditional on being approved by the committee – and being male. Despite its name, the Private

Chamber Music Society was public: anyone could join, regardless of gender, and its recitals were advertised in the newspapers.[11] Thus the event featuring Nielsen's quartet met the criteria to be considered a debut, but Nielsen was mistaken. It was not.

In fact, Nielsen's debut as a composer had taken place a few months earlier, on 17 September 1887, when his *Andante tranquillo e Scherzo* for string orchestra (CNW 31) was performed at the Tivoli Concert Hall under the baton of Balduin Dahl. It was at this event that Nielsen, who played in the orchestra, received his first public recognition as a composer, from both the audience and the press: the piece, 'extremely well instrumented and thoroughly well done, was received with great acclaim and the Scherzo had to be repeated'.[12] It seems that he had borrowed two previously composed movements for string quartet, which did not originally belong together, and with a slight reworking and the addition of a double bass part, had transcribed them for string orchestra. The fact that he did not later mention this concert as his debut may have been because, in retrospect, he did not consider the combination of the two movements to be a finished work.[13] When he was young, however, he had no doubt that it was his first performance, for he began a list of works in a notebook belonging to Emilie, which she continued until 1890. In it, he writes explicitly that the performance in the Tivoli Gardens was his 'debut as a composer' – and makes no mention of the String Quartet in F.[14]

Having a composer's debut concert in Tivoli was important to Nielsen, but it was only one step along the way. It is important to see the process as a gradual development from being primarily a musician who also composes to being a composer who is still a musician. In this context, it is revealing that during these years, when newspapers had to explain who the young composer was, they often referred to the fact that the public already knew him as a musician. Since his debut as a violinist, he had appeared several times in concerts where he had been noticed. But let's return to the beginning.[15]

Among Friends

Nielsen was already composing when he lived in Odense. In an interview in 1905, he reflected on this period and said:

> I wrote incessantly. And it was noticed, of course. Just the fact that one could put something together was great. By the way, what I produced was terrible! But my friends were happy about it. When we got together in the evening for a drink and so on, it was always: 'Have you composed anything new, Carl?' 'No, but I'm about to finish a duet.' And then we played it through … Well, it was a fun time anyway.[16]

Reading this account, it becomes clear that the starting point for these early compositions was the need for them: they are pieces composed to be played by the musicians he knew and cared about. So there was not much ambition involved, for there was no requirement that they should be innovative or original works. It was about being able to put something together in a way that worked. It is an activity akin to arranging a piece of music with a specific instrumentation in mind.

How, then, are we to understand Nielsen's early compositions? Carl Larsen, who taught Nielsen in Odense, believed that his former student was already a rare musical talent and that he had ambitions and high aspirations.[17] At Larsen's request, Marius Hegeland, who was Nielsen's colleague in the military band two years his senior, wrote down what he remembered from those days:

> Carl became an accomplished alto hornist, who often displayed excellent technique and tone on his instrument when now and then it had a solo passage. He also played the violin, but when he had eventually saved enough to rent himself a piano, it became his favourite occupation …
>
> That Carl also tried his hand at composition in this period goes without saying, but I was probably the only one who heard and saw his little pieces, of which probably most gradually ended up in the fire. The first composition I heard was a quadrille, which at least then I found exceptionally attractive. However, it was only the melody that he had written down and that he played for me on his violin; I thought he should see about getting it arranged, but it never came to anything. Later he often had a little romance or something like that to show me when I visited him, and as a rule it would be the little poems and sonatas in the *Illustrated Family Journal* that had inspired him, and which he set to music.[18]

Although Hegeland believed that Nielsen had ambitions even then, the actual description twenty-five years later suggests that Nielsen was composing, by trial and error on a small scale. The story of the quadrille shows that the tune and the instrumentation – if it was ever made – were referred to separately as an arrangement. Apart from the little songs set to poems that appeared in the weekly journal, it is also characteristic that Nielsen wrote for ensembles he knew. He composed a number of pieces for two, three and four brass players, which were performed by his regimental colleagues, and he wrote small pieces of chamber music. In both cases he was probably one of the performers.[19]

An early piece related to this period in Odense is the *Fantasy Piece for Clarinet and Piano* (CNW 66) 'dedicated to Mr M. Hansen', most likely Hegeland, who played clarinet and whose surname was Hansen until he changed it in 1904.[20] The piece survives in a neat transcription, although it is difficult to determine whether it is actually in Nielsen's handwriting – at least the dedication is definitely added by him.[21] The piece begins with Beethovenian pathos in the piano, and when the clarinet enters, the Viennese Classical inspiration becomes clear. It is a well-paced little piece that one can easily imagine being played among Nielsen's friends.

As a violinist, Nielsen would of course compose for violin and piano. During his time in Odense, he presented some of his pieces to Olfert Jespersen, who was visiting the city as the pianist for a singing troupe. Jespersen was a versatile musician and composer who later became the director of the concerts at Copenhagen Zoo. According to his recollection, they met in a bar called 'Det blaa Øje' (The Black Eye), from where he went home with Nielsen. In Nielsen's tiny room, where the piano and the bed took up most of the space, they played through the pieces. Jespersen explicitly remembers a sonata in G, composed with a touch of early Mozart. This agrees with the style of the surviving Sonata in G major for violin and piano (CNW 62).[22] The sonata is in three movements and is entirely in the Viennese Classical style, so much so that it can hardly be called anything other than a pastiche. The music works well, but is devoid of originality. The most successful is the final movement, a Scherzo with an energetic fugal theme that is introduced successively in the different parts. Nielsen must have seen potential in this movement, for he later reworked it as a string quartet movement, in which the fugal entries are given their due.

Among the early works are two pieces for violin and piano, both entitled Romance. They are good examples of the uncertainties surrounding the early works. One is in G major (CNW 60), which has survived in a transcription with a personal dedication 'To Mr Carl Larsen most sincerely from Carl Nielsen'.[23] The second is in D major (CNW 61) in Nielsen's own hand. The latter Romance is complete, although only the first page has been copied in ink. The rest is a mixture of pencil and ink.

It is known that Nielsen played a romance as an encore at a concert in the Odense Music Society in October 1888. It was not the first time he had come to Odense to introduce himself to the city's audiences, but this time he did so as both a violinist and a composer. As a composer, Nielsen conducted his own *Suite for String Orchestra*, and as a violin soloist he had excelled with Hubert Léonard's *Souvenir de Haydn*, a typical bravura piece in which an introduction is followed by a theme and a series of variations. The piece allowed Nielsen to show off his technical skills and elicited 'a veritable storm of applause' from the audience. As an encore, he played 'one of his own compositions, a fine and beautiful Romance', which received equally enthusiastic applause.[24] Larsen, his old teacher, was a key figure in the management of the Society and was obviously instrumental in making the concert happen. But does this mean that the Romance was the one dedicated to Larsen? The real answer is that we do not know.

The Romance in G major is an unconvincing work. The violin part is rather ordinary, and the piano part is decidedly uneven, with sudden shifts in style and genre. It is clear that Nielsen had not yet mastered the art of writing a well-functioning piano part. One possibility is that the piece was composed during Nielsen's early days in Odense, and that he played it at the concert out of veneration for his mentor Larsen. However, it is not possible to establish whether Nielsen added the dedication on this occasion, as it is also possible that he gave the copy to Larsen at another event.[25]

The Romance in D major is not a great work either. The melody may fit the description of 'fine and beautiful', but this is not enough to determine whether the work was performed on the occasion mentioned. The piano part is simpler and composed in a less dramatic vein. Had this been the piece he played in Odense, it would have fulfilled its function in the concert in an appropriate manner. A Romance requires an emotional and expressive performance and would naturally follow a virtuoso solo piece.[26] Thus, Nielsen the composer conceived a piece that met the needs of Nielsen the musician.

Under Rosenhoff's Tutelage

Until the end of the 1880s, Nielsen composed pieces for musicians who were his immediate colleagues. One such work is *Fantasy Pieces for Oboe and Piano*, Op. 2 (CNW 65). The piece is dedicated to Olivo Krause, who was an oboist in The Royal Orchestra. The collection has become part of the international repertoire of oboe pieces and is still widely known and played by musicians all over the world.

Nielsen began the composition in the autumn of 1889, when he had just joined The Royal Orchestra. The first evidence of the work is found in Emilie's notebook, where she writes that an Andante for oboe and organ was completed on 30 November, and the Intermezzo for oboe and piano on 9 March the following year.[27] These two movements became the *Fantasy Pieces for Oboe and Piano*.

In the summer of 1890, Nielsen had gone on holiday to his parents' home on Fyn and left the two oboe pieces with Rosenhoff, who was to look them over and then send them to Wilhelm Hansen for printing. Nielsen wrote to Rosenhoff to enquire about the matter and to express his gratitude for what Rosenhoff had shown to him:

> Whenever I have been with you, I have always had a clear feeling that I could achieve great things in the world. And what's remarkable is that this feeling was almost strongest when you didn't like my things; so it's not your praise but the inspiring way you approach things that gives energy.[28]

As in his letter to Emilie almost three years earlier, Nielsen emphasises Rosenhoff's ability to speak his mind honestly in a way that strengthens the private student's confidence as a composer. The respect is evident: he still addresses Rosenhoff using the deferential third person plural. Two days later, Rosenhoff replied that he had made small changes to the piano score and that he would like to see the pieces again when the publishers sent them for proofreading.[29] Comparing the different versions that have survived, it is clear that the piano part has been altered the most – it was here that Nielsen needed the most help. At the end of the year, Rosenhoff also read through Nielsen's corrections to the piano pieces Op. 3 before sending them to Wilhelm Hansen, and it was Rosenhoff who decided on the title, *Five Piano Pieces*.[30]

It shows a considerable degree of trust that Nielsen not only had the pieces proofread by Rosenhoff but also asked him to send them directly to the publishers, including any changes. It also shows how, as late as 1890, Nielsen relied on Rosenhoff as an advisor and as the final authority on whether a work could be considered finished and ready for publication.

In September 1890, Nielsen embarked on his first long foreign journey. In the middle of the month he was in Dresden, where he proofread the oboe pieces he had received from the publisher. A few days later he performed them at a private party, where he himself played the oboe part on the violin and Victor Bendix played the piano.[31] This was the beginning of the tradition that the work could also be played for violin. The original version for oboe and piano was published by Wilhelm Hansen in 1890, and two years later an arrangement of the first movement for violin and small orchestra was published under the title *Romance*. This piece was later published in a version for violin and piano, thus fulfilling the same function in concerts as the early romances.[32] It has also been performed several times in a version for oboe and organ, an idea that goes back to the earliest version of the movement.[33]

Even before the oboe pieces were fully completed and proofread in late 1890, there had been several performances of one or both movements. The official premiere, however, was to take place at the first of four chamber music soirees performed by members of The Royal Orchestra; but Olivo Krause fell ill, and it was not until 11 March 1891 that the pieces were presented in their final form to the people of Copenhagen.[34] Nielsen was still travelling and did not attend the event himself.

The two *Fantasy Pieces* were performed in a concert with an ambitious programme, including Beethoven's late String Quartet Op. 130, which at the time was still considered a highly demanding and advanced work. As in Dresden, Victor Bendix accompanied on the piano. By the time the printed edition appeared, the movements had been given their final titles, Romance and Humoresque. The pieces were generally well received, although one reviewer found them strange, noting their 'searching, almost morbid' harmony and consequently unnatural melody.[35]

This was a common view among critics of Nielsen's music at the time, and revealed that his harmonic imagination, in particular, went further than audiences were used to. Listening to the music with today's ears, the Romance can be characterised as having the atmospheric and slightly dreamy tone that one expects from an instrumental romance. The Humoresque is lively and varied, and Nielsen succeeded in making the piano an equal partner and not just an accompanying instrument.

Suite for String Orchestra

Nielsen's *Suite for String Orchestra* (CNW 32), which was to become his Op. 1, is a good example of how the process of achieving a finished result with which he was satisfied could be a protracted one. The four hallmarks of the post-academy period all come to the fore: first, the work was composed for musicians with whom he had direct contact: the strings of the Tivoli Orchestra. As with the *Andante tranquillo e Scherzo* of the previous year, it was Nielsen's contact with Balduin Dahl that led to the first performance of the Suite, and Nielsen himself was a member of the orchestra. Secondly, one can clearly see Rosenhoff playing a decisive role in the various stages of revision and completion of the work up to its printing. Thirdly, the Suite was performed several times and in several versions, allowing Nielsen to hear the effects of the various revisions. And fourthly, it was the earliest composition to be given an opus number and published.

The first version of the Suite was premiered at a prominent event during the Nordic Industrial, Agricultural and Art Exhibition of 1888: the Second Nordic Concert at Tivoli on 8 September. Nielsen later describes how Dahl accepted the piece for performance after a brief review a week before the concert, although it could hardly have been done so carelessly when the work was to be performed at such a high-profile concert. Dahl had to be sure that the piece was of such high quality that it could be performed alongside works from the other Nordic countries.[36] The concert was reviewed in several newspapers and the new work received considerable attention. Of the three movements, the audience were particularly enthusiastic about the second, which they insisted be played as an encore, and after the concert the composer was called to the stage three times.[37] Overall, it was a success, although Nielsen was not entirely satisfied with the result and the Suite underwent several revisions after the Tivoli performance.

In its final form, the Suite consists of three movements: a rather short, slow opening Prelude, followed by a light and elegant dance movement reminiscent of ballet music, which develops into a waltz in the middle section. The third movement, which is the length of the first two movements combined, has a slow introduction that recalls the melody at the beginning of the first movement. This is followed by a fast and lively section.

At the first performance at Tivoli, the third movement was entirely different. It had no slow introduction and there is much to suggest that it was completely reworked. A pencil sketch has survived which includes the third movement but without the slow introduction, and although it begins in the same way, it develops differently.[38]

The titles of the movements have also been changed. In the printed version, the movements have rather neutral titles: Präludium, Intermezzo and Finale. Nielsen's final manuscript, which was used as the printing manuscript, includes similar neutral titles, but in French.[39] At the first performance in Tivoli, however, the movements were given mythological titles: 'The Danaids', 'The Dance of the Charites' and 'The Procession of Bacchus'. According to Dahl, this was mythological nonsense and asked for them to be removed, but Nielsen left them in. The official Tivoli programme does not give the titles, only that it was a 'Suite for String Orchestra, in three movements (new)'.[40]

The titles must already have been known, for one reviewer heard the first movement as 'heavy, plaintive, hopeless: it was the Danaids who were to fill their bottomless vessels.'[41] With titles like these, the three movements give the impression of being character pieces. The critics also noted two things, which are quite accurate. First, that the Suite was immediately appealing and had the character of well-functioning dance movements. Second, that it balanced somewhere between classical models and a more modern harmony. The latter was an observation echoed in many of the following reviews, whether meant positively or negatively.

As mentioned above, the Suite was played again at the concert in Odense about a month later. It was then performed at the G Major Society in January 1889.[42] Shortly afterwards, Nielsen had a meeting with Wilhelm Hansen, who had expressed a wish to publish the Suite, but it was now clear that Nielsen was not satisfied with it. They therefore agreed that only the first two movements should be published. He also seems to have been concerned with the titles of the movements, for it was at this time that he thought that the two movements should be called Prélude and Intermède, the same French titles that he used in his final manuscript. He considered naming the second movement something with graces or sylphs. However, he did not want the Finale to be printed, 'as I'm not satisfied with it', as he wrote to Emilie.[43]

He began to rework the Finale, and in mid-April he told Emilie that it was almost finished. A week earlier, he thought he was done, but then he had the idea

> of letting the very first theme in the whole Suite (i.e. of the first movement) suddenly break through towards the end of the Finale, and the thought took hold of me so completely that I had to revise the entire conclusion. Now I think it's really good. Rosenhoff says the same, so I'm satisfied, my sweetheart.[44]

The revised Suite was performed on 28 April in the Hall of the Workers' Association as part of its series of Popular Concerts, at which Nielsen had previously appeared

a) First movement, bars 3–6

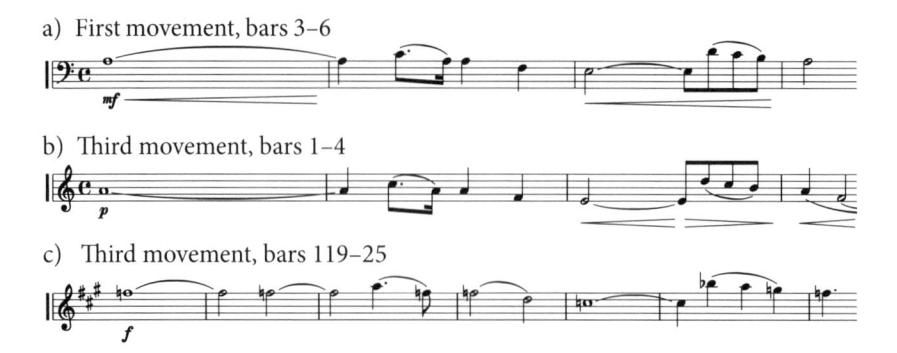

b) Third movement, bars 1–4

c) Third movement, bars 119–25

MUSIC EX. 1: Carl Nielsen, *Suite for String Orchestra*, Op. 1. The theme that Nielsen uses to create coherence across the movements appears in the cello part in the third bar of the first movement. At the beginning of the slow introduction to the Finale, the same theme is introduced in the second violin. The tempo is the same as in the first movement. Towards the end of the development section, the theme from the first movement reappears in the violins. Now it appears in note values twice as long, but because the tempo – in the fast section of the Finale – is just over twice as fast, it is easily recognisable to the listener. In the final version, the passage corresponds to bars 119–49, where the reprise begins. Here the Finale's own themes resume, and the piece ends with a coda at an even faster tempo.

as solo violinist. The Suite still did not include a slow introduction to the final movement, as one reviewer pointed out that the Finale's 'bold opening' was too difficult for the orchestra, which was partly made up of amateurs.[45]

A month later, another performance took place at Tivoli, and now the slow introduction was included, using the theme from the first movement that he had now inserted in the Finale. The work had reached its final form. With the reappearance of the theme in two prominent places in the Finale, he had created a link between the first and last movements, making the work seem more like a unified whole. The concert took place on 25 May 1889 to mark the return of the famous polar explorer Fridtjof Nansen from his last great expedition to Greenland. It was a highly publicised event. On this occasion, Nielsen himself conducted the Suite and the movements were announced as Prelude, Scherzino and Finale.[46] The change was so striking that the critics remarked that the Finale had been reworked.[47] A week later the piece was performed again at the same venue. It was now approved and Wilhelm Hansen could publish it, this time with all three movements.

However, it took about a year before it was published in the spring of 1890. The Suite was not issued by Wilhelm Hansen in Copenhagen, but by their German subsidiary in Leipzig. The reason for this was not that the publishers had Nielsen's international breakthrough in mind, although an instrumental work for strings could easily find interested buyers in Germany, but rather that Denmark had not signed the Berne Convention of 1886, the first international agreement on the protection of artistic rights. This did not happen until 1904, and it was only later, in 1912, that it was incorporated into Danish law. The Danish side initially saw an advantage in the fact that foreign books, articles, musical works and images could continue to be copied and published in Denmark without restriction, a practice that was very common. On the other hand, foreign publishers could also copy Danish publications without any problems. For music publishers such as Wilhelm Hansen, this matter was solved by setting up a branch in Leipzig, the European centre of the music trade. The work was therefore published under the German title *Kleine Suite für Saiteninstrumente* and with movement titles common in Germany: Präludium, Intermezzo and Finale.[48]

That it was not such a bad idea to publish the Suite in Leipzig is shown by the fact that it was given three performances in Dresden in the autumn of 1890. The fact that Nielsen himself was in the city must also have played a part.[49] The same is true of a performance at the end of December at the popular concerts of the Berlin Philharmonic, made possible by the Danish flautist and conductor Joachim Andersen.[50]

The work was dedicated to Rosenhoff, who had been involved throughout the process and had probably made the final corrections during the proofreading stage. From the letter Nielsen wrote to Emilie, it is clear that he had sent the revision of the Finale to Rosenhoff for approval. As mentioned above, Rosenhoff also played a key role in the *Fantasy Pieces for Oboe and Piano*, Op. 2, and the *Five Piano Pieces*, Op. 3, which, like others of Nielsen's early publications with Wilhelm Hansen, were also published in Leipzig.

Subsequently, however, it is evident that Rosenhoff's role begins to change. Nielsen still kept Rosenhoff closely informed of what he was composing, although in time Rosenhoff no longer needed to approve his work. By the end of 1890, all he had to do was imagine what Rosenhoff would say and envisage what Rosenhoff would do:

> When I have composed something, yes, even during my work, I think of you, of what you would say about this or that, and when I myself think that it's good, I can suddenly see you nodding along gently, with a quiet expression on your face; then I know the rest, and I'm proud.[51]

In the summer of 1892, the situation had changed: Nielsen played a theme from his First Symphony to Rosenhoff and was pleased that he liked it.[52] But now the decisions were his own. They kept in touch until Rosenhoff's death in 1905, but there are no surviving letters in which they discussed Nielsen's works. The apprenticeship had ended.

Mastering the String Quartet Genre

The first work in which Nielsen stands entirely on his own is the String Quartet in F minor, Op. 5 (CNW 56). Indeed, one senses that he felt more at home in this genre than in those with which he had worked during those years. It is not surprising, therefore, that the string quartet was the first genre in which he emerged with maturity and confidence as a composer in his own right.

String quartet playing was an activity in which Nielsen had already been well trained in Odense. He had received professional violin tuition from Carl Larsen, and he had formed a string quartet with colleagues from the military band.[53] It is possible that Nielsen also played chamber music in the circles of the city's musical life in which Larsen was active. This meant that Nielsen had both intimate knowledge of quartet playing and access to try out the pieces he had written.

The string quartet is a musical form in which the focus is on making music – that is, on well-functioning and entertaining ensemble playing itself. It is this ensemble playing that is very much in evidence in Nielsen's early quartets. Nielsen's sense that it should be enjoyable for the musicians to have melodies and motifs passed from one musician to another is clearly evident. It is music, in other words, composed to amuse the musicians themselves as well as to delight the audience listening to it.

Until well into the nineteenth century, string quartet playing was a semi-private activity cultivated by musicians and well-educated amateurs of the musically interested bourgeoisie. They played a wide repertoire of string quartets that functioned in this context. Peter Heise's six string quartets from the 1850s, for example, were composed for such musical evenings in private homes.[54] With the exception of one season in the mid-1850s, string quartets were not included in the repertoire of Musikforeningen's concerts in Copenhagen, and it was not until the 1870s that they became a regular feature of public concert life.[55]

When Nielsen composed his earliest surviving string quartet, the D minor (CNW 49), it was in connection with the fact that he had begun to play in a string quartet with his colleagues in Odense:

> I thus got to know Haydn's, Mozart's, Pleyl's, and Onslow's quartets, and was so fascinated by them that I resolved to compose one myself. A month later it was finished. I still have this work and cannot imagine how I could have put it together, not having any kind of theoretical knowledge at that time. For this quartet (in D minor) is very well formed, and the Scherzo even has a correctly executed canon. It has no originality, of course, but is fresh and vivid.[56]

Nielsen's assessment of his own work is not entirely wrong. The Scherzo he mentions is the movement from the violin sonata mentioned above, which he reused in the quartet. In this case, it is the ensemble playing that lifts the movement above the ordinary, as the theme is passed from one musician to the next. It is a pleasure both to play and to listen to.

When Nielsen mentions that he and his companions played quartets by Haydn, Mozart, Pleyel and Onslow, the latter two in particular should be noted as they were major suppliers of decent quartets in the Classical style. It was not primarily the works of the great masters that he played and knew, but rather a repertoire in need of new, though not necessarily highly innovative, pieces. Nielsen's D minor quartet is a fine work that fits well into this context. The Viennese Classical tonal language is clearly dominant, and if you do not know the composer, it is difficult to guess.

In his memoirs of 1927, Nielsen emphasises that he still had the quartet in his possession, revealing that it was a work with which he had a special relationship. It is the only complete quartet from his early years that he kept. The manuscript is in a careful transcription entitled 'Quartetto No. 1' and appears to be the same work that he took to Copenhagen to present to Niels W. Gade. The Andante, the second movement that Gade looked at, reveals Nielsen as a young musician who knew his craft rather than a promising and innovative composer. Indeed, he mastered the string quartet genre, as his quartet works well and sounds good, in contrast to his piano writing, which reveals an awkwardness and weakness.

There is a clear progression from this early work to the String Quartet in F minor, Op. 5 – a work that marks his public appearance as a fully qualified composer in the demanding genre. The common thread is, firstly, his intimate experience of quartet playing, which gives him a musician's knowledge of how to compose so that it functions for the ensemble. Secondly, during his early years, Nielsen worked continuously with the string quartet genre, and in addition to the surviving complete movements, there are also sketches for a number of unfinished ones.[57] The early String Quartet in F, mentioned in his Christmas letter of 1887 to Emilie, should be included in this context, as should the debut work, *Andante tranquillo e Scherzo* for string orchestra, which was a revised set of quartet movements.

During the same period he also worked on the String Quartet in G minor (CNW 55), later published as Op. 13. Little is known about its genesis or why he waited so long to publish it. Three of the movements are dated, so we know that it was composed in the winter of 1887–88. The quartet was first performed at the Private Chamber Music Society on 26 March 1889 and again at The Chamber Music Society later that year. It was also performed at least three times during the 1890s, before he revised it in February 1898 in preparation for a recital of his own works. The revisions can be regarded as adjustments, with short passages omitted, added or altered, but not to such an extent as to change the fundamental character of the work. The positive reception of the quartet at the concert in 1898 – at the expense of his more recent works – may have confirmed his view that it was worth publishing. Two years later, Wilhelm Hansen published the work.[58]

With the G minor Quartet, Nielsen has achieved a compelling mastery of the genre that transcends pastiche. There is fullness and sonority, momentum and energy, and variety without detracting from the whole. The first movement presents two themes, first an energetic one in the violin and later a cantabile and melodic theme played first by the cello. After the middle section's treatment of the motifs, the two themes return in reverse order at the end of the movement. Although it is much more mature than the early quartets, its Viennese Classical origins can still be heard. Hearing it for the first time, the listener could be forgiven for thinking that this is an unknown quartet by Beethoven.

The second movement of the quartet is slow and entitled Andante amoroso. It begins in a rocking 9/8 time signature, giving it a dreamy, romantic character. One of Nielsen's revisions was to include the first theme twice at the beginning, making it more assertive. The third movement, a Scherzo, is probably the most successful, with the theme sweeping the listener along with great energy, only to be contrasted by some hesitant passages. There is a sense of energy juxtaposed with thoughtfulness. The middle section of the Scherzo is reminiscent of Norwegian folk music in the Grieg tradition. The last movement is an energetic Finale in which the lower parts emphasise the offbeats, as in the tradition of Slavic dances. One possible reason for Nielsen's initial reluctance to publish the quartet may have been its stylistic breadth, which points to existing stylistic worlds rather than to a style in which one could discern Nielsen's personal hand.

His continuing interest in the genre is evident in a letter he wrote to Emilie in mid-April 1889, shortly after the first performance of the G minor quartet:

> I did think about writing some solo pieces for violin, which [Anton] Svendsen has said several times I should do; now though, I think it will probably be a [string] quartet. I can't seem to get away from my quartets, sweetheart.[59]

Whether this was the F minor Quartet he already had in mind is uncertain. In the summer of 1890, he was certainly making good progress on it, for in July, as he was preparing for his trip abroad, he wrote to Rosenhoff from Fyn that work was progressing well and that he hoped to finish the quartet before he left. He also explained that he would make a fair copy of it, and that if he had not left a few of the pages at home, he would have sent Rosenhoff the first movement long ago.[60] At the end of August, when he had still not left, he visited Rosenhoff before starting on his European journey. He was not finished, and in July he had apparently embellished the truth about how far he had got with the composition.[61]

The first few weeks of the trip were not devoted to composing, but from the end of September he found the time. On Friday 26 September, he noted in his diary that an extension of the first subject had occurred to him, which he went back to his room to notate and included it in his composition. He was thus still working on the first movement. The following day he continued composing, but without the piano as he was not allowed to play after 10 p.m. By Monday he had finished the third movement, the Allegretto,[62] and by mid-October he was still working on the quartet, as he confided in his diary:

> I worked well today. I think I've got my own sound, though; through the whole F minor quartet I've become clearer about what it is.[63]

Nielsen was in Berlin in mid-October and seemed to be at a standstill. The slow second movement in particular caused him problems. He routinely calls it 'Andante', although in the printed version he uses the slightly slower tempo 'un poco adagio'. At the beginning of November he writes: 'Today I finally got on with the Andante of the Quartet, which I had been stuck on for a long time.'[64] A week later, however, he finished the final movement and remarked: 'I wonder if it will be understood?'[65] The following week he worked again on the second movement, and when he finally finished it, he revealed in a letter of 23 November how difficult it had been:

> Also, I've finished my new Quartet [i.e. F minor, Op. 5]. How I've worked on that piece! I scrapped the Andante three times, and I worked on some bars in the finale for months.[66]

While in Berlin, Nielsen arranged with the famous violinist Joseph Joachim for the quartet to be performed in one of Joachim's classes at the Academy. The audition of the piece took place on 18 December, and the members of the quartet were Nielsen on first violin, his fellow Copenhageners Fini Henriques and Frederik Schnedler-Petersen on second violin and viola, and his new German acquaintance Paul Morgan on cello.[67] The first rehearsal in preparation for the audition took place on 22 November, and the next day he was in a daze:

> today I could weep for joy. I saw what a deep impression my Quartet made yesterday, and I felt that … but no, it's too ridiculous![68]

The letter, which Nielsen wrote to a particularly close friend in Copenhagen, Emil Sachs, reveals that it was a great emotional release for him to hear the quartet for the first time and to witness the reactions it provoked. He was not entirely satisfied, however, for on 28 November he made another note in his diary: 'I finished the Andante in the quartet today. At last! What this piece has cost me!'[69] So he had to make one more revision before he was satisfied.

The most detailed account of the performance of the work in Joachim's class, which was well attended, is Nielsen's letter to Rosenhoff in January 1891. By this time, the experience had already taken place some time ago, and Nielsen had time to reflect on the event:

> we played my Quartet for Joachim … We had five rehearsals, and yet it still went very mediocrely; it's extremely difficult to play well, because there are so many modulations and enharmonic business that have to be played absolutely in tune, so that half of that difficulty would be enough. If you add to that the fear of playing for Joachim, you can appreciate that it didn't go particularly well. As I said, his judgment consisted equally of praise and blame. He found that I had an unusual fantasy, invention and originality, but that there were so many 'frightful' radical transitions that it would be a great pity if I didn't move away from this direction.
>
> I was with him the following day, and he said that he had thought a lot about my Quartet and would advise me to revise the places he showed me in the score! Isn't it remarkable that with one exception where he was right about a trivial point, it was all the things I myself like best?[70]

Nielsen was adamant that he would not change anything. He was afraid that the quartet would lose its character, which suggests that he identified with what others found strange.[71] In this context, his statement about whether he believed he had found his own personal tone gives the impression that his self-awareness as a composer had reached a new level. On the other hand, some critics and listeners around this time may have sensed a Nielsen who insisted on features in his music that some found exaggerated. A certain youthful defiance may also be at play.

The F minor String Quartet has a characteristic full-bodied quartet timbre. Compared to the earlier quartets, this one appears as a sonorous whole. The parts complete the tonal space. Nielsen has now abandoned the Viennese Classical inspiration in favour of a compositional style that belongs to the late nineteenth century. This is especially true of the first movement. He places great emphasis on thematic work that moves between the parts, and all the parts have important melodic phrases – including the viola, an instrument that is often neglected. It may have been a factor that Nielsen also played the viola.

The second movement, with which he had so much difficulty, is slow and dreamy. He places great emphasis on timbral expression, for example by specifying that the melody is to be played on certain strings of the violin. In addition, in the combination of which instruments are to play certain melodic phrases, Nielsen creates a soft timbre in which the primary melodies are notated in the low register. The third movement is lighter and more playful and, like the Finale, is driven by a strong motoric impulse. The Finale balances this with long cantabile phrases and again the timbre is complete. The overall structure is easy to follow through all four movements.[72] The more sophisticated sections lie in the finer details and in the use of timbre.

The first performance took place in Copenhagen on 8 April 1892 at one of The Royal Orchestra's soirees; the musicians were Anton Svendsen, Holger Møller, Christian Pedersen and Frits Bendix. The work had not yet been published, and the programme listed it as his Op. 6. Most critics heard the work as confirmation of Nielsen's new maturity. *Politiken* wrote: 'none of his works has shown this as clearly as this quartet, which, in addition to the most youthful boldness, contains more will and knowledge than most of the works of our other quite young people.'[73] *Berlingske Tidende* also sees the work as a major step forward, noting 'the passionate, dark central mood of the piece, which sometimes appears in rather garish colours and almost overburdens the four instruments'. Although the piece is a little long and lacks formal clarity in places, 'it gives the impression of coming from a composer who has something to say'.[74]

The quartet was repeated on 28 April at Nielsen's composition soirée in Koncertpalæet, where he presented a selection of his works. *Berlingske Tidende* noted that on a second hearing the quartet seemed even more convincing, and that it 'can be regarded as a rather unusual work by a young man in his mid-twenties'.[75] *Morgenbladet* wrote that, compared to his string quintet, which was a few years older and performed at the same event, the quartet was far more interesting 'in both form and content'.[76] The general consensus was that the quartet showed that the composer had reached a new level.

After the two concerts in the early summer of 1892, Nielsen was in close dialogue with the publisher Wilhelm Hansen to prepare the quartet for publication. At this stage he reworked a number of details and introduced some minor changes he had made in the parts during rehearsals. The most thorough revision concerned the second movement, where he seems to have replaced an entire passage.[77] The practical experience gained from the two performances thus had an impact on the finished work. A heated argument ensued when Nielsen discovered that Wilhelm Hansen had not intended to publish a score, but only the parts. It was important to Nielsen that it should be possible to study the work in detail, which required access to a score. Otherwise it would only be possible to study one part at a time. 'It would be almost like publishing a play in the form of parts for each role! … Would you be so kind as to answer me immediately, because this matter is close to my heart?'[78]

The request seems reasonable, since it was common practice to publish a score as well. If Nielsen insisted so passionately, it was because the quartet had to be taken seriously as an artefact. It should not only be heard, but also studied. Another reason was that a score was necessary if the piece was to be promoted for performance. Nielsen also had his career in mind. He did not receive a prompt reply, for after he had reminded the publishers twice, they did not reply until August, and then with a refusal.[79] In the autumn, however, the matter was resolved and a printed score was available by the end of the year.[80]

The dispute with Wilhelm Hansen over the score is one of several indications that Nielsen was at this time making a determined effort to lay the foundations for a career as a composer. This is what he would now prioritise as his main task. However, it would require him to be able to make ends meet. His work as a member of The Royal Orchestra was the foundation, a job he had no intention of giving up. As an orchestral player, he used his musicianship and did not need to devote all his creative energy to the job. This approach is probably the reason why he remained at his desk as second violinist until 1905, without advancing in the ranks of The Royal Orchestra. What he needed to succeed was to be able to spend the rest of his time without too many commitments.

One of Nielsen's initiatives was that he and Anne Marie should visit his in-laws at their farm Thygesminde in the autumn of 1892. They asked her father for help, and got it. He promised 400 Kroner a year from May 1891, but at the same time urged the couple to be prudent and moderate, and to keep a tight rein on their finances. In the letter confirming his promise, the father also referred to a statement warning against pride, for during their visit Nielsen had compared himself and Anne Marie to Anne Marie's brother Poul, who was considering taking over the parents' farm, saying 'we can achieve something in the world and prosper'.[81] In the father's letter, written in German as most of his letters were, this particular sentence is indeed in Danish, presumably to emphasise their own formulation. The statement suggests that Nielsen saw both himself and Anne Marie as artists with careers ahead of them – if they had the means.

During that autumn, Nielsen received recommendations from the most important figures in Danish musical life, C. F. E. Horneman, Johan Svendsen, Victor Bendix and J. P. E. Hartmann, and in the spring of 1893 he enclosed their recommendations with his application for a Civil List annuity, that is, as a composer with a fixed annual sum. Again, Nielsen's main argument is his need to make ends meet in such a way that he has time to compose. He introduces himself in the letter as 'the under-signed, composer Carl Nielsen' and explains that if he had to take on pupils again, as well as being a musician in The Royal Orchestra, there is 'so little time left over for [him] to follow [his] actual vocation that it counts for nothing'.[82] Nielsen now describes himself as a composer without any hesitation. That is now how he identifies himself.

The First Symphony

With his String Quartet in F minor, Nielsen had made his mark as a composer of chamber music – all he needed was a similar breakthrough as a composer of orchestral music. He achieved this with his Symphony No. 1 in G minor (CNW 25), premiered at one of Johan Svendsen's prestigious Royal Orchestra Concerts in 1894. The road to his first symphony, however, was not a straight one.

The inspiration to compose a symphony came during his stay in Berlin in November 1890 and, interestingly, came directly from the energy of experiencing the sound of his F minor Quartet at its first rehearsal. In the same letter to Emil Sachs, in which he describes how deeply impressed he was by the quartet, he continues:

> today I'm the happiest person on earth; I could kiss the whole world, and I have a feeling of strength and power that is ravishingly beautiful. It's remarkable that every time I complete a major work I have the feeling that I'm only now really beginning.[83]

However, Nielsen's draft of a symphony while in Berlin was not his first attempt at the genre. When he described his ideas as a new symphony in 1890, it was because he had been working on a symphony for some time. The first movement survived and became the *Symphonic Rhapsody* (CNW 33). On this occasion, Victor Bendix was his main sounding board.

Later, Nielsen added the date 1888 to the fair-copied score of *Symphonic Rhapsody* and wrote the label on the front of the binding with the amusing spelling: 'Symfonisk Rapshodi. … Comp. 1888.'[84] However, according to Emilie's notebook, which carefully reproduces what Carl wrote to her, the completion is dated 27 September 1889, which is probably the correct date.[85] Nevertheless, there is no doubt that this is Nielsen's first attempt to compose a full symphony. The first page of music is simply marked 'Symphony'. In his sketchbook, which contains several pages of drafts of both the surviving first movement and unused ideas, Nielsen uses the term symphony several times and even 'Symphony No. 1'.[86]

In any case, the movement was completed by the summer of 1890, by which time it had been sent to Bendix for appraisal, and when their meeting was apparently cancelled, Nielsen received Bendix's comments in writing. Nielsen did not know Bendix very well at the time, so it must have been a deliberate act to ask for an assessment. It is clear that they both refer to the movement as the first part of a symphony, and Bendix praises both the craftsmanship and the instrumentation, although he feels that the motifs lack originality:

A little more originality and sincerity and it would be a masterpiece. The spirit in it is thoroughly healthy … As for the 'way of doing it' (the Gemach), I don't hesitate to say that it is impressively excellent, except perhaps for a few swirling octaves here and there. It sounds great from start to finish and will certainly be very effective. If I had to point out anything in particular, it would be the variety of treatment in which the first subject returns …[87]

The final sentence, which must be understood as a positive statement, refers to the fact that the first subject at the beginning of the movement is orchestrated differently when it reappears later.

Bendix maintained his positive opinion of the *Symphonic Rhapsody*, for on 26 February 1893 the movement was premiered in Copenhagen as an independent work at a so-called 'Popular Concert' that Bendix gave in the large auditorium of Koncertpalæet.[88] It seems that it was Bendix rather than Nielsen who insisted that the work be performed. After one of the rehearsals, Nielsen remarked somewhat ambivalently: 'It sounds very good, and although it seems a bit naive now, there is so much of my own and such a good attitude in the piece that I think it is quite good after all.'[89] Nielsen never attempted to complete the other movements. Bendix was so committed that, after a tepid reception at the premiere, he included the *Symphonic Rhapsody* again in the programme the following week. In fact, it was played twice at the second concert to give the audience a chance to familiarise themselves with it. This led to Bendix's dismissal as conductor of the Popular Concert series.[90] It was not the original purpose of the concert series to perform the same work several times at the same event – but was it really a musical work worth being dismissed for?

It is not a harmonious and complete work, and the audience expected more to follow. It was clearly a first movement, and Nielsen admitted that it was not suitable as a complete work per se. When the work was performed the following week, the title given in the programme was 'Symphonic Fragment for Orchestra'.[91] It was not played again until 1918, although it was not a work of which Nielsen was ashamed. In the years that followed, he included it whenever he had to list his most important works.[92]

So what kind of work did Nielsen's first attempt at composing in the symphonic genre produce? In *Symphonic Rhapsody*, Nielsen places great emphasis on the treatment of motifs, and in places this seems to get out of hand at the expense of form and coherence. One example is the figure of repeated thirds notated in quavers, which first appears in bar eight in the second violin. The idea is already apparent in the very first sketch. It is imperceptible at first, but becomes a characteristic element that unfolds throughout the movement.

If the first subject is rather ordinary, the second is successful. After a short transition, the oboe introduces a theme that has a genuinely good, dance-like character.

a)

b)

c)

MUSIC EX. 2. Carl Nielsen, *Symphonic Rhapsody*, bars 1–6. Indeed, as Bendix noted, the first subject of the *Symphonic Rhapsody* is not particularly original; nevertheless, it is remarkable to see how Nielsen has worked with it, giving it more prominence. In the first version in the sketchbook, the first eight bars are in place, but the melody in bars five and six uses only the notes of the chord. It is a D major seventh chord that briefly touches E♭: C D E♭ | D C A (example a). By employing visible corrections in the next version in the sketchbook, it becomes clear how the composer worked his way to the version he finally used. The melody has taken on a more independent form: C D E♭ | E♭ D C♯ (example b).[93] Below is the corresponding passage in the final version.

It seems to contain an element of folk music, as the theme consists of a very constant and elegant dance rhythm. It is also possible to hear it as more related to the balletic dances that he would later compose and include in his opera *Maskarade*. The movement contains several elements that appear much later in other works. Clear associations with folk music are rare in Nielsen's works, but a similar theme with obvious references to folk music is a fugal subject in the second movement of Nielsen's Symphony No. 5. Experimental sections in terms of timbre also occur when he creates a 'ghostly' ambience of something that does not belong to the mundane world. This is most evident at the beginning of the development section and towards the end.[94]

The structure is rather traditional. It consists of an exposition, in which the subjects are introduced, a development, in which they are worked out, and a recapitulation, in which they return. The recapitulation begins at the letter G in the score. Bendix particularly praised the return of the subject, which Nielsen had orchestrated differently from its first appearance in the exposition. However, the recapitulation is somewhat hampered. Because of the change in instrumentation, it is difficult for the listener to perceive the recapitulation as a reappearance of the beginning, and it loses some of its impact.

It is interesting to note that at this time Bendix was partly Nielsen's mentor in symphonic music, partly conducting some of his works and participating as a pianist. It is also striking that the symphonic piece – which Bendix promoted so strongly and which has a similar style of instrumentation to Bendix's own – does not become normative for the future Nielsen. Instead, he decided to make a fresh start by composing what would become his First Symphony.

At the end of the above-mentioned letter to Sachs, he states what had inspired him in November 1890:

> What do you say to this idea: a symphony with the title: 'From earth thou art come, to earth thou shalt return'? Dark and primeval at the beginning, where everything still lies in millennial hibernation. Then gradually movement and life, but as yet still half unconscious, then rising and rising to the maximum joie de vivre. Then back again to the 'black mould' which wraps us all up in its soft, dense robes; where we go to sleep for all eternity – eternal oblivion.[95]

The next day he wrote in his diary:

> Symphony: 'From earth thou art come, to earth thou shalt return'. It shall be the great work of my life, if I live long enough to become skilled and good enough to perform it. ... Today in the street the first theme of the new C minor symphony came to me. Perhaps it would be better if it were in C sharp minor; that key is almost more sombre.[96]

There are several remarkable things about these statements. The idea of a symphony depicting the circle of life as one great unified movement is surprisingly close to his later symphonic ideas. One might be led to believe that it was a programme idea for his Fourth or Fifth Symphonies. His description of the idea for the *Helios Overture*, which he composed thirteen years later in Athens, is also very close to what he presents in the above statements.[97] Indeed, it suggests that he had a primary conception of the symphonic to which he returned several times in his life. In 1922, when confronted with the fact that his Fifth Symphony was very different from the previous ones, he replied that he could not hear it himself. On the contrary, he believed that the titles of the earlier symphonies were merely different words for the same idea – that is, the only thing that music can ultimately express: the inactive forces as opposed to the active. He also mentioned his Symphony No. 1 in this context, although it has no title.[98]

Nielsen's diary gives the impression that he began jotting down ideas for his new symphony immediately after the rehearsal of the quartet, and on a blank page in the manuscript of the String Quartet in F minor there is indeed a theme that is used in the symphony. It is tempting to conclude that this may have been the first theme that occurred to him in the street, and that he therefore scribbled it down on a page of the string quartet that he was carrying around with him in Berlin at the time. It does not resemble a theme in C minor, but with a stretch of the imagination and an eye to Nielsen's penchant for eccentricity, it could very well be interpreted in that key.

Before getting carried away by the good story, however, it is important to study the sources. This is where the careful descriptions of the manuscripts on which the *Carl Nielsen Edition* is based prove their worth. The actual music folio with the symphony's theme belongs to the final revision of the second movement of the Quartet in F minor – a revision that Nielsen apparently made after the quartet's performances in April 1892.[99] The folio was added to the manuscript later and was therefore not part of it when he carried it around in Berlin. Rather, the theme scribbled on the folio proves that he worked on the first movement of the First Symphony between May and June 1892.

However, the fact that Nielsen thought of a theme for a C minor Symphony while walking in the streets of Berlin shows that he had been inspired to make a start. He also noted on 20 December that he had 'started very well on the Finale of the symphony' and at the end of January he confided in his diary that he had 'started on the Andante of the D flat major symphony'.[100] None of the keys he mentions, however, corresponds to the movements found in his Symphony No. 1. Rather than claiming that he immediately set to work on what would become his first symphony, it is more likely that he discarded these ideas and made a fresh start, working on it only after his return.

It is difficult to determine exactly when Nielsen began work on his First Symphony. He returned to Denmark in the summer of 1891 and began to set up a home with Anne Marie. From then until the end of May 1892, there are no sources that mention the symphony. The first evidence of the work is the motif he wrote on the page of the manuscript for the String Quartet in F minor, where he revises a passage in the second movement, which he embarked on at the beginning of June 1892.[101]

By the end of July, Nielsen is well into the symphony. He composes a theme for the 'second part of the symphony', which he plays for Rosenhoff:

> He says that it's the most beautiful thing I've written. I have never been so moved as the night I wrote it. I got shivers down my spine, and I was almost getting sick from agitation.[102]

Work on the symphony continued until early 1894. In August 1893, Nielsen is in Skovshoved, north of Copenhagen, and the letter reveals that he is working on the symphony: 'How is your work going, my love? I've scrapped the subsidiary motif in my Finale and made a new and better one out here.'[103]

Allegro orgoglioso (𝅗𝅥 = 104)

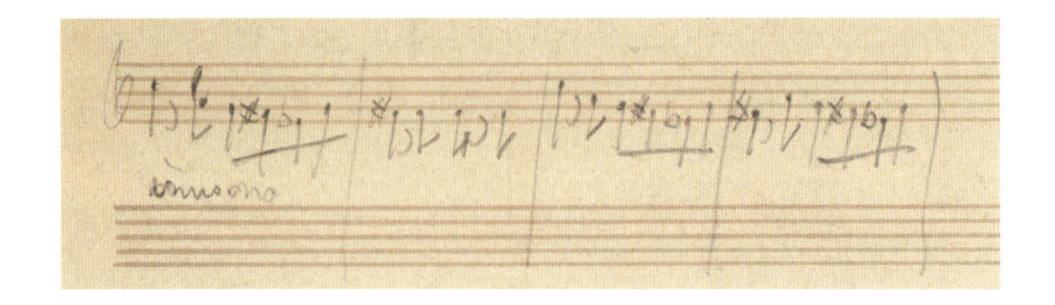

MUSIC EX. 3. Nielsen's sketch of a theme for his First Symphony, added to a page in the pencil sketch of the second movement of the String Quartet in F minor, Op. 5.[104] The theme in the manuscript for the string quartet is not the opening theme of the symphony; rather, it is the theme in the form that recurs after the return of the first subject following the development section (bars 233–36). If a first subject is notated in this way in the manuscript of another work, it is because the idea is to be retained and not lost. Compared to the opening bars of the symphony's first subject, shown below, the theme here is partly reversed and partly 'displaced', with an augmented interval between the fourth and fifth notes. The instruments all play in unison. In the finished symphony, flutes, oboes, violins and viola play the theme at this point over a bass playing the note A. The theme has a number of characteristic features that suggest something about Nielsen's musical world. It is a powerful unison theme and the unison aspect is already notated as part of the idea. The theme contains an augmented interval, which is a common feature of Nielsen's music.

In the autumn he suffered a heart attack; on 20 October he went to the doctor and was told to rest for three weeks, and he feared that the symphony would not be finished in time. He was absent from The Royal Orchestra for some time, but his heart condition did not improve. On 3 November he was taken by ambulance to hospital. When he was discharged three weeks later, he was able to work again, and by 4 December he had completed the fair copy of the first movement.[105] The other movements were completed on 11 December, 19 December and 14 January.[106] In February 1894, Nielsen wrote to Bendix that he was in a hurry to complete the instrumental parts, and on 14 March the symphony was premiered at one of The Royal Orchestra's symphony concerts. For the occasion, the orchestra was extended 'with the best musicians outside the orchestra', thus almost doubling the string section.[107]

The audience was treated to something new. With one of his characteristically ambiguous beginnings, Nielsen's symphony in G minor begins with a C major chord. Thus, in the first movement, he creates a small structure of two types of inner conflict that balance each other. One element is the introduction of two keys, with C major at the point where the key is expected to be established, on the first stressed beat, while G minor is the starting point of the melody, after the first four bars. The second element is to use minor when major is expected and vice versa. If the key is C major, the normal continuation would be G major, but in this case it is minor. If the key is G minor, the normal chord would be C minor, but Nielsen uses C major. By doing the opposite of what the audience anticipates, Nielsen prevents them from confirming their expectations. He keeps things open.

At the same time, the first movement has a distinct form. First comes the introduction with its two themes, the powerful first subject at the beginning and a cantabile second subject. The repetition of the first part of the movement comes as a sudden jolt back to the C major/G minor introduction, which makes the form clear to the listener. After a repetition of the introduction, the themes of the middle section are worked through until a clear gesture returns to the first subject and the original tempo (bar 185), where the overall sequence of the form begins again. At this point, the first subject clearly returns in G minor. He is thus still working within a classical model: 'conflict – resolution', and in this case the solution is that the internal conflict between the two keys of the theme presented at the beginning is now resolved. From then on, the movement continues in G minor until the end. The key is now stable.

The construction of a symphonic movement in which the opening evokes an image of the instability of modernity is intended to create a starting point full of energy and possibilities.[108] It is an image of modernity as a condition that has abandoned safe ground. For Nielsen, it is not a matter of establishing an order that then collapses. On the contrary, the very tension and uncertainty provoked by the opening chord is meant to create a sense of unpredictable and constant development, of rhythmic momentum and the risk that it might all fall apart. It is the combination with the strict formal constraints that holds it together.

A symphony of this type concentrates its energy and potential at the beginning of the movement and unfolds as the individual elements are allowed to develop their inherent possibilities. The emphasis is therefore felt to be on the opening of the movement rather than on a triumphant, emphatic ending. Nielsen's endings can be experienced as rhetorical rather than as the culmination of a purposeful process: when the material and energy, and possibilities introduced at the beginning are exhausted, it is time to round off the movement. The structural emphasis has shifted from the symphony's conclusion to its opening gesture.[109]

With a symphony such as this, Nielsen had entered the grand stage. As well as being a compelling musical statement, it also shows how he came to terms with composing for the large orchestra. His earliest orchestral work, *Andante tranquillo e Scherzo*, clearly bears the stamp of having been composed for four members of a string quartet. In the *Suite for String Orchestra*, his compositional style has changed so that the strings, which have no melody, together form a well-functioning orchestral background. *Symphonic Rhapsody* makes use of the large orchestra, but seems a little rigid in its orchestral treatment. It is mainly the strings that carry the movement, with doublings or fillings in the winds. In other cases, the woodwinds play the melody, or it alternates between strings and winds. The overall picture becomes somewhat uneven. By the time he reaches Symphony No. 1, it sounds as if it had been composed and intended for orchestra all along. Things have fallen into place.

Chapter 9

THE RADICAL AND INTELLECTUAL ENVIRONMENT

During his early years in Copenhagen, Nielsen matured not only as a musician and composer, but also as a person. His exposure to new intellectual and cultural environments he had not known before broadened his horizons and influenced his view of the world. Emilie Demant Hatt, née Demant Hansen, met Nielsen in the summer of 1887 and witnessed at first hand his experience of the new environment. Her memoirs describe their meeting as the experience of a lifetime – not only because they fell in love, but also because Nielsen's personality and outlook on life were so different from the values with which Emilie herself had been brought up:

> … he was a 'freethinker' – Yes, something as terrible as a freethinker! – A word worse than the devil himself. But the devil was recognised, as it were; he belonged to religion, but a freethinker was completely outside religion – he had sunk deeper than the devil incarnate. – I was confused. Could such a person look like 'little Carl'?[1]

Emilie also explains how her religious mother ('they were all common people') was deeply outraged and 'spoke sternly to the young godless human being'.[2] That the question of religion was an issue in their relationship is also evident from a letter Nielsen wrote to Emilie on Christmas Eve 1887:

> You write that your mother often thinks of me. Believe me, that's been a great Christmas gift. I hope she may always be fond of me. I know only too well that she has had her doubts about me concerning religion; but I have promised her that I shall never shake her dear little daughter's faith, and I shall keep to that.[3]

Nevertheless, Nielsen managed to shape Emilie's thinking during those years. As she writes, he brought into her life not only his personality, his opinions and his music, but also a different kind of literature from what she was used to. Together they cultivated the modern poets Jens Peter Jacobsen and Emil Aarestrup, whose poems Nielsen also set to music.[4]

The picture Emilie paints of the young Nielsen is not exactly the simple, rural man we know from his memoirs, *My Childhood*. On the contrary, she describes him as someone who brought her world into contact with the Copenhagen of the socio-cultural movement known as the Modern Breakthrough. In the eyes of Emilie and her family, Nielsen represented an intellectual and dangerous metropolitan phenomenon: freethinking.

Religious criticism was, of course, not a new invention in the 1880s, but it was given new life by Georg Brandes and his supporters, who advocated a free and modern outlook on life. The problems of society and family life were no longer to be suppressed in art and literature, but were to be discussed. This meant a break with bourgeois customs and their authorities, including religion.

The movement caused a stir in Copenhagen's political, academic and artistic circles. Politically, the Brandesians were part of the Liberal Party, Venstre; they represented the European-oriented intellectual wing of Venstre, which seceded from the party in 1905 to form the Social Liberal Party, known as Det Radikale Venstre. In academia, the movement put issues such as religious criticism, Darwinism and women's liberation on the agenda and led to new associations and new circles of individuals. Brandes's ideas also had a major impact on art and literature, contributing, for example, to a wave of realism and naturalism in the 1870s and 1880s.

The liberation of traditional gender roles also became a central element of the movement. By the mid-1880s, a fierce debate was raging over gender equality and morality, with women's right to free sexual expression high on the agenda. When love was no longer seen as a sublime, divine quality, it was instead linked to the biological urge. The sensual and the erotic thus became important themes in the art and literature of the time, in which women's love was often depicted as consuming and deadly to men.[5]

Emilie Demant Hansen met Nielsen a few years after he had moved from Odense to the capital to study at the Academy of Music. He must therefore have soon become part of some of the social circles in Copenhagen where the new radical ideas were in vogue. One place that Emilie describes as significant for Nielsen's spiritual development during these years was the Rosenberg family's home on Pile Allé. The literary historian and lawyer Carl Rosenberg lived here with his large family of children until his death in 1885. Two of the children, Vilhelm and Margrete, had started at the Academy of Music the same year as Nielsen. They became some of his closest friends and Nielsen was a frequent guest at the family home. Emilie writes of the importance of the home as an intellectual sanctuary for him:

> There, Nielsen's sense of humour was given free rein. There they wrote 'nonsense novels' and competed to be the worst babbler. There they read old and new literature. They were all musical. They were interested in art, philosophy and religion. There, 'free thinking' was practised in every respect.[6]

ILL. 1. Harald Slott-Møller, *Georg Brandes on the university rostrum*, 1889–90. Nielsen's association with the Brandes milieu in Copenhagen helped to broaden his intellectual horizons in the period around 1890.

The latter shows that 'freethinking' was not just about religion, but an outlook that was possible and relevant in many ways. It is clear that Nielsen's approach to religious and artistic issues during these years was shaped by his visits to the Rosenberg family. The discussions in the home are also described in some of Margrete Rosenberg's memoirs. She remembers how Nielsen would sit and absorb everything that was being discussed, even though the topics were often foreign to him. When the discussion was over, he would frequently ask for permission to borrow books on the subject to take home, or ask for explanations of foreign words he did not understand. And it often drew laughter from the family and from Nielsen himself when he demonstrated his cultural gaps or joined in the conversation with a sing-song Fyn dialect.[7]

The memoirs give the impression of a cultural encounter between young people, among whom Nielsen gradually made his way into the linguistic and cultural norms that characterised an intellectual home in Copenhagen in the 1880s. In the process, he undoubtedly acquired a knowledge of modern trends in thought and literature. Early on, Nielsen also came into contact with others in his immediate social environment who identified with the new ideas – and who, moreover, had a close personal connection with the events at the heart of the Modern Breakthrough in Copenhagen. But what kind of intellectual environment did he come into contact with in the years following his arrival in the capital?

Radical Copenhagen

When the drama surrounding Brandes began in the 1870s, the scene was not the outer Copenhagen that was then rapidly expanding beyond the old ramparts into the working-class districts and suburbs. On the contrary, one of Brandes's greatest connoisseurs, Jørgen Knudsen, has described the scene as 'the academic bourgeois Copenhagen, a small, completely open scene, sharply separated from the rest of the city'.[8] The so-called 'scene' was more or less geographically confined to the Latin Quarter of the inner city, but the separation was also very much social: 'shareholders, merchants, theologians, lieutenants, students and their wives and children – that is, the social framework of the scene'.[9] This meant that some districts were inherently part of the environment, while others were not. One consequence of the sharp separation from the rest of Copenhagen was that almost everyone in the milieu knew each other well: 'There all the enemies meet in the same barber shop, as [Bjørnstjerne] Bjørnson puts it.'[10]

In addition to everyday meeting places such as the barber's shop and the pavements, a number of institutions in the city were particularly important for the cohesion of the milieu, among the most important being the University of Copenhagen on Frue Plads, the natural centre of the Latin Quarter. The university provided the setting for the opening of the 'drama': Brandes's series of lectures on the main trends in nineteenth-century literature. From 3 November to 16 December 1871, he gave twelve lectures in the university's Auditorium No. 7, and with each lecture the audience grew in numbers – and in indignation.[11] The problem for Brandes's opponents was indeed the accusation that Danish literature was unrefined in comparison with other European nations as well as his demand that literature must address a wide range of contemporary social issues. But what particularly offended the audience was his positivist presentation of his views as pure fact.[12]

The split between the conservative and the new radical cultural establishment also gradually became visible in the associations. In 1882, The Students' Association (Studenterforeningen) in Holmens Kanal, which had long been an important academic meeting place in the city, found a rival in The Student Society (Studentersamfundet). At the beginning of the 1870s, the opposition group comprising adherents of Brandes in The Student's Association was so small that it could sit on the window sill to the left of the speaker's rostrum. Gradually, however, it had grown large enough to turn its back on the old association and set up its own.[13]

For the first twelve years, The Student Society had modest quarters in a few basement rooms in Badstuestræde, a couple of hundred metres from Frue Plads. It then moved to Nørre Voldgade, conveniently situated between the Latin Quarter, where both the University of Copenhagen and the old halls of residence were located, and the new rampart district, where the Polytechnic had recently moved and where many young students rented rooms.[14] Finally, in 1901, The Student Society moved to a new purpose-built residence on Bispetorvet, right next to Frue Plads and the University of Copenhagen. The event was celebrated with a grand opening on 1 June, the highlight of which was the performance of a cantata with words by Holger Drachmann and music by Nielsen.

Immediately after its foundation, The Student Society established the framework that had not been possible in The Student's Association: female students were admitted, and every week political speeches were organised, followed by discussions with the speaker.[15] In addition to its political activities, the society also had social and cultural aims. In December 1882, the Student Society's Evening Classes for Workers was founded, and a few years later, the Society's Legal Aid for the Needy was established. In the 1890s, two cultural institutions were also established under the society's auspices: The Free Theatre of the Student Society in 1891 and the Workers' Concerts of the Student Society in 1897. The aim of the former was to stage plays of literary interest that were neglected by other theatres.[16] In this society, the Brandesian assertion of artistic freedom was indeed of paramount importance. The Workers' Concerts, on the other hand, were conceived more as a social and educational enterprise; the intention was 'to spread the knowledge and understanding of good music among the workers of Copenhagen and others living under the same conditions'.[17] In other

ILL. 2. The first premises of The Student Society in Badstuestræde in the inner city. The society was an important meeting place for the radical environment, where young students could discuss literature and politics with prominent figures such as Georg Brandes and Harald Høffding. Afterwards, they could continue their discussions in a more relaxed atmosphere at Café Bernina on the corner of Vimmelskaftet and Badstuestræde.

words, the activities of The Student Society also reflected an emerging alliance at the time between freethinkers and socialists.[18] In The Student Society's 1907 jubilee publication, Julius Schiøtt described the movement that led to its founding as 'currents of a radical social spirit'.[19]

The radical movement also had its own mouthpieces and discussion forums in the city press. In the 1870s these included the newspaper *Morgenbladet*, which was the mouthpiece of the Liberal Party in the capital, and the cultural periodical *Det nittende Aarhundrede*, published 1874–77 under the editorship of Georg and Edvard Brandes. In 1884 the newspaper *Politiken* and the periodical *Tilskueren* were founded, both of which became central platforms for the radical movement in Copenhagen.

Finally, more informal social interaction also played an important role in the milieu. This took place partly in private homes and partly in the city's cafés, where the Café Bernina in particular became a well-known meeting place for radical intellectuals and bohemian artists.

Georg Brandes and His Associates

The first Brandesians were members of The Literary Society, founded in 1872. After the publication of his lectures entitled *The Emigrant Literature* in February 1872, Brandes came under fierce attack from the conservative cultural establishment, which at the time was also concerned about the newly emerging political movements of socialism and the Liberal Party. The establishment of The Literary Society was an attempt to show support for Brandes, who had been deeply shocked and distressed by the campaign waged against him.[20] The society was also called 'The Association of Freethinkers', and its members may give us an idea of what parts of cultural life belonged to Brandes's circle – also in the following decades.[21] The small group in the society can be broadly divided into three: one with the young avant-garde poets, which at the time included Holger Drachmann, Sophus Schandorff and Jens Peter Jacobsen. The second was a group around the Danish teacher and writer Kristian Arentzen and some of his students, the journalist Otto Borchsenius, the philosopher Harald Høffding and the writer Vilhelm Møller. The third circle consisted of Brandes's Jewish relatives and friends: Edvard Brandes, Frits Bendix, Carl Julius Salomonsen, Herman Trier, Ludvig Bing and Herman Bing.[22]

Through his work as a composer, Nielsen came into contact with several of the poets in Brandes's circle: in the 1890s he set texts by Jacobsen and Drachmann, both of the Modern Breakthrough, and later he worked with poets such as Johannes Jørgensen and Jeppe Aakjær, who represented the modern in the milieu around the turn of the century. Nielsen's personal connection to the radical environment, however, was mainly through the latter group: Brandes's Jewish relatives in Copenhagen. The cellist Frits Bendix, a cousin of Brandes, was one of the founders of The Literary Society. Like Nielsen, he was a member of The Royal Orchestra, and there are several indications in Nielsen's letters and diaries that they also met privately. For example, they spent much time together in Paris in the spring of 1891, where they were both part of the city's community of Scandinavian artists.[23]

However, it was two of Brandes's other cousins – the businessman Emil Sachs and the composer Victor Bendix – who were to play an important role in Nielsen's association with the radical environment in the years following his arrival in Copenhagen. A third important link to the milieu was the zoologist and composer Rudolph

ILL. 3. The businessman Emil Sachs was a cousin of Georg Brandes and a central figure in the radical environment.

Bergh, who was one of Nielsen's most ardent supporters on the musical scene at the turn of the century. These three acquaintances each influenced Nielsen in their own way during the period when he was establishing himself as a musician and composer in Copenhagen.

Emil Sachs

Emil Sachs, who was ten years Nielsen's senior, probably met him through Albert Sachs, Emil's cousin. Albert Sachs lived in Odense and was one of those who made Nielsen's studies at the Academy of Music possible by supporting him financially.[24] When Nielsen left Odense, Albert Sachs arranged for his family in the capital to contact the young musician, and Emil Sachs thus became one of Nielsen's earliest acquaintances in Copenhagen. In the 1880s, Emil Sachs still lived in his father's house on Gråbrødretorv, as later described by one of Emil's colleagues:

> The father was extremely interested in politics and society. The home therefore became a meeting place for many men, such as the future prime minister Neergaard, who helped to reshape our political life, and many young artists, such as the composer Nielsen, who found a refuge here in the young and difficult years when they were struggling to make a name for themselves. All in all, it was a highly cultured home that Sachs came from, and he had none of the artistic blood in his veins that made some of his relatives so famous.[25]

Emil Sachs was a trained businessman who ran an exclusive fashion boutique in Copenhagen for many years. In 1902 he became headmaster of The Business School, a position he held until his death in 1920. He was also involved in a number of social and artistic projects from which The Business School also benefited. His colleague Marius Vibæk described how Sachs was able to draw on his considerable network in Copenhagen's artistic and literary circles for the school's concerts and lectures: 'Georg Brandes and Harald Høffding have spoken here, Herman Bang has recited, and which of our greatest artists has not sung and played for us?'[26]

A commemorative publication from 1923 dedicated to Emil Sachs is another testimony to his many acquaintances in Copenhagen's cultural life. It contains poems by L. C. Nielsen and Jeppe Aakjær and articles by former prime minister C. Th. Zahle and Nielsen, among others. The essays must, of course, be read with the caveat that they are a tribute to the recently deceased Sachs, and that they describe events that took place a long time ago, and in some cases were not even experienced by the authors themselves. Nevertheless, the publication is interesting in that it paints a picture of Emil Sachs in which two characteristics stand out, which may also say something about his relationship with Nielsen: firstly, his interest in and work for the welfare of youth, and secondly, his strong commitment to the social and artistic movement that Brandes supported.

An article by his friend Cathinka Olsen describes how Emil Sachs's admiration for Brandes began in childhood. Brandes had been a source of support for Emil and his brothers when their mother, Julie Bendix, a sister of Brandes's mother, died of illness in 1865. In the 1870s Emil was sent to Holbæk as an apprentice and resented being excluded from the exciting events in the capital. In Holbæk he was also beaten for attending a meeting of the Liberal Party. When he returned to Copenhagen, he was happy to spend time with Brandes and listen to him in the aunt's living room. He is reported to have told Olsen that he owed Brandes so much 'that for me he is above all rules. If he killed a man, I'd still like him.'[27]

Emil Sachs's admiration for his cousin and his ideas would influence many of his artistic interests and social commitments. Throughout his life he was deeply interested in the visual arts, music, architecture and literature, and was particularly fond of Jens Peter Jacobsen's poetry. Jacobsen was an acquaintance of the Brandes brothers and one of the writers from whom they had the greatest expectations. As a young man, Emil Sachs had met the writer at his cousin Edvard Brandes's house, and in the days when Jacobsen was dying of tuberculosis, he anonymously sent him a precious orchid every day. According to Olsen, Sachs's enthusiasm for Jacobsen was partly due to the poet's ability as a portrayer of nature, but also to his importance as an artist of the Breakthrough:

> The reason why Sachs admired Jacobsen so much was that he was not only a great artist but also the poet who had described the feast of Breakthrough of the 1870s in his 'Niels Lyhne'. The 'jubilant joy of the seventies', as Sachs himself called it on the day of his first speech in 'The Liberal Youth' – the joy that [Sachs] wanted a new youth to feel, understand and preserve. In that bonfire he himself had lit his torch, which he never let go. He reported for duty to the crowd who in the seventies and eighties fought with such ardour and tirelessness to make J. P. Jacobsen's words 'Light over the Land' come true. The leader of the seventies, Georg Brandes, was the man who had the most profound influence on [Sachs's] life.[28]

Emil Sachs was probably in Holbæk at the time when The Literary Society was founded, although he later became involved in other central societies of the left-wing intellectual scene: The Progress Club (Fremskridtsklubben), The Liberal Youth (Frisindet Ungdom) and The Student Society (Studentersamfundet). In the latter, he was admitted as a member without being a student.[29] In The Student Society he was deeply involved in workers' education, and in 1897, together with his cousin Frits Bendix and the social democrat A. C. Meyer, he founded the society's Workers' Concerts, in which he was actively involved for the rest of his life.[30]

Several reports from the student society underline Sachs's keen interest in the welfare and education of young people. Zahle describes Sachs's role vis-à-vis the young students as that of an indulgent older friend, or a kind of loving uncle, who was concerned with helping them find and develop their unique abilities.[31] Testimonials from The Business School emphasise the same quality; they also stress that Sachs was able to offer them not only career advice, but also guidance in more fundamental matters of life:

When he became the great leader of the throngs of young people who have flowed through The Business School in such abundance over the years, it was not because he sought to develop their qualities as merchants, but because he made them understand that life – even for merchants – has values that are not determined by stock exchange quotations or momentary market conditions.[32]

He played a similar role for Nielsen: as a kind of mentor who gave no explicit instructions, but managed to stimulate thoughts in the young man that were important for his spiritual development. Nielsen reflects on this in his essay in the commemorative publication:

I've owed Emil Sachs a great deal since my youth. This is still quite astonishing. What was it? Did he teach me music, or did he make me acquire new skills? No … Did he perhaps lavish me with gifts and exquisite dinners? No … What he gave, then, was something comprehensive, something conclusive, born of a deep desire to live spiritually in the whole, to understand as much as possible, so that in his loving way he could pass on the values he had acquired to other people who were hitherto outside and hungry.[33]

In the same essay, Nielsen also describes in more detail how Sachs was able to make an impression and pass on certain values. For example, in his youth, when they were visiting an exhibition together or discussing a new book, Sachs might notice something that was seemingly ordinary, but which somehow touched the heart of the matter and which Nielsen could therefore remember many years later.[34] He also stresses that Sachs's education had nothing to do with knowledge and skill, but rather with the ability to think independently and help others to do the same.[35]

It is obvious that Sachs had an influence on Nielsen's interest in the poet Jacobsen.[36] During his stay in Berlin in the autumn of 1890, when Nielsen was working on a piano piece inspired by a poem by Jacobsen, he consulted Sachs in a letter about the wording of the poem: 'The Arabesque is new and composed with Jacobsen's poem "Arabesque" in mind … How do the first two lines of Jacobsen's poem go? I think it's: "Have you gone astray in the deep forest? Do you know Pan?"'[37] Nielsen was clearly fascinated by the poem, which has a clear erotic undertone. It is one of the places in contemporary literature where female sexuality is portrayed as poisonous and deadly:

She was like Jasmine's sweet-smelling snow,
Poppy blood ran through her veins,
The cold, marble-white hands

Rested in her womb
Like water lilies in the deep lake.
…
Of the poisonous lilies
Dazzling lime
She intoxicated me;
…[38]

Nielsen may have been accustomed to discussing Jacobsen's poetry with Sachs and felt well equipped to introduce Emilie to the author in the late 1880s. Jacobsen's poems thus had a profound effect on Nielsen's early activities as a composer, and in the early 1890s he published two collections of lieder setting the text of Jacobsen's poems. Nielsen contributed to the European wave of musical settings of Jacobsen's poems that followed the posthumous publication of the poet's *Digte og Udkast* (*Poems and Sketches*) edited by Vilhelm Møller and Edvard Brandes in 1886.[39]

Victor Bendix

During the same period, Nielsen formed a close relationship with another Brandesian: the composer Victor Bendix. Exactly when and how the two met is unclear. In addition to both being part of Copenhagen's musical life, they had several mutual acquaintances in the 1880s who may have introduced them to each other. Bendix was the cousin of Nielsen's friend Emil Sachs and the brother of Frits Bendix, who played with Nielsen in The Royal Orchestra from 1889. He was also a good friend of Nielsen's theory teacher at the Academy of Music, Orla Rosenhoff.[40] In her memoirs, Bendix's daughter refers to Nielsen as her father's pupil,[41] but it was more of a mentoring relationship, with Bendix giving Nielsen feedback and otherwise using his position in musical life to promote Nielsen's works.[42] This was particularly true in relation to Nielsen's first attempt to compose a symphony, the first movement of which became *Symphonic Rhapsody*.[43]

The letter Bendix wrote to Nielsen in June 1890, in which he assessed the movement, is the earliest evidence of their relationship. Bendix concludes the letter with the hope that they will meet in Dresden when Nielsen leaves on his European tour, and notes that Nielsen could obtain his address through his wife or Sachs.[44] The following letter also introduces Sachs as the link between the two. Nielsen writes to Bendix in August that he and Sachs are going to Berlin and plan to make a detour to Dresden to visit Bendix. However, Sachs was prevented from going, so Nielsen cautiously asks if he can still visit: 'How long will you be in Dresden? Will you have time to see me when I get there?'[45] Although the modest tone of the letter seems exaggerated, one senses that Nielsen was nervous about taking up his older colleague's time, and that the visit was not quite so obvious if Sachs would not be joining Nielsen. However, Bendix responded kindly to the letter and the two ended up spending a lot of time together in Germany. After almost two weeks in Dresden, Nielsen wrote home to Sachs that he saw Bendix every day and found their time together very valuable. He also gives the impression that much of the time was spent exploring musical subjects: 'and as a rule he plays something or other for me, which is both extremely instructive and fruitful.'[46]

Bendix was among the musicians in Copenhagen with the closest ties to the city's radical and liberal-minded milieu.[47] Bendix's daughter also writes that both her parents were freethinkers, and for her father, 'who had grown up in the Brandesian circle and had experienced the revolution of spiritual liberation, the rejection of all authorised religion was a perfectly natural development'.[48] In his memoirs *Levned*, Brandes describes how, as a young man in the mid-1860s, he spent some time with Bendix when he became interested in 'the musical element of language'[49] and sought his younger cousin's guidance in music theory:

> With the assistance of a young musician, Bendix, later known as a composer and first principal violinist, I immersed myself in the mysteries of figured bass and even wrote down the entire theory of harmony. I learned to express myself in the savage language of musicians, to speak of scale-like minor-ninth chords, to understand what enharmonic ambiguity meant. I studied voice leading, permissible and forbidden octaves, but did not find what I expected. I composed some little melodies which I found very beautiful, but for which my young teacher laughed at me with good reason, and one evening he parodied them with exuberant gaiety at the piano for a large party of guests. It was an embarrassing moment for the composer of the melody.[50]

Bendix, a boy between thirteen and fourteen, played an important role in Brandes's musical education. His disappointment at the lack of connection between music theory and language and his own musical limitations probably contributed to the fact that music never became a major interest of Brandes's cultural criticism. When Bendix later told his daughter about his association with Brandes, it was not Brandes's lack of musical ability that he focused on. According to her recollection, they discussed subjects other than music theory when they were young and 'walked the ramparts night after night'.[51] Indeed, Brandes introduced Bendix 'to the mighty conflicts, the storms, that swept through his mind before his thoughts and ideas found their form and full clarity. Those nights, Dad believes, were crucial to his – Dad's – formative years'.[52] Bendix had told the story to his daughter when

Brandes had become a cultural celebrity, something Bendix would not have known at the time of the incident. The significance of the meetings may therefore have been greater in his retelling of the event than it actually was. There is little doubt, however, that Bendix was one of the musicians in Copenhagen closest to Brandes and the circles that supported him.[53] This is also the impression given by Bendix himself in a letter to Ludvig Bing in 1912, in which he mentions his involvement in The Student Society:

> In the past – in those politically turbulent times – when it was often something of a sacrifice to support 'The Society', I – perhaps alone among musicians – have repeatedly shown my sympathy for it. I have both written cantatas for its events and played for its members.[54]

On this basis, it is not surprising that Bendix also offers a suggestion as to what a musical counterpart to Brandesianism might be. In an unpublished draft of a memoir, he remarks: 'For as I was in my youth, I was all that one was not supposed to be in Copenhagen at the time: that is, a Wagnerian, a liberal, a freethinker, a Darwinist'.[55] On the surface, it may be difficult to see how Wagner's music could be interpreted as a realistic reflection of society, as Brandes demands of art, and therefore the connection between Brandesianism and Wagner worship must be found by detour. If, instead of trying to translate Brandes's ideas into musical qualities, one looks at the musical alliances around 1860, it becomes clear that a common agenda of Brandesianism and Wagner worship was indeed the struggle for progress. The great musical battle of these years was between a position that cultivated the New German movement, represented by Wagner and Liszt, and a position that cultivated a Classicist faction, represented by Brahms. For the former, the assertion of progress was central, while the latter insisted that music depended on eternal laws and that progress was therefore not necessarily beneficial in a musical context.[56]

Given the musical positions of the time, it is therefore understandable why it made sense for a Brandesian to be a follower of Wagner. At the same time, Bendix's remark also gives the impression that a common denominator of his political and artistic values was that they challenged established fundamental positions. In the 1870s and 1880s, Wagner's absence from the mainstream of the Danish concert repertoire may have been an important reason for his promotion among the Brandesians.[57]

It is obvious that Bendix played a role in Nielsen's Wagner enthusiasm in the early 1890s, for it is striking that the admiration for Wagner arose while Nielsen was in Dresden with Bendix. After hearing *Das Rheingold*, he noted in his diary: 'Wonderful! Any musician who doesn't find Wagner great is himself little.'[58] Later, Nielsen's feelings towards Wagner became more lukewarm, but in those days in Dresden, when he spent every day with Bendix and experienced the four operas of *Der Ring des Nibelungen* for the first time, he was unreservedly enthusiastic. In general, the time Nielsen spent with Bendix in Dresden seems to have filled him with ideas and new inspiration. It was therefore a frustrated Nielsen who wrote in his diary when the intense interaction came to an end on 28 September 1890: 'Bendix left at 8.30 this morning. On the way home I could not contain my sorrow. Ridiculous!'[59] Back in Copenhagen, Nielsen and Bendix resumed their close relationship, and Bendix also used his position in musical life to promote Nielsen's music.

Rudolph Bergh

The composer and zoologist Rudolph Bergh was a third link between Nielsen and the radical milieu in Copenhagen. He was part of Nielsen's circle of friends and one of his most loyal supporters in musical life. He is an interesting figure in his own right, as he was part of both the scientific and the musical milieu in the city. Until 1903 he was associated with the University of Copenhagen, and his musical activities were a sideline. He had received private tuition in music theory from Rosenhoff, and in the spring of 1892 he was one of Rosenhoff's students who organised a concert of his own works in honour of their teacher. Nielsen was also on the programme, so it is possible that the two met on this occasion. This corresponds with Nielsen's first mention of Bergh in a letter to the writer Johannes Jørgensen dated 24 May 1892 – less than two months after the concert. In the letter, Nielsen invites Jørgensen to visit him a few days later and informs him that if he arrives at noon, he will meet one of his acquaintances: Dr R. Bergh.[60] The letter documents that Nielsen and Bergh were acquainted with Jørgensen at this time, who in turn was unaware that Nielsen and Bergh knew each other. Their connection at this time suggests that the relationship was relatively new.

The relationship between Bergh and Jørgensen is worth exploring for a better understanding of Bergh's links with radical circles. In his memoirs, Jørgensen describes how, as a young man in the 1880s, he was an ardent freethinker and Darwinist – and while Brandes was a role model in philosophical and artistic terms, Bergh seems to have been so in a scientific context. In addition to his literary activities, Jørgensen studied zoology and remembers how he and several of his fellow students gathered around their young, admired tutor, Bergh.[61] With his 'Lectures on the General History of Evolution', Bergh was the first university lecturer in Denmark to base his teaching on Darwin's principles of evolution, which he gave from 1885 and which Jørgensen attended.[62] The lectures were published in 1887 and later translated into German and Russian.

Rudolph Bergh was the son of the famous doctor and researcher of venereal diseases, Rudolph Bergh, and the grandson of the Royal Musician Hans Sophus

Simonsen. In his memoirs, his father's younger colleague, Oluf Jersild, described the Bergh family home in Stormgade as an important meeting place for the radical circle in Copenhagen:

> Just as in the middle of the last century the Heiberg House had a reputation as a meeting place and a centre of artistic and intellectual education ... so too the Bergh House was a place where one felt honoured to come. For here everything that was important to the learned and the free-minded met, and of course Georg Brandes shone as the banner around which all gathered.[63]

According to Jørgensen, Rudolph Bergh junior, just like his father, was closely connected with the city's radical circles, and Bergh's first wife, Emma Brandes, was a cousin of Georg Brandes. During the years when Jørgensen studied zoology, Bergh lived on the first floor of a villa on Amicisvej in Frederiksberg, where the ground floor was occupied by Harald Høffding, a professor of philosophy. Bergh's and Høffding's homes provided the setting for evenings of discussion with Jørgensen and other students who were freethinkers and Darwinists.[64] As in Bendix's memoirs, Jørgensen's account of Bergh suggests a connection between Brandesianism and the early Wagnerian cult in Copenhagen:

> Even then he was practising the art that was to dominate his life: he was a music lover and a musician. Together with Karl Gjellerup – from whom he was now separated by his break with Brandesianism in the 'Year of the Wandering' – he was one of the first and most ardent admirers of Wagner in this country. I remember that one day he played Wagner to my rather deaf ears. It was slow and solemn, and R. S. Bergh played with an expression of care, reverence and affection that made a deep impression on me ...[65]

Both Bergh's and Bendix's positions in cultural life suggest that there were close links between the musical environment and Brandesianism in Copenhagen. Nielsen experienced these connections at first hand in his youth, and they also influenced his artistic interests. His diary from the end of May 1893 mentions that he had 'composed Jacobsen's *Solnedgang* (Sunset) afresh'[66] and that a few days later he visited Brandes, who made an impression on him: 'We talked for a long time about Napoleon, Voltaire, Christ and the Home Mission. Brandes's gift is of the sparkling, igniting kind. He's constantly on the alert.'[67] The following year, he used his connection with Brandes to arrange for himself and Anne Marie to meet Max Klinger, who was exhibiting in Leipzig at the time.[68]

Freethinking in the 1880s

The central idea of Brandesianism was the assertion of the 'free thought'. It was consolidated in Brandes's famous inaugural lecture of 1871, printed in *The Emigrant Literature* the following year: 'I consider it a duty and an honour to pay homage to the principles to which I subscribe, to the belief in the right of free enquiry and in the final victory of free thought'.[69] But what did Nielsen really mean when he identified himself with the freethinker movement in the years around 1890?

In the first years after the lectures, Brandes did not have many followers, but during the 1880s the number of followers increased, and the fear of freethinking grew with it. In order to determine the position of the free thought movement around 1880, two texts from different factions should be examined: Edvard Brandes's apology 'I believe in Logos' (1880) and the theologian Otto Møller's 1881 essay 'Understanding and Judging the Freethought of the Present'. The latter essay begins with the warning that 'a storm of freethinkers is about to rise over the country' and that, based on experience, it is to be expected that the capital will be the breeding ground from which it will spread through the population. The struggle must therefore be expected to take place in Copenhagen.[70] Møller's main argument is that it is important to take the movement seriously if it is to be opposed – even if its supporters appear young and inexperienced:

> It all bears so many of the hallmarks of boyish pranks that it might be tempting to close your eyes and assume it is all a false alarm. … But the point is that it is not a new thing, but a very old and very familiar thing; they are playing with fire, and it is as dangerous as the hands that play with it – the more dangerous, I suppose, the smaller the hands and the more fumbling they are.[71]

The essay also contains a chapter on the main types of freethinking, of which Møller emphasises that it is among those who are the worst off that the most powerful form of freethinking is to be found: the denial of God, and materialism. This type represents the final stages in what Møller calls the evolutionary course of freethinkers. The first stage is the denial of the historical Christ; the second stage is generally the denial of divine government; the third stage is the denial of a personal God, from which one quickly slides into the final stage, which is raw materialism.[72] Møller goes on to point out that although the final stages are rarely defended scientifically, they are the ones practised by the general mass of people – and therefore freethinking in real life is the same as materialism and the denial of God.[73]

This distinction between a so-called mild intellectual form and a vigorous form of freethinking, which prevails among the masses, can also be detected in Edvard

Brandes. However, he regards the latter form as a misunderstanding of the concept. His speech 'I Believe in Logos' was given in defence of his election to Parliament in response to complaints from some voters of the Conservative Party who felt that the election should be considered invalid because Brandes had declared himself an atheist during the campaign.[74] In his speech, Brandes said in part:

> I have been called a freethinker. Well, if a freethinker means nothing more than a seeker after truth ... then I'm a freethinker, like many others in this country. If by an atheist one understands only a human being who is neither a follower of the Jewish religion nor of the Christian religion, then I'm an atheist; but then we are also a good many atheists in this country. But the fact is that these words mean something quite different. By these terms – freethinker and atheist – is meant ... a person who lives in the most extreme materialism, who has no ideal view of existence, and who – and this is the main point – recognises no morality.[75]

The debate of the 1880s about freethinking explains why Emilie Demant Hansen's family was so concerned that Nielsen was a freethinker – and how they too may have had a different experience of what it meant than he did.

By the late 1880s, when Nielsen and Emilie were a couple, the movement had become more successful. Perhaps the movement was even at its height during these years, as the publication of the journal *Fritænkeren* (The Freethinker) in 1887–89 seems to suggest. In his review of a collection of poems by Sophus Claussen from September 1887, Edvard Brandes writes a kind of victory speech about the emergence of the freethinker movement in the cultural and political landscape:

> Three times in the last two decades a literary youth has burst forth here in Denmark. And it is worth noting that in the history of Danish literature, the young family is never referred to as a united army. The first time was the great movement which, at the beginning of the seventies, wrote 'Free Thought' on its banner. It knew little of politics, not even of eroticism. By the beginning of the eighties, when a new generation came of age ten years later, the free-thinking literature had already become left-wing in the political sense. And now, five years later, when very young voices mix with those of the old, these new poets, the Latter-Day Saints and freethinkers, are just as they should be. Last year it was Mr Stuckenberg, this year Mr Johannes Jørgensen and now Mr Sophus Claussen. And there will be no other young literature in Denmark than a freethinking Left. Those who want to mourn can order the black mourning crape immediately.[76]

By the 1890s, then, there was a sense – at least among the movement's own adherents – that freethinking was the most important movement in culture, no longer merely an assertion of free thought but also a political movement and a worship of the erotic, as seen in the writers who debuted in the second half of the 1880s.

Nielsen's view of freethinking is most clearly expressed in a letter he wrote to Emil Sachs while in Berlin in late 1890. He describes how he came up with the idea for a symphony when the completion of his String Quartet in F minor had filled him with new energy. Following the description, he links the idea directly to freethinking. It is worth noting that he suggests to Emil that he himself might be the first composer to turn the freethinker's idea into a musical work:

> What do you say to this idea: a symphony with the title: 'From earth thou art come, to earth thou shalt return'? Dark and primeval at the beginning, where everything still lies in millennial hibernation. Then gradually movement and life, but as yet still half unconscious, then rising and rising to the maximum joie de vivre. Then back again to the 'black mould' which wraps us all up in its soft, dense robes; where we go to sleep for all eternity – eternal oblivion. But I must first be much more competent. It shouldn't be programme music. I haven't yet found a work that has taken on the Freethinkers' ideas.[77]

At first glance, it may seem strange that the title of Nielsen's symphony is a phrase borrowed from Christian burial rites. But used as a framework for the process Nielsen describes in the letter, it is consistent with a central idea of freethinkers: that one should not expect eternal life in heaven, but that life ends with death and thus on earth. Human beings must therefore strive to find joy in earthly life. It is in earthly life that man will 'ascend and ascend to the highest joy of life', whereas after death man will attain nothing but 'eternal oblivion'.

The first article in *Fritænkeren* (October 1887) deals with this very subject under the title 'The Belief in Immortality or Life after Death'. The essay highlights the paradox of describing the afterlife as pure paradise, while most people cling to earthly life as long as possible: 'Even the most pious and truly faithful would rather remain a little longer in the earthly vale of tears than take their place in heaven; if it were only a transition to a higher form of life, man would hardly fear the majesty of death so much.'[78]

It is tempting to suggest that Nielsen may have been inspired by the works of J. P. Jacobsen, best known for the two novels *Fru Marie Grubbe* (1876) and *Niels Lyhne* (1880), the latter of which was originally to be called 'The Atheist'.[79] Both novels deal with the question of what happens after death. In *Niels Lyhne*, the freethinker's idea that there is no heaven or hell after death is described by the protagonist as a relief:

'Do you not understand what kind of nobility it will spread over humanity when it is free to live life and die death without fear of hell or hope of heaven, but fearing itself and hoping for itself?'[80] In the other novel, *Fru Marie Grubbe*, the theme is touched upon when Ulrik Christian Gyldenløve talks to a priest on his deathbed:

> The sick patient looked around in confusion, 'I want nothing,' he muttered, 'I want nothing; I have nothing to do with your hell or your heaven; I want to die, only to die, and nothing else.'
>
> 'Ye shall surely die,' said the priest, 'but at the end of the dark passage of death there are but two gates: one to the joy of heaven and one to the misery of hell; and there is no other way to go, indeed no other way at all.'
>
> 'Yes there is, priest, yes there is – isn't there? Answer me! Is there not a deep, deep grave close by for those who have gone their own way, a deep, black grave down to nothingness, no worldly thing at all?'[81]

Nielsen's portrayal in the symphony of a life that begins and ends in the 'dark soil', where one finally falls asleep in 'eternal oblivion', is also a subject discussed in the modern literature of the time. Many years later, Nielsen had *Fru Marie Grubbe* in mind for a new opera project, so he must have been interested in the novel and felt that it had musical potential. However, the project was abandoned when the librettist, Einar Christiansen, objected to the idea.[82]

Freethinking is not clearly present in Nielsen's letters and diaries. In fact, only in the one letter to Sachs does he use the word explicitly. However, it is alluded to several times, suggesting that he experienced some problems and frustrations associated with not being a believer. In his diary of 4 December 1890, for example, he writes: 'I have received a letter from Ottilie that she is not well. If I believed in a God I would pray to Him ... but I cannot.'[83] In a letter to Emilie, written after receiving the news of her engagement, he also gives the impression that life would be easier if one believed in God:

> I wish I could tell you how much I want you to be happy all your life. But you will be, for you have a God to turn to when misfortune comes; and I agree with you, it is best for all men.[84]

Nor was it always easy for him to defend his views to others who were not part of the radical movement. In a letter to Emilie in January 1889, for example, he describes a visit to Niels W. Gade:

> Then we spoke for a long time about music and art, and it was so interesting. He also got around to religion, and he asked whether I had any interest in the mod-

ern faith; to which I answered that I couldn't deny it. Then you should have heard him. He rushed up and down in the room and fumed. [According to him] it was all accursed filth, and I, as a composer, should damned well know that there was something divine, something spiritual within us, which could not die. I had to draw in my horns and said that it was possibly just a phase that everyone has in their youth. Then he calmed down. He showed me several sketches for new works, which I was obviously happy to see.[85]

The letter confirms Møller's suspicion that many dismissed freethinking as a kind of boyish prank – at least Nielsen was shrewd enough to know that he could use his youth and consequent naivety as an excuse to allay Gade's indignation.

Holger Drachmann's *Snefrid*

Nielsen became more closely associated with the activities of the radical movement in early 1893, when he was commissioned to compose the music for Drachmann's melodrama *Snefrid*, which was to be staged at The Student Society's Free Theatre. The commission combined a number of factors characteristic of the environment represented by Copenhagen's radicals and intellectuals. It was modern theatre, written by one of the authors of the Modern Breakthrough. The music was to reflect this, and one of the central scenes takes up the theme of eroticism. It was Nielsen who was to provide the love music to enact what was not shown on stage.

Nielsen received the request from Erik Skram, who was on the board of The Free Theatre, and it was apparently Victor Bendix who persuaded Nielsen to accept the project.[86] As already mentioned, The Free Theatre was founded in 1891 with the aim of 'staging plays of literary interest which have been rejected or neglected by the ordinary stages';[87] it was modelled on the Théâtre Libre in Paris, which opened in 1887, and the Freie Bühne in Berlin, which opened two years later.[88] In its early years, the theatre succeeded in staging a number of national and international modern plays, such as Gustav Esmann's *The Widower*, Émile Zola's *Thérèse Raquin* and Gustav Wied's *A Wedding Night*; the latter caused a real scandal when chaos broke out among the audience after a scene in which a woman tries to kill her grandchild.[89] Carl Behrens, one of the members of the board, wrote in his memoirs: 'It seemed as if the protesters had forgotten that they were in a free theatre.'[90]

By this time Drachmann had had a turbulent relationship with the Brandesians. He had joined the circle in the 1870s, but distanced himself from the movement in the following decade – only to return in the early 1890s. He had written *Snefrid* during a stay in Berlin in the autumn of 1892, and in a letter of December 1892 to Peter Nansen, who was on the board of The Free Theatre, he mentions that the play was 'good poetry'. It is set in Viking Norway (*c.* 900) at the court of King Harald Fairhair. In Act One the king is captivated by Snefrid, the daughter of the rich Finnish chieftain Svase. The king wants Snefrid as a gift, but Svase refuses, and he therefore agrees to marry her. By Act Two, Snefrid is dead, but the king will not acknowledge it, and keeps a vigil over her bed as his kingdom falls apart. Eventually the king is brought out of his delusion by the minstrel Gunnar, and Snefrid's body can be carried to the pyre.[91]

One of Nielsen's tasks was to describe the wedding night of the king and Snefrid from a musical point of view. Two days after Erik Skram's visit, Nielsen's diary reads: 'I have started on the love music for "Snefrid" and I think it is quite good.'[92] Three days later he writes that he has 'finished the love music for Snefrid. It is a very good piece and intensely felt.[93] A few days later, he played it for Rudolph Bergh, who 'blushed at the sensual character of the music and praised both the piece and the prelude to the first act'.[94] It is tempting to regard Nielsen as a musical counterpart to the modern poets who cultivated eroticism around 1890.[95] Indeed, it seems that he was keen to create a strong sensuality through musical effects – and that he succeeded.

Nielsen's 'Love Music' lasts only about two minutes, but within that time there are major musical shifts, giving the audience a very intense experience. It was performed as an epilogue to Act One, after the king had led Snefrid into the bridal chamber and the minstrel Gunnar had sung his wedding song to the couple, ending with the words: 'When the last fire of the pit is quenched here in Finne-Stuen – then yonder will a torch blaze, double, through the Christmas night – there where Harald raises the treasure he found in Svase's earthen hut!'[96]

The sensuality of the music is created by the many changes of mood and large dynamic fluctuations that occur intensely within a few minutes: from light, playful quavers and quivering trills at the beginning, to more powerful and insistent elements in the middle, to light 'sighing' semitones with pauses to end the movement.

Much to his annoyance, Nielsen never got to try out his music in front of an audience at The Free Theatre, as a disagreement between Carl Behrens and the director of the Dagmar Theatre, C. Riis-Knudsen, resulted in the latter cancelling the contract that allowed the Dagmar Theatre's actors to take part in The Free Theatre's productions.[97] The music itself was instead performed at a Drachmann matinee at Koncertpalæet the following year, where it was well received. It was not until December 1899, when *Snefrid* was performed at the Dagmar Theatre, that Nielsen's music was included in the play.[98] Thus, being asked to provide the music was initially more important to Nielsen than to the wider public. It showed that he was taken seriously in the circles that cultivated the new ideas.

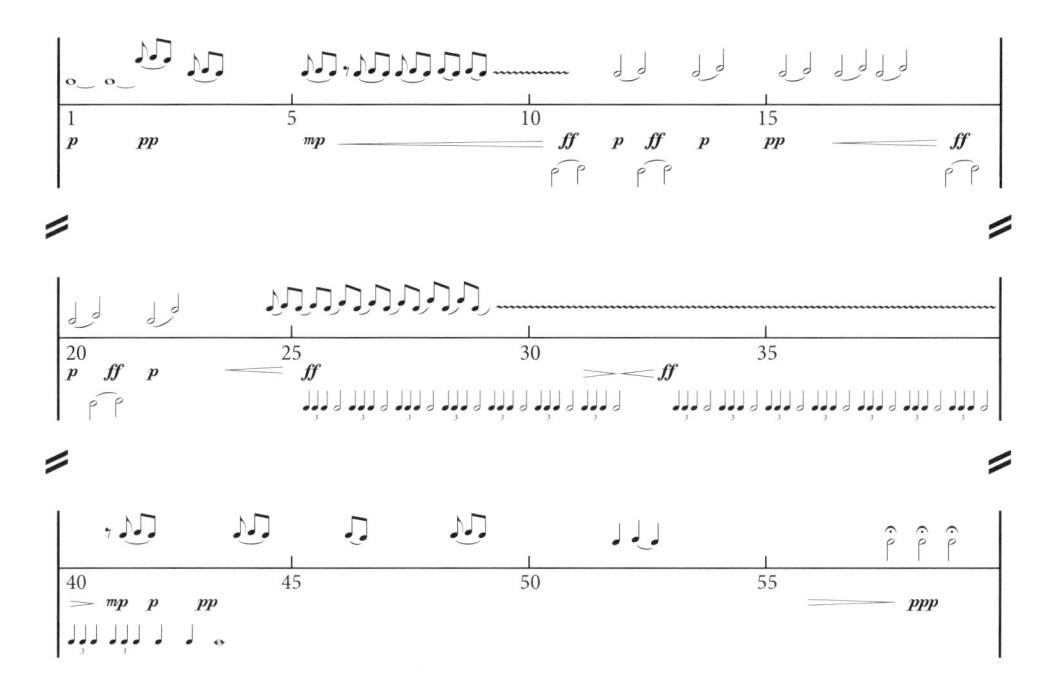

ILL. 4. Carl Nielsen, Music for Holger Drachmann's Melodrama *Snefrid*, No. 12, Postlude, referred to by Nielsen as love music. The piece begins softly in *p*, with a long note in the horn and the flute playing a motif consisting of a slightly oscillating motion in the interval of a major second; after a few bars, the flute plays in duet with the first violin. A few bars later, a crescendo creates an intensification, supported by trills in the oboe, and extends the seconds to thirds in the oscillating motif of the first violin. From bar 11, there follows a frenetic passage in which powerful and gentle motifs alternate rapidly. The intensification then continues, culminating in a sixteen-bar *ff* beginning in bar 25, where the flute and strings play lilting quavers. The development of the oscillating motif from seconds to larger intervals in this passage, together with the rhythmic and dynamic devices, means that the motif, which seemed light and playful at the beginning, becomes insistent and suspenseful. Two bars of rapid diminuendo and crescendo (bars 31–32) lead to a sharp drop in intensity, but otherwise the momentum continues with sustained force. From bar 40, the piece begins to slow down, and in the final bars of the diminuendo, the flute plays gentle, swaying crotchet motifs, while the first violin moves quietly upwards in perfectly light semitones, until the piece finally dies away in a *ppp*.[99]

The Great World

The spiritual horizon that Nielsen gained from the radical environment can be seen as part of a coherent process of formation. His childhood, youth and early adulthood are a time of learning, education and experience. This happens in all aspects of life.

Nielsen's view of the world and other people is formed in childhood. He learns what it is like to grow up in a family with many children in the countryside, but certainly not in the back of beyond. He learns to accept people for who they are, not for their social status or position. From an early age, he learns to be surrounded not only by farmers from Fyn, but also by German migrant workers. He learns to be useful and to appreciate the recognition that comes from fulfilling the expectations of others. He encounters the self-organised free school environment early on and sees how to build a movement from scratch. His mother instils in him the fundamental belief that it is possible for anyone to do well in the world if they really want to and work hard. His father gives him the foundation of musicianship and the joy of solving musical problems.

Odense marks a significant shift in backdrop. It is the province's most important cultural city and a modern industrial and commercial centre with links to Europe. Joining the military band at the age of fourteen, Nielsen receives a thorough training as a professional musician. Here he meets experienced Danish and German colleagues and takes part in the musical life of the city, both on and off duty. At concerts in the town they play marches, overtures, excerpts from popular operas and festive gallops. He also plays in a string quartet and performs at masques and parties. He acquires a repertoire whose essence belongs to a common northern European musical culture.

Moving to Copenhagen is a leap into the unknown. Nielsen encounters a growing city and has to adapt as a newcomer. He is accepted as a violin student at the Academy of Music and is trained as a musician at the highest level. He becomes part of Copenhagen's musical community and works hard to establish himself as a professional. Success crowns his efforts when, at the age of twenty-four, he becomes a permanent member of The Royal Orchestra. The professional approach to the musician's craft, established in his childhood, will remain with him throughout his life.

Nielsen has been composing since his youth, and in Odense it is customary for regimental musicians to arrange and compose music. At the Academy he attends classes in music theory, but it is only in the years after graduation that he receives instruction in composition, with Rosenhoff as his teacher and mentor. By the early 1890s he is able to present himself to the public with fully completed works such as the String Quartet in F minor, Op. 5, and Symphony No. 1. Only then is he ready to commit himself fully to a career as a composer.

Nielsen's education is not only about music. In Copenhagen, where he will spend the rest of his life, he will get to know the city and its music and cultural institutions. Copenhagen is a centre of power and a European cultural city that likes to show off. Through the places he lives and visits, he experiences the city's growth and modernisation. Through the Academy of Music, he becomes part of the city's musical community and establishes himself as a professional. But it is also through his new social contacts that Nielsen broadens his horizons. Through his fellow students and their families, as well as his connections to cultural and artistic circles, he becomes part of Copenhagen's intellectual and radical milieu. It is there that he undergoes a decisive change and adopts freethinking and oppositional attitudes rooted in the Modern Breakthrough. As in other fields, he is able to be fascinated without being completely absorbed. The breadth of his vision takes on a new dimension. His world has expanded in every way. Now he is ready to conquer the world.

II

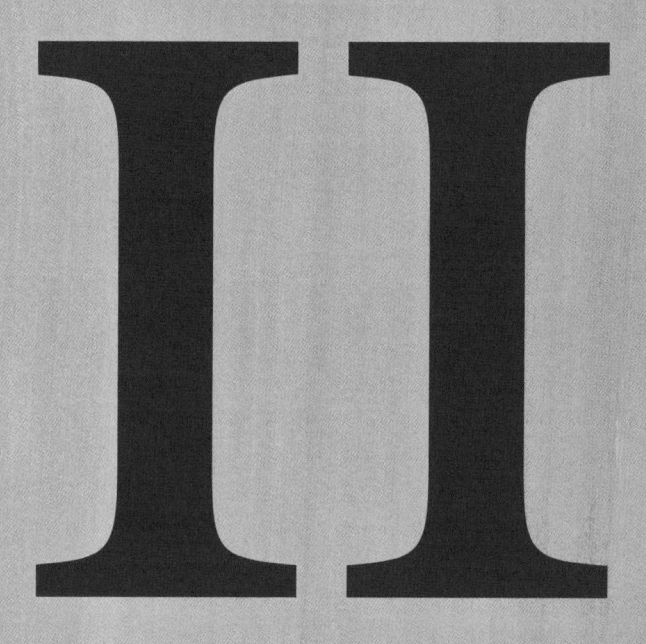

THE TURN-OF-THE-CENTURY CULTURE

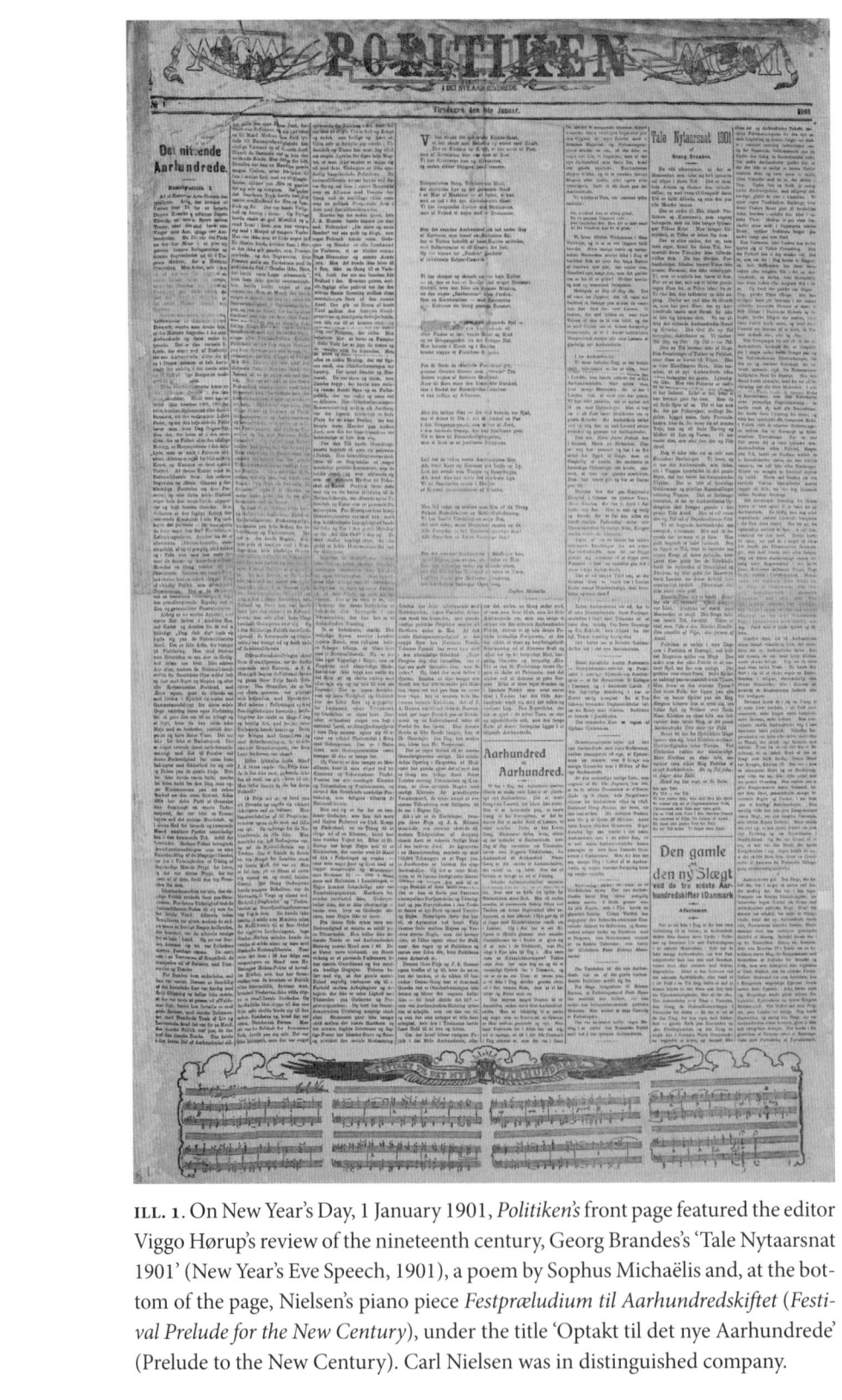

ILL. 1. On New Year's Day, 1 January 1901, *Politiken*'s front page featured the editor Viggo Hørup's review of the nineteenth century, Georg Brandes's 'Tale Nytaarsnat 1901' (New Year's Eve Speech, 1901), a poem by Sophus Michaëlis and, at the bottom of the page, Nielsen's piano piece *Festpræludium til Aarhundredskiftet* (*Festival Prelude for the New Century*), under the title 'Optakt til det nye Aarhundrede' (Prelude to the New Century). Carl Nielsen was in distinguished company.

Chapter 10

TURN-OF-THE-CENTURY CULTURE

> We who live in the darkness of midwinter, and those who live these days in high summer under the sky of the Southern Cross, meet in the imagination that something old has ended, something new is in the making. No one alive remembers anything like it … We who partake of such a rare event are more than ever urged to think back and to think forward.
> 'Aarhundredskiftet' (The Turn of the Century), *Dagbladet*, 1 January 1901

The fascination of a turn of the century is the expectation that something new is about to happen, even though we do not yet know what it is. The shift marks a transition between two periods, which can create a sense that all options are open and is therefore not only a point in time but also a metaphor for a time of transition. It is preceded by a period of anticipation, when something new is about to happen, and then it takes a while to see which innovations have become permanent. It marks a period of a few years on both sides and sets the scene for a time characterised by a particular mentality. Thus a special turn-of-the-century culture emerges.

As part of the musical life of Copenhagen at the turn of the century, Nielsen became associated with a group of younger composers who were experimenting with new forms of expression and positioning themselves internationally. He was thus not an isolated figure in the music scene. Furthermore, his extensive travels in 1890–91, funded by the scholarship Det Anckerske Legat, had given him considerable first-hand knowledge of European musical and cultural life. Through Anne Marie, whom he married in 1891, he had close links with Copenhagen's artistic milieu, which, like the rest of Europe, was in a period of great upheaval. When Anne Marie visited the World Exposition in Paris in the autumn of 1900, she wrote home to her husband: 'Modern art is interesting, but there is no single direction in modernism.'[1]

The culture of the turn of the century represents an unpredictable and changing situation, in which there is a common awareness of 'the new' without it being clear what this 'new' entails. Such a view of the period as one of openness and belief in progress – but also of insecurity and uncertainty – offers a different understanding of the culture to which Nielsen belonged from those narratives that take as their starting point the certainty of posterity as to where it is heading. Indeed, uncertainty and fragmentation are characteristic of the cultural and historical period around 1900.

This situation did not arise because of the turn of the century itself, although the transition to the twentieth century obviously helped to reinforce the sense of progress into a new era. A well-known example is Freud's *The Interpretation of Dreams*, published in 1899 but dated 1900 as Freud believed the work belonged to the future.[2] Similarly, in his 1901 New Year's speech, Georg Brandes sought to place the achievements of his own generation in the new century: 'We have never been the men and women of the nineteenth century. The concept *A New Age* enchants and excites us. We cry out: *Hail, New Age! New time – our time.*'[3]

Copenhagen's turn-of-the-century culture was closely linked to that of Europe, partly because the great central European metropolises of the late nineteenth century served as models for Copenhagen's art and architecture. It is also important to bear in mind that the Danish capital did not simply seek to emulate Paris or Vienna; rather, turn-of-the-century culture should be understood as a European phenomenon that manifested itself differently from place to place. Modern trends transcended national boundaries and were the product of a time when internationalisation and migration were shaping the art world.[4]

More specifically, Copenhagen occupied a dual position as both a peripheral and a central cultural city in Europe at the end of the nineteenth century. On the one hand, the North's geographical location on the periphery of Europe was reflected in the cultural imagination of the time. On the other hand, in the 1880s, Georg Brandes articulated a modern trend in the North that influenced a large number of Central European artists.[5] Brandes helped launch a form of cosmopolitanism that introduced new cities – including Copenhagen – onto the European cultural map.[6] That the Danish capital was indeed important is emphasised by international studies such as the literary historian Carl E. Schorske's influential *Fin-de-Siècle Vienna. Politics and Culture in Vienna*, which points to the lack of a comprehensive account of culture and politics in Copenhagen around 1900.[7]

Using Schorske's understanding of turn-of-the-century culture, it becomes clear that the uncertainty and openness of the period are indeed central. There has long been a debate in the academic literature as to whether the period around 1900 should be understood as an offshoot of nineteenth-century Romanticism or as a precursor to twentieth-century modernism. However, one could argue, as Schorske does, that it is a period in its own right, characterised by openness and awareness of the unknown.

Schorske explains that in creating a framework for understanding nineteenth-century culture, he was able to draw on a number of descriptive categories – for example, rationalism and Romanticism, individualism and socialism, realism and naturalism. This method, however, only works up to the end of the century. From then on, European culture seems to be characterised by pervasive fragmentation and an endless vortex of renewal. It is thus impossible for modern historians to define the changes of the period in terms of a single style.[8]

A similar picture is presented by the historian Alan Bullock in relation to the role of literature in the cultural climate of Europe around 1900. He points out that no single trend became dominant; rather, there was a constant debate about what the new might be to replace the old. It is a period full of counter-movements and contradictions, as in any cultural period when old patterns break down. What is unusual is that there is no new order ready to replace the past.[9]

Looking at the situation more specifically from a music-historical view, the picture is no clearer – at least not if one follows the music historian Carl Dahlhaus's reflections on the period around 1900. He argues that there has been a tendency to use terms from other art forms to characterise the musical works of the period – terms such as *Art Nouveau*, Symbolism, Naturalism, *Fin-de-siècle* and Late Romanticism. Nor does he believe that any of these terms are useful as an overall category for the turn-of-the-century period in music history. As an alternative, he proposes 'modern' as a label for the period, arguing that from around 1890 there was an emerging contemporary consciousness of being modern. Dahlhaus finds evidence for the emergence of such a new self-consciousness at this time in Vienna, where Hermann Bahr published his essay 'Die Moderne'. The essay, published on New Year's Day 1890, argues that a new generation is on the verge of a new beginning.[10] Dahlhaus argues that in music, too, 'modernism' represents a mood of change that is stylistically open. Accordingly, turn-of-the-century modernism is not an early form of the type of modernism that would take hold in the following century, but rather a reflection of the self-consciousness of the time.[11]

In other words, the period must be defined in terms of the shift in consciousness itself: 'What these radical new changes – in art, thought, literature and science – have in common is their consciousness of the future.'[12] The culture of the turn of the century is thus a shared consciousness of modernity – a consciousness of being in the process of creating something new!

Chapter 11

A MUSICAL TURNING POINT

Writing an essay on the state of music for the anthology *Danmarks Kultur ved Aar 1900* (Denmark's Culture around 1900) must have been a challenge for the music historian Angul Hammerich. No clear picture emerged, although it was clear that something was happening:

> Nowadays, it is not the national but the international connections that predominate, especially the strong stimuli from Richard Wagner and, more recently, from France. The young Danish school has turned away from the lyrical and is testing its strength mainly in large commissions: Louis Glass, Fini Henriques and Carl Nielsen. Chamber music is represented by Axel Gade, Robert Hansen and Gustav Helsted. This period stands in marked contrast to the preceding national period. There is no such thing as a 'school'; rather, it is the individuals who lead the way, young forces seeking new directions, preferably along untrodden paths, often impressionistic and revolutionary, sometimes with an eye to times long past, always full of restless ferment. The overall picture is quite varied. Where is it pointing? No one can say – we live in a decidedly transitional age. However, life is on the move, and where there is life, there is power.[1]

The book was presented in a French translation along with similar publications from, among others, Sweden and Norway at the Paris World Exposition in 1900.[2] The concept of the book was that specialists in each area of cultural life would write about conditions at the beginning and end of the nineteenth century, thus 'bringing out the contrast'.[3] In many areas of music there had been great progress for Hammerich to write about. This was particularly true of concert life, for by the end of the nineteenth century, Copenhagen's long-established main music societies, Musikforeningen and Cæciliaforeningen, had been joined by a number of other concert enterprises. They focused on providing space for the performance of newer works and also had a social aim, offering concerts at a lower price. This gave the broader Copenhagen public the opportunity to enjoy quality music.[4] Educational opportunities in music had improved considerably, and a number of newer associations helped to secure artistic and economic conditions for musicians.[5]

ILL. 1. The anthology *Danmarks Kultur ved Aar* 1900 (Denmark's Culture around 1900) was prepared in a French translation for the World Exposition in Paris in 1900.

Yet in Hammerich's essay it is not entirely clear if there was any progress at the turn of the century. Hammerich argues that it was not until the middle of the nineteenth century that a real 'Danish school' emerged, led by the composers Niels W. Gade and Johan Peter Emilius Hartmann, around whom other Danish composers gathered for a long time.[6] Hammerich, on the other hand, saw the period at the end of the century as one of transition, marked by international currents and a mixed picture. Nevertheless, there was potential for progress, for something was happening, even if no one could point to a single direction among the younger Danish composers. Hammerich sums up the feeling with two key concepts: there was life and there was power.

Hammerich was the foremost authority of his time on Danish music history, and his understanding of the situation must therefore be taken seriously. It clearly makes sense to see the group of younger Danish composers at the end of the nineteenth century, including Glass, Henriques, Nielsen, Helsted, Hansen and Gade, as a counterpart to the modern, European-oriented groups in other art forms that were opposed to the established, national cultural institutions. One argument in favour of this view is that around the same time as Den Frie Udstilling (The Free Exhibition) and Det fri Teater (The Free Theatre) were founded, the group of composers also formed a number of new associations to create space for the young and the new, which were not included in the programme elsewhere.

The image of a generation gap, in which younger composers struggled against the older, more conservative members of the musical community, is also confirmed by the article 'Om Musik og Musikere' (On Music and Musicians) in the magazine *Vagten* (1899–1900). The article is signed by 'L – – s', who may well be the composer Louis Glass.[7] The author discusses the conditions in musical life that hampered the development of young Danish composers, and the critics' lack of understanding of new music is identified as a particular problem:

> What is not to the advantage of our musical relations is the reserved and cool attitude of the older [composers] towards the new in art. There is no age limit at which the older musician finds it decent to give way to the young. … What we musicians and composers lack most of all is an understanding and talented critic. *When are we going to get our 'Georg Brandes'?* What momentum such a man would give to our musical life; with him a new era would begin. How glorious is the thought that there might be someone who understood us; who saw clearly what we wanted; who could answer all the thousand questions that the young artist is confronted with; who could alert; who could show the way; who could put into words what the creative musician felt and thought.[8]

The call for a Brandes of musical life clearly indicates that the debate is taking place within a self-image that views itself as part of the Modern. The image of a young generation of modern composers confronted with a conservative musical life – including the music press – is, however, somewhat simplistic. In some cases, it was the critics who were accused of only wanting to hear modern music in concert halls. The fact that critics were perceived as both conservative and radical in their tastes was, of course, partly due to differences between critics, but also to the fact that there were different ideas at the time about what the 'modern' in music was. The very nature of the modern was up for debate.

The article also points to another fact that is crucial to understanding the development of musical life: it was not only the composers who determined the direction of Danish music. Just as Georg Brandes had proved in literature and Emil Hannover in art, the ability of music critics to draw attention to certain works rather than others and to put the trends of the time into words was also crucial. Similarly, the programming by conductors and the boards of the various concert institutions helped to determine the development of musical life. It was not enough for new music to be available. It also had to be performed, talked about and discussed in order to have an impact.

It is therefore useful to take a closer look at the societies and forums that provided a home for young composers – here they themselves could play an active role in creating spaces where their music could be heard. It also makes sense to follow the debates about programming policy and the degree of aesthetic radicalism – that is, discussions about 'the young' and 'the new'. The debate is taking place both within the societies and in the public sphere, and part of it is about whether it should be primarily Danish composers who are performed, or whether new foreign music should be included on an equal footing. Another part focuses on whether it is important that the music is 'young' and 'new', or whether it should first be given a stamp of quality. The discussion is particularly interesting because it opens up the perspective that audiences also accept the premise that they attend in order to hear the 'new' and are not guaranteed in advance that it will be a success. This approach is also to be found in a sharper form after the First World War, when a new wave of societies emerges that explicitly want to create space for new music that cannot be heard in the general music environment.

The Young and the New

By the time Hammerich identified the young Danish school of music prior to the Paris Exposition in 1900, this group of composers had already been active for more than a decade. The six composers mentioned were born between 1857 and 1867, and thus in their thirties and early forties at the turn of the century. As Hammerich points out, the group was not united around a common stylistic or aesthetic trend – but because they were all considered experimental and chose to collaborate in bringing their works to an audience, their names became associated with a movement that represented the 'young' and 'new' in Danish music in the 1890s.

Symphonia

The foundation of the 'movement' was the establishment of the society Symphonia in the spring of 1889. Three of the composers mentioned, Helsted, Glass and Nielsen, were on the society's board and all six were on the concert programmes in the early years.[9] The founder and fourth member of the board was Robert Henriques, a cellist and composer in the late 1880s and a music critic in the 1890s.[10] He was a relative of Fini Henriques mentioned by Hammerich.

Nielsen had a relatively close relationship with Robert Henriques in the late 1880s. In a letter to Emilie Demant Hansen in December 1888, Nielsen mentions among other things that Robert Henriques was one of the friends who wanted to promote him.[11] According to Henriques's later account, it was around this time that Symphonia was founded with the aim of bringing Nielsen's works – and those of other young Danish composers – to an audience:

> The occasion was quite accidental. One winter evening in 1888, Carl Nielsen and the present author were sitting at Nimb's, which at that time had rooms in Erichsen's mansion. Nielsen had just composed his String Quintet, which had been played several times in private, and the young musician complained that the work could not be performed in public. I was enchanted by the piece, so I said resolutely: 'Let's found a society for the quintet. It shall be played in public.' The society, which I called 'Symphonia' to suggest its high aims, was subsequently organised, and I approached the musicians Gustav Helsted and Louis Glass and asked them to join the board with Carl Nielsen and myself.[12]

The piece by Nielsen quoted as the immediate reason for the founding of the society is his String Quintet for two violins, two violas and cello (CNW 59), a rather unusual instrumentation. It was one of the first of Nielsen's works to be performed in public. The quintet was composed in the autumn of 1888, completed on New Year's Day and premiered at Kammermusikforeningen (The Chamber Music Society) on 13 February 1889. Due to the private nature of this society, it was not considered a public concert; however, the first performance that took place in Symphonia shortly afterwards was a public event. On both occasions Nielsen played second violin. It was a piece that he stood by, even though it was not published. He included it in a concert when, three years later, he arranged a soiree with a programme consisting entirely of his own works at Koncertpalæet in Bredgade.[13]

The piece employs the five string instruments in such a way that they sound as a whole. Especially in the first two movements, Nielsen exploits the softer and fuller sound of two violas. In the third movement, the musician's delight in ensemble playing takes over when Nielsen demands such rapid repetitions of notes that they are almost impossible to execute: this is where the musicians get to perform. It was a fitting piece if Nielsen wanted to present himself as one of the young people who were breaking new ground.

The other three board members of Symphonia, Henriques, Helsted and Glass, all came from musical homes in Copenhagen and were therefore well connected in musical circles. Robert Henriques's childhood home at 19 Vimmelskaftet in the centre of Copenhagen was for many years a musical meeting place with weekly quartet evenings, where Franz Neruda, Niels W. Gade and Edvard Grieg were frequent guests.[14] Gustav Helsted was the son of the Royal Musician Carl Helsted and the nephew of the ballet composer Edvard Helsted. He worked for many years as an organist and composed symphonies, chamber music and choral works, including Jens Peter Jacobsen's *Gurresange*.[15] Louis Glass had studied piano at his father's music academy in Frederiksberg, an institution he later took over. Glass was a year older than Nielsen, and in many ways the two followed parallel paths as composers. Both cultivated the symphony and larger instrumental forms, completing their first symphonies in 1894.[16] They also composed songs to Jacobsen's poems in the early 1890s, as did a number of their contemporaries.[17] Nielsen's earliest mention of Glass is in December 1888, when he explained that he was unlikely to receive the scholarship Det Anckerske Legat for which he had applied. For, as Nielsen explains, 'there's a composer called Louis Glass who's much older than I am and who has been trying for many years, and it would be entirely fair if he were to get it'.[18] As predicted, Glass won the scholarship in 1889 and Nielsen the following year.

Symphonia's first concert took place on 28 April 1889 in Hornung & Møller's concert hall in Bredgade. The new society was well received by the public, 'although the season, day, hour and weather were definitely more conducive to a walk in the woods than to a concert'.[19] Among the audience were professors J. P. E. Hartmann, Niels W. Gade and Otto Malling, and of course the music critics of the Copenhagen newspapers.[20]

The concert opened with a sonata for cello and piano by Glass, performed by himself and Robert Henriques, and 'received with great approval by the largely expert audience'.[21] Next on the programme were songs by Robert Henriques – including one set to Jacobsen's poems 'Det bødes der for' and 'Pagen højt paa Taarnet sad', poems that Nielsen would also set to music a few years later. The songs received mixed reviews from the critics, but also great applause. Olivo Krause and Glass then performed Robert Hansen's *Fantasy Pieces* for oboe and piano, followed by Helsted's settings of poems by Christian Winther. Charles Kjerulf, the critic for *Politiken*, found in Helsted's songs 'many beautiful and poetic details, which, however, do not manage to free the songs from the enormous burden of reflection and through-composition, which makes it possible for them to sink under their own weight'.[22] Fortunately, the final piece, by Nielsen, managed to redress the balance: 'An extraordinarily fresh and enjoyable String Quintet in G by the very young composer, Mr *Carl Nielsen*, showed a healthy and fertile talent for instrumental composition.'[23] The quintet was also praised in *Berlingske Tidende*, which emphasised its 'pleasing melodiousness, a closed form and original inventiveness in harmony'.[24]

In addition to the individual works, the music critics also reflected on the project itself that Symphonia represented. Although the society was generally well received, some scepticism was expressed. In *Dagens Nyheder*, the reviewer pointed out that the opportunities for younger composers to have their works heard had already improved considerably in recent times – partly because of the positive attitude towards the works of young composers at Koncertforeningen (The Concert Society), Tivoli Gardens and the so-called 'Kapel Soirées', that is, chamber recitals played by members of The Royal Orchestra. According to the reviewer, this did not mean that the society's existence was unjustified, but that the board of governors had to ensure that only the best works by younger composers were included in the programme.[25]

> The new society offers no such guarantees for the time being, for the management is anonymous, and last Sunday's matinee programme was a random mixture of good and bad. It may be that a circle of good acquaintances among our young composers have agreed to form a society to enable their works to be performed – a very sensible, useful and praiseworthy thing in itself. If, however, the whole is based on a private agreement between the parties concerned, without any expert hand to weigh and reject, the matter is in its nature more private than public.[26]

Unsurprisingly, the Radical faction of *Politiken* was very positive about the new society, celebrating the young talents in music. In the newspaper, Charles Kjerulf's review of Symphonia's first concert was supplemented by a presentation of the society. Unlike the reviewer in *Dagens Nyheder*, Kjerulf argued that the society was justified precisely because it created a framework in which it was acceptable for works to lack the maturity and perfection required to be included in a programme elsewhere. In return, audiences were allowed to experience new aspects of Danish music:

> Modestly and without fanfare, Symphonia gave its first concert last Sunday morning. The new society, which was quietly formed in late winter, seems destined to play an important role in our national musical life. It will provide a platform for the growth of young people in Danish music, take good care of the germination of new seeds, arouse the public's interest in talented artists who are making their way, and resume work that has been successful elsewhere but has since been abandoned. As you can see, this is a goal that requires application and connection. In reality, we have long been short of a place where the young can invite the public to judge their work. It is said that there are enough music societies. True, but they are societies that only open their doors to people who have already made a name for themselves, not ones that offer a battleground for people who want to win a name. And rightly so, because no one would accept paying four or five Kroner to attend a music or concert society's soiree, only to be regaled with immature and fumbling works by beginners. So far, only Balduin Dahl, who occasionally has premiered new instrumental works at the Tivoli Concert Hall, has taken care of the young. Thus, the creation of Symphonia will be greeted with joy in the world of young people, and its development will be followed with interest by all those who lend an ear to the new that is emerging.[27]

As Symphonia had no choir or orchestra, their concerts were limited to chamber music.[28] Soon after the success of 28 April, however, the board entered into an agreement with the Tivoli Gardens for a concert featuring works by young composers, thus providing them with an opportunity to conduct their own orchestral works for a wider audience.[29] The concert took place on 25 May 1889, and the programme featured the four composers on Symphonia's board who had also been on the programme for the new society's first concert. *Politiken's* reviewer, Kjerulf, was still positive about the project, beginning his review with the words: 'It was a good and worthy idea that Tivoli put into practice for the first time last night – that is, to let young Danish composers conduct their own works in the "symphony" section of the programme.'[30] Kjerulf praised Nielsen in particular, and he also noted something that was to be a recurring theme in references to Nielsen for many years to come, namely Nielsen's youthful charisma:

> The second composer on the programme, Mr *Carl Nielsen*, seemed to have won over the audience with his astonishingly young but amiable appearance. When he took the baton with a sure hand, victory was already his, but when his 'Suite for Strings' also revealed its most talented and delightful content, the audience surrendered completely.[31]

> **De Unges Koncert**
> **i**
> **Tivoli.**
>
> Det var en god og følgeværdig Idé, Tivoli i Aftes for første Gang realiserede, den at lade unge danske Komponister i „Symfoni-Afdelingen" dirigere egne Arbejder.
>
> At Ideen ikke blot tiltalte Komponisterne selv, men ogsaa i høj Grad Publikum, viste den enorme Trængsel inde i Salen, hvor hver eneste Fodsbreds Plads var optaget en rum Tid, før Afdelingen begyndte.
>
> Det var de samme fire Komponister, der præsenteredes ved „Symfonias" første Koncert, som iaftes mødte op. Først Hr. *Gustav Helsted* med en *Valse lente* og *Adagio*. Som naturligt var, blev den „langsomme" Vals saa temmelig hurtig under Trykket af Debut-Nervøsiteten; mere til sin Ret kom Adagioen, som Komponisten havde givet Undertitlen: *Scene d'amour*, — et flydende og kønt Musikstykke, med bløde, fine Konturer. Betydeligt over disse Ting stod dog den Violin-Romance af samme Komponist, som Hr. kgl. Kapelmusikus *Axel Gade* udførte paa et senere Stadium af Koncerten. Der var her et overordenlig sympatetisk Følelses-Element tilstede i Musiken, der tilmed klædte Instrumentet særdeles nydeligt. Æmnet var dog nok spundet noget for langt ud. Sin væsenlige Andel i det smukke Resultat havde selvfølgelig Hr. Gades fortræffelige Spil. Baade han og Komponisten fremkaldtes gentagne Gange.
>
> Den anden Komponist i Rækken, Hr. *Carl Nielsen* indtog aabenbart allerede paa Forhaand Publikum for sig ved sin forbløffende unge, men elskværdige Apparition. Da han med sikker Haand greb Taktstokken, var Sejren ham allerede vis, — men da hans „Suite for Strygeinstrumenter" oven i Købet aabenbarede sit højst talentfulde og fornøjelige Indhold, overgav Tilhørerne sig ganske. Vi har tidligere udførlig omtalt Hr. *Carl Nielsens* lovende Begavelse, just i Anledning at den samme Suite og kan ganske henholde os dertil. Finalen var bleven omarbejdet for denne Lejlighed, men skønt vi for vort personlige Vedkommende nok saa gærne havde hørt den i dens gamle Form, gjorde den ingenlunde noget Skaar i Forsøjelsen. — Atter gentagne Fremkaldelser.
>
> Hr. *Robert Henriques*' kønt og naturligt malede „Solnedgang" og den paafølgende livfulde „Gnomen-Tans" øgede yderligere Stemningen. Begge Stykkernes Virkning er sikkert beregnet og Udførelsen var det bedste, Orkestret præsterede denne Aften. — Atter Fremkaldelser og Bifald af fuldt Hjærte.
>
> Hr. *Louis Glass*' noget tungt tænkte, men med ikke ringe Dygtighed skrevne „Tarantelle" sluttede Koncerten. Man føler stundom ligesom Savnet af et „Program" til dens overvejende tragiske Indhold, men selv uden dette faar man Respekt for Arbejdet.
>
> Koncerten endte med stor Tilslutning fra Publikums Side.
>
> *Ch. K.*

The group of young composers thus got off to a promising start in their project to bring their music to the Copenhagen concert scene. After only a few concerts, however, disagreements arose about the core mission of the society. The original aim was to promote music by younger Danish composers who had difficulty getting their works performed elsewhere, but also to make room for relatively unknown works by older, more established Danish composers.[32] The 1891–92 programmes included works by August Winding, Peter Erasmus Lange-Müller, Niels W. Gade and Christian Frederik Emil Horneman, which did not go down well with some of the critics who saw the society as a forum for 'young' music. After the concert in March 1891, for example, Kjerulf objected that Lange-Müller and Winding did not need a society like Symphonia to have their works performed, and the reviewer Schytte of *Berlingske Tidende* remarked after the concert in April 1892 that the society had changed its character.[33]

It was during this period that Nielsen resigned from the board, as did Robert Henriques in the autumn of 1892. In their place, music publishers Jonas and Alfred Wilhelm Hansen joined the board and, together with Glass and Helsted, the society began to change course. In the 1893–94 season, the board programmed newer foreign works by Franck, Liszt and Dvořák alongside Danish works, possibly in an attempt to attract more concertgoers.

Nielsen does not seem to have been enthusiastic about the new direction – at least not as he noted in his diary two days after the first concert of the season, which featured works by Franck, Alfred Tofft and Glass: 'I read in "Politiken" about great maritime accidents on the west coast of Jutland. It also says that Fini Henriques has joined the board of Symphonia. If this is true, he is a characterless wimp'.[34] Robert Henriques

ILL. 2. On the day after the concert, Kjerulf published a review of the young composers' concert, including one of the first of his countless reviews of Nielsen's music in the following years, *Politiken*, 26 May 1889.

also reacted to Symphonia's new direction in an article in *Dannebrog* the day after the concert. He pointed out that the original purpose of the society, to create an interest in Danish music, had been its legitimation and the reason why it had been able to compete with the other music societies in the capital. He therefore warned against the regular inclusion of works by foreign composers in the society's programmes; the new board, however, did not follow this advice.[35]

Symphonia's new focus was explicitly stated in a printed leaflet in 1894. Symphonia is now 'the only music society in Copenhagen that performs only new works' by Danish and foreign composers.[36] The disagreements among the members of the board, which had characterised the society almost from the beginning, were thus mainly about whether the Danish or the modern was the most important. For some, the main objective was to create a forum for Danish music, while others were more concerned with creating a society that cultivated the latest music – including foreign music.

The concert on 4 May 1895, however, was again a purely Danish programme. Moreover, the works were all first performances, and it was once again the 'young' composers of Symphonia whose works were played: Helsted, Glass and Nielsen. The critics, or at least the part of the press that belonged to the radical segment, seemed to like this basis. *Politiken*'s review was by 'B.', who might possibly be identified as the music historian and critic William Behrend. The review began with a tribute to the cause itself that Symphonia, and this concert programme, represented:

> It is always a pleasure to attend a Symphonia concert. The programme, which almost invariably includes – as was the case last night – *'all compositions being performed for the first time'*, is met with anticipation. Neither novelty nor initiative have been the hallmark of our musical life … But in this 'Young People's Society' there is a desire for the new, a courage to take a stand, no fear of frightening or offending; here they meet among our young musicians who have the most to share, here it is felt that if there is growth in Danish music, it has the will, the ability and the energy to assert itself.[37]

Sophus Andersen, who was a reviewer for the newspaper *København*, also referred to Symphonia as the 'Young People's Music Society'. Andersen reveals that he saw the society as comparable to the new institutions in art and theatre, although it did not enjoy the same public support. He writes: 'While the interest in contemporary art easily attracts people to The Free Exhibition and The Free Theatre, the public seems to take a more reserved attitude when it comes to music.'[38] The observation may also be seen as a comment on the fact that at the time there was an awareness of 'contemporary art' that transcended the arts and that revolved around the very fact of being 'young' and 'new', and was thus not tied to any particular aesthetic or stylistic direction.

As mentioned above, the conservative part of the press was also in favour of the idea of a forum for new Danish music. The disagreement, however, lay in the question of whether being 'young' and 'new' was in itself a quality of the music, and if so, whether fulfilling these qualities meant that the demands for quality could be lowered. *Politiken*, on the other hand, suggested that audiences must attend with a different approach, as the criteria for listening to and judging music are different when one enters a society for young people's music:

> One should not pay too much attention to the fact that the leadership may occasionally make a mistake, that the works performed are not always of *equal* importance, and that the performance *may* have its flaws. One must commend the rare zeal of the labour that the concerts of *Symphonia* bear witness to … It was not an 'exemplary concert' – no 'masterpiece' was played – … but everything was new, fresh, bursting with vitality, with the will and the right to be and to come forward.[39]

Andersen took a similar view, suggesting that the purpose of the society was to include those who represented the 'new' in Danish music:

> The society does not seem to have many composers – it is more or less the same names that recur: Gustav Helsted, Carl Nielsen and Louis Glass. However, to the credit of the young art, these three composers are each exceptional and gifted representatives of the new music that is trying to work its way up from the traditional.[40]

This was the basis on which the reviewers considered the works. Nielsen's piano work *Symphonic Suite*, Op. 8 (CNW 82), performed by Louis Glass, was described as 'marked by a reckless energy that seems more impressive than convincing'.[41] *Politiken* has the same ambiguous opinion of the Suite, calling it 'a work from which sparks fly as from a chisel hammer' and 'apparently too much a work of will'.[42] Yet in the context of Symphonia, these qualities seemed justified.

Indeed, the piece itself sets the stage for such an interpretation, with a first movement, Intonation, in which chords are hammered out at full volume, with the doubling of octaves in both hands. In the following three movements, the melodies are also doubled in octaves for long stretches in both hands, a technique that emphasises the strong, contrapuntal lines. In part, the technique is reminiscent of a Bach two-part movement with the volume turned up. It seems urgent, insistent and not particularly pianistic, although this is undoubtedly intentional. The reviewer –

who summarised that the 'grand counterpoint ... seemingly chaotically taunting its bold harmonies, surely needs to be heard several times to be fully understood' – was onto something.[43] The statement suggests that the piano piece struck the audience as provocatively new.

The article in *Politiken* concludes by saying that a thorough critique 'would hardly allow all that was presented last night to pass unchallenged – but on the whole one must acknowledge the talent, the courage, the will – and the promises for the future'.[44] These, however, were not immediately fulfilled – it was Symphonia's last concert.

The Music Society of 14 March 1896

Symphonia was dissolved in September 1895, on the grounds that its original purpose of promoting young Danish music had been fulfilled, since its work had given composers easier access to the city's major concert venues.[45] However, Glass and Helsted must have felt that Copenhagen still lacked a forum for the cultivation of modern music, for within six months of Symphonia's closure, they and William Behrend founded a new society: Musikselskabet af 14. Marts 1896 (The Music Society of 14 March 1896). The inaugural meeting, held at Glass's music academy in Frederiksberg, was attended by some twenty-five people, including Nielsen, Axel Gade, Frits Bendix and the music critic Gustav Hetsch. However, there is no evidence that Nielsen took an active part in the society's activities thereafter.[46]

The aim of the private music society was 'to perform modern music unknown in this country in its original form or in suitable arrangements'.[47] Thus, the new society was not intended to serve the interests of young Danish composers. Rather, it was a place where music lovers could become acquainted with new music from abroad – including symphonies by Bruckner and Mahler, largely unknown in Copenhagen at the time, performed in versions for four-hand piano or two pianos.[48]

Danish Concert Society

However, it was not many years before the need to improve conditions for Danish music was again raised, and in 1900 Dansk Komponistsamfund (Danish Composers' Association) was formed. At the top of the society's agenda was the search for solutions to promote the performance of the works of Danish composers, and this led to the establishment of the Dansk Koncert-Forening (Danish Concert Society) in June 1901.[49] The need for such a society was emphasised in an article published in *Berlingske Tidende* on 24 June 1901: 'Our musical art lacks an institution whose purpose is to perform Danish musical works, especially the larger forms (orchestral and choral works).' Helsted was elected chairman of the society, with Nielsen and Glass as members of the board. There was thus a clear link between the Dansk Koncert-Forening and Symphonia.[50] However, while Symphonia was perceived as a 'young people's society', the Dansk Koncert-Forening was clearly focused on the national aspect.

Reading the society's mission statement and the reports of the first concerts, it is clear that this was not just an attempt to solve the problem of having the works performed. The concerts were intended to be a meeting place for those interested in Danish music, and the foundation was also a response to the need to identify a direction for Danish music after the deaths of Gade and Hartmann.[51] Two years earlier, Hammerich had described the existing Danish school as heterogenous, but after the first concert he expressed an enthusiasm that made it possible to compare different Danish works and thus identify trends over time:

> So beautifully, the Dansk Koncertforening strives. So skilfully and promisingly it began. … Gade, Horneman and Gustav Helsted each represented their respective lineage and school of Danish music, past and present, and perhaps a piece of the future. And Emil Poulsen, who recited, Carl Nielsen, Gustav Helsted and Vilhelm Rosenberg, who conducted, the young, fresh and beautiful voices that sang, the large and absolutely excellent choir that was formed at a stroke. Everything showed skill, talent and energy.[52]

In the early seasons, Nielsen must have been one of the society's central figures. At the inaugural concert on 23 January 1902, he conducted a piece by Lange-Müller written for the occasion and which contained 'numerous quotations from the ballad and other well-known tunes', followed by Gade's overture *I Højlandene* (*In the Highlands*).[53] The next concert featured his own choral work *Hymnus Amoris*, while the first concert of the second season premiered his Second Symphony. However, it was not long before Nielsen distanced himself from the society, for in a letter written in Athens in April 1903 to his friend Svend Godske-Nielsen, he remarked: 'I can assure you that I had already decided to resign from the board of the Dansk Koncert-Forening before we left.'[54]

Much of Nielsen's early works were thus performed in societies that he helped to establish and that contributed to the debates of the time about the 'young' and the 'new' in Danish music. The activities of the societies reveal the various interests at stake, both among the founders and among the critics who assessed the societies' achievements. For some, the composers around Symphonia were interesting as they embodied the young Danish school of composers, while others were attracted by their enthusiasm for new music. Those who appreciated new music became involved in The Music Society of 14 March 1896, and it was here that the new, foreign music was cultivated. On the other hand, the intention of the Dansk Koncert-Forening was to create a forum for Danish music where, by juxtaposing newer and older Danish works, it would be possible to gain an impression of the development of the Danish school – and perhaps even to look into the future in this regard.

Radicalism and Modernity

Debates about new music did not only take place in the newspapers in connection with public concerts. An example of how modern music was discussed in the semi-public sphere at the time is found in the memoirs of the medical doctor Oluf Jersild. From 1897 to 1901 he worked as a registrar at Vestre Hospital, in the same department as the renowned senior doctor Rudolph Bergh, whose son was a good friend of Nielsen's. This was the beginning of a long friendship between the younger Jersild and the older Bergh. At the same time, Jersild began to cultivate music privately. He bought a grand piano so that he could study at home for the operas he planned to attend. He also took cello lessons and gradually began to gather professional musicians and amateur colleagues for evenings at his studio apartment in Tietgensgade. His memoirs describe how the medical doctor Jørgen Møller, once a member of the Student Choral Society, often sang at these events:

> One evening he turned up with a printed edition of Nielsen's settings of lyrics by J. P. Jacobsen [Op. 6]. He opened the first song in the volume and said to Kirstein: 'Play that'. Then [Møller] continued in numerical order with song nos. 2, 3, etc. To an ordinary musical ear in those days, Nielsen's music was almost a cacophony – at least his music seemed strenuous and tiring. When we had had a sufficient number of songs, and the volume still seemed to contain some, I became annoyed, which was apparent when Jørgen had just finished singing 'Silkesko over gylden Læst' (Silken shoe over golden last), a song that J. M. was not able to perform with lightness and roguishness. I interrupted the performance with the mild remark: 'that's a nasty piece of nonsense, that lyric, what does "Silkesko over gylden Læst" mean?' Jørgen gave me a sharp look and said, 'surely you must understand. It's a festive prelude. I continued, 'nonsense, "læst" is something with which the shoemaker straps the shoes. It's shoemaker's poetry. I'd understand it better if it said silk shoes with a high instep'. Jørgen ended in a huff with these words: 'I'm not singing any more', and he retired to the sofa and sulked until we got him to sing something by Wagner, like Siegfried's Forging Song.[55]

It is not certain that the details of this anecdote, written down many years later in Jersild's memoirs, correspond exactly to what actually happened that evening. One thing, however, can be assumed to be true: Nielsen's music at the turn of the century was considered by many to be strange and cumbersome, while Wagner had become part of the general public's taste.[56] The printed volumes of Nielsen's Jacobsen songs support the impression of the composer as inaccessible, which differed from the very early view of the *Suite for String Orchestra* and the chamber music of the late 1880s.

Hetsch's description of Nielsen's artistic development in the context of a concert in February 1898 gives us an idea of these changes in the early reception of Nielsen. According to Hetsch, Nielsen had passed 'from a relatively natural freshness and immediacy' through 'a period of ferment in which the composer made his life miserable with challenges, reflections and experiments'. Only recently, with the choral work *Hymnus Amoris* of 1897, had he achieved 'a pleasant clarity'.[57]

Judging from the reviews of Nielsens music, his 'period of ferment' began in the early 1890s. Indeed, it is from this period that the music began to be described as knotty and bizarre. An example of this perception can be found in the reviews of two concerts on 17 and 18 March 1891. The first was the chamber music soiree at which Nielsen's *Fantasy Pieces for Oboe and Piano*, Op. 2, was premiered. The newspaper *Dagbladet* commented:

> These are two strange, almost odd little pieces which, although they have a certain charm, do not seem to have sprung from a simple spirit. They are intensely mannered, almost neurotic in their choice of harmonies, and the melody twists and turns, often quite unnaturally, to suit these chords.[58]

The same view of Nielsen's music as strange and inaccessible was expressed in the newspaper *København* in connection with the following evening's concert at Symphonia. The concert featured Robert Henriques's Suite for Oboe and Piano: 'Mr Henriques has, in our opinion, been more successful in his composition than Nielsen, whose Fantasy Pieces were performed at the second Kapelsoirée the other day. His work is less bizarre and more accessible.'[59] The review also shows that it was common to compare the works of younger composers. When the critics and other concertgoers listened to Henriques's composition on 18 March, several of them still had Nielsen's oboe pieces from the previous evening in their ears.

Some of the early concerts featuring Nielsen's works were chamber music evenings in smaller concert halls and received relatively brief newspaper coverage. By contrast, the premiere of his First Symphony, on 14 March 1894, took place on a grand scale, which also provided an opportunity for more detailed consideration of the music by the critics. The reception was a triumph for Nielsen, with extremely positive reactions, but it is also interesting how words such as 'daring' and radical' recur in the reviews.

Nielsen's symphony opened the first of Johan Svendsen's symphony concerts with The Royal Orchestra, which was a reorganisation of The Philharmonic Concerts of 1883.[60] The concert took place in the main hall of Koncertpalæet, and the rest of the programme consisted of Brahms's Violin Concerto, Otto Malling's *Oriental Suite* and Wagner's Prelude to *Die Meistersinger von Nürnberg*.[61] It was an important event, and in order to perform the demanding programme satisfactorily, a large number of additional musicians had been recruited from outside of The Royal Orchestra.

Nielsen played in the orchestra during the concert and made a note in his diary afterwards: 'On 14 March 1894 my first symphony (G minor) was performed at Koncertpalæet by the entire Royal Theatre Orchestra and the best musicians outside the orchestra under the direction of Johan Svendsen. The Symphony was a great success, and I was called onto the stage three times after the final movement.'[62] The symphony was also well received by the critics, who emphasised the bold and radical nature of

ILL. 3. Robert Henriques's review of Nielsen's First Symphony in the newspaper *Dannebrog*, 15 March 1894.

the music. As Robert Henriques noted in *Dannebrog*: 'The composer does not follow well-trodden paths. He is bold, truthful and knows exactly what he wants.'[63] Henriques was particularly intrigued by the symphony's opening with a powerful C major chord, which seemed surprising in a symphony in G minor: 'This beginning is a happy find, especially as the rest of the symphony keeps what the beginning promises.'[64] The newspaper *Social-Demokraten* remarked that there was 'youth and boldness' in the music, and that the audience was greeted by a 'young prince of music'.[65]

Several critics noticed the radical or reckless nature of the music. Hammerich wrote in the *Nationaltidende*:

> It is written in a distinctly radical manner, something like César Franck's stuff. ... At first glance, one notices a number of effective ascents, well-adapted exits that bring the turbulent content to a harmonious conclusion, as well as many peculiarities and insignificant motifs. It is not immediately clear whether artistic imagination or constructive combinations have the upper hand. The young composer still owes us some of that which is immediate, which is musical for its own sake. If this is the case, the musical-aesthetic confession is, of course, quite unimportant. If we only perceive that there is 'music' in it, then both Radicalism and Conservatism must be allowed to stand their ground and have their right. With Mr Carl Nielsen we are still waiting for that 'something'. It is always a good sign that he is looking for it, and searching far and wide, going his own way.[66]

Hammerich described the music as 'restless' and 'radical', and also gave the impression that Nielsen had not yet landed musically, as the symphony had a searching and experimental character. The restlessness and boldness of the music was also emphasised in Kjerulf's unreservedly positive review in *Politiken*:

> Restless and reckless in harmony and modulation, yet wonderfully innocent and unconscious, like a child playing with dynamite. And yet, most importantly, from beginning to end: genuine and without pretence, an exact and faithful expression of this very particular, extraordinary young artistic personality.[67]

In the light of these reviews, it is not surprising that the radical circle around Georg Brandes saw in Nielsen's works an appropriate musical expression of the visions of the milieu at the turn of the century. Nielsen first provided the music for *Politiken's* celebration of the turn of the century on 1 January 1901, and later that year he wrote the music for *Cantata for the Inauguration of the Student Society Building* on Bispetorvet. This must be seen as an indication that radical circles were able to associate Nielsen and his musical style with the values and visions for the future of the milieu. The daring, reckless and explosive nature of the symphony and Nielsen's ability to 'get going without beating about the bush'[68] must have seemed a natural musical counterpart to the radical milieu's understanding of modernity.[69]

Nielsen was also explicitly associated with radical and modern currents in other areas of cultural life. In his review of Nielsen's book of art songs, *Songs and Verses by J. P. Jacobsen* (1893), Robert Henriques remarks:

The equally pretentious and affected cover picture of the publication is strikingly reminiscent of some of the stanzas in 'Politiken' and the pictures at The Free Exhibition – a society that J. P. Jacobsen would gladly have refused to join. The same goes for Mr Carl Nielsen, if his undoubted and natural talent does not get lost in the sand. In any case, he does not succeed in enriching our national song repertoire in the way laid out in these songs.[70]

A similar comparison is made in Hammerich's review of Nielsen's Violin Sonata in A major, Op. 9 (1895), only this time it is the music itself: 'Is it Willumsen's success in the camp of Symbolism that have tempted the young musician? Last time, in his piano pieces, it was this current he subscribed to, and in the violin sonata too.'[71] In both cases, the reviews seem almost a warning to Nielsen not to be led astray by the circle around *Politiken* and Den Frie Udstilling.

In the years leading up to the turn of the century, there are several examples of other younger composers being compared to Nielsen when they became too 'modern'. This is the case in Hetsch's review of Axel Gade's composition evening in January 1898: 'Modernism – or to be more precise, Carl Nielsen – has got into him.'[72] For some, Nielsen had become almost synonymous with 'modernism', and a review of some piano pieces by Fini Henriques says the same:

How many would have the courage to put up with the first piece, which piles chord upon chord like Pelion upon Ossa! Fini Henriques seems to have gone all Carl Nielsen here, and it is certainly not to his credit.[73]

Both here and in Hammerich's aforementioned review of Nielsen's Violin Sonata, it is probably Nielsen's piano piece *Symphonic Suite* that is being referred to. There is much to suggest that the radical circles who asked Nielsen to write a piece for the turn of the century also associated his radicalism with the work. In any case, the sharp and energetic piano style of *Symphonic Suite*, with powerful, massive chords in the treble and deep, wandering octaves in the bass, recurs in Nielsen's *Fest-Præludium ved Aarhundredskiftet* (CNW 84) – the work that was printed on the front page of *Politiken* on New Year's Day under the title *Prelude to the New Century*. A few months later, Wilhelm Hansen published the piano piece dedicated to J. F. Willumsen.[74]

The *Festival Prelude for the New Century* has often been compared to the *Symphonic Suite*, which is not to its advantage. It should be noted, however, that the two works were composed for very different purposes. The Suite requires a professional pianist, whereas the *Festival Prelude* was a commissioned work based on a very specific outline that Nielsen had to take into account. The scope was limited to a few staves of music at the bottom of the front page of *Politiken*, with the intention that amateur pianists among the readers could rehearse the work on their own, thus creating the sound of the turn of the century. In return, the work potentially had a much wider circulation than the *Symphonic Suite*. Around 1900, *Politiken* had a circulation of around 23,000.[75] The celebration was thus instrumental in associating the sound of Nielsen's music with radical currents in the arts.

Looking at the music societies of the 1890s and the reception of Nielsen's music during this period, it is clear that he belonged to a group of young Danish composers who were compared with modern trends in other art forms. Nielsen was likened to Willumsen, and Symphonia was seen as a musical counterpart to Den Frie Udstilling and Det fri Teater.

It would be a mistake, however, if this account gave the impression that the discourse took place exclusively in Copenhagen. The discussions of musical modernity in the capital were closely related to the musical-aesthetic debates taking place elsewhere in Europe, especially in Germany. The European context plays a crucial role, and for Nielsen it was already a lived experience in the early 1890s, when he embarked on the first of his many journeys in Europe.

Chapter 12

ON THE THRESHOLD OF THE MUSICAL MODERN

In September 1890, the 25-year-old Nielsen set off on a long European journey that was to be of crucial importance for him. The first part of the journey, in Germany, was an encounter with contemporary European musical life at the highest level. He experienced first-hand both the latest trends and performances of the contemporary repertoire by leading orchestras and opera houses. The second part of his tour took him to Paris and Italy, where he had a very different focus. He had been awarded the Anckerske Legat – a travel grant given each year to two visual artists, a poet and a composer – and a year's leave of absence from The Royal Orchestra. The grant had no specific requirements as to what the recipients should do abroad; the aim was to provide a basic education by travelling around Europe.[1]

Germany was the most popular destination for composers who received the grant. This was also true in Nielsen's case, and he spent almost half a year in Germany from 3 September 1890 to 25 February 1891. The time was divided between three important musical centres: Dresden, Berlin and Leipzig. Dresden was then one of the world's leading opera cities, while Leipzig was home to the famous Gewandhaus Orchestra, founded in 1743. In Berlin, the conductor, Hans von Bülow, and the violinist, Joseph Joachim, were at the forefront of a rapidly developing musical life.

Nielsen had extended stays in all three cities, although he also travelled back and forth between them when he needed to meet someone or attend a particular event. As well as experiencing musical life, he used his travels to make professional contacts and to present his music to some of Europe's most important music entrepreneurs. As in Copenhagen, it was important to be where the action was.

The day after his arrival in Germany, Nielsen was by chance introduced to the elderly composer Theodor Kirchner, and on the last day of his stay he met the young Richard Strauss. In the great controversy of the time between classicism and the New German School, Kirchner and Strauss were on opposite sides. Strauss belonged to the new generation of composers who, at the turn of the century, were regarded as modern representatives of the post-Brahms and post-Wagner era. In other words, it was the living history of music that was unfolding before Nielsen's eyes – and ears – as he toured through Germany.

He left at a time when the idea of a new era was taking hold, and the new was to become the musical modernity of the turn of the century. The mood of upheaval is reflected in the fact that there were two equal views on how to understand the question of progress in music. On the one hand, since the 1850s, European musical life had been sharply divided between two parties: the followers of Wagner and Liszt represented a direction that was seen as an indication of progress, while the supporters of a classicist aesthetic took as their starting point Hanslick's work *Vom Musikalisch-Schönen* (*On the Musically Beautiful*), which argued that beauty depended on eternal laws.[2] The debate was still going on in 1890, and Nielsen took an active part in it during his travels.

On the other hand, there was an emerging perception that this discussion was outdated. The new had to be found in a younger generation that saw itself and was seen as being 'after Wagner and Brahms' – even though Brahms was still alive. This did not mean that the two parties no longer existed – indeed they did, both as aesthetic positions and in their choice of repertoire – but they no longer represented the latest. They had been overtaken. Apart from Mahler, this new generation was represented by Strauss, and Nielsen heard several of Strauss's works during his travels in 1890–91. He was right where it was happening.

Travel Plans

Travelling was a natural part of an artist's life. For Nielsen, the European tour of 1890–91 was the first of many trips abroad. They were an opportunity for respite and inspiration in terms of his compositional work, but they were also an important part of creating an international network. If he wanted his music to be performed throughout Europe, he had to make an effort to find people who could make it happen. Nielsen's teacher at the Academy of Music in Copenhagen, Niels W. Gade, was a good example of how great success could be achieved by going abroad. As a young man Gade went to Leipzig in 1843, met Mendelssohn, became his successor as director of the Gewandhaus Orchestra and achieved fame in Germany and Denmark. When Nielsen left in 1890, Gade was still the central figure in Danish musical life, with all the important international connections.

It was also Gade with whom students had to ingratiate themselves if they wanted to be considered for the travel grant of the Anckerske Legat. The scholarship had been awarded since 1861, and from the outset Gade and Johan Peter Emilius Hartmann were responsible for shortlisting composers. It was the largest scholarship in music, and almost all the major Danish composers of the last decades of the nineteenth century had received it.[3] Nielsen must therefore have felt a great sense of recognition when, on his second application in 1890, he was awarded 1,800 Kroner.[4] It

3.9.90–8.10.90	Dresden	12.4.91–13.4.91	Basel
8.10.90–10.10.90	Leipzig	13.4.91–14.4.91	Luzern
10.10.90–19.10.90	Dresden	14.4.91–15.4.91	Flüelen
19.10.90–1.1.91	Berlin	15.4.91–16.4.91	Lugano
1.1.91–2.1.91	Leipzig	16.4.91–18.4.91	Milan
2.1.91–11.1.91	Berlin	19.4.91–15.5.91	Florence
11.1.91–17.1.91	Leipzig	15.5.91–21.5.91	Rom
17.1.91–19.1.91	Berlin	22.5.91–30.5.91	Florence
19.1.91–23.1.91	Leipzig	30.5.91	Pistoja, Bologna
23.1.91–25.1.91	Dresden	30.5.91–13.6.91	Venice
25.1.91–15.2.91	Leipzig	13.6.91	Padua, Verona
15.2.91–25.2.91	Berlin	13.6.91–14.6.91	Bolzano
26.2.91–12.4.91	Paris		

TABLE 1. According to his diary Nielsen toured through Europe from September 1890 to June 1891. The longer stays were spent in Dresden (3 Sept. to 19 Oct. 1890), Berlin (19 Oct. 1890 to 11 Jan. 1891), Leipzig (11 Jan. to 15 Feb. 1891), Paris (26 Feb. to 12 Apr. 1891) and Florence (19 Apr. to 15 May 1891). The last part of the journey home from Italy is not documented.

was a considerable sum, equivalent to a year and a half's salary as a member of The Royal Orchestra.

Before leaving on Wednesday 3 September 1890, Nielsen made thorough preparations by visiting a number of people who could advise him regarding the tour. On Saturday he visited his former theory teacher Orla Rosenhoff, on Monday he spent the day with Robert Henriques and Heinrich Hirschsprung, and in the evening he went to the Tivoli Gardens with Anton Svendsen. After receiving the Anckerske Legat a few years earlier, Henriques had spent time in Germany and France, and Anton Svendsen had studied violin in Germany with Joseph Joachim. Hirschsprung was an art collector and probably told Nielsen about the European art scene. On Tuesday, the day before his departure, he spent the whole day with Niels W. Gade, who gave him letters of recommendation for his international contacts.[5]

The preparations were crucial for Nielsen in gaining access to the right people in Germany – and perhaps even the opportunity to have his music performed in the famous German concert halls. At the start of the tour, he also had an important supporter in Victor Bendix, who was already in Germany. Before leaving, they had corresponded by letter and Nielsen had asked if he could visit Bendix in Dresden. It would be a detour from Berlin, where he had planned to spend the first few months. Bendix, however, had a different suggestion:

> I suppose there is no concert life in Berlin yet, so you might as well come to Dresden, where they have an excellent opera and, above all, an orchestra that you will have to look long and hard for – and there is beauty both inside and outside the city, which is also worth something at this time of year.[6]

Nielsen took the advice and changed his plans. From the station in Berlin, he went straight to Dresden, where, apart from a short trip to Leipzig, he spent the first month and a half of his stay abroad. Bendix met him at the station.

Dresden

In his diary, Nielsen describes Dresden as 'a charming city, cosy and friendly everywhere'.[7] He stayed in a hotel in the old town, south of the River Elbe. While he was there, the waters rose and caused flooding – an event that clearly fascinated him: 'The River Elbe has burst its banks, and several streets are under water. Fantastic sight!'[8] In general, he was enthusiastic about the city and the surrounding nature, which he immediately sensed in a musical way:

> Could you imagine composing like this: going out into a beautiful mountain landscape at sunset on a summer's day, following the beautiful lines drawn by the mountains with your eyes, and letting the musical thought or mood rise and fall accordingly? That is at least an idea! Nothing is more plastic than mountains.[9]

At the beginning of his stay, Nielsen stayed close to Bendix, who had spent a lot of time in Germany and therefore had many connections. The very day after his arrival, Nielsen was thus introduced by Bendix to the composer Kirchner, who became his first real encounter with German musical circles:

> Was with Bendix at Kirchner's. Resembles Beethoven and is a very original personality. … He had dreamed of playing Brahms's role in modern Germany, but bowed to the greater talent, and is therefore bitter.[10]

Kirchner had a long career as an organist and composer. As a very young man in the 1830s, Schumann had been his model and his idol.[11] He had been educated in Leipzig and, from 1843, held a number of posts in Switzerland and Germany while pursuing a distinguished career as an organist and pianist. He found it increasingly difficult to make ends meet and in 1883 he accepted a position as a teacher at the Academy of Music in Dresden, although he did not give many lessons and had serious financial problems. The following year, however, a group of friends – including Brahms, Gade and Grieg – managed to raise 30,000 Marks to pay off his debts.[12] In 1890, disillusioned, Kirchner gave up his post in Dresden and moved to Hamburg, where he lived until his death in 1903.

Nielsen and Kirchner met several times before Kirchner left Dresden at the end of September 1890. Nielsen's diaries show that he had a great sympathy for the mature composer, although he understood well why Kirchner had struggled for success:

ILL. 1. Theodor Kirchner.

> Spent all day at Bendix's. He played through everything of Kirchner's for me. There are many beautiful things among his songs, but they are lacking originality and virility. He has become hypnotised by the 'sweet' side of Schumann.[13]

Nielsen may have been inspired by listening to piano music all day. On the same day, he wrote in his diary that he had composed the piano piece 'Folketone' (Folk Tune), which was to become part of his *Five Piano Pieces*, Op. 3.[14] A month later, he came up with the idea of publishing the piano pieces in the form of small travel letters, with slanting staves and an envelope around them, so that they could be directly linked to the impressions of the European tour.[15] However, he was unable to convince the publishers of this idea and the pieces were published in the traditional way the following year.

The climax of Nielsen's acquaintance with Kirchner was a musical party at which Nielsen performed his *Fantasy Pieces for Oboe and Piano*, Op. 2, with Bendix at the piano and Nielsen playing the oboe part on the violin. It was the first time that Nielsen performed his music abroad, and Kirchner was not just anybody; throughout his career, he had moved in the inner circles of European musical life. Also present was the pianist Hermann Scholtz, who, like Kirchner, had been trained in Leipzig and was associated with the Dresden Academy of Music. Nielsen described the performance as 'really the greatest triumph I ever had. Scholz and Kirchner looked tired and indifferent at first, but before the pieces were over they were all on fire. I shall not easily forget *this* evening.'[16]

Two days later, Kirchner left Dresden. The departure, which marked Kirchner's final retirement from German musical life, left a deep impression on Nielsen:

> Last dinner with Kirchner. He is leaving for Hamburg tomorrow as he is unhappy with his position here. I wish him luck. It's a pity and a shame that the government

does not take better care of its important men. He said to me the other evening that the human being is generally ungrateful to death; he thinks it's a blessing. Thus said the man whom Schumann calls a genius![17]

Nielsen's reflections on Kirchner's fate must be understood in the light of the musical conflict between Romantic Classicism and the New German School, which had long dominated music in Germany and Vienna. When Nielsen remarked on his first meeting with Kirchner that he had 'dreamed of playing the role of Brahms in modern Germany' he meant that Kirchner would have liked to be seen as the most important modern representative of a classical trend in music.[18] Throughout his life Kirchner had tried to continue Schumann's line, but he was unable to foster innovation within a classicist tradition in the way that Brahms had. In the end he had to admit defeat, as Nielsen witnessed. Nielsen's view that Kirchner deserved a better fate in German musical life should probably be seen as an acknowledgement of Kirchner's human qualities and musical abilities. It should not, however, be taken as an expression of Nielsen's own adherence to a classical trend in music. Indeed, it was during this period of meeting Kirchner that his fascination with Wagner began.

Nielsen's early enthusiasm for Wagner can be directly linked to his attendance at the complete *Ring des Nibelungen* at Dresden's Semperoper from 10 to 15 September 1890. The circumstances must have been almost perfect, for the orchestra under Ernst von Schuch was renowned for its high standards, and Nielsen also had a knowledgeable Wagnerian at his side in Bendix. At the age of nineteen, Bendix had been employed as a rehearser at The Royal Theatre, and in 1870 he had helped to prepare the first Danish production of Wagner's opera *Lohengrin*. Two years later he assisted in the production of Wagner's *Die Meistersinger*, and that summer he attended the laying of the foundation stone for Wagner's Festspielhaus in Bayreuth, where Wagner conducted Beethoven's Ninth Symphony. For the first performance of the complete *Ring* in Bayreuth in 1876, Bendix was again present, this time with colleagues Christian Barnekow and Orla Rosenhoff. In his memoirs he recalls how this reinforced the impression that Wagner was 'like a giant among dwarfs, the only adult in the nursery of modern composers'.[19]

When Nielsen had the opportunity to attend all four operas of *Der Ring des Nibelungen* in Dresden, the effect was apparently as intense as it had been for Bendix fourteen years earlier. After attending the final opera, *Götterdämmerung*, he wrote enthusiastically in a letter to his friend Emil Sachs:

> I heard Wagner's complete *Nibelung* cycle this week. What a guy! Good God, what a giant in our times. It's incomprehensible that there are people who can't stand his music. I myself wasn't nearly so enthusiastic about him before I came here.

ILL. 2. The Semperoper on Theaterplatz in Dresden, *c.* 1900. From 1882 to 1914, the opera was directed by Ernst von Schuch, who was able to assemble an orchestra of the highest calibre and was extremely ambitious in his programming. He introduced German audiences to the Italian operas of Verdi and Puccini and also had a strong focus on contemporary German composers such as Brahms, Bruckner, Mahler and Strauss. Among the opera house's former conductors were the composers Carl Maria von Weber and Richard Wagner.

> But then I'd only heard *Tannhäuser* and *Lohengrin*, plus some excerpts from the later operas; but now I can't find words strong enough to praise him. He's a mighty genius. Hats off![20]

As already mentioned, the worship of Wagner was linked to a musical aesthetic that saw progress as essential to the justification of art. That this was also the case for Nielsen is evident from the way he assessed his other musical impressions in Germany. When he attended Mozart's *Die Zauberflöte* a few weeks after the *Ring des Nibelungen*, he noted in his diary that 'the whole scene of the "Gates of Terror" was beautiful and very unique to Mozart; but it must be enjoyed "historically". Wagner! Wagner!! what have you done!'[21]

Berlin

Nielsen had been working on his String Quartet in F minor throughout the trip and was finally able to complete it during his stay in Berlin. The timing was ideal, for in the German capital he was to meet one of the world's most famous quartet players: Joseph Joachim. Nielsen had received a recommendation from Gade and visited Joachim soon after his arrival. He must have heard a lot about him, for Joachim had taught several of Copenhagen's most prominent violinists, including Valdemar Tofte, Nielsen's teacher at the Academy. Tofte used Joachim's techniques as faithfully as possible in his own teaching, so Nielsen was very familiar with Joachim's style of playing. However, it was something else to see the master himself.

As a musician, Joachim was known for his ability to evoke an almost overpowering experience in his listeners. He took an austere approach to musical interpretation, submitting to the composer rather than demonstrating his own virtuosity.[22] Beethoven was almost always on the concert programme, and contemporary sources describe how many concertgoers felt that Beethoven's spirit was brought to life through Joachim's playing.[23] Nielsen's account of his first concert with the Joachim Quartet also speaks of an overwhelming experience:

> They played Beethoven in G major, Schubert in D minor and a Brahms quintet with the perfect mastery I could only dream of. When Joachim really 'goes for it', it is as though Zeus himself was shaking his mighty lion's head, and he can play as much *piano* as you can imagine, and yet he hovers above it all the time. Quite wonderful![24]

By this time, Joachim's musical career had already spanned half a century. In 1843, at the age of twelve, he had made his debut as a violinist with the Gewandhaus Orchestra in Leipzig, and in the following years he trained with the orchestra under the tutelage of Mendelssohn. After Mendelssohn's death in 1847, he studied with Liszt in Weimar. However, when he joined the circle of Brahms and Schumann a few years later, he distanced himself from Liszt and the New German School. In 1868 he settled in Berlin, where he became a key figure in the musical life, founding the city's new Academy, the Hochschule für Musik, and becoming deeply involved in concert life as a conductor, musician and organiser.[25]

String quartet playing had long been an important part of Joachim's activities. In Berlin, he immediately seized the opportunity to form his own quartet in conjunction with the Academy and a regular concert series at the city's Singakademie. The quartet quickly became a success, giving Joachim a platform to promote his favourite classical chamber music repertoire: Beethoven first and foremost, but also Haydn, Mozart and Brahms.[26] He also conducted Berlin's new Philharmonic Orchestra from

ILL. 3. The Joachim Quartet in Bonn, May 1890. At this time the quartet consisted of Joseph Joachim on first violin, Robert Hausmann on cello, Emanuel Wirth on viola and Heinrich de Ahna on second violin.

1884 to 1887, when Hans von Bülow took over. Joachim thus became a key figure in the transformation of Berlin into a major cultural city after it became the capital of the unified German Empire in 1871.[27]

The Academy and the new world-class orchestra also made Berlin attractive to travelling musicians such as Nielsen. He was not impressed by the city itself, however: 'I can't like Berlin, no matter how hard I try. No style, no atmosphere, no matter where you go.'[28] But Bülow's concerts and the surroundings of Joachim's Hochschule had a stimulating effect on him. He spent many evenings in the Philharmonie and wrote enthusiastically of Bülow's conducting skills in a letter to Rosenhoff: 'Good Lord, how he handles an orchestra.'[29] Through Joachim, Nielsen also had access to rehearsals and lessons at the Academy. He thus became part of the musical milieu around the famous violinist.

For Nielsen, the trip was not just about absorbing impressions. It was at least as important to use his stay abroad to promote his works in an international context.

The private performance of the oboe pieces for Kirchner in Dresden had been a milestone, but an even greater achievement was the performance of his String Quartet in F minor for Joachim on 18 December 1890. On that day, Nielsen made a brief note in his diary:

> Rehearsal of the quartet. Played it at four o'clock for Joachim in the Hochschule. (Many present) Thought there was a lot of 'horror' in it but praised me a lot for the parts he liked. There was enough imagination and talent, but the way it was presented was too radical for him.[30]

The next day Nielsen and Joachim had another opportunity to discuss the work, with Joachim repeating his praise but also suggesting improvements. Nielsen rejected these, however, as the places Joachim thought needed reworking were the ones Nielsen liked best.[31] Several months later, the incident was still fresh in Nielsen's mind, and in a letter to his friend Holger Møller, he recalled how Joachim had criticised the quartet's 'terrible radical harmonies, abominable modulations' and 'hideous modern tendencies'.[32] The Hochschule saw itself as a bulwark against modern tendencies, and Nielsen's account is not the only example of the school referring to new works in such terms, where aesthetic objections slipped into moralising rejection.[33] The letter also gives a detailed account of the discussion that followed the performance:

> So, when we had played the first Allegro he praised and found fault in equal measure. Afterwards he asked if Gade had seen this movement, and when I answered no, he added that it surely wouldn't have been to Gade's taste. I replied I was certain of that too, the more so because Gade couldn't get on with Brahms, Wagner et al. Then he got worked up and said that '*my friend Gade* told me that he likes Brahms very much and has performed his F major Symphony [No. 3] several times'. I answered that this was the only piece Gade liked and that he had told me shortly before my trip that Brahms's music was only a game of patterns. Now it so happens that Joachim is the only one at the Conservatoire who fights for Brahms. All the others – Bargiel, Spitta and so on – hate him. And that's why he went crazy when he heard that even his friend Gade was of their number, and that came back to bite me.[34]

Nielsen had thus turned Joachim's argument about Gade's hypothetical attitude to the quartet on its head by saying that Gade 'could not even' put up with Wagner and Brahms. In other words, according to Nielsen, Gade could not even appreciate the composers who had paved the way for today's modern music. At the same time, the remark had the effect of making Joachim feel even more alone in his admiration for

Brahms, which he thought he at least shared with Gade. Nevertheless, Nielsen admits in the letter that he probably should have handled the situation differently: 'I wasn't as careful as I should have been, and it was my fault that he got irritated for a moment and judged the passages he didn't like harsher than he otherwise would have'.[35] For Nielsen, it was not just about winning the argument; he also wanted to make a good impression and perhaps get the chance to have his work performed by the famous Joachim Quartet. As he travelled, he had to constantly adapt to the people he interacted with in order to increase his chances of achieving what he wanted.

A few days after the quartet's performance, Nielsen received a momentous piece of news about the domestic situation:

> Paul Morgan came and told me that Gade is dead. This news had a terrible effect on me. I simply can't imagine that he's dead – this healthy, fresh-spirited man and great artist, our pride! Our Gade! Gade is dead![36]

The news that the leading figure in Danish music had died came as a shock to everyone. Gade had continued his work right up to the end. In November he had conducted his own work, *Psyche*, at Musikforeningen in Copenhagen, and in December he had directed, together with Hartmann, the Academy's annual entrance examinations. On Sunday 21 December, Gade had played the organ at Holmens Kirke in the morning, as usual, and then stopped by the Viennese Café at Hotel Kongen af Danmark to greet Edvard and Nina Grieg. At midday he suddenly began to cough and gasp for breath. The doctor was called a few hours later, but there was nothing to be done.[37]

In the days that followed, Nielsen was deeply affected by the situation. On 23 December he writes in his diary that he is 'sick with grief and cannot eat or sleep'. He also reflected on Gade's importance while he was alive: 'He gave us others light and warmth, and now it is all over, he no longer stands in the foreground as a role model, as a shining example.'[38] For Nielsen, Gade was an example of what could be achieved as a musician and composer, and in Germany he had experienced firsthand how internationally recognised Gade was. Almost every newspaper Nielsen could find in Berlin reported Gade's death, and several memorial services were held for the composer. For Nielsen, being a Danish musician in Germany suddenly took on a special significance, as he was asked for information about Gade and invited to memorial services.

In a 'musical letter from Germany' which appeared in the newspaper *Nationaltidende* on 11 February 1891, Nielsen wrote home about the overwhelming tribute to Gade that had taken place in German musical life. The 'crown of all' had been Joachim's memorial concert at the Hochschule on 17 January, with works by Mendelssohn, Schumann and Gade. After the concert, Nielsen recalls, Joachim said with tears in his eyes: 'He was such a dear master.' Nielsen also took the opportunity to report on other performances of Danish music, in particular Bendix's success with the Symphony No. 1, *Fjeldstigning*, in Dresden. Finally, he noted that the interest in Danish music that Gade had stimulated in Germany was still alive, and that it was up to younger composers to maintain this interest.[39] He did not, of course, mention his own achievements, although that was exactly what he was trying to do at the time.

Yet Nielsen's immediate reaction to Gade's death was one of sadness and recognition of Gade's importance, and it must have aroused other feelings in him as well. Both he and others in his close circle had long felt that Gade's dominant position was problematic for Danish musical life. Bendix, in particular, had felt this as he had not received the appointments and performances of his music that he had been promised. Gade had originally been his mentor, but after Bendix had been in Germany and had begun to approach the New German School in terms of style, there had been a gradual drifting apart and the relationship had become cooler.[40] For Bendix, Gade's death meant that he could once again hope for a more central position in musical life.

Nielsen and Bendix could hardly have avoided discussing Gade's role in musical life, as they had been together in Dresden on a daily basis a few months earlier. Bendix was thus able to write to Nielsen on 25 December: 'It was, I suppose, with strangely mixed feelings that you heard of Gade's death? Something like that always makes an impression!'[41] Here Bendix seems to be suggesting that it is positive that Gade will no longer be in charge of everything, but that a passing is of course always sad. The same ambivalence characterises Nielsen's letters after Gade's death, although he seems more emotionally affected than Bendix. In a letter to Sachs dated 27 December, for example, he writes:

> Gade is dead! Although I can perfectly well see that Gade held things back in many respects, the fact that he is gone is still a great and irreplaceable loss. After all he was still Gade; and you understand that properly only when you've been abroad and seen what effect the mere mention of his name has in Germany.[42]

Nielsen was clearly conflicted. On the one hand, Gade was a role model, showing how to leave home and then return as a celebrity. Moreover, it was more or less thanks to Gade that Nielsen was in Germany at the time and had access to the right connections in the music world. On the other hand, he agreed with Bendix that Gade represented a musical conservatism that needed to be challenged. This was confirmed when, in mid-January, he took up residence in the city that had done more than any other to shape Gade musically: Leipzig.

Leipzig

Leipzig's fame as a city of music goes back to Telemann and Bach, but it was Mendelssohn who created the model for the city's musical life that was to influence the whole of northern Europe. In 1835 he took over the management of the Gewandhaus Orchestra, and in 1843 he founded the Leipzig Academy of Music. By the middle of the nineteenth century, the city had become a model for musical life in much of Europe, combining an academy that attracted students from Anglo-Saxon countries and northern and eastern Europe, a first-class orchestra and the home of the world's leading music publishers and music journals.[43]

Nielsen had made short trips to Leipzig during the tour, but from 11 January 1891 and for the next month he made the city his base. Leipzig was still an almost obligatory destination for musicians at this time, but Nielsen's impression of Leipzig and its famous orchestra was not very positive: 'It's terribly boring here in Leipzig, and I'm afraid I can't stand it. The Gewandhaus under Carl Reinecke is terribly backward; it's much worse than the Music Society [in Copenhagen] under Gade'.[44] He must have experienced a place that had once been a thriving centre of music in Europe but had failed to keep up with the times. He describes a rehearsal at the Gewandhaus as 'a really soporific concert',[45] and of Carl Reinecke's conducting of Beethoven's Eighth Symphony he remarks that it was 'played very well; but when I think of Bülow's performance, it was not played at all'.[46] Nielsen's arrival in Leipzig was clearly an anticlimax for him. Yet there were cracks in Leipzig's dullness and musical conservatism:

> In the evening, we went to a concert in Albert Halle. These concerts are a kind of opposition to the conservative Gewandhaus, and the programme was also quite 'radical'. Berlioz's 'Symphonie fantastique', Liszt's 'Tasso' and the final scene of 'Parsifal'. Full house, great enthusiasm; but the orchestra is still far from good.[47]

The Albert Halle hosted the Liszt Society's concerts, and it was here that Nielsen heard the 'radical' works of the New German School as a counterbalance to the conservative programme of Reinecke's Gewandhaus. Nielsen's view of the event shows that he made a distinction between aesthetic positions and musical ability. He had done the same in Dresden with Kirchner, whom he criticised for being too old-fashioned and set in his aesthetic ideals, although at the same time he admired his musical talent.

In Leipzig, Nielsen was to meet two prominent figures in musical life. One was, of course, the director of the Gewandhaus Orchestra, Reinecke, for whom Gade had given Nielsen a letter of recommendation. Reinecke was born in Altona, a town near Hamburg, which was part of Danish territory until 1864, so he had close connections with both Danish and German musical life. He was court pianist in Copenhagen from 1846 to 1848 and was appointed conductor in Leipzig in 1860 after Gade refused to return to his earlier position. Reinecke was known for his conservative views and, as director of the Gewandhaus Orchestra, made it his mission to uphold the tradition of classical composers.

On 13 January Nielsen visited Reinecke, who received him very kindly. They had met briefly at a Joachim concert a few weeks earlier, but now they had a better chance to talk properly. After the visit, Nielsen wrote in his diary: 'I would call him "a very nice and good old man" who wouldn't hurt a cat.'[48] Neither Reinecke's conducting skills nor his personal temperament made much of an impression on Nielsen. The experience was not particularly bad, but it did not set anything in motion. He already knew that Reinecke was extremely conservative, so his expectations of the meeting were probably not very high. For Gade, on the other hand, it was the meeting with the leader of the Gewandhaus Orchestra – Mendelssohn at the time – that launched his international career. Not so for Nielsen.

A particularly inspiring encounter was with the Russian violinist Adolph Brodsky. Nielsen paid him a visit after he had been with Reinecke and noted that he seemed 'a cheerful and free-spirited man'.[49] Brodsky was a professor at the Academy and the leader of the famous Brodsky Quartet, the only quartet to rival Joachim's in reputation. His house in Leipzig was a cultural meeting place and his close friends included Tchaikovsky, Brahms and Grieg.[50] Nielsen describes the house as 'a true artist's home!', where he could come and go as he pleased.[51] Here he met other musicians and composers, played music and discussed artistic matters. From Brodsky's house he often went to the opera or to concerts in the city. In short, it was a very stimulating environment to be a part of.

Nielsen had received a recommendation for Brodsky from Bendix, but he had also made contact with the Norwegian composer Christian Sinding, whom he had met in Berlin during the Christmas holidays. Nielsen played his new string quartet for Sinding shortly after the New Year. Sinding soon left for Leipzig and had managed to mention the quartet to Brodsky before Nielsen himself arrived in the city.[52] Nielsen had the parts copied for Brodsky and was offered the prospect of including the quartet in his programme.[53]

The Quartet in F minor thus gave Nielsen access to not one, but two of the world's leading string quartets. They were powerful ambassadors, whether or not they themselves included the quartet in their repertoire. The last note Nielsen wrote in his diary before leaving Leipzig, full of expectation, was that he had been promised a performance: 'My first quartet accepted for performance in the Lisztverein!'[54] However, it was not performed there – instead, to his surprise, he was later told that it had been performed in Nice.[55]

Sinding came to Germany for the same reasons as Bendix – because he felt that the musical conditions at home were too conservative. He had graduated from the Leipzig Academy and studied composition with Reinecke, so he was trained in the classical tradition. In the early 1880s, however, he received a new impetus in Munich, where he became acquainted with the works of Liszt and Berlioz. When Sinding returned to Leipzig, he was disappointed by the Gewandhaus Orchestra, which 'had such a traditional programme that [he] didn't bother to go'.[56] On the other hand, he met Brodsky, who became an important supporter of Sinding. It was thanks to Brodsky that Sinding made his international breakthrough in 1889 when his Piano Quintet was performed at the Gewandhaus by the Brodsky Quartet with Ferruccio Busoni as pianist.[57]

By the time Nielsen met Sinding in Berlin, Sinding had developed a kind of personal post-Wagnerian style which Nielsen also noticed.[58] When Sinding played him some themes from his new piano concerto, he made notes in his diary: '… it seems, however, that he has his own tone, although the influence of Wagner is evident.'[59] In a letter to Emil Sachs, he even remarked that Sinding was perhaps one of the greatest composers of the time and praised his ability to break free: 'He blows all the rules out of the water and puts his meaning into practice. Otherwise it's usually the case that people appear courageous when they break rules and forms, although they cannot completely free themselves from them.'[60] In other words, for Nielsen, Sinding represented an attempt at a new music that took its cue from Wagner by incorporating his musical innovations, but Sinding was also able to break away and be himself.

On his last evenings in Germany, Nielsen must also have experienced being on the threshold of musical modernity: he attended the Berlin premiere of Richard Strauss's tone poem *Tod und Verklärung*. Strauss was only a year older than Nielsen but was already making a name for himself in the music world. This was not least due to his tone poems of the late 1880s, the programmatic qualities of which helped to mark an aesthetic turning point in relation to his earlier classical orientation. *Tod und Verklärung* in particular, with its overwhelming public and critical success, was a major breakthrough for him. With this work he was well on the way to fulfilling the role of Wagner's successor – and at the same time signalling that a new generation was on the way.[61]

On 23 and 24 February 1891, Strauss himself conducted the tone poem with the Berlin Philharmonic. Nielsen attended both the rehearsal on 22 February and the concerts on the following evenings. At the rehearsal the work made a 'powerful impression' on him, and at the concerts his enthusiasm grew.[62] After the first evening, he wrote in his diary: 'Strauss's work seemed to me this time, if possible, even more significant, and he conducts like a Bülow.'[63] The next evening, Nielsen attended the concert with Sinding, and it was a musical highlight for both of them. In a letter to the composer Frederick Delius, Sinding described the tone poem as the only work of the season that had managed to move him. He was particularly impressed by Strauss's ability to have great ideas and to express them musically.[64] For Nielsen, too, the performance was an important event that must have made him think about the future of music. After the concert, he wrote in his diary: 'He's already a great composer. I was introduced to Strauss and talked to him about his work. His face is very original and not easy to forget.'[65]

The day after the concert, Nielsen was accompanied to the station by some of his Scandinavian travelling companions and boarded an overnight train to Paris. Meeting with the young, pioneering Richard Strauss was one of Nielsen's last musical impressions of his nearly six-month stay in Germany in the winter of 1890–91.

Epilogue 1894

In 1894 Nielsen made another trip to Germany, this time including Vienna. There, four years later, it became clear that the young Strauss represented a new generation about to take power – in other words, Nielsen's generation. Nielsen had been granted a two-month sabbatical from 9 October and was to use the trip to promote his works.[66] He wanted to follow up on the contacts he had made during his first visit to Germany. At the same time, the trip gave him an opportunity to assess how German musical life had developed in the meantime.

Although only a few years had passed since that first trip, much had changed on a personal level. Nielsen had married and had two children, so he was in a very different place in his life. Whereas on the first trip Nielsen had been the young man embarking on his long educational journey, this time he was a family man and the trip was primarily a business one. His career as a composer had also progressed since his last trip abroad. He now had several concerts and publications behind him, and his First Symphony had been performed to great acclaim in Copenhagen in the spring. It was indeed this symphony that he had gone to Germany and Austria to promote. In Vienna he managed to arrange a personal meeting with Brahms. Finally, he had developed his views on the musical aesthetic positions of the time, particularly with regard to Wagner.

The fact that Nielsen spent the first weeks of his 1894 journey in Berlin and Leipzig with his publisher, Alfred Wilhelm Hansen, suggests that it was a business trip. In a letter to his wife Anne Marie, he explains that they had a lot of work to do on the symphony in Berlin and notes that 'it was great that [Alfred Wilhelm Hansen] came, and we're hoping for a result.'[67] Of the many contacts Nielsen made, Jean Louis Nicodé in Dresden proved crucial, for although Nicodé was initially unfamiliar with Nielsen's symphony, it was at Nicodé's concerts that Nielsen conducted its first international performance in March 1896.[68] Nielsen also wrote that he did not intend to stay very long in Munich and Vienna, 'only as long as is necessary for the sake of the Symphony'.[69] In other words, he had set specific goals for the trip, and once these were achieved, he could return home.

Munich and Vienna were new destinations for Nielsen, and it was here that he was able to meet some of Europe's greatest musical personalities. His stay in Munich was short, but not because he had achieved what he wanted in terms of promoting the symphony. On the contrary, he soon realised that there was little to be gained there. When he left for Vienna, he wrote home to Anne Marie: 'I've been in Munich for four days to no avail, which I'll tell you orally. I've done what I could for my things so far, and I shall do what I can here.'[70]

His disappointment with Munich was probably linked to his meeting with Strauss the day after he arrived in the city. As mentioned above, he had already spoken briefly to Strauss in 1891 and remarked afterwards that Strauss was already a great composer. A few weeks before the Munich meeting, he had heard Strauss conduct the Berlin Philharmonic again. Here he had praised Strauss's musical abilities, but also noted that his gestures were 'terribly ugly and ill-shaped'.[71] Either way, he must have been delighted to meet one of the most controversial composers of the day, who was about his age and had already achieved great success. The meeting, however, did not go as expected:

> Went to see Richard Strauss at 2.30 and found him at home. To me he's a very unpleasant person, an upstart who already wants to play the great man. His whole being was extremely stupid and affected, his handshake effeminate and flabby, as though it was only gristle, and when you add that his face is plebeian and ordinary my antipathy is surely justified. He treated me with extreme condescension, and I went away again straight away. I don't know if I've ever met anyone, I find more repulsive.[72]

This might suggest that Nielsen did not have time to present his symphony to Strauss, although this must have been his intention before the visit. That Nielsen found Strauss arrogant and condescending implies that Strauss showed no interest in hearing the symphony – if Nielsen mentioned it at all. Later, Strauss's music came to represent everything Nielsen could not stand. In 1904, he wrote to his good friend, the composer Julius Röntgen, that he found the trend represented by 'Richard Strauss with his dilettante philosophy and timbral problems' unsympathetic.[73] Personal dislike seems to have had a strong influence on Nielsen's attitude to the music.

On the other hand, Nielsen was now determined to make the most of his stay in Vienna. Progress was already being made, as he was able to tell Anne Marie: 'I had the good fortune to meet Dr Schiff, a friend of Brahms, a man of great character, who is coming to see me tomorrow at 11 o'clock so that we can go together to B. with my things.'[74] Brahms was not an 'upstart' like Strauss; he was one of the greatest living composers and had a major influence on European music. Born in Hamburg, he had settled in Vienna as a young man to further his musical career. In the early years he moved frequently, but by 1872 he had settled in a small furnished apartment at 4 Karlsgasse, where he remained until his death.[75] It was here that Nielsen visited him.

The meeting with Brahms was a success. Nielsen wrote: 'So now I've seen this man whom I've admired for so many years and still admire so highly.'[76] He immediately made a note in his diary to remember the visit in detail, and the event is repeated in a letter to Anne Marie. Nielsen could hardly wait to tell his wife in person.

The visit took place on 7 November, when Dr Schiff accompanied Nielsen to the apartment. The girl opened the door, and they entered a corridor leading to several rooms. Schiff knocked on one of the doors, but as there was no answer, they opened the door themselves. They entered Brahms's bedroom, which was sparsely furnished with a mahogany bed, a wardrobe and a chair. There was a printed portrait of Bach on the wall. Schiff knocked on the next door and a loud voice answered 'enter'. Nielsen remained in the bedroom until Schiff's introduction to Brahms was over. Then, with his heart pounding, he entered the living room of the famous composer.

> Now he and Schiff began to talk about everything under the sun, without paying the slightest attention to me, which was fine by me, because I could then look at him in peace and quiet and get a proper impression of him, which one can't do so easily when one is preoccupied with what one should be saying. Brahms is a man of medium stature, very stocky, well-built and thick-set. He stands firmly and solidly on his feet and gives the impression of having a really good constitution. He is very short in the neck and slightly stooping, and if you look at him from behind, his head sits down between the shoulders, and his back isn't free from round-shoulderedness. The expression on his face varies as he talks, and sometimes his eyes have a sarcastic, almost evil look, which soon changes back to something infinitely warm and good.[77]

After a while, Brahms suddenly turned to Nielsen and asked him how Thorvaldsen's Museum was getting on. Brahms was referring to his visit to Copenhagen in 1868, when he had attended a party at Gade's. Danish relations with Prussia were still estranged after the defeat of 1864, which had resulted in the loss of the duchies of Schleswig and Holstein. It did not go down well when Brahms began to praise Bismarck and the German victories at the party. There are several interpretations of the conversation, but one is that Gade's mother-in-law reached for her glass and

ILL. 4. Brahms in his apartment at 4 Karlsgasse, Vienna, where Nielsen visited him in November 1894.

exclaimed, 'I drink to Bismarck's death', to which Brahms replied, 'we can talk about that when Thorvaldsen's Museum is in Berlin'. The episode quickly reached the Copenhagen newspapers, which wrote of Brahms's 'tasteless impertinence'.[78]

The story shaped the perception of Brahms in Denmark for many years to come, and Brahms must also have assumed that Nielsen had heard it. Some may have been offended that he had brought up the embarrassing story again, but Nielsen had simply replied that the museum was still there.[79]

The conversation between the three of them gradually became more and more animated, and eventually Brahms had asked Nielsen if he could keep his works for a few days. He had to go to Frankfurt but wanted to discuss the music with him on his return to Vienna. Nielsen was naturally delighted and, as he wrote to Anne Marie, it was also a good enough reason to stay a little longer in the city: 'You can understand that I cannot leave here until I've seen him again.'[80]

Unfortunately, a new meeting could not be arranged. After eight days Nielsen had to leave, even though Brahms had still not returned to Vienna. It must have been a great disappointment, but he had not completely given up hope of getting an assessment of his music from Brahms. A month later, when he was back in Copenhagen, he wrote a draft of a letter to Brahms, reminding him of their meeting and gently asking for his opinion of the works he had left in the apartment in Vienna. It must have been an overwhelming experience to have to send such a letter. He had the letter posted on Christmas Day, but there is no record of a reply from Brahms.[81]

On the other hand, Brahms remembered Nielsen's symphony when he was interviewed a year later by the Danish music critic William Behrend. Brahms had asked about young composers in Denmark and Behrend had mentioned some names. At first Brahms did not recognise them, but then he suddenly remembered something: 'Well, that's true. I know of a new Danish symphony that was good – by a … a Hansen … in G minor.' Behrend, of course, knew who had recently composed a symphony in G minor and corrected him: 'Oh, the doctor seems to mean – Nielsen, Carl Nielsen.' To which Brahms replied: 'Yes, I suppose it could be – Nielsen? Well, perhaps! It was good. But the title page was strange. I don't forget that easily!'[82]

Before leaving Vienna, Nielsen had time to see Wagner's *Tristan und Isolde* at the Court Opera. Nielsen found the performance itself excellent, but his opinion of Wagner was not as positive as it had been a few years earlier in Dresden:

> The Prelude is first-rate, and the entire first half of the second act until where the King enters and surprises the lovers is, I have to confess, written by a great master and is one of the most beautiful lyrical outpourings in music. But as a whole I'm still as far as ever from being a Wagner enthusiast; there's such mass of poor taste and empty effect in this, as in almost all his operas – perhaps with the exception of *Meistersinger* – that I can't do otherwise than take offence at it.[83]

Nielsen's notes from the two journeys show that between 1890 and 1894 there was a marked change in his musical ideals, particularly in his views of Wagner. This change also affected his views of his own music. Around the time of his journey in 1890–91, he was working on his first book of settings of texts by Jens Peter Jacobsen. When the songs were to be published in 1892, however, Nielsen withdrew the art song *I Drømmenes Land* (*In the Realm of Dreams*). He wrote to Behrend in 1895:

> In one of my compositions (a great poem by J. P. Jacobsen) I was able to trace Wagner's spirit; but when I realised it, I asked my publisher – who had bought it and had it engraved – not to publish it, and now the proof is in my drawer.[84]

Exactly what caused him to change his mind about Wagner in the early 1890s is hard to say. Apparently it had something to do with the fact that the idea that the new belonged to the generation after Wagner and Brahms had taken hold. For Nielsen, Wagner no longer represented progress, and he was henceforth highly critical of composers who wrote in the Wagnerian style: 'especially his copycats', as he called them, he had little use for.[85] He did not want to be associated with them. On the other hand, his fascination with Wagner would flare up again. In 1912, when he wanted to conduct *Tristan* as Kapellmeister at The Royal Theatre, he wrote to the theatre director about 'Wagner's most marvellous work alongside *Die Meistersinger*, namely *Tristan und Isolde*, where the most concentrated emotional life of Romanticism has found its most beautiful expression. … For any musician it has to be Wagner's finest and most remarkable work, which one constantly comes back to.'[86]

Similarly, his visit to Brahms did not mean that he had become a Brahms disciple. Rather, the visit reflected the enormous respect in which Brahms was held and the importance of having his recommendation if one wanted to be recognised in Vienna. The timing of the visit coincides with a shift in the perception towards the evaluation of new directions in music history in those years. By 1894, the sense of something new that Nielsen had encountered on his 1890–91 journey had become palpable. It was the beginning of what we now call turn-of-the-century modernism.

The German and Austrian musical centres thus became places where Nielsen could gain an impression of the state of European music and work purposefully to promote his own music. But the journey of 1890–91 also had another purpose, one that was to have at least as great an impact on his future as his encounter with German musical life. We left Nielsen on the platform of a station in Berlin in 1891: he was about to board the train to Paris – a stay that was to change his life.

Chapter 13

MEETING *FIN-DE-SIÈCLE* PARIS

When Nielsen arrived in Paris by night train on 26 February 1891, he must have had a clear idea of the city he was about to visit. As well as being an important artistic centre in Europe, Paris was also known at the time as a city of entertainment – a place to have fun and experience modern city life. Much of the city's international reputation was built on the World Expositions, which had been held regularly in Paris since the mid-nineteenth century.[1] The most recent had been held in 1889 – the centenary of the French Revolution – and saw the opening of famous attractions such as the Eiffel Tower and the Moulin Rouge. During the exhibition, a number of Danish-language guides to Paris were published, and Danish newspaper correspondents regularly reported back home about the many spectacular attractions to see in the city – from oriental processions and electric beams of light from the top of the Eiffel Tower to famous and royal guests from all over the world.[2]

It is typical of many accounts of Paris at the time that not only selected sites were highlighted as worth seeing, but also the city itself and its inhabitants. Writing in an American art magazine in 1893, the author notes that Paris's position as the centre of artistic life can hardly be attributed to any real French superiority in the arts. Rather, its pre-eminence was due to the decorative tastes of the French people, which found expression in everything Parisian: in its architecture and its lighted avenues, as well as in the city's gastronomic perfection or the coquettish grace with which the simplest shopgirl sways her skirt.[3] Not only was the city the host of the World Expositions, it had become an exposition in itself: Paris was a place to experience.[4]

It was certainly this vision of the city that attracted many Scandinavian artists and writers in the last decades of the nineteenth century. The prospect of studying with the French masters and viewing both ancient and modern art in the city's many exhibitions was, of course, an important motivation for the visiting artists, just as many writers were interested in the new French literature. But they were also undoubtedly attracted by the lifestyle and atmosphere of the modern French metropolis itself, as Jens Ferdinand Willumsen's memoirs of his first encounter with the city in the autumn of 1888 attests:

> I was fascinated by Paris, which at that time was much more developed than Copenhagen. I loved everything I saw and encountered, the beautiful houses and

the strange life of the streets and cafés. One curious thing I remember is the strange, soft sound late at night, when people and horse-drawn carriages passed over the wooden pavement, unfamiliar to me. I still remember this sound. It was so different from back home where the carriages rumbled loudly and noisily over the badly paved streets. I went straight to the Louvre and the old art, but I was not as fascinated as I should have been. None of these masters reproduced life, the rich, vibrant life I was looking for. The people these artists had painted neither looked nor acted like living people. Nor did the colours correspond to those I saw around me. They were dark and unnatural, the very thing I had come to work away from.[5]

Prior to his trip, Willumsen had seen an exhibition of recent French art in Copenhagen, and his main reason for visiting to Paris was most likely a desire to study art.[6] In the end, however, the sights and sounds of the modern metropolis were far more inspiring to Willumsen than the art museums. Nielsen's diary contains similar examples of how city life itself fascinated him in Paris. On 2 March 1891, for example, he writes: 'Got up at 10, went shopping and looked at the beautiful boutiques, which you never get tired of because everything is stylish. Saw two cabs smash each other to pieces. Went to the Les Grands Magasins du Louvre to look at the magnificent display of life on the first day of the spring season.'[7]

It is not clear what Nielsen's more formal purpose was in staying in Paris as part of his study tour of Europe. It is noteworthy, however, that according to his itinerary for Det Anckerske Legat – the travel grant he had been awarded – Paris was the city in which he intended to spend the most time, despite the fact that he had not stated a specific study-related purpose for his stay.[8] However, as he ended up staying almost six months in Germany instead of the three to four months he had planned, the money was not enough for three months in Paris, which he regretted after spending a few days in the city.[9] He managed to spend just over a month and a half in the French capital.

The Scandinavian Colony

Nielsen was accompanied from Berlin to Paris by his friend Emil Sachs. During his stay, Nielsen had a room at the Hotel des Beaux Arts, near the Seine in the Saint-Germain-des-Prés district of the sixth arrondissement.[10] The diaries give the impression that he explored much of the city on foot, in the company of Sachs and other Scandinavian travellers he met during his stay. On his first day in Paris, he wrote:

> Arrived in Paris at 6.45 p.m. after a delightful journey through Germany, Belgium and France. Saw the cathedral at Cologne this morning. Magnificent! Dined with Emil at the 'Hotel de Molte' in Rue de Ruhdin. Walked up and down the boulevards and immediately got a vivid impression of life here. On Place Vendôme where thousands of torches almost threw one off balance. Rue de Rivoli, magnificent! At the Café de la Régence, where we met Hans Nicolai Hansen and the Norwegian [Axel] Maurer. In bed at 12 a.m. Vive Paris![11]

The Café de la Régence was primarily a café and chess club, but it was also a meeting place for Scandinavians in Paris. It was located in the centre of the city, diagonally opposite the Théâtre-Français and close to the Louvre and the Tuileries. In his book about Paris in the 1890s, Henrik Cavling devotes an entire chapter to the café, writing:

> Place du Théâtre-Français is the Scandinavian centre of Paris, and the Café de la Régence is the first place the newly arrived Northerner sets foot. At the tables in front of the café, he finds himself among a crowd of gentlemen and ladies reading Scandinavian magazines, and through the buzz of conversation he hears his own language. Then he enters his name in the Scandinavian address book and, if he has been in the café for some time, he is tacitly admitted to the permanent but ever-changing colony.[12]

Willumsen's memoirs describe the café as a meeting place for Scandinavians, and he says that he and Peder Severin Krøyer went there one evening in February 1889.[13] It was also at the Café de la Régence in early 1889 that Krøyer met the painter Marie Triepcke, to whom he became engaged a few months later.[14] Both Cavling and Willumsen recount an urban legend that was told in the café at the time, that in 1793 chess was played with such passion that even when Marie Antoinette was led past the windows of the café on her way to the scaffold, the guests did not leave their seats.[15]

It was thus not a new idea when Nielsen and Sachs decided to spend their first evening in Paris at the Café de la Régence. The diary reveals that it was there that they met the Danish painter and draughtsman Hans Nikolaj Hansen, who was to become one of the people with whom Nielsen spent most of his time in Paris. The next day they met again at the café, where 'Hans N. Hansen gave an interesting talk on modern French painting and the turmoil therein at the moment'.[16] The following day Nielsen wrote to his friend Holger Møller that he had been to the Louvre 'and had an excellent guide in Hans Nicolai Hansen, who is here for the winter. Berlin and the Dresden galleries are not on a par [with the Louvre]'.[17] Unlike Willumsen, Nielsen was very enthusiastic about the museum and returned several times. He was particularly fascinated by the paintings of Leonardo da Vinci and the famous Greek sculpture *Venus de Milo*.[18] Together with Hansen, he also visited art exhibitions at the Musée du Luxembourg, the Pantheon and the École des Beaux-Arts.[19]

Hansen was twelve years older than Nielsen and must have known the city and French art well. He was part of a wave of young Danish painters who went to Paris in the late 1870s to study with the French artist Léon Bonnat. The wave of students had begun when Laurits Tuxen became Bonnat's pupil in 1875 and was later followed by Theodor Philipsen, P. S. Krøyer and Joakim Skovgaard. For these young painters, their stay in Paris was often motivated by the desire to further their education in a different direction from that of the Copenhagen Academy of Fine Arts, which still cultivated an idealised treatment of the motif.[20] In Paris it was possible to apply to the official French Academy of Fine Arts, the École des Beaux-Arts, but it was difficult to gain admission, both because of the requirements and the lack of professors.[21] In addition, the artistic ideals and educational model of the Academy were not far removed from those of Copenhagen, as were the many master studios in the city that functioned almost as branches of the Academy. As a result, many Danes opted for private, independent art schools.[22]

ILL. 1. Hans Nikolaj Hansen was a Danish painter, draughtsman and illustrator who was twelve years older than Nielsen.

Although there were several renowned private schools in Paris, Léon Bonnat was practically the only artist to accept Danish students in the years around 1880, and his school was therefore of great importance for the new orientation towards French art that took place in Danish painting in the 1880s.[23] With his artistic style, Bonnat occupied an intermediary position in relation to the tensions that had long existed in French art between the Academy as an institution and independent artists. These tensions became apparent when the Salon des Refusés was founded in 1863 as a protest by artists whose work had been rejected by the official Salon de Paris exhibition organised by the Academy. By the 1870s, the polarisation of French art had become even more pronounced with the breakthrough of Impressionism. Bonnat was not an Impressionist, but became an important representative of a naturalistic style in which he sought to capture the characteristics of the model rather than to produce a detailed rendering.[24] His combination of tradition and innovation made him more palatable to the Academy than many other independent artists of the time, and in 1878 he was elected as the non-academic artists' nominee to the Salon jury, becoming a professor at the Academy a few years later.[25]

Hansen had studied with Bonnat in 1878–79 and, after spending most of the 1880s in Copenhagen, he returned to Paris in 1890. According to a letter he wrote to Amalie Skram in January 1891, he found that his renewed stay had a positive effect on his art. He explained to her that in Paris he enjoyed rejecting contemplation and calculation and instead indulged in the ecstasy of simply reproducing in his own form and colour what was presented to him.[26] A series of thumbnail sketches of the Moulin Rouge and the Parisian cafés – in the style of the famous posters of the same period by Henri Toulouse-Lautrec, who had also studied with Léon Bonnat – date from this visit.[27] According to his letter to Skram, it was not only his art that was influenced by the atmosphere of the city – he also found himself personally changed during his stay:

> And next I'll tell you something about 'Now in Paris', as the blessed J. P. Jacobsen says:[28] yes, it's very pleasant to be here; one becomes young again – at least I think so – even in appearance. I'm like most people who are not naturally very talented (in outward appearance, of course), a little vain, and sometimes I look in the mirror and see myself. Like a slim, well-built gentleman, I can count my ribs, my hair no longer falls out, I take care of my moustache, I perfume myself with an extra-fine extract – just like ten years ago – and all in all I'm very well.[29]

This new confidence and attention to appearance was obviously visible to the outside world. Indeed, about a week and a half after meeting his new travelling companion, Nielsen writes about him:

> He is a good companion, and of a very amiable nature; but he is not deep in thought or feeling, and loves to talk of beautiful women, good food, and at dessert of poetry when ladies are present. His clothes fit him well, and his beard and hair are always in the best order.[30]

Nielsen also seems to have tried to adopt the elegant French style during his stay – he certainly bought a hat and a 'paletot' (a light overcoat) the day after he arrived, when he strolled the boulevards with Sachs, and he bought a nice dark blue tie with dots in the shop next to the Café de la Régence.[31] His diary gives the impression that, just as Hansen, he had a very pleasant time in Paris:

Saturday 7 March 1891
Lunch with Clement. Met Ballin at the Café de la Régence. He is a man of youthful enthusiasm for everything he finds great and beautiful. Went to the bodega together and drank wine. Later, all three of us ran in desperation to find a urinal. A funny scene with the old man who had forgotten to button his trousers.[32]

Sunday 8 March 1891
… Dinner at Bendix's, after which the whole party went to the Moulin Rouge, where we had a good time. Later, around the town till 4 a.m. with Ballin.[33]

Monday 9 March 1891
Slept with shame till 11.30 p.m. … In the evening to the Hungarian concert at the Oriental.[34]

The diary gives a sense of how the Scandinavian circle in the city socialised and with whom Nielsen spent time during his stay, in addition to Sachs and Hansen. Mogens Ballin and Gad Frederik Clement, both painters and slightly younger than Nielsen, had gone to Paris together on a study trip in 1891. In Copenhagen in the early 1890s they became part of the symbolist movement, together with the author Johannes Jørgensen and others. In 1893–94 Ballin designed the covers and vignettes for Jørgensen's important journal *Taarnet*, for which he also wrote several articles.[35]

Frits Bendix was a cellist and brother of the composer Victor Bendix, with whom Nielsen had recently spent some time in Germany. Frits Bendix and Nielsen were colleagues in The Royal Orchestra, so they already knew each other. Bendix was virtually the only musician Nielsen spent time with in Paris, although at the Scandinavian Society he met the pianist Johanne Stockmarr, whom he knew from his time at the Academy, and the Norwegian violinist Arve Arvesen.[36] Nielsen wrote of this evening at the Society that after dinner there was

> music by the Norwegian Arvesen (violin) who played an awful composition by Ole Bull and some other things that were completely unmusical. I played my piano pieces, which were a success. Then there was dancing, and I had a very good time until 12 o'clock, when Sachs and I accompanied Miss Dohlmann home in the most beautiful weather …[37]

It was one of the earliest performances of Nielsen's *Five Piano Pieces*, Op. 3, that were completed a few months earlier in Berlin.[38] There Nielsen had written in a letter to Sachs that 'all musicians find the pieces highly original and "märchenhaft" [fairy-tale-like], and a young gifted Finnish composer, Järnefelt, said one day that the Arabesque was something completely new in music'.[39] Nielsen must have felt confident that the pieces would be well received in the Scandinavian Association in Paris.

Nielsen's experiences testify to the strong social cohesion of the Scandinavian artists' community in Paris at the time. A Danish visitor would certainly have met Scandinavian artists at the Café de la Régence or the Scandinavian Association, as well as at other private events, and explored the cultural life of the city. The community must also have been characterised by the meeting of artists interested in modern European trends. In many ways, the Scandinavian artists' milieu in Paris can be seen as an extension of that in Copenhagen, a network that continued to have an impact when the artists returned home. Thus it becomes clear that Copenhagen's turn-of-the-century culture was an integral part of a modern European cultural movement.

Musical Life in Paris

Although music was not Nielsen's main focus in Paris, as it had been in Germany, he nevertheless had many musical experiences in the city, both in and out of the concert halls. In a speech at an official luncheon in Paris in 1926, for example, Nielsen recalled a concert given in honour of the recently deceased composer César Franck at the Société Historique on 11 March 1891. He also attended an event on 1 March 1891 at the Société des Nouveux Concerts, a society founded in 1881.[40] It was also known as the Concerts-Lamoureux, after the founder and conductor of the society, Charles Lamoureux. He was a great admirer of Wagner and was particularly well known for his central role in promoting Wagner in France. In his concerts, he often performed entire acts from Wagner's operas, which demanded a great deal of the audience's imagination and patience, as there was no staging.[41] The concert Nielsen attended included Wagner's Overture to *Die Meistersinger* and works by Goldmark, Schumann and Saint-Saëns.[42] In his diary, Nielsen wrote of the experience: 'At the Lamoureux concert, which included Schumann's Symphony in E flat major and the Overture to *Die Meistersinger*. He plays excellently, but I miss the passion and power I'm used to from Bülow. The air is stale here.'[43]

Although he was less impressed by Lamoureux than by Hans von Bülow, whom he had recently heard in Berlin, his characterisation of the French conductor is in some ways consistent with other, more enthusiastic descriptions of the time. In an article published in *The Musical Times* (1896), the writer notes that Lamoureux is hardly a 'great' conductor in terms of sympathy, insight and inspiration, but that he rehearses with the orchestra so often and with such discipline that he achieves a musical performance that is close to perfection.[44] For French poets such as Paul Valéry and Stephane Mallarmé, the concerts had almost cult status, revered as a

ILL. 2. Charles Lamoureux founded his famous concerts in Paris in 1881, which he led until 1897.[45]

sacred ritual with Lamoureux as the supreme authority proclaiming the divine laws of music.[46] This consensus of the time, that something almost otherworldly was going on at Lamoureux's concerts, is confirmed by Willumsen's memoirs of the winter of 1888–89:

> I spent what little money I had left on concert tickets. … I attended Charles Lamoureux's famous concerts, and at the Cirque d'Été on the Champs-Élysées, where I often took a gallery ticket for one franc, I heard both Wagner and Beethoven for the first time. Beethoven's Ninth Symphony had an otherworldly effect on me. After the concert, when we left the gallery, or 'Le Paradis' as it was called, we would usually line up at the main entrance to see the fashionable people (tout Paris) in the boxes and on the floor leaving the building. Among those I particularly remember was the dancer Cléo de Mérode, with her beautiful narrow face framed by the peculiar coiffure of the Romantic period.[47]

Willumsen's description of the fashionable guests indicates the particular social characteristics associated with Cirque d'Été concerts at the time. They were hardly accidental, for Lamoureux was very conscious of the image of his concerts and was therefore strategic in the way he programmed and staged them. Similar to other major Parisian concert societies, he was concerned with ensuring reliable ticket sales in competition with the city's other concert venues. However, whereas his colleague Éduard Colonne attracted audiences by appealing to the general public – especially women and families – by offering a broad repertoire and by encouraging audience participation, Lamoureux's aim was to attract members of the Parisian elite who preferred to mingle with others of the same social class.[48] He therefore played only 'serious' works and demanded complete silence from his audience.[49] It was also customary not to play encores. In contrast to Colonne, Lamoureux's concerts were based on creating a sense of exclusivity.[50]

Many of Nielsen's musical experiences in Paris were of a more informal nature. During his stay, he also took advantage of some of the most modern and popular entertainments of the time: the Parisian café concerts and the dance halls of Montmartre. According to contemporary guidebooks, there were around two hundred venues in Paris where café concerts were held, making them easily accessible for an evening out. The cafés did not charge for the concerts, but made a profit on the sale of beer and wine – often the first drink of the evening was more expensive, compensating for the cost of the ticket.[51] One of the venues for café concerts in the city was the Café Rouge on Boulevard Saint-Michel, where Nielsen once drank beer with Sachs and Hansen.[52] In those years, the café hosted nightly concerts with a five-piece orchestra, attracting many students because of its proximity to the Sorbonne.[53] Nielsen also wrote twice in his diaries about attending a concert at the Café Oriental 'where some Hungarians played quite excellently'.[54]

Often, the orchestral music performed at the café concerts was interspersed with pieces sung by vocal soloists and various artistic elements – a way of organising entertainment that was also used in the popular dance halls of Montmartre. The Mou-

ILL. 3. Henri de Toulouse-Lautrec, *La Goulue* (1895). Today, the turn-of-the-century Moulin Rouge is often associated with a line of dancing girls performing the famous cancan, although this only became common from the 1920s.[55] By the 1890s, the cancan was associated with solo dancers, and the painter Toulouse-Lautrec helped promote the Moulin Rouge's biggest stars of the day with his famous posters of La Goulue (1891) and Jane Avril (1893).

lin Rouge had opened for the World Exposition in the autumn of 1889, so it had only been in existence for a year and a half when Nielsen arrived in Paris. Yet it had already become one of the city's most famous attractions, mentioned in guidebooks alongside the Louvre and the Eiffel Tower.[56] It had become a fierce competitor to the city's older dance halls, such as the Élysée-Montmartre. Nielsen's diary describes an evening in the dance halls of Montmartre:

MEETING *FIN-DE-SIÈCLE* PARIS 249

In the evening to the Laundress' Ball [at] the 'Elysees montmartre', where I danced with Miss Brodersen. Later at the 'Moulin Rouge'. Then the 'cancan' danced by a famous (infamous) girl and some men, and the so-called belly dance. Got home at 2.30 in the morning.[57]

Nielsen's musical experiences in Paris were varied, but each reflected aspects of the city's modernity in the 1890s: from the exclusive Lamoureux concerts on the Champs-Élysées, to the popular café concerts in the Latin Quarter and the erotic performances in the dance halls of Montmartre.

A Crucial Encounter

The most significant event for Nielsen in Paris was undoubtedly meeting his future wife, the sculptor Anne Marie Brodersen. She was a few years older than Carl, and when they met she was on her second extended stay in Paris. Italy was usually the preferred destination for sculptors at the time, but as Anne Marie was also part of the wider artistic circles in Copenhagen, Paris must have seemed an important city to experience and study in.[58] She must also have known that the opportunities for female artists to study in Paris were better than in Copenhagen at the time. She discovered this in 1882 when the sculptor Vilhelm Bissen turned her down on the grounds that he did not accept female students.[59] Instead, from October 1882, she took lessons from the sculptor August Saabye. This was supplemented by studying with Agnes Lunn, who also became a friend and with whom Anne Marie went on her first study trip to Paris in 1889.[60]

Lunn had already studied several times in Paris, including in the studio of Léon Bonnat and with the painter and sculptor Jean-Léon Gérôme.[61] Like Anne Marie Brodersen, Lunn had grown up with farm animals and was fascinated by depicting their movements, especially those of horses.[62] Travelling together, they interrupted their journey to study art in the Netherlands and Belgium, and when they arrived in Paris they were particularly interested in the older art in the Louvre and the work of Auguste Rodin.[63]

In 1890 Anne Marie Brodersen received a grant and had the opportunity to travel again.[64] This time she went with the painter Augusta Dohlmann, who had previously studied at L'Académie Julien in Paris and had been one of the driving forces behind the founding of the Art School for Women in Copenhagen in 1888.[65] Before she left, Anne Marie Brodersen wrote a letter to Harald Slott-Møller about her plans for the trip:

> First to Paris to attend the studios and museums, then to Italy. You said that Italy is cold and uncomfortable in the winter months and that Paris would be a better place

to work. If possible, I'll draw in the same studio as Mrs Ancher and Mrs Krøyer – where Raphaelli and, if I'm not very much mistaken, Rodin did their corrections … Then perhaps I'll do a bust or something else in the way of a portrait. If a perfectly good group of travellers to Italy should turn up, I might change my mind.[66]

As well as arranging to travel with a colleague who had good connections in Paris, Anne Marie Brodersen also took note of where other prominent women artists went and used them as a guide. She may be referring in her letter to the studio of the French painter Pierre Puvis de Chavannes, a friend of Rodin's who had taught both Anna Ancher and Marie Krøyer in the spring of 1889. Puvis de Chavannes played a prominent role in Symbolism at this time and became a model for many of the Danish artists who were in Paris in the spring of 1890, including Johan Rohde and Willumsen.[67] Hans Nikolaj Hansen also sought inspiration in Chavannes's studio during his stay in Paris in 1890–91, although the two were stylistically very different. In the letter to Skram mentioned above, he wrote:

> Here I am in the middle of the morning – painting in Puvis de Chavannes's studio. He comes once a week, is very kind and at first praised me a lot. Now we talk more sensibly, and I find him very pleasant. He is old, but young in his art. His last paintings in Luxembourg shine above all the others. Although they are strictly decorative and calculated, they outshine all other realistic art, just as electric light above gas candelabras. He thinks I'm an Impressionist. He asked me if I knew Renouard [Renoir] (I did not), said I resembled him in drawing as in painting; and then, which was a very great compliment, he criticised my work and tore it to pieces.[68]

It is difficult to know whether Anne Marie Brodersen came into contact with Puvis de Chavannes's studio during her stay. According to her memoirs, during her stay in Paris, she visited Rodin, who, to her great surprise, remembered her two figures of calves that had been exhibited at the Nordic Industrial, Agricultural, and Art Exhibition in Copenhagen in 1888 and at the World Exposition in Paris the following year.[69] She also spent some time with Willumsen, whom she apparently met for the first time during her stay.[70] The two must have known of each other before, however, as they were both associated with the group of artists who, according to art historian Emil Hannover's memoirs, called themselves the 'clique'. In addition to Hannover, the 'clique' included Johan Rohde, Rasmus Christensen, Agnes and Harald Slott-Møller and Sofie Holten.[71] It was within this circle of artists that Den Frie Udstilling (The Free Exhibition) in Copenhagen was founded in 1891, modelled on the Salon des Refusés and as an alternative to the Charlottenborg Exhibition.

In the year before the founding, Anne Marie Brodersen and Willumsen had each been involved in different ways in the preparations. Anne Marie Brodersen had met Agnes and Harald Slott-Møller at an artists' party in the winter of 1889–90. The three decided to spend the early summer of 1890 together in Sønder Stenderup, near Kolding. Anne Marie Brodersen put them up at her parents' farm.[72] It was there that Harald Slott-Møller painted a portrait of Anne Marie Brodersen, which was exhibited at The Free Exhibition the following year. It was also at her parents' home that the planning for the exhibition got underway. During the 1880s there had been various attempts to create an artistic alternative to the Charlottenborg Exhibition, but it was not until the summer of 1890 that the Slott-Møllers, together with Rohde, gave impetus to the establishment of a new artistic forum. Harald Slott-Møller describes the process in his memoirs:

> Johan Rohde was living in Ribe that summer, and as the discussions about an exhibition independent of Charlottenborg continued, we asked him to come to us in Stenderup, as the correspondence on the subject was becoming too extensive. And it was there that the seeds of the 'Free Exhibition' conspiracy were sown.[73]

They subsequently approached several other Danish artists about the project and received support from the Skovgaard brothers, Marie and Peder Severin Krøyer, and Willumsen, who later emphasised the importance of the event in his memoirs:

> It was a break with the conservatism in Danish art, with the darkest narrow-mindedness, which can be compared with the unrest and moods that prevailed in all parts of Europe and which were reflected in Scandinavian art life in Edvard Munch's Norwegian meeting and the formation of the 'Svenska Konstnärsförbundet'.[74]

The Free Exhibition opened on 26 March 1891 and was an immediate success, attracting large crowds and media coverage. As might be expected, the exhibition met with resistance from some of the art critics of the time, and Willumsen's etching *Frugtbarhed* (*Fertility*) in particular was the subject of disparaging comments, to which Emil Hannover subsequently responded.[75] Anne Marie Brodersen did not exhibit the first year; however, she became a member the following year and continued to exhibit at The Free Exhibition for the rest of her life.[76]

Anne Marie Brodersen and Willumsen were thus part of a modern artistic breakthrough when they met in Paris in the winter of 1890–91. The meeting is mentioned in both their memoirs. Anne Marie Brodersen describes how the two sculptors experimented with ceramics in her stove: 'We stuck a pipe out of the window and lit a good fire. The landlady came in and was very astonished and horrified, so we had to stop for a while, but we had made some amusing firings.'[77] Willumsen recalls another episode from their collaboration, which shows that both artists had terrible tempers. He had agreed to sit for her for a bust, but the work was difficult and progress slow. Willumsen tried in vain to persuade Anne Marie Brodersen to abandon the project, and one day when Nielsen visited her studio while she was working, Willumsen lost his patience:

> Maybe I was in a bad mood and at the same time I thought enough is enough. I had no time to sit there any longer. In short, I scolded. Miss Brodersen cried, and the little musical shrimp of a man, who looked like a newly confirmed youngster, exclaimed: 'Woe to thy wrath, Thor, let not the source of thunderbolts thunder.' Shortly afterwards I left the studio and Miss Brodersen smashed her bust on the floor. I must add, however, that several years later, and until the death of Carl and Anne Marie, the three of us were united in a warm friendship.[78]

According to Willumsen, the incident took place a day or two after Carl and Anne Marie had met at a dinner at Frits Bendix's, which Willumsen also attended. The dinner took place on 2 March 1891 and is described in Nielsen's diary, where he remarks that 'Miss Brodersen is actually very pretty'.[79]

In the following days, Nielsen and Anne Marie met several times in the company of others from the Scandinavian circle, and nearly two weeks later the diary reads: 'Slept well: but awoke with a strange indeterminate feeling in the morning. Marie Brodersen!'[80] The following day he writes: 'In the evening I found the one for whom I've had a whole range of feelings all the time, and we shall live our lives together, be happy, and nothing shall cause me to doubt anymore.'[81]

From then on, Nielsen's diary entries became more sporadic. He was too preoccupied with his new love to continue his diary. However, it seems that he spent the following period with Anne Marie Brodersen at the Eiffel Tower, the Arc de Triomphe and the theatre.[82] They also visited the museum of medieval art, the Musée de Cluny, which made a great impression on the couple.[83] Brodersen later used the motif of one of the Cluny tapestries when she designed the title page of Nielsen's *Music for Five Poems by J. P. Jacobsen*.[84]

On the day of his visit to Cluny, 31 March 1891, Nielsen wrote in his diary: 'At the mayor's with Dr Tscherning; can't get married before the 16th!'[85] Only four weeks after their first meeting, they were already planning their wedding. Nielsen had joined forces with Danish ophthalmologist Marius Tscherning to organise it. Tscherning had grown up on Fyn but had been a researcher at the Sorbonne since 1882 and also ran a large eye clinic in Paris. He had good contacts and knew the system in

ILL. 4. A tapestry from the series *The Lady with the Unicorn* (*c*. 1480) in the Musée de Cluny in Paris was the source of inspiration for Anne Marie Carl-Nielsen's title page for her husband's *Music for Five Poems by J. P. Jacobsen* (1892). Five of the six tapestries in the series are commonly interpreted as allegories of the five senses. The motif used by Anne Marie is interpreted in this context as a representation of 'taste'. On the title page, 'Irmelin Rose' is written in the lady's veil, and the collection of art songs is dedicated to Anne Marie.

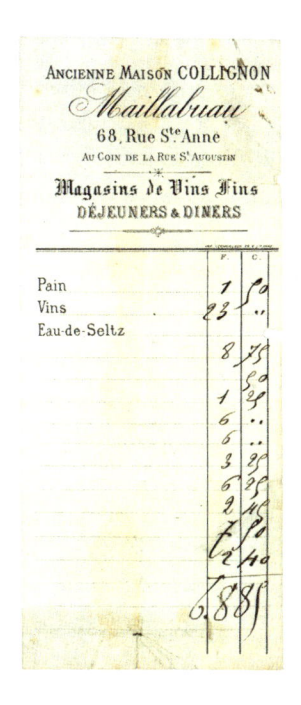

ILL. 5. Anne Marie and Carl's wedding party took place in a restaurant at 68 Rue Sainte-Anne; Nielsen kept the receipt in his wallet. The total bill for dining with seven people was just over 68 francs, today about 2,400 Kroner. About a third was spent on wine, which may explain Nielsen's remark in his diary: 'Very funny. – Followed two ladies who approached a policeman to our great amusement. Had I drunk a bit too much?'[86]

the city, so he was a good companion when they had to visit 'le maire', the mayor.[87] Tscherning's apartment was in the same arrondissement as Nielsen's hotel, just a few hundred metres from the town hall. However, it seems that Nielsen and Brodersen did not have the patience to wait in Paris for the necessary papers to be drawn up, as they were on their way to Italy. Instead, they decided to hold a private wedding ceremony on 10 April, which they considered to be their wedding day.

The wedding was held in a restaurant in Rue Sainte-Anne. The invited guests were Marius and Arnak Tscherning, Frits and Anna Bendix, and Hans Nikolaj Hansen.[88] Less than a month later, Nielsen wrote to Victor Bendix to explain the reasons for their hasty marriage: 'The fact is simply that when two people like each other to the extent that they can't do without one another's company, why should they sit and wait? Apart from this there's the fact that we were both due to travel to Italy, and that could only happen, if we wanted to show consideration for our families, as a married couple.'[89] Apparently, Anne Marie was the only one to tell her family in advance. She sent a letter and a telegram about the wedding plans, and her father, rather surprised, replied with a long letter. He welcomed the new, unknown son-in-law and hoped that they would come home and celebrate the wedding there.[90]

The day after the wedding they visited the exhibition Salon des Indépendants, where they saw paintings by Willumsen and Vincent van Gogh, among others, and in the evening they were received at the Tschernings to the strains of Felix Mendelssohn's Wedding March from *A Midsummer Night's Dream*.[91] They must have kept in touch with Tscherning afterwards – he was one of the godparents at the christening of their first child, Irmelin, who was born in Copenhagen eight months later.[92]

Two days after the wedding, they left Paris for Italy, where they were officially married in St Mark's English Church in Florence on 10 May.[93] They spent two months in Italy before returning to Denmark in mid-June.

Chapter 14

ANNE MARIE

Anne Marie Brodersen was born in the Duchy of Schleswig. She grew up on a large farm in a wealthy family, which gave her a good foundation of self-confidence and firmly rooted moral concepts. At the age of nineteen she moved to Copenhagen to train as a sculptor and succeeded in gaining both national and international recognition at a time when it was difficult for women to pursue a career on an equal footing with men. Throughout her life, travelling abroad was an important part of her work as an artist. When she met Carl Nielsen in Paris in 1891, she was more established as an artist than he was.

From then on, Anne Marie was one of the poles in a tense relationship between two equal artists. This relationship had a decisive influence on the marriage and on the profound crisis – and later reconciliation – that the couple went through. It is important to know Anne Marie's background and her relationship with art in order to understand her influence on Carl Nielsen and the nature of their relationship.

Family Background and Upbringing

Anne Marie was born on 21 June 1863 on the farm Thygesminde near Sønder Stenderup on the south side of Kolding Fjord, an area that had been part of Schleswig since the Middle Ages. Her father, Paul Julius Brodersen, had moved there as a young man and bought the large farm in 1853.[1] He had grown up in the marshes south of Højer on the west coast of Jutland, where his father had been the Royal Dyke Inspector in the area of Old Frederikskog, also known by its German name as Friedrichskoog.[2] The word 'kog' means reclaimed marshland, and the dyke inspector's farm was in the middle of the marshland. Old Frederikskog was reclaimed in 1692. In 1861 the rest of the area at Højer sluice was reclaimed and became New Frederikskog.[3] The new land, which was created by building dykes to protect the land from the North Sea, was an 'oktrojeret kog', that is, chartered reclaimed marshland. It belonged to the Kingdom of Denmark and not to the Duke of Schleswig. Paul Julius's father, Hans Hinrich Brodersen, was a royal official and therefore conducted the census of 1835, according to which six families lived in Frederikskog, including himself, his wife Anna Maria, six children and five servants.[4]

ILL. 1. Thygesminde estate was Anne Marie's childhood home on the south side of Kolding Fjord. Here the family is gathered on the steps leading to the garden. At the top are her parents and at the bottom are Anne Marie, her sister Julie and her brother Paul.

Anne Marie's paternal family was predominantly German-speaking, and Paul Julius continued to write letters in German to his daughter after she moved to Copenhagen.[5] She thus grew up in a bilingual home where German and Danish were spoken, which was a resource for her in later life. However, there is no evidence that her father was pro-German in the sense that he wanted a German or Schleswig-Holstein government. It may well have been the opposite, for as the son of a royal civil servant rather than a Schleswig official, he was likely to have believed in the United Monarchy and therefore to have been loyal to the king.

Paul Julius Brodersen was born in 1827 and not much is known of his early life except that the family lived in the marshes. His mother died in 1837 and his father did not remarry until 1845, dying almost three years later in 1848. The family left the farm, which was demolished a few years later. There were considerable assets in the estate and Paul Julius's inheritance, which included about eleven hectares of marshland, was valued at about 4,000 Rigsdaler. The land was sold in 1853 and he was able to buy the farm in Sønder Stenderup.[6] He must have been an enterprising and competent man, for

ILL. 2. Anne Marie's parents, Paul Julius and Frederiche, give the impression of respectable and traditional people with their fine, slightly old-fashioned clothing.

he was only in his mid-twenties when he established himself as a farmer and became a respected man in the area and was a member of the parish council for several years.[7]

The war of 1864, when Denmark had to cede the duchies of Schleswig and Holstein to Germany, brought great changes to the region. At the end of the war, when an armistice was signed, it was agreed that the border would be adjusted so that the so-called royal territories in Schleswig would be exchanged for other areas of land. It was already clear that, in addition to the region around Ribe and the island Ærø, which belonged to Schleswig, the area south of Kolding would be transferred to the Kingdom of Denmark; the only issue that remained was the exact demarcation of the border. A commission was set up and completed its report in the spring of 1865 – the result was that Sønder Stenderup became Danish territory.[8] Anne Marie was not yet two years old.

Anne Marie's mother, Frederiche Johanne Kirstine Gylling, came from the area between Ribe and Kolding. She grew up the daughter of a farmer and a midwife and was employed as a housekeeper at Thygesminde estate before marrying the owner in 1856.[9] Frederiche's father, Niels Friederichsen, came from Gylling in the Aarhus region and was a soldier in the Royal Guards in Copenhagen, where Frederiche's mother, Marthe Magdalene Wallstedt, trained as a midwife. They were married in

Copenhagen in 1822 and shortly afterwards moved to South Jutland, where Frederiche was born in 1825.[10] This part of the family was Danish-speaking.

Religion played an important role in Anne Marie's upbringing. Although she did not express any religious beliefs as an adult, growing up in a religious environment gave her some firmly rooted moral concepts, which she later defined as her sense of honour. A particular circumstance of her baptism reveals a connection with a devout evangelical congregation centred around the German pastor Johann Christoph Blumhardt in Bad Boll, Württemberg, in southern Germany. Unlike her siblings, who all had local godparents, they asked the pastor and his wife, as well as her uncle Theodor Brodersen, to be Anne Marie's godparents. However, at the christening they were not present, so local people stood in for them. Anne Marie's father must have been keen to ask the couple to act as godparents, for he travelled all the way to Bad Boll to visit his brother and the Blumhardts.[11] It is uncertain what prompted Paul Julius to seek this sponsorship. It is clear, however, that the connection was made through Paul Julius's brothers, Theodor (two years his junior) and Emil (nine years his junior), who both became part of the inner circle of the Bad Boll congregation. And perhaps it all began with a bad knee.

Johann Christoph Blumhardt was a well-educated theologian who represented an ecclesiastical movement that grew out of Pietism, with affinities to the Moravian Society. The substance of his message was a strong belief that the kingdom of God was imminent, that the Second Coming of Jesus was near. In addition, his experiences as a young pastor in the village of Möttlingen in the Black Forest in southern Germany had given him a strong conviction about the power of prayer. He had witnessed a small family of orphans being tormented, first by a poltergeist and then by what they understood to be a prolonged demonic possession of a young girl, Gottliebin Dittus. After almost two years of struggle, during which Blumhardt prayed for the girl's healing, the spirit disappeared just before New Year's Day 1843 with the cry 'Jesus is the Victor'. It was an intense event witnessed by the whole village.

The healing sparked a great revival, first in the region and then further afield, which meant that Blumhardt's small vicarage was almost besieged by visitors. As the situation became increasingly untenable over the years, the pastor raised funds to take over Bad Boll, an abandoned health resort with 129 rooms. In 1852 it became the home of his congregation, with accommodation for the many travelling guests.[12] After her recovery, Gottliebin Dittus became part of the Blumhardt family, and although she was the same age as the pastor's wife, she considered herself a daughter of the house. After moving to Bad Boll, which received more than seven hundred guests a year, she was in charge of the household and her very presence was living proof of the power of prayer.

With a bad knee, Theodor Brodersen arrived in Bad Boll on crutches in 1852. After a year he was well enough to be employed as a manager and gradually became

Blumhardt's assistant, also for correspondence and prayers. In 1855 he married Gottliebin and they had three children.[13] Later, his younger brother Emil also came to Bad Boll, where he married Blumhardt's daughter Maria in 1862, and they eventually took over the guesthouse, providing food and accommodation for the many visitors.[14]

We know that the Nielsen family sometimes talked about Pastor Blumhardt and had contact with the part of the family that lived in Bad Boll.[15] When Nielsen was looking for lodgings in Copenhagen in August 1892, he wrote to Anne Marie at Thygesminde that he had been reading the Bible and when he read about miracles, Blumhardt came to his mind.[16] Anne Marie's two siblings, Lucie and Poul, had spent a few weeks in Bad Boll a few months earlier.[17] Her family was thus associated with Pietist circles, and although her father did not give his children a strict religious upbringing, there is no doubt that Anne Marie was brought up in an environment of clear and strong moral standards. This was to have a profound effect on the way she dealt with the crises in her marriage.

Anne Marie's family also had contact with the Moravian community in the nearby village of Christiansfeld, where her father's youngest sister Marie had attended boarding school for five years.[18] Anne Marie's eldest brother, Hans Heinrich, was also a boarder at the Moravian school. It is unclear why he was enrolled at the school in Christiansfeld, which was then on the German side of the border. It may have been a desire for a German-speaking school and the broad and high-quality education it offered. Although Hans Heinrich was admitted in January 1871, he only attended for a few months, for at Easter that year he was killed by a collapsing wall at home on his parents' farm.[19] It was a great bereavement for the family and the loss of her brother affected Anne Marie deeply.

Poul, the younger of Anne Marie's elder brothers, did not attend the Moravian school, although he is the most obvious candidate to represent the religious vein of the surviving siblings. He later became a priest of the Catholic Apostolic Congregation in the town of Kolding. This was a denomination related to the Pietist movements and originated in the United Kingdom. When the denomination was founded, twelve 'apostles' were appointed to spread the word of the Gospel throughout the world; the congregation considered itself Catholic in the sense of 'general' or 'ordinary' because it had a strong ecumenical idea of uniting the whole of Christendom. However, it remained a small denomination.

Anne Marie and her younger sister Lucie were taught at home. Anne Marie remembers that the two sisters had a governess and that they at one point were schooled with the pastor's daughters in Sønder Stenderup.[20] In those days it was common for larger farms to have a tutor, perhaps even one shared by several farms. Anne Marie does not say more about the nature of the schooling, but it was part of the general compulsory education at the time.

Arts Education

Anne Marie's art training began in the autumn of 1880, when, at the age of seventeen, she attended a three-month course at Christian Carl Magnussen's woodcut school in the town of Schleswig. Magnussen was a well-trained painter from Bredstedt on the west coast of the Duchy of Schleswig and had studied privately with Herman Wilhelm Bissen in Copenhagen.[21] After long stays in Rome and Hamburg he moved to Schleswig, where he founded his school in 1875. He was interested in the techniques of the old masters and had a large study collection of North German woodwork, which took up space in the school's main building. Magnussen taught drawing, while assistants took care of the woodcarving. Anne Marie says that she learned mainly drawing and modelling.[22]

In Anne Marie's case, the training in woodcarving should not be taken too literally, although surrounded by the study collection and imbued with Magnussen's enthusiasm for it, she may have acquired a sense of the stylisation and simplification that characterise the old art. If Anne Marie had continued her training at the school, she might have become part of a Schleswig-Holstein or North German artistic milieu. A certain affinity with the slightly younger Ernst Barlach can be seen in some of her sculptures.[23] It is probable that the Schleswig starting point of her training may have influenced her in this direction.

It seems that Anne Marie's encounter with the art of woodcarving sparked her interest in playing with the various degrees of two- and three-dimensional forms known as reliefs. Many of her later works are indeed reliefs, and one of the commissions for which she received the most recognition was the painted copies of Greek reliefs she made during her stays in Athens in 1903–5. The rediscovery of the original colouring of Greek art preoccupied art historians throughout the world during these years, and Anne Marie supplied coloured copies to many of the major European museums.[24]

Finally, it should not be forgotten that there was a group of artists in Copenhagen, including Herman Wilhelm Bissen, who originally came from the province of Schleswig. The fact that Magnussen trained with Bissen may have played a role in Anne Marie's attempt to be accepted as a pupil by Bissen's son, Vilhelm. After her time at the Schleswig school, she wanted to continue her studies, but her father initially refused:

> I grieved and wanted to know more. But that was out of the question. ... I remember one Christmas I asked him if I could learn something that was real. No, my father said, he would not give his daughter or his money to something without knowing the outcome. And then my father slapped me and told me to stop nagging.[25]

ILL. 3. In the autumn of 1880, Anne Marie Brodersen was a student at Christian Carl Magnussen's woodcarving school in Schleswig. She is standing with another student in the school's studio, holding a modelling stick. The school taught in German.

Eventually she was allowed to travel to Copenhagen with some acquaintances from Kolding, the building inspector Winstrup and his wife. According to Anne Marie, Winstrup took her first to Bissen's studio, where she was rejected because he did not accept female students, and then to the sculptor August Saabye, who agreed to give her lessons.[26]

She therefore moved to Copenhagen in the autumn of 1882, where she enrolled at the Tegne- og Kunstindustriskolen for Kvinder (School of Drawing and Art Industry for Women) and became a private pupil of Saabye. She also paid for lessons with Agnes Lunn, thirteen years her senior, who was very important to Anne Marie, both as a role model as a female artist and as a support during her early years in Copenhagen. Together with Lunn, Anne Marie made her first visit to Paris in 1889, using the money she had received when she won the Neuhausen Prize in 1887. The task had been to draw a design for a fountain. She won the prize of 600 Kroner, one of her first official awards.[27]

Anne Marie seems to have continued to study privately with Saabye until 1888, when he was hired as a teacher at the newly established Kunstskole for Kvinder (Art School for Women). It was affiliated to The Academy of Fine Arts, where she was admitted with a free place from March 1889 to January 1890. She only stayed at the Academy for a year to prepare to compete with the graduating students for the Academy's gold medal. Although Anne Marie did not win the prize, she was awarded a travel grant and went to Paris in 1890–91. It was there that she met her future partner, Carl Nielsen.[28]

As well as the Neuhausen Prize, Anne Marie won recognition elsewhere. From 1884 to 1891 she exhibited every year at the prestigious Spring Exhibition of the Academy of Fine Arts at Charlottenborg in Copenhagen, where she had to pass a censorship. Also of great importance were two bronze calves that were chosen to represent Denmark at the 1889 World Exposition in Paris, where they won a bronze medal. The exhibition at Charlottenborg and the one in Paris brought her considerable public recognition. The two calves were also exhibited at the Nordic Industrial, Agricultural, and Art Exhibition in Copenhagen in 1888. This event also included an exhibition of French art, to which the brewer and patron of the arts Carl Jacobsen had invited the leading French painters to Copenhagen. On this occasion, Anne Marie took part in an excursion that included Auguste Rodin, whom she met again in Paris.[29]

Anne Marie's brother congratulated her on her birthday in 1886, saying that she was 'a favourite guest of several of Copenhagen's leading families'.[30] She was well established and making a name for herself as an artist before she met Carl in Paris in 1891. Anne Marie was thus well connected when they returned to Copenhagen to build a life together as an artistic couple.

Stormy Years

Anne Marie and Carl were not very young when they met in Paris. In March 1891, Carl was twenty-five and Anne Marie two years older. It seems that neither of them had made any serious plans to start a family before this time, although Nielsen, at least, had had serious crushes. He already had a child who grew up without close contact with his father.[31] Nevertheless, Anne Marie and Carl behaved like teenagers. They fell madly in love and were married in Paris on 10 April at a hastily arranged artists' wedding, although the documents were not in order. Exactly a month later, they married again in a legal ceremony in the English Church in Florence.[32] On their return to Copenhagen, they moved into their first apartment in Nyhavn, and nine months after they met, on 9 December 1891, their first daughter, Irmelin, was born.

What was it about Anne Marie that fascinated Carl? It is obvious that he was attracted to strong and independent women. But above all he must have been fascinated by Anne Marie as an artist and as a person who believed in herself and in her abilities as an artist. He had found an equal partner, and from that came the strength that kept them together in the long run, despite everything.

A dissertation, which also formed the background to the major retrospective exhibition of Anne Marie Carl-Nielsen's work at the Glyptotek in 2021, offers a new understanding of her position as an artist. She is presented not only as a role model for other female artists, who with 'strength, tenacity and skill … demonstrated a productivity and talent of international stature', but also as an artist who took a strategic approach to securing a career in a male-dominated environment.[33] The argument is that by consciously engaging with the contemporary notion that, as a woman, she was particularly connected to nature and animals, Anne Marie managed to create a position in which she could be accepted as an artist. She could then use this position to pursue her own goals of an international career.[34]

It was Anne Marie's work copying ancient Greek sculptures in Athens from 1903 to 1905 that gave her the international breakthrough she was looking for. In an environment dominated by male museum curators, she managed with incredible tenacity and perseverance to complete her coloured copies in the most impossible working conditions and to establish herself as the one who delivered them to the leading museums of Europe. She knew nothing of female modesty, nor did she let her ambition get the better of her, and her bilingual background made it easier for her to operate professionally in the German-speaking, international and professional environment. It should be emphasised that the very act of travelling was a prerequisite for achieving the career she wanted. And she did not return home until it was absolutely necessary, despite Carl's urging in 1905.[35] She did not want to give in – it would only have

ILL. 4. The image of Anne Marie when she was young shows her as a confident woman.

confirmed Bissen's sardonic remark when he rejected her as a student: 'It never works out with women anyway – they get married.'[36]

The tension between two great artists and their ambitions created at the same time the strong bonds that united them and the major conflicts that brought their relationship to the verge of crisis. The greatest and most profound crisis in their marriage occurred in 1914 and led to a separation that lasted several years, during which they did not live together. The separation was rooted in Nielsen's infidelity, but more importantly in his persistent dishonesty about it. The underlying layer of the conflict lay in his inability or unwillingness to recognise the significance of what Anne Marie experienced as an abysmal breach of trust.[37] Worst of all, it was a pattern that repeated itself. They had gone through a similar crisis in 1905 and Anne Marie had believed Carl's assurances that it would never happen again. The infidelity was bad enough. But what was worse was that she had fundamentally lost faith in him and could no longer trust him – and that was affecting her work.

With whom and when Nielsen was unfaithful will never be known in every detail, nor is it of any great importance. Even if all the sources were available, we would not know the lies and concealments. In terms of their relationship, it is Anne Marie's experience of betrayal that is crucial, and in this context the best source is what she herself writes in letters, diaries and notes not intended for others.

The crisis of 1914 was provoked when Anne Marie returned from a long stay in Germany to discover that Carl was having an affair with a pupil. Since October 1913, Anne Marie had been working intermittently in Celle on the horse that was the model for her largest and most prestigious commission: the equestrian statue of Christian IX. After a brief visit to Copenhagen in the spring of 1914, she became suspicious and wrote to Carl asking if he had been faithful to her during the winter. He swore that he had.[38] But it was a lie. She discovered the truth on her return from Celle on 6 June 1914. That day she wrote in her diary: 'Es wühlt ohne Hinterlassen in meinem Gebein [It gnaws constantly at my bones] … What I despised, what others endured, has been presented to me and has been presented to me for a long time.'[39]

This time it was Nielsen's relationship with his pupil Anine Koch that was revealed. She was married to the lawyer who advised Nielsen in his negotiations with The Royal Theatre. Anne Marie noted on 11 June: 'Talked to Carl in the evening / I can't rest, can't work, my strength is gone, betrayed and yet I can't free myself.'[40] Two days before her birthday on 21 June, she returned the ring Carl had given her for her birthday the previous year. On her actual birthday, Carl had gone to see Svend Godske-Nielsen and stayed there. A few days later she wrote in despair: 'Dear Carl / Now you're gone …' and ended the letter:

> I can't save myself from myself or run away from myself. Self-disgust is sitting beside me like a nightmare. I try to think of all the good times together with you, but it almost makes the pain stronger. I beg of you to burn this letter. Your Marie.[41]

In mid-July, Anne Marie went to Norway alone to sort out her thoughts. She explains her feelings in her notebook:

> Today is a year and a month since we were in Norway and Carl put the ring on my finger. Once again I hoped but now I'm back to square one, only I'm more destroyed and paralysed, physically my heart too; my desire to work and my strength have sunk together through the sleepless nights and self-torment.[42]

Then she returns to how it all began in 1905:

I can't work anymore. I can't smile. When I came home from Greece and Carl and I got through what had been, I was able to smile again as it seemed to be all behind me. Sadly, it was a deception, and that is what I have grieved and suffered about for the last year and a half, that … some of the most beautiful, softest and best moments of our life together was a lie. The relationship started before Carl met me in Greece in a warm and happy mood the first time I was there, I was deceived when I met him with my whole heart and he was not honest, which I believed so strongly at the time! Everything would have been over and done with. Now it has tormented and tortured me so much, and in my unhappiness I tried to evade myself in Harzen. One may be numbed by weariness, but one cannot run away from oneself, one's grief and one's shame.[43]

She explains that she had mourned for a year and a half, that what she thought they had left behind in 1905 had continued. In the spring of 1913 she discovered or learned something that made her realise that Carl had only told part of the truth eight years earlier.[44] She too had been away for a long time in 1905. Anne Marie had gone to Athens in January 1903 and Carl had joined her a month later; it had been an enriching trip for both of them. On 1 November of the following year, Anne Marie travelled to Greece again to complete her work on the copies of the sculptures.[45] Carl stayed in Copenhagen with Marie Møller, Anne Marie's close friend, who looked after the children, and Maren, who did the housework. But Nielsen had also begun an affair, which he kept secret from Anne Marie – and according to her account in 1914, it had begun before he visited her in Greece for the first time.

By March 1905 the situation was critical. There are a number of letters and telegrams between Copenhagen and Athens, some of which crossed paths, complicating the situation. Carl had resigned from The Royal Orchestra and was considering a new start abroad. He desperately needed someone to talk to and he needed Anne Marie.[46] She kept him waiting and tried to cheer him up by suggesting that he visit her in Greece, explaining that she would not be able to come home until May. She also relied on Marie Møller to keep the Nielsens' house in order.[47] Nielsen was beside himself with despair and anger. On 23 March he wrote to her that he could no longer stand it and that they had to start the divorce proceedings they had talked about.[48]

On the same day, Marie Møller wrote to Anne Marie that if she loved her husband, she had to put him, the children and the house before her work, for 'these things (especially the husband) are not worthy of second place and they will slip away from you'.[49] This letter in particular – which ends 'I'll always be your friend / M.M.' – has taken on added significance, for it reveals the depth of the betrayal Anne Marie is experiencing. Marie Møller was her best friend, to whom she had entrusted house and home, children and husband, in order to complete her work. Anne Marie was unwilling to sacrifice her career as an artist for the role of mother and wife. And she did not want a divorce. She sent a telegram home on 28 March, followed by a long letter, and left for Copenhagen in early April.[50]

In 1905 they survived the crisis and avoided divorce. Carl must have admitted at the time that he had been unfaithful, but not that it had lasted for several years. This lie seems to have been discovered in 1913. Now, when Anne Marie came home in June 1914 and discovered that he had lied to her once again, everything fell apart. Carl, for his part, seems to have had a crucial lack of self-awareness. Shortly before she left for Norway in mid-July 1914, he wrote to her from the estate Damgaard as if all was well again:

> My darling! Thanks for everything you still are for me and for us all. You must believe that things will be good for the two of us now. I wish that I might be able to live my life together with you all over again; then I should know what is great and high in it and what is low and mean, and I could then live according to that and be so much more for you than has been possible for me up to now.[51]

He then made an association that makes it sound as if his infidelity was caused by the same sense of being carried along by a force greater than himself that he experienced when composing his best works:

> Things have been so strangely sinister with me for a long time; as though everything was happening without my really having any idea about it before it was too late to get a firm grip on things. But I also want to explain something to you: when I've been creating best and most potently I've had this feeling to a similar degree. I've talked with you previously about this. At such times it's as though my personal will vanishes or is so slackened that it's the thing that takes me over to such an extent that I – i.e., the person I am – am dissolved … It's curious that my highest and lowest moments have this in common: that my ego vanishes and I become like an empty room, where there is neither good nor evil. If only I could explain everything and my true nature to you.[52]

As Nielsen saw it, there was something in his nature over which he had no control. He appealed to her understanding, but Anne Marie felt otherwise. During her stay in Norway, her crisis came to a head and she confided in her diary that she had come to a realisation:

> I've hardly slept and cried a lot … A few days ago, something dawned on me. Now I see everything in context. That Carl could accuse me of lacking confidence!

[He] had the heart to let me into such a foolish trick of pretence and falsehood. ...
There is something in pieces that I can't bring back.[53]

Anne Marie had realised that Marie Møller, who had accompanied her to the ferry twelve days earlier as if nothing had happened, had played a leading role in the whole affair. There is no doubt that Marie Møller was one of the women with whom Nielsen had a relationship at some point, although it is unclear when. Carl admitted the relationship to Anne Marie in January 1915 at the latest.[54] And apart from being one of Carl's lovers, Marie Møller knew everything that was going on – and kept quiet. Despite Carl's protestations to the contrary, his infidelity had never stopped. It had continued behind Anne Marie's back, or rather, right under her nose.

As soon as Anne Marie returned from Norway, she called Marie Møller and asked her to give her the keys to their house, and she went to Svend Godske-Nielsen, one of her and Carl's oldest friends, and told him everything.[55] She wanted Carl to come home from Damgaard, and he wanted her to come over, but now a war was interrupting. Instead of meeting up with Carl, Anne Marie boarded the last train to Berlin on the night between 31 July and 1 August 1914. The First World War was about to break out and she had to be in Celle to secure the equestrian statue. Once again, work came first.[56]

It is clear from reading her diary, written during her stay in Germany, that she did not accept his excuses:

I cannot get away from the fact that Carl wanted me to go on living a lie. I see [Marie Møller's] thieving, bitchy eyes licking up and down at him. ... Yesterday I read some of Carl's letters from last winter and had to cry, because they were lies too, maybe in a way they are not, but where is his personality?[57]

Carl, for his part, continued to write to Anne Marie, explaining that everything was going to be all right.[58] The conflict continued unresolved for the next few years, during which they led almost parallel lives.

In March 1916 it was twenty-five years since they had met in Paris, and it gave them both pause for thought. 'All that sun and joy of 25 years ago', Nielsen wrote to Anne Marie on 2 March, swearing by all that mattered to him – his life and whatever might remain of his art after his death – that he had never loved anyone but her. 'I can', he wrote,

assure you that in a deeply human sense I have never been unfaithful to you. I have never given myself to any other woman as I have to you. ... Please don't leave me. ... I don't think I entirely deserve that you should let me go under. For I am doing that, and it's certain that I shall never spend another happy hour if you won't have anything to do with me.[59]

Although it was he who broke the trust, he makes it sound as if he is the one to be pitied. Anne Marie had been away too long, he had been left alone, and he seemed to think he deserved to be forgiven for his indiscretions. In the end, it did not matter, he thought. For Carl, the good in their relationship had to outweigh the bad.

For Anne Marie, it was about the breach of trust, yet it was also about what she calls her 'code of honour': she found it undignified for someone to stay in a relationship after being betrayed, and once she had asserted this view to others, it had to apply to herself.[60] Her upbringing in a family with strong moral standards plays a crucial role in this. Although she was not religious, in a later letter to Carl in which she called for truthfulness and sincerity on his part, she referred to honest Christian people. If they have done wrong, they sincerely and wholeheartedly confess their mistakes to their God and do their utmost not to repeat them. 'That's how it is with us people in miniature', she wrote, 'when we really are something for one another and not just for show.'[61]

Things took another turn in April 1916. Two of the couple's oldest friends, Svend Godske-Nielsen and Henrik Knudsen, distanced themselves from Anne Marie because she had confided in another of their close friends, Ove Jørgensen, and his mother.[62] The situation became increasingly unbearable. In May she went alone to Søndervig on the west coast of Jutland, arriving on the seventh, three days before their official silver wedding anniversary. She decided to assess the situation: 'I've made a cold decision to make things right for him and for myself; perhaps then I'll be able to look at the whole matter more calmly and less confusedly.'[63] These notes, in which she weighs up the advantages of staying with him against those of leaving him, survive in several versions among her papers. In what seems to be the final version, she lists the following advantages:

Advantages of leaving
1) To be able to work again when I'm rested
2) Be a better mother and friend and more harmonious.
3) Won't have to take responsibility and will feel free.
4) Get my finances in order
5) Can manage my time. Could not stand going to bed late.
6) Will not be tormented by the half-day it takes to get the house going. Extravagance is irresponsible with my working hours.[64]

The argument is clear: she needs peace and quiet to return to work. Three of the six points are about work and one is about the children. In other words, she needs to get

Carl out of the house. It takes a couple of weeks and several drafts of a letter before, on 29 May, she pulls herself together and writes to him that she has made up her mind:

> We don't belong together anymore and have to divorce. ... I previously experienced a similar condition. That was in Greece when I received word about how things stood in my home; then I left behind all my artistic and financial advantages – the archaeological congress, which interested me intensely, the commission for my Typhon from the British Museum and two from America – and travelled home. At the time I believe faithfully in your assurances and promises, and that we could build up our marriage again. That you were deceiving me then, in the brightest and best moments of our life together, that's what has been the most painful thing of all. I was a fool! A poor, sympathetic fool. I was used as a convenient folding screen through the years, already then.[65]

During the summer they discussed the divorce and Nielsen was told to leave their home on Frederiksholm Kanal.[66] But the process dragged on, he lived there for long periods and she failed to send the papers. It was not until August 1919 that they were officially separated.[67] In the years that followed, Nielsen led a roaming life. He spent long periods at Damgaard, near Fredericia, and from November 1920 he lived with his daughter Irmelin when he was in Copenhagen.[68] In general, his two daughters, Irmelin and Anne Marie, known as Søs, became his confidants during this period, and much of our knowledge of what went on in the family comes from the daughters' correspondence with their parents and from their letters to each other. There is no doubt that Nielsen loved his children very much and that they meant a great deal to him, but it was primarily as a family and not in relation to his professional life that they played a role. This was also true of his son Hans Børge, whose development was stunted by a childhood illness and who spent time in institutions and foster homes from an early age.[69]

It also became a focal point for Nielsen that both daughters started families at this time. In 1918, the youngest daughter, Anne Marie, married the Hungarian violinist Emil Telmányi, whom she had known since the autumn of 1912, when he gave some concerts in Copenhagen. She found him attractive and was impressed by his violin playing.[70] They saw each other occasionally, and after a break in their relationship, they met in Malmö, Sweden, in the autumn of 1917, after which Telmányi proposed to Anne Marie in a telegram.[71] They were married on 6 February 1918, and shortly before the wedding Emil sent a long letter to Nielsen explaining his long-held wish to become the family's son-in-law.[72]

In the years that followed, Telmányi also became a valued adviser to Nielsen on musical matters. He played an important role in preparing Nielsen's Fifth Symphony for publication in 1926 and, with Nielsen's approval, added a single bar to the Sixth Symphony. But Telmányi was not given the central role in managing Nielsen's musical legacy that he had inferred from a letter Nielsen had written in 1925. Nielsen, still thrilled by Telmányi's performance of the A major Violin Sonata the day before, had written that 'when I die, I shall place my soul into your hands and ask that you alone be the true champion and judge of my works'.[73] This should be read more in relation to the performances of the works, for Telmányi, who was not a composer, never had the same direct influence on the creation of the works as, for example, Nancy Dalberg, who, after having been his student, was entrusted with the orchestration of *Springtime on Funen*.

The eldest daughter, Irmelin, married the doctor Eggert Møller on 14 December 1919, and both he and his mother, Frida Møller, became Nielsen's confidants. Frida Møller's late husband owned a pharmacy on Nørrebrogade, and the family lived in the apartment next door at no. 20. This was Nielsen's address from November 1920. At the same time, he spent long periods in Gothenburg as a conductor. In May 1922 he returned to Copenhagen and shortly afterwards suffered a serious heart attack. He was put to bed at Frederiksholm Kanal, and this led to Anne Marie taking him back into the household.[74] What was it that caused such a strong bond between them that they finally decided to live together again?

Sharing the Art

Apart from the fact that, after Carl's heart attack, Anne Marie accepted that he could not do without her and gave her life with him a second chance, she also missed something herself.[75] It is worth noting what Anne Marie wrote on the paper with her list of arguments for staying married. In a nutshell, her concerns about leaving Carl in 1916 boiled down to 'if I leave: 1) be lonely, 2) miss his view of art, 3) have to do everything myself, 4) lose friends?'[76] From the opposite point of view, that of staying, she had developed a slightly longer version:

Advantages of staying
1) Avoiding gossip
2) More comfortable at the moment, no critical encounters
3) Better [and] easier for the children
4) Keep the few friends I have left
5) Can talk to him about work.[77]

It is remarkable that most of the points are about herself, and only one is about what she will miss about Carl if he is not there: being able to talk to him about art. This had been such an important part of their life together – and indeed an important part of her life as an artist – that she feared losing it. It was not that she would miss him as such, but that it had been essential for both of them to have someone with whom they could discuss the prevailing and most important issues that preoccupied them as artists. They were, in the truest sense of the phrase, an artist couple. On the occasion of Anne Marie's eightieth birthday, symbiosis also came to the fore when, in an interview, she was asked to explain what, in her view, was central to all art forms.[78] In a phrase borrowed from Carl Nielsen, she said that although she was a sculptor, she used musical metaphors to express her ideas:

> There is rhythm and the contrapuntal, the balanced, which plays a role in all art. … There is a rhythm through all art: the living. I once asked my husband, 'what is the most important thing in art?' He thought for a moment, 'the living', he said, 'that life lives in it'. I would like to quote him here: 'Music is life, and as such it is inextinguishable' – you can say that about all art.[79]

When Anne Marie made Carl her spokesman, it was not because she could not articulate it herself. It was more an expression of the fact that, in retrospect, she saw their shared understanding of art as fundamental and, now that he had passed away, she had the energy to emphasise what had been at the heart of their life together as artists. She had come to terms with what divided them.

What she is alluding to are their conversations about art. The specific phrase refers to the motto of Nielsen's Fourth Symphony, *The Inextinguishable*: 'Music *is* life, which is inextinguishable.' It originates from a programme note in which Nielsen explains that music is particularly suitable when an artist needs to express life in the abstract. This can only be understood in the sense that all art is challenged to be an abstract expression of life. It is something common. And thus he is able to explain what he means when he elaborates on his understanding of life: 'Life is indomitable and inextinguishable, it is fought, broken, begotten and consumed today as yesterday, tomorrow as today, and everything returns.'[80]

Anne Marie's art was also interpreted as an expression of life and power. When the art critic Emil Hannover reviewed the sculptors' contributions to the exhibitions at Den Frie Udstilling (The Free Exhibition) and at Charlottenborg in 1906, he was highly critical. Virtually none could live up to what he described as the raison d'être of sculpture: the work was based on 'the silent, beautiful play of lines (light and shadow), which is the only valid plastic expression and the only valid testimony to the real and true soul of the sculptor.'[81]

But there was one who could, and that was Anne Marie Carl-Nielsen, for Hannover singled out her colour reproductions of important figures from ancient Athens,

ILL. 4. Anne Marie Carl-Nielsen's painted copy of the best-preserved male head from the Typhon sculpture group, *Blåskæg* (*Blue Beard*), was one of the very few contributions to Den Frie Udstilling of 1906 to find favour with the art critic Emil Hannover. The copy shown here was kept in the family home and today belongs to Museum Odense.[82]

such as the *Typhon* and the *Bull's Head* – the sculptures she had worked so hard to complete. Hannover praised her for her 'understanding of the Cyclopean beauty of this ancient art, with its barbaric beauty, its wild and daring colours, and its almost brutal devouring of the living form – as if a cry of the primeval artist's creative joy were released by these steaming bulls and this three-headed Typhon'.[83] In other words, she had mastered the primeval force.

There is one point on which Nielsen's formulation in the context of *The Inextinguishable* must be challenged – namely, when he asserts that the ability to express life in the essence of art is particularly present in music. Anne Marie was his equal in this respect, and by no means only in terms of her Greek reproductions: her sculptures of animals, and indeed of power-wielding humans, show the vital as part of the expression and not merely as a motif. Other examples are her small sculptures of athletes, which similarly express the power of deployment throughout their design.

What Anne Marie and Carl have in common is that they see the essence of art as a life force – not just a representation of something living. The expression of life is at a deeper level than what the music or art represents or relates to. The commonality of the arts is seen in the interplay of lines and shapes, in the layer of art that lies behind or in front of the subject. Anne Marie spoke of this principle, which in music is called counterpoint, the interplay of independent melodic lines. Nielsen would call the essence of sculptural form 'the true, organic play of forms and lines' when it came to formulating what he also saw as common to all art.[84] It was in their shared understanding of the essence of art that they needed each other.

Chapter 15

ROYAL MUSICIAN

Nielsen joined The Royal Orchestra as a violinist in 1889, at the age of twenty-four. He already had some experience, having assisted in the orchestra during the busy music summer festival of 1888 and the following season. At the audition for the post at the end of August, he played Wieniawski's 'lovely Polonaise'[1] in A major, Op. 21, one of those brilliant violin pieces which he himself had promoted in the concert halls. It gave him the opportunity to demonstrate both his technique and his mastery of the instrument's sound.

Nineteen participants were invited to audition for one viola and two violin positions. The happy result was that Nielsen and two of his closest friends, Holger Møller and Kristian Sandby, won the places and became colleagues at the Theatre. In a letter to Emilie the next day, Nielsen described how nervous he had been and that he had only been allowed to play the beginning of the piece before they announced 'enough'. He had seen Johan Svendsen nod approvingly to Frederik Rung, and it was reassuring that both Kapellmeisters looked pleased. Perhaps it helped that they already knew him. But he was still surprised when he was called up to the theatre director and told that he had been shortlisted.[2]

The Royal Orchestra was the country's finest symphony orchestra and the most prestigious workplace for classical musicians. It is considered the oldest orchestra in the world, tracing its history back to King Christian I's Corps of Court Trumpeters, founded in 1448, although, of course, it was not a symphony orchestra at the time. It has functioned as a court orchestra in various forms throughout history, and since 1770, when it was associated with The Royal Theatre's first building on Kongens Nytorv, it has served as its orchestra. When Nielsen joined the orchestra, it had about fifty members, which was the size of a full symphony orchestra at the time. Svendsen had been appointed Kapellmeister in 1883, and it was he who introduced the idea of the orchestra also giving symphonic concerts. This allowed them to play the symphonic repertoire at Kapelkoncerterne (the Royal Orchestra Concerts).[3] Nielsen benefited from this when they premiered his First Symphony in 1894.

However, the orchestra was first and foremost a theatre orchestra, whose role was to play at all the performances that required music, including operas, ballets and theatrical plays. This has left its mark on the orchestra. Unlike a symphony orchestra, where the musicians can concentrate on the long lines of the music, the theatre musicians and their conductor always have an eye on what is happening on stage. Everything has to be coordinated, it has to work immediately, and the effects the music is intended for have to be conveyed. It is a different approach to music, where the effect is part of a larger whole aimed at a theatre audience.

Unlike other orchestras in the city, the musicians were permanent, and as the theatre had a large repertoire, the performances could change almost every night. Playing in the orchestra was therefore a regular job and they got a lot of practice performing all kinds of music, both old and new, that was part of the theatre's repertoire. In 1874, the Theatre had moved to a new building on Kongens Nytorv. With its large stage it was particularly suitable for opera and Bournonville's ballets, which required a large number of performers. From 1889, Nielsen spent the next sixteen years here as an orchestra musician, taking part in rehearsals and performances.

The Experience

Crucially, what Nielsen gained from this experience as a musician and composer was a profound knowledge of the repertoire; of the effect of different types of orchestral movements and instrumentation; of the function of music in relation to singers, actors and dancers; of the theatrical effects of music; and, not least, of how the many different elements, resources and entities in a large theatre house worked together. He became an integral part of the theatre machinery. This came in handy when he had to compose incidental music and his two operas and, of course, when he became Kapellmeister.

As an indicator of the level of activity in Nielsen's early years, a normal season would include around thirty-five different plays, fifteen different operas and five or six ballets. In his first seasons, the theatre presented about 265 performances a year, of which about twenty-five were ballets, ninety were operas and the rest were plays. In terms of numbers, plays clearly outnumbered operas, although for an orchestral musician ballet and opera were the most important events. By the end of the 1890s, the number of ballet performances had doubled, the number of opera performances had risen to over a hundred, and the total number of performances reached 296 in 1902–3.[4] There was plenty to do.

The fact that Nielsen occasionally complained about his work is not the most important aspect – that is a common human trait – such as when he felt it was taking up all his attention, leaving him no time to compose. In 1896 he wrote to Anne Marie: 'Otherwise there's nothing new here without constant rehearsals in the theatre. I'd so much like to go to my work now, but it's not possible with this damned theatre.'[5] A few days later he added: 'The rehearsals at the theatre have got even worse. Rehearsals every day and today, for example, we had three rehearsals and tonight [Gounod's] "Faust" …' – and two days later he called the theatre his 'slave labour'.[6] It was hard work at times.

ILL. 1. The Royal Theatre's new building on Kongens Nytorv, inaugurated in 1874, is now called the Old Stage, although at the time it was a very modern theatre building that could accommodate all the theatrical arts. The new and larger stage made it possible to produce major operas and other spectacular performances. Under the Kapellmeisters Paulli and later Svendsen, opera and The Royal Orchestra flourished. Ballet stagnated somewhat, confined to the Bournonville tradition, which on the other hand had the advantage of keeping the ballet tradition intact. The large stage, however, was less suited to the naturalistic and realistic theatre that was becoming popular at the time. The greater physical distance from the audience was more of a barrier. In fact, the stage was one of the largest in Europe, which required the actors to use a special 'imposing style', even when performing naturalistic theatre. However, there was not much space in the pit, the musicians' daily workspace. The orchestra is seen here with the conductor Georg Høeberg.[7]

It should also be remembered that a large and demanding part of the work took place during the day, out of sight of the public. Edvard Fallesen, the theatre's director until 1894, replied to criticism that there were too few new productions by saying that, although only about three-quarters of the way through the season, the theatre had performed twenty-five plays, six operas and six ballets. This had required 286 major rehearsals, in addition to ballet rehearsals, choral rehearsals and piano rehearsals with soloists.[8]

And Nielsen did his job. In 1905, during his negotiations for a permanent position as Kapellmeister, he wrote to his old friend Klaus Berntsen in frustration at being told

ILL. 2. The Royal Orchestra 1899. Nielsen played with some of his closest friends and fellow students from the Academy, as well as some of his role models. In the third row, far left, are Julius Borup and Carl Nielsen; in the middle are the two Kapellmeisters, Frederik Rung and Johan Svendsen, flanked by the leaders, the violinists Anton Svendsen and Frederik Hilmer; on their right is Axel Gade, and on the far right is Georg Høeberg. Just below Nielsen is Kristian Sandby, who was employed at the same time as Nielsen and Holger Møller in 1889; third and fourth in the row are Johan Amberg, with whom Nielsen shared a desk, and Frits Bendix. Holger Møller left the orchestra in 1896 to take over the family farm Østrupgård on Fyn, where Nielsen's inner circle of colleagues met every August to spend their holidays and play music.[9]

he was unfit to be a civil servant: 'From my 24th to my 39¾ years I've been employed at The Royal Theatre, and there you'll be able to ascertain with the greatest ease all my circumstances, and there's absolutely nothing to be said of negligence or wrongdoing. ... my relations to duty and work I venture to set as an example to many others.'[10]

Nielsen rarely comments on the music he plays as a member of The Royal Orchestra. Thus the extent of Nielsen's first-hand knowledge of the music he played has been somewhat overlooked, mainly because it was an integral part of his everyday life and not something he needed to record in writing. He sometimes mentioned that he was not interested in the music being played, although one should not read too much into this.[11] Rather, it should be emphasised that he was thoroughly familiar with the music.

Of the sixteen years that Nielsen was in The Royal Orchestra, he spent almost twelve as violinist, not counting the periods when he was on leave. Nielsen was on sabbatical for the whole of the 1890-91 season, when he travelled in Europe as a recipient of Det Anckerske Legat (Anckerske Scholarship). In 1894 he spent two months on leave – from 9 October to 9 December – in Germany and Austria.[12] In 1896 he was granted ten days' leave to conduct his First Symphony in Dresden, and the following September he was granted leave for the first two weeks of the month to finish the harvest at Thygesminde, his parents-in-law's farm.[13] In August 1899 he was granted sabbatical for the whole of the following season, partly to complete *Saul and David* and partly because he had been awarded a travel grant. In December 1902 he applied for leave for the remainder of the season but did not receive confirmation until early February 1903. He was granted leave from 5 February 1903 and immediately left for Greece via Berlin. In August he applied for an extension of his leave until the New Year but returned to duty on 15 December 1903.[14]

The period from April 1904, when Nielsen became acting Kapellmeister, until his final resignation at the end of the following season in June 1905, must also be excluded. On 9 April 1904, he took up the position of substitute Kapellmeister for Rung and Svendsen at one day's notice, which meant that he conducted virtually all the performances for the remainder of the season.[15] For the following season it was agreed that he would be available as a substitute Kapellmeister and not as a violinist.[16] In fact, his activities as second violinist ended in April 1904, although he did not resign until the following spring, at the end of the season.

The Repertoire

Considering Nielsen's experience as a Royal Musician provides a very different picture of his musical horizons and European outlook from the traditional narrative of Nielsen as a local. It is therefore interesting to study the Theatre's repertoire in detail and compare it with the music he played during his employment. This gives us a fairly clear picture of the music he knew.[17]

Looking at the Theatre's repertoire during the sixteen years that Nielsen was employed, and subtracting the time he spent on leave, it is clear that he played in operas some 1,050 times. To this must be added the music for all the ballets and plays, as well as all the rehearsals. Even if he was occasionally absent or ill, the fact remains that he knew and played the repertoire offered by the Theatre. For example, if there was an opera on the programme, it would be performed several times, so a few days' absence would not be significant in the overall picture. The following figures therefore mainly tell us what we can expect Nielsen to have played over the entire period of his service as a violinist in The Royal Orchestra.

The opera repertoire at The Royal Theatre during Nielsen's employment was divided into four broad groups of almost equal size according to nationality: German, French, Italian and Danish composers – other countries played virtually no role in terms of opera.

German opera was the most popular, with just over 300 performances. These are concentrated on a few composers, with Gluck, Wagner and Mozart dominating, and a single opera by Marschner, *Hans Heiling*. Nielsen performed in works by Wagner almost a hundred times, with *Lohengrin* being the most frequently performed (nearly forty times); *Tannhaüser* and *Die Walküre* were each performed nearly twenty times; *Die Meistersinger*, which he was to conduct in 1913, was performed fourteen times; and productions of Wagner also included *Der fliegende Holländer* and *Siegfried*. Mozart's four operas *Don Giovanni*, *Le nozze di Figaro*, *Die Zauberflöte* and *Die Entführung aus dem Serail* received almost as many performances. Gluck's *Orfeo ed Euridice*, composed in 1762, became extremely popular after its premiere at the Theatre in 1896 and was performed almost ninety times during Nielsen's tenure.

In terms of the number of performances (*c.* 300), French opera is the second largest category, although it includes a slightly wider range of composers than the category of German operas. The most frequently performed opera of all during Nielsen's time is Bizet's *Carmen*, with over ninety performances. This is followed by Gounod's *Roméo et Juliette* and *Faust*, the latter with around seventy performances. The rest is spread over a wide range of composers, showing that the theatre was deeply rooted in the French operatic tradition: Auber, Boieldieu, Bazin, Delibes, Isouard, Ambroise Thomas, Meyerbeer, Massé, Adolphe Adam and Offenbach. Many of these composers also provided the overtures and popular excerpts for the concerts that Nielsen knew from his time in Odense.

The group of Danish operas is somewhat smaller, with just over 250 performances. On the one hand, the Theatre was obliged to produce national classics that had a permanent place in the repertoire, such as Johan Peter Emilius Hartmann's *Liden Kirsten* and Peter Heise's *Drot og Marsk*, both of which were performed almost fifty times during the period. August Enna's works were also frequently performed, as they were in the rest of Europe, with almost seventy performances of five works in all, including *Heksen* (*The Witch*) and *Kleopatra*.

On the other hand, the Theatre was also obliged to produce new Danish operas; among these, Nielsen played in Horneman's *Aladdin* and Alfred Tofft's *Vifakanda* between ten and twenty times each. Other works were performed less frequently. The composers included Johan Bartholdy, Julius Bechgaard, Peter Erasmus Lange-Müller, Axel Grandjean, Ludvig Schytte and Viggo Kalhauge – all names from the generation before Nielsen. The point of listing these composers is not that they are necessarily unjustly forgotten, but rather that Nielsen was familiar with the range of new works that were appearing, whether they remained on the programme or not.

The last group is made up of Italian operas, with around 170 performances. In this group, four composers in particular – Leoncavallo with *Bajadser* (*Pagliacci*), Mascagni with *Cavalleria rusticana*, Rossini and Verdi – account for the majority of the works. Of the latter, *Aida* and *Il trovatore* are the most performed Italian operas, although *Falstaff*, *Otello* and *La traviata* are also part of the repertoire.

The overall picture reveals the repertoire with which Nielsen was thoroughly familiar as a musician: on the whole, Gluck is closely followed by Wagner as the composers whom Nielsen played most often during the period in question; Mozart, Gounod and Bizet come next. While Wagner, Verdi and August Enna are represented by a large number of works, most of the other composers appear only once or twice in the Theatre's repertoire. Nielsen therefore knew his Wagner and Verdi and was familiar with a wide range of other works from the three great opera nations of Germany, Italy and France. He also had a profound knowledge of the Danish repertoire.

And that is only opera. Nielsen also played in many ballets, including around 200 Bournonville productions, such as *Fjernt fra Danmark*, *Livjægerne paa Amager* and *Sylfiden*, *Et Folkesagn*, *Thrymskviden* and *Napoli*. New productions of the latter three – with music by Niels W. Gade and J. P. E. Hartmann, and *Coppelia* with music by Léo Delibes – helped to increase the proportion of ballet in the repertoire. Since its premiere in 1896, Nielsen took part in more than eighty performances of *Coppelia*. Many of the operas also had ballet parts, so he had a keen sense of music that supported the dancing.

Many plays contained music in the form of incidental music, interludes and song interludes. Some of the most frequently performed plays at the Theatre were almost entirely made up of music, such as Holger Drachmann's adventure comedy *Der var engang –*, with music by Lange-Müller, and *Elverhøj*, with music by Friedrich Kuhlau. As a member of the orchestra, Nielsen performed these two plays at least sixty and ninety times respectively.

There are also a number of plays that are particularly significant because they represent forms of theatre music with which he would later work. From 1899 onwards, Nielsen took part in at least twenty performances of Mendelssohn's music for *A Midsummer Night's Dream*. It should also be noted that in 1891–92 he must have taken part in the last performances of Adam Oehlenschläger's *Aladdin*, with music by Frederik Rung based on Kuhlau's – that is, the play for which Nielsen would later write one of his most extensive scores. In the same year, the orchestra – and thus Nielsen – performed Rung's music for *Hagbarth and Signe*, based on a text by Oehlenschläger, which Nielsen was to set to music in 1910.

In all these areas, Nielsen gained extensive experience of what worked in a theatre, how to compose music for the stage and how to use the theatre's resources. One of the general arguments for keeping the theatrical arts together in one building was precisely that they worked together. Nielsen used this approach when writing for the Theatre. Had *Maskarade* not been composed specifically for The Royal Theatre, it seems unlikely that the opera would have included a ballet, large choruses and lots of street life. He must have known that these were the means at his disposal.

The Resignation

The end of Nielsen's employment as Kapellmeister was indeed triggered by the fact that he felt pressured to resign in the spring of 1905. His position as substitute Kapellmeister in the spring of 1904 had given him a taste for conducting – an activity that will be discussed in a later chapter. Now, the following year, he was asked to take his place again as second violinist. Although Nielsen had enjoyed a good relationship with Rung when he was younger, by this time they had become decidedly estranged, and gradually his trust in Johan Svendsen had also waned.[18] Svendsen was getting old, he was in his seventies, and in February 1904 Nielsen remarked: 'Svendsen gets weaker and weaker, and he now makes so many technical mistakes that it's beginning to become obvious; but he *was* once a really outstanding artist.'[19] It also meant that Svendsen's influence on the Theatre, which Nielsen had enjoyed over the years, was diminishing.

Shortly afterwards, Nielsen wrote a letter to Vilhelm Herold, the world-famous opera tenor who was his confidant at the time – and at a comfortable distance from the local conditions in Copenhagen. In the letter, he revealed that he had decided to resign in the autumn: 'Under no circumstances will I be there any longer.'[20] But that was more than a year before he actually resigned. One of the main reasons for staying on was that he needed the money. In the autumn of 1904, when he was even more exhausted, he did his accounts and concluded: 'So I can't do without the salary but will probably have to bite the bullet.'[21] Another reason for his perseverance seems to have been the prospect of taking over from the ageing Svendsen. At the end of the season, in the summer of 1904, he received a letter from Herold, who had heard about his great efforts:

> Well, you've probably done a good job at home! You see, I was right when I predicted that you would be Svendsen's heir! Now it's just a question of time![22]

The agreement between Nielsen and The Royal Theatre was along the same lines. They proposed an offer whereby Nielsen would receive his full salary for the whole of the next season in return for his availability as 'extra Kapellmeister'.[23] He was thus relieved of his duties as violinist. In a letter to Herold, he explains: 'I'm comfortable with it. It gives me time to compose and frees me from the sordid title of third Kapellmeister, which could easily prejudice things later.'[24] Nielsen foresees the situation that if he becomes Kapellmeister, he will not be subordinate to Rung. In this case, however, it would not matter.

Being a temporary replacement proved to be a double-edged sword. Rung and Svendsen led all but two performances of Nielsen's *Saul and David* in the following season.[25] And when Nielsen was not at the Theatre on a daily basis, it was difficult to exert an influence. When he wrote to Anne Marie in March 1905 that he felt compelled to resign, he had in fact been away from the Theatre for several months:

> My enviers and opponents at the Theatre – first and foremost I suppose the two Kapellmeisters – have been working quietly so that today I received my resignation, or rather was compelled to send it in. I've been sitting attending to my work in my room for months now and haven't been to the Theatre. But people have been digging and digging, and now the ground has given way beneath me. They couldn't reconcile themselves to the thorn in the flesh I have become and have demanded that I should either play the violin in the orchestra like a harmless private soldier and be their subordinate or take my leave.[26]

However, there were other things going on at the same time. In the autumn of 1904, Nielsen had 'many irritations with the Theatre' and was at odds with director Einar Christiansen over the new production of *Saul and David*, which was 'postponed and postponed again'.[27] The opera had been performed nine times in the first season of 1902–3, and it was not restaged until December 1904, and then only twice. Given that Christiansen had provided the libretto for the opera, it is not surprising that Nielsen took the lack of support for a revival as a rejection of their collaboration.

Thus, when he submitted his resignation on 11 March 1905, he had every reason to feel overruled, both as a composer and as a conductor. Within a week, the Ministry accepted his resignation with effect from the end of the season.[28] He had expected support from the Theatre, but now faced a serious problem. There was no immediate prospect of Svendsen handing in his notice. To return to his desk as a mere violinist would be humiliating. He could see no other way out but to resign. The decision also plunged him into an existential crisis, which he openly discussed with Anne Marie:

But what now? If you with your capital and income can take care of yourself and the children, I shall henceforth try my luck abroad from scratch.[29]

It was in this situation that Nielsen begged Anne Marie to come home from Athens – and where their marriage experienced its first serious crisis.[30] As already mentioned, there was an intense exchange of letters and telegrams between the two in March, when Nielsen's resignation from the orchestra was a major reason for the precarious situation. He felt that she did not take his situation seriously, and perhaps she did not understand the extent to which the orchestra had been his firm support, both financially and professionally as a musician. She returned home in April and their marriage survived. In a way, he was in the same position as when he left Fyn as a young man, uncertain whether he would be accepted at the Academy. Once again, Nielsen was faced with a leap into the unknown. Leaving The Royal Orchestra was an end, but it was also a new beginning.

Chapter 16

MUSIC FOR EVENTS

For centuries, music had been an integral part of public events in Copenhagen, as in the rest of Europe, from Renaissance pageants in the streets at royal weddings to the funerals of statesmen in the city's churches. The role of music was to act as a sonic scenography around the assembled people. Music was essential as a sensory part of the staging of the event, making the experience more powerful. The contribution of music depended on the situation, of course, and in some cases people sat and listened as if it were a concert. The important difference, however, was that the music supported the action and the story. It was not about itself. The effect of the music had to be adapted to the nature of the event, and the composer had to consider how the music could support the action unfolding before the eyes and ears of those present. In other words, it was a task that required not only imagination and a sense of the occasion, but also great artistic talent and compositional skill.

An event differs from an occasion and is defined in the academic literature on the subject as the study of '*planned, staged events*'.[1] It refers to somewhat larger, public events or performances with a large number of participants. Accordingly, it is important that they are both planned and staged: someone has an intention for the event, and a framework and a course of action have been devised. Writing music for such events is a significant moment in a composer's presence in the public consciousness, as was the case with Nielsen.

The use of the title 'music for events' rather than 'occasional music' is deliberate. Not only does occasional music imply an inferior work – a work to be performed only once – it also gives the impression that the work has no lasting significance, unlike works that can be included in a concert repertoire and thus have a permanent presence in musical life. Music composed for a particular occasion is therefore often seen as secondary or peripheral to a composer's oeuvre. It is important to change this perspective and realise that events have a vital function and that composing music for events can be of great importance. But this alone does not make the difference.

The central point about shifting the focus to the event is that it is not the musical work that is at the centre, as in a concert. The music is part of the whole staged event. Similarly, those present are not listeners or spectators, but participants. The participants have a co-creative position and are actors in the event.[2] They come to be there, and it is important for them and for others that they are there. It is the participants who can later recall the event in their memory and thus preserve its value, and who can refer to it in their interaction with others and keep its meaning alive – and negotiate the content of that meaning.[3] No participants, no event.

The perspective of the participants is vital because it is through their memory or reference to a piece of music performed at an event that the music has a lasting effect. Such an effect may even be more immediate and reach a wider audience than a concert performance. Although a work that becomes a permanent feature of a concert may have greater significance in the long term, music for an important event may have greater contemporary significance and be associated with a particular situation for a number of years. The opening ceremony of the Student Society is a good example.

The Inauguration of the Student Society Building

On 1 June 1901, Frue Plads in the centre of Copenhagen was full of people. At exactly two in the afternoon, trombones sounded from the balcony of the new home of the Student Society on Bispetorvet, opposite Frue Kirke, and the building was officially inaugurated. Inside, the banqueting hall was packed with guests standing close together in the summer heat. A considerable number of the capital's political and cultural elite had arrived and sat in reserved seats in front of the lectern. Among the invited guests were the university's chancellor, 'in a black coat and without a chain', and the brewer Carl Jacobsen, 'in an impressive tail coat hung with medals'.[4] Also present were the professors Harald Høffding and Kristian Erslev, the painter Viggo Johansen, the art critic Emil Hannover, the music director Frederik Schnedler-Petersen and the writers Amalie Skram, Peter Nansen and Jeppe Aakjær.[5] After the first speakers had welcomed the audience and presented the new building and the Student Society's vision, a choir and a small orchestra took their places in one corner of the hall. Nielsen stepped in front of the musicians and raised his baton. 'Now it begins. An electric crackling goes through the hall … A prelude in march tempo, pompous as Lohengrin, festive, cheerful.'[6]

The *Cantata for the Inauguration of the Student Society's Building* (CNW 104), with words by Holger Drachmann and music by Nielsen, was considered by many to be the highlight of the inauguration ceremony at Bispetorvet. The music was a central element of the event and made a great impression on those present. When the last words had been sung 'and the last rhythmic, crackling, jubilant, slowly waning octaves had been played, the students seized Carl Nielsen and carried him shoulder-high in stormy enthusiasm'.[7] Nielsen's music had thus succeeded in arousing the enthusiasm of the young members of the Student Society, and the next day the newspapers were full of praise.

ILL. 1. The Student Society's building on Bispetorvet in Copenhagen, as it looked at the inauguration in 1901. Trombone fanfares sounded from the balcony to the crowds gathered in the square. The music could also be heard inside the building, where the city's cultural elite and members of the Student Society sat in the banqueting hall. There, the new building was celebrated with speeches and Nielsen's music, the sound of which was associated with youth and progress – notions that the Student Society also stood for.

However, it was not just the music that was reviewed, but the whole event. The attention paid to the event by those present and by the newspapers, the careful description of the participants and of the event as a whole, show that the inauguration was a social and cultural occasion to which great importance was attached. There are 'spectators' outside who are not allowed in, there are insiders – that is those who have been invited – and there is a carefully orchestrated process in which participants are aware that they are taking part in the event and not just watching. They also attend in order to be seen, to see others and to have the opportunity to report from the place so that others know they have been there. It was important to be able to say that you had been there, or at least experienced the inauguration from the outside, or read about it, so that you could talk to people about the experience.

As the composer who had provided the music for such an occasion, Nielsen was at the centre of attention. The sound of his music had reached a wide circle of leading figures in social and cultural life, creating a sonic reference that they could recall when commemorating the inauguration. The cantata therefore played an important role in how those present imagined the nature of 'the new' at the turn of the century. It was the work that participants remembered when they thought of the Student Society as representing youth and progress.

The Sound of Youth and Progress

From the eighteenth century onwards, composers often wrote cantatas to mark special events. A cantata consists of a series of alternating movements in which instrumental sections are combined with sections comprising text. A cantata is therefore ideal for creating a sequence that suits a particular event. A special feature of the form is that it allows for a sermon towards the end if it is a church cantata, or a speech if it is for a secular occasion. The music then continues with a final section that rounds off the event. A cantata is therefore a good choice if you want to tell a story and enhance the impact of a speech as part of a momentous occasion.

Nielsen had received the request to compose the music for the cantata from his friend Emil Sachs, a cousin of Georg Brandes and a close associate of the Student Society and the radical milieu. The importance Nielsen attached to the commission is shown in a letter he wrote to Sachs after the inauguration ceremony in June 1901:

> You may imagine that I'm glad to have done this work, and it's because of you that I'm once again in your debt, both as an artist and as a human being. There's something so good and festive about you, dear Emil, that when you make such a request, one feels a desire, because it becomes, as it were, a beautiful task for one

to do the thing as well as one can. I had this feeling right up to the last rehearsal, when I still had to make one improvement in the cantata.[8]

At the time, Nielsen had only recently begun to compose music for events. He had only completed the music for one other cantata, the *Cantata for the Lorenz Frølich Celebration* (CNW 103), for the celebration of the artist's eightieth birthday six months earlier. It had been a major event, and everything from the menu to the many artistic contributions had been described in detail in the newspapers. Brandes was the principal speaker, and a large part of Copenhagen's cultural life was present, so it can be assumed that there was quite an overlap between the participants at the birthday party and the inaugural event at the Student Society. The celebration for Frølich was one of the rare occasions when Nielsen himself played the piano in public. The music is written for piano and a vocal soloist who alternates between melodramatic recitative and song. The cantata ends with a march-like song in 3/4 time with a strong rhythmic touch in the piano. Nielsen must have felt that this was partly the same mood he wanted to capture in the new cantata; in any case, much of the opening and closing sections of the cantata for the Student Society and the ending of the cantata for the Frølich celebration are almost identical.[9]

The Student Society was founded in 1882 as a left-wing offshoot of The Students' Association. It became an important meeting place for students and intellectuals from the radical milieu, with Brandes as its central figure. By the turn of the century, however, when the Student Society moved to its new building on Frue Plads, Brandes and the other key figures in the radical milieu were advanced in years. New forces were soon needed to ensure the youthful struggle for freedom and progress that was at the heart of radical thought. It was for this new youth that Drachmann was asked to write the text of the cantata, which therefore appears in both its structure and content as a transmission of the struggle against conservative dogma to a new generation.[10]

Musically, Nielsen emphasised the transmission from the older to the younger generation by using the young male choristers of the Student Choral Society to sing the festive, victorious sections at the beginning and end, as well as the march; however, opera singers Emma von Holstein-Berg and Helge Nissen and actor Emmanuel Larsen were responsible for the more serious sections, in which the text is addressed directly to young people at several points. The rest of the cantata was composed for French horns, string quartet and piano, for which some of Nielsen's colleagues from The Royal Orchestra had joined him that day.[11]

Let us imagine what happened on that June day in the new building. The cantata begins and the audience is greeted by the first piece, the Introit. The movement is in 3/4, a time signature that Nielsen liked to use when he wanted a piece of music to be firm and pompous.[12] The first four bars effectively underline this mood, as all the instruments – horns, strings and piano – play the same rhythmic motifs, consisting first of a repeated, festive motif, followed by a bar of quavers, then the first motif again.

As the chorus enters, it is accompanied by rhythmic motifs reminiscent of the opening, but with the sense of something growing, as the undulating quaver motif lengthens with each introduction. Now the listener's attention has been captured, and what they may not yet know is that the rhythmic motif becomes an important building block for the rest of the movement, giving the whole cantata the same basic mood. The motif becomes the young people's signature.

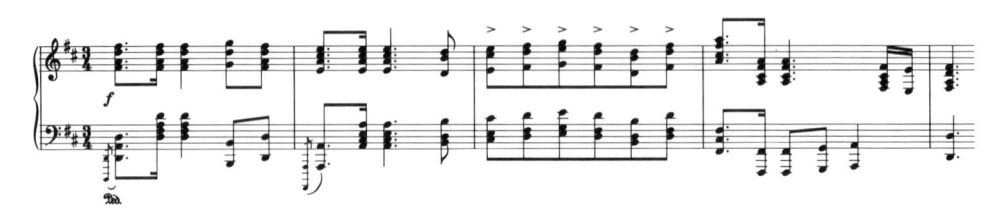

MUSIC EX. 1. Carl Nielsen, *Cantata for the Inauguration of the Student Society's Building*, No. 1, bars 1–5. The instrumental introduction to the cantata sets the mood. All the instruments play the same rhythmic motifs, consisting first of a small festive motif with a dotted quaver on the first beat in two bars, followed by a bar with quavers in a stepwise up and down motion, and then returning to the same rhythm as in bars 1–2. This is the motif of youth throughout the cantata.

The introductory text describes the free and heated debates that could arise in the Student Society – 'Peace on the house – free speech in the hall, fight at the wide tables as much as you want!' and at the same time includes an invitation to let 'the others' fall, to take the argument out into the public. The stanza describes who 'the others' are – that is, the opponents of the modern and free spirit that characterised the environment of the Student Society: 'And there are even enough of the "others" – ah yes! Enough of princes, enough of clerics, enough of those who make all sizes fit – enough of those who turn down our courage …'. The opponents were the institutions of the old society and, in general, the forces that hindered the development of the individual and wanted everyone to conform to the old, rigid norms.

The music therefore changes character in the strophe. In a gradual transition, the grandiose 3/4 is abandoned and replaced by 4/4, which, together with a change from D major to A minor, gives the piece a more serious expression. The chorus is now silent and 'opera singer Helge Nissen sings solo as a thoughtful bass'.[13] The piece almost takes on the character of a political speech about the injustices of society –

and those responsible for them. This effect is emphasised musically in a number of ways, including the use of shifting accents in the instruments, which occasionally fall into the gaps between the singer's phrases – for example, a strong one falls after the phrase 'And there are even enough of the "others" – enough of princes, enough of clerics', where the subsequent accents almost sounds like a response from the audience (similar to 'Hear, hear!' or 'Yes!').

Nielsen was aware of the harmonic and dynamic means he could use to support the structure of the 'speech'. In the first stanzas of the text, about 'the others', the music modulates several times as it moves dynamically from *f* to *mp* and back to *f*. When 'enough of those who turn down our courage' is sung, the dynamic suddenly drops from *f* to *pp* on 'down' and then gradually rising to *ff*, so that the intensity – or anger at these 'others' – is at its height when 'as we stare down into the pit, filled with the sacrificial blood of kin' is sung. After the preceding modulations, the four-bar crescendo rests on a dramatic C minor with tremolo. First a minor sixth, then a major sixth is added to the chord, effectively announcing that something is at stake. For the audience in the hall, this passage must have felt like an intensification. The anxious tremolo of the strings and the tense chords are used to create a mood.

The antistrophe now suggests that it is among the young that an army must be formed against the conservative forces. The text addresses the youth directly with the words 'you young, talented man and woman'. The antistrophe thus responds to the disturbing nature of the music. It is meant to give hope for the future, despite all the 'others' in the strophe. Tonally, there is a shift from A minor to A major, and the soprano takes over from the bass singer with the words 'but of the young, proud and strong, rally round the guard that shall one day win the victory'. The youthful lightness is emphasised as the piano recedes, giving way to the sound of the bright soprano voice and wavering quavers in the strings playing *p*. At the same time, the horns hint at a rhythmic motif derived from the beginning of the cantata. Thus, in addition to the new sonority, Nielsen gives the audience a piece of something musically recognisable. This foreshadows the spirit and celebratory mood that captured the listener's attention at the beginning of the cantata.

A march begins and the male choir enters. It becomes almost a battle cry as the choir takes over from the soloists, the change emphasising the youthful vigour. Studying the score, the section sung by the male choir appears almost banal. But imagining the theatrical performance in the banqueting hall, it must have seemed powerful:

> Young blood – and young courage
> Save the good forces;
> Steady forward – on a firm footing:
> There's much to be done!

ILL. 2. Drawing of the inauguration celebrations in the Student Society in *Politiken*, 2 June 1901. At the top are the speakers: politician Eduard Larsen, former president Herman Trier, and then president of the Student Society Ivar Berendsen. Below is the musical line-up during the cantata: Nielsen holding the baton, with soprano Emma von Holstein-Berg and bass singer Helge Nissen. Next to them is actor Emmanuel Larsen, who performed the recitative, and in the background are some musicians from The Royal Orchestra on the left and the young choristers of the Student Choral Society on the right.

We must face our destiny calmly
Where and what it bids,
But do not venture into your own game,
Until the right battle cry is sounded!

Musically, the march recalls the style and motifs of the cantata's introduction. But where the introduction was in D major, the key is now F major, and rhythmically the march is simpler. The choir and instruments follow each other with distinct crotchets and quavers, and dynamically the piece remains in *f* and *ff*. Nielsen thus creates a constant momentum and a sense of singing a choral battle cry. This is followed by a recitative that ends with a series of powerful chords that conclude the first part of the cantata.

It was here that the former president of the Student Society, Herman Trier, addressed the assembly. He ended by saying: 'Let this house be a lookout from which to watch the dawn of the day. Let there be a listening, a watchful youth who can do their part to help our little nation take its place in the great community of mankind.'[14] The speech was greeted with a standing ovation, and then the cantata's 'final apostrophe' sounded. Now the music returns to the theme of the introduction, and the text elaborates on the importance that the Student Society can have for the youth of the future: 'Peace on the house – atmosphere through the hall: there, where young families endure so much strife! There, where the woman rises, the man yearns: *freedom* to the house that holds the spring of *future*'.

Since the beginning of the cantata, the key has moved up a whole tone, from D major to E major. First we hear the grandiose opening of the cantata again, and then the choir enters. The two stanzas of the final apostrophe are similar to the stanzas of the opening movement, but the piece also contains a middle section which helps to build tension towards the final stanza. Here the two soloists sing in canon: 'If every day is used, milestones are moved,' as the dynamics build from *p*. Rhythmically, there is an intensification, with the first part of the middle section marking quavers, followed by a passage of quavers against triplets. Shortly afterwards, the triplets take over completely. This is an entirely new rhythm, never before heard in the cantata, and it signals the triumph of quick, youthful rhythms. It is a carefully considered touch on Nielsen's part, and one that is clearly audible.

The end of the cantata suggests that the grandiose motif of the beginning represents youth. If the listener had not already understood this, the ending reveals it. Nielsen had to make sure that the listener could relate to the music immediately. Contrasts and strong effects were important and accepted. The final phrase, '*freedom* to the house that holds the spring of *future*', is repeated *f* in long notes and the rhythmic motif accompanying it.

The reactions immediately after the performance and in the newspapers show that the music fulfilled its purpose of staging the event. The newspaper *København* said:

> Mr Nielsen has set Drachmann's words to music, and it would be difficult to find more beautiful, fresher, more youthful, more festive tones. There was a roar of courage and defiance in this festive cantata, there were tones of the most tender lyricism, and there was a triumphant mood in the march so grandiose and incendiary that it brought the audience to its feet in jubilant applause.[15]

The radical writer and journalist Ove Rode also saw Nielsen's music as a highlight of the celebrations, stressing that music, more than speeches, had the ability to awaken the youthful spirit that was crucial to ensuring progress and renewal in society:

> In many beautiful and strong words the nature and will of the Student Society, its wishes and aims, were explained and affirmed. But no speech about what youth should be could find a deeper and richer expression than Nielsen's beautiful music to Drachmann's poem. With such a rhythm in the life of our youth, with such a rhythm in its progress, with such a proud and manly joy in its being, it would soon succeed in transforming the Danish society of habits.[16]

Rode's subsequent remark suggests that the celebration left an impression on the guests that was entirely in keeping with the nature of the modern and free-spirited milieu: 'Thus the most lasting impressions of the dedication of the new home of the Student Society were pure impressions of beauty – not a lazy and dreaming beauty, but a struggling, a proud beauty.'[17] The decisive factor in the music's modernity was therefore not whether it was based on completely modern compositional techniques, but that it could produce the sharp sound of progress and willpower – as opposed to the sound of a romantic, dreamy world. The fact that Nielsen's music was able to do this was the very prerequisite for it being able to excite and arouse identification in its listeners in the radical milieu at the turn of the century. Nielsen provided the sound of a modern youth ready to fight for its ideals.

Ambitious Cantatas

Nielsen composed music for events from 1900 to 1930, on average one work a year. It was part of his identity as a composer that he could contribute in this way to the celebration of events in the society of which he was a member. The works were not only an important source of income for him. He often regarded the works as significant, often put a great deal of effort into them and took the task of composing them seriously so that he could deliver music of a high artistic standard.

Many of these works continue in the cantata tradition of Nielsen's earliest works of this type, the *Cantata for the Lorenz Frølich Celebration* and the *Cantata for the Inauguration of the Student Society Building*. In all, he composed thirteen cantatas of varying length. His music for events also comprises a handful of instrumental works, among them an impressive composition written in connection with the commemoration of the loss of the Titanic. There are also a dozen songs and choral works, most of them for school and college events, and music for five plays, including three celebrating Shakespeare, Holberg and Hans Christian Andersen.[18] The music for the events can therefore be of a very varied nature.

Nielsen had both artistic and practical ambitions with his music for events. This is reflected in the zeal with which he often worked and the time he spent composing this type of work. He was keen to immerse himself in the task at hand in order to understand what the role of the music should be. When one considers his reflections on how the music should affect the listener, one gets the impression that he tried to adapt his compositions to the wishes of the organisers. He was concerned that the music should be artistically satisfying and at the same time make a convincing impression on the participants, whether they were the audience or the performers.

One of Nielsen's most ambitious compositions for an event was *Cantata for the Opening Ceremony of the National Exhibition in Aarhus 1909* (CNW 107), premiered in 1909. The work ended up being a monumental cantata for symphony orchestra, choir and soloists in seven movements, composed in collaboration with Emilius Bangert. It was not obvious, however, that it would be a cantata of this size. Before agreeing to the task, Nielsen discussed with the librettist Laurits Christian Nielsen what he expected of the work. 'What is the overall plan for such an opening ceremony, in which a work of art like a cantata by you and me is supposed to be the central point?' he asks. They need to know if 'the audience will be in the right mood and prepared to listen properly and to know that it is having an artistic experience'. Nielsen wanted to avoid the speakers of the day using the 'usual banal toasting jargon' and would only attend if the whole thing had 'a dignified atmosphere'.[19]

Nielsen's concerns are an expression of his attempt to imagine the whole situation in which the music would be played. If he wrote pompous music when the audience was only in the mood for a toast, things would fall apart. There is also the impression that Nielsen took the commission seriously and had artistic ambitions in fulfilling it. He wanted to get to know the audience as listeners who might not be used to attending concerts with his music on the programme. It was important to him to know what the people who were paying him to compose had in mind. He expected the music to be an attraction and was certainly not prepared for it to play a secondary role at the event.

Nielsen also maintained his artistic integrity when composing for other occasions. When the Chancellor of the University of Copenhagen asked him in 1907 to compose the *Cantata for the Annual University Commemoration* (CNW 105), he was allowed to attend the annual celebration in order to familiarise himself with the process and the physical conditions of the university's banqueting hall. The cantata was structured with two interspersed speeches: a celebratory address after the first part, and the chancellor's official presentation following the middle section. In addition, musicians and singers had to be accommodated in the narrow gallery just below the ceiling.[20]

A few days after attending the celebration, Nielsen wrote to Professor Frants Buhl, the musically knowledgeable member of the university's cantata committee, believing that the committee – and Buhl in particular – were 'so musical that one can easily imagine a flowing sequence of purely elementary sound effects, and this moment is so important on such an occasion as an annual festival'. In the letter he describes his ideas for making the best possible use of the difference between soloists and large or small choirs, between types of voice and between recited and sung sections. It was important to Nielsen to be sure that his ideas met the expectations of the committee, and he took the task seriously, declaring: 'I intend to deploy everything in my power to place my stamp on this work, and it *shall* be as good as my gifts can manage.'[21] Together with those who commissioned the music, he tried to imagine how the music could best contribute to the event.

Nielsen was concerned not only with the overall effect, but also with how the music would work in the situation. To Niels Møller, who had written the lyrics for the cantata, Nielsen wrote of his thoughts on the final song, 'which in some ways I'd always been a bit anxious about, because it's more a matter of luck than anything else whether such a song turns out as it should do: that's to say catchy, unambiguous and yet with a certain sweeping character'. In order to get an impression of whether his ideas were having the desired effect, Nielsen revealed that he had been used to 'experimenting on listeners, first with my three children, then with other unprejudiced musical people (which I shall try out here this evening). The point is that I've discovered that professional musicians are often the most unreliable judges, because they tend to see the thing from a purely artistic point of view, and I don't need that here.'[22]

He described a way of listening to music that was not professional, but spontaneous. It is a listener who is able to be present at an event and experience it as a sensuous whole, of which the music is only one part. When he writes that the final song should be 'catchy', distinctive and 'yet with a certain sweeping character', it fits well with the idea that the music should be appealing and immediately understandable. It should frame and enhance the mood of the event and be effective in the present. To be remembered, however, it must also be memorable.

The cantata composed for the annual celebration of the university had a different structure from works intended for a single performance. The idea was that the work would become an integral part of the annual celebrations and would be repeated every year. Nielsen was aware of this premise from the outset, which may be why he spoke of placing his stamp 'on this work'.[23] Thus he took the criticism of the work after its premiere at the anniversary celebrations on 29 October 1908 seriously.

The criticism, mainly directed at Møller's text, was expressed in its harshest form in *Kristeligt Dagblad*, which spoke of 'Darwinian evolutionary mysticism' and a 'hostile relationship with Christianity'. The discussion continued in the university's academic council and resulted in some changes to the text before the next anniversary celebrations. Nielsen was nervous that the work would be shelved altogether. The changes reveal the crux of the criticism: 'when we marched out of the fate of the beast, … towards the high stars' became 'when we marched out of the valley of darkness …'. And as for 'knowledge': 'often the prisoner sat under the power of princes / for the hard church heavily it had to serve', the reference to princes and church is removed, so that it simply reads 'locked in a cage as a prisoner sat …'.[24]

The original text celebrates a scientific view of life and criticises the old authorities. When compared with the most positive reviewer's description of Nielsen's music as full of 'strength, manliness and health' and the ending as 'a hymn to youth, which is life-renewing and *must* guard the fire and lift the torch', it is clear that both authors were inspired by the Student Society's cantata.[25] The fact that one of the soloists, Helge Nissen, was the same only reinforced this impression, especially for the audience present at both events.[26] Nielsen and Møller had originally wanted to pay tribute to free science and free thought – and had come up against conservative forces who criticised the text. The cantata survived with minor changes and was performed at the annual celebrations for decades to come.

In 1930 Nielsen wrote *Digtning i Sang og Toner ved Svømmehallens Indvielse* (*Poetry in Song and Music for the Inauguration of the Public Swimming Baths*) (CNW 115) to celebrate the opening of Copenhagen's first indoor public swimming pool, now known as Øbro-Hallen. In such cases, the commission of a cantata marks events of national importance. The inauguration took place in Øbro-Hallen itself, with music, speeches and a swimming display in the presence of Prime Minister Thorvald Stauning and King Christian X.

The cantata was performed by the male choir Bel Canto, recited by the actor Svend Methling, and a small wind band consisting of clarinets, bassoons, horns and a trombone. The choice of the darker sounding wind instruments was probably due to the acoustics of the hall. The cantata consisted of three parts: an introductory chorus sung a cappella by Bel Canto, and two longer movements in which the wind band, in almost chamber-like instrumentation, provided the background for the reciter's description of the importance of sport to mankind from ancient Greece to the present day. The last two movements ended with the choir singing the same melody as at the beginning, and as a final effect the choir was accompanied by the wind band. Nielsen used the melody of 'Morgenhanen atter gol', which he had composed a few years earlier.[27]

The recycling shows that Nielsen was less concerned with the specific melody than with its character and effect on the performance of the cantata in the spacious building. The powerful male voices intoned 'swim to be strong and free and happy' in the resounding acoustic, and the reciter described the short Danish summer in picturesque terms, noting heroically: 'But today the dream has triumphed! We have stopped you in your flight, blocked the sea and the sun, held back the mighty wave.' The swimming pool became a symbol of humankind's control over nature, and the grandiose and festive cantata staged this victory.

Nielsen took the commissions seriously, but still felt that music for events had a different status from concert music. He was therefore surprised when, a few weeks after its premiere in 1917, concert plans were made for further performances of the *Cantata for the Centenary of the Chamber of Commerce* (CNW 111). After the concert, which was then repeated three days later, he wrote to his daughter Irmelin that he felt 'somewhat embarrassed by the situation, for it is and will be only an occasional composition without any great effort, but the musicians say it is nevertheless something new, and besides, a deliberate break has been made with the usual cantata form'.[28] Thus Nielsen evidently saw the work as intimately connected with the event and did not imagine that it would have an afterlife in the concert hall.

The concerts on 1 and 4 June in the concert hall of the Tivoli Gardens were sold out. *Nationaltidende's* critic shared Nielsen's view of the ambiguous status of the genre, writing after the concert that composing a cantata was not an easy task, for 'artistically, the composer has not chosen his subject himself and therefore … cannot give free rein to his imagination – and practically, because his work is tied to a specific event and he has little hope that the perhaps important work he has put into it will be rewarded by subsequent performances'.[29] That a concert performance was arranged, nevertheless, shows that those who attended the original event did not think in fixed categories. Their concern was not whether it was occasional music, but whether the music worked, whether it was well written and whether it had merit. Although music for events can be seen as music of the present, some works transcended this immediate definition.

A Wide Range of Assignments

A characteristic feature of the music Nielsen wrote for special occasions is that he adapted the music to support the event. However, events can be very different in character and commissions can be approached in many different ways. As a result, Nielsen's music for events appears as a diverse group of compositions. His varied output of music for events reflects a gifted composer who was able to produce music of high quality in many different contexts.

The versatility is reflected in the range of his works. He composed short songs, which became important to those who sang them, and large choral and orchestral works, the scale of which corresponded to events, sometimes of a national character. It is not always easy to determine whether music was composed for an event. A good example is the work composed by Nielsen in 1912 to commemorate the loss of the Titanic, which was to be performed at a concert in May by a wind band of 250 musicians. Shortly afterwards, the King died, a national period of mourning was declared and the planned concert was cancelled. When the work was finally performed three years later, the context had changed, although the original idea was still at the heart of the piece's structure.

The planned event was described as a giant 'monster concert'. It was to be a celebration in which a specially assembled wind band was to fill the former Central Station of Copenhagen with music.[30] It is not known how Nielsen was commissioned, but it is clear that the work was intended to draw attention to the tragic event. In form, it is a straightforward depiction of the incident in which the Titanic, *en route* to America, hits an iceberg with a tremendous crash in *ffff* in all brass and percussion – Nielsen's instructions in the manuscript read 'gong, gran cassa etc. all that is available'.[31]

Listening to the music in detail, it is clear that the impact must have been enormous. After a soft, almost lyrical introduction, the entire wind band breaks in at this point with a deafening diminished triad. The contrast between the previous passage in *ppp* and now *ffff* is extreme. Some of the musicians, such as the trumpeters, are required to play rapid tremolos, and they spit out sharp, pointed notes at the audience as hard as they can. The hammering of the snare drum and kettledrum hits the audience like a wall of noise. At the same time, the woodwinds begin to play rapid chromatic figures that descend bar by bar. The volume gradually decreases, the instruments fading away at a steady pace, until the kettledrum alone describes the ship's silent fate at the bottom of the ocean. The chorale 'Nearer, My God, to Thee', said to have been the musical farewell played by a string quartet aboard the Titanic in its final minutes, rises solemnly from this horrific scene.

ILL. 3. The ocean liner Titanic sank on 14 April 1912, and the news of the disaster sent shock waves around the world. The Copenhagen Orchestra Association decided to organise a concert in aid of the families of the musicians who had lost their lives on board. Nielsen composed a work for the occasion, *Nærmere Gud til dig* (*Nearer My God to Thee*), Paraphrase for Wind Orchestra (CNW 37).

In the summer of 1915 there were renewed plans for a 'monster concert' of Nielsen's work. The tragic event of 1912 was no longer relevant, as attention was now focused on the First World War and the economic difficulties it caused. The Copenhagen Orchestra Association planned a concert with the proceeds going to the association's pension fund. The event thus had nothing to do with the sinking of the Titanic, but rather with improving the living conditions of the association's members. Nielsen agreed to have his work on the loss of the Titanic performed at an open-air concert in Copenhagen's Rosenborg Gardens, attended by at least 25,000 people. Nielsen conducted the band of two hundred musicians.

The guests in Rosenborg Gardens were unaware of the context of Nielsen's composition and must have listened to the music without any concrete idea of whether it had been composed for a particular event. One reviewer, however, noted that it was 'an effective soundscape with a very realistic depiction of a storm at sea'.[32] Perhaps it had been revealed what the music was originally intended to depict, for the explosive passage in the middle may have been an unwitting comment on the ongoing war. The final chorale was probably crucial in linking the music to the loss of the Titanic, particularly if listeners remembered the newspaper reports published three years earlier about the hymn played by the quartet on board the ocean liner.[33]

It is easier for some works for events to enter the mainstream concert repertoire than others. Two good examples are the orchestral works Nielsen composed for official occasions, the *Rhapsodic Overture* subtitled *En Fantasirejse til Færøerne* (*An Imaginary Journey to the Faroe Islands*) (CNW 39) and the *Bøhmisk-Dansk Folketone* (*Bohemian-Danish Folk Song*) (CNW 40). Both works were commissioned for concerts in Copenhagen, of which the former was performed twice at The Royal Theatre for festive occasions attended by visitors from the Faroe Islands. When Nielsen received the commission in January 1927, he professed to be interested in the work and to be well paid.[34] The event was postponed until November due to an influenza epidemic. In an interview, he lowered expectations by saying that the composition was 'an occasional work … that is, a kind of craftsmanship'.[35] He then goes on to describe in detail the sea voyage to the Faroe Islands that the piece depicts, which ends on arrival with a party of folk songs and dancing. Nielsen also says that he has been interested in Faroese folk songs for many years and uses them to set the mood for the overture. The contrast between Nielsen's initial reluctance and his fascinating description of the piece shows that he shared the ambivalent attitude of his time towards music composed for a specific occasion, but that he also allowed himself to be carried away and immersed himself in the work.

The same was true of the second piece, which was performed in 1928 to mark the tenth anniversary of Czechoslovakia's independence. The music was written for a concert with a Czechoslovakian programme performed by the Danish Radio Symphony Orchestra. As a sign of the solidarity between the two nations, Nielsen combined a Danish and a Czech folk tune in the work.[36] Thus, for both of these events he was able to relate the music clearly and with simple techniques to the cultures being represented. The newspaper *Nationaltidende* wrote of the performance: 'Everything is composed with taste, harmony and the hand of a master, although it is probably only an occasional work.'[37] To devalue works simply because they were composed for specific events shows a lack of enthusiasm for the qualities of music that work in the moment.

Being purely instrumental and composed as orchestral works in a single movement, the two pieces could easily be included in many concert programmes where the genre – that is, short, narrative or programmatic orchestral pieces such as the *Helios Overture* – was already a regular feature. The narrative quality is also found in other of Nielsen's orchestral works, including *Saga Dream* and *Pan and Syrinx*. The references to folk music in the works have the character of programmatic elements, referring to a nation and its folk life, without the audience necessarily knowing the specific event for which it was commissioned. It is characteristic of the genre that the specific reference to an event can be generalised and passed on as a general reference to a nation and a journey, or to the idea of solidarity.

In other instances, Nielsen composed music in smaller forms for local events, similar to the function of the cantata, which celebrated the anniversary of the University of Copenhagen each year; in the same way, a secondary school might have its own special work to be performed each year on the occasion of the school's anniversary. Such works are the two school songs 'Blomsterstøv fra Blomsterbæger' (Flower pollen from profusion; CNW 343) and 'Nu er for stakket Tid forbi' (It's over for a short respite; CNW 344), which Nielsen composed for mixed four-part choir in 1929. They were composed for the annual graduation ceremony at Birkerød Statsskole. The music teacher, Knud Malmstrøm, who commissioned the songs, wrote to Nielsen that they were 'in some ways priceless in existing currency'.[38] It was of great importance to the school that Nielsen had done them the honour of contributing the melodies.

In 1926, Aarhus Katedralskole also asked Nielsen to write a melody for the institution on the occasion of the 400th anniversary of the school's former headmaster, Morten Børup's death. Nielsen wrote the melody to a translation of Børup's Latin poem 'In vernalis temporis' (Springtime, springtime breaking through; CNW 353). The same Latin text was the starting point for *Morten Børup's Song of May* (CNW 375), which Nielsen composed together with 'Kom blankeste Sol!' (Come, glistering sun; CNW 374) for Kolding Almenskole, who wanted to use the song at their traditional May festival. These songs are all strophic and similar to the popular songs Nielsen wrote during these years, aimed at the general public. As commissioned works, the songs, just as the popular ones, are marked by the fact that Nielsen composed them with the singers' musical abilities in mind.

The commissioned works include little songs that Nielsen was able to compose in a short time and without much effort. However, this is no trivialisation of the importance of the songs to the people who would mostly use them. In both 1911 and 1915 he wrote songs for the Children's Welfare Day, an annual celebration held since 1904 to raise funds to improve the living conditions of children. The two contributions, *Child Welfare Day Song* (CNW 293) and *Childen's Song* (CNW 301), are simple strophic songs that describe a good childhood and encourage care for the little ones: 'Fill the child's mind with joy, that's your and everyone's business', read the lyrics to the latter. It was important to make Children's Welfare Day visible to the public, so the organisation allied itself with artists and public figures. Nielsen's songs were published and sold to raise funds, and thus the songs became part of the promotion of the cause.

It is debatable whether such songs can still be considered music for an event, that is as part of a planned and staged programme. It may well have been the case in local contexts that the songs were used every year at the opening of Children's Welfare Day, as a song is more flexible than a large-scale work and can easily be incorporated into an event and become part of a local tradition. A similar example is *De unges Sang* (*Song of the Young*) (CNW 291), which Nielsen composed in 1909 as a song for the young gymnasts of the N. H. Rasmussen Gymnastics Institute to celebrate its twenty-fifth anniversary. From then on, the song could live on when the gymnasts met, but it also gained general recognition when it was included in *The Folk High School Melody Book*.

Some of Nielsen's works were composed for festive performances celebrating a great artist. These include three compositions in honour of Shakespeare on the 300th anniversary of his death in 1916 (CNW 15), Ludvig Holberg on the 200th anniversary of the first Danish theatre performance in 1922 (CNW 20) and Hans Christian Andersen with the festive play *Amor og Digteren* (*Cupid and the Poet*) (CNW 23) at the Odense Theatre in 1930. The first two works were the prologue and epilogue of a play, while *Cupid and the Poet* must be regarded as true incidental music.

The same is true of the music for the play *The Mother* (CNW 18). After the referendum regarding the question of North Schleswig's affiliation in early 1920, there was a desire to celebrate the result with music. In June 1920 the new border was drawn north of Flensburg and thus southern Jutland became Danish again. After the end of the war in 1918, members of the Artists' Association of 18 November had already expressed the wish to organise a celebration of the peace negotiations. The celebration was to be held in the summer of 1919 at the Open-Air Theatre at Dyrehaven, north of Copenhagen, and 100,000 guests were expected. A committee was set up, and in the spring of that year Nielsen and the poet Helge Rode were invited to take part. Less than two weeks later, the two had sketched out a national 'Te Deum' for soloists, choir and orchestra, divided into movements with a speech in the middle. A hymn-like song was to be sung at the beginning, and the experienced composer imagined the final part of the work 'with an alternation of men's, women's and children's choirs, which would finally merge into a great concluding apotheosis, in which the simple melody now known from the introductory march would break out again with a text of general, all-encompassing content, which the whole assembled crowd could join in singing.'[39]

This large-scale project never came to fruition. The plans were shelved, partly because it was considered impossible to transport so many people to Dyrehaven. However, the idea of a celebration was taken up by The Royal Theatre, which persuaded

Nielsen and Rode to continue their collaboration, this time on the play *The Mother*. Although it is possible to see reminiscences of the original sketch in the music for the play – an introductory march, simple and singable melodies – it does not make much sense to regard the new composition as the realisation of the original idea. It is the idea of writing a play to mark and celebrate the reunification that recurs. Thus the play is conceived as an event of national character, both officially and in terms of the authors. Nielsen was quite clear about this in his letter to the theatre director, asking for a decent fee, since it was the state that had commissioned the work.[40]

The premiere at The Royal Theatre on 30 January 1921 was an event in which the participants were part of a deeply rooted community celebrating the national event. However, the response was influenced by the fact that the major public celebrations had already taken place in the summer of 1920 and most newspapers were concerned that the production of the play had been delayed. The event had run out of steam and the newspapers did not give it as much coverage as one might have expected. *Nationaltidende* was the only paper to take the opportunity to report on public reaction, which showed that 'the great joy of reunification … is still as alive and warm among the people as it was during the great days of celebration' the previous summer.[41]

The event was not the popular festival that Nielsen and Rode had originally envisaged. The play did indeed run thirty-one times at The Royal Theatre until April 1922, giving a large number of people the opportunity to hear the music. However, the theatre performances must have been very different from the huge open-air celebration that had been the original idea. Subsequent performances were similar to ordinary ones, with an audience and tickets.

Nielsen also made efforts to bring the music to a wider audience. Before the premiere he had piano arrangements of some of the music published, including the instrumental piece *Taagen letter* (*The Fog is Lifting*) and the songs 'Min Pige er saa lys som Rav' (Like golden amber is my girl) and *The Song to Denmark*, thus ensuring that parts of the incidental music had a popular breakthrough. If the performers who used these versions knew the original context, they may have had reunification in mind. Today, these excerpts are rather played and sung as part of the common Danish repertoire.

In 1910 Nielsen wrote an instrumental work to which he attributed a significant and lasting importance. It was a movement for string quartet, *Ved en ung Kunstners Baare* (*By the Bier of a Young Artist*) (CNW 36), composed within a few days of hearing of the untimely death of the painter Oluf Hartmann. Nielsen knew Hartmann from his stays at Fuglsang manor on the island of Lolland, where Hartmann's sister Bodil Neergaard lived. The music was composed for the interment at the cemetery of Holmens Kirke. Nielsen later arranged the composition for string orchestra and had it performed several times in concerts. For Nielsen, the composition was more than a memorial to a deceased acquaintance. It was an instrumental work with universal qualities that could be performed alongside his First Symphony, excerpts from the incidental music to the play *Aladdin* and the Overture to the opera *Maskarade*, as was the case at a concert with the Swedish Radio Orchestra in Stockholm on 7 December 1928.[42]

Although *By the Bier of a Young Artist* was obviously written for a specific occasion, it is an example of a work whose basic character as an instrumental lament is capable of underpinning the mood of mourning among those present at any funeral. The work has qualities that are universally understood. The opening of the piece immediately sets the mood. The melodic character of the movement is marked by descending plaintive semitones, almost like intense sighs. The outer voices are melodic, and because the bass is not the harmonic fundament, the listener experiences a world of sound without a clear tonal direction. The register of the middle voices is reversed, forcing the second violin to employ the melancholy G-string, while the viola pushes the sound forcefully into the high register – all aspects that contribute to the music's intense expression. In view of this pathos, Nielsen's son-in-law, Emil Telmányi, thought it an obvious choice to play the work at Nielsen's funeral in Vor Frue Kirke in Copenhagen on 9 October 1931. This was indeed a major event, with thousands of people in the streets and reports in all the newspapers. The work had repeated its function as a funeral hymn on a higher level.

Chapter 17

THE LIED COMPOSER

The European lied tradition is the starting point for Nielsen's production of songs. In one of the earliest surviving letters, dated May 1888, he wrote at length to his girlfriend Emilie that he had become interested in how to write songs and had therefore begun to study the great German masters – above all Schubert. He was fascinated by Schubert's ability to penetrate deeply into the spirit of the poem and express it in music. He was particularly interested in Schubert's introduction of the through-composed lied, in which he does not repeat the same melody for each stanza, but lets the music follow the development of the poem.[1]

In general, a lied can be defined as a solo song with an independent piano accompaniment. It makes sense, therefore, to regard a large part of Nielsen's songs as lieder. From his earliest song compositions and in his first collections setting poems by Jens Peter Jacobsen (Opp. 4 and 6) and Ludvig Holstein (Op. 10), he composes such songs. The ideal is for the pianist and singer to interpret the poem together. Some of these songs are through-composed, in which Nielsen narrates stanza by stanza, shaping the melody and piano accompaniment according to the content and development of the text. Others are basically strophic, in which the melody is repeated, but the details of the delivery or piano accompaniment can be varied.

One of the functions of the piano in the genre of lied is to provide introductory as well as closing musical sections that introduce and round off the stanzas. The introduction sets the key, tempo and mood, prepares the audience and allows the singer to enter on the right note and at the right time. The ending rounds off the stanza, but in strophic songs it also has the important function of leading into the next one so that the tempo and key remain the same. The ending often has a harmonic relationship with the beginning, providing coherence between the stanzas. In addition, the piano can support the changing moods along the way, commenting on or illustrating the development in various ways.

Although Nielsen gradually simplified his method of composing songs, *Strophic Songs*, Op. 21, the two volumes of *En Snes danske Viser* (*A Score of Danish Songs*) (1915, 1917) and the 1926 collection *Ti danske Smaasange* (*Ten Little Danish Songs*) were also published for voice and an independent piano accompaniment that does not just double the voice in the upper part. Nielsen's approach to song composition follows the lied tradition, thus continuing his work in this genre. Many of these songs were subsequently reworked into versions in which the piano follows the melody part, in order to support their use in communal contexts, as in *Folkehøjskolens Melodibog* (*The Folk High School Melody Book*). However, this does not alter the fact that they were conceived as songs to be performed by a soloist. The simplification is an expression of Nielsen's wish to make the songs known to a much wider audience.

In the simple, strophic songs, the functions of the piano part in supporting the introduction and transition or epilogue may be simplified to almost nothing, yet it is still there. Even in those songs that have been reworked for use in the community, with the vocal melody in the piano part, one can often see a reminiscence of this function, typically a small piano figure at the end of the movement, maintaining the tempo and signalling when the next stanza begins. Elements of the lied tradition live on here.

Nielsen's Lied Production

Singing lieder requires considerable skill on the part of both the singer and the pianist. The singer must be able to carry the vocal part alone, without relying on the melody in the piano's upper part, which is required when singing communal songs. This is a demanding task, especially when it comes to the large format. And that is exactly what Nielsen does when he takes on this genre.

Nielsen's early songs must be regarded as ambitious lied compositions. They are solo songs with extended piano accompaniment, in which he was able to experiment with various effects, both vocal and instrumental. At the same time, working with lieder was a way for him to explore poetry as a composer. He composed most of his lieder of this type between the late 1880s and 1896, some of which were published in the three song collections *Music for Five Poems by J. P. Jacobsen* (Op. 4, 1892), *Songs and Verses by J. P. Jacobsen* (Op. 6, 1893) and *Songs by Ludvig Holstein* (Op. 10, 1897). He was particularly interested in the latest poetry of the time, and it became a feature of many of his early songs that they were based on the poetry of the Modern Breakthrough.

By the time Nielsen was composing songs to texts by Jacobsen, the poet was part of the European high fashion and his poems were set to music by numerous composers, especially in the German-speaking countries. Indeed, Nielsen had a selection of his own Jacobsen songs published in a German-language edition, *Lieder von J.P. Jacobsen*, in 1895. Composing lieder in the European tradition was encouraged by his composition teacher, Orla Rosenhoff, who himself cultivated the genre, and it was common among the young composers in the society Symphonia, where Jacobsen was highly regarded.[2] In this respect, Nielsen was following a trend of the time. Such lieder were concert music and a deliberate trademark in the encounter with the public. Nielsen's songs were performed in recitals by professional musicians and singers and discussed publicly in the daily press.

The collection *Strophic Songs* (Op. 21) followed in 1907, its title signalling a move towards a simpler form of song. Posterity has read the title as a programmatic statement, pointing to the ideal of the popular song that would prevail ten to fifteen years later. However, this is a rather exaggerated interpretation. The collection does not represent a significant break with the lied tradition. Moreover, in the early song collections some of the pieces were strophic – that is, the melody is the same in several stanzas. However, there are variations in the piano part, as well as in the details of phrasing, dynamics and expression in the performance of the song. This is also the case in *Strophic Songs*, where some of them make great demands on both the pianist and the singer. A song such as 'Den første Lærke' (The larks are coming) is decidedly virtuosic. Even in a song like *Jens Vejmand* (*John the Roadman*), which is characterised by its deliberately simple style, each stanza is written out with precise instructions as to how it should be performed. Thus Nielsen indicates that the song is intended to be performed by a soloist as if it were a narrative, and that as a composer he wants to retain control over the details of expression.

When Nielsen later published songs in a simpler and more popular style – as in volumes 1 and 2 of *A Score of Danish Songs* (1915 and 1917) and including *Ten Little Danish Songs* (1926) with 'Jeg ved en Lærkerede' (Two larks in love have nested) and 'Solen er saa rød, Mor' (Look! The sun is red, mum) – he kept to his basic approach. In these collections the accompaniment is much simpler, yet the idea that the piano and the vocal part as a whole should carry the text is maintained. He also used this approach when composing popular songs for a wider range of musicians and audiences. Even when writing for ordinary people who could sing, his compositions were based on his extensive experience as a lied composer.[3]

Late in life he resumed to compose songs in the large format, though to a lesser extent. He composed *Studie efter Naturen* (*Study on Nature*) (CNW 303; 1916), *Balladen om Bjørnen* (*Ballad on the Bear*) (CNW 315; 1923) and 'Det är höst' (Autumn's near) (CNW 335; 1929), all of which are through-composed songs performed by professional singers in concerts. The first of these was performed more than a hundred times during Nielsen's lifetime, suggesting that he regarded lieder as an independent genre with which he could still identify, and that he still found it relevant to compose for the professional singer who, accompanied by a pianist, could perform contemporary texts at private events or in public recitals.[4]

Lied Studies

In the letter to Emilie of May 1888, mentioned above, Nielsen describes his new interest in lieder, explaining that he wanted to learn 'how to set poetry' to music.[5] The ideal was Schubert's lieder, and Nielsen was also interested in how the master approached the task. He had heard that Schubert 'read his texts through again and again until he was completely absorbed by the poem's spirit and mood'. Only then did he compose 'his beautiful music to it'. He told Emilie that learning a poem could be a slow process, but that it was important before starting work. His eagerness to tell Emilie about it suggests that the poem was important to him as a work of literary art, and that this was an interest that Emilie understood. It refers to the time they spent together reading poetry. In her memoirs, Emilie describes Nielsen's visit to her and her parents at Selde in Salling in northern Jutland, probably in the summer of 1888:

> Carl and I had the lunch hour all to ourselves in the cosy three-bayed sitting room. It happened that Carl sat at the piano and worked with notes and sounds while I read. It was Aarestrup and J. P. Jacobsen who mostly influenced us. Carl composed the music for 'Alle de voksende Skygger' (All the developing shadows) and gave it to me, so it was never published.[6]

Emilie points out that poetry absorbed them both, and it was an intense preoccupation that left its mark. Many years later, Nielsen was still able to recite Lord Byron's poem 'My Soul is Dark', a text that Nielsen set to music in the years following his studies at the Academy of Music.[7] Thus the aim was not only to set the lyrics to music, but also to read and understand them.

The domestic environment of the living room was one of the social spaces in which Nielsen's interest in poetry and song developed. The study of lieder was one of the educational ideals of the time, and it became a way of developing an appreciation of poetry and music.[8] This way of spending time together is comparable to the European salon culture of the time, where solo songs accompanied by piano were a kind of 'domestic music', often played for a closed circle of invited guests.[9] Schubert gave his name to this type of gathering, later known as *Schubertiades*. In the private homes of the Viennese bourgeoisie in the early 1820s, friends and acquaintances met in an informal atmosphere and held a salon with readings, music, dancing and wine. Schubert participated as a pianist, playing his lieder and other compositions for the guests.[10]

Indeed, the connection with Schubert is even more tangible, for not only did Nielsen draw inspiration from Schubert's lieder: in the letter to Emilie, he also described Schubert as the innovator of the lied genre. Schubert composed over 600 lieder, songs that only in the generations after his death achieved the status of being highly innovative. From the 1860s onwards, his compositions became increasingly accessible, and after the first major biography in German appeared in 1865, his importance to the genre was widely recognised.[11] The fact that this happened only gradually in Denmark is shown by a portrait in *Søndags-Posten* in 1869. In a section entitled 'Famous Composers', the journal made a slightly apologetic reference to Schubert, stating that the musical world had 'only recently' become aware of him.[12]

The image of Schubert as an innovator of the lieder genre, as Nielsen puts it to Emilie, was thus the result of a rather new perception. It began with the German biography of 1865 and was only consolidated towards the centenary of Schubert's birth in 1897.[13] In Denmark the event was marked by the first monograph on Schubert in Danish and an extensive article on his songs.[14] Both accounts draw heavily on the German biography, and both describe Schubert as the 'greatest and most brilliant master' of German lieder.[15]

The through-composed form in particular is new with regard to Schubert. It is a form that does not reflect the stanzaic structure of a poem, but seeks to depict the development of its content. In practical terms, this means that the melodic aspect of a through-composed lied is constantly evolving, rather than having the same melody for every stanza – as in a strophic or communal song. In a through-composed lied, the description of the text is more important than its form.

In his letter to Emilie, Nielsen notes the consequences of the through-composed form for the musical treatment of the text: when Schubert composed in this way, 'every single word in the poem took on its own meaning and the poet's thought received its highest expression through music; whereas formerly the text had been considered as something quite subordinate'.[16] Although the last sentence about the status of the text for lied composers before Schubert is somewhat exaggerated, it does show that it was natural for Nielsen to regard the text as central.

Nielsen was so interested in how music could treat a poem that he set out to investigate Schubert's working process. He took the composer's already iconic lied *Erlkönig*, based on Goethe's poem, which was inspired by the Norse ballad 'Elveskud'. Goethe's version tells the story of a father who rides through the night with his dying son in his arms. In Schubert's lied, Nielsen found the treatment of the poem so compelling that he had to explain it to Emilie. Although he was using a lied that was now over seventy years old, he was aware that it represented a new way of dealing with poetry.

Nielsen must have had the music in front of him; he must have read, played and perhaps sung the piece several times to gain an impression of how the music treated the text. His detailed descriptions of the song's plot reveal that he studied the work intensively and read the poem thoroughly. To Emilie, he describes the introduction to the song as a visual experience: 'Hear the horse's thundering hooves and the sinister rustling in the wood at night; you even seem to see the moon's cold, magic beams.'[17]

Reading the music – or playing or listening to the insistent repetition of the notes – at the beginning of Schubert's lied does not tell us that it is an imitation of horseshoes. Only the question in the first stanza – 'Wer reitet so spät?' ('who is riding so late?') – makes it clear that it is a rider on the move. The text does not describe the

ILL. 1. Illustration of Goethe's *Erlkönig* in a painting by Moritz von Schwind. The painting was used as a template for contemporary postcards in large print runs.[18]

horse, nor does it mention the forest or the moon. Nielsen, like Schubert, must have read the text repeatedly, and with his vivid imagination he must have imagined the setting in which Goethe's story unfolded. Moreover, Schubert's evocative description must have contributed greatly to Nielsen's mental images. He may have seen one of the countless illustrations that were in circulation at the time, often depicting father and son in a moonlit forest.

The music itself does not reveal the plot, but together with the poem and the reader's imagination, the song opens up an overall description. When Nielsen retells the story to Emilie, he is highly influenced by all three – the music, his reading of the poem and his imagination. In the letter, he attributes many details that do not appear in Goethe's text, and which seem to be the result of a kind of holistic experience of reading the poem and the music.

It is interesting to see what features of Schubert's treatment of the poem Nielsen observed, as they may help us to understand his compositional approach to songs. In two passages that he describes in the letter, he notes how the registers of the voice can be used for dramatic effect and how the piano accompaniment can mark changes of mood.

THE LIED COMPOSER

Of the dialogue between the child and the father, Nielsen explains that the child's outburst is anxious, while the father's is reassuring. Schubert's treatment of the dialogue supports Nielsen's interpretation of the text. The same singer performs both characters, and in order to make the dialogue clear, Schubert has deliberately given the two characters different expressions. The child's lines are in a high, haunting register, rising one note with each new line from the middle of the song. The piano accompaniment is very dissonant in these passages, adding to the unsettling mood. In contrast, the father's phrases are in a lower register, accompanied by familiar harmonic turns and balanced cadences that give the father's lines a balanced and authoritative feel.

Of the end of the song, Nielsen remarks that 'the father spurs his steed, which flies through the air.' He senses an intensification, and although Goethe does write that the father now rides fast, the description of the situation is Nielsen's own. Schubert has intensified the horse's hooves at this point. The motif of the introduction is now more sonorous. By studying the connection between text and music, Nielsen has formed strong mental images of the situation. He describes the father to Emilie as 'he dismounts the shaking creature', a detail that is also absent from the song.

The intensive study of Schubert's songs also led Nielsen to study other composers:

> Recently I got hold of some songs by Schumann and Brahms, which I am studying whenever I have a free moment. When I have really immersed myself in the stirring, peculiar harmonies of these masters, I often get a strange feeling, because it always sets me thinking why I myself should actually want to compose at all, when so much wonderful music already exists. But fortunately that lasts only a short while, and then I can't refrain from it anyway.[19]

Nielsen's studies of German lieder thus raised existential questions about his own role as a composer and about the purpose of composing new songs. Yet the studies were an artistic driving force for him, giving him not only the desire but also the urge to compose and work with the poems he knew so well. He probably unconsciously had something in common with Brahms, who was interested in poetry from an early age and also composed lieder. Brahms regarded literature and poetry as works of art in their own right, and before the idea of setting a text to music, the text had to be studied on its own terms.[20] Brahms's pupil Gustav Jenner is reported to have said that Brahms expected composers of vocal music to know the text perfectly and to be able to recite it aloud to themselves before composing.[21]

Content-Saturated Composition

The lied was a genre in which a composer could experiment in a concentrated form. Nielsen's three published collections from the 1890s contain sixteen songs, which appear as saturated and rich compositions. The shortest songs are about twenty bars, the longest no more than seventy. The songs require only a singer and a pianist, and the manageable scale of the genre made it ideal for a young composer learning to master different compositional techniques. Nielsen's lieder clearly show that he was conscious of the relationship between singer and pianist, and that he used the piano in many different ways. The harmonic devices employed in the music also testify to his experimental approach to the lieder. In order to gain a better understanding of how Nielsen works as a composer, it is worthwhile taking a closer look at some of his lied compositions. What compositional means does he use, and how does he achieve the musical effects that the listener encounters?

Nielsen's involvement with the genre began some years earlier, and immediately after his studies at the Academy he composed lieder as part of his music studies with Orla Rosenhoff (CNW 276–287). He presented his drafts to Rosenhoff, who followed them with interest 'growing up, from sketches to completion'.[22] It may well have been his teacher who encouraged Nielsen to try his hand at the lied genre. Rosenhoff had composed songs himself and therefore knew the genre well. Remarkably, there is a considerable overlap in their choice of poems. Rosenhoff had composed lieder to texts by Emil Aarestrup, among others, and English poems in Danish translation by Caralis.[23] It was these that Nielsen set to music for the first time. In particular, 'My Soul is Dark' (CNW 279) in Caralis's translation of Lord Byron's poem was one of his very first lieder and can be seen as Nielsen's start in the genre.

'My Soul is Dark' is strophic in form and marked with repeat signs in the notes, so that the two stanzas are sung to the same music. This results in a simple two-part form in which the short introduction is reused as a conclusion. The music in the piano part is composed in the low register, and the dark sonorous quality captures the idea of the text and has a mood-setting effect. The accompaniment is rhythmically insistent, although not melodic, and is secondary to the singer. The song makes use of Romantic harmony, with a bold modulation in the middle marked by a powerful crescendo. This has only a brief effect, and the movement soon returns to the main key.

The small form can accommodate only a few effects. It is easily saturated and there is a danger of overburdening it. If this lied is seen as an exercise by Nielsen, it is clear that he was concerned with taming the development of the material while still allowing its potential to be expressed. Despite the strict framework, the vocal part manages to create contrasts between the quiet, almost recitative opening and the melodically energetic places where the piano stops and the poem's protagonist calls for singing. The whole is carefully structured according to the three paired lines of the poem's stanza. In other words, the structure of the poem dictated the composition. Three other early lieder, *Til mit Hjertes Dronning* (*To the Queen of my Heart*) (CNW 276), *Serenade* (CNW 277) and *Tag jer iagt for Anna* (*Bonnie Ann*) (CNW 278), are also based on translations by Caralis. They have essentially the same strophic characteristics as 'My Soul is Dark'.

Nielsen takes a completely different approach to composition when setting Jens Peter Jacobsen's poem 'All the developing shadows' (CNW 282) – the lied that Emilie mentions in her memoirs of the summer in Selde. The piano part is more than an accompaniment, more than just setting the mood. It goes far beyond Schubertian scoring and gives the piano a more independent role in the style of Schumann's or Brahms's lieder. The semitone of the introduction in the bass and later in the upper part of the piano blurs the tonality of the movement, which reflects the twilight mood. The text describes in concentrated form nature at dusk, when the dew has fallen, as an anonymous observer would sense it. At the point when the singer tells of the lone star shining pure in the sky, the piano sets a new mood. The highest note of the song is reached at the word 'lyser' (shines), and a crystal-clear piano figure played in the high register embellishes the pure ray of the star in sound. There is only one star, so the musical figure is played only once. It is a clear musical statement, for it is a figure that, with its somewhat sudden caprice, might otherwise have deserved more attention – an attention it was not to have, for in Jacobsen's poem the star is eclipsed, the clouds gather, and the viewer sees the flowers and hears the evening wind instead. Musically, it remains the art of suggestion.

It is a strong, sensuous poem in which impressions change rapidly. The lied not only sets the mood but is also a 'reading of the text'. The music thus represents Nielsen's intense engagement with the poem. He has read it repeatedly, pondered its meaning and found connotations in its statements that could be translated into sound. The music is therefore not simply a reflection of the poem. It is an interpretation of the text – and as saturated as the poem is in its content, so is the music.

This lied, which is the earliest Jacobsen poem that Nielsen set to music, was not included in his two collections of Jacobsen texts. Emilie kept the only copy that Nielsen gave her. Yet it illustrates the potential of Jacobsen's poetry and why it fascinated not only Nielsen but also a large number of European composers at the turn of the century. Its rapidly changing moods, its sensuousness and its delicate and rich descriptions were details that were noticed in the European reception of Jacobsen. In Vienna, Jacobsen's work was seen as an expression of modernity, understood as the 'nervous art'.

MUSIC EX. 1. Carl Nielsen, 'Alle de voksende Skygger' (All the developing shadows), bars 7–10. Nielsen has given the piano an independent role in the description of Jacobsen's poem. There is a clear change of character in bar 8, which becomes the transition to a tone-painting passage. Up to this point, while the text is about the growing shadows, the piano has been playing in a low register. In bar 8, both the register and the character of the accompaniment change to a light and twinkling sound. On the singer's long note on 'lyser' (shines) in bar 10, the piano plays a simple yet catchy figure. In the pianist's left hand, two high notes are notated in the treble clef, and the pianist's arms must cross to represent the lone star.

When Nielsen moves from his early chamber music into Jacobsen's universe, he encounters poems that challenge him. They are delicate and nuanced, but they are also very different, and now he has to relate to something beyond himself – unlike the instrumental music he had been working on earlier. In trying to understand it as 'nervous art', it is important to see it as Nielsen's attempt to empathise with the nuanced and differentiated world of the poems and to bring this into play in the music.

Hermann Bahr, the Austrian equivalent of Georg Brandes, summed up the characteristics of the new age in Vienna in 1890, using the concept of 'the modern', which he saw as the overcoming of naturalism.[24] In this context, he considers what the new is that is to replace it. First there was psychology, which turned everything upside down, but also introduced the precise observation and description of human states of mind. His prediction is that naturalism will be overtaken by what he calls a 'nervous romanticism' or, perhaps better, a 'mysticism of the nerves'. To emphasise that this does not mean a return to Romanticism, he insists that it is a new sensibility trained by the achievements of naturalism: 'Naturalism may be regarded as the high schooling of the nerves: a sensibility for the finest and most delicate nuances.'[25] It is precisely in this version that the idea of the modern as a 'nervous art' becomes specific: a delicate, hypersensitive capacity for observation and expression, as found in Jacobsen's work.

If the notion of modernity in Vienna was so closely associated with Jacobsen, it was because he was seen as the ultimate naturalist, whose special qualifications as an educated natural scientist, combined with his long illness, made him extremely sensitive. The result is a sensibility that combines a specific, detailed description of nature with a differentiated emotional naturalism.[26] The essence of Jacobsen's special quality is 'his highly developed sensitivity and receptivity to all that is fine, delicate, half-finished, to colours, scents and sounds, the faintest nuances of which he becomes aware, to the silent melancholy of the lonely, finally to longing, the great, agonising, trembling, never dying longing'.[27] According to this interpretation, Jacobsen embodies a link between naturalism and 'romanticism of the nerves', which might otherwise seem unrelated. The latter is naturalism transcended, not negated.

To explain what in music corresponds to a romanticism of the nerves, one might describe it as an ever-greater refinement of the faculty of perception and expression through gradation. The highly discriminating and constantly varying and changing soundscape corresponds musically to the highly refined play of the nerves – of the receiver as well as the sender.

In the art of the lied, this is expressed above all in the contrast between the scoring of the piano part and the refinement of the means of expression. Instead of striving for a uniform mood, the vocal part and the accompaniment follow even the slightest fluctuations in the universe of the text. In this way, it may be natural to distinguish between textual universes that are capable of something different. In a realistic and contemporary universe, a sensitive registration with nerves in a state of extreme preparation is a means of showing us the intensity and degree of the impressions and emotions described by the song.

In a number of Nielsen's songs set to Jacobsen's poems, there is a tendency for the music to reflect a delicate, seismographic and therefore formally distorted or fragmented perception. In the first collection, *Music for Five Poems by J. P. Jacobsen* (Op. 4), this characteristic fits *I Seraillets Have* (*In Seraglio Garden*) (No. 2), *To Asali* (No. 3) and 'Har Dagen sanket al sin Sorg' (If day has gathered all its woe) (No. 5); it also fits the song intended for Op. 4, but which Nielsen withdrew, *I Drømmenes Land* (*In the Realm of Dreams*).[28]

In 'If day has gathered all its woe', the delicate nuance is particularly evident in the use of tonal fluctuation, which, within the poem's basic mood of melancholy, suggests that three different realities are at play. The song may serve as an example of how Nielsen used tonal ambivalence as a subtle means of conveying his reading of Jacobsen's poem.[29]

If day has gathered all its woe	Har Dagen sanket al sin Sorg
And wept it into dew,	Og grædt den ud i Dug,
Then night reveals the heavens, though,	Saa aabner Natten Himlens Borg
With boundless sadness, silent woe.	Med evigt Tungsinds tavse Sorg.
And one by one	Og en for en
And two by two	Og to og to
The guardian spirits will emerge	Gaa fjerne Verd'ners Genier frem
From heaven's vague and distant verge.	Af Himmeldybets dunkle Gjem.
On high, over worldly dolour and pleasure,	Og højt over Jordens Lyst og Elende
With candle stars in hand, at leisure,	Med Stjernekjerter højt i Hænde
Striding along they cover the heavens.	Skride de langsomt hen over Himlen.
They change their bearing,	De Fodtrin skifte
And sorrow seizes.	Med Sorg i Sinde.
Strange is the flaring	Underligt vifte
In space, in icy breezes,	For Rummets kolde Vinde
Candle stars and their flickering flashes.	Stjernekjerternes flakkende Flammer.[30]

Similar to 'All the developing shadows', the text should be imagined as the sensations of an anonymous observer of a situation they are experiencing. The poem describes an incident that takes place in the borderland between day and night, but at the same time it seeks to express the basic mood of sorrow, longing and hopelessness that is gathered in the sensation of nature: day has gathered all its sorrow and turned it into nature's tears: dew. In contrast to the end of the day, in the third line of the text, night opens up to the sensory experience of a new universe in which the mood is even more sombre: here the silent sorrow of eternal torment reigns. With the transition to night, the harmonic range also shifts with a subtle jolt to E flat minor. One must imagine that the observer now focuses on the dark starry sky. In the distance, two genii, a kind of ghosts of light, appear hesitantly, and after some uncertainty about the key, the middle section of the lied ends in A flat major. The shift to the major, with a marked change in both melody and accompaniment, emphasises that the universe has shifted again: the ghosts of light must be a vision, a detail imagined by the observer, which momentarily distracts from the melancholy and offers a glimpse of hope. But even when they change their bearing, 'sorrow seizes', and here both melody and accompaniment return to the place where the lyrics speak of eternal melancholy, again in E flat minor.

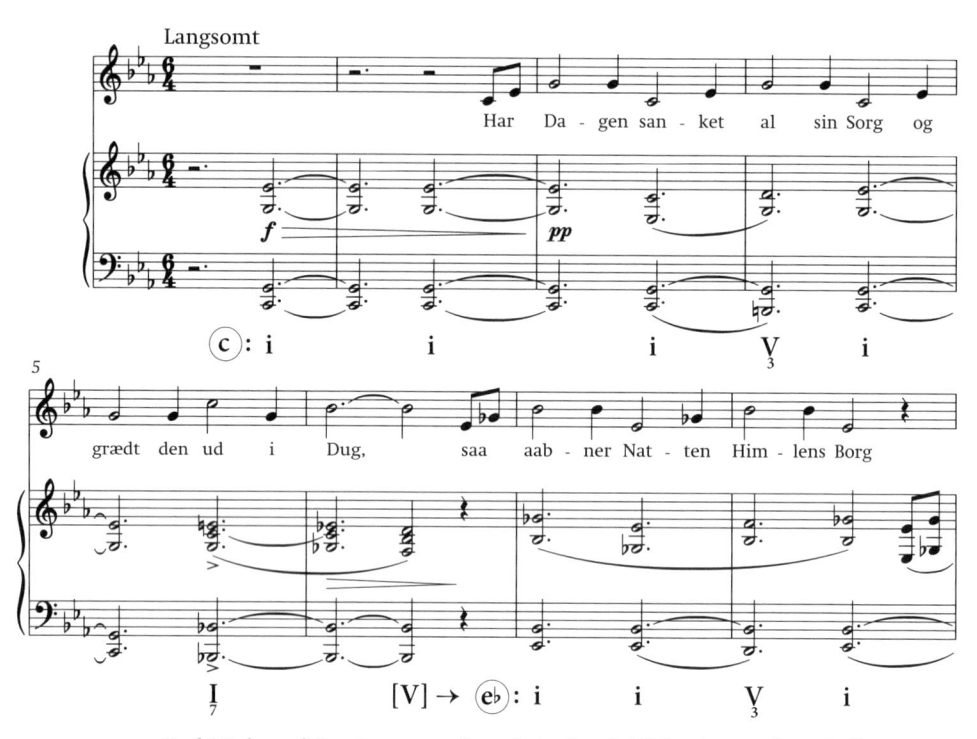

MUSIC EX. 2. Carl Nielsen, 'Har Dagen sanket al sin Sorg' (If day has gathered all its woe), Op. 4, No. 5, bars 1–8. The music begins on an unaccented beat with a C minor chord, which is repeated and faded out, then the vocal part enters, confirming the C minor. The C minor piano chords are played in the middle of the bars, which helps to set a suspended mood, creating uncertainty. The emphasis is on 'Sorg' (woe) in the middle of bar 4. In the next bar, C minor becomes C major with a seventh, which would normally suggest a modulation to F minor. Instead, the notes of the upper part simply descend in steps, so that what sounded like the beginning of a major-minor shift is actually a B flat chord. It then shifts to E flat minor, which sounds like a sudden jolt to a new tonal level. The earthly experience of nature is thus shifted to the observation of the celestial sphere. At the same time, the keys of C minor and E flat minor are linked in that they can be interpreted as relative keys, albeit as a variant, since E flat is a minor rather than a major key. They can thus symbolise two separate yet related parallel universes, the natural earthly universe and the distant celestial universe. Both convey a contemplation of nature, while the following middle section of the song in A flat major, which appears as a dreamlike vision of two ghosts of light moving across the sky, also provides a musical contrast.

The elements introduced at the beginning of the song return one by one at the end of the piece. After the return of the E flat minor phrase, both the melody and accompaniment of bars 3–4 return, but now in the piano, while the singer wonders, with a directionless melodic line, whether the starlight strangely 'is the flaring in space, in icy breezes'. The bass remains on C, while the other notes in the piano part gradually rise until they end on E flat, this time in the major key. Is E flat major a kind of mediation between the tonal planes of earth and heaven? This ambiguity is kept alive until the last note of the song. In the piano's postlude, it sounds as if E flat major is to be confirmed as the actual key of the piece, but at the very end we realise that we are returning to C minor, with the addition of the note C in both the low register of the bass and the high register of the treble. We are back in earthly reality, but so subtly and only hinted at that it is doubtful whether the observer in the poem is fully aware of which reality is the real one.

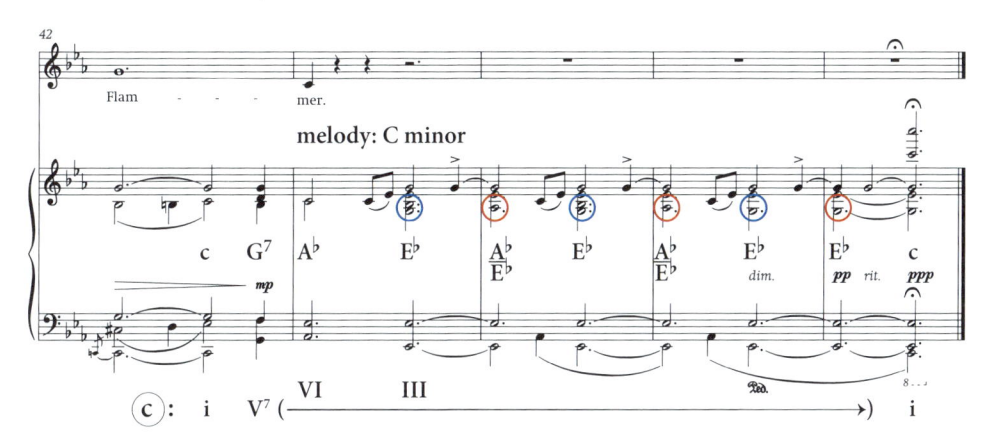

MUSIC EX. 3. Carl Nielsen, 'If day has gathered all its woe', bars 42–46. It is only in bar 42, in the middle of 'Flammer' (flashes), that the music has returned to C minor, and the final chord, a clearly placed G⁷ harmony, suggests that the C minor key is being confirmed. Instead, a so-called interrupted cadence appears in bar 43, reintroducing A flat major alternating with E flat major; at the same time, the melody in the right hand of the piano part quotes the beginning of the melody, which, taken in isolation, is C minor. The first chord in bars 44 and 45 is rather a combination of A flat major and E flat major. But in the next bar, E flat major seems to be the goal, as the A♭, previously in the low register of the piano's right hand, is now replaced by a G, part of the E flat major chord (marked in red). It is only at the very end, in the second half of bar 46, that C is added in the extreme high and low registers on either side of the existing chord. Now it is C minor, subtly prepared by omitting the B♭ that is part of the E flat major chord in bars 43 and 44 (marked in blue). However, the B♭ is not present when the chord is struck in the middle of bar 45, when the accompanist has to use the sustain pedal so that the notes continue to sound until the end. Thus Nielsen subtly alternates between the tonal universes present throughout the movement.

In Romantic lieder it was common to use the relative keys, for example C minor and E flat major, and thus shift between major and minor, to contribute to musical conflict. Similarly, tonal ambiguity and modulation were familiar devices used in the course of a movement. Nielsen, however, chooses to maintain the tension and uncertainty right to the end, building this ambiguity into the aural experience.

For Nielsen, the experimental element of the lieder was that he could try out different musical effects that would translate his reading of the poems into sound. He did not take existing models as a starting point, but created musical progressions that followed the lyrics. Some of the techniques of Schubert, Schumann and Brahms are at work, although Nielsen drew inspiration from many others – including outside the lieder repertoire. It is important to remember that Nielsen's lieder are not only linked to German models, but that his studies also gave him an artistic drive that allowed him to shape his lieder in his own way. Like his contemporaries Robert Henriques, Alfred Tofft, Gustav Helsted, Elisabeth Meyer and Louis Glass, who were all composing lieder to Danish texts around the same time, Nielsen composed his works on the basis of the lyrics and his personal interpretation of the poem. Thus the lied became an experimental genre, certainly influenced by persuasive models, but in which each composer's contribution to the genre was highly personal.

Lieder in Public

In the 1890s there was a renewed interest in lieder in the musical life of Copenhagen, and Nielsen's collections of lieder were intended for the general public. Here he encountered the problem that the ability of the audiences and critics to listen to the music on first hearing was in stark contrast to the intensive study of the poems that Nielsen himself had experienced. This was, of course, a problem that affected all first performances. However, it is worth considering whether a song was intended to be understood immediately, or whether a performance was to be intended as an introduction to a new song, to be returned to time and again, to be experienced as a work of art. What were the expectations of Nielsen's songs when they were presented to the audience?

Four of Nielsen's settings of texts by Jacobsen were performed at a concert in the small hall of Koncertpalæet on 28 April 1892.[31] The songs were published that year as part of *Music for Five Poems by J. P. Jacobsen*, Op. 4, but presumably not until after the concert.[32] The reviewers therefore had to make an assessment after only one hearing. If they knew the poems beforehand, they would obviously have a better chance of engaging with the music, and it was normal for the lyrics to be printed in the programme.

One reviewer said of *Solnedgang* (Sunset) and *Irmelin Rose* that they had 'much melodic invention and beauty of form' – both lieder have strophic features and thus a recognisable structure. The other two songs, 'If day has gathered all its woe' and

In Seraglio Garden, were 'less inspired and less clearly structured than the previous ones';[33] they are through-composed, and thus their structure is constantly evolving. The reviewer points out that Jacobsen's poems for the two songs are 'very fragmentary'.[34] Unlike the first two, they have irregular prosody. The 'leaping form of the fragment and the sketch, as well as the persistent presentation of the difference between dream, language and nature' was a characteristic of Jacobsen's poetry.[35] Brandes emphasises this characteristic as something absolutely positive and an expression of Jacobsen's modernity: 'A fixed form, regular metre would be impossible for Jacobsen. He is too modern.'[36] Nielsen's setting of the poems reflects precisely this fragmented character. The reviewer's observation that the lieder can seem unclear in their structure is formulated as a criticism, but it suggests that the reviewer had an ear for something new and challenging. It is Nielsen's empathy with the modernity of the poems that is evident in the reviewer's reservations.

Three years later, the five lieder from *Songs and Verses by J. P. Jacobsen*, Op. 6, were performed at Koncertpalæet, a recital organised by the society Symphonia. The five songs were performed at the end, and the critics' view of Nielsen's abilities as a composer seems to have changed. Compared to the instrumental works performed at the same event, the songs evoked 'fine and unique moods' and were seen as 'proof that Carl Nielsen can still feel the urge to capture the hearts of music lovers'.[37] Another reviewer points to *Genrebillede* (*Genre Painting*), Op. 6, No. 1, as the song that undoubtedly stood out the most.[38] These were not the same lieder that had been reviewed at the recital three years earlier, but it still shows that perhaps the view of his lieder had changed.

The composer Robert Henriques, who also made his living as a critic, had worked with the same texts, and in his review of Nielsen's *Songs and Verses by J. P. Jacobsen*, he took issue with Nielsen's interpretation of the poems. The critique thus provides an interesting insight into the two friends' views of the role of a composer of lieder. Henriques thought that Nielsen was forcing the style of the lieder and striving 'to be original, to compose differently from everyone else'.[39]

Indeed, when Henriques reviewed the published score, it was not a performance or a first glance at the publication that formed the basis of his assessment. He had had the opportunity to study the music in great detail. Yet Henriques's answer to the question of how Jacobsen's poems should be set to music was an argument for counterbalancing the subtlety of the poetry:

> Carl Nielsen generally took Jacobsen's dark poems too seriously. Whoever wants to set Jacobsen to music must certainly try to lighten up the beautiful stanzas with a transparent, folk-like tone that can bring them to the lips of the people.[40]

Henriques takes a different view from Nielsen, who hardly thought at the time that Jacobsen's songs should be on everyone's lips. On the contrary, Nielsen's early lieder were composed according to ideals suitable for professional musicians. Nielsen's aim was to empathise with and indeed emphasise the poem's uneasy and unresolved tensions.

The Art of Simplicity

After Nielsen's first two collections of lieder, new poets come on the scene, and he set six poems by Ludvig Holstein, published in 1897. The poems are sensuous in content and in this respect comparable to those of Jacobsen. However, the textual universe is different, focusing on scenes from nature, and the form is simpler, with a regular metrical structure. The lighter and more immediate style of the poems seems to be reflected in Nielsen's musical expression.

The tendency towards simpler expression is most evident in the two publications entitled *Strophic Songs*, published in 1907. They contain a total of seven solo songs with a wide range of stylistic approaches, from the expressive and through-composed *Høgen* (*Hawk*) with lyrics by Jeppe Aakjær to the strophic and introverted 'Skal Blomsterne da visne' (Shall flowers, then, all wither), which originally appeared in Helge Rode's play *The Fights in Stefan Borg's House*.

The seven songs were composed over a period of six years, five of them within a few months in the summer of 1907. The dedication on the title page suggests that Nielsen may have had a particular performance in mind when he completed the collection, which is dedicated to Bodil Neergaard.

Bodil Neergaard lived at Fuglsang Manor on the island of Lolland, where Nielsen often spent his summer and Christmas holidays from 1904.[41] Neergaard was the daughter of the composer Emil Hartmann, son of Johan Peter Emilius Hartmann, and she and her husband Viggo de Neergaard made their manor a meeting place for their musically talented friends. The Dutch composer Julius Röntgen, who had been staying at Fuglsang since 1893, was responsible for organising the soirees, where guests played and sang for each other. These private gatherings were part of the European salon culture that also promoted Schubert's lieder. Nielsen undoubtedly saw his new strophic songs in relation to this form of social gathering. Although these performances were not public, they were an important part of musical cultural life, where families of musicians, wealthy citizens and the old aristocracy met. Nielsen knew the tradition from the musical milieus of Odense and Copenhagen, and Bodil Neergaard represented the milieu that had the means and connections to organise high-quality musical gatherings.

Röntgen's son remembered the summers at Fuglsang, where the days were filled with music. From 11 to 12 in the morning, the musical programme for the evening was decided, and the afternoon was free for excursions into the countryside, with boat trips and outdoor life. The son describes how he and his siblings made music together with their father, who was the driving force behind the concerts.

> We were back for dinner at six o'clock, and then the concert began at exactly half past seven. The repertoire we played in those years included much of the chamber music literature. As we grew and developed as musicians, we participated more actively. Playing in the large hall with the two grand pianos was ideal. Bodil de Neergaard sang every evening, accompanied by my father.[42]

Bodil Neergaard was an accomplished amateur singer who had taken lessons from Asger Hamerik and the soprano Lola Artôt-Padilla in Paris.[43] Neergaard did not perform in public, but singing was important to her relationship with others. When she was in Copenhagen, she often visited Nina Grieg, also a singer, so that they could perform together.[44] For Bodil Neergaard, the musical evenings at Fuglsang were indispensable. She expressed this in a letter to her brother in September 1905, when all the summer guests, including Nielsen and Röntgen, had returned home: 'It is always with a heavy heart that we say goodbye to them … They also leave a deep loss [in my heart] – just the thought of not hearing the sound of music! We fall into hibernation and become sleepy in the evening.'[45]

Nielsen's daughter Anne Marie has described the musical evenings as she experienced them at the age of fifteen or sixteen. She gives the impression that the performances were shrouded in an atmosphere of seriousness.[46] It was not just entertainment. The evenings were conducted according to Röntgen's careful plans. In addition to instrumental music, songs by Schubert and Brahms were central. Nielsen's 'lieder' had also been on the programme since his first visit in 1904, often together with Schubert's.[47] Exactly which pieces were sung is not known, but it is interesting that Röntgen, as programme organiser, and Neergaard, as soloist, readily perceived Nielsen's songs in relation to the German lieder.

Also in the summer of 1907, Nielsen and his family were to visit Fuglsang. However, in August, less than half a year before his new strophic songs were to be published, Nielsen had to write to Neergaard with his regrets that he could not come. The letter ends with the words: 'I've a number of new songs that I'd have liked to have had you sing through.'[48] There is no doubt that it was the draft of *Strophic Songs* that he intended to bring with him. Five of the songs had been composed in June and July 1907 and were therefore completely new.

One of them is *John the Roadman*, which was to become Nielsen's greatest success, with a popular impact far beyond what he could have ever imagined. It was probably not his intention to write a catchy tune. In view of the collection's close relationship to the lied genre and Nielsen's approach to the poems, it is possible to understand the setting of Aakjær's poem as a staged ballad. *John the Roadman* may be viewed as a pastiche of a broadside ballad rather than a folk song to be taken at face value. Nielsen has a built-in distance from the sentimental tone that dominates the lyrics. Given Nielsen's experience with incidental music, it is possible that he envisaged an actor singing the piece, a characteristic feature of which is that, despite its basic strophic form, the original version contains precise instructions as to how each stanza should be expressed by the performer. One must imagine a trained singer who has perfected their technical skills, who has mastered every vocal expression and who is able to use their voice to tell a story. A study of the music reveals the exaggerated articulation with which Nielsen expected the song to be performed. In the second stanza, the hammering is illustrated by an expressive, dynamic alternation between *p f p*. In the last stanza, the tempo is slowed and the song is sung in *pp* for the first time: the roadman is now dead and the visitor to his grave realises how unfairly the roadman was treated. In other words, the song was written in the lied tradition, where the story is vividly described in sound by professional musicians for a listening audience.

Although the collection was in many ways a new development, it still comprised songs intended for the public. As with his previous song collections, Nielsen presented this new one at a 'composition evening'. The event took place at Odd Fellow Palæet in Copenhagen on 30 November 1907, with Johanne Kraup-Hansen singing the seven songs, accompanied by Henrik Knudsen.[49] Just as fourteen years earlier, a reviewer commented that 'the simplicity and straightforwardness of many of these songs came across as refreshingly natural' after the tortuous instrumental pieces.[50] Another reviewer took the opposite view, finding that Nielsen's new String Quartet in F major, Op. 44, also been performed at the event, had become 'milder' and had a wit comparable to Haydn's, while the songs failed to live up to expectations. The text was 'excellently chosen', but otherwise they did not offer much. It is interesting to note that what the reviewer misses is the central features of the lied:

> Carl Nielsen is strangely old-fashioned in his songs. He mainly uses a purely supporting piano accompaniment, rarely elaborates on the lyrics, but sets them to a melody that may be both original and slightly characteristic – but by no means feels like the only one, the one especially for this poem.[51]

A comment by another reviewer emphasises that what one was used to hearing in the concert hall was the through-composed 'Kunstlied', from which Nielsen's strophic songs were different. In 1907, therefore, it was still expected that Nielsen's lieder would be judged in relation to a European lied tradition. It was a tradition that audiences and critics knew and recognised, and in which it could not be taken for granted that a move towards simpler, strophic solo songs would be viewed positively.[52]

Up to and including *Strophic Songs*, Nielsen structured his lied collections in such a way that it was clear that they were aimed at an audience that cultivated the genre. The parallel publication of a selection of Jacobsen's songs in German in 1895 also shows that Nielsen was not only aiming at a Danish audience, but also at the German-speaking musical world, where the lied was in great demand. This is also true of the two subsequent song collections, the *Songs by Ludvig Holstein* (1897) and *Strophic Songs* (1907), both of which appeared in first editions with parallel Danish and German texts and bilingual titles. Indeed, the songs were intended for a European audience from the very beginning. This changed after 1907, when Nielsen almost always published his first editions in Danish, although translations were still possible.

Until the 1920s, however, Nielsen held on to the ideals of the lied genre when composing new songs. A central idea he retained was that the poem should be the

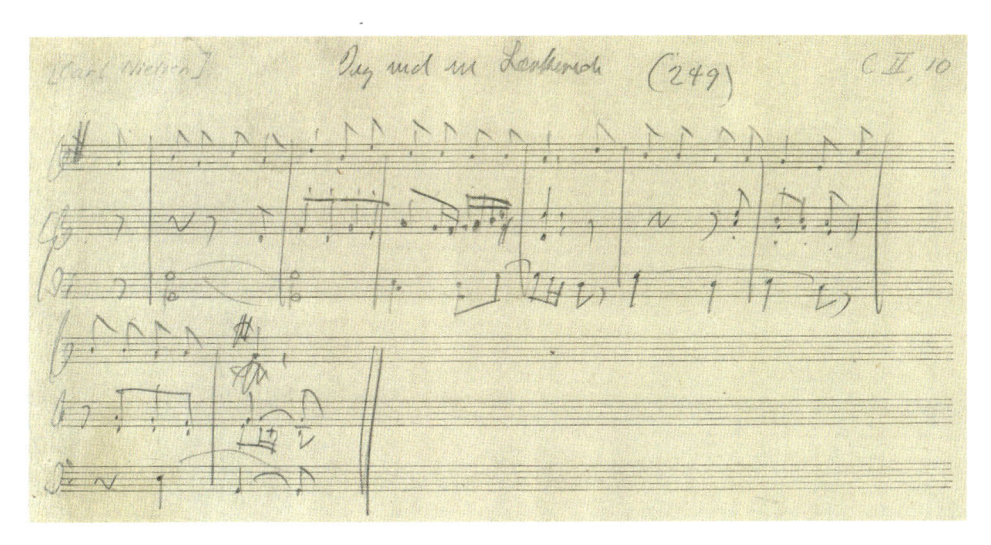

ILL. 2. Nielsen's manuscript, CNS 173a, for 'Jeg ved en Lærkerede' (Two larks in love have nested). Nielsen first composed the song in a version for two-part girls' choir. It begins as a catch, with the two voices singing in canon. Nielsen transfers this idea to the piano accompaniment where the singer enters alone, and the piano imitates the first line of the piece. The piano part then continues with a small ascending motif in bar 3, imitating the song of the lark and its flight across the sky. The pianist's left hand rounds off the first half of the stanza with a small musical figure that continues the rapid motif in the right hand that sounds like the lark's song. The final figure is used again at the end, after the last word has been sung. This brings the whole piece together and at the same time the figure sets the scene for the beginning of the next stanza.

starting point for the musical composition – he took seriously that it was a matter of setting a poem to music. Even in a song such as 'Two larks in love have nested', published in 1926 in the collection *Ten Little Danish Songs*, he insisted that the accompaniment should both express his interpretation of the poem and support the mood of the text.

The qualities of the song have made it a popular monophonic lullaby; however, this does not alter the fact that Nielsen took great care in working out the setting. The singer acts as a narrator, telling what they have seen, but also involving the listener in the need to keep the location of the lark's nest a secret. The following stanzas list all the dangers lurking for the little lark couple and their nest. Nielsen emphasises the delicate lightness of the song by dotting the notes in the piano's upper part – that is, instructions for a staccato performance. This also adds to the feeling that the singer is telling the story with bated breath. If someone happens to speak too loudly, the secret may be revealed. With simple and precise means, Nielsen delivers a perfect strophic lied in miniature.

Chapter 18

THE SYMBOLIST

In his biography *Carl Nielsen. Danskeren* (The Dane), Jørgen I. Jensen clearly states that 'Carl Nielsen's art, in short, comes from a symbolist culture; it is musical symbolism.'[1] With this astute formulation, he emphasised Nielsen's deep roots in the modern European culture of the 1890s. His observation is important, and his book was one of the first to see Nielsen in a European perspective. Yet his statement needs to be qualified and delimited if it is to be successful in understanding Nielsen's development. Nielsen was not a symbolist in all respects. He participated in a number of different European modern trends – at different times and in different ways – but he rarely accepted them unreservedly, and he could engage with several of them at the same time without them necessarily fitting together. This does not alter the fact that Nielsen's art is very much rooted in the symbolist culture of the 1890s.

A good starting point for a more precise definition of what might characterise Symbolism is to see it as currents in cultural life which, from around 1890, reacted against the rationalism of the Modern Breakthrough based on the experience of naturalism. Naturalism had sharpened the powers of observation of both physical and psychological conditions, and the scientific realisation that nerves were not spirits but electrical impulses meant that the idea of 'the modern' could be understood as a 'nervous art', expressed in a highly nuanced representation of natural impressions, moods and emotions. It was a version of 'the modern' that Nielsen also cultivated in some of his early lieder set to poems by Jens Peter Jacobsen.

The Symbolists recognised the achievements of naturalism, but they were opposed to rationalism based on science. If everything is nature, there is no place for the spiritual, the divine and the mental. They felt that the spiritual dimension had been lost and insisted that art should convey a sense that there was something beyond everything that realistic representation could not capture. The symbolist culture of the 1890s thus emerged as a reaction to the fact that the realist and naturalist art and literature that had preceded it had become too austere. From the Symbolists' point of view, it had lost the sense that something existed beyond concrete reality.

Symbolism is one of several movements that recognised that the Modern Breakthrough and its cultivation of the rational had promoted progress and art, but at the same time the movement found that the rational had left humanity in a void. If God is dead, as Nietzsche argued, humans are left to their own devices. Crucially for the symbolist movement, it sought to reintroduce a spiritual dimension that could either point upwards to something spiritual or divine, or inwards to the mental and unconscious layers of human consciousness. Either way, it opens up to aspects beyond the rational.

Hermann Bahr, who in 1890 had defined the period as 'the modern', set out his views on how to understand Symbolism in 1891. He wrote an article entitled 'Die Décadence' on the French Symbolists. Having lived in Paris, he had first-hand knowledge of French literature. In the article he discusses a group of critics, painters and poets around Huysmans, Verlaine and Mallarmé, and Bahr concludes that they had three things in common. First, they dismissed naturalism and shared the Romantics' quest for the infinite and their worship of the indeterminate and obscure. Unlike the Romantics, however, the Symbolists do not seek to reproduce emotion but rather 'mood' – a key concept of Symbolism. The second characteristic is a preference for the artificial and a conscious distance from the natural. The artist creates an artificial universe and deliberately keeps reality at a distance. Features such as stylisation, refinement and archaisation come into play, where the representation of reality is abandoned in favour of the representation of the sign or symbol. A third characteristic they share is a tendency towards the mystical and towards obscure, allegorical images that reveal their deeper meaning only to the initiated. They are preoccupied with the mysteries of the Middle Ages and the hallucinations of dreams.[2] These three main approaches, the worship of atmosphere, stylisation and the mystical and dreamlike, can be used as a starting point to shed light on Nielsen's approach to Symbolism.

Mood

When Jørgen I. Jensen published his biography of Nielsen in 1991, it was only recently that writers and art historians had begun to take an interest in turn-of-the-century Symbolism, which had otherwise been suppressed by cultural history and museums for many years.[3] The neglect of Symbolism must be part of the explanation for the fact that Nielsen had not previously been interpreted from a symbolist point of view. However, it may also be due to several features of Symbolism that run counter to the traditional image of Nielsen. In the Danish context, the symbolist movement originated in the European-oriented artistic milieus of Copenhagen. It was therefore difficult to reconcile with the idea of a national music that bore the stamp of the composer's Fyn roots. Moreover, Symbolism is associated with the mood worship of the 1890s, which contrasts sharply with the image of Nielsen's music as healthy, simple and natural. Jensen is indeed aware that the interpretation of Nielsen's works as musical symbolism does not necessarily fit in with the popular image of the composer, and points out that 'this view may sound strange at first, but the problem lies in a single word: mood'.[4]

It must be emphasised that the concept of mood in Symbolism does not correspond to our normal understanding of the word, for it is a concept whose meaning is difficult to grasp. One of the characteristics of Symbolism is that it actually defies rigid definitions. Jensen stresses that the term should not be understood as a fleeting state of mind or an immediate whim – in this way Symbolism differs from Impressionism, which seeks to reproduce the immediate sensation of a phenomenon. Jensen explains that, on a more general level, mood is more concerned with what in music is called form.[5]

However, this is not a clear definition either, as the term 'form' is usually employed to refer to the overall process of music. Mood lies somewhere between the transience of the moment and the totality of the whole. It is best thought of as a synthesis or a 'merging of atmosphere and emotional expression'.[6]

At the same time, a mood denotes a particular kind of temporality: it has a certain extension and appears relatively stable within its duration. A characteristic feature of the symbolist use of mood is the attempt to create the impression that it carries meaning, which is done by maintaining and prolonging its extension in time.[7] Thus the sense of time passing, which characterises most musical sequences, is nullified. Time is momentarily brought to a standstill.[8]

By maintaining a mood for a while, a series of inherently stable musical sections emerges. As a result, a symbolist work of art can consist of a continuous series of sonorous units that appear as musical conditions that replace one another. This establishes a formal progression that does not appear as a continuous development, and the temporal dimension functions differently. It breaks with the idea of musical development as an organic process in which a musical logic, such as harmonic cadences or modulations, binds the progression together. Instead, the process consists of sonorous building blocks or 'moments', each with its own characteristic manifestation and musical identity, expressing a 'mood'.[9]

Understood in this way, mood can indeed be associated with features in Nielsen's works. In a song such as 'Har Dagen sanket al sin Sorg' (If day has gathered all its woe), Op. 4, No. 5, discussed in Chapter 17, it is evident that, on one level, the extremely fine depiction of the emotional fluctuations of the text and the changes in the emotions of the anonymous observer characterise the song as modern 'nervous art'. At the same time, on another level, one can hear how the symbolist cultivation of mood is expressed in a series of alternating 'conditions'. The three different tonal levels, each representing a universe in the song – the earthly nature, the nocturnal celestial space and the spiritual space where the spirits of light appear – follow one another, but Nielsen does not convey the transition between them. One mood lasts for a while, and then the music abruptly shifts to a new one.[10] While the first two levels are related in terms of expression and key affinity, the transition to the universe of the spirits is also a shift in style and type of movement.

Moreover, on a more general level, the entire musical dress of the song is the expression of a 'mood' that maintains a basic tone of deep melancholy, floating indeterminacy and lack of momentum in the interpretation of the poem, consistently avoiding the confirmation of any tonal level as the actual one.[11] The instability of the movement and the harmonic parallel universes reflect the unstable state of mind of the protagonist.

Nielsen also works with a kind of timeless mood in two other early songs in Op. 4, *Solnedgang* (*Sunset*) (No. 1) and *Til Asali* (*To Asali*) (No. 3). The poems are thematically related, as the adored Asali appears in both. In *Sunset*, Nielsen takes his starting point from the text's image of 'floating clouds', in which the piano begins in a high, middle register with a figure that evokes a hazy cloud moving across the sky, gradually changing its contours. The song begins with the same melodic motion as the piano, only right on the beat. Harmonically, almost nothing happens in the first four bars. The impression is that the personal pronoun 'I' of the poem is lying on his back, looking at the clouds, thinking of his beloved, with whom he hopes to be united in a love so strong that he forgets everything else. As there are two stanzas, the floating clouds return musically both in the middle and at the end of the song, revealing that he is probably still dreaming of something that has not happened.

In the song *To Asali*, the frame similarly creates an atmosphere of contemplative serenity, as the singer contemplates Asali but remains inactive. Here the thoughts are associated with the night, which is musically related to the tranquillity at the beginning and end of the movement. Every night he has dreamed that he has won Asali's heart; by comparison, the day has been depressing and hollow. Now, however, he dreams that he has lost her. Thus there is a great contrast, where the music to the last line of the poem must be played energetically, with sustained and full chords to the lyrics 'how bright and clear is the day', making it clear that the bright daylight is hell. The music leads back into the darkness of the night, where he can hope to see Asali again in his dreams.

Stylisation and Archaisation

It is also possible to approach Symbolism by defining it as an art that uses stylisation and archaisation. This interpretation is particularly appropriate for those of Nielsen's songs, which are based on medieval themes and the world of folk tales. There is a clear parallel with the stylised depictions of folk tales and historical motifs from the Middle Ages by the artist Agnes Slott-Møller, which are among the most important

ILL. 1. The cover of Nielsen's *Viser og Vers af J. P. Jacobsen* (*Songs and Verses by J. P. Jacobsen*) (1893) is drawn by Anne Marie Carl-Nielsen. The motif is a clear expression of stylisation. The way the woman holds the instrument gives the impression of light and spherical music, and her attention is focused on something above her. The picture has similarities with Renaissance depictions of angels playing music that Anne Marie and Carl may have seen in Florence.[12]

works of Danish Symbolism. In contrast to the National Romantic and historicist use of such motifs, Slott-Møller's depictions always have an air of detachment, and the figures do not appear heroic, but rather introverted and often doubting or powerless. Together with her husband, she was a leading figure in Danish Symbolism and a close friend of Anne Marie Carl-Nielsen, who also became interested in the movement in the 1890s.[13]

Anne Marie's cover illustration for Nielsen's Op. 6, *Viser og Vers af J. P. Jacobsen* (*Songs and Verses by J. P. Jacobsen*), is a clear example of how the motif is not intended to show a realistic musical situation, but a stylised representation of the motif. The woman is surrounded by golden wings, a deep blue sky and something resembling stars or a halo. The decorative elements, the colour effects and the treatment of the subject convey a mood rather than a reference to reality. It is clear that Anne Marie is at least as much at home here as Nielsen himself.

In the spring of 1893, The Free Exhibition included a large section with pictures by Gauguin and van Gogh, which Nielsen visited several times.[14] The poet Johannes Jørgensen, a central figure in Danish Symbolism, published a review of the exhibition, which is one of the first to address this style of art in a Danish context. Later that year, Jørgensen began to publish the journal *Taarnet*, a forum for Danish poets and an introduction to the French Symbolists in particular.[15] In his review of the exhibition, Jørgensen considers how to understand the term symbolism, which is used primarily in relation to Gauguin. Unlike Impressionism, which insisted on the way in which a subject reveals itself to the painter at a given moment, Symbolism was not concerned with the representation of reality, and its art was therefore also an expression of a dissociation from the detailed realism that characterised naturalism. Instead, Jørgensen notes the use of distance and stylisation, an art akin to hieroglyphics: 'For him, forms and colours are simple, clear, fixed. He simplifies, stylises, works decoratively.' As Jørgensen sums it up: 'A Symbolist would be nothing other than someone who expresses oneself through signs.'[16] With key words such as these, it makes sense to associate Nielsen with this type of Symbolism.

The cultivation of detachment, stylisation and the archaic is particularly evident in Nielsen's treatment of poems associated with ballads and the Middle Ages. An obvious example is the composition of Jacobsen's poem *Irmelin Rose*, which must have been of central importance to Carl and Anne Marie, as they named their eldest daughter Irmelin. Nielsen uses a number of devices that deliberately distance the song from the modern harmonies of the time and places it alongside older stylistic models. The way he does this is not by imitating the old style, but by referring to it, so that the music functions as a sign. This may sound somewhat puzzling, so it is worth taking a closer look at how Nielsen achieves this effect.

MUSIC EX. 1. Carl Nielsen, *Irmelin Rose*, Op. 4, No. 4, bars 3–6, 11–13. The composition begins with a melody that gradually descends through an A minor scale before returning to the starting point. The piano accompanies in parallel octaves. After a repetition of the same phrase, the singer arrives at the refrain 'Irmelin Rose, Irmelin Sol', with the piano imitating the sound of the harp. The refrain is always the same. However, the four stanzas are designed so that the accompaniment changes as the narrative progresses. In the second stanza, the words 'cheerful splendour' are followed by a small, festive figure, and in the third stanza, Irmelin's many suitors are depicted by the piano, imitating the vocal line in a displaced manner, as if the suitors were appearing in several rows.

The song *Irmelin Rose* begins with the piano playing an identical figure in several octaves; the voice begins in the same way – that is, as simple as possible: a melody that descends stepwise through a scale before ascending again to the starting point. The accompaniment is equally simple, with the piano just following the melody in octaves until it reaches a plain cadence. The beginning of the lyrics 'Se, der var en Gang …' (Look, once upon a time …) suggests a singer telling a story. It is clear that the situation represents a bard reciting the song as a ballad, accompanied on the harp.

Jacobsen's poem *Genrebillede* (*Genre Painting*) (Op. 6, No. 1; CNW 121), about the page who cannot find the words to his poem, similarly conveys a medieval scene. When Nielsen set *Genre Painting* to music, he emphasised Jacobsen's poetic irony and self-reflection on the role of the poet. The text does have a narrator, although not as clearly as in *Irmelin Rose*. As the lied progresses, the poet – that is, the page – becomes

THE SYMBOLIST

ILL. 2. Agnes Slott-Møller, *Tristan* (1907).[17] Agnes Slott-Møller depicts a scene in which Tristan, like the page in Jacobsen's poem, reaches for his hunting horn. The pose does not show him as a hero, but rather as a somewhat resigned, thoughtful figure expressing his thoughts in music. The melancholy mood of the picture is often seen in symbolist art.

MUSIC EX. 2. Carl Nielsen, *Genrebillede* (*Genre Painting*), Op. 6, No. 1, bars 25–31. At the end of Nielsen's *Genre Painting*, the page gives up trying to make the poem succeed and takes up his horn instead. At this point the lied is harmonically stable, with an accompaniment that remains on the same chord, imitating horn music with so-called horn fifths. The singer descends resolutely, step by step and with great accumulated strength, until the energy dissipates and doubt reappears. The final figure in bars 28–30, associated with longing and love, later appears as a recurring motif in Nielsen's Fifth Symphony, where it concludes the first movement in a similarly longing manner in a clarinet solo.[18]

increasingly frustrated at his lack of success. This is imitated in the harmony, which is characterised by a lack of tonal stability.[19] Nielsen also emulates the increasingly fragmented form of the lines, in which the poet 'sat and groped' for the right words. The poet tries, but the melodic line is fragmented by rests, causing the rhythm to go against the otherwise regular beats. After another attempt, the poet is still not satisfied with the words 'stars' and 'roses', which unfold in the lied with an almost feverish series of pitches. It illustrates the futility and becomes an almost comic depiction of the poet's failed efforts. The singer thus becomes not only a mediator of the text, but also a personification of the poet who appears in the text. The coincidence of the music with the poet's state of mind leads us to believe that it is the poet himself who is telling us the story.

There is another level to the text, where the crucial impulse is not to finish the poem, but to express what lies behind it, the poet's 'lust for love'. As the writing of the poem comes to a standstill, the repressed energy accumulates until it is suddenly released through music rather than words. The page 'then desperately put the horn to his mouth' and 'blew his love over all the mountains'. At this point (bar 25) the melody follows a powerful descending line as the piano imitates the hunting horn, until the song melancholically fades into a characteristic series of pitches.

Nielsen's approach to the poem is to treat it with detachment. In his view, it is a medieval motif that can carry a meaning. Robert Henriques, who had set the same poem, found Nielsen's arrangement affected:

> Originality is indeed a beautiful thing, but only if it seems to be a natural expression of the artist's personal mood and feelings. Otherwise it can easily come across as affectation.[20]

Henriques formulates a version of the popular aesthetic view that composers must express themselves. For Nielsen, however, it was not a question of expressing himself but of interpreting the text. In Nielsen's version of the lied, the soloist personifies the poet, the struggling artist, as a common figure. He is observed with detachment and deliberate distance. Just as Jacobsen was in control of the poem's irony, Nielsen was fully aware of his musical mastery of the poem. In the final bars of the song, the motif's yearning series of notes becomes a fixed figure, a sign pointing beyond itself. From now on, this musical figure can stand for longing and love.

Mystery and Inspired Nature

It is also possible to see Symbolism as 'a contribution to the understanding of the turn-of-the-century mentality with its attraction to the unrecognised forces of spiritual life'.[21] From this point of view, Nielsen's interest in the spiritual or psychological, which is clearly expressed in his diaries and works from around and after the turn of the century, becomes significant and must be stressed as another feature that links him to the symbolist current of the time.

Johannes Jørgensen's best-known article on Symbolism, published as a kind of manifesto in his journal *Taarnet* in December 1893, focuses on Symbolism's idea of a correspondence between the symbolic sign or work of art and the human soul:

> All true art is and remains symbolic. Throughout the great masters one finds nature understood as an outward sign of an inner spiritual life.[22]

This is the basic idea of mysticism that Jørgensen had already anticipated in his article in *Politiken* a few months earlier. The purpose of a symbolist work of art, he insisted, was 'to evoke in the soul of the beholder a mood corresponding to that with which the artist was filled at the moment of creation'. A work of art is 'a synthesis of two souls – that of the artist and that of nature'.[23] Art achieves its effect through a correspondence between the object and the soul. Similarly, the manifesto states that 'the soul and the world are one.'[24] And alluding to Nietzsche's *Also sprach Zarathustra*, it concludes emphatically:

> They will ... accuse me of mysticism. I plead guilty in advance. Moreover, it is my firm conviction that a true worldview must necessarily be mystical. The world is profound. And only shallow minds fail to understand it.[25]

In other words, it is a concept of Symbolism that focuses on the spiritual and the mystical, and a view of art as a medium that, through correspondences between the symbolic signs of art and the world, is able to open up insights that are otherwise inaccessible.[26]

Nielsen's preoccupation with metaphysical mysticism is not his most distinctive feature, although he sometimes expresses thoughts along these lines. In 1892, for example, he wrote to Anne Marie after reading the Bible for several days in a row:

> Have a go at reading the beginning of St John's Gospel. Don't you think it's wonderfully deep and mystical? Just the first verses. I especially like: 'And the light shineth in darkness, and the darkness comprehended it not' [John 1:5]. But overall there's a special kind of muted mysticism throughout the whole thing. I came to think of the wood in Botticelli's 'Primavera'. The trees are half human, half plants, and when they talk to one another it sounds like a mixture of rustling and human voices.[27]

It is striking that Nielsen reads the Bible as literature, and rather than making religious associations he thinks of Botticelli's painting *Primavera* (c. 1480) – a painting he may have seen with Anne Marie in Florence. It shows a group of people in a forest with trees laden with fruit; the flat composition and stylised character are similar to many symbolist paintings. As he looks at the picture, he can hear the trees in conversation.[28]

A lied in which the fascination with the mystical is particularly evident is *Erindringens Sø* (*Lake of Memories*) (CNW 127) from Op. 10, which consists of songs set to texts by Ludvig Holstein. The song begins almost vegetatively, with quiet undulating movements in the piano without harmonic fluctuations. The key and character are reminiscent of the beginning of the lied *Sunset* from Op. 4, which is also set in an indefinable and inactive mood. From then on, the music slowly begins to drift up and down in different keys without a clear direction. The music leads to the climax of the stanza, 'and slumbering therein' – that is, in the lake – 'a mysterious apparition of darkness appears …'. Here the voice is lowered to *pp*, while the piano part is reduced to a series of chords that seem enigmatic: each is simple and stands alone as a sound to be explored. The lake is a reservoir of memories and experiences that, when sought, make one sad and melancholy, but also irresistibly drawn to it. It is the partially forgotten that has slipped into the subconscious or subliminal layer of consciousness. In the lake you can find everything that once was and that the artist, as a spectator, can draw on: 'Seers have seen and known what it holds, and have awakened it from its slumber and raised the treasure of art.'

Such explicitly symbolist statements as those found in the text of *Lake of Memories* are relatively rare, although Nielsen would occasionally return to them, as when he wrote a poem some ten years later that is clearly related to Holstein's text. His poem is about a dialogue with someone who is grieving and has sad memories. Together, however, they can find solace in the depths of memory: 'So deep is the bottom of the sea / And the peace of souls. … A comfort to follow and to seek together / The land of memories.'[29]

In other cases, the texts refer indirectly to the harmony between the world and the soul in the form of inspired nature. This idea is found in the song *Æbleblomst* (*Apple Blossom*), Op. 10, No. 1, which begins with a question to the apple blossom, although from then on it is the blossom that does the talking. The apple blossom is loved, loves itself and dies as it scatters its petals – 'my white flower, my wedding garland' – over the grass. Even a song such as 'Sænk kun dit Hoved, du Blomst' (Lay down, sweet flower, your head), Op. 21, No. 4, has this mood of quiet dialogue with a nature that seems to have a consciousness of its own.

Poems and Dreams

Nielsen not only read poetry – he also wrote poetry. The earliest surviving poem is from 1887, in a letter to Emilie. It is about the poet's own thoughts and desires, which must remain sacred and secret. There is no doubt that Emilie understood that it was a love poem.[30] Twenty years later, in 1907, he wrote a series of poems which he even considered publishing.[31] The plan did not come to fruition, but eighteen poems survive from this period.[32] They are very different, but not bad, and come from a period when he was composing the last five songs of *Strophic Songs*, having completed the opera *Maskarade* the previous year. At the same time, he wrote music for Laurits Christian Nielsen's play *Willemoes* and Holstein's play *Tove* in the autumn. This was a period in which he worked mainly with songs, apart from incidental music consisting of introductions and melodramatic passages.

Nielsen was also interested in dreams throughout his life. He wrote diary entries about them in the autumn of 1893 while he was in hospital, and as early as 1889 he explained to Emilie that he believed they could, for example, give premonitions of death.[33] His diaries and letters to Anne Marie contain many descriptions of his dreams, large and small.[34] He later became very interested in their interpretation and acquired several of Freud's books in German, the earliest of which was published in 1916. He also owned the 1920 Danish translation of two of Freud's essays on psychoanalysis and on dream, entitled *Det Ubevidste* (*The Unconscious*).[35] It was at this time that his daughters also became involved in sharing dreams with each other and with their parents; Nielsen in particular involved his daughter Anne Marie in interpreting them: 'I had a strange dream last night, and I know you like to hear about dreams,' he wrote to her, describing an eerie dream in which he held a small, trusting bird that was being fed by its mate, but ended up being crushed to death by his hands. 'What do these dreams mean? Ask Emil and let me have your opinion.'[36]

Nielsen's most important composition in terms of dreams is the choral work *Søvnen* (*Sleep*), Op. 18 (CNW 101), composed in 1903–4 and premiered in 1905. He was still working on it in 1907, reading the final proof of the score in January before it went to print. He was also preoccupied with the song 'Sænk kun dit Hoved, du Blomst', published in *Strophic Songs* that autumn. He had composed the song in 1903 to accompany the poem that Jørgensen had provided as a first draft of the text for *Sleep*.[37] That same autumn, Nielsen began work on *Saga Dream*, Op. 39, which was completed in the spring of 1908.[38] There is no doubt that both poetry and dreams played an important role for him during this period.

The urge to begin *Sleep* came immediately after the completion of *Helios*, which he composed in Athens in the spring of 1903; however, the idea was older, for in late April he wrote to Julius Lehmann asking if he had a text ready for *Sleep*. They had discussed the idea before Nielsen's departure in February, and now that he had almost finished *Helios*, he wanted to get on with *Sleep* immediately: '… this is especially because the idea of 'Sleep' is completely opposite to what I've just composed … For God's sake let me have it! Or write and say no; in that case I'll try it myself.'[39]

Before he left, Nielsen had written down his first idea for the work, which from the start was to describe the contrast between some waking creatures personifying dreams and a violent nightmare vision: '… the whole world is shaking and everything seems to be about to explode. Some rage with murder and blood.'[40]

No text came from Lehmann, and shortly after Nielsen's return to Denmark in July, he wrote to Johannes Jørgensen asking for help. The idea that *Sleep* is an explicit counterpart to *Helios* becomes more tangible here: whereas *Helios* is a hymn to the protagonist of the day, the sun, the new work is to be a depiction of 'Sleep in music – a kind of hymn to its glory'. Nielsen continues:

> Sleep heals all wounds and soothes all torments; it's the greatest good for all living beings and the blissful condition where nothing is hard and tangible but everything swims away in a long, golden eternity. But Sleep has its dreams, both good and bad ones. Yet they in turn must retreat, each to its place; for Sleep may certainly be disturbed but never murdered (*Macbeth*). So it has to be a poem somehow in three parts. … So … I. Some words to evoke the bliss of Sleep / II. Some that disturb it / III. The first mood, but with an allusion to Death.[41]

In order to clarify his idea, Nielsen included in the letter a draft in three sections, describing the course of the composition in verse. The first part relates how the sun sets and 'everything opens up and draws long, deep breath' – a description that is closely akin to how *Helios* ends. In the second part, the dreams are interrupted, first the joyful ones, then the evil and finally the terrifying ones, until it ends with a cry: '… Help!' The nightmare is still central. In the final part, the dreamer calms down again and the 'sleep's great gentle waters flow out over the whole world'.[42]

The way Nielsen approached and arranged Jørgensen's poems shows him as a composer determined to realise his own artistic visions. In October 1903, Jørgensen sent Nielsen four poems that Nielsen thought were very beautiful but not suitable for *Sleep*. He replied that he had something more objective and universal in mind and asked to set the poems as songs instead. It is not known exactly which poems he was given, but 'Lay down, sweet flower, your head' was among them.[43] In the beginning of December he composed it as an independent song.[44]

On 21 November Jørgensen sent Nielsen a new draft of the text,[45] and a few weeks later he had 'truly begun on "Søvnen"'.[46] The text Jørgensen had sent him consisted of three poems, corresponding to the three-part structure Nielsen wanted. The first, 'Great Sleep, Our Gentle Mother', had a more general tone in its description of sleep as he had requested. He used the beginning and end of the poem, but changed the first line to 'Gentle Sleep, Our Great Mother', which has a more striking effect. This emphasises the all-encompassing gentleness of sleep, making it appear as a healing and benevolent force.

Jørgensen's second poem, 'Men i de mørke Skove' (But in the dark woods), describes a person who has poisoned his friend and is now wandering around in despair. It has the character of a bad dream but is not explicitly called that. Nielsen does not use the poem, and at some point he must have asked Jørgensen for an even clearer description of a nightmare, which he got with 'An agony, a heaviness … woe is me, am I awake?' It describes in detail a person being chased, trying to escape through some dark and damp subterranean caves, until 'Help me! I'm suffocating! A fear of death will crush me! … Almighty, o, save me! I'm dying!' The final exclamation puts into concrete form Nielsen's original idea of ending with a cry for help; it is probably his own addition, as these lines do not appear in Jørgensen's published version of the poem.

In the last part of *Sleep*, Nielsen uses an adapted version of the third poem Jørgensen sent him, 'Drømme svinde, Syner falme' (Dreams vanish, visions fade), with the crucial difference that where Jørgensen thanks sleep for the peace and rest he has regained, Nielsen leaves it as an unfulfilled prayer. When Jørgensen says: 'Thank you for the peace and the rest! We have found in your heart new strength, new smiles', Nielsen's version reads: 'Give me peace and rest again; let me, let me, our gentle mother, find new strength in your heart'. At the end of the work, parts of the text from the first poem are repeated.[47]

In November 1904, when Nielsen was finishing his work, Jørgensen published in the journal *Illustreret Tidende* the three poems he had sent to Nielsen the previous year entitled *Søvnen. En Hymne* (Sleep. A Hymn).[48] They were printed without Nielsen's changes to the text and included the poem that Nielsen had not used. When Jørgensen later published the seven poems in the complete cycle 'Søvnen' (1907), it was his original text, albeit with some minor changes.[49] It is thus reasonable to assume that Jørgensen was not involved in Nielsen's revision of the poems.

Sleep is very much composed with the musical nightmare at its centre. Nielsen's aim in revising the text, which had not improved poetically, was to sharpen the contrast between the gentle sleep and the terrifying nightmare. He stuck to his original basic idea, and when Jørgensen's drafts did not meet Nielsen's expectations, he commissioned new drafts or composed them himself.

The piece begins with a subdued instrumental introduction, the mood of which is reminiscent of *Helios*. When the choir enters, it sings a fine and well-balanced polyphonic chorale, accompanied throughout by the orchestra, forming a harmonious whole. The middle section is in stark contrast, introduced by sharp tremolo figures in the strings and built around pursuit and apprehension, culminating in a cry for help. Here the instrumental parts of the orchestra envelop the choir, which is left to fend for itself, giving us a musical sense of man surrounded by hostile forces. After the nightmare, the beautiful polyphonic choral singing returns and the composition ends as it began, with the quiet orchestral music fading away.

When *Sleep* was first performed at Musikforeningen on 21 March 1905 under Nielsen's baton, the critics were generally sceptical. Angul Hammerich was one of those who recognised its qualities.[50] He wrote about the first and last parts of the work:

> They have all the best qualities of the Carl Nielsen style. And, moreover, there is that touch of musical archaism which runs so easily through his pen and gives his artistic personality an increased originality! It is the masters of the Palestrina age to whom this Danish composer is spiritually related. … In the treatment of the stanza 'Pious sleep, our gentle mother', in the last section, one is reminded of none younger than Josquin des Près.[51]

In *Sleep* Nielsen creates a contrast by juxtaposing 'archaic' polyphonic choral music inspired by the masters of the Renaissance with late Romantic and dissonant sounds. Thus the very act of composing it as polyphonic choral music can stand as a symbol, a sign, pointing beyond the individual feeling to something greater and more communal. In the first and last parts of the choral work, which are characterised by polyphony, there is a web of independent choir parts. They describe the gentle, peaceful sleep, while the middle section portrays the nightmare of fear of death and the feeling of being hunted. During the nightmare, the voices are treated homophonically and in some places with sharp dissonances.[52]

Nielsen's intention was to describe the phenomenon of sleep in all its aspects. However, the intense experience of the nightmare has the effect that the contrasting musical means are perceived as dominant. It was the dissonant sounds in the middle section that caught the attention of most critics; the newspaper *Dannebrog* argued that 'in this work one finds some of the gifted composer's strange, twisted and pronounced tendency to accumulate discordant sound effects'.[53] The reviewer in *Dagens Nyheder* thought that Nielsen had fallen into 'his eagerness to paint with sufficiently strong colours' and called the work a radical composition and a characteristic of Nielsen.[54]

Nielsen's use of musical effects in *Sleep* meant that the contrasts evoked by the principle of depicting the condition in all its forms had a stronger effect on the listener than the desire to describe the universality of sleep. It is the contrast between gentle sleep and bad dreams that comes to the fore when listening to the work. In the middle section, with its sharp dissonances and the lyrics 'An agony, a heaviness … woe is me, am I awake?' and later 'Help me! I'm suffocating! A fear of death will crush me! … Almighty, o, save me! I'm dying!', the interpretation appears psychological and is immediately difficult to reconcile with the ideal of giving the work an objective, universal character.[55]

However, it was precisely this ideal that puzzled Nielsen. He was very explicit about this in his instructions to Jørgensen when he received the first drafts of the text for the work and wanted something different:

> Yet I'm also very unhappy. Because I fear I can't use it at all. I was thinking of something quite objective. Do you remember Macbeth's words on sleep in Act 2,

Scene 3 [*recte* Scene 2]? I was thinking of something in that direction, something applicable to all living beings at all times. ... as song texts they're really just right for me. But a choral work is something quite different. When people come to sing in a choir it must be something quite different from when they're singing each for themselves. Singing together, one can praise God's greatness and goodness through all eternity, or the light of the sun, the power of love, and other powers on which we depend, and whose force keeps us going. Therefore a few lines would have been enough for me, just as 'Gloria in excelsis' or 'Credo' were for the old church composers.[56]

There is much to suggest that Nielsen saw polyphonic sacred music as an objective and universal expression of human feeling. His views on Renaissance sacred music, and Palestrina in particular, are the subject of a later chapter, but in essence he saw polyphonic choral music as music in which the individual voices are raised to a higher level, representing the sum of human emotion. This is true of choral music in general, but it is especially true of polyphonic choral music of the early sacred style, which consists of individual choral parts, each with its own text and melody. On the other hand, in homophonic choral music, in which the voices follow each other and simply have their own pitches in the harmonies, the singers may also sing together, albeit the result can be seen as a potentiation of the actual subjective feeling they share in the singing. Early church music was sung by voices of equal importance: that is, there was no principal voice. The use of polyphonic choral music, which in itself gives the music an archaic character, points as a symbol or sign to something greater and universal, beyond the individual. Rather, the nightmare is personal and subjective, and the reconciliation in the embrace of gentle sleep is common to all.

When Nielsen revisited the idea of depicting a dream in his orchestral work *Saga Dream*, Op. 39 (CNW 35), in 1907–8, he employed a different strategy of generalised description. The story is taken from the Icelandic Njál's Saga, in which the exiled Gunnar falls asleep during a journey and has a nightmare. He dreams that he and his companions are attacked by a pack of wolves and that a companion is killed. Instead of describing the nightmare, Nielsen chooses an outsider's view of the dreamer. He takes a sentence from the saga, in which Gunnar's companions consider waking him but decide to let him dream and uses it as the work's motto: 'Now Gunnar is dreaming; let him enjoy his dream in peace'.[57] Thus *Saga Dream*, like *Helios* and *Sleep*, both shaped like an arc with a peaceful beginning and end, becomes less contrasting. Gunnar's dream is not a subjective account of the dream, but a description of his disturbed sleep as seen from the outside. The listener experiences the reflection of a dream through the troubled sleeper. The most innovative feature is a musical cadenza in the middle of the work, in which the wind instruments play related melodies one after the other, but without any tempo coordination. The conductor pauses and the parts are allowed to play in parallel *ad libitum*. The suspension of a common sense of time is an aural impression of the unreal world of dreams.

The Literary Shift

In Holstein's poems, symbolist features can be found in the worship of mystical and unworldly nature. The worship of nature continues in *Strophic Songs*, published by Nielsen in 1907, although there is a real literary shift regarding the poets chosen. In addition to Jørgensen's 'Lay down, sweet flower, your head', the collection contains a song by Helge Rode, 'Skal Blomsterne da visne' (Shall flowers, then, all wither), three by Jeppe Aakjær, *Høgen* (*Hawk*), *Jens Vejmand* (*John the Roadman*) and 'Den første Lærke' (The larks are coming), and two by Johannes V. Jensen, *Husvild* (*Vagrant*) and *Godnat* (*Good Night*). Although the songs continue the lied genre, they mark an interesting change in Nielsen's choice of lyrics.

The songs are all based on texts by contemporary poets. Compared to Jens Peter Jacobsen's poems, they are characterised by a greater simplicity and straightforwardness. Aakjær and Jensen express this tendency, which is at the same time a simpler literary form and draws its themes from a different part of reality. Similar to the motifs of the Fyn painters, the connection of the poems with Jutland not only broadened the geographical horizon, but also opened up to new social classes in the population. Nielsen recognised this reality from his upbringing, but it was only now that he began to use it as a starting point for his art.

It was therefore significant that Nielsen's first public performance of *Strophic Songs*, especially those set to Jutlandic lyrics, was so effective that several of the songs were sung as encores.[58] Jensen's *Vagrant* and *Good Night* are from his novel *The Fall of the King* and are written in the Jutlandic dialect. In the novel, the wandering fiddler Jakob, who brings the deaf girl Ide with him, sings both songs, the first of which he hums on the road one day:

> Thus they came to Skagen, where Ide saw the great sea. The sand here was the whitest and finest she had ever seen. And when they had reached the very end of Grenen, Jakob sang the ballad he had written about himself and Ide. Their only audience was the seagulls that flew near them. Jakob laughed and waved his hand at them as he sang. Ide saw the white birds open their beaks, but she heard nothing, nor did she hear the sea whirling and growling in the good weather.[59]

The song portrays Jakob as an unpretentious and self-deprecating wanderer who, at 'the end of the world', feels called to ask the universe for shelter. Later in the novel, when he has a mental breakdown and decides to take his own life, he sings the second song as a farewell to the world. Nielsen does not simply describe the poems. He reads them into the plot in which they appear and relates them musically to the characters' traits as they appear to a reader of the novel. Through music he tries to express the situation in which Jakob finds himself.

In both songs Nielsen uses stylised expressions that clearly indicate that we are not in a realistic universe. The first piece is in a dance form that could go on indefinitely. Each strophe ends with 'Gi Husly!' (Give shelter!) with a simple broken triad on the dominant. The piano imitates the figure, almost like the fiddler's own echo on the violin. The second song is accompanied by broken chords in the piano, as if to imitate the sound of a harp. The lied is meant to represent the bard accompanying himself.[60] In order for the singer to illustrate the situation, Nielsen instructed that the song should be 'sung with a certain tired, sardonic humour'. The staging of Jakob's collapse in the poem thus becomes the focus of the lied.

The opening up to new poets, and thus to a new literary universe, is the beginning of a movement away from the symbolist starting point. There is no sudden break, and poets such as Aakjær and Jensen can be seen as continuing the cultivation of nature as the abode of meaning. Aakjær's publication of *Rugens Sange* (Songs of the Rye) in 1906 and Johannes V. Jensen's *Digte* (Poems) from the same year also mark the beginning of the alliance between the Fyn painters and the Jutland poets that has been called the Popular Breakthrough. Yet it is important to remember that Aakjær and Jensen came from the same radical circles around the Student Society in Copenhagen before they presented themselves as Jutlandic poets, and that the decisive meeting between Jensen and the Fyn painters took place in his apartment in Copenhagen. It was indeed in the spring of 1907, before Nielsen had composed the last five of the *Strophic Songs*, that a criticism of the dominance of the Fyn painters at The Free Exhibition developed into the feud known as the Farmer-Painter Dispute. It appears to be an attack by the Symbolists on the Fyn painters, but in fact it shows that the symbolist movement had lost its support in the art world.[61] From then on, the Symbolists were relegated to a marginal position in art history, a situation that only changed with the revival at the end of the twentieth century. On the other hand, the growing interest in Danish nature itself, anticipated by Symbolism's more abstract worship of nature, points to the image of Denmark that was to become central to the renewal of the repertoire of the Folk High School Songbook.

Chapter 19

WRITING OPERA AROUND 1900

Nielsen wrote only two operas in his entire career, although he considered other operatic projects at various times. In 1926 he read Ben Jonson's drama *The Silent Woman* and reflected on whether he should compose an opera based on the text. He worked on the project for several years, but it never progressed beyond jotting down some musical ideas. It would have been interesting to see how he would have approached it, as it would have been a companion piece to Richard Strauss's opera *Die schweigsame Frau* (1935), on the same text. In 1911 he had planned to write an opera based on Jens Peter Jacobsen's novel *Fru Marie Grubbe*; in 1908 he wrote a note for an opera based on Holberg's *Julestue*; and in the early 1920s he wrote a single musical sketch for *Kilderejsen*, another text by Holberg. In 1898, before beginning work on his opera *Saul and David*, Nielsen abandoned a collaboration with Sophus Michaëlis on what would have been his first opera, based on Shakespeare's *The Merchant of Venice*. Also from this period are some early sketches for an opera inspired by the Old Testament's story of Judith and notes for a plot based on the story of *Amor og Psyche* (Cupid and Psyche).[1] Thoughts of opera thus preoccupied Nielsen throughout his life. He completed only two operas, both from the turn of the century, *Saul and David* and *Maskarade*.

The Royal Theatre had a tradition and a duty to stage new works by Danish composers. It seems natural, therefore, that Nielsen should have thought of writing an opera for the theatre when he was establishing himself as a composer in the late 1890s. Having an opera performed would be an important step in his career. He teamed up with Einar Christiansen, an experienced playwright who also wrote librettos and had good connections with The Royal Theatre.[2] With a theme from the Old Testament, the ominous and dramatic subject of conflict is at the centre of *Saul and David*. However, Nielsen's next opera, *Maskarade*, which premiered in 1906, is based on one of Holberg's comedies of a more playful and carefree nature. The fact that he was able to use the conventions of comic opera, with parodic scenes and the confusion inherent in masquerades, does not mean that there are no serious themes in this work. The success of *Maskarade* laid the foundation for Nielsen to distinguish himself from his fellow composers and to achieve a position where he would eventually be regarded as the new national composer.

By 1899, when Nielsen began his first opera, *Saul and David*, he had been a member of The Royal Orchestra for ten years and was familiar with a wide repertoire of

German, French, Italian and Danish operas. With his experience as a musician in an opera orchestra, he knew how opera music worked and what was effective in achieving certain dramatic effects. He understood the wide range of musical solutions to dramatic music and the resources available to an opera house such as The Royal Theatre. This influenced his approach to the assignment.

Dramatic Music

Some of Nielsen's reflections have survived in a manuscript of a lecture he held in 1905 on Gluck, Haydn and Mozart, and show that he gave careful thought to the composition of dramatic music. Nielsen singles out Christoph Willibald Gluck, one of the most important opera composers of the eighteenth century, and says that Gluck really understood drama as something other than plot. At the heart of drama are relationships between people, and the dramatic is found in the reaction to the words and actions of others.

Another consideration that reflects Nielsen's deep understanding of the dramatic is his focus on direct address to the audience, similar to that of the busker. Nielsen explains that Gluck, already well trained musically, had gone to Prague to study; however, Gluck was financially challenged and had to support himself by singing in churches and on the streets:

> In the end he went from place to place, singing and playing for the people. ... In other words, I think that Gluck ... became such an eminent *dramatist* ... primarily because of his experiences among the *people*. As he wandered about, he must have been forced to take note of the temperaments and feelings of different people when he practised his art. Indeed, no one had sent for him. He had, as it were, to conquer his audience at close quarters, to weigh the chances, to estimate the receptivity of his audience, and to adapt himself accordingly. Thus he acquired an immense knowledge of human nature and judgement, and this is probably the most important thing for a dramatist, whether he be a poet, a painter, a sculptor, a musician or an actor.[3]

The ideas about drama that Nielsen draws from his work with Gluck are indeed his own insights and reflect his awareness that theatrical and dramatic effect is of paramount importance to an opera composer. Basically, Nielsen sees opera as theatre. Theatrical music must have a sense of immediate effect and, before it can have its impact, it must capture the attention of the audience as a prerequisite for achieving that effect.

This is not to say that he does not attach great importance to the musical aspect. Nielsen has an eye both for the immediate effect of the moment and for the large-scale formation of musical relationships as well as for the proportions by which the individual sections work together.[4] The more or less unconscious experience that the overall form of the piece makes musical sense gives the listener satisfaction on a level other than the immediate.

In the 1760s, Gluck promoted a radical reform of the operatic genre in Germany, so that the action – though still operatic – seemed more natural and logical, and the music and singing more in tune with the dramatic situation. Nielsen points out that Gluck had learned that

> for something to function properly, it must first of all be in its natural relationship to what precedes and follows. It must, so to speak, grow out of the inner instinctive logic and restraint and be subject to the laws of cause and effect.[5]

He maintains that Gluck introduced a greater naturalness to declamation and that the first work in which this pioneering reform took hold was *Orfeo ed Euridice* in 1762.[6] It was an opera well known to Nielsen and to the Copenhagen audiences, having been a staple of the repertoire since its premiere at The Royal Theatre in 1896. The emphasis on these particular qualities suggests that they corresponded to Nielsen's own ideas of how best to compose opera.

Although Nielsen's background is very different from Gluck's, his observations reflect some of his own early experiences. The immediacy and contact with the audience was part of his musical upbringing as he played with his father at balls and parties. It should also be remembered that his experience of theatre music was not confined to The Royal Theatre. Some of his earliest orchestral works were written for theatres, and it is likely that he was already assisting in the theatre orchestra when he lived in Odense. He had a sense of the role of music in the theatre from an early age.

Late in life, Nielsen returned to the question of opera composition, insisting in a letter to the Swedish music historian Gunnar Jeanson that even at the time he composed *Saul and David*, he had a clear sense of the dramatic. In retrospect, he placed more emphasis on the elements of musical form and unity – elements that make a work last – than on the immediate musical representation of the action:

> I can tell you that before I began to compose my first opera, *Saul and David*, I was already clear about how the term 'dramatic music' should be understood, so far as I was concerned. Early on I was of the clear opinion that there should be a distinction between theatrical music and dramatic music. Spontini, Meyerbeer, Gounod and to some extent Wagner had convinced me that the danger for a dramatic composer lay especially in two areas, namely the *lyrical* and the *pic-*

torial. I felt instinctively that music's dramatic tension should reside in a certain symphonic (purely musical) unfolding. In other words: only according to absolute-musical inner laws could music's art have a true and permanent dramatic effect. What would it matter if I could depict storm and stillness, or moonlight and thunder, if the music wasn't alive and tensely animated in and of itself and from its own nature or couldn't awaken or seize the interest as a self-sufficient, independent art?[7]

Nielsen distinguishes between what is usually called dramatic and what is actually dramatic:

I had learned that what one is used to calling 'dramatic' was on the contrary in the long run undramatic … Therefore I saw how correct it was that the music first and foremost should unfold itself according to its own nature and its own laws, and I strove in every situation to create a certain symphonic-musical form for the various scenes, without too many breaks, even if the text was tempting me to invent new musical motifs. I considered that the dramatic element in music should be sought in the development of simple themes and not in a naturalistic illustration of the individual verses or scenes on stage.[8]

Although Nielsen's emphasis is different from his earlier statements, he retains the central idea that there must be, on the one hand, an immediate theatrical effect and, on the other, an underlying musical form beyond the current action on stage. Central to his statement is his rejection of naturalistic illustration in the detail of text or action. He imagines the individual scenes as entities.

This view is underlined by a remark in a letter to Niels Møller, who had written the text of the *Cantata for the Annual University Commemoration*. Nielsen argues that unlike the text of a cantata, which must be inspiring in itself, the libretto of an opera is not quite so decisive: 'In operas it's better when there's less content in the text, because if one can't get inspired by the verse then one can compose according to the stage situation and imagine a background of, for example, mime, pastoral mood, etc.'[9] His approach is thus to imagine the situations and scenes that make up the opera and to give each its own mood and musical form, rather than to follow the text and plot down to the last detail.

Nielsen describes a similar approach when asked candidly in an interview, 'How do you compose an opera?' and replies in a manner similar to a recipe:

You take a text and read it carefully. Then you navigate and evaluate it. From here to there you have to be in one mood, and there you have to replace it with a new one. In Act One of *Maskarade*, I have grumpy bassoons describing the dark, sultry room until Leander opens the shutters and the light streams in and makes the music clear.[10]

The formulation has features in common with Nielsen's approach to composing lieder, in which a careful reading of the text precedes the shaping of the music. He then makes a plan and sketches a course before beginning the work. Rather than entering the compositional process by simply following the text or the action on stage, he works with the concept of 'mood', which describes the character of the music over a longer sequence and continues until a change occurs. Although he is referring to *Maskarade* in the interview, his description is very similar to how the music for *Saul and David* functions.

Nielsen's work on his first opera came at a time when opera composers throughout Europe were looking for new compositional models to replace Wagnerian music drama and traditional Italian opera. There was a general feeling that the genre was in crisis, and Verismo, a new and more naturalistic style, had emerged from Italy in the 1890s. Works such as Mascagni's *Cavalleria rusticana* and Leoncavalli's *Bajadser* (*Pagliacci*) were extremely popular and soon became part of the opera repertoire in Copenhagen. Nielsen, however, wrote himself into another European movement that sought alternatives to naturalism. He looked to the past, to what he called the 'tragically sublime'.[11]

Undoubtedly Rome's historic surroundings and ancient history provided a setting that was inspirational for Nielsen's work on *Saul and David* during a significant phase in the spring of 1900. He and Anne Marie had both been awarded travel grants, which enabled them to spend six months in Italy, concentrating on their work and drawing inspiration from the nature and the country's impressive cultural treasures. During the day, Anne Marie studied at the French Academy with the sculptor Victor Ségoffin, while Nielsen worked on his opera.[12]

Saul and David

The idea of composing an opera based on the story of *Saul and David* (CNW 1) seems to have arisen during a conversation between Einar Christiansen and Nielsen in 1898. In a much later memoir, Nielsen mentions that when the idea was presented to him, it struck him like a bolt of lightning, where he was 'seized by its Old Testament atmosphere. The grandeur of it all, so far removed from "reality" and everyday life, captivated me in a special way.'[13] The subject undoubtedly captured Nielsen's imagination, and in the reference to the mood of the material, its sublimity and distance from reality, some of the characteristic keywords of Symbolism echo. This may explain his choice of form, which in places seems to be tableaux rather than continuous action, and also the major role he gives to the chorus and choral sections, leading one critic to remark that the audience should expect 'an oratorio rather than a musical drama'.[14]

At Nielsen's request, Christiansen wrote the libretto in January 1899. It seems likely that it was finished when, at the end of January, and by his own admission quite unprepared, Christiansen was appointed artistic director of The Royal Theatre from the following season. This did little to diminish the play's chances of being accepted and performed.[15] In the spring, Nielsen applied for – and received – a travel scholarship, explaining that he wanted to study the art of singing in Italy and compose *Saul and David*. In August he was granted leave from The Royal Orchestra for the whole of the coming season to pursue this plan.[16] He began composing in the summer of 1899, and by the time he left for Italy in late December he had completed the first act and begun the second, which is essentially the part of the opera he composed while in Rome.[17]

According to his grant application, Nielsen's purpose in going abroad was to study the Italian vocal tradition in addition to composing.[18] It is not clear, however, whether he was referring to an older or a newer tradition – in any case, Italy gave him the opportunity to experience alternatives to Wagner and German opera, which were often used as models by Danish composers at the time.[19]

There was a small Danish colony in Rome, which became the social circle of Carl and Anne Marie. In particular, the composer and organist Thomas Laub stayed in the city, and his correspondence with friends and family is one of the most important sources for Nielsen's activities in Rome. The circle also included the art historian Vilhelm Wanscher and the painter Hans Nikolaj Hansen, whom Nielsen knew from his stay in Paris in 1891. Laub had travelled to Italy to continue his studies of early Italian music, which he had begun during his first visit there in the early 1880s. He was not particularly impressed by contemporary Italian music. On the other hand, like Nielsen, he appreciated getting to know the country's people, nature and, above all, art.[20] His letters show that he cherished his time with Nielsen. In a letter of 20 April he describes how on some excursions there was 'a cruel crowd of Danes who always had a lot to say; Carl Nielsen was my consolation in all the hustle and bustle'.[21] Another letter describes how Laub and Nielsen had spent the rainy February evenings playing almost all of Mozart's sonatas for violin and piano for their Danish friends in the city.[22] In a third letter, dated 18 January, Laub tells his friends in Denmark how the day had passed with almost nothing to do, but still had been fruitful for him. He had got up late and after breakfast had had coffee with Carl and Anne Marie. Then they had gone out for lunch together, and in the afternoon he had gone with Carl to see the town, while Anne Marie had gone to her lessons and then rejoined them later. In other words, they had done little but talk.

> But it's possible that such idle days can be just as useful and productive as other working days. *In this way we are indeed obliged to deal with our art – and also with our outlook on life (they are, however, connected)*; all around us we have great art *en masse*, which forces us to compare, and which raises our ideas and demands on our own art – at least in my case and I think in his too – they are rising, and that must be good …[23]

Laub's comments reveal that the spring of 1900 was a time when he and Nielsen discussed the big questions about the tendencies of their art and also their views on the development of art in the wider sense. The stay in Rome, in many ways Nielsen's third great formative journey, became a period in which he had time to immerse himself in great art and architecture. Rome was explored as thoroughly as Leipzig, Berlin and Paris had been on his earlier journeys. At the same time, it becomes clear that there are people in his immediate environment who have high expectations that he would also fulfil their own visions of the future of art.

A week before this 'idle day' in Rome, Nielsen had received a letter from his friend Rudolph Bergh about conditions back home in Copenhagen. In the letter, Bergh expressed his frustration with the music critics William Behrend and Charles Kjerulf and their 'laziness towards all old music'.[24] Bergh himself had recently tried to understand the modern trends in music, but to no avail. On the other hand, he had high hopes for Nielsen's chances of making a breakthrough with his new opera and becoming an influential composer: 'How I wish you to succeed and be able to ignite the love of mankind! Let's hope so; for that you'll write some noble and good music, I need not wish it.'[25]

For Laub, too, the meeting with Nielsen in Rome helped to raise hopes of change in Danish musical life. Laub saw the advantage of Nielsen being married to a sculptor who could give him a special insight into older art, and Laub and Nielsen shared many views on the problems of more modern music.[26] As well as discussing their views on art, they also cultivated their mutual interest in Mozart by playing all his violin sonatas, as mentioned above. Laub must have felt that he had met a kindred spirit in Nielsen, and so he expected that their shared musical ideals would be reflected in the opera that Nielsen was working on during his stay. As it turned out, this was only partly true.

The plot of *Saul and David* echoes the story of the Old Testament.[27] It also follows the basic structure of a tragedy: a fateful event occurs at the beginning, after which there is no turning back, and in the end the inevitable happens.[28] In *Saul and David*, this event occurs at the beginning of Act One, when Saul, as king and commander-in-chief, faces a crucial dilemma. The Philistine army is approaching, and unless Saul moves out with his own army and takes up the fight, he risks losing the war. He waits for Samuel, for according to Jewish law it is unthinkable to go to war without first offering a burnt sacrifice to God, and the prophet Samuel is overdue to light the pyre. Saul finally decides to light it himself, breaking the pact with God.

This first scene begins without any real prelude, and the general mood is one of anxious waiting for Samuel. When he arrives, he curses Saul and prophesies his downfall. Saul launches into a long, melancholy monologue, and David is summoned to comfort him by playing the harp. The act ends with David sitting in the dark with Saul's son Jonathan and daughter Michal. David and Michal fall in love and sing a love duet, ending 'for death is not stronger than love'.

In Act Two, the Philistine army has closed in and challenges Saul to send his best man to duel with the giant Goliath. David volunteers, goes out, wins the battle and returns victorious. The people, represented by the chorus, hail him. First they sing a powerful choral section, with the singers singing in unison 'Hallelujah! Hallelujah! Let us honour God's name'. It is staged as an approaching procession. The house is filled to capacity for the celebration, and finally Saul, David and the soldiers arrive. This is followed by the first large, polyphonic choral section, with the chorus singing 'Saul slew thousands. David ten thousands!' Up to this point, the audience has experienced the whole story as spectators of this event in Saul's royal house; the war and David's victory over Goliath is something they have only heard about from afar. The whole story is told to the audience as a narrative, and if they were looking for drama on stage they would have been disappointed, for not much happens. It is not only the important role of the chorus, but also the nature of the narration that gives the opera an oratorio feel.[29]

It is this part of the second act of the opera – that is, from the moment when David's victory over Goliath is proclaimed, up to the great tribute to David, who has defeated tens of thousands – that was written in Italy. This entire middle section of Act Two is notated on a type of music paper that Nielsen never used before or after, so it seems likely that it was obtained while in Rome. Nielsen's approach to both Acts One and Two was to write a short score in pencil, which he then orchestrated and reworked in one go. In the middle of the Act Two, when the unison chorus begins, he added to the manuscript: 'Song of praise E flat major / Pompei 19 May 1900', and in a note on the instrumentation he wrote to himself that horns and trumpets should accompany the chorus. At the corresponding point where the chorus resumes the unison praise, he added another note on the instrumentation: 'Trombones and winds [that were] spared earlier!!' Thus, from the outset, Nielsen planned for the return of the chorus to be even more impressive than the first time the audience heard it. The dating, and the fact that the use of the different music paper belongs to the place where the chorus's 'Saul slew thousands' has just begun, suggests that the account of the duel and the ensuing tribute scene are the main results of the stay in Italy.[30] The fair copies of Acts One and Two were completed in Denmark in the autumn of 1900, and the last two acts were finished the following spring.

When the chorus hails David as the victor, the opera changes character. It is at the end of the second act that Nielsen comes closest to realising the ideals of the truly dramatic that he had formulated in relation to Gluck. For the first time, the characters begin to respond to each other and to the reactions of the people surrounding them. Saul repeats the basic phrase 'Saul slew thousands. David ten thousands!' and each time he hears it, his jealousy and anger increase. He breaks up the party and dismisses David.

In Act Three, David sneaks into Saul's camp to prove that he can kill him and steals the spear and water jug from a sleeping Saul. Saul eventually forgives David, and their reconciliation is celebrated with the first of the magnificent polyphonic choral passages: 'God is our witness, wows have been plighted again.' Nielsen has structured this section so that the chorus sings first, then the five main characters – the soloists – and finally, as a climax, 'first the chorus, then all *ff*, as Nielsen added in the manuscript. Once again, it is clear that he had planned the musical effect of his composition. The action continues with the appearance of the dying Samuel and the anointing of David as the new king, after which Samuel passes away which Saul then uses to reclaim the throne and drive out David and Michal, threatening to kill them.

The prelude to Act Four begins with a gesture reminiscent of a Vivaldi concerto, followed by a very different scene in which Saul seeks out a sorceress to conjure up Samuel so that Saul can speak to him again. Samuel appears but is stubborn. The scene is interrupted as the army searches for Saul. The great battle against the Philistines is about to begin. For this scene, Nielsen has composed an impressive, mainly orchestral piece of music that depicts the war in such a way that this time the audience experiences it – or at least has the illusion of experiencing it. With 'War Music behind the Curtain' and the chorus off-stage with an extra brass section, the audience can follow the action. As in a radio drama, the audience hears how the battle progresses and how Saul's army is finally defeated: 'Let us fly!' The battle fades away and the curtain rises again. The opera ends with Saul dying by his own hand. At the moment of Saul's death, David returns and is hailed, this time as the new king. It is at this point that the last great polyphonic choral movement appears, set to the text "'Tis thou, 'tis thou who art our trust and our hope', a dialogue with the three surviving soloists, which is brought to a grand finale.

ILL. 1. The premiere of Nielsen's *Saul and David* was a grand production that made full use of The Royal Theatre's extensive stage facilities. The Theatre's large stage was well suited to mass performances, where the opera chorus could fulfil its role both scenically and vocally.

The premiere took place on 28 November 1902, after a hectic autumn in which Nielsen rehearsed both *Saul and David* and completed his Second Symphony, which premiered three days later. The opera had already been accepted the previous summer, following Johan Svendsen's very positive review of the music, as documented in the Theatre's censorship protocol:

> A very interesting work, with the stamp of an independent and gifted artist throughout. There is no borrowing from elsewhere. The composer goes his own way, clearly and surely. Without looking to the right or to the left, he pursues his goal: to give musical character to the dramatic action in an original way.[31]

In mid-September 1901, Nielsen was informed that the opera had been accepted and that rehearsals would begin at the opening of the following season.[32] Niels Juel Simonsen and Vilhelm Herold took the leading roles, while Emilie Ulrich and Helge Nissen were cast as Saul's daughter Michal and son Samuel. The sorceress was played by another of Nielsen's friends, Elisabeth Dons.

Part of the audience gave Nielsen an almost ostentatious ovation at the premiere, while others may have found the opera uninteresting. The newspaper *København* mentioned that 'the opera's main flaw is that it is anything but funny'.[33] Explaining his objection, the reviewer argued that there was no conflict in the meeting between the characters. They do what they are supposed to do, but the audience already knows the story, so there is no surprise. The reviewer for another newspaper, *Social-Demokraten*, bluntly states that *Saul and David* is

> a very talented Danish opera, which will unfortunately be stranded by an unimaginative subject and a dull text. ... Last night's performance was a success, even a great success. ... The only misfortune is that there is too little of importance to captivate and hold the audience. ... It was not enough to set the two opposites against each other, we had to be interested in them, we had to see them in conflict, struggling with each other. But this does not happen, and therein lies the dramatic weakness of the opera. The emphasis is on Saul's character. ... and David, on the other hand, is too insignificant, too lyrically diluted, light and affectionate, sweet and melodious. ... In other words, the drama itself is not achieved. ... What remains is the setting, the frame, the scenery. And here Carl Nielsen shows himself to be the excellent and independent musician that he is.[34]

The reviews are interesting because they address Nielsen's own definition of drama and find that it fails: the audience is bored, and the drama does not come from the characters reacting to each other. One objection, however, might be that the critics ignored the important ending of Act Two. Perhaps more importantly, both reviews assume that the plot of the opera is a conflict between the two main characters, Saul and David. This is a reasonable view, although in reality it is not David who is Saul's opposite. He is merely the one needed to fulfil the prophecy: he defeats Goliath and is anointed and hailed as Saul's successor. He has done nothing himself – it is God's decision.

The real action, arising from the resentment between Saul and Samuel, is what triggers the events, and Saul's confrontation is not with David but with Samuel, who represents the old religious authorities. The dramatic conflict takes place externally between the secular and religious powers and internally within Saul alone.[35] This reading is confirmed by the fact that Nielsen musically links the opening waiting for Samuel ('Is he come. See ye the Prophet?') with Saul and Samuel's first confrontation in the second scene of the opera, and further links them to their respective keys, with Saul's D minor gradually destabilised and taken over by Samuel's C major, which concludes the work.[36]

In this light, the structure and character of the opera make perfect sense. With the right expectations, it is easier to get an ear for its qualities. For this, the audience could rely on William Behrend, who pointed out in his review that the audience should expect an oratorio rather than a musical drama. He goes on to explain his address to the audience:

> If you want to take advantage of and enjoy Mr Carl Nielsen's new opera, do not go there expecting an ordinary dramatic opera, do not expect to be overwhelmed by effects, but be prepared to meet a stern, serious, zealous musician …[37]

Behrend was thus in line with Nielsen's own statements that he wanted to avoid the theatrical and superficial and achieve an elevated character.

Among the enthusiastic audience, and one who could see these qualities, was Rudolph Bergh, whose expectations, expressed in a letter to Nielsen two years earlier, were indeed fulfilled.[38] Bergh published a review of Nielsen's Second Symphony and *Saul and David* in the journal *Tilskueren*, in which he emphasised Nielsen's 'outstanding ability to assimilate elements from all the great composers, classical and modern, without weakening his originality in the least'.[39] This is followed by his commentary on *Saul and David*, in which he emphasises the role of the choral movements:

> With *Saul and David*, Carl Nielsen has also succeeded in creating a quite unique work, which differs in the highest degree from all other modern operas that we have heard. The style of the opera, the composer's melodies, harmonies and counterpoint are all his own, and the large part he gives to the choruses, together with the highly polyphonic treatment of them, give the opera a somewhat unfashionable, if you like, more oratorio-like character. This is not to say that it is undramatic, but it is the grandeur of Bach and Handel that the composer aims for in the most powerful parts of the opera, not as an imitation but as a renewal … It is to Carl Nielsen's credit that he has blazed a new trail for opera in our time. In many unexpected places in *Saul and David*, the word 'renaissance' comes to mind.[40]

A similar observation is made in the article 'Saul and David. A Breakthrough', published in the newspaper *København* a week after the premiere. The critic 'J.H.' writes in the introduction: 'Carl Nielsen must be regarded with the greatest interest after his new opera. With *Saul and David* he has broken new ground for the music of the future.'[41] For the reviewer, what was new was precisely the function of the chorus in the opera, which was different from its usual use in modern opera:

> It is especially the choruses that give it its value. No instrument possesses such beauty as the human voice, and nothing is capable of expressing such ebullient mood and such powerful pathos as the harmonious unison of human voices. Here in *Saul and David* the chorus has acquired a new position in that it sings music

first and foremost – it is there for the musical effect. ... It makes a powerful and sublime impression to hear these fixed, fugal stanzas in the old oratorio style – instead of the usual chorus singing to give the soloists a rest, and at the same time to fill the stage with pilgrims, returning soldiers, ghosts, and so on.[42]

The choruses play a crucial role in the central sections of the opera. In Act Two, the chorus's powerful singing in unison sets the mood for the ritual and solemn procession as David and the warriors return from their victory over Goliath. The chorus also sets the mood with the magnificent anthem of joy 'Saul slew thousands. David ten thousands!' until Saul interrupts the celebration. Bergh's reference to the grandeur of Bach's and Handel's manner is indeed apt for this kind of choral music, which also recalls Gade's choral pieces in which the voices follow one another with the same text. And one should not forget the large polyphonic choral sections in Acts Three and Four, where the choral parts each have their own text and rhythm. They are all based on the polyphonic style of the Renaissance, in which the individual parts form a magnificent whole. These sections have clear forms, with Nielsen using instrumental effects in the repetition of previous passages, and at the same time they form part of the action – a feature which, despite the many oratorio-like qualities, asserts *Saul and David* as an opera.[43]

Another quality that has received less attention is the inclusion of instrumental pieces. The Prelude to Act Two, which is similar in character to the *Symphonic Suite*, has taken on a life of its own as an orchestral piece and was performed as such at a concert in November 1900. It is notable, however, that neither the Prelude to Act Four, which is of reasonable length and forms a self-contained whole, nor the large-scale war music behind curtains in the final act were performed as independent pieces. The war music is in many ways a highly innovative solution, enhancing the experience of the great battle scene by blinding the sense of sight. It is like listening to film music without having access to the moving images.

The Way out of the Thorn Bushes

When Laub finally heard the finished opera, about two years after his discussions with Nielsen in Rome, he had to admit in a letter to Nielsen that his hopes had only been partially fulfilled:

Since my 'conversion' (from modern Romantic music) I've been looking for 'the dawn of the new day' – and I've always been disappointed: the new did not come, only the rubbish of the old, worse and worse. ... Then I finally gave up waiting. When I say that there's something about your music that has raised my hopes,

> I'm really paying you a huge compliment, one so huge that it should be able slide down the coarseness that goes with it: the music that has awakened my hopes is at the same time so opposed to me ...[44]

This is how you start a letter when you want to tell someone your honest opinion. It should be noted that Laub uses the terms 'old' and 'new' in a particular way in the letter to Nielsen. The 'old' refers to Romanticism and its 'modern' echoes, while the 'new' is what Laub expects to happen but has not yet happened. The phrase expresses the culture of the turn of the century as an open situation in which there is great expectation of something new, not yet known. Nielsen's music has raised hopes for this 'new', but in Laub's view it is only fulfilled in certain elements of the music:

> The excellent side, as I said before, is the rhythmic one, if one understands not only the rhythm of the music itself (in the themes), but also the rhythm of the articulation and the polyphonic interplay of the voices. The embarrassing side is the tonal, also understood in three ways: the tonal system of the melodies, the modulations, the harmonic composition of the notes. It speaks a language that I don't understand and, even worse, don't believe in.[45]

According to Laub, Nielsen's music has only partially succeeded in freeing itself from the problematic features of contemporary music. From dealing specifically with *Saul and David*, Laub shifts focus to a more abstract level in the rest of the letter, explaining how he imagines a new music might emerge and how it will relate to contemporary music:

> There has been music before, in transitional periods, which in a way could be called new, but which on closer inspection was rather an exaggerated extension of the old ... The manure which smells strong, which has intense colours and large masses, is not the new: it's the dead parts without coherence, parts of what has been; the sprout which is small and pale, without smell, is the new because it's the whole, the coherent, it's what is to come. And that's how I think the new comes in music, simply, clearly and completely.[46]

Laub believed that Nielsen shared his views on contemporary music, so in the letter he tried to find an explanation for the 'discrepancy' in the different roles they played in this matter:

> I'm aware that it's very different for a producer to stay free of the diseases of time than it is for a watcher. You must necessarily be bound to your time in many ways.

WRITING OPERA AROUND 1900 361

And it's as you work your way out that you and the rest of us feel the connection. It takes time to free yourself. But what I feel compelled to argue is: if I'm right, as I once said, that your music is like someone working his way out of a thicket of thorns, then it's a matter of keeping the two things separate in one's musical conscience: the thorns and the work out of them. There must be a sharp distinction between good and evil. We mustn't be tempted by the morbid tendency of our times to call the thorns good. I'm afraid some of your admirers worship the very thorns. The good man is the one who works on himself, and at the end he must stand clear and clean, quite apart from the thorns, which must be a thing of the past.[47]

For Nielsen, Laub's disappointment must have been a hard blow. In any case, it took several months before Laub received an answer:

Now to myself, poor man, whom you have mistreated and wrestled with. What is it you actually want of me? A fresh and completely new shoot, without any connection or relationship whatsoever to all other music? Or do you want a music that consciously archaicises and simplifies and keeps red human blood in check and cuts off tendons and muscles every time they show a sign of tightening themselves into life and passion? You are certainly right that our age has reached the limit of sentimentality and so-called passion in art; but the reaction certainly won't come in the shape of a little new shoot that the sun would burn up if it was standing completely alone, but rather as a mighty sucker root up through the fertilizer, nourished by it, whipped by nettles in the wind, protecting itself from all the rubbish around it, and yet sucking the same stuff from the earth, instructed and enriched by the weeds which it couldn't avoid, in order eventually to become a good and proper tree – absolutely not a new or remarkable one – finally, perhaps, to bear a little fruit and rejoice if that in turn should take root.[48]

Laub and Nielsen agree that there is something to be learned from the inspiration of classical art, but not how to achieve it. Laub speaks as a 'true classicist', asserting eternal ideals of beauty, who in his own practice takes a much more ascetic and retrospective approach to what it means to cultivate classical ideals. Laub's approach to renewal is conservative in this sense: he wants to change in order to preserve or, if it is too late, to revive. Nielsen, on the other hand, believed that there was much to be gained from the principles of classical art, but that it was certainly not an ideal to be copied or imitated. At the end of his letter to Laub, Nielsen says frankly that even the best late antique imitations of early Greek statues make him nauseous. And while their inspiring conversations in 1900 took place in Rome, surrounded by great art, the letter of reply was written three years later in Greece, where Anne Marie was in the process of rediscovering the archaic ferocity of the colouring of Greek antiquity and doing away with the ideal of white, serene antique sculpture.

When it came to the question of how a creative artist should relate to the glories of the past, Nielsen had to distance himself from Laub. He could not feel bound by the rules of the music of the past and thus 'archaise', nor could he help being nourished by the 'weeds' of his own time. It was a discussion that Laub and Nielsen would continue over the next decades, but one that did not prevent them from embarking on new projects. There were issues on which they would never agree, but they respected each other and their friendship could accommodate their common views as well as their differences. Nielsen ends his letter in a way that shows that while he insists on retaining his artistic freedom, he wants to keep the way open for their friendship to continue:

> I can't alter my way of working, or try to think about what I'm doing, or rationalise which modulations or harmonies I dare to use. I can't do without that rushing of the streams of notes that lead me on and which I can at best just regulate now and then; but I can promise that in the future, as up to now, I shall give the best I can, and I have already realised a lot of things, and even though your letter hasn't shown me any specific path, in its spirit there is still something that teaches me, refreshes me and inspires me not to rest content but constantly to purify myself, to get through, and finally to free myself entirely from the 'thorns'.[49]

Maskarade

Nielsen took a very different approach to his next opera. Instead of aiming for noble grandeur and seriousness, he composed a comic opera on a grand scale. His work at The Royal Theatre had given him a thorough knowledge of the operatic repertoire, and by writing with that Theatre in mind, he was able to draw on his knowledge of how the staging of an opera worked in practice and what resources were available. There would hardly have been any ballet elements if there had not been a ballet company in the Theatre, and the music suits The Royal Orchestra without employing unusual instruments and without the need to increase its size. Nielsen also said that he composed with the theatre's permanent singers in mind.[50] He was writing for an opera house that he knew inside out.

The idea of composing an opera to a libretto based on a text by Holberg was not surprising, as Holberg's comedies were well known and popular. Holberg had written his play for the theatre in Lille Grønnegade, which from 1722 staged plays in Danish with Holberg as the driving force. It is considered the birth of Danish theatre.

Holberg wrote the comedy *Mascarade* in 1724, but the theatre had to close temporarily the following year and permanently a few years later.

Masquerades were the latest fashion among the new theatre audiences; however, they were banned in Copenhagen in 1724, and thus debates about their beneficial or harmful effects were of great interest at the time. Holberg's theatre was typical of the Enlightenment's desire to debate current issues, and the celebration of reason was high on the agenda. Nielsen thus reached back to a time when the ideals had much in common with the circles he knew in the Modern Breakthrough in Copenhagen.

Watching Holberg's play today, it is striking how all the characters are constantly arguing without the play coming to an obvious moral or conclusion. It is a play in which the struggle between different opinions and arguments is evident, although the playwright never clearly states who is right. However, this has not prevented later interpreters from believing that it was, of course, the representatives of progress and youth that were right, and that Jeronimus was an old fool. Yet there is something to be said for his arguments, and it is, after all, part of the Enlightenment mentality that the audience must make up their own minds on the basis of their own reasoning. Holberg's play is therefore extremely verbose. It was a challenge to turn it into a usable opera libretto.

Holberg's plays had been an integral part of The Royal Theatre's repertoire since the middle of the eighteenth century, with hundreds of performances and over twenty different plays premiered within a few years. *Mascarade* was first staged at the Theatre in 1748, and by the time Nielsen wrote his opera, Holberg's comedy had been performed almost two hundred times, most recently in the spring of 1897, when Nielsen played in the orchestra.[51] He could therefore rely on the audience knowing Holberg and being familiar with Holberg's characters, which recur in several of his comedies. Nielsen could also draw on the Theatre's long tradition of using music to accompany Holberg's plays.[52]

The desire to write another opera of a different kind arose shortly after the premiere of his *Saul and David* in November 1902.[53] However pleased he was with his first opera, he must have realised that it would have difficulty in reaching a wider audience. It was a good omen that on 11 November 1905 – exactly one year before the premiere of *Maskarade* – excerpts from his forthcoming opera, which he had included in a concert of orchestral works, were very well received. The programme included the Prelude to Act Two, 'Hanedansen' (Dance of the Cockerel) and 'Magdelone's Dance Scene', as well as *Helios*, *Søvnen* (Sleep), excerpts from *Saul and David* and his Second Symphony. These were major works, premiered between 1902 and 1905. After the concert, it was generally agreed that with *Maskarade* he had embarked on a new direction, one that was more popular and no longer subject to being seen as erudite or artificial. It was spontaneous and accessible music, and Angul

Hammerich wrote in the newspaper *Nationaltidende* that the excerpts from *Maskarade* showed 'Carl Nielsen with a whole new face. Not only *is* he popular, he is now also *writing* popular music!'[54]

In an interview in October 1905, after the submission of *Maskarade* to the theatre for evaluation, he was asked why he had chosen this particular text:

> Well, it was the interlude, the masque-like comedy that interested me. And then the character Henrik from *Maskarade*! I think he is so great. And he is basically quite modern in his feelings; he even says socialist things. The opera's Act One is almost entirely Holberg. The second act begins with the night watch. We took the liberty of making the interlude Act Three, in which the denouement takes place.[55]

The basic structure of Holberg's story is simple: Act One takes place the day after a masquerade, between Acts One and Two there is another masquerade in the evening, and Act Two takes place the following day. The two main themes of the play are discussed throughout: the moral implications of masquerades, especially for young people, and the question of arranged marriages in relation to true love. Relationships between generations and relationships with authority are also explored. By denouement, Nielsen means the unmasking and the point at which the plot of the play is revealed: Leander and Leonora, who are in love, are the same people who were promised to each other by their parents.

How did Nielsen approach the task of turning the story into an opera? He could use Holberg's model for interpreting the story in song, although he had to get to the heart of it, because a libretto needs far fewer words than a play. He used the ploy that since two of Holberg's acts take place after a masquerade the night before, it is possible to move scenes and performances from Act Two of the play and place them in the opera's Act One. Firstly, he chose the scenes that he found most obvious and entertaining, and which had the greatest potential for musical development. Secondly, he had to use texts for arias, duets and larger ensembles that did not exist in Holberg's play. They could not be left out of an opera. Some of them were inspired by passages in Holberg's play, while others had to be invented for the occasion. And when the opera chorus had to act as masquerade guests, they also had to sing. The third element is the masquerade itself. In Holberg's play, the interlude between the two acts, where the masquerade itself takes place, is described in just a few lines:

> Interlude. Where the masquerade is introduced, Leander appears as being in love with a mask worn by Leonora, the daughter of Leonard. They both take off their masks, talk to each other and give each other their rings. When this introduction has lasted a quarter of an hour, the curtain is lowered.[56]

In Holberg's comedy, therefore, the central scene for Nielsen is not a play but a pantomime, which is not described in detail. The performance would be similar to those staged at the Pantomime Theatre in the Tivoli Gardens. Fortunately, Nielsen had other sources of information. The Royal Theatre had a tradition of how the interlude should be performed when the play was on the programme. In addition, masquerades were still a living tradition in Copenhagen's entertainment venues. As an established part of society, the masquerade was not just a costume party. It followed a fairly common standard, where participants knew how things worked, which enabled them to participate. After all, Nielsen himself had known and played at masquerades in his youth, when he was a musician in Odense.

Nielsen needed a librettist but did not know who to turn to. When Nielsen saw the literary historian Vilhelm Andersen participating in the student comedies at Folketeatret, he seemed to be the right person to approach. He asked Andersen if he would write a libretto for an opera, which surprised Andersen at first, but when he heard that it was to be based on a text by Holberg, he replied: 'Yes, that is another matter. Provide me with a plot.'[57] They began collaborating around the turn of 1903–4, and by April Andersen had produced a libretto based on Nielsen's plot and Holberg's text.[58]

In Act One, Nielsen gathers together the scenes in Holberg in which music appears and the plot is established. At the beginning, the two young men, Leander and his servant Henrik, have slept most of the day. In his sleep, Henrik sings and dances the 'Cotillion' of the masquerade the night before. This is followed by the story of how Leander fell in love at the event, but is promised to another woman; then, as a play within a play, Henrik performs an imaginary 'Tamperret', a court for matrimonial cases, demonstrating what will happen to Leander if he breaks off the engagement. In her dance scene, Magdelone, who is Leander's mother, confesses that she too would like to go to a masquerade and shows that she can still dance, ending with a Folie d'Espagne. Leander's father, Jeronimus, enters and it is now revealed that Leander has fallen in love. Leonora's father confides that the same thing has happened to his daughter. Jeronimus blames the masquerades and orders no one to leave the house. Along the way, there is a song or aria for each of the three main characters. In the beginning, Leander sings an aria, enjoying the evening sun through the window. In the middle, Mr Jeronimus remembers the peace of the old days, singing 'Fordum var der Fred i Gaden' (Time was when our street was silent); and towards the end, Henrik sings about the need to have fun when you live in a country where it is dark for eleven months of the year. Act One ends with a finale in which everyone sings at once about attending a masquerade.

As a prelude to the finale, Henrik has another aria in which he elaborates on his argument, and it is to this point that Nielsen alludes when he mentions that Henrik

ILL. 2. Magdelone's dance scene from *Maskarade* became one of the opera's most popular pieces and was issued in a number of arrangements and piano excerpts so that it could be played at home, in restaurants or at popular concerts. At the premiere, Jeronimus was sung by Karl Mantzius, his wife Magdelone by Jonna Neiiendam, Leander by Hans Kjerulf and his servant Henrik by Helge Nissen.

expresses almost socialist sentiments. The argument is borrowed from Holberg and transformed into a song text:

> We are born in poverty, we are starved,
> we live on want and by sighs
> …
> we struggle and labour and make ourselves slaves
> that we may not die of hunger.
>
> Then the colourful masked procession whirls
> with freedom and equality
> with the richest king and the poorest commoner
> what a wonder if *we* join in!⁵⁹

Nielsen's statement hardly implies that the opera's message should be interpreted as socialist propaganda. Henrik is concerned with social differences and the injustice and distress they cause, and it is clear that Nielsen sympathises with him. Freedom and equality are democratic ideals that he himself espouses. Henrik's main point is that the masquerade is a space of freedom, a counterbalance to the social realities of everyday life, where one can experience the liberty and equality he sings about. The masquerade assumes the character of a utopia in which the ideals of the Enlightenment acquire a specific form. Social hierarchies are abolished for a while. However, this is only temporary, and the unmasking in Act Three is also the moment of truth. Here we return to reality.

Act Two of the opera is based on the theme that the farmhand, Arv, is on sentry duty, but is frightened and the way is open for everyone to join the masquerade. The act functions as an interlude, albeit with a different content from Holberg's. From a plot point of view, nothing happens except that all the characters cross the street to the comedy house. However, the act gives way to one of the musical highlights, when Leonora and Leander meet and perform a grand and lavishly orchestrated love duet that could have found its way into a Puccini opera or one of the great Viennese operettas. Nielsen shows his mastery of different styles, contrasting the grand, romantic and extended rendezvous of the children of the bourgeoisie with Henrik and his girlfriend Pernille, two servants who get straight to the point and sing about the same thing in a simple, ballad-like style.

In Act Three, Nielsen and Andersen had to invent a story. One of the sources of inspiration was that both attended a carnival in the Casino in Copenhagen in February 1904.[60] Nielsen's own experience, however, came directly from Odense, where he had played in masquerades and where the dancing could go on for most of the night.[61] From the end of January, the city's clubs and innkeepers organised masquerades in such numbers that the Odense Theater was forced to announce that it was impossible to hire the theatre's costumes.[62] From his time in Odense, Nielsen must also have been familiar with the performance of *Kalifen paa Eventyr* (*The Caliph on an Adventure*), which was a great success in the spring of 1883. Act Two of *The Caliph* took place during an artists' carnival in a 'splendidly decorated and illuminated ballroom in Copenhagen', and this act includes an interlude which is supposed to be the entertainment, presented during the masquerade.[63] The interlude was considered so important that the theatre advertised the individual pieces in the newspaper, which included some ten numbers, including 'Eight Unnamed Masks', a 'March of the Cockerel', and finally 'An Express Locomotive', 'Grand Quadrille' and 'Finale'.[64] The newspaper made special mention of how the audience cheered 'the splendid arrangement of the artists' carnival with its endlessly amusing dance of the cockerel'.[65]

Nielsen's idea of including a cockerel's dance in the opera may thus have been inspired by the inserted musical numbers, as was the construction of an interlude illustrating a masquerade. There are also a number of elements from Act Two of *The Caliph* that recur in Act Three of *Maskarade*. In the first scene, a quartet sings: 'Long live Prince Carnival! Free is his kingdom, all are friends, and all are equal. Happy we dispel … all duress', which is similar to Henrik's statement. Later there is a song full of jaunty rhymes in the style of the Tutor's aria in *Maskarade*, and the act ends with a chorus that is clearly a 'Kehraus', the final dance of a party: 'Now off, off, follow all! A well-provided table awaits us near.'[66] This very specific reference to a known practice appears in an advertisement from the Odense Club: 'Masquerade. The unmasking takes place at Midnight. Buffet and a well-provided table available.'[67]

The score of *The Caliph on an Adventure* has survived and may provide us with another thread to tie the story together. August Rasmussen, who was director of the Odense Theater during Nielsen's time there, became director of the Casino in 1884, which is where the score ends up. *The Caliph on an Adventure* was an immensely popular production in Copenhagen and was staged from 1857, reaching almost 250 performances by 1905.[68] But rather than trying to reconstruct in detail whether Nielsen might have known of it and possibly borrowed from it, it is more important to understand the coincidences as indicating that masquerades, with the music used and the entertainment that appeared as 'interludes', were a familiar model to which Nielsen could refer and from which he could draw.

Another source of inspiration for Act Three may well have been the music and structure of the interlude when Holberg's comedy *Mascarade* was staged at The Royal Theatre. The ballet master August Bournonville organised the sequence, which was apparently intended to be performed by ballet dancers. By the mid-nineteenth century, the music consisted of an 'Introduction' and six other movements: 'Cotillon', 'Menuetto', 'Dance of the Cockerel', 'The Scotch Sextour', 'Chiaconne' and finally 'Finale, Kehraus!'[69] As a member of the orchestra, Nielsen played this music in 1897. In the opera *Maskarade*, three of the dances – the Cotillon, the Dance of the Cockerel and the Kehraus – are included in an identical sequence. Nielsen may have been inspired by some of the musical details, but he was aware that his colleagues in the orchestra and the audience knew the incidental music, so he avoided the most obvious borrowings.[70]

Act Three of the opera begins with a chorus of soldiers, students and young girls, as well as all the guests at the masquerade. The scene is one of extraordinary activity. Then the Master of Masquerades announces the first dance: the Cotillon. When Leander meets Leonora, they sing another love duet in high style, promising each other eternal fidelity. This is followed by Henrik and Pernille's 'Canzone parodica', a parody of the pompous circumlocutions befitting the finer circles. In the next scene, Mr Leonard flirts with Magdelone, followed by an interlude announced by the Master of Masquerades: the Cockerel's Dance. Henrik has spotted Jeronimus dressed as Bacchus, the god of wine and intoxication, and to get rid of him Henrik sings a long aria in which he explains the whole story to the Tutor – a man of learning – who promises to get Jeronimus drunk. The next entertaining feature is a ballet scene in which the dancing master and his girlfriend perform 'Mars and Venus' also called 'Vulcan's ruse'. Venus loves Mars but fears that her husband Vulcan will appear; it seems likely that they are alluding to Mr Leonard, Magdelone and Jeronimus. In the background, Jeronimus becomes increasingly intoxicated, prompting the Tutor to sing a ballad interpreting the morale of the ballet scene. It culminates when Jeronimus gets the hiccups and the chorus of students responds: 'Oh, you ludicrous old fellow, oh why did you choose to play the part of Bacchus?'

It is at this point in the libretto that Andersen makes his mark most clearly, replacing Holberg's text with his own puerile verbosity. The addition of the Tutor and the many students makes the plot more elaborate, but it also emphasises a theme close to Andersen's heart, namely the Dionysian. In his book *Bacchustoget i Norden* (The Bacchus Procession in the Nordic Countries), published in 1904, he argues that Dionysus (Bacchus in Greek) is the most ancient and primal divine force, the life force that is 'the very thing that grows'.[71] It is clear that he probably saw the masquerade as a release and worship of the creative force, and that the Dionysian was the force behind both the return of life in spring and creativity, the ability to create art. It is a way of thinking close to Vitalism that defines the Dionysian as 'the point of life' where opposites meet, where 'spirit and nature', 'the high and the low, the horrifying and the laughing' are united.[72]

Another aspect can be traced back to Andersen: he sees the students and their drinking parties as an image of the Dionysian return to European culture after a long absence. The reappearance of intoxication is positive, and in his book he quotes a Swedish drinking ballad that could be the model for Jeronimus's hiccup aria.[73] But Andersen adds another layer to his interpretation, arguing that Bellman's Swedish drinking songs express an inherent seriousness: 'Empty your glass – death is awaiting you.'[74] This corresponds to the seriousness with which the Master of Masquerades appears at the end of Act Three, as Corporal Mors, that is, Death, who brings a huge urn. The opera takes up the 'memento mori' of the drinking song (remember, you must die), at which point the music changes entirely. Nielsen first composes a ritual prelude in E flat minor, in which Corporal Mors, accompanied by low strings and brass, introduces the unmasking. This is followed by a mournful and reflective choral setting in *ppp*, as the group slowly pass the urn and drop their masks. This is followed by the 'denouement', in which everyone recognises the context of things, and immediately by a finale, the festive and almost manic Kehraus, which celebrates dance across all social divides.

Even at the premiere, Nielsen seems to have had problems with the balance between the serious and the festive aspect at the end, as he shortened Captain Mors's warning to the guests to be serious during the unmasking. As a result, the unmasking is not given the importance it was originally intended to have. The contemplativeness is toned down, and the end is heard more as a festive finale to the masquerade. Perhaps Nielsen wanted to avoid the depth and element of reflection that he had originally envisaged for the premiere in order to ensure a positive reception for the opera. It is impossible to know, although he stuck to the shorter version in all performances during his lifetime.[75]

Rehearsals began in May and sixty-five were held before the premiere on 11 November 1906. The final changes were made in the last hectic week. On 3 November, the theatre rehearsed all the acts with orchestra for the first time, and that night, on his return home, Nielsen scribbled the last notes of the overture.[76] Two days later he composed an additional scene for Pernille in Act Two. On 7 and 8 November there were rehearsals for all acts, and on Friday 9 November there was a dress rehearsal. Frederik Rung conducted these three days so that Nielsen could follow the action from a distance. The final dress rehearsal was held on Saturday 10 November, during which several possible cuts in Act Three were tried out, and the premiere took place the following day. The process reflects Nielsen's method of working, which ultimately resulted in the final structure of the opera.[77]

At the premiere, the cast included Helge Nissen and Emilie Ulrich as Henrik and Leonora, and Hans Kjerulf as Leander. Karl Mantzius was Jeronimus, whose wife Magdelone was played by Jonna Neiiendam, while Peter Jerndorff took the part of Leonard. With the exception of Margrethe Lendrop, who was substituted by Ida Møller as Pernille on the opening night, Nielsen had the whole team of singers he had imagined the year before.[78] This allowed him to tailor the roles to the individual actors, some of whom, such as Karl Mantzius, were not opera singers. The ballet master Hans Beck played the role of the dance master.

The opera was almost unanimously considered a musical success, and Act One in particular was praised by the critics. However, there were doubts about Andersen's libretto, and Hammerich wrote in *Nationaltidende*:

> The main result of last night's premiere is easy to judge. It was a complete success, with rapturous curtain calls at the end to the composer, who thanked the audience from the conductor's stand. ... Act One seems excellent. After this experience, one could swear that Nielsen was born for the *opéra comique*. So light, so skilful, so quick in change, so apt in line, with fine phrases and amusing fancies, in the

treatment of the text, in the vocal parts, in the instruments of the orchestra equally apt. ... In the musical structure it is a complete master who holds the pen; one is inclined to think of Verdi in 'Falstaff' to find a counterpart. ... This is the first authentic *opéra comique* in Danish.[79]

This places Nielsen at the top of the European league of opera composers. On the other hand, at the time of its premiere there was no definitive interpretation of the work as a Danish national opera. This was to come about ten years later.[80] Nevertheless, it must be said that the production and reception of *Maskarade* marked a change in the perception of Nielsen. It laid the foundations for his future status as the country's undisputed leading composer.

Chapter 20

PROGRAMME MUSIC

One of Nielsen's most often cited essays is his 'Ord, Musik og Programmusik' (Words, Music and Programme Music). It first appeared in the journal *Tilskueren* in 1909 and later in his book *Levende Musik* (*Living Music*) (1925), which for many years served as a kind of music-aesthetic manifesto for his followers. In the essay he explains that music cannot and will not 'bind itself to any particular content of thought; its very nature is completely opposed to this'.[1] For this reason, Nielsen was widely regarded as an opponent of programme music.

At the same time, Nielsen was extremely good at expressing himself verbally, including the ideas associated with his music.[2] There is no doubt that he was often strongly inspired by something he had seen or imagined while composing. On several occasions he even gave his works a title or motto that could obviously be interpreted as a programme idea, as in his Second Symphony, *The Four Temperaments* (1902), or the orchestral works *Helios Overture* (1903), *Saga Dream* (1908) and *Pan and Syrinx* (1917). So how are we to understand Nielsen's relationship to programme music?

To understand this question, we must first look at the situation in his time. During the period in which he was active as a composer, programme music went from being a recognised and natural part of modern music in Europe to being condemned by leading composers and critics.[3]

In the second half of the nineteenth century, programme music was one of the central points of contention in the split between the New German School and Romantic Classicism. A crucial debate concerned music's ability to accommodate meanings that lay outside of the music itself. Was it acceptable for a poem or an idea expressed in a title to be part of the musical work itself? The debate was prompted by Wagner's essays from around 1850, in which he developed his ideas of the 'Gesamtkunstwerk' and presented music as a fundamentally expressive art form. In 1852, in response to Wagner's ideas, the music critic Eduard Hanslick published his book on musical beauty, in which he advocated absolute music. He argued that instrumental music could not refer to anything outside itself and that the beauty of music lay in the musical structures themselves. The next edition of Hanslick's book, which appeared six years later, was an attack on both Liszt and Wagner, as Liszt had now composed his programme symphonies, providing a musical counterpart to Wagner's writings. In 1860, Brahms was one of the signatories of a manifesto by a group of 'serious musicians' protesting against the New German School, and was thus at the centre of the dispute between the two factions that became known as the Brahmsites and the Wagnerians.[4]

In the 1890s the conflict was still very much alive. This is evident in Nielsen's letters and diaries from his long tour of Europe in 1890–91, one of which, written in Berlin to his friend Emil Sachs, reads: 'Here I'm surrounded by some young musicians from the Academy, and of course we are always arguing about Wagner and Brahms.'[5] But the situation was also changing at this time. A new generation of German and Austrian composers was emerging, and by the turn of the century they had become representatives of modernity: notably Richard Strauss and Gustav Mahler – and, a little later, Max Reger. Strauss, with his tone poems of the late nineteenth century, can be seen as the perpetuator of the New German trend towards programme music, while Reger was one of those who continued the classical tradition.[6]

In its 1905–6 issue, the Danish music journal *Programmet* published portrait articles on Reger and Strauss, explaining their different modern positions. The one on Reger included a quotation from Hugo Riemann, who associated Reger with a classical aesthetic: 'Reger owes his reputation to those works in which he maintains a close relationship with Bach, Beethoven and Brahms, but in which his own nature nevertheless finds expression in the most unconstrained, developed way.'[7] The journal describes Strauss as the most controversial of all contemporary composers, with at least as many fanatical opponents as ardent admirers. It goes on:

> As a composer, Strauss seeks to renew the movement to which he belongs ... Unlike Liszt, he is not content with large, impressive sketches, he gets down to the details and wants to give images of the soul and developments rather than external events. In a sense, he wants to be a philosopher in his music, and Strauss's rare technical mastery is very much to his advantage. His counterpoint and his instrumentation, which finds new and surprising sounds and combinations even after Liszt and Wagner, make Strauss appear as a most modern and refined orchestral virtuoso, a master of nervously energetic power, ecstatically delicate rendering and glowing colour.[8]

Strauss represented a new version of programme music, and his international breakthrough was linked in particular to programmatic orchestral works such as *Also sprach Zarathustra* and *Till Eulenspiegel* from the 1890s, which deal respectively with a philosophical text and as a theme of the musically precise portrayal of tricks. The description also points to many of the characteristics associated with the modern, New German trend in music at the turn of the century: technical mastery, surprising sounds and intense use of timbre.

It was in this context that Nielsen contributed several works of programme music, which must be seen as evidence that his attitude to the genre was not – as posterity has otherwise seen it – unambiguously negative. His statements about programme music, together with the musical statements – that is, his works – must be seen in a more nuanced light than we are used to. Many of his claims must also be seen in the context of who they were addressed to and in what context they were made. It was not by chance or with a guilty conscience that Nielsen composed programme music. It was important to him, however, not to be associated with the trend of Strauss, and he was aware that it was not good manners to identify oneself explicitly as a programme musician. For this reason, many of his statements were accompanied by assurances that they were not in fact dealing with programme music, at least not in the sense that the term was understood at the time.

The Four Temperaments

There are a number of examples of Nielsen giving his works some form of programme title. The *Humoresque-Bagatelles*, Op. 11 for piano (1897) have titles such as 'Snurretoppen' (The Spinning Top) and 'Spilleværket' (The Musical Clock), and the movements of his *Suite for String Orchestra* originally had the mythological titles 'The Danaids', 'The Dance of the Charites' and 'The Procession of Bacchus'. When Nielsen was in Berlin in 1890, he thought of a symphony that would have programmatic associations from the outset. He imagined the title 'From earth thou art come, to earth thou shalt return'. He had a clear picture in his mind of a progression from something dark and foreboding, steadily rising to the highest joie de vivre, and finally ending in the black earth. At the same time, he emphasised that the symphony should not be programme music, and thus felt the need to distance himself from the concept, even though the idea is clearly programmatic.[9]

The work that became his First Symphony was not given a title, but the next three were. His Second Symphony, *The Four Temperaments* (CNW 26), is undoubtedly the one that comes closest to a programmatic tradition, referring to the doctrine of the temperaments, which originated in antiquity with the Greek Hippocrates. The theory posits that there are four bodily fluids: blood, black bile, yellow bile and phlegm, each of which is associated with the four temperaments and the four elements: air, earth, fire and water. When out of balance, they can cause illness, but they also indicate different personality types. The sanguine temperament is optimistic, the melancholic sad, the choleric bad-tempered, while the phlegmatic is indifferent.[10]

The Second Symphony was composed during a productive period for Nielsen. The opera *Saul and David* was completed on 20 March 1901, and in the spring he had also completed the cantata for the Student Society, which was premiered on

1 June. It is not known when he began work on the symphony in 1901, but the first movement was completed on 28 December. The second movement was completed in the summer of 1902, and to finish the work he made a final push in the autumn, finalising the last movement on 22 November 1902. This coincided with the final rehearsals of *Saul and David*, which premiered on 28 November. Three days later, on 1 December, Nielsen conducted the first performance of his new symphony, entitled *The Four Temperaments*, at Dansk Koncert-Forening (the Danish Concert Society).[11]

The four movements are named after the four temperaments: *Allegro collerico, Allegro comodo e flemmatico, Andante malincolico* and *Allegro sanguineo*. By beginning with the choleric, Nielsen is able to open the symphony with a violent burst of musical energy that, within a few bars, introduces the central material of the movement. The opening is reminiscent of that of his First Symphony. The choleric temperament is characterised by powerful and fiery passages in a turbulent sound. In a contrasting section, the choleric realises that the outburst was excessive and regrets the anger until it becomes extreme again. The phlegmatic reveals an imperturbable calm in which all impressions seem to fade away, while the melancholic is characterised by a sad seriousness. The last movement presents the sanguine, the incorrigible optimist who carries on regardless of what happens. The mood anticipates the overture to *Maskarade*, which expresses the same kind of celebration and joy. Surprisingly, just before what could have been its celebratory conclusion, the movement breaks off and plays the second subject in a slow version, allowing a link with the two middle movements. The passage serves as a moment of reflection. The symphony ends with a stately march.

The structure of the work, with two slow middle movements framed by the active outer ones, as well as the design of the individual movements, follows the model of a traditional symphonic form. However, the way in which Nielsen uses the titles to create a link between the idea and the music meant that several critics questioned the genre designation of the work after its first performance at the Dansk Koncert-Forening. Writing in *Politiken*, Julius Schiøtt argued that the idea of basing a symphony on the four temperaments, while original and seemingly appropriate, was problematic. The temperaments represent four different types of personality, not one individual in four different moods. According to Schiøtt, the organic connection between the movements could not be achieved, nor could the development and sense of unity required by the symphonic genre. However, if this shortcoming is ignored and the work is conceived as a symphonic suite, 'the task is not only amusing and good, it is also to a great extent skilfully conceived and solved'.[12]

By suggesting that the genre designation should be 'symphonic suite' rather than 'symphony', Schiøtt's review comes across as an obvious programmatic interpretation of the work. A characteristic of the suite is precisely that it usually consists of individual pieces whose identity is partly derived from something external, and that it may have programmatic associations indicated by titles.[13] That the symphony should be regarded as programme music is also suggested by several other reviewers, who also point out that it would have been more correct to call it a symphonic suite – for example, the reviewer in *Berlingske Tidende*, who is positive about Nielsen and the work, but clearly does not regard it as absolute music:

> The concert hall is his true field, and although the new symphony does not seek its strength in the beauty and weight of its musical content, this symphonic suite – as it is would be called in the musical terms still in use – is an attractive work for its individuality and for its developed orchestral language.[14]

A similar view can be found in *Dannebrog*, whose reviewer Leopold Rosenfeld uses a vocabulary similar to that employed to describe the New German trend of the time:

> Carl Nielsen's new work might be better described as a suite of moods for orchestra than as a symphony. But beyond the name, this new piece by the celebrated composer is yet another positive testimony to its composer's exceptional ability to create characteristic tonal expression through the use of extensive orchestral technique. Whether one really dares to call these ingeniously constructed orchestral sounds music is another question. What is particularly fascinating about this illustrator of music is the composer's ability to blend colours, which never fails to captivate the listener's ear. Sometimes, however, the colours are rather brutal, and their ugliness easily crosses the line of beauty.[15]

The work is perceived not simply as a symphonic suite but as a 'suite of moods for orchestra', and the music is described with phrases such as 'characteristic tone painting', 'constructed orchestral sounds', the 'illustrator of music' and the 'ability to blend colours', which are indeed similar to those used about the works of Richard Strauss. The reviewers do not use these terms as part of a criticism of Nielsen – on the contrary, they are generally positive. This is also true of Gustav Hetsch's review in *Nationaltidende*, which explicitly defines the work as programme music and sees it as typical of its composer: 'The very idea of depicting the four temperaments in music is very Carl Nielsenian – off the beaten track, even on a different path than programme music usually takes. It is the traces of scholastic psychology that are trodden in this work.'[16]

Nielsen's friend Rudolph Bergh took a different view in his critique of the work, which appeared in *Tilskueren* a few months after the premiere. Like other writers, Bergh was generally enthusiastic about the symphony, but his minor objection to the work was quite the opposite of theirs: he felt that the programme title was unnecessary, and that the symphony was best understood as absolute music:

> Let it be said that the title 'The Four Temperaments' is somewhat naive and rather superfluous ... Fortunately [the symphony] is not conceived in the way that programme music usually is, but as strict, absolute music. ... His new symphony, considered as absolute music, is a masterpiece ...[17]

A major complaint against programme music in contemporary debates was that musical form had been neglected in favour of external factors, and that the programme was necessary because the inner coherence of the music was not working.[18] Nielsen's symphony thus lands in the middle of the argument between programme music as a quality in itself and the view that a symphony, even if it has a programme, should rise above it and appear as a musical entity in its own right. A common strategy in later years for highlighting Nielsen's qualities as a symphonist was to emphasise the elements that gave the work coherence within and across movements. On the other hand, it is also possible to take seriously the fact that character pieces for orchestra were a well-known and recognised genre in Nielsen's time. It is worth noting that some of those who say that this is an orchestral suite or a series of character pieces emphasise that they are successful.

From a programmatic, aesthetic point of view, other characteristics of the movements than internal coherence are evident, as is the perception of 'the characteristic' as a quality. Interestingly, the two approaches are reflected not only in reviews or reactions to the work, but also in orchestral culture and in conductors' interpretations. A conductor may choose to emphasise the distinctive features of the performance, exaggerate the theatrical expressions and say musically, 'Ha, wasn't that just right!' It is also possible to downplay the features in favour of a performance that emphasises melodiousness and the purely musical, non-narrative qualities. Today, the latter way of playing symphonies dominates, but in 1902 the performance of character pieces was still part of orchestral culture. It is striking that, in a review in a German journal the following year, the author took it for granted that the characteristic features should be heard: 'It must be admitted that he has, on the whole, succeeded very well in drawing the desired picture of the character in a clearly recognisable way.'[19]

Although Nielsen certainly knew how to create musical coherence in his works, especially in his symphonies, he often chose the characteristic over the neat when it came to deciding. As a listener, you can try to detect the qualities yourself, which makes for a different experience. The work comes to us in a different way depending on how we choose to hear it. It is similar to listening with two different sets of ears.

Character pieces will communicate directly with the audience. Symphony movements, on the other hand, communicate primarily with themselves and each other. They refer to themselves as an entity and their attention is directed elsewhere. Both aspects are present in a work such as *The Four Temperaments*.

The means by which Nielsen combines these two considerations is to regard each movement as a living being with a character that it must reflect. Thus the music can have an internal coherence and at the same time express a programmatic idea. During his work on the symphony, Nielsen recounted how far he had come in treating the movements as independent beings:

> Now the idea was that the Sanguine [Temperament] would come sweeping in one day. As yet I have no idea how the beast will take shape. The Phlegmatic now has a fine tail on him and is thus completely finished and won't get any better in this draw.[20]

On several occasions Nielsen described how he personally saw the relationship between the programme idea and the music – an approach that is repeated here. The most detailed description appears in a programme note from October 1931, which begins by repeating the caveat that the remarks should in no way be understood as a programme, but rather as a private matter between the composer and the music.[21] Nielsen first explains how the idea came from a picture of the four temperaments he had seen in a village inn. It was a funny, coloured picture with four motifs, one for each of the four temperaments. It was this picture that planted the idea in his head, even though he found it silly at first. If the incident is true, and not just a literary device to provoke the reader's interest, it seems strange that he waited thirty years to reveal it. The story is strikingly reminiscent of Mahler's programme note for his First Symphony, in which he says that the third movement was inspired by the well-known parody of *The Hunter's Corpse* from an old children's book, in which the animals carry the hunter to his grave.[22] Nielsen then discusses the four movements and their relationship to the programmatic titles. He writes of the first movement, the Choleric, that it 'behaves sometimes wildly and violently, like a man about to die, sometimes in a gentler mood, like one who regrets his irascibility'.[23] It should be noted that Nielsen is talking about the music, and that it is the music that has these qualities. The human being is only included to better explain what the music does.

The programme of 1931 does not necessarily reflect Nielsen's view at the time of its composition; unfortunately, no personal statements have survived from the period when he was working on the symphony. There is, however, another work that can also be said to have programmatic features: the *Helios Overture* of 1903.

Helios

Nielsen's *Helios Overture* was composed during his stay in Athens in 1903 and is inspired by the sun's movement across the sky. Nielsen had been granted leave from The Royal Orchestra and went to Greece to visit Anne Marie, who was working on her copies of Greek reliefs. He had access to a study room at the music academy. Over the course of a few weeks, he composed the overture and completed it on 23 April.[24]

Through Nielsen's letters and diaries, it is possible to follow his thoughts during the composition process. On 27 March 1903, he wrote home to his friend Svend Godske-Nielsen: 'Helios is burning all day long, and I'm writing away at my new "solar system" [the *Helios Overture*]; I've finished a long introduction with sunrise and a morning song, and I've begun the Allegro.'[25] Barely a month later, on 24 April, he had completed the work and was able to describe it in detail to his friends Julius and Dagmar Borup:

> Yesterday I finished my new composition. It's precisely an overture in praise of the sun, and it's called *Helios* (the sun). It begins from absolute silence, with some long notes in the bass, and little by little various instruments come in, and some horns then sing a semi-solemn morning song. Then it grows and grows until midday's quivering light nearly blinds you, and everything lies in a pool of light that makes virtually every living thing dozy and lethargic. Finally it descends again and sinks slowly and majestically behind the distant mountains turning blue far out to the west. Have I succeeded? I only know that I've been tremendously absorbed in carrying out this idea, which lends itself well to musical treatment and takes shape naturally as an organic entity.[26]

On the same day, Nielsen wrote a letter to his friend Hother Ploug, in which he on the one hand explicitly linked the musical effects to the idea and, on the other, expressed scepticism about programme music:

> Yesterday I finished my new overture. I've been very absorbed with this idea, which is highly suitable for musical form. … It begins with some long notes in the bass and gradually horns and violins emerge into a solemn morning song, which then grows and grows in the Andante (Introduction). The Allegro – when the sun is high – breaks out in E major and stays more or less in this key until towards the evening, when the Andante motif comes back in C major, finally laying itself to rest in this tonality. But stuff and nonsense with programmes! If the thing can't stand on its own two feet, then it's all wrong. But I just think that a title or a hint is justified. Don't you think so? One may dare to go so far, but no further.[27]

When Nielsen wrote to Thomas Laub the following day, he was even more reticent about a programmatic understanding of the overture:

> If you'd like to write me a note, I should be very happy. But in that case, you should do so soon because the post is slow, and we may soon be going on to Crete. Then you could give me your opinion about so-called programme music. To what extent do you think a programme is legitimate, and so on? This is of some interest to me, because I've just composed such a thing. That's to say: no detailed programme. My overture represents the sun's progress across the sky from morning to evening; but it's just called *Helios*, and no explanation whatsoever is necessary. What do you say to that? A programme title of this kind isn't bad, I suppose. After all, light, darkness, sun and rain almost correspond to Credo, Crucifixus, Gloria, and so on.[28]

The letters seem to imply that Nielsen was completely absorbed in his idea of describing the power of the sun in Greece and its orbit across the sky, and that only afterwards did he think about the problem of programme music. In any case, it seems contradictory that on the one hand he describes enthusiastically and in detail how the idea is expressed musically, and on the other hand he has to emphasise that the music needs no explanation. At the same time, the letters are examples of his awareness of whom he is addressing: to his friends he describes the idea of the work without reservation; to Ploug he emphasises how well the idea lends itself to musical form; and in the letter to Laub, who he knows does not like programme music, he almost asks for absolution, but adds bluntly: 'I've just composed such a thing.' He knows he is writing programme music.

Although Nielsen had already stated in the days following the completion of *Helios* that the music could stand alone without a programme, the work was accompanied by a motto when it was performed by Johan Svendsen and The Royal Danish Orchestra at the first symphony concert of the season on 8 October 1903:

> Stillness and darkness – Then the sun rises to joyous songs of praise – Wanders its golden way – quietly sinks in the sea.[29]

The motto was conceived by Nielsen himself and developed by Einar Christiansen, with whom Nielsen had just collaborated on *Saul and David*.[30] The motto was quoted by several reviewers, who used it as a basis for judging the extent to which Nielsen had succeeded in expressing the idea musically. Alfred Tofft, for example, noted that the dusk at the beginning and the twilight at the end had been best described, while the dazzling climax of the sun had failed: 'The sun does not warm.'[31] Leopold

b. 215
Fugue subject group

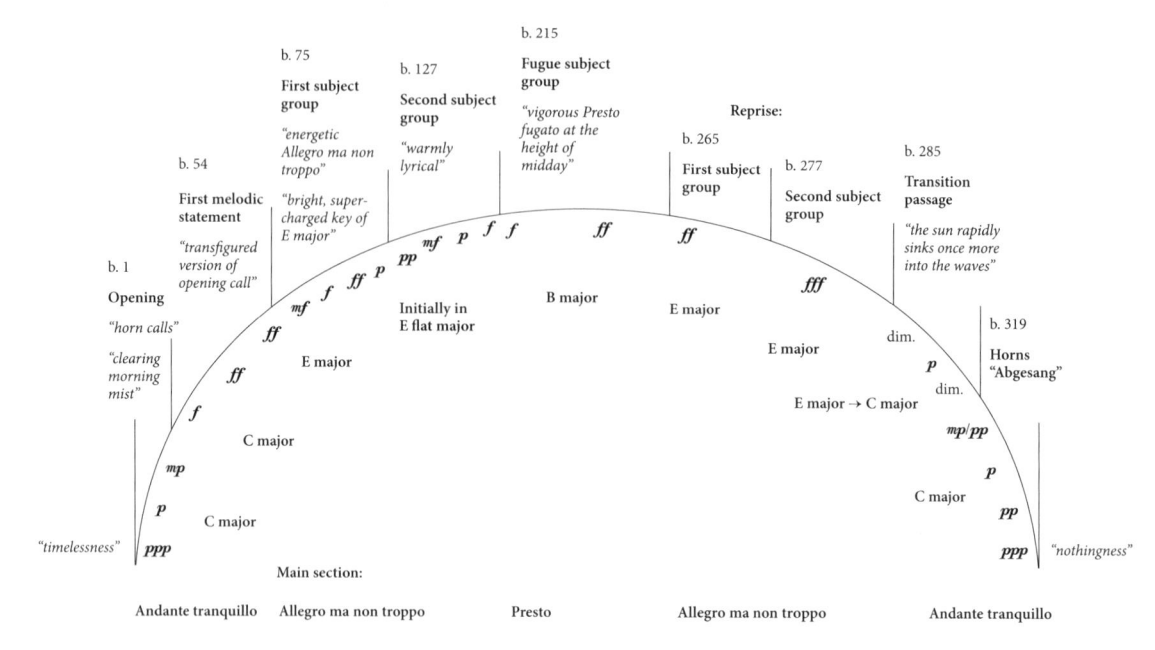

b. 127
Second subject group
"vigorous Presto fugato at the height of midday"

b. 75
First subject group
"energetic Allegro ma non troppo"
"bright, super-charged key of E major"

Reprise:
b. 265
First subject group

b. 285
Transition passage
"the sun rapidly sinks once more into the waves"

b. 54
First melodic statement
"transfigured version of opening call"

b. 277
Second subject group

mf *p* *f* *f*
pp
ff *ff* *ff*

b. 1
Opening
"horn calls"
"clearing morning mist"

Initially in E flat major

B major

E major

fff

b. 319
Horns
"Abgesang"

dim.
E major
p
dim.
E major → C major
mp/pp

ff
f
E major
ff
f
C major

mp
p
C major
ppp

p
C major
pp
ppp

"timelessness"   "nothingness"

Main section:
Andante tranquillo   Allegro ma non troppo   Presto   Allegro ma non troppo   Andante tranquillo

ILL. 1. Graphic representation of how the musical parameters of Nielsen's *Helios Overture* follow the idea of the sun's orbit across the sky. The illustration is based on Grimley's review and analysis of the work.[32]

Rosenfeld made the same assessment in the newspaper *Dannebrog*: 'One waits in vain, the sun does not warm up and shine as well as the dawn.'[33] Rosenfeld also pointed out, as he had done with the Second Symphony, that the genre designation for the work did not seem appropriate: 'Carl Nielsen's new work is an "overture" in name only. The piece has no such character. Rather, it gives the impression of a character piece for orchestra.'[34]

Looking at the music, it is not surprising that critics used the motto as a starting point for their assessment. The musical parameters that have the most immediate effect on the listener illustrate the symmetrical arc formed by the sun's course across the sky. Dynamically, the music moves gradually from *ppp* to *fff*, back to *ppp*, while tonally, the movement proceeds from C major to E major, culminating in B major, before returning to E major and ending in C major. The tempo moves similarly from Andante tranquillo to Allegro ma non troppo, then to Presto and back again. However, the thematic treatment in the Allegro section suggests an absolute musical principle of form, with a first and second subject, followed by a fugal Presto, and finally a recapitulation and coda.[35]

It could be argued that the music works without the programme, but both the musical effects and Nielsen's letters suggest that the overture was strongly inspired by his experience of the sun in Athens. Since it is clear that Nielsen was in no way associated with the New German School at the turn of the century and did not wish to follow such a programmatic musical trend, it is worth examining what he wrote on the subject. Between 1905 and 1909 Nielsen was a prolific writer and lecturer. It was during this period that he clearly began to formulate the musical aesthetic views that were to have a decisive influence on his posterity. Nielsen's music and essays became part of the debates about music in Copenhagen's musical life, and these debates in turn influenced Nielsen's own reflections on music.

Music and Words

In his 1907 lecture on Greek music, Nielsen set out his view of the relationship between music and words: 'It is quite impossible to speak of music and give an impression of it through words.'[36] He develops the same idea in more detail in his essay 'Word, Music and Programme Music', written the following year for publication in January 1909. Indeed, the essay contains only a relatively short passage on programme music at the end. The rest is a reflection on the nature of music and its relationship to language and words. The author is concerned with the nature of music as an art form and medium, and how it manages to create an effect on the listener.

Nielsen spends the first part of the essay refuting Herbert Spencer's thesis, outlined in 'The Origin and Function of Music' (1857), that music has its origins in language; this, along with Darwin's writings, helped shape the debate on the origins of music and was translated into Danish in 1882. Darwin argued that the origin of music was a mating call and thus had nothing to do with the origin of language. Spencer, on the other hand, maintained that the two were closely related, as both were produced by certain muscle movements. According to Spencer, when strong emotions or tensions are involved, larger intervals are typically used, while the voice becomes more tremulous. Since music makes greater use of the powerful muscular movements that produce tremors and large intervals, music must have originated as a kind of idealised speech, giving heightened expression to emotions.[37] Nielsen completely disagreed with this view. For him, the opposition between music and language was absolute: 'It is, of course, the most elementary purpose of language and speech to be a practical aid to people in understanding each other, but music in this sense has not the slightest grain of intention or purpose.'[38]

This view of the difference between language and music is echoed when Nielsen has to explain what music can articulate when combined with words, as in opera. He gives some specific examples of dramatic music in which the music seems to be quite specific in terms of expression. Yet he points out that it is a mistake to think of it in this way: 'These tones could just as easily be a cry for help or a warning in the hour of danger, and the "no" in Orpheus could be an equally effective "yes".'[39] Nielsen's point is very clear: music can create the effect of a certain feeling or state better than anything else described in words, although this does not suggest that it signifies or corresponds to that feeling or state. The combination of words and music may be important for how we perceive it, but it still has nothing to do with the music itself and what it expresses. This is the key point that Nielsen develops in his central argument:

> But music cannot and will not bind itself to any particular content of thought; its very nature is opposed to this. It wants to be free, and although it serves and sounds, it does so only because it enjoys itself in this way and rejoices in the flexibility of its being, like the sea lion in the water or the swallow in its flight. The less one tries to bind it and the more one lets it follow its nature and its own strange laws, the better it serves and the richer it proves itself. And if it cannot, as architecture, show anything in particular, or, as the art of poetry, painting and sculpture, give information about what we call nature and reality, it can, above the other arts, illuminate, emphasise, anticipate and clarify with lightning certainty the most elementary emotions or the tensest situations.[40]

At the end of the essay, Nielsen discusses programme music, and it is these statements that have had a major influence on how his works have been interpreted in the literature:

> Since music can in no way express specific thoughts or actions – and its relation to the word can never be more than decorative-illuminatory – it can neither express a whole, long, coherent programme. And yet, at the present time – especially in Germany, the resting place of the metaphysicians – there are many composers who cultivate this trend. It would be very interesting to know what different listeners would make of a piece of programme music to which the key had been withheld. One thing is certain: none of them would guess right.[41]

However, Nielsen also opens the door to the possibility that a title can be appropriate under the right conditions. It is clear that he is also involved in the defence of his own works, which critics have on several occasions interpreted as programme music:

> But with so many artists – and so many talented ones among them – dealing with the idea of programme [music], is there really nothing to it? Yes, but only few know how to draw the right line between dream and possibility. What about

music? If we confine ourselves to a brief allusion or title, music can illuminate and emphasise from many sides and in many ways, as we have seen in its relationship with words. Of course it can. But the programme or title itself must contain a motif of mood or movement, but never a motif of thought or specific action.[42]

In this context, it is worth considering whether Nielsen is entirely consistent in his reasoning. He seems to stay within his own boundaries when he structures the movements of his Second Symphony around the four temperaments, or when he provides the *Helios Overture* with a motto of four lines depicting the sun's orbit across the sky. But in 1918 he also wrote a work such as *Pan and Syrinx* (CNW 38), subtitled *Pastoral Scene for Orchestra*. It has a clear plot, which was also printed in the concert programme: the forest god Pan sees the nymph Syrinx and pursues her; she manages to escape by taking refuge in a forest lake and is transformed into a reed. It is quite easy to follow the action and to hear Syrinx represented by flute, oboe and English horn in turn, while the lurking Pan is the solo cello and, during the chase, a clarinet.[43] Moreover, reading Nielsen's letters and diaries, it is clear that his ideas for works often originate from something he has experienced or imagined. Nielsen seems to have found it useful to combine music and words, both for his own creativity and to guide his listeners.

There are a number of possible explanations for this. Firstly, it must be acknowledged that Nielsen was not always rigorous in his positions. He was never the type to commit himself completely to a particular philosophy or ideology and use it as the starting point for everything he did. One keen observer has described Nielsen's musical thinking as 'homespun' at best, because he was extremely well informed, although he combined ideas from many sources.[44]

Secondly, it is important to be aware of the historical context of Nielsen's works and statements. When he wrote his early works in the late nineteenth century, it was common to give orchestral suites and symphonies titles and mottoes; ten years later, programme music was in sharp decline.[45] When Nielsen wrote in 1909 that there were composers, especially in Germany, who were following the trend of composing programme music, it shows that he still considered the subject relevant at that time.[46] However, a wider consensus had emerged in the musical world that programme music had no place in the musical renewal that might be under way. It had become easier and more obvious to argue against its relevance. Yet it is also possible to read Nielsen's essay, written at a time when programme music might be dying out anyway, as a defence that if one understood how to use programme ideas appropriately, as he did, then programme music still had a justification.

Thirdly, it is reasonable to assume that Nielsen was not particularly concerned with the question of absolute music and programme music. For him, and probably for other composers of his generation, the problem seemed to be different. For many years it had been common to ask what the meaning of music was, and this is what Nielsen challenged.[47] According to Nielsen, music could not have a meaning that might be adequately described in words. Instead, he saw music as a form of expression on a par with language, and the one could not correspond to the other as they were different in nature. This is not to say that music combined with words cannot have an effect; for Nielsen, it is this quality of music to illuminate or clarify elementary emotions when accompanied by words that has often been confused with specific thought content:

> At such moments, music can indeed envelop and penetrate the word or situation with such expansive force that it seems to speak, and of course it does, albeit in its own language, although it is not a language. It is rather a constant floating in and out, up and down, among the words, sometimes far from them, sometimes close to them, yet without touching them; sometimes accelerating, sometimes lingering, but always in a living oscillation.[48]

To Nielsen, what matters most is the effect of the music and the fact that it speaks to us.

III

CLASSICITY AND LIFE

ILL. 1. One of Anne Marie Carl-Nielsen's finest sculptures portrays a musician blowing an aulos, using his entire body in the physical exercise of playing. Similar to the oboe, the aulos requires great physical effort, and when looking at the sculpture it is almost possible to hear the intense sound of the instrument as the body radiates the energy invested in playing.

Chapter 21

CLASSICITY AS A SOURCE OF INNOVATION

Nielsen's view of the relevance of classical ideals at the turn of the century is reflected in an autobiographical text he sent in February 1905 to Knud Harder, who was preparing an article on Nielsen.[1] Nielsen's description of his musical position reveals his admiration for the masters of the past and the classical ideals, but also his curiosity about the open situation in which music found itself, which meant that it could move stylistically in all possible directions and come closer to the ideal of the future:

> As far as my musical point of view is concerned, I am convinced that Palestrina, Sebastian Bach and Mozart are essentially the composers who have reached the highest peak of all. … Of course, I do not mean that these masters should be our ideals. I believe that music is still far from reaching its zenith in its ability to express human emotions and moods, but the direction in which it will develop is impossible to say at present.[2]

The composers that Nielsen highlights as models do not belong to the same stylistic period, but represent a kind of clarified completion of the period that they represent. It is clear, therefore, that Nielsen does not regard them as stylistic models or as a reference to a particular stylistic period. He is addressing a deeper level of ideality, that is, the principles that underlie the fact that they can be seen as classical models. In other words, it is their classicity – the qualities that make them classical – that he admires. At the same time, he makes it clear that he is not thinking in terms of imitating old models and continues:

> This much is clear to me, however, that there is an enormous amount of potential in harmony and modulation, and I should be very wrong if the future does not reject our modern major and minor keys as inadequate to express the thoughts and feelings of modern humans.[3]

For Nielsen, 'classical' meant something that was exemplary and perfect according to the criteria of its time. In this context, he was not just talking about classical music in the broad sense, or about Viennese Classical music as a style. So what were the characteristics he emphasised when explaining what he meant?

One aspect that appealed to him about classical music and art was that it had a universal and objective quality that enabled it to express universal human emotions and conditions or phenomena that had an effect on human beings. This was one of the ideals he emphasised in Mozart, and which also fascinated him in Renaissance and ancient art. In his own works from the years around the turn of the century, these ideals are particularly evident in his thinking and elaboration of choral works.

Another aspect is Nielsen's preoccupation with finding a balance between complete freedom in musical ideas and a high degree of rigour in their realisation. Again, he looked to Mozart as a model, not in a stylistic sense, but in Mozart's ability to reconcile these opposing tendencies:

> The fact is that Mozart is at once extraordinarily strict, logical and consistent in his voice-leading and modulations, and at the same time more free and uninhibited in his form than any other of the classical masters who have used the ... so coveted and difficult sonata form ...[4]

In both cases, Nielsen's ideal of classicism is a matter of principle and generality rather than style, and the veneration of classicity should be seen not as a retrospective trend but as a desire to use classicism as a source of renewal.

The Mozart Anniversary, 1906

In the years leading up to the 150th anniversary of Mozart's birth in 1906, there was talk of a Mozart renaissance as a European phenomenon. It was manifested in an increasing number of performances of his music and solidified his status not only as one of the great classical composers, but also as a possible model for future developments. Discussions began across Europe about how Mozart could be seen as a role model and whether the qualities he represented could lead to a renewal of Western art music.[5]

When Nielsen wrote his essay 'Mozart og vor Tid' (Mozart and Our Time) in 1906, he was contributing to a development that was taking place throughout European musical life. Taking as his starting point what young composers could learn from Mozart, he set the stage for a forward-looking reassessment of Mozart's position. Nielsen's reflections on classicism as a source of inspiration were particularly intense in the years leading up to 1906 and were brought to the fore by the Mozart anniversary, which gave him the opportunity to formulate his ideas in a more fully developed way. Nielsen must therefore be seen as one of those European composers who helped to form a new image of Mozart, and his ideas are characterised by the broader context in which they were set. It is therefore useful to see his contribution as part of a larger picture.

Looking at the European reception of Mozart in these years, there is a tendency to call for a 'return to Mozart', even if no specific source for such a claim can be identified. This trend combines two different approaches. On the one hand, there is a movement throughout the nineteenth century to change the perception of Mozart from primarily a Rococo composer to a Classical composer. In other words, the image of Mozart changed from being associated with something light, entertaining and amusing to something substantial, sublime, exemplary and universal. On the other hand, this reverence for Mozart is accentuated at the turn of the century because it takes place in a context in which Mozart is used as a counter-image to Wagner. This perception is influenced by Nietzsche's turning from Wagner worshipper to Wagner critic and thus has a Nietzschean connotation. But while Nietzsche elevates Bizet and the opera *Carmen* to a new model, this role in the wider musical public is left to Mozart. This leads to an intense worship of Mozart, which can be summed up in the concept of 'serenitas': the qualities of a sublime, superhuman, supremely smiling ('cheerful') and almost divine being are ascribed to him. As a result of this setup, the exalted and partly fictitious figure of 'Mozart' can, in the years leading up to the 150th anniversary, serve as a synonym for various forms of distancing from Wagner and for various attempts to turn to a 'classical' model as a starting point for future developments.[6] In this way, it is not Mozart's music per se, but what he symbolically stands for that becomes the decisive factor in the new wave of Mozart worship.

It was a development that took place in stages over several generations. The use of the terms 'classical' or 'classic' to refer to Mozart and Haydn, among others, in the sense of the highest rank or the exemplary, had been in use since the end of the eighteenth century, and the qualities associated with the idea of the classical were applied to their works for most of the nineteenth century. This was the case, for example, with Schumann, who, in an 1834 review associated Mozart's school with what he considered to be the most important characteristics of ancient works of art: cheerfulness, serenity and grace.[7] In the same year, Raphael Georg Kiesewetter's history of music was published, in which he retrospectively described 'the age of Haydn and Mozart' as the 'Viennese School' and 'the perfection of instrumental music' as the historical culmination.[8]

Franz Brendel's seminal history of music, published in 1852, emphasised the contrast between Gluck, Haydn and Mozart on the one hand, and the era ushered in by Beethoven on the other. It was based on a conception of history that identified three epochs in the history of music: the 'sublime' period culminating in Bach, the 'beautiful' or 'objective' phase represented by Gluck, Haydn and Mozart, and the 'subjective' period initiated by Beethoven. The references to 'beauty', to his 'classical' status and to his 'universality' as an artistic genius were central to the reception of Mozart in the nineteenth century.[9]

In Brendel we find the model that Nielsen also draws on, in which the Classical is associated with the objective and the Romantic with the subjective. At the same time, we see the beginning of a development in which the concepts of the Classical and the Romantic appear as antagonistic opposites, rather than as an understanding of the relationship between them as a gradual development in music history. It was not until the latter part of the nineteenth century that the concept of the Classical emerged as a real counter-concept to Romanticism. This was due to musicians and writers who argued that Romanticism was becoming dominant in music. They argued that this led to an over-emphasis on individualism and an increasingly unrestrained use of the musical devices. In contrast, the concept of the Classical takes on the character of a battle cry, expressed in the emphasis on classical beauty as a counterweight to the excesses of Romanticism. In culturally conservative circles, it was also seen as a bulwark against what was perceived as the erosion of universally accepted norms.[10]

Nielsen does not share the approach to the cult of the classical that manifests itself in a deep cultural pessimism and the idea that all modern development is an expression of decadence and decay. He does not belong to the reactionary wing – he is too deeply rooted in the modern currents of his time for that. On the contrary, he is one of those who see the cultivation of classical ideals as a source of renewal. He wanted something new, but on a different basis from the Romantics.

In this context, it is important to note that the view of classical ideals in Copenhagen's musical life was not only linked to the Central European musical aesthetic positions of the time. A renewal of the understanding of antiquity in terms of art and philosophy also helped to shape the perception of the classical. This was particularly evident in the reappraisal of ancient Greek art, a development that Nielsen was able to witness at first hand. Indeed, in the years leading up to the Mozart jubilee, Anne Marie worked on the replicas of the coloured reliefs in Athens, which Emil Hannover later praised for their 'barbarically beautiful, wild and daring colours' when they were exhibited in Copenhagen in the spring of 1906.[11] Together with Nielsen, Harald Høffding and Georg Brandes, Anne Marie was a founding member of the Greek Society in 1905, where Nielsen gave a lecture on Greek music in 1907.[12] The year before, the art historian Vilhelm Wanscher published his important book *Den æsthetiske Opfattelse af Kunst* (The Aesthetic Perception of Art), in which he emphasised the formal and aesthetic qualities of art, using the classical ideals of antiquity and the Renaissance as a model for what he later called 'The Great Style'.[13] Wanscher was one of the Danes whom Nielsen met in Rome in 1900. The worship of the classical in music at the turn of the century should thus also be seen in the context of the renewed interest in antiquity stimulated by the Hellenistic and Vitalist movements of the time.

ILL. 2. In the summer of 1904, Nielsen met the Dutch composer Julius Röntgen for the first time during a visit to Bodil Neergaard at the Fuglsang Manor. In addition to playing quartets with Röntgen's son Engelbert on the cello and Gerard von Brucken Fock on the viola, the discussions between Nielsen and Röntgen about the development of modern music became an important source of inspiration.

Mozart as a Paragon

Nielsen's most important contribution to the discussion on classicism was 'Mozart and Our Time'. The essay was written on the occasion of Mozart's 150th birthday at the request of Ove Rode with a view to publication in *Politiken*. The assignment kept Nielsen busy, and the text ended up being longer than agreed; it was published in the March issue of *Tilskueren* instead.[14] However, Nielsen was not without resources when he had to write it, for the view that the Classical and the Romantic should be seen as opposites, and that Mozart should be emphasised as the opposite of Wagner, was already to be found in the music debate in Copenhagen. Nielsen could rely on his friend Rudolph Bergh, who in 1900 had published a paper on the state of contemporary music in which he contrasted Wagner and Mozart in order to give the latter the status that Bergh believed he deserved.

In his *Nogle Betragtninger over Musik og musikalske Tilstande i vor Tid* (Some Reflections on Music and Musical Conditions in our Time), Bergh attempts to find 'the root of the evil' and states that 'the original guilt lies with Richard Wagner'.[15] The problem, according to Bergh, was not in recognising Wagner's greatness as a composer, but rather in proclaiming his style to be 'the music of the future' and using his judgements about the music of other composers, both newer and older, as a guide. Wagner's influence meant that it was now legitimate to call Mozart boring and to complain when his music was on the programme.[16] Bergh adds that as a young man, he was more enthusiastic about Wagner than Mozart, thus associating the ability to appreciate Mozart's music with the education and maturity that comes with age: 'The radiant clarity, the perfect purity that one finds in Mozart's music is indeed in many cases not obvious to the young. … One is more easily dazzled by a splendid external apparatus.'[17]

The last part of the sentence is close to Nielsen's comments on the direction of German music in the wake of Wagner.[18] In an important letter to Julius Röntgen in 1905, there is a passage in which Nielsen criticises the virtuoso instrumentation of German orchestral music represented by Richard Strauss as superficial and a delusion:

> I'm amazed at the technical facility the Germans have these days, and I can only believe that all this complexity will soon exhaust itself. I envisage a whole new kind of art of the purest archaic stamp. What do you say to a monophonic music?[19]

The crux of Nielsen's criticism is that this kind of music lacks essence and core, leaving the listener with a feeling of emptiness. At the time, he described this type of music as modern and not his own. In a slightly later letter to Anne Marie, he says:

> I often feel uncomfortable when I hear or see modern art. It may dazzle, impress, startle or astonish, and for a moment awaken one's admiration, but then you suddenly feel empty inside, and everything then seems so cold and poor, much worse than before.[20]

The idea also appears in the Mozart essay, where he writes: '[Mozart] did not tear down our houses around our ears and build palaces that impressed us, but in which we froze.'[21]

In contrast to the tendency to continue Wagner's path, Nielsen sees a 'movement towards the classics'.[22] He uses this expression in the letter to Rode explaining why the article was longer than agreed. It is precisely the argument about the topicality of the 'classics' in relation to the latest music that he uses as justification:

> The fact is that not only because of my personal great admiration for Mozart, but also with regard to the trend towards the classics in the most recent German music – see Max Reger Op. 89 – I feel compelled to dwell somewhat on an investigation into how far Mozart's art is of significance for today's musical life and how it may thereby acquire significance for that of the future. It's precisely from such a starting point that a longer article about Mozart is justified, and only in this way will the project interest me.[23]

The reference to Reger points to Julius Röntgen as another source of Nielsen's reflections. Röntgen and Nielsen met for the first time in the summer of 1904 at Bodil Neergaard's Manor, Fuglsang, and their stimulating conversations led Nielsen to study the latest German music. In this connection he obtained a sonata by Reger.[24] Nielsen's subsequent correspondence with Röntgen gave him the opportunity to compare Reger and Richard Strauss, and in this context Reger was to be preferred: 'His aims are still far more sympathetic to me.'[25] But it was precisely his effort that Nielsen recognised, for he was never a great fan of Reger's music. What is important is that his preoccupation with Reger gave him the opportunity to reflect on the 'movement towards the classics' which Reger represented and which was current, since Reger was at that time recognised as a 'fashionable composer', as Röntgen writes. Hence Nielsen arrived at his above-mentioned striking and original formulation, in which the Greek inspiration is also evident: 'I envisage a whole new kind of art of the purest archaic stamp.' And he concludes by emphasising: 'We must go back – not to the Old, but to the Pure and Clear.'[26]

In Nielsen's article on Mozart, it is not primarily Wagner but Beethoven who is used as a contrast to Mozart. It is important to understand how Nielsen treats them as models. They are not juxtaposed as representatives of different periods in music history, but rather as representatives of two fundamentally different approaches to art – which can be found in all periods of music, literature and art history from the ancient Greeks onwards. Mozart represents classical principles that can be applied to all times, and Beethoven represents romanticism as a similar, ahistorical phenomenon:

> The matter can thus be presented as a choice between two aesthetic ideals: a sublime, clarified 'classical' versus a more subjective and obscure 'romantic' art form, and correspondingly a pursuit of the melodic or linear element at the expense of the harmonic, vertical aspect.[27]

Nielsen, Mozart and the Future

Like Bergh, Nielsen went from being a Wagner enthusiast in his youth to being sceptical of the composer and his admirers.[28] Nielsen's view of Mozart also changed markedly. In his diary of his educational journey in October 1890, he noted that Mozart should be enjoyed 'historically';[29] however, in 1906 he wrote the article 'Mozart and Our Time', in which he emphasised that Mozart was still relevant to contemporary music. This shift in opinion is described in the article, with Nielsen noting that his main aim was to 'examine whether [Mozart's] works can still relevant for today's music students and thus for the music of the future.'[30]

The article is partly based on a lecture on Gluck, Haydn and Mozart that Nielsen gave twice. It is worth noting that on both occasions he addressed young people. On 22 November 1905 he gave the lecture as part of the series 'Tyskland i Frederik den Stores Tidsalder' (Germany in the Age of Frederick the Great), which formed a module of the teaching at Borups Højskole,[31] while on 18 December 1906 he gave the presentation at Frisindet Ungdom (The Liberal Youth), albeit with a new introduction.[32] The Liberal Youth was founded in December 1904 as a spiritual refuge for young 'freethinkers' in Copenhagen's radical circles who were not students and therefore could not be members of the Student Society. The lecture was probably organised by Nielsen's friend Emil Sachs, who was one of the driving forces behind the society.[33] Both the lecture and the article give an impression of how Nielsen perceived the ideals of classical music, and can therefore contribute to an understanding of how he related to these ideals in his own works from the years around the turn of the century.

In these texts, Nielsen uses contrasts to argue for the value and relevance of the older music.[34] However, the central point of the article, in terms of Mozart's relevance to the music of today and tomorrow, is the balance between the subjective or lyrical and the objective or epic in music:

> There are always examples in Mozart's works from which we can learn. And I have no doubt that when the wheel of time has turned a few more rounds, Mozart's best symphonies will stand, while most of Beethoven's will fall. This is because in Mozart's art there is a better balance between the lyrical, the subjective and the epic-artistic than in Beethoven's works. In spite of his marvellous ability to construct, Beethoven is really only a lyricist. In creative art, however, the all-too-individual is first to fall. Our time *feels* more when listening to Beethoven's works; but in a hundred years' time one will feel quite differently, and art, which is thus mainly based on feeling, will be superfluous if it does not contain in it some of the conditions and rules which apply to all times ...[35]

In other words, it is Mozart's universality that means that his music will continue to be valuable.[36] Nielsen writes of the literature on Mozart that it fails to explain his genius, although he refers to Otto Jahn's Mozart biography of 1856 as a work that 'is otherwise highly meritorious'.[37] For Jahn, however, it is precisely Mozart's universality and ability to depict the common that constitutes his genius:

> Everything that moves man, he feels musically, and every emotion he shapes as a work of art … The universality for which Mozart is rightly praised is not confined to outward appearance … His universality is reached only at the limitations of human nature …[38]

In his lecture on Gluck, Haydn and Mozart, Nielsen makes an observation that is very similar to Jahn's formulation, for in connection with Mozart's operas he writes: 'In his works, all human emotions and passions have found expression in notes.'[39] Thus, in both the article and the lecture, the universal – the common to all humanity – of Mozart's music is a quality that is strongly emphasised.

As mentioned above, Nielsen wrote a new introduction for his lecture at The Liberal Youth. For the series of lectures at Borups Højskole on German culture during the reign of Frederick the Great, he had begun with the words: 'The three figures I'm going to talk about today are among the greatest in the history of German culture in the eighteenth century.'[40] It was clearly intended as a historical presentation as part of an educational programme.

For The Liberal Youth, a place where issues of a spiritual and social nature were discussed, Nielsen chose a different angle for his lecture, introducing the musical culture of the eighteenth century in relation to the present: 'If we compare the musical life of the [eighteenth] century with the music of today, we must unfortunately admit that we are far behind in many respects.'[41] On the one hand, he warned against forgetting the old works, which could easily be drowned out by the vociferous publicity given to the newer orchestral music. On the other hand, he also recognised an emerging 'healthy and fresh reaction' against this development, which must refer to the movement towards the classics that he mentioned in his letter to Rode.[42] And he clearly hoped that his lecture would encourage this movement.

Choral Music as a Description of the Universally Human

As for Nielsen himself, his interest in choral composition at the turn of the century seems to have been linked to a general effort to represent the 'universally human' in music. It was precisely the universal that could be represented musically by drawing on models from polyphonic choral music. In his above-mentioned review of Nielsen's opera *Saul and David,* Bergh had pointed out that the prominent role of the chorus and the polyphonic treatment of the choral sections gave the work a grandiosity in the style of the old masters – not as imitation, but as innovation.[43]

A portrait of Nielsen, published in the music journal *Programmet* on the occasion of the premiere of *Saul and David*, included a passage regarding what Nielsen wanted the music to express – a passage that he presumably helped to formulate. It is remarkable how, in his choice of words about the great, contrasting emotions, he anticipates formulations that he would use much later about his Fourth Symphony:

> And what is it that he is primarily trying to describe in his music then? It is the great, simple, fundamental emotions: grief, joy, hatred, love, enthusiasm, despair. He has always been opposed to making the small, finely minced, highly specialised emotions the subject of musical treatment.[44]

There is some evidence to suggest that, for Nielsen, choral music was a powerful means of doing just that: expressing great, simple and fundamental emotions. This seems to have been one of the central ideas to which he returned time and again. His first choral work, *Hymnus Amoris* (1896), is a tribute to one of the fundamental emotions: love.

Hymnus Amoris

The idea for *Hymnus Amoris* (CNW 100) came to Carl Nielsen while he and Anne Marie were on their honeymoon in Italy in the spring of 1891, seeing Titian's fresco *Miracolo del marito geloso* (*Miracle of the Jealous Husband*, 1511) in Padua.[45] In the foreground of the painting, a woman is killed by her husband, who mistakenly believes that she has been unfaithful to him. Afterwards, the husband regrets his deed and seeks the help of St Anthony of Padua, who brings the woman back to life, as can be seen in the background. According to Carl and Anne Marie's daughter Irmelin, the painting had made a deep impression on both of them, and Anne Marie had the idea of creating a relief depicting love in all its forms. Unrequited love was to be symbolised by a woman hanging herself, although it would be difficult to show that the woman was driven to the act by this particular kind of love.[46] Anne Marie never completed the relief, but Nielsen later used the idea in *Hymnus Amoris*.

Hymnus Amoris is composed for vocal soloists, children's choir, mixed choir and orchestra and describes love at all ages: childhood, youth, adulthood and old age. The text was written by the folklorist Axel Olrik and translated into Latin by the philologist Johan Ludvig Heiberg. In the preface to the printed score of 1898, Nielsen justifies the Latin translation in terms that make it clear that the portrayal of love as something common or universal was central to him:

> I think I can justify my choice of Latin on the grounds that it is a monumental language, and that it elevates one above overly lyrical or personal sentiments, which would be out of place when the aim is to describe such a universal human force as love through a grand polyphonic choir.[47]

Nielsen's distinction between objective and subjective art, which he later developed in his article on Mozart, is clearly visible in this argument. He associates the objective and universally human with the polyphonic style and the Romantic and subjective with the homophonic style. The article makes the important point that Beethoven's music would not last as long as Mozart's because it is too lyrical and expresses only individual feelings. He wanted to avoid this in his choral work on love. Instead, he sought to portray the emotion as a 'universal human force', to which the large polyphonic choir and the Latin text would contribute. Another text, possibly intended for a German performance of the work, suggests what other musical devices Nielsen used to emphasise the universal aspect:

> Just as love is a common feeling for all people of all ages, a single musical motif underlies the whole structure of this work, and just as in life the different ages flow imperceptibly into each other, so in this hymn there are no particular sections or pauses. Everything continues in one long, coherent movement.[48]

The opening motif of the children's chorus with the text 'Amor mihi vitam donat, adolesco in fasciis eius' (Love gives me life and I grow in its arms) is repeated throughout the rest of the work, expressing the common feeling of love, which can vary from person to person and through the stages of life, although it is essentially the same for all humans.[49] In order to create a sense of coherence, Nielsen had also chosen not to pause between movements. The work was thus to be seen as a continuous development of the feeling of love throughout life, rather than as four separate emotions.

The first part of the work, 'Childhood', consists of three stanzas, the first and last of which are sung by the children, while the middle stanza is sung by a 'Mothers' Choir'.[50] The children's first stanza consists of a simple homophonic movement, which is answered by the women's choir, gradually introducing the polyphonic style that pervades the rest of the work.[51] Of the transition to the third stanza, Nielsen writes: 'The children now repeat their chorus again, but this time more developed, as if taught and enriched by their mothers.'[52] It is clear that it is the polyphony of the Mothers' stanza, the main section of which is a fugue for four female voices based on the love motif, which for Nielsen creates this sense of something more learned and enriched.[53] The next sections, 'Youth' and 'Adulthood', are also fugal choral movements with variations on the main subject.[54] There is a strong contrast some way into 'Adulthood', when the powerful male choral fugue is suddenly interrupted by the introduction of a solo soprano singing – or almost screaming – 'Love is my pain. Nothing has wounded me like love.' Of this section Nielsen writes:

> The men sing of achievement and strength, and in order to best express the joy of the work and the feeling of power, the composer has chosen the manly fugal style. It now continues in a strict four-part, fugal movement, but is suddenly interrupted by a woman who utters a cry of pain … This section casts a shadow, as it were, over the rejoicing at the price of love that had hitherto been the basic tone …[55]

Nielsen retained the early idea of symbolising unrequited love through a woman in pain, probably inspired by the woman in Titian's painting. The soprano is gradually disturbed in her song of suffering by a bright female choir, which leads to a repetition of the male choir's stanza. This is followed by the stanza on old age, with a fugue for three male voices (tenor, baritone and bass). Finally, the work culminates in a final chorus in which 'both the heavenly and the earthly are gathered together in a great common hymn of rejoicing in honour of the power that embraces all that lives and breathes, a hymn of rejoicing in praise of Love!'[56]

Hymnus Amoris was premiered on 27 April 1897 at a concert given by Musikforeningen in the concert hall of Koncertpalæet. The programme also included a symphony and some songs by the recently deceased composer Brahms. Angul Hammerich spent the first part of his review reflecting on the audience's reaction to the music and their alienation from Brahms. Better off, however, was Nielsen, who was called upon twice after conducting his new *Hymnus Amoris*.[57] The work was generally well received in the newspapers. Nanna Liebmann remarked that Nielsen had written 'beautiful, natural and poetic music, which must have immediately appealed to the listeners in last night's performance'.[58] This was quite a change from the way his new music had been described in recent years as contrived and difficult for the audience to understand. Charles Kjerulf also praised the music, but he had little sympathy for the choir singing in Latin. He found it affected, and ridiculed Nielsen:

> Dear me – why must the little, Danish-born Carl Nielsen, who only a few years ago was still a military musician in the town square of Odense, playing on the bugle or striking the triangle at the changing of the guard – why must he absolutely first set his feelings down in Latin in order to set a love hymn to music?[59]

Hammerich's review, however, was of a different, serious tone. He took Nielsen's efforts seriously, and during the concert had particularly noted Nielsen's polyphonic treatment of the choral parts, which he thought could suggest a completely new direction for music:

> It is interesting to note this latest phase in the path of musical development. The great 'homophonic' period in the history of music seems to be coming to an end. Now the movement returns to the starting point of art music, towards the 'polyphonic' period, modified in many ways, of course, as the means of art itself have changed. A motet by Josquin, for example, and Carl Nielsen's latest work are obviously very different, but not so much as to hide a kinship beneath the surface.[60]

In the second half of the nineteenth century, Niels W. Gade and Johan Peter Emilius Hartmann were the central representatives of a Danish choral tradition with a clear stylistic link to the German Romanticism of the Mendelssohn tradition.[61] The polyphonic style of *Hymnus Amoris* must have been very different from the choral music that audiences were accustomed to hearing in Musikforeningen.[62] Yet Hammerich does not see this move towards the older music heard in Nielsen's works as an artistic regression. On the contrary, he sees it as the beginning of a new phase in music, which also suggests a close relationship with the modern tendencies in the visual arts:

> It is also interesting to see the connection between the various modern art forms in this area. Now music, the art of composing, is about to move into the place where painting has been for the longest time. Carl Nielsen's music and the young Skovgaard's paintings are going the same way.[63]

That year, Den Frie Udstilling opened on 27 April – the same day as Musikforeningen's concert took place. It is tempting to imagine that Hammerich also visited the art exhibition before writing his concert review, which appeared two days later in the newspaper *Nationaltidende*. Den Frie Udstilling included a number of studies from Greece by Joakim and Niels Skovgaard, which combined the architectural style of antiquity with a modern sense of colour.[64] It is perhaps these paintings that Hammerich had in mind when he wrote that Nielsen's music went in the same direction as the young Skovgaard's paintings. This version of the 'classical', inspired by the styles of antiquity and the Renaissance, seems to have had a more refreshing effect on the public than Brahms. It also had a clearer connection with modern artistic trends.

Hymnus Amoris is a good example of how Nielsen worked with the idea of choral music as an expression of the universally human, and how he found inspiration in classical models without falling into imitation of the music of earlier times. *Hymnus Amoris* is almost a pedagogical presentation, in which the children begin in a simple way before learning from their mothers to sing polyphony with individual parts. The work is also an example of how Nielsen combines these ideas with the notion that music should describe the profoundly simple and fundamental emotions that at the same time reflect the great contrasts and basic layers of human life.

In choral music, the idea of the universally human is particularly associated with polyphony, in which the voices follow their own independent course, and in which all the individual voices are combined into a supra-individual, universally valid expression. No single voice leads the way; all the voices as a whole describe the overall mood. Nielsen also employs this approach in the last two acts of *Saul and David*, where large polyphonic choral movements, reminiscent of Renaissance music, form the climax of the people's celebration of the restoration of the covenant with God and the election of David as the new king. And in *Søvnen* (*Sleep*), composed shortly afterwards, the outer movements describe sleep as a general phenomenon. They are also written in the form of polyphonic choral music, while the individual nightmare allows all the choral parts to intensify a communal musical expression, so that it appears as an enhanced version of the individual. It seems obvious that the same approach lies behind his decision to compose *Hymnus Amoris* for polyphonic choir.

De-Romanticisation

Nielsen's scepticism about the trends that were considered modern in contemporary European parlance at the beginning of the century does not mean that he was unconcerned with them. His acquaintance with Röntgen gave him the impetus to study the latest music, and he emphasised this in a letter to Röntgen of 1904: 'Don't you think we also have to do our duty by our contemporaries? In this respect I want to be a worthy pupil of yours.'[65] Their correspondence mentions works such as Hans Pfitzner's opera *Die Rose vom Liebesgarten* (1901), Strauss's *Sinfonia domestica* (1903) and some of Hugo Wolf's compositions, as well as works by Reger.[66] In a letter to Carl Johan Michaelsen in 1906, Nielsen also explained: 'I know several of Mahler's works, and last year I founded a little (private) society consisting mostly of my pupils, where we obtained most of the new music that is being published. There we also played Mahler's symphonies.'[67] Thus they studied scores and played piano excerpts for two or four hands. It shows that Nielsen also insisted that his pupils be familiar with the latest music.[68]

In a context where most of these composers were described as 'modern', while a composer such as Reger was referred to as representing a new 'movement towards the classics',[69] it is not surprising that Nielsen at this time did not present himself as a modern composer, but rather as part of the counter-movement. Yet his interest in Reger also shows that he was familiar with what was being composed and discussed in European musical life.

The correspondence between Nielsen and Röntgen may have served to compensate for the previously mentioned discussions with Thomas Laub, as Nielsen tried to find his own way forward. It is almost possible to read it as a hidden dialogue between Röntgen and Laub, when Nielsen writes to Laub, after Laub's criticism of the style in *Saul and David*, that the new must grow out of the strong fertiliser of contemporary music. On the other hand, Nielsen suggests that Röntgen should consider whether it would be possible to achieve a monophonic music: 'We must go back – not to the Old, but to the Pure and Clear.'[70] This central formulation was not written for Laub, who would read it as an expression of agreement, but was addressed to Röntgen in a search of other answers as to how such an idea could be realised. Nielsen's formulation must be interpreted as a statement of intent to move forward. He wants to arrive at something new on the basis of having reached – not returned to – the pure and the clear on which to build further. He wants to get to the substance, and that substance lies in the pure and powerful lines of the music.

It is in this context that Nielsen was delighted to come across the term 'de-Romanticisation' in an article by the Swedish composer Ture Rangström in 1909. Rangström's article, published in three parts in the newspaper *Svenska Dagbladet*, had introduced the concept when discussing the subject of modern song composition: 'The name Carl Nielsen does indeed raise a current musical question of deep and far-reaching significance: the question of, shall we say, the de-Romanticisation of music.'[71] For Rangström, this question, with its deep and far-reaching consequences, arises from his encounter with Nielsen's music, which makes it easier for Nielsen to accept the concept than if he had said it himself. In a letter to Rangström, he enthusiastically acknowledged the expression:

> When I read them [i.e. the articles] for my wife she exclaimed, 'that's perfectly correct', several times over, and the term 'de-Romanticising' struck us both as a fitting, indeed completely convincing expression for everything – not just in music, but also in the other arts – that is '*af nöden*' [of need] at this moment.[72]

In Rangström's argument, de-Romanticisation is an expression of a movement away from the trend that builds on Wagner, and he sees Nielsen as the strongest advocate of such an oppositional endeavour. Rangström's statement is therefore an opportunity for Nielsen to look at himself from the outside and to gain a greater clarity about what he represents.

De-Romanticisation is a more concrete concept to relate to than when Nielsen talks about renewal based on antiquity or classical ideals. It denotes a way of relating to the immediately preceding music and is therefore not the same as seeking specific models in the past or working with abstract notions of classical ideals. Although it is a negatively defined term, it can be understood as a strategy for working away from Romantic stylistic traits. Working towards the pure and clear can be done by omitting certain things that can be seen as superimposed on the musical core.

Nielsen is therefore someone who takes his statements to Laub seriously: he does not want to sever the connection with the immediate past, that is, the present, but to work his way out of it. It is not a radical and sudden break with the past, but a movement away from it. Within the framework of the ideals of classicism as a general standard, according to which concepts such as clarity and balance in form and melody can be maintained, de-Romanticisation can be seen as a compositional strategy in the specific work of putting these ideals into practice. There is also a great difference between such de-Romanticisation as a process and the far more 'doctrinaire' rejection of Romanticism expressed in some of the anti-Romantic movements of the 1920s.

The concept of de-Romanticisation fits in well with the principle of linear musical thinking.[73] The explanation for this lies in the juxtaposition of two ways of understanding music: if Romanticism is associated with harmony, beautiful surface, over-decorated and lavish orchestration, and vertical musical thinking, then de-Romanticisation is a focus on melody, the essence of music, simplicity, audible structure and horizontal musical thinking. The result of the latter is music that emphasises melodic polyphony, transparency and form as a process.

For Nielsen, the return to the essential is a counterbalance to what he perceives as the worship of appearances, of elegant superficiality. Instead, he turns his attention to the intrinsic values of music, to its core and substance, and thus a focus on the structural elements of the musical texture. Nielsen concentrates on the inner workings of the music rather than on the outer clothing.[74] If he is sometimes criticised for not working on his orchestration on a par with his French and German colleagues, it is because that is not his focus. He wants the audience to be able to hear what is going on internally in the music.

In this light, it is not surprising that Ferruccio Busoni also became a partner in the dialogue that led to a new understanding of how contemporary music could be renewed.

A Kindred Spirit

Nielsen and Busoni had originally met during Nielsen's first major trip abroad, in Leipzig in February 1891. Nielsen attended a concert by the Brodsky Quartet, who played Busoni's Violin Sonata No. 1 in E minor of 1890 with the composer at the piano. Nielsen's attention was drawn to Adolph Brodsky, to whom he wanted to present his new String Quartet in F minor.[75] However, Nielsen's account of the meeting also shows that he immediately appreciated Busoni, who was a year younger than Nielsen and had already embarked on an impressive career. As a child he had been a celebrated piano virtuoso, and by the age of fifteen he had also trained as a composer. By the age of twenty-two he had become professor of piano in Helsinki, and in 1890 he was appointed professor at the Moscow Academy of Music. At the same time, Nielsen had a year's service as second violinist in The Royal Orchestra and had just been granted leave for his first European tour. Despite the slight age difference in Nielsen's favour, Busoni was the more experienced colleague.[76]

With his German-Italian background from the then Austro-Hungarian Trieste, Busoni was a citizen of the world. From 1894 he was based in Berlin, except for the years during the First World War when he was in Switzerland, refusing to play in any of the belligerent countries. Despite all the acclaim, he was too Italian to be recognised as a German and too German to be an Italian national composer. Nor did he want to be. Whereas for Nielsen becoming a national composer was a role he grew into and could not escape, Busoni remained above the national and would hardly have been allowed to become a national composer if he had wanted to. However, this was not an issue that played a major role in their relationship.

More importantly, they shared many of the same views and could see themselves reflected in each other. In a letter to Busoni in 1904, Nielsen wrote that it was indeed the fruitful and inspiring nature of their conversations that he missed when they did not see each other.[77] It was also important for the relationship that Nielsen was one of those who, at least from their second meeting in 1894, fully recognised Busoni as a composer and not just as a pianist. Busoni seems to have particularly valued colleagues who did this.[78]

It seems that Busoni was looking for interlocutors who would honestly try to understand what he himself considered important. Busoni found himself in a position where it was difficult to be fully accepted. In addition to the ambiguity of his national allegiance and the widespread suspicion of his lack of substance as a composer, with which virtuosos were generally met, he also encountered a lack of understanding of his aesthetic positions. In his writings Busoni often expressed himself with a radicalism that his own works do not seem to live up to. What is often overlooked is that even when Busoni was interested in the most advanced compositional tech-

ILL. 3. Ferrucio Busoni became one of Nielsen's closest conversational partners when it came to reflecting on the renewal of music. The picture shows Busoni around the time Nielsen first met him, although it was taken in the USA during one of Busoni's many concert tours.

niques, he was fundamentally arguing for a radical renewal rooted in tradition. At the time, his writings were therefore often read with the assumption that radicalism must necessarily lead to atonality or to avant-garde provocation, but this is not the case with Busoni.[79]

A work that has had an overwhelming impact on posterity is Busoni's *Entwurf einer neuen Aesthetik der Tonkunst* (*Sketch of a New Esthetic of Music*), published in 1907. It is in this book that later readers have encountered many of the phrases that are supposed to show Busoni as a proponent of the modernist or avant-garde future. However, two factors must be taken into account. The first is that the book had a very limited circulation, since it did not become popular until 1916, when the revised edition was published in large numbers by the prestigious publishers Inselverlag. At that time, the situation in music history was very different from that of 1907. The text was now read in the light of subsequent events, when atonality and other experiments with quarter-tones, for instance, had already been developed. In 1916, his essay was read as a specific prophecy that was already being fulfilled, rather than as the opening of a new way of thinking that could unfold in many ways.

Busoni's essay also became embroiled in a perfidious discussion of modern art by a number of highly conservative individuals, in which he was targeted by those who believed that modern music had become incapable of creating on the basis of genuine inspiration. The discussion was strongly encouraged by Hans Pfitzner, who published a pamphlet in 1917 entitled *Futuristengefahr* (*The Danger of the Futurists*).[80] It was further fuelled in Pfitzner's supplement, in which he spoke of the aesthetics of modern music as musical impotence and as a symptom of decay.[81] At the heart of the debate was the relationship between divine inspiration and craftsmanship in the creation of new music, but the controversy made Busoni appear as a radical subverter of all that existed.

One specific example that has led to Busoni's being construed as a harbinger of the future comes from a passage in which he considers the potential of working with each whole tone by dividing it into three parts instead of the usual two semitones. By combining two series of thirds of a tone, it is possible to obtain one series of sixths of a tone. In the same passage, Busoni considers how this could be done, referring to the fact that he had just read in an American magazine from 1906 about the invention of an electronic instrument called the dynamophone, which could produce any pitch and could be seen as the precursor of the synthesiser.[82] Interestingly, Nielsen was occupied with similar thoughts when he wrote the above-mentioned short autobiography in 1905, reflecting on quarter-tones as a way of creating a more finely nuanced tonal system, which he claims he would have liked to use somewhere in his First Symphony.[83]

It is not only their shared openness to new ideas that links Busoni and Nielsen. Reading Busoni's main message in *Sketch of a New Esthetic*, one finds formulations about the freedom of music that have a great affinity with Nielsen's way of expressing himself. Busoni speaks of music as the child among the arts:

> The child – it floats! Its feet do not touch the ground. It is not subject to gravity. It is almost incorporeal. Its matter is transparent. It is sounding air. It is free.[84]

Nielsen concludes his essay 'Words, Music and Programme Music' (1909) in a similar vein:

> If music were to take shape and explain its nature, it might say something like this: I am everywhere and nowhere; I leap over the wave and the top of the forest; I sit on the throat of the savage and on the foot of the black person and sleep in the stone and in the sounding ore. No one can seize me, all can grasp me; I live ten times stronger than all living things and die a thousand times more profoundly. I love the great expanse of silence, and it is my greatest desire to break it. I know neither sorrow nor joy, neither happiness nor tears, but I can rejoice, weep, laugh and lament at the same time and endlessly.[85]

Busoni's concept of free music is not formless, but neither is it tied to existing, inherited forms. Busoni sees the well-known opposition between absolute music and programme music as two forms of constraints imposed on music from the outside; rather, music must find its form by following its own laws of development at a higher level, beyond the framework of traditional forms. He sees each musical motif as a seed that contains the germ of a whole plant that will unfold according to the rules laid down in it, like a genetic code. The places where one can observe music behaving in this way are in preludes and transitions; here the music has no predetermined form.[86] When Busoni summarises what such a strictly free and organically structured music might look like, he quotes Tolstoy's story 'Lucerne':

> Neither on the sea, nor in the mountains, nor in the sky a single straight line ... everywhere movement, irregularity, arbitrariness, diversity, an incessant merging of shadows and lines, and in all of this the calm, gentleness, harmony and necessity.[87]

Busoni's formulation of the marvellous coincidence of the individual parts in a whole, indeed of each part moving according to its own laws, is strikingly reminiscent of Nielsen's description of the sheep driven through a fence or of the course of a stream. In the essay 'Musikalske Problemer' (Musical Problems) of 1922, Nielsen writes of an organic rhythm that behaves as

> a turbulent sea, a rolling cornfield, or a forest during a storm. When I was a child, I often saw a flock of sheep with thick fleeces being driven through a gate or a narrow portal. It is a rhythmic celebration … It is the irregular and the regular that have come together to form a beautiful and living whole … The rhythm must be organic, it must develop as consistently and naturally as the flow of the stream, the snowdrift through the air, or the little feather that sails up the chimney in small rhythmic steps.[88]

Nielsen speaks of rhythm here, although this is not fundamentally different from his understanding of the organic development of motifs, melodic lines or formal elements. In the same way, he works from an understanding of form in which that of music is the result of the unfolding and development of the individual sections according to the 'inner' or 'inherent' rules of the musical material. The many analogies to natural phenomena that he used to explain musical relationships indicate that he perceived music as a kind of nature that unfolds according to its own set of rules, and that he therefore perceived musical regularities as a kind of natural law that was built into the musical material. A motif, a theme or even an interval contained the seeds of a development, and the composer's task was to follow these laws and unfold the potential already present in the material.[89]

There are many similarities between Nielsen's and Busoni's musical reasoning, suggesting that they shared a way of thinking about music at the beginning of the twentieth century. Although they were not in contact for long periods of time, they seem to have been kindred spirits who understood each other immediately and were able to engage in a fruitful dialogue. Their formulations reflect a way of thinking that is not concerned with questions of tonality or atonality, nor with the idea that the development of music necessarily represents a historical progress. Instead, they focus on how to reconcile the free expression of musical invention, of individual creativity, with music's own laws of logical and consistent development. In their view, musical form emerges as the result of a musical process that follows the logic of the development of the material itself.

Continuing this line of thought, Nielsen wrote to Rangström in 1920:

> For the task now and in the future is surely to work towards a unification of the greatest possible *freedom* in the unfolding of personal content and the greatest possible *strictness* with regard to organic interconnection. The first (the content) must be made to grow and blossom by ourselves and the gods in conjunction; the second (the organism) we can learn from the old masters …[90]

There is no doubt that Nielsen and Busoni regarded Mozart as one of the old masters to be emulated. After professing his devotion to Mozart, Busoni continues: 'I am a *worshipper of form*! But I demand – no, the organic nature of art demands – that every idea take its own form.'[91]

Similarly, Nielsen turns to form as a result of rigour and freedom to articulate the essence of what young composers can learn from Mozart. In the process, his Mozart essay elaborates on what has been quoted above:

> The fact is that Mozart is at once extraordinarily strict, logical and consistent in his voice-leading and modulations, and at the same time more free and unbound in his form than any other of the classical masters … He loosens all restraints and says everything that comes to his mind in the most convincing and natural way. … Never before or since has there been such a perfect and fine elaboration, such a flexible and yet convincingly strict form, such a ravishing sweetness and harmony in the melody and intellect, indeed such wisdom in counterpoint.[92]

What may be learned from the old masters are the laws of musical coherence, and coherence is defined as organism, or perhaps more precisely, organicity. When music behaves like a piece of living nature, it is at the same time most freely and completely bound by nature's musical laws. The old masters represent such a perfect correspondence between a musical substance and the logic that governs the musical process. In this sense, their perfection, their classicity, is exemplary.

Chapter 22

TIME

Time is music's primary medium. Music happens in time. Simultaneously, music is being expressed through time. Consequently, we have the opportunity to experience a passage of time that takes shape through music. When we listen to Nielsen's music, we can follow how he plays with time – and thus with the listener, with our experience of time.

Nielsen was very preoccupied with temporal relationships, and in his essay 'Musikalske Problemer' (Musical Problems) he defined rhythm as 'the division of time' – before it is anything else.[1] He is at pains to explain that it is a much more complex phenomenon than a mechanical division of time into equal parts. He distinguishes between the superficial rhythm provided by a clock or metronome, which he finds uninteresting, and the living, organic rhythm found in nature, which he defines as the rhythmic life in the passage of time.

To explain what he means, Nielsen compares the phenomenon of rhythm to the sight of an undulating cornfield, a turbulent sea or a flock of sheep being driven through a gate. An artist, he says, should be inspired by the rhythmic phenomena of nature, 'the rhythmic sources of life … draw from them and organise the thousands of movements into a whole'.[2] In other words, he sees rhythm as a temporal phenomenon, consisting of a series of simultaneous movements organised into a larger whole, taking place simultaneously on many levels.

One of the basic ways of making time perceptible is to divide it. Pulse, time and metre are all expressions of the division of time. The first thing Nielsen does when he wants to create a musical passage of time is to establish a basic division it. Similarly, one of the conditions for the listener to experience a musical passage is to find or recognise a sense of time. This is one of the most important approaches to listening to a piece of music.

For most of the music we listen to, this is not a problem. The division of time is clear and unambiguous, and the listener is immediately engaged. But when the composer begins to play with the sense of time, and thus with the listener's perception of it, it gets interesting. This requires the listener to sharpen their attention and adds a subtle element to the experience. This is often what elevates a song or piece of music above the ordinary.

In the tradition of classical music, it is the standard practice for a piece of music to begin with an indication of metre, time and key, so that the listener can immediately

MUSIC EX. 1. Beethoven, Symphony No. 3, *Eroica* (1803), first movement, bars 1–8. Bars 1 and 2 mark the metre and key with two clear chordal beats in E flat major, and the regular metre is confirmed when the cellos stress the first beat in bar 3 and continue this regular basic feel in the following bars. From bar 3 we notice that we are in triple time, as the melody is clear at this point. The key is also confirmed, as the motif in the cellos is based on an E♭ major triad. We are therefore on safe ground for the first six bars, and the starting point for listening has been both introduced and confirmed. Against this background, the first dramatic note, the C♯ of the melody in bar 7, makes a great impact, so that we immediately realise that something is happening that will certainly have consequences. The listener is in suspense as to what will happen next.

recognise the point of departure. Beethoven's *Eroica Symphony* is a prime example of this emphasis.

A hundred years later we come to Nielsen. He belongs to a generation of European composers whose music reflects the fact that the modern world is no longer so clear-cut. And one of the ways of being modern is to keep the listener in metrical uncertainty – an uncertainty that sharpens the senses and challenges the intellect.

Nielsen's Third Symphony, *Sinfonia espansiva*, is in many ways his most Beethovenian. It opens with the same gesture that Beethoven uses in his Third Symphony, with powerful chordal strokes on what we interpret as being a major key. But Nielsen plays with our sense of time. It is not until bar 15, when the wind instruments enter with the first subject, that we get a clear sense of metre and time, and only then does a motif appear that explicitly establishes the key and the triple time. At first we think we have understood the basic rhythm, then we are left in

MUSIC EX. 2. Nielsen, Symphony No. 3, *Sinfonia espansiva* (1911), first movement, bars 1–23. At the beginning of *Sinfonia espansiva*, a metrical sense is established with the strong chordal beats, all of which play the note A. The first two appear at a well-defined distance, although it is not revealed to the listener what that distance entails. The third and fourth chordal beats confirm that this is the basic metre by splitting it in two. The fifth and sixth chords leave us somewhat confused, because we are lacking the repetition of the first accented beat; however, in return we get the information that we are in triple time. This impression is immediately disrupted, for the rhythm is then contracted into something that sounds as if in duple time: two notes, two rests, two notes, two rests – clearly at odds with the triple time we thought we had just heard. Then the rhythm continues until suddenly, with a jolt, it is confirmed that we are indeed in triple time when the first subject enters in bar 15. It turns out that the whole passage is designed to keep the listener in a state of alert suspense, deliberately postponing the moment when metre and key are established in the listener's consciousness.

doubt, and finally we are given a clear answer. Nielsen plays with time and with our perception of it.

A variation of this is the transition from uncertainty to certainty. In Nielsen's Symphony No. 6, *Sinfonia semplice*, there are first four delicate chimes that introduce a metrical sense – and that is all the listener knows. There is a rhythm, but we do not know the underlying time. Studying the score, it becomes apparent that the music begins in the middle of a bar, although this is not audible. You could hear it as if it were four genuine chimes of a clock, an element of real sound that does not need to be coordinated with anything other than itself. It can be perceived as a quotation from the real world of sound. The violins enter at an indeterminate point in the bar, while the clarinets and bassoons are also metrically atypical in their efforts. It is not until bar 8 that a decisive statement is made: in a clear metre and key, with an emphasis on the first beat and a melody whose rhythm can only be interpreted in one way.

MUSIC EX. 3. Nielsen, Symphony No. 6, *Sinfonia semplice* (1925), first movement, bars 1–8. The four chimes on the note D do not in themselves reveal where we are in the bar. The violin subject begins after a rest on the first quaver of the bar, and just by listening, without being able to establish the first beats of the bars, it is difficult to guess where we are metrically. If attention is paid to the melodic aspect, it is natural to interpret that the emphasis, and thus the beginning of the bar, is on the fifth note of the violins (G). The melody ends on the root of the chord, and the implied harmonic shift would typically be at the beginning of a new bar. The entries of the clarinet and bassoon seem to confirm the accentuation of this beat of the bar, since they enter at a regular distance after the G and naturally accentuate their first note. However, these notes are on the weak beats of the bar, contrary to the notes of the chimes. Finally, it emerges that the composer deliberately avoids all the accentuated beats until the first note of bar 8, and that the four chimes begin in the middle of a bar and their D was not the root after all but rather the fifth.

At the beginning of Nielsen's Fifth Symphony, there is a further intensification of the metrical uncertainty. It begins with a very faint, oscillating figure in the violas. They play so faintly that the listener is unsure of when the figure actually began, and consequently there is some doubt as to which of the two notes was played first. It is also impossible to determine aurally where in the bar the motif begins and how many notes are in each bar. Furthermore, the tempo is adjusted in such a way that it is aurally uncertain whether it is a melodic motion or a sound consisting of a minor third. The tempo is precisely balanced between the two points of melodic motion and sound. It is only when the bassoons enter that a sense of metre and time is established. Once again, the audience is kept in suspense, for it seems that the second note of the bassoons marks the beginning of a bar. It is only further on in the melody that it is possible to determine the strong beats of the bars, and hence we are now on safe ground.

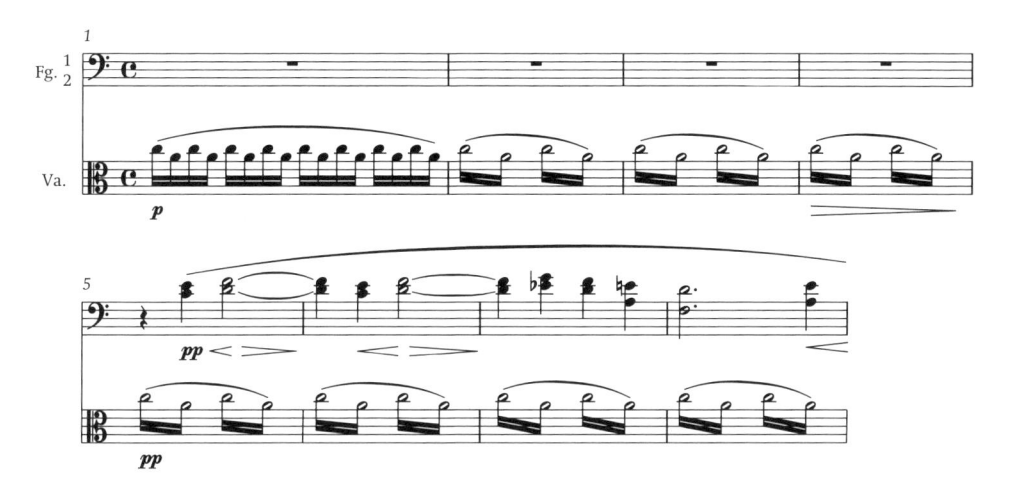

MUSIC EX. 4. Nielsen, Symphony No. 5 (1922), first movement, bars 1–8. The symphony begins with a small oscillating motif in the violas. They play a descending minor third, C–A. The interval has no apparent tonal significance, as it does not define an obvious key in the same way as a major third or an ascending fourth, and indeed not when the top note is the one emphasised. Nielsen provides the movement with the metronome marking of one hundred beats per minute. The experience of the oscillating motif is thus on the borderline between being heard as a melodic movement, C–A–C–A–C–A–C–A, and being fused into the harmony C–A. Rhythmically, too, it remains in a state of flux, since the motif is heard as a continuum of sound rather than as a metrical division. It is only in bars 5 and 6 that a melody in the bassoons gives the impression of time, although the accent on the consonance in the middle of the bar initially suggests that the bars begin here. Only in bar 8 does it become clear that the melody does not enter on an upbeat to a new bar, but rather as an upbeat to the middle of a bar.

The same way of establishing ambiguity at the beginning is found in some of Nielsen's accompanied songs, where the piano often opens with a short introduction before the soloist enters. These introductions are instances where Nielsen frequently plays with the listener's perception. Although the purpose of the introduction was to establish a basis for listening to a song, Nielsen often chose to create an ambivalent one. In 'Har Dagen sanket al sin Sorg' (If day has gathered all its woe) from the first collection of settings of Jens Peter Jacobsen's poems, Nielsen consciously plays with the arrangement of the piano accompaniment in such a way that it presents the middle of the bars as if they were the opening, when in fact it is the vocal line that marks the beginning. Indeed, the melody clearly establishes both the metre and the time. Rather than simply letting the melody dominate the accompaniment and give the listener a clear metrical sense, Nielsen maintains the ambiguity of the balance between a strong and a weaker metrical sense. This is a way of shaping the hidden uncertainty that is part of the expression of modern music.

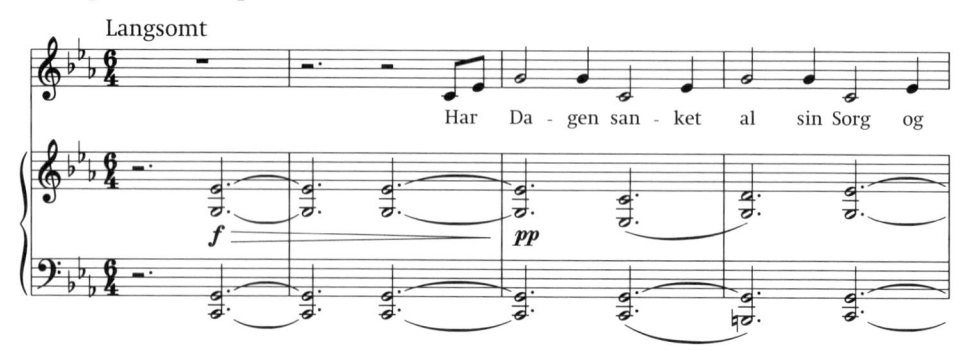

MUSIC EX. 5. Nielsen, 'Har Dagen sanket al sin Sorg' (text: J. P. Jacobsen), Op. 4, No. 1 (1892), bars 1–4. Nielsen gives the listener the illusion of beginning on the strong beat of a bar with an energetic piano chord, which is repeated more subduedly in the middle of the following bar. A metre is established, but not a time, and although we get a sense of the length of the metre, it is displaced in relation to how it functions in the melody. It is only when the melody enters that we have a clear understanding of where the bars begin and that they are in duple time with six beats per bar. However, the composer leaves a little doubt by placing the tonic chord in the middle of bars 3 and 4, while the irregular chord is on the first beat of bar 4, where the opposite would normally be expected. This creates an uncertainty between the harmonic sense of where the bars begin and the metre of the melody. As well as maintaining an element of ambivalence, it also makes the rhythmic sense more subtle, as it lightens the accented part of the bar and avoids over-emphasising the tonic chord. If the tonic C, the C minor chord and the first accented beat of the bar were to coincide, the experience would have a very strong unambiguous effect, which is neutralised since the melodic, harmonic and rhythmic accents create a balance between the different levels of accentuation.

An even more pronounced version of this ambivalence appears in Nielsen's song 'Tidt er jeg glad' (Oft am I glad), one of the songs from the second volume of *En Snes danske Viser* (*A Score of Danish Songs*). In this song, the composer goes one step further, for he not only introduces an ambivalence at the beginning, but deliberately maintains the tension between two ways of hearing the metre. This creates an intensity of listening as the audience tries to grasp which of the two possibilities is appropriate. The ambiguity is very much in keeping with the lyrics and message of the song, which is constantly about conflicting emotions: 'Oft am I glad, still may I weep from sadness' is a rhetorical figure that recurs throughout Ingemann's poem. The metre of the melody is also ambiguous. Both the natural accents of the text and the three initial notes of each phrase sound as if they lead to the beginning of a bar. Yet each time, the accented words seem to be placed in the middle of the bar. Thus, even on a metrical level, a sense of ambivalence is maintained throughout.

MUSIC EX. 6. Nielsen, 'Tidt er jeg glad' (text: B. S. Ingemann), *En Snes danske Viser* (*A Score of Danish Songs*), vol. 2 (1917), bars 1–5. Nielsen begins with a distinct bass note on the first beat of the first bar, although the rhythm of the melody, including the three short notes 'Tidt er jeg' (Oft am I), has a marked gesture, as if they were an upbeat to the strong beat on the fourth note ('glad'), which coincides with the natural stress of the text. Similarly, the harmonic emphasis is placed in the middle of the bar, where the F minor tonic chord appears, creating an ambiguous beginning – that is, the accompaniment sounds like an emphatic opening on the tonic chord in the root position and the beginning right on the accentuated beat. It turns out to be an illusion: the chord is not the starting point of the key, but, like the melodic rhythm, points to the chord in the middle of the bar. This ambivalence is maintained throughout most of the song and corresponds to the constant duality of the lyrics. Each new line is constructed according to the same model. Although the song shifts harmonically, it is always in the middle of the bar that Nielsen touches the new temporary key.

Noticing such details reveals some patterns in Nielsen's use of metre. Particularly in instrumental music, he often chooses to start in the bar rather than employing the strong beat that emphasises a clear beginning. On the other hand, he sometimes makes surprising and sudden openings that make it difficult for the listener to maintain the pace. Nielsen does this, for example, in his Fourth Symphony, *The Inextinguishable*, when he starts right on the first beat of the bar, but so much happens at once that it takes a while to realise how it all fits together.

This approach is also found in Nielsen's songs, although here, as in the two examples above, he often prefers a metrical ambiguity. His avoidance of placing the accents of the text, and thus of the melody, on the strong beats is indeed deliberate. The idea can also appear as a shift between the harmonic centres of gravity and the accents of the text or the time. There is thus a tension between two or more metrical levels, which is not necessarily a struggle but rather a nuance that creates a balance between valid rhythmic levels. It also provides subtle nuances in the presentation of a song when the accents of the levels do not coincide. It may be described as a kind of polymetric polyphony in which the centres of gravity keep each other alert.

Ambiguity is more interesting than clarity. The technique is to retain a dynamic condition, allowing a sentence to be interpreted in several ways or to be led in multiple directions. Ambivalence, ambiguity, is an aesthetic position that corresponds to the uncertainty of the modern world. It is not to be understood as a negative term, but as a potential opportunity to choose points of departure that have potential because of their ambiguity. Rather than establishing closure and creating certainty, a musical situation can be pregnant with a whole range of possibilities, all of which are valid. This is also a way of composing music that corresponds to the worldview of modernity.

Chapter 23

THE VITALIST

Around 1900, the cultivation of the vital and vigorous emerged as a trend in Danish and European cultural life. This art movement – Vitalism – may be regarded as a fight against some of the central characteristics of Symbolism. The latter's adherents worshipped the evocative and the presentiments, which were supposed to point to the beyond and the subliminal, and they used stylised ballads, dreamy inwardness and distant contemplation as motifs for their art. Around the turn of the century, this provoked a reaction that turned away from the otherworldly and away from Symbolism, which was now considered an anaemic, powerless or even decadent art.

The symbolist culture of the 1890s was itself a reaction against the realist and naturalist art and literature that had preceded it. The Symbolists criticised it for being too rational and for having lost the sense of the spiritual and metaphysical that they considered essential. Naturalism and realism, on the other hand, had their origins in the modernist criticism of Romanticism for being out of touch with reality. There is thus a pendulum swing between trends that focus on social reality and trends that emphasise the more intangible aspects of existence. With the breakthrough of Vitalism, the pendulum swung back towards the concrete and the real. However, this should not be seen as a step backwards. Although it is a reaction against what has gone before, Vitalism is not reactionary. Rather, it represents an evolution and a self-criticism on the part of the major players in cultural life. There is a constant forward movement, with each new trend building on the experience of the previous ones.

Nielsen was one of the artists who became part of the new movement. Like many others who became involved, he had a background in the symbolist culture of the 1890s, but he also had early contact with the circles that laid the foundations for the new vitalist movement.

One of the first manifestations of a new way of life can be found among the 'Hellenes' of Refsnæs. From 1894, this group, which only survived for a few years, tried to establish an artists' colony in the steep coastal hills near Kalundborg on the west coast of Zealand, where they practised outdoor activities, naturism, art and sport based on an idealised Greek past.[1] The aim was similar to that which led to the revival of the Olympic Games in 1896.

The Hellenes were a loosely organised group, whose inner circle consisted of students of the painter Kristian Zahrtmann. Their standard-bearer was Gunnar Sadolin, who painted the group of naked men in the hills, naming the image *The Hellenes at Refnæs*. Another common point of reference was the gymnastics teacher Niels Hansen Rasmussen. It was at his gymnastics institute that the idea of an open-air colony was born.[2] Several of the artists who had a looser connection with the group were associated with The Free Exhibition and thus belonged to Anne Marie and Carl's circle. When the couple moved to Vodroffsvej in 1908, they became Rasmussen's neighbours.

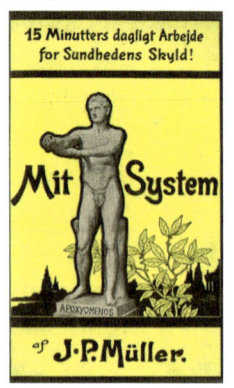

Carl and Anne-Marie also took part in the practical cultivation of body and health. In 1904, Jørgen Peter Müller's book *Mit System* (My System) was published, which prescribed daily gymnastics with carefully planned exercises. When Anne Marie had travelled to Athens in January 1905, Carl described his daily exercises and his own perseverance: 'I do and have always done the system of bathing, rubbing and so on, and my muscles and body have become so beautiful and strong, if I may say so myself.'[3] In Athens, Anne Marie also used the system daily to keep herself slim and in shape.[4]

ILL. 1. Nielsen's private copy of Jørgen Peter Müller's *Mit System: 15 Minutters dagligt Arbejde for Sundhedens Skyld!* (My System: Fifteen Minutes of Daily Exercise for the Sake of Health!). The correspondence between Carl and Anne Marie shows that they both already knew and used Müller's exercises in the same year as the book was published.

Nature and Vitality

The vitalist movement contained important elements of Symbolism, which in some ways can be seen as a preparation for Vitalism.[5] One example is the new movement's central idea that there is a force in nature, a life force, which brings everything to fruition and is the seed of all life and development. Naturalism had provided a basis in the form of the scientific understanding that humans are part of nature and that it is not a god that governs the world, but biology. The Symbolists opposed this view and insisted that there is also something divine, or at least something beyond the biological, that gives direction to evolution and does not leave humans alone and abandoned. Vitalism combines these two views in the idea that there is an elemental force in nature, a life force that lies behind everything and in which the human being, as part of nature, has a share.

A number of Nielsen's central works from the turn of the century can be understood in the light of the vitalist idea of life force.[6] Reading Nielsen's works and writ-

ILL. 2. Nielsen, here in 1912, was no stranger to the vitalist idea of outdoor life.

ings from this period, there is no doubt that he thought in terms of Vitalism: he used language and ways of thinking in which the concept of life and the notion of an underlying life force play a central role. This is clearest and most explicit when he writes about his Fourth Symphony, *The Inextinguishable*, with the motto 'Music is life, like this inextinguishable'. When Nielsen articulated the vitalist idea of the life force as 'the elementary will to live, the driving force, the great movement behind everything', it was linked to this symphony.[7] An equally striking manifestation of vitalist language is the title of his collection of essays *Living Music*, published on his sixtieth birthday in 1925, which became an aesthetic manifesto that significantly shaped subsequent perceptions of Nielsen.

On this basis, there is no doubt that Nielsen can be regarded as a central figure in a Danish vitalist movement. The literary scholar Anders Ehlers Dam, who has made significant contributions to the understanding of Danish Vitalism, uses Nielsen's thoughts on *The Inextinguishable* as the starting point for his own account of Vitalism: 'The notion of an inextinguishable force, as described by Nielsen, is at the centre of the vitalist trend',[8] he writes, referring to one of Nielsen's letters of 1920:

> The music is supposed to give expression to the most elementary forces as manifested between people, animals and even plants. We might say: if the whole world was destroyed by fire, flood, volcanoes etc., and all living things were destroyed and dead, then Nature would still begin again to beget new life, and to assert itself

with the strongest and finest powers that are to be found in the material itself. Soon plants would begin to form, and the coupling and screeching of birds would be heard and seen, along with people's aspirations and desires. It's these powers that are 'inextinguishable' and that I have sought to represent.[9]

Nielsen was not a highly ideological person, and it would be problematic to make him the spokesperson for an entire movement. Yet, it is true that he provided some of the most striking formulations of how to understand the central idea of Vitalism, and not least how to think about it in relation to music. However, it is crucial to understand that the very idea of Vitalism itself changes over time. It is therefore necessary to consider what kind of Vitalism is at play.

Vitalism may be divided into two phases, the first of which achieved a breakthrough around the turn of the century and may be described as a positive and life-affirming version. It emphasised all the positive qualities of energy and the fulfilment of life's potential. Around 1914 the understanding of the central concept of Vitalism, 'life', changed. From representing those ideas that create life and growth, it became a concept that embraced all aspects of life, both positive and negative. The vitalist idea of life became all-encompassing.

Nielsen's programme note quoted above is an expression of this expanded understanding of Vitalism after 1914. The positive attitude and optimism that characterised early Vitalism has been replaced by a disillusioned but no less powerful view that life embraces the whole. Life contains both good and evil, joy and sorrow, creation and destruction, and the recognition of this is a condition of life. Life, accordingly, is the never-ending great cycle of life and death. In Nielsen, this version of Vitalism comes to full fruition in his Fourth Symphony, which will be discussed later. However, Nielsen is also a full representative of the early version of Vitalism, which is the focus of the following discussion.

Positive and Life-Affirming Vitalism

What does it take for a musical work to be perceived as vitalist? There is no easy answer, as 'vitalism' is not merely about specific musical elements. A parallel with art history may help.

One of the central events in Danish cultural life that reintroduced the concept of Vitalism into the understanding of Danish art history was the exhibition 'Livslyst' (Passion for Life), which was shown at two Danish art museums in 2008. In the accompanying catalogue, Sven Halse provides a central reflection on what it takes for a work of art to be considered vitalistic:

> Is it enough that there are a group of children bathing on the beach and that the picture was painted in the 'vitalist period'? I think not. As far as I can judge, there has to be an explicit or implicit reference in a picture to the basic vitalist idea of *life as an autonomous force that exists in nature and in which humans strive to maintain their participation*. ... The analysis must argue in what way and with what intensity vitalist thoughts and ideas are present in the work of art.[10]

Adding more specific features to the vitalist idea of life – that is, as *an autonomous force that exists in nature and in which humans strive to maintain their participation* – it is possible to summarise some basic characteristics. Life is understood as 'elementary, physical and specific', some things are understood as 'life-enhancing', others as 'life-inhibiting', and human beings are regarded as 'part of life' and experience themselves as such. Moreover, art is supposed to be life-giving, and life can thus be 'a source of religiosity'.[11] The latter does not necessarily have to be seen in relation to a god, but may also take the form of a secularised worship of nature or life as such. The preoccupation with these ideas translates into a worship of the vital, the healthy and the strong, and into a preference for certain motifs such as athletes, warriors, muscular men, bathing children, strong animals and energetic scenes of nature.

Jens Ferdinand Willumsen was one of the central artists who, like Nielsen, participated in the change from Symbolism to Vitalism. His association with Anne Marie and Carl Nielsen goes back to their meeting in Paris in 1891, and they remained in contact thereafter.[12] One of the motifs Willumsen worked on most intensively was that of lively children bathing on the beach. He painted this motif several times and it is possible to follow the development of the vitalist characteristics, which became more pronounced each time. The final version, *Sol og Ungdom* (*Sun and Youth*) (1910), is considered a major work of Danish Vitalism. The previous year, Willumsen had painted the same motif with the title *Bathing Children on Skagen Beach*. Interestingly, the idea for this painting dated back almost ten years, and he used the modern techniques of the time in his preparations. In 1904 he was in Amalfi in southern Italy, where he photographed three boys running into the water. They are clearly the models, both when he presents them as children on the beach at Skagen in 1909, and for the central figures in *Sun and Youth*.[13]

Similarly, when it comes to music, a way must be found to make a concrete connection between the idea and the work of art. It is easy to find an association with life in a work of art. But it is not enough. Yet it is important to avoid falling into the trap of pretending that the vital is tangible and easily identifiable in the music. Thus, on the one hand, it is necessary to articulate the qualities associated with the notion of vitality; in other words, it is important to examine which features are emphasised when speaking of the vital in art. On the other hand, it is necessary to define some of

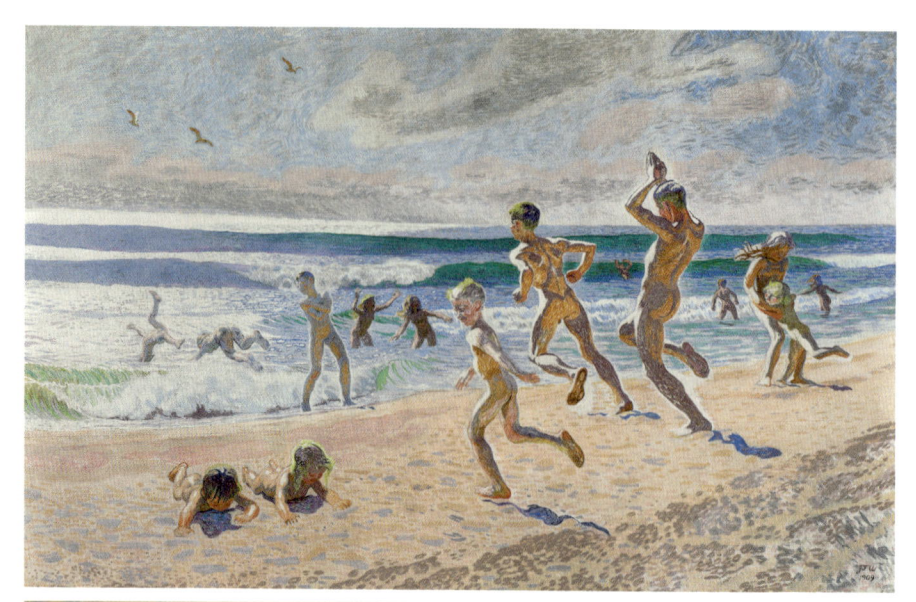

ILL. 3. Jens Ferdinand Willumsen, *Badende Børn på Skagens Strand* (*Bathing Children on Skagen Beach*) (1909) and *Sol og Ungdom* (*Sun and Youth*) (1910). Although the subject is the same, there is a clear difference between the two versions of the painting. In the first, the sun-drenched boys on the beach at Skagen are in full motion and seem quite natural in their preoccupation with running towards the sea. The 1910 painting has an even clearer focus on the muscles, body and movement. The title *Sun and Youth* removes the painting from its specific location and from the associations of the Skagen painting. The sunlight has been reduced and the blue shadows make the colours of the bodies resemble those of the sea. The strength of the muscles created by the light and the human body as part of nature are emphasised.

the musical characteristics associated with the qualities emphasised as vitalist. Thus, there must be elements in the music that can be associated with the qualities that are considered vitalistic.

One of the instances in which Nielsen shows a clear connection with the early phase of Vitalism is the *Helios Overture* (CNW 34). The work was composed in 1903 and was discussed in an earlier chapter in connection with Nielsen's relationship to programme music. However, the introduction to the work is also a good example of how music can be specifically linked to the idea of the life-giving force of nature.[14]

Nielsen names the piece 'an overture in praise of the sun', and it is clear that it is not only about describing the sun's path across the sky, but also about the sun as the source of life: 'It has tempted out everything from the earth that has the slightest root.' He calls the motif of the French horns a 'semi-solemn morning song' and makes the piece seem like a hymn or praise to the sun.[15] In the letter from which these phrases originate, he indicates that he understands that people have worshipped the sun, and continues:

> In Norway there are still traces of sun worship. In the narrow valleys where the sun's rays rarely penetrate there's a festival day when it finally gets to shine on the house, and the farmer then puts a pat of butter on the window sill, which the sun melts. It's a sacrificial offering.[16]

The work can thus be seen as an expression of secularised religion, in which the vital force of the sun and nature is worshipped or praised as a force beyond or behind the purely biological and physical. But is it also possible to link the idea of life as an autonomous force found in nature with specific musical features in the work?

The introduction begins with a single note in the lower strings. It begins very softly, increases in intensity a little, and fades away. There is a fermata on the last note, indicating that its duration is *ad libitum*. The figure is then repeated in the same way, sounding like the breathing of a dormant creature or large organism, and is to be interpreted as nature sleeping. The listener has no sense of the temporal division of the piece other than the length of the pulsating rhythm of the breath.

When something breathes, there is life, and from bar 5 the French horns enter with some long, hymn-like notes that linger over the low strings. The lowest pitch is C, and the notes that are slowly added are part of the harmonic series rooted in that C – that is, the pitches produced by a natural horn without valves. The series is also known as the natural harmonics, which creates a symbolic link between the notes played and the concept of nature. Moreover, the fact that the notes are played on a French horn is indeed a reference to nature, derived from the hunting horn. It is a direct reference in that it evokes something that can be heard in nature, and an indirect one in that horns were often used in orchestral music when the audience needed to be reminded of the forest or nature.

There is a reference to nature, but how can there be a musical reference to the life force inherent in nature? The harmonic tension of the G in the bass, descending to C in bar 5, activates the energy that initiates the development. As it falls, an impulse is released that sets the horns in motion, building up the sound that symbolises nature. The slow addition of more and more energy is a consequence of the rising sun. When the movement comes to an end, the energy level has returned to its lowest point. The sun has set and nature is back in its dormant state, but still breathing.

MUSIC EX. 1. Nielsen, *Helios Overture*, short score, bars 1–23, 339–42. The introduction begins with a metrically indefinite pulsating sound in the low strings on G. In bar 5, the bass descends to C, revealing that the starting note was the fifth and that the key of the piece is based on C. This confirms to the listener that the opening note was not entirely without energy, although it was played softly. The G represents a harmonic tension as the dominant to the C. In bars 5–18, a timbre is slowly built up, based on the harmonic series rooted in C. A characteristic but natural feature of the series is that its seventh, in this instance B♭, is low, which distinguishes it from what a C major introduction would sound like. When the strings enter with the melody, the low seventh is still sounding. For the listener, this is a distinctive soundscape that can be associated with the concept of nature. From bar 339 the overture ends in the same way as it began, now on C, confirming the listener's perception that C is the true tonic on which everything then settles. The energy is now fully released.

Firstly, with this introduction Nielsen creates an emblematic association between the force of nature and natural harmonics, and with the sound of the French horns as a specific reference to nature. Secondly, he creates a reference to the vitalist principle that nature unfolds from an inherent life force, which in this case is specifically brought to life prompted by the sun. The life force is present in the organic breath, which represents the resting state of nature, and in the harmonic tension – albeit modest – inherent in the downward leap in the bass. There is not only an abstract reference to an idea of life and life force, but also an explicit use of musical elements that can be related to the idea of life as an autonomous force found in nature.

Sinfonia espansiva

Another work associated with this first phase of Vitalism is Nielsen's Third Symphony, *Sinfonia espansiva* (CNW 27). Composed between 1910 and 1911, it is perhaps the clearest expression of Vitalism in Nielsen's output, representing a 'positive, life-affirming line in which the active, the vital, the simple and healthy, the vigorous and lively are celebrated'.[17] The first movement was composed in the spring of 1910 and is end-dated 13 April. He then worked on the incidental music for *Hagbarth and Signe*, which was staged in June in the Open-Air Theatre at Dyrehaven, north of Copenhagen. The second movement of the symphony was composed in July and finished in early November, while the last two movements were completed in January and April 1911.[18]

Nielsen has argued in terms that certainly imply that the symphony may be regarded as an expression of vitalist ideas.[19] *Espansiva*, which in Italian denotes something that expands, is itself a metaphor for vitality. In addition, the word has a connotation of something extroverted, suggesting something that unfolds per se because of an inherent force. However, at the first performance at Odd Fellow Palæet on 28 February 1912, when Nielsen conducted The Royal Orchestra, the symphony was simply named *Symphony for Orchestra*.[20] This is clear from both Nielsen's pencil score and the ink fair copy used as the printer's manuscript. In both sources, the title *Sinfonia espansiva* was added after the music had been notated, and the tempo marking of the first movement was changed from Allegro to Allegro espansivo.[21] Once the title was in place, however, it also conveyed to Nielsen the essence of how the symphony was to be interpreted.

Within a month of the premiere in Copenhagen, Nielsen was to conduct the symphony at the Concertgebouw in Amsterdam. He wrote a programme note for the occasion and was quite explicit about the title and its meaning:

> The symphony is named after the character of the first Allegro. This first movement begins with some strong unison jerks, which gradually take on a rhythmic form, until the following subject leaps forward as if by violent pressure:[22]

Thus the reference to the term *espansiva* is the key to the whole symphony and a description of how the beginning is meant to be an inhibited force unleashed in the first subject. Shortly before his death in 1931, Nielsen wrote another programme note for the work in which his vitalist formulation is even clearer:

> The first movement is intended to be a burst of energy and passion for life out into the wider world, which we humans not only want to know in its diverse activity, but also wish to conquer and appropriate.[23]

Nielsen's descriptions suggest an irrepressible force expressed in music. This is supported by the musical effects he employs. At first we hear only the rhythmic beats of the whole orchestra playing the same note in several octaves. In terms of time, they are liquefied, like energy gathering behind a dam. When the dam bursts, the first subject of the symphony emerges immediately from the last note of the rhythmic motif.

MUSIC EX. 2. Nielsen, *Sinfonia espansiva*, first movement, bars 1–23. The introduction to *Sinfonia espansiva* is about energy. In the first bars, and rhythmically, the energy is intensified with increasingly dense chordal beats. When the first subject enters in bar 15, the harmonic tension of A (a fifth in the D minor key, heard at the beginning of first subject) is released. Incidentally, Nielsen employed the same device in the opening of the *Helios Overture*. He adds further rhythmic and melodic energy at the beginning of each new phrase; this begins in bar 15 with an upbeat. The next phrase is intensified by beginning in bar 19 with two crotchets as an upbeat; and leading up to the upbeat of bar 23, Nielsen uses three accented quavers. Not only does the flow of energy continue – it is also given an extra push forward each time.

The upbeat to bar 15 serves as the final note of the opening chords, as well as the first note of the first subject. There is no pause in the flow. Only much later – that is, more than a hundred bars into the movement, after renewed bursts of energy – is there a climax on *ffff*, followed by the rhythm of the opening bars played retrograde in trumpets, trombone and timpani. The energy of the remaining instruments is brought to a close in a large diminuendo. But even at this point, the work does not come to a standstill. Rather, a new beginning is established from this low level of energy. Here Nielsen introduces his second subject, the starting point for a new, long and uninterrupted flow of energy. In this way, he musically emphasises the movement as 'a burst of energy and passion for life out into the wider world'.

As to the symphony's final movement, the programme note of 1931 reads:

> The Finale, on the other hand, is straightforward: a hymn to the work and a healthy portrayal of everyday life. It is *not* a pathetic tribute to life, but a certain expansive joy at being able to participate in the work of life and of the day, and to see activity and skill unfolding on all sides around us.[24]

The caveat only applies to the word 'pathetic', because it is precisely a tribute to daily life and the active, persistent work that keeps things going. The expression 'a certain expansive joy' refers to the satisfaction of making a daily contribution to the continuity of society.

Nielsen wrote about the same movement in 1912:

> The Finale is the apotheosis of the work! The composer wanted to show the healthy morality that lies in the blessing of work. Everything moves towards the goal. The first subject
>
> is much used and the character of the movement is maintained with as much vigour and energy as possible.[25]

Here, too, Nielsen is in tune with vitalist language. The term 'apotheosis of the work' is a reference to Beethoven's Seventh Symphony, which Wagner called 'the apotheosis of the dance'. For Nielsen, it is the work that is to be celebrated and glorified.

The character of the display of energy is different from that of the first movement. In contrast to the harmonic and rhythmic build-up of tension in the first movement, the Finale begins immediately with a melody in a bold, progressive duple metre. In the first movement, Nielsen develops the intense force that, once broken through, continues as a wave of energy throughout the movement; in the last movement, however, the focus is on the daily, steady and persistent work done with desire and energy. It is reminiscent of Nielsen's remark in *My Childhood* that his father was perhaps most at ease after a long and regular day's work when he had lent a hand on one of the farms during the harvest.[26] This work, which in other interpretations might be seen as unrelenting drudgery, is praised as the contribution of ordinary people, not only for their own good but also for the common good.

In 1912, Nielsen described the two middle movements in rather neutral terms. According to Nielsen, the second movement, Andante pastorale, depicts peace

MUSIC EX. 3. Nielsen, *Sinfonia espansiva*, fourth movement, bars 1–17. The character of the melody emphasises the steady but calm momentum of everyday work. As in many of Nielsen's melodies for communal singing, the subject is divided into two sections, each beginning with the same rhythm. Apart from the ending, which closes more openly than a song melody would, the subject appears aurally as an instrumental version of a sound also found in Nielsen's popular songs. The tenuto on the notes in the lower part indicates that they must be held for their entire duration, and the accents in the upper part help to maintain the energy and momentum.

and tranquillity in nature, 'interrupted only by the voice of a few birds, or whatever you like'. He then assigns the subjects to the three entities that interact in the movement, namely 'the landscape … the voices of nature … and the strong *feeling* of humans therein'.[27]

The most interesting aspect of this movement is the use of two human voices, one male and one female, interwoven with the orchestral texture in the second half of the movement. This is a specific example of the vitalist idea of humans as part of nature. The two soloists sing without text and so softly throughout that they do not draw attention to themselves as individuals.

Remarkably, it is not the singers who present the theme that expresses the human feeling for the landscape and nature. That is the task of the orchestra. Rather, the singers appear as an integral part of the sound of the 'scenic calm and depth', which Nielsen describes at this point as 'more condensed'.[28] The pencil score shows that Nielsen added the two vocal parts at the bottom of the page after completing the movement, initially giving them a simple text, 'All thoughts vanished. I lie beneath the heavens.'[29] He subsequently abandoned the text, leaving them to sing only the sound 'aaa –'. In this way he achieves that the voices are not conspicuous, but rather part of the overall orchestral sound, representing the landscape and nature, and therefore not manifesting themselves as human beings. In doing so, Nielsen gives a concrete musical expression to the vitalist idea of humans as a part of nature, *striving to maintain their participation* in it.

Looking at the symphony as a whole, it could be argued that it articulates the celebration of the expansive life force, human participation in nature and the healthy, industrious drive to action as three different aspects of the life-affirming version of Vitalism.

In 1912, Nielsen's description of the two middle movements was not characterised by vitalist language. In the 1931 programme note, however, all the movements of the symphony were included in a vitalist understanding, suggesting that the concept had changed in the intervening period. In the early phase of Vitalism, when the focus was on the active, healthy and positively life-affirming, it was not obvious to include the two introspective movements in a vitalistic description. In 1912, he therefore described them as contrasting with the two outer movements which expressed the positive representation of life.

By the time he wrote about his Third Symphony in 1931, the broader understanding of Vitalism had taken hold. Now all aspects of life are part of life, and therefore the whole symphony is seen as an expression of vitality. This is already clear from the opening sentence: 'The work is the result of different forces.' Now the second movement is not excluded, for it is indeed part of the description of life, since it is 'the absolute opposite' of the first movement. Life contains the greatest contradictions. The movement expresses 'the purest idyll, and when the human voices are finally heard, it is only to emphasise the peaceful atmosphere that could be imagined in paradise before the fall of our first parents, Adam and Eve'.[30] The third movement can now also be described in vitalist terms. Whereas in 1912 Nielsen merely noted that the movement 'ends as it began, in an ambiguous mood, between major and minor',[31] in 1931 it is regarded as 'a matter that cannot really be characterised, because both good and evil make themselves known without any real decision.'[32]

The programme note of 1931 must be read as an expression of the fact that at this time, shortly before his death, Nielsen still regarded the *Sinfonia espansiva* as a work that embodied vitalist concepts. The note also reveals that he viewed the entire symphony – in retrospect – within the framework of an expanded concept of Vitalism that had since been established. Last but not least, it shows that in 1931 he still believed that music should express life in all its breadth and illustrate the force behind and beneath it all.

It therefore makes sense to think of Nielsen as a vitalist. Yet it is equally important to remember that this is only one of the elements that define him. He participates in many of the trends of the time without being entirely absorbed by them. He may be completely taken with an idea or a school of thought for a short or long period of time, but he does not want to be pigeonholed.[33] Nielsen lives with the cultural trends of the time, uses them, identifies with them in whole or in part, but he can also leave them again or be content to take elements of the way of thinking with him into his further life. Vitalism is one of the trends that leaves its mark on his thinking and further activities.

Chapter 24

THE COLLABORATION WITH LAUB

Nielsen often collaborated with other composers and musicians when working on his pieces. One particular collaboration in which he appeared to the public as one half of an artistic pair was the fruitful partnership with the organist Thomas Laub. This resulted in the song collections *En Snes danske Viser* (*A Score of Danish Songs*), volumes 1 and 2 (1915 and 1917), which consisted of solo songs with piano accompaniment and were intended for experienced amateurs. They were the result of Nielsen's and Laub's desire to write good songs to quality texts that could be used by a wider audience.

Many of the songs became popular and were further disseminated as communal songs, so that they are now known by a large part of the population. However, this was not part of their original plan. They wanted to write melodies in the tradition of Johann Abraham Peter Schulz – that is, simple lieder with a touch of the seemingly familiar, and thus suitable for performance in the many homes with a piano. For Nielsen, the songs should therefore also be seen as part of the simplification of his lied style that he began in the collection *Strophic Songs* of 1907.

Laub was full of initiative and was used to tasks that involved not only composing music but also disseminating knowledge about music – in other words, he was strategically aware of how music should be presented to the general public. So when Nielsen and Laub began their collaboration, it was not just about composing songs and giving each other advice on the pieces. For Laub, it was also about how to get the songs out to the singers.

It was not the first time that Laub had embarked on a song project. Since the 1880s he had worked extensively on church hymns, and in the following decade he also began to explore the old Danish ballads and, in collaboration with the philologist and folklorist Axel Olrik, he attempted to reconstruct them. Both Laub and Olrik were interested in the ballads as poetry and sought to promote knowledge of them to a wide audience by performing them as songs. And this is where the story begins, for Laub's work with the ballads encouraged the idea that quality songs could again be presented to the general public in the form of Laub's and Nielsen's new collections of popular songs.

The Ballads

In May 1898, the citizens of Copenhagen flocked to the small hall of Koncertpalæet in Bredgade for an extraordinary musical evening: a performance of ballads. The audience was first introduced to six songs, including one with fifteen stanzas that told of the betrayal of King Erik Klipping and his murder at Finderup. Royal actor Peter Jerndorff sang the stanzas, while a chorus of ten women from Cæciliaforeningens Madrigalkor (the Madrigal Choir of the Cecilia Society) sang the refrain, 'for the country stands in peril', in unison. The ballads, in full length and with interpolated choruses, gave the audience the opportunity 'to hear them in the form in which they were originally performed' in the Middle Ages, as one of the newspapers put it.[1] The second part of the concert featured Laub's choral arrangements of the ballads, sung by the madrigal choir under the direction of Frederik Rung.[2] One reviewer found the choral music a 'lyrical echo' to the more historical section of the concert.[3] During the evening, Olrik gave a lecture on the work of reconstructing the old Danish ballads.[4]

The recitals were preceded by a long collaboration between Olrik and Laub. For years they had both been interested in Danish ballads – the medieval oral tradition of songs that Olrik and Laub believed to have originated among the common people. It is now thought that they originated in the upper classes of society.[5] Olrik and Laub were concerned with the roots of the ballads and, in particular, with their original form. They agreed that the texts represented a poetic art that deserved to be disseminated to a wider audience. Laub's work on the ballads was seen as an attempt to reconstruct the tunes 'and restore them to their pristine musical form'.[6] Laub omitted elements that had been added in later times, while Olrik, who together with Svend Grundtvig had worked on the publication of the ballad texts based on sixteenth-century sources, revised the texts. It was described as 'a great and laborious academic collaboration', but in fact the new ballad tunes were based on Laub's personal idea of how they would have sounded. There were no sources for the tunes as they had been sung in the Middle Ages, and Laub's starting point was the documents collected in the nineteenth century and published by Rasmus Nyerup and Andreas Peter Berggreen.[7]

Laub wrote an article in 1904 describing his work on the ballads and his view of those that had survived:

> The old tunes were in ruins. The original outlines were still visible, but the details were so damaged that the whole thing would fall to pieces if you tried to touch it in order to clean it. Some tunes, however, were so intact that I tried to save them from the flames: it would just have been too sad to give them up. As I set these

tunes to the words, stanza by stanza, I realised that things were indeed not so bad: in one sense I had still been prejudiced by a modern view of the ballads, which prevented me from seeing the matter as it really was.[8]

Laub's perception of the original form of the tunes concerned their rhythmic sequence, tonality and the connection between text and music. He believed that the ballads had evolved from 'Gregorian chant, the cultural stream from which all art music in Europe originated'.[9] With this conviction, Laub had before him an infinite amount of musical material from which he believed he could adapt Berggreen's versions of the ballads into a 'mode of singing [that] is many times closer to the spirit of the original than the usual one'.[10]

In May 1897, when Laub and Olrik had ideas about performing the ballads in public and publishing them, Laub began to think strategically.[11] He was assigned tasks that he and Olrik could not solve. Laub spoke to the composer Peter Erasmus Lange-Müller, who became involved in the project and would try to persuade Jerndorff to sing the songs.[12] Lange-Müller also spoke to the philologist and folklorist Ernst von der Recke, who was involved in editing the lyrics.[13] Lange-Müller also found it be useful to have the music publisher Henrik Hennings on board. He had experience as an impresario and was responsible for organising the recital at Koncertpalæet, where the ballads were to be premiered. The press had to be made aware of what was coming, and Olrik was put in touch with the newspaper *Politiken*.[14] In the weeks leading up to the recital, Hennings expected a lot from the events and got Laub to make statements to the newspapers *Dannebrog* and *Nationaltidende*.[15]

Tickets were sold out before the day of the recital, and a second performance was organised four days later at the same venue. At the end of the month, the main hall of Koncertpalæet was again used for an evening of ballads. The interest was so great that the following year Olrik and Laub opened the summer with another recital of ballads, after which Jerndorff took it upon himself to visit the folk high schools in Ollerup, Vestbirk and Ry to present the songs.[16] Around the same time, after more than a year and a half of work, the music for fourteen ballads was published as *Danske Folkeviser med gamle Melodier* (Danish Ballads with Old Tunes).[17] Five years later, a second volume with fourteen more songs was issued.

Nielsen followed Laub and Olrik's project on the side. Axel Olrik and his wife Sofie were close friends of the Nielsen family, and their shared interest in ballads had inspired Nielsen to compose the music for the song about Mr Thorben in 1897.[18] Anne Marie, as well as artists such as Lorenz Frølich, the Skovgaard brothers and Agnes Slott-Møller, was also interested in ballads – an interest that would later find expression in Anne Marie's art. She designed the title page for the printed piano version of her husband's ballad melodrama *Hr. Oluf han rider* – (*Sir Oluf He Rides* –)

ILL. 1. Joakim Skovgaard designed the title pages for Laub and Olrik's publication of old Danish ballads and included motifs inspired by them. The collection was issued in two volumes in 1899 and 1904.[19]

(1906), and created an imposing monument to Queen Dagmar (1913) in Ribe, which has a bronze relief of a scene inspired by the ballad on its granite base.

According to Nielsen, he was introduced to Laub by the Olriks.[20] At the end of March 1898, when Laub and Olrik were about to finish the lyrics and tunes, Olrik wanted to invite Nielsen, Laub and the music historian Hortense Panum to dinner.[21] It is unclear whether this took place, but it is possible that the project was discussed among the friends. A month later Olrik gave Anne Marie and Carl Nielsen free tickets, for which Anne Marie thanked him by saying that she was 'looking forward to the ballads'.[22] In other words, it seems very likely that the Nielsens were present in Koncertpalæet that May evening.

Nielsen and Laub

Nielsen first met Laub through the musical circles in Copenhagen, although their friendship developed during a stay in Rome in 1900.[23] There they enjoyed each other's daily company, 'talking and talking' and making music together.[24] Laub found that the Italian art that surrounded them stimulated their own 'ideas about and demands on' their own art.[25] The many Danes in Rome did, however, interfere with Laub's experience of Italian culture, for in a travel letter to friends and acquaintances he explains that he enjoyed Nielsen's company as a counterbalance, thus revealing that it was a relationship of trust.[26] The focus of their time together was the conversation of art and attitudes to life, and under the southern skies they must have discussed Laub's work on the ballads.

Laub was keen to communicate his ideas not only to colleagues and music lovers, but also to the general public. Fundamental to his work was a desire to influence the way people used and understood music. In a short essay entitled *Vor musikundervisning og den musikalske dannelse* (Our Music Education and Musical Literacy) (1884), he argued that music education should not only develop the ability to produce and perform music, but also the ability to listen to music and that music education could therefore be achieved through skilled listening.[27] One of the criteria for success of the ballad project – as for Laub's reform ideas regarding church hymns – was that the people should acquire a specific repertoire of melodies. This was to be achieved through widespread dissemination in writing and speech, in singing and in music.

Laub showed renewed vigour when he and Olrik repeated the ballad recitals for the Copenhagen audience in 1902. Newspaper reviews of the earlier recitals had been extremely positive, focusing on the extensive work that had gone into reconstructing the ballads. By 1902, Laub and Olrik's efforts were still highly regarded, but the viability of Laub's approach to the restoration was questioned musically. A reviewer in *Social-Demokraten* stated that everyone would be captivated 'by the mood, the naive art of the words and music, the melancholy, mischievous, touching or poignant mood', and pointed out that the value lay in the overall experience rather than in the music alone.[28] Other reviewers went further, suggesting that the music itself was of no importance. The music critic Gustav Hetsch felt that he had been miscast for the task of reviewing the event, which he felt 'was much more of a literary, general aesthetic or Nordic philological nature'.[29] The same view was expressed by Leopold Rosenfeld, who argued that 'from a musical point of view, it is certainly boring to hear the same monotonous melody in an infinity of stanzas with an endless monotonous refrain, sung by featureless voices'.[30] The anonymous reviewer in *Aftenbladet* did not mince his words either, describing the songs as 'insidiously dull ballads'.[31]

Was Laub risking the demise of the whole project with these comments of the press, and would his years of work on the project have been in vain? Only a counter-offensive could dispel the criticism, which Laub felt was misguided. At this point, Nielsen had nothing to do with the organisation of the recitals, and he was now brought into the fray as an impartial supporter. It was not difficult to persuade Nielsen to join the cause. He had attended the recitals, followed the work and knew the background to the project, and for his efforts Nielsen was given two tickets for the next ballad recital evening.[32]

Laub knew that he and Nielsen had a common interest in the ballads, and in the letter in which Laub tried to persuade Nielsen to support the project, he emphasised the recitals as a central part of the presentation of the ballads to the general public. Newspaper criticism might discourage those who attended: 'There are many under-age and innocent people who would like to enjoy the ballads, but who are afraid to do so now that they have read that it was really a boring nonsense.'[33]

In an article in *Politiken* a few days later, Nielsen gave his unreserved support to Laub. According to Nielsen, the melodies of the ballads, as Laub had recreated them, were fully in keeping with the texts. Nielsen urged readers to attend the next recital, which was to take place the following evening, and the reason was clear: not for Laub's sake, 'nor for the sake of the ballads – they will survive – but it is of the greatest importance that as many as possible should share in the best'.[34] The polemical tenor of the newspaper article revealed Nielsen's disappointment at the opposition Laub had encountered in other contexts. The text could be interpreted as a defence of the person, not the cause. This was noted by the music critic Charles Kjerulf, who in a response in *Politiken* the following day suggested that Nielsen had overreacted to the cautious criticism of the recitals by some of the reviewers: 'I really do not understand what you want to help [Laub] with and for, dear Carl Nielsen.'[35]

Although Nielsen's defence of Laub was heartfelt, it was a natural part of their friendship to allow for differences of opinion. A few weeks after the newspaper debate, and after having attended a performance of *Saul and David*, Laub wrote: 'My soul is as full of *contradictory* impressions which your music has made on me'. His argument was that 'all your music seems to me, at one and the same time (seen from two sides), excellent and utterly wrong, poignant and contrary to sound sense (mine anyway).'[36] Laub did not mince his words. It is clear that Nielsen felt hurt, for a few months later he replied: 'Dear Friend! … You mean a great deal to me, and I value your friendship and interest very highly. But I suppose it's human nature to think most of the evil one does and hardly of the better.'[37] It shows the strength and depth of their friendship that they were able to discuss their views on music without reservation. Their differences were productive and helped to sharpen their views.

Their opinions of the folk tunes also differed. While working on *Folkehøjskolens Melodibog* (*The Folk High School Melody Book*) in 1922, Nielsen recalled Jerndorff's performance of the ballads, which 'was nice, cultivated and stylish, like the pretty mahogany furniture in a well-bred and well-to-do Copenhagen home. But there was really very little of the rawness, force and cruelty that are often found in the texts, and occasionally also in the notes (at least they *can* always be inflected in that direction).'[38] Nielsen was never a fan of neatness. Two decades had passed since he had defended the ballad project in *Politiken*, and Nielsen's view was influenced by the fact that a new kind of European interest in folk tunes had emerged in the meantime. In the same letter to Thorvald Aagaard, who published *The Folk High School Melody Book* with Laub, Nielsen and Oluf Ring, he suggested that Laub should have gone to Hungary to visit Bartók and Kodály, who were collecting folk tunes from the common people. Their approach to the subject was, in Nielsen's new opinion, better than Laub's.

From Ballads to Popular Songs

The question of how to define and understand popular songs was a concern for both Laub and Nielsen, and for Laub his engagement with the ballad genre was closely linked to efforts to revive what he saw as the popular songs of earlier times. A central argument for the current interest in ballads in this context was their poetic value. With a similar starting point, Laub tried to persuade Nielsen in late 1914 to join him in a new project to compose new tunes to poems by Danish poets, and together with Laub, Nielsen was to bring his experience as a lied composer to his work on popular songs. The result of Laub and Nielsen's collaboration in composing new popular songs was two volumes of *A Score of Danish Songs*.

It was on a Wednesday evening in early December 1914 that Laub first described to Nielsen his ideas for working together to publish a collection of songs. The aim was 'to give people good *words* to sing to good *folkelige* melodies'.[39] Laub's idea was that the collection should not be aimed at the usual musical audience, but at the common people. Recognising that the Romantic songs of the nineteenth century were not suitable for the general public to sing, Laub believed that they should compose songs that could be performed without any special requirements. A basic feature of the tunes was to be recognisability, despite their novelty.

In an attempt to characterise his approach to composing tunes suitable for popular singing, Laub drew on a term formulated in the late eighteenth century. He cited Johann Abraham Peter Schulz's concept of the 'Schein des Bekannten' ('the seemingly familiar'), coined in Schulz's *Lieder im Volkston* (1785).[40] Schulz argued that the secret of the 'Volkston' lay in the familiar.[41] Whereas Schulz was influenced by a Herderian understanding of 'the popular' as the expression of the spirit of the people, Laub seems more determined to emphasise that the songs were intended for the people: they were to be sung by the people. The popularity of the songs was to be defined by the fact that they could be used by the general public, who had only a limited musical training, but who could be encouraged to sing quality songs.

Nielsen was not hard to convince, and a few days after Laub proposed the idea, he set to work. His diary shows that the drafts came in dribs and drabs throughout December, and within a few weeks he had set fifteen poems to music.[42] The collaboration was now well underway and would result in two publications, both entitled *En Snes danske Viser* (1915 and 1917). The first collection contained twenty-three

ILL. 2. Johann Abraham Peter Schulz was a renowned and sought-after composer and Kapellmeister who worked in Germany and Denmark. Besides being a versatile musician, Schulz was also composer and organiser, and his main interest was songs. Shortly after the publication of his first two volumes of *Lieder im Volkston*, he was appointed Royal Kapellmeister in Copenhagen in 1787, where he published the third volume in the series. He stated that his aim was to be called 'Liedermann des Volkes' – the people's singer.[43]

songs; twelve of them were by Nielsen and eleven by Laub. The second collection continued the numbering of the first volume, adding another twenty-two texts with eleven songs each by the two composers.

Laub and Nielsen used the phrase about the familiar, 'Schein des Bekannten', as a lever for the project, and it was indeed to become the motto for *A Score of Danish Songs*. They attached such importance to Schulz's motto that they reproduced a translation of a distilled extract from Schulz's *Lieder im Volkston* as the preface to their collection, without giving any further explanation. They discussed how to render Schulz's German words in Danish, as no translation existed. Their discussion revolved around the subtleties of 'Schein', with Laub arguing that the Danish word 'skær' (a tinge) in the sense of light emanating from an object, had a false connotation. Rather, it should be understood as the passive 'to seem', which better captured the idea that the tunes had a 'quality of the seemingly familiar'.[44] However, it was not only Schulz's preface that inspired them; his collection of songs that they studied was also important.[45] This, as well as other collections by Schulz, contained simple art songs in a plain popular style with modest piano accompaniment.[46] This style became a guideline for Laub and Nielsen's work.

Calling their songs 'viser' (ballads) was also a way of distancing themselves from the repertoire of professional musicians. Although a ballad was not clearly defined as a genre, it was more akin to popular singing than concert hall music. Laub explained to Nielsen that they 'should be simple tunes' by which he did not necessarily mean something plain and ordinary, but rather something pure, reliable and precious. Rather, it is clear from his characterisation of the lyrics that he believed that 'the best is not good enough'.[47]

Nielsen later described the melodies that resulted from his collaboration with Laub as 'so straightforward that any child could sing them straight away'.[48] If a child was the yardstick for the quality of the melodies, it shows that the popular element was not just about Schulz's so-called 'familiarity', which of course presupposes that people already have a relationship with it. It was also about immediacy and of simple melodies. They are songs composed for anyone with only a basic understanding of music, regardless of gender or age. Nielsen described the essence of the tunes to the composer Julius Röntgen, whom he knew from his stays at Fuglsang:

> They are kept so 'simple' that a child can play and sing them; and there is no prelude or postlude. Now we shall see whether the people will receive these modest little children as they are intended, namely, as a gentle discourse on good poetry, and as a guide away from the modern 'lieder', which often consist of a passionate and difficult piano part, with which words and melody must fight a desperate battle.[49]

Nielsen exaggerates, for there are small epilogues in some of the songs, and in the second volume there are also examples including short introductions for the piano before the singer begins to sing. The pieces are still composed in the lied tradition, in which the piano and the vocal parts are independent, thus they enter into a musical dialogue without the piano including the vocal part. To Röntgen, Nielsen emphasises that his intention with the songs was not to write lieder in the grand style that he had used earlier.

It was also important for both to stage the idea that the songs were intended for a wider audience. They were to be presented to the Copenhagen public in Odd Fellow Palæet, as Koncertpalæet was now called. To challenge the notion that this was ordinary concert music, the singers appeared in their everyday clothes. Throughout the evening they sat on the edge of the stage, relaxed and waiting their turn, as if they were in a living room listening to family members making music. It was an important message to get across, which is why, as part of the carefully planned marketing strategy, Nielsen mentioned in an interview in *Nationaltidende* a few days before the first recital that the event would show traces of 'the mark of something homely, something bourgeois-cosy'.[50]

ILL. 3. Niels Skovgaard who, like his brother Joakim and Anne Marie Carl-Nielsen, was associated with Den Frie Udstilling (The Free Exhibition), designed the title page for Laub's and Nielsen's ballads. The illustration depicts Poul Martin Møller's poem 'Rosen blusser alt i Danas Have' (The rose is blooming now in Dana's garden), the first stanza of which ends: 'The stallion proudly forages on the graves of the ancestors, the boy picks from the red berries.'

Although it was the popular element that was to be expressed in the common ballads, this did not mean that they were simple songs in terms of content. Stylistically, the collection is composed using a number of different devices that Laub and Nielsen must have found recognisable.[51] Some melodies have a romance-like concept, such as Laub's 'Paa Mark og Eng i Skovens Læ' (On fields and pastures in lee of the forest) and Nielsen's 'Hvor sødt i Sommer-Aftenstunden' (How sweet, as summer day is fading) (CNW 215). Nielsen must have thought it suited the slightly Romantic style of Oehlenschläger's poem, and Laub has no objections. He makes explicit reference to Nielsen's melody, calling it one of his favourites.[52]

Other ballads are in an anti-Romantic style, using modal harmony and melody. Laub's 'Ja, I Sønner af Kæmpeæt' (Yes, ye sons of giant lineage) seems to be a deliberately archaic setting of selected stanzas from Grundtvig's *Nordens Mytologi* (Nordic mythology).[53] Similarly characteristic melodic passages are also found in Nielsen's 'Naar Odin vinker' (As Odin beckons) (CNW 206), which plays with a soundscape of Norse mythology with its harp-like piano chords. Other songs feature minimal use of effects, with small melodic fluctuations, frequent repetition of motifs and simple piano accompaniment. This can be seen, for example, in Nielsen's 'Vender sig Lykken fra dig' (Fortune has lately left you) (CNW 207).

Nielsen's letters to Laub have not survived and consequently Nielsen seems today to have been unintentionally silent. It is clear that Nielsen often followed Laub's ideas, but this is only what the surviving correspondence reveals. To what extent the influence went in the other direction is uncertain.

In his letters to Nielsen, Laub repeatedly raises the question of the role of the piano, and by looking at how each composer shaped his accompaniments, it is possible to gain an impression of their specific compositional collaboration. One example is the song 'Nu er da Vaaren kommen' (At last the spring's upon us) (CNW 214), which Laub uses as an opportunity to express some basic views on how the accompaniment to a ballad, in which the piano plays an independent role, must not collide with the melody. In the letter, he reproduces Nielsen's version of the accompaniment, explaining that when the piano is used to accompany, it should not follow the melody; rather, the piano's role is to 'fill out the melody more than to follow it, and not to collide with it'.[54] Laub therefore suggests a modified accompaniment in which the right-hand figure is divided into two parts every other bar. Laub's suggestion is supported by relevant arguments, and the new version is indeed better than the original.

The role of the piano in the performance of the songs is both important and subordinate to the voice, and Laub as well as Nielsen were aware that its role in the prelude and postlude could overshadow the song. In December 1914, when they were working on the songs, they discussed how to solve the individual cases. Laub criticised Nielsen's piano setting of 'Farvel, min velsignede Fødeby!' (Farewell, my respectable

ILL. 4. In his letter to Nielsen of 2 August 1916, Laub reproduces Nielsen's original accompaniment to the song 'Nu er da Vaaren kommen' (At last the spring's upon us) and comments: 'Now look! In the second bar we have an almost painful clash – the acciaccatura ("Vå-ren") E to F♯–D♯, at the same time as the figure is being pieced together from two chords'. His point is that while the singer sounds an E on the first syllable of 'Vå-ren' (the spring), the piano has the two notes on either side of that note (F♯ and D♯), both of which are dissonant or 'clash' with the singer's note. Instead, Laub suggests that the piano's right hand omit the middle note of bar 2 and change the penultimate note from the harsh, dissonant D♯ to the softer F♯, and then use this model throughout the song. Thus according to Laub: 'to perform what is necessary consistently, to use the motif that the circumstances provide, with awareness'.[55] It is clear that in the final version of the song, Nielsen follows Laub's suggestion and implements it throughout the setting.

native town) (CNW 211), in which the postlude, according to Laub seemed 'dramatic-representational', which was 'indeed contrary to the style'.[56] In Laub's view, the epilogue 'in no way develops from the melody itself' and contradicts the idea that the piano accompaniment should only have 'plain "supports" that have nothing of their own to say'.[57] This is one of the instances where an explicit aesthetic for the songs emerges. Nielsen took the criticism to heart and the postlude was omitted from the printed version of the song. The draft criticised by Laub has not survived.

By contrast, we know the postlude to 'De Refnæs-drenge, de Samsøe-piger' (The boys of Refsnaes, the girls of Samsoe) (CNW 202), which Laub found appropriate. Here one gets the impression that the piano accompaniment unfolds the concluding rhythmic motif of the melody with renewed energy over a few bars after the vocal part has ended in a restrained tempo. Laub believed that 'the last notes of the accompaniment simultaneously support the last note of the vocal part and are also organically connected to the ballad tune and therefore do not stand alone.'[58] The accompaniment must support the soloist, yet not overshadow the song. It is still the singer who must sing the melody independently, and of course the accompaniment provides a harmonic and tonal foundation; it does not interfere, but helps to move the song forward. Similarly, 'Nu er Dagen fuld af Sang' (Now the day is full of song) (CNW 213) has a postlude, derived from the punctuated rhythm of the melody, which prepares the transition to the next stanza.

To see how the ideal of the accompaniment, which is to carry the vocal line forward without attracting too much attention, is put into practice, it seems appropriate to examine in detail one of Nielsen's best-known songs, 'Nu er Dagen fuld af Sang' with text by Jeppe Aakjær.

Nu er Dagen fuld af Sang,	Now the day is full of song,
og nu er Viben kommen,	And now arrives the peewit,
Bekkasinen Natten lang	While the snipe works all night long
haandterer Elskovstrommen.	His drum of love in free fit.
Plukke, plukke dugget Straa,	Picking, picking dewy straw
plukke, plukke Siv ved Aa	Picking, picking rush galore,
plukke, plukke Blomster.	Picking, picking flowers.[59]

One immediately striking feature is Nielsen's use of a particular rhythm that closely follows the rhythm and structure of the poem. The first two lines of the stanza have the same structure as the last two, each structured so that lines 1 and 3 of the Danish poem end with words consisting of a single stressed syllable; lines 2 and 4, on the other hand, end with a multi-syllabic word that ends unaccented. The dotted rhythm

MUSIC EX. 1. Nielsen, 'Nu er Dagen fuld af Sang' (Now the day is full of song) is probably known to most Danes from songbooks such as *Højskolesangbogen* (The Folk High School Songbook). However, it was composed for *A Score of Danish Songs* (1915) as a solo song with piano accompaniment, just like the other songs in the collection. The mixed interplay between singer and pianist shows the ideal of Nielsen and Laub on which the collection is based. In the opening bars, the performers are in unison and in octaves, but from the end of bar 2 the singer must (and without hesitation) continue with the upbeat to the next stanza. The first few bars are therefore not only a support for the singer, but also an effective common introductory line. For the rest of the song, the piano provides only occasional support for the voice, leaving the singer to perform the vocal part independently throughout. The passage of bars 5–12 corresponds to Laub's surviving proposal (CNS 196d) for a more polyphonic accompaniment, in which the piano creates a contrary motion to the voice. Nielsen's fair copy shows that he followed Laub's suggestion after transcribing the piece in ink, for he carefully erased the original music and wrote a new setting in the fair copy (CNS 196a). Yet he does not follow Laub's suggestion when it comes to changing the melody.

Med jævn og rolig Glæde
mf
Nu er Da - gen fuld af Sang, og nu er Vi - ben kom - men,
mf
5
Bek - ka-si - nen Nat - ten lang haand - te - rer El - skovs-trom - men.
9
p roligt
Pluk - ke, pluk - ke dug - get Straa, pluk - ke, pluk - ke Siv ved Aa
roligt
p
13
pluk - ke, pluk - ke Blom - - ster.
pp

at the beginning of each bar is a clever device that makes the song easy to learn, at least rhythmically. And where the rhythm is not in the voice, it is in the piano, as in bar 7. It is only in the final bars, where we have a two-syllable word, that this rhythm is omitted, so that the song can be phrased naturally. Moreover, the two notes that end 'Elskovstrommen' (The drum of love) are carefully prepared in the piano part on 'kommen' (arrived). Thus, there is a close and logical connection between the words and the music.

On closer inspection, the connection between the rhythm and the words is quite advanced. The words that would normally be emphasised ('Dagen' and 'Viben') are placed on the second beat, and with the melody starting on the first beat 'nu' and 'fuld' are musically accentuated. There are two levels of accentuation: 'nu' stressed by the music and 'Dag' stressed by the lyrics. All in all, this creates a special rhythm that could be compared to the sarabande, a Baroque dance.[60] It is also very similar to the rhythm of the Minuet from *Elverhøj*. The refrain, however, alters the time signature so that 'Plukke, plukke dugget Straa' is in duple time, which seems natural as the inflection of the language is strong and the accompaniment changes character. At the end, Nielsen composes a postlude that returns to triple time, so that the singer is introduced to the original rhythm before the next stanza begins.

If Nielsen and Laub work from an ideal in which the piano and vocal part have independent roles, the beginning of 'Now the day is full of song' is all the more effective. It is a powerful underlining of the opening motif that the piano and the voice occasionally proceed in unison and in octaves. For the rest of the song, the accompaniment alternates with and against the melody in a polyphonic structure, with the piano rhythmically complementing the vocal part. This is how the song appears in the printed version of *A Score of Danish Songs*; however, it is indeed the result of the compositional partnership between Nielsen and Laub. Nielsen had originally written a homophonic four-part accompaniment for the refrain, but he adopted Laub's idea of changing the opening bars into a more chamber-music-like piano structure.[61]

It was in this collaborative exchange of ideas that the songs were born. It was Laub who was the organiser and driving force behind the project. He liaised with the publisher, suggested the format and layout of the publication and was generally very interested in how the project was presented to the public. Laub saw each volume as a unified whole, with the songs arranged in a logical or aesthetically justified order.[62] The volumes were conceived by both composers. Although either Laub's or Nielsen's initials were added above each song, they are the result of a true collaboration. The route from idea to final result was not a circuitous one from pen to press. Both had an influence on the whole, and the songs can undoubtedly be described as a joint effort to create a new popular song tradition.

Chapter 25

THE THEATRE COMPOSER

Composing incidental music for the theatre was an activity that Nielsen pursued throughout his career. In all, he wrote music for twenty-two stage productions, from his very first attempt at the genre with a prelude and a final chorus for *En Aften paa Giske* (*An Evening at Giske*), which premiered at Dagmarteatret in January 1890, to the music for *Grundtvig-Paaske-Aften* (*Grundtvig Easter Evening*) at The Royal Theatre in the spring of 1931. The scale of his contributions ranges from a single song heard faintly in the background to one of his most ambitious scores, the music for *Aladdin*, which premiered in 1919.

A characteristic feature of the incidental music is that it was tied to specific productions, which, during Nielsen's lifetime, often received only a single series of performances at the theatre where they were premiered. The exceptions were *Hagbarth and Signe*, written in 1911 for the Open-Air Theatre at Dyrehaven north of Copenhagen and restaged in 1930; the incidental music for *Moderen* (*The Mother*) (1921) celebrating the reunification of southern Jutland with Denmark after the First World War, which went on an extensive provincial tour after the performances at The Royal Theatre; and Einar Christiansen's *Fædreland* (*Native Land*), which went to Aarhus after its performances at The Royal Theatre in 1916. Finally, *Aladdin*, with Nielsen's incidental music, was revived at the Deutsches Schauspielhaus in Hamburg in 1929.[1]

Nielsen's early incidental music up to 1901 is all associated with Dagmarteatret. A busy period followed from 1906, having resigned as a Royal Musician the previous year, composing for five theatre productions until 1909. From 1910, he took a keen interest in the Open-Air Theatre at Dyrehaven, and until 1921 he also composed major works for The Royal Theatre. After 1921 he wrote a single work for the Open-Air Theatre, a song for a play at Aarhus Teater and music for the tributes to Holberg, Hans Christian Andersen and Grundtvig.

A common feature of incidental and occasional music is that they are rarely performed again in their original form. On the other hand, there were ample opportunities for employing these songs and orchestral pieces in other contexts, and thus for them to take on a life of their own, independent of the play for which they were originally conceived. Nielsen consciously cultivated this possibility, and he often published songs from plays in small collections or individual prints in direct connection with the theatre performances. A number of his best-known songs have their origins as incidental music, as do some of Nielsen's most popular instrumental works, such as *Aladdin Suite* or *Taagen letter* (*The Fog is Lifting*) from *The Mother*.

There is no doubt that incidental music played an important role in Nielsen's development as a composer. In letters and interviews, he repeatedly stated that he had to experiment and try out new ideas in order to achieve the right effect with his incidental music. In other words, the task of creating music for specific dramatic situations helped stimulate his creativity and made him aware of musical effects that he could later use in other genres.

Music's Role in the Theatre

Incidental music is essentially dramatic music, composed with the stage in mind. Nielsen was therefore aware of how the music could support the play or have a dramatic effect in itself. He was able to draw on his extensive experience as a theatre musician, which probably began in Odense, but really took shape when he began to substitute in The Royal Orchestra in 1888. In addition, his years as Kapellmeister gave him an extensive knowledge of what worked in a theatre.

The genre of incidental music includes several categories that fulfil different functions in a play. A general distinction can be made between off-stage music – such as overtures, preludes and entr'actes, which create a particular atmosphere – and music that is part of the spoken dialogue. In the latter case, there is a distinction between background music and songs and music pieces that were incorporated into the drama as an actual presence of what the actors heard or performed themselves – for instance, songs sung on stage or music played at a wedding or other events that were part of the plot. The second type of music used in the dialogue scenes themselves is melodramatic music, where the actors recite between sections of music or with the music as a background; that is, the music acts as an underlay, creating a pervasive feeling or dramatically supporting or commenting on the action.[2]

Nielsen usually composed music for new plays, which he produced in collaboration with modern playwrights such as Holger Drachmann, Helge Rode and Otto Benzon. However, he also composed music for Adam Oehlenschläger's *Hagbarth and Signe*, *Sanct Hansaftenspil* (*Midsummer Eve Play*) and *Aladdin or The Wonderful Lamp*, all of which were written during the golden age of the nineteenth century. These plays were all reinterpretations of Romantic works, so there was already an established tradition – both dramatic and musical – to which the new production had to relate.

Often it was the genre and style of the play that determined how important a role the music played in the drama. Nielsen's incidental music ranges from a single song in *Atalanta* and *Kampene i Stefan Borgs Hjem* (*The Fights in Stefan Borg's House*) to extensive orchestral scores in works such as *Hr. Oluf han rider* – (*Sir Oluf He Rides* –), *Tove* and *Aladdin*. The plays of theatrical realism do not need a lot of music because they are meant to describe the real world, and too much music can be distracting. People do not spontaneously burst into song. When music is used, it is integrated into the plot in a meaningful way, as in Jeppe Aakjær's social-realist drama *Ulvens Søn* (*The Wolf's Son*), to which Nielsen contributed two songs. One of them, *Kommer I snart, I Husmænd!* (*Now is the Time, Smallholders!*) is sung by the main character, Goj, when in one scene he has to persuade a group of day labourers to leave the manor house where they are working.[3] It is a kind of workers' song, an extension of Goj's political speech, and serves to incite protest against social injustice – not only among the day labourers, but among the audience as well.

Yet some of the pieces Nielsen worked on were based on legends or tales, which required a very different approach to the music, so that it could truly unfold and help to create the illusion of being in another time and place, far away from the trivialities of everyday life. In general, when the drama is full of activity that cannot be expressed by spoken lines, the music must help. In such situations, it is often the stage directions rather than the lines that the composer has to deal with.

The Literary Stage

The theatre could be both an intellectual and a popular place. It was very much a platform for modern trends – yet also a place where people went to be entertained in an age before television. Each theatre had its own identity, and therefore the choice of venue was significant. Three institutions were particularly important to Nielsen: Dagmarteatret, The Royal Theatre and the Open-Air Theatre.

In the last decades of the nineteenth century, the theatre scene in Copenhagen underwent drastic changes. Firstly, there were major conflicts between the old romantic, idealising tradition and the new realism and naturalism. Herman Bang and Edvard Brandes both fought for a new type of dramatic play that offered a realistic and psychological portrayal rather than the glorified one that had been the norm until then.[4] Secondly, three private theatres had opened in the centre of Copenhagen – the Casino in 1848, Folketeatret in 1857 and Dagmarteatret in 1883 – creating a new situation in theatre life, enabling a larger audience to attend theatres and playwrights the opportunity to have their plays performed in theatres other than The Royal Theatre.[5]

Initially, private theatres were subject to a number of conditions determining which plays they could stage. However, the situation underwent a transformation with the passing of a new Theatre Act in the spring of 1889. Prior to this, The Royal Theatre held the exclusive right to stage serious plays, while private theatres were allowed to perform serious pieces only with permission of The Royal Theatre. The new law meant that the monopoly would no longer apply if the drama had not been performed by The Royal Theatre within the previous ten years. It was now possible to give The Royal Theatre stiff competition. It was during these years that Dagmarteatret in particular established itself as a cultured and important theatre.

Even before the new legislation, Dagmarteatret had begun to take on the role of a literary theatre, performing dramas by modern playwrights such as Bjørnstjerne Bjørnson, Henrik Ibsen and Edvard Brandes.[6] This was a different direction from the Casino and Folketeatret, which both mostly performed plays in popular genres such as comedy, operetta and variety. Dagmarteatret's real heyday, however, was between 1889 and 1909, when the law provided a freer framework for programming under the auspices of the prominent directors Christen Riis-Knudsen (1889–97) and Martinius Nielsen (1897–1909). Under the latter, Dagmarteatret became known as the 'guilty conscience' of The Royal Theatre, as it programmed a large number of pieces by contemporary Danish playwrights.[7]

An Evening at Giske

It was during this period that Nielsen wrote his earliest theatre music. He made his debut as a composer of incidental music on 15 January 1890, when a new production of the Norwegian playwright Andreas Munch's *An Evening at Giske* (CNW 3) premiered at Dagmarteatret. Nielsen composed a prelude and a final chorus for the play. Not much is known about the circumstances, but it seems reasonable to assume that he received the commission from his friend Vilhelm Rosenberg, who was the theatre's conductor.[8]

It was the first time that Nielsen had his music performed by a full orchestra. It is surprising that he does not mention this event, and that the music was not rediscovered and linked to its composer until twelve years after his death.[9] This may be due to the fact that the piece was not a great success, with only a few performances. It is also possible that, some years later, he found it difficult to fully appreciate the music, which is composed in a more grandiose and late-Romantic style than that with which he is usually associated. However, there are also features that clearly reveal the composer of the work, in particular his playful alternation between major and minor keys, creating abrupt and surprising shifts in the music.

It is easy to imagine that the Prelude, with its melancholy theme in a minor key, would have had a powerful effect as a sonic backdrop to Munck's drama, set in the Viking Age on Giske, a small island off the west coast of Norway. The Norwegian sound was particularly emphasised in the only review to mention the music. It stated: 'For the play, the Royal Musician Carl Nielsen had written a short prelude, the Norwegian character of which was apparently modelled on Grieg.'[10] It must have seemed natural to make this comparison, for a few years earlier Henrik Ibsen's play *Peer Gynt* had its Danish premiere at Dagmarteatret with Grieg's music.

In addition to *An Evening at Giske*, Nielsen composed music for four dramas performed at Dagmarteatret at the turn of the century: Drachmann's aforementioned *Snefrid* with its striking love music, Helge Rode's *The Fights in Stefan Borg's House*, Gustav Wied and Jens Petersen's *Atalanta* and Ludvig Holstein's *Tove*. Nielsen thus worked with some of the most prominent modern writers of the time. In particular, *The Fights in Stefan Borg's House* and *Tove* are, in their own way, expressions of trends that characterise the European currents at the turn of the century.

The Fights in Stefan Borg's House

The Fights in Stefan Borg's House from 1901 (CNW 5) was a contemporary drama in the style of Ibsen's plays, which were Helge Rode's role models. The plot revolves around Stefan Borg, a power-hungry man who cynically gets rid of three people in order to achieve his goal, his young stepdaughter, Helen.[11] Borg's ideal of masculinity is inspired by Nietzsche, and Rode's characterisation reflects the 1890s' cultivation of the individual rather than the sociable man, which was the focus of Georg Brandes's Modern Breakthrough.[12] On the other hand, the setting is realistic, as it had been in previous decades, in that the action takes place within the confines of the middle-class home. In other words, this is not a drama that requires extensive use of music, and Rode had no plans for music to create a mood or for the actors to suddenly break into song or dance. Rather, the music is limited to a single passage: at the beginning of Act Four, when Helen and her mother faintly hear someone singing 'Skal Blomsterne da visne' (Shall flowers, then, all wither) from an adjoining room.

Nielsen wrote the song a few weeks before the premiere on 7 February 1901. It was the first time that Nielsen and Rode had collaborated, and Rode was well aware that the task was not the most attractive for a composer who wanted his music to be promoted. In a printed copy of the play he wrote a dedication to Nielsen:

Thank you for the music! I told you it was an ungrateful task. On stage it turned out to be even more ungrateful than expected, as the song had to be sung from the theatre ceiling in order to work as the situation demanded. I hope you're not too upset about having made the beautiful melody. Yours HR.[13]

The desire to create a realistic effect in the drama took precedence over the ability to hear the music properly. It was not the music itself that was important, but the dramatic effect of hearing a beautiful melody in the distance. This is the kind of play where the drama clearly takes priority over the music. Nevertheless, Nielsen derived some benefit from the commission. The following year the song was printed as a music supplement in *Illustreret Tidende*, and it was subsequently included in his collection of songs, *Strophic Songs*.[14]

Tove

Ludvig Holstein's *Tove* (CNW 10) was published as a 'drame à lire' in 1898 and first performed as a play at Dagmarteatret in 1908. As a book it was subtitled *Et Kærlighedsdrama* (*A Love Drama*), while as a play it was entitled *Et Sommersagn i 5 Akter* (*A Summer Tale in Five Acts*). The play was based on the traditional ballad about Tove and King Volmer and was stylistically part of the Symbolism of the 1890s. Holstein was inspired by the French writer Maurice Maeterlinck, whose first symbolist drama, *La Princesse Madeleine* (1889), has a similar plot to *Tove*. Both plays depict the sad fate of a lovesick couple when the young woman is killed by a queen who disapproves of their relationship. In Maeterlinck's play, the queen is driven by the desire to marry her own daughter to the prince, while in the Danish ballad it is the queen's husband, King Volmer, who has fallen in love with the young Tove. Tove must therefore be disposed of.[15]

In Holstein's symbolist, traditional ballad universe – with its landscapes endowed with spirits and erotic undertones – music could play a much more important role than in Rode's cynical contemporary drama. The correspondence between Holstein and Nielsen also demonstrates a genuine collaboration between playwright and composer, with Nielsen's musical contributions influencing the play. In a letter to Nielsen a month and a half before the premiere, Holstein wrote:

> Bear with my lamp fever, and don't be angry with me for sending you what is still lacking – a tripping waltz behind the stage (Act 1), Mrs Boredom, and a little music in the final scene of Act 5. Whether the latter is necessary I leave to your best judgement. But shouldn't there be some music *before* the curtain rises??[16]

Holstein had a clear idea of how the music should be incorporated into the piece, but he also knew that Nielsen had a much better musical sense than he did. He had to trust Nielsen's judgement. This realisation is also evident when Holstein mentions in the letter the parts of the music that Nielsen had managed to finish: '… I think you have found the sound of my piece. Only "Song of the Larks" I haven't managed to get hold of, which is undoubtedly my fault.'[17] The song he is referring to is 'Det er Lærkernes Tid' (It is the time of the larks), performed in the play by a girls' choir.

Holstein's eagerness to have the music shows how important it is for this kind of play, which is imbued with much more activity than can be experienced on stage. For instance, at the end of Act One, the meeting between Tove and Volmer is accompanied by an Andante (No. 4) which, after six bars, marks a shift from the real world to a symbolic fairy-tale world that Volmer wants to show Tove. Specifically, the scene is about the king's seduction of Tove, although in the fairy tale it is described through erotic symbols, which the musical effects help to illustrate.

The scene is framed as a recitative, with actors reciting and music in the background. Tove begins by asking Volmer: 'Oh, Lord, why are you looking at me like that?' He replies that he is thinking of a fairy tale and asks her to follow him. During these first lines, the music is powerful and intense, with long notes in the French horn and tremolo in the upper strings, while the lower strings play pizzicato. In each bar, the horn and lower strings begin on the second beat rather than the first, challenging the listener's sense of time. Harmonically, the parts move stepwise in a downward motion without it being clear where the piece is going tonally. This gives the listener a sense of an uncertain situation awaiting a resolution.

Towards the end of the passage, the music begins to soften, and just before Volmer begins the tale with the words 'It was a lovely evening in May', the strings begin to play gentle background music in *p*, while the time signature changes from 4/4 to the lighter 3/4, and the andante is to be played *espressivo*. Paradoxically, it is only when the adventure begins that the music seems 'real': the music finally reaches a G major harmony, the key's root chord, and the strings play a distinct theme in contrast to the hesitant tremolo and pizzicato of the opening bars. The soft strings, interspersed with a brief flute motif, transport Tove – and the audience – into Volmer's sensuous fairytale world, where a bachelor meets a maiden just as the cherry blossoms are bursting forth.

In the death scene in Act Four, when the queen has locked Tove in the bathhouse, the music (No. 11) again helps to mark the transition to another world. At the beginning of the scene, when the curtain rises and Tove is kneeling in despair in the bathhouse, the music emphasises the eerie situation and Tove's fear. First there is the sound of dripping water in the form of violins playing a single note in pizzicato on the crotchets in 3/4 time. A few bars later, the lower strings begin to tremble softly in a tremolo, consisting of an interval of a fifth, and shortly afterwards the horns are introduced softly with a motif in thirds, alternating between short and long notes. After eleven bars, the music stops and Tove exclaims: 'Die! Die, so young and loved, it is cruel.'

When the music resumes, Tove has already started calling for her dead mother. The time signature has changed to 4/4 and the imitation of dripping water in the violins has stopped. The focus is no longer on the specific situation in the bathhouse, but on Tove's attempts to make contact with the other side. Tove talks of being afraid, while a short rhythmic pattern is heard repeatedly. It appears first in the winds and then in the strings, and the constant short rests in this context create a nervous and breathless feeling. Dynamically, the music is still subdued. But when Tove has fallen silent after calling her mother, there is a dramatic crescendo with tremolo in the strings and timpani rolls, leading to a passage with powerful swirling movements in the woodwinds and strings. The connection with the other side has been established.

After a few bars, her mother's voice is heard, 'You called, child', followed by a conversation between mother and daughter about salvation and the opening of the gates to eternity. Tove stretches out her arms up towards her mother, and then the scene goes dark and Tove lets out a final, piercing cry: 'Volmer!' Silence follows, and from now on Tove is neither seen nor heard on stage. However, the music begins to play again in powerful swirls, allowing the audience to imagine Tove accompanying her mother in death into the realm of eternity. Only when the music fades out with a diminuendo eight bars later, and Tove has spiritually travelled to another world, does the death scene end.

In these scenes, *Tove* stands as a clear example of the symbolist theatre production of the time, in which sound and music were often used to describe the connection to a symbolic world after death or outside the real world. Around 1908, when *Tove* was first performed at Dagmarteatret, realism as a dramatic style was beginning to look old-fashioned, while Symbolism was becoming the dominant trend among modern Scandinavian playwrights.[18]

The 1910s also saw the emergence of several other trends in theatre that departed from the style of realist naturalist style. At The Royal Theatre, Johannes Poulsen's imaginative productions represented a break with the realism of previous generations, and when the Open-Air Theatre was founded in 1910, it was part of an international movement against the intimate performances in small, enclosed theatres of the previous period.

Nielsen was involved in both trends, but before that, in 1906, he began a long series of commissions to write incidental music for plays at The Royal Theatre.

The Large Productions

Nielsen wrote incidental music for nine dramas staged at The Royal Theatre. The most extensive in terms of music were *Sir Oluf He Rides* – (1906) and *Aladdin or The Wonderful Lamp* (1919). With these pieces, Nielsen began to move into an area that had already been musically explored by famous Danish composers such as Niels W. Gade and Christian Frederik Emil Horneman. The works also showcase the large-scale theatre technology that was used for the productions at The Royal Theatre. Opening nights were major events in Copenhagen's cultural life, and there was often intrigue behind the scenes.

By the time Nielsen began composing incidental music for The Royal Theatre, he was already intimately familiar with the institution. Between 1889 and 1905, he was employed as second violinist in the orchestra and also acted as substitute Kapellmeister. His two operas, *Saul and David* and *Maskarade*, were premiered at the Theatre in 1902 and 1906 respectively. It was while Nielsen was putting the finishing touches to *Maskarade* that he was asked to compose the incidental music for Drachmann's melodrama about Sir Oluf.

Sir Oluf He Rides –

Drachmann's play *Sir Oluf He Rides –* (CNW 7) was inspired by the ballad 'Elveskud', which tells the story of Sir Oluf, who is seduced by an elf maiden on the way to his wedding. The legend of the elf maidens had already been interpreted in several famous works. The text for Gade's popular choral work *Elverskud* (*The Elf-King's Daughter*) (1854) was based on the two ballads 'Elveskud' and 'Elvehøj'. The latter was also the basis for Johan Ludvig Heiberg's play *Elverhøj* (*Elves' Hill*) with music by Friedrich Kuhlau (1828), which was the most frequently performed play at The Royal Theatre. Hans Christian Andersen had also written an interpretation in the form of the fairy tale *Elverhøi* (1845). In other words, it was a story that was well known and part of the national identity.

However, it was not only the old Danish ballads that inspired Drachmann. In letters to the censor of The Royal Theatre, Otto Borchsenius, Drachmann refers to Shakespeare as his 'great master and teacher',[19] and also notes that: 'You see, Borch, it's not only the old ballad of Sir Oluf that is being dramatised: no, it's the very "drama of the Danish summer night" that I've tried to bring to life on the stage.'[20] It is very likely that Drachmann imagined *Sir Oluf He Rides –* as a kind of a Danish counterpart to Shakespeare's famous *A Midsummer Night's Dream*.

Drachmann had originally asked Peter Erasmus Lange-Müller to write the music, but he had refused and suggested Nielsen instead, who eventually accepted the commission.[21] Nielsen and Drachmann had previously collaborated on the melodrama *Snefrid* and the *Cantata for the Inauguration of the Student Society Building*, and they knew each other as they both moved in the same cultural circles in Copenhagen. Drachmann had a reputation for being rather vain and self-absorbed, and Nielsen seems to have resented him. After attending a party at which Drachmann was present in 1897, Nielsen wrote in a letter to Gustav Wied: 'I don't like Drachmann; he doesn't seem to be a real man. This long spiral with a voice like a castrato.'[22]

The new melodrama was planned as part of the celebrations for Drachmann's sixtieth birthday on 9 October 1906. In April, Drachmann had personally approached the director of The Royal Theatre, Einar Christiansen, with the idea, and Nielsen joined the project at the end of May. Now began the hectic process of getting the work ready for the autumn birthday. Drachmann struggled to meet his deadlines, and Christiansen had to cut the text drastically, asking Nielsen to reduce the musical sections as well.[23]

Christiansen was the coordinator of the project, and in a letter to Nielsen in July 1906 he asked him to prioritise the sections of the music that were most important for the rehearsal of the play. Christiansen made a distinction between the sections of music that were relatively independent of the staging, and background music – the melodrama – that is closely linked to with the dramatic structure:

> If the play is to be performed 9 October, I must have two piano scores for the Theatre at the beginning of September – at least as far as all the melodramatic music is concerned. The songs and the introductory pieces to the Acts can wait.[24]

Nielsen took his work on the incidental music seriously, and six days later he wrote to his friend Henrik Knudsen: 'The project interests me, and if one could elevate the art [of incidental music] a little bit there would be no harm in that; most composers consider this kind of task from a kind of costume-maker's point of view.'[25] To complete the music and the fair copy, which was further delayed by changes to Drachmann's text, Nielsen had to involve both Knudsen and Julius Röntgen. It was not until 21 September – two and a half weeks before the premiere – that the orchestral material was completed.[26]

The music for *Sir Oluf He Rides* – consists of five preludes and twenty-three sections that occurs throughout the play. A small number of these are directly part of the action; for example, Sir Oluf and several other characters sing songs, and there is music in the wedding scene in the form of music for the organ, fanfares and party music. However, most of the music in the dialogue scenes is background music, and in these cases it is clear that the music has a very specific function: to accompany the supernatural elements of the play.

The use of music to emphasise supernatural phenomena in the theatre dates back to medieval religious drama. Since the Reformation, however, it has mainly been characters from pagan superstition who have been accompanied by music in plays.[27] This is also the case in *Sir Oluf He Rides* – which most often features what might be termed 'fairy music'. Mendelssohn's overture (1826) and incidental music (1842) to Shakespeare's *A Midsummer Night's Dream* provided a powerful model for this musical genre. Mendelssohn's fairy music is characterised by a fast tempo with woodwinds playing staccato and swirling, fluttering motifs in the strings that alternate between the instruments.[28]

When Nielsen was a member of The Royal Orchestra, *A Midsummer Night's Dream* was one of the most frequently performed pieces.[29] It is not certain that Niel-

MUSIC EX. 1. The opening of (a) Nielsen's fairy chorus 'Ud og ind – ind og ud' (Out and in – in and out) from *Hr. Oluf han rider* – (*Sir Oluf He Rides* –) is similar to the beginning of (b) Mendelssohn's Scherzo from *A Midsummer Night's Dream*, one of the pieces of music that helped create a model for fairy-tale music, with fast, staccato motifs in woodwinds and strings.

sen was consciously inspired by Mendelssohn's music for the play, but the style of the fairy music for *Sir Oluf He Rides* – suggests that it was common at the time to imagine the sound of the supernatural in this way. In Nielsen's work, the bright woodwinds in particular dominate the soundscape, but the strings also play an important role; as in Mendelssohn's work, they play mostly fast, flighty motifs with frequent use of staccato and pizzicato.

The Dance of the Elf Maidens (No. 15) stands out musically from the other supernatural sections of the melodrama. The thematic material is in the strings and the music is powerful and grandiose, involving much of the brass section. Part of the explanation may be that the elf dance was orchestrated by Röntgen, who, like Nielsen, stayed at the Fuglsang estate in the summer of 1906. For the dance itself, Nielsen reused his little piano piece 'Elf's Dance', and as he was short of time, he asked his friend for help.[30]

However, there may also be musical explanations for the difference in style. For one thing, this is dance music, which is more conducive than melodrama to the use of a full orchestra. It could also be argued that the nature and behaviour of the elf maidens is different from that of the elves and goblins who appear in other scenes with supernatural music. The effect of the supernatural is still maintained through the use of swirls and pizzicato, but the small whirling and fluttering movements that the fast woodwind motifs illustrated in other sections are replaced here by magnificent string motifs that match the sensual, dancing movements.

The elf music in particular has been criticised by several reviewers for failing to live up to the musical models for supernatural music. In *Dannebrog*, for example, it was said that 'Carl Nielsen's fairy kingdom is too heavy and substantial, and one thinks nostalgically of Kuhlau, Mendelssohn and Gade, who spontaneously created a fairy kingdom that one could touch and feel.'[31] According to the reviewer, the reason why Nielsen does not succeed in characterising the elf maidens is 'perhaps precisely because he wanted to create a completely new fairy-genre'.[32] In other words, the observation signals that the music was marking something new. What the reviewer was expecting in the scene was probably the airy sounds of the staccato woodwinds, as in Mendelssohn, or the bright, light motifs in woodwinds and strings accompanied by triangle, as in Gade's elf music for *Elverskud*.

A similar argument is made in *Berlingske Tidende*: '… one of the music's central points, the "Elf Dance", was only partially successful, the reason being that it can only be attributed to the composer's very pronounced concern not to emulate the examples of Mendelssohn's "A Midsummer Night's Dream" and Gade's "The Elf-King's Daughter"'.[33] Thus, as a composer, it was not easy to get away with creating a new musical fairy style.

The play's five preludes stand out in that they do not accompany the action, but rather set the mood while the curtain is down. They are scored for full orchestra and can therefore function as concert music in their own right. In the play's opening prelude, Nielsen uses a device also employed by Grieg in his famous piece *In the Hall of the Mountain King* from *Peer Gynt*: that is, to introduce a magical landscape by having the strings play a slow motif in pizzicato, giving the impression of small, cautious tiptoeing feet of goblins or elves. Nielsen also draws the listener's attention right from the outset by creating a bright pedal point in the oboes in the first twenty-two bars of the prelude.

In addition, some of the effects of the supernatural music are repeated in the preludes to acts in which something magical is about to happen. This is particularly true of the prelude to Act One, 'I Rosenlunden' (In the Rose Garden). It is framed by a light oboe motif consisting mainly of staccato semiquavers, occasionally supplemented by the piccolo flute. The motif is accompanied by staccato and pizzicato playing in the strings, adding to the lightness of the music.

In the music associated with the human characters, the soundscape is different. In the style of Mendelssohn's famous Wedding March from *A Midsummer Night's Dream*, in which the trumpet fanfares end in a festive march for the whole orchestra, Nielsen has composed the prelude to the wedding scene in *Sir Oluf He Rides* – as a powerful orchestral movement in march tempo with fanfare-like triplet motifs. Nielsen also introduces a very special instrument into the music that accompanies the songs or speeches of the humans in the action: the harp. Both Sir Oluf's and Helleliden's songs are accompanied by the harp and the wanderer's recitative at the beginning is accompanied by harp playing and a motif in the brass instruments. In addition to the harp's association with the past, when bards recited epic quatrains, it also functioned as an instrument capable of establishing contact with the supernatural, as when the wanderer in Act One summons the fairies with the sound of a few strokes on the harp. Throughout the history of music, the harp has been symbolically associated with the otherworldly, either as an image of transfiguration in the sense of the transition from the earthly to the heavenly, or as a symbol of the state attained in the afterlife.[34]

In the time preceding the premiere, expectations were high for Drachmann's new play. As one critic observed, it was a very special evening in Copenhagen's cultural life:

> Sitting there, from floor to ceiling, filling every seat in the large room, is the Copenhagen first-night audience, fully mobilised. They are dressed for the occasion, in a festive mood, expectant. What is expected is not an honest, entertaining evening at the Theatre. It is an *event*. It is something that can fit into a historic moment.[35]

The extreme expectations probably also contributed to the disappointment of the performance. Although most critics agreed that Nielsen's music was successful, the drama itself was not well received. According to the critics, Drachmann was too much of a lyricist and not enough of a dramatist.[36] After nine performances at The Royal Theatre, the play was removed from the programme with no plans to stage it again. Later, there was talk of staging it at the new Open-Air Theatre in Dyrehaven, but this did not materialise either.[37] This must have upset Nielsen, who had invested a great

ILL. 1. *Politiken*'s drawing from the premiere of *Sir Oluf He Rides* – on 9 October 1906. The illustration shows that people were interested not only in what was happening on stage, but also in what took place among the audience. In addition to a review of the play, *Politiken* gave a full description of what happened before, during and after the performance, and of the prominent guests who were seen in the parterre.[38]

deal of effort into the music. It would be more than a decade before he would again be involved in writing music for one of the national theatre's major productions.

Aladdin or The Wonderful Lamp

Nielsen's incidental music for *Aladdin or The Wonderful Lamp* (CNW 17) is only surpassed in length by the two operas.[39] When he worked on this project in 1918-19, he had already received great acclaim for his Third and Fourth symphonies and was thus more culturally recognised than when he wrote his earlier incidental music. This probably also meant that he had the courage to protest publicly when the framework for the incidental music to *Aladdin* did not turn out the way he wanted.

Nielsen began composing the music for *Aladdin* in July 1918. In September he was told that the musicians were not to be placed in the orchestra pit but backstage. This worried him as the music would be more subdued and therefore less effective. In addition, the music was cut and there were several changes in the way it was incorporated into the play that he did not like. Firstly, he was unhappy that the order of the dances in the wedding scene had been reversed and that one of the dances had been removed altogether. Secondly, he was also outraged that the final dance had been called 'The Dance of Love' without his permission, and that the music had been accompanied by erotic choreography. He had intended the piece to be a universal hymn to love and goodness.[40]

Shortly before the premiere in February 1919, Nielsen almost withdrew the incidental music in protest at the way it was being treated in the production. He was saved, however, by having his name removed from the programme. In the days after the premiere, he also had a press release issued in all the major Copenhagen newspapers to draw attention to the situation:

> Announcements about the production of 'Aladdin' have stated that the music was composed by me. Due to the position and limitations of the orchestra and the way in which the production has generally used my compositions, I therefore disclaim any artistic responsibility for the musical accompaniment to 'Aladdin'.[41]

To understand what Nielsen was trying to do with the incidental music to *Aladdin*, we need to broaden our perspective. The decades around 1900 were a time when major composers such as Grieg, Debussy and Sibelius were producing extensive symphonic music for the theatre.[42] There was no question of looking at the music 'from a kind of costume-maker's point of view', as Nielsen had earlier remarked.[43] Several composers had indeed become famous for their incidental music, which was regarded as fully cast musical works. Nielsen's followers had hoped that the music for *Aladdin* would make him famous. They believed it had the potential to have the same significance for Nielsen as the music for *Peer Gynt* had for Grieg.⁴⁴ And while that may not have been the case in the long run, the music was a huge success at the time – especially outside the walls of the theatre.

The story of Aladdin was originally taken from the Arabian Nights, but the new piece was based on Adam Oehlenschläger's 1805 version, one of the most important works of Danish Romanticism. As with *Sir Oluf He Rides –*, this was a story that was important to the national self-perception and had familiar musical models. In 1839 an abridged version of the story was produced for the Theatre, with music by Friedrich Kuhlau, Peter Ferdinand Funck and Gade. This version was last performed at The Royal Theatre in 1902. Horneman also produced an opera based on *Aladdin*, which was premiered in 1888 and staged in a revised form in 1902–4. As a Royal Musician, Nielsen must have been involved in the performance of both works.⁴⁵

It was the actor and director Johannes Poulsen who instigated a new theatrical version of Oehlenschläger's work in 1917. A few years earlier, his production of Hofmannsthal's *Det gamle Spil om Enhver* (Everyman) had marked a new artistic trend in the Theatre, a trend he formulated in a letter to Borchsenius in connection with the play. He expressed the view that 'the realistic-naturalistic period with the Brandes brothers is now *over* … We, who are young now, will and must and shall bring forth a *new* and an *old*, large-scale, passionate and fantastic, realistic Romanticism.'⁴⁶

In Poulsen's imaginative staging, it was natural to include musical elements that could contribute to the festivities. For example, it was crucial to the effect of the festive procession in front of the palace that it be accompanied by a grand march played by brass and percussion instruments (No. 11). For the scene of Aladdin and Gulnare's wedding, Nielsen composed a series of short dances with different expressions – from the chromatically coloured 'Chinese Dance' (No. 14), in which the agile oboe is accompanied by intense, staccato afterbeats in the violas, to the powerful, sharp dissonances in the 'Prisoners' Dance' (No. 15) and the gently rocking strings in the 'Hindu Dance' (No. 16).⁴⁷

The most creative element from Nielsen's hand is in the scene 'A Beautiful Square in Ispahan' (No. 7), where he experimented with finding musical instruments that could create the colourful experience of standing in a marketplace with different sounds coming from all sides. His solution was to divide the large orchestra into four smaller ones, each playing in a displaced manner in different time signatures and keys. The first orchestra consisted of woodwinds, horns and a triangle; the second of strings; the third of horns, trumpets and four untuned timpani, with the timpanists singing at the same time; and the fourth of piccolo flutes and a gong.⁴⁸

For the performance, Nielsen wrote detailed instructions for the conductor, including how to create the effect of the special acoustic conditions in a market square: '… the four different groups now play on separately, without worrying about each

ILL. 2. A stage picture from the performance of *Aladdin* gives an impression of the opulent and grandiose style with which Johannes Poulsen renewed The Royal Theatre's repertoire when he was appointed stage director in 1917. The picture also illustrates the problem that there was no room for the musicians on stage, so they had to be placed under the grand staircase where they could hardly be heard.

other. The conductor signals one orchestra, then another, to play louder or softer, just as if the wind in the square were emphasising one group or the other.'[49] For Nielsen, it was not just a question of composing the right music for the situation, but also of playing with the sounds and dynamics of the instruments to create just the right effect. In this light, it is easier to understand why he found it so difficult to accept that the musicians should be hidden behind the stage.

As in *Sir Oluf He Rides* –, the incidental music for *Aladdin* played an important role when something supernatural happened on stage. In the latter, this happens when the Genie of the Ring or the Genie of the Lamp appears. Poulsen had some ideas about how to achieve the right effect: the Genie of the Ring always appeared after a gust of wind and therefore had to be accompanied by 'music that imitated the wind'.[50] The Genie of the Lamp appeared after thunder, and in this case Poulsen simply noted that there should be music.[51] Nielsen composed a rather distinctive musical motif, alternating between dramatic crescendos in timpani and brass and a powerful unison chorus of bass singers representing the Genie of the Lamp.

THE THEATRE COMPOSER   463

MUSIC EX. 2. The musical motif in *Aladdin* that accompanies the Genie of the Lamp in the musical numbers 6, 9, 10 and 21.

In order to include as much of Oehlenschläger's drama as possible, Poulsen divided the play into two evenings. It was a lot of work to change all the set pieces for each section, so the first one was performed several times in a row, starting on 15 February, while the second section was performed the following week.[52] A remark in *Social-Demokraten* the day after the premiere suggests that Nielsen was right in his accusations: 'Unfortunately, the music was almost inaudible – see the following statement by the composer, Carl Nielsen.'[53] But things apparently improved. When Nielsen had attended the first section a few times, he wrote to his friend Wilhelm Stenhammar with relief:

> The production has turned into a splendid film which all Copenhagen has to see; but there's not much that's artistic about it. The music can hardly be heard because Poulsen forgot to make space for the orchestra. Now the orchestra spends most of the evening under a stairway. I had to make a public protest and so on (big row!!) so that now it's a little better, and for the second 'evening' it sounds good.[54]

The performance was praised by several reviewers, but also criticised for deviating too much from Oehlenschläger's version.[55] There was also disagreement over whether the grandiose staging was appropriate or not. Sven Lange of *Politiken* wrote enthusiastically after the first section: 'Such a sumptuous splendour of colour in costumes and décors has hardly ever been seen in a Copenhagen theatre before, and all the details came together to form a convincing picture of oriental life.'[56] For the reviewer, the play was a sensation and a demonstration of the Theatre's ability to create scenic effects. *Nationaltidende*'s Valdemar Vedel was less impressed, concluding his critique: 'There was, of course, wild applause for all the poetic images. But, as I said, in the end one was somewhat saturated by all these Eastern "shimmering flowers without fragrance".'[57]

After fifteen performances of both sections, the piece was taken off the bill to make room for other productions. But the music soon took on a life of its own outside the Theatre. After a few years, Nielsen arranged an *Aladdin Suite*, which was performed numerous times in Denmark and abroad during the 1920s, including in Stockholm, Dresden and Paris.[58] The suite consists of seven movements from the play, but in a different order suitable for a concert suite: first the 'Oriental Festive March', followed by 'Aladdin's Dream' and the 'Dance of the Morning Mists', and then four distinctive dances placed two by two on either side of the 'Square in Ispahan'.[59]

Despite the problems surrounding the premiere, the music for *Aladdin* was ultimately a success, and the overwhelming number of performances of the orchestral suite, or excerpts from it, during Nielsen's lifetime show that it became one of his most popular works. This is underlined by the fact that a significant number of the performances took place at the summer concerts in the Tivoli Gardens, which had a wide appeal. The fate of the incidental music reflects the duality that characterised Nielsen's relationship with The Royal Theatre. On the one hand, the Theatre was one of the most important venues for his activities and provided the setting for considerable success. On the other hand, it was a place where he often felt he had to compromise his artistic ambitions.

Nielsen's protests about the treatment of the incidental music to *Aladdin* should probably also be seen in the light of his involvement in another theatre project in the 1910s: the Open-Air Theatre. Here he was the main musical driving force, with the authority to decide how best to use the music in the productions.

The Open-Air Theatre

In the early decades of the twentieth century, open-air theatre experienced a worldwide renaissance. Four Greek-inspired open-air theatres were built in California, while in Europe it was mainly the so-called 'natural theatres' that were built for open-air productions in those years.[60] Unlike the sculptural Greek theatres, natural ones were designed to blend the stage and audience into the surrounding landscape, usually forests or mountains. Nature therefore became an important part of the theatrical experience, providing backdrop and soundscape. The most famous of these was the open-air theatre in the German mountain town of Thale, founded in 1903, and few years later, a natural theatre opened in the south of France, followed by another one in Hertenstein near Lucerne in Switzerland in 1909.[61] When the Open-Air Theatre in Dyrehaven, north of Copenhagen, opened on 4 June 1910, it was part of a wider international trend at the time.

Among its founders were the actor Adam Poulsen and the journalist Henrik Cavling. Both had attended outdoor theatrical plays staged at the new natural theatres abroad and had an idea of what an open-air theatre could look like.[62] The decision to establish the new theatre was made at a picnic in Dyrehaven in October 1909, which Nielsen attended.[63] The importance of the event was emphasised the following year in the theatre committee's report:

> None of those present will forget the atmosphere and the enthusiasm with which the decision to build the Open-Air Theatre was immediately taken. Here, in the most beautiful part of the woods, where the beeches stand in their most manly strength, where the ancient oaks are a living memory of a bygone age, where the acoustics finally allow the human voice to sound with particular eloquence – here was to be built the new temple of the art of acting, here was to be revived the great national drama.[64]

The report shows that the Open-Air Theatre was a project that sought renewal through both ancient and national Romantic models. The circle met several times after the picnic, and at the inaugural meeting on 5 February Nielsen was appointed member of the theatrical committee. The extensive preparations for the opening of the theatre began.[65]

Hagbarth and Signe

The Open-Air Theatre's first production was Oehlenschläger's ballad-inspired tragedy *Hagbarth and Signe* from 1815, with incidental music by Nielsen (CNW 12). The play was premiered in 1910. The plot is about Hagbarth, the son of the Norwegian king. He falls in love with Signe, the daughter of the Danish king, whose brothers Hagbarth has killed in battle. Hagbarth is captured and Signe promises to follow him to his death. On his way to the scaffold, he hangs his cloak from a tree as his last wish, and when Signe sees it, she takes poison and sets fire to the maiden's cage in which she is imprisoned. She is saved from the flames, but in the meantime Hagbarth has killed himself, and Signe, having poisoned herself, eventually dies next to his body.[66]

The production made full use of the different skills of the theatre's committee members. These included Vilhelm Andersen, who wrote the introduction to the programme, and Poulsen, who played the male lead.[67] Jens Ferdinand Willumsen designed the fifteen-metre-wide stage, which was framed by two large wooden fantasy birds, known as 'Willumsen's ravens'. During the performances, a fire burned from the bowls placed on the ravens' heads.[68]

Cavling, editor of *Politiken*, took care of the marketing and published a series of articles about the theatre in the spring of 1910. Readers were told of an impromptu rehearsal on 12 May, attended by several well-known cultural figures, including 'on horseback, below the stage, the composer Kapellmeister Carl Nielsen and his young daughter, who, tall and slender on horseback in her two-part skirt and with her sunny yellow hair under her black velvet jockey cap, looked like spring itself.'[69]

As the only musical professional on the committee, it seemed natural that Nielsen should compose the music for *Hagbarth and Signe*. Part of his task was to find out how to ensure the best possible musical experience in the special acoustic conditions of the Open-Air Theatre. He spoke about this in an interview in *Politiken* the day before the premiere:

> The whole thing is an experiment of great musical interest to me, and from an acoustic point of view it is of the utmost importance to experience how to deal with music in this particular way. I have been to Ulvedalene [in Dyrehaven] several times. The other day the students sang for me from the stage, and even though I went to the back seats, I could hear the finest *piano* and every word of the lyrics that evening. But it is very different from day to day how it sounds out there and it is very strange to study the conditions.[70]

As later with *Aladdin*, *Hagbarth and Signe* prompted Nielsen to experiment not only with musical issues but also with sound and acoustics. The conditions in Dyrehaven and the character of the piece meant that he eventually decided to compose for wind instruments alone, with a single movement for harp. There were nine movements in all: first a short introduction, followed by four mood-setting pieces of music, then a series of movements and songs that were part of the plot, and finally some more mood-setting music to support the tragic events at the end.[71] In the interview, Nielsen explains how he had approached the task:

> I did it in a style I had never worked with before. I tried to give the whole thing a certain distant ballad-like melancholy and a sound of the poetry of the natural harmonics. The lurs (four) are used in the introduction and also in the funeral music at the end of the final act, where they suddenly appear. Otherwise, the music is made with as few means as possible.[72]

The lur was an important national symbol, and around the turn of the century it became the subject of renewed interest. In the 1890s, the music historian Angul

ILL. 3. *Dannebrog* published an evocative drawing on 5 June 1910, showing two of the four lur players performing the overture to *Hagbarth and Signe*.

Ouverturen. Lurblæserne ved Willumsens Ravnefigur. I Baggrunden Fangetaarnet.

Hammerich had organised lectures and concerts on the Bronze Age instrument, which he saw as a symbol of the beginning of Danish music history.[73] At the same time, the painter Lorenz Frølich had the idea of erecting a column with a figure of a lur player on the Copenhagen Town Hall Square, and Siegfried Wagner's monument *The Lur Players* was placed on the site in 1914. Nielsen's use of the lur was thus part of a wider trend, and the critics seem to have found the instrument entirely appropriate in this context. Carl Behrens wrote of his impressions after the premiere:

> It is not the individual outdoor performances at Dyrehaven that will be remembered, but the overall effect: the deep sound of the lurs echoing through the woods announcing that the Norwegian Vikings have landed, the roar of battle that comes from between the trees, and the battle that ensues as one giant after another bites the dust.[74]

The premiere was a great success, and many critics agreed with Behrens that it was the sensory impressions rather than the drama and acting that made the performance a success. Julius Clausen, for example, notes that the picturesque elements and the musical are the theatre's two most important features, and that 'art and nature are fused into one'.[75] Nielsen made the same observation in his diary:

> The premiere of 'H. and S.' went very well. It is especially the natural setting of the whole thing makes the effect. It's impossible to do without the music here. It's the visual and auditory effects that matter, rather than the content.[76]

ILL. 4. The premiere of *Hagbarth and Signe* in Dyrehaven on 4 June 1910 was a box-office success. Nielsen's daughter Irmelin had attended the dress rehearsal the day before and described the performance and her impressions in detail in a letter to her sister: '… then they began to play and it was quite marvellous, nothing has ever touched me in such a way; it seemed so harmonious and magnificent with that Oehlenschlägerian pathos between the broad green crowns and the dark trunks. The stage was covered with brown, withered leaves, and here and there a broken branch and a little green thorn … Miss Brincken acted Signe, and I thought she did it so warmly and beautifully that one could not help crying; and then, at the end of the play, they brought torches, and Signe's maiden cage was in flames; one did not see the flames, only vapour and light shining on the dark green leaves, for it was already quite dark at that time, and then, at the end, Hagbarth's and Signe's bodies were carried away to a lurid sound. The music in general sounded brilliant. It was an enormous success.'[77]

In other words, the Open-Air Theatre was a form in which music was not subordinate to the drama, but was essential to the experience.

After the inaugural season, Nielsen continued to be involved in the theatre's activities as a composer, organiser and conductor. He was particularly involved in the theatre's innovations.[78] In 1913 he wrote seven short pieces of music for Oehlenschläger's *Midsummer Eve Play*, which was divided into two parts, one preceding and one following Heiberg's vaudeville *Recensenten og Dyret* (*The Reviewer and the*

Animal). Both plays are set in Dyrehaven, serving as the theme of 'Dyrehavsspil'.[79] Two years later, Nielsen was the artistic director for the two new productions of the season, Johan Peter Emilius Hartmann's opera *Liden Kirsten* and Gade's choral work *The Elf-King's Daughter*. He introduced a completely new concept to the theatre's audiences: open-air opera. It was a great triumph for Nielsen, and one reviewer remarked after the premiere that 'one is tempted to say that the music is the very life of the Open-Air Theatre, and that it is precisely through the sound that the atmosphere is created which some of the earlier plays had difficulty in bringing to life'.[80] Finally, in 1925, he wrote the score for Harald Bergstedt's open-air play *Ebbe Skammelsen*, specially composed for the stage in Dyrehaven.[81]

For Nielsen, composing incidental music was not merely a peripheral activity; it was a central part of his production, which he took seriously and which gave him musical ideas and impulses that he could apply in other contexts. This included his experiments with four orchestras playing independently of each other, which he drew on when writing his Sixth Symphony. In the world of theatre, music is always linked to what is happening on stage and must have an immediate effect on the audience. This sense of immediacy is also conveyed by Nielsen when he composes in other genres, giving the feeling that the music is communicating directly with the listener. His lifelong association with the theatre, both as a musician and conductor, gave him a wealth of experience and a good feel for what worked on stage and what effect a particular piece of music would have.

Music for the theatre is inherently linked to the specific context in which it is performed. Yet much of Nielsen's incidental music, whether in the form of songs or orchestral pieces, achieved great popularity independently of the performances for which it was written. In this way, the music – often with a slight reworking or adaptation – continued to live on as part of the familiar repertoire of Danish songs or as concert music. In many cases it is no longer common knowledge that a song comes from a play, while in other cases, such as in the *Aladdin Suite*, it is precisely the making of the movements into independent works that keeps the consciousness of the great works of theatre alive. Without the theatre and its need for music, the incidental music would not have existed at all, and the challenge of composing music to meet new and untried musical expectations was a great source of inspiration for Nielsen.

Chapter 26

COMPOSER OF HYMNS

In the spring of 1914, Nielsen was deeply absorbed in composing hymns. He sat at the grand piano in his home on Vodroffsvej in Copenhagen and played his new tunes. Perhaps he also hummed along, trying to get a feel for the impressions the music gave. It seems that working with the hymns was therapeutic for Nielsen. Anne Marie was away for the first few months of 1914, and at the same time he was experiencing major problems at The Royal Theatre, where the conductor Frederik Rung had died and Georg Høeberg had been appointed as his successor against Nielsen's wishes. Composing hymns did not require much writing, but was mainly a matter of conceiving the music and playing with the details; it allowed him to put aside his quarrels at the Theatre. He wrote revealingly to Anne Marie: 'I've been so occupied with my hymns and it's been good to feel love for something completely different'.[1]

The invitation to compose hymns had come from the Grundtvigian free-church minister Valdemar Brücker, perhaps when Nielsen visited him in 1911. Nielsen did not set to work immediately, but he must have found the idea tempting, for in the course of a few months in early 1914 he composed some fifty-two tunes. Brücker was surprised to hear that Nielsen had made a good start, as he had assumed that Nielsen had given up on the project.[2] Most of the songs were published in 1919 in the collection *Salmer og aandelige Sange. Halvhundred nye Melodier for Hjem, Kirke og Skole* (*Hymns and Spiritual Songs. Fifty New Melodies for Homes, Church and School*) (CNW 153–201). More than half of them were set to texts by Grundtvig.

Although a hymn tune generally had to be short and clear, Nielsen's attention was focused on creating an intimate connection between words and music. He wrote to Anne Marie about his tune for Grundtvig's hymn 'Under Korset stod med Smerte' (Neath the cross of the departed):

> I really think the melody has turned out well and suits the anguished words. But hymn composition is somehow tricky. The thing is that one's subjective feelings have to be suppressed to some extent, and the choice of notes is really limited.[3]

It was a task he took seriously, and he did not shy away from problems, for composing hymns was a source of fulfilment for him. Since Anne Marie had left after a short visit home, he had composed three hymns, of which two are among the very best, and one is probably the most beautiful I have yet composed. I'm so happy with this melody, and I'm playing it over occasionally for myself; it's so natural that you will probably think when you first hear it that you've known it from your tenderest infancy. Both the melody and its harmonies came straight away, entirely of themselves.[4]

The tune in question was 'Forunderligt at sige' (How wonderful to ponder) – a tune that was also used to Hans Adolph Brorson's original text, 'Mit Hjerte altid vanker'. Anne Marie sensed that the hymns were very important to him and she looked forward to hearing them when she returned home.[5]

Nielsen did not work on the hymn tunes just for his own pleasure or for Brücker's sake. He was deeply concerned that the tunes should be useful, for he knew that there was a lack of good tunes for many hymn texts. At the same time, he was interested in solving the challenges that hymn singing had been facing for decades. Here Thomas Laub and the organist Paul Hellmuth influenced his views, but as an independent observer of hymnody Nielsen made his own choices in the setting of the melodies.

Grundtvigian Hymn Singing

From 1887 to 1929 Valdemar Brücker was minister of the Grundtvigian Free Church in the village of Aagaard, north of Kolding.[6] From 1899 to 1922 he was also headmaster of the Aagaard Folk High School, which had been founded in 1863.[7] Brücker belonged to the Grundtvigian left wing and was at the time known for his liberal approach to the Bible. His strong opinions often brought him into conflict with people in his own circle. He was also interested in Darwinism and saw these ideas as a possible framework for interpreting the Bible.[8] *Højskolebladet,* the journal of the folk high schools, often devoted space to Brücker's contributions, which had a significant influence on the journal's rapidly growing number of subscribers in the decades around 1900.[9]

In 1909 Brücker argued in *Højskolebladet* for the establishment of a state college based on Grundtvig's ideas of a popular educational institution for the general public.[10] The college should attract the best young people who did not wish to pursue an academic career, but who would be given a position of trust in society. One particular argument that provoked a strong reaction was Brücker's realisation that 'a man can be an excellent popular educator even if he is not a Christian'. The most important thing was that teachers were competent and could inspire enthusiasm for their subject. The idea for Brücker was that Christianity would still be the predominant religion, but it was essential that the pupils were given the opportunity to form an independent judgement without coercion.[11]

Brücker was a well-known figure in the Kolding area, and Nielsen met him during one of his many visits to Anne Marie's birthplace. A mutual friend was Elise Konstantin-Hansen, a painter who taught drawing and art history at Aagaard Folk High School.[12] She frequented the same artistic circles as Anne Marie, and they also met privately. Among them was Marie Møller, who had worked as a domestic servant for Rev. Jakob Knudsen and later for Brücker before moving to Copenhagen and joining the Nielsen family in 1897.

Hymn singing occupied an important place in the environment of Aagaard electoral congregation and the folk high school. From the very beginning, the Grundtvigian congregations throughout the country preferred to use Grundtvig's *Fest-Psalmer* (Festive Hymns) as their hymnal, rather than the authorised one, *Salmebog til Kirke og Huus-Andagt*. In the second half of the nineteenth century, several supplements to the festive hymns were published on private initiative; the selection was growing, and it was impractical for them to be scattered in too many different anthologies. Realising that some of the original festive hymns were not being used, Brücker and Knudsen had the idea of creating a new, complete hymnal. Its title was *Salmebog for Kirke og Hjem* (Hymnal for Church and Home), which differed only in spelling from the new authorised *Psalmebog for Kirke og Hjem*, published in 1899 and based on a draft from 1885. Brücker and Knudsen's hymnal was used in several congregations in South Jutland.[13]

Many of these hymns were sung to existing but incompatible melodies. Brücker found this unsatisfactory, and his request to Nielsen was therefore very specific: to compose music for those texts that did not have their own tunes. At first it seemed to be a purely private project, and Brücker was pleased that Nielsen was able to send him the music gradually as the tunes were completed. He even had a prioritised list of the songs he felt were 'most urgently needed: nos. 76, 110, 4, 99, 30, 93';[14] the hymns are 'Utallige Blomster paa Jorderig gro' (Though countless the flowers), 'Maria sad paa Hø og Straa' (The Virgin Mary sat in hay), 'Fred med dig' (Peace with you), 'Guds Engle i Flok!' (God's angels, unite), 'Korsets Tegn og Korsets Ord' (The sign and the word of cross) and the above-mentioned 'How wonderful to ponder'. The numbers corresponded to Brücker's own hymnal, and soon Nielsen had composed all six tunes.

Disputes over Hymn Singing

Nielsen adopted Brücker's argument that there was a need for new tunes. But he also linked the task to discussions that had been going on in church circles for decades. It was felt that church singing was poor and that congregations needed to be trained to sing better. This was not a new viewpoint, as Johann Abraham Peter Schulz had already suggested it in 1790 when he became the king's advisor on musical matters.[15] In the nineteenth century, the song commissioners Rudolph Bay and Andreas Peter Berggreen had tried to improve the singing skills of the population. Bay saw the problem as a pedagogical challenge and advocated a reorganisation of the way in which singing was taught.[16] Berggreen set himself the goal of eliminating the secular tunes, while more recently Thomas Laub attempted to improve the singing in churches by reusing the Reformation melodies in their original form.[17] In a letter to Julius Röntgen, Nielsen made himself the spokesman for the cause for which many before him had fought:

> Our hymn singing in this country has declined and is getting worse. If I could play even a small part in bringing it back, I would be delighted.[18]

Nielsen had never worked as a church musician, and he rarely attended church, to judge from the few mentions in his diaries and letters.[19] Nevertheless, he had contact with one of the battlegrounds in Copenhagen where passions ran high in the decades around 1900 when church singing was discussed: Holmens Kirke, where Laub was the organist. Laub's closest colleague was the cantor Viggo Bielefeldt, who in 1900 had published a new chorale book with tunes for all the hymns in the latest authorised hymnal, *Psalmebog for Kirke og Hjem*. Bielefeldt was a highly respected singer and teacher who had been a much sought-after soloist in Copenhagen concert life since the 1870s. As a cantor, he had been a colleague of Niels W. Gade until the latter's death in 1890, and Nielsen knew Bielefeldt since he was head of the obligatory course in choral singing classes at the Academy of Music.

Laub had worked for decades to improve church singing, and when he was appointed without notice as Gade's successor at Holmens Kirke in 1891, it caused consternation.[20] Laub's idea was to change the hymn tunes and, in the case of the Reformation tunes, to try to restore them to their original form. In 1887 Laub set out his objections to the hymn singing in *Om Kirkesangen* (On Hymn Singing), advocating a revival of 'the old tunes of the Reformation'. The aim was to 'purify [the tunes] from the "improvements" of an … un-churchly time'.[21] By the end of the seventeenth century the practice had developed that all notes in a hymn tune should be of equal length, which was further established as the ideal for hymn singing in Niels Schiørring's chorale book *Kirkemelodierne* (*The Hymn Tunes*) (1781).[22] For Laub, the melodies had thus lost 'what little life was still left in them', and since then the chorale books had favoured what Laub systematically began to call 'the rigid chorale'.[23] To accommodate the modernised hymn texts used in churches, Laub had to rework the tunes he found in the historical sources.[24] He published his first attempts in 1888 in the monophonic anthology *80 rytmiske Koraler* (*Eighty Rhythmic Chorales*).[25]

Another of Laub's objections to the church singing at the time was the use of tunes in the *romance* style. Tunes that either were taken from secular songs or used effects from art songs had no place in the church, he believed. In Laub's view, the tunes had to be kept in such a style that the music did not obscure the message. A central aspect of his criticism was mood: 'Without mood, a service is indeed nothing, but mood must not be made the object of deliberate presentation, otherwise you get idolatry, self-contemplation, instead of worship'.[26] Therefore, music should not contribute to 'evoking or producing moods'.[27]

Laub's attempts were not without controversy. In 1900, when Bielefeldt published his chorale book to accompany the recently published *Psalmebog for Kirke og Hjem*, he attempted to reconcile conflicting considerations and showed himself to be a diplomat.[28] He tried to include the tunes that were in use, so that the book would contain 'the central or the average number of tunes that make up the church hymns of our time'.[29] He also included tunes that he personally did not like, in the hope that church singing throughout the country would 'gain in firmness and uniformity'.[30] On the whole, Bielefeldt continued the established tradition of notating the chorales with note values of equal length, although he had also included versions of tunes in their 'older rhythm'.[31] He reproduced these tunes in a rhythmic form similar to the versions favoured by Laub. Bielefeldt thus recognised the value of the fact that congregations throughout the country had begun to follow Laub's song reform.

Laub was convinced that when the congregation became acquainted with the restored old tunes, they would 'receive them with joy because they recognise the spirit in them'.[32] Sometimes, however, persistent work was required, for which Laub resorted to a rather robust pedagogy. Every Wednesday evening he rehearsed the old hymns with the congregation in Holmens Kirke.[33] Laub suggested that the tunes should be practised with the lead singer beating the pulse rhythmically – not in the 'modern way with the conductor's gestures in the air, but with very audible strokes (with a ruler against the edge of a table or something similar)'.[34] Nielsen's approach to the dissemination of new tunes differed from Laub's. For him, it was up to the congregations themselves to adopt the songs.

New Tunes

In connection with the publication of *Hymns and Spiritual Songs* in 1919, Nielsen wrote a preface that was ultimately not used. He emphasised that 'it is quite unfruitful to try to reform by coercion'.[35] The hymns should be cultivated in the congregation and 'nourished by the simplest means'. When the tunes left Nielsen's study, it was left to others to transform them into 'live singing'. He believed that his task as a composer was fundamentally different from that of a church musician. Unlike Laub and Bielefeldt, who as assistants to the congregation had to encourage the singing, Nielsen's task was to compose the tunes. Nevertheless, Nielsen stressed in his preface that his intention with the collection was to contribute to 'improve the singing of hymns', which had often made his 'soul tremble'. He was concerned with the use of the tunes, emphasising how the settings could be applied in different contexts, performed 'on organ, harmonium, piano or by a four-part mixed choir'.[36]

The unpublished preface and the late date of publication suggest that Nielsen was hesitant about how to handle the publication in relation to Laub. In 1924 he explained to his publisher, Asger Wilhelm Hansen, that Laub had suggested to him that he should publish his hymns with Laub's, but that 'since I didn't want to, he asked me to wait until his had appeared before publishing mine'.[37] He writes openly that he did this 'out of friendship for Laub' and because they had worked so well together on the two volumes of *En Snes danske Viser* (*A Score of Danish Songs*). Laub's collection of hymns, *Dansk Kirkesang. Gamle og nye Melodier* (*Danish Church Singing. Old and New Melodies*) was released in 1918 and as a songbook including the hymn tunes as well as a chorale book. Nielsen must have realised that he would be compared to Laub in terms of hymnody if he and Laub published their hymns in the same volume. There are no direct references to Laub in Nielsen's preface of 4 December 1919. Yet indirectly he acknowledges Laub's thinking when he writes that the melodies are based on a detailed study of church singing after the Reformation and that he has tried to make the structure 'as clear and simple as possible – from a certain point of view even uninteresting'. The music should not obscure the text, and at the same time he implicitly refers to Brücker's original impulse when he writes that 'Danish composers should try to recapture Grundtvig in new notes'.[38]

A few days later Nielsen wrote a statement on 'Thomas Laub's significance for church singing and folksong in this country', which he sent to Laub. It has the character of a public statement, although – like the preface – it was not published. The statement fully acknowledges Laub and his great importance to church singing, and emphasises how he had observed Laub and his work ever since the dispute over Laub's appointment in 1891. It is not known whether the statement was intended for use in connection with the publication of *Hymns and Spiritual Songs*, which took place around the turn of the year.[39]

Nielsen was anxious that the publication should not be seen as a rejection of Laub, not least because he had realised in advance that Laub could not accept the style in which Nielsen had composed the hymns. Laub wrote to Nielsen in 1917, referring to a discussion they had had two years earlier about Nielsen's hymns. According to Laub, neither of them had changed their views on the matter during the two years, which he did not find strange in view of their fundamental beliefs:

> The reason why you, in my opinion, have missed the target, comes, I think, from the *path* by which you have come to the task. A hymn composer must be *a child of*

the house [*barn af huset*], by which I don't mean that he must have a patented faith – his faith may be small, may even be wrong – but he must be at home in it, i.e. he must have lived with community song from his childhood on and must know it from its *use*. It must be his religious means of expression; he must know and love all its treasures – by which I mean *not least* its hymn-*poems* – and must lament its shortcomings. His goal must be to repair its faults by means of using its treasures.[40]

For Laub, writing hymn tunes was literally a sermon, a religious practice that had to be based on both historical knowledge and the experience of practical church life. He denied Nielsen this ability, but the letter also shows that they were equally stubborn. That the discussion was known in the circle around Laub and Nielsen is evident from the fact that Nielsen involved Erik Dalberg – married to Nielsen's former student Nancy Dalberg – and allowed him to comment on Laub's letter. In letters to Thorvald Aagaard, Laub also refers to the question of 'being a child of the house'.[41] In this light, Nielsen could not publish a preface referring to his years of study of church hymns, nor would it make sense to publish an endorsement of Laub. The hymns, however, had to be published, and Nielsen hoped that his tunes would help to raise the standard.

It was hardly as if Nielsen had not studied the question in depth. He was well aware that it was not easy to reform hymn singing, and he also recognised the division of labour in the church. Indeed, organists and choirmasters did not have a great deal of influence in the churches. In connection with the paper 'Aanden i Musik' (The Essence in Music), which he presented several times in 1917 and 1918, he gave examples of what he deemed to be exemplary and bad hymn tunes, and on a sheet of music he had jotted down the old tunes for two of the hymns for which he had composed new ones. In an unusually vehement formulation, he had written on the same piece of paper: 'The priests decide the tunes. It is a hellish torture to be an organist in a Christian church.'[42] It is easy to imagine how Laub spent Sunday after Sunday in Holmens Kirke, playing Romantic and secular tunes to the hymns dictated by Rev. Fenger, who preferred to be spared for Laub's reforms.[43] Thus, when a minister such as Brücker finally approached Nielsen and asked for new tunes, there was a chance that they would be used.

Early in his friendship with Laub, Nielsen realised that they had different points of view. Laub had been composing melodies since the late 1880s, and of *Salmemelodier i Kirkestil* (*Hymn Tunes in Church Style*) (1902), which included seven of Laub's melodies, Nielsen wrote: '[Your hymns] have long delighted me more than any other music by new composers.'[44] But he also had a different focus from Laub. Nielsen was concerned only with the musical content of the hymns and did not comment on the texts or whether the hymns were suitable for church singing. He got straight to the point, writing to Laub: 'There are some harmonies I don't like, and strangely enough it's precisely those harmonies that make me waver with the tonal aspect.'[45] The criticism went both ways.

Even when Laub's *Forspil og Melodier. Forsøg i Kirkestil* (*Preludes and Melodies. Attempts in Church Style*) was published in 1909, Nielsen was a critical reader. This prompted Laub to write a letter outlining the main principles on which his church style was based. His starting point was that 'one must take the style as it is in the existing works'.[46] Particularly in the hymns and in what he called simple chorale arrangements, that is, four-part harmonisations, he followed the style strictly. Nielsen must have questioned Laub's approach to composing the hymns, for Laub replied that he had 'followed the rule' by imitating a style that he had found in the old works. The argument was so obvious to him that Nielsen's question puzzled him; Laub replied: 'You seem to have doubts, I don't understand why – the cases you mention are completely normal in style'.[47] For Laub the answer was self-evident, but for Nielsen, it was a matter for the composer having to decide.

To Compose Hymns ...

Nielsen was deliberate in his approach to the composition of hymn tunes. Influenced by Bielefeldt's pragmatic view of hymnody and Laub's reform ideas, Nielsen chose a third path. He distanced himself from the Romantic tradition, but at the same time sought an alternative to Laub's line. Nielsen thus became an independent interpreter of the church song. However, he did not carry out this task alone. As a matter of course, he showed his drafts to his family, friends and colleagues. He was interested in their opinions to test whether he had found the optimal solution, and he was willing to take advice. Particularly important was his relationship with the organist Paul Hellmuth, who must be regarded as Nielsen's co-composer on several of the hymns.

While working on his chorales in 1914, Nielsen discussed the details of the harmonisation with Hellmuth. In 1907 Hellmuth took lessons from Nielsen, from 1909 he was organist at Skt. Thomas Kirke and from 1914 he was a popular theory teacher in his own right.[48] He lived nearby in Frederiksberg and he and Nielsen kept in touch. Hellmuth had also taken lessons from Laub and acted as a substitute for him at Holmens Kirke. He was thus a key figure in the community and had the practical experience that Nielsen lacked. Hellmuth was an ideal advisor.

It may seem surprising that Nielsen involved Hellmuth in the preparation of the hymn 'How wonderful to ponder', for after the first draft Nielsen wrote to Anne Marie that both 'the melody and its harmonies came straight away, entirely of themselves'.[49] That he nevertheless asked Hellmuth for advice shows the depth and quality of their collaboration. Nielsen had already composed a four-part chorale and was interested to hear how Hellmuth would harmonise the melody. In order not to in-

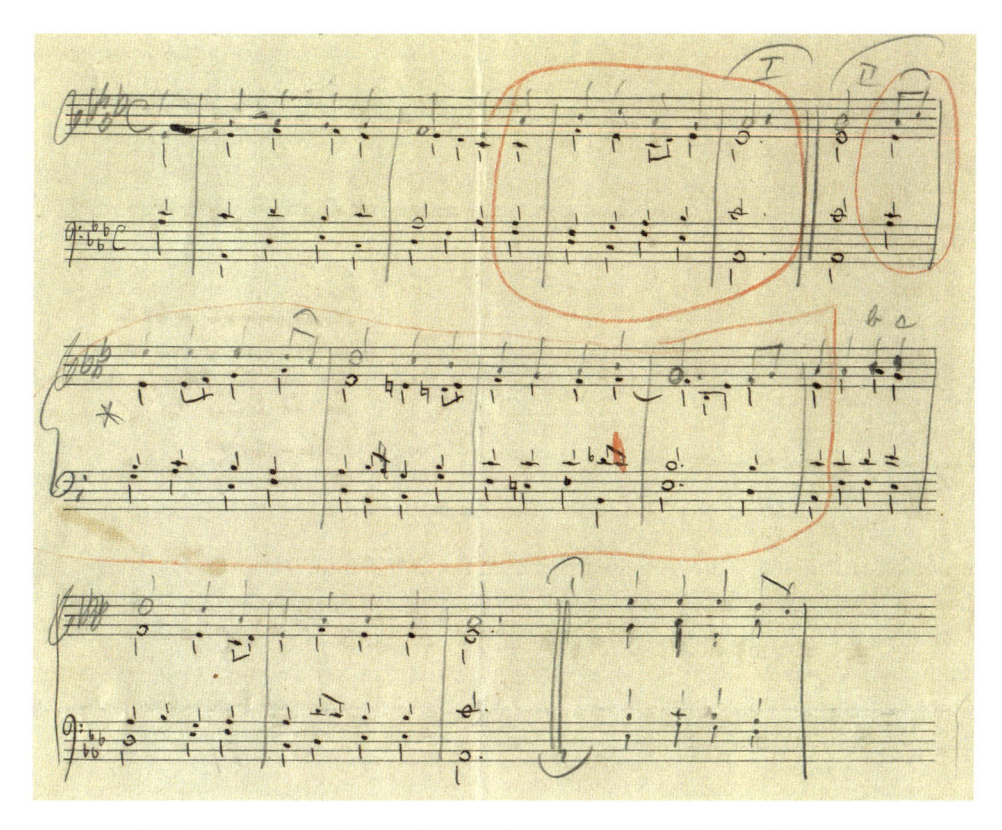

ILL. 1. Nielsen had first jotted down his own harmonisation of 'Forunderligt at sige' (How wonderful to ponder) (CNS 217c) with a reference to the number in Brücker's hymnal. He then notated the tune in pencil on a new sheet of music, shown above (CNS 145b), which Hellmuth employed to draft his proposal for a four-part harmonisation in ink. The red markings indicate which parts of the proposal Nielsen considered suitable for inclusion in the final version, with the exception of the two cancelled quavers in bars 6 and 7. The last bar after the double bar line is Nielsen's attempt to provide an alternative to Hellmuth's harmonisation of bar 5; however, Nielsen ultimately rejected his own proposal.

fluence Hellmuth beforehand, Nielsen only gave him the melody, hiding his own harmonisation from him. Hellmuth came up with a completely different solution from Nielsen's, and now he had something to work with. It was Nielsen's decision as to what the chorale would become, and the version that was finally printed is a combination of both proposals.

Nielsen chose his own path. What Nielsen and Hellmuth aimed for together was a modal harmonisation of the hymn tunes, but unlike Laub, it was not to achieve complete conformity with the style of the old hymns. Laub's principle was to give priority to chords in the root position, that is, the fundamental note of the harmony

MUSIC EX. 1. Nielsen's tune to Caspar Johannes Boye's hymn text 'Dybt hælder Aaret i sin Gang' (Well on the wane the passing year) contains final cadences on the Danish 'Lund' and '-stund'. In the transition between the other lines of the stanza, Nielsen chooses a dissonant ninth chord on 'Gang', where the note F of the preceding chord is retained, forming a dissonance that is not resolved until the first word of the next line, while a first inverted chord is placed on 'Sang'. The lines are thus linked in pairs.

placed in the bass, and to make limited use of dissonances.[50] He followed this ideal, which is clearly reflected in the settings in his above-mentioned book of chorales, *Dansk Kirkesang* (1918). By comparison, Nielsen was freer in his harmonisations. This is particularly evident in the transitions between the phrases of a tune, for Nielsen would use first inverted chords (that is, chords with the third in the bass), where, unlike chords in root position, there is no harmonic weight to give a concluding effect.[51] Sometimes he would use a dissonance on the last chord of a line of a stanza, just at the point where the singer would take a breath before continuing. The dissonance is thus left unresolved, contrary to the rule observed in the older works.[52] For Nielsen, this was a simple and effective way of ensuring coherence, as he sought to create a musical connection across the transitions between phrases. Some phrases would end with the usual cadence, marking the end of a textual unit. Other phrases would try to counteract a pause and attempt to link two lines. In other words, first inverted chords and dissonances became Nielsen's means of structuring his tunes and creating intimate connections between text and music.

With his four-part chorales, Nielsen sought to provide a solution to the problems that had plagued church singing. In this context, Hellmuth's experience as a church organist was important in determining whether the chorales would work as intended.

The way the settings are framed shows that Nielsen used the harmonisations to create a sense of momentum. Too many chords in root position created too much weight, and rests during the phrase divided the melodic lines into small fractions. By prioritising coherence between the phrases and between stanzas, the music is given direction and a natural sense of being in constant motion.

... and Spiritual Songs

Hymns were more than just about church singing, as they were also used in domestic and educational contexts. The statement that hymns should be used 'in church, school and home' is evidenced in the first Danish, royally authorised hymnbook of 1569.[53] It was a fundamental Lutheran idea that hymns were a constant element in the life of every Christian at all stages of life and in all social contexts. Since the Reformation, hymn writers had consciously recognised that some hymns were closely associated with worship, while others were intended for private devotion.

Throughout the nineteenth century, hymnals made a distinction between hymns and spiritual songs in an attempt to provide guidance on the use of songs within or outside the auspices of the church.[54] Brücker combined these types in his *Salmebog for Kirke og Hjem* (1892), while the authorised *Psalmebog for Kirke og Hjem* (1899) has a section at the end entitled 'Spiritual Songs'. These are texts that the Hymnal Commission did not want to exclude, but also did not want to put on an equal footing with the hymns.[55]

In terms of content, there is often a difference between hymns and spiritual songs. Grundtvig's 'Der sad en Fisker saa tankefuld' (There sat a fisherman deep in thought) tells of Peter's fishing and his call to discipleship. Grundtvig called it 'Aandelig Fiskervise' (Spiritual Fisherman's Song).[56] These are biblical-historical songs in which the interpretation is central, surrounded by accounts of Christian life. From a theological point of view, spiritual songs were therefore seen as the counterpart of the 'hymn', which in a narrow definition had to be confessional and preaching.[57]

In 1919 Nielsen wrote a tune to Grundtvig's text about the fisherman and had it published in the journal *Højskolebladet*.[58] As a spiritual song, it was linked to the ideals of popular education of the folk high school movement. Today it is one of the few of Nielsen's spiritual songs to be included in the hymnal. Similarly, Nielsen chose to publish 'The Virgin Mary sat in hay' in the same journal before publishing it in *Hymns and Spiritual Songs*.[59] It was a Bible story in sound: Christian teaching in the form of song.

The title *Hymns and Spiritual Songs* reflects Nielsen's view that religious songs had different purposes. The title indicates that the publication included both songs for the church and devotional songs that could be used outside the church. The sub-

MARIE SAD PAA HØ OG STRAA

CARL NIELSEN.

Ma-ri-e sad paa Hø og Straa i Stald ved Nat-te-ti-de, i Krybben Je-sus-bar-net laa i Svøb med Fag-ter bli-de.

En Engel kom med Krone paa,
den var af Guld det røde,
deri som mange Sole smaa
man funkle saa og gløde;

Som Bøg i Skov han raged op,
som Pilen rank til Skue,
hans Vinger gik fra Taa til Top,
som Lyn i Lyn, i Bue!

Saadan med et den Engel stod
for Hyrderne i Vange,
da gyste det i deres Blod,
de blev saa grumme bange!

Vær aldrig bange, sagde han,
og I maa ikke græde!
Jeg kommer fra det skjulte Land
med Julesang og Glæde!

Jeg kommer fra Guds Paradis
med Sang til Folkemunde:
Guds Søn er født paa Barnevis
til Frelser fra det onde.

Det Jesusbarn, i Krybben lagt,
i Bethlehem I finde,
han vil med eder gaa i Pagt,
saa Himmerig I vinde!

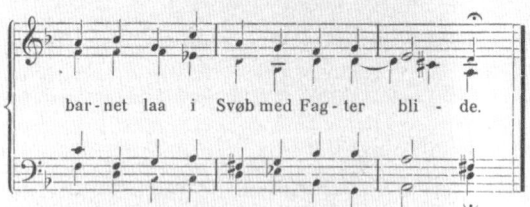

Og der kom Barneengle smaa,
som Stjernerne saa mange,
med Kroner og med Vinger paa,
med klare Julesange!

Til Dagskær og til Morgengry
de sang paa Hyrdemaalet,
de sang i Kor, de sang i Sky,
af Himmelglans omstraalet.

»Nu Ære være Himlens Gud,
som troner i det høje!
Paa Jorden Fred! med Julebud
sig Mennesker fornøje!«

Halleluja, Halleluja
for Frelseren den spæde!
Saa lød det alle Vegne fra
til evig Juleglæde!

De takked Gud af Hjertensgrund
og det med Fryd og Gammen,
det gør med dem i allen Stund
vi Kristne allesammen.

N. F. S. GRUNDTVIG.

ILL. 2. Nielsen's melody to Grundtvig's 'Marie sad paa Hø og Straa' (The Virgin Mary sat in hay) was first published in the Grundtvigian *Højskolebladet*, before it was included in *Hymns and Spiritual Songs*. In the journal, the more popular form of the name 'Marie' is used for the mother of Jesus, which emphasises its character as a religious song. In *Hymns and Spiritual Songs* her name is changed to the common form used in church for the Virgin Mary, 'Maria'.

title suggests that Nielsen was fully aware of the theological minefield he was entering. By calling the songs 'for home, church and school' he had reversed the usual order, so that the church was not the first priority. He wanted to position himself as an innovator in popular religious song, irrespective of where the performance took place. Yet we are left with a collection of hymns that was not really a success. Only a few central melodies have survived and become part of the hymnal tradition: 'How wonderful to ponder' (CNW 165), 'God's angels, unite' (CNW 170), 'Guds Fred er mer end Englevagt' (God's peace is more than angel guard) (CNW 171), 'Min Jesus, lad mit Hjerte faa' (My Jesus, let my heart obtain) (CNW 184) and 'Nu Sol i Øst oprinder mild' (Now sun arises in the East) (CNW 186), all of which are included in the authorised chorale book of 2003.

When the collection was issued, it passed almost without comment in the daily press, and Laub's criticism of Nielsen for not being a '*child of the house*' was allowed to stand as a fact, even though it was not a criticism that was published at the time.[60] Perhaps Nielsen was not a child of the house in the sense that Laub required of a hymn composer. He was, however, as Jørgen I. Jensen put it, a child of 'a wider stream of tradition, a deep and broad religious-Christian wave in Danish history, of which the church is a part, but at that time not the only expression.'[61]

Perhaps the fact that the criticism is still referred to is more an expression of the authority that Laub and his followers enjoyed in later church music circles than of the quality of Nielsen's hymns. Nielsen never attended a folk high school and was never a teacher, apart from the few lectures he gave at folk high schools. Nevertheless, no one would argue that his songs for the folk high school lacked relevance and quality, or that they were not suitable for the context in which they were sung. On the contrary, they have become the norm that others must try to live up to.

Chapter 27

THE AESTHETIC-SENSORY

When Nielsen tries to explain what aesthetic sense is in his essay 'Ord, Musik og Programmusik' (Words, Music and Programme Music) (1909), he uses a metaphor. It is the sense of immediate receptive impressions, of being able to recognise aesthetic qualities *before* a thing is imagined. It is the sensory impression itself that he associates with the aesthetic:

> One morning, the farmer walks across his freshly harrowed field. He bends down, picks up a strangely shaped natural stone from the ground, turns it in his hand, feels it and examines it from all sides. Then he walks on, taking his find with him to add to the other *strange* stones in his garden.[1]

It is the shape of the stone itself, its peculiarity, that Nielsen emphasises: it is 'mærkelig' (literally: strange). However, he uses the word 'mærkelig' in an older sense, meaning 'remarkable' or 'striking' – the stone has the quality of being noticed. And he emphasises that it is precisely 'the original sense of plasticity': plasticity as sculptural form that is at work when one does not immediately imagine that it resembles some kind of animal:

> This simple fact, that the thing is not supposed to mean or represent anything at all, but yet attracts our attention and wonder simply by the truthful, organic play of forms and lines, are primordial formations in what we call the life of our soul.[2]

Nielsen also gives another example to explain what he is trying to say. If you see a yellow flag over blue water and are startled by the experience of the colour combination, he writes, it is a sure sign that 'you are filled with the pure, original basic sense, that is, of the desire of the eye'.[3] Again, it is the immediate experience of the juxtaposition of colours that is at play. He describes this as the opposite of recognising and being moved by the red and white of the Danish flag abroad. The latter he considers as a sentimental, conceptual association without any particular aesthetic value.

That Nielsen himself was susceptible to such aesthetic experiences is evident at several points in his *My Childhood*. Even when he recalls an experience from many years ago, the immediacy of the sensory impressions shines through in his language. He describes how their pig was stabbed and slaughtered:

> The blood squirted at first on to Mother's hands, but she at once caught the thick jet in the pail. … Turning to go back to the cottage, I saw that the sun had risen. It was blood-red, and my eyes dazzled with all the red I had seen.[4]

Nielsen's concept of the aesthetic draws on older notions of aesthetics from the eighteenth century, which focused on sensory experience and the immediate sense of pleasure, while the nineteenth-century concept was dominated by a work-oriented approach that emphasised beauty.[5] Although these older notions do not stand alone in Nielsen's work, they form a deep layer of his thinking that he maintained throughout his life.

Similarly, in the introduction to *My Childhood*, he points to the core of his self-understanding as a human being and as an artist when he says that 'poetic talent, I imagine, is fundamentally the faculty, the gift, of distinctive observation and perception'.[6] It is an ability, he says, that the child has and that is only rarely preserved in adults. It is found in great poets, thinkers, naturalists and artists. He thus relegates the true artistic gift to the faculty of observation. The ability to be receptive to strong and immediate sensory impressions and to retain them in memory is the prerequisite for the creation of art.

To have this ability does not per se make one an artist; rather, it is a prerequisite for becoming an artist. Without the ability to absorb impressions, there is nothing to express. The next step, producing a work of art, is a craft that can be learned, according to Nielsen. The aesthetic sense is a *primordial* faculty, and the artist is the one who preserves its originality.[7]

Nielsen is one of those who retain the spontaneous fascination with sound of his childhood. The older he got, the more explicitly he referred to the sensuous experience of sound as something that preceded the experience or creation of music. In some of his diary entries from 1923, he explains how he is inspired by the immediate, sensuous pleasure of experiencing sound: 'Everything has music in it: a grain of sand, the rustling of a newspaper, cannon-fire etc.' – and he enjoys and notices the sounds: 'Observe all the sounds we hear in the course of our work. Here I'm sitting with my pen and writing. What variety …'.[8] He absorbs impressions that he can use later.

To create music is to mould such sensory impressions into one's own aesthetic expression. However, the purpose of creating art is not to express oneself, but to create something that can give other people an aesthetic experience. What is important, then, is that the music can make an impression on others, can create a sensory experience for the listener. In the same way, music – as when Nielsen himself listens to the sounds around him – must attract attention and provide a sensory experience. The nature of music is 'sound, life and movement, which break silence into pieces',[9] and the task of music is to do this 'in such a way that it arouses the attention, wonder and enthusiasm of other people'.[10]

With such formulations, Nielsen echoes another premise of a pre-Romantic conception of aesthetics, that is, that music must attract the listener's attention in order to be perceived. This idea is a key to understanding late eighteenth-century music. At a time when there were no concert halls and a concert culture that demanded silence and concentration even before the music began, the music itself had to arouse and hold the listener's attention. It had to begin in a manner that made the audience listen attentively, and it had to continue in such a way that they would not become bored or distracted. The many technical instructions of the time for composing were tools for creating variety, surprise and thought-provoking wonder, mixed in a good balance with the joy of repetition.[11]

Although composition was no longer practised in the same way in Nielsen's day, he was still concerned that the prerequisite for music was sounds that attracted attention. This approach is also an essential quality of good musicianship, something that Nielsen, as a performing musician, had in his bones: Nielsen knew that it was the musician's job to capture and hold the listener's attention – whether at a concert, at a ball or when the regiment played in the town square. The musician must communicate with the person using or listening to the music.

In this context, aesthetics can be defined as a sense of immediate sensual pleasure or experience that is not yet linked to a concept or a specific idea. And this is precisely what Nielsen emphasises as the true nature of music, that it cannot be put into a concept or say anything concrete.[12] Music is in a place where, when it is entirely itself, it gives access to an aesthetic, sensuous experience without having to be conceptualised beforehand. It is the effect of the artistic means, their clashes, their proportions, their interaction and their overall effect that ultimately constitute a work. And it is the listener's receptivity to sensory impressions that makes possible the communication of which the musician is the transmitter.

Chapter 28

'MUSIC *IS* LIFE'

The work that best represents Nielsen's vitalist conception of music is his Fourth Symphony, *The Inextinguishable* (1916). The title itself refers to the fundamental force that underlies all life, including not only human life, but also that in nature and the regenerative power of all nature. The life force is the fundamental urge to live that fills nature and defies destruction. Every time a living being withers, dies or is destroyed, new life is born. Not only is Nielsen inspired by this fundamental idea, he also believes that expressing it is the most important and appropriate function of music.

The symphony shows how Nielsen's concept of Vitalism entered a new phase around the start of the First World War. As already mentioned, at the beginning of the century he had cultivated an understanding of the vital as an expression of the positive and life-affirming elements in both life and art, as expressed, for example in Symphony No. 3, *Sinfonia espansiva*. Around 1914 the concept was redefined to reflect life in its very broadest sense – that is, in all its facets, including all its positive and negative aspects. Vitalism becomes an all-encompassing concept because life is a unified force that permeates everything.

In a sense, the idea of writing music to express the great cycle of life and death was present in Nielsen from his youth and remained a central part of his worldview until his death. This idea was already in play when, in Berlin in 1890, he conceived of a symphony based on the 'Freethinkers' idea' and entitled 'From earth thou art come, to earth thou shalt return'.[1] He found the material suitable for a musical form in which the music begins in silence and darkness, before rising to the highest joy of life and finally sinking into darkness to eternal rest. On the one hand, the freethinkers' idea is present in the non-transcendent: we have only one life, and when it is over, nothing more happens. The third part of the Danish funeral ritual, 'and from dust thou shalt rise again', is not included. On the other hand, the concept is expressed in that man is nature, a biological creature. When people are buried, they become black humus, the nutrient-rich layer of soil from which new life can spring.

It must be stressed, however, that there is a crucial qualitative difference in the way this idea was formulated in the 1890s and at the beginning of the new century compared with the period after 1914. Nielsen's new and all-encompassing idea of life, and of music as an expression of life, is much broader than the early version. In 1890, he envisioned a simple arc shape, akin in many ways to his description of the sun's passage across the sky in the *Helios Overture* of 1903. Similarly, in the context of his Third Symphony, Nielsen clearly focused on the life-affirming elements in statements formulated before 1914. It was only in later texts that all the movements of the symphony were included in a universal vitalist reading, revealing that it was in fact a new understanding that led Nielsen, while working on his Fourth Symphony, to arrive at his central formulation: 'music *is* life'.[2]

In 1916, Nielsen presented the European public with a symphony in which all his experience as a human being and a composer was brought to the fore.[3] Both the conception and the shaping of *The Inextinguishable* (CNW 28) is in many ways a synthesis of everything he had done up to that point. It is in this context that the idea of music as life is strongly emphasised by the use of italics twice in the programme for the first performance:

> The composer, in using the title 'The Inextinguishable', has attempted to suggest in a single word what only music itself has the power to express fully: the elementary will to life. Faced with a task such as this, that is, to express life abstractly … there and only there is music at home in its primal region, at ease in its element, simply because by being only itself, it has performed its task. For it *is* life there, where the others only represent and write about life. Life is indomitable and inextinguishable; the struggle, the wrestling, the generation and the wasting away go on today as yesterday, tomorrow as today, and everything returns. Once more: music *is* life, and like it inextinguishable.[4]

The range and depth of Nielsen's formulations in 1916 are very different from earlier, and one can even see how, in the period after the first performance, Nielsen continued to reflect further on his new symphony and sharpen his formulations even more. By 1920, in a letter to Julius Röntgen quoted earlier, the description has taken on almost apocalyptic qualities, and the power of the life force seems even stronger as a result:

> The music is supposed to give expression to the most elementary forces as manifested between people, animals and even plants. We might say: if the whole world was destroyed by fire, flood, volcanoes etc., and all living things were destroyed and dead, then Nature would still begin again to beget new life, and to assert itself with the strongest and finest powers that are to be found in the material itself. Soon plants would begin to form, and the coupling and screeching of birds would be heard and seen, along with people's aspirations and desires.[5]

There are truly primal forces at work here. Humans are part of nature, as are plants and birds, and the urge to create new life, to procreate and multiply, is shared by all.

The force is nature's and its power cannot be extinguished. It is thus a symphony that seeks to express the idea of an all-embracing Vitalism.

But the quote also contains a key to how Nielsen thinks it can be expressed musically. The creative force by which 'Nature would still begin again to beget new life' is explained by the phrase, 'to assert itself with the strongest and finest powers that are to be found in the material itself'. Nielsen's use of these words is very close to the kind of formulation he employs when he wants to explain how music develops organically from the forces that lie like a seed in a theme or a motif. Here, in the musical material itself, there is a parallel to nature's ability to germinate and grow according to its own innate dispositions. This is why Nielsen, in his programme note of 1916, can state emphatically that music does not represent or depict life, but it '*is* life' because it has fulfilled its task 'simply … by being only itself'.[6] Music is like life. It is itself an unfolding of life, and therefore expresses life in the moment when it is most itself: it is music.

This, however, requires an understanding of what Nielsen thinks music is when it is most itself. We need to return to his idea of organic development, introduced in Chapter 21. Nielsen saw the rules of musical development as a kind of natural law, an inherent part of the musical material, which the composer had to follow. A musical motif should be regarded as a seed, the development of which the composer should bring to fruition. This idea is rooted in nineteenth-century musical thought, where it is used as a metaphor for thematic work and as an image of musical forms resulting from the logical unfolding and shaping of musical elements. But something crucial had happened in the meantime. Whereas in the nineteenth century it was taken for granted that in general music was based on the traditional types of forms and rules of composition, which could be questioned but not overturned, by the beginning of the twentieth century organicity had acquired such a high status that it was able to override the hitherto valid rules. Organicity, understood as the inner musical coherence of the structure, became the supreme commandment that could obscure other received rules.[7]

Nielsen's definition of organism as coherence is a juxtaposition of the two concepts, 'organism – coherence', by which he links the world of nature and that of music.[8] The quote is from a letter to Ture Rangström in 1920, written the day after the abovementioned letter to Röntgen, and reinforces the view that the definition must be understood in relation to 'the strongest and finest powers that are to be found in the material itself'.[9] In this sense, Nielsen is able to understand music in its purest form as music that develops completely freely according to its own organic laws of development, without having to conform to any external requirements, either in the form of a programme or a predetermined musical form. On the other hand, these musical laws must be strictly observed. They are inherent in the musical substance, and when it unfolds according to its own rules, the form emerges as a result of the organic development.

This is, of course, an ideal that Nielsen has formulated here. A number of factors come into play in the actual compositional work process, which also influence what the final work will look like. Yet it provides a key to understanding one of the central layers of Nielsen's musical thinking, which may be present to a greater or lesser degree, and which is very much present in his Fourth Symphony. It is the very idea that the symphony seeks to express.

It is interesting to follow the details of how Nielsen's idea for the symphony underwent adjustments in its formulation.[10] Firstly, it is clear that from the beginning he had the idea that it should be a symphony expressing life. Before he had even started, he wrote to Anne Marie in May 1914:

> ... I have an idea for a new work [Symphony No. 4], which has no programme but which is meant to express what we understand by the life-urge or life-manifestation; that's to say: everything that moves, that craves life, that can be called neither good nor evil, neither high nor low, neither great nor small, but simply: 'That which is life' or 'That which craves life' – I mean: no definite idea about anything 'grandiose' or 'subtle and delicate' or about warm or cold (powerful, maybe) but simply Life and Movement, yet varied, very varied, but holding together, and as though always flowing, in one large movement, in a single stream.[11]

At this early stage – that is, before he started working – the idea is still rather vague, although it is clear that he is talking about life in an all-encompassing sense and does not distinguish between positive and negative elements. Everything is included, big and small, good and bad, and the music must 'express' manifestations of life or simply life. It is also clear that he decided from the outset that it should be a symphony 'in one large movement, in a single stream' – that is, without separate movements. In July, when he was staying at Damgaard near Fredericia and had begun work on the symphony, he wrote almost identically to Emil Holm, emphasising that he was talking about '"Life" in the broadest sense ... Everything can be subsumed under this term.'[12]

As Nielsen progressed with the symphony, his focus shifted from the depicting of life to trying to describe the deeper layer of what makes life. He now emphasised more strongly that it was the life force itself that he wanted to give express musically. In 1915 he writes to Röntgen:

> I have sought to depict everything that has the will and the urge to life, which cannot be kept down. *Not* such that I would devalue my art to the imitation of Nature, but that I want to let it try to express what is behind the cries of birds, the cries of pain and joy of animals and people, their growling and shouting amid hunger, struggle and coupling, and what all this most elementary quality may be called.[13]

That it is about 'the elementary will to life' is repeated in the programme note for the first performance, and when he wrote a more detailed version of the note after the premiere, he was even more explicit:

> The symphony describes the most primordial sources of life and the origins of the feeling of life, that is: what lies behind human, animal and plant life ... It is ... a non-programmatic grasp down to the still semi-chaotic and completely elementary layers of emotional life. ... It is, as it were, a totally unconscious expression of that which, without any explanation, makes the birds cry, the animals roar, bleat, run and fight, and the people wail, groan, rejoice and shout. The symphony *does not* describe all this, but rather the basic feeling that lies *beneath* it all.[14]

Previously in connection with *Hymnus Amoris*, Nielsen had expressed the view that what he wanted to describe in his music were above all 'the great, simple, fundamental emotions: grief, joy, hatred, love, jubilation, despair'.[15] The difference is that Nielsen now wants to include them all, rather than describe them one by one. It is the emotions in their extreme and pure form, in their contradictory nature, that together make up life. When Nielsen refers to such contradictions, and when in his letter to Anne Marie he speaks of life as 'neither evil nor good', it is hard not to hear an affinity with Nietzsche. There is no evidence that Nielsen studied or read Nietzsche, but Nietzsche's thoughts and writings were known and certainly discussed in the Copenhagen circles in which Nielsen moved.[16]

In summary, it is evident that Nielsen sharpened his formulations not only during but also after the composition of the symphony. Whereas his early ideas revolved around portraying life and what is meant by the manifestations of life – that is, the result of the underlying forces – in his later texts he emphasised that it is precisely the underlying life force itself that the music should express. Music can reveal this 'most elemental' if we hold the view that music *is* life, that the very act of *being* music gives us insight into the principle of life. The metaphorical link between music and life is raised to a higher and more abstract level. If the force that governs the development of musical material is the same as that behind organic development in nature, then by gaining insight into one area it is possible to gain insight into the other.[17] Life and music are linked by this mysterious correspondence.

The Inextinguishable

What does all this mean for the understanding of a work like Nielsen's Fourth Symphony? Is it possible to explain how such an idea is articulated in specific terms? The paradox is that while in Nielsen's *Sinfonia espansiva* the specific musical features that correspond to the idea of life-affirming, positive forces, expressions of energy and expansion, are indeed visible, the all-encompassing, sharpened formulation 'music *is* life' loses its specificity. If the very fact of being music – and here in the sense of absolute music in its purest form – is an expression of a vitalist aesthetic, then it is difficult to find anything specific in the music on which to pin the idea. Then it is all life.[18]

A different approach is therefore needed. On the one hand, this could be done by considering whether the music lives up to the ideals of organicity and organic development; on the other hand, by considering whether music is also capable of accommodating and representing the full range of contradictory impulses and emotions that constitute the full range of life. Finally, it is useful to consider that there is still a composer involved who plans a strategy for their work.

As mentioned above, the concept of organic development as an overarching principle is an ideal that cannot stand alone. In his extended version of the programme note, Nielsen also juxtaposes the description of the sources of life-emotion with his own work as a composer. It is not, he says, simply a matter of letting the material unfold, for 'the construction of the various sections and the arrangement of the musical material is the result of a consideration on the part of the composer, just as when an engineer constructs dikes and sluices to keep the water out during a flood'.[19] The composer sets forces in motion, but also tries to control them.

From the very first bar of the symphony, Nielsen establishes an ambivalence or an interaction between major and minor by having the triad appear first as D minor and then as D major within the first few seconds. Nielsen was keen to establish this powerful, mutually contradictory motivic material at the beginning of the symphony. From the outset, Nielsen emphasises that the symphony must be able to accommodate contradictions. That he was less concerned with whether it would be heard immediately is confirmed by Launy Grøndahl, the long-time conductor of the Danish Radio Symphony Orchestra, who spoke to Nielsen during a rehearsal at one early performance of the work. They discussed whether the opening motif, the two triads in the first bar, was audible, and Nielsen admitted that it was barely perceptible. Grøndahl was surprised that Nielsen did nothing about the problem before the symphony was printed, revealing that for Nielsen it was more important to have the central motif in order to work with the material than for the audience to be able to hear it.[20]

Unlike the Third Symphony, where the opening chordal beats build up energy that is released when the first subject is introduced, the Fourth Symphony begins with a high level of internal and sustained energy. There is a lot of internal energy, like a boiling cauldron. The opening theme contains a number of elements that are used throughout the symphony: the alternation between major and minor keys, the brief upbeat, the central role of the timpani and the energetic drive of the triplets.

MUSIC EX. 1. Nielsen, Symphony No. 4, *The Inextinguishable,* first movement, bars 1–15, short score.[21] The symphony begins in the same way as the previous three, with a powerful burst of energy that immediately sets in motion a host of developmental possibilities. The entire opening is in the form of an unfolding dominant chord, a D minor/D major chord with the seventh C in the bass and the ninth, E♭, in the melody of the following bars. The brief upbeat in the bass is a B, confirming that the chord is to be heard as a dominant in a G key, introduced in the melodic motion within the G minor scale from bar 6 and confirmed with a clear tonal cadence on G major in bar 12.

Equally characteristic is that the first subject material turns out to be less significant. Throughout the first part of the movement, the second subject slowly takes control and comes to dominate the introductory first subject. It turns out that Nielsen is preparing the listener for the fact that the second subject will become the most important one in the entire symphony. The movement's second subject first appears in the clarinets in bar 51, before emerging in a surprising march version in bar 97, and finally returning as a climax in the fully orchestrated *fff* from bar 121 (see Music ex. 2, a–d).

Although Nielsen constructs the chain of events as a single movement, an underlying four-movement framework is indeed audible. The framework is familiar, and the audience acquainted with the symphonic form would have recognised it. Thus, the first movement is a fast movement and structured as a sonata form; the second movement is a dance with a contrasting middle section; the third is a pathos-filled slow movement and the fourth movement is a fast finale. In terms of formal structure, Nielsen can anticipate that the listener will have expectations of what might happen

a) First presentation, bars 51–56, played by two clarinets (in A), A major.

b) Presentation in duple time, bars 97–100, tutti (entire orchestra), march tempo, E major.

c) Culmination of the introduction, now without upbeat, violins 1–2, bars 121–26.

d) Second part of the culmination, bars 129–36, theme descending two octaves, A major.

e) Reappearance as 'recapitulation', in the full orchestra, bars 387–94, descending two octaves, E major.

f) Reappearance of the second subject at the end of the 'final movement', bars 1140–44, E major.

MUSIC EX. 2. Nielsen, Symphony No. 4, versions of the second subject.

and will be able to compare them with what actually does occur. It is therefore useful to speak of four movements. Nielsen achieves the linking of the movements into an overall sequence by letting the music ebb and flow in the first three movements rather than leading it to a conclusion, and when the energy has been drained from the system, he creates a bridge that leads directly to the next movement.

As the first movement progresses, the many elements of the first subject emerge and are developed, but in a fragmented form, with individual sections of the subject appearing separately. For example, in bar 2 the beginning introduces a figure of a few short chirps, which appears from bar 144 in a melodically transformed form, now sounding like birds; it returns several times in the middle section, but without any distinctive form. The triplet motif also returns in increasingly unremarkable versions, until the reappearance of the first subject in bar 341, when the expected form, the recapitulation, is presented in the original key, in a recognisable instrumentation, and even with the lowest note in the bass as the root. This time the tonality seems stable, although after only six bars the music moves in different directions from its first appearance, so that the recapitulation lacks prominence.

In contrast, the second subject returns in the recapitulation at bar 387, fully orchestrated and in E major, whereas in the exposition it was in A major. In the recapitulation, the second subject is presented in the form it had at the end of the introduction, in bar 129, where it gradually descends two octaves, ending on the root of the scale (see Music ex. 2, d and e). This section of the recapitulation seems brief, as Nielsen immediately bridges to a passage in which the energy of the music fades away to almost nothing. The final presentation of the movement's first and second subjects in the recapitulation thus seems strangely unfinished and psychologically unsatisfying, as the listener would have expected an emphatic conclusion in keeping with the introduction.[22] This unfulfilled expectation is realised in the final movement of the symphony, when the second subject reappears.

If Nielsen had intended four single movements, the first one would have seemed amputated, but by linking it with the other movements he is able to compensate for this imbalance. However, he avoids another imbalance often found in symphonies, which is that the interesting material is exhausted in the first movement, and the symphony is thus balanced by a peaceful centre and a festive conclusion, which creates balance primarily on the formal level. The shift of musical emphasis to the beginning of the symphony, mentioned in connection with the First Symphony,[23] is also present here, but by saving some of the material and tension for the end of the work, Nielsen avoids the risk of idling at the end.

The second movement opens in the woodwinds with an elegant, rococo-like dance that contrasts sharply with the previous movement. It is in a classical form with an interlude. The third movement begins with great pathos as a dramatic recitative in the strings. In bar 584, a small motif appears which is to have great significance in the rest of the movement. The descending figure, a minor third followed by a major second, is clearly audible in the flute. However, it has already appeared in the preceding passage in the cello and viola.

From this point on, Nielsen begins to build up to the great synthesis at the end of the symphony. The small motif becomes a key figure in the rest of the movement, where it can appear in forms that change the direction of the intervals or the order

a) 'Key motif' (x) consisting of the interval structure, a minor third–a major second, bars 584–85 (first noticeable appearance in the 'third movement').

b) First appearance of 'the threatening motif', bars 603–6, played in unison by the woodwinds.

c) Key motif intensifies, bars 633–34, in all woodwinds.

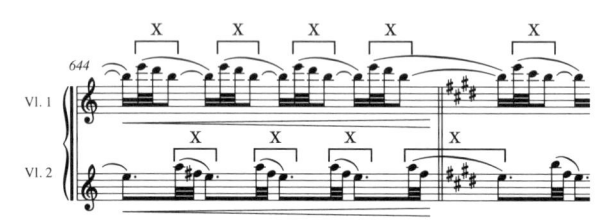

d) The key motif becomes omnipresent, here in violins 1–2, bars 644–45.

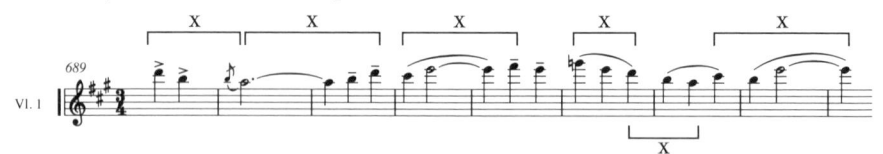

e) The first subject of the fourth movement, bars 689–96, with the 'key motif's' combination of a minor third and a major second as a recurring element.

MUSIC EX. 3. Nielsen, Symphony No. 4, the little 'key motif' and its reappearance in different guises.

of the notes, although the same interval structure is always used: a minor third and a major second. This motif is opposed by a 'threatening motif' – played first by the woodwinds – which was also prepared by the rhythmic figure of the viola in the first movement; this in turn is linked to rolls on the same pitch in the timpani.[24] The two motifs enter into an increasingly intense dialogue or battle. The presence of the key motif intensifies until it becomes an ever-present element in several layers of instruments simultaneously. After a diminuendo and an intense transition to the fourth movement, it is revealed that the new first subject of this movement is composed entirely of the intervals of the key motif in various combinations (see Music ex. 3, e). The entire symphony is permeated by internal motivic and thematic connections that weave the symphony into one great 'organism – coherence'.[25]

The timpano also enters in the third movement, supporting the restlessness and anticipating the role it will play at the end. Nielsen has designed the performance for two sets of timpani, and in the score he has, rather remarkably, prescribed a particular orchestral arrangement in which the second set is placed directly opposite the first one, 'thus at the far end of the orchestra, near the audience'.[26] Although the instruction is not entirely clear, it seems plausible that the first set is in its usual place to the right of the orchestra, and that the two sets are thus to be heard and seen separately. Their function is also made clear in Nielsen's footnote at the beginning of the fourth movement, when the sets of timpani first appear: 'From here and until the end the timpani, although *piano*, should retain a certain menacing character'.[27] Nielsen thus intended the timpani sets to function as a duel rather than a dialogue. The fact that the sets are tuned in two different tritones, the first in F and B and the second in D♭ and G, supports this idea.

The entire final movement is structured as an increasingly chaotic and conflicted affair. It begins with the new first subject, consisting of a march-like two-part opening figure, which continues in triple time with the subject's principal melody. If the timpani have taken on the role of the menacing element, then the melody of the new first subject has taken on the role of the little 'bird chirping' which began in the woodwinds of the first movement and which might be associated with the little key motif introduced by the flute. Soon after, the timpani duel begins. Surrounded by accented string figures, brass signals and melodic material from the movement's first subject, the timpani lay the foundations for a long build-up that culminates in a section labelled 'Glorioso'. The movement then thins out as the hymn-like section intensifies. A transition follows, and the melodic material of the first subject is heard very faintly again, in a fugal form that pulls all the threads together. The second subject from the first part of the symphony then reappears, before the timpani duel returns. Finally, the real climax of the movement and the symphony is reached: the second subject reappears in glorious E major in its most perfect melodic and orchestral form, like a resolution after all the conflicts.

It is reported that Nielsen once told the violinist Thorvald Nielsen that the duel between the two timpanists had 'something to do with the war'.[28] The remark was made during a walk and only became public knowledge fifty years later. It has been suggested that Nielsen revealed what the symphony was really about: the First World War – but also the war-like conditions on the home front and in relation to The Royal Theatre.[29] Although the war was undoubtedly part of the context in which he worked on the piece, it makes more sense to emphasise the consistency of the many statements he made at the time, and to believe that he really meant what he said.

There is no reason to doubt that 'life' – in the sense that Nielsen insisted was inherent in the symphony – was also about conflict. From the very first bar, the symphony is full of conflicts, and these are clearly played out throughout the work. A reasonable interpretation is to see the reappearance of the second subject in the fourth movement as the element that first of all brings order to the chaos and secondly balances the unresolved tension left by the brief and unfinished recapitulation in the first movement.[30] In addition, it seems reasonable to regard the various elements as expressing either positive forces – the second subject, the key motif and the first subject of the final movement – or as negative ones: the 'threatening motif', the timpani duels and the elements of chaos. One conclusion might be, as David Fanning puts it, to see the whole symphony as a battle between good and evil, and Nielsen's musical message as 'an impassioned defence of those values against inimical forces'.[31] Thus the triumphant reappearance of the second subject at the end of the symphony must be understood as an expression of the triumph of good.

Another interpretation, more in line with Nielsen's central formulations, would be to emphasise that good and evil are all part and parcel of music and life, and that neither is ultimately victorious. Firstly, it is worth considering whether the second subject, in its final appearance, actually carries the weight to make it victorious. Although the second subject returns for the first time in its full and original rounded melodic form, it is not an extended passage. Secondly, the symphony lacks the constant sense of momentum and direction found in the Third Symphony, where there is a constant sense that the music is moving forward. In the Fourth Symphony there is a lot of motion, although there is no progression. There are passages of great energy and many forces at work at once, and there are corresponding passages where the energy seems to be drained from the system. Perhaps the message is that it is all there all the time. In that case, the meaning of the symphony is to be found in seeing it in its entirety, not in looking at its end: life is the struggle, not the victory.

The symphony was premiered by Musikforeningen on 1 February 1916 at Odd Fellow Palæet; like all the society's concerts, it was an event for members only. Nevertheless, it received a great deal of attention in the press, which generally agreed that Nielsen had composed a work of lasting importance. Emilius Bangert went so far as to speak of a 'great work in the music of Denmark, indeed … of Europe', comparing Nielsen's achievement with that of Strauss, Saint-Saëns and Debussy. Although, according to Bangert, they may be more technically accomplished, Nielsen's symphony is carried by a 'different, profound feeling for the original' and therefore rises above the time-bound.[32] It was also the most performed symphony abroad during his lifetime: Stockholm, Berlin and Oslo in 1917; Gothenburg and Stockholm in 1918; Gothenburg again in 1919, 1925, 1928 and 1929; Amsterdam in 1920; Bremen, Vienna and Berlin in 1922; Karlsruhe and London in 1923; Oslo and Bergen in 1926; Munich in 1927; Stockholm in 1927 and 1929; Schwerin in 1928 and Königsberg in 1928 and 1930.[33]

In Denmark, the Symphony was also the work that truly established Nielsen as the country's greatest contemporary composer. It was a work that set in motion the trend that would lead to his general recognition as the national composer at the expense of Niels W. Gade, who was still regarded as the most prominent composer in the overall picture of Danish music.[34] Charles Kjerulf, the critic for the newspaper *Politiken*, who for many years had both praised and criticised Nielsen, now capitulated completely. At the premiere, he referred to the programme and remarked that the inextinguishable life 'fought for, broken, bred and consumed' had indeed shown itself in the 'sea of flames of sound that the composer ignited with tremendous willpower and considerable creative ability'.[35] After hearing the second performance of the symphony at a public concert in Odd Fellow Palæet on 14 April, including excerpts from *Saul and David* and the Violin Concerto with Peder Møller as soloist, Kjerulf wrote in retrospect:

> The writer of these lines has followed this composer, work by work, since his first efforts, often with enthusiasm and joy, but just as often with displeasure and regret ... This work is his crowning achievement, a breakthrough. For the first time, he not only promises, but fulfils ... almost everything he has promised before. For the first time, he has succeeded in creating a great work that reaches for the clouds, but that at the same time has both feet firmly planted on the ground.[36]

With this symphony, Nielsen established his name once and for all, but he also launched his musical thinking and the central concept of music as life as something to which the musical world began to refer. The vitalist aesthetic, in its all-encompassing version, finds its strongest musical expression in *The Inextinguishable*, where the concept embodied in the statement 'music *is* life' becomes both the starting point of the composition and the message to the audience. In the decade that followed, he did not abandon this starting point, but complemented it with other and new approaches to composing music. It is one element among many in Nielsen's musical thinking. Sometimes it seems to be qualified, as Nielsen adapts his compositions to the specific tasks that need to be solved. Yet there are clear features in the works of the 1920s, which show that he continues essential parts of his thinking about music as an art form in which the organic in the development and throughout the music, understood as inner coherence, is crucial to how the music unfolds. This is no less true if the actual works sometimes contradict each other or appear on the surface to be anything but harmonious. But if everything is life, then the organic is not necessarily harmonious. It can also be chaotic, held together at a deeper level.

IV

MODERNITY AND POPULARITY

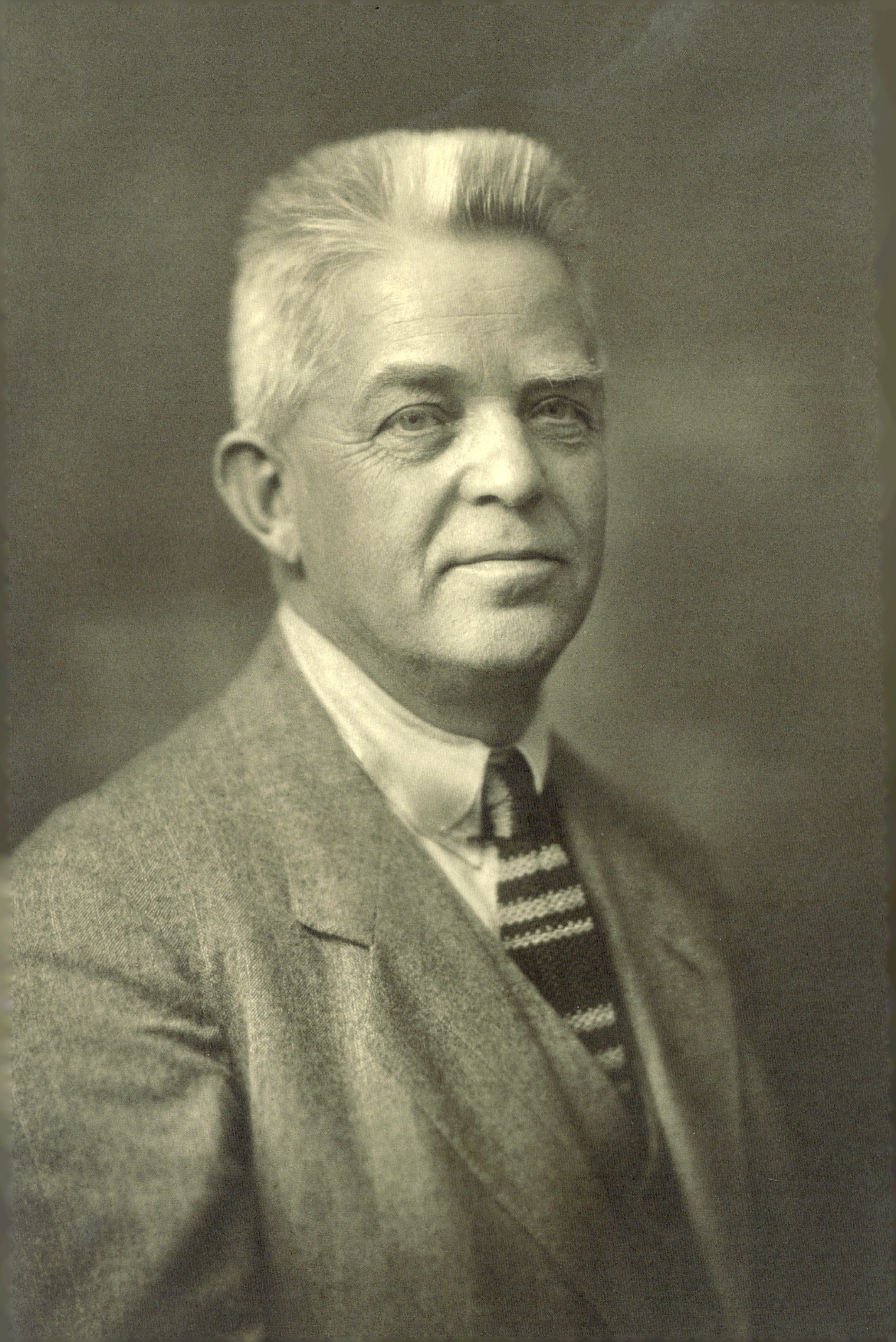

Chapter 29

THE POPULAR AND THE MODERN

One question that has puzzled many who have studied Nielsen's music is how, towards the end of his life, he seemed to move increasingly in two different directions. In the first of these we find his gradually growing interest in writing popular songs and melodies that could be used to raise the musical level in schools, in the folk high school environment and in all the different circles that use the Folk High School Songbook. The same goes for his contribution to the renewal of church singing and music education. As for the other direction, he is regarded as a composer whose symphonies, concertos and instrumental works are increasingly moving towards a form of modernism that is difficult for the common people to approach and understand. How can these two directions be part of the same composer's work?

One reason why this question is so difficult to answer is that it is asked in an imprecise manner. The premise seems to be that a composer's oeuvre must be coherent by virtue of stylistic unity. The centenary of Nielsen's birth in 1965 saw a huge focus on his entire œuvre, and yet the impression was left that his late compositions were absent from the picture presented. Critics argued that Nielsen had become a mythological figure associated with a stylistic ideal in which his late works had no place. One explanation given was that they were 'so stylistically uneven that this alone deprives them of a consistent description. They are characterised by a fragmentation that makes them unsuitable as a basis for dogmatics'.[1] There is, however, no reason to establish a dogmatic view of how Nielsen should sound.

There is only one Carl Nielsen, so the question should be asked differently. If it is not a question of style, then the question should be: what is his approach to the many tasks he undertakes, and how does he solve them in terms of composition? Indeed Nielsen does not solve all tasks in the same way. He brings all his experience and craftsmanship to bear when considering how best to solve a particular problem. And if his music does not always sound the same, that is a deliberate choice.

In the 1920s, Nielsen was preoccupied with two major questions that determined the direction of the projects in which he became involved. One was the question of the future development of music: where was contemporary music heading, and how could he help to shape its development? In 1920 he began to compose his Fifth Symphony, working intensely with the development of motifs and shaping the symphony with such rigour that the whole symphony emerged as a single organism. In 1922 he tried a different model with his Wind Quintet, and shortly after that there followed a series of new attempts to give voice to all the contradictions of modern life. All the time he insisted on trying out new solutions. His desire for a new music, and the fact that he did not quite know how it might turn out, became part of the music's objective. Nielsen is thus clearly one of the modern composers of the 1920s in Europe.

Nielsen's second concern was to renew and improve the public's relationship with music. His work on songbooks, popular songs and, last but not least, the comprehensive reform of the song programme of the folk high school are projects to which he is wholeheartedly committed. The same is true of his contribution to church music and the musical education of piano students. Each of these tasks is carried out in its own way, according to the principle he proposed in 1922: 'The greatest beauty of form' depends on the fact that, through use, things are fully adapted to the purpose for which they are intended.[2]

Chapter 30

THE GREAT REFORM PROJECT

The publication of the tenth edition of *Højskolesangbogen* (The Folk High School Songbook) in 1922 marked a crucial breakthrough: in addition to the textbook, the first edition of *Folkehøjskolens Melodibog* (*The Folk High School Melody Book*) was published, containing piano settings of all the tunes. The melody book was organised by Thorvald Aagaard, a teacher at the folk high school in Ryslinge, Oluf Ring, a lecturer at the teacher's college in Ribe, Thomas Laub and Carl Nielsen. The purpose of the book was to fulfil the singers' wish for a good and up-to-date collection of tunes. The four, with Aagaard at the head of the project, were to be the guarantors of quality.

The melody book, which had its roots both inside and outside of the folk high school circles, became very important for the singing and included many different tunes, both old and new. For the first time there was a complete music edition of all the pieces collected in the Folk High School Songbook. The music not only provided the tunes, but also comprised piano settings in versions suitable for accompanying communal singing. A number of new songs were included for which the editors had composed tunes, many of which became part of the basic repertoire in the many later editions of the songbook. In addition, many of the older texts were given new melodies or an alternative one alongside the original. There was thus a reform of both the content of the songbook and, more importantly, the melodic material. The new tunes were a major step away from the Romantic melodies and were rather more simple, straightforward and singable – the kind of tunes that are associated with folk high school songs today.

A standardised melody book meant that everyone throughout the country had a common basis for choosing tunes, as well as the key in which they were to be sung. The carefully prepared piano accompaniments also contributed to a common aesthetic in continuation of Nielsen's and Laub's ideals for popular singing. The piano part was to support the vocal line, not overpower it. Previously, folk high school singing could be rather chaotic with people performing the tunes as they knew them best. Now it became an ideal that they should be sung as notated. In this sense, a common, nationwide melody book was a mass medium.[1] It served the same function as the national broadcasting corporation, Danmarks Radio, since from 1925 it was possible to listen to a common version of standard Danish throughout the country, according to the received pronunciation. The melody book thus established a norm, which meant that people adapted to a more uniform way of singing from then on.

However, the ambitions were greater than simply renewing the content of what was sung in the folk high schools. By establishing a common vocal range, the melody book was also an attempt at a nationwide reform of singing. The favoured vocal range meant that most people had to make an effort to sing in a different way. People had to stand up straight and use their diaphragm support, and the result was that the communal singing took on a more beautiful tone and sound. Similar efforts were made to improve the quality and style of singing in schools. Folk high school singing was an important element, although not the only one, in a wider effort to improve the singing culture. Nielsen participated wholeheartedly in this great reform project, and a few years after the publication of the *Folk High School Melody Book* he declared that it was one of the most important things he could contribute to. In connection with the publication of another songbook, *Sangbogen 'Danmark'*, he said:

> My major symphonies are one thing; but the popular, simple song is closest to my heart, and if this new book of melodies can help to improve the taste in the schools, I shall consider it my greatest triumph.[2]

The Prelude

The reform of folk high school singing, which took place gradually during the first decades of the twentieth century, was reviewed by Harald Balslev, the headmaster of Ubberup Højskole, in 1922 – that is, the same year as the melody book was published. The occasion for the review was that the association of folk high schools, Foreningen for Højskoler og Landbrugsskoler, had just published the tenth edition of its songbook, *Folkehøjskolens Sangbog*, as well as *The Folk High School Melody Book*:

> In the last ten to fifteen years it has become more stimulating to teach singing at the Folk High School than it used to be. In the past it was basically the same from year to year as far as the tunes were concerned: there was little that was new; there was usually no choice; the established tunes were known, but by no means were they all sung correctly. And many of them were not very rich in musical content. Then a renewal began in many areas of the songbook.[3]

In fact, the songbook, including the lyrics, had changed very little over the last three editions. From the seventh edition in 1913 to the tenth in 1922, only about thirty new ones had been added, and compared to the 685 lyrics in the tenth edition, this was a very minor adjustment.[4] The period has therefore been described as the 'quietest in the history of the book'.[5] The major change that Balslev traced in the last decade was a reform of the singing. The renewal was a result of the introduction of new tunes, and he referred in particular to those of Laub and Nielsen, which replaced many of the old ones.

Communal singing at the folk high schools was a living tradition based on how each individual learned the tunes. Many of them were not performed correctly, partly because the songbook was a textbook, with only brief references to the tunes to which the texts were to be sung, either in the form of the composer's name or the first line of a tune's lyrics. In the seventh edition of 1913, for example, a reference above the first stanza of Jakob Knudsen's 'Tunge, mørke Natteskyer' (Heavy, gloomy clouds of night) indicates that it could be sung to three different *romance* melodies composed for other texts. If the tunes were unknown, the music had to be found elsewhere, such as in Heinrich Nutzhorn's anthology of 1904, which was the first collection of music adapted to the Folk High School Songbook.[6] As with most collections of the time, this one contained only unison melodies, and if a piano accompaniment was needed, the pianist might find it in *Danmarks Melodibog* (*Denmark's Melody Book*), published in five volumes comprising 1,500 songs. The first volume was issued in 1895, the year after the first edition of the Folk High School Songbook; the contents of the volumes, however, were not coordinated with those of the songbook.[7] In general, during the first decades of the songbook's existence, the available anthologies, including the tunes, were based on a nineteenth-century repertoire, which Balslev found to be inadequate.

Just like Balslev, the organist Thorvald Aagaard also felt the need for new songs through his work with the electoral congregation in Ryslinge and as a teacher at Ryslinge Højskole.[8] Aagaard had been associated with the school since 1905, and three years later, in an article entitled 'Folkelig Sang' (Popular Singing), he proposed that an anthology of tunes should be prepared for the Folk High School Songbook to make up for the neglect of singing practice that he had experienced. The repertoire, Aagaard thought, was like a disorganised lumber room containing only a few popular tunes. No wonder 'people's ideas about tunes [were] generally quite confused'. The short-term solution was an anthology of tunes to facilitate a more accurate performance of the songs, but Aagaard's vision went much further. He wanted to weed out the tunes and retain those that 'bend and conform to the needs of the text and make no great demands on the voice or musical development'.[9] Many of the nineteenth-century tunes could be used, but new ones were also needed.

Aagaard's proposal to compile an anthology of tunes did not come to fruition at first, and he was later glad that it was delayed.[10] In 1912 he turned down the editors of the Folk High School Songbook when they asked him to take charge of a melody book.[11] If the anthology had been published then, some of his work would have been wasted. He realised that it was not only a question of having a complete edition of music, but also of providing the communities with good singable tunes. This required a reform of singing practice, not just a collection of tunes. In June 1919

Aagaard felt that the conditions had not yet been met, although important steps had been taken in the right direction. Johan Borup and Erik Spur, both involved in the folk high school movement, had already published songbooks with new tunes by Laub, Nielsen and their pupils. Borup's songbook was also accompanied by a melody book edited by Nielsen. Spur was reticent about his parallel project, describing his songbook as 'an attempt to break new ground, a beginning'.[12]

Balslev had been on the editorial board of the Folk High School Songbook since October 1916,[13] and in the autumn of 1919 the board must have tried again to persuade Aagaard to take on the task of publishing a melody book. He accepted, and in November he presented to Balslev his vision for organising the work.[14] The following year, the board of the association of folk high schools was able to announce the news of the forthcoming melody book:

> It will be of the greatest importance for the future of the popular culture of singing of our country if we get a really sound and up-to-date anthology of tunes, which has long been lacking in all secondary schools and in many homes. A number of people who have a high level of musical education and are well acquainted with our popular poetry and songs have responded to our encouragement to remedy this deficiency with desire and diligence. They are preparing an anthology of harmonised melodies for use in schools and in the many homes which have recently acquired pianos and harmoniums. Such an anthology will undoubtedly benefit many more people than if it had been an ordinary collection of only unison melodies.[15]

In the 1908 article, Aagaard mentions two of Nielsen's tunes as prototypes for popular songs: 'Du danske Mand' (*Danish Patriotic Song*) and *Jens Vejmand* (*John the Roadman*) are 'based on the same pattern, and these two good songs will therefore find their way into wide circles'.[16] Nielsen composed neither 'Du danske Mand' nor *John the Roadman* as communal songs, but they had become popular with the general public, and for Aagaard their quality lay in the fact that they were regular and simple tunes. When Aagaard highlighted them in his article in 1908, they were new and were not yet associated with a Danish song heritage. Nielsen composed the tune to Holger Drachmann's 'Du danske Mand' for a summer revue in the Tivoli Gardens in 1906, which was performed by the play's main character as part of the plot. The song soon became well known, and an arrangement with piano accompaniment was printed by the publishers Wilhelm Hansen at the request of the revue's author, Anton Melbye.[17] It also became very popular as a song for men's choir. Nielsen composed the music to Jeppe Aakjær's text about John the Roadman as a solo song with piano accompaniment and published it in the anthology *Strophic Songs* (1907), which was a continuation of the solo songs he had written in the previous decades.

Without having taken the initiative himself, Nielsen thus became part of an incipient reform of singing practice. Although he had not composed the songs for communal singing, they were included in a small booklet, *Enstemmige Sange til Brug for Højskoler, Gymnastik og Skytteforeninger* in 1909, a year after Aagaard's comment.[18] And the text of 'Du danske Mand' was included in the seventh edition of the Folk High School Songbook (1913), with the words 'melody by Carl Nielsen' printed above the first stanza. In the same edition, Grundtvig's hymn text *Paaske-Liljen* (*The Daffodil*) was included with a reference to Nielsen's tune from 1910. The subsequent editions show that his tunes were far from unknown in folk high school circles. In the eighth edition (1917), eight of his tunes are mentioned in the songbook, seven of them from the first volume of *En Snes danske Viser* (*A Score of Danish Songs*) (1915), a clear sign that the songs in this volume were rapidly becoming popular. The ninth edition in 1920 added ten more tunes, including Nielsen's 'Heavy, gloomy clouds of night', which had been published in *Højskolebladet* three years earlier.

Two paths intersected in this development: the popular breakthrough of the tunes and Nielsen's work in composing songs. The reform was largely driven by those who sang and those who led the singing, but it also had an impact on Nielsen's work. It was particularly decisive for him when, in 1914, he was included in one of the milieus where singing was practised. This was in collaboration with Johan Borup and indeed before Laub approached Nielsen with the idea of composing *A Score of Danish Songs*. It was as editor of the tunes for Borup's songbook that Nielsen first became directly involved in the work of reforming the folk high school singing.

Borup's Songbook

In 1891 Johan Borup founded the school, which from 1916 was known as Borups Højskole and was first located at 9 Vestre Boulevard, where the Borup family lived.[19] In 1926 the institution moved to 24 Frederiksholms Kanal, where it has been ever since – today known as Johan Borups Højskole. Borup became almost a neighbour to Nielsen, who from 1915 lived two houses down the street in the honorary residence that Anne Marie had been awarded.

Borup was a keen observer of and participant in the development of Danish folk high school singing. His collaboration with Nielsen began in connection with the preparation of his *Dansk Sangbog*, which Borup published in 1914. Borup needed an editor for the companion melody book, which contained the tunes without accompaniment. Nielsen was chosen and thus became active in the ongoing singing reform.

Johan Borup probably knew Nielsen through Borup's brother Julius as they had been fellow students at the Academy of Music and had both been members of The Royal Orchestra from the late 1880s. Julius and his wife Dagmar were also close

ILL. 1. The official title of the melody book was *Nye Melodier til de nyere Sangtekster i Johan Borup's Dansk Sangbog redigeret af Carl Nielsen* (*New Melodies to the Latest Song Texts for Johan Borup's Danish Songbook Edited by Carl Nielsen*), although it was known as *Carl Nielsen's Melody Book*. On the left a bound copy of the melody book, on the right an advertisement from *Maanedsblad for Borups Højskole*, April 1916.[20]

friends of the Nielsen family. Dagmar helped look after the children when Anne Marie was away.[21] Their relationship also originated from the music lessons that Nielsen and Dagmar Borup gave at her home in 1903.[22] It was also under the auspices of Borups Højskole that Nielsen delivered a lecture on Gluck, Haydn and Mozart in 1905 as part of a series of lectures on eighteenth-century German culture.[23]

In 1916, when Borup looked back on his twenty-five years as headmaster of the folk high school, he recalled the literary discussions of the 1870s and '80s and the labour movement that had 'stirred up the minds' of the young people.[24] Borup was a central figure in the Grundtvigian milieu of theologians and educators, part of the intellectual circles in Copenhagen where it was important to take a stand on the current issues of the day.[25]

Having attended his uncle Ernst Trier's lectures at Vallekilde Højskole as a young man, Borup wanted to give the citizens of Copenhagen a folk high school where they could 'learn something useful and something new ... under free and uninhibited forms'.[26] As a prerequisite for this education, Borup offered his students freedom of speech and regarded the individual's opinion as inviolable. There had to be trust between teacher and pupil: teachers had to be able to present their material without prejudice and see the matter from all sides, and the pupils had to feel safe enough to form their own opinions.[27]

However, Borup realised that a folk high school in Copenhagen had to be different from those in the provinces. In his anniversary publication, *Højskolen og København* (The Folk High School and Copenhagen), he tried to explain why his school was still relevant after twenty-five years in the capital. He saw the history of the Danish adult education as a history of adaptation and stated that it was Grundtvig's idea that 'the folk high school should never have any other method, form or shape than that of life or the moment; rather, its method is that it has none, but must constantly invent it anew'.[28] Such a school in the capital therefore had to be adapted to the conditions of the city, and Borup recognised that there were crucial differences between the city and the rural areas. Copenhagen has

> its customs, its language. The air, the light, the food, the clothes, the houses and the pace are different. We have noise where the country has silence; we have streets and alleys for roads and fields; we are many where the country people are few; and above all, we live in tenements where they have houses and farms. Thus they are steady where we are transient; they are slow where we are fast; they stay at home while we go out; they build on the traditions of families while we cling to the new.[29]

In other words, the adult education system in Copenhagen had to be able to do something different from the folk high schools around the country, which, as Borup realised, also had their own special conditions. Having started by organising lectures attended by the city's upper classes, he attracted the working class by offering trade union members a fifty per percent discount on fees.[30] And his college gained momentum when he realised that it could meet the needs of the workers. It was not lectures on a historical subject that attracted the workers, who initially preferred to enrol for basic courses in writing, arithmetic and spelling; however, Borup was aware that this was only the beginning. Later, he introduced programmes in which students could debate various topics in which anyone could participate: what is education or what is the relationship between men and women?[31] The purpose of these dialogues was not 'to find a solution, but simply to refresh the thoughts so that they can be better disentangled'.[32] The individual's ability to relate to the world around them was more important than consensus. The composition of the class was also diverse. Joakim Skovgaard's art history lectures were attended by a shoemaker as well as a baroness.[33]

History, literature, art and music were subjects taught at Borups Højskole and were highly valued. Borup lectured on literature, Skovgaard on art history and Laub on music history.[34] Music evenings were held on Saturdays in Borup's apartment at the school. In the 1920s, Borup's son Hans was responsible for organising intimate recitals in private surroundings, which, according to one student, made them much more pleasant than those held in a public concert hall.[35] In everyday life, too, music played an important part in creating a sense of community between teachers and students. There was great joy in singing, with one student describing how communal singing was a natural part of being together in the premises on Vestre Boulevard: 'The rooms may be cramped, but life is so much richer: here we are building the Denmark of the future. And all the time we have moments to sing.'[36]

It was the students at the school who wanted a new songbook. This is the explanation given by Hans Borup, who succeeded his father as headmaster.[37] Johan Borup supported the students, and he probably thought it was only natural that the school should have its own songbook, just as he had seen at Vallekilde Højskole.[38] The songbook became a means of promoting solidarity at the school. The student magazine, *Maanedsblad for Borups Højskole*, described the new situation when *Dansk Sangbog* was introduced in 1914: 'We who previously sat silent next to each other, closed off from each other, now feel that when we sing together, the separation disappears and the song unites us.'[39] Until then, singing had been an important part of the school day, but a songbook gave the students something to gather around. The book represented a unifying 'we'.

Johan Borup wanted the students to sing new tunes that reflected their own times. In 1917 he defended this point of view in the article 'Vore Sange' (Our Songs), which first appeared in the school's monthly journal and the following week in *Højskolebladet*. His contribution thus became part of the nationwide debate on the reform of folk high school singing. Borup argued that 'the living generation must also sing in their own language, in their own spirit',[40] and he also responded to criticism that the songbook was displacing the old patriotic tunes. According to Marius Sørensen, a college teacher from Jelling, the new ones 'will put people in an aesthetic relationship with the country's nature rather than in a historical relationship with their native land'.[41]

In his criticism, Sørensen formulated what was at the heart of a new interpretation of the national identity. It was indeed the traditional patriotic sense of nationhood that was challenged by the nature-bound relationship to Danishness that became the characteristic feature of the new folk high school songs. As an example, he cited Aakjær's song 'Jeg lægger mig i Læet her ved Storrugens Rod (I take shelter at the root of the tall rye), the second stanza of which reads: 'The chimes of the tops of the summer rye –

that is the dear Danish sound with which we grew up.' A horror scenario for Sørensen would be if 'a peasant at the folk high school learns to have such an aesthetic relationship with his work that he lies down for hours "at the root of the tall rye" and listens to the "chimes" of the rye instead of cutting it with the scythe'.[42] The objection was not new. In the mid-nineteenth century, the poet Bernhard Severin Ingemann had already warned against Grundtvig's idea of a school for the people. If pupils learn anything at all there, they will want to learn more and will be unwilling to do peasant work. This could have repercussions for society as a whole, Ingemann believed, and 'the Danish people cannot tolerate all the bright young peasants sitting down to their books'.[43]

For Borup, the criticism was misplaced. Essentially, he believed that the old and the new tunes could do something different. The patriotic tunes were important, but they 'are our festive tunes and it is not appropiate to wear them out on a daily basis; normally we just need some tunes in everyday clothes that can stand the wear and tear'. Of course, Borup's plea to spare the patriotic ones was not for the sake of the tunes. He was concerned with those who sang; he argued that in everyday life, 'when we come home from work, tired, dizzy', then 'the powerful tunes', the old patriotic ones are not suitable.[44]

Borup's solution was 'songs of daily life'. Rather than dealing with common issues and 'resounding with dissatisfaction with work', these are tunes that 'take us out of the intimate reality of everyday life, if only an inch above it'.[45] The songs could point to meaningful connections in life through recognisable situations, and by acknowledging this, the song could have a beneficial effect on the performer. In this respect, Borup felt that Aakjær's ballads were exemplary. For the students who came from the working class, Aakjær's ballads about farmers were not realistic depictions of their daily lives, but images of the toil and labour of like-minded people. Even if the specific stories of farm work could not be directly applied to themselves, Borup found that the songs made sense to those who sang them.

Tunes of Daily Life

It is evident that Borup was the driving force behind the decision to collaborate with Nielsen on the new melody book. His correspondence with Nielsen indicates that he had already prepared the songbook before asking for assistance in composing the tunes to the lyrics. Either Nielsen set about composing them, or he asked his pupils and colleagues for help. Shortly after their collaboration began in the spring of 1914, Nielsen asked Aagaard for advice on the ideal form for the songbook. Aagaard recommended that the new tunes should be printed in a separate booklet, a solution that Borup accepted.[46] It did not seem important to him that the songbook and the melody book should be published at the same time, and in the summer of 1914 he set about completing the songbook, even though the new tunes were not yet available. In the course of this work he agreed with Nielsen that the composers' names should be placed above each song text.[47] By this time, Nielsen must have received commitments from his students and colleagues as to which new tunes they should write.

The songbook went to press in December 1914, but changes regarding the tunes were made later. In the songbook, the name of the composer Ove Scavenius, Nielsen's pupil, appears above Steen Steensen Blicher's text 'Det er hvidt herude' (It is white out here). However, it was Laub who eventually composed the tune, as can be seen from a correction published on a cancel page at the back of the songbook.[48] In the time that followed, several changes were made to the list of participating composers. For example, four songs that Nielsen had assigned to himself ended up with new tunes by others when the anthology was published in the spring of 1916.[49]

Jeppe Aakjær was one of those who had high hopes for the new melody book. After receiving the newly printed songbook in December 1914, he wrote to Borup: 'When the new tunes arrive and are disseminated throughout the country by your pupils, we will have a renewal of our popular singing culture that can usher in a new era'. Aakjær obviously had great confidence in Nielsen's abilities as an editor. He called him 'the leading force in our vocal music' and recalled how Nielsen had 'taken such good care of my poems'.[50] So far Nielsen had composed two songs for his play *Ulvens Søn* (*The Wolf's Son*) and the three songs *Høgen* (*Hawk*), *John the Roadman* and 'Den første Lærke' (The larks are coming), published in *Strophic Songs* in 1907 – the kind of songs to which Aakjær was referring.

It is easy to understand Aakjær's expectations for the publication, and a glance at Borup's songbook shows that Borup was well aware that the singing in the folk high schools also needed a musical revision. New lyrics meant new tunes, so of the 244 lyrics in the songbook, 53 were given new tunes.[51] Thus the songbook also reflects the new ideal of communal singing that Borup and his students were promoting. This is evident in a section of thirty-two songs under the heading 'songs of daily life'.[52] These include Blicher's 'Ud gaar du nu paa Livets Vej' (Now you must find your path in life), Carsten Hauch's 'Vender sig Lykken fra dig' (Fortune has lately left you) and Aakjær's song about John the Roadman, all three with tunes by Nielsen.[53] Also included is Jens Peter Jacobsen's 'Det bødes der for i lange Aar' (You suffer throughout an age of pain), surprisingly sung to Nielsen's melody, an elaborate lied published in 1893.[54] At first glance, the lied seems to have been composed far from the ideals expressed in the new reform. However, the melody has some features that make it recognisable and suitable for communal singing by those with good vocal skills. Aakjær's *Gamle Anders Røgters Sang* (*Song of Old Anders the Cattleman*) contains a reference to Nielsen's melody composed for *Ulvens Søn* in 1909 and shows that Borup borrowed pieces from outside the usual repertoire of communal songs.[55] And

MUSIC EX. 1. Jacobsen's text 'Det bødes der for i lange Aar' (You suffer throughout an age of pain) is included in Borup's songbook. A note above the text indicates that the tune is by Nielsen. It appeared in the anthology *Viser og Vers af J. P. Jacobsen* (*Songs and Verses by J. P. Jacobsen*, Op. 6, 1893) with an extended piano setting, which shows that it is a solo song related to the lied genre. However, if one looks only at the vocal part, it is clear that it is comparable to the communal songs. A characteristic feature is the strophic structure of the melody, and the rhythmic figure of paired quavers on weak beats is a consistent element that makes the melody easy to memorise. This gives it a natural flow that is easy to follow when people sing together in groups. The shape of the melody is organised in a traditional A A' B form, in which a varied repetition of the A section creates a transition to the contrasting B. A similar procedure is at work at the beginning of *John the Roadman*, 'Underlige Aftenlufte' (*Homesickness*) and many others. If Nielsen had composed 'You suffer throughout an age of pain' with communal singing in mind, he would probably have tried to avoid the large downward leaps in the last part of the song (down to the Danish words 'Sorg' and 'Harm'). These are difficult intervals for an untrained singer.

yet it also demonstrates a breadth in Borup's understanding of what folk high school singing could be.

As editor, it was important for Nielsen to take a critical approach to the content of the melody book. He would collect the tunes, copy them neatly onto large sheets of paper and thus get an overview of the material. At the same time he would go through them and perhaps sing them to get a feel for whether they were good. In Nancy Dalberg's melody for 'Ja, i Bølgetoner bløde' (Yes, you soft sound of waves) there was a problem with the distribution of the lyrics, and with a pencil he suggested corrections in his fair copy of the melody. He probably gave his suggestions to Dalberg, and to solve the problem she recomposed the last line.

Work on the tunes for Borup's songbook was not isolated from other projects. Shortly before the songbook was issued in late 1914, Laub, who had provided

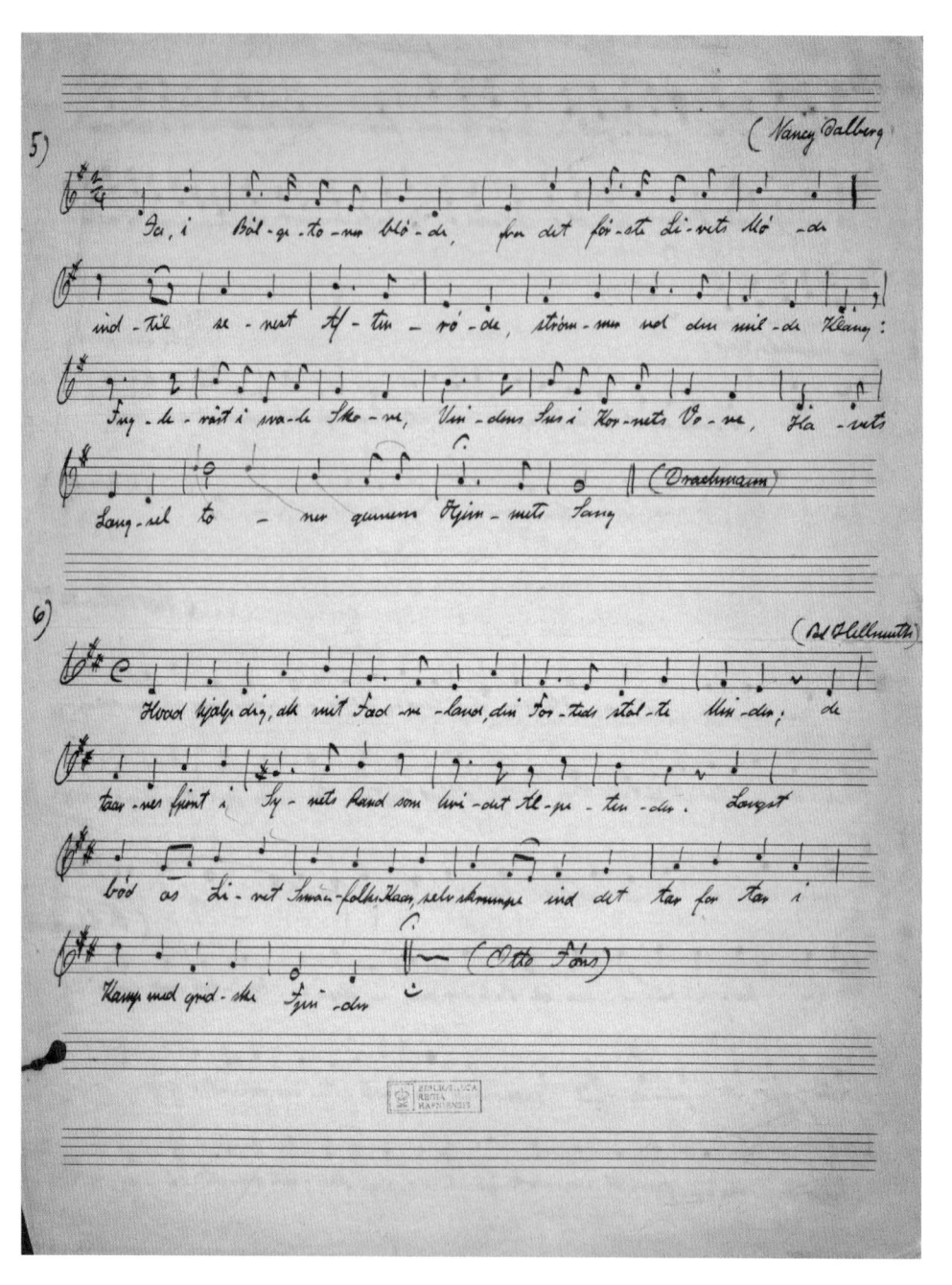

ILL. 2. As part of his editorial work, Nielsen transcribed his colleagues' melodies for Borup's songbook. This illustration shows two tunes, one by Nancy Dalberg and the second by Paul Hellmuth. Nielsen's pencil corrections, which Dalberg chose to follow, can be seen at the end of her tune in the middle of the page.[56]

two new tunes, sent a proposal to Nielsen suggesting that they collaborate on a selection of ballads that would eventually be published in the two volumes of *A Score of Danish Songs*. Laub was critical of Borup's approach, and he and Nielsen, who were to compose the music, would be able to choose the lyrics themselves. Thus it was Borup's songbook that provided the impetus for Laub's and Nielsen's new joint project.[57]

Nielsen set to work immediately as soon as he had finished composing the tunes for Borup's songbook. He did not consider the lyrics to be a problem: seven of them he was to set for Borup he also composed for *A Score of Danish Songs*.[58] The distinction between the two projects can be observed in the composition of the respective publications: Borup's melody book comprises only unison melodies, whereas *A Score of Danish Songs* features solo parts with piano accompaniment. For Nielsen, there was thus an overlap in the ideals that characterised the two projects: that is, a good popular tune could be used both as a communal song and as a solo song. The combination of the actual work on the melodies in the two projects is revealed by a diary entry dated 28 December 1914, in which Nielsen wrote: 'Thus finished "Viserne" and Borup's Songbook.'[59] Three days later, he could celebrate New Year's Eve with the Borup family with a clear conscience.[60]

The Folk High School Melody Book

It was a coincidence of circumstances that led Nielsen to work on *Folkehøjskolens Melodibog* (*The Folk High School Melody Book*). He had already composed tunes that people liked and that could be used for communal singing – although some were intended for other purposes. He published some of the songs himself, making them available to the public; but even unpublished songs became known and used throughout the country. The editors of songbooks referred to Nielsen's tunes in new publications, thereby branding them as popular. This had a cumulative effect, and when Nielsen became the editor of Borup's melody book, which the public saw as a new direction for song practice in the folk high school environment, he became actively involved in the reform of singing culture. When Aagaard expressed the wish that Nielsen should take part in the editorial work on *The Folk High School Melody Book*, he naturally did not want to disappoint his friend.

Nielsen had known Aagaard's family, who lived at Rolfstedgaard in Ferritslev on Fyn, about fifteen kilometres east of Nr. Lyndelse, since his childhood. Aagaard's father, Anders Hansen, was the manager of Rolfsted Øvelseshus,[61] Fyn's second oldest community centre, where Nielsen and his colleague Julius Borup gave a concert in 1888.[62] Nielsen remembered his initial encounter with Hansen, which occurred when he was eleven or twelve. This took place at a wedding in Ferritslev, where he and his father were playing music. It may have been Hansen's own wedding in September 1876.[63] Thorvald was born nine months later.

As the first born, Thorvald was expected to take over the farm, but he had a keen interest in music. Together with his father, he visited Nielsen in 1898 to get his opinion on whether he was suited to become a musician.[64] Although Nielsen openly explained that it was better 'to be a good farmer … than a skilful musician', Aagaard decided to settle in Copenhagen in 1899, where he took lessons from the pianist Dagmar Borup and music theory from Nielsen.[65] He applied to the Academy of Music and studied from 1900 to 1902.[66] He then received additional tuition in composition from Nielsen and in music history and church music from Laub. With a recommendation from both Nielsen and Laub, he returned to his home region in 1905 and was employed as organist at the Ryslinge electoral parish.[67]

When Aagaard asked Nielsen in 1919 if he would participate in the publication of the melody book as the companion to the Folk High School Songbook, Nielsen replied in the affirmative – that is, on condition that Laub also be involved. Aagaard had asked Laub, whose answer depended on Nielsen's.[68] Ring and Aagaard had already agreed to work on the edition.[69] The group of four was now complete. Ring and Aagaard did most of the work, selecting the tunes and arranging them for piano.[70] Laub took care of arranging the piano settings of the hymns, while Nielsen was responsible for his own tunes, which he made sure met Aagaard's expectations in terms of accompaniment. In a letter of February 1921, Nielsen posed a number of questions to Aagaard about what the music should contain 'so that the book could have a uniform, truly "edited" appearance'.[71] Nielsen did indeed take his role as editor seriously, so that the tunes would be conveyed to the performers in the best possible way.

A good piano part was an important means of supporting the singer. One ideal on which Aagaard and Nielsen seemed to have agreed was that the piano settings should be simple and 'not too difficult'. They should be playable and suitable for a wide range of pianists, including amateurs.[72] They must have had in mind that the *Folk High School Melody Book* would be used in a variety of contexts, in meetings and associations, and not just in folk high schools where there were trained teachers. This was an important signal for Nielsen, and when the four editors had to formulate the preface to the melody book, Nielsen added a passage about the piano part. In the final version of the preface, the editors state that 'the settings are the composers' own or based on them. Where we had none, we have arranged the tunes as simply as possible.'[73] In his previous collection, *Tyve folkelige Melodier* (*Twenty 'folkelige' Melodies*), Nielsen elaborated: 'I have tried to keep both the melodies and their harmonic clothing as simple and easy as possible'.[74] Simple also meant a score without phrasing, character designations, dynamic markings and characterising titles.[75] When he emphasises the simplicity of the piano part, also in terms of harmony, it seems to be because he has the accompanist in mind.

MUSIC EX. 2. The piano setting of the well-known song 'Jeg bærer med Smil min Byrde' (I bear with a smile my burden), as published in *Folkehøjskolens Melodibog* (1922). Nielsen composed it on 20 December 1914 and included it in the melody book for Borup's songbook as well as in the first volume of *A Score of Danish Songs*. The setting shows the care with which it was adapted for use as an accompaniment to communal singing. The melody is always clear and distinct in the upper part. The rest of the setting is kept as simple and straightforward as possible. There are three, and in some places only two, parts, yet both the harmonic progression and the independent contrary motions to the melody that Nielsen has incorporated in the other parts, are clear. This is no mere harmonisation. All the compositional subtleties that Nielsen put into the version for solo voice are included, and the setting retains the lightness that corresponds to the text's message of the joy of physical labour in nature. Even in this form, the piano part is a small work of art.

The purpose of the melody book was to support the culture of singing. It is clear that in selecting the tunes the editors took into account the existing strong traditions of communal song practice. They retained a very large number of Romantic melodies, that is, those which had been well practised and which the singers wished to keep. Aagaard and Laub discussed the matter in their correspondence in the autumn of 1920 and agreed that it was acceptable to publish the tunes that people used. The ideal was also to preserve the tunes composed for the particular lyrics.[76] This was in contrast to the widespread tendency in nineteenth-century popular song culture for new lyrics to be sung to existing tunes. New texts required new tunes, so that the melody could bend and shape itself to the needs of the text, as Aagaard put it in his article on popular song in 1908.

The new melody book was not intended to be a completely new anthology, and it was indeed the question of old tunes versus new ones that led to what on the surface might appear to be a compromise. In fact, it was a deliberate choice. Aagaard discussed the issue again with Ring in the spring of 1921, who replied that if 'people miss too many of the old favourites, it will affect the sales potential of the book and thus its distribution'.[77] In order to accommodate as many as possible, the editors decided to offer new tunes as alternatives to many of the more familiar ones. More than fifty texts were thus assigned two tunes, indicated in the melody book by the letters 'a' and 'b', for the singers to choose from. It was mainly hymn texts to which Laub had composed new tunes or provided new ones as an alternative to the Romantic melodies. He thus combined the song traditions with the new approach he had been advocating within the church for decades, and which had last appeared in the choral book *Dansk Kirkesang* (1918). In two cases the editors also used the double numbering, that is, including the letters 'a' and 'b', for two new tunes: for the text 'Naar Nat udvælder fra sorten Sky' (*The Flood*) with tunes by Laub (No. 215a) and Nielsen (No. 215b) and 'Der gaar et stille Tog' (There is a quiet procession) with tunes by Ring (No. 568a) and Aagaard (No. 568b).

a)

b)

MUSIC EX. 3. Nielsen's and Weyse's tunes were both commonly employed to the lyrics 'Paa det jævne, paa det jævne' (Simple-rooted, simple-rooted). Right from the start, Nielsen's tune (a) has a different aim. Unlike Weyse's, Nielsen's tune was composed specifically for the lyrics, which thus enabled him to create a clear link between the tune and the lyrics as Aagaard had requested. While Weyse's melody (b) emphasises 'Paa' (on), Nielsen uses a weak upbeat to shift the focus to 'jævne' (simple), which is at the heart of Kaalund's emphasis on the importance of everyday life. The tune thus accentuates the message of the lyrics and is kept in a simple style, only gradually expanding in scope, limiting the melodic leaps and maintaining a steady, forward-moving pulse. With its brisk march tempo, the tune represents the individual's zest for life and pride in existence. Weyse's melody, on the other hand, is in a grandiose, dramatic and solemn style, worthy of the king, the key figure in the poem, for whom the melody was composed. Nielsen's tune sounds like one of the everyday songs that Borup had fought for.[78]

As the editors of the melody book were composers, it was obvious that they would contribute tunes to the anthology. Aagaard drew up a list of texts for which new ones were required and distributed them among the four members of the team. Laub contributed sixty-three melodies, Nielsen thirty-three, Aagaard twenty-three and Ring nineteen. In January 1921, Nielsen was able to write to Aagaard that he had now composed nine of the songs Aagaard had 'marked with a cross'. Ten days later he had composed four more. Among them was 'Paa det jævne, paa det jævne' (Simple-rooted, simple-rooted), Hans Vilhelm Kaalund's text, previously sung to Christoph Ernst Friedrich Weyse's melody for 'Paa den Dag Kong Kristians Øje', which described the heroism of Christian IV at the Battle of Kolberger Heide in 1644.

That the new melody had a positive effect can be seen from Harald Balslev's review of the publication, in which he explains that for him the tune had 'refreshed the text'.[79] This is remarkable, for he must have known the text well, having sung it several times to Weyse's melody, and yet a new one could open up a different understanding of the content of the text.

After the anthology was published, Aagaard was criticised for the fact that most of the new tunes were composed by the four members of the editorial team. They should have asked for tunes from other Danish composers, suggested Jens Laursøn Emborg, a vocal tutor at Vordingborg Teacher's College.[80] Aagaard replied diplomatically that the publishers had 'always regarded the anthology as a transitional form' and that other tunes might be included in later editions. For Aagaard, the ultimate question was whether the songs would be accepted by the people.[81]

Nielsen, too, was aware that public's opinion was crucial to the success of a tune, and so he made great efforts to promote the new ones. While working on the anthology, he decided to publish many of them in *Twenty 'folkelige' Melodies* (1921). Although they were intended for the melody book, he thought it would be an advantage if they were distributed before the anthology was published. Nielsen also tried to get *Højskolebladet*, which was a central medium for many singers throughout the country, to publish his tunes.[82]

The team did not fully agree on how to produce the book. The four members met only a few times, and most of their work was based on agreements reached by letter exchange. Aagaard was the coordinator, while the others consulted him and expected him to make decisions about the editorial line. Ring did a considerable amount of work, including liaising with the publisher as well as proofreading at various stages.[83] There is some evidence that Laub tried to work in tandem with Aagaard, bypassing Ring and Nielsen. When the final result became available in June 1922, Laub was very critical and wrote the following to Aagaard:

Such a work of 'popular education' should first and foremost be conscientious. And it is not. You and I are to some extent, but the other two are not.[84]

Laub's view that the team was divided is contradicted by both Nielsen and Ring. Ring was eager to complete the project in collaboration with Aagaard, and there is no indication in his letters to Aagaard that he shared Laub's views on the final outcome. In June 1922 Ring wrote to Aagaard that the book had arrived and that the rest was now up to the critics. He had clearly not expected the criticism to come from within the editorial group.[85] Nielsen also expressed his satisfaction with Aagaard's work, suggesting that Laub was alone in his criticism.[86] The design of the melody book must therefore be seen as a product of the deliberate priorities of the editor-in-chief, Aagaard, supported by Nielsen and Ring, and strongly influenced by Laub.

The intention of the project was not only to cultivate the song tradition, but also to improve it. The reform was intended to radically change and transform the communal singing culture. People were to be taught how to use their voices and thus develop their vocal skills. One specific approach was to set the songs in a tessitura that most people could join in with a little practice. It should not be too high and there was no point in setting the tunes too low.

The thirty-three tunes that Nielsen contributed had all been published before. Twenty-five were reproduced in the same key, while eight were transposed down, usually by a minor or major second, which did not necessarily mean accepting the lowest common denominator. One example is 'Vi Sletternes Sønner' (We, sons of the plains). When it was first published, the melody was in G major, notated in a high tessitura. In *The Folk High School Melody Book*, however, it is transposed down a major third to E flat major. The original key implies that the song was originally composed as incidental music for the play *Tove*, which was premiered in 1908 and was performed by a professional singer accompanied by an orchestra. The key of G major suited the soloist well, allowing a brilliant performance in a dramatic tessitura. The song was then included in Borup's melody book, edited by Nielsen, in the same key. In principle, the key was not important, as the collection of tunes was only intended to reproduce the vocal line. A singer could therefore use any suitable key for a performance without the piano accompaniment. In other words, the key in Borup's melody book was variable. In *The Folk High School Melody Book*, where the tunes were harmonised and to be played on the piano, it was important that the accompaniment was notated in a suitable key. For communal singing, the most suitable one was E flat major, with most of the tune in the middle tessitura. A short, well-prepared high E♭ note at the end of the song is the melodic climax that most people who are used to singing can achieve.

Surprisingly, there is one instance where one of Nielsen's songs is reproduced in a higher key. In the 1927 supplement to *The Folk High School Melody Book*, Nielsen's

'I solen går jeg bag min plov' (*Song behind the Plough*) is in D major. In his anthology *Songs by Ludvig Holstein* (1897) it is in C major, a major second lower. In each case, the editors considered how the song should be presented in order to realise the ideals behind the great reform project.

In other words, *The Folk High School Melody Book* was intended to help its performers to rejoin communal singing and was the culmination of a reform that was already underway. At the same time, it was an important milestone that served from then on as a tangible ideal for the cultivation of popular singing, codified and standardised so that a suitable vocal range would allow as many individuals as possible to participate and simultaneously establish a higher standard. The melody book represented more than just a new songbook. It was a new way of singing together. Three criteria were now established: to sing well, in time and correctly.[87] The emphasis was not only on the tunes themselves, but also on the culture of singing together, which was judged by a new standard.

The reform of song practice was a long project with an end goal that may have been clear to the composers, but could not be achieved by strategic planning or diligence alone. Success depended on the interest of the singers. *The Folk High School Melody Book* was an important step in this direction, but the reform was not yet over. In 1923, 1927 and 1928 supplements were added to the melody book, and Nielsen contributed a further eighteen tunes. Together with the composer Hakon Andersen, Nielsen also took on the task of editing the *Melodier til Sangbogen 'Danmark'* (*Melodies for the Songbook 'Denmark'*), which was published in 1924 with 305 melodies, of which forty-four were by Nielsen, and which introduced 'Jeg ved en Lærkerede' (Two larks in love have nested) and 'Solen er saa rød, Mor' (Look! the sun is red, mum) to the public for the first time. When asked to contribute to the second edition of Borup's songbook, Nielsen passed the task on to his pupil Adolf Riis-Magnussen; the anthology was released in 1926 with Nielsen contributing sixteen melodies. In addition to these collections, he preferred to publish his own melodies in independent anthologies: *Four 'folkelige' Melodies* appeared in 1925 and *Ti danske Smaasange* (*Ten Little Danish Songs*) the following year, both of which included previously published tunes. For Nielsen, the 1920s was a productive decade in the service of cultivating the popular song tradition.

Chapter 31

MODERNISM AND MODERNITY

By the time Nielsen's Fifth Symphony was premiered in 1922, the yardstick for what was considered modern had changed significantly from what had gone before. It was a change that had begun in the 1910s. At the beginning of the century, Nielsen had used Richard Strauss as a benchmark, when he referred to contemporaries who were considered modern. Now it was Arnold Schoenberg who had taken over that role. And this was not only a generational change, but a qualitative leap, for to speak of Schoenberg as modern was to speak of a more radical form of modernism than that represented by Strauss. What was decisive was Schoenberg's break with tonality.

In 1907–8 Schoenberg had written his first atonal music, and although very few had heard it, many were aware of it. The works, by their very existence, created the basis for a shift in consciousness comparable to Einstein's introduction of the theory of relativity. Now, for the first time, music existed outside the world of tonality, which had hitherto been taken for granted as an obvious prerequisite for the existence of music.

At the time, composers who took the step from tonality to atonality were considered the most radical modernists. One consequence was that composers were faced with a choice. A composer such as Strauss, who had until then been among the most modern because he had challenged the boundaries of tonality without going beyond them, for example in the opera *Salome* (1905), was reluctant to take the next step and leave the realm of tonality. In a progressive musical culture, therefore, he had to cede his place as a representative of those at the forefront of music-historical developments to people like Schoenberg. The 'modern' of the early 1920s meant something different from the modern music of the turn of the century. The frames of reference had changed.

In this situation Nielsen, like everyone else, had to consider how to deal with the question of tonality and atonality. In some respects he shared Schoenberg's views, and some of the compositional techniques used in early atonal music can also be found in Nielsen's works. Where their paths diverged was in the Schoenberg School's idea that music history was moving forward along a single path that took the form of a progressive, inexorable development. This path consisted of an increasingly chromatic music from Wagner onwards – that is, an ever greater degree of inclusion of all twelve semitones of the scale, until a point was reached where all the notes were present at all times and the music became atonal. Nielsen did not share this view.

When he moved away from the major and minor keys, it did not mean that the direction was necessarily through chromaticism.[1] On the contrary, he retained the diatonic. Nor did he believe that the history of music followed a rigid historical logic that could only lead in one direction.

By the early 1920s, Nielsen had reached a point where the question of tonality or the absence of tonality was no longer decisive for him; it was not a question of either/or. Because he did not see the development of music as a one-track or fixed progressive process, where each advance should be followed by new steps in the same direction, he did not need to answer the question of whether he should leave the basis of tonality forever. Instead, he looked at the situation with a spaciousness in which many new possibilities were available, and in which he could effortlessly make use of them when he found it appropriate. For many years now he had been working in such a way that he could begin a movement in one key and end it in another, and move freely between keys as he wished – either as modulations at the detailed level or at the overall level of musical form. For him, this new situation was an expression of freedom.

Symphony No. 5

On the occasion of the first performance of his Fifth Symphony, which took place on 24 January 1922, Nielsen gave an interview to the newspaper *Politiken* in which he explained how he saw his new symphony in relation to the earlier ones. When asked what he called the work, he replied: 'Nothing!'[2] This was followed by an explanation which revealed that it was something he had thought about carefully:

> My first symphony had no name either. But then came 'The Four Temperaments', 'Espansiva' and 'The Inextinguishable', which are really just different names for the same idea, that is, the only thing that music can ultimately express: the resting forces as opposed to the active ones. If I were to find a name for this, my fifth and new symphony, it would express something similar. I have not been able to find the one word that is at once characteristic and not too pretentious – and so I have left it alone. …
>
> I have been told that my new symphony is not like my previous ones. I cannot hear it myself. But perhaps it is true.[3]

In the interview, Nielsen goes on to explain the basis of the form. He says frankly that the problem he is trying to solve is the feeling that everything important is said in the first movement. That is why he has 'changed the form this time and decided on two parts instead of the usual four movements'.[4]

It was important for him to emphasise that he saw the new work as a continuation – a continuity – of the earlier symphonies. It may have sounded different, but it was essentially a new expression of the same thing. He speaks as if he had always held the same fundamental belief that symphonies exist to express the only thing that music can express: an interplay of musical forces unfolding. In this respect, his formulation is an extension of the arguments he used when trying to explain what he meant by 'The Inextinguishable'. And it is also striking how he finds it crucial that it can be expressed in a single word.[5]

This may have something to do with Nielsen's constant insistence that his symphonies should not be regarded as programme music that 'depicts' something. Even when there is no question that the audience can hear something going on in the music, he holds back. This is because he wants the audience to adopt a certain attitude while listening – to listen to the development of the music, rather than sit and think about what the music might represent: 'Long explanations and instructions … distract the listener and destroy absolute absorption.'[6] He wants the audience to listen to the symphony as absolute music.

However, it is not as if Nielsen did not have a word in mind when he composed the work. In the pencil draft for the symphony, at the top of the first page, after the Roman numeral 'I', marking the first movement, he added '(Vegetatio)'.[7] As in his Third Symphony, he could have chosen to elevate this word to a higher level by using it as the title of the work. The word literally means something that grows, and it has a clear affinity with organic growth in nature – as does the word vegetation. 'Vegetatio' is related to both 'espansiva' and 'the inextinguishable' as a metaphor for the process that emerges from the vital force of nature.

Nielsen began composing the symphony during 1920, and by October he was well under way.[8] During the summer he had worked on the incidental music for Helge Rode's play *The Mother*, and at the same time he was warming up for his next major composition. It was not unusual for him to have a certain 'incubation period', in which he would let his thoughts circle around a future work before starting on it, and this seems to have been the case here. In August he was able to write to his son-in-law Emil Telmányi: 'I'm now turning my attention to the great things.'[9]

What he was preparing can be linked to the two letters of February 1920 mentioned in Chapter 28, when on the Sunday he wrote to Julius Röntgen about the 'strongest and finest powers that are to be found in the material itself', referring to 'The Inextinguishable', and the following day to Ture Rangström that what was important now and in the future was the greatest possible combination of freedom and rigour with regard to 'organism – coherence'.[10] These thoughts can be read, perhaps unconsciously, as a preparation for his Fifth Symphony, as well as a reflection on the Fourth. The 'vegetatio' of the draft and the specific beginning of Nielsen's Fifth point

MUSIC EX. 1. Nielsen, Symphony No. 5, first movement, bars 1–9 in the pencil draft of the symphony (CNS 66b), compared with the final version (bars 1–8). The symphony begins with almost nothing, a single interval, the descending minor third C–A, played *piano* in the violas. By choosing a minor third rather than a major third, which would give the impression of a major key, and by choosing a descending interval rather than an ascending one, which would confirm the lowest note as the tonic, he leaves as many possible interpretations open in terms of tonality. He deliberately keeps it floating and undecided. When the bassoons enter, the lowest one begins on the same note as the violas, C, but moves in the opposite direction, through D up to E♭ in bar 7. The interval C–E♭ is an inversion of the minor third C–A.

in this direction, for here we find one of the most remarkable realisations of the idea that everything must grow from a small germ in an organic growth according to the strict rules inherent in the substance itself.

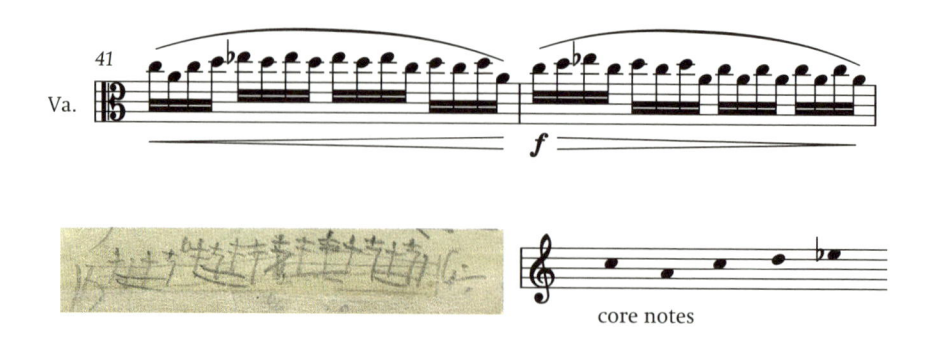

MUSIC EX. 2. Nielsen, Symphony No. 5, first movement, bars 41–42, contains the core motif that grew out of the symphony's first intervals. Nielsen notated it in pencil in the margin of the first page of the draft (CNS 66b). The first five notes of the motif repeat the structural element that was extended over the first seven bars of the symphony: C–A–C–D–E♭, forming a symmetrical figure in which the minor third is mirrored around C.

The symphony begins with a single interval, a minor third, played only by the violas, and when the bassoons enter in bar 5, the lower bassoon part mirrors the descending interval in the viola with an ascending minor third. The first two notes form the seed from which the symphony grows, and the symmetrical mirroring of the interval from the same initial note creates the closest possible organic relationship between the notes. That this is the structural core of the symphony's motivic material is confirmed by what follows. In the bottom right-hand corner of the first page of the pencil draft, Nielsen has noted the central motif that results from this mirroring. He could see where it might lead and made a note of it in the margin. Thus he had it ready when he arrived at the place where it was to be used. It takes him forty bars to get there.

When this core motif first appears in bars 41–42, it is clearly presented as a motif for the listener to remember. The indeterminate thematic material of the opening has now coalesced into a significant motif. At the same time, the snare drum is heard for the first time, linking the sound of the percussion to this motif. In the following passage, extensive melodies are heard in the strings, constantly building around the symmetrical intervallic structure of the core motif, moving up and down by shifting the central note in which the others are reflected. The central note moves up a fourth each time, once in the first wave, another fourth upwards in the second wave, and three times a fourth up in the third melodic wave.[11] It could not be more tightly woven.

The movement unfolds in ever new waves of organic development, first with the extensive melodies in the strings, and then in a march-like version in which the de-

MUSIC EX. 3. Nielsen, Symphony No. 5, first movement, bars 59–62, shows the melodic ascent, which begins the third wave of the unfolding of the extensive melodic lines. The structure of the core motif – a major second and a minor third mirrored around a central note – unfolds first around G, then around C, then around F and finally around B♭. Each time the central note is the point from which the symmetrical structure begins, and each time it moves to a new level, the structure is established a fourth higher. The four middle notes (G–C–F–B♭) form a stack of fourths and have nothing to do with traditional scale structures that repeat each time an octave is reached. In a major scale the notes are the same in every octave. In the system that Nielsen constructs, the first E and the eighth note E♭ are both a constituent part of the diatonic grid of pitches. The music is an example of how Nielsen works with the organic development of small motivic germs, and does so consistently and with such strict logic that a new way of constructing the tonal system emerges. It is very much an expression of the desire to achieve 'organism – coherence'.[12]

scending minor third is in the bass, accompanied by a considerable amount of percussion. This is followed by a further development in which a small figure consisting of the first three notes of the core motif, a minor third and a major second, begins to take on an independent significance. Finally, this three-note figure lies as a constant band of rapid triplets in the woodwinds, while the bassoons' initial motif returns. It takes about ten minutes for this whole continuous development to reach its conclusion in the middle of the movement, in which the intervals and rhythm become increasingly diluted, until only a few sharp repetitions of notes remain in the violins, interacting with the snare drum and tambourine.

At this point, in the middle of the first part of the symphony, a new subject is introduced in slow triple time, with well-balanced melodic phrases. This beautiful, cantabile subject provides an almost exaggerated contrast in sound and expression to the intense display of power the listener has just heard. Although it may sound as if a new movement is about to begin, this is not the case. Instead, the second subject begins. Up to this point, the music has been building on the main thematic material from the opening of the symphony, and only now is a second subject presented. Here begins a new great coherent unfolding in which the second subject is almost besieged from all sides as elements from the first part of the movement surround and challenge it in ever more extreme forms. The second subject's response is to strengthen its appearance in firm and resilient forms until, at the end of the movement, it seems to assert itself as the victor. It breaks through all resistance and stands alone, and after the great display of power it fades out with a long major chord. Above it, a solitary clarinet, accompanied by a snare drum, muses melancholically over the core motif until they both disappear in the distance.

During the siege of the second subject, Nielsen introduces a device that has never before been heard in the symphonic repertoire. By the time the second subject has established itself in the brass, and all the woodwinds and strings alternately attack it from opposite positions with the core motif from the first part of the movement, it seems unlikely that the intensity can be increased any further. At this point, Nielsen allows a snare drum to enter at its own pace contrary to the rest of the orchestra, explicitly noting in the score that the musician should play 'as though determined at all costs to obstruct the music'. A little later, the musician is asked to improvise, still at their own tempo: 'The side drummer now improvises entirely freely with all possible fantasy, although from time to time he must pause.'[13] That Nielsen was serious about this is evident when he heard that the conductor Wilhelm Furtwängler was to perform the symphony in Germany in 1926, he wrote to him: 'During previous performances I've noticed that the player has always been nervous about letting go, starting from the place (unfortunately I don't have the score out here in the country) where he has to play in free time. He should be completely obsessed with his determination to destroy the song in the orchestra, with all possible figurations'.[14]

On top of the snare drum's fury, the trumpets now begin to play fanfare figures. The effect is an enormous build-up of energy, culminating in the second subject, which unfolds in a balanced and concluding manner, as if the sun is finally breaking through. But, as already mentioned, it does not end here: the core motif reappears, getting the final say as a solo played by the clarinet.

Form and Narrative

When Nielsen was asked in the interview what thought or idea was behind the nameless symphony, he replied:

> Yes, how can I explain it? I roll a stone up a hill, using the forces within me to bring the stone to a high point. There, the stone lies inert, the forces are bound up in it – until I give it a kick, the same forces are released and the stone rolls down again.[15]

This should be viewed as an elaboration of the fact that music can only express 'the resting forces as opposed to the active ones'.[16] But the formulation is interesting because it clearly refers to the physics concept of kinetic and potential energy, the former denoting motion and the latter the kind of energy stored in a tensioned spring, a dammed body of water or a stone lying on a slope. It also reveals that Nielsen was well informed about the latest discussions in German-language literature, in which August Halm and Ernst Kurth used such concepts to understand the music of Bach and Bruckner. In his book on Johann Sebastian Bach's linear counterpoint, Kurth argued that music should be understood as a play of forces, with melodic forces perceived as kinetic energy and structure as the result of the interaction of opposing forces.[17]

In an interview a few days earlier, Nielsen elaborated on his thoughts about the form of the symphony in two major parts. He argues that it is intended as a juxtaposition of the vegetative, passive relationship with nature in the first part and the unfolding of active forces in the second.[18] It is difficult to hear the whole symphony in this way, but it makes sense if one thinks of it as the starting point for the two parts of the symphony. In *The Inextinguishable*, the four linked movements are clearly audible in a sequence behind the larger form, but in the Fifth Symphony Nielsen does something different.

The first part of the symphony corresponds to a first movement in which the presentation of the subjects and their development are folded together so that the development takes place simultaneously with and as part of the exposition. Nielsen is thus able to develop the material of the first subject and then let the second subject unfold in one long motion under the siege of material from the first part of the movement. The two large, coherent sequences of building up and releasing energy are satisfying because the listener experiences a balance between the amount of energy that is built up and the forces that are released.

The second part of the symphony presents an integration of the three movements usually used in the traditional version of the remainder of a symphony: two middle movements and a fast finale. The middle movements, a fast Presto that unfolds as a fugue in increasingly frantic strettas, and a calm and cantabile Andante poco tranquillo, are embedded in the Finale. Nielsen begins the last movement in an energetic triple metre, which has a very distinctive and different sound from the first part of the symphony in that the interval that permeates it is the fourth. The melody moves in fourths in all parts.

The fugue is remarkable in that it is one of the few instances in Nielsen's oeuvre where he borrows from the fiddler's repertoire. The theme is reminiscent of the tune known in Denmark as 'Den lille Englænder' (The little Englishman), which was used for folk dancing.[19]

The Andante is a surprise, as the violins take up the subject of the introduction with the fourths, but now in a completely different guise and form, so that at first the listener is not even aware that it is the same melodic material. Then the opening of the Finale returns in a shorter version, leading to a haunting ending that may seem a little abrupt.[20]

It is clear that the symphony was composed to allow the audience to hear it as Nielsen would have wished – that is, to hear the musical development. The subjects and the elements are easily recognisable and recur several times. Along the way, they undergo transformations that the listener can follow. The small core motif of the first movement, initially played rather discreetly but clearly audible on its own, appears in increasingly violent versions until it ends quietly as part of the clarinet's final phrase. This plays an important role in the aural experience, as the listener is able to follow what the recognisable themes undergo and 'experience', and how they interact with each other. This gives the music an explicitly narrative character. It appears as a storyline. For the same reason, Nielsen's Fifth Symphony also has a more explicit focus than *The Inextinguishable*, as the narrative is constantly moving forward.

Nielsen was well aware that the musical landscape had changed after the First World War, and he actively used this to promote his new symphony. In the interview before the premiere, he spoke to this new reality when he said of his symphony that it was difficult to play and not 'quite easy to understand', adding: 'Some have even thought that Arnold Schoenberg could now pack up his disharmonies. Mine were worse. But I don't think so.'[21] Nielsen could count on the readers of a Danish newspaper to know that atonal music existed and that Schoenberg was its architect.

The view that the first movement was the most successful was echoed in the reviews, which also seemed to indicate that Nielsen's reference to Schoenberg had borne fruit, for the critics seized the opportunity to make a comparison that turned out in Nielsen's favour.[22] Yet something else also happened that made the reference to Schoenberg both topical and concrete, for several of Schoenberg's works had been performed in Copenhagen in the preceding months. Overall, in the early 1920s, Copenhagen was one of the leading European musical cities, alongside musical metropolises such as Vienna, Frankfurt, Berlin and Paris, when it came to hearing new and radical compositions.[23]

The Music-Historical Context

Until the end of the First World War, the new music for which Schoenberg and his like-minded contemporaries were responsible had little chance of being performed because the traditional music world would have none of it. After the war, however, there was a great interest throughout Europe in hearing the new and radical music that rejected the old world of the pre-war era. There was a mood of curiosity and openness towards a new generation of composers. At the same time, in reaction to the nationalism of the war years, there was a new interest in international cooperation, also in the terms of music.

Denmark was at the forefront, and in 1920–21 three societies were established to organise concerts of contemporary music in Copenhagen. These were parallel institutions to the societies and concert series in which Nielsen had been active in his youth, in order to get the new compositions of his generation performed. The Unge Tonekunstneres Selskab (Young Composers' Society) and Dansk Filharmonisk Selskab (the Danish Philharmonic Society) were founded in 1920, and Foreningen 'Ny Musik' (The Society 'New Music') the following year. The latter had its roots in the environment of the Academy of Music, and at its foundation the pianist Christian Christiansen was elected chairman, and a censorship committee was set up to plan the programme; among its members were Nielsen's close colleagues of the younger generation: Rudolph Simonsen, Thorvald Nielsen and Knud Jeppesen. In 1922, the organisation co-founded the ISCM, the International Society for Contemporary Music.[24]

The creation of new societies and European networks was important because it created the infrastructure for contemporary music to be performed throughout Europe. It was a prerequisite for this music to be accessible and to have a specific presence in the musical world. It is not enough for a work to have been composed if only the composer is aware of it. When writing about music history, it is therefore crucial to alternate between two perspectives. On the one hand, the development of music can be seen as a history of composition, in which a work is written into the history at the time of its creation. On the other hand, the history of musical life must be kept in mind, as it is in this context that it is possible to examine what kind of music was available, performed and discussed. The two approaches interact in the sense that a work must be composed before it can be performed, while it cannot have an impact until it is recognised.

This is important if we are to understand the music-historical context in 1922. In some respects it was similar to the situation at the turn of the century, in others it was quite different. The common point was a general desire to get to know the new. The music performed in the new Copenhagen societies for contemporary music in 1920–22 was, however, very diverse. There was music by Schoenberg, Stravinsky, Bartók, Ravel, Reger and Rued Langgaard, but also by Nielsen's contemporaries such as Glazunov, Sibelius and Louis Glass, and the Danish Philharmonic Society also performed major orchestral works by Scriabin, Debussy, Mahler and Paul von Klenau.[25]

At the beginning of the 1920s, as at the turn of the century, the situation was open in the sense that no one knew where it would end. When one spoke of atonal music, one could only refer to free atonal music in which no system of the twelve-note series ruled. It was not until 1923 that the first twelve-note music composed according to the serial principles were published.[26] It was only two or three years later that a clearer picture emerged, showing that Schoenberg, Stravinsky, Hindemith and Bartók represented different directions within a contemporary music to which one could relate.

On the other hand, it was not an open situation in the same sense as at the turn of the century, when there was a stylistic permissiveness and a space of possibility for different forms of music that represented modernity and youth. After the advent of atonal music, there was 'a before' and 'an after' that composers could not ignore.

At the end of October 1921, the townspeople of Copenhagen were able to hear Schoenberg's First String Quartet in the Society 'New Music'. A month later, one of the other societies, the Danish Philharmonic Society, performed two of Schoenberg's works, *Verklärte Nacht* (1899) and *Pierrot Lunaire* (1912).[27] The latter piece, in particular, fulfilled the expectations of those who wanted to hear atonal music, with *Sprechgesang* and a highly unusual soundscape. Nielsen's reference to Schoenberg in January 1922 thus had a particular resonance, for the *Pierrot Lunaire* concert was an event that had received widespread press coverage. The reviews show that there was an interested audience for this music in Copenhagen, but also that the work was regarded as being outside of the conventional boundaries typically associated with the concept of music: 'A strange stream of sounds, of detached moods held for a moment, of unfamiliar, foreign pitches. It was not music at all, it was something completely new, something that cannot be given a name.'[28]

What is important in this context is not what people believed or thought they knew about Schoenberg, or whether they liked his music, but that it was relevant for the Copenhagen music public in 1922 to refer to him when dealing with Nielsen – and that Nielsen was aware of this. Thus, new perceptions of what was considered modern music at the time had taken hold.

The interesting question is how Nielsen related to and acted in this new reality. How did he approach questions of tonality and atonality, and how did he deal with the challenges he faced as a composer?

Away from the Keys?

Nielsen had long been interested in how counterpoint and modal harmonisation could be used to find alternative approaches to harmonising and modulating to new keys in other ways than what he had learned at the Academy. Although Orla Rosenhoff's theory lessons emphasised the relationship between the outer voices and included modulations to distantly related keys, it was fundamentally the harmonic progression that governed the framework. Even as a student, Nielsen took a keen interest in the counterpoint lessons he was given, where, after tireless work with systematic exercises, he gradually realised that there were entirely different possibilities if one concentrated on the course of the lines rather than on the vertical aspect of chords and harmonies. It was an approach that he insisted on passing on to his students as a teacher. While working on the *Hymnus Amoris*, he revisited exercises in four-part counterpoint, training the ability to control four independent voices, whose movements create the harmonic progression. In 1909, in a review of a music theory textbook, he even formulated as a dictum that 'every good musician should be able to modulate using pure triads'.[29] This shows his desire to get away from the usual harmonic phrases and to exploit the possibilities that lay in the use of the voice-leading instead.

In 1913, Nielsen commented on some of the wording in an introduction written by Henrik Knudsen to Nielsen's *Sinfonia espansiva,* and continued:

> We ought to move away from the keys for once, and yet at the same time make a diatonically convincing effect. That's the thing; and here I feel in myself a striving for freedom.[30]

The phrase seems to point to a rather central element in Nielsen's relationship to tonality, and thus to his understanding of the direction in which he believed music should move in the future. The 'we' at the beginning of the sentence suggests that he is not just talking about himself, but about music as such.

But how should we interpret his view? It is one of those maxims that are often quoted and discussed in the Nielsen literature, although it is clear that the statement is ultimately not very specific.[31] Yet it is also one that goes to the heart of one of the central issues that musicians, composers and the music world as a whole had to deal with at the time: the question of the status of tonality in contemporary and future music.

Nielsen's formulation suggests that for him it was not a choice between composing tonally or atonally, but that it was crucial to be able to relate freely to the tonalities, as long as it was diatonically convincing. Basically, diatonic means working in scales consisting of an intervallic combination of whole tones and semitones. Assuming that an octave is divided into seven notes, many different scales can be constructed from a diatonic principle. All major and minor scales are diatonic, as are the modal scales. By combining scales and creating new combinations, it is possible to be diatonic without resorting to the familiar major and minor keys. The idea of 'getting away from the major and minor keys' can thus be achieved by utilising the means contained in other scales. By adhering to the basic principle of diatonicity, Nielsen distanced himself from the chromatically based twelve-note series and strict atonality.

In 1913, when Nielsen made his comment, the awareness of the emergence of atonal music was widespread in musical circles, but it did not yet play a significant role in musical life. With very few exceptions, it was not until around 1918 that atonal music was performed and heard throughout Europe. It is therefore not clear that Nielsen had specific atonal music in mind when he commented on Knudsen's formulation in 1913.

Knudsen begins his introduction to Nielsen's Third Symphony, issued in German by the Leipzig publishers who printed both score and instrumental parts, by noting that when it comes to absolute music, it is not so much a renewal of form or a profound programme that makes the difference: 'If you want to break new ground you have to look for new expansions and perspectives in the tonal field.'[32] He goes on to say that he is not only concerned with the new symphony:

> This applies, for example, to the key relationships. Carl Nielsen was acutely aware of the limitations of the traditional style. Therefore, one notices everywhere in his works the urge to break through them. Sometimes it is as if the twelve major and the twelve minor keys or the church modes did not exist at all, but had been put into a mortar and processed into a single tonality.[33]

For this reason, Knudsen argues that Nielsen's music often contains sections that cannot be assigned to a particular key, and he notes that Nielsen does not maintain the usual key relationships either within movements or between them. Knudsen then emphasises Nielsen's preference for strong diatonicism and that Nielsen avoids chromaticism as much as possible – an aspect that also characterises his modulations, which are 'short, powerful, convincing, and achieved frequently by means of pure triads'.[34]

Knudsen could, of course, only speak of the music Nielsen had already composed at the time. In his discussion of Nielsen's music up to and including the Third Symphony, the notion of music that breaks with key relationships may refer to sections of the music where, temporarily – through bold modulations or polyphonic passages – no firm tonal ground is felt. Knudsen may also be referring to instances, such as at the beginning of the First Symphony, where Nielsen balances between two keys, or where a movement ends in a different key than it began. When Knudsen says that it is as if all the keys are being processed into one, he is not talking about atonality, but about all-tonality: all the keys at once.

When Nielsen takes up the idea in Knudsen's text, however, he thinks further ahead. First he asks, somewhat critically, whether there is not a contradiction between talking about diatonic relationships, which he believes are linked to scales, and the fine image of all the keys in a mortar. But then he synthesises the two concepts and arrives at his succinct formulation about abandoning the keys and still sounding diatonically convincing. He imagines how this might be achieved in the future. In Nielsen's case, the phrase comes across as a vision of a music that has not yet been composed.

In his efforts to realise his ideas, Nielsen resorts to two strategies that can be combined. One is a continuation of a tendency, already present in twentieth-century music, to keep the key uncertain or wavering for long stretches by refraining from confirming a particular key as the dominant one. This technique has much in common with Schoenberg's approach in his early atonal compositions. The second strategy is to exploit the possibilities of moving freely between keys through modal chord relationships and strong, contrapuntal lines.

The Technique of Avoiding

Around 1907–8, Schoenberg composed some of the first pieces of music that may be described as atonal. Schoenberg's approach can be compared to Nielsen's compositional technique, which he employs at the beginning of the Fifth Symphony: the music consists mainly of minor thirds and other intervals that do not have clear tonal associations, and accents are placed to counteract the establishment of a key. The early atonal pieces by Schoenberg, including the *Three Piano Pieces*, Op. 11 (1909), work in such a way that he consistently avoids chords, chordal relationships and melodic twists that might confirm a particular tonality, thus eliminating the sense of key. The music is in 'no key'. It is known that Nielsen was familiar with these pieces.[35]

MUSIC EX. 4. Schoenberg, *Three Piano Pieces*, Op. 11, No. 2, bars 1–3. Schoenberg abandons the sense of tonality by avoiding the confirmation of any key. Similar to the opening of Nielsen's Fifth Symphony, Schoenberg begins in the piano's left hand with a downward movement of the minor third. By using a particular time signature (12/8, in which the bar is divided into four times three notes), he achieves an almost perfect balance as the emphasis alternates between F and D. If the ear is inclined to hear the lowest D as the fundamental (as in D minor), he counteracts this by placing an F below it in the bass. However, this F is deliberately notated low and is struck very softly and only once, so that it does not assert itself as the fundamental. The balance is maintained. And just as a sense of tonality is about to emerge in bar 2, Schoenberg deliberately adds three notes – first a D♭, then an A and finally an E♭ in the right hand – to cancel out the sense of key that is about to emerge.

When Schoenberg and his students argued for the development of atonal music, they, like Nielsen, spoke of organicity and coherence as the overriding principle governing the development, explaining that when the inner coherence of the music had become strong enough to support itself, then the keynote, and thus tonality, was no longer necessary. It could be dismantled like a scaffolding that was no longer needed. When Schoenberg abandoned free atonal music in the early 1920s in favour of composing with twelve-note series, he saw this as a logical continuation and fulfilment of this development. Another view that the Schoenberg School shared with Nielsen was that one should avoid the superfluous and focus on the essential. The free, atonal pieces were therefore often very short and concentrated.[36]

If we take Nielsen's 1913 formulation as a programme for a future music, then the way in which Nielsen composes his Fifth Symphony could be a suggestion for its realisation. As shown above, in the first part he creates long melodic lines in which the symmetrical intervallic structure of the core motif forms the starting point for all the notes in the gradual unfolding of the melody. The effect of this technique is to create a tonal system in which the same interval structure is repeated, but not – as in major-minor or modal scales – at octave intervals, but each time ascending by a fourth. There is no evidence that Nielsen planned or imagined in advance that he would end up with a systematically organised structure – and he may not even have been aware that this was happening. He followed the logic of the notes within a diatonic framework and ended up with such a structure. The fact that this results in a diatonic tonal system, established according to a strict logic derived from a core motif, is an expression of music that has got 'away from the tonalities' and yet is 'diatonically convincing'.[37]

Yet it cannot be concluded that Nielsen generally wanted to abandon the existing diatonic scale structures in favour of a completely new tonal system. The passage in the Fifth Symphony is a special case. But it shows how, by working intensively with motifs and their inner context, he can achieve a result where a key is no longer necessary.

Free Modulations and Counterpoint

Another way of seeing Nielsen's vision realised is to continue Knudsen's concluding remark in the quoted passage, referring to Nielsen's modulation practice. Knudsen emphasises that the transitions between keys are 'short, powerful, convincing', often using only pure triads.[38] Knudsen obviously knew that he was referring to the ideal that Nielsen had formulated in 1909. The ideal of modulating with pure triads – and thus avoiding letting the flow of the music be determined by major-minor harmonic shifts, especially dominant seventh chords – points in the direction of a modal harmonisation practice in which the individual voices control the harmonies and not the other way around.

The rejection of major-minor tonal effects opens up new possibilities while maintaining a triad-based harmony. In this sense, too, it is possible to 'to move away from the keys for once, and yet at the same time make a diatonically convincing effect'.[39] This is also a key to understanding why Nielsen saw no contradiction between major-minor tonality and the new modal way of thinking. They were both based on diatonic scales and triads; the difference was in the extent to which the harmonies could move freely.

Another way of realising Nielsen's vision might therefore be a radical use of modal harmony, in which the harmonic movements are not tied to a particular tonal framework. In terms of time, such music is closer to Nielsen's 1913 statement than the Fifth Symphony. An interesting example is the modal harmonies that Nielsen and Paul Hellmuth worked on in 1914, when most of the anthology *Salmer og aandelige Sange* (*Hymns and Spiritual Songs*) was composed.

What Nielsen and Hellmuth aimed for together was a modal harmonisation of the hymns. The style is characterised by sequences of triads conditioned by natural melodic lines in all four voices. In contrast to Romantic harmony, which favours chromatic relationships, extended timbres and dominant chords, the modal style is characterised by minimal means. Every melodic movement must be justified, every departure from the modal scales must have consequences. In Nielsen's own words, the setting must be 'as clear and simple, from a certain point of view as uninteresting as possible'; yet he wants the user to dwell on each individual tune, to see how the notes follow one another and how they relate to the words.[40] There are many possibilities within this framework. Some of the hymns, such as the one mentioned in Chapter 26, 'Dybt hælder Aaret i sin Gang' (Well on the wane the passing year), move effortlessly through several keys within the short format.

The fact that Nielsen talks about making a diatonically convincing effect and at the same time recognises modulation must mean that he attaches importance to keys. Modulation is moving from one key to another, so the concept has no substance if there are no keys to relate to. On the other hand, the keys are not limited to major and minor, since modal harmony has its origins in the church modes. A modulation practice based on this principle, working through pure triads, therefore has a wide range of possibilities to work with. In this sense, it can be experienced as a compositional freedom.

The starting point is very much in line with the idea that if all the keys are put in a mortar, the result is an 'all-tonality' in which all the keys are present at once. In this context, Knudsen spoke explicitly of major, minor and modal scales. When moving in such a musical universe, the aim is to avoid being tied to one key and to be able

MUSIC EX. 5. Nielsen, *Thema med Variationer* (*Theme and Variations*), Op. 40, bars 1–16. Working on the theme interested him greatly, Nielsen wrote to his daughter Irmelin, and he was particularly interested in the modulations. He described ending the theme in a different key from the one in which it began as a deliberate device to make each new variation, with its return to the original key of B minor, seem like a new beginning.[41] The theme moves from B minor via a half close in A minor (with the E major chord in bar 8) to F minor, and then back via D flat major to G minor, and then beginning again in B minor. An astute analyst would explain the marked change of key in the middle of the theme – from the final chord of the phrase, E major, to F minor – in terms of functional harmony, although it is not the experience of a difficult and complicated transition that meets the ear. Rather, one hears the convincing stepwise movement in the middle voice, continued by the bass: in bar 8, the notes E–F♯–G♯–A are heard, followed by A♭ in bar 9. Since G♯ and A♭ sound the same, a small rotational movement is formed, G♯–A–A♭. This, combined with the upward leap of a fourth in the melody, corresponding to the beginning of the theme, gives the listener a coherent impression that we have now safely landed in a new key. The final downward diatonic scale of the melody is an example of Nielsen's ability to modulate melodically by effortlessly combining several familiar scales: A♭–G–F–E♭–D♭–C–B♭–A–G.

to move freely between several related ones. The means – the use of modulation through pure triads – is based on the idea that linearity is the most important element in music. It is the linear aspects and not the dissonances of the chords that determine the harmony. Thus the diatonic – and not the chromatic – becomes essential.

A realisation of this principle is apparent in Nielsen's piano work *Thema med Variationer* (*Theme and Variations*), Op. 40 (CNW 87), composed in 1917. He works with a theme that is harmonised with rich but simple triads that underpin the melody in the right hand, while the left hand accompanies with strong and distinctive lines that are doubled by an octave in the final section. It is the interplay between the two outer voices that determines the course of the piece.

The theme is an example of modal harmonisation and of a movement that shifts between tonal levels through the progression of the melodic lines. The melody of the first phrase forms a very simple and regular arc, while the bass part accompanies it discreetly. The second phrase of the melody begins in a similar way, but now the movement in the bass leads in an energetic, upward line to a half-cadence, from which it continues up to the middle voice in the right hand. The third phrase begins with an upward leap followed by two descending notes, then the same figure is repeated one note higher; the fourth phrase repeats the upwards motion, after which the melody descends an octave stepwise. In the last two phrases of the melody, the bass part follows downwards, descending stepwise through one and a half octaves, before turning and continuing upwards as a contrast to the descending melody towards the end.

Formally, the variations build gradually to a first climax at the end of Variation 6. Nielsen then breaks off and reintroduces the theme, now in a new harmonisation, with only linked modal chords and in long, calm note values, retaining only the characteristic rhythm of the opening figure. Nielsen uses almost exclusively pure triads in root position and in stepwise motion. It is clearly audible that the tonal universe is now different and is in contrast to the first harmonisation. The difference is particularly evident as there is less rhythmic motion and no contrapuntal part in the bass. The audience listens to the harmonies and the melody because there is nothing else to listen to. When Nielsen builds on the new harmonic design in the following three variations, the difference is particularly clear.

Theme and Variations was premiered by Alexander Stoffregen at a recital in Odd Fellow Palæet on 29 November 1917. Earlier that year, on 13 April, he had also given the first performance of Nielsen's earlier piano work, *Chaconne*, Op. 32 (CNW 86). The work was composed over the course of a month during New Year 1917.[42] *Chaconne* begins with a single melody in the bass, which forms the basis of the entire work. Here too he builds into the theme and its movements, even in its single melodic form, the possibility of moving freely between several keys.

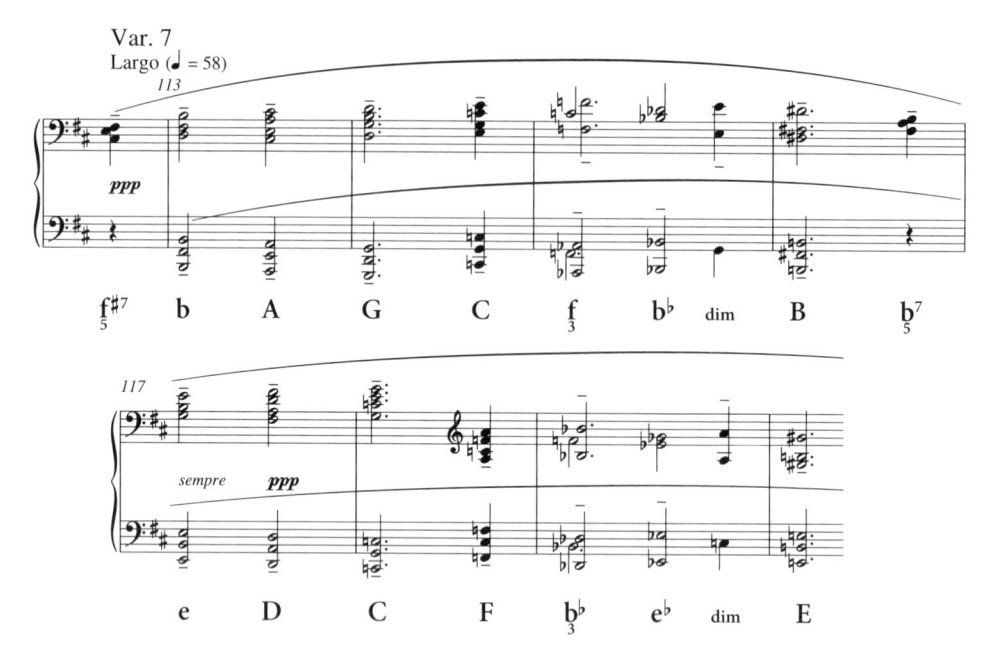

MUSIC EX. 6. In *Theme and Variations*, Variation 7 (bars 113–20), Nielsen reintroduces the theme, but this time in a new and completely modally harmonised form, using almost exclusively pure triads in the basic form. The rhythmic tension is replaced by notes of equal length. The melody is harmonised with a simple counterpoint between the outer voices with stepwise connected chords in the root position: B minor, A major and G major. The first four bars are then repeated a fourth higher, with the corresponding notes harmonised: E minor, D major and C major. The only reminiscence of a dominant seventh chord is the sound of the opening upbeat, which is a reference to the original theme. In the second half, the melody returns to its range, with slight variations in the melody.

Freedom and Tonality

Nielsen's freer approach to tonality is reflected in his compositional practice. When he drafted the introduction to his Fifth Symphony in 1920, he began by notating it with a single flat key signature, indicating that he had conceived the beginning in D minor. However, he then cancelled the signature and had the entire first movement notated without one. When working on the first page of the draft of the second movement, he was also in doubt and noted 'E major key signature? A major?' and added in capital letters 'A major key signature!'[43] The question 'E major key signature?' refers to how the music should be notated.[44] These examples show that it was not important to Nielsen that the notation should determine the key of the

Tempo giusto (♩ = 96)   Op. 32

MUSIC EX. 7. Nielsen, *Chaconne*, Op. 32, bars 1–8. The first five bars of the monophonic theme suggest G minor, after which the next three bars present an upward movement in C major. In the penultimate bar, with the tie to the last note giving a sense of lingering on the note A, Nielsen reinforces the sense that the key is momentarily F major.

music – perhaps the intention was sometimes to obscure it. In any case, it is possible to conclude that he did not have a 'heartfelt' relationship with tonality in such situations.

Similarly, in the pencil draft of his Sixth Symphony, he began the notation with the key signature of G major, corresponding to the symphony's introduction. Later, he cancelled the accidental and added 'to be notated (without key signature)' at the top of the page.[45] And in a programme note for his Flute Concerto, composed in 1926, he could easily describe the first movement: 'The movement does not end as it began; on the contrary, it settles down gently in G flat major, whereas it began dissonant and in no key.'[46] None of the introductions to these movements are atonal in the sense that they use all twelve semitones of the scale or have negated any sense of tonality.

Not that Nielsen was incapable of devising a subject containing all twelve notes – he does so in the third of the *Three Piano Pieces* (CNW 90), composed in 1928. It contains a fugal subject that includes all twelve semitones and is often used as an example of Nielsen's ability to compose atonally when he wanted to.[47] However, this is not the most relevant way of interpreting the subject. The defining feature of this piece is not its atonal quality, as it contains all twelve notes of the scale; rather, it is the coherence of the subject – due to its powerful internal musical relationships and the strong contrapuntal effect of the two outer voices – which effectively expand it in a fan-like manner. The musical logic and the strength of the voicing are so convincing that there is no need for a tonality as a musical framework. It can carry itself.[48]

Nielsen's approach to tonality and atonality is therefore not about whether the step from the one to the other should be taken. Such a formulation of the problem is rooted in a progress-oriented understanding of history in which there was only one way forward, which was not part of Nielsen's way of thinking. He was looking

MUSIC EX. 8. The fugal subject of the third of Nielsen's *Three Piano Pieces*, Op. 59 (1928), bars 90–93. The subject contains all twelve notes of the chromatic scale, and thus formally fulfilling the requirement of being a twelve-note theme. Nor is it in any key. However, the two times twelve notes do not occur equally often, nor do they form a twelve-note series.

for a new freedom, also beyond the traditional tonal framework, which he found restrictive. Yet he would have found it equally restrictive not to be able to use tonal frameworks whenever he wanted.

One way of achieving the freedom was to strive for ever greater coherence in the internal relationships of the music, so that it no longer needed an external framework of a fixed tonality to make sense. Another way was to deliberately leave the field open, refraining from establishing or confirming a particular key in favour of an ambiguous and indeterminate musical landscape in which to move. These strategies of moving away from tonality as a necessity can also be seen in Schoenberg's compositions as he worked towards his early atonal pieces. Starting from a chromatic tonal material, Schoenberg arrived at a kind of atonality in which the twelve individual notes are constantly kept in a balance, so that none of them is given more weight than the others. Nielsen, on the other hand, stuck to the diatonic tonal material, in which there are always notes that act as local centres of gravity, although these centres need not always be the same. Nielsen did not want to abolish tonality, but rather to be able to move freely between the keys.[49] The inner coherence of the music and the strict musical logic of its development were decisive for him.

Equally important was Nielsen's experience of counterpoint, which also enabled him to create musical coherence. His lifelong interest in working with the individual musical voices and their mutual harmony as a result of linear movement enabled him to compose harmonic progressions based solely on the melodic lines of the voices. He could choose to compose freely in counterpoint or to rely on modal harmonies. Both provided an opportunity to move away from the Romantic tradition, where the emphasis on harmony was paramount. The combination of organic coherence in the musical material and powerful, independent lines that depended on counterpoint were tools that allowed him to depart from the basis of tonality when he chose to do so.

In Nielsen's day, it was widely believed that those composers who took the plunge into atonalism were the most radical modernists. Nielsen's answer to this question, however, is perhaps at least as radical and sets an entirely different agenda: for him, the question was not crucial as long as the music was coherent and diatonically convincing. Music could be tonal, it could move through keys and it could leave the keys, as long as it made sense. He transcended and left behind the question of whether to be tonal or atonal. Instead, he achieved the freedom to move beyond traditional tonal and harmonic frameworks – including the freedom to decide for himself if and when he wanted to do so.

Chapter 32

THE KAPELLMEISTER

One of the moments when Nielsen felt that his career and international recognition had received a decisive boost was when he was made a member of the Prussian Akademie der Künste in Berlin in 1923. The news of his membership reached him in early March, while he was staying in Menton in the south of France, after conducting some very successful concerts in Germany.[1] The decision had been taken on 27 January 1923 by the music section of the Akademie der Künste, which appointed its own members. Five new members had been nominated at the meeting, two of whom were considered residents of Prussia as they lived and worked in Berlin: Nielsen's old friend Ferruccio Busoni and the Austrian composer Franz Schreker. The three 'foreign' members were Nielsen from Copenhagen, Alexander Glazunov from St Petersburg and Walter Braunfels from Munich.[2] Nielsen was in excellent company. It was only two years since his colleague Jean Sibelius had become a member, and it was not until 1927 and 1928 respectively that Arnold Schoenberg and Igor Stravinsky were admitted.[3]

The appointment had to be confirmed by the Academy's leadership and the Prussian Ministry of Science, Art and Education, so it was not until March that Nielsen's new title was announced and reached his ears. As part of the process, he was asked to complete a document outlining his life and achievements. It is interesting to note that although he was accepted in his capacity as a composer, in his self-presentation he places great emphasis on his activities as Kapellmeister and conductor. He mentions his employment as a Royal Musician since 1889, but begins the list of public appointments, without being quite sure of the exact dates, with that of Kapellmeister at The Royal Theatre. He states that he was employed at the Theatre in 1906, although it was in 1908. In detailing his career, Nielsen emphasises, with some exaggeration, that from that time until 1914 he 'conducted almost all the music and opera performances since my excellent colleague, Fr. Rung, was constantly ill.'[4]

On the front page of the form, Nielsen listed his current main occupation as 'director and conductor of Musikforeningen (The Music Society) in Copenhagen' and 'director' of the Royal Danish Academy of Music – although in reality he was only a member of the board, which he correctly notes on one of the following pages. As a composer, he gives a brief list of his major works: the two operas, four string quartets, two violin sonatas, curiously only the first four symphonies, despite his Fifth having been premiered over a year earlier, and his *Salmer og aandelige Sange* (*Hymns and*

ILL. 1. In his biography for the Akademie der Künste in Berlin, Nielsen writes of his public duties: 'From 1906 [recte: 1908] to 1914, Court Kapellmeister of The Royal Orchestra. From 1915 to the present, manager and conductor of The Music Society's concerts in Copenhagen. From 1915, member of the board of the Royal Academy of Music in Copenhagen. During the years 1916-17 [recte: 1918-20] and 1921-22, also active as manager and Kapellmeister in Gothenburg (Sweden), where I have conducted about 60-70 symphony concerts. I have also conducted various concerts (of my own compositions and those of others) in Amsterdam, Dresden, Berlin, Bremen, Stockholm, Kristiania [i.e. Oslo], Helsinki, Karlsruhe, Stuttgart, London, etc.'[5]

Spiritual Songs) as well as 'lieder, cantatas and minor works' in general.[6] This may suggest that he did not see his being a composer as a real job, but rather stressed the importance of the functions that earned him a living. It also implies that he identified with his activities as a conductor and did not regard them as secondary.

Royal Kapellmeister

Nielsen had conducted before he was appointed Kapellmeister at The Royal Theatre in 1908, but his experience was limited. Apart from the early performances of the *Suite for String Orchestra*, which he led, his debut as a conductor was on 7 January in 1893, when he conducted Saint-Saëns's Violin Concerto and Beethoven's *Egmont Overture* at a concert in Copenhagen. Johan Svendsen had recommended Nielsen for the job and he was very nervous. Although the soloist skipped a bar and a half and Nielsen himself did not think the concert went well, he still concluded in his diary: 'I have a definite feeling that I have abilities as a conductor.'[7]

Until 1904 he had conducted mainly performances of his own works, and in connection with The Royal Theatre this included only his first opera, *Saul and David*. However, he had not regularly conducted works by other composers. It was therefore a great turning point for him when, in the spring of 1904, he was asked to replace the Theatre's two conductors, Frederik Rung and Johan Svendsen, literally at a day's notice. On 8 April, Svendsen was ill and Rung had to take over the evening's performance. However, Rung was not feeling well either, so he conducted only Siegfried Salomon's opera *Kain*, which was given its first performance, while the second work of the evening, *Orfeo ed Euridice*, was conducted by the orchestra's leader, Anton Svendsen. On the same evening, Nielsen was asked to conduct the popular *Elverhøj* (*The Elf Hill*) the following day. *Elverhøj*, a play by Johan Ludvig Heiberg with an overture and incidental music by Friedrich Kuhlau, is today considered the first Danish national play.[8]

It was a real baptism of fire. On Saturday 9 April, Nielsen conducted *Elverhøj* in a performance attended by both the British royal couple and the Danish royal family. Now there was no stopping. The following days Rung and Anton Svendsen shared the duties, but on Tuesday it was announced that Rung had been granted leave for the rest of the season. On Thursday, Nielsen led the rehearsal of Mozart's *Don Giovanni*, which was performed the following day under his direction, with both the Danish and British royal couples in the audience. For the rest of the spring, Nielsen conducted all the major performances, while Anton Svendsen as leader took over the more routine tasks, such as ballets and plays, which the orchestra had performed countless times before. In addition to *Don Giovanni*, Nielsen was responsible for performances of *Lohengrin*, *Carmen*, *La dame blanche* and rehearsals of *Roméo et Juliette* in April and May. Rung conducted a single performance of *Mignon* despite being on leave, and Johan Svendsen returned at the end of May to conduct a single performance of *Il trovatore* and *Le nozze di Figaro* before the end of the season.[9]

For the following season, Nielsen had agreed to act as 'Deputy Kapellmeister' replacing Rung and Johan Svendsen when they were indisposed. However, they carried out all the duties throughout the season except for the rehearsals and two performances of *Saul and David*, which Nielsen conducted. His hopes of working his way up to the position of Kapellmeister and being the obvious successor to Johan Svendsen were dashed. Instead, he retired from The Royal Orchestra at the end of the season.

Nielsen did not break off contact with The Royal Theatre, however, and in 1906 he was responsible for the production of his next opera, *Maskarade*. At the same time, on 9 October 1906, his extensive music for *Hr. Oluf han rider* – (*Sir Oluf He Rides* –) (CNW 7) was premiered under his baton. The work was a tribute to Holger Drachmann's sixtieth birthday, but it was not a success. The Theatre's journal noted that 'after the final curtain there was faint applause'.[10] The play was performed ten times, three of which were conducted by Nielsen. The music was composed in July and August, although changes were made right up to the premiere.[11] Nielsen then set to work on the last missing part of *Maskarade*: the overture. He was busy rehearsing before the first performance on 11 November 1906. The opera was presented twenty times in the first season, and Nielsen conducted the twenty-fifth performance in March 1908.

In the spring of 1908, Nielsen had the opportunity he had been waiting for. Johan Svendsen had handed in his resignation around New Year, with effect from the end of the season, and Second Kapellmeister Rung was now to be promoted to First Kapellmeister.[12] This was not surprising, as Rung had extensive experience as a conductor, having led performances alongside Johan Svendsen for many years. During the spring, Rung conducted most of the performances, assisted by the Theatre's choirmaster, Axel Grandjean, and he also made great efforts to mark his and the Theatre's capabilities with the Wagner repertoire: from January to May, *Lohengrin*, *Die Walküre*, *Siegfried*, *Götterdämmerung*, *Die Meistersinger von Nürnberg* and *Das Rheingold* were performed under his direction. In other words, all four parts of Wagner's *Der Ring des Nibelungen* and two other major Wagner productions were staged in Copenhagen that spring.[13]

On 31 March Johan Svendsen reported that he was ill, and in early April Rung took over the operas for which Svendsen had been responsible, such as *La traviata* and *Carmen*. Assistance was now needed, and on 12 April Nielsen conducted *Cavalleria rusticana* and *Bajadser* (*Pagliacci*) and two days later *Carmen*, both evenings with Vilhelm Herold as guest soloist. In May, Nielsen also conducted *Et Folkesagn* (*A Folk Tale*) and was allowed to conduct the production of *Il barbiere di Siviglia*. On 31 May there was a farewell performance for Johan Svendsen, who conducted for the last time. The Theatre's journal, which includes summaries of each performance, notes that 'the newly employed were … Mr Carl Nielsen, Kapellmeister. Mr Rung, First Kapellmeister.'[14]

The somewhat odd title of address was due to the sequence of events leading up to the appointment, during which Nielsen was anxious not to be given the title of Second Kapellmeister, which would have placed him formally below Rung. Both Johan Svendsen and Nielsen's staunch supporter Klaus Berntsen were instrumental in bringing Nielsen into play for the position. In early March, Berntsen wrote to Nielsen that he had heard through his contacts that the Theatre expected Nielsen to accept the offer of Second Kapellmeister and urged him to do so.[15] Nielsen noted how the process had come to a head in mid-March with some dramatic negotiations. He had reached a verbal agreement with the theatre manager, Count Danneskjold-Samsøe, on 10 March at the 'important and decisive meeting'. On the same day, Nielsen conducted *Maskarade* for the twenty-fifth time, which was celebrated with a large party in the evening.[16]

The matter was still not settled, however, and it was not until two months later that Nielsen was able to sign a contract. The issue was whether his position should be equal to Rung's. A compromise was reached, but it did not solve the problem: they were to be placed on an equal footing, but retained their titles. Nielsen's contract reads 'Second Kapellmeister', but the Theatre announced in a press release that the titles of 'First Kapellmeister' and 'Second Kapellmeister' had been abolished. The salaries reflected a similar ambivalence. Rung and Nielsen would both receive 4,500 Kroner a year, with Rung receiving an additional bonus of 1,500 Kroner.[17]

Nielsen's contract further specified the rights and duties he had negotiated. He was thus required to conduct 'all plays with music, Singspiele, ballets and overtures', with the exception of a number of lighter genres and ballets for which no original music had been composed. In return, he was entitled to conduct a selection of the current operatic repertoire, 'preferably of the Opéra Comique genre', including *Don Giovanni* and *Die Meistersinger*, as well as a third of the new and newly rehearsed works.[18] Grandjean would continue to handle some of the more routine conducting duties alongside Rung and Nielsen.

The discussions were not only about rank, but also about the theatre director's doubts regarding Nielsen's ability to do the job. This is reflected in Danneskjold-Samsøe's letter to the Ministry, in which he suggested that Nielsen should receive his salary from an account for shorter engagements, since 'it is not known with certainty whether Mr Nielsen is able to give adequate satisfaction as Kapellmeister in the position offered to him'.[19] The fact that Rung fell ill on 2 September 1908 – the day after the start of the season – and did not return until a month later was therefore a crucial event for Nielsen. Throughout September, Nielsen, with some help from Grandjean, conducted all the rehearsals and performances, including major works such as *Lohengrin*, *Carmen*, *Aida*, *La traviata* and Gounod's operas *Faust* and *Roméo et Juliette*. When Rung returned, Nielsen's duties for the next two months consisted mainly of conducting Beethoven's *Leonore Overture (No. 3)*, which was used as an introduction to a play.

On 10 December, Nielsen conducted *Die Meistersinger* for the first time. Three days later, while also leading rehearsals for *Maskarade*, he was to conduct the French opera *Mignon* for the first time. During the performance, an incident occurred of which there are several interpretations. The Theatre's journal records that on 13 December, towards the end of Act One, Nielsen fell ill and, after the end of the act, he declared that he could not continue. Rung was called in and took over the rest of the performance after a slightly prolonged interval.[20] Criticism of Nielsen's performance had already begun to appear in the press after *Die Meistersinger*. In the case of *Mignon*, Nielsen seems to have felt that he could conduct the work virtually without rehearsals, since he was familiar with the opera from the old days. However, his knowledge of the opera was limited. As a member of the orchestra he had played it a few times during his first season in 1889–90, and perhaps twice in the spring of 1904.[21] He seems to have overestimated himself, and according to the recollections of those present, his beat was off, with the result that both chorus and orchestra were out of time in Act One.[22] The following day Nielsen had a full rehearsal of *Maskarade*; two days later he conducted *Die Meistersinger* again, and on 18 December he conducted the restaging of his own opera. Two days later he reported that he was ill. He was absent for a week.[23]

There is evidence to suggest that the relationship between Rung and Nielsen was one of conflict rather than cooperation. Nielsen's first six months alternated between periods when he was left alone with almost all the tasks and a few months with only limited duties. Whether Rung deliberately tried to exploit doubts about Nielsen's abilities is impossible to say. There were periods, however, when Nielsen was overburdened with new tasks he had never performed before. At the performance of *Die Meistersinger* on 10 December, one of the works mentioned in Nielsen's contract, Rung felt disregarded and wrote to the Theatre that he would be away for a week as they had not taken him into account – he 'who was employed as the opera's manager'. In the letter, Rung threatened to resign if he did not have a person at his side 'who is really up to the task'.[24] There is no evidence that Rung deliberately called in sick to demonstrate his indispensability, but there is no doubt that he had a hot temper and that there was intense rivalry on his part.

In a letter written in 1917 to his Swedish colleague and friend Wilhelm Stenhammar, Nielsen looks back on his time as a conductor at the Theatre. He mentions his 'tale of woe' and explains how he was persecuted by Rung's followers. It should be emphasised that the letter was written as part of Nielsen's attempt to get himself into a position to substitute for Stenhammar as conductor in Gothenburg, so he was obviously trying to show himself in a positive light. The letter is interesting, however, mainly because Nielsen reflects on the criticism he had received and admits that there might be something to it. Nielsen's presentation in the letter is in the third person, although he is writing about himself.

Nielsen reports that his friends were surprised at a 'certain strange outward sloppiness in his manner of working and conducting. He apparently didn't acquaint himself properly with things and didn't seem to be taking trouble', before going on to list some of the occasions when he conducted erratically. This could be due 'brain fatigue', that is, overexertion and lack of rehearsal. He also points out that in these cases the orchestra had continued to play on its own.[25] It is likely that, as an experienced Royal Musician, he recognised that the musicians knew the repertoire and that he could rely on the orchestra when necessary. But it was not ideal. Charles Kjerulf's criticism of Nielsen in *Politiken* points in the same direction, for in *Die Meistersinger* Nielsen 'beat time according to The Royal Orchestra playing the music, rather than them obeying his baton'.[26]

It also points to another character trait, for Nielsen mentions his ambitions with the music as something that could cause it to fail: 'Now and then he would suddenly get a strong urge to show the whole world that he was an artist, and therefore in the middle of a performance he would try to make the whole thing become more lively, more soulful, warm and animated.' He admits that it took him some time to learn 'that when an opera is rehearsed by someone else, one should let it run on the tracks it is already on, until by means of a new preparation, or in any case a number of rehearsals, one can make one's mark on the whole thing.' The fact that he had not led the rehearsals was true of almost all the productions when he accepted the post, and it was also true of the production of *Die Meistersinger*, the rehearsals for which had been conducted by Rung. On the other hand, when Nielsen did succeed as conductor, the audience would find that *Die Meistersinger* or *Die Walküre*, for example, 'were performed under his direction as never before or since', as he writes.[27]

What does this say about Nielsen as a conductor? To understand this question, it is useful to take a closer look at another source that describes Nielsen's conducting style. Shortly before the 'accident' with *Mignon*, Nielsen conducted a concert at The Music Society in Kristiania (Oslo) on 5 December. The programme included his Second Symphony and Victor Bendix's Piano Concerto with Henrik Knudsen as soloist. The Norwegian newspaper *Verdens Gang* reported on the rehearsal and described Nielsen as a conductor. The essay presents Nielsen as seen by a detached observer who was not part of the musical environment in Copenhagen:

> Carl Nielsen is unlike any other conductor I have ever seen. He is not one of those heavy, confident people who conduct with quiet little turns of the hand, who conduct more with their eyes than with their hands; nor does he resemble the elegant pirouetting conductors or the restless, pushing types who look like foil fencers. In fact, Carl Nielsen is very much like an American bandmaster – in the best sense of the word. He has the energetic setting in motion, in his hands, in his head and in his body; being of small stature, he often has to stand on tiptoe and then slash diagonally across the music stand. Or he conducts high above his head, something he learned from conducting opera. He often uses his left hand, but instead of

catching the notes neatly between his forefinger and thumb, he grasps them with his whole fist and hurls them away again with a whizzing stroke.[28]

It is clear from the description that the author is trying to capture Nielsen between the very lively and gesticulating type of conductor, on the one hand, and the calm and somewhat heavy conductor, with emphasis on eye contact, on the other. In a European context, Nielsen's style was somewhere in the middle, between that of Hans von Bülow, who worked with great musical contrasts and took liberties, and that of the more subdued and conservative conductors, who conscientiously reproduced what was notated in the score.[29] It seems that Nielsen conducted with his right hand and used his left to shape the expression and phrasing of the music. He conducted with his arms quite high and appeared physically energetic. Most unusual is the reference to an American bandmaster – perhaps Nielsen's time in the military music band left its mark on his behaviour?

It is difficult to say that Nielsen belonged to any particular tradition in terms of his conducting. On the one hand, he had played under the baton of Johan Svendsen, who was one of those who used small movements and conducted with his eyes.[30] On the other hand, he had listened with enthusiasm to Bülow in Berlin, but was critical of Bülow's protégé, Richard Strauss, whose 'gesticulation' he found 'terribly ugly and ill-shaped'.[31] It is important to note that the modern, full-body style of conducting had not yet become generally accepted, even with Bülow or Strauss. Conductors had rather small podiums and the music stand was placed at chest height, so movement was concentrated in the upper part of the body, with emphasis on eye contact.[32] Could one of his models – also in this context – have been Niels W. Gade, whom the young Nielsen had seen conducting at Musikforeningen? In a short essay from 1930, Nielsen gives an interesting characterisation of how he perceived Gade as a conductor:

> I've been asked to say a few words about N. W. Gade as a conductor. It really could be said in one sentence: as a conductor he was in perfect harmony with himself. … But how did he behave? Well, he corrected, shaped, produced and improvised incessantly, both verbally and mimetically. He composed, rehearsed and created the work on the spot and in every second, so to speak. … A delightful naturalness marked his whole figure as he gave himself to the music, and the performers were invariably affected by it and, without being aware of it, gave the best they could.[33]

The description suggests that Nielsen's emphasis was not on outward technical ability, but on empathy with the music. This may also typify his own ideals as a conductor. Nielsen never experienced Brahms conducting, although there is a characterisation of Brahms as a conductor that is remarkably close to Nielsen's description of Gade.[34] Even if Nielsen did not know the description of Brahms before writing about Gade, it is at least an expression of shared ideals of how a conductor should perform. Whether Nielsen himself lived up to these ideals is a matter of opinion. It seems to depend as much on the eyes that see as on Nielsen's preoccupation with the work, and on how large and complicated the task was.[35] Both Nielsen and his critics agreed that the technical side of conducting was not his strong point, but that he had a resilient will and the ability to get the musicians to follow him in his passion for expressing the music's emotions.

From the spring of 1909, after a tumultuous first six months, work at The Royal Theatre settled down and the collaboration with Rung became more tolerable. The public had the opportunity to compare the two conductors' productions of Mozart in February, when they were able to attend Rung's new production of *Così fan tutte* and, the following day, the season's only performance of *Don Giovanni*, conducted by Nielsen. *Don Giovanni* was the second of the two operas specifically mentioned in Nielsen's contract, and one of those he had conducted as a substitute in the spring of 1904. This did not settle the dispute, however, as neither performance was a great success. The press found the plot and libretto of *Così fan tutte* impossible, though they praised the music and Rung's steady baton. Similarly, they found it difficult to understand why the Theatre staged *Don Giovanni* with poor singers.[36] The newspapers did not call for more Mozart. The biggest event of the spring, however, was undoubtedly the first complete performance of the *Der Ring des Nibelungen* in Denmark, with all four parts of Wagner's monumental work performed in one week under Rung's direction.[37]

During his six years as Kapellmeister, Nielsen was responsible for the musical production of ten operas. Prior to his appointment, he had rehearsed Boieldieu's *La dame blanche* as a substitute (spring 1904), *Il barbiere di Siviglia* (spring 1908) as well as his own two operas, *Saul and David* and *Maskarade*. In the 1909–10 season he led *Les noces de Jeannette*, *Les contes d'Hoffmann* and *Et Eventyr i Rosenborg Have* (*A Fairy Tale in Rosenborg Gardens*) which received a considerable number of performances, although only Offenbach's *Les contes d'Hoffmann* gained a permanent place in the repertoire after Nielsen's departure. In the following season he conducted *Ungdom og Galskab* (*Youth and Madness*) and in 1911–12 *Maître Pathelin*. Apart from *Et Eventyr i Rosenborg Have* with music by Weyse, these productions were part of the Theatre's French repertoire. It was in his last two seasons as Kapellmeister that he really left his mark on the standard repertoire with new productions of *Die Meistersinger*, *La traviata* and *Faust*, and the ballet *Sylfiden* (*La Sylphide*).[38]

It was also during Nielsen's last two seasons that Georg Høeberg began conducting at the Theatre. The 1912–13 season began as planned, with Nielsen and Rung sharing the work, and Grandjean taking on some of the lighter duties. In mid-September, however, Rung was suddenly taken ill during a performance of *Le nozze di*

Figaro, and the leader Ludvig Holm, who occasionally filled in as conductor, had to take over Act Four. Rung took sick leave and Nielsen was left alone with all the duties. In October it became clear that Rung would be absent for a long time, and on 17 October Høeberg became acting Kapellmeister during Rung's illness. That evening, Høeberg conducted one of the major performances, *Aida*, for the first time, and unlike Nielsen, who left the orchestra pit in 1904 to become a substitute, Høeberg was given the title of Kapellmeister from the start. Høeberg was also in charge of new productions and was allowed to lead the new production of *Tosca* with the guest tenor Vilhelm Herold. It was usually Nielsen who conducted the prestigious performances in which Herold took part.[39]

Nielsen was no doubt aware that he had gained a competent colleague in Høeberg. This certainly had its advantages. In January 1913, Nielsen was able to accept an offer to conduct his Third Symphony in Stuttgart, as Høeberg was now able to take over the responsibilities of Kapellmeister. The same was true when he was allowed to travel to Berlin in December 1913 to attend the performance of his Third Symphony there.[40] However, he also soon realised that Høeberg was a potential rival.

In Nielsen's last season as Kapellmeister, Høeberg conducted most of the performances. Only a few of them were conducted by Rung, who was on permanent sick leave from the beginning of November. He died on 22 January 1914 at the age of fifty-nine, having worked at the Theatre since 1877 and as conductor since 1884.[41] This did not come as a surprise and, in the autumn, negotiations began for Rung's replacement. By the start of the 1913 season, however, the Theatre was under new management: Karl Mantzius and Permanent Secretary Andreas Peter Weis, who had been director and theatre manager respectively since 1909, were replaced by Otto Benzon and Frands Brockenhuus-Schack.[42] Nielsen had to negotiate and work with new people.

While Rung was ill in October, Nielsen initially stepped in, but it was also decided that Høeberg would take on some of Rung's duties. For example, Høeberg was tasked with rehearsing and performing *La muette de Portici*, with the unusual stipulation that it was 'at the manager's discretion'.[43] It was with the new management that Nielsen discussed who should rehearse the production of Wagner's *Tristan und Isolde*. Nielsen had long wanted to work on the opera, which he felt he had been promised.[44] On 8 October, Nielsen was told that Benzon had assured Høeberg that he would lead the production of *Tristan*. On the same day, Nielsen wrote that he had already spoken to Benzon about this in the spring and threatened to hand in his resignation within two hours if Høeberg was given Rung's assignment.[45] Now it was Nielsen who pulled rank as Kapellmeister:

> The legitimate relationship is the one that best serves the Theatre: if the First Kapellmeister is ill, I take charge; when I'm ill, the next takes charge ... May I say

to you once more, as clearly as I can: if the management decides that Mr Høeberg is to be Mr Rung's deputy in any of The Royal Theatre's opera affairs without my consent, then not only will I *ask* for my resignation within the two hours I have mentioned, but I *have* it.[46]

Benzon replied the same day that the situation was 'quite desperate' and that the Theatre needed extraordinary assistance because of Rung's prolonged illness. He also referred to the strained relationship between Rung and Nielsen, which was why it was advisable to have Høeberg replace Rung. Benzon also mentioned the importance of having a Kapellmeister who could play the piano, which was an argument for giving Høeberg the task of rehearsing the production of *Tristan*.[47] That hurt. The next morning, Nielsen called Benzon and announced that, after reading the letter, he was 'laying down the baton' and that Høeberg would have to take over the evening's performance.[48] Nielsen took a few days' sick leave to have his way. On 15 October he sent his resignation to the Theatre, but was persuaded not to forward it to the Ministry immediately.[49]

Nielsen was aware that he was contractually obliged to stay on for the rest of the season, and the Theatre had also been kind enough to grant him leave to conduct two concerts, one in Helsinki and another in Stockholm later in the month. On 23 October he conducted a concert at the Finnish National Theatre, including his Third Symphony, *Helios* and Dvorak's Cello Concerto, while on 31 October in Stockholm he conducted his Third Symphony, *Helios*, the Violin Concerto with Peder Møller as soloist, *Saga Dream* and two movements from *Suite for String Orchestra*.[50] For Nielsen, both concerts were important because they confirmed foreign interest in his music. But just as importantly, their success confirmed that he was an able conductor. Of the Helsinki concert, he wrote to Anne Marie of the great applause and that he 'was truly celebrated both as a composer and as a conductor'.[51] Similarly, he wrote to Robert Henriques about the rehearsals in Stockholm that as 'a conductor I was instantly acknowledged'.[52]

The same was true in February 1914, when Nielsen was invited to Gothenburg for the first time to conduct his own works.[53] As in Stockholm, the programme included the Violin Concerto, Symphony No. 3, *Helios* and *Saga Dream*. The event was an unqualified success.[54] From Gothenburg he wrote to Johannes Nielsen, who was to take over as director of The Royal Theatre from the following season; Nielsen drew a connection between the recognition he had received abroad and the question of the position of Kapellmeister. This was shortly after Rung's death, and once again the question of the equality between the two Kapellmeisters arose. Nielsen now believed that he should be the First Kapellmeister with the same authority as Rung. He did not want Høeberg to be on an equal footing when decisions had to be made.[55] The letter of resignation was still in the theatre manager's desk drawer.

Shortly afterwards, Nielsen received a letter from the theatre director stating that the Ministry had approved Høeberg's appointment as Kapellmeister on a par with Nielsen.[56] Together with his advisor, Jørgen Hansen Koch, Nielsen held further talks with the Theatre, but on 12 March the resignation was forwarded to the Ministry and two weeks later Nielsen was granted his resignation at the end of the season.[57]

This left Nielsen without a permanent position, but on the other hand he was a recognised orchestral conductor outside the Theatre. As Kapellmeister, Nielsen had to act as both conductor and organiser of the Theatre's rehearsals and operations. Although he had already been employed at The Royal Theatre for many years and, as a musician, was familiar with many of the musical works, it was quite another matter to get the huge machinery of the Theatre and the many people involved to work together smoothly. It was a great challenge in the early years. But by 1914, when Nielsen left the post of Royal Kapellmeister after six difficult years, he was an experienced man, both as a conductor and as the head of a large institution.

Conductor of Musikforeningen

The position of Kapellmeister had not only given Nielsen an influential and important position in Danish musical life, it had also provided him with a steady income, in contrast to the uncertain and fluctuating one he had as a composer. As a composer, he also received a permanent state stipend, albeit only 1,200 Kroner, which was not enough to live on. It is not surprising, therefore, that in 1915 Nielsen applied for the post of conductor of Musikforeningen, when it became vacant following the death of Franz Neruda. Nielsen was also appointed to the board of the Royal Danish Academy of Music. In both places he followed in the footsteps of Niels W. Gade, and both helped to consolidate the view that Nielsen was on his way to becoming one of the central figures in Danish musical life.[58]

Musikforeningen was founded in 1836 and was one of the most important musical institutions in Copenhagen from the beginning of its activities in 1843. In 1850 Gade became director and conductor of the society's concerts, a position he held until his death in 1890. In the nineteenth century, the society was Copenhagen's most prestigious concert institution, usually offering four subscription concerts a season. Membership of Musikforeningen was required to attend the events, and there were sometimes long waiting lists to secure entry to the coveted concerts. To accommodate as many people as possible, the concerts were repeated.[59]

During Nielsen's time as conductor, the concerts were held in Odd Fellow Palæet and the orchestra was Københavns Filharmoniske Orkester (Copenhagen Philharmonic Orchestra), consisting of the musicians from the Tivoli Concert Hall Orchestra who did not play during the winter. It was a well-trained orchestra – perhaps not on

ILL. 2. There are not many images of Nielsen conducting and this one seems to have been a staged situation in honour of the photographer. The picture was taken in connection with the art convention at Forum in Copenhagen in 1929.

a par with The Royal Orchestra, but it had solid experience and many talented musicians. Regarding Musikforeningen, the orchestra performed only four times a year.[60]

Membership peaked in 1901, when Musikforeningen had just over 2,000 members. It then fell steadily to just over 1,000 in 1913, after which the repetition of concerts was discontinued. By 1915 the number of members had fallen further to 898. The financial situation of the society became increasingly difficult. From 1907 they received a state subsidy of 2,000 Kroner a year, which was increased to 3,000 in 1915 and 4,000 four years later. It would be no exaggeration to say that when Neruda died in the spring of 1915, the society was in a state of crisis. His death also triggered a major change in the leadership of Musikforeningen, with Angul Hammerich elected chairman and Nielsen's long-time colleague in The Royal Orchestra, leader Anton Svendsen, becoming vice-chairman.[61]

One of the reasons for the society's decline was competition. Palæ-Koncerterne (Concerts of Koncertpalæet) began their concert series in 1895, the Dansk Koncert-Forening was established in 1901 and even The Royal Orchestra gave symphonic concerts. The special feature of Musikforeningen was its choir, which was the mainstay of the society's activities, not least among its members. This was due to the fact that the it was based on a model common in many northern European cities. Local choral societies were at the heart of the musical life of the towns, working closely with the local orchestra. The choirs were usually quite large, made up of able but not professional singers. This was also the case in Copenhagen. In 1886 the choir had 125 members. There was thus a close connection between the music life and the city's bourgeoisie, who not only bought tickets but also took an active part in the choir's rehearsals and concerts. Many families were therefore closely involved in the society's activities, both socially and musically, as part of the cultural life of the city.[62]

But it also meant that the repertoire had to be organised in such a way that the choir could participate, and that Musikforeningen was dependent on the quality of the choir. The singers were furthermore very loyal and many of them were in their prime. The choir was the backbone of the society, but in some ways also its weakness, as it was obliged to take part in all concerts.[63]

Among the eight candidates who applied for Neruda's post were Nielsen's fellow composer Louis Glass and the slightly younger composers Peder Gram and Ludolf Nielsen. Due to the special structure of the society, the choir was also able to propose candidates, and seventy-one members of the choir had signed a petition stating that that they wanted Georg Høeberg as conductor. This was crucial, as it brought the dispute that had led to Nielsen's resignation from The Royal Theatre into Musikforeningen.

Nielsen was present at the beginning of the decisive meeting of Musikforeningen in May 1915 to promote his candidacy and to discuss the matter. It is evident that the circumstances at The Royal Theatre were a contributing factor in this situation. Høeberg had made it clear that he would accept the post if the society approached him, but it was not clear beforehand whether the Theatre would approve of Høeberg taking on the additional post. This was the deciding factor in the appointment of Nielsen. The reason for the unanimous decision for Nielsen was that he was unlikely to accept being nominated as second choice, given what had happened at the Theatre the previous year. Furthermore, the press release, drafted as a vote of confidence in Nielsen, shows that the very criticisms levelled at him – namely his lack of experience and focus on the job – had been discussed, yet he was offered the position, 'in confidence of the experience that this gifted musician has gained as a conductor, and in the expectation that the more limited work of the position will allow him to concentrate his energy undiminished'.[64]

Nielsen had great ambitions when he assumed the post and one of the first things he did was to reorganise the choir. Formally, the choir was disbanded in 1917 and then re-established with all members having to pass an examination if they wished to continue in the choir. At the same time, new singers could be admitted. In his letter sent to the choir members, Nielsen explained that Musikforeningen was making progress and had set itself important goals. In the spring of 1919 the new choir of the society performed Beethoven's Ninth Symphony with the grand choral finale, which was such a success that it was repeated in two public concerts.[65]

In the early years of Nielsen's tenure as conductor, the society did indeed make progress. After the first season, membership had risen to over 1,000 and the season had turned a profit for the first time in many years. From 1919 the number of regular concerts increased again to four, and in 1920–21 membership reached a peak of 1,250.[66]

Nielsen applied for leave of absence in 1920–21, so that he only conducted the first autumn concert. Emil Robert-Hansen, his long-time colleague from the society Symphonia, substituted for Nielsen. It was not a success, however. Nielsen had to step in for the final concert of the season in April to restore his reputation. Although it was customary for the conductor to lead only the final rehearsals, delegating the first ones with the choir to a choral conductor, both Nielsen and Robert-Hansen were criticised for not taking enough responsibility for preparing the performances. It was hardly the fault of the conductors alone when things did not go well. In several cases, the combination of the choir's demands for participation and its singing ability meant that the result did not match their ambitions.[67]

It was Nielsen's responsibility as director of the concerts to decide the programmes in collaboration with the board. This sometimes led to conflicts, both in terms of repertoire and practical and financial arrangements, but Nielsen thought carefully about how to produce a good concert programme. In a letter to Frants Buhl, Vice-President of the Society's Board of Governors, Nielsen wrote in 1918:

> My experience – not only as conductor at the Music Society but as an audience member at concerts in general – is that placing the Romantics (Mendelssohn, Schumann, Gade et al.) together with Brahms, Wagner or modern composers is the worst thing one can do. It's completely fatal for the Romantics. On the other hand one can certainly put Classical and very modern things together, or Romantics and very old Classical things (Bach) in the same programme. But from the artistic point of view, the most elegant way is to stick with the separate eras.[68]

Nielsen cultivated the Classical repertoire favouring Mozart, Beethoven and Haydn, although Brahms and Johan Peter Emilius Hartmann were also played regularly. Gade's works appeared twice on the programme, and Nielsen conducted only one of these concerts. In January 1918 he made an effort to introduce works by his Swedish colleagues, which was followed a year later by a concert featuring Wilhelm Stenhammar as composer, soloist and conductor. French music also featured prominently in the programmes, with works by Berlioz, Franck, Debussy, Ravel and Milhaud, including the Danish premiere of Debussy's *La Mer* in 1919.[69]

Musikforeningen was also an important platform for Nielsen himself. *Hymnus Amoris* (1897), *Søvnen* (*Sleep*) (1905) and *Saga Dream* (1908) had earlier been premiered and performed under his baton. As the director of the society, he was able to schedule the premieres of his Fourth Symphony (*The Inextinguishable*, 1916) and his Fifth Symphony in 1922. The little piece in memory of his predecessor, *Franz Neruda in Memoriam* (CNW 109) for orchestra and recitation, and the fine *Hymne til Mindefesten paa Niels W. Gades 100-Aardag* (*Hymn for the Commemoration of the Niels W. Gade Centenary*) (CNW 110) were also composed for performances at Musikforeningen. In addition, he included his Third Symphony, *Fynsk Foraar* (*Springtime on Funen*), the Flute Concerto, the Violin Concerto and another performance of the *Hymnus Amoris*, which he conducted himself.[70]

Nielsen continued as conductor until 1927, but the final years were marked by decline. The Danish Radio had started broadcasting in 1925, which has often been blamed for the decline of Musikforeningen, although it had been in crisis for a long time. By the end of the 1925–26 season, membership had fallen to around 800, and Nielsen had to accept a twenty per cent pay cut. He conducted only the first two concerts of the following season, and on 8 March 1927 he resigned for health reasons, leaving the last two concerts to the regular choirmaster Christian Christiansen. That spring it was decided to appoint the composer Ebbe Hamerik as the new conductor.[71]

Gothenburg Orchestral Society

When Nielsen conducted in Helsinki, Stockholm and Gothenburg in 1913 and 1914, it was mainly with his own works that he enjoyed success. However, it was also an opportunity to get to know the orchestras and musical life of the cities. It is clear that he was preoccupied with the possibility of leaving The Royal Theatre. When he conducted in Gothenburg, there was clearly good chemistry between Nielsen and the orchestra: 'In the orchestra you have won all the hearts, and the musicians' eyes shine when they speak of you', wrote Stenhammar after the concert.[72]

In 1917, Wilhelm Stenhammar, the permanent conductor in Gothenburg, visited Copenhagen. He spoke to Nielsen about the possibility of taking a leave of absence for a year or two. Nielsen was clearly open to new opportunities:

> So what would you say to my taking over the position for a season as your deputy for a year? I should like to get away from the Conservatoire here, but can't do so without having a suitable reason. This could be that I needed to live in Gothenburg for a season. I could probably still conduct the three Music Society concerts here. ... I need to be in a new environment for a while.[73]

He followed up soon after:

> As conductor of the Music Society I've garnered nothing but recognition and triumph, but in a way that's of no account, since it's at the opera, after all, that I've shown my best qualities as a conductor. So I can't possibly fail in Gothenburg, if I devote all my gifts to the matter, and I shall and *will* do that. I can work for eight to ten hours a day as a conductor if needs be. I've often done that at the Theatre ...[74]

It ended with an agreement that Nielsen would take over a third of Stenhammar's concerts in Gothenburg during the 1918–19 season in return for a third of Stenhammar's fee, which amounted to 4,000 Kroner. Nielsen conducted twelve concerts during the season, eleven of which took place between 30 October and 18 December, and the last in April. This was a private arrangement between Stenhammar and Nielsen, so there was no official contract with Gothenburg Orchestral Society. The following year, Nielsen received a similar agreement to conduct twelve concerts, five from 22 October to 5 November and seven in the first half of February.[75]

Nielsen regarded the Gothenburg Symphony Orchestra as one of Europe's leading orchestras, and after his first autumn he was able to report that 'both the orchestra and the city's musical circles were delighted with my conducting'.[76] At the start of the next season, he was equally clear that the respect was mutual: 'I've just had a rehearsal with the orchestra, and it's a great artistic satisfaction to play with these people, for they obey my slightest hint and show me so much respect that I'm almost ashamed of it.'[77]

The orchestra's level of activity was high, with around seventy concerts per season. The concerts were organised in three series, with the subscription concerts being the least frequent but also the most ambitious. There was a parallel series of symphony concerts on Wednesdays and popular concerts on Sundays. The division was similar to that of the Berlin Philharmonic Orchestra. Nielsen conducted all three types of concerts when he was in town. They took place in the city's concert hall, which had a capacity of almost 1,300. Gothenburg was a city with a strong concert life.[78]

In 1920-21 Nielsen failed to secure an appointment to conduct in Gothenburg, but the following year was his most extensive engagement. The agreement seems to have been that he would conduct from November to New Year and then again from the end of March until he had given twenty concerts:[79] nine concerts from November to mid-December, four in February, two in March and five in April. After this season, he only conducted in Gothenburg on three occasions, when his own works were on the programme.[80]

In Gothenburg, Nielsen had no administrative duties, but he did have an influence on the programme. He made suggestions for programmes and often took the opportunity to include works that he also conducted at Musikforeningen in Copenhagen. Works performed under his direction at both societies were Brahms's Second Symphony and Berlioz's *Roméo et Juliette*, which he chose for his inaugural concert in Gothenburg in 1918.[81] Other works included Debussy's *La Mer* and Sibelius's *En Saga*. Overtures were a regular feature of the programmes, along with occasional excerpts of operas, many of which were from those that Nielsen had conducted at The Royal Theatre. This allowed him to make the most of his preparation and perform works with which he was already familiar.

However, the programme did not exclude works that were new to both him and the audience. In Gothenburg, Nielsen cultivated the Nordic and Swedish repertoire in particular. It is clear, nevertheless, that he used the concerts – as well as those at Musikforeningen in Copenhagen – as a platform. *Pan and Syrinx, Saga Dream* and, shortly after its premiere in Copenhagen, his Fifth Symphony were all performed in Gothenburg during his tenure. If we include the concerts he conducted in the city before and after his regular engagements, more than a third of the Nordic works performed in Gothenburg were his own.[82]

Throughout his life, Nielsen continued to conduct his own compositions, both in Denmark and abroad. A total of about 350 performances under Nielsen's baton have been recorded, although some of them took place at the same event. In addition to conducting his own operas, it was his symphonies as well as engagements abroad that added to the numbers. The first climax came in 1912 and 1913 with seven performances of the *Sinfonia espansiva*, combined with concert tours to Helsinki and Stockholm. During these two years he conducted one of his own works more than twenty-five times. In 1918, 1922 and 1923 he reached a new peak, conducting one of his own compositions almost twenty-five times a year. In 1918 it was his Fourth Symphony, *Pan and Syrinx* and the staging of his two operas at The Royal Theatre that made the difference. In 1922, in addition to the two major concerts in Berlin in December, it was the performances in Gothenburg that increased the numbers. In 1923, his own works were performed in two major concerts at Odd Fellow Palæet and in concerts in Berlin, Karlsruhe and London.[83]

Although Nielsen had been examined by a German cardiologist in Bad Nauheim in April 1926 and had received explicit medical advice not to conduct, it was not until the following spring that he resigned from Musikforeningen.[84] Later that spring, his heart was examined again and his condition, which had been considered quite serious the previous year, had improved somewhat, although he was still not well.[85]

According to Nielsen, the doctor's advice did not mean that he should stop conducting: 'I … know what I can do and what I should leave undone. I can't take on a whole evening, especially not with a choir, but I can do a single piece with ease, especially a piece that I've conducted so often at home and abroad.'[86] 1926 was indeed the year in which he conducted one of his own works most often, although the vast majority of performances took place in January and February – so he was apparently listening to his doctor. For the next three years his level of activity was almost the same as in 1922 and 1923. During these years he undertook many concerts, especially abroad, and he did not limit himself to conducting only one work on each occasion. In 1927 he led performances in Kiel, Helsingborg, Bremen and Gothenburg; the following year in Gothenburg and Stockholm; and in 1929 again in Gothenburg, as well as at some major concerts at Forum in Copenhagen and Fyns Forsamlingshus (Fyn's Community Hall) in Odense.[87]

Thus conducting remained a central part of Nielsen's identity and public persona, even in the last years of his life. But despite occasionally toying with the idea of pursuing a career abroad, he never followed through. Nor did his health allow it. In the absence of regular engagements as a conductor or Kapellmeister in his latter years, Nielsen increasingly conducted his own works, and his activity as a conductor served primarily to enhance his reputation as a composer.

Chapter 33

MUSICAL PROBLEMS

The Wind Quintet, Op. 43, marks a new departure in Nielsen's output and in many ways it also occupies a special position. Begun at the end of February 1922, shortly after the first performance of Nielsen's Fifth Symphony, it was a deliberate attempt to move in a different direction. The quintet was completed within a few months and premiered privately in Gothenburg on 30 April 1922.[1]

The *Quintet for Flute, Oboe, Clarinet, French Horn and Bassoon* (CNW 70) is Nielsen's most clearly neo-classical work. It is said that Nielsen was inspired to compose the quintet when, during a telephone conversation with Christian Christiansen, he heard members of the Copenhagen Wind Quintet practising Mozart's *Sinfonia Concertante for Oboe, Clarinet, Horn, Bassoon and Orchestra in E flat major* in the background.[2] Nielsen's work is influenced in a different and much more direct way by the tonal and formal language of the Viennese Classicism than Nielsen had addressed in his 'Mozart og vor Tid' (Mozart and Our Time) of 1906. In the article he considered Mozart's exemplary classicism on a more abstract level.

Once again, Nielsen was taking part in a current development in European musical life, for around 1920 there was a new interest in composing music inspired by classical forms and styles. In 1920, Stravinsky had composed his *Pulcinella Suite* by recomposing and re-orchestrating eighteenth-century music, and in 1923 he wrote his *Octet for Wind Instruments*, which is related to Nielsen's Wind Quintet in its distinct chamber music sound and deliberate use of traditional forms. In the same year as Nielsen, Hindemith also wrote an entertaining neo-classical wind quintet, *Kleine Kammermusik*. In addition, other composers began in these years to reconsider established formal models in order to create a recognisable structure for their compositions.

A letter from 1920 shows that Nielsen was interested in such ideas at the time. In the same letter to Ture Rangström, in which Nielsen defines 'organism' as coherence, he also introduces another idea that preoccupies him. He believed that there might be an unexploited potential in using classical architectural forms combined with a modern tonal language. This idea may have been in the back of his mind as something to try out for himself when he finished his symphony:

> Believe me! It's of the greatest importance that people like you understand and treasure Gluck's (and Handel's?) architectural works. What might modern music

become if it could bind together these eternally valid ground-plans with a new and richly faceted means of expression and personal features, though without exaggeratedly subjective sensations in the details? In my mind's eye I foresee a new kind of musical generation, which will draw from the sources – not like shady thieves with careful hands, but as open and dauntless artists, who consider everything that is and has been as their natural property.[3]

These are formulations that openly acknowledge the borrowing and reuse of traditional forms, and also openly declare that it is acceptable to hear them. Nielsen shows that he is responding to the European trend of the 1920s, known as Neoclassicism. The word carries a negative connotation of imitation and stylistic copying, and so in the late 1990s an attempt was made to reintroduce this movement as 'Classicist Modernism'. The concept emphasises that this is a forward-looking trend. The central argument for such a reappraisal echoes Nielsen's quote above, namely 'that there is at least as much potential for innovation in the productive reflection on earlier art as in a strictly progress-oriented pursuit of the materially "new"'.[4] According to this view, it is indeed a tendency within aesthetic modernism to seek renewal through the critical and reflective use of elements from earlier periods.

A Unique Work

How did Nielsen manage to work within this framework? There is a big difference between, for example, taking the sonata form and using its basic model to create a framework, as Nielsen did in many of his works, and taking a specific style as a model, which was the neo-classical strategy.

In the Wind Quintet, the Mozartian inspiration is most evident in its thoroughly entertaining and conversational character. In the first movement, Nielsen comes closest to realising the notion of classicism he attributed to Mozart in 1906, when he wrote that 'Mozart is at once extremely strict, logical and consistent in his voice-leading and modulations, and at the same time more free and unbound in his form' than others who use the 'so coveted and difficult sonata form'.[5]

In the first movement, Nielsen does indeed use the sonata form, but allows the movement to be permeated by an organic development of the melodic material employed. The periods seem perfectly logical, but their lengths are flexible, right down to the use of individual bars that are longer than the others. Thus he sees no contradiction between the cultivation of 'organism' as coherence and the use of traditional forms as eternal blueprints. The linear force of his melodic lines is so strong that it penetrates the old forms, and the development of the music therefore proceeds organically across the sharp divisions of the architectural forms into sections. Such a

ILL. 1. At its inception, the Copenhagen Wind Quintet consisted of Aage Oxenvad on clarinet, Knud Lassen on bassoon, Paul Hagemann on flute, Svend Christian Felumb on oboe and Hans Sørensen on the French horn. In this constellation they premiered Nielsen's Wind Quintet.

working process is not entirely unprecedented, for the same organic cohesion across a fixed form is also found in Nielsen's *Suite for String Orchestra*, Op. 1.

The second movement of the Wind Quintet is more closely related to a predetermined form with a fixed framework. The movement is a minuet, a dance that maintains the regular structure of the form in periods of four bars, which are combined into sections of eight, twelve and sixteen bars. The melodic development is linked across the sections of the form. Although the movement sounds distinctly Mozartian, it is also Nielsenian in its fine rhythmic design, with the elegant phrasing discreetly emphasising the two-beat counterbalance to the regular triple metre.

The third movement is a set of variations in which the theme Nielsen has used is his hymn 'Min Jesus, lad mit Hjerte faa' (My Jesus, let my heart obtain), which appeared in *Salmer og aandelige Sange* (*Hymns and Spiritual Songs*). It is one of Nielsen's most successful hymn tunes and one that undoubtedly meant a great deal to him. In the variations he made a virtue of letting each soloist speak as an individual, and in a programme note he emphasised that he had 'tried to give the various instruments their character. Now they all speak at once, now completely alone.'[6] He makes full use of the characteristics of a wind quintet in that the five instruments are distinctly different in sound and character.

In contrast to all this Classical eloquence is the Prelude that precedes the variations based on the hymn. Because the rest of the music is in the neo-classical style, the Prelude represents a stark contrast in style, featuring distinctive, dissonant chords that slowly dissolve into recognisable chordal inversions. The Prelude has a tripartite form, with a middle section that uses some closely related chords over which the flute and the English horn plays melodic melismas. The dissonant introduction is then repeated, but now a whole tone lower.

The Prelude has been the subject of considerable analytical attention in an attempt to understand why it sounds so markedly different from the rest. The short conclusion is that the movement neither behaves like tonal music nor follows atonal structures.[7] Such a negative result of a detailed analysis may seem disappointing, but it is nevertheless instructive, for it reveals that if analytical questions are posed based on the assumption that the essence of the matter is to determine whether Nielsen's Prelude is tonal or atonal, then we will not get an answer. Something else must be at work here.

It turns out that the issue Nielsen is concerned with in this instance is the opposition between the Classical and the Romantic. Analysing the music from this point of view, the sound of the Prelude can be seen as the result of the use of advanced Romantic harmony. The perception of a violent opposition between two musical expressions, one of which is emphatically Classical, turns out to be based on a juxtaposition of Classical and Romantic compositional techniques.

Thus Nielsen does something unexpected: he composes in a Romantic vein. He also adds extra, dissonant notes that are placed in the opening chords for the sole purpose of further sharpening the contrast. They cannot be explained as anything other than additional dissonances, introduced precisely to be dissonant.[8] Nielsen deliberately wanted to emphasise this contrast between the two sound worlds.

The fact is that Nielsen has composed a wind quintet in which the Classical element dominates most of the work, and in which the marked contrast in the Prelude represents an advanced, Romantic harmony. When asked what the Sixth Symphony was about, Nielsen replied: 'only *purely musical* problems'.[9] Similarly, the 'musical problem' with which the work is concerned is the opposition between Romanticism and Classicism – this time in a neo-classical framework. The question of how to deal with the Romantic in relation to the Classical, and how to use Classical models of style and form in order to move away from the Romantic, was one that preoccupied Nielsen at this time. The work is a musical contribution to the previously mentioned debate about how to achieve a de-Romanticisation of music.

MUSIC EX. 1. Nielsen, *Quintet for Flute, Oboe, Clarinet, French Horn and Bassoon*, Op. 43, third movement, a) bars 1–4 and b) bars 27–30. Nielsen seeks to create the greatest possible contrast between the freely dissonant melodic lines as well as the Romantic harmonies of the Prelude and the Classical sound in the harmonisation of the hymn tune.

'Musikalske Problemer' (Musical Problems) was also the title of an important article published in the August 1922 issue of *Tilskueren*. In a letter prior to the publication, Nielsen points out that the preparatory work for the article goes back several years.[10] The ideas were thus formulated before the composition of the Wind Quintet and may have influenced it.

The article is concerned with two issues, both of which can be seen as a rejection of the legacy of Romanticism. One is a critique of the overloaded and unnecessarily ornate, which Nielsen contrasts with an ideal of the complete fusion of form and function. He discusses an adaptation of the form of the utilitarian object, the ideal and unattainable realisation of which 'ends only at the threshold of the divinely purposeful'.[11] This also applies to the forms of art. The formulation is remarkable, as he juxtaposes a critique of a Romantic art form with an equally idealistic and almost art-religious emphasis on the concept of beauty in applied art. What he achieves is an ideal that can be applied as much to the simplest songs as well as to great works.

If that is the goal, then the next step is to find the way. To get there, he argues, one must reflect on the most fundamental and elementary nature of art. One must return to its original elements, which are to be 'sought in the primordial soil, where the seeds of what we call art have scarcely appeared'.[12] Here Nielsen continues the thoughts associated with his Fourth Symphony. The elements he finds in the primordial soil are intervals and rhythm. He then contrasts Mozart and Wagner and their use of intervals. Again, this is clearly a contrast between the Classical and the Romantic. He quotes a motif of Wagner's which he describes as ugly, outdated, unhealthy and unbearable. This is opposed to Mozart as a representative of the classicism from which we can learn something.

That the whole approach, and not just the criticism of Wagner, is rather a rejection of Romantic musical thinking becomes clear when one realises that harmony is not a topic Nielsen addresses at all in the article. Harmony is at the heart of Romantic music, but he only mentions the concept once, and then in the Greek sense of the word, referring to the equilibrium of all things.[13]

The essay is an expression of the fact that what Nielsen is concerned with in 1922 is the relationship between the Classical and the Romantic. It is not a question of either tonality or atonality. With regard to the Wind Quintet, he addresses the question in music and lets the quintet illustrate it. It is in the contrast between the Romantic harmony of the Prelude and the Classical style of the rest of the quintet that the work is to be understood.

In the light of Nielsen's overall production, however, it is not the Prelude but the rest of the Wind Quintet that stands out. In the essay, he emphasises, as he has done many times before, that he does not want to return to the music of earlier times and that he does not want to copy and imitate styles.[14] Nielsen's Wind Quintet is a discussion in music about Romanticism versus Classicism, and thus the Classical tonal language has a clear function. In this context, Nielsen found it legitimate to compose in a Classical style. However, sounding like Mozart was not the way forward in the long run.

This may explain why Nielsen, despite all the unmistakable qualities of the Wind Quintet, did not continue with new works in this vein. On the other hand, he had acquired a taste for using the clarity of chamber music, in which the wind instruments are clearly audible, and for cultivating the uniqueness of the instruments, expressed in their individual sound character and playing style. It was a forward-looking approach that he would continue to pursue.

Chapter 34

THE CREATIVE PROCESS

A basic requirement for a composer is to invent something that does not yet exist. The creative process of producing a work is complex, and the composer's task is one of mental and technical management of creativity. On the one hand, the composer must provide an external framework for their work, so that ideas and impulses can emerge, and on the other hand, the composer must master the technical skills to organise the ideas and to promote creativity.

Henrik Knudsen says of Nielsen that when 'the spirit was upon him, he did not care for food or rest, but played his piano and wrote music day and night'.[1] The process described as a spiritual inspiration was due to the composer's ability to combine ideas and solve problems. Nielsen was aware of his abilities and skills, which shows a composer who was able to capitalise on his creativity. It also shows a composer who approached tasks differently depending on the situation and used different solutions from work to work. This emphasises the complexity of his creativity and the contradictory nature of his compositional work.

Creativity

Nielsen's creative moments were integrated into his daily life, and his daily routines were in turn intertwined with his creative work – for better or for worse. He could isolate himself in his study to concentrate on his composing, where inspiration could be fuelled by craftsmanship. But inspiration could just as easily come from interaction with the outside world, often beyond his control. The moment when new motifs or ideas materialised in his mind could happen at any time. He said that it could be on a walk, on a tram or on a boat trip.[2]

For the creative artist, it is a matter of seizing the whim of the situation. From the outside, leaving the study might seem like an act of procrastination, but for Nielsen it was sometimes a strategy to create a mental space in which inspiration could take hold. He admitted that the ideas he could get on the move were often useless as material for larger works, but at the same time he recognised that sensory impressions in nature had a strong influence on him and set his imagination in motion.[3]

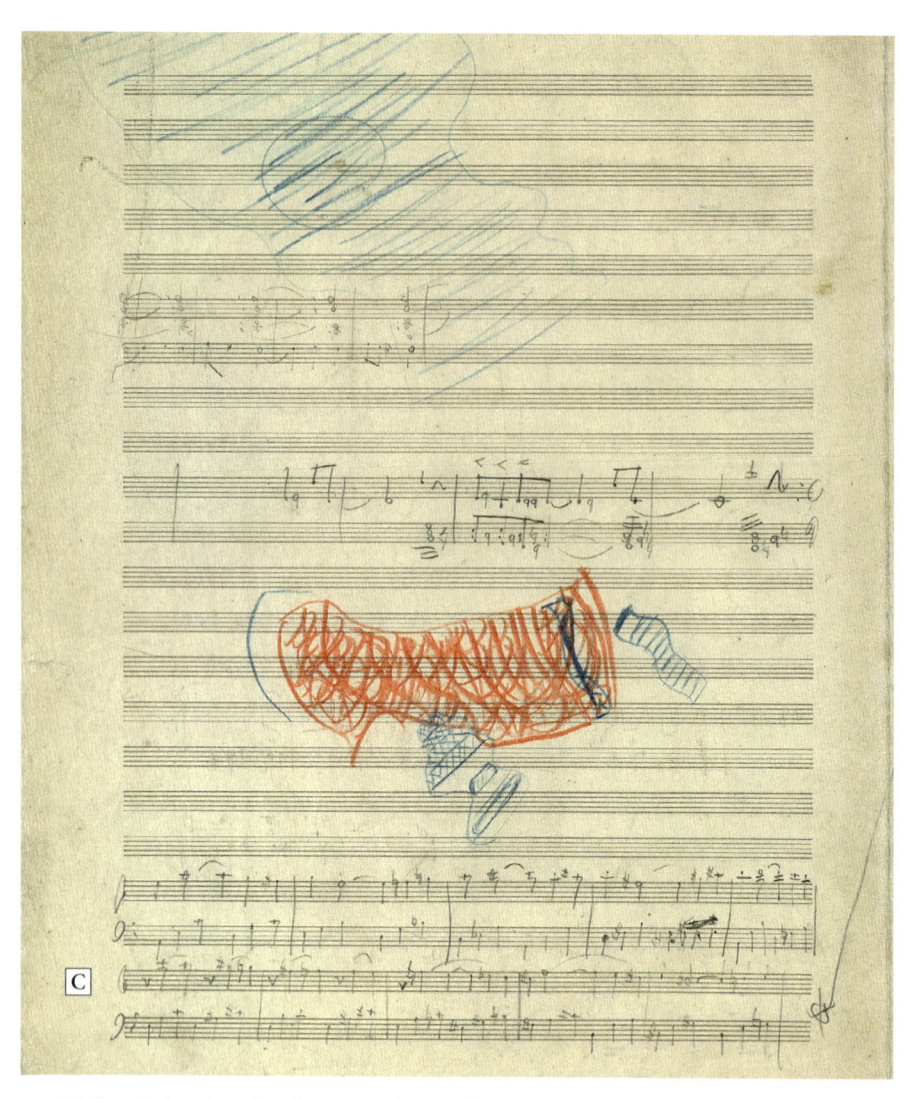

ILL. 1. Nielsen's sketches for the Second Symphony, second movement (CNS 63b part 3). Nielsen's manuscripts are probably the closest we can get to being in the composer's workshop. However, they reveal only a small part of his creative process. When he composed the Second Symphony, he used large sheets of music, each sheet comprising four pages; the images show an opening with the two centre pages. There are a few scribbles written upside down, including sketches for the third movement. Something has also been drawn in red and blue crayon. Is it himself or one of his children who drew this? The pages suggest that he was working on several different themes at the same time. Presumably, he began at the top of the right-hand page with a single-line motif that would eventually become the first subject of the movement from bar 3 (**A**). This is the only place where he notates both the time and the key signatures. Usually this is done at the very beginning to remind him that it applies to the whole page. The first subject is still unfinished. He only knows that it must end with a motion towards F, harmonised in 'F minor', as he notes. Then comes the some-

what more detailed elaboration of the first subject (**B**). He imagines the flute and first violins playing, and notates a second part. In addition, he had obviously prepared to compose two or three more instrumental parts, for he draws the bar lines across four or five staves. He then abandons the further development of the first subject because ideas have arisen for another theme: a theme derived from motifs in the first subject. It will probably be used for something later in the movement. In order not to forget it, he notates it at the bottom of the left-hand page (**C**). In a two-part progression, the gist of the melodic and harmonic ideas is outlined. Soon the paper runs out, and he marks where the passage continues with two coda signs resembling wheel crosses connected by a line (**D**). Having sketched the two passages, he moves on to the material that will connect them (**E**). He then returns to work on the first subject, now in a four-part setting (**F**). At the bottom of the right-hand page, he ends by adding the 'beginning' (**G**). The sketches on these two pages provided the material for the first fifty bars of the movement.

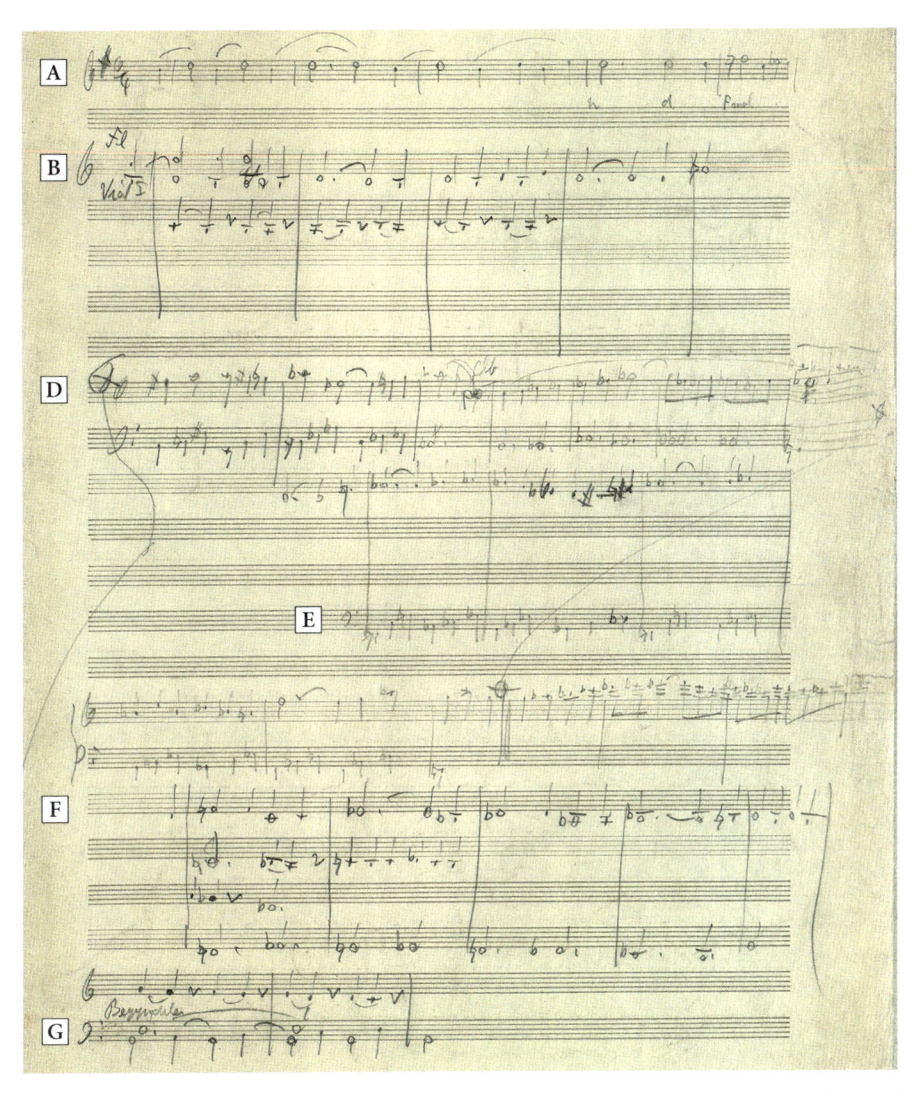

THE CREATIVE PROCESS

There is no doubt that inspiration could arise spontaneously: a newspaper or the cuff of a shirt could be used for a musical sketch in an emergency.[4] Thus, activities not directly related to music were important in the creation of a new work, and it is not surprising that during periods of musical productivity, letter writing, hiking and knitting were also part of his daily routine.

While changing activities can be productive in daily life, it can also be disruptive at the most inopportune times. Occasionally, therefore, Nielsen felt the need to seek out places that could act as a break from everyday life. Particularly during the last twenty years of his life, he was approached by many seeking advice and guidance, and received many letters demanding his attention. After a month's stay in Gothenburg in 1922, he returned home to twenty-eight unread letters waiting to be answered.[5] Home, then, was a place that was not always compatible with creative work.

When asked where he composed best, he replied in 1925:

> At Mrs Thygesen's, a good friend of my wife and me. She lives at 'Damgaarden' by Lillebælt. It is the home of the old chamberlain Thygesen, and everything there is just as it was a hundred years ago … no telephone, rural peace and quiet! I often work there. It was also there that I found the motif for my next symphony, which is now almost finished …[6]

It seems clear that he needed to be in quiet surroundings that were conducive to his work. Damgaard, as well as the manor Fuglsang on Lolland and his holiday home in Skagen, were welcome havens where he could concentrate on the kind of composing that required special attention. But the stays in these places were more than just an escape. Damgaard and Fuglsang also demanded social engagement with his hosts and other guests, which were nevertheless important moments in the creative process.

Indeed, composing is a creative practice that involves the outside world and thus becomes also a social activity.[7] The composer does not work alone in inspiring isolation, but is dependent on others, from suppliers of the basic necessities of creative labour, such as dealers in instruments, music paper and writing implements, to close collaborators who actively contribute to parts of the compositional process. Many of them were involved in the process from the initial idea to the first performance of the work. He asked colleagues and friends for their opinions on his thoughts, and along the way he could get help with the fair copying, instrumentation, proof-reading and transcribing the parts. He could also get feedback by listening to the musicians rehearsing on the piece, and after a performance he might get ideas for improvements or changes that were then incorporated into the final version of the piece. Thus many of his works are the result of intensive collaboration and dialogue with others.

Resistance

Was it just a matter of making the situation as favourable as possible for creativity to flourish? No, far from it. Composers use acquired techniques to organise their material and to balance possibilities and constraints. The techniques define the composer's professionalism and ability to channel their creativity in a particular direction so that the material is organised in the most fruitful way. For Nielsen, working with music involves an interaction between the freedom of ideas and the rigour of elaboration. Composers must be unrestricted in their musical ideas, but they also need a guideline for consistency in musical logic. A framework must be established within which this freedom can unfold, and composers must therefore constantly challenge themselves in their creative work.

For a composer who has to produce a new work and who is working in this way, there will inevitably be resistance in the process. And for Nielsen, resistance was conducive to creativity, because problems require solutions. This seems to be the situation he described during a stay at Damgaard when he was working on the Clarinet Concerto:

> I've been working a lot here and it's going fairly well, although it's a very difficult task I've set myself: a composition for solo clarinet and orchestra. The fact is that for me at least it's easier to compose a symphony or another freely composed piece than constantly to have to think of a solo part and to take pains that it can sing out from the instrument's only soul. And yet, that's precisely why it's interesting to do; because overcoming difficulties, as we all know, has its own charm.[8]

In contrast to a solo concerto, he presents a symphony as an example of a free composition, with fewer specific demands on the composer's approach. While working on the Clarinet Concerto, he was amused when it was difficult to achieve a satisfactory result. This kind of resistance was productive in that it pushed him to find new solutions.

External pressure could also be productive. He was usually at ease with commissioned works for events, where the framework was often fixed and predetermined. In these cases there was a kind of resistance in the external framework regarding the use of the composition. He had to write a piece that would have an immediate effect on the audience when they heard it for the first (and often only) time. The fact that he was comfortable with this kind of commission indicates a high degree of professionalism. It is also shows that he sometimes worked well under time pressure, for many of his pieces were completed just before the first performance. In other words, deadlines were productive for him because they insisted on a solution.

One of the tasks of the composer is to organise his time. The temporal aspect of Nielsen's approach to composing also shows the inherent complexity and unpre-

ILL. 2. The manuscript CNS 176b contains the earliest surviving sketch for *Jens Vejmand* (*John the Roadman*). The source is remarkable in that it simultaneously reproduces the tune, the important movement in the middle part in bar 2, and the harmonic effect on the last note in the same bar. The process of notating it illustrates that not only the tune, but also the basic design of the movement came to Nielsen when he had a creative idea to solve a musical problem.

dictability of creative processes. For example, it may take him only a single day to write and complete a piece, such as many of the songs, which were manageable in scope and easy to finish in a short time. However, the scope of the composition does not seem to be the determining factor in terms of time taken. Other songs were reworked several times. The text for Jeppe Aakjær's *Jens Vejmand* (*John the Roadman*) required 'probably more than fifty unsuccessful attempts' before Nielsen arrived at a satisfactory tune, he claimed in 1918.[9] The relatively large chamber music work *Serenata in Vano* (CNW 69) took him only a few days to compose.[10]

Creativity can flourish in many processes at the same time, and so the notion that the works came regularly – one after another, like pearls on a string – must be abandoned. Nielsen often worked on several compositions simultaneously, for example in 1920 when he was preparing the incidental music for *The Mother* and started on the Fifth Symphony. Before the symphony was finished, he had to put it aside to compose *Fynsk Foraar* (*Springtime on Funen*). In between, he also wrote a number of songs for *The Folk High School Melody Book*. Thus a composer must have a strong sense of self-discipline in order to be able to control various compositional processes within in a short period of time.

But work could also be carried out in a state of continuous, uninterrupted activity. Nielsen said of his approach to composing: 'Once I have got into a strong mood, I can work day and night without getting tired – and I do it often and gladly. During such a period I'm always longing for my work and am of little pleasure to those around me.'[11] He explained to Anne Marie that while working on *Maskarade* he sometimes felt that he was 'like a large drainpipe through which a stream was running that I couldn't do anything about'.[12] Nielsen explains that he was deeply absorbed in his work. He would not be disturbed and was in complete control of his work. In this situation, time and the time of day did not matter.

Chapter 35

THE TEACHER

One of the ways in which Nielsen influenced the development of Danish musical life was as an educator. From his earliest years as a professional musician, Nielsen was also a teacher, and it is clear that he took this task very seriously. He instructed pupils in piano, violin, music theory and composition, and after many years with a varying number of private pupils, he became a teacher at the Academy of Music from 1916 to 1919. He then continued to teach students privately, while at the same time serving as a member of the Academy's board of governors. He had a profound influence on his students, not only because of the knowledge he passed on to them, but also because they were able to experience his musical ideas and principles first hand. Nielsen was also willing to make the extra effort to help his students whenever he could.

In a wider sense, too, music education was part of his identity and what he cared about. Spreading knowledge of music was not just a matter for his own pupils and his own teaching. He had a strong desire to improve musical education in society as a whole, which is reflected both in his involvement in the founding of the Musikpædagogisk Forening (The Society for Music Education) where he was active in various ways right up to the end of his life, and in his preoccupation with projects to disseminate quality music for teaching and domestic use, as well as in his sixteen years as a member of the board of the Academy, where he was responsible for the training of professional musicians. Teaching was thus an essential part of his life and a lifelong occupation, culminating in his appointment as director of the Academy in 1931.

At the end of the nineteenth century, anyone could call themselves a music teacher, as it was not a protected title. Thus, private music lessons were widely available, often at a low professional level. It was difficult for the general public to know which teachers were worth taking lessons from. This situation led the music historian Hortense Panum and the composer Louis Glass to take the initiative of founding the Musikpædagogisk Forening in 1898. The aim was to create an association of professionally trained music teachers and to guarantee the qualifications of its members through professional examinations. Nielsen became a member of the Society shortly after it was founded and participated in its work. From 1898 he was a member of the examination board for violin teachers, and in 1901 and for a number of years thereafter, he was vice-chairman of the board.[1]

For a long time, those trained in the profession had been aware of the professionalism of teaching. The establishment of the Society, however, signalled the importance attached to improving the quality of music education and making it available to the general public. In Germany, music teachers' associations already existed, admitting members who had passed an approved examination, and especially around 1900 there were discussions among German teachers about whether the state should take over responsibility for training music educators.[2] The Musikpædagogisk Forening followed these discussions and from the very beginning worked towards accredited professional examination. Initially, the examinations were assessed according to the Society's own rules, but from 1940 onwards the Ministry of Education's executive order established the framework for the music pedagogy examination.[3] From then on, it was possible to obtain the title of certified music teacher.

In the late 1920s, a new generation of music teachers came to the fore, and the education of young people became more important than before. As part of this work, *folkemusikskoler* – that is, popular music schools in the sense of music schools for the people – were established and new pedagogical methods were developed for the education of children and young people. The election of the composer Finn Høffding as chairman of the Musikpædagogisk Forening in 1929 marked this generational change. In the last years of his life, Nielsen participated in this work, composing music that was both popular and modern. This is particularly evident in the collection *Klavermusik for Smaa og Store* (*Piano Music for Young and Old*) (1930), which combines modern stylistic features with pedagogically structured pieces that present music appreciation on a contemporary basis.

Private Pupils

Nielsen had many private pupils. It is possible to name between twenty and thirty, but there were probably more who left no trace in his letters and other written sources. The number of students is also uncertain for other reasons, as at some point it became tempting for people to claim to have studied with Nielsen. In 1912 this led the Swedish composer Bror Beckman, who was Nielsen's age, to question the definition of a pupil-teacher relationship, wondering why Ture Rangström called himself a pupil of Nielsen's: 'In that case I'm also a pupil of yours', Beckman replied, referring to the fact that he had never taken lessons from Nielsen, but that in their close correspondence they had often discussed each other's works.[4] There is no doubt that being a pupil of Nielsen's in 1912 was important.

Nielsen had private pupils in the early years after graduating from the Academy. The number varied, and after his employment at The Royal Orchestra he had to fit the lessons into his busy schedule. This was undoubtedly difficult, and during his tour of Europe in 1890–91 he lost some of his pupils who had found other teachers in his absence.[5]

Private pupils did not provide Nielsen with a steady source of income, but rather a supplement to his commitments as a musician. When he lived with the Bauditz family in Frederiksborggade from 1885 to 1887, he was obliged to teach the family's daughter Agnes piano and violin as part of his rent.[6] Even later, the provision of private tuition was a financial matter, as can be seen from his application to the Ministry of Church and Education for a fixed annual sum for his work as a composer.[7] His argument was that with a grant he would not need to teach. On other occasions, however, Nielsen found it worthwhile to teach, as he appears to have given some pupils free lessons. If a pupil began a more extensive programme of regular tuition, Nielsen would charge a fee. In 1905, after writing an article about Nielsen, Knud Harder began taking private lessons from him.[8] At first the lessons were free, but later he had to pay 20 Kroner a month.

To attract students, Nielsen placed advertisements in the daily press. In 1891, for example, he offered violin and ensemble lessons;[9] and in 1903, together with the piano teacher Dagmar Borup, he encouraged 'young ladies from more affluent families' to attend courses in music, including music theory.[10] Later, the acceptance of new pupils was probably largely spontaneous, especially after he had established his name as a composer. In 1903 he was on leave from The Royal Orchestra and had time to teach, but in the years around 1910, when he was Kapellmeister and at the same time busy composing incidental music and his Third Symphony, the situation was quite different, for he had to admit that he did not have time to take on pupils. It was a necessary decision, although he would have liked to teach more. He did make an exception for the Swede Torsten Boheman, whom he found 'unusually gifted in all respects and perhaps above of all as a musician'.[11]

Nielsen taught mainly music theory and composition, usually in his own home. However, when it came to teaching composition, he could also instruct the student by post, although he did not feel comfortable commenting on the student's work in writing, as evidenced by a letter to Knud Harder, who lived in Munich and sent his compositions to Copenhagen:

> In your manuscript I've put some NBs in a light blue pencil, where I think the voice-leading is poor. Ah, I'm sitting here feeling like a thousand-year-old pedant! But I give you full license to hit back and not give a damn; especially if you stick to the tonality! Well! This sermon is going on a bit.[12]

Written feedback was clearly not an optimal teaching method for Nielsen, who felt that it was about more than just providing instruction in compositional technique.

It was equally important for him to get to know the pupil, to relate to the context of the composition and, not least, to have the opportunity to justify his comments and to hear the pupil's reactions.

As Nielsen mainly gave private tuition to his pupils, very little evidence has survived of how it was structured. His students Poul Schierbeck and Knud Jeppesen told the music historian Torben Meyer in the 1940s that their studies with Nielsen 'took place under fairly free forms', which probably meant that the content of the lessons was not organised in advance, but took into account the needs of the pupil:

> He was not systematic, as that was not his nature, and he generally stuck to his personal conception of the music. In his lessons he was lively and amusing, yet strictly objective, using many apt comparisons, and could talk about anything between heaven and earth.[13]

Beginning in the autumn of 1915 and continuing for several years, Jeppesen was Nielsen's private pupil in counterpoint and composition. Jeppesen described the tuition he received as 'strangely conservative, even for those days', and explained that Nielsen taught counterpoint exactly as he had learned it from Orla Rosenhoff, whose approach he seems to have adopted because Rosenhoff was a 'very fine critic, with a rare ability to pounce on all the weak points at once and to clarify where the weakness lay'.[14] Another approach that Nielsen had learned was one he also used when teaching Jeppesen:

> Thus my first assignment was to copy a string quartet by Mozart in such a way that I invented new themes after Mozart, but otherwise followed the modulation and, above all, the form exactly. Strange as it may seem, I actually gained something from this rather mechanical task. But it was not until my next assignment, which was to write a new string quartet – this time free from my own head – that C. N.'s abilities as a teacher really dawned on me. … He was particularly interested in the form, and anything that could not be read in a textbook, he could tell you about.[15]

It may be difficult to understand what it meant for Nielsen to be concerned with the form of the quartet when the outline of the composition had been set in advance. But looking at the preparatory papers for the string quartet, in which Jeppesen noted the teacher's comments, it is clear that form should be understood as the shaping of the individual parts, their mutual effect and the way in which they create the transitions between the thematic constructions. Nielsen was concerned with the length and proportions of the themes, musical consistency and the continuation of what had been started.[16]

That teaching could be about many different things did not mean that he was unambitious on behalf of his pupils. On the contrary. He put his students to the test and made sure that they were regularly engaged in composing. To Ove Scavenius, who was Nielsen's private pupil for several years around 1903, he described his expectations: 'I'd like you to write at least one song a week, and to choose such poems in which the strophic treatment is the most natural, as well as the usual contrapuntal tasks'. Nielsen thought it important that the work be continuous, preferably daily, and that the student should solve different kinds of tasks. The letter goes on to urge: 'I hope to receive a large roll [of music paper with new compositions] one of these days'.[17] Nielsen thus saw his role not only as one of encouragement and stimulation, but also as one of providing critical feedback to the pupil. The way in which Nielsen phrases the letter suggests that it was important for teacher and pupil to discuss the work at regular intervals.

In 1911 the music publisher Wilhelm Hansen issued three songs by Scavenius at Nielsen's request, and Nielsen wrote to him: 'They're indeed three fine songs that have now been published, but it's far too easy to rest on your laurels. I tell you in advance, my dear Scavenius, that I want to see a lot when you come to town, otherwise I shall lose the desire to work with you.'[18] He may have been praising his pupils, but he was also demanding more compositions from them so that when they next met they would have something to look at together. Nielsen's demand that Scavenius submit new works shows that, given his busy schedule around 1910, teaching his pupils was a priority.

The theory lessons that Nielsen had received at the Academy became a model for his own teaching.[19] Exercises in counterpoint were important, and with his pupil Judith Ahrendtsen he practised Fux's five species of counterpoint as he had learned them when he was a student, even giving her the manuscript textbook that he had used during his studies.[20] His pupils Emilius Bangert and Jeppesen were taught according to Bellermann's book on counterpoint.[21] The emphasis on counterpoint exercises was probably because they were designed to support the pupil's progress by training the essential rules. Indeed, Nielsen insisted that his pupils first learn to master the basic setting before moving on to freer compositions. To Scavenius he wrote:

> I'd like to have another setting soon, and now you can compose in a freer form, as long as you're careful to avoid too many leaps; in other words, let the imagination run more freely, but still under control. Try a minuet, a scherzo or a little half-merry allegretto.[22]

The letter reveals that even what Nielsen describes as freer forms had the character of an exercise. A framework could be established for a free form which, under the name of scherzo, could describe a piece in triple time, at a fast tempo and with a playful character. This forced the pupil to consider which musical ideas, melodic structures, harmonic phrases and timbral expressions were appropriate to the basic character of the piece. If the pupil did not master the basic skills, it was impossible to complete such a task.

The alternation between set and free exercises continued even after the pupils had produced their first independent compositions. After teaching Harder for a number of years, Nielsen wrote to him: 'It's just a question of continuing to work, and especially of studying voice-leading and counterpoint – not so as to become learned or complicated, but on the contrary in order thereby to achieve greater power and simplicity.'[23] From the pupil's point of view, these may have been perceived as skills to be learned, but from the teacher's point of view, it was a pedagogical goal to practise contrapuntal techniques, as it could still help to develop one's artistic potential.

Nielsen's relationship with his pupils was not limited to private tuition, and he often used his contacts to promote them in public. In 1907 and 1912, he organised student concerts for them so that they could hear their own compositions. The idea of students presenting their works in concerts had only become popular in European academies in the 1880s.[24] This was not yet the case at the Academy of Music in Copenhagen, and in the 1880s Nielsen himself had to arrange for his own works to be performed. Rosenhoff had suggested that Nielsen's string quartet could be performed in a society that Rosenhoff wanted to establish; however, he did not organise student concerts. On the other hand, Rosenhoff's students arranged a concert in the spring of 1892 to publicly express their disappointment that Rosenhoff would no longer be teaching at the Academy.[25] Nielsen was clearly thinking of Rosenhoff's helpfulness when he organised his own student concert in April 1907, featuring compositions by his pupils Hans Berg, Svend Godske-Nielsen, Paul Hellmuth, Gudrun Bergh, Adolf Riis-Magnussen, Emilius Bangert and Thorvald Aagaard.[26] It was also a benefit concert, with the proceeds going to 'the widow of a celebrated deceased musician'. The musician is not mentioned by name in the advance announcement of *Nationaltidende*, but from Nielsen's correspondence with the newspaper's reporter and the letter of thanks from the widow, it is clear that the musician in question was Rosenhoff.[27]

The student concerts show that Nielsen was keen to help his students progress in musical life. One way he did this was by writing letters of recommendation. He had certainly experienced the importance of Gade's letters of recommendation when he visited Germany in 1890–91. With his many contacts in the music cultural environment, Nielsen was now in a position to be the teacher who helped open doors for his pupils. On behalf of Scavenius and Gunnar Ågren, Nielsen contacted the publishers Wilhelm Hansen and encouraged the firm to print their compositions.[28] In the case of Scavenius, this was necessary if anything was to happen as, in Nielsen's words, Scavenius was 'so immensely modest and shy' that he did not want to try himself.[29] As for the works by the Harder, Nielsen tried to persuade his colleagues in Copenhagen to perform them. Nielsen showed some of his songs to the singer Vilhelm Herold and his string quartet to Johan Svendsen and Axel Gade.[30]

Even after the lessons had ended, Nielsen remained interested in his pupils' progress. In 1915, when Scavenius was no longer receiving lessons, Nielsen wrote to him: 'You know so much that you're able to work on your own; but should you have the desire and the urge to exchange ideas with me in a meeting, you know that I'll always welcome you with open arms.'[31] Their relationship continued even though formal teaching had ended. Nielsen also kept in contact with Harder after the actual teacher-student relationship had ended, and Harder continued to send him his new compositions. In reply to a letter from 1909, Nielsen wrote encouragingly: 'I like the two songs; they're the best I've seen from your hand and I'll follow your development with interest', and he used a similar formulation in 1913 about Harder's new string quintet.[32] When Harder settled in Aarhus in 1925, he wished to resume contact, writing to Nielsen: 'Basically, I've been quietly waiting for an encouraging word or action from you for many years, thinking that you were spiritually rich enough to find the right thing to do.'[33] Harder's formulation suggests that he still saw himself in a teacher-student relationship, although it had evolved into an equal one in which they corresponded as colleagues about Harder's role as Kapellmeister.

Nielsen often had a personal and trusting relationship with his pupils and considered several of them to be his friends, including Svend Godske-Nielsen. He had been teaching him since 1902, and when he and Anne-Marie were in Athens, Godske-Nielsen took care of some of the Nielsens' private affairs in Copenhagen. It was a practical arrangement as they lived in the same house on Toldbodvej.[34] Nielsen's relationship with Carl Johan Michaelsen, to whom he taught music theory in 1903–9, also developed into a close friendship, which especially in the 1920s meant that Michaelsen, now a wealthy businessman, supported Nielsen financially. The student Nancy Dalberg and her husband also became friends with the Nielsen family. Such personal ties with students led to many private moments together, such as in the spring of 1920, when Nielsen travelled to Spain with the Dalbergs and the Michaelsens.

Nielsen enjoyed a professional relationship on an equal footing with some of his pupils. Together with Emilius Bangert, Nielsen composed the *Cantata for the Opening Ceremony of the National Exhibition in Aarhus 1909* (CNW 107) and the incidental music for *Willemoes* (CNW 8), of which Bangert was responsible for the main part. Nancy Dalberg was a great help to Nielsen when he was busy and had no time to transcribe or orchestrate his compositions. It was not merely due to a lack of time, however, for he had complete confidence in Dalberg's skills. Thus it was a matter of trust when Nielsen gave her the task of orchestrating his works *Aladdin* and *Fynsk Foraar* (*Springtime on Funen*).[35] His relationship with Paul Hellmuth shows a similar development, with advice and guidance now going in the opposite direction, from student to teacher – that is, from Hellmuth to Nielsen. When Nielsen was working on *Salmer og aandelige Sange* (*Hymns and Spiritual Songs*), Hellmuth made suggestions for the harmonisations of many of the songs.

The Academy of Music

In the years following his graduation in 1886, Nielsen had no formal connection with the Academy until three decades later, and from then on the institution remained a focal point of his educational work until his death. Much had changed since the 1880s, not least in terms of premises: the Academy had moved twice, first to a newly built property in Vester Voldgade and then to the new, large building on what is now H. C. Andersens Boulevard, where the institution was housed from 1905 to 2008. In 1902, King Christian IX became the institution's patron, and since then it has been known as the Royal Danish Academy of Music.

In 1915 Otto Malling, the director of the Academy at that time, died. His place on the board had to be filled and Nielsen was elected. The members of the board had to act as censors for the entrance examinations and tests, so the board had to select members who were experienced teachers, who had significant artistic careers and who knew the musical cultural environment thoroughly.

At the same time as his appointment to the board, Nielsen was hired as a teacher, and from January 1916 he took over Malling's instruction in instrumentation and form theory. Malling's theory and ensemble classes were divided between Nielsen and the other teachers. In all, he taught fourteen hours a week in the first year, a considerable amount compared to his colleagues at the Academy. In the following years this was reduced to eleven, ten and then eight hours.[36] In his theory classes he continued the line he had followed as a student at the Academy, with counterpoint based on species theory and Rosenhoff's exercises in four-part setting.[37]

Nielsen was able to take on the board position and the many hours of teaching because he had resigned from his employment as Kapellmeister at The Royal Theatre in 1914. But when he became deputy conductor to Wilhelm Stenhammar at the Gothenburg Orchestral Society in the autumn of 1918, Nielsen was overwhelmed with work. After the summer holidays in 1918, he entrusted some of his theory lessons at the Academy to his private pupil Jeppesen, paying him out of his own pocket.[38] He also occasionally had Christian Christiansen or Rudolph Simonsen give ensemble instruction, and recommended Jeppesen as a substitute in that capacity.[39] In this way,

ILL. 1. The board of the Royal Danish Academy of Music in 1917, from left: The lawyer Godfred Hartmann; the Royal Musician and leader, Axel Gade; the director Anton Svendsen; the permanent secretary of the Ministry of Church and Education, Andreas Peter Weis; and, on the far right, Carl Nielsen. Both Gade and Svendsen had been Nielsen's colleagues as members of The Royal Orchestra, and while Nielsen was Kapellmeister, Gade and Svendsen were both leaders of orchestra. Weis was the manager of The Royal Theatre until summer 1913. There were thus close ties between the Royal Academy of Music and The Royal Orchestra, and also with Musikforeningen, where all five members of the Academy's board were involved in the management.[40]

Nielsen promoted his own pupil, and when he resigned as a teacher at the end of 1919, Jeppesen was permanently on the payroll and taught music theory until 1946.

The work of the board was very important to Nielsen and he was conscientious, although he often complained in his letters about spending full and half days attending exams. The seriousness with which he took his duties at the Academy was demonstrated by his wholehearted participation in discussions on how to improve the institution's programmes. With the chairman of the board, Anton Svendsen, Nielsen discussed in detail the form and content of his own teaching, and Svendsen also consulted him on the planning of the curriculum.[41] In September 1916, Nielsen proposed to the board that the Academy should make it possible to take the organ examination without prior enrolment and tuition, subject to payment of a fee. He wrote to Svendsen: 'This matter is very close to my heart, and I believe that the Academy has both the right and the duty to exercise some control in this important area, one of the most important in musical life at the present time'.[42] There had previously been a loose arrangement for private students, but Nielsen's proposal laid down a plan for the scope of the examination and the new system became a permanent part of the Academy's examinations. Among the first private students to take the organ examination in December 1916 were Knud Jeppesen and Mogens Wöldike, two of Nielsen's private students.

The chairman of the board had the title of director of the Academy. Anton Svendsen took over from Malling, and after Svendsen's death in December 1930, Nielsen became director – a position he held until his death in October the following year. Rudolph Simonsen, who had been on the board since 1926, was next in line for the directorship. It was a foregone conclusion that Nielsen would take over from Svendsen. In fact, Svendsen had already asked him in 1926 if he would be his successor. A written agreement was drawn up, stating that a future director must first and foremost be a renowned artistic person who 'by virtue of their musical qualifications occupies a particularly prominent and respected place in our musical life'.[43]

The agreement meant that the day-to-day management would be handled by other members of the board. This was in recognition of the fact that Nielsen was the right person to succeed Svendsen as director of the Academy, but it was also out of consideration for Nielsen's failing health. After the agreement was reached in December 1926, he wrote frankly to his daughter: 'I'm giving up practically all my work at the Conservatoire – though they desperately want to keep my name.' With the prospect of no tests and entrance examinations, he continued: 'From the New Year my whole situation is easy … I'm actually looking forward for the first time in my life to living and going wherever I please in the whole wide world. Not because I shall necessarily do that, but just to have the feeling! Ha! This is good!'[44] However, this did not stop him from taking part in examinations and other tasks in the future. In January 1931, when the agreement was due to be implemented, he was reluctant to be elected because of the workload and his health, but he kept his promise. He took comfort in the fact that the administrative tasks would be carried out by Simonsen and the long-serving secretary of the board, Godfred Hartmann.[45]

Pedagogical Commitment

Nielsen's interest in music education was to improve the individual's experience of music. His participation in debates on academic literature and educational issues, such as in 1909 when he raised the idea of rethinking the teaching of harmony, was linked to his efforts as a teacher to present the material to his students in the best possible way.⁴⁶ Although he did not write any textbooks, his participation in the debates shows that his way of thinking about music was informed by a fundamental educational interest.

This is particularly evident in the preface Nielsen wrote in 1928 to Gustav Smith's book *Om Musikkens Dobbelt-Virkning* (On the Dual Function of Music). One of the themes of the book is to point to a functional urge, which Nielsen explains as 'the work the individual does to come into direct contact with the piece of music'.⁴⁷ For Smith, it was not just a matter of listening to music, of experiencing it aurally. He distinguished between an acoustic acquisition, which is simply hearing the music, and a mental acquisition, in which the listener is immersed in the music. In the first case, the music may have been played brilliantly, but it may not have left a deep impression on the listener. In the second case, the listener can hash their way through a piece of music on the piano with considerable deficiencies and still have a musical experience by playing and understanding it themselves. The author's criticism was that concert life and much of musical practice focused on the acoustic. He believed that the value for the individual lay in the mental urge to function, that is, in the practice of the active, inner involvement in music.⁴⁸ In his preface, Nielsen states that the book should appeal to all music teachers, for 'it is they who, through their teaching, must instil in their pupils a sense of the living musical values and thereby awaken their *urge to function*. This should be the greatest task of music education.'⁴⁹

The fact that Nielsen wrote a preface to the book shows that he was interested in what the individual could gain from music. The great reform project to promote popular communal singing was also an educational project. His many contributions of songs to the melody book for Borup's songbook and *The Folk High School Melody Book* show that he saw music as an educational tool in itself, in the sense that those who perform the music receive a musical education.

In his later years, Nielsen also composed pieces with a more direct educational purpose, aimed at music students. These include his contribution to *60 danske Kanoner* (*60 Danish Canons*), a collection of songs published in 1930 by the chairman of the Musikpædagogisk Forening, Finn Høffding, together with Hakon Andersen. The collection was subtitled 'for schools and colleges of education' and was therefore explicitly intended for educational use. It is clear that his forty-four small choral settings for one to three equal voices included in *Melodier til Sangbogen 'Danmark'* (*Melodies for the Songbook 'Denmark'*) (1924) were a precursor and that the accompanying songbook was explicitly 'for schools and homes'. The short piece *Allegretto for to blokfløjter* (*Allegretto for Two Recorders*) (CNW 72), published in Carl Maria Savery's recorder school in 1931, the same year that Savery founded the Frederiksberg Folkemusikskole, also shows that Nielsen was involved in the educational trend of the time, working with music for young people.⁵⁰

The establishment of *folkemusikskoler,* popular music schools, was inspired by Germany, where Høffding and Jørgen Bentzon, among others, had attended the music festivals of the German Youth Movement and the popular music schools in Berlin. In November 1931 they opened Københavns Folkemusikskole, which in the following years became an important factor in the renewal of musical education, with many young composers contributing as teachers or with musical pieces. There was a need for both arrangements and new music to meet the needs of the schools. Six weeks after Nielsen's death, the first collective presentation of so-called 'Gebrauchsmusik', newly composed short pieces for educational use, took place, with Nielsen's recorder duet opening the programme. These works are examples of how new compositions had important didactic purposes. They were both popular and modern.[51]

Nielsen's most important contribution to modern educational music was *Klavermusik for Smaa og Store* (*Piano Music for Young and Old*), Op. 53 (CNW 92), published in two volumes in 1930. It shows how his interest in music education led not only to this rather large collection, which he took so seriously that he gave it an opus number, but also to his support of the new initiatives of the Musikpædagogisk Forening. Høffding was the driving force behind the renewal of music education when he became chairman in September 1929, at the head of a completely new board.[52]

A lecture given by Nielsen at Borups Højskole on 18 December 1929 sparked the debate about music for educational purposes. It also provided the impetus for a competition in which a number of other composers took on the task of writing piano music for beginners. At the meeting organised by the Musikpædagogisk Forening, Nielsen stressed the importance of the teacher's role in relation to the pupil. The teacher's most important task, he said, was 'not to give the young pupils a stone for bread, but to provide them with fresh spiritual food with vitamins. "Vitamin" comes from "vita": life, that is, living art'.[53] Nielsen believed that teachers had a great responsibility to choose the right material for their pupils, quality works that would both help them progress in their mastery of their instrument and lay the foundations for an aesthetic sense. It should not be music that was simplistic and lacking in artistic content in a misguided consideration of the pupil's abilities; on the contrary, it had to be music that could combine pedagogical sense with modern aesthetic ideals.

The lecture included a specific endorsement of the Musikpædagogisk Forening's initiative and supported the call for composers of the time to write contemporary music for educational use. Nielsen immediately began composing piano pieces, and by the end of January he had composed the planned twenty-four piano pieces, one in each major and minor key – plus one extra, making a total of twenty-five.[54] He had set himself a difficult task from the outset. Firstly, they had to be five-tone pieces, with each hand placed in such a way that the performers did not have to move their hand positions while playing the piece. Secondly, he wanted to explore all the keys.[55]

By the spring of 1930, the two volumes were ready for publication and he offered them to the music publishers Wilhelm Hansen, who turned them down.[56]

At the same time, the publishers had begun to collaborate with the Musikpædagogisk Forening on a competition for educational music – an idea that had emerged from the lively discussion that followed Nielsen's lecture.[57] The terms of the competition were based on the same starting point as Nielsen's settings, in that one of the categories was five-tone pieces. The competition was divided into three categories: '1) pieces that do not exceed the difficulty of Kuhlau's sonatinas; 2) pieces that are even slightly easier and 3) pieces for beginners (regarding the five-tone pieces).'[58]

Nielsen, who had composed his pieces before the competition was announced, had them published by Borups Forlag in September 1930.[59] Later that year, Wilhelm Hansen published music from the competition in *Vor Tids Børnemusik* (Contemporary Music for Children), which included pieces by Niels Otto Raasted, Beate Novi, Oluf Ring, Ejnar Jacobsen, Herman Koppel, Otto Mortensen and Jørgen Bentzon, but not Nielsen. The preface emphasised that the intention was that the pieces should be in a contemporary style, so that the children would 'become acquainted at an early stage with the feelings and forms of expression of their own time'.[60] The emphasis on contemporary music was carried on from the announcement of the competition, which was to reward the best 'contemporary children's piano music'.[61] A selection of Nielsen's pieces were premiered at a concert at the Academy on 27 October, while the pieces from the competition were performed at a concert at Det unge Tonekunstnerselskab (Young Composers' Society) in December.[62]

As chairman of the new board of the Musikpædagogisk Forening, Høffding played a central role both in the discussions at the meeting and in the subsequent organisation of the competition.[63] Since 1928, Høffding had been interested in German music education based on the work of the music pedagogue Fritz Jöde and the composer Paul Hindemith. The latter had been in Copenhagen in March 1930 to present a number of his works 'to play and sing' for amateurs, and the previous year he had published a collection of easy five-tone pieces entitled *Kleine Klaviermusik. Leichte Fünftonstücke*, in which the composer emphasises the contemporary tonal language in very simple settings. There is no doubt that Høffding had Hindemith as one of his sources of inspiration when he sought to renew the concept of five-tone pieces for children.[64]

However, the idea of using five-tone pieces for teaching purposes was not new. It was a familiar pedagogy that had been used in works such as Czerny's *Les cinq Doigts* (published *c.* 1846), Diabelli's *28 Melodische Übungsstücke* (published *c.* 1855) and Rosenhoff's *Smaastudier paa fem Toner for Piano* (published *c.* 1870). Looking at the music from the pupil's point of view, the pedagogical starting point is clear: the performers keep their hands fixed on the keyboard so that the five fingers naturally span a fifth. The basic idea is that each finger is assigned to a key. In this way, the hands are immobile and the pupil only has to concentrate on the movement of the fingers.

Compositions limited to five notes in each hand inherently have a limited range of possible sounds. In Diabelli's and Czerny's pieces, the limited number of notes resulted in simple tonal movements in which the hand spans from the root to the fifth, that is, a chord in root position. Rosenhoff's little pieces, on the other hand, show that the content can be made complex and interesting within the restricted framework. Bartók also explores the didactic strategy of giving priority to content-rich piano pieces for beginners. In his collections *For Children* (1908–9) and *Mikrokosmos* (1926–40), which also includes five-tone pieces, he demonstrates that didactic aims do not stand in the way of the use of modern stylistic features. This approach, which marks a shift in the perception of educational music, also characterises Hindemith's *Kleine Klaviermusik*. In this collection of twelve short five-tone pieces, Hindemith exploits the possibility of using the intermediate semitones within the limited range of the hands, writing twelve pieces each based on one of the twelve notes of the octave. Both ideas are echoed in Nielsen's collection.

Nielsen was clearly inspired by the rigid framework. When he finished the last pieces, he wrote to his son-in-law Emil Telmányi, explaining: 'It interests me like nothing before, because the task is so circumscribed that it's going to be very difficult.'[65] Nielsen enjoyed the challenge of overcoming the limitations with as much imagination as possible. He composed a piece in every major and minor key, which in itself creates variety – a principle also familiar from Bach's *Das wohltemperierte Klavier*, showing that the collection covers the whole musical spectrum. Why Nielsen chose to compose two pieces in G major, bringing his total to twenty-five, remains a mystery.

So how does Nielsen approach the task? It is obvious that he takes great pains to vary the pieces so that they differ in sound, type of movement, tempo and expression. Some of the pieces are simple two- or three-part settings, in which he economises on the use of intermediate semitones, so that there is a definite sense of key. In other pieces he has carefully considered the placement of the two hands in a displaced position, so that each has its own range of notes within the key, giving him a greater freedom in which to work.[66] In others he approaches a kind of free two- or three-part counterpoint that sounds like freely imagined parts unfolding in dialogue with each other.

With these variations, the fixed hand position becomes a recurring feature throughout the collection, and on this premise he resorts to many different compositional solutions. It seems that he always had the pupil in mind and worked with a stylistic breadth and a variety of settings that could promote the pupil's development. He conceived all the pieces as tonal and organised them according to a simple system.[67] The first two pieces have no key signatures (that is, C major and A minor), the next two have a key signature with one sharp (G major and E minor) and so on up to five sharps. The second volume contains the key signatures with one to six flats (G flat major and E flat minor). This was also a didactic strategy, as the pieces have a deliberate progression in complexity.

Despite this systematic approach, Nielsen is not limited by the tonal range chosen. This is clearly reflected in his choice of hand placement. In the first four pieces, both hands have the same range of a fifth, offset by an octave. In the following pieces Nielsen experiments with the effect of how the two hands are placed in relation to each other. In the old piano methods of five-tone pieces, the two hands are in the same position, which clearly defines the key. The fact that he deliberately abandoned this approach shows his willingness to try something new and experimental.

For Nielsen as a composer, the pieces become a kind of exercise, just as when he taught composition to his students. Nielsen's approach to music pedagogy is not only a tailored learning of technical piano skills, but also an introduction to musical thinking – in this case, his own. It is therefore interesting to examine more closely what it is that Nielsen presents to the pupil.

The pieces show many different solutions within the strict framework. One option was to use not just five diatonic steps, but indeed all eight chromatic steps within the fifth – a technique also employed by Hindemith. This approach breaks the pattern of tonal thinking and allows Nielsen to move beyond a simple diatonic major-minor tonality within each piece. This is demonstrated by simple means in the first piece. It begins in C major, until the introduction returns in C minor eight bars later. At the end, the two keys are juxtaposed, each represented by its own hand. A similar structure characterises No. 2 in A minor, although the juxtaposition of the major and minor keys becomes a recurring feature throughout the collection. Other movements exploit the chromatic possibilities without any underlying tonal strategies. In No. 18 in C minor, all the chromatic notes are used, and the right hand is extended by an extra note outside the range of a fifth. The piece is notated on a single stave, with the hands alternating after two notes, resulting in a unison flow of notes that seems chordal but lacks tonal direction.

The strict focus on the two hands means that most of the pieces seem polyphonic. For the student, each hand becomes its own protagonist, with one or more independent parts that Nielsen shapes with an eye to how they work together. The result is that each hand has a strong independence in its musical material. Even in those settings where the upper part has a clear melodic profile that stands out in the sonic landscape, the lower part has its own character. In the G minor piece (No. 16), the lower part begins with a stepwise motion that works its way upwards. It is no coincidence that the upper part has a downward motion. The two parts begin at opposite ends of the hand position – the left hand with the little finger, the right hand with the little finger – and then move inwards towards the thumb with different rhythmic and melodic figures. This gives the student a physical sense of the contrary motion of the two parts and their independent contribution to the polyphonic texture.

In some movements the contrapuntal element is disguised, but it is still fundamental. The piece in D minor (No. 14) has a clear melodic profile in the upper part, while the lower one at first seems to be accompanying and therefore subordinate. After seven bars, however, the roles change and for the rest of the movement the contrapuntal aspect is incorporated into a dense dialogue between the two parts. A similar approach is taken in the humorous D flat major piece (No. 21) entitled Marcia di goffo, a clumsy march that begins with an unimpressive bass repeating the same few notes in the lower part. But this is only the beginning of a part whose melodic qualities Nielsen has carefully prepared.

A recurring technique is imitation, in which the parts emulate each other – one might say that they mirror each other's qualities and develop in the reflection. Nielsen reveals one of his contrapuntal models with the performance instruction 'Alla Bach' added above the piece in A flat major (No. 19). Stylistically, there are few references to Johann Sebastian Bach, although the first eight notes correspond to the subject in the well-known Toccata and Fugue in D minor. The similarities lie rather in the treatment of the subject: first in the upper part, then in the lower part, then forced into a dialogical complementary rhythm, then in successive sequences or short excerpts of the subject that follow each other in imitation. Finally, the two parts meet in a rhythmic climax in which they both have fast note values – just as Bach would have done towards the end of a fugue. What they have in common, then, is their treatment of the material and the way in which they work the subject with contrapuntal techniques. Nielsen's piece also serves as an introduction to Bach's music.

When Nielsen composed the piano pieces, he was aware that they were both modern and educational. He wrote in the preface that the pieces could 'meet a common need of the time', namely to enable children, young people and adults to better understand 'the great repertoire of music'.[68] This was an important social task which he wanted to solve and which he was able to achieve with his didactic insight.

Composing didactic music was only one way in which Nielsen contributed to music education. He also did so through his lifelong activity as a teacher, from his youth, when he paid his rent by teaching, to his position as director of the country's most prestigious music education institution, the Royal Danish Academy of Music. His enormous commitment to the strengthening and development of the popular song was also an educational project in the sense that it was intended to contribute to the improvement of musical education and to spread active participation in musical culture on a sound basis to as many people as possible. Ordinary people should have access to both participating in and listening to quality music. Nielsen's influence as a teacher extended far beyond his own pupils.

MUSIC EX. 1. Nielsen, Piano Piece No. 22 in B flat minor from the collection *Klavermusik for Smaa og Store* (*Piano Music for Young and Old*). The piece has structural similarities to No. 21, 'Alla Bach', and uses some of the same techniques. The small notes following the key signature on the first stave indicate the range of each hand. The subject, presented from the beginning and kept within the range of a fifth, is in two parts: a three-note motif followed by a two-note oscillating figure. The subject is somewhat unusual in that it is presented twice in unison, but it has a clear pedagogical function: rather than being a copy of a Baroque fugue, it is a piece of music that trains the student in polyphonic thinking. The contrapuntal structure is built up gradually. When the two hands play together for the first time, the beginning of the subject appears in the left hand and the end in the right hand. The treatment of the subject begins from this point. The oscillating figure is rhythmically shifted in the right hand in bar 7, the interval becoming smaller with each undulation. The left hand imitates the technique in bar 9, but now in the original rhythm. A third voice is introduced at the same time, creating a fuller sound. Throughout the rest of the piece, similar techniques are used to shorten, lengthen and shift the subject and its individual sections, taking into account that both hands contribute equally to the development of the movement.

As his status in musical life grew, so did his educational efforts and musical views. Not only his own students, but generations of music teachers and musicians have used his music in their tuition, referred to something he wrote or told anecdotes about Nielsen's deeds and sayings. Phrases from *Levende musik* (*Living Music*) and stories from *My Childhood* became aesthetic statements that influenced the development of Danish musical culture in the decades after his death. At gatherings, when it came to choosing a song from the Folk High School Songbook, people knew that one by Nielsen was something special. The piano teacher also knew that Nielsen's little piano pieces were not only suitable for pupils, but also an introduction to a particular aesthetic and an opportunity to say something about Nielsen and his place in music history. Nielsen's students and followers had a great influence on Danish musical life, not least because they were able to follow in the footsteps of Nielsen himself.

Chapter 36

THE LEGACY OF PALESTRINA

The Italian composer Giovanni Pierluigi da Palestrina is known for his contributions to the revival of polyphonic church music in the period following the Council of Trent (1545–63). According to tradition, he succeeded in persuading a critical group of clergy, who were on the verge of abolishing polyphonic vocal music in the Church. This story was crucial to the revival of interest in Palestrina's music in the nineteenth century and to the canonisation of his sacred works as expressions of a universal musical ideal.[1] The fact that Palestrina was perceived as the paragon of the noblest polyphony of the Renaissance also left its mark on Nielsen's musical thinking. In an autobiographical sketch of 1905, he wrote: 'As far as my musical point of view is concerned, I am convinced that Palestrina, Sebastian Bach and Mozart are the composers who have reached the highest of all.'[2]

In 1897, the author Hortense Panum summarised the prevailing views on Palestrina in the *Illustreret Musikhistorie* (Illustrated History of Music), based on the fourth volume of *Geschichte der Musik* (History of Music) by the Austrian music historian August Wilhelm Ambros, which was devoted to Palestrina's time. Panum sought to explain why Palestrina's music was held up as an ideal, with the justification centred on his polyphonic art:

> When they spoke of the new style created by Palestrina, they did not mean it literally. Palestrina's style was still largely based on the old Dutch polyphony. He alone knew how to bring greater clarity to this tangle of intertwined melodies, and to give it all a timbre that cannot be described in words, but which shows that in him we have a truly brilliant master who created in complete independence, without borrowing from others. The imitative 'arts' still appear in Palestrina, but only as a means to an end, never as an end in itself. Palestrina's music can be described as the ideal of early polyphony, and then it becomes immediately apparent that this is one of the reasons why it is so difficult for our modern audience to understand. Palestrina's music, like that of the Dutch, moves exclusively in the medieval church modes, which are foreign to us. As with all polyphony, it must be regarded as a melodic rather than as a harmonic art. According to Ambros, the aim of this music is not harmony, but only the accidental result of several melodies sounding together at the same time.[3]

ILL. 1. Statue of Palestrina by the Florentine sculptor Arnaldo Zocchi. The statue stands in his native town of Palestrina, outside Rome.

Panum argues that Palestrina's style, although based on existing models, was exemplary in its clarity and a distinctive sonority achieved through contrapuntal means. As a logical consequence, she, like Ambros, considers the linear structures of the compositions, that is, the melodies, as the basic constituents, while the vertical harmonies, the chords, were a consequence of this.

The question of whether melody or harmony is the basis of Palestrina's music is a theoretical discussion at an abstract level. Discussions of Renaissance and Baroque counterpoint were renewed in the decades after the turn of the century by European musicologists such as Ernst Kurth, who explored the concept of linearity in Bach's music, and Jeppesen, who took up Palestrina as a response to Kurth. What they had in common was an understanding of linearity as the primary structural principle. This was a viewpoint that distanced itself from the Romantic aesthetics' cultivation of harmony. The renewed interest in linearity left its mark on much of early twentieth-century European music, including Nielsen's.

For the composer who wishes to use contrapuntal techniques, melody and harmony are not opposites but interacting elements. The interest in linearity cannot stand alone without an understanding of the vertical effect. Nielsen therefore cultivates both sides, often with a subtle sense of the linear. His understanding of the effect of the line was undoubtedly shaped by the stylistic conventions of Renaissance music. However, he composed with the awareness that he was employing techniques and aesthetic concepts that merely referred to Renaissance music.

Nielsen's familiarity with Palestrina's music goes back to his time at the Academy, where Palestrina's counterpoint was the backbone of the theory classes. It provided a foundation for his compositional work and became a recurring feature of his musical thinking from his first to his last works. Throughout his life, however, he was preoccupied with learning to understand counterpoint better, and his relationship with Knud Jeppesen was crucial to his renewed interest in Palestrina's music in the 1920s. Jeppesen played a central role not only for Nielsen but for the whole international reception of Palestrina. Nielsen had learned counterpoint from Orla Rosenhoff using the traditional method of exercises according to certain rules, and Nielsen himself had taught Jeppesen according to the same rules when he was his pupil from 1915. This laid the foundation for Jeppesen's further studies until he received his doctorate in Vienna in 1922 with his thesis *Palestrinastil med særligt henblik paa Dissonansbehandlingen* (*The Style of Palestrina and the Dissonance*). When he published this and later also a textbook, Nielsen studied both carefully and in this sense became Jeppesen's student. Thus, when Nielsen resumed his counterpoint studies in the 1920s, it was a different Palestrina that he encountered.[4]

It makes sense, therefore, to focus in particular on how Nielsen related in various ways to the counterpoint of the Palestrina era and how he used it in his musical thinking and in his compositions. In some cases he talks about it himself, so we have his own formulations to draw on. In many cases, however, it is a matter of what is termed 'compositional reception', that is, it is important to study Nielsen's working process.[5] He could consciously compose his works without having to express verbally how he approached them or why he went about it the way he did. Tacitly, he made active choices as well as choices of rejection in his understanding of Renaissance polyphony. By studying his creative process, it is possible to trace some of the strategies he used in composing new works.

It is clear from this approach that his use of elements from the contrapuntal techniques of the Palestrina period changed over the years. In his early years, the contrapuntal element played a central role in his compositional style, with strong independent melodic lines serving as the musical framework. In his later years, he also began to use larger forms and stylistic features from existing Renaissance works as a source of inspiration for artistic innovation.

'Power and Simplicity'

From an early stage, Nielsen's music was associated with counterpoint.[6] In a portrait review appearing in the German journal *Die Musik* in May 1906, Knud Harder highlighted Nielsen as a great contrapuntist in comparison with other contemporary composers. Harder described Nielsen's music as strong and pure in its linear aspect, striving for contrapuntal rigour, terms used at that time to describe the music of the Palestrina era. Harder's observation that this approach to musical thinking in terms of melodic lines also celebrates a 'modern intellectual trend in the freest sense of the word' indicates that the Palestrina aesthetic was also perceived as a potential catalyst for artistic renewal.[7]

Nielsen did not attempt to imitate Palestrina; rather, he consciously employed the techniques and aesthetics of early music, from which he derived a craftsman's approach to composition and which provided him with a framework for thinking about music, a thinking which he had in common with the vocal polyphony of the Renaissance. At the time, before Jeppesen's stylistic studies, this approach was mediated both by the systematic counterpoint exercises in the textbooks and by the status of Palestrina as the embodiment of the Renaissance musical style.

Nielsen also associated contrapuntal skills with concepts such as clarity and purity. In 1897 he advised his Swedish colleague Bror Beckman: 'Do a lot of practice in counterpoint and modulation. That will purify, mature and solidify your talent.'[8] By strengthening his technical skills, his work with free compositions could unfold better. Perhaps it was like solving a crossword puzzle and being forced to think about synonyms, grammar and puns. The aim of the exercises was not to achieve a certain level of technical mastery. It was about gaining insight into the possibilities of the techniques. This is the impression one gets when Nielsen encourages Harder to study 'voice-leading and counterpoint – not so as to become learned or complicated, but on the contrary in order thereby to achieve greater power and simplicity.'[9]

One way of gaining insight into the technical possibilities of counterpoint was to do the short exercises using Fux's method, which Nielsen knew from the Academy. Even after completing his studies, Nielsen often returned to the counterpoint exercises. Individual exercises can be found in his compositional sketches, indicating that while working on a piece he benefited from practising counterpoint in parallel.[10] The exercises seem to have been a way of refreshing techniques that were not directly related to the material he was working with. The strategy in this instance was to become aware of the substance with which the simple exercises were concerned, that is, the progression and interrelationship of the individual parts.

The reason for working on these exercises may have stemmed from Nielsen's desire to achieve 'greater power and simplicity', that is, the ability to compose in a simple and effective manner. During his work on *Hymnus Amoris* in 1896, when he wanted to celebrate love in a large polyphonic choral work, he prepared up to 200 counterpoint exercises following Fux's instructions.[11] He kept the exercise book, which reveals the systematic approach he took to the task. He worked through different subjects in different keys, with different numbers of parts, alternating the subject between all the parts.[12] In this way he was able to practise and explore the possibilities of a subject.

There is no direct connection between the exercises and *Hymnus Amoris*, and there was no intention to include material from the exercises in the work. Based on his understanding of the music of the Palestrina era, Nielsen chose the ideals by which he wanted to mould his own music. *Hymnus Amoris* is characterised by a recurring four-note motif which, in various rhythmic forms, serves as the beginning of the work's subjects. Working with such a concentrated core, Nielsen set himself the task of using contrapuntal techniques to unfold the material. It was a question of technical skills.

The exercises were also a way of practising harmonisation using only major and minor triads. The notebook contains eighty-four exercises in four parts, and at least three of the parts are in the simplest of the textbook models: Fux's first species in long note values. They are almost dogma exercises: only pure triads are allowed, no modulations or accidentals, and each part notated on its own stave, thus maintaining the focus on linearity. For Nielsen, the exercises functioned as an almost endless study of how to join four parts without thinking about chordal relationships, which encourages novel harmonic progressions that may differ from a major-minor tonal tradition and Romantic harmony. This kind of modal harmony within a diatonic scale allows almost any chordal relationship, and thus practising the four-part exercises is a way of renewing harmonic thinking. It allows the possibility of thinking of new chord relationships as a consequence of linearity. Moreover, if the starting point is pure triads, the soundscape is cleansed of the kind of tension-filled chords that often occur in Romantic harmony. The order of the chords can now create different tensions and make room for new harmonic relationships. Linear thinking becomes a renewal of the vertical.

Although the exercises he wrote while working on *Hymnus Amoris* left no tangible mark, they contributed to his awareness of how he composed. Nielsen explained this in 1909 when describing his interest in modulation on a theoretical level:

> Every good musician should be able to modulate by means of pure triads, and the pupil should be warned, indeed forbidden, to rave about or jump from one key to another in the usual crude and unartistic manner.[13]

The usual way, which Nielsen challenged here, was to modulate with dominant seventh chords, the most common way of changing key in major-minor tonal music. The chord was not, he believed, the 'only beatifying aid'; other chords could do the job.[14] Thus he paved he way for modal harmony, in which the order of chords is determined not by major-minor tonal patterns but by the movement of the individual parts. The description that a student should be able to modulate using only pure triads is essentially an exercise in controlling four individual parts, just like a Fux exercise.

Nielsen's idea of modal harmony was based on Palestrina's music, although it developed into a new harmonic ideal, detached from the Renaissance style. *Hymnus Amoris* contains many modal harmonic features, and it seems characteristic of many of his later works that he consciously strove to achieve a harmonic expression that corresponded to the simple triad-based aesthetic he had formulated in 1909. In his *Salmer og aandelige Sange* (*Hymns and Spiritual Songs*), composed in 1913–15, Nielsen sought advice from Paul Hellmuth on the harmonisation of the hymn tunes, and adopted a modal approach, which is evident in its extreme form. Rather than deriving the individual parts from chordal progressions, as was previously the case, the harmonies are now the result of strong melodic lines.

A similar approach was used in his already mentioned piano work *Theme and Variations*, Op. 40 (CNW 87) of 1917. He employed stepwise chordal progressions whose linear relationships could justify the harmonic shifts, and with a clear direction in the individual parts, the transitions could become the kind of 'art of modulation' that he anticipated would be possible with the pure triads.[15] With a strict focus on linear effects, he learned to master harmony to such an extent that he could compose harmonic progressions simply by using good linear treatment. He could compose freely in terms of counterpoint or be guided by modal harmony. In any case, it was a contrast to Romantic compositional practice, which accorded primacy to harmony. In Nielsen's work, linear thinking was detached from its origins in Palestrina and became an aesthetic norm from which the composer's actual work could be derived.

By considering a bass line as a discrete entity, composers shift their attention away from the bass as a mere consequence of chord progression. This distinction was indeed crucial for Harder's assessment of Nielsen as a contrapuntist. Harder recognised these characteristics in Nielsen's works and claimed that Nielsen never composed rhythmically or melodically bland bass parts.[16]

The independent, linear role of the bass is evident in *Symphonic Suite* (1894), which Harder considered to be an example of Nielsen as the greatest and most brilliant contrapuntist of his time. The first movement superficially sounds like a series of monumental chords, suggesting a basic harmonic way of thinking. However,

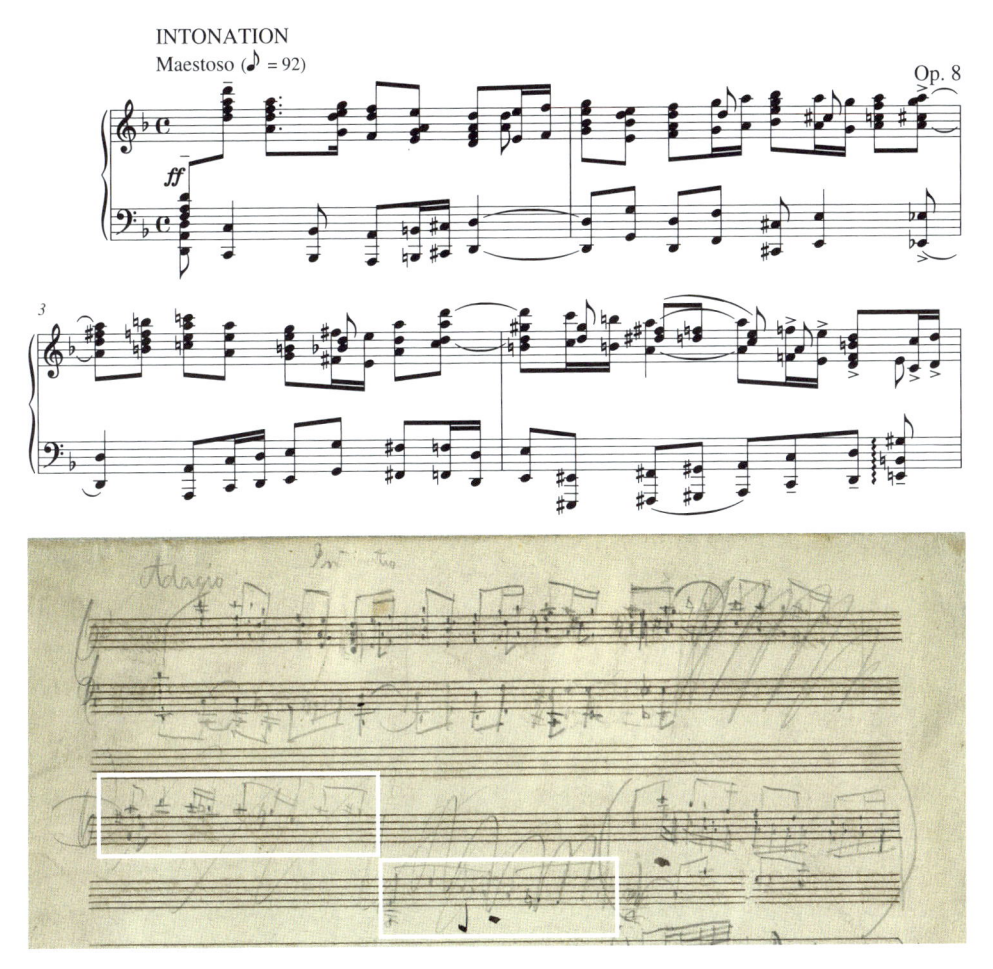

MUSIC EX. 1. Nielsen's sketch for the beginning of the first movement of the *Symphonic Suite* (CNS 17b) below the finished composition. The detail shows a set of two staves, the upper one being the most elaborate, with full chords. The cancelled bars, which differ from the final version, reveal the compositional approach. Nielsen began with a two-part framework and added the full chords later. The cancelled bars also show that the two parts were equally important to him. The two framed sections in the lower stave show that Nielsen sometimes started with the upper part and sometimes with the lower part before composing the other. By shifting the focus between the parts, he created two equal parts, the result of linear structures.

its outward features conceal rigorous contrapuntal lines. Nielsen's sketches for the movement reveal that his approach was to devise a two-part sequence, a lower and an upper part, to which a rich chordal sound was later added. These two parts thus become the primary parts of equal importance. As a composer, it is sometimes possible to start with an upper part and add a lower, and sometimes the other way round. Both approaches produce bass parts that appear as independent melodic lines.

Counterpoint could also be used in a more concrete way – that is, as a starting point for compositional work. In a letter to his colleague Wilhelm Stenhammar, Nielsen writes:

> Don't bother waiting for the right mood. Just begin with long minims, like dry *cantus firmi*, like wooden beams that lie there giving the basic form of a house, like basic crude cornerstones around which one can build. You are after all a master in counterpoint as well, so use that. Begin in unison for 50 bars if needs be! ... In short: just begin! It can *never* be bad, even though you may feel not the slightest inclination!! I'm telling you![17]

Nielsen's advice is to start with the basic techniques. When the framework is simple polyphony, the independence of the bass part becomes the hallmark of the composer's linear thinking. In music based on harmonic principles, on the other hand, the function of the bass is to support the structure: in other words, it is dependent on the upper parts.

Counterpoint was thus present from the outset as one of the elements that gave Nielsen's music its special character and contributed to the sense of powerful forces at work in his music. As well as providing the raw material for the composition of powerful, independent parts that can carry the setting like a skeleton, it is also a way of renewing the harmonic language. This was noted at the time, and it is still a way to understand the central features of Nielsen's musical thinking. At the same time, however, it is important to focus on how the perception of the linear aspect of music changed in the final decades of Nielsen's life. This was a development that took hold particularly after the First World War and affected not only Nielsen but European musical culture as a whole.

The Culture of the Line

It was Jeppesen who used the concept of 'Linjens Kultur', the 'culture of the line' in the preface to his textbook *Kontrapunkt (Vokalpolyfoni)* (*Counterpoint. The Polyphonic Vocal Style of the Sixteenth Century*), published in 1930. The book was based on his dissertation on Palestrina's style and on his experience of teaching the subject in music theory at the Academy. In the preface he explains why Palestrina was the ideal starting point for learning the counterpoint technique:

> I believe, as a long line of theorists over the centuries have believed before me, that his style is the one from which one can best learn what has always been the true goal of the teaching of counterpoint: the independence of voice leading, the culture of the line.[18]

Jeppesen's work reflects the interest of the time in understanding the linear treatment, the movement of the individual parts, as the determining factor. He was inspired by another buzzword of the time, formulated by the music theorist Ernst Kurth, who in 1917 published a groundbreaking book on the music of Bach that included the concept of 'linear counterpoint' in its title. Jeppesen and Kurth were both interested in the unfolding of the parts and their relationship to each other, and in the guidelines that could be derived from the music of their great models. They did not imagine that Bach or Palestrina composed according to rules, but rather that their fine musicality and aesthetic sense led them to choose the best possible solutions from which others could learn. In the belief that these composers represented the pinnacle of a style, there was much to be learned from the principles behind them. But while Kurth took Bach's eighteenth-century Baroque style as his starting point, Jeppesen thought it more appropriate to look at the music of the sixteenth-century Renaissance.

Kurth's theory was based on the idea that the melodic line should be understood as a movement and a flowing force that does not pass from note to note, but through notes. He used the works of Bach as a starting point to demonstrate his idea of the kinetic energy of melodic motion. Kurth argued that Bach's polyphony consisted of linear counterpoint, that is, the interaction between the motions of the individual melodies.[19] This was in contrast to the prevailing view since the nineteenth century that Bach's music was composed on the basis of harmony.

Kurth's position influenced Jeppesen, who, after his private lessons with Nielsen and with Angul Hammerich at the University of Copenhagen, had begun a systematic study of Palestrina's music. Jeppesen realised that despite the importance of Palestrina's music, the surviving works had not been sufficiently studied. Jeppesen combined his interest in the linear aspects of Palestrina's music with a systematic stylistic analysis to see how his music was composed.

In musicology, style analysis was a young discipline, pioneered by the Viennese professor Guido Adler, who published *Der Stil in der Musik* (Style in Music) in 1911.[20] Adler did not see style as something that could arise by chance. On the contrary, he emphasised the art of music as an organism consisting of musical works that interact and depend on each other to form a whole. A style is thus perceived almost as an independent entity, giving the impression that it is the music itself that develops according to its own laws. It was these laws that Jeppesen sought to uncover.

Jeppesen's style-critical studies of Palestrina's music were based on Adler and marked a new departure in the conception of Renaissance counterpoint. In his dissertation, *Palestrinastil med særligt Henblik paa Dissonansbehandlingen* (*The Style of Palestrina and the Dissonance*), Jeppesen presented his systematic mapping of stylistic features in Palestrina's music, comparing them with other composers of the time and with an eye to Renaissance theoretical writings. He concluded by emphasising that the linear writing of Palestrina's style emerged as a reaction to the pressures of an increasingly vertical approach, and that the result was a 'perfect balance between the two dimensions'.[21]

In early 1922 Jeppesen submitted the dissertation to the University of Copenhagen. Immediately prior to this, Hammerich had resigned from his position as lecturer in music history, and the university replied to Jeppesen that they did not have sufficient expertise to evaluate the work. He therefore submitted a German translation of the dissertation to Adler at the University in Vienna, where he defended it in the summer of 1922.[22]

Jeppesen's study of the Palestrina style was more than a music-historical project. It had clear didactic potential, and he turned it into a textbook, published in 1930. Jeppesen's books earned him an international reputation and also contributed to the recognition of Adler's approach to stylistic history. Counterpoint, he argued, could now be taught on the basis of academic insights into style.[23] In a narrower sense, the book was intended to introduce future musicians and composers to the counterpoint that Jeppesen taught at the Academy. His model was Palestrina, because he 'starts out from lines and arrives at the chords'; he felt that this was the ideal approach for those who were to learn it.[24]

The essence of the textbook is reflected in the concept of the 'culture of the line', suggesting that Jeppesen viewed the concept from the perspective of an educational ideal. It is possible to learn to cultivate and nurture the melodic line so that it can reach a stage that is elevated and desirable. In this sense, it has a life of its own and acts according to its own rules. Only by understanding this autonomy can one appreciate counterpoint: an understanding of the linear aspect is an indicative marker of musical education.

In the textbook, which elaborates on melodic aesthetics, Jeppesen describes Palestrina's musical style as if it were an independent being with its own consciousness:

> The linear treatment of the Palestrina music reveals a marked inner coherence and an understanding of what is, in the truest sense, organic, which is indeed sought after in every style species. It abhors the rough and inelegant and rejoices in the free and natural. It avoids strong, unduly sharp accents and extreme contrasts of every kind and expresses itself always in a characteristically smooth and

pleasing manner that may seem at first somewhat uniform and unimposing but that soon reveals the richly shaded expression of a superior culture.[25]

This way of writing about music is also found in Nielsen, who speaks of music as governed by its own laws, which the composer must follow. He therefore appreciated Jeppesen's objective and systematic description of Palestrina's music, which he associated with a de-Romanticisation of the approach to musicology. In his review of the dissertation, Nielsen praised Jeppesen for a new way of writing about music. He contrasted the strongly emotional with the more rational, and in this light he saw Jeppesen's study as a rejection of 'Romanticism's revelling in and arousing its own strong emotions'. The book takes the reader 'to the musical works themselves', so that one can 'feel their pulse and hear their language behind the author's penetrating analysis and loving understanding'.[26]

Nielsen saw potential in Jeppesen's studies, because they identified aesthetic norms of a universal nature. After reading the book, Nielsen wrote to Jeppesen:

> Amazing to think that so far as I can see 16th-century music is finally being explained in a refined way and held up as an indispensable starting point for all art music, not by means of assertions or fanatical enthusiasm, but with proof wrestled from the actual nature of the art, indeed certainly more than that, because a truth or a law in one area surely also applies to another.[27]

Nielsen extends Jeppesen's argument about the importance of the melodic line in the Palestrina style to all art music, or perhaps even all art. When Nielsen emphasises Jeppesen's evidence based on 'the actual nature of the art', he is referring to the way in which Jeppesen almost personifies the melody, attributing human traits and behavioural patterns to it as an organism. With Jeppesen, the Palestrina style had once again become an ideal for Nielsen. Not stylistically or technically, but aesthetically.

Three Motets

Jeppesen's work gave Nielsen the impetus for a renewed interest in Renaissance music. One result was the *Three Motets*, Op. 55 (CNW 345–47), composed between the beginning of April and the end of August 1929.[28] It was then that he began to study the works of the old masters, and in a letter to Anne Marie in May he explains that he is 'very busy studying the old [polyphonic] masters, not only at the piano, but also by writing them out, which forces one to be thorough.'[29] Jeppesen may have been an inspiration, for the following year, when Nielsen saw that Jeppesen had dedicated the textbook to him, he felt that he could not live up to it. However, he took it as a

ILL. 2. Nielsen often describes how an idea or a theme could come to him in all sorts of situations. The following is an example of an idea he needed to try out immediately (CNS 308d): on a newspaper dated 21 June 1929, he jotted down the two subjects of the last of the three motets (*Benedictus Dominus*), beginning with the first and middle sections of the piece. His approach was to experiment with the material. In this case, he sketched the two subjects and explored their possible combinations. He wanted to know if together they could produce a satisfactory effect. This may be an idea of how the third part of the movement might begin, where the text 'Benedictus' and its first subject return, corresponding to bar 83 of the finished motet. The passage was not used in the form scribbled on the newspaper, but he learned from testing the subjects. Through his investigation he realised that this was not the way to use the two subjects in the last part of the movement.

challenge and an incentive to revisit Palestrina's music. He wrote to Jeppesen that he would rise to 'the occasion through work and creative joy, which I also believe the book will give me'.[30] The embrace of Palestrina's music provided new inspiration.

Nielsen dedicated the *Three Motets* to Mogens Wöldike and the Palestrina Choir. Wöldike was a central figure in the musical life of Copenhagen, first as cantor at Holmens Kirke, where Thomas Laub was organist, and later as Laub's successor. For a short time he was also a student of Nielsen's. Wöldike, who had founded the choir in 1922 to perform Renaissance choral music on a professional level, told that he had suggested to Nielsen that he should compose a work for the choir. Nielsen had heard one of the choir's recitals in Glyptoteket's Central Hall in the spring of 1928 and afterwards expressed his admiration for their repertoire of Renaissance motets.[31] The choir's ability had impressed him, and he was delighted when they won both first prize and an honourable mention at an international choir competition in Milan later that year.[32] He heard the choir again at a recital in March of the following year, and soon began composing the motets.[33]

Work on the motets went hand in hand with the study of old compositions, as the sketches for the motets include copies of music by sixteenth-century composers.[34]

MUSIC EX. 2. The subject of *Dominus regit me* (CNW 346) bears striking similarities to the melodic aesthetics of the Palestrina style, as described in Jeppesen's book. The subject begins in a stepwise motion, the most favoured one in the Palestrina style. When an upward motion is interrupted by a leap, there is a rhythmic deceleration, a point of rest, before the upward motion continues. This corresponds to the principle that the highest note in an upward motion has the longest rhythmic value. The same is true when the new apex (the note E) is reached. The fact that it does not occur a third time is entirely in the nature of the style. Sequences are not used. The three crotchets, the first of which briefly touches the note F, now proceed in a stepwise motion downwards, ending on an accented beat, in keeping with Palestrina's rhythmic ideals. All in all, the subject is well balanced in terms of its one octave range, ending on a fifth above the opening note. This gives the impression of a perfectly proportioned subject.

The pieces imitate the outward framework of a Renaissance motet. They are four- and five-part movements composed for a cappella choir to Latin texts. They are distinctly polyphonic in conception, with highly individualised voices. Throughout the pieces, Nielsen uses imitation between the voices in a way that mimics his models in form. The connection with the Renaissance motet is obvious, but the compositional technique makes the link even clearer.

Nielsen approached the task with the ideal of creating something permanent, 'something of that metal which at any time can be placed on the scales without losing value'.[35] The motets were to have a transcendental character, and to achieve this he resorted to contrapuntal techniques. Although ostensibly similar to Renaissance music, Nielsen's three motets are stylistically innovative and do not adhere to Jeppesen's prescriptions for the Palestrina style. It was not intended to be a pastiche. It was the idea of the culture of the line that was a common starting point for both Palestrina and Nielsen.

During the composition process, Nielsen wrote to Anne Marie that he had begun, although he had not yet chosen the lyrics.

> I'm already working on my new work [*Three Motets*] (without text, which in fact can always be found and underlaid in Latin). What's needed is just a very few words in each piece, because it's just the basic mood that counts: 1) pain and lamentation, 2) peace and wellbeing, 3) thanks and jubilation (hymn).[36]

As in *Søvnen* (*Sleep*) and *Hymnus Amoris*, Nielsen emphasises that the music must express a basic human mood and that, although it is a choral work, it is the music rather than the text that guarantees this effect. At the same time, he believes that polyphonic choral music is particularly suited to creating such an expression. He was thus able to treat the task as a compositional challenge in which he could work without the lyrics. The basic mood of each motet had to be distinct, and this could be achieved musically without a text. Studying the way in which he composed the pieces, one gets the impression that the contrapuntal tools were fundamental to the working process. It was a means of experimentation and a way of achieving the desired expression.

ILL. 3 Sketch of the opening bars of *Benedictus Dominus* (CNS 308c). The early sketches show Nielsen testing the potential of the subjects, refining their form and recognising their potential for development.

One of the earliest sketches for *Benedictus Dominus*, described in his letter to Anne Marie as 'thanks and jubilation', begins with a two-part introduction in quick note values compared to the previous two motets. In the sketch, Nielsen develops the material by erasing and altering the pencil notation in order to refine the details of the vocal lines. This method of working is based on the principle that the subject and its counterpoint must be perfectly worked from the very beginning. In this respect, the sketches can almost resemble theoretical exercises. In this last motet, Nielsen has set the text from the outset, and it is hard to believe that he did not have the words in mind when he designed the subject, which fits them perfectly.[37]

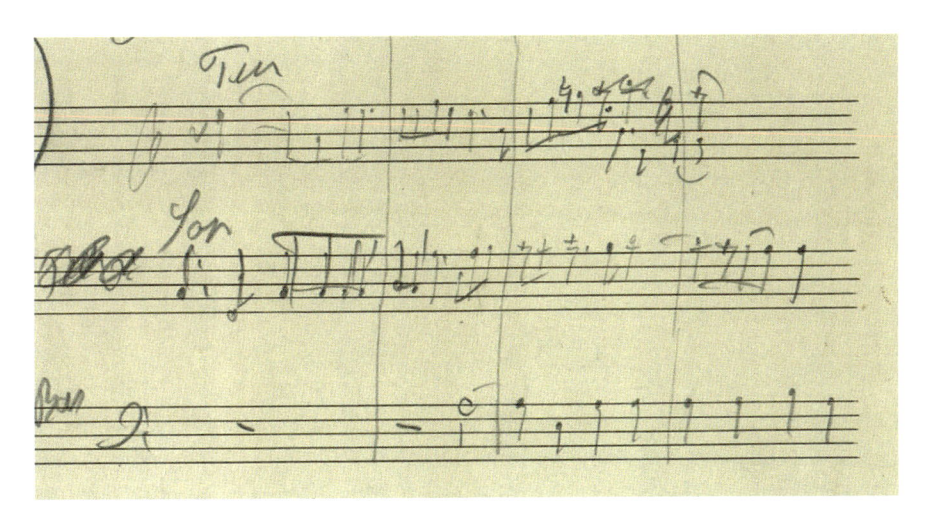

ILL. 4. While preparing the first sketch, Nielsen suddenly stops and changes his working method. There follows a passage in which he tests how the subject might be combined in a stretto in two different voices (CNS 308c).

Later in the same sketch, Nielsen experiments with the subject. He did not use the result until seventy bars later, but at this early stage in the process it was important for him to familiarise himself with the possibilities of the material. He even experimented with adding longer note values to the subject in a third voice, an effect he did not use in the final composition; however, it was important for him to test it.

Nielsen was very pleased with the result. After completing the second motet, he wrote to Anne Marie: 'I'm very proud of this work, which stands entirely on its own two feet, yet with the old masters constantly in mind.'[38] When he had made a fair copy of the three pieces in August, he elaborated on what he thought was particularly successful, namely that he had managed to rise above the purely subjective and achieve a universal and pure expression. He believes, he wrote, that 'this time I've got into something in art that lies above everything we call temperament, feeling, sensation, fashion and surprise, and (taking everything into consideration) also enthusiasm. There's no personal stamp on these pieces'.[39]

The motets were performed at a recital with the Palestrina Choir on 11 April the following year. According to *Politiken*'s critic Hugo Seligmann, Glyptoteket's Hall was filled to capacity with the elite of Copenhagen's musical life. The programme was arranged chronologically, starting with works from the Renaissance, moving on to Heinrich Schütz and then moving directly to Nielsen. According to Seligmann, Nielsen's motets were dressed up in the costume of the old masters, and only the

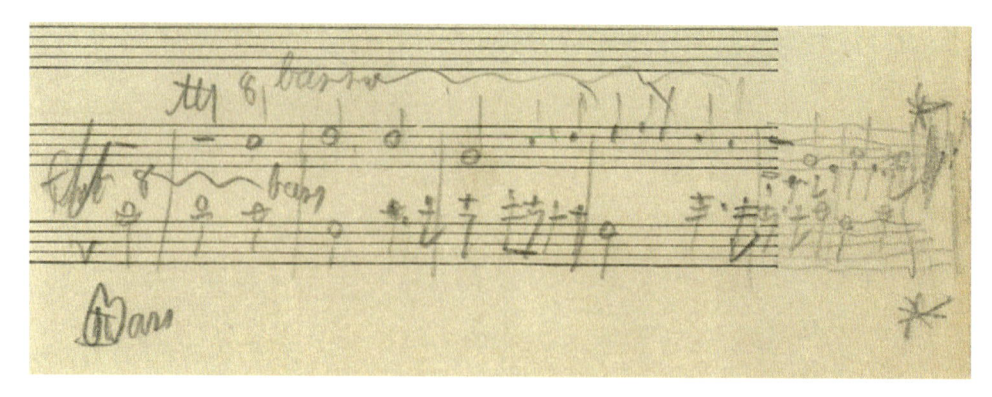

ILL. 5. Another sketch for the middle section of *Benedictus Dominus* shows Nielsen working on a stretto of the subject (CNS 308b), which is identical to the one he experimented with on the newspaper (Ill. 2). The sketches form the basis of three different passages. First, he used an exact repetition of the stretto exercise at the beginning of the middle section of the movement (from bar 46), where the first two voices begin an octave apart, and the third voice enters a fifth above, which appears on the pencilled section of the stave. He then transposed the exercise down a fifth (from bar 66), where it is used in a similar way. Finally, he composed a passage using the exercise with the counterpoint on the lower fifth, that is, the second voice begins five notes below the first (from bar 90). In this instance, Nielsen uses the technique known as double counterpoint, where the second voice can be used in two ways, either above or below the subject. Nielsen could easily work out that the voices would work because he had designed the subject according to the guidelines on double counterpoint from Bellermann's textbook – a treatise he knew from his studies at the Academy.[40]

greatest could succeed in making the music 'resurrect itself through the composer's own personality'. Mozart was able to do this, but not Mendelssohn, and certainly not Reger – but Nielsen did:

> These three motets ... are undoubtedly the mightiest vocal polyphony that has been written in Denmark. Each one is an organic whole and of a thematic concentration that cannot be surpassed. And although they are audacious in their modulations, which makes for almost insuperable difficulties especially in the first motet, they never for a moment come across as wilful, but possess the inexorable logic of the perfect masterwork – just so, and no other way![41]

Nielsen's expectations and pride in the pieces were fulfilled. The power and simplicity, or, in the words of the newspaper *Politiken*, the 'refinement of spirit and the primeval force of temperament' that he wanted to achieve reached the audience. Palestrina's legacy was transformed here into a technical approach that ensured a composition of lasting value. The motets are the result of an idea that Nielsen had formulated to his son-in-law Emil Telmányi the year before he began writing them. The secret of the artistic value lies not in the material, but in the way it is treated:

> A brilliant idea isn't worth the slightest if the artist lacks the character necessary to really develop the whole, and I'm certain that the *enduring* value of a work of art depends 99 percent on [mental] concentration. What is a theme of Bach? Or Palestrina? Just a few notes that any decent musician could come up with, and with Palestrina it's often just 4–6 notes borrowed from Gregorian chant.[42]

Nielsen's relationship to the music of the Palestrina era is characterised by a pendulum swinging between the aesthetic ideals attributed to pure and powerful music and the technical execution that influenced the actual compositional work. Over the years, Nielsen experienced a shift in the perception of Palestrina that also affected his approach to Renaissance music and his own works. Having been influenced by the Romantic cult of genius, the reception of Palestrina was now replaced by a systematic stylistic analysis that focused on a horizontal linear approach rather than the vertical harmonic one in an attempt to understand the core of Palestrina's music. This knowledge of style became a specific impulse for Nielsen's creative work, leading to a conscious use of the stylistic features of early music, and his new approach led to new artistic solutions to specific compositional problems. Counterpoint became an important means of composing modern music.

Chapter 37

MECHANICAL MUSIC

In Nielsen's time, the concept of mechanical music – music stored on a medium or transmitted by a device – was defined as the antithesis to all music performed live. Thus, mechanical music includes phonogram rolls and other early media, but the two most culturally significant forms were the gramophone and the radio. The earliest Danish sound recordings were made on an Edison phonograph in the 1890s and are part of the Ruben Collection.[1] Gramophone records appeared around the turn of the century, although the only existing recording of Nielsen performing his own music was made on a phonograph cylinder. It is a private recording made in the home of Carl Johan Michaelsen, a good friend of Nielsen's, sometime in the early 1920s. Unfortunately, the machine was set up incorrectly, resulting in a recording on which the sound is very faint. However, thanks to a meticulous restoration process carried out in a Ukrainian sound laboratory, who were capable of amplifying the sound, the recording is now audible. It is still difficult to hear anything other than that Nielsen is a rather mediocre pianist, clunking his way through 'Puppet March' from *Humoresque-Bagatelles* and 'Som en Rejselysten Flaade' (*The Song to Denmark*) from *The Mother*, after which he improvises a little to make use of the last bit of the phonograph's wax cylinder.[2]

Due to Nielsen's lack of interest in recording, there is not a single one with an orchestra under Nielsen's baton, despite his extensive activities as a conductor. In fact, in 1920 he demanded that a contract with Wilhelm Hansen be amended so as to cancel the publishers' right to allow gramophone recordings to be made.[3] The few times Nielsen mentions the gramophone favourably in his letters are in connection with ethnographic sound recordings from Greenland and the Balkans.[4] Otherwise he associates it mainly with low-quality popular music.

The mechanical medium with which Nielsen was primarily concerned was radio. His view of radio was ambivalent, shaped by the contemporary relationship with new media: on the one hand, mechanical music was seen as part of modern progress, and radio in particular was promoted as democratising access to culture and education, not least music. This was also the view of the Danish Radio when it was founded in 1925 as Statsradiofonien (Danish Broadcasting Corporation, today DR), with Emil Holm at its head, a director who insisted on bringing high-quality speech and music radio to the general public, and who insisted on live music broadcasts. He strongly opposed the broadcasting of gramophone music and, when it was introduced in

1929, it was limited to half an hour a week in a special programme. Holm was a professional musician and held the title of Royal Court Singer, which he had earned while he was a bass singer at the Stuttgart Opera.[5] Nielsen had known him since his youth and, during his time in Stuttgart, Holm had made great efforts to help promote Nielsen's music in Germany.[6]

On the other hand, mechanical music was perceived as a threat, not least by musicians and the established music scene. In the higher cultural circles, the radio concerts in particular were seen as a dangerous competitor to concert life, and the crisis experienced by Musikforeningen (The Music Society) and Palækoncerterne (Concerts in Odd Fellow Palæet) in the 1920s was largely blamed on the radio. At the popular end of the cultural spectrum, it was the gramophone in particular that threatened the livelihood of the entertainment musicians, as many small pubs and music venues switched to gramophone music. In Tom Kristensen's contemporary novel *Hærværk* (*Havoc*), the protagonist Jastrau of *Politiken* goes down to the Bar des Artistes, where the guests dance to gramophone music in the smoky, reddish room.[7]

Nielsen has something of the same ambivalence. On the one hand, he was actively involved in choosing the best broadcasting equipment for the newly established Danish Broadcasting Corporation, and radio became an important source of dissemination for his music in the second half of the 1920s. On the other hand, he was conductor of Musikforeningen until 1927 and experienced the increasingly difficult conditions of the live concert scene. As a musician and composer, he was always a strong advocate of live music.

Nielsen signalled the importance of this debate when, in April 1931, he wrote a foreword to Karl Larsen's collection of newspaper chronicles, *Levende Musik – Mekanisk Musik* (Living Music – Mechanical Music) which included contributions by Jørgen Bentzon and Finn Høffding.[8] It is possible that Nielsen may have encountered scenes similar to those in *Hærværk* on his way through the city, when he mentions the misplaced music in the foreword: 'From being a spiritual value around which we all gathered, it has become a harlot who offers herself out of open doors and windows, from cellar alleys and stinking low-end jazz pubs.'[9] At the same time, he urged radio managers not to give in to the listeners' demands for more popular music, but to preserve 'the educational moment that mechanical music can contain'.[10] He thus recognised the cultural and musical democratic potential of radio. In an interview a few months earlier, he elaborated on his views:

> Music from the radio and the gramophone is, so to speak, lacking in vitamins. Yet it is possible that in the long run radio will be beneficial to musical life. You have to give it some time before you make a judgement. Incidentally, could one of the reasons for people's indifference not be that we are gradually getting far too much

music? There is music in restaurants, there are radios or gramophones in homes, and if you are sailing on a steamship on a nice, quiet evening, then, God help me, the latest hits are being played!'[11]

Nielsen saw both sides of the situation, but he was also genuinely concerned with influencing developments and exploit the opportunities offered by the medium of radio. The foreword to the debate book ends with the sentence: 'It is less our task to fight the inferior than to promote the best'.[12]

Here he agreed with Holm. As a co-founder of the Danish Artists' Union in 1918, Holm was also an organiser who was concerned not only with the quality of the music, but also with the employment and pay conditions of the musicians. In his memoirs, Holm makes a virtue of the fact that he always managed to avoid conflict with the musicians' unions by reaching agreements on tariffs, the use of professionals and the payment of fees to composers for the broadcasting of their music. His first priority was to organise the content and technical standards of radio in such a way as to ensure the best possible artistic reproduction of music and speech: 'the accuracy of the sound image'.[13]

In 1926, when it was time to decide on the permanent equipment for the Danish Broadcasting Corporation, Holm arranged for Nielsen, the composer Poul Schierbeck and a radio engineer to travel to Munich on a commission. From there they went to a hotel a hundred kilometres away to listen to various radio stations and assess the sound quality. Holm needed Nielsen's authority, and the commission insisted on purchasing equipment similar to that of the radio station who had broadcasted from Prague.[14] Nielsen was committed to the task and noted in his diary: 'Prague 16th: for the first time I heard violin passages as *violin* music.'[15]

When Nielsen returned home, he gave an interview in which he explained the possibilities he saw in radio: 'It is truly amazing what has been achieved and how powerful the development of radio has become. It also fascinated me as an artist – imagine the audience you can reach now that everyone has their own little receiver.' He countered critics of radio by emphasising the development of technology, which had now reached a stage where orchestral music could be heard as it actually sounded.[16] At the time, there was optimism and faith in radio's potential to democratise access to culture and quality music.

From the very beginning of radio, Nielsen was a major contributor to the music played on the air and thus also benefited from the reach of the new medium. From the founding of the Danish Broadcasting Corporation until the memorial concert in his honour shortly after his death, Nielsen was represented by a work or a feature some 800 times and his music was played in more than 500 programmes.[17] On average, a work, song or programme featuring Nielsen was heard two or three times a week.

```
Torsdag den 30. April 1925.

            Kjøbenhavns Radiofonistation (775 m).

Kl. 7.30.   "Radio Uge Revue", Programavis.

Kl. 8.      Carl Nielsen - Aften.

            Indledning.              Kgl. Kammersanger Emil Holm.
            Kvintet for Blæsere. Opus 43.
                    a. Allegro.  b. Menuet.  c. Præludium-Tema med
                    Variationer.
                                     Københavns Blæserkvintet:
                    Holger Gilbert Jespersen        (Fløjte)
                    Kgl. Kapelmusikus Sv. Chr. Felumb (Obo)
                    Kgl. Kapelmusikus Aage Oxenvad   (Klarinet)
                    Kgl. Kapelmusikus Hans Sørensen  (Horn)
                    Kgl. Kapelmusikus Knud Lassen    (Fagot)

            Sange.
                    Underlige Aftenlufte. (A. Oehlenschlæger).
                    Tidt er jeg glad og vil dog gerne græde. (B.S.Ingemann)
                    Sang bag Ploven. (Ludvig Holstein)
                                        Koncertsanger Vilhelm Michelsen.

            Sonate. Opus 35. Adagio.   Violinvirtuos Emil Telmányi.
                                        og Komponisten Rudolph Simonsen.

            Sange.
                    Sænk kun dit Hoved, du Blomst. (Johannes Jørgensen)
                    Jeg bærer med Smil min Byrde. (Jeppe Aakjær)
                                        Koncertsanger Vilhelm Michelsen.

            Fantasistykker for Obo. Opus 2.
                    a. Romance.  b. Humoresque.
                                        Kgl. Kapelmusikus Sv. Chr. Felumb.

                    Ved Flyglet:  Komponisten Rudolph Simonsen.
```

ILL. 1. Statsradiofonien (the Danish Broadcasting Corporation) had only just begun transmitting their programmes when they filled the airwaves with a Carl Nielsen evening on 30 April 1925.[18]

Nielsen's involvement in radio predates the advent of public broadcasting. The official inauguration of the Danish Broadcasting Corporation on 1 April 1925, when the new Radio Act came into force, should not be seen as a sharp demarcation. The Finance Committee did not approve the Act until 3 April, and the first document in the radio archives is the programme for 21 April.[19] The private radio associations, which the Danish Broadcasting Corporation was replacing and of which Holm was chairman of one, were already active, transmitting concerts almost daily. A reader of *Politiken*'s radio column would not have noticed that anything significant had happened in April, as the same types of transmissions continued on the same stations.

Nielsen's first radio appearance was on 24 January 1925, when he gave a radio lecture entitled 'The composer Nielsen talks about good and bad music'.[20] And on

31 March, the private station Ryvangen Radio broadcast Musikforeningen's concert from Odd Fellow Palæet, where Nielsen conducted Mozart's *Eine kleine Nachtmusik* and Haydn's *Die Schöpfung*.[21] A few days later, Nielsen reported that the positive reception prompted Musikforeningen to repeat the concert: 'It was broadcast all over the country, and within half an hour we received telegrams of thanks, even from as far away as Jutland, asking for a repeat performance.'[22]

On 30 April, shortly after the official launch, the radio service broadcast an entire Nielsen evening with the Copenhagen Wind Quintet, the pianist Rudolph Simonsen, violinist Emil Telmányi and the singer Vilhelm Michelsen performing Nielsen's Wind Quintet, Violin Sonata No. 2, the *Fantasy Pieces for Oboe and Piano*, and five songs.

On a number of important occasions, Nielsen led performances of his own works. On 25 November 1925, for example, there was a test transmission of opera – and it was no coincidence: it was the fiftieth performance of the opera *Maskarade* at The Royal Theatre. On 11 October the following year, the fourth anniversary concert of the Dansk Koncert-Forening was broadcast, with excerpts from Nielsen's *Aladdin*. And on 14 January 1927, the Radio Symphony Orchestra, which on that occasion consisted of eighty-three musicians, gave its first ever symphony concert. The event, held at Odd Fellow Palæet, included the Prelude to Act Two of *Saul and David*, the second part of his Violin Concerto and his Third Symphony. The concert was part of a major initiative by Holm to organise three major concerts to demonstrate the potential of radio as a cultural institution and the need to establish a permanent full-scale radio symphony orchestra.[23]

In June 1931, Nielsen conducted his Flute Concerto in a transmission from Tivoli Gardens, and on 1 October the stage was set for another major celebration with the inauguration of the new radio studio called Stærekassen. Nielsen was to conduct his Violin Concerto with Peder Møller. Unfortunately, the audience missed this event as Nielsen was taken to the hospital the same evening. He died two days later.

A number of Nielsen's important works from the 1920s were presented to radio audiences. In December 1928, Nielsen's Clarinet Concerto was broadcast from the Dansk Koncert-Forening's concert at Odd Fellow Palæet. In 1927, the premiere of *En Fantasirejse til Færøerne* (*An Imaginary Journey to the Faroe Islands*) at The Royal Theatre was broadcast; in August 1929, the *Cantata for the Centenary of the Polytechnic College* was premiered at Forum, and in October, *Hymne til Kunsten* (*Hymn to Art*), commissioned for the opening of the Forum Art Convention, was premiered at the same venue. In 1930 the radio studio transmitted the premiere of the work *Iceland* on the occasion of the millennium celebrations of the Icelandic parliament Altinget, and in May 1929 the entire opera *Saul and David*, performed at The Royal Theatre, was broadcast on the radio.

The importance of the radio in the dissemination of Nielsen's major works should be emphasised: the three concertos, the first three symphonies, the Wind Quintet and a number of first performances of music for events were broadcast throughout the country. On the other hand, it must be said that the most frequently performed instrumental works contributed to the image of the popular Nielsen, with numerous transmissions of excerpts from *Maskarade* and *Aladdin*, Prelude to Act Two of *Saul and David* and *Suite for String Orchestra*. With almost a hundred performances, the songs to texts by Jeppe Aakjær were clear favourites; around forty were with texts by each of Ludvig Holstein, Jens Peter Jacobsen and Helge Rode. A number of popular songs were repeatedly performed, including 'Sænk kun dit Hoved, du Blomst' (Lay down, sweet flower, your head) with lyrics by Johannes Jørgensen and Drachmann's 'Du danske Mand' (*Danish Patriotic Song*); the latter appeared as a song with piano accompaniment, a choral piece, a communal song and in several orchestral arrangements.

Nielsen took an interest in the transmissions when he himself was broadcast on the radio. In 1929 he invited his friends to turn on the radio or to visit Frida Møller, Irmelin's mother-in-law, who apparently had a particularly good receiver.[24] They were transmitting a concert from Gothenburg; and on 23 May, when the Danish Radio broadcast *Saul and David*, they also used Møller's radio. Damgaard, where Nielsen was staying at the time, was not equipped with the latest technology, so the receiver was transported across the Storebælt (the Great Belt) with great difficulty so that he could listen to the performance there.[25]

When he conducted again in Gothenburg on 12 February 1930, the concert was transmitted on Swedish radio, and Nielsen wrote home to Irmelin in Copenhagen: 'Listen carefully to the Flute Concerto! The acoustics here are dull, but perhaps it will be good for the broadcast'.[26] Apparently the transmission went well, and Anne Marie, who had been at Irmelin's to listen to the concerto on Frida Møller's device, writes: 'Beethoven sounded especially good, you could hear all the notes. I thought the flautist had a very beautiful tone and also played with passion.'[27] Both sound quality and musical expression were commented on.

By 1927, the Danish Broadcasting Corporation was practically nationwide, and by 1930 the number of radio licences had reached more than 437,000.[28] In addition, radio could be heard across borders. At least 200 times during his lifetime, Nielsen's music was broadcast by a foreign radio station.[29] As a medium, radio had a much wider reach than concerts, both geographically and socially. Although it was also a medium where his great works could be heard, radio, even more than live concerts, had the format to disseminate and maintain the image of the popular Nielsen throughout the country.

Chapter 38

ORGAN MUSIC

Nielsen's association with the production of organ music is not extensive; however, at the end of the 1920s he was engaged in the discussions of the time about organs and organ music. The result was two large and distinct organ works, each aimed at a different audience. One is a collection of organ preludes, *29 Little Preludes*, intended for daily use in church services, and the other is a large concert work, *Commotio*. However, Nielsen had already been writing for the organ, for one of his earliest compositions, *Fantasy Pieces for Oboe and Piano*, was originally conceived as a piece for oboe and organ, and an arrangement of the first movement for violin and organ was performed on several occasions.[1] In 1913 he was inspired to compose for the organ again when the famous organist and cantor of St Thomas' Church in Leipzig, Karl Straube, visited Copenhagen. Straube was one of Johann Sebastian Bach's successors as Thomaskantor and was known as a great interpreter of Bach's music, and he took part in the discussions of the German organ revival movement, which promoted a rejection of the organs of Romanticism and their aesthetic ideals.[2] After the visit, Nielsen wrote: 'I feel like writing a Fantasy for organ and have already begun. It's tremendous how an organ can sound when a great master is handling it.'[3] He did not get very far, as only eleven bars survive in some sketches for the play *Sanct Hansaftensspil*, which he composed in the same year.

The Organ Revival Movement

In Denmark, the organ revival movement had strong supporters from the 1920s onwards, with Mogens Wöldike and Povl Hamburger as central figures. They built on Thomas Laub's ideas, published in his book *Musik og Kirke* (Music and Church) in 1920. Laub advocated the introduction of organ music into the church service in a style that 'fits modestly into the framework without asserting itself in its own right'.[4] The approach was the same as when he set out his ideas for accompaniment of secular, popular songs. The word should be the centre of attention. He found models for this style of organ performance in the music of the sixteenth and seventeenth centuries such as that of the German Baroque composer Johann Pachelbel. Laub envisioned the task of writing organ music to be undertaken by a future 'brilliant composer who would be able to combine the serious organ style of Pachelbel with

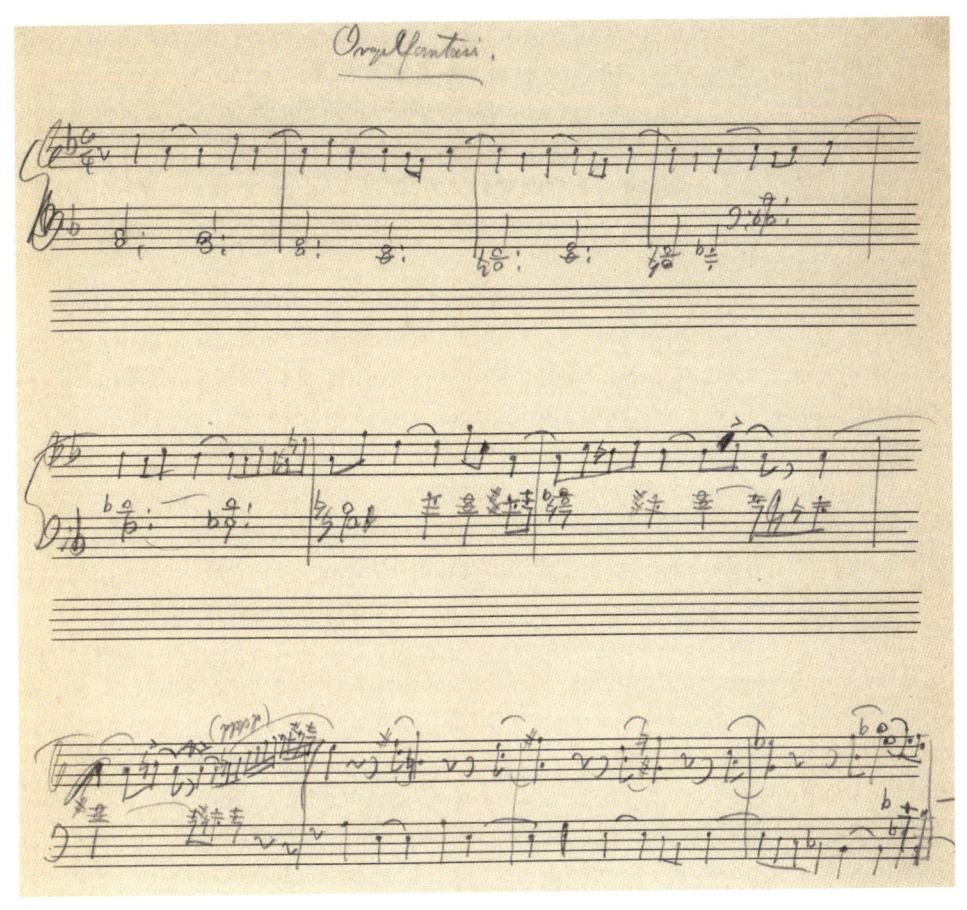

ILL. 1. The sketch (in CNS 347f) shows that Nielsen had an idea suitable for an organ fantasia in which a subject can develop gradually. He begins with a subject in the right hand which is a single oscillating interval of a fourth, while the left hand descends in parallel thirds. A bright timbre seems to expand gradually, giving the impression that Nielsen had the sound of the organ in mind. The subject slowly becomes more animated, and the left hand ascends until, in bar 8, it interrupts the process with a rapid passage in the right hand, marked *pppp*. This is followed by a repetition of the subject, now in the lower part of the left hand. The first two bars of this passage follow the subject exactly, until the third bar, when it begins to move off on its own. What happens next is a matter of conjecture.

the pure sound of Palestrina'.[5] The phrase was an expression of the almost impossible task that Laub believed it would be to arrive at a satisfactory style.[6]

Mogens Wöldike was a key figure in the debate about organ music. Firstly, he found suitable organ works from the seventeenth century, which he published together with Hamburger.[7] Secondly, he followed the reforms in organ building that were gaining ground in Germany, which in Denmark were known as the 'new organ movement'.[8] The Romantic organ, which was designed to imitate an orchestra, fell out of favour. In the 1920s the organ builder Sybrand Zachariassen of Marcussen & Son in Aabenraa was inspired by the new ideas and was responsible for building the first large organ in Denmark constructed entirely according to the new principles. It was placed in Nikolaj Kirke in Copenhagen and inaugurated in 1931, and of course Wöldike was involved.[9]

The ideal for the organ revival movement was the Baroque organ of the type known as the mechanical slider chest. The instrument's wind-chest, in which the air is distributed to the pipes, is built according to the old principles, which were otherwise considered inadequate during the nineteenth century and therefore fell into disuse. The new organ movement brought new technical solutions to the construction of the wind-chest, which was improved to such an extent that it was considered superior to all other types.[10] The organ movement was not only an attempt to approximate historical models, but also to improve the art of organ building.

The movement also drew inspiration from Baroque organs in another way, by looking at how the registers, the sets of pipes that produce different timbres and from which the organist can choose, were arranged at that time. Baroque organs often had very different types of registers rich in harmonics, and the pipes were also designed to produce a brighter and fresher sound than was common in Romantic organs. The stops in Baroque organs were often divided into a number of sections, that is, Hauptwerk, Oberwerk, Brustwerk, Rückpositiv and Pedalwerk, named after their function or position in relation to the performer. Each section was a separate organ, which meant that an instrument with, for example, three keyboards and pedal had four corresponding sections, each with its own distinct registers rich in harmonics and timbres, making the instrument ideal for performing the polyphonic organ music of the Baroque period.

The transparent, polyphonic style of writing, which was the ideal for what Laub saw as organ music suitable for worship, required organs whose sound made it possible to hear the independent voices of the composition. This was exactly what the new type of organ could do, and the organ builders who now followed the organ revival movement became preoccupied with refining the timbre of the instruments. The ideal was to achieve a purity of sound suitable for the polyphonic repertoire. The organ in Nikolaj Kirke has been described as having 'a transparent clarity', suggesting that the ideal of sound should support the desire to hear every detail of the music.[11]

When Nielsen began composing little preludes for church services in early 1929, he had probably never heard one of the new organs. However, he was undoubtedly aware of Laub's thoughts and wanted to contribute to the solution of the problem, not as a great genius, but on the basis of Laub's more modest admonition: 'If we only approach the matter *modestly*, we are probably going in the right direction'.[12] Nielsen's path to the kind of organ music that Laub and others had been seeking since the early 1920s was guided by Wöldike, who introduced Pachelbel's organ works to Nielsen and gave him the opportunity to play the instrument in Christiansborg Slotskirke, the church at the Christiansborg Palace.[13] The organist Peter Thomsen, a pupil of Laub's, also contributed by lending Nielsen scores of organ repertoire of sixteenth and seventeenth centuries.[14]

So when Nielsen composed the little preludes, he used the same approach as when he composed his *Three Motets*. The studies of the old masters seem to have given Nielsen different ideas for the organ pieces. The *29 smaa Præludier* (*29 Little Preludes*) (CNW 96) vary stylistically from toccata-like pieces to strictly fugal ones. Some appear predominantly homophonic, but Nielsen always takes the individual voices into account and allows them to influence the development of the piece. Counterpoint and his interest in early music are here used to renew organ music in the church.

Nielsen came to regard Thomsen as an advocate of the new organ style and as 'one of the most solid and gifted of the young church musicians'.[15] It was Thomsen who was responsible for the first performance of all the preludes on 19 March 1930, so Nielsen sought his advice when, the following year, he was asked by the editor of the journal *Vor Ungdom* for his thoughts regarding the use of the preludes in the church. Nielsen felt that Thomsen's views, which he had sent in a letter to Nielsen, could not be 'better or more clearly expressed',[16] so he reproduced Thomsen's words in his reply, which was then published in the journal.

Nielsen follows Thomsen's assessments of his own pieces fairly closely, admitting that some of them are definitely not suitable for church use, although a number of them are.[17] Nielsen also admits that it was not his primary aim in composing the pieces to fulfil the Laubian ideals. Nevertheless, Nielsen reproduces verbatim Thomsen's formulation of the main requirements for an objective organ style – in which the music is not 'the speech or observations of a single man', but the means to achieve this style – was a 'linear manner of writing'. By this he meant a polyphonic style in which the parts flow independently and 'are not stopped by period structures', such as formal breaks in terms of form in which all the parts pause. The linear style of composition results in music in which the audience listens for the individual phrases of each part. The strong focus on the progression of the parts should also limit the composer's use of modulation. At the end of his article, Nielsen approves of the concept of 'striving for the crystal clear values hidden in the self-will of the tones, above all kinds of sensations' – that is, a recognition of the aesthetics he saw in Renaissance and Baroque music.[18]

MUSIC EX. 1. Nielsen, *29 smaa Præludier* (*29 Little Preludes*), No. 14, bars 1–6. Thomsen points out that the characteristics that he had defined for the correct instrumental style in terms of sacred music are prominent in the E flat major Prelude. The linear writing is not developed by fugal techniques or by imitation between the parts. On the contrary, the setting is consistently in four parts. The way in which Nielsen achieves a polyphonic texture is by giving space to the individual parts, as only one is usually moving at a time, and it is therefore possible to follow each one in the polyphonic progression when listening to the music. When approaching a heavy beat of the bar, Nielsen allows all of the parts (or most of them) to move, giving it a sense of weight and the listener a sense of metre. However, this does not become a fixed pattern, and to prevent the parts from being forced into a fixed metre, Nielsen often uses syncopation, which is particularly effective in the outer parts. An example of this can be heard in bars 3–4 and 5–6, where the bass note is tied across the bar line. This creates a shift in the way the metre is perceived, suggesting that it is not important to listen to the first beat of the bar, but rather to the progression of the part. From bar 5, the upper part resembles Palestrina's melodic aesthetic: first the opening figure (C–B♭–G–C), followed by the top note E♭, which deliberately lingers on a weak beat before continuing downwards. Again, syncopation is a means of achieving metrical displacement, but the rhythm is determined above all by the melodic development of the upper part. It is a linear style of composition that takes into account the individual needs of each part.

No. 14 was one of the two preludes that Thomsen emphasised as an example of the qualities he considered ideal for a sacred instrumental style. It is therefore not surprising that it is one of the least Nielsenian preludes. On the other hand, it is clear from bar 4 of Prelude No. 1 that this is a piece composed in a 'contemporary' style, with phrases that Nielsen often used. Although the apparent form of the pieces resembles older models, they often behave quite differently from music in the older Baroque style. It was never Nielsen's intention to imitate the style. However, Nielsen later wrote two more preludes for Thomsen (CNW 98), which seem to meet the strict requirements of a church organ style.[19]

This seems to support the fact that Nielsen did not share the strict Laubians' quest for a style that, in Hamburger's words, recreates 'the objective, "supra-personal"

MUSIC EX. 2. Nielsen, *29 smaa Præludier* (*29 Little Preludes*), No. 1, bars 1–4. The prelude is regular, beginning with an F in the right hand and an imitative answer on B♭. In bar 4, however, the E heard in bar 3 is lowered to an E♭, while the right hand retains the E. Nielsen seems to be sticking his neck out, despite his assertion that in such pieces he tries to suppress his personal taste and let the notes follow their own will.

austerity' of early sacred music.[20] In his review of Nielsen's preludes, Hamburger thus denies the pieces any value as church music, with the exception of the two mentioned by Thomsen, Nos. 14 and 29. Furthermore, Hamburger felt that Nielsen had failed to 'keep his own individuality sufficiently in check' and even warned against thinking that the collection was suitable for church use. Nielsen should rather have called the pieces 'studies for organ'.[21] Yet Hamburger saw them as a natural extension of the polyphonic writing and imaginative richness he also found in Nielsen's symphonies. Even Johannes Hansen, Thorvald Aagaard's brother-in-law, who had originally encouraged Nielsen to write some small, simple preludes, did not find the pieces quite what he had in mind. Others, however, heard the collection in a very different way.[22] When Poul Schierbeck gave the first performance of twenty-eight of the preludes on the new Frobenius organ in Skovshoved Kirke, the critic August Felsing wrote that it seemed as if Nielsen was giving 'a retrospective presentation of himself' covering his entire output, from *Saul and David* to the symphonies and the popular songs to the Clarinet Concerto.[23]

Commotio

The twenty-nine preludes were a kind of preliminary study for the large organ work *Commotio* (CNW 99), which was inspired by the Baroque organ style and which according to Nielsen consists of two fugues framed by an introduction, middle sections and a coda.[24] The work is thus directly linked to the organ revival movement. In a letter to Emil Telmányi, Nielsen states that the work on *Commotio* was also an evaluation of the new organ type:

> None of my works has demanded such great concentration as this: it's an attempt to rebuild the one and only truly valid organ style, namely the kind of polyphonic music that is especially suited to this instrument, which for long time has been considered as a kind of orchestra, which it *isn't at all*.[25]

Nielsen employed concepts from the organ revival movement. The organ should not imitate an orchestra, but should have clear registers capable of articulating the polyphonic music. He believed that his task as a composer was to compose works in the style demanded by Wöldike and Thomsen, although it is notable that the argument is also that the music should be suitable for the new type of organ. *Commotio* was not intended for use in church services, but as a concert piece in keeping with the new ideals. The connection with the organ revival movement could hardly be clearer.

Nielsen explains that *Commotio* is 'movement [*Bewegung*], also spiritually' and cryptically states that it is to be understood in the sense of 'self-objectification'.[26] From the description, it seems that this means that the musical and emotional activity that the work is intended to show should be 'observed with the ear rather than embraced with the heart'; that is, the listener should observe the feeling and motion rather than be immersed in it. Again, Nielsen advocates an objective musical style that requires 'detachment rather than emotion'.[27]

Nielsen began composing the work in 1930 and completed it on 27 February 1931, the day before the inauguration of the new, innovative organ in Nikolaj Kirke.[28] As he stayed at Damgaard to finish the work, he was therefore unable to attend the event. However, Wöldike wanted Nielsen to hear the new organ and asked the organist Finn Viderø to play *Commotio* twice for an intimate audience in Nikolaj Kirke on 14 June. Nielsen had already heard the work once, when Thomsen had played it in a private performance in Christiansborg Slotskirke on 24 April.[29] About a week after Viderø's performance in June, Emilius Bangert played it in Roskilde Cathedral, before presenting the first public performance of the work at a concert on 14 August in Aarhus Cathedral. This performance was not in keeping with the ideals of the organ revival movement, as the cathedral's instrument was a large and sonorous Romantic organ.[30] The following performance in Lübeck, where Bangert played *Commotio* at an important organ festival three days after Nielsen's death, meant that it received international recognition in influential circles.

Nielsen liked his new work and wrote to Anne Marie that it was 'made with more skill than any of my other things'.[31] When he wrote a draft for the concert programme in Lübeck, he was adamant that he did not want the work to appear as an organ fantasia: 'I don't want to include anything about "improvising" ["*phantasierende*"]. After all the work is so strict in its form and part-writing that I can't imagine doing anything more solid.'[32] However, the structure of the work appears as an organ fantasia of large dimensions, and the very fact that Nielsen rejects it is a sign that the thought had crossed his mind. Hamburger comes as close as one can without using the word: 'The work appears in a rather free form, whose closest models seem to be the great improvisational forms of the Baroque.'[33] *Commotio* (that is, movement) is an apt expression for the flow of music that runs through the entire work, with virtually no pauses other than the large, form-shaping incisions that mark the beginning of the fugues and the continuation of the second fugue as the end.[34] Yet the proportions of the individual formal sections seem to correspond to the large format, where the introduction, over a sustained pedal point, lasts more than three minutes. The static and the dynamic elements are balanced.[35]

Nielsen did not comment on the performances he attended or on the organs on which *Commotio* was played. For Hamburger, it was important that the work should be played on 'at least a moderately modern organ', by which he meant one built according to the principles of the organ revival movement, 'so that its character is fully acquired'.[36] The most perfect performance during Nielsen's lifetime was thus the recital that Wöldike organised with Viderø in Nikolaj Kirke. At this event, Nielsen and the limited audience were able to hear the new work presented on one of the few organs that could do justice to the work in terms of sound.

Chapter 39

A SERIOUS GAME

Nielsen's late orchestral works of the 1920s show a marked change in character from those he had composed up to the beginning of the decade. There is something much more playful and a new lightness in his approach to the art of composing. Although the music still deals with important issues and can seem both experimental and fragmented, it is now more about telling stories and depicting the diversity of life. Nielsen has now achieved a clarity and a new approach, striving for something new and working directly with the sound. All the conflicts are still present in the music, but it is as if he has accepted that they are part of life. They can be portrayed and discussed, but not necessarily resolved or removed from the world. In this respect, the two late concertos for flute and clarinet are related to the Sixth Symphony: they also have the character of a serious game and an action set out in music.

'Music is Sound'

One of the most fascinating things about Nielsen is that he was never satisfied with what he had achieved. In the years leading up to 1925, when he turned sixty, he was still longing for a 'new music' that was not simply 'modern' in the sense of already known or fashionable. He was familiar with a wide range of modernist and avant-garde ideas, even if he was reluctant to apply them directly to his art. This intellectual receptiveness led to new ways of understanding the concept of 'notes', which were more than just beautiful and precise pitches of musical instruments.

On the day of the premiere of his Sixth Symphony, 11 December 1925, an interview with Nielsen was published in the newspaper *Politiken*, in which he made a striking statement: 'Music is sound'. He arrived at this observation through his fascination with some grey paper wrapped around a painting he had recently received. The paper 'crackled most amusingly', and Nielsen continues: 'Telmányi and I enjoyed ourselves for ages playing with that paper. There are modern composers who want to employ that grey paper directly in the orchestra. I would prefer to transcribe its sounds for one of our known instruments.'[1]

It is notable that at this point in his life Nielsen was able to fundamentally rethink the concept of what music consists of. As late as 1922, in a seminal text entitled 'Musikalske Problemer' (Musical Problems), he maintained his previous position that the essence of music was the intervals. An oft-repeated quotation from this article is his anti-Romantic remark that there was no cure against Wagner's 'exuberant' and unhealthy themes but to cultivate the basic intervals: '… a melodic leap of a third should be treated as a gift from God, a fourth as an experience and a fifth as the supreme joy.'[2] Thus, in 1922, Nielsen still spoke of music as something consisting of relationships between musical notes with fixed pitches.

Nielsen's 1925 statement 'Music is sound', however, suggests that he had adopted a new approach to composition. He was now composing based on the sound. In the 1925 interview he tries to explain that he had always thought in this way, without realising it. Inadvertently, he came to express the opposite: 'I began by composing with the piano and then later orchestrated the music. The next stage was to write my score directly for the instruments. Now I think out from the instruments themselves – almost as though I'm creeping inside them.'[3]

Contrary to what he claims, this is a radical change from thinking of music as a structure of notes, which are then given colour by orchestration, where the surface of the music is generally regarded as a secondary element while the structure is crucial. Now he was working directly with sound, at least in the sense that the result is a musical structure made up of sounds, and sometimes in such a way that the sound is more important than the actual pitch. For example, when he enjoys the wonderful sound of the lowest possible note on a bassoon, the low B♭, which is the final note of his Sixth Symphony, one gets the impression that it was sometimes more important for Nielsen to hear this particular *sound* than whether it was a B♭ or an A.

Nielsen's change of attitude towards composing took place around 1923, when he was preparing, albeit unconsciously, for his next major work. This was noted by Jan Maegaard in a commentary on the programme for the Carl Nielsen Festival in 1953, which he criticised for maintaining a traditional view of Nielsen. Maegaard drew attention to a significant change in Nielsen's approach to composing. The first time it is heard is in the introduction to the variations in Nielsen's Wind Quintet (1922), in which, according to Maegaard, Nielsen was directly inspired by the sound of the English horn rather than having an abstract or programmatic idea: 'I would go so far as to suggest that after 1922 he heard and conceived music in a significantly different way than before.'[4]

In his pocket diary for 1923, Nielsen made some important notes about this change in perception. They do not relate to the specific dates of the pages on which they appear, although the reference to the sound of a threshing mill suggests that they were added after the harvest, when he was staying at Damgaard in early October:

> Observe all the sounds we hear in the course of our work. Here I'm sitting with my pen and writing. What variety: (the pen, the inkwell, the paper, the sand). And new sounds are coming in with machines (threshers, automobiles).[5]

This situation is probably a reflection on the current soundscape, as Nielsen sits by an open window on the Damgaard estate, a place where many of his works have been composed, with agricultural machinery in operation outside. Immediately afterwards, however, he pulls back from his own thoughts and adds on the following page: 'All this should not be enjoyed aesthetically, God preserve us from such affectation!'[6] But the reader should be aware that this is one of those cases where Nielsen is *not* to be trusted. He is intimidated by the far-reaching implications of his thinking, but the switch to an *aesthetic* way of listening to everyday sounds is exactly what he is doing. Another note reveals Nielsen: 'Everything has music in it: a grain of sand, the rustling of a newspaper, cannon-fire etc. To be developed.'[7] When he uses the phrase 'to be developed', he is implying that it was a thought he wanted to retain in order to work on it further.

These new experiences have implications. On the one hand, they open up the view that sound that can be used for aesthetic purposes is not limited to traditional musical sounds, such as pitches emitted by a singing voice or musical instruments. On the other hand, it makes Nielsen realise that not only can music be composed using all kinds of sounds, but that musical instruments intrinsically also 'sound' – they do not merely produce musical pitches.

At the same time, this new approach is rooted in a continuity of his thinking at a deeper level. Nielsen maintains his basic view of the roots of music: it arises from man's fascination with sound events. In his article of 1922, Nielsen argues that the fundamental elements of music are to be found in its origins: 'The joy of [primitive] human beings in hearing their own voice cannot be compared with the joy and wonder that is felt when a note is produced on a bell stone, an ox horn, or when strumming a string stretched over a tortoise shell.'[8] Wonder is the key word.

Similarly, Nielsen's fascination with 'sound events' was already present in a passage from a 1909 book review, in which his reflections lead to a fundamental consideration of the musician's task:

> What exactly are we setting out to do? And why and for whom? Our whole tragedy and endeavour is ... to break the silence, to cut and chop it in such a way that it arouses the attention, wonder and enthusiasm of others ... the street boy whistling, the coachman cracking his whip for no reason, the bully amused by the crash of the stone through the window pane ... they are in reality musicians like us ...[9]

Musicians are human beings who create remarkable sound events, and any sound that attracts attention is essentially a form of music. It is an approach that allows Nielsen to remain a truly innovative composer in the 1920s.

Sinfonia semplice

In the spring of 1923, Nielsen enjoyed some of his greatest successes with concerts and official recognition abroad. On 5 March he wrote to Anne Marie from Karlsruhe, where he was to conduct a major concert that evening, that it was almost too good to be true:

> Isn't it strange that now finally my cause and my life's work are so appreciated, so that I now stand here absolutely aimless. Is this the beginning of a time when the line [of my career] will start to fall, do you think?[10]

The period between this and the composition of the Sixth Symphony, *Sinfonia semplice* (CNW 30), is not one of great output. In 1923 he composed *Prelude, Theme and Variations*, Op. 48, for solo violin in the spring and *Balladen om Bjørnen* (*Ballad on the Bear*) at the end of the year.[11] In the following spring he was busy composing tunes for the *Songbook 'Denmark'*, nine of which were also published in the collection *Ti danske Smaasange* (*Ten Little Danish Songs*).[12]

On the one hand, this period is marked by a number of major concerts abroad and in Copenhagen. In December 1922, Nielsen had conducted the Berlin Philharmonic Orchestra in two concerts in Berlin, including the Violin Concerto with Peder Møller as soloist, the overture to *Maskarade*, Symphonies Nos. 2, 3 and 5, the *Aladdin Suite*, *Saga Dream* and four of his lieder in an orchestral version. The following week, Georg Høeberg conducted Nielsen's Fourth Symphony in Berlin, which he had also done in Vienna in October. In February, Møller was in Vienna, playing the Violin Concerto in the large hall of the Musikverein, and, according to the rumours that reached Nielsen, 'to wild applause'.[13] This was clearly an exaggeration, but no one told Nielsen.[14]

The concert programme in Karlsruhe in March consisted of the Violin Concerto and the Fourth Symphony, accompanied by two short orchestral pieces, *Pan and Syrinx* and 'Dance of the Cockerel' from *Maskarade*. It was this constellation of works that gave Nielsen the feeling of a major international breakthrough. He presented virtually the same programme at a concert in Copenhagen in February and at a prestigious concert in London in June, with Emil Telmányi as violin soloist. Thus Nielsen himself helped to create the image, that alongside the 'early', slightly awkward Nielsen, there was also the 'great' Nielsen, characterised by the symphonies Three, Four and Five, the popular orchestral pieces and the brilliant Violin Concerto.

However, Nielsen also feels that he is at a crossroads and does not really know what to do. He seems to have doubts about how to follow up his great successes. From Karlsruhe, he travelled to the south of France, where he wrote to the music historian William Behrend: 'In the past year or so I've thought much about this question and have therefore begun an article on it, which I hope to have finished in this next fortnight.'[15] There is no sign that his plan came to fruition. Instead, the solo work for Telmányi takes priority in the spring and is completed on 28 May.

In 1923, Nielsen was not yet working on his Sixth Symphony. In August of that year, on his way home from Damgaard, he wrote to Nancy Dalberg that he was not working on any composition: 'I've no work to do and can't conceive of anything either; I haven't seen a note all this time.'[16] He told her that at that moment he had no desire to do anything but read. He had written to Oluf Ring a few days earlier in the same vein:

Everything to do with art is in chaos these days, and it seems that – like in a shipwreck – it's every man for himself trying to reach land. Even the best musicians nowadays seem to have been seized by the anxiety of being considered too 'old-fashioned'.[17]

October is almost certainly the time when he scribbled the aforementioned entries in his pocket diary on music as sound. If read as an unconscious preparation for his forthcoming symphony, they may explain why he begins to imagine music that is very different from what he has done before.

By the following summer his mood had changed. In July and August 1924 Nielsen was in Skagen, and now the desire to compose had returned. He writes to his daughter that he is at present 'feeling a strong creative urge and yet somehow can't get going with anything', yet he is still able to describe his vision:

A new symphony, completely idyllic in character. I mean quite different from any time-bound taste or fashion, but just a subtle and deeply musical abandonment to the notes, in the same way as the old *a cappella* musicians; yet still using the resources of our time. Well, what do I know, when as yet I'm only sensing a vague and obscure instinct for something in this direction?[18]

Two days later, on 14 August, he is composing and has 'begun to work on a new charming, playful symphony'.[19] These descriptions may well apply to the beginning of the first movement of the symphony, and one should not read more into them than they can bear.

In October 1924, Nielsen had returned to Damgaard, where he had made a good start, and was now able to say a few words about the symphony: 'So far as I can tell, it will be of a different overall character from my others – more amiable, more flowing, or whatever; but it's not good to say, because I don't yet have any idea what currents may arise during the voyage.'[20] He wrote to his daughter Anne Marie two days later:

> God knows how it will turn out! ... little Nielsen can't keep going in the same damned way, with temperament and all that. This time it will be considerably boring and respectable.[21]

The statements are not particularly precise, and perhaps there is a certain amount of affectation in them, for he must have been quite far along with the first movement, which he finished four weeks later, on 20 November, again at Damgaard.[22] The second movement was completed on 28 January 1925, the third on 18 April, and after a summer of stalling, he finally got going again at the end of August. The fourth and last movement was completed on 5 December, six days before the premiere.[23]

There are no surviving statements that shed any light on the two middle movements, except that Nielsen remarks that they are quite short. In the spring of 1925, he was approached by a journalist while crossing Rådhuspladsen, the Town Hall Square. On that occasion, Nielsen remarked: 'The finale will be a series of variations, a cosmic chaos whose atoms will clear up from the dark to the light and come together to form a planet.'[24] It was a vision, however, for he was still working on the third movement.

Most of these early statements were either formulated before he began on the project, or couched in vague and sometimes contradictory phrases. In terms of the finished symphony, however, it is remarkable that Nielsen remained steadfastly committed to his original idea of composing an amiable and playful work. In an interview published two days before the premiere, he said:

> I have given it the name of 'Sinfonia semplice', because its main character is of a lighter colour than in my other symphonies – there are cheerful things in it.[25]

This does not correspond to the common perception that the symphony is a difficult work to listen to. Even a composer like Maegaard, an expert on Schoenberg's music and thus accustomed to contemporary music, heard it quite differently:

> The Sixth Symphony is the culmination of incomprehensibility; ... probably only those who are thoroughly acquainted with Carl Nielsen's life and music will understand the tragic combination of all three parts [i.e. joke, seriousness, sardonic humour] of which the symphony is an expression, and will therefore forgive its undeniable weaknesses. For better or worse, it is a bleeding wound that exposes its composer in the harshest light ...[26]

So how are we to understand what Nielsen is saying? He firmly rejects the idea that the symphony reflects his own moods. It is not about him. It is worth trying to take at face value what he says when asked in the same interview: 'What are you presenting in the new symphony?' His answer is: 'Just *purely musical* problems.'[27] He then goes on to explain what happens in the second movement, the Humoresque. It is a playful narrative in music, which on the one hand is light and cheerful, and on the other hand must be understood as a serious game. In contrast to his earlier statements, he is quite specific:

> On one side I have placed a group of two clarinets, a piccolo and two bassoons; on the other side there is a glockenspiel, a snare drum and a triangle; and finally a trombone. The Humoresque begins with the three small percussion instruments – the glockenspiel, the snare drum and the triangle – agreeing to wake the other, bigger instruments that are asleep. These three small creatures do not have a lot of brains, rather they are very childish, sweet, innocent little ones, and they now begin with their *bimme-limme-bim* and their muted *boom-boom-boom* … they become more and more eager, and finally they arouse the others to play … the clarinets, the piccolo and the bassoons. But the small, innocent instruments do not like this modern music – they pound away to themselves: *Stop it, stop it,* they say … and then the modern music is soon over. But then a clarinet begins to play, it is a little childish melody, and the small instruments are silent and listen. The trombone, that great instrument, yawns and says: *Baah, kid's stuff!* The other instruments join in, there is a quarrel about the music, it sounds a bit out of tune and confused – and in the end it all comes to nothing.[28]

It is a story in music and about music. In the interview that appeared the same day, Nielsen explains his approach in more general terms. He repeats that he chose the title *Sinfonia semplice* because 'in this work [he] has sought to achieve the greatest possible simplicity', and continues: 'This time the starting point is the character of the instruments and I have tried to portray them as independent characters.'[29] What happens in the Humoresque are instruments

> fighting for taste and favour. Times change, of course. Where will contemporary music take us? What will remain? We do not know! You will find out in my little Humoresque, which is the second movement of the symphony, and in the last movement, which is the theme and variations, where things get very cheerful. There are more serious, problematic issues in the first and third movements, but overall I tried to make the symphony as lively and cheerful as possible.[30]

When Nielsen speaks of music that deals with musical problems, this should not be understood in a derogatory sense, but as matters that require thorough consideration. He has the instruments act as characters or persons in a play, and in the Humoresque it could even be a puppet theatre. There – in music – is a discussion about the ends and means of music. This is the starting point when trying to understand the symphony as simple: 'What you hear is what you get'. In the Humoresque, the music acts out the discussion and the uncertainty about where music should go.

Paradoxically, because the symphony represents in music the uncertainty and disagreement about how the new is to be understood in the future, the conditions of modernity are particularly evident: the symphony becomes an expression of the unresolved state of affairs that the question of modernity and renewal poses to composers. The symphony becomes truly modern because it reveals that the composer does not know the solution. The conflicts are present in the music, but Nielsen has now accepted that they are part of life. The problems can be described, discussed and debated, but the conflicts do not necessarily have to be resolved, overcome or brought to an end. This is a new view of Nielsen's modernity, where dissonance is not seen as a problem or a flaw, but as one of the qualities of music.

At the same time, if one listens to the symphony with an open mind, the work can be interpreted as Nielsen achieving a new level of mastery over the means he uses. He is now able to float smilingly above the waters, using all the artistic and compositional tools at his disposal to realise his conception of sound. He has reached that exalted state from which he can see the conflicts from a broader perspective and let them play out in music as if it were a theatre.[31] If ever he appears as the idealised figure of Mozart, able to reconcile freedom and constraint in the tonal language of his own time, it is here.

The new approach to instruments as individual 'sound beings' and to music as composed of sound(s) leads to an unprecedented independence for the percussion, allowing them to act on an equal footing with the melody instruments. It is the percussion in the role of small, innocent beings in the Humoresque, and it is the triangle and the snare drum that take the lead. The melody instruments – flute, bassoon and clarinet – initially play just a single note, a chirp or a honk, pretending to be 'sound makers' too. A little later, when they are supposed to be playing a 'modern' piece, Nielsen adopts sounds reminiscent of atonal music.[32] The story that he is telling is clearly audible.

By giving the percussion such a central role and allowing the melody instruments to act as sound generators, Nielsen reduces the distinction between the instrumental groups to a difference of degree. Nielsen makes a decisive contribution to the historically significant development of recognising the percussion as an independent section of orchestral instruments on a par with the others. In the fourth movement,

ILL. 1. The party at the restaurant Nimb after Stravinsky's concert in Copenhagen on 2 December 1925. Nielsen, who had cancelled all other engagements for those days in order to finish his Sixth Symphony, is sitting in the middle with Stravinsky.

a theme and a set of variations, he includes one variation for the percussion, augmented by some low pitches from a tuba and a bassoon, which is one of the first examples in the history of music that functions on the percussion's terms. The composer Edgard Varèse is generally regarded as the leading figure in this development, but Nielsen's approach is equal to Varèse's seminal work *Hyperprism* of 1923 – a work with which Nielsen had little opportunity to familiarise himself.[33] Nielsen is at the forefront of the development of contemporary music in the twentieth century.

But he was not entirely without role models. The playful approach, in which the winds in particular stand out clearly as individuals 'playing characters', is also found in Stravinsky, not least in a work such as *Petrushka* (1911). Stravinsky's music was well known in Copenhagen, for in the summer of 1924 he had performed his latest piano concerto while Nielsen was in Skagen.[34] And when Nielsen was working on the Humoresque in January 1925, he attended a performance of *Petrushka* at the Danish Philharmonic Society, which had been programmed together with Nielsen's Violin Concerto.[35]

At the end of 1925, shortly before the premiere of Nielsen's symphony, Stravinsky was in Copenhagen for the second time, performing works with musicians from The Royal Orchestra and with Nielsen at the subsequent celebrations. The programme included the *Pulcinella Suite*, *Ragtime* for eleven instruments, Stravinsky as soloist in his new piano sonata, his orchestral suite and, last but not least, *Histoire du soldat* with Stravinsky at the piano, Peder Lynged on violin and Aage Oxenvad on clarinet. When asked what impression Stravinsky had made on him, Nielsen replied: 'I had a *wonderful time*.'[36] Reflecting a few months later on Stravinsky's visit, Nielsen said: 'He is genius, a little impudent, but lively and strong.'[37] From October 1925, *Petrushka* was also performed as a ballet at The Royal Theatre in Mikhail Fokin's production, bringing Stravinsky to a wider audience.[38]

Not surprisingly, some critics thought of Stravinsky when they heard Nielsen's Sixth Symphony for the first time. In the newspaper *København*, the comparison was in Stravinsky's favour, and *Berlingske Tidende* thought that Nielsen was 'too personal and idiosyncratic' to imitate Stravinsky.[39] *Politiken* described the sixty-year-old Nielsen as 'an innovator' and stressed his unwillingness to rest on his laurels: 'No, he wants to be the living present itself.' And so he was:

> We have just heard a Stravinsky. We have also seen the new man in him and admired him for it. How much greater should the admiration be for Nielsen, who was new when he came along a lifetime ago and remains so to this day.[40]

Nielsen and Stravinsky stood side by side as representatives of a new music.

Order or Chaos

Although Nielsen says that more serious things are going on in the first movement of the symphony, it also has the quality of a musical narrative that carries the form and is strong enough to compensate for the lack of overall unity on the tonal level that many have been concerned with.

A recurring feature in the structure of this movement is that Nielsen works on the basis of a narrative model in which an apparently simple and easily understood motif is presented, which is then undermined, losing its innocence, before being replaced by a new version of an expression of purity. Then another cycle begins in which the new expression can be degraded and corrupted in order to reach a new representation of something simple – and so on. Against this background, the American musicologist Jonathan Kramer sees the expression of the symphony as fundamentally pessimistic. According to Kramer, simplicity and straightforwardness are the positive aspects that are constantly being undermined and must ultimately be

MUSIC EX. 1. Nielsen, Symphony No. 6, *Sinfonia semplice*, first movement. The movement's opening of first subject material with its characteristic elements are: a) the repeated note in the glockenspiel and the central theme in the violins from bar 3, and b) the 'innocent' melody in the violins from bar 8. All three elements are presented in a delicate and subdued form, somewhat hesitant and without a clear metrical and tonal structure, until the melody of bar 8 confirms both the key of G major and the time signature of 4/4. In bar 21, the flute presents c) the second subject of the movement, again delicate and expressive, with a contrapuntal phrase in the violin that also provides material for the rest of the movement. The third subject, d) the energetic fugal theme, appears for the first time in bar 54. Although it seems to contrast sharply with the second subject, the first three notes of the latter two subjects share the same intervallic structure: a minor third combined with a major second. Beneath the surface of contrast, there is a high degree of internal musical coherence throughout the movement.

seen as untrustworthy. It is music, he argues, that has lost its innocence, and he thus attributes an element of fatalism or nihilism to Nielsen's symphony.[41]

The narrative model makes sense when you listen to the music. It is essentially a variation on the familiar principle of musical development in symphonic movements: to present a subject, develop it, before landing on solid ground again. Traditionally, the solid ground has been understood as being deeply rooted in tonality. In Nielsen's version, the model is transformed into an expressive shift between simplicity and complexity, order and disorder, without necessarily being linked to tonality.

This need not be seen as an expression of pessimism. Nielsen describes some of the subjects as small and innocent, as naive as children, and it could also be seen as positive if they grow up and become wiser, less naive and more inclusive with age.

Rather than hearing it as destructive when disruption disturbs the idyll, one can hear the fine, small and idyllic subjects as the backbone of the movement, which, when they return, use the opposite rhetoric to the common triumphant reprises of the traditional symphonic form. As an effective alternative, Nielsen's music softens its voice as the subjects reappear in an almost finer form than before. In this sense, there is a strong continuity between Nielsen's Fourth, Fifth and Sixth symphonies. In the *Sinfonia semplice*, the idea is realised in a new form that if 'all living things were destroyed and dead, then Nature would still begin again to beget new life, and to assert itself with the strongest and finest powers that are to be found in the material itself'.[42]

This is not to say that the music does not make its voice heard along the way. All the central subjects appear in the movement in forms in which their rhythmic contour is unchanged, but in which the melody, the degree of intensity and the instrumentation are emphasised to such an extent that one might describe it as a brutalisation of their character.[43] In this way, even in the midst of tumult and chaos, they are able to assert themselves and participate in the musical discussion.

To counterbalance the rough surface, the music has a very high degree of internal coherence between subjects and motifs throughout the movement. The first three notes of the fugal theme contain the same intervals as the beginning of the second subject of the movement, the minor third and the major second, and the sound of these intervals characterises the whole movement. The network of internal musical relationships is similar to that found in the first movement of the Fifth Symphony, but unlike there, they are not directional. The relationships in the Fifth emerge through a forward development that can be followed as a process of organic growth. In the *Sinfonia semplice*, the network is formed by connections across time and space.[44]

Despite its fragmented form, the first movement is easy to follow. The individual subjects are presented in such a way that they are immediately recognisable and characteristic. In the introduction, Nielsen works with the familiar model of presenting a first subject consisting of several different elements, followed a little later by a lyrical theme that clearly stands out as a second subject. Thus Nielsen has established the contrast that the listener expects in a symphony. The two groups of subjects form a contrast between something naive, expectant and simple in the first group and a more dreamy expression in the second. A third one is a fiery fugal theme that appears three times in the course of the movement, breaking things up each time.

The development that follows the first fugue ends surprisingly with the introduction of an entirely new, innocent theme, presented quietly in the strings at bar 129, accompanied only by a glockenspiel, piccolo flute and triangle – the three instruments that

MUSIC EX. 2. Nielsen, Symphony No. 6, first movement, a) bars 129–31, b) bars 171–72. After the first subject, second subject and the first fugue, elements of the latter two are combined and developed in a longer passage that concludes with a new, seemingly innocent theme in bars 129–31 that will play a crucial role in the subsequent development. It reappears after the second fugue and, with great energy, creates the dynamic that, in bars 171–72, first establishes the climax of the movement before leading to a collapse in bar 189.[45]

play a crucial role in the Humoresque. This section is followed by the second fugue appearing in the woodwinds, which is combined with motifs from the first subject. The passage leads to the climax of the movement, where the small, seemingly innocent theme suddenly bursts through in the brass, while the other winds play the first subject and the strings speed away in rapid runs. It all ends with a big, complex chord in *fff* in the full orchestra, before two notes that form a semitone remain as a jarring dissonance. There is no great, triumphant climax as might be expected – it is more like a collapse.

The collapse is not permanent, however. The first subject returns, quietly beginning a build-up that leads to the movement's third fugue. The first movement ends as quietly as it began with the first subject of the introduction, but now based on A♭ rather than G. The expectation that the symphony might return to its tonal starting point is not fulfilled.

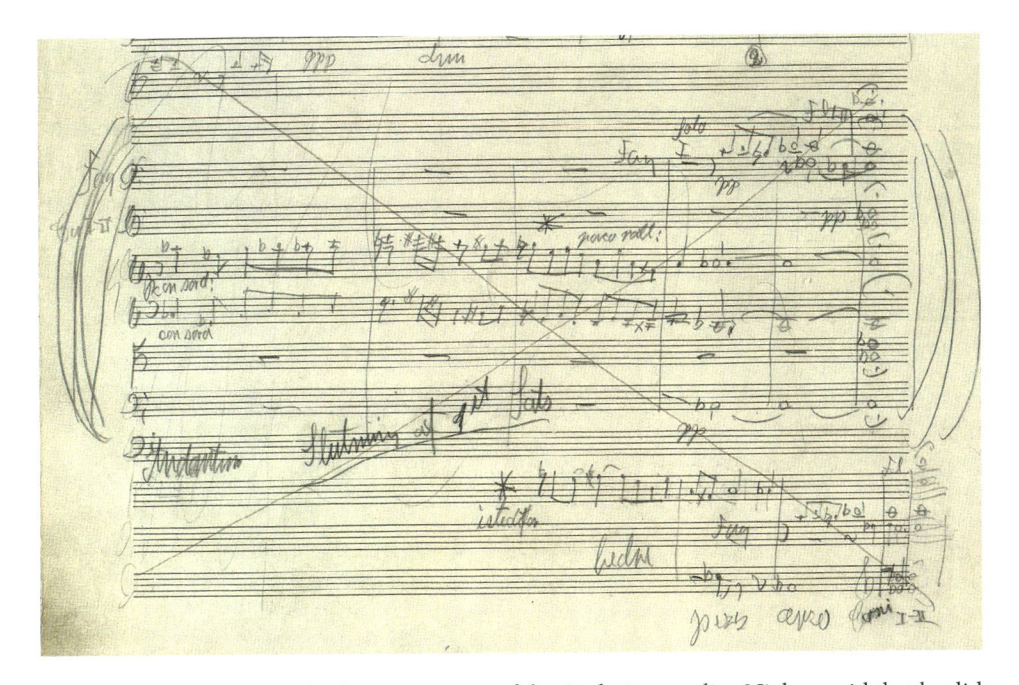

ILL. 2. When composing the first movement of the *Sinfonia semplice*, Nielsen said that he did not know what 'currents might arise during the voyage,'[46] but at the same time he was sure of how he wanted to end the movement. On page six of the pencil draft of the score (CNS 67b), Nielsen had reached the point where he was about to begin the first fugue; here he had already added a sketch on the lower part of the music paper for the 'end of the 1st movement'. He decided to end in A flat major or minor, and including the additions he made, marked 'instead of' and 'better' at the bottom of the page, the sketch contains all the essential elements of the ending. In the final version, he added two bars to the opening passage, as well as the glockenspiel, and extended the use of the small three-note motif in the antepenultimate and penultimate bars.

One way of interpreting the movement, then, is to hear it as a narrative in which the overall structural order – both in the music and in the world outside – is no longer intact. Accordingly, the ending in A♭, prepared after the collapse, is the consequence of the breaking of the thread running through the symphony. Although the fugal theme is initially perceived as the most aggressive, it does not cause the collapse; it is the new, seemingly innocent theme introduced in bar 129 that does: rather than being perceived as the stripping away of its innocence, this theme is the very element of destruction that, in its brutal version from bar 171, causes the final collapse. At first, the theme attracts the listeners' attention and invites them to take sides, making them believe that it is one of the 'good' elements with which to sympathise. However, the listeners are deceived and later realise that it was a wolf in sheep's

A SERIOUS GAME

clothing that they should have been wary of. The theme is the perpetrator, not the victim.[47] According to this interpretation, it is not a negative outcome that the symphony collapses when the new theme is about to win. The collapse paves the way for hope, as the first subject of the movement is allowed to develop again.

The fourth movement consists of a theme and nine variations, but it is more than that. It also functions as a narrative, with a number of independent characters appearing along the way. The structure, consisting of an introduction – that is, a theme introduced by a clearly audible solo bassoon – and the first variations, has much in common with the theme and variations of the Wind Quintet. Both introductions share a common sound as the same combination of instruments – flute, clarinet, oboe, bassoon and French horn – is heard until the string section enters in variation 2. The next three variations take the music in new directions before pausing to present the melody in an elegant waltz time in Variation 6. After two repetitions, the fun begins: first with the flutes playing at their own pace, mocking at the dance music like street urchins, then a full brass band joins in at a different tempo while the dance musicians try to keep their beat. After a slow, meditative contrast, a variation for the percussion reminiscent of the Humoresque appears, which is interrupted by a completely unexpected fanfare, as if to announce the arrival of someone important. This leads to a conclusion in which the winds evoke the theme, followed by a transition to an ironic umba-bumba rhythm, before arriving at the end, the lowest note of the bassoon.

Nielsen's Sixth Symphony shows that a decisive change had taken place in the early 1920s. The work represents a different kind of modernity from the one that is based on an organic development and waves of energy. It should rather be interpreted as an interplay and an interaction of musical characters, each with their own identity, enacting their parts. The music thus expresses several characters rather than just one, each having its say, and, as Daniel M. Grimley argues, as a complex, carnivalesque play of identities. The carnivalesque implies not only the abolition of the social divisions and norms of a certain limited period, as in a carnival or masquerade, but also that the humorous, caricatured and absurd episodes bring to the surface what is otherwise repressed. The meaning of Nielsen's statement is that the symphony should be understood as a game – but a serious game. As listeners, we must learn to relate to this 'playfulness', to Nielsen's delight in a theatrical staging with musical actors.[48]

Aurally, the first movement is a dramatised narrative and the Humoresque a puppet show, while the fourth movement is reminiscent of a carnival procession; or the listener may imagine that they are standing in a square, an orchestra is playing a waltz on a bandstand, street urchins are interfering and a brass band is marching past. Nielsen had already anticipated this idea in *Aladdin* in the scene 'Torvet i Ispahan' (The Marketplace in Ispahan). The spontaneous fanfare towards the end interrupts the action in the same way as the Master of the Masquerade in the opera *Maskarade*, announcing that something else, more important is about to happen.

Even at the premiere, some saw a connection between the *Sinfonia semplice* and the carnival in *Maskarade*. Hugo Seligmann of *Politiken* heard the symphony, for all its modernity, as 'a synthesis of Holberg and Fyn'. In the last movement, he experienced a completely new sound that 'we do not recognise, a new *Maskarade*, if you like.'[49] There is also a touch of sardonic humour at the end. After Variation 9, the short section for percussion supported by tuba and bassoon, comes the surprising fanfare, leading to a forced and relatively short ending. This is 'playful' music, but it is perhaps not entirely credible as an ending – at least not if it is meant to suggest that everything has now fallen into place. Rather, it ends up in a state of limbo, an expression of comic irony rather than negativity.[50] But again, one could draw a line back to the opera *Maskarade,* where the final Kehraus conveys a similar sense of a forced, exaggerated joie de vivre that is also not entirely credible. There is also an air of desperation about the opera's ending.

Narratives

Others of Nielsen's late works also have the character of musical narratives. An obvious example is the Concerto for Clarinet and Orchestra, Op. 57 (CNW 43), which Nielsen composed in 1928. The work was composed for Aage Oxenvad, the clarinettist of the Copenhagen Wind Quintet, and is thus linked to Nielsen's Wind Quintet, which was composed with these musicians in mind. Nielsen had originally intended to write a concerto for each member of the quintet, but only completed the Flute and Clarinet concertos.[51] Oxenvad had been a member of The Royal Orchestra since 1909, so Nielsen undoubtedly knew him and his musical abilities well. And Oxenvad was no ordinary person. When Nielsen composed the work, Oxenvad had participated in the performance of one of Schoenberg's most advanced works, *Pierrot lunaire,* in Copenhagen in 1921, and had played under Schoenberg's baton during his visit in 1923 and with Stravinsky in the performance of *Histoire du soldat* in the version for clarinet, violin and piano in 1925.[52]

The clarinet was one of the instruments to which Nielsen attributed an individuality early on, using it as a 'character' in his works. In an interview about his Sixth Symphony in 1925, Nielsen spoke of the soul of the instruments and said of the clarinet that it 'can be warm and downright hysterical at the same time, mild as balm or screeching like a tramcar on poorly greased rails'.[53] In the Fifth Symphony, the clarinet already plays an important role, and its hysterical outbursts are heard several times throughout the work. In particular, at the end of the first movement, the clari-

MUSIC EX. 3. Nielsen, Concerto for Clarinet and Orchestra, bars 1–9. The first subject of the concerto is a small, regular melody of eight bars. In the same way that Nielsen composes popular songs, he uses a fixed rhythmic pattern, of which bars 1 and 2 are identical, and the rhythm of the first four bars is repeated in 5–8. Unlike a melody for a song, however, the subject is distinctly instrumental, with the emphasised pause between the second and third notes providing a little jump that skilled musicians are able to bring to life musically. With its repetitive melodic formulae and distinctive rhythmic shape, the subject is already fixed in the listener's mind after the first hearing, but to be on the safe side, Nielsen has the low strings play it twice. Then the clarinet takes over and embellishes and varies the subject, whose elements recur throughout the work, holding the music together as a whole across the movements and the many imaginative inventions along the way.

net plays a key role alongside the snare drum, another of the symphony's prominent protagonists, both of whom fantasise wistfully about the symphony's central motif until it fades into the distance. Both characters reappear in the Clarinet Concerto.

In the Clarinet Concerto the snare drum and the clarinet resume their intimate partnership, with the snare drum having almost as large a solo part as the clarinet. Almost every time the clarinet appears with free solo passages – apart from the two large solo cadenzas in the first and third movements – it is in dialogue with the snare drum. It is almost a concerto for clarinet and snare drum. Nielsen is well aware that the instrument must have a very special sound, and in the first edition of the score he advises that it should be the smallest possible drum with the lightest sound.[54] He also reduced the instrumentation to a string section, two bassoons and two French horns in addition to the two soloists. Thus it sounds like chamber music for an orchestra, with the result that everything is clearly audible at all times. That these aspects were important to Nielsen during his work on the concerto is evidenced by a letter he wrote to Telmányi the day after the completion of the concerto:

> I've taken a lot of trouble over this work, striving in particular for clarity and rigour, also in the instrumentation. ... The small drum is also handled individually.[55]

MUSIC EX. 4. Nielsen, Concerto for Clarinet and Orchestra, a) bars 547–55; b) bars 720–28. The ending is based on the motif, described by Nielsen as 'folkish-childlike', which introduces the final movement of the concerto (bars 549–55). The snare drum accompanies the clarinet and is the instrument that, with a little solo of its own, invites the listener to pay attention to the new subject. At its final reappearance, the subject's intervals become increasingly small, until only a single note remains; and from bar 720, the rhythmic motion also stops, while the snare drum fades into the background and the violins disappear into the air with very high flageolet notes.

The Clarinet Concerto is structured in four continuous movements that flow effortlessly into one another. It begins with a regularly constructed eight-bar subject, which sounds like a perfect, simple melody, yet is formed in such a way that it is slightly out of shape. This subject becomes the starting point for the entire concerto, appearing in all conceivable places and forms. Its clear form and recognisable elements strengthen the musical cohesion, and every time the small rhythmic introductory motif appears, the listener feels the joy of recognition.

A few weeks before completing the concerto, Nielsen wrote a letter to his daughter describing his method of working. The description makes it clear that Nielsen was thinking in terms of musical narratives, much as he had in his Sixth Symphony:

> My Clarinet Concerto will soon be finished. The instrument (solo) and the orchestra parts are treated as individuals (as far as possible), but towards the conclusion the clarinet discovers a light and almost completely folkish-childlike motif (as though by accident) and when the other instruments hear it they fall on it and

express their happiness with it in a forceful and yet cheerful tutti: 'this is something we understand'. But it doesn't end (the concerto, I mean) in this world; it's just a 'social' episode.[56]

The example he describes is the introduction to the fourth movement, the Rondo, in which the opening subject is presented in this way in the clarinet and then eagerly taken up by the rest of the orchestra. As befits a rondo, the subject returns several times, but each time in a transformed form.[57] Finally, the music fades away into thin air and, as in the Fifth Symphony, the two protagonists withdraw into the faintest nuances of a long, decreasing diminuendo until the sound dies away.

Unlike the arguments, disputes and battles of the Sixth Symphony, foreshadowed by the timpani duel in the Fourth Symphony and the snare drum running wild in the Fifth, the idea of the Clarinet Concerto is not to present a quarrel. Rather, the musical action is concerned with a full and varied presentation of the clarinet's personality. The instrument and its companion, the snare drum, are locked in battle, and it is their individual personalities that are to be displayed. It is not about either winning a battle or coming to a conclusion, for when they are finished, they leave the stage without much hesitation.

Nielsen anticipated this final gesture in another work, *Theme and Variations*, Op. 40, in which he similarly refers to the music as if it were taking place on a theatre stage. Writing to Julius Röntgen, Nielsen explains why the piece has an 'ordinary conclusion' rather than an effective one:

> if we consider Variation 15 as a wild defence of a man who is fighting with his back to a mountain of ice and who finally, as if drunk … and deafened by the battle, stumbles away, then it's right that the entire conclusion should be 'uninteresting', just like a character (in a play) who, having fought to the end and gone away, no longer should attract the main interest to himself …[58]

The Clarinet Concerto was premiered on 14 September 1928 by musicians from The Royal Orchestra at a private concert at Carl Johan Michaelsen's home. Four weeks later, on 11 October, they gave the public premiere of the Concerto at Odd Fellow Palæet. Four more performances followed over the next year – in Stockholm, Gothenburg and twice in Copenhagen, each time with Oxenvad as soloist.[59]

The Violin Concerto also had its regular soloists, Peder Møller and, from 1920, Emil Telmányi. Compared to the Clarinet Concerto, this is a more traditional one. The soloist is indeed the musical protagonist, and the work gives the soloist the opportunity to display all their technical and musical skills, supported by the orchestra, although it remains essentially a violin concerto. There is little of the soloist's character as a fictional musical figure in this piece. If Nielsen programmed it so often in the 1920s, it is probably because it fits into the large, international repertoire of violin concertos. There is no doubt that Nielsen considered the work important, and that he considered it as his contribution to one of the great European concerto genres.

The Concerto for Flute and Orchestra (CNW 42), composed in 1926 for Holger Gilbert-Jespersen, is by contrast a narrative work. It was composed under great pressure in August and September to be premiered in Paris on 21 October.[60] The work is in two movements. The nature of the musical action is a series of dialogues, as if the flute were on a journey, meeting and conversing with a number of characters along the way. The most prominent interlocutors are the clarinet, bassoon, bass trombone and timpani, and occasionally a viola or oboe. The strings rarely stand out as individuals. Sometimes there are several that interrupt the conversation, or one notices that the flute has been startled.

The instrumentation is limited to strings, timpani and two of each of the winds, which together with the flute constitute a wind quintet, supplemented by a bass trombone. Of all the instruments, the trombone stands out for its sound. It is played on a slide trombone, which, as in Nielsen's Sixth Symphony, is able to produce sneering glissandos, reinforcing the idea that that the trombone is meant to stand out as a character in its own right.

As with the Clarinet Concerto, the one for flute was composed with the character of the solo instrument in mind. In a programme note for the Gothenburg performance in 1930, Nielsen explains:

> The flute cannot deny its nature, it belongs to Arcadia and prefers pastoral moods; the composer must therefore adapt to its gentle nature if he does not want to risk being labelled a barbarian.[61]

This is not to say that the concerto takes place exclusively in an idyllic universe, or that the flute does not reach every corner of its expressive potential. Rather, it means that this is the space in which it feels most at home, most comfortable and most in tune with its identity. Nielsen is aware that a flautist does not have the same technical possibilities for varying his playing as a violinist: the concerto 'lasts about sixteen minutes: that is enough for a flute', he wrote after completing the work.[62] Nor does the flute have the same expressive range as the clarinet. It is therefore a deliberate choice that the Flute Concerto is the shortest of them all.

In the programme note, Nielsen says that the instruments should be perceived as individuals that act in relation to each other and react to what the others do:

> The solo flute … enters into a little conversation with a solo clarinet and a bassoon. Then a strong crescendo bar drives the solo instrument to some more passionate remarks, but they are not meant so harshly, and we slip back into peaceful conditions … But then it seems as if the instruments are beginning to get bored and take up a more prominent, fugal theme, which is suddenly interrupted by the timpani: [musical notation] *ff* and chasing a solo trombone out of its previous mood. The solo flute gets nervous and screams … and now things are coming to life.[63]

The place he speaks of in the first movement leads to a passage in which the trombone and timpani enter into a long, intense dialogue with the flute. At the end of the second movement, the trombone and timpani again take the stage as the most independent individuals. After the first two performances, the Flute Concerto was given a new and extended conclusion, in which Nielsen assigned a central role to these two instruments in the final version of the story. The fact that it is the timpani and the trombone that return at the end suggests that it was the notion of a serious game that Nielsen wanted to emphasise.[64]

In the middle of the second movement, an elegant melody in 6/8 begins in a calm march tempo. As the rest of the orchestra is about to move away from the melody, the trombone suddenly joins in with it, before entering on the flute's terms, playing an expressive contrapuntal part to the flute. This leads to an excited flute solo, accompanied by vigorous rhythms from the timpani and with a single sneering comment from the trombone. The march melody returns in the full orchestra, the flute and timpani take a final solo and, after a few more comments from the trombone, the movement comes to an end, the orchestra fading away. The movement thus ends not with an exclamation mark but with a disarming gesture.

As in the Clarinet Concerto, the musical discussions seem to end without any real decision. Even if the concerto is heard as the flute's pastoral universe, an idyll lost in the modern world, it seems appropriate to hear the playful dialogue between flute, trombone, timpani and orchestra that concludes the concerto as an expression of reconciliation with the state of things. The characters of the piece have come to terms with the idea that the idyll cannot be restored, and review everything with a slightly nostalgic, indulgent gaze.[65]

In his last orchestral works, Nielsen reached a pinnacle, both in terms of the complexity of the works and, paradoxically, in their directness. He achieved a brilliance in his technical mastery of compositional means that allowed him to compose literally with the sound of the orchestra. He treats each instrument as a character in a musical theatrical play and is not afraid to be banal at times. His compositions are like a game, but a serious one. Not for fun, nor out of desperation, although the works are full of contradictory ideas, little quirks, big emotional outbursts and interruptions in continuity. They are musical stories about life in the modern world, where nothing is as it seems any longer.

The works are thus fully modern in that they reflect on the conditions of modernity, posing questions and debates rather than providing answers. The fragmented surface, the dissonant passages and the absence of a unifying tonal framework have been taken as expressions of frustration or negativity. Rather, it is a more playful approach to the world, a reconciliation with its conflicts and a fundamental belief that the small and powerful forces of Nature and music will eventually bring life back, no matter what. At this point, Nielsen is able to see things more from above, and to look at music and life from a more universal perspective.

V

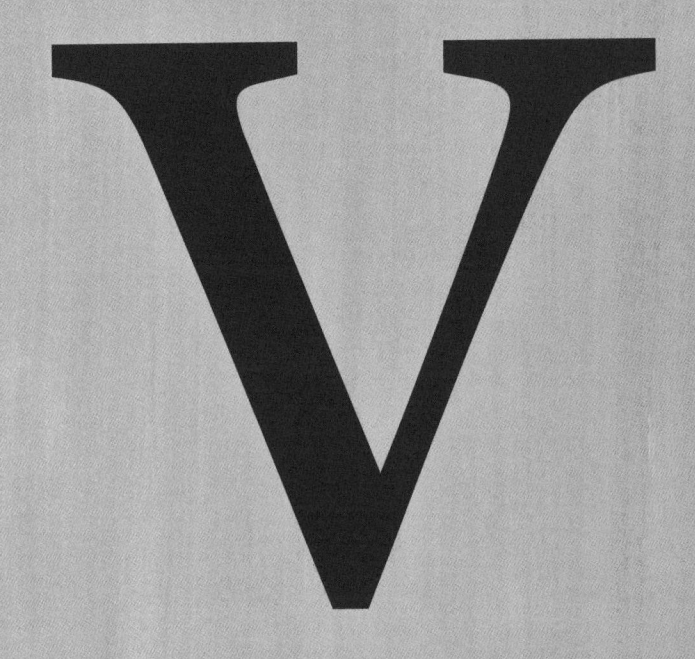

LEGACY

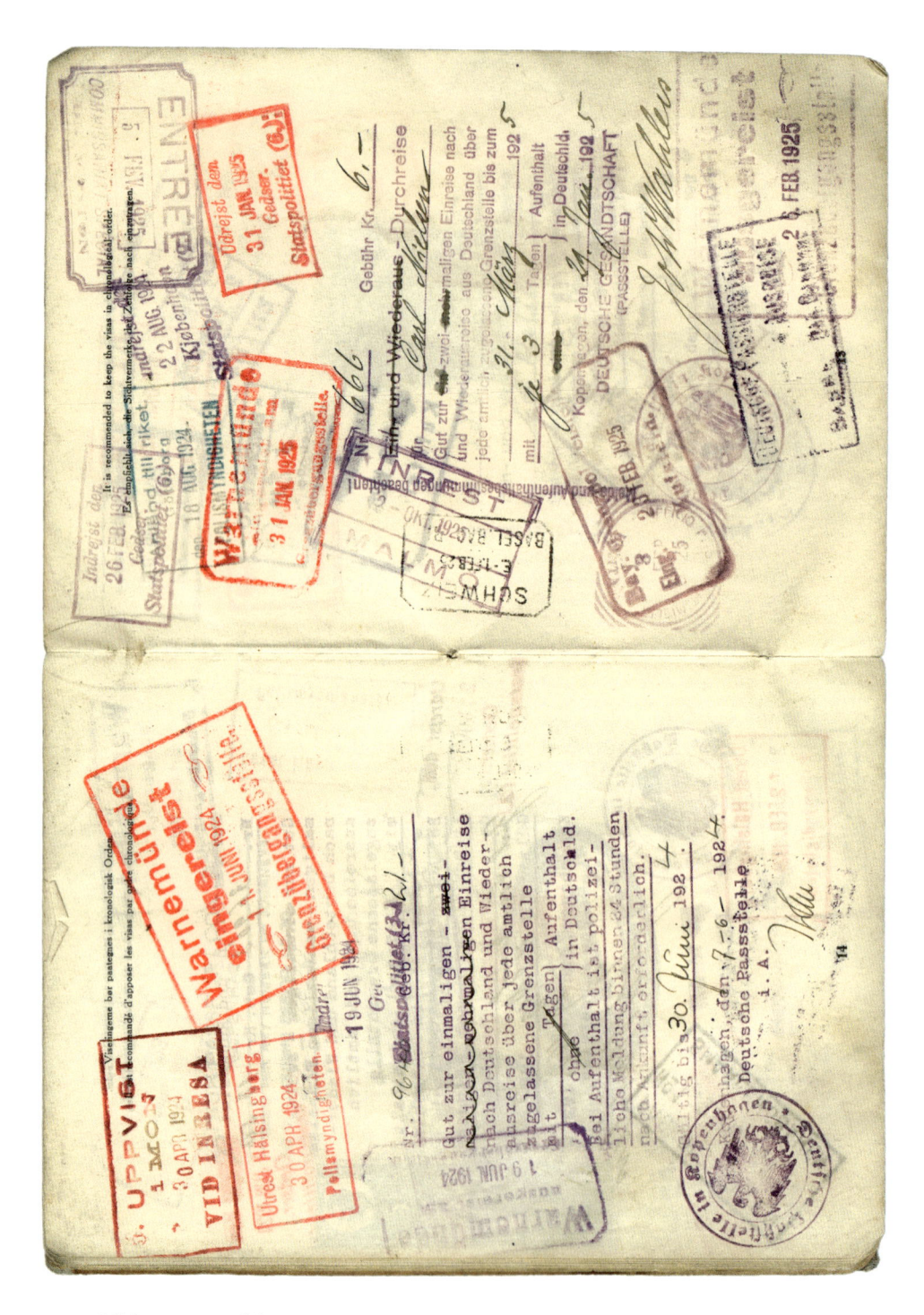

ILL. 1. Nielsen was widely travelled. His passport from the early 1920s reveals multiple visits to Sweden and continental Europe.

Chapter 40

REPUTATION

It seems not enough to focus on the environments and contexts in which Nielsen participated and made contributions during his lifetime. To get a fuller picture of his role and significance, it is crucial to ask: what is the image of Nielsen that has been passed on to posterity? This requires a change of perspective, focusing on how he was perceived by others. At the same time, it is important to recognise that he himself was very much involved in creating the narratives that set the tone for posterity. Establishing his legacy was a complex process – and one that indeed did not begin with his death.

Part of this process was the evolution of Nielsen's image, as he was gradually accorded a higher status by influential opinion leaders and the general public. At the beginning of the new century, Nielsen was increasingly regarded as the most important composer of his generation, and by 1920 this development had reached the point where he had replaced Niels W. Gade as the Danish national composer in the public consciousness. This process was primarily one of how Nielsen was received over time. It involved a change in the way Nielsen was perceived by others, and in the qualities and status attributed to him.

The second part of the process was his own active contribution to the creation of posterity's image of him, which was also well underway in the last 10–15 years of his life. The management of his legacy, which in particular became the responsibility of his students and followers after his death in 1931, was based on perceptions that he himself had largely helped to shape through his music and the publication of articles, interviews and memoirs.

In this context, it is not important whether his position as a national composer was more or less deserved, or whether it came too late or too early. The crucial point is to recognise the interplay between his increased status and his ability to assert his aesthetic and views in musical life. It is precisely because of the reputation he achieved that his music, his opinions and his articles had an impact that continues to this day.

The starting point was not the best. In the spring of 1914, Nielsen had resigned from one of the most prestigious positions in the country, that of Kapellmeister at The Royal Theatre, without having a steady income to rely on. He found himself in a situation where he had to find a new livelihood as a composer. He was also in the midst of a marital crisis which, from the summer of 1914, led to a year-long break in his relationship with Anne Marie. What at first seemed an extremely precarious situation and a leap into the unknown turned out to be an important step on the ladder to wider recognition.

As a composer, Nielsen received a permanent, annual state grant of 1,200 Kroner, which was just under a quarter of his salary as a Kapellmeister. This was increased to 2,000 Kroner in the Finance Act of 1918–19 and to 3,600 Kroner three years later, although it should be noted that the inflation caused by the First World War had pushed prices up to about two and a half times their pre-war level.[1] This was not enough for him to sustain the family. As a composer, he was now dependent on the income from his compositions and also had to accept a number of well-paid conducting engagements.

It is therefore worth examining in some detail how this rise in status took place and what factors contributed to securing the position he achieved by the time of his death. This is the subject of the following two chapters. On the one hand, it is important to understand the course of events as a historical process because it allows us to nuance the oft-painted picture of him as predestined to become 'our great composer'. It was not a foregone conclusion, and it could have turned out differently. After all, the local newspaper *Fyens Stiftstidende* was not in a position to announce on 10 June 1865: 'Yesterday the great composer Carl Nielsen was born in a cottage outside the village Nr. Lyndelse.'

On the other hand, the development offers insight not only into how Nielsen gained an increasingly central position in musical life, but into how the very perception of what it meant to be a Danish national composer was changed in the process. The development has succeeded in changing the understanding of what 'Danish' sounds like. As a result, when listening to Nielsen today, many people recognise what they perceive as the sound of Danish music. This is due both to his orchestral sound, which many identify with the soundscape of Danish nature, and to his songs, which have become the core of the concept of the 'Danish song'.

The image of Nielsen created in the 1920s also involved the canonisation of certain works at the expense of the whole. The development that saw a young Nielsen – whose music was described as vain, twisted, unnatural and idiosyncratic – replaced by a mature Nielsen – whose music was described as great, organic, natural and popular – was part of the canonisation process. The combination of the great Nielsen and the popular Nielsen gave him a platform that meant that his works as a whole could be heard as national, and that the features identified as typical of his music were perceived as the recipe for sounding Danish. The fact that this model of understanding resulted in some of Nielsen's late works being regarded as strange and out of place was for a long time remedied by simply ignoring them.

Given Nielsen was himself an active debater and opinion leader, this meant that he gradually exerted a significant influence on the standards by which his music was judged. He was very much involved in creating the image that has come down to us. Part of the price was that the canonised image of Nielsen could be experienced as a straitjacket not only for posterity, but also for Carl Nielsen himself.

Chapter 41

NIELSEN BECOMES THE NATIONAL COMPOSER

Becoming 'the national composer' is a long and complex process of gaining increasing status among the general public and eventually being undisputedly identified as the leading musical figure of the nation. This process can be understood as 'canonisation', adopting a term from the Catholic Church's naming of saints. There are a number of factors that make this recognition possible and that generate the public dialogue through which canonisation takes place.

In an analysis of the canonisation of Béla Bartók, the British musicologist Malcolm Gillies has systematised the factors involved in such processes, which can also be used to examine the Nielsen case. One factor is that Nielsen's music needs to be played and mentioned, and in this context performances that attract attention, allowing the public to discuss and relate to it, are essential. Other factors include the dissemination and availability of Nielsen's music through its publication. It is also important that renowned orchestras and soloists at home and abroad include the music in their repertoire, and that recognition abroad enhance his status at home. Finally, professional musicians and musicologists play a role when Nielsen and his music become the subject of articles, books and academic studies. All of this serves to raise his status.[1]

This approach, which focuses as much on the preconditions for canonisation as on whether and how it materialised, allows us to draw a nuanced picture of the process by which Nielsen achieved his status as 'the national composer'. At the same time, it is possible to assess the opportunities offered by this particular type of status – the combination of high status and identification with being 'Danish'. But it also reveals where it reached its limits and was, in a sense, a double-edged sword.

The Canonisation of Nielsen

Writing about Nielsen in 1917, Gerhardt Lynge explained that it was Hans Christian Andersen's fairy tale *The Ugly Duckling* all over again:

> ... now he holds the position as the conductor of Musikforeningen, succeeding Gade and Neruda; as a member of the board of the Royal Academy of Music and as a teacher of composition and theory at the same institution; as a member of the

scholarship committees of Ancker, Berggreen and Wexchall; as a Knight of the Order of Dannebrog; as a member of the Swedish Academy; and as his country's most distinctive – and most controversial – contemporary composer.[2]

It is correct that in 1917 Nielsen had accepted a number of positions in which he had specifically succeeded Niels W. Gade. This was true both of the post he took over as conductor of Musikforeningen in 1915, following the death of Franz Neruda, and of Nielsen's election to the board of the Academy of Music in the same year. From January 1931 he also held the title of director of the Academy. Like Gade, he taught music theory and form theory at the Academy for a number of years from 1916.[3] In 1914 he succeeded Gade as one of the two members of the scholarship committee for the Anckerske Legat, which Nielsen himself had received in 1890.[4]

The development described by Lynge took place over a period of ten to fifteen years. From the middle of the first decade of the twentieth century, Nielsen became increasingly recognised as a leading figure, first among his peers and later as the foremost of all Danish composers. In the years around the turn of the century, however, Nielsen was still perceived as part of a group of young Danish composers who represented a new direction. Louis Glass, Robert Henriques, Emil Robert-Hansen, Gustav Helsted and Carl Nielsen, all more or less of the same age, had been working together since the late 1880s to promote their own music and that of others in societies such as Symphonia, and were the driving force behind many new initiatives in the capital's musical life.

Twenty years later, the situation was very different. The composers who had been Nielsen's comrades-in-arms felt increasingly marginalised and were labelled 'late Romantics', a term that was not meant in a positive way. It implied that they had all been swept aside by the anti-Romantic movement that Nielsen represented, in favour of the next generation of young composers. They lost their position at the forefront of developments and as representatives of the new and the modern. Being a late Romantic had become a dead end. It was a conceptual framework that also influenced the historiography of Danish music and has left its mark to this day.

Some, like Glass, whose output was in many ways comparable to Nielsen's, fought for their position and their views, while others slipped more quietly into the margins. As early as 1907, Glass expressed his feelings of marginalisation: 'It's a bit difficult for me to understand that I, who so much wanted "the new", should sit back, half perplexed, hardly feeling the desire to join in the dance'.[5] He elaborated on this in a letter to Nielsen in 1923:

> Moreover, the ideas I represent can no longer be said to belong to the present. I'm the keeper of the natural inheritance of the forefathers, but also the innovator in a

deeper sense ... Thus, I represent a musical culture whose refinement and uniqueness can only be recognised by those who are at the pinnacle of it ... Since it's now you – dear Carl Nielsen – who stands in the common consciousness as our first man in Danish music ...[6]

By the 1920s, Nielsen had attained a prominent status and was regarded as the most important Danish composer, even from a historical point of view. He inherited the role of the Danish national composer from his predecessor and teacher, Niels W. Gade. When Nielsen was a young man in Odense, it was almost impossible for him to afford a picture of Gade: Nielsen had to skip dinner to buy one at Braunstein's music shop at 26 Overgade. Remembering the incident many years later, he recalled the picture 'was one ... that particularly captured my imagination, and that was, of course, because I knew that he was still alive and living in Copenhagen, so there was a possibility that one day I might actually be able to see him and perhaps even to talk to him.'[7] He never dared to dream that he would succeed him.

A National Composer?

It is not possible to become '*the* national composer', unless the person is recognised as '*a* national composer'. It should be emphasised that the two concepts are not the same. Separating them requires further reflection, for how should the difference be understood? Nielsen mused on whether art can be national and what it takes to make it so. This is adressed in an interview on the occasion of his sixtieth birthday:

> Nielsen has been described as a distinctly *national* artist, and he protests against this. 'There's nothing more destructive to art than nationalism and formal religion,' he says. 'Patriotism is the last resort of the scoundrel, and it's impossible to make national music on commission. If you try, you're not an artist but a dabbler. If music becomes national, it's because those who take it to heart make it national ...'[8]

This statement has often been interpreted as Nielsen rejecting the idea of being 'a national composer'; yet Nielsen's point is rather that it is not a quality one can ascribe to oneself. Being 'a national composer' does not depend – or at least only partly depends – on whether it is the composer's intention: a composer may well aim to write a national song or tune, and by following familiar models he or she may increase the chances of success. This is precisely what Nielsen did with some of his songs and incidental music. The key to recognition as a national composer, however, is a question of reception in the broadest sense: whether those who hear the music embrace it and identify with it through a national conceptual framework. It is a question of whether they say to themselves and to each other: yes, this is Danish, and this is our music, because we are Danish. Nielsen recognises that this is occurring in a historical process in which the listener adds qualities to music or other national symbols that are subsequently identified as Danish, because, as he continues:

> The Overture to *Elverhøj* was not originally particularly Danish, but it has since been established as such by *associations*, just as when the flag is unfurled: the white cross on the red field is not in itself typically Danish, it is the associations and habits that determine everything.[9]

Nielsen has thus a rather modern view of the national in music. 'Danish' is not merely a static quality: if music is commonly accepted as Danish, the composer of that music may also be recognised as a composer of national music. This is what happened to the German-born Friedrich Kuhlau who composed music for the national play *Elverhøj*.

But being recognised as 'a national composer' is only one step on the road to becoming 'the national composer'. It is a vital prerequisite, albeit only one element in a larger package. To be labelled 'the Danish national composer' requires that not only specific compositions, but also Nielsen himself, be granted a status according to which his music represents and is identified with the nation.

In trying to understand how Nielsen became 'the national composer', it is therefore necessary to shift the focus away from the question of whether he composes employing specific national qualities. Rather, the attention must be given to how he is perceived, and how his music is ascribed qualities that are subsequently identified as uniquely Danish. The process of becoming 'the national composer' is a long one, in which the person is recognised and identified with the musical attributes that characterise the nation. It is essentially a question of Nielsen being accorded increasing status, both by specialists and other cultural authorities, as well as by a large part of the general public, until the process reaches a point where he can emerge as the national composer: the one who is regarded as the most important representative of Danish music, and the one whose music is associated with the sound of Danishness. This is due to the fact that 'those who take it to heart make it national'.[10]

Spectacular Performances

One of the factors that plays a major role in determining the status of a composer is performances that attract attention – that is, a performance that is so out of the ordinary that many people are able to relate to it and to articulate their views, which, in this context, may be upheld or revised. A critical body of opinion is generated, which may lead to a re-evaluation of the composer. It is possible to trace such changes in views of Nielsen and his music shortly after the turn of the century.

The first examples of interest in Nielsen at the expense of his contemporaries appear as early as 1903: 'The symphonic composers among Carl Nielsen's contemporaries in this country appear almost as talented epigones of Wagner, Bruckner and the Russians. And to an even lesser extent originality has influenced the contemporary opera composers …'[11] In this light, Nielsen is celebrated with words such as greatness and genius:

> If this musical season is of so much more importance to us than so many others, it is because of one man in particular, whose sharply defined figure stands above all his contemporaries among Danish musicians. For some time now it has been clear to many that Carl Nielsen is by far the greatest and most supreme composer we have today: the main, the manliest, the mightiest, the most self-reliant, the most monumental constructing, the most firmly moulding, the one who possesses the strongest will and the greatest skill. This judgement, moreover, has been confirmed by what has been heard this autumn. There are indeed those who believe that no living person whose works have been performed in Denmark has equalled him in importance, grandeur and genius. Hardly any of his previous works – with the exception of the Hymnus Amoris heard last year – has achieved the clarity, the immediate beauty of the sound, as in his last two works: the opera 'Saul and David' and the symphony 'The Four Temperaments'.[12]

This was not a widely held view at the time, but that of a few, referred to as a clique, and one reference suggests that this included a small group of descendants of old Liberal luminaries such as Hother Ploug (Carl Ploug's son), Ove and Helge Rode (Orla Lehmann's grandchildren) as well as Nielsen's friend Rudolph Bergh, the author of the above quotation.[13] In other contexts, this clique of sworn followers is often referred to as Nielsen's 'fire worshippers'.[14]

The success of Nielsen's opera *Maskarade* in 1906 brought about a decisive change in the public's perception of the composer. In the previous year, when Nielsen had presented the most important of his recent works together with excerpts from his forthcoming opera at a concert on 11 November, several critics had already noticed

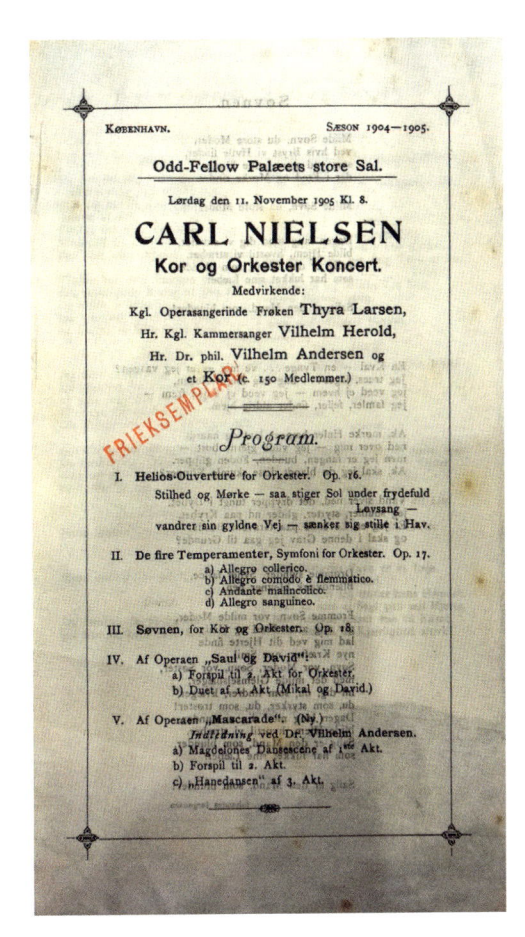

ILL. 1. The concert on 11 November 1905, with excerpts from *Maskarade* combined with some of his latest major works, is an example of an event that attracted so much attention and publicity that it managed to change the general image of what kind of music Nielsen should be identified with.

that a change was taking place. For them, the excerpts they had heard from *Maskarade* indicated a change of direction in Nielsen's music. Angul Hammerich remarked: 'Not only *is* he popular, he is now also *writing* popular music!'[15] Characteristic is the critique in *Berlingske Tidende* in which Alfred Tofft maintained his view that works such as the *Helios Overture*, *Søvnen* (*Sleep*) and *The Four Temperaments* were not generally accessible:

> The composer, gifted in so many ways, often goes beyond the limits of the music in his admittedly exaggerated fear of becoming banal. In any case, he regularly crosses the boundaries of beauty, and that can never be a musical or aesthetic pleasure. On the whole, his music – including the symphony 'The Four Temperaments' – suffers from an almost overly nervous turning away from the broad, natural singing out of the melody. ... It is often difficult for music authorities to

follow him, but to amateurs the vagueness often seems profound, and indeed it is revealing that Carl Nielsen has his greatest and warmest admirers precisely outside the ranks of professional musicians.[16]

More broadly, Tofft saw the excerpts from *Maskarade* as evidence that Nielsen had realised that his previous course was unsustainable:

> There were clear signs tonight that a clever artistic personality like Nielsen will not be satisfied with this in the long run, as he seems to want to change course with the only new thing on the programme. The musical excerpts from his new opera 'Maskarade' fully demonstrated that he can express himself in a natural language … Magdelone's dance is written with a lightness and grace that had a beneficial effect after the rather irritating unnaturalness [of the other pieces] … thus it is conceivable that he himself would regard much of his earlier music as belonging to experiments that perhaps should have remained in the study folder.[17]

The premiere of *Maskarade* was widely acclaimed by the critics and this was certainly new. Although there were critical objections, they agreed that Nielsen had found his way to a wider audience. The reviews note that the audience enjoyed themselves and mention 'sure hits' such as 'Tamperretten', 'Magdelone's Dance Scene' and Jeronimus's song.[18] The focus is not so much on the large overall effect of the opera, but rather – as in the previous year's concert – on the fact that the striking individual movements could also be successfully performed as concert pieces or at home on the piano. Thus, in terms of opera reception, there is an interaction between the appreciation of the stage production as a complete work and individual pieces whose impact outside the staging could have a reciprocal effect on the opera's popularity. Excerpts such as 'Dance of the Cockerel', the *Maskarade Overture* and 'Magdelone's Dance Scene' were performed in more than 500 concerts during Nielsen's lifetime, and the dance scene was also published in arrangements for salon orchestra and piano trio. Together with six other songs from the opera, it was published as a separate print for voice and piano in 1906.[19] Nielsen had become truly popular.

However, this does not imply Nielsen had suddenly become *the* Danish national composer,[20] for Charles Kjerulf in *Politiken* does not associate Nielsen's music with a particularly Danish tone, but contrasts it with the possibility of drawing on the rococo style of the Holberg era, concluding that 'it is still his own language, not that of earlier times'.[21] Robert Henriques, on the other hand, expresses a purely national framework of interpretation: Nielsen, with 'his new work … has won fresh territory for national music. All the stylised arias and songs sound so quintessentially Danish, and the precious scene in which Jeronimus and Leonard meet could only have been written by an artist on whom Danish culture has left its mark.'[22] Hammerich's critique strikes a balance between the two views, for although he ascribes to the opera a 'light, yet so nationally Danish – not French – conversational tone', by which he presumably means Holberg's style, he concludes that it is the 'first authentic *opéra comique* in Danish'. He does not say that it is the first authentic Danish *opéra comique*.[23]

Popularity and Danish Nature

Jens Vejmand (*John the Roadman*), published in the collection *Strophic Songs* in 1907, became a hit both as a solo song with piano, which could be performed at concerts and in private homes, and, from 1909, through its distribution in songbooks for communal singing. It also appeared as a single sheet in large print runs and was played in all kinds of different arrangements.[24] Its popularity gave rise to anecdotes such as the one about the man who was grinding *John the Roadman* on the street organ when Nielsen passed by. 'A little faster', said Carl, and the next day a sign was put up on the organ: 'Pupil of Carl Nielsen.' Another song that brought Nielsen national fame was 'Du danske Mand' (*Danish Patriotic Song*), written for a summer revue at the Tivoli Gardens in 1906, but immediately circulated throughout the country in versions for voice and piano and, not least, for men's choir.

These songs established the idea that not only was Nielsen a well-liked composer but he could also be popular, and one even finds the phrase 'beloved by the people' applied to *John the Roadman* when *Strophic Songs* was premiered at a composition recital on the evening of 30 November 1907. This was linked to the view that the character of the song could also be heard in Nielsen's latest String Quartet in F major, Op. 44, which was premiered at the same event.[25]

It would be some years, however, before the idea that Nielsen's songs were generally popular became widespread. It was first established in connection with the publication of the two volumes of *En Snes danske Viser* (*A Score of Danish Songs*) in 1915 and 1917, which the critics in Copenhagen considered to be genuinely popular – a term they associated with the simpler and more pristine life that they typically linked with rural communities. The two volumes were reprinted numerous times in the following years.[26] The new songs were not at first perceived as communal songs, and Gustav Hetsch wrote in *Nationaltidende* that they would be best conveyed to the listener if they were presented by a 'musically and poetically inclined amateur with a decent voice and song culture and a good Danish heart in the right place'.[27] He saw them as songs to be listened to and associated them with a certain Danish quality.

A few years earlier, in 1912, something decidedly new happened in connection with the premiere of Nielsen's Third Symphony, *Sinfonia espansiva*. There was a general tendency in the reviews to ascribe nature-like qualities to the work, an interpretation suggested by Nielsen's own programme notes. At the same time, this quality was strongly linked with the idea that the music was a genuine manifestation of Danishness.

This coupling of Danish music and Danish nature as two sides of the same coin shows that a changing understanding of what it meant for music to sound uniquely Danish was taking hold. The nineteenth-century National Romanticism associated with Gade was based on the idea that the Danish sound was linked to the qualities of old ballads and national tales. Gade's First Symphony, which used his own ballad-like tune for 'På Sjølunds fagre Sletter' about King Valdemar's hunt as its first subject, was therefore the perfect representation of Danish music in Gade's time. Gade had composed the tune based on his teacher Andreas Peter Berggreen's instructions on what characterised the Danish sound in folk tunes, before using it as a subject in his symphony.[28]

In Nielsen's time, at the beginning of the twentieth century, this idea of the Danish sound was replaced by another in which nature, the landscape and the character of the people were central. And then the wonderful thing happens: not only does the music sound like nature, but Nielsen's music is indeed identified with Danish nature. Nielsen's descriptions of this landscape thus form the basis for a new perception of what defines the Danish musical tone. Similarly, the sound of the new tunes Nielsen composed for the Folk High School Songbook, as did Oluf Ring and Thorvald Aagaard, is much more closely associated with lyrics about Danish nature than with historical heroes and ballad themes.

In 1906, when Robert Henriques heard Jeronimus's and Magdelone's 'stylised arias and songs' from *Maskarade* as being distinctly Danish, he was indeed not talking about nature, but about a particular culture, a theatre tradition that had its origins in Holberg.[29] The new perception, which promoted the notion that Nielsen's music sounded like Danish nature, was, however, recognised in the 1910s, for in 1912 critics argued regarding the *Sinfonia espansiva*:

> Ah, this world really is Denmark … Summer sunshine under a cloudless sky: only the thunder roars and rolls on the horizon. How Danish Nielsen is in his music, as so often before … but his Danish colours are not the red and white of Hartmann-Gade – no, the blue – and green – and yellow of the Danish landscape: water and forest and fields.[30]

Thus wrote Kjerulf in *Politiken*, and his wording reveals that he was aware that a new image of Danish national music was being expressed in 1912. He explicitly contrasts Nielsen's new, musical Danishness with the National Romantic version of Gade and Hartmann. Ten years earlier, Nielsen was not even considered as representing a Danish sound: at the premiere of *The Four Temperaments* in 1902, Henriques pointed out that, in contrast to Nielsen's symphony, Lange-Müller's cantata composed for the Nordic Exhibition of 1888 and performed on that occasion, consisted of 'notes that warm the heart by their Danishness'.[31]

Legends

Although Nielsen's music gradually became associated with Danish nature and perceived as popular, his path to becoming the national composer also took parallel route. This is evident in his preoccupation with incidental music for plays, the plots of which are based on popular legends and historical events. This placed him in a position where he is identified as the provider of music for national narratives, thus enabling the general public to be reminded of Nielsen when they think of Danish music with national themes. This seems to be as a strategic move, similar to that of Anne Marie Carl-Nielsen, when she took on the role of a female artist with a close connection to nature in order to strengthen her career, also managing to change the role from within.[32] Similarly, Nielsen approaches the tradition of Gade and Hartmann with eyes wide open, and thus has created the opportunity to change the perception of what is associated with national music, without this necessarily being an expression of conscious career planning.

It was at the Open-Air Theatre in Dyrehaven that Nielsen began to work with drama that had strong national connotations. He was involved in the founding of the theatre in 1909 and, as composer, stage director and conductor, was undoubtedly its most important musical driving force. He was a central figure in the theatre's production of plays that consciously drew on traditional National Romantic notions of the national as linked to the world of the old ballads and historical narratives. With a setting in the middle of nature, and with Jens Ferdinand Willumsen's two ravens placed on either side of the stage, it was hard to imagine anything other than a Grundtvigian link to a historical and mythological past as a symbol of Danishness. This provided Nielsen with a platform where his music was associated with a national quality, which subsequently was developed into the notion that the composer himself embodied such a quality.

The first production of the Open-Air Theatre in 1910 – Oehlenschläger's *Hagbarth and Signe* – was based on the legends of the Nordic kings and the old ballads, and Nielsen responded by aiming for 'a certain distant ballad-like melancholy' in the music, using four lurs as a specific reference to the past. The allusion to the melancholic character of the ballads was prompted by Berggreen's 1842 preface to the first volume of his comprehensive publication of folk songs, in which he speaks of 'a trait

ILL. 2. In 1915, Nielsen led the production of the opera *Liden Kirsten* at the Open-Air Theatre in Dyrehaven, with a text by Hans Christian Andersen and music by Johan Peter Emilius Hartmann. Now Nielsen not only had the role of conducting works by other composers, but was also responsible for the actual staging.

of melancholy that runs through all the Nordic songs'.[33] Nielsen is thus directly in line with the traditional view of a national tone, since Berggreen's formulations in the preface were related to a National Romantic programme.

As early as 1908, Nielsen had scored music to a similar theme for Dagmarteatret's production of a play by Ludvig Holstein, based on the ballad of King Volmer and Tove. In this case, Nielsen did not use the ballad in his music for the drama, entitled *Tove*, but focused on the romanticism of the forest and the hunter, and on music's ability to convey what lies outside true reality. He said that he was looking for a musical tone in the piece that expressed 'Zealand's grace and warmth', and that his friends heard in it 'a new, particularly Danish moment that [he] had not shown so strongly before'.[34]

Two years earlier at The Royal Theatre, Nielsen had set the music to Drachmann's *Hr. Oluf han rider* – (*Sir Oluf He Rides* –) in which the ballad about Sir Oluf played a central role. One way of emphasising the connection to the Middle Ages and the ballad was simply to imitate the tune at several points in the play. This was an approach that Kuhlau had used in *Elverhøj*.[35] It was Drachmann's wish that the ballad should be incorporated into the music, and although Nielsen was initially against it, he later relented. The tune was noticed by several critics, and it was clearly a device that helped to reinforce the feeling that this was a national play.[36]

Drachmann seems to have liked Nielsen's music for its ability to be modern while maintaining a link with the tradition of National Romanticism and ballads. Drachmann also identified the music with nature, as is clear from one of his letters to Otto Borchsenius:

> As for the music, the part I've heard is excellent. … *He follows in the footsteps* of Gade (one might say), working reverently and yet with an utterly modern awareness of the tone of the ballad – its nature-fresh simplicity and its mysterious, captivating power: like a strong scent of foliage and heath and moor and meadow at nightfall.[37]

With such contributions Nielsen joined the tradition of Gade and Hartmann and the National Romantic conception of Danish music, and the opening of the Open-Air Theatre with *Hagbarth and Signe* in 1910 provided further opportunities to develop in this role. The production was repeated the following year, and in 1913 he composed music for Oehlenschläger's *Sanct Hansaftenspil* (*Midsummer Eve Play*). In 1914 the main production of the year was *Elverhøj*, which was repeated the following year, along with two productions for which Nielsen had the overall responsibility: Hartmann's opera *Liden Kirsten* and Gade's choral work *Elverskud*, with the dramaturgy by Nielsen. Taking a closer look at the repertoire of the Open-Air Theatre, it is clear that Nielsen was part of a context associated with national performances.[38]

With *Liden Kirsten* and *Elverskud*, which were performed at the same event, Nielsen took on a new role as far as theatre production was concerned. He was used to being involved in the planning of plays for which he had composed the music, but in this instance he was in charge of the entire production – and that was his primary role, as he had not composed the music. In the programme for the performance, Nielsen makes a direct link from his own production and the world of ballads to Hartmann and Gade, who Nielsen introduced in the official programme for the performance:

> *Gade* and *Hartmann*, 'Elverskud' and 'Liden Kirsten' are names that most Danes know and love. The names and the works contain in sound everything that the people have dreamed of for centuries. It is the very *spirit of the Danish ballad* which, as if for the first time, has looked at itself in the mirror and recognised its own nature in larger and newer forms.[39]

With this last sentence, Nielsen sets the scene for an interpretation in which the connection to the past is not made directly through the ballads, but through a self-reflexive recognition of what lies behind them. It is not the ballads themselves, for they do not appear in any of the works; it is 'the spirit, the feeling, the manner of expression that is so Danish'.[40]

In an article in the theatre magazine *Masken*, published on the day of the premiere, Nielsen focused on the musical worship of nature promoted by the open-air theatre. The audience had read both texts and would have been able to relate the Danish National Romanticism with the intense worship of nature, adding a new dimension to the experience of the works:

> We have all experienced the occasional beautiful evening – in the forest, on the lake or in the mountains – and we have learned that music is the only art that manages to merge perfectly with nature at rest. The sound of a horn in the forest, a song on the lake or in the mountains when everything is quiet, is enough to explain what I mean.[41]

The widespread impact of the performances helped to strengthen Nielsen's position and reputation, and he was recognised as the driving force behind the project.[42] This helped pave the way for the critics' unanimous view that, with the Fourth Symphony, *The Inextinguishable*, in 1916, he had now achieved a position that no living Danish composer could match.

The Outcome

The premiere of *The Inextinguishable* on 1 February 1916 raised Nielsen's status to a new level. A consensus had been reached on the great value of his music, and he was now associated with a profound originality in his creative authority, with phrases such as 'secrets drawn from deep down in the primordial ground of music' and that 'his musical nature grows out of a primordial time'.[43] Such comments echo Nielsen's own formulations in programme notes, articles and other statements, and thus show how they have come to carry more weight than before in the way others perceive his music. Increasingly, Nielsen is being measured against standards that he himself helped to create.

Kjerulf associates Nielsen's primeval musicality with his intimate contact with nature, and it is this combination that makes the symphony a national masterpiece: 'The Danish colours will prevail in this gripping, masculine, human and yet so strangely new music,' according to Kjerulf.[44] Seligmann adds that the symphony is constructed with a rigour and purity that rejects Romanticism and paves the way for 'a rebirth of our national music'.[45] Nielsen's status as the national composer was about to be established.

ILL. 3. The premiere of Nielsen's *Fynsk Foraar* (*Springtime on Funen*) at Kvægtorvet, the cattle market in Odense on 8 July 1922, was staged as a major national event. Georg Høeberg conducted the 800-strong choir gathered for the occasion. Nielsen was not present, but when the work was performed again at Musikforeningen in Copenhagen on 22 November, he himself held the conductor's baton.

With *A Score of Danish Songs* (1915–17), the idea of Nielsen's general popularity came into focus, and with the publication of *The Folk High School Melody Book* in 1922, his tunes for communal singing became the epitome of what popular Danish songs should sound like. The melody book became the standard for a reformed folk high school singing, and Nielsen's tunes are at the heart of those songs that have come to be identified with the concept of 'the Danish song'.

A crucial aspect of Nielsen's new position as the national composer is that his status extends to broad sections of the population who embrace him. His music is not reserved for an elite, but is recognised by 'all the people' – or at least by the majority of the leading authorities and the large number of ordinary people who sing the songs. The popularisation also includes the publication of his tunes for use in schools and at home, such as *Sangbogen 'Danmark'*, in which songs that almost every Danish child knows, 'Jeg ved en Lærkerede' and 'Solen er saa rød, Mor', were printed for the first time.

In connection with the premiere of *Fynsk Foraar* (*Springtime on Funen*) in the summer of 1922, Nielsen's association with Danishness was further strengthened, combining a celebration of originality and authenticity with popularity and his native region, Fyn. The premiere was also a national event. The work was performed at a national choir convention in Odense, attended by the royal couple. The entire city was decorated with flags and triumphal arches, and the newspapers carried detailed coverage with pictures. *Politiken* reported an audience of 6,000 and 800 active singers in the converted cattle market hall, and called the music 'simply brilliant' and 'some of the finest in the field of Danish popular music'.[46] In the reviews, the character of Fyn is transformed into an intensified representation of Danishness. Similarly, Axel Kjerulf's eulogy seems somewhat exaggerated when he, in connection with the subsequent performance in Copenhagen, speaks of 'Carl Nielsen's Danish tone, only here sweeter and truer than before'.[47]

It is almost impossible for the music to do justice to this, for it is not the composition into which Nielsen put the most effort. It was written in the summer of 1921, when he had to interrupt work on his Fifth Symphony because he had agreed to have *Springtime on Funen* ready for the choir convention. Aage Berntsen, Klaus Berntsen's son, had won the contest to provide the lyrics in 1917, but the plan for a choir festival in Odense was postponed until 1922. Within a few weeks Nielsen had composed the music with the help of Nancy Dalberg, who made the fair copy and orchestrated the work.[48]

The reception of Nielsen's Fifth Symphony in 1922 does not show the same emphasis on a national interpretation, although there was agreement that the symphony did demonstrate Nielsen's grandeur and originality. The music was associated with nature, and the first movement in particular was highly praised, to the point of being 'in harmony with the eternal in art'.[49] The new production of *Maskarade* in 1918, on the other hand, was very much linked to the fact that it was an opera by the national composer, and after the relaunch in 1931 the first act was described in *Dagens Nyheder* as 'a masterpiece in all opera art and a climax in Carl Nielsen's production'.[50]

From around 1920, Nielsen's status as the national composer was clear and undisputed. Yet some sought to elevate Nielsen beyond the status of being national composer to one of the great masters of music in general. That would be the ultimate canonisation, but for the time being he had to be content with his position as the national composer.

Publishing

Performances and the formation of public opinion were one element of the canonisation process, but there were other conditions that had to be met. To qualify for the status of national composer, his or her works must be accessible to musicians and music lovers. This means that they must be available in print from a publisher who is capable of disseminating the music at home and abroad. In addition, the publisher must be recognised – this also gives the printed music status. Despite approaches from others, Wilhelm Hansen, with offices in Copenhagen and a branch in Leipzig, became Nielsen's main publisher from the start, printing his first opus, *Suite for*

String Orchestra in the spring of 1890. The listing of Leipzig on the title page was important because the establishment of a branch in Germany enabled the firm and the composer to acquire and enforce copyrights to the works both in Denmark and on the European music market centred in Leipzig. It also meant that Nielsen's publications were available throughout Europe from the outset and that interested parties knew where to obtain them. Wilhelm Hansen was not only a national but also a large and respected European music publisher.[51]

Despite all the controversies – and there were many – Wilhelm Hansen remained Nielsen's main publisher throughout his life. After a meeting with Alfred Wilhelm Hansen in January 1903, Nielsen signed a permanent contract with the firm, which enabled him to receive regular advance payments.[52] The firm's ledgers, including the private accounts of Nielsen and other composers, reveal an almost symbiotic relationship between composer and publisher. They show not only how the individual works were sold, but also what Nielsen bought, such as music paper, music literature and printed music, and that Nielsen's account occasionally acted as an overdraft facility to pay his rent.[53] In a letter to Carl in 1926, Anne Marie explains that she had a long conversation with Asger and Svend Wilhelm Hansen, who had taken over the firm in 1923 after the death of their father, Alfred Wilhelm Hansen. They discussed how much Nielsen had received from the publishers over the years and reached a figure of 65–70,000 Kroner.[54]

On two occasions Nielsen signed contracts with publishers in Leipzig. The first time was in 1913, when his Third Symphony was issued by C. F. Kahnt. Nielsen sold it for 5,000 Marks, reportedly six times more than Wilhelm Hansen would have paid for the work. It remained an isolated incident and seems to have been an exception to the general profile of C. F. Kahnt, who preferred the marketable standard repertoire to new names.[55]

A more serious attempt to work with a new publisher seems to have been the agreement with C. F. Peters, with whom Nielsen came into contact in 1920 through Wilhelm Hansen.[56] This should not be seen as a defiance of his Danish publishers, but rather as a result of Wilhelm Hansen's financial problems in the years after the First World War.[57] Three years later, C. F. Peters published two works, the String Quartet in F major, Op. 44, and *Suite* for piano, Op. 45, followed in 1925 by *Prelude, Theme and Variations* for solo violin, Op. 48; these were suitable for publication by a foreign publisher as they were purely instrumental. The String Quartet, Op. 44 (CNW 58), was composed in 1906 and premiered in the same year at one of the private recitals at Fuglsang. It became one of his most frequently performed quartets both before and after its publication.

The *Suite* for piano (CNW 88) was composed in 1919 and consists of six movements in which sections alternate between Nielsen's 'characteristic' tonal language and violent outbursts and fluctuations. The overall development has an almost symphonic quality in the structure of the individual movements, each with its own distinct expression.[58] During Nielsen's lifetime, the work was played mainly by Johanne Stockmarr and Christian Christiansen, and was not performed very often, although it is perhaps one of his most elaborate and pianistic pieces, as *Politiken* noted in its review.[59] The *Suite* was dedicated to the famous pianist Artur Schnabel, whom Nielsen had known since at least 1919 and who made a considerable effort to disseminate knowledge of Nielsen's works.[60]

Prelude, Theme and Variations (CNW 46) was composed in the spring of 1923 for Emil Telmányi's recital in London that summer. It is a work designed to show off the soloist's technical and musical virtuosity, and during Nielsen's lifetime it was mainly Telmányi who performed it in Copenhagen and on his concert tours of Europe and the USA.

Nielsen undoubtedly hoped that the publication of these works by Peters would encourage more foreign musicians to include them in their repertoire, but this did not prove to be the case. Only these three were issued by the publishers, who did not offer Nielsen the opportunity to publish any more of his compositions.

Throughout the 1920s, Wilhelm Hansen continued to play an important role in publishing Nielsen's works, including the Wind Quintet and the orchestral piece *Pan and Syrinx*. However, Nielsen also had a number of important works that remained unpublished, the most important of which was his Fifth Symphony. The main point of contention with Wilhelm Hansen was not whether to print Nielsen's pieces, but rather the question of remuneration. In June 1924, Nielsen signed a contract for 1,200 Kroner for the publication of the Overture to *Maskarade*, the *Aladdin Suite* and *Pan and Syrinx* – a contract he later asked to be cancelled. The following year he negotiated with Wilhelm Hansen to print the Fifth and Sixth symphonies and two other works for a total of 7,000 Kroner to be paid over two years. This contract was not signed either.[61]

Instead, Nielsen made a deal with Borups Musikforlag, a new publishing house established in 1922. The founder was Hans Borup, the son of the folk high school principal Johan Borup. The firm was initially based in the family home at 9 Vester Voldgade, but moved to 2 Palægade in 1925. One of the investors was Carl Johan Michaelsen, who also supported Nielsen in other ways during these years. Instead of signing a contract with Wilhelm Hansen to print his last two symphonies, Nielsen had Borup publish his Fifth Symphony in 1926, and later *Ti danske Smaasange* (*Ten Little Danish Songs*) (1926), *29 Little Preludes* (1930), *Klavermusik for Smaa og Store* (*Piano Music for Young and Old*) (1930) and *Three Motets* (1931).

Another publishing company, Samfundet til Udgivelse af Dansk Musik (The Society for the Publication of Danish Music), became involved in some of Nielsen's late works, which were published posthumously. Since 1899, Nielsen had been a member of its board of directors, Samfundsrådet, whose members took it in turns every three years to decide which works to publish. The Society had already published four-hand piano scores of the *Helios Overture* and Symphony No. 2, and in 1929 they produced the score and orchestral parts for the Overture to *Maskarade*. The most important output was the posthumous edition of Nielsen's Clarinet Concerto. Later, the Society undertook to publish some of the compositions that had never been printed, including *Commotio*, Symphony No. 6, the Flute Concerto and *Three Piano Pieces*, Op. 59.[62]

One view, of course, would be that Nielsen was badly treated by his publishers, yet virtually all the works that anyone needed to be able to buy printed editions of were in fact published during his lifetime. Only the late and less accessible works had to wait for publication. There was no market for the printing of opera scores, pieces composed for special occasions or incidental music. It was the complete scholarly edition of Nielsen's music, the *Carl Nielsen Edition*, begun in 1994 and completed in 2009, that had to fulfil this task.[63] The fact that a complete edition was initiated and realised with public funding was indeed also a way of emphasising that Nielsen's status as the national composer remained undiminished at the turn of the twenty-first century.

Presence

A decisive factor in achieving the status of national composer is that the music be performed, and there is no doubt that Nielsen's music had gained a firm and stable place in the concert repertoire already during his lifetime. The online version of the Nielsen catalogue of works (CNW) lists 4,865 documented performances up to Nielsen's death in 1931, including about 500 abroad.[64] Such an inventory will never be complete, of course, but it shows that Nielsen's music was widely played, and it is clear that it was performed more and more often as he grew older.

If we consider for a moment what is included in such a list, the performances of major works, for which there are programmes and newspaper coverage, are almost completely recorded, while individual songs and minor pieces very often slip by unnoticed. In addition, all the music that was sung and played in private homes, churches, schools and community centres, and at all types of entertainment events, is virtually invisible. The figures therefore show almost 5,000 performances of such importance that they have left concrete evidence.

Furthermore, the presence of Nielsen's music in Danish radio programmes from 1925 onwards is of paramount importance. As already mentioned, more than 500 programmes on Danish Radio featured one or more of Nielsen's compositions. On special occasions, his larger and more advanced works were broadcast, while on a daily basis, the extensive repertoire of popular orchestral pieces and songs was often used in live performances by the radio orchestras and ensembles or with invited soloists. His music was indeed transmitted.

ILL. 4. An indication of Nielsen's international recognition are the orders and honours that he was awarded. Here is a selection, from left to right: the Order of St Olav from Norway (1927), the Order of the North Star from Sweden (1926), the French Legion of Honour, Légion d'honneur (1926), the Italian Order of the Crown, Ordine della Corona (1922) and the Order of the White Rose from Finland, Suomen Valkoisen Ruusun ritarikunta, which he was awarded in 1923 at the latest.[65]

Nielsen himself did much to promote his music. There is evidence that he conducted any of his own works 344 times, 121 of them abroad.[66] The main purpose of his trip to Germany and Austria in 1894 was to generate interest in his First Symphony, which had just appeared in print. His publisher, Alfred Wilhelm Hansen, accompanied Nielsen on part of the journey and together they used all their contacts in Berlin, Leipzig and Dresden to get the symphony included in concert programmes. At the same time, Nielsen was trying to promote his String Quartet in F minor, which was also available in print.[67] He systematically sought out conductors and Kapellmeisters who might be interested in the symphony: Franz Mannstädt and Karl Muck in Berlin, Jean Louis Nicodé in Dresden, Richard Strauss in Munich and Johannes Brahms in Vienna. Through a chance meeting, he also learned that the famous violinist Eugène Ysaÿe already knew his string quartet and was considering performing it.[68]

Another strategy for becoming known and recognised was to obtain coverage in foreign quality journals. While travelling, Wilhelm Hansen used his contact with the editors of *Allgemeine Musik-Zeitung* and agreed that William Behrend should write an article about Nielsen for the journal. Nielsen wanted Orla Rosenhoff to help, but Rosenhoff thought this was an improper approach: 'That W. Behrend and I should write an article at your instigation for a German publication, so that the very same article should later appear in the Danish papers as a *true* expression of what is said and thought in Germany about the composer Carl Nielsen – no, my dear friend, doesn't that leave you with a funny taste?'[69] The article did not appear, but the strategy was used again in 1905, when Nielsen supplied material to Knud Harder, who wrote a long introductory article for the influential journal *Die Musik*.[70] There are a small number of such articles aimed at German or Nordic audiences, such as Fritz Crome's article in the Swedish journal *Ord och Bild* (1924) or Ture Rangstrøm's series of chronicles 'Modern sångkomposition' (Modern Song Composition) (1909), in which Nielsen is the central figure. Although the number of articles was small, they carried weight and complemented the short introductions that usually appeared in concert programmes when his music was performed.[71]

Performances generating attention and articles are often linked and are mutually reinforcing. The performance of Nielsen's Fifth Symphony at the ISCM Festival in Frankfurt in the summer of 1927 attracted a great deal of international attention, including a mention in the leading Austrian journal for contemporary music.[72] In response, Jørgen Bentzon wrote an article for the journal *Melos*, entitled 'Carl Nielsen und der Modernismus' (Carl Nielsen and Modernism).[73] As the event was an international festival for contemporary music, it was a topic that was of interest to the German music public.

The story of the Frankfurt performance also illustrates how musical performances by the most eminent conductors could effectively enhance a composer's reputation. The renowned Wilhelm Furtwängler conducted the performance of the Fifth Symphony, which was repeated in October with the Gewandhaus Orchestra in Leipzig. Such concerts always attracted a considerable attention. It is also an example of how Anne Marie's excellent international network may have played a role, as she knew Wilhelm's father, the classical archaeologist Adolf Furtwängler. She had heard of his musical son as early as 1905 and promised Wilhelm's mother to send him some of her husband's compositions, which she did.[74] So Nielsen was not unknown to Furtwängler when he agreed to conduct the symphony. Shortly after the performance in Frankfurt, the symphony was played in Königsberg under Jascha Horenstein and in Amsterdam with Pierre Monteux conducting the Concertgebouw Orchestra. Nielsen's music was performed by the world's leading conductors of the time.

Such performances have a special significance and prestige due to the involvement of renowned conductors with the reputation of performing only music of the highest quality. The focus is thus shifted away from the fact that the composer is Danish. Equally significant for Nielsen's posthumous status is that in 1952 the world-famous violinist Yehudi Menuhin recorded Nielsen's Violin Concerto with the Danish Radio Symphony Orchestra led by Mogens Wöldike. It was noted that this was the first LP recording to be produced in Denmark by His Master's Voice.[75] It should also be mentioned that on 17 May 1965, after receiving the Léonie Sonning Music Prize, Leonard Bernstein conducted the *Sinfonia espansiva* with The Royal Orchestra, a performance that was both broadcast on television and recorded on LP. It was, as Nielsen's publishers wrote in their twenty-page report of Bernstein's visit, 'the most intense, the most overwhelming musical event to take place in the Danish capital in a lifetime'.[76] There are those who were present at the concert who can still bear witness to this.

There is a particular dynamic between international recognition and the status a composer achieves in their home country. On the one hand, the recognition as the national composer requires that foreign countries recognise the composer's qualities and contribute to his or her status through reviews and performances. It is therefore important to know whether Nielsen's music was actually played abroad on a regular basis, or whether there were only isolated instances. The answer is clear: the music was indeed performed abroad, as confirmed by the registration of the more than 500 performances, a third of which were conducted by Nielsen. It is also important to notice that, to an even greater extent than in Denmark, only performances that attracted public attention have left traces in Danish archives.

On the other hand, being a national composer is not an advantage per se if a composer is to achieve the very highest international status: to be one of the greatest of all composers. In Gade's time it was the other way round. In 1843 he arrived in Leipzig, the capital of musical opinion-forming, at a time when national movements were on the rise throughout Europe and people were longing for music that could represent their agenda. It was in Leipzig that a 'Nordic tone' was first heard in Gade's music, and it was because of this that he enjoyed an international career, quickly gaining recognition as a major European composer. To be a national composer was the highest praise a composer could achieve in the mid-nineteenth century and was widely respected throughout Europe. In a seminal German account of music history published in 1901, Gade had achieved such international status that he was dealt with in the central chapter on the music-historical era of Schumann and Mendelssohn, while all other Nordic composers were relegated to a sub-section of the chapter on national trends.[77]

For Nielsen's international impact at the beginning of the twentieth century, the label of the national composer was rather a disadvantage. By then, the idea that each nation had its own distinctive music had gained ground – that is, a music that was difficult for others to fully understand and with which they could not fully identify. Abroad, Nielsen came to be seen as a composer of a particular country, and thus was of less relevance to audiences of other states. In Germany and France it was possible to listen to Danish or Czech music with interest, but it was not their own.[78] Rather than strengthening Nielsen's position internationally, the perception of his music as distinctively Danish or Nordic tended to keep Nielsen on the margins of European music historiography.[79]

In the twentieth and twenty-first centuries, therefore, the means of being recognised as one of the great composers of all time is no longer to be identified as the musical representative of a particular nation, but to cease to be so. Only time will tell how this will develop in Nielsen's case.

A Man of Power

Yet another factor in achieving status is through official positions and titles. With the many positions Nielsen held and the high esteem in which he was regarded in Danish musical life and society in general, he also became an authoritative figure. And he was not afraid to use his influence. In December 1926, for example, Nielsen, as a member of the board of directors of the Academy of Music, single-handedly admitted a sixteen-year-old youngster, Vagn Holmboe, whose knowledge of music and music theory was inadequate. This was against the advice of the director, Anton Svendsen. Late in life, Holmboe told the story on several occasions. Carl Nielsen had showed him into Room A of the Academy and asked if he could play the piano:

> I confirmed. 'And the violin?' And of course I could. Then he looked at my quartet and said: 'Yes, you can consider yourself accepted.'[80]

The story sounds very similar to Nielsen's experience when he was accepted with a string quartet at Gade's behest, and that may be the point. It shows who had the authority and the ability to recognise the young man's great talent. The details cannot be verified, and as Nielsen was not teaching at the Academy at the time, there was no closer contact.

Nielsen was also able to award grants and scholarships to those he felt were next in line, although this sometimes caused him problems when applicants believed he had promised them a grant. In 1921 the organist and composer Christian Geisler wrote to Nielsen that he had once said of the Anckerske Legat: 'You'll get it, but not this year.' Geisler apparently never received it.[81] Niels Otto Raasted was more fortunate, however, and in a long and persistent letter to Nielsen in 1927 he told his version of the story of how he had been given the prospect of a scholarship several times.[82] Raasted received his share of the grant that year.

In addition to the three scholarships mentioned by Gerhard Lynge – that is, the Anckerske, Berggreenske and Wexchallske – Nielsen was also involved in the nomination of the scholarships of Det Kirsteinske Legat, Det Raben-Leventzauske Legat, from

1923 the Jonas and Alfred Wilhelm Hansen Mindelegat, Ernst Michaelsen's Legat in memory of the pianist Ove Christensen and the Vera and Carl J. Michaelsen's Legat.[83]

Through his positions on boards and committees and his roles in the Academy and in Musikforeningen, Nielsen had a huge network. He knew the relevant people when something needed to be organised. In 1912 the civil servant Andreas Peter Weis was promoted to permanent secretary in the Ministry in charge of cultural matters and was at the same time director of The Royal Theatre in 1909–13, the tenure of Nielsen as Kapellmeister. It was Weis who had signed the official announcement that Nielsen had been awarded the Anckerske Legat in 1890, and it was he who, on behalf of the Ministry, asked Nielsen to join its board of trustees in 1914.[84] At the same time, Weis sat with Nielsen on the board of both the Academy of Music and Musikforeningen.

Nielsen was not afraid to use his connections when he wanted to achieve something or needed help. In October 1913, Nielsen decided to hand in his resignation in protest at the conditions at The Royal Theatre, because Høeberg had been allowed to take over Rung's duties without Nielsen's consent. On this occasion, Nielsen noted in his diary the following day that he first visited Edvard Brandes, who was finance minister in the newly appointed Social Liberal government, then spoke with the Theatre's director and manager and agreed with them not to implement the resignation, and in the evening visited Klaus Berntsen, the recently resigned prime minister.[85]

In March 1914, when he submitted his resignation and it was accepted, he visited Weis to discuss his financial prospects and was advised to speak directly to the minister in charge of cultural matters, Søren Keiser-Nielsen. Nielsen asked if he should also visit the members of the Finance Committee himself.[86] The following year, he approached the finance minister, Edvard Brandes, in order to increase the subsidy for Musikforeningen, and received a confidential reply from the minister himself.[87]

During the work on this book, a small collection of Nielsen's letters was discovered, which shed light on another case where Nielsen used his influence and was crucial to the outcome: the appointment as organist at Vor Frue Kirke, the cathedral of Copenhagen, in 1924. The recipient of the letters was Niels Otto Raasted, whom Nielsen had known since the autumn of 1913, when Raasted accompanied Karl Straube, cantor at St Thomas' Church in Leipzig, on a concert tour to Denmark.[88] Raasted was studying with Straube at the time and became organist at the Frue Kirke in Odense in 1915. The letters, which were in the posession of the Raasted family, have now been transferred to The Royal Library.

On 5 July 1924, Nielsen wrote to Raasted that he had been to the Ministry the previous day but had not seen the minister. The secretary had told him that the minister was very pleased to hear that Nielsen was coming and that nothing would be decided until Tuesday, when the minister would be back. Nielsen would write to Raasted as soon as he knew anything.[89] On Tuesday a telegram arrived in Odense: 'Hurray, congratulations, letters will follow'. The same day Nielsen wrote a letter of explanation:

> It was very interesting to follow this matter through. … The case was hanging by a thread, albeit a strong one, because the minister favoured you. But he said that he would like support, and I replied that I would be happy to put my back into it if it was criticised … Then he said: 'I thank you, then, consider the matter settled, and let it now go to the chief clerk for finalisation.'[90]

The fact that the incident occurred shortly after Denmark had its first Social Democratic government, with Thorvald Stauning as prime minister, does not seem to have made Nielsen's access to the relevant ministers any more difficult. He had also known Stauning for a number of years, at least since 1918, when they had served together on a commission on musical matters set up by the Copenhagen City Council, of which Stauning was a member.[91]

When the Bill is Settled

Nielsen's recognition was both widespread and lasting. By 1916 he had reached a position where there was general agreement in influential circles about the fine quality of his music, while at the same time he was liked by large sections of the population. By the 1920s, he was undisputedly recognised as the leading Danish composer and was also gaining fame and recognition abroad as a prominent musical figure. The interaction between foreign recognition and national status, which is a prerequisite for becoming the national composer of a country, had taken effect.

All the conditions now seemed to be in place. Nielsen's music had found a secure and central place in the repertoire, and indeed a number of Danish soloists and musicians had made playing his compositions part of their professional profile. These were usually musicians with whom he had a personal relationship, and whom he knew from The Royal Orchestra, the Academy or as musical colleagues in general. Abroad, his music was performed by leading conductors and most of his works were available from reputable publishers.

But the recognition also had its limits. During his lifetime there was very little real academic literature on Nielsen. The part of the canonisation process that is based on his being taken seriously as a subject of musicological study is that of posterity. Nielsen was personally involved in some of the more detailed studies, such as Henrik Knudsen's introduction to the *Sinfonia espansiva*. Others he influenced only indirectly through a teacher-student relationship, such as Rudolph Simonsen's and Hugo Seligmann's discussions of Nielsen's symphonies. The only scholarly analysis of his music that he had the opportunity to read was Povl Hamburger's 'Formproblemet i vor Tids Musik' (The Problem of Form in the Music of Our Time), published in May 1931.[92]

In assessing the extent of the canonisation of Nielsen, Gillies's model also allows us to look at who he has been compared to. One category is when he is being measured against already recognised contemporary composers. In his 1916 review of Nielsen's *The Inextinguishable*, Emilius Bangert went so far as to call it a 'great work of Danish music, indeed … of European [music]' and compared Nielsen to Richard Strauss, Saint-Saëns and Debussy, thus making Nielsen, according to Bangert, one of the leading composers of his time in Europe.[93] In 1906, Hammerich wrote about Act One of *Maskarade* that he could only think of Verdi's *Falstaff* as a parallel, while Robert Henriques heard it on a par with Wagner's *Die Meistersinger*. It was major opera composers in the history of music with whom Nielsen was compared.[94] And when Finn Høffding, in his report on the ISCM Festival in Frankfurt in 1927, was able to highlight the triumvirate of Bartók, Stravinsky and Nielsen as 'masters of the so-called objective music', it was Nielsen who was emphasised as one of the leading innovators in Western compositional music.[95] But when Charles Kjerulf claimed in *Politiken* (1903) that there was talk of 'Beethoven – Mozart – Carl Nielsen', Nielsen had to protest against what he called a ridiculous comparison.[96] There could be no question of equating him with the greatest of them all.

Nor has it come to that. Nielsen has so far maintained a secure position as the leading Danish composer of all time. This secure status is based on a general recognition of the composer's originality, quality, longevity and popularity or resonance with a large audience. To go further requires a broad consensus on the universality of the composer, and in this context the perception of Nielsen as a national figure may stand in the way, but so may the perception that he is something quite unique.[97] It is an idea that can be found in an almost caricatured form in the early Nielsen literature:

> The directions of his journey as a composer are to be sought solely in Nielsen himself and his undeniable musical instinct. They cannot be attributed to impulses or influences from any other source, precisely because it is difficult to see where they could have come from. There were no similar currents abroad …[98]

It has not helped Nielsen's posthumous international reception – including Danish reception – that he has often been described as unique and unaffected by what was happening in European musical life around him.[99] Yet nothing could be further from the truth. Instead of believing that direct stylistic models are a prerequisite for an interaction with other European music, it is important to consider Nielsen's deep roots in the European culture of his time.

The European culture was an integral part of the culture to which Nielsen belonged, both on Fyn and in Copenhagen, and thus it becomes possible to understand why Nielsen's position as national composer does not prevent him from being an important European composer. We must distinguish between the way in which the Danish public and posterity have regarded him, and the background and deep empathy with the European culture of his time that characterised him and formed the basis of his approach to thinking and composing music.

Chapter 42

CURATING THE LEGACY

Nielsen's funeral service on Friday 9 October 1931 in the cathedral of Copenhagen, Vor Frue Kirke, was a public event that attracted enormous attention in all the country's newspapers. He died shortly after midnight on 3 October as a result of a heart condition, having been severely weakened during his last weeks.[1] Around 1,500 reports, reviews and tributes appeared in the newspapers in the days following his death, and on the day of the funeral around 30,000 people attended the events. The huge turnout shows that not only were the associations and institutions of the musical community, his family and friends affected by his death, but that ordinary people also felt the need to show their sympathy. Rarely had a cultural figure been given such a grand farewell.

The funeral was planned down to the last detail and the event was moved from Holmens Kirke to Vor Frue Kirke to accommodate the expected large number of participants. Admission tickets were issued and music was played both inside and outside the church. There were wreaths from the Royal Family, the University, the Academies of Music in Copenhagen, Aarhus and Odense, The Royal Theatre, the Danish Radio, the Danish Composers' Society, The Royal Theatre in Stockholm, the Swedish Academy, the Danish Choral Society, and the counties and towns of Fyn and Nielsen's native parish of Nr. Lyndelse.[2] The large turnout for the service and the large crowd gathering outside show the respect, popularity and recognition that Nielsen enjoyed from people of all walks of life in his last years.

It may seem that Nielsen's legacy was being formed at this moment, but in fact it had already been established. The celebration of his sixtieth birthday and the publication of *Levende Musik* (*Living Music*) in 1925 and *My Childhood* two years later played a major role in creating the image of Nielsen that was handed down to posterity. Yet there were threads that went back much further, for in his earlier presentations Nielsen actively contributed to creating a self-image of how he was to be perceived, and his firm foundation in Copenhagen's cultural life since his youth formed relationships that were still alive and active at the time of his death.

One example is the tribute by the Social Democrat Frederik Borgbjerg, who in 1931 was the Minister of Education and thus also in charge of culture. The morning after Nielsen's death, he received a phone call from the newspaper *Aftenbladet* and gave his immediate reaction:

ILL. 1. The crowd at Nielsen's funeral, which took place on 9 October 1931, six days after his death, causes traffic chaos outside Vor Frue Kirke.

> It moved me very much … He was the great master of Danish musical life in our time … the greatest since the days of Gade. We were the same age, so I was able to follow him from his earliest years. I remember with wistfulness how his first musical works spoke to me in a quite unique and moving way in those young years … I remember his cantata at the inauguration of the Student Society's new building at Frue Plads, his first songs, which were so genuinely Danish in tone and yet always an expression of the times – he was always both so Danish and so modern …[3]

Borgbjerg's account reveals the strong network Nielsen had had since his youth in the intellectual and cultural circles of the capital, where the leading political and cultural figures of the new century knew each other. The circles in which the political opposition to the country's conservative government gathered at the end of the nineteenth century consisted politically of the Liberal Party, Venstre, the Social Democratic Party and, from 1905, Det radikale Venstre, the Social Liberal Party, all of which were culturally closely linked to the environment of the Student Society. Borgbjerg and Nielsen had moved in the same circles since their youth.[4]

At the same time, Borgbjerg's reaction underlines how the Danish, the popular and the modern in people's perceptions of Nielsen were linked to the memory of significant cultural events. The impact of witnessing the inauguration of the Student Society's building in 1901 was still fresh in Borgbjerg's mind thirty years later, even though the music had only been performed on that one occasion.

Nielsen's Birthday in 1925

The celebration of Nielsen's sixtieth birthday on 9 June 1925 was a similarly momentous occasion in Copenhagen. In the morning he was awakened by a brass band, including musicians from The Royal Orchestra, playing music outside his window.[5] The fact that the newspaper *Politiken* took it upon itself to organise the official part of the celebrations shows how important Nielsen was to the population at large. They organised a party in Tivoli Gardens that lasted all evening and well into the night. First there was a concert in the Tivoli Concert Hall, featuring four of Nielsen's major works. The programme began with the *Suite for String Orchestra*, Op. 1, which had been premiered in the same venue many years earlier, followed by the Violin Concerto with Peder Møller as soloist, then his Fifth Symphony and finally *Fynsk Foraar* (*Springtime on Funen*). The concert was followed by a festive three-course dinner with wine and coffee at Nimb for those who managed to get one of the 332 tickets made available. As the organiser of the event, *Politiken* had a special reason to document the successful festivities and carefully listed all the prominent guests from the capital's cultural and intellectual circles in its report.

After speeches and the garlanding of Nielsen with a laurel wreath, a torchlit procession arrived at midnight, having marched through the city from Christiansborg's riding ground, led by a brass band and student singers. Along the way they sang 'Du danske Mand' (*Danish Patriotic Song*), 'Jeg bærer med Smil min Byrde' (I bear with a smile my burden) and *Jens Vejmand* (*John the Roadman*). The young and the common people were thus able to take part in the celebration of Nielsen. When the procession arrived, there were more speeches, followed by entertainment and finally dancing until dawn.[6] It was the great and popular Nielsen who was celebrated and honoured with the music chosen and in the many speeches.

By this time there was a generally accepted understanding of which works were identified with the so-called 'Nielsen sound', that is, those presented in the concert programme of the event and in the songs performed during the torchlit procession. This was part of Nielsen's legacy that was about to manifest itself. It was crucial for the reception of Nielsen's new works of the 1920s that they were compared not only with how his music had sounded in the past, but also with a normative understanding of how it should sound.

ILL. 2. On the evening of Nielsen's sixtieth birthday, a torchlit procession was organised in which hundreds of people took part. The route went from Christiansborg to Tivoli Gardens, where Nielsen and the invited guests interrupted the party at Restaurant Nimb to welcome the procession.

This is evident in connection with the first performance of the Sixth Symphony in December 1925, when Hugo Seligmann distinguished between 'the Carl Nielsen we know', whom he could hear in the first movement, although there were places where 'some force took him over and led him elsewhere than where he really wanted to go', and a Carl Nielsen who was 'a completely new person'.[7] Another reviewer, Gunnar Hauch, explains what he associated with the Nielsen sound. The new symphony seemed strange to him when he thought of Nielsen's 'greatest works, *Maskarade*, the broad field of the Espansiva Symphony, the passionate fantasy of "The Inextinguishable", the grand structure of the first part of the Fifth Symphony, the music for Aladdin'.[8] The image that it was this body of great works with which Nielsen was identified was partly created by Nielsen's own concert programmes as he presented his music at home and abroad in the years leading up to his birthday. Yet the image of 'Nielsen as we know him' also had an impact on his own opportunities for recognition when he chose other routes.

Living Music

A few days before Nielsen's birthday, the collection of essays *Levende Musik* (*Living Music*) was released, containing a small selection of articles published over the last two decades. Of the nine essays included, six were taken from the nearly one hundred texts Nielsen had previously published.[9] The preface and the last two essays were written for this occasion.

Through a clear selection and arrangement of the essays, *Living Music* came to be regarded his most important contribution. This meant that the collection, which deals with the interpretation of music and art, was treated by both his contemporaries and posterity as Nielsen's aesthetic testament. For many years, much of posterity's understanding of Nielsen was based on interpretations derived from this small collection, which was sold and reprinted many times over the following decades. The first edition sold out quickly, the second appeared in the same year, and the fifth edition was published by the time of Nielsen's death in 1931. A steady stream of reprints followed, remarkably at a time when little other literature by and about Nielsen was as readily available.

The publication of *Living Music* as part of the highly profiled sixtieth anniversary celebrations enhanced its importance, and the inclusion of the essays in a single edition changed their focus. They were now seen as part of a unified statement, and by virtue of the combination they were indeed so. The publication of the essays in a single volume, without informing the reader where the essays originally appeared, gives the collection a sense of contemporaneity. Read in this light, the monograph may be perceived as an aesthetic tract, suggesting that it be read ahistorically, that is, as a reflection of commonly held views.

Throughout the present book, the essays have been read as historical documents, describing Nielsen's views at a particular time and in relation to the context of the period in which they were written. This seems appropriate when dealing with Nielsen's views at certain points in time and the gradual development of those views. However, if the aim is to understand the impact of *Living Music* on posterity, as is the case in this chapter, it seems appropriate to read them systematically in order to gain an overall impression of Nielsen's aesthetic views. By bringing these essays together, Nielsen has composed a new text. Statements in one essay can be read as a continuation of an argument in an earlier essay in the collection, thus creating a narrative that the essays did not contain when read separately.[10]

Moreover, by using the collective title, *Living Music*, the edition appears as a distinctly vitalist programme, which is indeed evident as Nielsen emphasises his intention by inserting the motto from his Fourth Symphony as a vignette above the preface: 'Music is Life, like this Inextinguishable'[11] – an explicit reference to his insistence that music be understood *as* life and not merely as a representation of life. By including the concept of life in the collective title, the author makes this message central to his understanding of music in general.

What impression does the reader get from studying the essays in *Living Music* as a whole? Nielsen explains in the preface that he feels the urge to write when he encounters something that reflects an important aspect of the nature of music.[12] This is not a book about music theory or history. Thus he suggests that we should read the book in order to learn more about fundamental aesthetic issues.

The first essay, 'Mozart and Our Time', first published in 1906, contrasts Mozart with Beethoven, emphasising the former's clear and objective approach to music. 'Words, Music and Programme Music', published in 1909, attacks tone-painting and an approach to music intended only for delicate enjoyment. Comparing this type of music to hothouse plants, Nielsen criticises the tendency to mix art forms and to promote abominations, which he sees as an expression of decadence and cultural decay. As an alternative, he asserts the fundamental ability to observe and perceive aesthetic phenomena, such as the juxtaposition of two colours or a movement, which he calls 'the pure, original, basic sense' that underlies all genuine artistic perception.[13] He concludes by dividing composers into two groups, one dependent on the support of a text and the other group including those who feel free only when they are able to devote themselves entirely to sound. Although Nielsen does not name himself, it is clear that he belongs to the second category, and he ends with a pathos reminiscent of Busoni. Nielsen associates music with nature and freedom, and ends by letting the music express its character in order to make life more potent: 'I live ten times stronger than all living beings and die a thousand times deeper.'[14]

In the next article, 'Musical Problems' (1922), Nielsen's starting point is the utilitarian value of music, distancing himself from excessive ornamentation that goes beyond functionality. This leads to reflections on the origins of music, which Nielsen sees as the aesthetic fascination of the simplest intervals, such as those found in the call of the cuckoo. He finds this primal quality in the simple melodies of Mozart and, as a frightening example, he cites a motif from Wagner's *Ring des Nibelungen* that seems 'hideous and already obsolete' and unbearable.[15]

This is followed by three essays, all of which had previously appeared in *Politiken*: the first, 'Danish Songs' (1921) is a review of a small collection of songs by Laub; the second is 'Musicology' (1923), a review of Knud Jeppesen's book on Palestrina; and finally he includes a review of a book on Beethoven's piano sonatas (1923).

In a new essay, 'The Fullness of Time', Nielsen continues to describe the modern composers of the turn of the century, with their huge orchestras and quest for originality, as a phenomenon of the past. As this is presented as an idea taken seriously fifteen to twenty years before the 1925 essay, it is clear that Nielsen has composers such as Richard Strauss and works such as Mahler's Eighth Symphony in mind. However, what he now finds necessary is to reflect on 'the alpha and omega of music, that is, the notes themselves, the series of notes and the intervals'.[16] The final short essay is 'Den fynske Sang' (The Song of Fyn), which is a declaration of love for his childhood region.

Taken as a whole, *Living Music* is an extremely powerful document. Reading the essays in the order in which they appear, the general impression is that an overall argument emerges that can be interpreted as Nielsen's aesthetic credo: a worship of the objective and sublime rather than the subjective (1906) is linked to an experience of decadence (1909), which in turn is identified with Wagner (1922) and is now relegated to a bygone era of music history (1925). Vitality, vigour and health are formulated here as the opposite of decadence and the aftermath of Romanticism.

One striking detail is the way Nielsen works with binary oppositions throughout the book. On the one hand, there is the negative that needs to be fought: the Romantic, Wagnerian, Straussian and decadent, with its indulgence in sound, obscurity, chords and the over-refined. Wagner becomes the representative of the unhealthy, the unviable, the unattractive and the obsolete, in other words, of a Romanticism that has led to an unhealthy and unsustainable situation that must be overcome. On the other hand, there is the positive, the healthy, the fundamental, the organic, the natural and the linear culture, which is associated with the popular, the Danish and Fyn. Thus the book *Living Music* confirms and reinforces the notion that the real Nielsen is the one who composed *The Inextinguishable* and the popular songs. The problem, however, is that much of Nielsen's music does not sound 'as we know him' and is therefore difficult to understand within this framework. Even during his lifetime, he was confronted with the image of his own legacy. In other words, he helped to create an image in which he was then trapped.

Self-Curating

Throughout his life, Nielsen was conscious of how he presented himself to the world around him. It was not only his professional achievements that were presented in an inviting and individual way. Even small distortions of reality could be a means of projecting himself in the best possible light. As already mentioned, he maintained throughout his life his version of the story of his admission to the Academy of Music in 1883, even though it was not entirely true. Many of his early autobiographical statements were brief and factual for use in applications, but it is clear that he had thought about how he wanted to appear.

When Nielsen applied for the Anckerske Legat in 1888, he called himself a 'musician' but also wrote that he had been taught composition at the Academy by Orla Rosenhoff and Niels W. Gade, although the teaching was actually in music theory and music history. Gade, who sat on the committee and read the applications, was of course aware of this, but it was a way of signalling that Nielsen also considered himself a composer.[17] After Gade's death, when Nielsen had to introduce himself prior to the international premiere of his First Symphony in Dresden in 1896, he added that he had also been taught composition by Gade after his studies, but there is no evidence of this: Nielsen exaggerated.[18] For the Dresden audience, Gade was a familiar frame of reference, and Nielsen knew that Gade was a respected name. During his travels, he had experienced how a relationship with Gade could facilitate access to German musical circles. These external circumstances made it convenient for Nielsen to emphasise his connection with Gade.

In the Dresden letter, Nielsen's autobiographical statements already begin to take on the characteristics found in *My Childhood*. He explains that he began playing the violin at the age of six, that he made early attempts at composing little tunes, and talks about his father and his education in Odense. In 1905 he gave more detailed descriptions, some of which were used in a portrait published by Knud Harder in the German journal *Die Musik* and others in an article by Klaus Berntsen in *Søndagsbladet*. They appeared at a time when Nielsen was beginning to stand out from his peers and to be recognised as the most important name of his generation.[19] There is no doubt, however, that it was in the wake of the events surrounding his sixtieth birthday that the idea of writing his memoirs – and thus really leaving his mark on how others should see him – took shape.

My Childhood

The stories in *My Childhood* were important to Nielsen. When he gave his closing speech at the birthday party in 1925, he did not talk about everything he had achieved. *Politiken* reports:

> Deeply moved as the memories of his childhood flooded in, he spoke of the time he spent as a little herd boy at home in Nr. Lyndelse. He spoke quietly and movingly about his childhood. It was not a speech, it was a heart overflowing with gratitude for life, a new version of *The Story of My Life*.[20]

The newspaper's reference to the memoirs of another famous person from Fyn – that is, those of Hans Christian Andersen – set the tone, attributing literary quality to Nielsen's own recollections from the outset. It was apparently at the urging of his daughter Irmelin over the years that Nielsen began writing the memoirs in 1927.[21] Yet there may have been other factors at play. When Nielsen received the first volume of Klaus Berntsen's autobiography in 1923, he already toyed with the idea of writing his own memoirs in his letter of thanks to Berntsen: 'But if I ever write my memoirs …'[22]

Nielsen's introduction to *My Childhood* reflects on the writing of memoirs, and Nielsen is aware that it is not necessary to remember everything as it really happened, or to have experienced everything at first hand. He is also aware that it is a representation, a literary form, based on what he remembers.[23] His diary shows that he began thinking about the project in 1926. The actual writing took place over a period of four months in the spring and summer of 1927, when he was greatly assisted by his daughter Irmelin's mother-in-law, Frida Møller. Because of his heart condition, most of the manuscript was dictated, and then Møller, Irmelin and Margrete Rosenberg helped with the final editing.[24]

Nielsen was not the only cultural figure to write memoirs during this period. There seems to have been almost a wave of autobiographies in the 1920s: Klaus Berntsen, Martin Andersen Nexø and Jeppe Aakjær wrote memoirs, each offering a personal narrative of the great upheaval from the rural society of childhood to modernity. Such memoirs are always marked by a temporal duality between the time of remembering, childhood and youth, and the time of writing, where parts are selected, reflected upon, compared and emphasised. Memoirs are written from the perspective of the one who is reminiscing. Furthermore, autobiography is akin to the 'Bildungsroman', both of which focus on the central character's coming to terms with themselves and their lives.[25] In the introduction to his memoirs, Nexø formulates this aspect, which is indeed similar to Nielsen's occasional doubts about himself and his inner balance. Nexø writes:

> Am I really something to myself, just because I mostly feel like an affected person who has misunderstood the meaning of my existence? Throughout my life I have had the feeling that I was two things: one Self that no one could argue with, so sovereignly asserting itself above all doubt and criticism; and another Self of a terribly unsuccessful kind that *I* held in my hands and had to try to shape. ... Have I succeeded, over the years, in moulding myself, at least in part, in the direction of the structural lines that seem to be deeply rooted in me?[26]

In Nexø's case, it is a project in which a conscious and self-conscious superego has tried to get a grip on a subego – or, perhaps more accurately, on the potential inherent in its abilities or talents. But Nexø is an author and has the 'Bildungsroman' as a reference. With Nielsen, on the other hand, this kind of doubt is less evident in *My Childhood* than in the personal letters and public statements he makes at various points in his life. And yet, in an omitted passage at the end of the manuscript, where Nielsen tries to justify why the memoirs must end with the journey to Copenhagen, he writes:

> Here, then, begins a whole new chapter in my life, and here I must end, for I cannot explain the contradiction that lies in the fact that, to same extent I've had my wishes fulfilled – that is, to learn, to try, to hear, to see and to take part in the artis-

tic life in Copenhagen and other places – I've just as much longed for and missed all that and all those who had filled my childhood and early youth with rich and vivid impressions. … A voice in my heart asks in a restless whisper, has my later life been a disappointment?[27]

In the preface to *My Childhood*, Nielsen articulates his fascination with memoirs, arguing that they are valuable because 'the study of the [whole person is] the most important and interesting that we know … something we would wish to know, something which, in spite of all defects and imperfections, we will like once we look into it'.[28] Although he speaks in the third person, it is the legitimation of his own memories that is articulated here. One of the persons he wants to know is himself.

What is particularly characteristic of Nielsen's memoirs is that he writes best when he evokes sensory situations. He not only remembers and observes, he hears, smells, feels and tastes as much as he sees. Indeed, it is striking that the sounds are rarely in the foreground. With Aakjær, who published his childhood memoirs the year after Nielsen, it is the opposite, for he writes much more sensually when it comes to using words that evoke notions of sound. Aakjær's memoirs begin with a description of his childhood farm and an early experience of having to get out and hold on to the thatched roof when the wind was about to blow it away. The language is rich in sensory impressions of sound and movement:

> Naked and exposed to all winds, the farm was constantly shaken by the prevailing westerly gales. It sounded rather mournful to stand on its empty floors on such a stormy day, listening to the creaking and cracking of the wooden pegs and rafters as the storm squeezed its side legs.[29]

Nielsen's descriptions in *My Childhood* are also very sensuous, but unlike Aakjær he rarely focuses on sounds. Movements and colours are more important, and sometimes smells and heat are clearly discernible, as when he describes the children lying on the grass in the sun outside their childhood home, and their mother, Maren Kirstine, coming home with 'æbleskiver' (a kind of apple fritters) after harvesting at Bramstrup. When Nielsen depicts his neighbour kneading peat, he again draws attention to the sensory:

> It was queer to see him working … First he would remove the turf, next he would enclose a rectangular hole in the pit … and knead the mess with his bare feet. His trousers would be turned up to the thighs, and he would sweat and slog away for dear life.[30]

The story of Carl and his brother playing tunes on the woodpile outside their childhood home has been told since it took place in the 1870s. Nielsen tells it slightly differently at various times, and perhaps it is also a story told to him by his mother, who plays an important part in the narrative. She was talking to Langkilde, the lord of the manor, who had heard the sound of the boys' performance before he went to talk to Carl.[31] Nielsen could not have experienced this part of the story himself.

The story shows that Nielsen was musical and inventive from childhood, and this is how he used the story when he told it to William Behrend and Klaus Berntsen. One way of ascribing status to a composer is to argue that their talent was recognised early on. This function is still important in *My Childhood*, as it helps to support Nielsen's legacy. When Nielsen included the story in his memoirs, however, it was framed within a broader account of the family's attachment to the region where they lived, and in particular their relationship with the landowner, Langkilde, at Bramstrup. It was important for Nielsen to portray the social conditions in which he and his family members had grown up, and the dignity with which they were able to interact with the rich and poor in the area.

As with *Living Music*, *My Childhood* was a crucial element in establishing the image of Nielsen that has been handed down to posterity. Whereas the aesthetic tract gave us a picture of a stable and well-established aesthetic position, in contrast to Romanticism and its aftermath, *My Childhood* reinforces the view that the most important approach to understanding Nielsen is to deal with his childhood and upbringing on Fyn. Thus, Nielsen was a key player in the creation of his own legacy.[32] The image that was created is the basis for how posterity has understood Nielsen – and more than that, it has also influenced posterity's ability to see and understand Nielsen at all. The legacy established during his lifetime was an essential element in the entrenched views of posterity, called the Nielsen myth. The difference is that after his death he was no longer able to act as someone who could adjust the image in words or music. What would it have meant if Nielsen had pulled himself together and written a second volume of his memoirs, describing his youth as part of Copenhagen's musical, cultural and intellectual milieu?

The Nielsen Myth

The innovator of the Danish sound, the anti-Romantic, the ordinary man from the countryside – this is the image of Nielsen that has been dubbed the Nielsen myth. To label it a myth is not to say that it does not have the quality of being true. It articulates that a static image of who Nielsen was has been formed, that a mythologised and idyllic image of Nielsen has emerged and taken on a life of its own. A partly fictional figure of 'Nielsen' has been established, with which the real Nielsen, in all his contradictory behaviour, has had to compete in the attempt to understand him posthumously.[33]

The earliest explicit criticisms of such a Nielsen myth are probably to be found in Jan Maegaard's articles in *Dansk Musik Tidsskrift*, 'Den sene Carl Nielsen' (The Late Carl Nielsen) (1953) and 'Når boet skal gøres op efter Carl Nielsen…' (Settling the Estate of Carl Nielsen…) (1965).[34] The former discusses the programme for the Carl Nielsen Festival in 1953 and, like the views that had become established in 1925, is based on a distinction between 'Nielsen *as we know him*' – that is, 'the early Nielsen' and 'the great Nielsen' – and the modern Nielsen, which Maegaard did not find to be present.[35] He sees it as part of a wider trend that leads to the reproduction of the familiar image of Nielsen, which emphasises certain parts of his oeuvre and correspondingly neglects his late works in particular.[36]

Maegaard attempts to dispel the Nielsen myth in two ways. Firstly, by emphasising features in the music characterised by a schism and the composer's struggle with the material, thus giving a different impression of Nielsen's style from the usual narrative of the period. Secondly, by emphasising Nielsen's relationship with some of the Central European composers who were influential in his time, such as Mahler, Schoenberg and Wagner.

Maegaard's articles on Nielsen give the impression that there are two problems with the Nielsen myth. The first is that the portrayal of Nielsen has been unbalanced for years, obscuring certain aspects of the composer's personality and style. Maegaard goes on to say that eventually he realised that there was another Nielsen: 'the problematic one, the one who composed the Sixth Symphony, the works for solo violin, the Clarinet Concerto and the last three piano pieces.'[37]

If one problem was the one-dimensional understanding of Nielsen, Maegaard sees the other in the consequences for Danish musical life. Because of the Nielsen myth and the impact that the legacy of Nielsen's books, his music and that of his pupils had on musical life, the entire narrative of Danish music after Gade was built around Nielsen:

> The anti-Romantic, objectivity-cultivating attitude at the heart of this aesthetic meant that composers of Carl Nielsen's time and immediately after who were oriented toward Romanticism – including composers such as Louis Glass, Fini Henriques, August Enna, Hakon Børresen, Ludolf Nielsen and Peder Gram – were gradually forgotten.[38]

The marginalisation of composers other than Nielsen, which began at the beginning of the twentieth century, became, with the adoption of an anti-Romantic aesthetic, the very narrative of Danish musical life. A concrete example of how the Nielsen myth has influenced our understanding of Danish music history can be found in Kaj Aage Bruun's *Dansk Musiks Historie fra Holberg-tiden til Carl Nielsen* (1967). Even the title could be paraphrased as 'from Holberg's *Mascarade* to Nielsen's *Maskarade*'. Virtually all composers born in the second half of the nineteenth century – from Victor Bendix (b. 1851) and Nielsen's contemporaries to Rued Langgaard (b. 1893), Ebbe Hamerik (b. 1897) and Knudåge Riisager (b. 1898) – are treated under the heading 'Other Late Romantics'. They are thus juxtaposed with 'The Thomas Laub– Carl Nielsen Era' and 'Carl Nielsen' – the titles of the subsequent chapters.[39] In Nils Schiørring's *Musikkens Historie i Danmark* (1978) it is also clear that a long period of Danish music history is regarded as 'Nielsen-centric', since the chapters following the one on Nielsen are entitled 'Samtid og eftertid' (Present and Future) and 'For og imod Carl Nielsen' (For and against Carl Nielsen).[40] It is only in recent years that interest in these marginalised composers has been revived, and their works have begun to be performed and recorded.[41]

Maegaard's summary of the myth as the story of the 'cheerful son of nature', who 'in a personal way continued a classicist tradition in the footsteps of Brahms'[42] and opposed the Central European trends from Wagner to Schoenberg, is based largely on his own experiences as a young composer at a time when Nielsen was the paragon in musical life. Maegaard explains that when he was admitted to the Academy of Music in 1945, 'it was frankly oozing with Carl Nielsen'.[43] Maegaard's main point, however, is that the problem is not Nielsen himself, but rather the myth: 'His spirit, that is, the image that posterity has formed of him and presented to the youth.'[44]

However, a distinction must also be made, for Maegaard, who was born in 1926, belongs to a generation that did not have a personal relationship with Nielsen. The generation of young composers in the 1920s had a more nuanced experience. Nielsen was of enormous importance to these composers, and for an otherwise sober person like Finn Høffding, who in the late 1920s embraced Nielsen's anti-Romantic approach and combined it with a younger generation's involvement in current social issues, Nielsen's death is portrayed as the loss of a father figure. In the memorial issue of *Dansk Musik Tidsskrift* Høffding wrote:

> What did Carl Nielsen mean to me? ... He was one of the greatest melodists I know; at a time when no one else cultivated melody, *pure* melody, he devoted his finest energies to it. In an effeminate age, when the subtleties of the mind were pampered by tonal narcosis, he knew how to make a triad bright and deep. Where others were interested in rare plants, hothouse plants, he struck gold. ... His way of thinking was highly original, his mind was open but at the same time searching. Thus, even in his old age, he never came close to becoming narrow-minded. ... He is my starting point, he is my musical educator ...[45]

Reading Høffding's assessment of Nielsen's individuality, the echo of Nielsen's formulations show how strongly he influenced the perception of himself. Equally important is the emphasis on the fact that Nielsen was still a searching and open-minded person in his later years. Høffding was one of those who moved from a fascination with the new, modernist music of the early 1920s to a view of Central European Expressionism as the last turbulence of Romanticism at the end of the decade. Around the time of Nielsen's death, Høffding was one of those who, together with the editor of *Dansk Musik Tidsskrift*, Gunnar Heerup, advocated the formation of a new musical culture in which Nielsen and Béla Bartók were the new role models.[46]

It is Heerup who expresses most clearly that Nielsen was not just someone to be admired or who overshadowed others, but someone who created a free space in which the young generation to which he belonged could find room and air:

> We young people … found in him not a conventional, shoulder-slapping sympathy, but an immediate, warm, deeply human understanding, which we sought in vain in his lineage. We have lived under the protection of the respect that surrounded his name.[47]

It is clear that at the time of his death Nielsen was well on his way to becoming a myth for posterity, and that he was partly caught up in his own self-presentation during his lifetime. But it is just as evident that he also acted as a mentor to the next generation, who not only had his writings and the great and popular Nielsen to aspire to. They experienced Nielsen as a composer whose uncompromising and deeply varied music, depending on the task he was trying to fulfil, showed them that they should not take everything in *Living Music* at face value.

Chapter 43

INQUISITIVENESS AND TENACITY

One fascinating aspect of a composer like Nielsen is his inquisitiveness. Unlike many of his European predecessors and colleagues, he never settled into a particular style or remained within a limited musical universe. On the other hand, it must be emphasised that the diverse ways in which he solved very different assignments never led him to be considered an eclectic, that is, someone without a recognisable musical physiognomy of their own. So there must indeed be something that makes it all cohere.

The other fascinating aspect of Nielsen is his tenacity. He has a strong imagination and a strong will, and once he has set his mind on a particular sound, it is difficult to dissuade him from achieving it. In 1890, as a very young composer, he played his String Quartet in F minor for the famous violinist Joseph Joachim at the Music Academy in Berlin. When Joachim subsequently criticised the very parts Nielsen loved most, he made no attempt to follow Joachim's advice. Yet he was not rigid in his continuing work as a composer. For the theatre, for example, he complied with their specific requests for new pieces of music and revisions of musical contributions, and in his collaboration with Thomas Laub he usually followed Laub's well-founded suggestions as to how to improve the setting of the songs.

There are, of course, a number of common features in Nielsen's music, and yet it is impossible to characterise it as always sounding like these features. To claim that the music does indeed have a particular sound suggests that the argument is circular: if you take the phrase 'Nielsen as we know him' as a starting point and select certain recognisable stylistic features as expressions of Nielsen's style, the result is precisely 'Nielsen as we know him'. And that is indeed true, because everything that sounds different has been eliminated in advance. It is impossible to capture a particular Nielsen style by trawling through his entire output for the stylistic features of his music and boiling them down to a distillate without harming the composer. The only way to do this is to dismiss large parts of his work and not allow them to count as the real Nielsen. But why is this the case?

On the one hand, Nielsen composed his music according to the purpose for which it was intended. It could therefore sound very different depending on whether it was to illustrate a love scene in a play, a knightly procession in a lied or a landscape in a symphony. Nielsen retained the approach to music that he had learned as a trained musician, namely that music should work according to the situation. In this sense, he works like a craftsman who sees his professional inventory of compositional resources as a tool with which to solve a task. On the other hand, it is precisely Nielsen's tenacity that is one of the hallmarks of his music, which never does exactly what is expected, but almost always moves in a surprising way or continues in an unpredictable direction. Having learned to expect the unexpected, listeners are disappointed when it does not happen, and so they may conclude that the unexpected is one of the qualities for which Nielsen is known.

One of the features that make it difficult to get a grip on where Nielsen stands is the means by which he argues when he wants to explain his views on music. Firstly, his formulations are rarely very precise, as he often uses metaphors or narratives to deal with the subject, believing that words cannot be used to say anything precise about what music is. Often a statement only makes sense when compared to his actions, such as when he translates an idea into a musical work. Secondly, Nielsen tends to express himself in such a way that his statements appear to be eternal truths, or at least something he has always believed. This is problematic because it is obvious that his views can change over time. Statements such as 'study the old masters' or the many references to the counterpoint of the Palestrina era can mean anything until they are realised in his actual compositions.

To illustrate how this can be misinterpreted, consider the reaction of Thomas Laub when he had attended the performance of *Saul and David* in 1902. When Nielsen and Laub were both in Rome in 1900, they spent many hours together discussing the need for a reform of music based on classical ideals. We will 'have *to come to terms with our art – and also with our outlook on life*', Laub wrote during their stay, imagining that the demands on art made by being surrounded by the classical treasures of Rome had also had an effect on Nielsen.[1] They talked about how Romanticism and musical culture were in decline and that there was a need for renewal, starting from scratch.

When Laub heard the result, as presented in *Saul and David*, he admitted that he neither understood nor believed in Nielsen's musical language: the problem was 'the tonal system of the melodies, the modulations, the harmonic composition of the notes', in short, almost everything.[2] The difference was that while Nielsen wanted to innovate by returning to the *principles* of the old polyphonic art and then applying them to the tonal language of his own time, Laub imagined that Nielsen would arrive at a new art that respected the rules of the motion of the individual voices in the old music.

The confusion reflects the fact that they used the same words but meant different things. Nielsen's reply to Laub drew on his experience of growing up in the countryside, explaining the value of fertiliser and the need for new seedlings to develop, sheltered by the weeds if they were to survive. The friendship between Nielsen and Laub was a strong one, even though they were indeed completely at odds with each other and remained so for many years. *En Snes danske Viser* (*A Score of Danish Songs*) was a successful collaboration, but when it came to hymn tunes and chorale settings they were at variance. Nielsen's cautious criticism of Laub's *Forspil og Melodier. Forsøg i Kirkestil* (*Preludes and Melodies. Attempts in Church Style*) (1909) was not recognised by Laub, who did not realise that it was even possible to question whether he had followed the rules. However, Laub made no secret of the fact that Nielsen's *Hymns and Spiritual Songs* were beyond what he could accept. Nielsen's stubbornness and tenacity is revealed by the fact that not a single note of the music was changed, with the exception of those suggested by his former pupil Paul Hellmuth.

Nielsen's urge for renewal and the way in which he achieved it is rooted in the fact that, as a young man in the 1890s, he belonged to the group of composers who became the moderns of the turn of the century. From around 1890, the group identified themselves as a generation representing the music and art after Wagner and Brahms. When Nielsen changed his position from Wagner admirer to Wagner critic in the early 1890s, it was not because he had become a sworn follower of Brahms. Brahms, too, belonged to the past, and it was not in the immediate past that Nielsen sought renewal. He wanted a de-Romanticisation, but he went forward from Romanticism, which is one of the reasons why it is possible to misinterpret Nielsen's way of thinking: one must always bear in mind that the starting point is that Nielsen already belongs to the modern. He never became a reactionary.

Similarly, his reluctance in the 1920s to use the words 'modern' or 'modernism' to describe his own music may have been an indication that he was sceptical of these two terms in particular. In studying Nielsen's music, it is clear that his youthful insistence on the need to arrive at something new – and that it was better to try than to remain with the old – is intact. When he was asked in one of his last interviews whether he was a modernist, it was based on the interviewer's outlining how – since Nielsen's *Symphonic Suite*, Op. 8, from the 1890s – he had understood Nielsen as truly modern. In an insightful way, the interviewer sketched how Nielsen went beyond Bach into the 'deeper layers of the earth', and thence arrived at

> his unique tonality, his thoroughly independent rhythms, his almost 'homespun' polyphony, the obvious and compelling logic of his dissonances: hence his entire physiognomy as a 'modernist' in the best sense of the word.[3]

Nielsen's response is marked by his refusal to be pigeonholed: 'Am I really so "modern" …? … In any case, I have never done the slightest thing to be "modern", but have simply composed as I have had to.'[4] The argument he uses here is that it is a prerequisite to follow the musical logic for the legitimacy of music. Indeed, this is the key argument of many twentieth-century modernists. This principle could take him beyond the confines of the tonal system, as when he created diatonic melodies based on symmetrical intervallic structures in his Fifth Symphony, or when he embarked on wild experiments in his Sixth Symphony. The advice he gives to a fictional younger composer in the interview also applies to himself: if it is going to be ugly, he says, let it be so extraordinarily ugly 'that our ears will fall off'.[5]

In the search for a unifying thread that binds this wide range of music together, it is futile to look for a common style that is expressed on the surface. The link must be sought at a deeper level, below the surface. In a 1928 interview, Nielsen tried to articulate this idea when asked about the connection between the great and the small, popular works:

> If you penetrate into the basic unit of my compositions, you will certainly find that this unit is the same in both the great symphonies and the small ballads.[6]

A unit or a cell is something that lies within the structure of music and is not a superficial phenomenon. Just as Nielsen speaks of the powerful and subtle forces within the material itself, in this case he is speaking of the musical material, the tonal material with which he has created his works. Some of the characteristics of his music that enable the listener to recognise it lie in the material and in the combinations of intervals that dominate the sound of his music.

One specific element is Nielsen's preference for minor thirds, which have the property of being less tonally stable, or – more to the point – having a greater potential to move effortlessly between different tonal universes. For example, the minor third dominates the major third in the melodic lines of all his piano works except the last, the *Three Piano Pieces*, Op. 59.[7] Another characteristic is the frequent alternation between major and minor in his melodies. In the First and Fourth symphonies, he makes this duality a programmatic point, building it into the basic material presented in the very first bars.

The combination of minor third and major second is common to many of his works and gives them a particular tonal quality. At the same time they act as an 'escape mechanism', for the longer he can hold on to such intervals, which tend less to define a fixed tonality, the longer he can keep the free flow and range of possibilities open. Indeed, Rued Langgaard recognised something central in Nielsen, for when he came up with the idea of imitating Nielsen in his own Sixth Symphony, he imbued the music with the interval structure of minor third and major second, combined with augmenting a few intervals in the melody to create a surprising motion, and by leaving the interval structure unchanged when shifting a motif up or down.[8]

There is also Nielsen's predilection for repeated notes, often staged with rhythmic emphasis, so that it becomes an essential part of the music's expression. It functions not only as a rhythmic but also as a melodic element. If we take the interval of a perfect unison seriously, that is, two identical pitches and therefore not really an interval (the distance between the two pitches is naught), it can be regarded as one of the basic intervals on which Nielsen builds his music.[9]

Overall, Nielsen's subtle handling of the rhythmic and metrical layers of the music, playing with balance and imbalance and with the listener's sense of time, is an element of paramount importance in Nielsen's approach to composing. He often creates a slight shift in accentuation or placement in time that transforms what would otherwise be banal into an experience.

Many of the techniques Nielsen uses in his attempt to move away from Romanticism are, indeed, the devices of Romantic music. Alternations between major and minor, modulations by thirds, passages of fluctuating or indeterminate tonality and surprising key changes are all found in Romantic music. Nielsen employs such techniques and takes the consequences of where they lead him. Thus he also works his way out of Romanticism. Combined with Nielsen's profound mastery of counterpoint, which enables him to create compelling logical modulations without the use of harmonic devices, this gives him the freedom he says he strives for: the freedom to move away from familiar keys and still be diatonically convincing. The combination allows Nielsen to compose at will, using all possible compositional means, precisely because he does not share the notion that modernity is bound up with the idea of musical progress that can only lead in one direction. He is sovereign in the solutions he chooses to shape his music.

An important basis for Nielsen's approach was his background as a professional musician. He had initially trained as a bugler in the regiment in Odense, before continuing as a violin student at the Academy of Music in Copenhagen. He gradually became a composer, based on the theory lessons he received at the Academy and his own experience as a musician, although he only really established himself in the years after graduating from the Academy, when he took private lessons with Orla Rosenhoff.

As a composer, Nielsen accepted commissions of all kinds and genres. Although he felt a sense of freedom when composing symphonies, that is, composing without any extraneous constraints, he also found commissions with predefined frameworks and tight deadlines exciting and approached them to the best of his ability. He could often get deeply involved in composing, but that did not mean that he behaved like a genius sitting in an ivory tower. Rather, he acted more like a master craftsman, trained as a musician and educated as a designer or architect, posing the question: how should a given task be approached in order to maximise its impact and utility?

In this sense, composing music for events, for use in the church, to improve children's singing in schools, for piano lessons or for singing at home at the piano is no less important than composing advanced music for the concert hall.

Nielsen's tenacity, his ability and willingness to go his own way, should not be misconstrued as meaning that he is an unaffected, isolated loner in the history of European music. It undermines the deeper understanding of what composers are capable of. They are so extremely integrated into the musical culture of their time and its roots that it seems pointless to look for role models in order to trace an 'influence' from a particular piece of music. All the music Nielsen knew and had played, and all his training in music theory and composition, had given him the tools to create something new without having heard it elsewhere. If this were not the case, it would be impossible to compose new music. Musical culture and the culture of the musicians is a basis rather than as an influence. It makes sense, then, to see Nielsen as a composer who is able to interact with the cultural trends and music-historical issues of his time and to present his own ideas of how they can be set to music. Nielsen is a European composer.

VI

NOTES AND INDEXES

Notes

Foreword
1 See CNU, CNB, Samtid and CNW.

Introduction
1 Samtid, 263.

I

Chapter 1
A PLACE IN THE WORLD
1 Topographic map, Nørre Søby, drawn 1863, revised 1885 and published 1886 (historiskekort.dk).
2 MfB; Childhood.
3 Jeppesen, 'De rejste ud – om Carl Nielsens familie som udvandrere', 90.
4 Cadastral map, Nr. Lyndelse By, drawn 1859 and used until 1895 (historiskekort.dk). Copy of surveyor's drawing, Nr. Lyndelse Sogns Lokalhistoriske Arkiv, A 62, Uglehuset.
5 Cadastral map, Nr. Lyndelse By, 1809–1859 and 1859–1895; cf. topographafic map, Videnskabernes Selskab, Fyn Nord og Slesvig, 1st edn. 1782 and 2nd edn. 1810 (historiskekort.dk).
6 RA, Census 1870, Odense Amt, Aasum Herred, Nr. Lyndelse Sogn. The survey applies to the part that is registered as belonging to Sortelung, with the two other areas being Lumby and Nr. Lyndelse By.
7 MfB, 27; Childhood, 25.
8 'Efterskrift', in MfB, 211–12.
9 MfB, 17; Childhood, 15–16.
10 MfB, 19.
11 MfB, 16–21, 48–49, 80; cf. cadastral map, Nr. Lyndelse By, 1859–1895.
12 MfB, 27–28, 33, 47.
13 Cf. http://www.iisg.nl/migration/ziegler/. The database covers the period 1778–1869.
14 MfB, 28; Childhood, 26–27. The shift from Rigsdaler and Skilling to Kroner and Ører was decided in 1873, effective from 1 January 1875 (Nationalbanken.dk, Historie/1875-1907).
15 MfB, 40; Childhood, 39–40.
16 MfB, 40; cf. Census 1870 and 1890, Odense Amt, Aasum Herred, Nørre Lyndelse Sogn.
17 MfB, 43; Childhood, 43.
18 MfB, 43.
19 Larsen, 'Carl Nielsens fædrene familie', 14–16.
20 Bramstrup Godsarkiv, RAO, Jordebog 1870, fol. 26, gives details on the property Frydenlund, which includes: the brickworks, matr. 36r, and Uglehuset, matr. 36t, with Niels Jørgensen and Hans Jensen as tenants. Niels Jørgensen's lease is dated '11 June 1861', and Hans Jensen's '25 April 1859'; cf. the accounts in Niels Jørgensen's notebook, OBM.
21 RA, Census 1870, Odense Amt, Aasum Herred, Nørre Lyndelse Sogn, fol. 25, p. 241.
22 MfB, 17, 20.
23 MfB, 20–21, quot. on 20; Childhood, 17–18.
24 Cf. Madsen, *Carl Nielsens Fyn*, 17, and Hansen, *En fynsk bondeslægts historie*, 51–53.
25 Hansen, *En fynsk bondeslægts historie*, 49–52.
26 Larsen, 'Carl Nielsens fædrene familie', 22–23.
27 Interview with Kirstine Godske, neé Kristiansen, born 9 May 1866, sound recording in Nr. Lyndelse Sogns Lokalhistoriske Arkiv, L 12.
28 Cf. MfB, 80–81.
29 MfB, 70; Childhood, 72–73.
30 MfB, 84; Childhood, 88.
31 MfB, 95.
32 MfB, 87; Childhood, 91.
33 'Personalia. Degne og Skolelærere', Official Register for Nørre Lyndelse Skole (1901-1919), RAO, Nr. Lyndelse Skole, NLS-5.
34 MfB, 35, 70; CNB 9:97, 10:43.
35 MfB, 35; Childhood, 34.
36 Interview with Kirstine Godske, Nr. Lyndelse Sogns Lokalhistoriske Arkiv, L 12.
37 Copy of a page from an examination record from Nr. Søby Skole in Nr. Lyndelse Sogns Lokalhistoriske Arkiv, A 16 Carl Nielsen. It has not been possible to locate

the original; cf. Nørr, *Skolen, præsten og kommunen*, 370–73.

38 RA, church register for Nr. Søby Sogn, 1877-1891, p. 80.
39 MfB, 96–97.
40 Copy of a page from an examination record in Nr. Lyndelse Sogns Lokalhistoriske Arkiv, A 16 Carl Nielsen.
41 Copy of the land register transcript of the purchase contract and deed in Nr. Lyndelse Sogns Lokalhistoriske Arkiv, A7 Niels Jørgensen; cf. Larsen, 'Carl Nielsens fædrene familie', 7.
42 Niels Jørgensen's notebook with the accounts for 1873, OBM.
43 Larsen, 'Carl Nielsens fædrene familie', 24–25; cf. MfB, 97–101.
44 Larsen, 'Carl Nielsens fædrene familie', 25; cf. MfB, 140–41, 149.
45 MfB, 17–19, quot. 17.
46 Meyer and Schandorf Petersen, *Carl Nielsen*, vol. 1, 13; MfB, 93.
47 Larsen, 'Carl Nielsens mødrene slægt', 1–4.
48 Larsen, 'Carl Nielsens mødrene slægt', 4–7.
49 Larsen, 'Carl Nielsens mødrene slægt', 8–12.
50 Larsen, 'Carl Nielsens mødrene slægt', 13; quot. from Odense City Court's probate record, 19 March 1874.
51 MfB, 93; Childhood, 98.
52 Larsen, 'Carl Nielsens mødrene slægt', 11.
53 Larsen, 'Carl Nielsens mødrene slægt', 17.
54 Cf. MfB, 102.
55 Larsen, 'Carl Nielsens fædrene familie', 1–3.
56 Larsen, 'Carl Nielsens fædrene familie', 5–6.
57 Larsen, 'Carl Nielsens mødrene slægt', 17.
58 Conduct book for Maren Kirstine Johansen, OBM, CNM 1989/0015.
59 MfB, 77. Frederik Jørgen Briand de Crivecoeur was pastor in Nr. Søby, 1839–1885.
60 Conduct book, OBM, CNM 1989/0015.
61 Larsen, 'Carl Nielsens fædrene familie', 8–10.
62 Larsen, 'Carl Nielsens fædrene familie', 11–12. When Niels Jørgensen leaves Fangel, the pastor notes him as journeyman painter in the graduation list (RA, Fangel Sogn, Til- og Afgangslister 1853-1875, p. 178).
63 Larsen, 'Carl Nielsens mødrene slægt', 18.
64 Larsen, 'Carl Nielsens fædrene familie', 12–13. In MfB, 154, the place is identified as the present 21 Albanivej.
65 MfB, 154, identifies the house as the present 94 Albanivej.
66 MfB, 88; cf. Childhood, 93. Until the construction of the community hall in 1878, he gave his lectures in the 'friskole'; cf. letter from Mads Bødker, below n. 71; Berntsen, *Erindringer fra Barndom og Ungdom*, 116–17, 172.
67 Berntsen, *Erindringer fra Barndom og Ungdom*, 9.
68 Pedersen, 'Chresten Kold'.
69 Korsgaard, 'Fra stand til folk – med kolske friskoler', 12.
70 Berntsen, *Erindringer fra Barndom og Ungdom*, 116, 172.
71 Undated letter [1921–1926] from Mads Rasmussen Bødker, Årslev, to Klaus Berntsen, in Klaus Berntsens Privatarkiv, RA 05131; cf. Cook, 'Et kig i arkivet'.
72 Berntsen, *Erindringer fra Barndom og Ungdom*, 172.
73 CNB 8:305.
74 Niels Jørgensen's notebook, OBM; MfB, 90; CNB 3:939. A fair copy of the arrangement for wind band, dedicated to Klaus Berntsen, was discovered in the Tivoli Gardens' archives in 2023.
75 CNB 1:571; cf. MfB, 140.
76 Nr. Lyndelse Sogns Lokalhistoriske Arkiv, A 76 Hans Larsen Privatarkiv, 'Nr. Lyndelse Friskole m.m.'.
77 CNB 2:438, 3:463, 3:650, 3:697.
78 MfB, 88; Childhood, 93.
79 CNB 7:290.
80 Berntsen, *Erindringer fra Barndom og Ungdom*, 97–120; Klaus Berntsen, *Erindringer fra Manddommens Aar*, 135.
81 Berntsen, *Erindringer fra Barndom og Ungdom*, 144, 172–78; Berntsen, *Erindringer fra Manddommens Aar*, 83.
82 CNB 7:412; Prik., 'Carl Nielsens bror mindes sin rige fynske barndom'.
83 MfB, 21–22, 91, 114.

84 CNB 2:444; CNL 191.
85 MfB, 45–46, 51.
86 Vorre, 'Spillemænd på Midtfyn', 65.
87 MfB, 45, 53.
88 Berntsen, *Erindringer fra Barndom og Ungdom*, 85.
89 MfB, 71; Childhood, 74.
90 Koudal, 'Spillemandsbøger', 23–64.
91 MfB, 90; Childhood, 94.
92 MfB, 21; Samtid, 48; CNB 2:444; CNL 191.
93 MfB, 35, cf. 70; Childhood, 34, cf. 73.
94 Nicolajsen, *Sang i landsbyskolen*, 33.
95 MfB, 82, 85, 96.
96 RA, Census 1855, 1860; the church records consistently state 'painter' in connection with the children's confirmations in 1870, 1877, 1881, 1885 and at the death of Caroline in 1879.
97 CNB 1:318, 1:325.
98 Højby Lokalhistoriske Arkiv; cf. Ødegaard (ed.), *Højby Forsamlingshus*, 16.
99 Niels Jørgensen's notebook, OBM.
100 Pedersen, 'Spillemanden Blinde Anders', 28–29; Vorre, 'Spillemænd på Midtfyn', 68, 73–74.
101 Minutes for Højby Skytteforening, Højby Lokalhistoriske Arkiv.
102 Meyer and Schandorf Petersen, *Carl Nielsen*, vol. 1, 15–16.
103 Madsen, *Carl Nielsens Fyn*, 25; MfB, 52.
104 MfB, 75.
105 Vorre, 'Spillemænd på Midtfyn', 74–76. The story about the bugle signals is based on Sonja Sørensen, 'Musiker Mads Pedersen "Pæsen"', published on landsbyhistorier.dk.
106 MfB, 83.
107 MfB, 25–26.
108 Petersen, 'Musikforeningen Braga', 46–63, gives an account of the repertoire in those music books in Museum Odense, which can be attributed with certainty to Braga.
109 MfB, 51, cf. Vorre, 'Spillemænd på Midtfyn', 58. The society is mentioned for the first time in *Fyens Stiftstidende*, 6 August 1873.
110 MfB, 52; Childhood, 53.
111 Madsen, *Carl Nielsens Fyn*, 34–37; MfB, 99–101.
112 MfB, 101; Childhood, 105.

Chapter 2
SYMPHONIES ARE FICTION
1 Dahlhaus, *Between Romanticism and Modernism*, 3.
2 CNB 2:436; CNL 189.
3 CNB 7:314.
4 Cf. Fjeldsøe, 'Musik ist anders', 32–38.
5 Cf. Samtid, 162–64.
6 Burnham, 'A. B. Marx'.
7 One paradigmatic example could be Marx, *Die Lehre von der musikalischen Komposition*. Most of Marx's examples come from Beethoven, whom he considers the prototype of a composer combining musical progression with a form that, in return, obtains balance and unity through the progression.
8 Cf. Fanning, 'Progressive Thematicism in Nielsen's Symphonies'.

Chapter 3
MUSICIAN IN ODENSE
1 Samtid, 57; quoted in MfB, 232.
2 In MfB, 101, Nielsen writes that the audition took place in July or August.
3 MfB, 101.
4 Matthiessen, *Danske byers folketal*.
5 Boje and Nielsen, *Moderne tider*, 448; *Statistisk Tabelværk. Fjerde Række, Litra A, Nr. 3. Folkemængden i Kongeriget Danmark den 1ste Februar 1880*, 134–35.
6 Thomsen, 'Odense som garnisonsby', 141.
7 Boje and Nielsen, *Moderne tider*, 32–94.
8 Boje and Nielsen, *Moderne tider*, 110–32.
9 Anon., *Katalog over den almindelige fynske Industri- og Landbrugs-Udstilling i Odense 1885*.
10 Gregersen, 'Kvæghandel', 510–12; Rosted, *Fra Kyst til Kyst*; Kristensen and Poulsen, *Danmarks byer i middelalderen*, 181.
11 Trap, *Statistisk-topographisk Beskrivelse af Kongeriget Danmark. Amterne Odense, Svendborg og Maribo*, 27.
12 Boje and Nielsen, *Moderne tider*, 120–24.

13 Olsen and Topsøe-Jensen (eds.), *H. C. Andersens Dagbøger*, vol. 7, 387.
14 Cf. the timeline in Olsen and Topsøe-Jensen (eds.), *H. C. Andersens Dagbøger*, vol. 7, ix, xiv.
15 MfB, 132–33.
16 Kryger, 'Carl Lendorf'; Sommer, *Den danske arkitektur*, 25–31.
17 Larsen, 'Begyndelsen af Carl Nielsens musikalske karriere', 10–12. A shorter version of the text is included in Larsen, 'Optur fra sumpen'.
18 Larsen, 'Optur fra sumpen', 179.
19 Larsen, 'Begyndelsen af Carl Nielsens musikalske karriere', 11; MfB, 84.
20 Larsen, 'Begyndelsen af Carl Nielsens musikalske karriere', 11–12; MfB, 111.
21 In MfB, 120, Nielsen mentions that the field exercise at Hald took place during the summer of 1881. However, it was in the summer of 1880 that the Sixteenth Battalion participated in the exercise; cf. Jacobsen, "Fast i Nød", 202–4.
22 Larsen, 'Begyndelsen af Carl Nielsens musikalske karriere', 12–13; MfB, 113–14.
23 Larsen, 'Begyndelsen af Carl Nielsens musikalske karriere', 14–15; MfB, 113.
24 Myrtue, 'Carl Nielsens Odense', 101–4.
25 Bokkenheuser, *Blade af 16de Bataillons Historie*, 28–35; Friis, *Militærmusikken*, 19–22.
26 Their place of birth appears in the census for city of Odense 1870. The information is summarised in www.odensedatabasen.dk.
27 Numerous adverts appear in *Fyens Stiftstidende*, e.g. 15 August 1877 and 7 October 1882.
28 Schmidt, *Meddelelser om Skuespil og Theaterforhold*, 249.
29 Adverts in *Fyens Stiftstidende*, e.g. 7 October 1882.
30 Adverts in *Fyens Stiftstidende*, quot. 1 June 1872; *Fyens Stiftstidende*, 14 December 1875, 2 edn., and 13 October 1870.
31 *Fyens Stiftstidende*, 14 April 1877.
32 *Fyens Stiftstidende*, 17 May 1866.
33 MfB, 124.
34 MfB, 103.
35 RA, Fynske Livregiment (6. Regiment), 16. Bataillon, A. Indgående skrivelser, A85, 1880, 30. januar 1880.
36 Letter from Captain Jacobsen to the Sixteenth Battalion, RA, Fynske Livregiment (6. Regiment), 16. Bataillon, A. Indgående skrivelser, A85, 1880, 30. januar 1880.
37 Nielsen's connection to the Lance Corporal School is evident from his pedigree; cf. Vorre, 'Spillemand Carl August Nielsen', 51. The weekly timetables for the classes from 1 January 1880, showing the distribution of the subjects: RA, Fynske Livregiment (6. Regiment), 16. Bataillon, A. Indgående skrivelser, A85, 1880.
38 In MfB, 104, it appears that the teaching continued at least until the merging of the battalions 1 November 1880.
39 MfB, 104; Childhood, 109.
40 MfB, 132.
41 The regiment's instrumental parts are kept at RA, Fynske Livregiments Musikkorps, Fynske Livregiments Musikkorps, V. Nodesamling.
42 MfB, 106; Childhood, 111.
43 MfB, 106.
44 MfB, 121.
45 MfB, 120.
46 Anon., *Horn-Signaler*, 16, 24.
47 MfB, 107.
48 MfB, 126; Childhood, 128.
49 MfB, 107.
50 MfB, 111.
51 Roth, *The Radetzky March*, 23.
52 *Fyens Stiftstidende*, 27 May 1879.
53 The announcement is reported in *Fyens Stiftstidende*, 27 May 1879.
54 *Fyens Stiftstidende*, 27 May 1879.
55 Petersen et al., *Byens ansigt*, 24–36.
56 *Fyens Stiftstidende*, 27 May 1879.
57 See articles in *Fyens Stiftstidende*, 28 May and 10 June 1879.
58 Topp, *Dengang i Odense*, 68.
59 Dyrbye, 'Alfred Helsengreen's Samling', 56.
60 Cf. the announcements of the eleven concerts in the autumn of 1883 in *Fyens Stiftstidende*.

61 RA, Fynske Livregiments Musikkorps, Fynske Livregiments Musikkorps, V. Nodesamling, 26–29, stemmesæt R, stemmebog 23, nr. 42.
62 The Danish National Archives holds twenty-eight instrumental parts from the fifth regiment of which around half of them date to Nielsen's time in Odense and earlier. RA, Fynske Livregiments Musikkorps, Fynske Livregiments Musikkorps, V. Nodesamling.
63 *Illustreret Tidende*, 24 (1883), 418.
64 Grotjahn, *Die Sinfonie*, 143–54; Weber, 'The Rise of the Classical Repertoire'.
65 Cf. Hansen, 'Regimentsmusik i Odense', 156.
66 Weber, *The Great Transformation*, 208–31.
67 RA, Fynske Livregiments Musikkorps, Fynske Livregiments Musikkorps, V. Nodesamling, 26–29, stemmesæt I, 12–19.
68 RA, Fynske Livregiments Musikkorps, Fynske Livregiments Musikkorps, V. Nodesamling, 12–19, stemmesæt I.
69 The work is in the set of parts, Æ, in RA, Fynske Livregiments Musikkorps, Fynske Livregiments Musikkorps, V. Nodesamling, 39. The partbooks contain dates from October 1885 when Nielsen was no longer in the regiment.
70 The works are in the set of parts, T, in RA, Fynske Livregiments Musikkorps, Fynske Livregiments Musikkorps, V. Nodesamling, 31–32.
71 MfB, 127.
72 The works are in the set of parts, T and E, respectively.
73 MfB, 127; Childhood, 129.
74 MfB, 182–83.
75 Keyper, *Militair Musik-Skole*, foreword. On Keyper, see Thrane, *Fra Hofviolonernes Tid*, 269.
76 Keyper, *Militair Musik-Skole*, 18.
77 Kongsted et al., *Masser af messing*, 34.
78 Kongsted et al., *Masser af messing*, 35.
79 MfB, 103.
80 MfB, 106; Childhood, 110.
81 Keyper, *Militair Musik-Skole*, 67.
82 Keyper, *Militair Musik-Skole*, 67.

83 MfB, 114; Childhood, 117.
84 Cf. CNB 2:426; CNL 188.
85 CNB 5:574; CNL 400.
86 MfB, 115; Childhood, 118.
87 CNB 2:426; CNL 188.
88 MfB, 114.
89 Nielsen mentions that the lessons with Carl Larsen commenced after the field exercise at Hald (MfB, 127); cf. CNB 2:425; CNL 187.
90 Petersen, *Odense Musikforening*, 75–77.
91 Berntsen, *Erindringer fra Manddommens Aar*, 142–43.
92 Hanslick, 'Miszellen', 220: 'Zu den einflußreichsten und wohlthätigsten Mitteln musikalische Bildung zu verbreiten, gehören unstreitig die Musikalien-Leihanstalten.'
93 Hanslick, *Aus meinem Leben*, vol. 1, 40: 'mein musicalisches Futter'. Cf. Widmaier, *Der deutsche Musikalienleihhandel*, 9–11.
94 Lehrmann, 'Læseforening og lejebibliotek'.
95 A copy of Woldemar, *Varulven. Skuespil i 2 Akter*, was purchased in 1894 for Nyborg Klub og Sangforening, receiving the serial number 4,649.
96 Martino, *Die deutsche Leihbibliothek*, 318.
97 Martino, *Die deutsche Leihbibliothek*, 630.
98 Widmaier, *Der deutsche Musikalienleihhandel*, 154.
99 Widmaier, *Der deutsche Musikalienleihhandel*, 136–41.
100 Skjerne, *H.C. Lumbye*, 40–41.
101 Fog, *Musikhandel*, 69–70.
102 In 1873, the total number of music publications in Braunstein's rental library was 9,000, as shown in three catalogues from 1853, 1871 and 1873; cf. Anon., *Katalog des Musikalien-Leih-Instituts von Matthäus Wilhelm Braunstein*; Anon., *Catalog over C. Braunsteins musikalske Leiebibliothek i Odense*; Anon., *Første Tillæg til Catalogen over Musikalier, som erholdes tilleie eller tilkjøbs i C. E. Braunsteins Musik- og Instrumenthandel i Odense*.
103 Anon., *Handbuch der musikalischen Literatur oder allgemeines systematisch geordnetes Verzeichnis*; Fog, *Musikhandel*, 46–49.

104 Cf. http://www.hofmeister.rhul.ac.uk/2008/index.html.
105 Cf. foreword in Anon., *Catalog over C. Braunsteins musikalske Leiebibliothek i Odense.*
106 Fog, *Musikhandel*, 69.
107 Three printed catalogues of Gundestrup's assortment are preserved in KB: a main catalogue from 1869 comprising 1,292 titles, and two supplements from 1870 and 1871 listing 450 titles in all.
108 MfB, 114; Childhood, 117.
109 MfB, 128–29; Childhood, 130–31.
110 Yearly adverts in *Fyens Stiftstidende* from the end of January into March.
111 Schmidt, *Meddelelser om Skuespil og Theaterforhold*, 249; MfB, 183.
112 Fellow, *Vil Herren ikke hilse på sin Slægt*, 12–14; cf. 'Kasse Bog for Odense Theater Begyndt Juni 1865', RAO, Odense Teater GD001 Kassebog 1865-1950, 1865-1894.
113 Samtid, 49; Lynge, *Danske Komponister*, 93.
114 An index of the theatre orchestra's music archives, including overtures and the music that was employed as entr'actes, 'Odense Teater. Katalog over Musikalier. 1921', RAO, GD001. Odense Teater 1888-1947. Teaterkatalog 1888-1947 m.m. Music which was part of the theatre plays is, however, located among the material of the theatre companies. A large collection is preserved in RAO, Odense Teater 1796-1970 Musikforlæg. Cf. Regnskabsbog 1882-1883 for Thomas Cortes' teaterselskab, RAO GD001 Odense Teater 1854-1889. Regnskabsbog 1876-1889.
115 Cf. Odense Stadsarkiv, Odense Teater, Teaterprogrammer 1878-1879.
116 *Uddrag af Odense Byraads Forhandlinger*, (1880), 91; *Uddrag af Odense Byraads Forhandlinger*, (1882), 285–88. Cf. MfB, 195.

Chapter 4
DEPARTURE

1 MfB, 177. On Jespersen's and Nielsen's relationship, see CNB 2:220; CNL 151, and Samtid, 546–48. Cf. Jespersen, *Oplevelser*, 169–72.
2 CNB 2:425; CNL 187.
3 CNB 2:425; CNL 187.
4 MfB, 147. Concerning Schiørring and Tofte, see Bendix, *Af en Kapelmusikers Erindringer*, 17–20.
5 Petersen, *Odense Musikforening gennem et halvt Aarhundrede*, 88. The concert is mentioned in *Fyens Stiftstidende*, 8 October 1883.
6 Berntsen, *Erindringer fra Manddommens Aar*, 143.
7 MfB, 148.
8 Harder, 'Carl Nielsen'.
9 CNB 2:421, 2:422, 2:425, 2:426, 2:432, 2:440, 2:442; 2:445, 2:446; CNL 187, 188, 190, 192.
10 Harder, 'Carl Nielsen', 157.
11 CNB 2:444; CNL 191; jf. *Søndagsbladet. Ugeblad for Land og By*, 11 June 1905, 188–90.
12 MfB, 147.
13 MfB, 148.
14 MfB, 148–52.
15 MfB, 149; Childhood, 150.
16 MfB, 146–52.
17 Eskildsen, 'Nielsen and Gade', 149–50. However, in a biography from 1901 he explains that he visited Copenhagen in the autumn of 1883, CNB 2:193.
18 MfB, 146. Cf. CNB 2:444; CNL 191.
19 RA, Hæren (Infanteriet), Fynske Livregiment, E. Rapportbøger, E1, 1880-1885, Rapportbog 1883-1884.
20 RA, Det Kongelige Danske Musikkonservatorium, Elevsager/undervisning: Optagelsesprotokoller, 6, 1884-1894.
21 RA, Det Kongelige Danske Musikkonservatorium, Elevsager/undervisning: Anmeldte elever, 382, 1866-1885.
22 CNB 1:501; CNL 96.
23 CNB 1:533; CNL 109.
24 RA, Hæren (Infanteriet), Fynske Livregiment, G. Stambøger, G2, UOFF 1880-1913, '6. Regiment. Stambog for Underofficerer o.l. 1/11-1880 til 31/3-1892', fol. 86.
25 MfB, 150; Childhood, 151.
26 Fellow, *Vil Herren ikke hilse på sin Slægt*, 26–44.
27 MfB, 146; Childhood, 147.

Chapter 5
NIELSEN'S COPENHAGEN

1. Busck and Poulsen (eds.), *Danmarks historie*, 437. The chapter is a revised version of Engberg, *Carl Nielsen og århundredeskiftekulturen*, 79–95.
2. Busck and Poulsen (eds.), *Danmarks historie*, 267.
3. Zerlang, *Bylivets kunst*, 11.
4. Wassard, *Nørrevold, Østervold og Kastellet*, 79.
5. CNB 1:510; CBL 99.
6. Zerlang, *Herman Bangs København*, 63.
7. Jensen and Smidt, *Rammerne Sprænges*, 157–58.
8. Hvidt, 'Københavns Rådhus', 223.
9. Gnudtzmann and Linn, *Stor-København*, vol. 2, 19.
10. Røllum-Larsen, 'Træk af musiklivet i København', 8–9.
11. Gnudtzmann and Linn, *Stor-København*, vol. 2, 427.
12. Jørgensen, 'København', 743; Mortensen, 'Det uforfærdede øje', 23.
13. Jørgensen, 'København', 776.
14. Mortensen, 'Det uforfærdede øje', 24.
15. Meyer and Schandorf Petersen, *Carl Nielsen*, vol. 1, 57.
16. Hatt, *Foraarsbølger*, 154.
17. Fellow, *Vil Herren ikke hilse på sin Slægt*, 48.
18. Faber, *Frederiksstaden og Nyhavn*, 267.
19. Cf. *Kjøbenhavns Adressecomptoirs Efterretninger*, 20 November 1883; *Kjøbenhavns Adressecomptoirs Efterretninger*, 30 November 1883; *Kjøbenhavns Adressecomptoirs Efterretninger*, 18 April 1884.
20. Cf. Krack (ed.), *Vejviser for Kjøbenhavn og Frederiksberg for 1884*; Krack (ed.), *Vejviser for Kjøbenhavn og Frederiksberg for 1885*.
21. Bang, *Stuk*, 40.
22. Faber, *Frederiksstaden og Nyhavn*, 82.
23. Faber, *Frederiksstaden og Nyhavn*, 82.
24. Jørgensen, 'København', 761.
25. Fellow, *Vil herren ikke hilse på sin Slægt*, 49–51.
26. Cf. Krack (ed.), *Vejviser for Kjøbenhavn og Frederiksberg for 1881*; Krack (ed.), *Vejviser for Kjøbenhavn og Frederiksberg for 1884*.
27. *Kjøbenhavns Adressecomptoirs Efterretninger*, 14 February 1883.
28. Fellow, *Vil herren ikke hilse på sin Slægt*, 49–51.
29. Meyer and Schandorf Petersen, *Carl Nielsen*, vol. 1, 60.
30. Cf. Krack (ed.), *Vejviser for Kjøbenhavn og Frederiksberg for 1885*; Krack (ed.), *Vejviser for Kjøbenhavn og Frederiksberg for 1886*. Cf. Samtid, 116–19.
31. Jensen and Smidt, *Rammerne sprænges*, 178.
32. Christiansen, *Anne Marie Carl-Nielsen*, 41.
33. Jørgensen, 'København', 773.
34. Fellow, *Vil herren ikke hilse på sin Slægt*, 33.
35. Hatt, *Foraarsbølger*, 85.
36. Lange, 'Glade dage i 1890'erne', 47.
37. Clausen, *Mennesker paa min Vej*, 20.
38. *Berlingske Tidende*, 28 August 1891.
39. Faber, *Frederiksstaden og Nyhavn*, 11–14.
40. Cf. advert in *Dagens Nyheder*, 11 November 1891.
41. Jørgensen, 'København', 761.
42. Krack (ed.), *Vejviser for Kjøbenhavn og Frederiksberg for 1892*.
43. *Berlingske Tidende*, 10 September 1892.
44. CNB 1:347.
45. CNB 1:349.
46. Lange, 'Glade dage i 1890'erne', 52.
47. Wassard, *Nørrevold, Østervold og Kastellet*, 56.
48. Telmanyi, *Mit Barndomshjem*, 24.
49. Faber, *Frederiksstaden og Nyhavn*, 135.
50. Faber, *Frederiksstaden og Nyhavn*, 148–49.
51. Telmanyi, *Mit Barndomshjem*, 44.
52. Gnudtzmann and Linn, *Stor-København*, vol. 1, 229–30. Concerning the concerts, cf. Meyer and Schandorf Petersen, *Carl Nielsen*, vol. 1, 100–3, 153–54.
53. Jørgensen, 'København', 770.
54. Larsen, *Det gamle København*, 81.
55. Cf. Krack (ed.), *Vejviser*.
56. Krack (ed.), *Vejviser for Kjøbenhavn og Frederiksberg med Omegn for 1899*; Krack (ed.), *Vejviser for Kjøbenhavn og Frederiksberg med Omegn for 1900*; Krack (ed.), *Vej-

viser for Kjøbenhavn og Frederiksberg med Omegn for 1901.

57 Telmanyi, *Mit Barndomshjem*, 35–36.
58 Telmanyi, *Mit Barndomshjem*, 38.
59 From 10 May the address 5 Ny Toldbodgade appears in Nielsen's letters, so they probably moved on the third Tuesday in April, which was one of the two annual fixed days on which tenants could move.
60 Faber, *Frederiksstaden og Nyhavn*, 412; Telmanyi, *Mit Barndomshjem*, 64.
61 Cf. CNU I/1, xxvii–xviii.
62 Cf. Telmanyi, *Mit Barndomshjem*, 64. However, the actual work on the opera took place before the Nielsen family moved to Ny Toldbodgade.
63 Christiansen, *Anne Marie Carl-Nielsen*, 69.
64 Christiansen, *Anne Marie Carl-Nielsen*, 95.
65 Meyer and Schandorf Petersen, *Carl Nielsen*, vol. 1, 227.
66 An income of 4,000 Kroner a year was the minimum to be considered part of the upper middle class in Copenhagen at the turn of the century, cf. Lauring, *Københavnerliv*, 115.
67 Cf. note to CNB 2:165; CNL 142.
68 Cf. Nørtoft, 'Første Verdenskrig betød stigende priser'.
69 Christiansen, *Anne Marie Carl-Nielsen*, 140.
70 Bierlich, *Excentriske slægtskaber*, 136–38.
71 Christiansen, *Anne Marie Carl-Nielsen*, 187.
72 CNB 3:520.
73 Cf. note to CNB 3:520.
74 Gotved, *Barn i Gymnastikhuset*, 20.
75 Christiansen, *Anne Marie Carl-Nielsen*, 110.
76 Cf. Krack (ed.), *Vejviser*.
77 Telmanyi, *Mit barndomshjem*, 70.
78 CNB 3:657.
79 Telmanyi, *Mit barndomshjem*, 70.
80 RA, census, 1 February 1911, 53 Vodroffsvej (p. 103f.) also includes a transport behaviour survey.
81 Linvald, *Gammelholm og Frederiksholm*, 237.
82 Linvald, *Gammelholm og Frederiksholm*, 238.
83 Telmanyi, *Mit barndomshjem*, 105.
84 Telmanyi, *Mit barndomshjem*, 38.

Chapter 6
THE ACADEMY OF MUSIC

1 Sørensen, *Niels W. Gade*, 17–20, 69; Thrane, *Fra Hofviolonernes Tid*, 383.
2 Hetsch, *Det kongelige danske Musikkonservatorium*, 5; Schiørring, *Musikkens historie i Danmark*, vol. 3, 29.
3 Keld, 'Rids af Giuseppe Sibonis virksomhed', 57–78.
4 Hammerich, *Kjøbenhavns Musikkonservatorium*, 10.
5 Drachmann, *Hornung & Møller Aktieselskab*.
6 Hetsch, *Det kongelige danske Musikkonservatorium*, 30.
7 Røllum-Larsen, *Impulser i Københavns koncertrepertoire*, vol. 1, 56.
8 Hammerich, *Kjøbenhavns Musikkonservatorium*, 49.
9 *Illustreret Tidende*, 24 (1882), 112.
10 Thrane, *Fra Hofviolonernes Tid*, 323. The two pedagogical treatises are *Theoretisk-praktisk Violin-Skole for Begyndere* (København: C. C. Lose & Delbanco, 1838); *Fuldstandig theoretisk-praktisk Violin-Skole. Uddraget af Mozart's, Rode's og Kreutzer's store Violinskoler til Brug for Begyndere* (København: C. C. Lose, s.a.).
11 Phillips, *The Leipzig Conservatory*, 244; Wasserloos, *Das Leipziger Konservatorium*, 28–38, 85–89; Fjeldsøe, 'The Leipzig Model and Its Consequences'.
12 Schiørring, *Musikkens i historie i Danmark*, vol. 3, 84, 163.
13 Hammerich, *Kjøbenhavns Musikkonservatorium*, 39–41.
14 Hetsch, *Det kongelige danske Musikkonservatorium*, 25–26. Nielsen mentions that Gade himself suggested that he be admitted on a scholarship, cf. CNB 1:533; CNL 109.
15 Printed pamphlet with the title 'Kjøbenhavns Musikconservatorium', 1870: RA, Det Kongelige Danske Musikkonservato-

rium, Elevsager/undervisning: Elev- og lærerlister.
16 Letter from Viggo Bielefeldt to Angul Hammerich, in which he provides Hammerich with information about his affiliation as a teacher, RA, Det Kongelige Danske Musikkonservatorium, Almindelige korrespondancesager, 1866-1919.
17 Letter from Viggo Bielefeldt to Angul Hammerich, RA, Det Kongelige Danske Musikkonservatorium, Almindelige korrespondancesager, 1866-1919.
18 Hagen, 'Bielefeldt, Viggo Emil', 191.
19 Hammerich, *Kjøbenhavns Musikkonservatorium*, 18; Hetsch, *Det kongelige danske Musikkonservatorium*, 13.
20 Hammerich, *Kjøbenhavns Musikkonservatorium*, 23; Hetsch, *Det kongelige danske Musikkonservatorium*, 17–18.
21 CNB 1:139; CNL 30.
22 CNB 2:98, 2:234.
23 CNB 3:152; CNL 221.
24 Samtid, 489.
25 Quot. in CNU II/12, x.
26 RA, Det Kongelige Danske Musikkonservatorium, Elevsager/undervisning: Elevprotokoller, 13, 1883-88, protocols 1884–85 and 1885–86.
27 RA, Det Kongelige Danske Musikkonservatorium, Elevsager/undervisning: Elevprotokoller, 13, 1883-88, protocols 1884–85 and 1885–86. The teachers kept absence lists which show that Nielsen was ill or 'unwell' eight times in Matthison-Hansen's classes; in comparison he had only one single cancellation in three years in Rosenhoff's theory classes. RA, Det Kongelige Danske Musikkonservatorium, Elevsager/undervisning: Forsømmelsesprotokoller, May 1874–July 1885, August 1885–August 1894.
28 Samtid, 589–90.
29 RA, Det Kongelige Danske Musikkonservatorium, Elevsager/undervisning: Testimonier, 379, vol. 1, 1872-98, p. 79.
30 Allen, *August Jaeger*, 7.
31 KB, NKS 2052, fol.
32 Valdemar Tofte's book of remembrance kept at Nationalmuseet, Musikmuseet. Clara Tofte's sketches for a major biography of Valdemar Tofte in KB, NKS 2052, fol. Two violin bows were also presented to the museum (MMCCS D 124a and MMCCS D 124b), cf. Hammerich, 'Musikhistorisk Museum', 62–68. Thanks are due to curator Marie Martens, Nationalmuseet, Musikmuseet, for information on these materials.
33 *Kjøge Avis*, 10 September 1888.
34 Quot. in Clausen (ed.), *Til Minde om Valdemar Tofte*, 76. See also Røllum-Larsen, 'En dansk violinist i udlandet', 31–32.
35 Frederik Schnedler-Petersen's contribution to Valdemar Tofte's book of remembrance, 55, dated January 1916 (Nationalmuseet, Musikmuseet; underlining original).
36 Clausen (ed.), *Til Minde om Valdemar Tofte*, 25, 37. Tofte's music collection, which comprises 185 volumes according to a manuscript list, is housed in the library of Det Kongelige Danske Musikkonservatorium.
37 Schedule (presumably from 1867–69) prepared by Gade with the title 'Timetable for Mr Tofte': Valdemar Tofte's book of remembrance, 127 (Nationalmuseet, Musikmuseet). See also Tofte's teaching diary for 1867–69, in which he made notes on his students' progress: RA, Det Kongelige Danske Musikkonservatorium, Elevsager/undervisning: Undervisningsdagbøger, 376.
38 Sørensen (ed.), *Niels W. Gade og hans europæiske kreds*, letter no. 1208.
39 RA, Det Kongelige Danske Musikkonservatorium, Elevsager/undervisning: Elevprotokoller, 13.
40 Eskildsen, 'Nielsen and Gade, 154.
41 CNB 2:218.
42 Behrend (ed.), *Minder om Niels W. Gade*, 85. Cf. CNB 1:102, 1:139, 1:156; CNL 30, 35.
43 CNB 1:178; CNL 40.
44 CNB 1:109, 1:156, 1:162; CNL 35.
45 CNB 1:137, 1:165; CNL. 29.

46 CNB 1:166.
47 Samtid, 50.
48 Nielsen kept many of his written exercises from his time at the Academy. For an overview of their location, see the CNS catalogue (under CNS 359), which includes references to other locations.
49 See printed pamphlet entitled 'Kjøbenhavns Musikconservatorium', dated 1870: RA, Det Kongelige Danske Musikkonservatorium, Elevsager/undervisning: Elev- og lærerlister; Hammerich, Kjøbenhavns Musikkonservatorium, 38.
50 Behrend (ed.), Minder om Niels W. Gade, 83-84.
51 Hammerich, Kjøbenhavns Musikkonservatorium, 35. In a letter to Hammerich, Rosenhoff writes in more detail about his teaching: RA, Det Kongelige Danske Musikkonservatorium, Almindelige korrespondancesager, 1866-1919, letter dated 3 July 1891.
52 CNB 2:446; CNL 192.
53 RA, Det Kongelige Danske Musikkonservatorium, Elevsager/undervisning: Elevprotokoller, 13, 1883-88, protocol for 1884–85.
54 Nielsen's transcription in CNS 359.
55 Gebauer, Exempelbog til Harmonilæren.
56 Rasmussen, Exempelbog til Harmonilæren af Prof. JOH. CHR. GEBAUER; Lange, Kort Forklaring til 'Exempelbog til Harmonilære'.
57 Richter, Die Grundzüge der musikalischen Formen; Richter, Lehrbuch der Harmonie; Richter, Lehrbuch des einfachen und doppelten Contrapunkts.
58 Cf. introd. dated September 1882, Gebauer and Bondesen, Harmonilære af Ernst Fr. Richter.
59 Rosenhoff, 450 firstemmige Opgaver. The treatise was issued as three collections comprising two booklets in each. They do not include the year of publication, but the plate numbers suggest a possible dating, cf. Fog, Musikhandel, 215.
60 Cohn [Haste], Nøgle til Løsning af Orla Rosenhoffs firstemmige Opgaver.
61 Samtid, 140.

62 Nielsen numbered many of his exercises on the loose folios preserved in CNS 359. It is thus possible to find the following exercises from Rosenhoff's treatises: Collection 1, second booklet, nos. 43 and 44; Collection 2, first booklet, nos. 54 and 55; Collection 2, second booklet, no. 36; Collection 3, second booklet, nos. 40 and 41.
63 Museum Odense has two of Rosenhoff's Collections, which belonged to Nielsen: Collection 1, second booklet, and Collection 3, second booklet. The latter is the second edition from 1904 with a dedication 'To Carl Nielsen from his old, devoted friend Orla Rosenhoff / September 1904'.
64 Rosenhoff, 450 firstemmige Opgaver, introd. to Collection 1, booklet 1.
65 Rosenhoff, 450 firstemmige Opgaver, introd. to Collection 1, booklet 1.
66 Rosenhoff, 450 firstemmige Opgaver, introd. to Collection 1, booklet 1.
67 Menke, 'Generalbass'; Diergarten, 'Romantic Thoroughbass'; Moe, 'Tracing Compositional and Writing Processes in Sources'.
68 Weyse, Choral-Melodier til den evangelisk christelige Psalmebog harmonisk bearbeidet.
69 Weyse, Choral-Melodier til den evangelisk christelige Psalmebog harmonisk bearbeidet, third edn.
70 Private ownership.
71 CNS 359.
72 Richter, Lehrbuch des einfachen und doppelten Contrapunkts, 64–73; Richter, Lehrbuch der Harmonie, 150–56.
73 CNB 6:414; CNL 445.
74 Bellermann, Der Contrapunkt; Richter, Lehrbuch des einfachen und doppelten Contrapunkts.
75 Bellermann, Der Contrapunkt, xi; Richter, Lehrbuch des einfachen und doppelten Contrapunkts, 8–13.
76 The manuscript book is OBM, CNM/1980/0007. Here we have transcripts of Bellermann, Der Contrapunkt, 102, and Cherubini, Cours de contrepoint, 69–70.
77 Nielsen's transcription of the music examples from the manuscript book, CNS 359;

Nielsen recommended Bellermann's treatise to Knud Harder (CNB 2:516) and later named it, as well as the treatises of Cherubini and Fux, as monuments in the history of counterpoint theory (CNB 11:218; CNL 696).

78 Note added on the inside cover of the book, OBM, CNM/1980/0007.
79 I.e. Fux's Ionian, Dorian, and Phrygian subjects. Nielsen's exercises employing these three subjects are in CNS 359.
80 CNS 359.
81 CNB 3:285; CNL 225.
82 Sketches and fair copies to the Bach fugues in CNS 359. Cf. CNU IV/1, 271–80.
83 CNU IV/1, xxviii–xxix.
84 CNB 1:633; CNL 127.
85 Hetsch, *Det kongelige danske Musikkonservatorium*, 56.
86 CNB 1:557.
87 Eskildsen, 'Nielsen and Gade', 156–59; CNB 1:46.
88 Jensen, 'The Rosenhoff affair'; Hauge, 'Carl Nielsens første opus'.
89 CNB 1:13; CNL 6; Schnedler-Petersen, *Et Liv i Musik*, 19.
90 The printed list of members for the season 1886–87 shows 'Nielsen, Carl, musician'. This is confirmed by the list of members for the season 1888–89, referring to Nielsen as 'Royal Musician'. Cf. KB, Kontorchef Withs scrapbøger, including the lists.
91 On 13 February 1889, Nielsen joined Anton Svendsen, Christian Petersen, Kristian Sandby and Frederik Hansen in the performance of his own string quintet (CNW 59). On 18 December that same year, Nielsen played his string quartet Op. 13 (CNW 55) with Holger Møller, Kristian Sandby and Frits Bendix.
92 An advert in *Nationaltidende*, 2 October 1886, explicitly states that Nielsen played 'with permission of the Academy'.
93 Hetsch, *Det kongelige danske Musikkonservatorium*, 18, 56.
94 *Fyens Stiftstidende*, 21 August 1885.
95 *Fyens Stiftstidende*, 21 August and 22 August 1885.
96 *Fyens Stiftstidende*, 10 August 1886.
97 *Fyens Stiftstidende*, 12 August 1886.
98 David and Hermann (eds.), *Violin-Concerte von Louis Spohr. Concerto XI*.
99 *Fyens Stiftstidende*, 12 August 1886.
100 Fabricius, *Træk af dansk Musiklivs Historie*, 383; Røllum-Larsen, *Impulser i Københavns koncertrepertoire*, vol. 1, 58.
101 *Dagens Nyheder*, 13 October 1886.
102 Neiiendam, *Det kongelige Teaters Historie*, vol. 4, 145, 163; Krogh, 'L.C. Tørsleff'.
103 *Nationaltidende*, 12 October 1886.
104 *Nationaltidende*, 16 November 1887.
105 Hetsch, *Det kongelige danske Musikkonservatorium*, 150. On Minna Hohn, cf. https://www.odensedatabasen.dk/kilde/person/18639999021.
106 *Fyens Stiftstidende*, 28 December 1886.
107 Concert programme in *Fyens Stiftstidende*, 24 December 1886. On Nielsen's final exam at the Academy, see Eskildsen, 'Nielsen and Gade', 154.
108 Røllum-Larsen, *Impulser i Københavns koncertrepertoire*, vol. 1, 56; *Social-Demokraten*, 22 March and 20 April 1887.

Chapter 7
MUSICIAN IN COPENHAGEN

1 Anon., *Haandbog under Den nordiske Industri-, Landbrugs- og Kunstudstilling i Kjøbenhavn 1888*, 105, 110, 117–18, 121.
2 Bauer, 'Udstillingen 1888 og dens Forgængere', 2.
3 Quot. in Kristensen, *Georg Carstensen*, 188–89.
4 Bang, *Stuk*, 16.
5 Kristensen, *Georg Carstensen*, 187.
6 Fabricius, *Træk af dansk Musiklivs Historie*, 325.
7 Bang, *Stuk*, 18.
8 Guthmann and Melbye, *Tivoli*, 34 (italics in original).
9 The Tivoli Gardens had turnstiles installed, and at the beginning of each month the visitor numbers were published in the Copen-

hagen newspapers: *Dags-Telegraphen*, 2 August 1887, and *Nationaltidende*, 25 September 1887. To this must be added the number of subscribers which in 1887 totalled *c.* 3,600, cf. Guthmann and Melbye, *Tivoli*, 106. The population of Copenhagen was 261,360 in 1880 and 359,813 ten years later, cf. Matthiessen, *Danske byers folketal*, 13.

10 Engelbrecht, *Arven efter Lumbye*, 312.
11 Guthmann and Melbye, *Tivoli*, 108.
12 Engelbrecht, *Arven efter Lumbye*, 78.
13 Guthmann and Melbye, *Tivoli*, 34–35.
14 Fabricius, *Træk af dansk Musiklivs Historie*, 322.
15 *Nationaltidende*, 19 March 1886.
16 Fabricius, *Træk af dansk Musiklivs Historie*, 323.
17 Neiiendam, *Casino*, 17–19; Røllum-Larsen, *Impulser i Københavns koncertrepertoire*, vol. 1, 54.
18 *Illustreret Tidende*, 8 (1867), 190.
19 Hammerich, *Musikforeningens Historie*, 182; Schousboe, 'Koncertforeningen i København', 177.
20 The works are: CNW 41, 57, 58, 63, 64, 69, 82, 86, 87, 116, 117, 119, 121, 122, 123, 124, 125, 126, 128, 129, 131, 137, 138, 139, 150, 210, 212, 216, 217, 219, 221, 302, 303, 305 and 359.
21 A detailed floor plan by Carstensen and the architect H. C. Stilling was prepared in order to attract shareholders, cf. Kristensen, *Georg Carstensen*, 249–50. The plan identifies the individual rooms in the building ('Opstalt, snit og grundplan af Casino', KB, Billedsamlingen. Topografisk samling, København, 2°, Amaliegade, 1, lige nr., nr. 10, Casino); a floor plan for the Casino's large hall (KB, Billedsamlingen. Topografisk samling, København, 2°, Amaliegade, 1, lige nr., nr. 10, Casino).
22 Fabricius, *Træk af dansk Musiklivs Historie*, 324.
23 Røllum-Larsen, *Impulser i Københavns koncertrepertoire*, vol. 1, 56.
24 Fabricius, *Træk af dansk Musiklivs Historie*, 327–32.
25 Fabricius, *Træk af dansk Musiklivs Historie*, 331.
26 Fabricius, *Træk af dansk Musiklivs Historie*, 359.
27 Fabricius, *Træk af dansk Musiklivs Historie*, 361.
28 Fabricius, *Træk af dansk Musiklivs Historie*, 441.
29 Fjeldsøe and Groth, '"Nordicness" in Scandinavian music', 10–12.
30 Behrend, 'Den nordiske Musikfest'; Kjerulf, 'Musik i Ugen', 448.
31 Kjerulf, 'Musik i Ugen', 448.
32 Kjerulf, *Gift og Hjemfaren*, 324.
33 Behrend, 'Den nordiske Musikfest', 597.
34 KB, CNA I.C.1, notebook 1888.
35 Ketting, 'Carl Nielsen og Tivoli', 234.
36 This arrangement was also used in H. C. Lumbye's time as leader of the Tivoli Orchestra, cf. Hammerich, *Musikforeningens Historie*, 127f. Dahl's activity of renting out his orchestra to Musikforeningen is documented in the numerous invoices that he wrote to the Society (KB, Musikforeningens arkiv).
37 Friis, *Det Kongelige Kapel*, 155–56.
38 Skjerne and Bruhn, *Københavns Orkesterforening*.
39 Jonsson, *Københavns Orkester-Forening*, 9.
40 Jonsson, *Københavns Orkester-Forening*, 10.
41 Jonsson, *Københavns Orkester-Forening*, 13.
42 Jonsson, *Københavns Orkester-Forening*, 13–14. On the organisation of Danish music life, cf. Røllum-Larsen, 'Træk af musiklivet i København'; Fellow, 'Da danske musikere var blevne til børn igen'.
43 Jonsson, *Københavns Orkester-Forening*, 29.
44 Engelbrecht, *Arven efter Lumbye*, 110–11.
45 Nationalmuseet, Musikmuseet, Arkiv 287 Dansk Musiker Forbund: II. Forhandlingsprotokoller, love og medlemsfortegnelser for Københavns Orkesterforening (1876-1959), 18–19.
46 Musikmuseet, Nationalmuseet, MMCCS arkiv 249.

47 Among musicians playing in both orchestras in 1888 were Thorvald Hansen, Carl Skjerne, Emil Robert-Hansen, Julius Ferdinand Berg, Bernhard Rosenbaum, Poul Osvald Poulsen and Agnes Dahl, cf. photocollage of the Tivoli Orchestra, 1888 (Musikmuseet), and the list of Royal Musicians in Friis, *Det Kongelige Kapel*, 325–31.
48 CNB 1:5; CNL 2.
49 Samtid, 165–67, 228–29.
50 Schnedler-Petersen, *Et Liv i Musik*, 19–20.
51 KB, CNA I.C.1, notebook 1888.
52 Gottschalksen, *En glad Musikants Dagbog*, 78–79.
53 Behrend (ed.), *Minder om Niels W. Gade*, 124–25; Schnedler-Petersen, *Et Liv i Musik*, 22–23.
54 CNB 1:11; CNL 5. It was possibly a rehearsal for a concert on 5 March 1887 featuring Brahms's Third Symphony, cf. Falkencrone, *Musikforeningen*, app. 15, 10.
55 Samtid, 59; Glass relates the same story, cf. Behrend (ed.), *Minder om Niels W. Gade*, 100. It may have been at a rehearsal for Musikforeningen's concert on 14 March 1889, cf. Eskildsen, 'Nielsen and Gade', 156–57.
56 CNB 1:10.
57 Fabricius, *Træk af dansk Musiklivs Historie*, 444; Friis, *Det kongelige Kapel*, 191–92.
58 KB, CNA I.C.1, notebook 1888.
59 CNB 1:15; CNL 8.

Chapter 8
FROM MUSICIAN TO COMPOSER
1 For an overview of the surviving manuscripts, see CNS.
2 The early works, which have survived in a complete form, are published in CNU IV/1.
3 CNB 1:7; CNL 4.
4 CNU IV/1, xvi–xviii.
5 CNB 1:39; CNL 19.
6 CNB 1:7; CNL 4.
7 CNB 1:7; CNL 4.
8 Advert in *Berlingske Tidende*, 25 January 1888.
9 Meyer and Schandorf Petersen, *Carl Nielsen*, vol. 1, 63; Anon., 'Privat Kammermusik-Forening'.
10 CNB 4:531.
11 Røllum-Larsen, *Impulser i Københavns Koncertrepertoire*, vol. 1, 23–26; on the Private Chamber Music Society, see Schiørring, *Musikens historie i Danmark*, vol. 3, 79.
12 *Nationaltidende*, 18 September 1887.
13 CNU II/7, xi–xii; Samtid, 167.
14 Hatt, *Forårsbølger*, 89–92. The note was probably written in September 1888, as the two first entries are in Nielsen's hand while the following ones are by Emilie Demant Hansen.
15 Cf. e.g. *Kjøge Avis*, 10 September 1888; CNB 1:20.
16 Samtid, 59.
17 CNB 2:425; CNL 187.
18 CNB 2:426; CNL 188.
19 Meyer and Schandorf Petersen, *Carl Nielsen*, vol. 1, 41; MfB, 127; CNB 8:9; CNL 532. These pieces have not survived.
20 Larsen, 'Begyndelsen af Carl Nielsens musikalske karriere', n. 12.
21 The manuscript to *Fantasy Piece* (CNW 66) is digitally available on KB's website.
22 CNB 2:220; CNL 151; cf. MfB, 146; Jespersen, *Oplevelser*, 169–72.
23 CNS 416. The score, with the dedication added by Nielsen, is a careful fair copy, perhaps carried out by a scribe, although it could also be by Nielsen.
24 The concert took place 16 October 1888, cf. *Fyens Stiftstidende*, 10, 13 and 17 October 1888. He had previously given concerts in Odense on 23 August 1885 in Fruens Bøge (*Fyens Stiftstidende*, 21 August 1885), in Klubbens Festsal 11 August 1886 and again 27 December 1886 (*Fyens Stiftstidende*, 12 August and 28 December 1886) and in Ringe on Fyn on 2 January 1888 (*Fyens Stiftstidende*, 30 December 1887).
25 According to CNU IV/1, 286, the *Romance* in G major was not, like most early manuscripts, in Nielsen's estate but was acquired in 1993 by KB through the music dealer

Dan Fog. This suggests that it may have been in the possession of Carl Larsen. The violin part of CNS 416 was transcribed by a different, delicate and somewhat shaky hand, which also copied the dedication.
26 CNU IV/1, Add. 4.
27 Hatt, *Forårsbølger*, 92.
28 CNB 1:38; CNL 18.
29 CNB 1:39; CNL 19.
30 CNB 1:146, 1:162, 1:168.
31 CNB 1:63, 1:67.
32 Fog, *Carl Nielsen. Kompositioner*, 6–7.
33 Cf. CNW 60, Performances.
34 CNW mentions two performances at the Private Chamber Music Society and a single unrecorded performance of the second movement. Regarding the postponed performance, cf. *Nationaltidende*, 6 December 1890.
35 *Dagbladet*, 18 March 1891. Cf. *Berlingske Tidende*, 17 March 1891.
36 Samtid, 167. Knud Jeppesen relates a somewhat different version of the story in 'Carl Nielsen på Hundredårsdagen', 144.
37 Hauge, 'Carl Nielsens første opus', 230–31.
38 Facsimile of all the sources in Krabbe (ed.), *Suite for Strygeorkester*. It is not certain that the surviving draft is the version performed at Tivoli. The draft leads into an Adagio with the addition of a violin solo, of which only the first nineteen bars have survived. There is no evidence that there was such a violin solo in the Tivoli performance.
39 CNU II/7, xiv–xvii.
40 Samtid, 229, 791; Tivolis Programblad, 8 September 1888.
41 *Kjøge Avis*, 10 September 1888.
42 CNB 1:13; CNL 6; programme published in Hatt, *Forårsbølger*, 120.
43 CNB 1:16; CNL 9.
44 CNB 1:21; CNL 10.
45 *Politiken*, 2 May 1889.
46 Tivolis Programblad, 25 May 1889.
47 *Politiken*, 26 May 1889; *Dagbladet*, 29 September 1889.
48 Hauge, 'Carl Nielsens første opus', 227–30; cf. adverts in *Signale für die musikalische Welt*, 84 (March 1890), 415; *Berlingske Tidende*, 14 May 1890 (German title); *Dagstelegrafen*, 14 May 1890; *Nationaltidende*, 14 May 1890 (both 'Suite for Strygeorkester'); *Nationaltidende*, 23 May 1890 ('den lille Suite for Strygeorkester'); *Musikbladet*, 8, no. 4 (1891), 20.
49 CNB 1:74, 1:79, 1:144; CNW mentions three performances in Dresden: 2 October, 29 November and 4 December 1890, of which the first was led by Paul Hein while the two following ones were led by A. Trenkler.
50 CNB 1:134, 1:156, 1:192, 1:193; CNL 35. Cf. Muck, *Einhundert Jahre Berliner Philharmonisches Orchester*, vol. 3, 37. The popular concerts took place three times a week, conducted by Gustav Kogel and Joachim Andersen.
51 CNB 1:139; CNL 30.
52 CNB 1:342; CNL 58.
53 MfB, 127–28, 189; Meyer and Schandorf Petersen, *Carl Nielsen*, vol. 1, 40.
54 Fjeldsøe, introduction in Heise, *Strygekvartetter*, ix–xi.
55 Hammerich, *Musikforeningens Historie*, 104–6, 193–209.
56 MfB, 127; Childhood, 129.
57 Cf. CNU IV/1 and references in CNS, 42–47, 212–13, 217–18.
58 CNU II/10, xxiii–xxvii. The contract concerning the publication was apparently agreed in June 1896, cf. Schousboe, *Carl Nielsen. Dagbøger og brevveksling*, 127, who reproduces information from Nielsen's account books for 1895–96, OBM.
59 CNB 1:21; CNL 10.
60 CNB 1:38; CNL 18.
61 CNB 1:44.
62 CNB 1:71, 1:72, 1:74.
63 CNB 1:91.
64 CNB 1:115.
65 CNB 1:124.
66 CNB 1:137; CNL 29; cf. CNB 1:139; CNL 30.
67 CNB 1:226; CNL 46.
68 CNB 1:137; CNL 29.
69 CNB 1:143.

70 CNB 1:199; CNL 44; cf. CNB 1:165, 1:178; CNL 40.
71 CNB 1:167, 1:199, 1: 226; CNL 44.
72 Cf. Joseph, 'Structural Pacing', 470.
73 *Politiken*, 9 April 1892; CNU II/10, xxxiii.
74 *Berlingske Tidende*, 9 April 1892.
75 *Berlingske Tidende*, 29 April 1892.
76 *Morgenbladet*, 29 April 1892.
77 CNB 1:327, 1:330. Cf. CNU II/10, xxix.
78 CNB 1:331; CNL 55.
79 CNB 1:332, 1:334, 1:335; CNL 56, 57.
80 CNB 1:358; 1:382.
81 CNB 1:355.
82 CNB 1:398; CNL 68; cf. CNB 1:353, 1:354, 1:356, 1:357.
83 CNB 1:137; CNL 29; cf. CNB 1:135.
84 CNU II/7, 131–32.
85 Hatt, *Foraarsbølger*, 92. The letter has not survived but Hatt mentions that some of the letters from that autumn were burned, cf. Hatt, *Foraarsbølger*, 137–38.
86 *Symfonisk Rhapsodi*, fair copy, CNS 68a, and sketch book, CNS 358a, fols. 1v–5r. The sketch book was used from 1888 and to c. 1900 and is therefore not suitable for dating.
87 CNB 1:37; cf. CNB 1:41; CNL 20.
88 Cornelius, *Victor Bendix*, 80–81; *Dagbladet*, 25 and 27 February 1893.
89 CNB 1:385.
90 CNB 1:376, 1:385–391, 1:395. The piece received its first title shortly before the concerts. Cf. Dolleris, *Carl Nielsen. En Musikografi*, 37; Cornelius, *Victor Bendix*, 81.
91 CNB 1:387 og note for 1:394.
92 CNB 1:398, 1:533, 1:557, 1:565, 2:59, 2:94, 2:165; CNL 68, 109, 115, 142.
93 The sketch book, CNS 358a, fols. 1v and 3r, respectively.
94 The fugue subject is found in Nielsen's Symphony No. 5, second movement, from bar 410.
95 CNB 1:137; CNL 29.
96 CNB 1:138.
97 CNB 2:285; CNL 162.
98 *Samtid*, 257–58.
99 CNU II/10, xxix and 254–56.
100 CNB 1:166.
101 CNB 1:330; cf. CNB 1:327.
102 CNB 1:342; CNL 58.
103 CNB 1:419; CNL 75.
104 String quartet in F minor, CNS 38b, fol. D2^v, top stave. The folio is part of the manuscript to the second movement, which Nielsen mentions as 'Andanten', cf. CNU, II/10, 253. In CNU, I/1, 163, the work, CNS 38b, is specified as Source D^2 to Symphony No. 1.
105 CNB 1:426, 1:433, 1:452, 1:454.
106 CNU II/1, xii.
107 CNB 1:460; CNL 83; cf. CNB 1:458; CNL 82; CNU II/1, xii–xvi.
108 Grimley, *Carl Nielsen and the Idea of Modernism*, 55–56.
109 Grimley, *Carl Nielsen and the Idea of Modernism*, 58–60.

Chapter 9
THE RADICAL AND INTELLECTUAL ENVIRONMENT

1 Hatt, *Foraarsbølger*, 46. The chapter is a revised version of Engberg, *Carl Nielsen og århundredeskiftekulturen*, 96–120.
2 Hatt, *Foraarsbølger*, 46.
3 CNB 1:7; CNL 4.
4 Hatt, *Foraarsbølger*, 47–48.
5 Mortensen, 'Det uforfærdede øje', 29–33.
6 Hatt, *Foraarsbølger*, 84.
7 Meyer and Schandorf Petersen, *Carl Nielsen*, vol. 1, 55–56.
8 Knudsen, *Georg Brandes*, 199.
9 Knudsen, *Georg Brandes*, 200.
10 Knudsen, *Georg Brandes*, 200.
11 Hertel, *Det stadig moderne gennembrud*, 60.
12 Hertel, *Det stadig moderne gennembrud*, 61.
13 Henriques, *Svundne Dage*, 193–95.
14 Ottosen, 'Studentersamfundet', 5.
15 Schiøtt, 'Studentersamfundets Stiftelse og første Aar', 128.
16 Skram, 'Studentersamfundets fri Teater', 33.
17 Behrens, *Studentersamfundets Arbejderkoncerter*, 6.
18 Hertel, *Det stadig moderne gennembrud*, 70.

19 Schiøtt, 'Studentersamfundets Stiftelse og første Aar', 127.
20 Hvidt, *Edvard Brandes*, 57–58.
21 Hvidt, *Edvard Brandes*, 58–59.
22 Hvidt, *Edvard Brandes*, 58.
23 CNB 1:244, 1:247, 1:248, 1:252, 1:255, 1:272; CNL 49.
24 Fellow, *Vil Herren ikke hilse på sin Slægt*, 34.
25 Vibæk, *Foreningen til unge handelsmænds uddannelse*, 89–90.
26 Vibæk, *Foreningen til unge handelsmænds uddannelse*, 109.
27 Olsen, 'Minder og Breve af Malerinde frk. Cathinka Olsen', 97.
28 Olsen, 'Minder og Breve af Malerinde frk. Cathinka Olsen', 96.
29 Weiss, 'Nogle erindringer og Indtryk af Fr. Weiss', 69.
30 Behrens, *Studentersamfundets Arbejderkoncerter*, 5.
31 Zahle, 'Emil B. Sachs og Studentersamfundet', 62–63.
32 Hersom, 'Bidrag fra Købmandsskolen. V', 41.
33 Samtid, 283.
34 Samtid, 282.
35 Samtid, 280–82.
36 Hatt, *Foraarsbølger*, 47–48.
37 CNB 1:137; CNL 29.
38 Jacobsen, *Samlede Skrifter*, 223–24.
39 Cf. Bergsagel, 'J.P. Jacobsen and Music', 289–300; Villagomez, *Carl Nielsen og det musikalsk moderne*; Grimley, *Carl Nielsen and the Idea of Modernism*, 25–47; Reynolds, *Carl Nielsen's Voice*, 51–120.
40 Stampe-Bendix, *Fra mit livs tjørnekrat*, 37.
41 Stampe-Bendix, *Fra mit livs tjørnekrat*, 36, 90.
42 Cf. Cornelius, *Victor Bendix*, 102.
43 Cf. CNU II/7, xviii–xx.
44 CNB 1:37.
45 CNB 1:41; CNL 20.
46 CNB 1:60; CNL 28.
47 Fjeldsøe, *Kulturradikalismens musik*, 45.
48 Stampe-Bendix, *Fra mit livs tjørnekrat*, 52.
49 Brandes, *Levned*, vol. 1, 170. Digital edn. at https://georgbrandes.dk/texts.
50 Brandes, *Levned*, vol. 1, 170.
51 Stampe-Bendix, *Fra mit livs tjørnekrat*, 32.
52 Stampe-Bendix, *Fra mit livs tjørnekrat*, 32.
53 Fjeldsøe, *Kulturradikalismens musik*, 45–46.
54 Letter to Ludvig Bing, 5 November 1912, KB, NKS 4076, 4°.
55 Victor Bendix, 'Autobiografiske noter', Efterladte papirer, KB, NKS 2040, 2°.
56 Fjeldsøe, *Kulturradikalismens musik*, 45–47.
57 Fjeldsøe, *Kulturradikalismens musik*, 65.
58 CNB 1:54; CNL 23.
59 CNB 1:73.
60 CNB 1:328.
61 Jørgensen, *Mit Livs Legende*, vol. 1, 123.
62 Hjermitslev, 'Rudolf Sophus Bergh'.
63 Jersild, *Fars erindringer fra Højbroplads Nr. 15 Kronprinsessegade Nr. 2. Bind 2* [Oluf Jersild's memoirs], written 1946–48 and in 2013 transferred to Københavns Stadsarkiv, 33. https://kbharkiv.dk/permalink/post/18-2614.
64 Jørgensen, *Mit Livs Legende*, vol. 1, 124.
65 Jørgensen, *Mit Livs Legende*, vol. 1, 124.
66 CNB 1:412.
67 CNB 1:413; CNL 73.
68 CNB 1:523; CNL 106.
69 Knudsen, *Georg Brandes*, 214.
70 Møller, *Til Forstaaelse og Bedømmelse af Nutidens Fritænkeri*, 1.
71 Møller, *Til Forstaaelse og Bedømmelse af Nutidens Fritænkeri*, 16–17.
72 Møller, *Til Forstaaelse og Bedømmelse af Nutidens Fritænkeri*, 19–21.
73 Møller, *Til Forstaaelse og Bedømmelse af Nutidens Fritænkeri*, 20–21.
74 Brandes, *Politik, magt, ret*, 254.
75 Brandes, *Politik, magt, ret*, 256.
76 [Edvard Brandes], 'Literatur', *Politiken*, 25 September 1887.
77 CNB 1:137; CNL 29.
78 Anon., 'Udødelighedstroen eller Livet efter Døden', 3.
79 Jansen, 'J.P. Jacobsen', 15.
80 J. P. Jacobsen, *Niels Lyhne* (chapter 9), quot. in Jansen, 'J.P. Jacobsen', 16.

81 Jacobsen, *Fru Marie Grubbe*, 90–91.
82 Krabbe, 'Nielsen's Unrealised Opera Plans', 12–13.
83 CNB 1:150.
84 CNB 1:189.
85 CNB 1:16; CNL 9.
86 Cf. *Dannebrog*, 8 April 1894.
87 Skram, 'Studentersamfundets fri Teater', 33.
88 Neiiendam, *Det kongelige Teaters Historie*, vol. 6, 59. In order to avoid censorship, Det fri Teater was established as a society where only members could attend the performances, cf. Behrens, *Erindringer*, 166.
89 Behrens, *Erindringer*, 162–63.
90 Behrens, *Erindringer*, 163.
91 CNU I/6, xxi–xxii. On the the legend of King Harald Hårfagre and Snefrid, see Koht, *Harald Hårfagre og rikssamlinga*, 73–74.
92 CNB 1:372.
93 CNB 1:373.
94 CNB 1:375.
95 Cf. [Edvard Brandes], 'Literatur', *Politiken*, 25 September 1887.
96 CNU I/6, 56.
97 Cf. CNB 1:411 and *Dannebrog*, 8 April 1894; Behrens, *Erindringer*, 165–66.
98 CNU I/6, xviii–xix.
99 Nielsen's fair-copied score, CNS 331e, contains the original version. The edition in CNU I/6, No. 12, Postlude, reflects the version from 1899, with the changed instrumentation and minor discrepancies in the music.

II

Chapter 10
TURN-OF-THE-CENTURY CULTURE

1 CNB 2:163. The chapter is a revised version of Engberg, *Carl Nielsen og århundredeskiftekulturen*, 7, 11–17.
2 Jensen, *Død og evighed i musikken*, 17.
3 Brandes, 'Tale Nytaarsnat 1901'.
4 Bradbury and McFarlane, 'Preface to the 1991 Reprint', 13.
5 Grimley, *Carl Nielsen and the Idea of Modernism*, 25–26.
6 Wilkinson, 'They Fluttered like Moths', 62.
7 Wilkinson, 'They Fluttered like Moths', 62; Schorske, *Fin-de-Siècle Vienna*.
8 Schorske, *Fin-de-Siècle Vienna*, xix.
9 Bullock, 'The Double Image', 68–69.
10 Dahlhaus, *Nineteenth-Century Music*, 334. The term 'the modern' is phrased differently in the English edition, and the German edition has therefore been used: Dahlhaus, *Die Musik des 19. Jahrhunderts*, 279–80; cf. Bahr, 'Die Moderne'.
11 Dahlhaus, *Nineteenth-Century Music*, 334.
12 Bullock, 'The Double Image', 70.

Chapter 11
A MUSICAL TURNING POINT

1 Hammerich, 'Musik', 470. The chapter is a revised version of Engberg, *Carl Nielsen og århundredeskiftekulturen*, 137–58.
2 Carlsen, Olrik and Starcke, 'Forord', 10.
3 Carlsen, Olrik and Starcke, 'Forord', 10.
4 Hammerich, 'Musik', 461–64.
5 Hammerich, 'Musik', 464–66.
6 Hammerich, 'Musik', 469.
7 Cf. Albeck. 'Vagten', 615.
8 Glass, 'Om Musik og Musikere', 585.
9 Programmes are reproduced in Schousboe, 'Foreningen Symphonia', 162–65.
10 Brincker, 'Robert Henriques'.
11 CNB 1:13.
12 Henriques, 'Symfonia'.
13 CNU II/10, l–lv; Hatt, *Forårsbølger*, 92.
14 Hetsch, *Dur og Moll*, 33; Behrend, 'Robert Henriques'.
15 Bruun, *Dansk musiks historie fra Holberg-tiden til Carl Nielsen*, vol. 2, 284–85.
16 Røllum-Larsen, 'Louis Glass og Carl Nielsen', 592.
17 E.g. Alfred Tofft and Robert Henriques. Cf. Bergsagel, 'J.P. Jacobsen and Music', 288–89. See also Villagomez, *Carl Nielsen og det musikalsk moderne*.
18 CNB 1:13.
19 Ch. K. [Charles Kjerulf], 'En ny Koncertforening', *Politiken*, 30 April 1889.
20 Cf. Schousboe, 'Foreningen Symphonia', 157.

21 'Symphonia', *Berlingske Tidende*, 29 April 1889.
22 Ch. K. [Charles Kjerulf], 'En ny Koncertforening', *Politiken*, 30 April 1889.
23 Ch. K. [Charles Kjerulf], 'En ny Koncertforening', *Politiken*, 30 April 1889.
24 'Symphonia', *Berlingske Tidende*, 29 April 1889.
25 Rz., '"Sinfonia"', *Dagens Nyheder*, 30 April 1889.
26 Rz., '"Sinfonia"', *Dagens Nyheder*, 30 April 1889.
27 F., 'En ny Koncertforening [part 2]', *Politiken*, 30 April 1889.
28 Schousboe, 'Foreningen Symphonia', 157.
29 'Tivoliana', *Kjøbenhavns Adressecomptoirs Efterretninger*, 15 May 1889.
30 Ch. K. [Charles Kjerulf], 'De Unges Koncert i Tivoli', *Politiken*, 26 May 1889.
31 Ch. K. [Charles Kjerulf], 'De Unges Koncert i Tivoli', *Politiken*, 26 May 1889.
32 Cf. Røllum-Larsen, *Impulser i Københavns koncertrepertoire*, vol. 1, 115–16.
33 Schousboe, 'Foreningen Symphonia', 158.
34 CNB 1:451.
35 Schousboe, 'Foreningen Symphonia', 158.
36 Schousboe, 'Foreningen Symphonia', 159.
37 B. [William Behrend?], 'Koncert. Symfonia', *Politiken*, 5 May 1895.
38 S. A. [Sophus Andersen], '"Symphonia"', *København*, 7 May 1895.
39 B. [William Behrend?], 'Koncert. Symfonia', *Politiken*, 5 May 1895.
40 S. A. [Sophus Andersen], '"Symphonia"', *København*, 7 May 1895.
41 S. A. [Sophus Andersen], '"Symphonia"', *København*, 7 May 1895.
42 B. [William Behrend?], 'Koncert. Symfonia', *Politiken*, 5 May 1895.
43 *Avisen*, 5 May 1895, quot. in CNU II/12, xviii.
44 B. [William Behrend?], 'Koncert. Symfonia', *Politiken*, 5 May 1895.
45 Røllum-Larsen, *Impulser i Københavns koncertrepertoire*, vol. 1, 116.
46 Røllum-Larsen, 'Louis Glass og Carl Nielsen', 593.
47 Røllum-Larsen, *Impulser i Københavns koncertrepertoire*, vol. 1, 117.
48 Røllum-Larsen, 'Louis Glass og Carl Nielsen', 593.
49 Røllum-Larsen, *Impulser i Københavns koncertrepertoire*, vol. 1, 118–19.
50 Røllum-Larsen, *Impulser i Københavns koncertrepertoire*, vol. 1, 115.
51 Røllum-Larsen, *Impulser i Københavns koncertrepertoire*, vol. 1, 122.
52 A. H. [Angul Hammerich], 'Dansk Koncertforening', *Nationaltidende*, 24 January 1902.
53 A. H. [Angul Hammerich], 'Dansk Koncertforening', *Nationaltidende*, 24 January 1902; cf. note to CNB 2:201.
54 CNB 2:284.
55 Oluf Jersild, *Fars erindringer fra Højbroplads Nr. 15 Kronprinsessegade Nr. 2. Bind 2* [Oluf Jersild's memoirs], written 1946–48; in 2013 transferred to Københavns Stadsarkiv, 31–32; https://kbharkiv.dk/permalink/post/18-2614.
56 Fjeldsøe, *Kulturradikalismens musik*, 65; Dal, 'Danske Wagner-tilløb'.
57 -st-ts- [Gustav Hetsch], 'Koncert', *Nationaltidende*, 4 February 1898.
58 T., '2den Soirée for Kammermusik', *Dagbladet*, 18 March 1891.
59 C. B., 'Koncertsæsonen', *København*, 19 March 1891.
60 Cf. Røllum-Larsen, *Impulser i Københavns koncertrepertoire*, vol. 1, 26–28.
61 Concert advertisement in *Dannebrog*, 8 March 1894.
62 CNB 1:460; CNL 83.
63 R. H. [Robert Henriques], 'Det kgl. Kapels Koncert', *Dannebrog*, 15 March 1894.
64 R. H. [Robert Henriques], 'Det kgl. Kapels Koncert', *Dannebrog*, 15 March 1894.
65 'Kapellets Koncert', *Social-Demokraten*, 15 March 1894.
66 A. H. [Angul Hammerich], 'Kapel-Koncert', *Nationaltidende*, 15 March 1894.
67 Ch. K. [Charles Kjerulf], 'Det kgl. Kapel. Symfoni-Koncert', *Politiken*, 15 March 1894.

68 R. H. [Robert Henriques], 'Det kgl. Kapels Koncert', *Dannebrog*, 15 March 1894.
69 Cf. Grimley, *Carl Nielsen and the Idea of Modernism*, 51–54.
70 R. H. [Robert Henriques], 'Ny Musik. Carl Nielsen: Viser og Vers af J.P. Jacobsen', *Dannebrog*, 11 June 1893.
71 A. H. [Angul Hammerich], 'Koncerter', *Dagens Nyheder*, 17 January 1896.
72 -st.-ts.- [Gustav Hetsch], 'Koncert', *Nationaltidende*, 22 January 1898.
73 Coda. 'NY UDKOMMEN MUSIK', *Dagens Nyheder*, 23 December 1899.
74 CNU II/12, xxii–xxiii; *Politiken*, 1 January 1901.
75 Jørgensen, *Det danske anmelderis historie*, 185.

Chapter 12
ON THE THRESHOLD OF THE MUSICAL MODERN

1 Røllum-Larsen, 'Det Anckerske Legats rejsestipendier', 80–81; CNB 1:35.
2 Hanslick, *Vom Musikalisch-Schönen* (1854) was transl. into Danish after the sixth edn. as *Om Det Skjønne i Musikken. Et Bidrag til Tonekunstens Æstetik* (1885). The New German School was promoted in Brendel, *Geschichte der Musik*, which was published in numerous revised editions.
3 Røllum-Larsen, 'Det Anckerske Legats rejsestipendier', 75, 78.
4 CNB 1:12, 1:29, 1:31.
5 CNB 1:46. An important source for the course of the journey is his travel diary, which covers the period from 1 September 1890 (CNB 1:45) to 14 June 1891 (CNB 1:320).
6 CNB 1:42.
7 CNB 1:49; CNL 21.
8 CNB 1:49; CNL 21.
9 CNB 1:84.
10 CNB 1:48.
11 Fuller-Maitland, *Masters of German Music*, 199–201.
12 Würz, 'Kirchner, Theodor'; Sietz, *Theodor Kirchner*, 55.
13 CNB 1:56; CNL 25.
14 CNB 1:56; CNL 25.
15 CNB 1:106.
16 CNB 1:67.
17 CNB 1:68.
18 CNB 1:48.
19 Cornelius, *Victor Bendix*, 15–17, 43.
20 CNB 1:60; CNL 28.
21 CNB 1:78.
22 Borchard, 'Joseph Joachim'.
23 Leistra-Jones, '(Re-)Enchanting Performance', 87–88.
24 CNB 1:107.
25 Schenck, 'Die Ära Joseph Joachim'.
26 Riggs, '"Das Quartett-Spiel ist doch wohl mein eigentliches Fach"', 150, 154, 157.
27 Riggs, '"Das Quartett-Spiel ist doch wohl mein eigentliches Fach"', 158.
28 CNB 1:116.
29 CNB 1:139; CNL 30.
30 CNB 1:165.
31 CNB 1:178; CNL 40.
32 CNB 1:226; CNL 46.
33 Schenck, 'Die Ära Joseph Joachim', 50–52.
34 CNB 1:226; CNL 46, tr. adjusted.
35 CNB 1:226; CNL 46.
36 CNB 1:170; CNL 39.
37 Sørensen, *Niels W. Gade*, 282–84.
38 CNB 1:172.
39 Samtid, 29–30.
40 Cornelius, *Victor Bendix*, 23–26.
41 CNB 1:175.
42 CNB 1:178; CNL 40.
43 Cf. Fjeldsøe, 'The Leipzig Model and Its Consequences', 71–74.
44 CNB 1:199; CNL 44.
45 CNB 1:197; CNL 43.
46 CNB 1:228.
47 CNB 1:225.
48 CNB 1:196.
49 CNB 1:196.
50 Rugstad, *Christian Sinding*, 113; Anon., 'Adolph Brodsky', 227.
51 CNB 1:226; CNL 46.
52 CNB 1:188, 1:196.
53 CNB 1:226; CNL 46.
54 CNB 1:231.

55 CNB 1:358, 1:382. A performance did not occur in the Liszt Society as they ceased to play chamber music in 1891 (personal communication with Stefan Keym, 31 May 2022). Cf. Keym, 'Komplementarität und Pluralisierung', 157–62. Regarding Nice, CNB 1:488, 1:490; Meyer and Schandorf Petersen, *Carl Nielsen*, vol. 1, 84.
56 Rugstad, *Christian Sinding*, 100.
57 Rugstad, *Christian Sinding*, 114.
58 Rugstad, *Christian Sinding*, 153.
59 CNB 1:177.
60 CNB 1:178.
61 Werbeck, 'Richard Strauss's Tone Poems', 109.
62 CNB 1:239; CNL 48.
63 CNB 1:240.
64 Rugstad, *Christian Sinding*, 153–54.
65 CNB 1:241.
66 CNB 1:474. A main source for the journey is his travel diary, which covers the period from 12 October to 17 November 1894, cf. CNB 1:476 to 1:522.
67 CNB 1:486; CNL 91.
68 CNB 1:493, 1:494, 1:496, 1:562; CNL 94.
69 CNB 1:486; CNL 91.
70 CNB 1:509.
71 CNB 1:478; CNL 86.
72 CNB 1:505; CNL 97.
73 CNB 2:547; CNL 211.
74 CNB 1:509.
75 Ostwald, 'Brahms, Solitary Altruist', 27.
76 CNB 1:510; CNL 99.
77 CNB 1:510; CNL 99.
78 Commentary to CNB 1:510.
79 CNB 1:510; CNL 99.
80 CNB 1:511.
81 CNB 1:526, CNB 11:935A; CNL 107.
82 Behrend, 'Hos Johannes Brahms', 436.
83 CNB 1:513; CNL 101.
84 CNB 1:407; cf. Villagomez, '"In the Land of Dreams"'.
85 CNB 3:218; CNL 223.
86 CNB 4:500; CNL 302.

Chapter 13
MEETING *FIN-DE-SIÈCLE* PARIS

1 Schwartz, *Spectacular Realities*, 1. The chapter is a revised version of Engberg, *Carl Nielsen og århundredeskiftekulturen*, 58–78.
2 Cf. 'Verdensudstillingen', *Morgenbladet* (København), 10 May 1889; 'Verdensudstillingen i Paris', *Berlingske Tidende*, 23 August 1889, 2nd edn.
3 Anon., 'Notes on the Fin De Siecle Movement', 4.
4 Schwartz, *Spectacular Realities*, 1.
5 Willumsen, *Mine Erindringer*, 42–43.
6 Willumsen, *Mine Erindringer*, 42. Cf. Wivel, *Symbolisme og impressionisme*, 30.
7 CNB 1:248; CNL 49.
8 CNB 1:33.
9 CNB 1:246.
10 CNB 1:246.
11 CNB 1:243.
12 Cavling, *Paris*, 449–50.
13 Willumsen, *Mine Erindringer*, 48.
14 Svanholm, *Malerne på Skagen*, 115–16.
15 Willumsen, *Mine Erindringer*, 48; Cavling, *Paris*, 451.
16 CNB 1:244.
17 CNB 1:246.
18 CNB 1:245, 1:249.
19 CNB 1:247.
20 Frederiksen, 'Mødested Paris', 10.
21 Schultz, 'Danske Kunstnere i Paris', 455.
22 Frederiksen, 'Mødested Paris', 10.
23 Frederiksen, 'Mødested Paris', 11.
24 Frederiksen, 'Mødested Paris', 17.
25 Frederiksen, 'Mødested Paris', 14–15.
26 Zibrandtsen, *Hans Nikolaj Hansen*, 76.
27 Zibrandtsen, *Hans Nikolaj Hansen*, 80.
28 The sentence 'Now in Paris' introduces chapter 15 in Jacobsen, *Fru Marie Grubbe*, 259.
29 Letter from Hans Nikolaj Hansen to Amalie Skram, 4 January 1891, quot. in Zibrandtsen, *Hans Nikolaj Hansen*, 76.
30 CNB 1:256.
31 CNB 1:244. The tie is in OBM, CNM/1956/0087.
32 CNB 1:253.

33 CNB 1:255.
34 CNB 1:256.
35 Schultz, 'Danske Kunstnere i Paris', 495–96.
36 CNB 1:245.
37 CNB 1:245.
38 CNW 81.
39 CNB 1:137.
40 Samtid, 398. Cf. Schousboe (ed.), *Carl Nielsen. Dagbøger og brevveksling*, 50.
41 Pasler, *Composing the Citizen*, 469.
42 Cf. *Concert-Lamoureux (Société des Nouveaux-Concerts). Programme. Dix-Septième Concert (Série A)*, 1 March 1891, Bibliothèque historique de la Ville de Paris, Paris.
43 CNB 1:247.
44 Anon., 'Lamoureux Concerts', 314.
45 Bibliothèque Nationale de Paris.
46 Valéry, 'At the Lamoureux Concert'; Pasler, *Composing the Citizen*, 525.
47 Willumsen, *Mine Erindringer*, 48.
48 Pasler, *Composing the Citizen*, 469–72.
49 The programme for the concert of 1 March 1891, at which Nielsen was present, states that the audience was asked not to leave the hall during the performance of the works, cf. *Concert-Lamoureux (Société des Nouveaux-Concerts). Programme. Dix-Septième Concert (Série A)*, 1 March 1891, Bibliothèque historique de la Ville de Paris, Paris.
50 Pasler, *Composing the Citizen*, 469, 472.
51 Pasler, *Composing the Citizen*, 477, 480; Cavling, *Paris*, 49–50.
52 Pasler, *Composing the Citizen*, 680.
53 Pasler, *Composing the Citizen*, 680.
54 CNB 1:253.
55 Price, *Cancan!*, 20.
56 Hindson, *Female Performance Practice*, 93.
57 CNB 1:251.
58 Cf. Schultz, 'Danske Kunstnere i Paris', 507.
59 Christiansen, *Anne Marie Carl-Nielsen*, 34.
60 Christiansen, *Anne Marie Carl-Nielsen*, 42.
61 Munk, 'Agnes Lunn'.
62 Christiansen, *Anne Marie Carl-Nielsen*, 42.
63 Christiansen, *Anne Marie Carl-Nielsen*, 39.
64 Christiansen, *Anne Marie Carl-Nielsen*, 45.
65 Christiansen, *Anne Marie Carl-Nielsen*, 57.
66 Christiansen, *Anne Marie Carl-Nielsen*, 57.
67 Cf. Wivel, *Symbolisme og impressionisme*, 15, 30, 119.
68 Zibrandtsen, *Hans Nikolaj Hansen*, 78.
69 Christiansen, *Anne Marie Carl-Nielsen*, 39–40.
70 Cf. Willumsen, *Mine Erindringer*, 80.
71 Hannover, *Erindringer fra Barndom og Ungdom*, 162.
72 Apparently a disagreement between Harald Slott-Møller and Anne Marie Brodersen's family led to the couple leaving the farm and renting accommodation in Sønder Stenderup instead; cf. Christiansen, *Anne Marie Carl-Nielsen*, 46.
73 Quot. in Christiansen, *Anne Marie Carl-Nielsen*, 54.
74 Willumsen, *Mine Erindringer*, 76.
75 Willumsen, *Mine Erindringer*, 81–82.
76 Christiansen, *Anne Marie Carl-Nielsen*, 55. Cf. Bierlich, *Excentriske slægtskaber*, 130–32.
77 Christiansen, *Anne Marie Carl-Nielsen*, 58.
78 Willumsen, *Mine Erindringer*, 80.
79 CNB 1:248; CNL 49.
80 CNB 1:262.
81 CNB 1:263; CNL 50.
82 CNB 1:267; CNL 51.
83 CNB 1:268.
84 Christiansen, *Anne Marie Carl-Nielsen*, 62.
85 CNB 1:268.
86 Receipt in Nielsen's wallet, CNA I.C.1; CNB 1:272. In the diary Nielsen notes the address as Rue St. Anne 69.
87 Mons Lie, MS 'Dr. Tscherning i Paris', KB, Palsbo AB, fol. 5.
88 CNB 1:272.
89 CNB 1:284; CNL 52.
90 CNB 1:269.
91 CNB 1:273.
92 Irmelin Nielsen was born on 9 December 1891.
93 CNB 1:291.

Chapter 14
ANNE MARIE

1 RA, transcripts of Nørre Tyrstrup Herred's debt and mortgage registers (1835–70), p. 2106–7.

2 RA, parish register for Højer Sogn, 1817–1867, fol. 56.
3 Cf. Hansen, *Nørremølle*, 88–99. The exact location of the farm is shown in an excavation report from Museum Sønderjylland; see http://www.kulturarv.dk/fundogfortidsminder/Lokalitet/162770/, (location 2).
4 RA, census 1835, Tønder / Højer / Højer, oktrojerede koge, Højer. Cf. Rolfs, *Højer sogns og flækkes historie*, 379.
5 KB, CNA II.A.a.5.
6 Hansen, *Nørremølle*, 96.
7 Cf. photo at arkiv.dk from Kolding Stadsarkiv, B2035, informing that he was a member of the Sønder Stenderup parish council 1872–77 and 1882–87.
8 On the demarcation, see Schiøller, 'Aktstykker og Skrivelser', esp. 48.
9 Cf. the genealogical table at abcbellevue.dk/ABClausen/14594.htm. In the census of 1855 she is listed as housekeeper, RA, census 1855.
10 RA, 259 Fødsels- og Plejestiftelsen 1807–1837, Protokoller over jordemodereksamen, vol. 1820–1825, fol. 62; parish register for Garnisonskirken, marriages, 1819–1825, p. 193.
11 Ising (ed.), *Johann Christoph Blumhardt. Briefe*, vol. 5, 350. Cf. commentaries in Ising (ed.), *Johann Christoph Blumhardt. Briefe*, vol. 6, 290.
12 Ising, *Johann Christoph Blumhardt*, 74–309.
13 Ising, *Johann Christoph Blumhardt*, 322–26.
14 Ising, *Johann Christoph Blumhardt*, 327–28.
15 CNB 2:170, 2:347, 11:871. Cf. letters from the family to Anne Marie Carl-Nielsen, KB, CNA II.A.a.6.
16 CNB 1:345; CNL 60.
17 CNB 11:873.
18 Marie Brodersen is entered in the school's class register from the second term of 1856; according to the enrolment register, she graduated at Easter 1861. Brødremenighedens arkiv, Christiansfeld, Karakterprotokol A.A.R.6.B.2 [Mädchen 1845–57] and A.A.R.6.B.3 [Mädchen 1857–61], Indskrivningsprotokol A.A.R.7.B.3. Cf. Holdt, 'Elev-Fortegnelse', 125.
19 Brødremenighedens arkiv, Christiansfeld, Indskrivningsprotokol A.A.R.7.B.3. He is discharged with the remark: 'Ostern 1871 zuhause heimgegangen' (died at home at Easter 1871).
20 Cf. 'Anne Marie Carl Nielsens erindringer, 1920'erne', in Christiansen, *Anne Marie Carl-Nielsen*, 380.
21 Schlee, *Christian Carl Magnussen*, 10–11.
22 Schlee, *Christian Carl Magnussen*, 105–30; Christiansen, *Anne Marie Carl-Nielsen*, 31–33; CNB 1:417.
23 Compare e.g. Barlach's *Der Schebende Engel* in Güstrow with Anne Marie Carl-Nielsen's *Dronning Dagmar* in Ribe.
24 Cf. Bierlich, *Excentriske slægtskaber*, 134–38; Houby-Nielsen, 'Anne Marie Carl-Nielsen og det sene 1800-tals farvedebat'; Christiansen, *Anne Marie Carl-Nielsen*, 144–65.
25 'Anne Marie Carl Nielsens erindringer, 1920'erne', in Christiansen, *Anne Marie Carl-Nielsen*, 381.
26 'Anne Marie Carl Nielsens erindringer, 1920'erne', in Christiansen, *Anne Marie Carl-Nielsen*, 381–82.
27 Christiansen, *Anne Marie Carl-Nielsen*, 35–40, and 'Anne Marie Carl Nielsens erindringer, 1920'erne', in Christiansen, *Anne Marie Carl-Nielsen*, 383; Anne Marie Carl Nielsen's ledger for 1882–84, KB, CNA II.C.1.a. In Copenhagen Anne Marie had rented a room with Agnes Lunn's cousin on the first floor of the house in Østerbro with August Saabye living on the ground floor, cf. RA, census 1885, Petersborgvej nr. 6.
28 Christiansen, *Anne Marie Carl-Nielsen*, 42–45.
29 Christiansen, *Anne Marie Carl-Nielsen*, 38–42; CNB 1:413.
30 Christiansen, *Anne Marie Carl-Nielsen*, 41.
31 In 1888 Karen Marie Hansen, who was a maid in the same building where Nielsen lived with the Bauditz family, had a son Carl August Hansen, cf. Fellow, *Vil Herren ikke hilse på sin Slægt*, 51–55.

32 CNB 1:272, 1:291.
33 Bierlich, *Excentriske slægtskaber*, 126.
34 Bierlich, *Excentriske slægtskaber*, 129.
35 Bierlich, *Excentriske slægtskaber*, 135, 137–38. The study also documents to the extent of which Anne Marie Carl-Nielsen was able to sell her works abroad at high prices.
36 Christiansen, *Anne Marie Carl-Nielsen*, 34.
37 CNB 5, 115–46, commentaries on Anne Marie Carl-Nielsen's notebook and diary of these months.
38 CNB 5:53, 5:56; CNL 330, 331.
39 Notebook 1914, KB, CNA II.C.1.a.; cf. CNB 5, 115.
40 Notebook 1914, KB, CNA II.C.1.a.; cf. CNB 5, 13–15, 115–16.
41 CNB 5:91; CNL 337.
42 Notebook 1914, KB, CNA II.C.1.a.
43 Notebook 1914, KB, CNA II.C.1.a. The original reads: 'that was (not) some of the most beautiful …', where the brackets should be read as a deletion; cf. CNB 5, 129.
44 CNB 4:607, 4:629.
45 Cf. Anne Marie Carl-Nielsen's diary regarding the travel beginning on 1 November 1904, KB, CNA II.C.1.a.
46 CNB 2:451, 2:453; CNL 196, 197.
47 CNB 2:452, 2:455, 2:457.
48 CNB 2:460; CNL 198.
49 CNB 2:461. Cf. CNB 5, 376; Anne Marie Carl-Nielsen's notebook of 1916, 23 May 1916, KB, CNA II.C.1.a., in which she refers to this letter.
50 CNB 2:464 and commentary; CNL 199; cf. Anne Marie Carl-Nielsen's notebook 1904: 'Tuesday 28 March / Letter from Carl – and Marie Møller. I'm in despair, I cannot think. I'll telegraph 11.30 that Carl should come. He is out of his mind, poor dear boy.'
51 CNB 5:96; CNL 338.
52 CNB 5:96; CNL 338.
53 Notebook 1914, KB, CNA II.C.1.a., 27 July 1914; cf. CNB 5, 134.
54 In a letter to Ove Jørgensen in 1916 (CNB 5:336), Marie Møller claims that Carl wrote to her in January 1915 that he had now told his wife everything and quotes from a now lost letter. This does not rule out the possibility that Carl admitted it earlier, but not before Anne Marie returned from Norway in the summer of 1914.
55 Notebook 1914, KB, CNA II.C.1.a., 30 July 1914; cf. CNB 5, 135.
56 CNB 5:108 and commentary referring to her notebook.
57 Notebook 1914, KB, CNA II.C.1.a., 13 August 1914; cf. CNB 5, 141–42.
58 CNB 5:140, 5:141.
59 CNB 5:323; CNL 365.
60 Notebook 1914, KB, CNA II.C.1.a., 21 July 1914; cf. CNB 5, 128.
61 CNB 7:206; CNL 486.
62 Notebook 1916, KB, CNA II.C.1.a., 18 March 1916, reproduced in CNB 5, 335; cf. CNB 5:328, 5:329, 5:331, 5:333, 5:336, 5:339, 5:345; CNL 368.
63 Notebook 1916, KB, CNA II.C.1.a., 13 May, 14 May, 15 May, 17 May 1916; cf. CNB 5, 374.
64 Loose folios in KB, CNA II.C.1.a.
65 CNB 5:355; CNL 374; cf. letter draft from notebook CNB 5, 382–85.
66 CNB 5:376; CNL 378.
67 Cf. CNB 5, 575: The Prefect's Office granted the separation on 26 September 1919, following an application made on 18 June 1919.
68 The police records list his address from 1 November 1920 as 20 Nørrebrogade, 4th floor; cf. CNB 6:482 ff.
69 CNB 3, 21–22.
70 CNB 4:479.
71 Telmanyi, *Mit barndomshjem*, 115. Cf. CNB 5:13, 5:208, 5:241, 5:402, 5:405.
72 CNB 6:15; CNL 403.
73 CNB 8:479; CNL 571; CNU II/5, xi; Telmányi, *Af en musikers billedbog*, 162–65. Cf. Krabbe, 'Ebbe Hameriks påståede korrumpering af Carl Nielsens første symfoni', 138–42.
74 Introduction, CNB 7, 24.
75 CNB 7:236; CNL 490.
76 Loose folios in KB, CNA II.C.1.a.
77 Loose folios in KB, CNA II.C.1.a.

78 For a more detailed presentation, see Fjeldsøe, '"Music *is* Life"', 182–85.
79 J. S., '"Der er en Rytme gennem al Kunst"'.
80 Programme from the premiere on 1 February, quot. in CNU I/4, xiii–xiv.
81 Hannover, 'Udstillingerne III'.
82 Christiansen, *Anne Marie Carl-Nielsen*, 157.
83 Hannover, 'Udstillingerne III'.
84 Samtid, 125.

Chapter 15
ROYAL MUSICIAN

1 Meyer and Schandorf Petersen, *Carl Nielsen*, vol. 1, 76.
2 CNB 1:24 and commentary.
3 Engberg, *Det Kongelige Teater*, vol. 1, 92, 104, 428–29. Cf. https://kglteater.dk/om-os/kunstarter/det-kongelige-kapel?section=27735.
4 Leicht and Haller, *Det kongelige Teaters repertoire*, 17–33.
5 CNB 1:585.
6 CNB 1:588, 1:590.
7 Engberg, *Det Kongelige Teater*, vol. 1, 424–40, and 368: quot. by the theatre critic Frederik Schyberg i 1941.
8 Engberg, *Det Kongelige Teater*, vol. 1, 418.
9 The portrayed musicians are listed in Friis, *Det kongelige Kapel*, 223. Cf. Meyer and Schandorf Petersen, *Carl Nielsen*, vol. 1, 80–82.
10 CNB 2:438.
11 Meyer and Schandorf Petersen, *Carl Nielsen*, vol. 1, 104.
12 CNB 1:474 and commentary.
13 CNB 1:558, 1:650.
14 CNB 2:86; cf. CNB 2:59, 2:226, 2:242, 2:306, 2:325; CNL 171.
15 CNB 2:332, 2:336, 2:338; CNL 174. RA, Det kongelige Teaters Arkiv og Bibliotek, Journal, 1895-1904, p. 286ff. Some of the less demanding tasks were conducted by the orchestra's leader, Anton Svendsen.
16 CNB 2:339.
17 The lists of what Nielsen has played are based on Leicht and Hallar, *Det kongelige Teaters repertoire*. In the seasons when Nielsen was on partial sabbatical, the exact number of appearances in which he participated could not be determined, and thus a proportional estimate has been made.
18 Cf. commentary to CNB 2:130.
19 CNB 2:325; CNL 171.
20 CNB 2:328.
21 CNB 2:394; CNL 182.
22 CNB 2:337.
23 CNB 2:338; CNL 174.
24 CNB 2:339.
25 RA, Det kongelige Teaters Arkiv og Bibliotek, Journal, 1904-1911, season 1904–5.
26 CNB 2:451; CNL 196.
27 CNB 2:370; CNL 177.
28 CNB 2:450, 2:458; CNL 195.
29 CNB 2:451; CNL 196.
30 CNB 2:460; CNL 198.

Chapter 16
MUSIC FOR EVENTS

1 Eigtved, *På! Begivenhedskultur fra selfie til scenekunst*, 45.
2 Eigtved, *På! Begivenhedskultur fra selfie til scenekunst*, 46.
3 Eigtved, *På! Begivenhedskultur fra selfie til scenekunst*, 108.
4 Obs., 'Studentersamfundets Festdag. Indvielsen af det nye Hjem', *Politiken*, 2 June 1901. This and the following section is a revised version of Engberg, *Carl Nielsen og århundredeskiftekulturen*, 128–36.
5 Obs., 'Studentersamfundets Festdag. Indvielsen af det nye Hjem', *Politiken*, 2 June 1901.
6 'Studentersamfundet indvier sit ny Hus!', *Social-Demokraten*, 2 June 1901.
7 'Studentersamfundet indvier sit ny Hus!', *Social-Demokraten*, 2 June 1901.
8 CNB 1:176.
9 Cf. CNU III/2, 7-9, bb. 99–134.
10 Drachmann, *Breve*, vol. 4, 146.
11 CNU III/2, xii; cf. *Politiken*, 2 June 1901; *Demokraten*, 3 June 1901.
12 CNB 11:16.
13 'Studentersamfundet indvier sit ny Hus!', *Social-Demokraten*, 2 June 1901.

14 Obs., 'Studentersamfundets Festdag. Indvielsen af det nye Hjem', *Politiken*, 2 June 1901.
15 Chark., 'Studentersamfundets Hus. Indvielseshøjtideligheden', *København*, 2 June 1901.
16 Rode, 'Fest i Studentersamfundets nye Hjem', 562.
17 Rode, 'Fest i Studentersamfundets nye Hjem', 562.
18 Regarded as music for events are the instrumental works CNW 36, 37, 39, 40 and 84; the cantatas CNW 103–15; among the songs CNW 293, 294, 306 and 310 and the choir pieces CNW 343, 353, 354, 365, 374, 375 and 386.
19 CNB 3:539; CNL 244.
20 CNB 3:409; CNU III/2, xv–xix.
21 CNB 3:419 (original in italics); CNL 230; cf. CNB 3:409.
22 CNB 3:534; CNL 241.
23 CNB 3:419; CNL 230.
24 CNU III/2, xviii–xxiii, quot. *Kristeligt Dagblad*, 30 October 1908. Cf. Petersen, 'Censur på universitetet?'.
25 Hugo Seligmann, *Politiken*, 9 November 1908.
26 CNU III/2, xix.
27 CNU III/3, xxxiii–xxxiv; CNW 395.
28 CNB 5:512; CNL 391.
29 *Nationaltidende*, 2 June 1917.
30 CNU II/8, xix–xxi.
31 CNS 50b, p. 3, reproduced in CNU II/8, xxxvii.
32 *Nationaltidende*, 23 August 1915.
33 CNU II/8, xix–xxi.
34 CNB 9:449; CNL 611.
35 Samtid, 449. Cf. CNB 9:761.
36 CNU II/8, xxix–xxxi.
37 *Nationaltidende*, 2 November 1928, quot. in CNU II/8, xxx.
38 CNB 10:521; CNL 677.
39 Nielsen and Helge Rode typewritten MS 'National-Folkefest i Ulvedalene', RA, Komiteen vedrørende Afholdelse af en Nationalfest i Ulvedalene ved Sønderjyllands Tilbagekomst, Minutes of the meeting (forhandlingsprotokol) including a few letters (1919).
40 CNU I/9, xi; CNB 6:356.
41 *Nationaltidende*, 31 January 1921.
42 CNB 10:337, 10:348.

Chapter 17
THE LIED COMPOSER
1 CNB 1:11; CNL 5.
2 Villagomez, *Carl Nielsen og det musikalsk moderne*.
3 Reynolds, *Carl Nielsen's Voice*, 217–327.
4 List of performances in CNW.
5 CNB 1:11; CNL 5.
6 Hatt, *Forårsbølger*, 66–67. 'Alle de voksende Skygger' (CNW 282), in MS with text by J. P. Jacobsen, has been published in CNU; KB, HA, Emilie Demant Hatts samling.
7 Newspaper report from 1928, in which Nielsen 'by memory' quotes the entire first stanza, *Samtid*, 482.
8 Tunbridge, 'Introduction. Restaging German Song', 2.
9 Danuser, *Musikalische Lyrik*, 97–99.
10 Gibbs, *The Life of Schubert*, 74–76.
11 Kreissle von Hellborn, *Franz Schubert*.
12 *Søndags-Posten*, 18 April 1869.
13 Gibbs, 'German reception'.
14 Schou, *Franz Schubert*; Behrend, 'Franz Schubert'.
15 Schou, *Franz Schubert*, 94. Cf. Behrend, 'Franz Schubert', 839–40. Both are based on Kreissle von Hellborn, *Franz Schubert*, 485.
16 CNB 1:11; CNL 5.
17 CNB 1:11; CNL 5.
18 Bayerische Staatsgemäldesammlungen, Sammlung Schack München; cf. http://www.goethezeitportal.de/wissen/illustrationen/johann-wolfgang-von-goethe/erlkoenig.html.
19 CNB 1:11; CNL 5.
20 Loges, *Brahms and His Poets*, 4.
21 Loges, *Brahms and His Poets*, 6–7.
22 CNB 2:446; CNL 192.
23 Rosenhoff, *Fire Sange af Bernh. Sev. Ingemanns "Kunnuk og Naja"*; Rosenhoff, *Emilie*

Rosenhoff tilegnede. Fem Digte af Emil Aarestrup og Chr. Winther; Rosenhoff, *Digte efter det engelske ved Caralis*; Rosenhoff, *Fem danske Sange med Klaver*.
24 Bahr, 'Die Moderne'.
25 Bahr, 'Die Überwindung des Naturalismus', 202: '… daß der Naturalismus überwunden werden wird durch eine nervöse Romantik; noch lieber möchte ich sagen: durch eine Mystik der Nerven'; 'man kann den Naturalismus als die hohe Schule der Nerven betrachten: … eine Sensibilität der feinsten und leisesten Nüancen'.
26 Fels, 'Die Moderne', 194: 'Naturalist ist, wer die Außenwelt mit all ihren Details peinlichst sorgfältig nachzubilden sucht, indem er das ungeordnet Zufällige, Unwichtige und Zusammenhangslose beibehält; Naturalist ist, wer sich in die Innenwelt versenkt und mit ängstlichem Bemühen jeder kleinsten Nüanzierung seines Seelenlebens nachspürt'.
27 Fels, 'Jens Peter Jacobsen', 344: 'seine höchst gesteigerte Empfindungs- und Aufnahmsfähigkeit für alles Feine, Zarte, Halbe, für Farben, Düfte und Töne, deren leiseste Nuancen er gewahr wird, die lautlose Melancholie des Einsamen, endlich das Sehnen, das große, qualvolle, bebende, nimmer ersterbende Sehnen'.
28 Villagomez, '"In the Land of Dreams"'.
29 Cf. Grimley, *Carl Nielsen and the Idea of Modernism*, 31–38.
30 Jacobsen, *Samlede Værker*, 124.
31 *Morgenbladet*, 29 April 1892, and *København*, 30 April 1892.
32 CNU III/7, 24.
33 C.B., 'Kompositionssoirée', *København*, 30 April 1892.
34 C.B., 'Kompositionssoirée', *København*, 30 April 1892.
35 Andersen, 'J.P. Jacobsen'.
36 Brandes, *Det moderne Gjennembruds Mænd*, 159.
37 *Nationaltidende*, 7 May 1895, quot. in CNU III/7, 28.
38 S.A., 'Symphonia', *København*, 7 May 1895.
39 *Dannebrog*, 11 June 1893.
40 *Dannebrog*, 11 June 1893.
41 CNB 2:341, 2:346.
42 Quot. Sørensen, 'Musiklivet på Fuglsang', 230.
43 Röntgen jun., 'Musiklivet på Fuglsang'.
44 Cf. Sørensen (ed.), *Johannes Palmer Hartmann og hans kreds*, vol. 1, 339, 464, 473.
45 Sørensen (ed.), *Johannes Palmer Hartmann og hans kreds*, vol. 1, 484.
46 Telmanyi, *Mit barndomshjem*, 53. Her recollection probably dates back to a stay at Fuglsang in 1908 or 1909, cf. Sørensen, 'Musiklivet på Fuglsang', 227.
47 Manuscript concert programmes, KB, HA, acc. 2013/29.
48 CNB 3:371.
49 *Nationaltidende*, 30 November 1907.
50 *Dannebrog*, 1 December 1907. The instrumental pieces performed were String Quartet in F major, Op. 44, and *Symphonic Suite*.
51 S.A., 'Karl Nielsens Kompositions-Aften', *Dannebrog*, 1 December 1907.
52 A.T., *Berlingske Tidende*, 2 December 1907.

Chapter 18
THE SYMBOLIST
1 Jensen, *Carl Nielsen. Danskeren*, 92.
2 Bahr, 'Die Décadence'.
3 Wivel, *Symbolisme og impressionisme*, 7–8. The section includes revised text from Engberg, *Carl Nielsen og århundredeskiftekulturen*, 47–51.
4 Jensen, *Carl Nielsen. Danskeren*, 92.
5 Jensen, *Carl Nielsen. Danskeren*, 92–93.
6 Grimley, *Carl Nielsen and the Idea of Modernism*, 27.
7 Tange, 'Musikalsk symbolisme', 42; cf. Jørgensen, 'Feberen i blodet', 188.
8 Tange, 'Musikalsk symbolisme', 52.
9 Tange, 'Musikalsk symbolisme', 46; cf. the definition of 'moments' in Nielsen, *Rued Langgaard*, 100.
10 Grimley, *Carl Nielsen and the Idea of Modernism*, 36, quot. Reynolds, 'The Early Song Collections', 403.

11 Reynolds, *Carl Nielsen's Voice*, 100–1.
12 Cf. Hindsberg, *Enargeia-Energeia*, 10–15, 49–53.
13 Overgaard (ed.), *Agnes Slott-Møller*, esp. 17–74.
14 CNB 1:403, 1:405; CNL 70, 72.
15 Jansen (ed.), *Taarnet*.
16 Jørgensen, 'Foraarsudstillingerne'; cf. Jensen, *Carl Nielsen. Danskeren*, 93.
17 Overgaard (ed.), *Agnes Slott-Møller*, 90.
18 Cf. Fanning, *Nielsen: Symphony No. 5*, 21.
19 Grimley, *Carl Nielsen and the Idea of Modernism*, 42–44; Reynolds, 'The Early Song Collections', 411.
20 *Dannebrog*, 11 June 1893.
21 Jensen, *Carl Nielsen. Danskeren*, 91.
22 Jørgensen, 'Symbolisme', 56.
23 Jørgensen, 'Foraarsudstillingerne'.
24 Jørgensen, 'Symbolisme', 54.
25 Jørgensen, 'Symbolisme', 56. 'Die Welt ist tief' (The world is deep) occurs several times in 'Das Nachtwandler-Lied' in Nietzsche, *Also sprach Zarathustra*, 124, 129.
26 Cf. Grimley, *Carl Nielsen and the Idea of Modernism*, 28–31.
27 CNB 1:345; CNL 60; cf. Grimley, 'Carl Nielsen's Dreamscapes'.
28 www.uffizi.it/en/artworks/botticelli-spring.
29 Samtid, 650. The poem is dated 14 March 1907.
30 CNB 1:3; CNL 1. He also wrote small occasional poems during these years, cf. Hatt, *Forårsbølger*, 55–60.
31 CNB 3:298; CNL 226. Cf. CNB 3:305, CNL 227, and 3:295 regarding the agreement with The Royal Theatre.
32 Samtid, 648–81. As far as they can be dated, the poems are written in spring and summer 1907.
33 CNB 1:20, 1:21, 1:438, 1:440, 1:441; CNL 10, 78, 79.
34 CNB 1:93, 1:242, 1:438, 1:440, 1:441, 1:447; CNL 78, 79, 80, and in letters to Anne Marie: CNB 1:344, 1:419, 1:422, 1:496, 1:582, 1:659, 2:36, 2:110; CNL 56, 75, and in her letters to Carl: CNB 2:100, 2:472, 2:501. Cf. also CNB 2:21.
35 Nielsen's book collection, which includes Freud's *Vorlesungen zur Einführung in die Psychoanalyse, Massenpsychologie und Ich-Analyse, Kleine Beiträge zur Traumlehre* and *Det Ubevidste*, is housed at Museum Odense.
36 CNB 6:228; cf. CNB 5:241, 5:319, 5:376, 5:435, 5:443, 6:28, 6:328, 6:406, 7:137, 7:149, 7:158, 9:422, 10:56, 10:580; CNL 364, 378, 443, 475.
37 CNB 3:202; cf. CNB 3:247.
38 CNU II/8, xi.
39 CNB 2:282; CNL 161, cf. CNB 2:245, 2:285, 2:286; CNL 162, 163.
40 Samtid, 722; the text is an undated note added on the reverse side of a printed invitation to make a financial contribution to the decoration of the new City Hall of Copenhagen, dated June 1901.
41 CNB 2:302; CNL 166.
42 CNB 2:302; CNL 166, cf. CNB 2:294. A draft of the poem is written on the reverse side of the letter and fair-copied below the text of the letter.
43 CNB 2:312; CNL 167. Also No. 1 in Jørgensen's collection, 'Bag de fjærne Markers sidste Rand', is among the poems that Nielsen received.
44 MS end-dated 8 December 1903.
45 Petersen, 'Carl Nielsen, *Søvnen*', 406, 418–20.
46 CNB 2:321, 2:322; CNL 170. The fair-copied score is end-dated 27 November 1904 and the draft 10 November 1904, CNU III/1, 211.
47 Petersen, 'Carl Nielsen, *Søvnen*', 418–21. Jørgensen published all seven poems which belonged to his cycle of poems 'Søvnen', in the collection of poems *Blomster og Frugter*, 7–14.
48 Jørgensen, 'Søvnen. En Hymne', 82.
49 Jørgensen, *Blomster og Frugter*, 7–14. The seven poems are reproduced in their original version in Jørgensen, *Udvalgte Værker*, vol. 7, 177–80.
50 A. H. [Angul Hammerich], 'Musikforeningen', *Nationaltidende*, 22 March 1905.

The following section is a revised version of Engberg, *Carl Nielsen og århundredeskiftekulturen*, 205–8.
51 A. H. [Angul Hammerich], 'Musikforeningen', *Nationaltidende*, 22 March 1905.
52 Doctor, *Choral Music in Demark*, 61.
53 G. K. H., 'Musikforeningen', *Dannebrog*, 22 March 1905.
54 Coda, 'Musikforeningen', *Dagens Nyheder*, 22 March 1905.
55 Cf. Sørensen, 'Korværkerne', 105.
56 CNB 2:312; CNL 167.
57 CNU II/8, xi–xii.
58 A.T., *Berlingske Tidende*, 2 December 1907.
59 Jensen, *Kongens Fald*, 38–39.
60 Cf. Steensen, *Musik er liv*, 163.
61 Sørensen, 'Bondemalerstriden'.

Chapter 19
WRITING OPERA AROUND 1900
1 Krabbe, 'Nielsen's unrealised opera plans'; cf. CNB 2:15, 2:62, 4:74, 9:229; CNL 134, 138, 597. On *Julestue*, see CNB 3:538; CNL 243, cf. CNB 3:545; on *Kilderejsen*, see CNB 7:323; CNL 500 and CNS 82.
2 Christiansen, *Nogle Træk af mit Liv og af dansk Teaters Historie*, 112–37.
3 Samtid, 63.
4 Regarding the tonal relationships on a general level, see Reynolds, *Carl Nielsen's Voice*, 307–27; Reynolds, 'Nielsen's *Saul and David* as Tragedy', 240–41.
5 Samtid, 64–65.
6 Samtid, 65–66.
7 CNB 11:370; CNL 712.
8 CNB 11:370; CNL 712.
9 CNB 3:551; CNL 245.
10 Samtid, 158.
11 Samtid, 519; Muntoni, 'Nielsen's Saul and David and Italian opera', 73–74; cf. Sansone, 'Verismo'; Leicht and Hallar, *Det kongelige Teaters repertoire*, 130, 141.
12 CNU III/1, xiv–xv.
13 Samtid, 518.
14 W.B. [William Behrend], *Politiken*, 29 November 1902. Cf. McCreless, 'Strange Bedfellows', 111–14. The following section is a revised version of Engberg, *Carl Nielsen og århundredeskiftekulturen*, 168–70.
15 CNU I/4, xii; Christiansen, *Nogle Træk af mit Liv og af dansk Teaters Historie*, 142–43, 233.
16 CNB 2:70, 2:86.
17 CNU I/4, xiii; cf. CNB 2:80, 2:81.
18 CNB 2:70.
19 Muntoni, 'Nielsen's Saul and David and Italian opera', 76.
20 Hamburger, *Thomas Laub*, 74–75.
21 CNB 2:148.
22 CNB 2:133.
23 CNB 2:127.
24 CNB 2:122.
25 CNB 2:122.
26 CNB 2:127.
27 McCreless, 'Strange Bedfellows', 115–27; CNU I/4, xxv–xxviii.
28 Reynolds, 'Nielsen's *Saul and David* as Tragedy'.
29 Cf. McCreless, 'Strange Bedfellows', 109–15.
30 *Saul og David*, pencil MS, CNS 330b, cf. CNU I/2, 617–19. The different music paper was used for the notation of Act 2, bb. 518–859.
31 Censure by Johan Svendsen, dated 31 May 1901, Det kongelige Teaters censurprotokol, quot. in CNU I/4, xvi.
32 CNB 2:191, 2:213; CNL 148.
33 Sophus Andersen, *København*, 29 November 1902.
34 *Social-Demokraten*, 29 November 1902.
35 McCreless, 'Strange Bedfellows', 109–11.
36 Reynolds, 'Nielsen's *Saul and David* as Tragedy', 240–50.
37 W. B., *Politiken*, 29 November 1902, quot. in CNU I/4, xx.
38 CNB 2:122, cf. CNU I/4, xix.
39 Bergh, 'Fra Opera og Koncertsal', 175. The following section is a revised version of Engberg, *Carl Nielsen og århundredeskiftekulturen*, 191–92, 199.
40 Bergh, 'Fra Opera og Koncertsal', 176.
41 J. H., 'Saul og David. Et Gennembrud', *København*, 5 December 1902.

42 J. H., 'Saul og David. Et Gennembrud', *København*, 5 December 1902.
43 McCreless, 'Strange Bedfellows', 113–15.
44 CNB 2:225. The section is a revised version of Engberg, *Carl Nielsen og århundredeskiftekulturen*, 180–84.
45 CNB 2:225.
46 CNB 2:225.
47 CNB 2:225.
48 CNB 2:288; CNL 164.
49 CNB 2:288; CNL 164.
50 Samtid, 58.
51 Leicht and Hallar, *Det kongelige Teaters repertoire*, 224, 334–35.
52 Foltmann, 'Carl Nielsens "Maskarade" og Det Kongelige Teaters scenemusik'.
53 Samtid, 156.
54 CNU I/1, xvii, quot. *Nationaltidende*, 12 November 1905.
55 Samtid, 55.
56 Holberg, *Mascarade*, Act 1, sc. 11.
57 Samtid, 56. In a later interview from 1911 (Samtid, 156), Nielsen claims that he saw Vilhelm Andersen in the play 'Den krøllede Fritz'; however, that is most likely a lapse of memory, as it was played in 1901, cf. 'Studenterforeningens Forestilling', *Dagbladet*, 5 May 1901.
58 CNU I/1, xi–xii; CNB 11:939; cf. CNB 2:333, 2:334.
59 CNU I/1, *Maskarade*, Act 1, bb. 1063–86; cf. Holberg, *Mascarade*, Act 2, sc. 3.
60 Meyer and Schandorf Petersen, *Carl Nielsen*, vol. 1, 228–29.
61 MfB, 155–56.
62 *Fyens Stiftstidende*, 27 January 1883; there were many advertisements for masquerades around the time.
63 Bøgh, *Kalifen paa Eventyr*, 58; cf. *Fyens Stiftstidende*, 22 January 1883.
64 Advertisements were posted by Odense Theater in *Fyens Stiftstidende*; the production ran for twenty-five performances from 21 January to 17 February 1883.
65 *Fyens Stiftstidende*, 22 January 1883.
66 Bøgh, *Kalifen paa Eventyr*, 58, 77, 107.
67 *Fyens Stiftstidende*, 10 February 1879.

68 Schmidt, *Meddelelser om Skuespil og Theaterforhold i Odense*, 205–10. The score for *Kalifen paa Eventyr* is today at KB, preserved in the archives of the Casino. An overview of the Casino's productions is available at danskforfatterleksikon.dk.
69 Foltmann, 'Carl Nielsens "Maskarade" og Det Kongelige Teaters scenemusik', 374–75. The Royal Theatre's score is preserved at KB (DKT 258).
70 Foltmann, 'Carl Nielsens "Maskarade" og Det Kongelige Teaters scenemusik', 376–84.
71 Andersen, *Bacchustoget i Norden*, 53.
72 Andersen, *Bacchustoget i Norden*, 295–96.
73 Andersen, *Bacchustoget i Norden*, 104, 122.
74 Andersen, *Bacchustoget i Norden*, 134, quot. Bellman's Epistle No. 30. Cf. Jensen, *Carl Nielsen. Danskeren*, 236–39.
75 CNU I/1–3, *Kritisk Beretning*, 99, 103.
76 CNU I/1, xvii–xix; CNB 3:115; the overture (CNS 329a) is end-dated 4 November 1906.
77 CNB 3:119; CNU I/1–3, *Kritisk beretning*, 7; the insertion corresponds to Act 2, bb. 654–700. RA, Det kongelige Teaters Arkiv og Bibliotek, Journal 1904-1910.
78 CNU I/1, xix; Samtid, 56.
79 Angul Hammerich, *Nationaltidende*, 12 November 1906.
80 Thaning, *Nationalitetskonstruktioner*, 26–27, 39–41.

Chapter 20
PROGRAMME MUSIC

1 Samtid, 130. The chapter is a revised version of Engberg, *Carl Nielsen og århundredeskiftekulturen*, 159–67.
2 Cf. Kristensen, 'Carl Nielsen as a Writer'.
3 Kregor, 'Program Music', 208; cf. Dahlhaus, *Nineteenth-Century Music*, 360.
4 Kregor, *Program Music*, 2, 136–38, 145.
5 CNB 1:109.
6 Kregor, *Program Music*, 195.
7 Anon., 'Max Reger'.
8 Anon., 'Richard Strauss'.

9 CNB 1:137; CNL 29.
10 Cf. Schmitter, 'Ancient, Medieval and Renaissance Theories of the Emotions', section 3.
11 CNU II/2, xi–xii, cf. CNB 2:213.
12 Ch. K. [Charles Kjerulf], 'Dansk Koncert-Forenings første Koncert', *Politiken*, 2 December 1902.
13 Fuller, 'Suite'.
14 S. [H. V. Schytte], 'Dansk Koncert-Forening', *Berlingske Tidende*, 2 December 1902.
15 Leop. Rosenfeld, 'Dansk Koncertforenings første Koncert', *Dannebrog*, 2 December 1902.
16 -st-ts- [Gustav Hetsch], 'Dansk Koncertforening', *Nationaltidende*, 2 December 1902.
17 Bergh, 'Fra Opera og Koncertsal', 177–78.
18 Dahlhaus, *Nineteenth-Century Music*, 361.
19 *Signale für die musikalische Welt*, 62 (1904), 912, quot. in CNU II/2, xiii.
20 CNB 2:213; CNL 148.
21 Samtid, 621.
22 Floros, *Gustav Mahler. III: Die Symphonien*, 26.
23 Samtid, 622.
24 CNB 2:263; dating in CNS 65b.
25 CNB 2:270; CNL 160.
26 CNB 2:285; CNL 162.
27 CNB 2:286; CNL 163.
28 CNB 2:288; CNL 164.
29 CNU II/7, xxiii.
30 Meyer and Schandorf-Petersen, *Carl Nielsen*, vol. 1, 210.
31 A. T. [Alfred Tofft], '1ste Symfoni-Koncert af Johan Svendsen og det kgl. Kapel', *Berlingske Tidende*, evening edn., 9 October 1903.
32 Grimley, *Carl Nielsen and the Idea of Modernism*, 61–67.
33 L. R. [Leopold Rosenfeld], '1ste Symfonikoncert af Johan Svendsen og det kgl. Kapel', *Dannebrog*, 9 October 1903.
34 L. R. [Leopold Rosenfeld], '1ste Symfonikoncert af Johan Svendsen og det kgl. Kapel', *Dannebrog*, 9 October 1903.
35 Cf. Meyer and Schandorf-Petersen, *Carl Nielsen*, vol. 1, 211–12.
36 Samtid, 99.
37 Spencer, *Musikkens Vorden og Virken*, 31, 43–44.
38 Samtid, 128.
39 Samtid, 129.
40 Samtid, 130–31.
41 Samtid, 134.
42 Samtid, 135.
43 CNU II/8, xxi–xxiii; Samtid, 222.
44 Rowell, 'Carl Nielsen's Homespun Philosophy of Music', 45.
45 Kregor, 'Program Music', 204–5, 208.
46 Samtid, 134.
47 Jensen, *Carl Nielsen. Danskeren*, 184–85.
48 Samtid, 131.

III

Chapter 21
CLASSICITY AS A SOURCE OF INNOVATION

1 CNB 2:440; CNL 190; cf. CNB 2:421 and Harder, 'Carl Nielsen'. The introduction is a revised version of Engberg, *Carl Nielsen og århundredeskiftekulturen*, 170.
2 Samtid, 50–51.
3 Samtid, 51.
4 Samtid, 80.
5 Seedorf, *Studien zur kompositorischen Mozart-Rezeption*, xi.
6 Seedorf, *Studien zur kompositorischen Mozart-Rezeption*, 1–5, 19–21, 29–36; Sousa, 'Musical Controversies in Nietzsche and Kierkegaard', 246–48.
7 Daverio, 'Mozart in the Nineteenth Century', 178. The following section is a revised version of Engberg, *Carl Nielsen og århundredeskiftekulturen*, 172–73.
8 Webster, *Haydn's "Farewell" Symphony and the Idea of Classical Style*, 347–51.
9 Daverio, 'Mozart in the Nineteenth Century', 178.
10 Blume, 'Klassik', col. 1030. Cf. Dahlhaus, *Die Musik des 19. Jahrhunderts*, 18–20.
11 Hannover, 'Udstillingerne III'.

12 Samtid, 99–110.
13 Wivel, *Symbolisme og impressionisme*, 229; Wanscher, *Den æsthetiske Opfattelse af Kunst*.
14 Samtid, 78–86.
15 Bergh, *Nogle Betragtninger over Musik*, 8. Rudolph Bergh's text was originally a lecture read in the Student Society on 25 February 1900 and published in *Berlingske Aftenavis* on 26, 27 and 28 February. It was later issued as an offprint. The following section is a revised version of Engberg, *Carl Nielsen og århundredeskiftekulturen*, 188–89, 193–94.
16 Bergh, *Nogle Betragtninger over Musik*, 9, 14.
17 Bergh, *Nogle Betragtninger over Musik*, 18–19.
18 Cf. Fjeldsøe, *Den fortrængte modernisme*, 127–30.
19 CNB 2:547; CNL 211.
20 CNB 4:193; CNL 289.
21 Samtid, 86; cf. Samtid, 126.
22 CNB 3:3; CNL 212.
23 CNB 3:3; CNL 212.
24 CNB 2:350; CNL 175.
25 CNB 2:547; CNL 211.
26 CNB 2:547, in which Röntgen's letter is also summarised; CNL 211.
27 Fjeldsøe, *Den fortrængte modernisme*, 128.
28 Villagomez, '"In the Land of Dreams"', 4–5.
29 CNB 1:78.
30 Samtid, 80.
31 Cf. the printed programme for the school year 1905-6, in RA, Skoleplaner m.m. (1891-1974), Borups Højskole; Samtid, 754.
32 Cf. Samtid, 60.
33 Samtid, 754–55; Bjørner, 'Emil B. Sachs og "Frisindet Ungdom"', 78–79.
34 The following section is a revised version of Engberg, *Carl Nielsen og århundredeskiftekulturen*, 194–205.
35 Samtid, 84–85.
36 Webster, *Haydn's "Farewell" Symphony and the Idea of Classical Style*, 351; Daverio, 'Mozart in the Nineteenth Century', 173.
37 Samtid, 79.
38 Jahn, *W. A. Mozart*, vol. 2, 585: 'Alles was den Menschen berührt empfindet er musikalisch, und jede Empfindung gestaltet er zum Kunstwerk; … Diese Universalität, welche mit Recht als Mozarts Vorzug gepriesen wird, beschränkt sich nicht auf de äußerliche Erscheinung … Seine Universalität hat ihre Schranke in der Beschränkung der menschlichen Natur überhaupt …'.
39 Samtid, 76.
40 Samtid, 62.
41 Samtid, 60.
42 Samtid, 62.
43 Bergh, 'Fra Opera og Koncertsal', 175–76.
44 Anon., 'Komponisten Carl Nielsen'.
45 Roth, 'Carl Nielsen's Cultural Self-Education', 322. Cf. Mosorini, 'New Findings in Titian's Fresco Technique', 163–64.
46 Meyer and Schandorf Petersen, *Carl Nielsen*, vol. 1, 131.
47 Foreword, quot. in Meyer and Schandorf Petersen, *Carl Nielsen*, vol. 1, 130. Cf. CNB 1:617.
48 Meyer and Schandorf Petersen, *Carl Nielsen*, vol. 1, 132–33.
49 Meyer and Schandorf Petersen, *Carl Nielsen*, vol. 1, 133.
50 Meyer and Schandorf Petersen, *Carl Nielsen*, vol. 1, 133.
51 Doctor, *Choral Music in Denmark*, 43.
52 Meyer and Schandorf Petersen, *Carl Nielsen*, vol. 1, 133.
53 Sørensen, 'Korværkerne', 100.
54 Cf. Meyer and Schandorf Petersen, *Carl Nielsen*, vol. 1, 135–36.
55 Meyer and Schandorf Petersen, *Carl Nielsen*, vol. 1, 134.
56 Meyer and Schandorf Petersen, *Carl Nielsen*, vol. 1, 135.
57 A. H. [Angul Hammerich], 'Musikforeningen', *Nationaltidende*, 29 April 1897.
58 N. L. [Nanna Liebmann], 'Musikforeningens tredje Koncert', *Dannebrog*, 28 April 1897.
59 Ch. K. [Charles Kjerulf], 'Koncerter', *Politiken*, 28 April 1897.

60 A. H. [Angul Hammerich], 'Musikforeningen', *Nationaltidende*, 29 April 1897.
61 Sørensen, 'Korværkerne', 97.
62 Doctor, *Choral Music in Denmark*, 42.
63 A. H. [Angul Hammerich], 'Musikforeningen', *Nationaltidende*, 29 April 1897.
64 *Fortegnelse over Kunstværkerne paa Den frie Udstilling 1897*, Danmarks Kunstbibliotek, http://kunstbib.dk/samlinger/udstillingskataloger/samlingen/000218523; Henrik Wivel, *Symbolisme og impressionisme*, 237, 246.
65 CNB 2:350; CNL 175.
66 CNB 2:350, 2:374, 2:547; CNL 175, 178, 211.
67 CNB 3:152; CNL 221.
68 For a more detailed presentation, see Fjeldsøe, *Den fortrængte modernisme*, 127–30.
69 CNB 3:3; CNL 212.
70 CNB 2:547; CNL 211.
71 Rangström, 'Modern sångkomposition', part 2; cf. CNB 3:752.
72 CNB 3:753; CNL 256.
73 Fjeldsøe, *Den fortrængte modernisme*, 130.
74 Fjeldsøe, *Den fortrængte modernisme*, 132–33.
75 CNB 1:224, 1:226; CNL 46.
76 Fjeldsøe, 'Ferruccio Busoni og Carl Nielsen', 18–21, 36–37.
77 CNB 2:351; CNL 276.
78 Fjeldsøe, 'Ferruccio Busoni og Carl Nielsen', 37.
79 For a more detailed presentation, see Fjeldsøe, *Den fortrængte modernisme*, 143–47.
80 Pfitzner, 'Futuristengefahr'.
81 Pfitzner, 'Die neue Aesthetik der musikalischen Impotenz'.
82 Busoni, *Entwurf einer neuen Aesthetik*, 50–52.
83 Samtid, 51.
84 Busoni, *Entwurf einer neuen Aesthetik*, 12f.: 'Das Kind – es schwebt! Es berührt nicht die Erde mit seinen Füßen. Es ist nicht der Schwere unterworfen. Es ist fast unkörperlich. Seine Materie ist durchsichtig. Es ist tönende Luft. Es ist frei.'
85 Samtid, 136.
86 Busoni, *Entwurf einer neuen Aesthetik*, 14–17.
87 Busoni, *Entwurf einer neuen Aesthetik*, 55: 'Weder auf dem See, noch an den Bergen, noch am Himmel eine einzige gerade Linie … überall Bewegung, Unregelmässigkeit, Willkür, Mannigfältigkeit, unaufhörliches Ineinanderfließen von Schatten und Linien, und in allem die Ruhe, Weichheit, Harmonie und Notwendigkeit des Schönen.'
88 Samtid, 267–68.
89 Fjeldsøe, *Den fortrængte modernisme*, 134.
90 CNB 6:340; CNL 436.
91 Busoni, 'Offener Brief an Hans Pfitzner', 249: 'Ich bin ein *Anbeter der Form*! … Aber ich verlange – nein, das Organische der Kunst verlangt, – daß jede Idee ihre eigene Form sich selbst bilde …'.
92 Samtid, 80–84.

Chapter 22
TIME

1 Samtid, 266.
2 Samtid, 267.

Chapter 23
THE VITALIST

1 Oelsner, 'Den sunde natur', 159–63.
2 Oelsner, 'Den sunde natur', 159, 314–15.
3 CNB 2:424; CNL 186; cf. CNB 2:416.
4 CNB 2:464, 2:484; CNL 199.
5 Fjeldsøe, 'Carl Nielsen and the Current of Vitalism', 29–31. See also Jensen, 'Carl Nielsen: Artistic Milieu and Tradition', 59–64.
6 Fjeldsøe, 'Vitalisme i Carl Nielsens musik'.
7 Undated MS, KB, CNA I.D.3.a., including a draft of a programme note, which was presented at the premiere of Nielsen's Fourth Symphony on 1 December 1916, quot. in CNU II/4, xiv, n. 14.
8 Dam, *Den vitalistiske strømning*, 9.
9 CNB 6:339; CNL 435.
10 Halse, 'Den vidtfavnende vitalisme', 52.
11 Dam, *Den vitalistiske strømning*, 14–15.
12 Cf. CNB 1:273.

13 Jacobsen and Johansen, 'Med kunstneren på arbejde', 20, reproduces the photograph 'Børn på stranden ved Amalfi'.
14 The following is based on Fjeldsøe, 'Vitalisme i Carl Nielsens musik', 36–39.
15 CNB 2:285; CNL 162.
16 CNB 2:285; CNL 162.
17 Dam, *Den vitalistiske strømning*, 23.
18 CNU II/3, xi–xiii. Cf. CNB 3:882, 3:925; CNL 264, 268. In the first two years after its premiere, the Third Symphony received a further twelve performances.
19 The following is based on Fjeldsøe, 'Vitalisme i Carl Nielsens musik', 39–43.
20 Foltmann and Krabbe, 'Source material for Carl Nielsen's Symphony no. 3', 231.
21 CNS 064a and CNS 064x, which are respectively Nielsen's pencil draft and the ink fair copy that was sent to Leipzig as a printer's manuscript.
22 Samtid, 162.
23 Samtid, 595.
24 Samtid, 595.
25 Samtid, 162.
26 MfB, 87.
27 Samtid, 163.
28 Samtid, 164.
29 CNU II/3, xiii, cf. CNS 64a, second movement, p. 11.
30 Samtid, 595.
31 Samtid, 164.
32 Samtid, 595.
33 Cf. CNB 1:622; CNL 126.

Chapter 24
THE COLLABORATION WITH LAUB

1 N. L., 'Folkevise-Aften', *Dannebrog*, 4 May 1898.
2 Laub's arrangements in MS, *Seks gamle danske Folkeviser, udsatte for blandet Kor af Thomas Laub 1897-1898. Indrettet til brug for Ceciliaforeningens Madrigalkor*, KB, mu8902.1088.
3 'En Folkevise-Aften', *Nationaltidende*, 3 May 1898.
4 MS in KB, Dansk Folkemindesamling, Olriks samling.
5 Dahlerup, *Dansk Litteratur. Middelalder*, vol. 2, 113–233.
6 *Nationaltidende*, 3 May 1898.
7 Nyerup and Rahbek, *Udvalgte Danske Viser fra Middelalderen*; Nyerup, *Udvalg af Danske Viser*; Berggreen, *Folke-Sange og Melodier*.
8 Laub, 'Vore Folkevise-Melodier og deres Fornyelse', 194.
9 Laub, 'Vore Folkevise-Melodier og deres Fornyelse', 182.
10 Laub, 'Om udførelsen af viserne', 81.
11 Cf. letter from Laub to Olrik, 8 May 1897, KB, Dansk Folkemindesamling, Olriks samling.
12 Letter from Laub to Olrik, 8 May 1897, KB, Dansk Folkemindesamling, Olriks samling.
13 *Berlingske Tidende*, 5 May 1898, second edn.
14 Undated letter from Laub to Olrik, KB, Dansk Folkemindesamling, Olriks samling.
15 Letter from Laub to Olrik, 19 May 1898, KB, Dansk Folkemindesamling, Olriks samling. Cf. 'En Folkevise-Aften', *Nationaltidende*, 3 May 1898, and 'Folkevise-Aften', *Dannebrog*, 4 May 1898.
16 Advertisements in the daily press.
17 Cf. letter from Laub to Olrik, 31 October 1897, KB, Dansk Folkemindesamling, Olriks samling.
18 CNB 1:644.
19 Correspondence between Olrik and Skovgaard, KB, Dansk Folkemindesamling, Olriks samling.
20 Samtid, 426.
21 CNB 2:15; CNL 134.
22 CNB 2:19.
23 Cf. Meyer and Schandorf Petersen, *Carl Nielsen*, vol. 1, 175, 201.
24 CNB 2:127, 2:133.
25 CNB 2:127.
26 CNB 2:148.
27 Laub, *Vor musikundervisning og den musikalske dannelse*. Nielsen knew the tract, cf. CNB 2:178; CNL 145.

28 *Social-Demokraten*, 23 October 1902.
29 Gustav Hetsch [-st-ts-], 'Folkevise-Aften', *Dagbladet*, 23 October 1902.
30 Leopold Rosenfeld, 'Folkevise-Aften', *Dannebrog*, 23 October 1902.
31 'Toner, gamle og nye', *Aftenbladet*, 23 October 1902.
32 CNB 2:219.
33 CNB 2:219.
34 Samtid, 43.
35 Charles Kjerulf, 'Om Hr. Laubs Folkeviser, forhen de danske Folkeviser', *Politiken*, 7 November 1902.
36 CNB 2:225.
37 CNB 2:288; CNL 164.
38 CNB 7:240; CNL 491.
39 CNB 5:159; CNL 346.
40 Schulz, *Lieder im Volkston*, vol. 1, second edn., foreword.
41 Translation of Schulz's text, printed as foreword to *En Snes danske Viser*, vol. 1, 1915.
42 CNU III/7, 53.
43 Høgel, *Johann Abraham Peter Schulz*, 79-80.
44 CNB 5:188.
45 CNB 5:171; CNL 347.
46 Høgel, *Johann Abraham Peter Schulz*, 79-99, 184-91.
47 CNB 5:159; CNL 346.
48 CNB 6:19; CNL 404.
49 CNB 5:209; CNL 351.
50 Audivi, 'En ejendommelig Vise-Aften', *Nationaltidende*, 11 April 1915.
51 Cf. Reynolds, *Carl Nielsen's Voice*, 121-62.
52 CNB 5:384.
53 Cf. Grundtvig, 'Rim-Brev til Nordisk Paarørende'.
54 Letter from Laub to Nielsen, 2 August 1916, KB, CNA I.A.b. Breve, æske 15; the letter's introduction is cited in CNB 5:396.
55 Letter from Laub to Nielsen, 2 August 1916, KB, CNA I.A.b. Breve, æske 15.
56 CNB 5:171; CNL 347.
57 CNB 5:171; CNL 347.
58 CNB 5:171; CNL 347.
59 Transl. in CNU III/7, 222-23.
60 Reynolds, *Carl Nielsen's Voice*, 168-69, 173.
61 Schousboe, '"Det skulle være jævne viser...", esp. 171-74. Laub's draft to the corrections are in CNS 196d.
62 CNB 5:188, 5:205.

Chapter 25
THE THEATRE COMPOSER
1 CNU I/8, xix.
2 Cf. Savage, 'Incidental Music'.
3 CNU I/6, xlii-xliii.
4 Wiingaard, 'Den svære realisme', 36-38.
5 Rask, 'Privatteatrene 1848-57', 11.
6 Rask, 'Dagmarteatret', 50.
7 Rask, 'Dagmarteatret', 53.
8 CNU I/6, xiii.
9 Se CNU I/6, xiv-xv.
10 *Nationaltidende*, 16 January 1890.
11 Engberg, *En digters historie*, 100-1.
12 Engberg, *En digters historie*, 74, 103.
13 Dedication in Nielsen's copy of the printed edition in Museum Odense, quot. in CNU I/6, xiii.
14 CNU I/6, civ.
15 Stangerup and Jansen, *Dansk Litteraturhistorie*, vol. 3, 432-33.
16 CNB 3:455.
17 CNB 3:455.
18 Broad, *Nordic Incidental Music*, 61.
19 Drachmann, *Breve*, vol. 4, 274.
20 Drachmann, *Breve*, vol. 4, 272.
21 CNU I/7, ix.
22 CNB 1:622; CNL 126.
23 CNB 3:56.
24 CNB 3:53.
25 CNB 3:54; CNL 216.
26 CNU I/7, xii.
27 Savage, 'Incidental Music'.
28 Brittain, 'Music, Magic and the Supernatural', 134-35.
29 Leicht and Hallar, *Det kongelige Teaters repertoire*, 257.
30 CNU I/7, xii.
31 *Dannebrog*, 10 October 1906, quot. in CNU I/7, xiv.
32 *Dannebrog*, 10 October 1906, quot. in CNU I/7, xiv.

33 *Berlingske Tidende* (second edn.), 10 October 1906, quot. in CNU I/7, xv.
34 Hines, 'Hearing and Seeing Brahms's Harps', 77–82.
35 *Dagbladet*, 10 October 1906.
36 CNU I/7, xiii.
37 CNU I/7, xvi.
38 *Politiken*, 10 October 1906.
39 CNU I/8, xi.
40 Meyer and Schandorf Petersen, *Carl Nielsen*, vol. 2, 173.
41 *Berlingske Tidende*, quot. in Meyer and Schandorf Petersen, *Carl Nielsen*, vol. 2, 172–73. The advertisement was published on 16 February in *Berlingske Tidende, København, Nationaltidende, Politiken* and *Social-Demokraten*, and on 17 February in *Kristeligt Dagblad* and *Vort Land*.
42 Savage, 'Incidental Music', 11.
43 CNB 3:54; CNL 216.
44 CNU I/8, xi.
45 CNU I/8, xii; Leicht and Hallar, *Det kongelige Teaters repertoire*, 123–25. Cf. Sørensen, 'Indledning'.
46 Letter from Johannes Poulsen to Otto Borchsenius, 11 March 1914, quot. in Poulsen, *Johannes Poulsen som iscenesætter*, 9.
47 CNU I/8.
48 CNU I/8, 33–35.
49 Quot. in Meyer and Schandorf Petersen, *Carl Nielsen*, vol. 2, 177–78.
50 Poulsen, *Johannes Poulsen som iscenesætter*, 77.
51 Poulsen, *Johannes Poulsen som iscenesætter*, 76–77.
52 CNU I/8, xvii.
53 *Social-Demokraten*, 16 February 1919.
54 CNB 6:182; CNL 426.
55 CNU I/8, xviii.
56 *Politiken*, 16 February 1919.
57 *Nationaltidende*, 16 February 1919.
58 CNW 17.
59 CNU II/8a, 'Aladdin' Suite.
60 Cheney, *The Open-Air Theatre*, 30.
61 Cheney, *The Open-Air Theatre*, 64–70.
62 Bernsen, 'Friluftsteatret i Dyrehaven', 151.
63 Willumsen, *Mine Erindringer*, 180.
64 Anon., *Beretning om Friluftsteatret i Ulvedalene*, [1].
65 Anon., *Beretning om Friluftsteatret i Ulvedalene*, [3].
66 CNU I/6, xlix–l.
67 CNU I/6, xliv–xlv.
68 Bernsen, 'Friluftsteatret i Dyrehaven', 155.
69 *Politiken*, 13 May 1910.
70 'Nyt Musikværk', *Politiken*, 3 June 1910.
71 CNU I/6, xlix–l.
72 *Politiken*, 3 June 1910.
73 Hesselager, *Musik i Danmark*, 25.
74 Behrens, 'Friluftsspil', 592.
75 *Berlingske Tidende* (second edn.), 8 June 1919, quot. in Bernsen, 'Friluftsteatret i Dyrehaven', 161.
76 CNB 3:835.
77 CNB 3:838.
78 The repertoire of the Open-Air Theatre is listed in Bernsen, 'Friluftsteatret i Dyrehaven', 200–5.
79 CNU I/6, l–li; Bernsen, 'Friluftsteatret i Dyrehaven', 165.
80 *Teateret* (1915), quot. in Bernsen, 'Friluftsteatret i Dyrehaven', 166.
81 CNU I/9, xxxvii; Bernsen, 'Friluftsteatret i Dyrehaven', 173.

Chapter 26
COMPOSER OF HYMNS

1 CNB 5:43; CNL 329.
2 CNB 4:86, 5:58; cf. CNB 5:209; CNL 351.
3 CNB 5:12; CNL 324.
4 CNB 5:43; CNL 329.
5 CNB 5:16.
6 Lindholm, *Starup Sogn i Brusk Herred*, 80–82.
7 Hjermitslev, 'Georg Valdemar Brücker (1852-1929)'; Ottesen, 'Valdemar Brücker 1852-1929'.
8 Gregersen and Kjærgaard, 'Darwin and the divine experiment'.
9 Hjermitslev, 'Protestant Responses to Darwinism in Denmark', 288.
10 Brücker, 'Folkehøjskolen'. Cf. Grundtvig, *Skolen for Livet*.
11 Ottesen, 'Valdemar Brücker 1852-1929'.

12 Munk, 'Konstantin-Hansen, Elise'.
13 Malling, *Dansk Salmehistorie*, vol. 8, 351–52, 448–49.
14 CNB 5:58. The numbers Brücker mentions in his letter correspond to the second edition of the hymnal, published in 1908.
15 Schulz, *Gedanken über den Einfluss der Musik*; Bryndorf, 'Salmesang til orgelklang'.
16 Røllum-Larsen, 'Musikken i Holmens Kirke', 153–56; Arnfred, 'Sang bliver et skolefag'.
17 Glahn, *Salmemelodien i dansk tradition*, 39–56.
18 CNB 5:209; CNL 351.
19 Cf. CNB 4:372.
20 Hamburger, *Thomas Laub*, 51–58.
21 Laub, *Om Kirkesangen*, 1–2.
22 Glahn, *Salmemelodien i dansk tradition*, 28–34.
23 Laub, *Om Kirkesangen*, 78.
24 Hamburger, *Thomas Laub*, 41. The Danish sources that Laub must have had at his disposal are available at https://salmer.dsl.dk/. Cf. Moe, 'Salmesang på skrift'; Moe, '"Galopader af stavelser"'.
25 Laub, *80 rytmiske Koraler*.
26 Laub, *Om Kirkesangen*, 104.
27 Laub, *Om Kirkesangen*, 133.
28 Bielefeldt, *Melodier til Psalmebog for Kirke og Hjem*, first edn.
29 Bielefeldt, *Melodier til Psalmebog for Kirke og Hjem*, second edn.
30 Bielefeldt, *Melodier til Psalmebog for Kirke og Hjem*, first edn., foreword.
31 It concerns 'Gak under Jesu Kors at staa' (No. 64b) and 'Hvo ikkun lader Herren raade' (No. 94b).
32 Laub, *Om Kirkesangen*, 4.
33 Røllum-Larsen, 'Musikken i Holmens Kirke', 164.
34 Laub, *80 rytmiske Koraler*, 3–4.
35 *Samtid*, 684.
36 Samtid, 685.
37 CNB 8:74; CNL 539.
38 Samtid, 685.
39 CNB 6:305; CNL 432; the statement, which is dated 13 December 1919, is among Laub's papers, Musikmuseet. *Salmer og aandelige Sange* is advertised as a new publication in *Nationaltidende*, 23 January 1920.
40 CNB 5:546; CNL 394.
41 CNB 5:547, 5:551; CNL 395; cf. CNB 6:3.
42 *Samtid*, 203–18, the sheet is reproduced on 218.
43 Røllum-Larsen, 'Musikken i Holmens Kirke', 165.
44 CNB 2:288; CNL 164.
45 CNB 2:288; CNL 164.
46 CNB 3:812.
47 CNB 3:812.
48 Olesen, *Organistbogen*, 62–63; Schousboe, '"Barn af huset"', esp. 87–91.
49 CNB 5:43; CNL 329.
50 Cf. CNB 3:812.
51 Chords in first inversion and dissonances at phrase endings appear in V, bb. 2, 4; X, bb. 2, 5; XIV, b. 8; XV, b. 2; XXI, b. 10; XXIV, bb. 6, 12; XXV, b. 12; XXIX, b. 6; XXXI, b. 6; XXXIII, b. 6; XXXVI, bb. 6, 12; XXXVII, b. 4; XLII, bb. 10, 13; XLIII, bb. 6, 14; XLIV, b. 4; XLIII, 10.
52 In Laub's *Dansk Kirkesang. Gamle og nye Melodier*, which includes seventy-three of his own tunes, he only deviates in one single instance from a consonant chord in root position at a transition between phrases: 'Vor Aldersoms Trøst og Støttestav' (b. 2).
53 Cf. Thomissøn (ed.), *Den danske Psalmebog*, fol. d 4r.
54 Malling, *Dansk Salmehistorie*, vol. 8.
55 Jensen, 'Hvad er en salme?', 33.
56 Grundtvig, 'Aandelig Fiskervise'.
57 Jensen, 'Hvad er en salme?'
58 *Højskolebladet*, 44 (1919), cols. 1631–34.
59 *Højskolebladet*, 42 (21 December 1917).
60 CNB 5:546; CNL 394.
61 Jensen, *Carl Nielsen. Danskeren*, 290.

Chapter 27
THE AESTHETIC SENSORY
1 Samtid, 125.
2 Samtid, 125.
3 Samtid, 125.
4 MfB, 49; Childhood, 51.
5 Berger, '"Musik" nach Kant', 37.

6 MfB, 12–13; Childhood, 10.
7 MfB, 13.
8 CNB 7:384; CNL 506.
9 CNB 5:209; CNL 351.
10 Samtid, 143.
11 Riley, *Musical Listening in the German Enlightenment*, 7–9.
12 Samtid, 130–31.

Chapter 28
'MUSIC *IS* LIFE'

1 CNB 1:137; CNL 29; cf. CNB 1:138.
2 Fjeldsøe, 'Vitalisme i Carl Nielsens musik', 39–43.
3 CNU II/4, 121. The symphony is published with a title page in Danish, German and English, also including information on agencies in France, Belgium and the USA.
4 Programme note for the first performance on 1 February 1916, quot. in CNU II/4, xiii–xiv. Knud Jeppesen was responsible for the final version of the programme note, based on a draft by Nielsen.
5 CNB 6:339; CNL 435.
6 CNU II/4, xiii.
7 Fjeldsøe, *Den fortrængte modernisme*, 147.
8 CNB 6:340; CNL 436; the original Danish formulation is: 'den størst mulige *Frihed* i Udfoldelsen af det personlige Indhold og den størst mulige *Strenghed* med Hensyn til Organisme – Sammenhæng.' In CNB the important dash has been replaced with a hyphen.
9 CNB 6:339; CNL 435.
10 For a more detailed discussion, see Fjeldsøe, 'Vitalisme i Carl Nielsens musik', 43–47.
11 CNB 5:81; CNL 336.
12 CNB 5:104; CNL 339; cf. CNB 5:95, 5:98.
13 CNB 5:209; CNL 351.
14 Samtid, 194–95.
15 Anon., 'Komponisten Carl Nielsen'.
16 Cf. Fjeldsøe, 'Carl Nielsen and the Current of Vitalism', 34.
17 Fjeldsøe, 'Vitalisme i Carl Nielsens musik', 44–45.
18 Fjeldsøe, 'Vitalisme i Carl Nielsens musik', 46.
19 Samtid, 194.
20 Note added by Launy Grøndahl to the copy of the score belonging to the Danish Radio, dated 31 August 1951, quot. in CNU II/4, 123.
21 Fjeldsøe, 'Vitalisme i Carl Nielsens musik', 45.
22 Cf. Fanning, 'Progressive Thematicism in Nielsen's Symphonies', 188–91.
23 Cf. Grimley, *Carl Nielsen and the Idea of Modernism*, 60.
24 The motif of the viola appears the first time in b. 169.
25 CNB 6:340; CNL 436.
26 Printer's MS, CNS 65a, quot. in CNU II/4, xxiv.
27 CNU II/4, 84, note regarding b. 764.
28 Nielsen, 'Nogle personlige erindringer', 12.
29 Jensen, *Carl Nielsen. Danskeren*, 320.
30 Fanning, 'Progressive Thematicism in Nielsen's Symphonies', 188.
31 Fanning, 'Progressive Thematicism in Nielsen's Symphonies', 191.
32 Emilius Bangert, 'Musikforeningens 2den Koncert', *Hovedstaden*, 2 August 1916.
33 CNW 28.
34 Thaning, *Nationalitetskonstruktioner*, 32–45, 96.
35 Ch. K., *Politiken*, 2 February 1916.
36 Ch. K., *Politiken*, 15 April 1916.

IV

Chapter 29
THE POPULAR AND THE MODERN

1 Maegaard, 'Når boet skal gøres op efter Carl Nielsen…', 104.
2 Samtid, 263.

Chapter 30
THE GREAT REFORM PROJECT

1 Marstal, 'Gamle rammer, nye måder?'; cf. Bak, 'Fællessangstraditioner i Danmark ca. 1780-1960'.
2 Samtid, 318.
3 Balslev, 'Folkehøjskolens Melodibog ved Carl Nielsen, Thomas Laub, Oluf Ring og Thorvald Aagaard', 855.

4 For an overview of the contents of each issue, see: https://hojskolesangbogen.dk/om-sangbogen/historie-om-bogen/alle-udgaver/. Cf. Bak, *Højskolesangbogens historie*, 78–82.
5 Bak, *Højskolesangbogens historie*, 83.
6 Nutzhorn, *Melodier til Sangbog for Højskoler og Landbrugsskoler*.
7 The first editions of the five volumes were published in 1895, 1899, 1901, 1921 and 1928, respectively, and in several new issues along the way, cf. overview in KB, Dan Fogs Samling 23, 'Danmarks Melodibog'.
8 Balslev, *Thorvald Aagaard*, 41–43; Ring, *Thorvald Aagaard*, 48–52.
9 Aagaard, 'Folkelig Sang'.
10 Aagaard, 'En ny Sangbog'.
11 Ring, *Thorvald Aagaard*, 56–57.
12 Spur (ed.), *Viser og Sange*.
13 Bak, *Højskolesangbogens historie*, 81.
14 Ring, *Thorvald Aagaard*, 58.
15 Povlsen, 'Melodier til Højskolesangbogen'.
16 Aagaard, 'Folkelig Sang', 1166.
17 CNB 3:48. Cf. Fellow, 'Fædrelandssang med følger'.
18 Anon. (ed.), *Enstemmige Sange til Brug for Højskoler, Gymnastik og Skytteforeninger*.
19 RA, census for Vestre Boulevard, 1901.
20 *Maanedsblad for Borups Højskole*, 1/7 (1 April 1916), 56.
21 See e.g. CNB 2:83 and CNB 2:289.
22 Advertisement under the heading 'For unge Damer' (For young ladies), *Dagens Nyheder*, 23 September 1903.
23 Samtid, 60–77. The presentation took place in Industriforeningens Foredragssal, cf. the printed programme of lectures, *J. Borup's Læreanstalt. Videregaaende Undervisning for Herrer og Damer*, 15 (1905–6), RA, Borups Højskole, Skoleplaner m.m. (1891-1974).
24 Borup, *Højskolen og København*, 23.
25 Marstrand, *Johan Borup og hans kreds*, 59–70.
26 Borup, *Højskolen og København*, 28.
27 Borup, *Højskolen og København*, 38.
28 Borup, *Højskolen og København*, 20.
29 Borup, *Højskolen og København*, 27.
30 Borup, *Højskolen og København*, 31. By 1925, 11,000 students had attended the school, 4,000 of whom were from the working class, cf. Sørensen, 'Borups Højskole og Arbejderne'.
31 Borup, *Højskolen og København*, 31–35.
32 Borup, *Højskolen og København*, 35.
33 Borup, *Brogede Blade*, 14.
34 Laub, 'Et Indledningsforedrag'.
35 Carstensen, 'Vore Musikaftener'.
36 Thomsen, 'Vore Sange', 39.
37 Clausen, *Dansk Folkesang gennem 150 år*, 221.
38 The *Vallekildebog* was issued as Trier (ed.), *Sange for den kristelige folke-skole*. Cf. Bak, *Højskolesangbogens historie*, 57–60.
39 Anon., 'Bladet', 2.
40 Borup, 'Vore Sange' (*Højskolebladet*), cols. 321f. 'Vore Sange' was issued in *Maanedsblad for Borups Højskole*, 2/6 (1 March 1917).
41 Sørensen, '"Fædreland" eller "Fødeland"?', 3.
42 Sørensen, '"Fædreland" eller "Fødeland"?', 3.
43 Quot. in Schrøder, *Den nordiske Folkehøjskole*, 136.
44 Borup, 'Vore Sange', 322.
45 Borup, 'Vore Sange', 322.
46 CNB 5:77 and commentary; letter from Johan Borup to Nielsen, 2 May 1914, KB, CNA I.A.b.
47 Letters from Johan Borup to Nielsen, 27 May, 25 June and 29 June 1914, KB, CNA I.A.b.
48 Cf. CNB 5:154, 5:156.
49 The songs are 'Solen ler saa godt og mildt' (melody: H. V. Godske-Nielsen), 'Og spørger du mig' (Paul Hellmuth), 'En Sømand med et modigt Bryst' (Thomas Laub) and 'Der ligger Guld i Barrer' (Paul Hellmuth).
50 RA, Johan Borups Arkiv, Breve, alfabetisk ordnet (1828-1946), A-H, letter from Jeppe Aakjær to Johan Borup, 15 December 1915.
51 The number of new tunes in Nielsen (ed.), *Nye Melodier til de nyere Sangtekster i Johan Borup's Dansk Sangbog*.
52 Borup, *Dansk Sangbog*, 274–310.

53 *Dansk Sangbog*, 276, 285, 306.
54 *Dansk Sangbog*, 294.
55 *Dansk Sangbog*, 305.
56 The music manuscripts used for Johan Borup's melody book, KB, IA-2-A398 Musiksamlingen.
57 CNB 5:182.
58 The songs are 'Der dukker af Disen' (CNW 222), Song of Old Anders the Cattleman (CNW 151), 'Hør, hvor let' (CNW 223), 'Jeg bærer med Smil' (CNW 212), 'Nu er Dagen fuld af Sang' (CNW 213), 'Se dig ud en Sommerdag' (CNW 221), 'Ud gaar du nu' (CNW 203) and 'Vender sig Lykken' (CNW 207).
59 CNB 5:182.
60 CNB 5:184.
61 Frederiksen, 'Fynske Forsamlingshuse', 75, 83–84.
62 CNB 1:8; cf. CNB 10:6; CNL 630.
63 CNB 6:168; cf. Ring, *Thorvald Aagaard*, 12.
64 CNB 2:11; CNL 132.
65 CNB 2:65, 2:68; cf. Ring, *Thorvald Aagaard*, 39.
66 Hetsch, *Det kongelige danske Musikkonservatorium*, 170.
67 Ring, *Thorvald Aagaard*, 32–48.
68 Ring, *Thorvald Aagaard*, 58. Cf. CNB 6:296.
69 Ring, *Oluf Ring*, 98–99.
70 Cf. Aagaard, 'Folkehøjskolens Melodibog. I Anledning af Emborgs kritiske Bemærkninger'.
71 CNB 7:16.
72 CNB 7:11; cf. CNB 7:16, 7:27; CNL 455.
73 'Fortale', in Nielsen et al. (ed.), *Folkehøjskolens Melodibog*. Nielsen's draft is placed among Laub's letters to Aagaard, KB, NKS 4737 4°, Thorvald Hans Aagaard, I Breve, 1 Til Thorvald Aagaard, L-Mu.
74 Foreword to *Tyve folkelige Sange* (1921), quot. in CNU III/7, 66.
75 CNB 7:16.
76 Letter from Laub to Aagaard, postmarked 27 November 1920, KB, NKS 4°, Thorvald Hans Aagaard, I Breve, 1 Til Thorvald Aagaard, L-Mu.
77 Letter from Oluf Ring to Aagaard, 14 March 1921, KB, NKS 4737 4°, Thorvald Hans Aagaard, I Breve, 1 Til Thorvald Aagaard, R-Se.
78 The text is no. 221 in Borup, *Dansk Sangbog*, where it appears in the section 'Hverdagens Sange' (Everyday songs); however, Nielsen's tune was composed later; cf. Weyse, *Sange med klaver*, vol. 2, 158–60, 214.
79 Balslev, 'Folkehøjskolens Melodibog ved Carl Nielsen, Thomas Laub, Oluf Ring og Thorvald Aagaard', 857.
80 Emborg, 'Folkehøjskolens Melodibog. Kritiske Bemærkninger'.
81 Aagaard, 'Folkehøjskolens Melodibog. I Anledning af Emborgs kritiske Bemærkninger', 1084.
82 Cf. CNB 6:300.
83 Cf. Ring's letters to Aagaard 1920–2, KB, NKS 4737 4°, Thorvald Hans Aagaard, I Breve, 1 Til Thorvald Aagaard, R-Se.
84 CNB 7:235.
85 Letter from Ring to Aagaard, 3 June 1922, KB, NKS 4737 4°, Thorvald Hans Aagaard, I Breve, 1 Til Thorvald Aagaard, R-Se.
86 CNB 7:240; CNL 491.
87 Cf. Bak, 'Fællessang og danskhed'.

Chapter 31
MODERNISM AND MODERNITY

1 Fjeldsøe, *Den fortrængte modernisme*, 138–39.
2 *Samtid*, 257.
3 *Samtid*, 257–58.
4 *Samtid*, 257.
5 Jensen, *Carl Nielsen. Danskeren*, 307.
6 *Samtid*, 257.
7 CNS 66b, quot. in CNU II/5, xvi.
8 CNB 6:459; CNL 447; cf. CNB 6:453, 6:460; CNL 448.
9 CNB 6:435.
10 CNB 6:339, 6:340; CNL 435, 436.
11 For a detailed analysis, see Fjeldsøe, 'Organicism and Construction'.
12 Fjeldsøe, 'Organicism and Construction', 23–26; CNB 6:340; CNL 436.

13 CNU II/5, 50 and 55, at b. 351 and b. 367, respectively.
14 CNB 9:438; CNL 610; cf. CNB 9:447.
15 Samtid, 257.
16 Samtid, 257.
17 Grimley, *Carl Nielsen and the Idea of Modernism*, 111–13, 217–19; Kurth, *Grundlagen des Linearen Kontrapunkts*, 9–12, 62–67.
18 Samtid, 255–56.
19 Cf. roditraditionerne.dk/undervisningsmateriale/den-lille-englaender/#1457530055137-79d73dff-f980; according to Dansk Folkemindesamling (Axel Teich Geertinger), the melody corresponds to the song 'Blaydon Races', composed in England in 1862 by the author Geordie Ridley. It has since found its way to Denmark as folk dance tune entitled 'Den lille Englænder'.
20 Grimley, 'Modernism and Closure', 150–51, 166–69.
21 Samtid, 258.
22 Fjeldsøe, 'Carl Nielsens 5. symfoni', 61–64.
23 Fjeldsøe, *Den fortrængte modernisme*, 20–26, 40–44.
24 Fjeldsøe, *Den fortrængte modernisme*, 59–63; Fjeldsøe, 'Organizing the New Music'.
25 Fjeldsøe, *Den fortrængte modernisme*, 301–2, 311–12, 316–17.
26 Schoenberg's *Fünf Klavierstücke*, Op. 23, his first published work based on the twelve-note series, was issued by Wilhelm Hansen in Copenhagen in 1923.
27 Fjeldsøe, *Den fortrængte modernisme*, 316.
28 L-m-., 'Schönberg-Koncerten', *B.T.*, 10 November 1921.
29 Samtid, 141.
30 CNB 4:708; CNL 313.
31 Cf. Rowell, 'Carl Nielsen's Homespun Philosophy of Music', 45–46.
32 Knudsen, *Sinfonia espansiva*, 4: 'Wer Neuland erwerben will, muß neue Erweiterungen und neue Gesichtspunkte auf tonalem Gebiete zu gewinnen suchen.'
33 Knudsen, *Sinfonia espansiva*, 4: 'Da sind z.B. die Tonartenverhältnisse. Carl Nielsen hat die Schranken ihrer Begrenzung stark empfunden; man merkt daher überall in seinen Werken den Drang, sie zu durchbrechen. Es ist manchmal in seiner Musik, als ob die zwölf Dur- und die zwölf Molltonarten oder Kirchentonarten überhaupt nicht existierten, sondern als ob sie in einen Mörser gekommen und zu einer einzigen Tonart verarbeitet worden wären.'
34 Knudsen, *Sinfonia espansiva*, 4: 'seine Modulation ist kurz, kräftig, überzeugend und geschieht häufig nur mittelst reiner Dreiklänge.'
35 CNB 7:1; CNL 452.
36 Fjeldsøe, *Den fortrængte modernisme*, 137–40.
37 CNB 4:708; CNL 313.
38 Knudsen, *Sinfonia espansiva*, 4.
39 CNB 4:708; CNL 313.
40 Samtid, 685.
41 CNB 5:488; CNL 387.
42 CNB 5:453; CNL 384; cf. CNB 5:465; CNL 385.
43 CNS 66b, cf. CNU II/5, 160 and xvi.
44 Fjeldsøe, 'Carl Nielsens 5. symfoni', 56–58.
45 CNS 67b.
46 Samtid, 543.
47 See e.g. Meyer and Schandorf Petersen, *Carl Nielsen*, vol. 2, 266–70.
48 Fjeldsøe, *Den fortrængte modernisme*, 140.
49 Fjeldsøe, 'Carl Nielsens 5. symfoni', 57–58.

Chapter 32
THE KAPELLMEISTER
1 CNB 7:442.
2 Akten betreffend ordentliche Mitglieder, 1923-1924, Archiv der Akademie der Künste, Berlin, PrAdK 708, Blatt 38–40. Nielsen, Glazunov and Braunfels were 'auswärtige', that is, from outside Prussia, yet 'ordentliche', ordinary members.
3 Membership database for Akademie der Künste, Berlin, at adk.de.
4 Personalnachrichten Musik, Carl August Nielsen, PrAdK, Archiv der Akademie der Künste, Berlin: 'bis 1914 alle Musik- und Opernauführungen an den Theater so zu sagen beinahe allein leitete, da mein treff-

liche Kollege, Fr. Rung, fortwährend krank war.'
5 Personalnachrichten Musik, Carl August Nielsen, PrAdK, Archiv der Akademie der Künste, Berlin.
6 Personalnachrichten Musik, Carl August Nielsen, PrAdK, Archiv der Akademie der Künste, Berlin.
7 CNB 1:367; cf. CNB 1:360–366; CNL 62–63.
8 Journal, 1895-1904, 8 April 1904, RA, Det Kongelige Teaters Arkiv og Bibliotek; cf. CNB 2:332; CNL 154.
9 Journal, 1895-1904, RA, Det Kongelige Teaters Arkiv og Bibliotek.
10 Journal, 1904-1910, 9 October 1906, RA, Det Kongelige Teaters Arkiv og Bibliotek.
11 CNU I/7, ix–xii.
12 Meyer and Schandorf Petersen, *Carl Nielsen*, vol. 1, 271–72.
13 Journal, 1904-1910, RA, Det Kongelige Teaters Arkiv og Bibliotek.
14 Journal, 1904-1910, RA, Det Kongelige Teaters Arkiv og Bibliotek.
15 CNB 3:463; Christiansen, *Nogle Træk af mit Liv*, 233.
16 CNB 3:464; cf. CNB 3:465–469.
17 CNB 3:488; CNL 237; Meyer and Schandorf Petersen, *Carl Nielsen*, vol. 1, 293.
18 Nielsen's contract dated 10 May 1908, CNB 3:488; CNL 237.
19 Letter to the Ministry of Church and Education, 14 May 1908; see commentary to CNB 3:488.
20 Journal, 1904-1910, RA, Det Kongelige Teaters Arkiv og Bibliotek; Christiansen, *Nogle Træk af mit Liv*, 234.
21 Regiprotokol, 1874-1896, p. 118, RA, Det Kongelige Teaters Arkiv og Bibliotek.
22 Meyer and Schandorf Petersen, *Carl Nielsen*, vol. 1, 296–97; Clausen, *Mennesker paa min Vej*, 166–68; Hansen, *En kgl. kapelmusikers erindringer*, 38–39.
23 Journal, 1904-1910, RA, Det Kongelige Teaters Arkiv og Bibliotek; Nielsen was on sick leave from 20 until 27 December, when he resumed conducting in the evening.
24 Christiansen, *Nogle Træk af mit Liv*, 234–35, quotes a letter from Rung, 10 December 1908.
25 CNB 5:574; CNL 400.
26 *Politiken*, 11 December 1908.
27 CNB 5:574; CNL 400.
28 Samtid, 123.
29 Frisch, 'As Conductor', 96.
30 Clausen, *Mennesker paa min Vej*, 166.
31 CNB 1:478; CNL 86; cf. CNB 1:240.
32 Holden, 'The Conductor', 189.
33 Carl Nielsen, [Niels W. Gade som dirigent], MS in private ownership, probably written as a contribution to Behrend (ed.), *Minder om Niels W. Gade*, which, however, was published without Nielsen's essay. Reproduced by kind permission of Steen Chr. Steensen.
34 Niemann, *Brahms*, 166; cf. Frisch, 'As Conductor', 95.
35 Foltmann, 'Dirigenten Carl Nielsen og Musikforeningen', 302–13.
36 Cf. 'Det kgl. Teater', *København*, 14 January 1909; 'Det kgl. Theater', *Dannebrog*, 14 January 1909; 'Det kgl. Teater', *Social-Demokraten*, 8 February 1909.
37 Journal, 1904-1910, RA, Det Kongelige Teaters Arkiv og Bibliotek.
38 Leicht and Hallar, *Det kongelige Teaters repertoire*, 407.
39 Journal, 1911-1916, RA, Det Kongelige Teaters Arkiv og Bibliotek.
40 Cf. CNB 4:500, 4:528–45, 4:840, 4:844–47; CNL 302, 304.
41 Journal, 1911-1916, 22 January 1914, RA, Det Kongelige Teaters Arkiv og Bibliotek.
42 Leicht and Hallar, *Det kongelige Teaters repertoire*, 10–11.
43 Journal, 1911-1916, 26 September 1913, RA, Det Kongelige Teaters Arkiv og Bibliotek.
44 CNB 4:500; CNL 302.
45 CNB 4:764, 4:765; cf. CNB 4:596, 4:598.
46 CNB 4:765.
47 CNB 4:766.
48 CNB 4:767; CNL 317.
49 CNB 4:774–76 and commentary, and 4:779, which is the theatre's minutes of

their negotiations, which Nielsen has also signed.
50 CNB 4:778–808; CNL 318; cf. CNB 4:733.
51 CNB 4:795; cf. CNB 4:788, 4:790, 4:811.
52 CNB 4:799; CNL 318.
53 CNB 5:17.
54 Hauge, 'Carl Nielsen and the Gothenburg Orchestral Society', 11.
55 CNB 5:19; CNL 326; cf. CNB 5:14, 5:20.
56 CNB 5:30, 5:31; CNL 327; cf. CNB 5:33.
57 CNB 5:63; cf. CNB 5:52.
58 Foltmann, 'Dirigenten Carl Nielsen og Musikforeningen', 283. Cf. note to CNB 2:165.
59 Hammerich, *Musikforeningens Historie*, 135–83; Foltmann, 'Dirigenten Carl Nielsen og Musikforeningen', 279–80.
60 Foltmann, 'Dirigenten Carl Nielsen og Musikforeningen', 280–81.
61 Falkencrone, *Musikforeningen*, 51; Foltmann, 'Dirigenten Carl Nielsen og Musikforeningen', 279–81, 284–85.
62 Cf. Lotzow, *Das Sinfonische Chorstück im 19. Jahrhundert*, 31–64; Foltmann, 'Dirigenten Carl Nielsen og Musikforeningen', 279–80. Regarding the choir, see Hammerich, *Musikforeningens Historie*, 226–28.
63 Falkencrone, *Musikforeningen*, 55–56; Foltmann, 'Dirigenten Carl Nielsen og Musikforeningen', 296.
64 Falkencrone, *Musikforeningen*, 34–35; Foltmann, 'Dirigenten Carl Nielsen og Musikforeningen', 281–83.
65 Falkencrone, *Musikforeningen*, 35–36, quotes Nielsen's letter to the choir members of Musikforeningen, dated 31 August 1917; Foltmann, 'Dirigenten Carl Nielsen og Musikforeningen', 286–87.
66 Foltmann, 'Dirigenten Carl Nielsen og Musikforeningen', 285–86, 289–90.
67 Falkencrone, *Musikforeningen*, 39, cf. commentaries to CNB 7:46 and 7:47; Foltmann, 'Dirigenten Carl Nielsen og Musikforeningen', 288–89.
68 CNB 6:40; CNL 406.
69 Foltmann, 'Dirigenten Carl Nielsen og Musikforeningen', 295–302, 315–40.
70 Foltmann, 'Dirigenten Carl Nielsen og Musikforeningen', 283–84, 295–302.
71 Falkencrone, *Musikforeningen*, 40–42, Foltmann, 'Dirigenten Carl Nielsen og Musikforeningen', 292–93.
72 CNB 5:21.
73 CNB 5:559; CNL 396.
74 CNB 5:569; CNL 398.
75 Hauge, 'Carl Nielsen and the Gothenburg Orchestral Society', 12–16, list of concerts 29–35.
76 CNB 6:163; cf. CNB 6:168.
77 CNB 6:279.
78 Hauge, 'Carl Nielsen and the Gothenburg Orchestral Society', 7–11.
79 CNB 7:133; CNL 470.
80 Hauge, 'Carl Nielsen and the Gothenburg Orchestral Society', 30–35.
81 CNB 6:121; CNL 415.
82 Hauge, 'Carl Nielsen and the Gothenburg Orchestral Society', 25–27.
83 Extraction of the CNW database.
84 CNB 9:126.
85 CNB 9:562; cf. CNB 9:563.
86 CNB 9:565.
87 Extraction of the CNW database.

Chapter 33
MUSICAL PROBLEMS
1 CNB 7:198, 7:219; CNU II/11, xxxv–xxxviii.
2 Cf. Meyer and Schandorf Petersen, *Carl Nielsen*, vol. 2, 214.
3 CNB 6:340; CNL 436; cf. Fjeldsøe, *Den fortrængte modernisme*, 153.
4 Danuser, 'Einleitung', 13.
5 Samtid, 80.
6 Samtid, 634.
7 Parks, 'Pitch Structure in Carl Nielsen's Wind Quintet', esp. 562–89.
8 Fjeldsøe, *Den fortrængte modernisme*, 154–57, cf. Kirkegaard-Larsen, *Analytical Practices in Western Music Theory*, 297–304, and Kirkegaard, 'The Course of the Brook'.
9 Samtid, 378.
10 Samtid, 262–72; CNB 7:272; CNL 494.
11 Samtid, 263.
12 Samtid, 263.

13 Samtid, 268.
14 Samtid, 265–66.

Chapter 34
THE CREATIVE PROCESS

1 Meyer and Schandorf Petersen, *Carl Nielsen*, vol. 1, 173.
2 Samtid, 225.
3 Samtid, 225–27.
4 CNS 308d; Samtid, 226.
5 CNB 7:229.
6 Samtid, 332.
7 Cook, *Music as Creative Practice*.
8 CNB 10:118; CNL 638.
9 Samtid, 226.
10 Meyer and Schandorf Petersen, *Carl Nielsen*, vol. 2, 95.
11 Samtid, 226.
12 CNB 5:96; CNL 338.

Chapter 35
THE TEACHER

1 Berg, *Træk af Dansk Musikpædagogiks Historie*, 35–45.
2 Limbach, 'Musikerziehung und Musikpflege als staatliche Aufgaben', 24–26.
3 Nielsen, 'Statens overtagelse af den musikpædagogiske eksamen'.
4 CNB 4:248.
5 CNB 1:398; CNL 68.
6 CNB 1:1.
7 CNB 1:398; CNL 68.
8 CNB 2:526; CNL 209.
9 *Dagens Nyheder*, 11 November 1891.
10 Advertisement under the heading 'For unge Damer' (For Young Ladies), *Dagens Nyheder*, 23 September 1903.
11 CNB 4:177.
12 CNB 3:285; CNL 225.
13 Meyer and Schandorf Petersen, *Carl Nielsen*, vol. 2, 104.
14 Jeppesen, 'Carl Nielsen paa Hundredaarsdagen', 142.
15 Jeppesen, 'Carl Nielsen paa Hundredaarsdagen', 142.
16 Hansen, 'Carl Nielsen and Knud Jeppesen', 123–27.

17 Letter in RA, 3 September 1907, quot. in Krabbe, 'Ove Scavenius', 40.
18 Quot. in Krabbe, 'Ove Scavenius', 45.
19 Meyer and Schandorf Petersen, *Carl Nielsen*, vol. 1, 225.
20 Odense Bys Museer, CNM/1980/0007.
21 Meyer and Schandorf Petersen, *Carl Nielsen*, vol. 1, 225; Hansen, 'Carl Nielsen and Knud Jeppesen', 118–29.
22 Quot. in Krabbe, 'Ove Scavenius', 41.
23 CNB 3:285; CNL 225.
24 Weber, 'Concerts at four conservatories in the 1880s', 343–49.
25 Jensen, 'The Rosenhoff Affair', 60–63. The concert took place on 1 April 1892, cf. *København*, 31 March 1892.
26 'En Velgørenhedskoncert', *Nationaltidende*, 4 March 1907.
27 CNB 3:237, 3:277.
28 CNB 2:428, 2:429; Krabbe, 'Ove Scavenius'; un-dated note in the letter archives of the music publishers Wilhelm Hansen, KB, æske 42, I. Breve til forlagene (Ne–Nielsen, Carl S.).
29 Krabbe, 'Ove Scavenius', 42–43.
30 CNB 3:693, 3:761; CNL 257.
31 Quot. in Krabbe, 'Ove Scavenius', 52.
32 CNB 3:693, 4:665.
33 CNB 8:297.
34 CNB 2:242, 2:247–250, 2:266, 2:267; CNL 156, 157, 159.
35 CNU III/1, xxviii.
36 Annual reports and programmes for *Det Kgl. danske Musikconservatorium* (København: Det kgl. danske Musikkonservatorium, 1916–1919) and RA, Det Kongelige Danske Musikkonservatorium, Regnskaber: Lærerhonorar (1909-1948).
37 CNB 6:56.
38 CNB 6:56, 6:196.
39 CNB 6:109.
40 Foltmann, 'Dirigenten Carl Nielsen og Musikforeningen', 314.
41 Cf. e.g. CNB 5:456, 5:575, 6:109.
42 CNB 5:424A.
43 Minutes from the Academy's board meeting on 23 November 1926, quot. in Samtid, 575.

44 CNB 9:419; CNL 609.
45 Samtid, 575-80. Cf. CNB 10:805-814.
46 Samtid, 140-41, 148-49.
47 Samtid, 489.
48 Fjeldsøe, *Kulturradikalismens musik*, 90-91; Smith, *Om Musikkens Dobbelt-Virkning*.
49 Samtid, 489.
50 Savery (ed.), *Blokfløjten*.
51 Fjeldsøe, *Kulturradikalismens musik*, 439-54.
52 Fjeldsøe, *Kulturradikalismens musik*, 223.
53 Samtid, 534.
54 CNB 11:32; cf. CNB 11:2-33.
55 CNB 11:28; CNL 690.
56 CNB 11:145; CNL 693.
57 CNB 11:206; cf. CNB 11:65. Cf. foreword to Anon. (ed.), *Vor Tids Børnemusik*.
58 Anon., 'Konkurrencen om den bedste børne-klavermusik', 99.
59 CNB 11:259.
60 Foreword to Anon. (ed.), *Vor Tids Børnemusik*.
61 Anon., 'Konkurrencen om den bedste børne-klavermusik', 99.
62 DUT's concert, 11 December 1930, cf. *Dansk Musik Tidsskrift*, 5 (1930), 172 and 6 (1931), 24.
63 Krarup, *Finn Høffding*, 69-70.
64 Fjeldsøe, *Den fortrængte modernisme*, 194-99.
65 CNB 11:28; CNL 690.
66 CNB 11:28; CNL 690.
67 CNB 11:28; CNL 690.
68 Samtid, 558.

Chapter 36
THE LEGACY OF PALESTRINA

1 Garratt, *Palestrina and the German Romantic Imagination*, 42.
2 Samtid, 50.
3 Panum and Behrend, *Illustreret Musikhistorie*, 140. Cf. Ambros, *Geschichte der Musik*, vol. 4, 49.
4 Hansen, 'Knud Jeppesens Kontrapunkt – og de andres'.
5 Cf. Hohmaier, "Ein zweiter Pfad der Tradition", esp. 30-39.
6 E.g. in review of *Symphonic Suite*, Op. 8, *Avisen*, 5 May 1895.
7 Harder, 'Carl Nielsen', 156: 'Hiermit ist der musikalische Standpunkt Nielsens ganz kurz bestimmt: die Grösse und Reinheit der Linien, die kontrapunktisch Strenge anstrebend, wodurch die Arbeiten der genannten Meister ausgezeichnet sind, huldigt er gleichzeitig einer modernen Geistesrichtung der freiesten Art.'
8 CNB 1:633; CNL 127.
9 CNB 3:285; CNL 225.
10 The theory exercises are included in CNS 353c (fuga a 2, fuga a 3 and five four-part Fux exercises in sketches for *Scherzo* (CNW 31), 1887); CNS 355g (fuga a 2 in sketches for a song with lyrics by J. P. Jacobsen and String Quartet (CNW 50), c. 1887); CNS 39c (fuga a 3 in sketches for String Quartet, Op. 13, 1887-88); CNS 295 (four-part harmonisation exercises and four-part Fux exercises in sketches for *Græshoppen sidder på Engen* (CNW 372), 1898).
11 Meyer and Schandorf Petersen, *Carl Nielsen*, vol. 1, 132.
12 CNS 310c.
13 Samtid, 141.
14 Samtid, 141.
15 Samtid, 149.
16 Harder, 'Carl Nielsen', 161: 'Als der grosse Kontrapunktiker, der er ist, schreibt er z. B. nie rhythmisch und melodisch nichtssagende Bässe, wie man sie selbst bei hochbegabten Komponisten findet; vielmehr teilt er ihnen oft eine bedeutende Rolle zu.'
17 CNB 7:133; CNL 470.
18 Jeppesen, *Kontrapunkt*, iii.
19 Kurth, *Grundlagen des linearen Kontrapunkts*; Rothfarb, *Ernst Kurth: Selected Writings*, 22-26; Rothfarb, *Ernst Kurth as Theorist and Analyst*, 11-14.
20 Adler, *Der Stil in der Musik*.
21 Jeppesen, *Palestrinastil med særlig Henblik paa Dissonansbehandlingen*, 291.
22 Hansen, 'Danske doktordisputatser i musikvidenskab', 243, 245-48; Hansen, 'Konkurrencen om musik-docenturet i 1924'.

23 In addition to the dissertation, which was soon translated into German and English, the textbook is also available in at least seven other languages and has been issued in numerous editions, cf. Hansen, 'Knud Jeppesens *Kontrapunkt*', 36–37.
24 Jeppesen, *Kontrapunkt*, v.
25 Jeppesen, *Kontrapunkt*, 58.
26 Samtid, 287.
27 CNB 11:218; CNL 696.
28 CNU III/7, 116–19, cf. CNB 10:487, 10:774. According to the dates in the diary, No. 1 was finished on 15 June (CNB 10:582), No. 2 on 26 May (CNB 10:555) and No. 3 on 28 June (CNB 10:613), which is also noted in the autograph draft. Wöldike received the work shortly before 28 August, CNB 10:774.
29 CNB 10:533; CNL 680.
30 CNB 11:218; CNL 696.
31 Meyer and Schandorf Petersen, *Carl Nielsen*, vol. 2, 318; cf. CNB 8:322.
32 CNB 10:176.
33 CNB 10:473, 10:486.
34 CNU III/7, 117.
35 CNB 10:709; CNL 685.
36 CNB 10:547; CNL 681.
37 CNB 10:565, cf. CNB 10:557; CNL 682.
38 CNB 10:557; CNL 682.
39 CNB 10:709; CNL 685.
40 Bellermann, *Der Contrapunkt*, 236–83.
41 H. S., 'Palæstrinakorets Koncert', *Politiken*, 12 April 1930.
42 CNB 10:265; CNL 655.

Chapter 37
MECHANICAL MUSIC
1 Nielsen and Byrith, *Danmarks ældste lydoptagelser*.
2 *Carl Nielsen spiller Carl Nielsen. Tre fonografvalser fortæller*, SBCD 05 (Aarhus: Statsbiblioteket, 2003).
3 CNB 6:488.
4 CNB 3:235, 7:240, 9:153; CNL 491, 587.
5 Michelsen et al. (eds.), *Stil nu ind…*, 13–21, 153–58.
6 CNB 4, 9–11.
7 Kristensen, *Hærværk*.

8 Larsen, *Levende Musik – Mekanisk Musik*.
9 Samtid, 596.
10 Samtid, 597.
11 Samtid, 587–88.
12 Samtid, 598.
13 Holm, *Erindringer og Tidsbilleder*, vol. 2, 75.
14 Holm, *Erindringer og Tidsbilleder*, vol. 2, 77–80. Cf. CNB 9:306, 9:314.
15 Quot. in commentary to CNB 9:307. Cf. CNB 9:327.
16 Samtid, 400.
17 The following is based on a survey of the Danish Broadcasting Corporation's digitised archives of actual broadcasts in the database larm.fm; the documents are now available on dr.dk/alletidersprogramoversigter. A large part of the repertoire is documented in Ketting, 'Carl Nielsen and the Radio', 79–87.
18 Radio programme, 30 April 1925, dr.dk/alletidersprogrammer.
19 *Politiken*, 4 April 1925; larm.fm.
20 'Radio', *Politiken*, 24 January 1925.
21 Ketting, 'Carl Nielsen and the Radio', 62–63. Cf. Foltmann, 'Dirigenten Carl Nielsen og Musikforeningen', 327.
22 Samtid, 324.
23 Granau, *Holms vision*, vol. 1, 73.
24 CNB 10:484, 10:487.
25 CNB 10:543, 10:556.
26 CNB 11:52.
27 CNB 11:55.
28 Michelsen et al. (eds.), *Stil nu ind…*, 19.
29 Ketting, 'Carl Nielsen and the Radio', 75–78, 85–87.

Chapter 38
ORGAN MUSIC
1 Hatt, *Forårsbølger*, 92.
2 Cf. Anderson, *Karl Straube*, 266–77.
3 CNB 4:761; CNL 316.
4 Laub, *Musik og Kirke*, 169.
5 Laub, *Musik og Kirke*, 170.
6 Hamburger, 'Kirke og Orgel', 20.
7 Hamburger and Wöldike (eds.), *Orgelmusik til Gudstjenestebrug*.
8 Hamburger, 'Vor Tid og Orgelkunsten', 84.

9 Prip, 'Om den danske orgelbevægelse', 61.
10 Lund, *Orglets ABC*, 14.
11 Møller, 'Et nyt mekanisk Orgel i Nicolai Kirkesal', 34.
12 Laub, *Musik og Kirke*, 170.
13 Meyer and Schandorf Petersen, *Carl Nielsen*, vol. 2, 317.
14 Schousboe, *Carl Nielsen. Dagbøger og brevveksling*, 578.
15 Samtid, 600.
16 CNB 11:513.
17 Samtid, 599–600; CNB 11:504.
18 Samtid, 600; CNB 11:504.
19 CNU II/12, xlviii.
20 Hamburger, 'Ny Orgelmusik til Gudstjenestebrug', 165.
21 Hamburger, 'Ny Orgelmusik til Gudstjenestebrug', 167.
22 CNB 11:168.
23 CNU II/12, xliv–xlv.
24 CNB 11:759; CNL 736; Samtid, 640.
25 CNB 11:492; CNL 723.
26 CNB 11:759: 'Bewegung, auch geistig'; CNL 736.
27 Samtid, 640.
28 Fair copy (CNS 1b) end-dated 27 February 1931, although in his diary Nielsen writes that he has finished the work on 1 March, CNB 11:510; cf. CNB 11:512; CNL 725.
29 CNB 11:640; Schousboe, *Carl Nielsen. Dagbøger og brevveksling*, 611.
30 Michelsen and Licht (eds.), *Danmarks Kirker, Århus Amt*, vol. 2, 581–94.
31 CNB 11:512; CNL 725.
32 CNB 11:759; CNL 736.
33 Hamburger, 'Carl Nielsen som Orgelkomponist', 28.
34 Grimley, *Carl Nielsen and the Idea of Modernism*, 226.
35 Grimley, *Carl Nielsen and the Idea of Modernism*, 231.
36 Hamburger, 'Carl Nielsen som Orgelkomponist', 32.

Chapter 39
A SERIOUS GAME
1 Samtid, 379.
2 Samtid, 265.
3 Samtid, 378.
4 Maegaard, 'Den sene Carl Nielsen', 76.
5 KB, CNA I.C.4, diary 1923, cf. CNB 7:384; CNL 506. The notes are written in a pocket diary on the pages from 6 January to 1 March, and it was only used for diary entries from 1 October to 13 November 1923. Nielsen erroneously wrote 'salt' instead of 'sand'.
6 KB, CNA I.C.4, diary 1923, cf. CNB 7:384; CNL 506.
7 KB, CNA I.C.4, diary 1923, jf. CNB 7:384; CNL 506.
8 Samtid, 264.
9 Samtid, 143.
10 CNB 7:435; CNL 509; cf. CNB 7:429, 7:436–441.
11 CNB 7:501, 7:579; CNL 526.
12 Cf. CNB 7:592, 8:61 and 8:136 with commentary.
13 CNB 7:448; cf. CNB 7:434.
14 The concert with Hans Seeber van der Floe as conductor took place on 24 February 1923, at 9 p.m. in Musikverein's large hall; Peder Møller and Ellen Overgaard were soloists, see e.g. *Neue Freie Presse*, 24 February 1923; *Neues Wiener Tagblatt*, 26 February 1923.
15 CNB 7:451; CNL 511.
16 CNB 7:542.
17 CNB 7:539; CNL 520.
18 CNB 8:126; CNL 546.
19 CNB 8:134; CNL 547.
20 CNB 8:165; CNL 549.
21 CNB 8:169; CNL 550.
22 CNU II/6, xii, the first movement in both draft and fair copy is end-dated 20 November 1924.
23 CNU II/6, xii; cf. CNB 8:217, 8:267, 8:425; CNL 558.
24 Samtid, 324. The following day Nielsen had an addendum published in the newspaper, 'Carl Nielsens nye Symfoni', *Politiken*, 4 April 1925.
25 Samtid, 375.
26 Maegaard, 'Den sene Carl Nielsen', 75.
27 Samtid, 376.

28 Samtid, 376.
29 Samtid, 378.
30 Samtid, 379.
31 Cf. Grimley, *Carl Nielsen and the Idea of Modernism*, 252, 277.
32 Krebs, 'Tonal Structure in Nielsen's Symphonies', 246–47.
33 Fjeldsøe, *Den fortrængte modernisme*, 161–64.
34 CNB 8:98; CNL 542; Ravnkilde, 'Stravinsky i København'. On the reception of Stravinsky, see Fjeldsøe, *Den fortrængte modernisme*, 73–75.
35 CNB 8:197.
36 Samtid, 377. Concert programme, Musikmuseet, Nationalmuseet.
37 Samtid, 391.
38 Leicht and Hallar, *Det kongelige Teaters repertoire*, 239.
39 CNU II/6, xv, quot. *København* and *Berlingske Tidende*, 12 December 1925. The concert was originally scheduled for 27 November 1925, cf. CNB 8:454.
40 H. S., 'Det kgl. Kapels Festkoncert for Carl Nielsen. Den nye Symfoni', *Politiken*, 12 December 1925.
41 Kramer, 'Unity and Disunity', 294, 322–23, 341–42.
42 CNB 6:339; CNL 435; cf. Grimley, *Carl Nielsen and the Idea of Modernism*, 256.
43 Fanning, 'Progressive Thematicism in Nielsen's Symphonies', 196–200.
44 Kramer, 'Unity and Disunity', 321, 323.
45 Cf. Tarrant, 'Breakthrough and Collapse', 35.
46 CNB 8:165; CNL 549.
47 Tarrant, 'Breakthrough and Collapse', 41–44.
48 Grimley, *Carl Nielsen and the Idea of Modernism*, 293.
49 H. S., 'Det kgl. Kapels Festkoncert for Carl Nielsen. Den nye Symfoni', *Politiken*, 12 December 1925.
50 Tarrant, 'Breakthrough and Collapse', 47.
51 Meyer and Schandorf Petersen, *Carl Nielsen*, vol. 2, 259.
52 Fjeldsøe, *Den fortrængte modernisme*, 74, 316–17.
53 Samtid, 379.
54 Fjeldsøe, *Den fortrængte modernisme*, 163. Cf. the score, Samfundet til Udgivelse af Dansk Musik, 3. serie nr. 32 (1931).
55 CNB 10:286; CNL 661.
56 CNB 10:270; CNL 656.
57 Meyer and Schandorf Petersen, *Carl Nielsen*, vol. 2, 297–98.
58 CNB 7:1; CNL 452.
59 CNW 43.
60 Cf. CNB 9:287, 9:297, 9:361; CNL 602.
61 Samtid, 543.
62 CNB 9:361.
63 Samtid, 542–43.
64 CNB 9:449; CNL 611; Petersen, 'Carl Nielsen's Flute Concerto', 209–12.
65 Ross, 'Nielsen's Arcadia', 300.

V

Chapter 40
REPUTATION

1 Commentary to CNB 2:165; CNL 142; Nørtoft, 'Første verdenskrig betød stigende priser'.

Chapter 41
NIELSEN BECOMES THE NATIONAL COMPOSER

1 Cf. Gillies, 'The Canonization of Béla Bartók'.
2 Lynge, *Danske Komponister i det 20. Aarhundredes Begyndelse*, 144.
3 Anon., *Det kgl. danske Musikconservatorium. Aarsberetning for 1916*, 8–9.
4 CNB 5:23; cf. CNB 11:959; Røllum-Larsen, 'Det Anckerske Legats rejsestipendier', 77.
5 Røllum-Larsen, 'Louis Glass og Carl Nielsen', 593, quot. letter to Edvard Grieg, January 1907; cf. Engberg, *Carl Nielsen og århundredeskiftekulturen*, 18–19.
6 CNB 7:520.
7 Samtid, 535–36.
8 Samtid, 354.
9 Samtid, 354.
10 Samtid, 354.
11 Bergh, 'Fra Opera og Koncertsal', 175.

12 Bergh, 'Fra Opera og Koncertsal', 175.
13 *Middagsposten*, 29 November 1902, quot. in CNU I/4, xix.
14 Meyer and Schandorf Petersen, *Carl Nielsen*, vol. 1, 213–15.
15 *Nationaltidende*, 12 November 1905, quot. in CNU I/1, xvii.
16 A. T., *Berlingske Tidende*, 13 November 1905.
17 A. T., *Berlingske Tidende*, 13 November 1905.
18 *Aftenbladet* (København), 12 November 1905.
19 Fog, *Carl Nielsen. Kompositioner*, 15–17.
20 Thaning, *Nationalitetskonstruktioner*, 26–27.
21 Ch. K., *Politiken*, 12 November 1906.
22 Thaning, *Nationalitetskonstruktioner*, 27, quot. Robert Henriques, *Vort Land*, 12 November 1906.
23 Angul Hammerich, *Nationaltidende*, 12 November 1906.
24 Meyer and Schandorf Petersen, *Carl Nielsen*, vol. 1, 272–74.
25 Thaning, *Nationalitetskonstruktioner*, 27, quot. Robert Henriques, *Vort Land*, 1 December 1907.
26 Foltmann, 'Musikforlaget Wilhelm Hansens Arkiv', 33.
27 Thaning, *Nationalitetskonstruktioner*, 29, quot. *Nationaltidende*, 14 April 1915.
28 Schwab, 'Guldalderens musik og danskhed', 63–70.
29 *Vort Land*, 12 November 1906.
30 Charles Kjerulf, *Politiken*, 29 February 1912.
31 Thaning, *Nationalitetskonstruktioner*, 26, quot. *Vort Land*, 3 December 1902.
32 Bierlich, *Excentriske slægtskaber*, 127–30.
33 Berggreen's Foreword, *Folke-Sange og Melodier. Fædrelandske og Fremmede*, vol. 1 (1842), quot. in Koudal, 'Musikken. På sporet af "originale nationaltoner"', 107.
34 CNB 3:486.
35 Krogh, 'Omkring Elverhøj-Musikens Tilblivelse'.
36 CNB 3:51; CNU I/7, xiii.
37 Drachmann, *Breve*, vol. 4, 276.
38 Bernsen, 'Friluftsteatret i Dyrehaven', 200–2.

39 *Samtid*, 188.
40 *Samtid*, 188; cf. Sørensen, *Niels W. Gade*, 166.
41 *Samtid*, 191–92.
42 *Politiken*, 7 June 1915.
43 Thaning, *Nationalitetskonstruktioner*, 32–35; Emilius Bangert, *Hovedstaden*, 2 February 1916.
44 Ch. K., *Politiken*, 15 April 1916; Thaning, *Nationalitetskonstruktioner*, 33.
45 Seligmann, 'Carl Nielsen og hans sidste Symfoni', 5.
46 *Politiken*, 9 July 1922; Thaning, *Nationalitetskonstruktioner*, 41–45.
47 *Politiken*, 22 November 1922.
48 CNB 6:17 and commentary; CNU III/1, xxvii–xxx; Meyer and Schandorf Petersen, *Carl Nielsen*, vol. 2, 204–9.
49 August Felsing, *Musik*, VI/2 (Febr. 1922), 26; Thaning, *Nationalitetskonstruktioner*, 36; Fjeldsøe, 'Carl Nielsens 5. symfoni', 61–64.
50 Thaning, *Nationalitetskonstruktioner*, 35–41; *Dagens Nyheder*, 27 September 1931.
51 Cf. CNB 1:487; CNL 92.
52 CNB 2:229, 2:246; CNL 155; Ketting, 'Helios og Typhonen', 167. Receipts from the years 1903–1911 on account payments in KB, Musikforlaget Wilhelm Hansens brevarkiv, æske 42.
53 Foltmann, 'Musikforlaget Wilhelm Hansens Arkiv', 33. The material is currently located at RA, Viborg.
54 CNB 9:231.
55 CNB 4:587 and commentary; CNB 4:860; Foltmann and Krabbe, 'Source material for Carl Nielsen's Symphony no. 3'; Deavill, 'The C.F. Kahnt Archive in Leipzig'.
56 CNB 6:426, 6:434, 6:437.
57 CNU II/12, xxxiii.
58 CNU II/12, xxxii and 243–44.
59 Ax.K., *Politiken*, 15 March 1921.
60 CNB 6:255, 6:422, 6:486, 7:383, 8:234.
61 CNB 8:72, 8:74; CNL 539; Foreword, CNB 8, 50–54.
62 Petersen, 'Carl Nielsen og Samfundet til Udgivelse af Dansk Musik 1899-1931'.
63 Krabbe, 'The Carl Nielsen Edition'.

64 From the database CNW (accessed 28 April 2023). Around five per cent of the records are not linked to a location, and the performances in southern Jutland up to 1920 are counted as Danish.
65 Nielsen's orders and honours, Museum Odense.
66 CNW.
67 The process can be followed in CNB 1:476–523, dairy and letters from the journey.
68 CNB 1:494; CNL 94.
69 CNB 1:501; CNL 96; cf. CNB 1:496.
70 Harder, 'Carl Nielsen'; CNB 2:440; CNL 190; Samtid, 48–52.
71 Crome, 'Carl Nielsen'; Rangstrøm, 'Modern sångkomposition'; for an overview, see Miller, *Carl Nielsen. A Guide to Research*, 29–48.
72 Paul Stefan, *Musikblätter des Anbruch*, 9/7 (1927), 271.
73 Bentzon, 'Carl Nielsen und der Modernismus'.
74 CNB 2:416, 2:489, 3:43.
75 Re-issued on *Carl Nielsen on Record. Vintage and other historical Recordings* (Danacord: DACOCD 801–830, 2015); *Politiken*, 29 September 1952.
76 Anon., *Leonard Bernstein*.
77 Riemann, *Geschichte der Musik seit Beethoven*, 270–72, 535–40; cf. Matter, *Niels W. Gade und der "nordische Ton"*, esp. 25–97.
78 Fjeldsøe, 'The Leipzig Model and Its Consequences'.
79 Grimley, *Carl Nielsen and the Idea of Modernism*, ix.
80 Michelsen, *Det dybe og det rene*, 48.
81 CNB 7:140.
82 CNB 9:762; cf. letter from Nielsen to Niels Otto Raasted, 4 September 1916, KB, HA, acc. 2020/41.
83 CNB 4:854, 7:136, 7:486, 7:521, 10:691, 11:281, 11:337.
84 CNB 1:31, 5:23.
85 CNB 4:776.
86 CNB 5:61.
87 CNB 5:276.
88 CNB 4:753; cf. CNB 4:760, 4:761; CNL 316.

89 Letter from Nielsen to Niels Otto Raasted, 5 July 1924, KB, HA, acc. 2020/41.
90 Telegram and letter from Nielsen to Niels Otto Raasted, both dated 8 July 1924, KB, HA, acc. 2020/41. Cf. Højlund, *Nu siger jeg lige noget*, 100.
91 Holm, *Erindringer og Tidsbilleder*, vol. 2, 11–12.
92 Knudsen, *Sinfonia espansiva*; Seligmann, 'Carl Nielsen og hans sidste Symfoni'; Simonsen, 'Carl Nielsen som Symphoniker'; Hamburger, 'Formproblemet i vor Tids Musik'.
93 Emilius Bangert, 'Musikforeningens 2den Koncert', *Hovedstaden*, 2 February 1916.
94 Angul Hammerich, *Nationaltidende*, 12 November 1906; Robert Henriques, *Vort Land*, 12 November 1906.
95 Høffding, 'International Musikfest i Frankfurt am Main', 211.
96 Charles Kjerulf, *Politiken*, 9 October 1903; Samtid, 46.
97 Gillies, 'The Canonization of Béla Bartók', 297–98.
98 Dolleris, *Carl Nielsen. En Musikografi*, 14.
99 Reynolds, *Carl Nielsen's Voice*, 45.

Chapter 42
CURATING THE LEGACY

1 CNU 11, 39–43.
2 'Carl Nielsens slorslaaede Bisættelse', *Middelfart Avis*, 10 October 1931.
3 'Minister Borgbjergs Mindeord om Carl Nielsen', *Aftenbladet*, 3 October 1931.
4 Cf. CNB 1:404; CNL 71. In the Copenhagen city council election in 1893, Nielsen voted for the opposition, that is, the joint list of Social Democrats and the Liberals, which won a majority for the first time, cf. https://trap.lex.dk/1850-1920_i_K%C3%B8benhavn.
5 Telmányi, *Af en musikers billedbog*, 162.
6 *Politiken*, 10 and 11 September 1925, quot. in CNB 8, 30–43.
7 H. S., *Politiken*, 12 December 1925.
8 Gunnar Hauch, *Nationaltidende*, 12 December 1925, quot. in Thaning, *Nationalitetskonstruktioner*, 38.

9 Samtid, texts 1-100 are published up to and including his sixtieth birthday.
10 Fjeldsøe, 'Vitalisme i Carl Nielsens musik', 50-53.
11 Samtid, 339.
12 Samtid, 340.
13 Samtid, 125.
14 Samtid, 136.
15 Samtid, 265.
16 Samtid, 243-44.
17 CNB 1:12.
18 CNB 1:557.
19 CNB 2:438, 2:440, 2:444; CNL 190, 191; cf. CNB 2:425, 2:426, 2:446; CNL 187, 188, 192. The early autobiographies are collected and published in MfB, 225-35.
20 Andreas Winding, 'Symposiet for Carl Nielsen', *Politiken*, 11 June 1925, quot. in CNB 8, 43.
21 Telmanyi, *Mit Barndomshjem*, 161.
22 CNB 7:291; CNL 496.
23 MfB, 12-13.
24 'Efterskrift', MfB, 210-19.
25 Yde, *Nexø*, 315, 323.
26 Nexø, *Erindringer (1932-1939)*, quot. in Yde, *Nexø*, 315-16.
27 MfB, 150.
28 MfB, 11; Childhood, 9.
29 Aakjær, *Fra min Bitte-Tid*, 11.
30 MfB, 20; Childhood, 18.
31 MfB, 43.
32 Cf. Grimley, *Carl Nielsen and the Idea of Modernism*, 14-18.
33 The section is a revised version of Engberg, *Carl Nielsen og århundredeskiftekulturen*, 30-47. On myth-making, see Brincker et al., 'Beethovenmyten', *Gyldendals Musikhistorie*, vol. 2, 44-50 and Burnham, *Beethoven Hero*.
34 Maegaard, 'Den sene Carl Nielsen'; Maegaard, 'Når boet skal gøres op efter Carl Nielsen…'.
35 Maegaard, 'Den sene Carl Nielsen', 74.
36 Maegaard, 'Den sene Carl Nielsen', 74; cf. Miller, 'Introduction', 17.
37 Maegaard, 'Ung komponist i Carl Nielsens skygge', 21.
38 Kullberg, *Nye toner i Danmark*, 2.
39 Bruun, *Dansk Musiks Historie fra Holberg-tiden til Carl Nielsen*, vol. 2.
40 Schiørring, *Musikkens Historie i Danmark*, vol. 3.
41 Kullberg, *Nye toner i Danmark*, 2; cf. e.g. the series 'Danske Komponister' published by Multivers.
42 Maegaard, 'Ung komponist i Carl Nielsens skygge', 20-21.
43 Maegaard, 'Når boet skal gøres op efter Carl Nielsen…', 104.
44 Maegaard, 'Ung komponist i Carl Nielsens skygge', 18-19.
45 Høffding, 'Carl Nielsen og de unge', 53.
46 Heerup, 'Vejen til den ny musik'.
47 Heerup, 'Carl Nielsen død', 177.

Chapter 43
INQUISITIVENESS AND TENACY
1 CNB 2:127.
2 CNB 2:225.
3 'Carl Nielsen og "Modernismen"', interview by Hans Tørsleff based on a conversation with Nielsen around 1927, Samtid, 617.
4 Samtid, 617.
5 Samtid, 618.
6 Samtid, 497.
7 Pedersen, *Carl Nielsens klavermusik*, 70-72.
8 Fjeldsøe, 'Rued Langgaard im Kontext anderer symphonischer Traditionen', 92-101.
9 Fanning, 'Nielsen, Beethoven and repeated notes'.

Bibliography

Standard Works

Childhood   *Carl Nielsen. My Childhood*, trans. Reginald Spink (Copenhagen: Wilhelm Hansen, [1972]); all quotations refer to this edition.

CNB   *Carl Nielsen Brevudgaven*, ed. John Fellow, 12 vols. (Copenhagen: Multivers, 2005–15). Searchable e-book available at multivers.dk. References are to volume followed by letter number, e.g. CNB 3:43.

CNL   *Carl Nielsen. Selected Letters and Diaries. Selected, Translated and Annotated by David Fanning and Michelle Assay* (Copenhagen: Royal Danish Library / Museum Tusculanum Press, 2017). References are to letter number, e.g. CNL 104.

CNS   *Carl Nielsens Samling. Katalog over komponistens musikhåndskrifter i Det kongelige Bibliotek*, ed. Birgit Bjørnum and Klaus Møllerhøj (Copenhagen: The Royal Library / Museum Tusculanum Press, 1992). References to Nielsen's manuscripts consist of 'CNS' and manuscript number.

CNU   *Carl Nielsen Værker / Carl Nielsen Works*, published by Carl Nielsen Udgaven / the Carl Nielsen Edition (Copenhagen: The Royal Library, 1998–2014). References are to series, volume, and page numbers, e.g. CNU II/5. The volumes are available at https://www.kb.dk/find-materiale/samlinger/nodesamlingen/nodeudgivelser-og-vaerkfortegnelser-fra-det-kgl-bibliotek.

CNW   *Catalogue of Carl Nielsen's Works*, ed. Niels Bo Foltmann, Axel Teich Geertinger, Peter Hauge, Niels Krabbe, Bjarke Moe and Elly Bruunshuus Petersen (Copenhagen: The Royal Library / Museum Tusculanum Press, 2016). Extended online version available at https://www.kb.dk/dcm/cnw/navigation.xq. References are to the online version and to works with CNW numbers.

MfB   Carl Nielsen, *Min fynske Barndom. Kommenteret udgave*, ed. Ejnar Stig Askegaard and Thomas Søndergaard Estrup Iversen (Odense: Forlaget Odense Bys Museer, 2015).

Samtid   *Carl Nielsen til sin samtid. Artikler, foredrag, presseindlæg, værknoter og manuskripter*, ed. John Fellow, 3 vols. (Copenhagen: Gyldendal, 1999).

Archival Material

The archival material employed is listed in the notes. The following abbreviations for archival institutions are used in the references:

KB   Det Kgl. Bibliotek / Royal Danish Library
RA   Rigsarkivet / Statens Arkiver / Danish National Archives
RAO   Rigsarkivet Odense, formerly Landsarkivet for Fyn / Danish National Archives, Odense
OBM   Museum Odense, formerly Odense Bys Museer, incl. Carl Nielsen Museet

Literature

The bibliography includes all literature referenced in the book. Exceptions are references to e.g. reviews and newspaper articles; these are listed in the notes.

Adler, Guido, *Der Stil in der Musik. Prinzipien und Arten des musikalischen Stils* (Leipzig: Breitkopf & Härtel, 1911).

Albeck, Gustav, 'Vagten. Efterskrift', in *Vagten. Udgivet af L. Mylius-Erichsen 1899–1900*. Fotografisk optryk med efterskrift og registre ved Gustav Albeck (København: Det danske Sprog- og Litteraturselskab, C.A. Reitzels Forlag, 1982), 607–21.

Allen, Kevin, *August Jaeger: Portrait of Nimrod. A Life in Letters and Other Writings* (London and New York: Routledge, 2000).

Ambros, August Wilhelm, *Geschichte der Musik*, vol. 4: *Geschichte der Musik im Zeitalter der Renaissance von Palestrina an* (Leipzig: F.E.C. Leuckart, 1878).

Andersen, Jørn Erslev, 'J.P. Jacobsen', *Arkiv for Dansk Litteratur*, https://tekster.kb.dk/text/adl-authors-jpjacobsen-p-root.

Andersen, Vilhelm, *Bacchustoget i Norden* (København: Det Schubotheske Forlag, 1904).

Anderson, Christopher, *Karl Straube (1873–1950). Germany's Master Organist in Turbulent Times* (Rochester: University of Rochester Press, 2022).

Anon., 'Adolph Brodsky', *The Musical Times and Singing Class Circular*, 44/722 (1903), 225–27.

Anon. [Komiteen for Dyrehavsspil], *Beretning om Friluftsteatret i Ulvedalene 1910* (København: Langkjærs Bogtrykkeri, 1910).

Anon., 'Bladet', *Maanedsblad for Borups Højskole*, 1/1 (1916), 1–2.

Anon., *Catalog over C. Braunsteins musikalske Leiebibliothek i Odense* (Odense: J.C. Dreyer, [1871]).

Anon., *Det kgl. danske Musikconservatorium. Aarsberetning for 1916* (København: Sophus Larsens Bogtrykkeri, 1917).

Anon. (ed.), *Enstemmige Sange til Brug for Højskoler, Gymnastik og Skytteforeninger* (København and Leipzig: Wilhelm Hansen, [1909]).

Anon., *Første Tillæg til Catalogen over Musikalier, som erholdes tilleie eller tilkjøbs i C. E. Braunsteins Musik- og Instrumenthandel i Odense* (Odense: J.C. Dreyer, [1873]).

Anon., *Handbuch der musikalischen Literatur oder allgemeines systematisch geordnetes Verzeichnis der bis zum Ende des Jahres 1815 gedruckten Musikalien* (Leipzig: Anton Meysel, 1817).

Anon., *Horn-Signaler* (Nyborg: V. Schønemanns Forlag, 1884).

Anon., *Haandbog under Den nordiske Industri-, Landbrugs- og Kunstudstilling i Kjøbenhavn 1888* (København: O. Prieme, 1888).

Anon., *Katalog des Musikalien-Leih-Instituts von Matthäus Wilhelm Braunstein, Instrumenten- und Musikalien-Händler in Flensburg* (Flensburg: A.S. Kastrups Buchdruckerei, 1853).

Anon., *Katalog over den almindelige fynske Industri- og Landbrugs-Udstilling i Odense 1885* (Odense: O. Prieme, 1885).

Anon., 'Komponisten Carl Nielsen', *Programmet* VI (1902–3).

Anon., 'Konkurrencen om den bedste børne-klavermusik', *Dansk Musik Tidsskrift*, 5 (1930), 99.

Anon., 'Lamoureux Concerts', *The Musical Times and Singing Class Circular*, 37/639 (1896), 314.

Anon., *Leonard Bernstein* (København: Wilhelm Hansen, 1965).

Anon., 'Max Reger', *Programmet. Udgivet af Dansk Tonekunstner-Forening*, 1905–6, no. 7.

Anon., 'Notes on the Fin De Siecle Movement in Parisian Art and Literature', *The Art Critic*, 1/1 (1893), 4–9.

Anon., 'Privat Kammermusik-Forening', *Orpheus. Fælles Organ for danske Musikere*, 1/3 (1892), 17–18.

Anon., 'Richard Strauss', *Programmet. Udgivet af Dansk Tonekunstner-Forening*, 1905–6, no. 5.

Anon., 'Udødelighedstroen eller Livet efter Døden', *Fritænkeren*, 1 (1887), 2–3.

Anon. (ed.), *Vor Tids Børnemusik. Klaverstykker*, 2 vols. (København: Wilhelm Hansen, 1930).

Arnfred, Knud, 'Sang bliver et skolefag. Træk af skolesangens historie i 1. halvdel af det 19. århundrede', *Årbog for Dansk Skolehistorie* (1971), 54–75.

Bahr, Hermann, 'Die Décadence' (1891), in Gotthart Wunberg (ed.), *Die Wiener Moderne. Literatur, Kunst und Musik zwischen 1890 und 1910* (Stuttgart: Philipp Reclam jun., 1984), 225–32.

Bahr, Hermann, 'Die Moderne', in Gotthart Wunberg (ed.), *Die Wiener Moderne. Literatur, Kunst und Musik zwischen 1890 und 1910* (Stuttgart: Philipp Reclam jun., 1984), 189–91.

Bahr, Hermann, 'Die Überwindung des Naturalismus' (1891), in Gotthart Wunberg (ed.), *Die Wiener Moderne. Literatur, Kunst und Musik zwischen 1890 und 1910* (Stuttgart: Philipp Reclam jun., 1984), 199–205.

Bak, Karl, *Højskolesangbogens historie. Et bidrag til den grundtvigianske folkehøjskoles historie* (København: Nordisk Forlag A/S, 1977).

Bak, Kirsten Sass, 'Fællessang og danskhed', in Jens Henrik Koudal (ed.), *Musik og danskhed. Fem faglige bidrag til debatten om nationalitet* (København: C.A. Reitzels forlag, 2005), 100–22.

Bak, Kirsten Sass, 'Fællessangstraditioner i Danmark ca. 1780-1960', in Stine Isaksen (ed.), *Fællessang og fællesskab – en antologi* (Herning: Sangens Hus, 2018), 15–48.

Balslev, Harald, 'Folkehøjskolens Melodibog ved Carl Nielsen, Thomas Laub, Oluf Ring and Thorvald Aagaard', *Højskolebladet*, 47 (1922), cols. 855–62.

Balslev, Povl C., *Thorvald Aagaard. Komponist og musikformidler i den folkelige sangs tjeneste* (Odense: Odense Bys Museer, 2009).

Bang, Herman, *Stuk* (København: J.H. Schubothes Boghandel, 1887).

Bauer, Adolf, 'Udstillingen 1888 og dens Forgængere', *Nationaløkonomisk Tidsskrift*, ny række, 6 (1888), 1–52.

Behrend, William, 'Den nordiske Musikfest i København 1888', *Tilskueren. Maanedsskrift for Litteratur, Samfundsspørgsmaal og almenfattelige videnskabelige Skildringer*, 5 (1888), 594–611.

Behrend, William, 'Franz Schubert. Den tyske Sangs Mester 1797-1897', *Tilskueren. Maanedsskrift for Litteratur, Samfundsspørgsmaal og almenfattelige videnskabelige Skildringer*, 14 (1897), 821–42.

Behrend, William, 'Hos Johannes Brahms. Et Rejseminde', *Tilskueren. Maanedsskrift for Litteratur, Samfundsspørgsmaal og almenfattelige videnskabelige Skildringer*, 4 (1897), 426–39.

Behrend, William (ed.), *Minder om Niels W. Gade. Kendte Mænds og Kvinders Erindringer* (København: J.H. Schultz Forlag, 1930).

Behrend, William, 'Robert Henriques', *Dansk Biografisk Leksikon* (2011), https://biografiskleksikon.lex.dk/Robert_Henriques.

Behrens, Carl, *Erindringer. Mennesker og Begivenheder* (København: H. Hirschsprungs Forlag, 1937).

Behrens, Carl, 'Friluftsspil', *Ord och Bild*, 11 (1910), 577–93.

Behrens, Carl, *Studentersamfundets Arbejderkoncerter 1897 – 15. September – 1922* (København: O.C. Olsen & Co. Bogtrykkeri, 1922).

Bellermann, Heinrich, *Der Contrapunkt oder Anleitung zur Stimmführung in der musikalischen Composition* (Berlin: Julius Springer, 1862).

Bendix, Frits, *Af en Kapelmusikers Erindringer. Miniaturportrætter fra Paullis Tid* (København: H. Hagerup's Forlag, 1913).

Bentzon, Jørgen, 'Carl Nielsen und der Modernismus', *Melos*, 6 (1927), 532–34.

Berg, Sigurd, *Træk af Dansk Musikpædagogiks Historie. Festskrift i Anledning af Musikpædagogisk Forenings 50 Aars Jubilæum* (København: Musikpædagogisk Forening, 1948).

Berger, Christian, '"Musik" nach Kant', in Michael Beiche and Albrecht Riethmüller (eds.), *Musik – Zu Begriff und Konzepten. Berliner Symposium zum Andenken an Hans Heinrich Eggebrecht* (München: Franz Steiner Verlag, 2006), 31–41.

Berggreen, Andreas Peter, *Folke-Sange og Melodier, fædrelandske og fremmede*, vol. 1 (København: C.A. Reitzel, 1842).

Bergh, Rudolph, 'Fra Opera og Koncertsal', *Tilskueren. Maanedsskrift for Litteratur, Samfundsspørgsmaal og almenfattelige videnskabelige Skildringer*, 20 (1903), 175–81.

Bergh, Rudolph, *Nogle Betragtninger over Musik og musikalske Tilstande i vor Tid* (København: Berlingske Tidendes Officin, 1900).

Bergsagel, John, 'J.P. Jacobsen and Music', in Frederik J. Billeskov Jansen (ed.), *J.P. Jacobsens spor i ord, billeder og toner* (København: C.A. Reitzels Forlag, 1985), 283–313.

Bernsen, Christina, 'Friluftsteatret i Dyrehaven', in Jeppe Tønsberg (ed.), *Fra Taarbæk og Dyrehaven. Lyngbybogen 1989* (Lyngby: Historisk-topografisk Selskab for Lyngby-Taarbæk Kommune, 1989), 143–214.

Berntsen, Klaus, *Erindringer fra Barndom og Ungdom. Bidrag til Folkelivets Historie paa Fyn* (København: V. Pios Boghandel, 1921).

Berntsen, Klaus, *Erindringer fra Manddommens Aar* (København: V. Pios Boghandel, 1923).

Bielefeldt, Viggo, *Melodier til Psalmebog for Kirke og Hjem* (København and Leipzig: Wilhelm Hansen, 1900).

Bielefeldt, Viggo, *Melodier til Psalmebog for Kirke og Hjem* (København: Wilhelm Hansen, 2. edn., 1901).

Bierlich, Emilie Boe, *Excentriske slægtskaber. En mobilitetsbevidst gentænkning af danske kvindelige kunstnere ca. 1880-1890* (Ph.D. diss., Københavns Universitet, 2019).

Bjørner, Louise, 'Emil B. Sachs og "Frisindet Ungdom". II', in L.C. Nielsen (ed.), *Emil B. Sachs. Et Mindeskrift* (København: Steen Hasselbalchs Forlag, 1923), 78–82.

Blume, Friedrich, 'Klassik', in *Die Musik in Geschichte und Gegenwart*, ed. Friedrich Blume, vol. 7 (Kassel: Bärenreiter, 1958), cols. 1027–90.

Boje, Per and Henning Nielsen, *Moderne tider. Odense 1868-1914* (Odense bys historie, 7; Odense: Odense Universitetsforlag, 1985).

Bokkenheuser, Christian, *Blade af 16de Bataillons Historie. 1747-1922* (Odense: Hagen & Sørensen, 1922).

Borchard, Beatrix, 'Joseph Joachim', rev. Katharina Uhde, *Grove Music Online* (2001), https://doi-org.ep.fjernadgang.kb.dk/10.1093/gmo/9781561592630.article.14322.

Borup, Johan, *Brogede Blade. Erindringer, Artikler og Taler* (København: Gyldendalske Boghandel, Nordisk Forlag, 1945).

Borup, Johan, *Dansk Sangbog* (København: Borups Læreanstalt, 1914).

Borup, Johan, *Højskolen og København* (København: Lehmann & Stages Forlag, 1916).

Borup, Johan, 'Vore Sange', *Højskolebladet*, 42 (1917), cols. 321–24.

Borup, Johan, 'Vore Sange', *Maanedsblad for Borups Højskole*, 2 (1917), 43–45.

Bradbury, Malcolm and James McFarlane, 'Preface to the 1991 Reprint', in Malcolm Bradbury and James McFarlane (eds.), *Modernism. A Guide to European Literature 1890–1930* (London: Penguin Books Ltd, 1976, repr. 1991), 11–16.

Brandes, Edvard, *Politik, magt, ret. Politiske erindringer og aktuelle indlæg 1863-1916*, ed. Claus Friisberg (Varde: Vestjysk Kulturforlag, 2010).

Brandes, Georg, *Det moderne Gjennembruds Mænd. En Række Portrætter* (København: Gyldendal, 2. edn., 1891).

Brandes, Georg, *Levned. Barndom og første Ungdom* (København: Gyldendal, 1905).

Brandes, Georg, 'Tale Nytaarsnat 1901', *Politiken*, 1 January 1901.

Brendel, Franz, *Geschichte der Musik in Italien, Deutschland und Frankreich. Von den ersten christlichen Zeiten bis auf die Gegenwart* (Leipzig: Bruno Hinze, 1852).

Brincker, Jens, Finn Gravesen, Carsten E. Hatting and Niels Krabbe, *Gyldendals Musikhistorie*, 4 vols. (København: Gyldendal, 1984).

Brincker, Jens, 'Robert Henriques', *Komponistbasen* (2010), https://komponistbasen.dk/node/1502#1.

Brittain, Francesca, 'Music, Magic and the Supernatural', in Benedict Taylor (ed.), *The Cambridge Companion to Music and Romanticism* (Cambridge: Cambridge University Press, 2021), 127–45.

Broad, Leah, *Nordic Incidental Music: Between Modernity and Modernism* (Ph.D. thesis, University of Oxford, 2017).
Bruun, Kai Aage, *Dansk musiks historie fra Holberg-tiden til Carl Nielsen*, 2 vols. (København: Stjernebøgernes Kulturhus/Vinten, 1969).
Brücker, Valdemar, 'Folkehøjskolen', *Højskolebladet*, 34 (1909), cols. 577–90.
Bryndorf, Bine, 'Salmesang til orgelklang. Orgelledsagelse af menighedssang – historisk og aktuelt', *Dansk kirkesangs årsskrift* (2006), 67–86.
Bullock, Alan, 'The Double Image', in Malcolm Bradbury and James McFarlane (eds.), *Modernism. A Guide to European Literature 1890-1930* (London: Penguin Books Ltd, 1976, repr. 1991), 58–70.
Burnham, Scott, 'A. B. Marx and the Gendering of Sonata Form', in *Sounding Values. Selected Essays* (Farnham: Ashgate, 2010), 55–78.
Burnham, Scott, *Beethoven Hero* (Princeton: Princeton University Press, 1995).
Busck, Steen and Henning Poulsen (eds.), *Danmarks historie – i grundtræk* (Aarhus: Aarhus Universitetsforlag, 2. edn., 2002).
Busoni, Ferruccio, *Entwurf einer neuen Aesthetik der Tonkunst. Kommentierte Neuausgabe*, ed. Martina Weindel (Wilhelmshaven: Florian Noetzel, 2001).
Busoni, Ferruccio, 'Offener Brief an Hans Pfitzner', in Busoni, *Von der Einheit der Musik. Verstreute Aufzeichnungen* (Berlin: Max Hesse, 1922), 247–50.
Bøgh, Erik, *Kalifen paa Eventyr. Sangspil i tre Acter* (København: Th. Gandrup, 1858).
Carlsen, J., Hans Olrik and Carl N. Starcke, 'Forord', in J. Carlsen, Hans Olrik, Carl N. Starcke (eds.), *Danmarks Kultur ved Aar 1900 som Slutning af et Hundredaars Udvikling* (København: Det Nordiske Forlag, Bogforlaget Ernst Bojesen, 1900), i–ii.
Carstensen, Valdemar, 'Vore Musikaftener', *Maanedsblad for Borups Højskole*, 6 (1921), 75–77.
Cavling, Henrik, *Paris. Skildringer fra det moderne Frankrig* (København: Gyldendal, 1899).
Cheney, Sheldon, *The Open-Air Theatre* (New York: Mitchell Kennerley, 1918).
Cherubini, Luigi, *Cours de contrepoint et de fugue* (Paris: Maurice Schlesinger, 1832).
Christiansen, Anne, *Anne Marie Carl-Nielsen født Brodersen* (Odense: Forlaget Odense Bys Museer, 2013).
Christiansen, Einar, *Nogle Træk af mit Liv og af dansk Teaters Historie* (København: Gyldendal/Nordisk Forlag, 1930).
Clausen, Julius, *Mennesker paa min Vej. Minder fra de unge Dage* (København: Gyldendal, 1941).
Clausen, Julius (ed.), *Til Minde om Valdemar Tofte ved Clara Tofte* (København: Langkjærs Bogtrykkeri, 1934).
Clausen, Karl, *Dansk Folkesang gennem 150 år* (København: Tingluti Forlag, 1975).
Cohn [Haste], Carl, *Nøgle til Løsning af Orla Rosenhoffs førstemmige Opgaver til Brug ved Undervisningen i Harmonilære* (København and Leipzig: Wilhelm Hansen, s.a.).
Cook, Marianne, 'Et kig i arkivet: Mads Bødker – en ildsjæl fra Årslev', *Midtfynsposten*, 21 December 2019.
Cook, Nicolas, *Music as Creative Practice* (New York: Oxford University Press, 2018).
Cornelius, Jens, *Victor Bendix* (København: Multivers, 2021).
Crome, Fritz, 'Carl Nielsen', *Ord och Bild*, 33 (1924), 315–18.
Dahlerup, Pil, *Dansk Litteratur. Middelalder*, vol. 2, *Verdslig litteratur* (København: Gyldendal, 1998), 113–233.
Dahlhaus, Carl, *Die Musik des 19. Jahrhunderts* (Neues Handbuch der Musikwissenschaft, 6; Laaber: Laaber Verlag, 2. edn., 1989).
Dahlhaus, Carl, *Nineteenth-Century Music*, tr. J. Bradford Robinson (Berkeley: University of California Press, 1989).

Dahlhaus, Carl, *Between Romanticism and Modernism. Four Studies in the Music of the Later Nineteenth Century*, tr. Mary Whittall (Berkeley: University of California Press, 1980).

Dal, Ea, 'Danske Wagner-tilløb', in Henrik Glahn et al. (eds.), *Hvad fatter gjør ... Boghistoriske, litterære og musikalske essays tilegnet Erik Dal* (Herning: Poul Kristensen, 1982), 130–42.

Dam, Anders Ehlers, *Den vitalistiske strømning i dansk litteratur omkring år 1900* (Aarhus: Aarhus Universitetsforlag, 2010).

Danuser, Hermann, 'Einleitung', in Hermann Danuser (ed.), *Die klassizistische Moderne in der Musik des 20. Jahrhunderts. Internationales Symposion der Paul Sacher Stiftung Basel 1996* (Winterthur: Amadeus Verlag, 1997), 11–20.

Danuser, Hermann, *Musikalische Lyrik. Vom 19. Jahrhundert bis zur Gegenwart – Außereuropäische Perspektiven* (Handbuch der musikalischen Gattungen, 8/2; Laaber: Laaber-Verlag, 2004).

Daverio, John, 'Mozart in the nineteenth century', in Simon P. Keefe (ed.), *The Cambridge Companion to Mozart* (Cambridge: Cambridge University Press, 2003), 171–84.

David, Ferdinand and Friedrich Hermann (eds.), *Violin-Concerte von Louis Spohr. Concerto XI* (Leipzig: C.F. Peters, [*c*. 1880]).

Deavill, James, 'The C. F. Kahnt Archive in Leipzig: A Preliminary Report', *Notes*, 42/3 (1986), 502–17.

Diergarten, Felix, 'Romantic Thoroughbass. Music Theory between Improvisation, Composition and Performance', *Theoria. Historical Aspects of Music Theory*, 18 (2011), 5–36.

Doctor, David Reinhardt, *Choral music in Denmark, 1900-1960 repertory and stylistic trends* (Ph.D. diss., University of Minnesota, 1976).

Dolleris, Ludvig, *Carl Nielsen. En Musikografi* (Odense: Fyns Boghandels Forlag, 1949).

Drachmann, Holger, *Breve til og fra Holger Drachmann. IV. 1894-1908*, ed. Det danske Sprog- og Litteraturselskab by Morten Borup (København: Gyldendal, 1970).

Drachmann, Povl, *Hornung & Møller Aktieselskab Kgl. Hof-Pianofabrik 1827-1927. Et Jubilæumsskrift* (København: Fr. Bagges Kgl. Hofbogtrykkeri, 1927).

Dyrbye, Martin, 'Alfred Helsengreen's Samling', *Magasin fra Det kongelige Bibliotek*, 8/1 (1993), 49–58.

Eigtved, Michael, *På! Begivenhedskultur fra selfie til scenekunst* (København: Samfundslitteratur, 2021).

Emborg, Jens Laursen, 'Folkehøjskolens Melodibog. Kritiske Bemærkninger', *Højskolebladet*, 47 (1922), cols. 1005–12.

Engberg, Hanne, *En digters historie. Helge Rode 1870-1937* (København: Gyldendal, 1996).

Engberg, Jens, *Det Kongelige Teater i 250 år. Til hver mands nytte*, 2 vols. (København: Frydenlund, 2. rev. edn. 1998).

Engberg, Katarina Smitt, *Carl Nielsen og århundredeskiftekulturen i København* (Ph.D. diss., Københavns Universitet, 2022).

Engelbrecht, Helge, *Arven efter Lumbye – musik og musikere i Tivoli 1843-1944* (København: Forlaget henrikengelbrecht.dk, 2020).

Eskildsen, Karsten, 'Nielsen and Gade. Landmarks of Musical Denmarks', *Carl Nielsen Studies*, 6 (2020), 147–66.

Faber, Tobias, *Frederiksstaden og Nyhavn* (København før og nu – og aldrig, 6; København: Palle Fogtdal, 1989).

Fabricius, Lars Børge, *Træk af dansk Musiklivs Historie m. m. Omkring Etatsraad Jacob Christian Fabricius' Erindringer* (København: Nyt Nordisk Forlag, 1975).

Falkencrone, Jan, *Musikforeningen København 1886-1937* (MA thesis, Københavns Universitet, 1992).

Fanning, David, 'Nielsen, Beethoven and repeated notes', *Carl Nielsen Studies*, 7 (forthcoming).

Fanning, David, *Nielsen: Symphony No. 5* (Cambridge: Cambridge University Press, 1997).

Fanning, David, 'Progressive Thematicism in Nielsen's Symphonies', in Mina Miller (ed.), *The Nielsen Companion* (London: Faber & Faber, 1994), 167–203.

Fellow, John, 'Da danske musikere var blevne til børn igen. Om den såkaldte Wüllner-strid og dens forudsætninger i Dansk Tonekunstnerforening fra Charles Kjerulf til Carl Nielsen og Louis Glass', *Fund og Forskning*, 38 (1999), 201–90.

Fellow, John, 'Fædrelandssang med følger. "Du danske Mand" i hundrede år', in Anne Ørbæk Jensen et al. (eds.), *Musikvidenskabelige kompositioner. Festskrift til Niels Krabbe* (København: Det kongelige Bibliotek, 2000), 457–77.

Fellow, John, *Vil Herren ikke hilse på sin Slægt. Brud-stykker af Carl Nielsens ungdomshistorie* (København: Multivers, 2005).

Fels, Friedrich Michael, 'Die Moderne' (1891), in Gotthart Wunberg (ed.), *Die Wiener Moderne. Literatur, Kunst und Musik zwischen 1890 und 1910* (Stuttgart: Philipp Reclam jun., 1984), 191–96.

Fels, Friedrich Michael, 'Jens Peter Jacobsen' (1891), in Gotthart Wunberg (ed.), *Die Wiener Moderne. Literatur, Kunst und Musik zwischen 1890 und 1910* (Stuttgart: Philipp Reclam jun., 1984), 344–45.

Fjeldsøe, Michael, 'Carl Nielsen and the Current of Vitalism', *Carl Nielsen Studies*, 4 (2009), 26–42.

Fjeldsøe, Michael, 'Carl Nielsens 5. symfoni. Dens tilblivelse og reception i 1920rne', *Danish Yearbook of Musicology*, 24 (1996), 51–68.

Fjeldsøe, Michael, *Den fortrængte modernisme – den ny musik i dansk musikliv 1920-1940* (Ph.D. diss.; København: Hr. Nilsson, 1999).

Fjeldsøe, Michael, 'Ferruccio Busoni og Carl Nielsen – brevveksling gennem tre årtier', *Musik & Forskning*, 25 (1999–2000), 18–40.

Fjeldsøe, Michael, *Kulturradikalismens musik* (København: Museum Tusculanum Press, 2013).

Fjeldsøe, Michael, 'Musik ist anders … aber wie?', in Kathrin Kirsch and Alexander Lotzow (eds.), *"Music is different" – isn't it? Bedeutungen und Bedingungen musikalischer Autonomie. Festschrift für Siegfried Oechsle zum 65. Geburtstag* (Kassel: Bärenreiter, 2021), 27–38.

Fjeldsøe, Michael, '"Music *is* life" – Carl Nielsen and the Idea of Vitality', in Anna Manly and Emilie Boe Bierlich (eds.), *Anne Marie Carl-Nielsen* (København: Ny Carlsberg Glyptotek / Strandberg Publishing, 2021), 180–91.

Fjeldsøe, Michael and Sanne Krogh Groth, '"Nordicness" in Scandinavian music. A complex question', in Tim Howell (ed.), *The Nature of Nordic Music* (Abingdon: Routledge, 2020), 3–19.

Fjeldsøe, Michael, 'Organicism and Construction in Nielsen's Symphony No. 5', *Carl Nielsen Studies*, 1 (2003), 18–26.

Fjeldsøe, Michael, 'Organizing the New Music. Independent organizations for contemporary music in Copenhagen, 1920–1930', in Niels Krabbe (ed.), *Music in Copenhagen. Studies in the Musical Life of Copenhagen in the 19th and 20th Centuries* (Musik & Forskning, 21; København: Musikvidenskabeligt Institut, 1997), 249–73.

Fjeldsøe, Michael, 'Rued Langgaard im Kontext anderer symphonischer Traditionen: Leipziger Klassizismus, Dredsner Romantik und Carl Nielsen', in Juri Giannini (ed.), *Rued Langgaard. Perspektiven* (Wien: Hollitzer Verlag, 2021), 87–103.

Fjeldsøe, Michael, 'The Leipzig Model and Its Consequences: Niels W. Gade and Carl Nielsen as European National Composers', *Studia Musicologica*, 59/1–2 (2018), 69–76.

Fjeldsøe, Michael, 'Vitalisme i Carl Nielsens musik', *Danish Musicology Online*, 1 (2010), 33–55.

Floros, Constantin, *Gustav Mahler. III: Die Symphonien* (Wiesbaden: Breitkopf & Härtel, 1985).

Fog, Dan, *Carl Nielsen. Kompositioner. En bibliografi* (København: Nyt Nordisk Forlag, 1965).

Fog, Dan, *Musikhandel og Nodetryk*, vol. 2: *Nodetryk efter 1750. Historie, trykteknik, datering* (København: Dan Fog Musikforlag, 1984).

Foltmann, Niels Bo, 'Carl Nielsens "Maskarade" og Det Kongelige Teaters scenemusik til Holbergs komedier', *Fund og Forskning*, 50 (2011), 371–85.

Foltmann, Niels Bo, 'Dirigenten Carl Nielsen og Musikforeningen', *Fund og Forskning*, 42 (2003), 277-340.

Foltmann, Niels Bo, 'Musikforlaget Wilhelm Hansens Arkiv på Erhvervsarkivet – en kilde til dansk musikhistorie', *Danish Yearbook of Musicology*, 24 (1996), 31-39.

Foltmann, Niels Bo and Niels Krabbe, 'Source material for Carl Nielsen's Symphony no. 3, Sinfonia espansiva, in Sächsisches Staatsarchiv', *Carl Nielsen Studies*, 2 (2005), 229-33.

Frederiksen, Finn Terman, 'Mødested Paris – Atelier Bonnat', in Finn Terman Frederiksen and Villads Villadsen (eds.), *Mødested Paris. 1880'ernes avant-garde* (Randers: Randers Kunstmuseum, 1983), 7-46.

Frederiksen, Svend, 'Fynske Forsamlingshuse', *Fynske Årbøger* (1976), 71-108.

Freud, Sigmund, *Det Ubevidste. Om Psykoanalyse – om Drømmen*, tr. Otto Gelsted (København, 1920).

Freud, Sigmund, *Kleine Beiträge zur Traumlehre* (Leipzig, 1925).

Freud, Sigmund, *Massenpsychologie und Ich-Analyse* (Leipzig, 2. edn. 1923).

Freud, Sigmund, *Vorlesungen zur Einführung in die Psychoanalyse*, 2 vols. (Leipzig, 1916).

Friis, Niels, *Det kongelige Kapel. Fem Aarhundreder ved Hoffet, paa Teatret og i Koncertsalen* (København: P. Haase & Søns Forlag, 1948).

Friis, Niels, *Militærmusikken. Blade af dens Historie. Minder om dens Mænd* (Viborg: Viborg Stiftstidende, 1941).

Frisch, Walter, 'As Conductor', in Natasha Loges and Katy Hamilton (eds.), *Brahms in Context* (Cambridge: Cambridge University Press, 2019), 88-97.

Fuller, David, 'Suite', *GroveMusicOnline*, https://www-oxfordmusiconline-com.ep.fjernadgang.kb.dk/grovemusic/view/10.1093/gmo/9781561592630.001.0001/omo-9781561592630-e-0000027091.

Fuller-Maitland, John Alexander, *Masters of German Music* (London: Osgood, McIlvaine & Co., 1894).

Garratt, James, *Palestrina and the German Romantic Imagination. Interpreting Historicism in Nineteenth-Century Music* (Cambridge: Cambridge University Press, 2004).

Gebauer, Johan Christian, *Exempelbog til Harmonilæren: Udarbeidet til Brug for Kjøbenhavns Musikkonservatorium* (København: Horneman & Erslev's Forlag, [c. 1870]).

Gebauer, Johan Christian and Jørgen Ditleff Bondesen, *Harmonilære af Ernst Fr. Richter* (København: Thorvald Petersens Bog- og Musikhandel, 2. edn., 1882).

Gibbs, Christopher H., 'German reception: Schubert's "journey to immortality"', in Christopher H. Gibbs (ed.), *The Cambridge Companion to Schubert* (Cambridge: Cambridge University Press, 1997), 241-53.

Gibbs, Christopher H., *The Life of Schubert* (Cambridge: Cambridge University Press, 2000).

Gillies, Malcolm, 'The Canonization of Béla Bartók', in Elliott Antokoletz (ed.), *Bartok Perspectives* (Oxford: Oxford University Press, 2000), 289-302.

Glahn, Henrik, *Salmemelodien i dansk tradition 1569-1973* (København: Anis, 2000).

Glass, Louis [L – – s], 'Om Musik og Musikere', *Vagten. Udgivet af L. Mylius-Erichsen 1899-1900. Fotografisk optryk med efterskrift og registre ved Gustav Albeck* (København: Det danske Sprog- og Litteraturselskab, C.A. Reitzels Forlag, 1982), 583-86.

Gnudtzmann, Albert and Helmer Lind, *Stor-København. Skildringer og Billeder af Byen og dens Liv i vore Dage*, 2 vols. (København: Gyldendalske Boghandel, Nordisk Forlag, 1907).

Gottschalksen, Carl, *En glad Musikants Dagbog* (København: Kunstforlaget Danmark, 1920).

Gotved, Helle, *Barn i Gymnastikhuset* (København: Rosinante / Munksgaard, 1992).

Granau, Martin, *Holms vision. Radiosymfoniorkestret 75 år*, 2 vols. (København: DR, 2000).

Gregersen, Hans V., 'Kvæghandel', in Erik Alstrup and Poul Erik Olsen (eds.), *Dansk kulturhistorisk Opslagsværk* (Åbyhøj: Dansk Historisk Fællesforening, 1991), vol. 1, 510-12.

Gregersen, Niels Henrik and Peter C. Kjærgaard, 'Darwin and the divine experiment. Religious responses to Darwin in Denmark 1859–1909', *Studia Theologica*, 63/2 (2009), 140–61.
Grimley, Daniel M., *Carl Nielsen and the Idea of Modernism* (Woodbridge: The Boydell Press, 2010).
Grimley, Daniel M., 'Carl Nielsen's Dreamscapes', *Carl Nielsen Studies*, 7 (forthcoming).
Grimley, Daniel M., 'Modernism and Closure: Nielsen's Fifth Symphony', *The Musical Quarterly*, 86/1 (2002), 149–73.
Grotjahn, Rebecca, *Die Sinfonie im deutschen Kulturgebiet 1850 bis 1875. Ein Beitrag zur Gattungs- und Institutionengeschichte* (Sinzig: Studiopunkt, 1998).
Grundtvig, Nikolai Frederik S., 'Rim-Brev til Nordisk Paarørende', *Nordens Mythologi eller Sindbilled-Sprog historisk-poetisk udviklet og oplyst* (2. edn., København: J.H. Schubothes Boghandling, 1832), iii–xii.
Grundtvig, Nikolai Frederik S., *Skolen for Livet og Academiet i Soer borgerlig betragtet* (København: Wahlske Boghandel, 1838).
Grundtvig, Nikolai Frederik S., 'Aandelig Fiskervise', *Nordisk Kirke-Tidende*, 6/29 (1838).
Guthmann, Axel and Anton Melbye, *Tivoli* (København: Ernst Bojesens Kunst-Forlag, 1888).
Hagen, Sophus. A. E., 'Bielefeldt, Viggo Emil', in C. F. Bricka (ed.), *Dansk Biografisk Leksikon* (København: Gyldendalske Boghandels Forlag, 1887–1905), vol. 2, 191.
Halse, Sven, 'Den vidtfavnende vitalisme. Om begrebet og fænomenet vitalisme i filosofi og kunst', in Gertrud Hvidberg-Hansen and Gertrud Oelsner (eds.), *Livslyst. Sundhed – Skønhed – Styrke i dansk kunst 1890-1940* (Odense: Fuglsang Kunstmuseum and Odense Bys Museer, 2008), 46–57.
Hamburger, Povl, 'Carl Nielsen som Orgelkomponist', *Dansk Musik Tidsskrift*, 7 (1932), 26–33.
Hamburger, Povl, 'Formproblemet i vor Tids Musik: med Analyse af Carl Nielsens Sinfonia espansiva (1. Sats)', *Dansk Musik Tidsskrift*, 6 (1931), 89–100.
Hamburger, Povl, 'Kirke og Orgel', *Dansk Musik Tidsskrift*, 5 (1930), 19–28.
Hamburger, Povl, 'Ny Orgelmusik til Gudstjenestebrug', *Dansk Musik Tidsskrift*, 5 (1930), 165–68.
Hamburger, Povl and Mogens Wöldike (eds.), *Orgelmusik til Gudstjenestebrug for Orgel uden Pedal eller Harmonium. 54 Orgelstykker fra det 17. Aarhundrede* (København: Wilhelm Hansen, 1931).
Hamburger, Povl, *Thomas Laub. Hans Liv og Gerning* (København: Aschehoug Dansk Forlag, 1942).
Hamburger, Povl, 'Vor Tid og Orgelkunsten', *Dansk Musik Tidsskrift*, 4 (1929), 81–90.
Hammerich, Angul, *Kjøbenhavns Musikkonservatorium grundet af P. W. Moldenhauer 1867-1892* (København: Kjøbenhavns Musikkonservatorium, 1892).
Hammerich, Angul, 'Musik', in J. Carlsen, Hans Olrik and Carl N. Starcke (eds.), *Danmarks Kultur ved Aar 1900 som Slutning af et Hundredaars Udvikling* (København: Det Nordiske Forlag, Bogforlaget Ernst Bojesen, 1900), 459–70.
Hammerich, Angul, *Musikforeningens Historie 1836-1886* (Festskrift i Anledning af Musikforeningens Halvhundredaarsdag, 2; København: Musikforeningen, 1886).
Hammerich, Angul, 'Musikhistorisk Museum', in Emil Hannover (ed.), *Det Danske Kunstindustrimuseums Virksomhed* (København: Det danske Kunstindustrimuseum, 1915), 62–68.
Hannover, Emil, *Erindringer fra Barndom og Ungdom*, ed. H. P. Rohde (København: Forening for Boghaandværk, 1966).
Hannover, Emil, 'Udstillingerne III', *Politiken*, 17 April 1906.
Hansen, Anton, *En kgl. kapelmusikers erindringer. Samlet og udgivet af Per Gade* (København: Quality Music Press, 1996).
Hansen, Jürgen, *En fynsk bondeslægts historie. Mads Hansens slægt på gårdene Marielund, Hestehavegaard, Kohavegaard og Arvensminde i Nr. Lyndelse Sogn* (Nr. Lyndelse: Nr. Lyndelse Sogns Lokalhistoriske Forening og Arkiv, 2019).
Hansen, Lorens, *Nørremølle – en bebyggelse i marsken og dens beboere* (s.l., 2007).

Hansen, Niels, 'Regimentsmusik i Odense', *Odensebogen 1998* (Odense: Byhistorisk Udvalg, 1998), 150–74.

Hansen, Thomas Holme, 'Carl Nielsen and Knud Jeppesen. Connections and Collaborations, Influences and Significances', *Carl Nielsen Studies*, 5 (2012), 107–47.

Hansen, Thomas Holme, 'Danske doktordisputatser i musikvidenskab – en fortegnelse og et tillæg i anledning af 100-året for Angul Hammerichs disputats', *Cæcilia*, 2 (1992–93), 233–64.

Hansen, Thomas Holme, 'Knud Jeppesens *Kontrapunkt* – og de andres. Nogle observationer vedrørende kildegrundlaget for et udvalg af lærebøger i vokalkontrapunkt fra det 20. århundrede', *Danish Yearbook of Musicology*, 28 (2000), 35–52.

Hansen, Thomas Holme, 'Konkurrencen om musik-docenturet i 1924 – en doku-soap med særligt henblik på Knud Jeppesen', *Cæcilia*, 5 (1998–2001), 53–110.

Hanslick, Eduard, *Aus meinem Leben* (Berlin: Allgemeiner Verein für Deutsche Litteratur, 3. edn., 1894).

Hanslick, Eduard, 'Miszellen. (Harm's Musikalien-Leihanstalt in Klagenfurt)', *Oesterreichische Blätter für Literatur und Kunst*, 38 (1853), 220.

Hanslick, Eduard, *Om Det Skjønne i Musikken. Et Bidrag til Tonekunstens Æstetik* (Bergen: Chr. W. Huuns Forlag, 1885).

Harder, Knud, 'Carl Nielsen', *Die Musik*, 5 (1905–6), no. 15 (Erstes Maiheft), 155–63.

Hatt, Emilie Demant, *Foraarsbølger. Erindringer om Carl Nielsen*, ed. John Fellow (København: Multivers, 2002).

Hauge, Peter, 'Carl Nielsen and the Gothenburg Orchestral Society 1914–31', *Carl Nielsen Studies*, 2 (2005), 7–35.

Hauge, Peter, 'Carl Nielsens første opus. Problemer omkring tilblivelsen og førsteopførelsen af Lille Suite', *Fund og Forskning*, 35 (2012), 223–37.

Heerup, Gunnar, 'Carl Nielsen død', *Dansk Musik Tidsskrift*, 6 (1931), 177.

Heerup, Gunnar, 'Vejen til den ny musik', *Dansk Musik Tidsskrift*, 4 (1929), 21–25.

Heise, Peter, *Strygekvartetter nr. 1-6*, ed. Michael Fjeldsøe (København: Dansk Center for Musikudgivelse, 2017).

Henriques, Axel, *Svundne Dage. Kaleidoskopiske Minder fra et langt Liv* (København: Gyldendalske Boghandel, 1929).

Henriques, Robert, 'Symfonia', *Dannebrog*, 30 September 1895.

Hersom, Paul, 'Bidrag fra Købmandsskole-Elever. V.', in L. C. Nielsen (ed.), *Emil B. Sachs. Et Mindeskrift* (København: Steen Hasselbalchs Forlag, 1923), 40–41.

Hertel, Hans, *Det stadig moderne gennembrud. Georg Brandes og hans tid, set fra det 21. århundrede* (København: Gyldendal, 2004).

Hesselager, Jens, *Musik i Danmark* (København: Multivers, 2022).

Hetsch, Gustav, *Det kongelige danske Musikkonservatorium 1867-1917 med en Fortegnelse over samtlige Elever* (København: Nordisk Forlag, 1917).

Hetsch, Gustav, *Dur og Moll. En Bog om Teater og Musik* (København: s.n., 1902).

Hindsberg, Lise Henriette, *Enargeia–Energeia: The Heavenly Sounding Image in the Italian Renaissance* (Ph.D. diss., Københavns Universitet, 2022).

Hindson, Catherine, *Female Performance Practice on the Fin-de-Siècle Popular Stages of London and Paris* (Manchester: Manchester University Press, 2007).

Hines, Jane, 'Hearing and Seeing Brahms's Harps', in Nicole Grimes and Reuben Phillips (eds.), *Rethinking Brahms* (Oxford: Oxford University Press, 2022), 70–88.

Hjermitslev, Hans Henrik, 'Georg Valdemar Brücker (1852-1929)', *Darwinarkivet*, https://www.darwinarkivet.dk/arkivet/danske-reaktioner/biografier/bruecker-georg-valdemar/index.html.

Hjermitslev, Hans Henrik, 'Protestant Responses to Darwinism in Denmark, 1859–1914', *Journal of the History of Ideas*, 72/2 (2011), 279–303.

Hjermitslev, Hans Henrik, 'Rudolf Sophus Bergh (1859-1942)', *Darwinarkivet*, http://www.darwinarkivet.dk/arkivet/danske-reaktioner/biografier/bergh-rudolf-sophus/index.html.

Hohmaier, Simone, *"Ein zweiter Pfad der Tradition". Kompositorische Bartók-Rezeption* (Saarbrücken: Pfau, 2003).

Holberg, Ludvig, *Mascarade*, in *Ludvig Holbergs Skrifter* (2015), http://holbergsskrifter.dk/holberg-public/view?docId=skuespill%2FMascarade%2FMascarade.page&brand=.

Holden, Raymond, 'The Conductor', in Morten Kristiansen and Joseph E. Jones (eds.), *Richard Strauss in Context* (Cambridge: Cambridge University Press, 2020), 182–90.

Holdt, Jens, 'Elev-Fortegnelse fra Christiansfelds Kostskoler 1775-1891', *Sønderjyske Aarbøger* (1944/1), 92–129.

Holm, Emil, *Erindringer og Tidsbilleder fra Midten af forrige Aarhundrede til vor Tid*, 2 vols. (København: Berlingske Forlag, 1939).

Houby-Nielsen, Sanne, 'Anne Marie Carl-Nielsen og det sene 1800-tals farvedebat', in *København-Athen tur/retur. Danmark og Grækenland i 1800-tallet* (København: Ny Carlsberg Glyptotek, 2000), 149–61.

Hvidt, Kristian, *Edvard Brandes. Portræt af en radikal blæksprutte* (København: Gyldendal, 1992).

Hvidt, Kristian, 'Københavns Rådhus – "et gesamtkunstwerk"', in Henrik Wivel (ed.), *Drømmetid. Fortællinger fra Det Sjælelige Gennembruds København* (København: G.E.C. Gads Forlag, 2004), 214–27.

Høffding, Finn, 'Carl Nielsen og de unge', *Dansk Musik Tidsskrift*, 7 (1932), 53.

Høffding, Finn, 'International Musikfest i Frankfurt am Main', *Dansk Musik Tidsskrift*, 2 (1926/27), 211–19.

Høgel, Sten, *Johann Abraham Peter Schulz. Den folkelige fællessangs far* (København: Multivers, 2020).

Højlund, Christian, *Nu siger jeg lige noget. En familiefortælling* (Sørvad: Forlaget Veivad, 2021).

Ising, Dieter (ed.), *Johann Christoph Blumhardt. Briefe. Band 5: Bad Boller Briefe 1852-1880. Texte* (Johann Christoph Blumhardt Gesammelte Werke, III/5; Göttingen: Vandenhoeck & Ruprecht, 1999).

Ising, Dieter (ed.), *Johann Christoph Blumhardt. Briefe. Band 6: Bad Boller Briefe 1852-1880. Anmerkungen* (Johann Christoph Blumhardt Gesammelte Werke, III/6; Göttingen: Vandenhoeck & Ruprecht, 1999).

Ising, Dieter, *Johann Christoph Blumhardt. Leben und Werk* (Göttingen: Vandenhoeck & Ruprecht, 2002).

J. S., '"Der er en Rytme gennem al Kunst", interview med Anne Marie Carl-Nielsen', *Politiken*, 19 June 1943.

Jacobsen, Hans Henrik, *"Fast i Nød". Fynske Livregiment 1614-1964* (Odense: Fynske Livregiment 1964).

Jacobsen, Jens Peter, *Fru Marie Grubbe. Interieurer fra det syttende Aarhundrede* (København: Den gyldendalske Boghandel, 1876).

Jacobsen, Jens Peter, *Samlede Skrifter* (København: Gyldendalske Forlag, 1948).

Jacobsen, Jens Peter, *Samlede Værker udgivet paa Grundlag af Digterens efterladte Papirer*, ed. Morten Borup (København: Det danske Sprog- og Litteraturselskab, Nordisk Forlag, 1928).

Jacobsen, Louise Bugge and Annette Johansen, 'Med kunstneren på arbejde', in Mette Bøgh Jensen and Annette Johansen (eds.), *I bølgen blå. Willumsen og de badende børn* (Aarhus: Aarhus Universitetsforlag, 2016), 13–34.

Jahn, Otto, *W. A. Mozart*, 2 vols. (Leipzig: Breitkopf & Härtel, 1867).

Jansen, Frederik J. Billeskov, 'J.P. Jacobsen, omrids af en digters værk', in Frederik J. Billeskov Jansen (ed.), *J.P. Jacobsens spor i ord, billeder og toner* (København: C.A. Reitzels Forlag, 1985), 9–18.

Jansen, Frederik J. Billeskov (ed.), *Taarnet. Udgivet af Johannes Jørgensen 1893-1894, fotografisk optryk med efterskrift og registre* (København: Det danske Sprog- og Litteraturselskab, 1981).

Jensen, Eva Maria, *Død og evighed i musikken 1890-1920* (København: Museum Tusculanum Press, 2011).

Jensen, Johannes V., *Kongens Fald. Vinteren* (København: Det Nordiske Forlag, 1901).

Jensen, Jørgen I., 'Carl Nielsen: Artistic Milieu and Tradition: Cultural-Historical Perspectives', in Mina Miller (ed.), *The Nielsen Companion* (London: Faber & Faber, 1994), 58–77.

Jensen, Jørgen I., *Carl Nielsen. Danskeren. Musikbiografi* (København: Gyldendal, 1991).

Jensen, Lisbeth Ahlgren, 'The Rosenhoff Affair', *Carl Nielsen Studies*, 3 (2008), 50–64.

Jensen, Sigurd and Claus M. Smidt, *Rammerne sprænges* (Københavns historie, 4; København: Gyldendal, 1982).

Jensen, Thorkild Borup, 'Hvad er en salme? Forsøg på en genrebestemmelse', in Thorkild Borup Jensen and Knud E. Bugge (eds.), *Salmen som lovsang og litteratur* (København: Nordisk Forlag, 1972), vol. 1, 9–62.

Jeppesen, Knud, 'Carl Nielsen paa Hundredaarsdagen. Nogle Erindringer', *Dansk Årbog for Musikforskning*, 4 (1964–65), 137–50.

Jeppesen, Knud, *Kontrapunkt (Vokalpolyfoni)* (København and Leipzig: Wilhelm Hansen, 1930).

Jeppesen, Knud, *Palestrinastil med særlig Henblik paa Dissonansbehandlingen* (København: Levin & Munksgaards Forlag, 1923).

Jeppesen, Torben Grøngaard, 'De rejste ud – om Carl Nielsens familie som udvandrere', in Ida-Marie Vorre (ed.), *I Fyn er alting anderledes... – en antologi om Carl Nielsen og hans fynske baggrund* (Odense: Forlaget Odense Bys Museer, 2015), 80–93.

Jespersen, Olfert, *Oplevelser* (København: Olfert Jespersens Forlag, 1930).

Jonsson, Alexis, *Københavns Orkester-Forening. 1874 – 25. April – 1924* (København: Københavns Orkesterforening, 1924).

Joseph, Charles M., 'Structural Pacing in the Nielsen String Quartets', in Mina Miller (ed.), *The Nielsen Companion* (London: Faber & Faber, 1994), 460–88.

Jørgensen, Bo Hakon, 'Feberen i blodet – om suggestion og symbol', in Bente Scavenius (ed.), *Grib tiden* (København: Gyldendal, 2001), 184–95.

Jørgensen, Johannes, *Blomster og Frugter* (København and Kristiania: Gyldendal/Nordisk Forlag, 1907).

Jørgensen, Johannes, 'Foraarsudstillingerne. Symbolismen', *Politiken*, 14 April 1893.

Jørgensen, Johannes, 'København', in Martinus Galschiøt (ed.), *Danmark i Skildringer og Billeder af danske Forfattere og Kunstnere* (København: P.G. Philipsens Forlag, 1893), vol. 2, 725–80.

Jørgensen, Johannes, *Mit Livs Legende*, ed. Elise Juul and Henrik Wivel, 4 vols. (København: Det danske Sprog- og Litteraturselskab, 2019).

Jørgensen, Johannes, 'Symbolisme', *Taarnet*, 1/2 (1893), 51–56.

Jørgensen, Johannes, 'Søvnen. En Hymne', *Illustreret Tidende*, 46 (1904), 82.

Jørgensen, Johannes, *Udvalgte Værker* (København: Gyldendal, 1915).

Jørgensen, John Chr., *Det danske anmelderis historie. Den litterære anmeldelses opståen og udvikling 1720-1906* (København: Fisker og Schou, 1994).

Keld, Jens Peter, 'Rids af Giuseppe Sibonis virksomhed i årene 1819-39. I anledning af 200-året for hans fødsel', *Dansk Årbog for Musikforskning*, 11 (1980), 57–78.

Ketting, Knud, 'Carl Nielsen and the Radio', *Carl Nielsen Studies*, 2 (2005), 60–88.

Ketting, Knud, 'Carl Nielsen og Tivoli', *Fund og Forskning*, 41 (2002), 233–60.

Ketting, Knud, 'Helios og Typhonen. Om Carl Nielsens og Anne Marie Carl-Nielsens ophold i Athen i 1903', *Fund og Forskning*, 40 (2001), 167–98.

Keym, Stefan, 'Komplementarität und Pluralisierung. Zur "zweiten Säule" der Leipziger Symphoniekonzerte im langen 19. Jahrhundert und ihrem Repertoire', in Helmut Loos (ed.), *Musikstadt Leipzig. Beiträge zu ihrer Geschichte* (Leipzig: Leipziger Universitätsverlag, 2019), 143–78.

Keyper, Franz, *Militair Musik-Skole* (København: J.D. Qvist, 1832).

Kirkegaard-Larsen, Thomas Jul, *Analytical Practices in Western Music Theory. A Comparison and Mediation of Schenkerian and Post-Riemanian Traditions* (Ph.D. diss., Aarhus Universitet, 2020).

Kirkegaard, Thomas Husted, 'The Course of the Brook: Rethinking Schenkerian and Riemannian Perspectives on Organicism in Nielsen's Music', *Carl Nielsen Studies*, 7 (forthcoming).

Kjerulf, Charles, *Gift og Hjemfaren. Erindringer fra Firserne* (København and Kristiania: Gyldendalske Boghandel, 1917).

Kjerulf, Charles, 'Musik i Ugen', *Illustreret Tidende*, 29 (1888), 448.

Knudsen, Henrik, *Sinfonia espansiva für Orchester von Carl Nielsen. Erläutert von Henrik Knudsen* (Leipzig: C.F. Kahnt, 1913).

Knudsen, Jørgen, *Georg Brandes. Frigørelsens Vej. 1842-77* (København: Gyldendal, 1985).

Koht, Halvdan, *Harald Hårfagre og rikssamlinga* (Oslo: Aschehoug & co, 1955).

Kongsted, Ole et al., *Masser af messing. En udstilling om trompetinstrumenter* ([København]: Musikhistorisk Museum, 1990).

Korsgaard, Ove, 'Fra stand til folk – med koldske friskoler', in Mette Havsteen-Mikkelsen, Laust Riis-Søndergaard and Birte Fahnøe Lund (eds.), *Friskolehistorie – en antologi* (Asperup: Dansk Friskoleforenings Forlag, 2016), vol. 1, 12–27.

Koudal, Jens Henrik, 'Musikken. På sporet af "originale nationaltoner"', in Palle Ove Christiansen (ed.), *Veje til danskheden. Bidrag til den moderne nationale selvforståelse* (København: C.A. Reitzel, 2005), 95–123.

Koudal, Jens Henrik, 'Spillemandsbøger og andre personlige dansenodebøger fra Danmark: En indføring', in Märta Ramsten et al. (eds.), *Spelmansböcker i Norden. Perspektiv på handskrivna notböcker* (Uppsala and Växjö: Kungl. Gustav Adolfs Akademien för svensk folkkultur / Smålands Musikarkiv, 2019), 23–64.

Krabbe, Niels, 'Ebbe Hameriks påståede korrumpering af Carl Nielsens første symfoni eller Om nytten af kildestudier', *Fund og Forskning*, 39 (2000), 121–47.

Krabbe, Niels, 'Nielsen's Unrealised Opera Plans', *Carl Nielsen Studies*, 6 (2020), 10–67.

Krabbe, Niels, 'Ove Scavenius (1884-1973) – elev af Carl Nielsen', *Magasin fra Det Kongelige Bibliotek*, 30/4 (2017), 37–54.

Krabbe, Niels (ed.), *Suite for Strygeorkester* (Udvalgte kilder til Carl Nielsens værker, 1; København: Det kongelige Bibliotek, 2000).

Krabbe, Niels, 'The Carl Nielsen Edition', *Carl Nielsen Studies*, 4 (2009), 88–106.

Krack, T. (ed.), *Vejviser for Kjøbenhavn og Frederiksberg* (København: J.H. Schultz, 1880-1900).

Kramer, Jonathan D., 'Unity and Disunity in Nielsen's Sixth Symphony', in Mina Miller (ed.), *The Nielsen Companion* (London: Faber & Faber, 1994), 293–344.

Krarup, Bertel, *Finn Høffding* (København: Multivers, 2022).

Krebs, Harald, 'Tonal Structure in Nielsen's Symphonies: Some Addenda to Robert Simpson's Analyses', in Mina Miller (ed.), *The Nielsen Companion* (London: Faber & Faber, 1994), 208–49.

Kregor, Jonathan, 'Program Music', in Morten Kristiansen and Joseph E. Jones (eds.), *Richard Strauss in Context* (Cambridge: Cambridge University Press, 2020), 200–8.

Kregor, Jonathan, *Program Music* (Cambridge: Cambridge University Press, 2015).

Kreissle von Hellborn, Heinrich, *Franz Schubert* (Wien: Carl Gerold's Sohn, 1865).

Kristensen, Hans Krongaard and Bjørn Poulsen, *Danmarks byer i middelalderen* (Aarhus: Aarhus Universitetsforlag, 2016).

Kristensen, Steen, *Georg Carstensen – Tivolis stifter. En historie om guldalderens forlystelseskonge* (København: Gyldendal, 2003).

Kristensen, Tom, 'Carl Nielsen as a Writer', in Mina Miller (ed.), *The Nielsen Companion* (London: Faber & Faber, 1994), 151–59.

Kristensen, Tom, *Hærværk* (København: Gyldendal, 1930).

Krogh, Torben, 'L.C. Tørsleff', *Dansk Biografisk Leksikon* (København: Gyldendal, 3. edn., 1979–84), https://biografiskleksikon.lex.dk/L.C._T%C3%B8rsleff.

Krogh, Torben, 'Omkring Elverhøj-Musikens Tilblivelse', *Dansk Musik Tidsskrift*, 17 (1942), 162–76.

Kryger, Karin, 'Carl Lendorf', *Weilbachs Kunstnerleksikon*, 4. edn. (1994), https://www.kulturarv.dk/kid/VisWeilbach.do?kunstnerId=8940&wsektion=alle.

Kullberg, Erling, *Nye toner i Danmark. Dansk musik og musikdebat i 1960'erne* (Aarhus: Aarhus Universitetsforlag, 2003).

Kurth, Ernst, *Grundlagen des linearen Kontrapunkts. Bachs melodische Polyphonie* (Bern: Drechsel, 1917; 2. edn. Berlin: Max Hesse, 1922).

Lange, Frederik and Johannes Wiel, *Kort Forklaring til "Exempelbog til Harmonilære"* (København: Wilhelm Hansen', [s.a.]).

Lange, Ole, 'Glade dage i 1890'erne', in Henrik Wivel (ed.), *Drømmetid. Fortællinger fra Det Sjælelige Gennembruds København* (København: G.E.C. Gads Forlag, 2004), 44–57.

Larsen, Jørgen, 'Begyndelsen af Carl Nielsens musikalske karriere i Odense 1879-83', author's version 2 April 2015, previously published at historienshus.dk.

Larsen, Jørgen, 'Carl Nielsens fædrene familie', author's version 19 November 2015, previously published at https://odenseleksikon.wordpress.com.

Larsen, Jørgen, 'Carl Nielsens mødrene slægt', author's version 22 May 2016, previously published at https://odenseleksikon.wordpress.com.

Larsen, Jørgen, *Det gamle København* (København: Gyldendal, 2010).

Larsen, Jørgen, 'Optur fra sumpen. Om Carl Nielsens mors familie og hans ophold i Odense 1879-83', *Odensebogen 2015* (Odense: Byhistorisk Udvalg, 2014), 166–83.

Larsen, Karl, *Levende Musik – Mekanisk Musik* (København: Levin og Munksgaard, 1931).

Laub, Thomas, *80 rytmiske Koraler (uden Harmonisering) samlede og indrettede til Menighedsbrug* (København: C.A. Reitzels Forlag, 1888).

Laub, Thomas, *Dansk Kirkesang. Gamle og nye Melodier* (København and Leipzig: Wilhelm Hansen, 1918).

Laub, Thomas, 'Et Indledningsforedrag', *Dansk Tidsskrift* (København: Vilhelm Trydes Forlag, 1899), 465–73.

Laub, Thomas, *Musik og Kirke* (København: Gyldendal, 1920).

Laub, Thomas, *Om Kirkesangen* (København: C.A. Reitzels Forlag, 1887).

Laub, Thomas, 'Om udførelsen af viserne', in Thomas Laub and Axel Olrik (eds.), *Danske Folkeviser med gamle Melodier* (København: Gyldendalske Boghandels Forlag, 1899), 81–82.

Laub, Thomas, 'Vore Folkevise-Melodier og deres Fornyelse', *Danske Studier*, 1 (1904), 177–209.

Laub, Thomas, *Vor musikundervisning og den musikalske dannelse* (København: C.A. Reitzels Forlag, 1884).

Lauring, Kåre, *Københavnerliv* (København: Gyldendalske Boghandel, Nordisk Forlag A/S, 2009).

Lehrmann, Ulrik, 'Læseforening og lejebibliotek. Elementer af skønlitteraturens formidlings- og forbrugshistorie i de fynske købstæder ca. 1870-1900', *Fortid og Nutid*, 31 (1984), 103–28.

Leicht, Georg and Marianne Hallar, *Det kongelige Teaters repertoire 1889-1975* (København: Bibliotekscentralens Forlag, 1977).

Leistra-Jones, Karen, '(Re-)Enchanting Performance: Joachim and the Spirit of Beethoven', in Valerie Woodring Goertzen and Robert Whitehouse Eshbach (eds.), *The Creative Worlds of Joseph Joachim* (Woodbridge: The Boydell Press, 2021), 86–103.

Limbach, Reinhard, 'Musikerziehung und Musikpflege als staatliche Aufgaben', in Hans Fischer (ed.), *Handbuch der Musikerziehung* (Berlin: Rembrandt-Verlag, 1954), 24–26.

Lindholm, Poul, *Starup Sogn i Brusk Herred. Et historisk-topografisk Forsøg* (Kolding: s.n., 1911).

Linvald, Steffen, *Gammelholm og Frederiksholm* (København før og nu – og aldrig. En billedkavalkade om København inden for voldene og søerne, 2; København: Palle Fogtdal, 1987).

Loges, Natasha, *Brahms and His Poets. A Handbook* (Woodbridge: The Boydell Press, 2017).

Lotzow, Alexander, *Das Sinfonische Chorstück im 19. Jahrhundert. Studien zur einsätzigen weltlichen Chorwerken mit Orchester von Beethoven bis Brahms* (Kassel: Bärenreiter, 2017).

Lund, Carsten, *Orglets ABC* (Jelling: Det danske Orgelselskab, 1980).

Lynge, Gerhardt, *Danske Komponister i det 20. Aarhundredes Begyndelse* (Aarhus: Erik H. Jung's Forlag, 1917).

Madsen, Herman, *Carl Nielsens Fyn* (Odense: Fyns Boghandels Forlag, 1950).

Maegaard, Jan, 'Den sene Carl Nielsen', *Dansk Musik Tidsskrift*, 28 (1953), 74–79.

Maegaard, Jan, 'Når boet skal gøres op efter Carl Nielsen…', *Dansk Musik Tidsskrift*, 40 (1965), 101–4.

Maegaard, Jan, 'Ung komponist i Carl Nielsens skygge', *Musik & Forskning*, 16 (1990–91), 18–24.

Malling, Anders, *Dansk Salmehistorie*, vol. 8, *Salmebøgerne* (København: J.H. Schultz Forlag, 1978).

Marstal, Henrik, 'Gamle rammer, nye måder? En undersøgelse af sangbogens institutionelle status i Danmark i det tidlige 20. århundrede', *Danish Musicology Online*, special issue 2018 'Musikkens institutioner', 29–48.

Marstrand, Even, *Johan Borup og hans kreds. Tids- og livsbilleder fra slutningen af det nittende og til begyndelsen af det tyvende århundrede* (Odense: Nyt Bogforlag, 1953).

Martino, Alberto, *Die deutsche Leihbibliothek. Geschichte einer literarischen Institution (1756-1914). Mit einem zusammen mit Georg Jäger erstellten Verzeichnis der erhaltenen Leihbibliothekskataloge* (Wiesbaden: Otto Harrassowitz, 1990).

Marx, Adolf Bernhard, *Die Lehre von der musikalischen Komposition, praktisch theoretisch*, 4 vols. (Leipzig: Breitkopf & Härtel, 1837–47).

Matter, Michael, *Niels W. Gade und der "nordische Ton". Ein musikgeschichtlicher Präzedenzfall* (Kassel: Bärenreiter, 2015).

Matthiessen, Christian Wichmann, *Danske byers folketal 1801-1981* (Statistiske undersøgelser, 42; København: Danmarks Statistik, 1985).

McCreless, Patrick, 'Strange Bedfellows. The Hebrew Bible and Wagner, in *Saul and David*', *Carl Nielsen Studies*, 4 (2009), 107–44.

Menke, Johannes, 'Generalbass', in Helga de la Motte-Haber (ed.), *Lexikon der Systematischen Musikwissenschaft* (Handbuch der Systematischen Musikwissenschaft, 6; Laaber: Laaber-Verlag, 2010), 146–48.

Meyer, Torben and Frede Schandorf Petersen, *Carl Nielsen. Kunstneren og Mennesket*, 2 vols. (København: Arnold Busck, 1947–48).

Michelsen, Morten, Iben Have, Anja Mølle Lindelof, Charlotte Rørdam Larsen and Henrik Smith-Sivertsen (eds.), *Stil nu ind… Danmark Radio og musikken* (Aarhus: Aarhus Universitetsforlag, 2018).

Michelsen, Thomas, *Det dybe og det rene. En biografi om Vagn Holmboe* (København: Multivers, 2022).

Michelsen, Vibeke and Kjeld de Fine Licht (eds.), *Danmarks Kirker, Århus Amt* (København: G.E.C. Gads Forlag, 1972), vol. 2.

Miller, Mina F., *Carl Nielsen. A Guide to Research* (New York & London: Garland Publishing, 1987).

Miller, Mina, 'Introduction', in Mina Miller (ed.), *The Nielsen Companion* (London: Faber & Faber, 1994), 16–25.

Moe, Bjarke, '"Galopader af stavelser". Musikalske virkemidler bag integrationen af tekst og toner i reformationstidens danske salmesang', in Jens Bjerring-Hansen, Simon Skovgaard Boeck and Eva Skafte Jensen (eds.), *Nogle betænkninger om dansk sprog og litteratur. Festskrift til Marita Akhøj Nielsen* (København: Universitets-Jubilæets danske Samfund, 2021), 463–85.

Moe, Bjarke, 'Salmesang på skrift: Om forholdet mellem levende sang og musikalsk notation i reformationstidens danske salmer', in Marita Akhøj Nielsen, Simon Skovgaard Boeck and Bjarke Moe (eds.), *Danske reformationssalmer i kontekst* (København: Det Danske Sprog- og Litteraturselskab, 2022), 167–93.

Moe, Bjarke, 'Tracing Compositional and Writing Processes in Sources to the Choral Works of Niels W. Gade', *Danish Yearbook of Musicology*, 43 (2019), 3–36.

Mortensen, Klaus P., 'Det uforfærdede øje', in Klaus P. Mortensen (ed.), *Uden for murene. Fortællinger fra det moderne gennembruds København* (København: G.E.C. Gads Forlag, 2002), 20–39.

Mosorini, Sergio Rossetti, 'New Findings in Titian's Fresco Technique at the Scuola del Santo in Padua', *The Art Bulletin*, 81 (1999), 163–64.

Muck, Peter, *Einhundert Jahre Berliner Philharmonisches Orchester. Darstellung in Dokumenten*, 3 vols. (Tutzing: Ernst Scheider, 1982).

Munk, Jens Peter, 'Agnes Lunn', *Weilbachs Kunstnerleksikon*, 4. edn. (1994), https://www.kulturarv.dk/kid/VisWeilbach.do?kunstnerId=2764&wsektion=alle.

Munk, Jens Peter, 'Konstantin-Hansen, Elise', *Dansk Kvindebiografisk Leksikon online*, https://www.kvinfo.dk/side/170/bio/512/.

Muntoni, Paolo, 'Nielsen's Saul and David and Italian opera', *Danish Yearbook of Musicology*, 41 (2017), 73–100.

Myrtue, Anders, 'Carl Nielsens Odense', in Ida-Marie Vorre (ed.), *I Fyn er alting anderledes… – en antologi om Carl Nielsen og hans fynske baggrund* (Odense: Forlaget Odense Bys Museer, 2015), 96–115.

Møller, Otto, *Til Forstaaelse og Bedømmelse af Nutidens Fritænkeri* (København: Karl Schønbergs Forlag, 1881).

Møller, Svend-Ove, 'Et nyt mekanisk Orgel i Nicolai Kirkesal', *Dansk Kirkemusiker Tidende*, 28/4 (1931), 31–34.

Neiiendam, Robert, *Casino. Oprindelse og Historie i Omrids. Udgivet i Anledning af Hundredaaret for Privatscenernes Oprettelse* (København: Morten A. Korchs Forlag, 1948).

Neiiendam, Robert, *Det kongelige Teaters Historie*, 6 vols. (København: V. Pios Boghandel, Povl Branner, 1921–30, vol. 6: Nyt Nordisk Forlag Arnold Busck, 1970).

Nicolajsen, Lissa, *Sang i landsbyskolen i 1800-tallet. Ej blot til lyst fik mennesket syngeevner* (Herning: Dansk Sang / Folkeskolens Musiklærerforening, 2006).

Nielsen, Bendt Viinholt, *Rued Langgaard. Biografi* (København: Engstrøm & Sødring, 1993).

Nielsen, Carl, Thomas Laub, Oluf Ring and Thorvald Aagaard (eds.), *Folkehøjskolens Melodibog* (København and Leipzig: Wilhelm Hansen, 1922).

Nielsen, Carl (ed.), *Nye Melodier til de nyere Sangtekster i Johan Borup's Dansk Sangbog redigeret af Carl Nielsen* (København and Leipzig: Wilhelm Hansen, 1916).

Nielsen, Steen Kaargaard and Claus Byrith, *Danmarks ældste lydoptagelser – Edisons fonograf i 1890'ernes København* (Aarhus: Aarhus Universitetsforlag, 2017).

Nielsen, Thorvald, 'Nogle personlige erindringer', in Jürgen Balzer (ed.), *Carl Nielsen i hundredåret for hans fødsel* (København: Nyt Nordisk Forlag – Arnold Busck, 1965), 7–17.

Nielsen, Thorvald, 'Statens overtagelse af den musikpædagogiske eksamen', *Dansk Musik Tidsskrift*, 15 (1940), 116–19.

Niemann, Walter, *Brahms* (Berlin: Schuster & Loeffler, 1920).

Nietzsche, Friedrich, *Also sprach Zarathustra*, vol. 4, Leipzig 1891. Online: https://www.deutsches-textarchiv.de/book/view/nietzsche_zarathustra04_1891?p=131.

Nutzhorn, Heinrich, *Melodier til Sangbog for Højskoler og Landbrugsskoler* (Nyborg: V. Schønnemanns Forlag, 1904).

Nyerup, Rasmus, *Udvalg af Danske Viser*, 2 vols. (København: Schultz, 1821).

Nyerup, Rasmus and Knud Lyne Rahbek, *Udvalgte Danske Viser fra Middelalderen*, 5 vols. (København: J.F. Schultz, 1812–1814).

Nørr, Erik, *Skolen, præsten og kommunen. Kampen om skolen på landet 1842-1899* (København: Jurist- og Økonomiforbundets forlag, 1994).

Nørtoft, Magnus, 'Første Verdenskrig betød stigende priser og rationeringer på brød og kød', Danmarks statistik (2018), https://www.dst.dk/da/Statistik/nyheder-analyser-publ/bagtal/2018/2018-11-09-foerste-verdenskrig-betoed-stigende-priser.

Oelsner, Gertrud, 'Den sunde natur', in Gertrud Hvidberg-Hansen and Gertrud Oelsner (eds.), *Livslyst. Sundhed – Skønhed – Styrke i dansk kunst 1890-1940* (Odense: Fuglsang Kunstmuseum and Odense Bys Museer, 2008), 159–97.

Olesen, Eva-Marie, *Organistbogen* (København: Dansk Organist og Kantor Samfund, 9. edn., 2005).

Olsen, Cathinka, 'Minder og Breve af Malerinde frk. Cathinka Olsen', in L. C. Nielsen (ed.), *Emil B. Sachs. Et Mindeskrift* (København: Steen Hasselbalchs Forlag, 1923), 88–120.

Olsen, Kåre and H. Topsøe-Jensen (eds.), *H. C. Andersens dagbøger, 1825-1875*, vol. 7 (1866–67), ed. Kirsten Weber (Det Danske Sprog- og Litteraturselskab, København: Gad, 1972).

Ostwald, Peter F., 'Brahms, Solitary Altruist', in Walter Frisch (ed.), *Brahms and His World* (Princeton, NJ: Princeton University Press, 1990), 23–35.

Ottesen, Doris, 'Valdemar Brücker 1852-1929', *Ågård frimenigheds jubilæumsskrift* (1987), http://www.oxenvad.dk/menigheder/Menigheder/Aagaard/brucker.html.

Ottosen, Johan, 'Studentersamfundet, stiftet d. 2. maj 1882', in *Det danske Studentersamfund og dets Virksomhed. Redegørelse ved det nordiske akademiske Møde i Kristiania* (København: Det nordiske Forlag, Ernst Bojsesen, 1896), 3–10.

Overgaard, Iben (ed.), *Agnes Slott-Møller. Skønhed er til evig glæde* (Aarhus: Odense Bys Museer/Skovgaard Museet, 2008).

Panum, Hortense and William Behrend, *Illustreret Musikhistorie. En Fremstilling for nordiske Læsere* (København: Det Nordiske Forlag, 1897).

Parks, Richard S., 'Pitch Structure in Carl Nielsen's Wind Quintet', in Mina Miller (ed.), *The Nielsen Companion* (London: Faber & Faber, 1994), 541–96.

Pasler, Jann, *Composing the Citizen. Music as Public Utility in Third Republic France* (Berkely: University of California Press, 2009).

Pedersen, Bendt Astrup, *Carl Nielsens klavermusik* (MA thesis, Københavns Universitet, 1960).

Pedersen, Ole, 'Chresten Kold, friskolen og 150 år', *Folkeskolen*, no. 18 (2002), online at folkeskolen.dk.

Pedersen, Paul Georg, 'Spillemanden Blinde Anders', *Højby Nyt*, 21/6 (2012).

Petersen, Christian M.K., *Odense Musikforening gennem et halvt Aarhundrede. Odense Musikforening 1866-1916 og dens Forgængere 1856-1865* (Odense: Odense Musikforening, 1916).

Petersen, Elly Bruunshuus, 'Carl Nielsen og Samfundet til Udgivelse af Dansk Musik 1899-1931', *Fund og Forskning*, 40 (2001), 199–228.

Petersen, Elly Bruunshuus, 'Carl Nielsen, *Søvnen*, opus 18. En musiktekst bliver til', *Fund og Forskning*, 43 (2004), 405–22.

Petersen, Elly Bruunshuus, 'Censur på universitetet? Carl Nielsen og Niels Møllers kantate til universitetets årsfest 1908', in Anne Ørbæk Jensen et al. (eds.), *Musikvidenskabelige kompositioner. Festskrift til Niels Krabbe* (København: Det Kongelige Bibliotek, 2006), 561–77.

Petersen, Jens Åge S. et al., *Byens ansigt. Historien om Odense Rådhus 1480-2005* (Odense: Byhistorisk Udvalg), 2005.

Petersen, Kirsten Flensborg, 'Carl Nielsen's Flute Concerto. Form and revision of the ending', *Carl Nielsen Studies*, 2 (2005), 196–225.

Petersen, Kirsten Flensborg, 'Musikforeningen Braga', *Fynske årbøger* (2001), 46–63.

Pfitzner, Hans, 'Die neue Aesthetik der musikalischen Impotenz. Ein Verwesungssymptom?' (1920), in Hans Pfitzner, *Gesammelte Schriften*, vol. 2 (Augsburg: s.n., 1926), 99–281.

Pfitzner, Hans, 'Futuristengefahr' (1917), in Hans Pfitzner, *Gesammelte Schriften*, vol. 1 (Augsburg: s.n., 1926), 185–223.

Phillips, Leonard M., *The Leipzig Conservatory: 1843–1881* (Ph.D. diss., University of Indiana, 1979).

Poulsen, Kirsten, *Johannes Poulsen som iscenesætter* (Rhodos, 1990).

Povlsen, Alfred, 'Melodier til Højskolesangbogen', *Højskolebladet*, 45 (1920), cols. 1385–86.

Price, David, *Cancan!* (London: Cancan Publishing, 2. edn., 2010).

Prik., 'Carl Nielsens bror mindes sin rige fynske barndom', *Politiken*, 3 February 1956.

Prip, Svend, 'Om den danske orgelbevægelse – et forsøg på sammenfatning og afrunding', in Per Kynne Frandsen, Svend Prip and Claus Røllum-Larsen (eds.), *Dansk Orgelkultur. Det Danske Orgelselskab 1970-1995* (Vanløse: Det Danske Orgelselskab, 1997), 55–76.

Rangström, Ture, 'Modern sångkomposition', *Svenska Dagbladet*, 29 June, 10 September and 11 September 1909.

Rask, Elin, 'Dagmarteatret. Nationalscenens "dårlige samvittighed"', in Kela Kvam et al. (eds.), *Dansk Teaterhistorie 2. Folkets teater* (København: Gyldendal, 1992), 49–54.

Rask, Elin, 'Privatteatrene 1848-57', in Kela Kvam et al. (eds.), *Dansk Teaterhistorie 2. Folkets teater* (København: Gyldendal, 1992), 11–16.

Rasmussen, Peter, *Exempelbog til Harmonilæren af Prof. JOH. CHR. GEBAUER*, 3. edn. (København and Leipzig: Wilhelm Hansen, [c. 1908]).

Ravnkilde, Svend, 'Stravinsky i København, sommeren 1924 – et strejftog med Finale 1924', *Dansk Musik Tidsskrift*, 56 (1981–82), 258–69.

Reynolds, Anne-Marie, *Carl Nielsen's Voice. His Songs in Context* (København: Museum Tusculanum Press, 2010).

Reynolds, Anne-Marie, 'Nielsen's *Saul and David* as Tragedy: The Dialectics of Fate and Freedom in Drama and Music', *Carl Nielsen Studies*, 5 (2012), 236–57.

Reynolds, Anne-Marie, 'The Early Song Collections', in Mina Miller (ed.), *The Nielsen Companion* (London: Faber & Faber, 1994), 399–453.

Richter, Ernst Friedrich, *Die Grundzüge der musikalischen Formen und ihre Analyse, als Leitfaden beim Studium derselben und zunächst für den praktischen Unterricht im Conservatorium der Musik zu Leipzig* (Leipzig: Verlag von Georg Wigard, 1852).

Richter, Ernst Friedrich, *Lehrbuch der Harmonie. Praktische Anleitung zu den Studien in derselben, zunächst für das Conservatorium der Musik zu Leipzig* (Leipzig: Breitkopf & Härtel, 1853).

Richter, Ernst Friedrich, *Lehrbuch des einfachen und doppelten Contrapunkts. Praktische Anleitung zu dem Studium desselben zunächst für das Conservatorium der Musik zu Leipzig* (Leipzig: Breitkopf & Härtel, 1872).

Riemann, Hugo, *Geschichte der Musik seit Beethoven* (Berlin: W. Spemann, 1901).

Riggs, Robert, '"Das Quartett-Spiel ist doch wohl mein eigentliches Fach": Joseph Joachim and the String Quartet', in Valerie Woodring Goertzen and Robert Whitehouse Eshbach (eds.), *The Creative Worlds of Joseph Joachim* (Woodbridge: The Boydell Press, 2021), 145–62.

Riley, Matthew, *Musical Listening in the German Enlightenment. Attention, Wonder and Astonishment* (Aldershot: Ashgate, 2004).

Ring, Frands Johan, *Oluf Ring. Et Liv i dansk Folkesangs Tjeneste* (Odense: Fyns Boghandel, 1961).

Ring, Frands Johan, *Thorvald Aagaard. Mennesket – Musikeren* (Odense: Fyns Boghandels Forlag, 1954).

Rode, Ove, 'Fest i Studentersamfundets nye Hjem', *Illustreret Tidende*, 42/36 (9 June 1901), 562.

Rolf, Claus, *Højer sogns og flækkes historie* (Højer: Fonden til Udgivelser af Egnsbeskrivelser for Højeregnen, 1998).

Rosenhoff, Orla, *450 firstemmige Opgaver til Brug ved den musiktheoretiske Undervisning* (København and Leipzig: Wilhelm Hansen), Collection 1, first booklet [1885], Collection 1, second booklet [1885–86], Collection 2, first booklet [1887], Collection 2, second booklet [1886?], Collection 3, first booklet [1887?], Collection 3, second booklet [1889].

Rosenhoff, Orla, *Digte efter det engelske ved Caralis* (København: Horneman & Erslev, 1868).

Rosenhoff, Orla, *Emilie Rosenhoff tilegnede. Fem Digte af Emil Aarestrup og Chr. Winther* (København: Horneman & Erslev, [1867]).

Rosenhoff, Orla, *Fem danske Sange med Klaver* (København and Leipzig: Wilhelm Hansen, [1902]).

Rosenhoff, Orla, *Fire Sange af Bernh. Sev. Ingemanns "Kunnuk og Naja"* (København: Horneman & Erslev, [1865]).

Ross, Ryan, 'Nielsen's Arcadia: The Case of the Flute Concerto', *Carl Nielsen Studies*, 5 (2012), 280–301.

Rosted, Kristian, *Fra Kyst til Kyst. Overfartstedet Sønderjylland-Fyn gennem Tiderne* (Assens: Plums Boghandel, [1930]).

Roth, Colin, 'Carl Nielsen's Cultural Self-Education. His Early Engagement with Fine Art and Ideas and the Path towards *Hymnus Amoris*', *Carl Nielsen Studies*, 5 (2012), 302–27.

Roth, Joseph, *The Radetzky March*, tr. Joachim Neugroschel (New York: Alfred A. Knopf, 1996).

Rothfarb, Lee A., *Ernst Kurth as Theorist and Analyst* (Philadelphia: University of Pennsylvania Press, 1988).

Rothfarb, Lee A., *Ernst Kurth: Selected Writings* (Cambridge: Cambridge University Press, 1991).

Rowell, Lewis, 'Carl Nielsen's Homespun Philosophy of Music', in Mina Miller (ed.), *The Nielsen Companion* (London: Faber & Faber, 1994), 31–57.

Rugstad, Gunnar, *Christian Sinding 1856-1941. En biografisk og stilistisk studie* (Oslo: Cappelen, 1979).

Røllum-Larsen, Claus, 'Det Anckerske Legats rejsestipendier for komponister 1861-1915', *Danish Yearbook of Musicology*, 30 (2002), 75–87.

Røllum-Larsen, Claus, 'En dansk violinist i udlandet. Johannes Schiørrings tidlige karriere', *Magasin fra Det Kongelige Bibliotek*, 30/4 (2017), 29–36.

Røllum-Larsen, Claus, *Impulser i Københavns koncertrepertoire 1900-1935. Studier i præsentationen af ny, især udenlandsk instrumentalmusik*, 2 vols. (København: Museum Tusculanum Press, 2002).

Røllum-Larsen, Claus, 'Louis Glass og Carl Nielsen. Modsætninger i dansk musik. Deres forhold belyst hovedsagelig gennem breve fra Louis Glass', in Anne Ørbæk Jensen et al. (eds.), *Musikvidenskabelige kompositioner. Festskrift til Niels Krabbe. 1941 – 3. oktober – 2006* (København: Museum Tusculanum Press, 2006), 591–602.

Røllum-Larsen, Claus, 'Musikken i Holmens Kirke. Orgler og organister', in Ulla Kjær et al. (eds.), *Holmens Kirke* (København: Gads Forlag, 2019), 144–73.

Røllum-Larsen, Claus, 'Træk af musiklivet i København i perioden 1890-1914, med særligt henblik på populærmusikken', *Danish Yearbook of Musicology*, 13 (1982), 5–41.

Röntgen jun., Julius, 'Musiklivet på Fuglsang', in Johannes Hansen (ed.), *Bodil Neergaard. Hendes Slægt og Virke skildret af Familie og Venner i Anledning af hendes 80-Aars Dag* ([København]: Thaning & Appels Forlag, 1947), 127–36.

Sansone, Matteo, 'Verismo', *Grove Music Online* (2001), https://doi-org.ep.fjernadgang.kb.dk/10.1093/gmo/9781561592630.article.29210.

Savage, Roger, 'Incidental Music', *Grove Music Online* (2001), https://doi.org/10.1093/gmo/9781561592630.article.43289.

Savery, Carl Maria (ed.), *Blokfløjten. Vejledning i at spille Blokfløjte og synge dertil* (København: Skandinavisk og Borups Musikforlag, 1931).

Schenck, Dietmar, 'Die Ära Joseph Joachim', in *Die Hochschule für Musik zu Berlin. Preußens Konservatorium zwischen romantischen Klassizismus und Neuer Musik, 1869-1932/33* (Stuttgart: Franz Steiner Verlag, 2004), 43–57.

Schiørring, Nils, *Musikkens historie i Danmark*, 3 vols. (København: Politikens Forlag, 1978).

Schiøtt, Julius, 'Studentersamfundets Stiftelse og første Aar', in Paul Læssøe Müller (ed.), *Studentersamfundet gennem fem og tyve Aar. Jubilæumsskrift* (København: Gyldendal, Nordisk Forlag, 1907), 127–46.

Schlee, Ernst, *Christian Carl Magnussen. Ein Künstlerschicksal aus der Kaiserzeit* (Husum: Husum Druck- und Verlagsgesellschaft, 1991).

Schmidt, Karl, *Meddelelser om Skuespil og Theaterforhold i Odense i Anledningen af Hundredeaarsdagen for den første danske Komedies Opførelse paa Odense Theater* (Odense: Fyens Stiftsbogtrykkeri, 1896).

Schmitter, Amy M., 'Ancient, Medieval and Renaissance Theories of the Emotions', *The Stanford Encyclopedia of Philosophy* (2021), ed. Edward N. Zalta, https://plato.stanford.edu/entries/emotions-17th18th/LD1Background.html#HipGalMed, section 3.

Schnedler-Petersen, Frederik, *Et Liv i Musik* (København: Forlaget Novografia, 1946).

Schorske, Carl E., *Fin-de-Siècle Vienna. Politics and Culture* (New York: Vintage Books, 1981).

Schou, Alette, *Franz Schubert. I Anledning af Hundredaaret for hans Fødsel (1797-1897). Frit efter Kreissle von Hellborn og flere andre. Med et Forord af Fru Erika Nissen født Lie* (København: Jacob Lunds Forlag, 1897).

Schousboe, Torben, '"Barn af huset" – ? Nogle tanker og problemer omkring et utrykt forord til Carl Nielsens "Salmer og aandelige Sange"', *Dansk kirkesangs årsskrift*, 21 (1969–70), 75–91.

Schousboe, Torben (ed.), *Carl Nielsen. Dagbøger og brevveksling med Anne Marie Carl-Nielsen*, 2 vols. (København: Gyldendal, 1983).

Schousboe, Torben, '"Det skulle være jævne viser…" Notater om et skelsættende samarbejde mellem Carl Nielsen og Thomas Laub', in Mette Müller (ed.), *Festskrift Henrik Glahn* (København: Musikvidenskabeligt Institut, 1979), 151–82.

Schousboe, Torben, 'Foreningen Symphonia', *Dansk Musik Tidsskrift*, 45 (1970), 156–68.

Schousboe, Torben, 'Koncertforeningen i København. Et bidrag til det københavnske musiklivs historie i slutningen af det 19. århundrede', *Dansk Årbog for Musikforskning*, 6 (1968–72), 171–209.

Schrøder, Ludvig, *Den nordiske Folkehøjskole. Bidrag til dens Historie* (København: G.E.C. Gad, 1904).

Schultz, Sigurd, 'Danske Kunstnere i Paris under den tredje Republik', in Franz v. Jessen (ed.), *Danske i Paris gennem Tiderne. Andet Bind. Andet Halvbind. 1870-1935* (København: C.A. Reitzels Forlag, 1938), 433–524.

Schulz, Johann Abraham Peter, *Gedanken über den Einfluss der Musik auf die Bildung eines Volks, und über deren Einführung in den Schulen der Königl. Dänischen Staaten* (København: Christian Gottlob Proft, 1790).

Schulz, Johann Abraham Peter, *Lieder im Volkston, bey dem Claviere zu singen*, vol. 1, 2. edn. (Berlin: George Jakob Decker, 1785).

Schwab, Heinrich W., 'Guldalderens musik og danskhed', in Jens Henrik Koudal (ed.), *Musik og danskhed. Fem faglige bidrag til debatten om nationalitet* (København: C.A. Reitzel, 2005), 59–74.

Schwartz, Vanessa, *Spectacular Realities. Early Mass Culture in Fin-de-Siècle Paris* (Berkeley: University of California Press, 1998).

Schøller, Frederik C. G., 'Aktstykker og Skrivelser betræffende den ved Wienerfreden af 30te October 1864 §§ V og VI nedsatte internationale Grændsereguleringe-Commission til Bestemmelse af Grændsen mellem Danmark og Slesvig m.m.', *Fra Ribe Amt*, 2 (1904), 37–112.

Seedorf, Thomas, *Studien zur kompositorischen Mozart-Rezeption im frühen 20. Jahrhundert* (Laaber: Laaber-Verlag, 1990).

Seligmann, Hugo, 'Carl Nielsen og hans sidste Symfoni', *Musik*, 1 (1917), 3–5, 105–9.

Sietz, Reinhold, *Theodor Kirchner. Ein Klaviermeister der deutschen Romantik* (Regensburg: Gustav Bosse Verlag, 1971).

Simonsen, Rudolph, 'Carl Nielsen som Symphoniker', *Dansk Musik Tidsskrift*, 2 (1926), 7–11.

Skjerne, Godtfred, *H.C. Lumbye og hans Samtid* (København: J.L. Lybeckers Forlag 1912).

Skjerne, Godtfred and Gottfried Bruhn, *Københavns Orkesterforening. 1874 – 25 April – 1899. Festskrift* (København: J. Henriksens Bogtrykkeri, 1899).

Skram, Erik, 'Studentersamfundets fri Teater', in *Det danske Studentersamfund og dets Virksomhed. Redegørelse ved det nordiske akademiske Møde i Kristiania* (København: Det nordiske Forlag, Ernst Bojesen, 1896), 33–34.

Smith, Gustav, *Om Musikkens Dobbelt-Virkning* (København: Levin & Munksgaards Forlag, 1928).

Sommer, Anne-Louise, *Den danske arkitektur* (København: Gyldendal, 2009).

Sousa, Elisabete M. de, 'Musical Controversies in Nietzsche and Kierkegaard', in Katia Hay and Leonel R. dos Santos (eds.), *Nietzsche, German Idealism and Its Critics* (Berlin and Boston: de Gruyter, 2005), 246–57.

Spencer, Herbert, *Musikkens Vorden og Virken*, tr. Thomas Sachs (København: F.H. Eibes Forlag, 1882).

Spur, Erik (ed.), *Viser og Sange* (København and Leipzig: Wilhelm Hansen, 1919).

Stampe-Bendix, Karen, *Fra mit livs tjørnekrat* (København: Hans Reitzels Forlag, 1960).

Stangerup, Hakon and F.J. Billeskov Jansen, *Dansk Litteraturhistorie. Bind 3. Fra Georg Brandes til Johannes V. Jensen* (København: Politikens Forlag, 1971).

Steensen, Steen Chr., *Musik er liv. En biografi om Carl Nielsen* (Frederiksberg: Fisker & Schou, 1999).

Svanholm, Lise, *Malerne på Skagen* (København: Gyldendal, 2001).

Sørensen, Carl, 'Borups Højskole og Arbejderne', *Borups Højskole. Medlemsblad for Foreningen til Højskolens Fremme i København*, 10/11 (1925), 180–81.

Sørensen, Inger, 'Introduction', in *C. F. E. Horneman. Aladdin. A Fairy-Tale Opera in Four Acts*, ed. Niels Bo Foltmann, Peter Hauge, Bjarke Moe and Axel Teich Geertinger (København: Dansk Center for Musikudgivelse, 2020), xvi–xxii.

Sørensen, Inger (ed.), *Johannes Palmer Hartmann og hans kreds. Familiebreve 1883-1930* (s.l.: Forlagsbureauet v. Ole Klitgaard, 2012).

Sørensen, Inger, 'Musiklivet på Fuglsang 1892 til 1931', *Fund og Forskning*, 52 (2013), 215–47.

Sørensen, Inger, *Niels W. Gade. Et dansk verdensnavn* (København: Gyldendal, 2002).

Sørensen, Inger (ed.), *Niels W. Gade og hans europæiske kreds. En brevveksling 1836-1891* (København: Museum Tusculanum Press, 2008).

Sørensen, Kurt Risskov, 'Bondemalerstriden', in Malene Linell Ipsen (ed.), *Du danske sommer. Fynbomalerne og de jyske forfattere i samklang* (Kerteminde: Johannes Larsen Museet, 2007), 39–46.

Sørensen, Marius, '"Fædreland" eller "Fødeland"?', *Sorø Amtstidende*, 22 January 1917.

Sørensen, Søren, 'Korværkerne', in Jürgen Balzer (ed.), *Carl Nielsen i hundredåret for hans fødsel* (København: Nyt Nordisk Forlag Arnold Busck, 1965), 97–109.

Tange, Esben, 'Musikalsk symbolisme. En indkredsning af symbolismen og en særlig musikalsk symbolisme inden for "det moderne"', *Dansk Årbog for Musikforskning*, 29 (2001), 37–56.

Tarrant, Christopher, 'Breakthrough and Collapse in Carl Nielsen's *Sinfonia semplice*', *Danish Yearbook of Musicology*, 41/1 (2017), 32–49.

Telmanyi, Anne Marie, *Mit Barndomshjem. Erindringer om Anne Marie og Carl Nielsen skrevet af deres Datter* (København: Thaning & Appel, 1965).

Telmányi, Emil, *Af en musikers billedbog* (København: Nyt Nordisk Forlag Arnold Busck, 1978).

Thaning, Fie Louise Skovsbøg, *Nationalitetskonstruktioner i receptionen af Carl Nielsen – en receptionshistorisk analyse* (MA thesis, Musikvidenskabeligt Institut, Københavns Universitet, 2005).

Thomissøn, Hans (ed.), *Den danske Psalmebog* (København: Lorentz Benedicht, 1569).

Thomsen, Carl, 'Vore Sange', *Maanedsblad for Borups Højskole*, 1 (1916), 39.

Thomsen, Jørgen, 'Odense som garnisonsby. Kasernen på Sdr. Boulevard 100 år', in *Odensebogen 1992* (Odense: Byhistorisk Udvalg, 1992), 137–54.

Thrane, Carl, *Fra Hofviolonernes Tid* (København: Det schønbergske Forlag, 1908).

Topp, Kylle, *Dengang i Odense. Min barndoms by i ord og billeder* (Odense: Lokalhistorisk Afdeling ved Odense Centralbibliotek, 1981).

Trap, Jens Peter, *Statistisk-topographisk Beskrivelse af Kongeriget Danmark*, vol. 4, *Amterne Odense, Svendborg og Maribo*, 2. edn. (København: Forlagsbureauet, 1873)

Trier, Ernst (ed.), *Sange for den kristelige folke-skole* (København: Karl Schønbergs Forlag, 1874).

Tunbridge, Laura, 'Introduction. Restaging German Song', in Natasha Loges and Laura Tunbridge (eds.), *German Song Onstage: Lieder Performance in the Nineteenth and Early Twentieth Centuries* (Bloomington: Indiana University Press, 2020), 1–9.

Valéry, Paul, 'At the Lamoureux Concert', in *The Collected Works of Paul Valéry. Volume 11: Occasions*, tr. R. Shattuck and F. Brown (Princeton: Princeton University Press, 1956), 199–200.

Vibæk, Marius, *Foreningen til unge handelsmænds uddannelse 1880-1930* (København: Chr. Christiansens Bogtrykkeri, 1930).

Villagomez, Nanna Staugaard, '"In the Land of Dreams": Carl Nielsen's Second Thoughts about Wagner', *Danish Yearbook of Musicology*, 44 (2020–21), 3–28.

Villagomez, Nanna Staugaard, *Carl Nielsen og det musikalsk moderne. Symphonias lieder i 1890'ernes København* (MA thesis, Københavns Universitet, 2022).

Vorre, Ida-Marie, 'Spillemand Carl August Nielsen', *Fynske minder* (2008), 49–63.

Vorre, Ida-Marie, 'Spillemænd på Midtfyn', in Ida-Marie Vorre (ed.), *I Fyn er alting anderledes… – en antologi om Carl Nielsen og hans fynske baggrund* (Odense: Forlaget Odense Bys Museer, 2015), 56–77.

Wanscher, Vilhelm, *Den æsthetiske Opfattelse af Kunst* (København: Gyldendal/Nordisk Forlag, 1906).

Wassard, Erik, *Nørrevold, Østervold og Kastellet* (København før og nu – og aldrig. En billedkavalkade om København inden for voldene og søerne, 10; København: Palle Fogtdal, 1990).

Wasserloos, Yvonne, *Das Leipziger Konservatorium im 19. Jahrhundert. Anziehungs- und Ausstrahlungskraft eines musikpädagogischen Modells auf das internationale Musikleben* (Hildesheim: Georg Olms Verlag, 2004).

Weber, William, 'Concerts at four conservatories in the 1880s: a comparative analysis', in Michael Fend and Michel Noiray (eds.), *Musical Education in Europe (1770-1914). Compositional, Institutional, and Political Challenges* (Berlin: Berliner Wissenschafts-Verlag GmbH, 2005), 331-49.

Weber, William, *The Great Transformation of Musical Taste: Concert Programming from Haydn to Brahms* (Cambridge, UK: Cambridge University Press, 2008).

Weber, William, 'The Rise of the Classical Repertoire in Nineteenth-Century Orchestral Concerts', in Joan Peyser (ed.), *The Orchestra: Origins and Transformations* (New York: Billboard Books, 2000), 361-85.

Webster, James, *Haydn's "Farewell" Symphony and the Idea of Classical Style* (Cambridge: Cambridge University Press, 1991).

Weiss, Frederik, 'Nogle Erindringer og Indtryk af Fr. Weiss', in L. C. Nielsen (ed.), *Emil B. Sachs. Et Mindeskrift* (København: Steen Hasselbalchs Forlag, 1923), 65-70.

Werbeck, Walter, 'Richard Strauss's Tone Poems', in Mark-Daniel Schmid (ed.), *The Richard Strauss Companion* (Westport, Conn.: Praeger, 2003), 103-44.

Weyse, C. E. F., *Choral-Melodier til den evangelisk christelige Psalmebog harmonisk bearbeidet* (København: Kongelig Vaisenhuses Forlag, 1839).

Weyse, C. E. F., *Choral-Melodier til den evangelisk christelige Psalmebog harmonisk bearbeidet*, 3. edn., ed. Johan Christian Gebauer (København: Th. Lind, 1877).

Weyse, C. E. F., *Sange med klaver*, ed. Sten Høgel, 2 vols. (København: Edition Samfundet, 2007).

Weyse, C. E. F., *Syv Aftensange af B.S. Ingemann* (København: C.C. Lose & Delbanco, 1838).

Widmaier, Tobias, *Der deutsche Musikalienleihhandel. Funktion, Bedeutung und Topografie einer Form gewerblicher Musikaliendistribution vom späten 18. bis zum frühen 20. Jahrhundert* (Saarbrücken: Pfau, 1998).

Wiingaard, Jytte, 'Den svære realisme', in Kela Kvam et al. (eds..), *Dansk Teaterhistorie 2. Folkets teater* (København: Gyldendal, 1992), 16-38.

Wilkinson, Lynn R., 'They Fluttered like Moths. Exile and Cosmopolitanism in the Work of Germaine de Staël and Georg Brandes', in Richard Hibbit (ed.), *Other Capitals of the Nineteenth Century. An Alternative Mapping of Literary and Cultural Space* (New York: Palgrave Macmillan, 2017), 51-67.

Willumsen, Jens F., *Mine Erindringer. Fortalt til Ernst Mentze med biografiske Oplysninger, Noter og Kommentarer* (København: Berlingske Forlag, 1953).

Wivel, Henrik, *Symbolisme og impressionisme* (Ny dansk kunsthistorie, 5; København: Forlaget Palle Fogtdal A/S, 1994).

Würz, Anton, 'Kirchner, Theodor', in Otto zu Stolberg-Wernigerode (ed.), *Neue Deutsche Biographie*, vol. 11 (Berlin: Duncker & Humblot, 1977), 663-64.

Yde, Henrik, *Nexø. Martin Andersen Nexøs liv og værk* (København: Lindhardt og Ringhof, 2019).

Zahle, Carl Th., 'Emil B. Sachs og Studentersamfundet', in L. C. Nielsen (ed.), *Emil B. Sachs. Et Mindeskrift* (København: Steen Hasselbalchs Forlag, 1923), 62-64.

Zerlang, Martin, *Bylivets kunst – København som metropol og miniature* (Hellerup: Forlaget Spring, 2002).

Zerlang, Martin, *Herman Bangs København* (København: Politikens Forlag, 2007).

Zibrandtsen, Jan, *Hans Nikolaj Hansen. 1853-1923* (København: Berlingske Forlag, 1953).

Ødegaard, Bent (ed.), *Højby Forsamlingshus 1878-2003* (Højby: Højby Forsamlingshus, 2003).

Aagaard, Thorvald, 'En ny Sangbog', *Højskolebladet*, 44 (1919), cols. 743-44.

Aagaard, Thorvald, 'Folkehøjskolens Melodibog. I Anledning af Emborgs kritiske Bemærkninger', *Højskolebladet*, 47 (1922), cols. 1080-84.

Aagaard, Thorvald, 'Folkelig Sang', *Højskolebladet*, 33 (1908), cols. 1161-68.

Aakjær, Jeppe, *Fra min Bitte-Tid. En kulturhistorisk Selvbiografi* (København: Gyldendal, 1928).

Index of Names

A

Abel, Johannes M. A. 57
Adam, Adolphe 282
Adler, Guido 603–4
Ahna, Heinrich de 227
Ahrendtsen, Judith 120 581
Alexander III 81
Amberg, Johan 280
Ambros, August Wilhelm 595–96
Ancher, Anna 251
Andersdatter, Helene 32–35
Andersen, Hakon 523 587
Andersen, Hans 33 46
Andersen, Hans Christian 38 54 297 305 447 455 654 664 687
Andersen, Joachim 153
Andersen, Niels 33
Andersen, Peder 36
Andersen, Sophus 209–10
Andersen, Vilhelm 99 366 368 370–71 466
Arentzen, Kristian 175
Artôt de Padilla, Lola 325
Arvesen, Arve 245
Auber, Daniel-François-Esprit 65–66 73 76 282
Avril, Jane 249

B

Bach, Johann Sebastian 69–70 74 121 123 210 231 236 359–60 374 389 391 531 561 590 592–93 595–96 603 611 618 696
Bahr, Hermann 199 317 330
Ballin, Mogens 245
Balslev, Harald 48 506–8 521
Bang, Herman 130–31 177 449
Bang, Margrethe 110
Bangert, Emilius 297 498 581–83 624 678
Bargiel, Woldemar 228
Barlach, Ernst 262
Barnekow, Christian 224
Bartholdy, Johan 126 283
Bartók, Béla 438 533–34 590 654 678 693
Bauditz, Agnes 89 579
Bauditz, Waldemar Sempill 89
Bauer, Adolf 128
Bay, Rudolph 474

Bazin, François 282
Bechgaard, Julius 283
Beck, Hans 371
Beckman, Bror 123 578 598
Beethoven, Ludwig van 46 50 111 122–23 127 147 149 156 222 224 226 231 248 374 391 395–96 399 412 429 548 550 560–61 617 678 685
Behrend, William 81–82 209 211 238 354 358–59 630 672 690
Behrens, Carl 189–90 468
Bellermann, Heinrich 120 581 610
Bellman, Carl Michael 370
Bendix, Anna 255
Bendix, Frits 159 175 178 180 211 245 253 255 280
Bendix, Julie 177
Bendix, Victor 149 160–64 166 175 180–84 189 221–24 230 232–33 245 255 552 692
Bentzon, Jørgen 588–89 613 673
Benzon, Otto 448 555–56
Berendsen, Ivar 294
Berg, Hans 582
Berg, Julius Ferdinand 137 139
Berggreen, Andreas Peter 70 117 433–34 474 655 662–64 675
Bergh, Gudrun 582
Bergh, Rudolph, jun. 96 175–76 183–84 190 354 359–60 377–78 393–94 396 398 658
Bergh, Rudolph, sen. 183–84 213
Bergstedt, Harald 470
Bériot, Charles-Auguste de 125–27
Berlioz, Hector 231 233 561 563
Bernstein, Leonard 674
Berntsen, Klaus 22 38–42 45 71 79–80 279 550 668 676 687–88 690
Berntsen, Aage 668
Bielefeldt, Viggo 110 474–75 478
Bing, Herman 175
Bing, Ludvig 175 182
Birkedal, Vilhelm 39
Bismarck, Otto von 236–37
Bissen, Herman Wilhelm 103 262
Bissen, Vilhelm 103 250 262 264 266
Bizet, Georges 282–83 391
Bjørnson, Bjørnstjerne 172 450
Blicher, Steen Steensen 514

Bloch, Anton 144
Bloch, Valdemar 124
Blumhardt, Johann Christoph 260–61
Boheman, Torsten 579
Bohlmann, Georg Carl 89
Boieldieu, François-Adrien 66 282 554
Bondesen, Jørgen Ditleff 116
Bonnat, Léon 243–44 250
Borchsenius, Otto 175 455 462 665
Borgbjerg, Frederik 680–82
Borup, Dagmar 94 380 509–10 518 579
Borup, Hans 512 670
Borup, Johan 508–17 519–20 522–23 587 670
Borup, Julius 89 94 124 144 280 380 509 517
Botticelli, Sandro 339
Bournonville, August 141 278–79 283 369
Boye, Caspar Johannes 480
Brahms, Johannes 15 140 182 215 219–20 222–26 228–29 232 234 236–39 314 316 322 325 373–74 400–1 553–54 561 563 672 692 696
Brandes, Edvard 42 174–75 178 180 185–86 449–50 462 676
Brandes, Emma 184
Brandes, Georg 42 170–78 180–85 196 198 202–3 216 290–91 317 323 392 451 462
Brandt, Morten Kisbye 54
Braunfels, Walter 546
Braunstein, Christian Emil 72–73
Braunstein, Matthäus Wilhelm 72–73 656
Brendel, Franz 391–92
Briand de Crèvecoeur, Frederik Jørgen 31 35–36
Brincken, Dagny 469
Brockenhuus-Schack, Frands 555
Brodersen, Anna Maria 257
Brodersen, Anne Marie, see Carl–Nielsen, Anne Marie
Brodersen, Emil 260–61
Brodersen, Frederiche, née Gylling 259–60
Brodersen, Julie 258
Brodersen, Hans Heinrich 261
Brodersen, Hans Hinrich 257
Brodersen, Maria, née Blumhardt 261
Brodersen, Paul Julius 160 257–60
Brodersen, Poul 160 258 261
Brodersen, Theodor 260
Brodsky, Adolph 232–33 405

Brorson, Hans Adolph 472
Brucken Fock, Gerard von 393
Bruckner, Anton 211 225 531 658
Brummer, Nicolai 36
Bruun, Kai Aage 692
Brücker, Valdemar 471–73 476–77 479 481
Brylle, Jens Rasmussen 33–35
Buhl, Frants 298 560
Bull, Ole 245
Bullock, Alan 199
Busoni, Ferruccio 233 404–10 546 685
Bülow, Hans von 219 227 231 233 246 553
Byron, Lord (George Gordon) 311 315
Bødker, Mads Rasmussen 40
Børup, Morten 304
Børresen, Hakon 691

C
Caralis (pseud. for Christian Preetzmann) 315–16
Carl-Nielsen, Anne Marie, née Brodersen 85 91 93–96 99–105 160 165 184 197 234–37 250–76 278 285–86 333–34 339 341 352–53 363 380 388 392 394 398 420 423 434–35 441 471–73 478 490–91 509–10 556 576 583 605 607–9 617 624 629 652 663 669 673
Carstensen, Georg 130 132
Cavling, Henrik 242 466–67
Chavannes, Puvis de 251
Cherubini, Luigi 120
Christensdatter, Karen 36
Christensen, Jørgen Christen 75
Christensen, Ove 676
Christensen, Rasmus 251
Christiansen, Christian 533 561 565 584 670
Christiansen, Einar 188 285 348 352–53 381 447 455–56
Christian I 277
Christian IV 521
Christian VII 95
Christian IX 100 103 267 584
Christian X 299
Clausen, Johannes 38
Clausen, Julius 468
Claussen, Sophus 186
Clement, Gad Frederik 245

Cohn Haste, Carl 116
Colonne, Édouard 248
Crome, Fritz 673
Czerny, Carl 70 589–90

D

Dahl, Balduin 132 135–40 145 150–51 207
Dahlerup, Vilhelm 91
Dahlhaus, Carl 199
Dalberg, Erik 477
Dalberg, Nancy 273 477 515–16 583 630 668
Dam, Anders Ehlers 421
Danneskjold-Samsøe, Christian Conrad Sophus 550
Darwin, Charles 170 182–84 299 383 472
David, Ferdinand 125
Debussy, Claude 461 498 533 561 563 678
Dehn, Friedrich Ludwig von 107
Delibes, Léo 282–83
Delius, Frederick 234
Demant, Hans 54 83
Demant, Ottilia 188
Diabelli, Anton 589–90
Dittus, Gottliebin 260
Dohlmann, Augusta 245 250
Dons, Elisabeth 357
Drachmann, Holger 141 173 175 189–91 283 288 291 296 448 451 455–56 459 508 549 617 664–65
Dvořák, Antonín 208 556

E

Edison, Thomas 612
Eggert-Møller, Irmelin 93 105 256 265 272–73 300 334 398 469 540 617 643 687–88
Einstein, Albert 524
Emborg, Jens Laursøn 521
Enna, August 282–83 691
Erik V Klipping 433
Erslev, Kristian 288
Esmann, Gustav 189

F

Fabricius, Jacob 135
Fahrbach, Philipp 66
Fallesen, Morten Edvard 279
Fanning, David 498

Felding Jørgensen, Jørgen 43–44
Felsing, August 623
Felumb, Svend Christian 567 615
Fenger, Hans Mathias 477
Fiorillo, Federigo 113
Fischer, Paul 129
Fokin, Mikhail 635
Franck, César 208 216 246 561
Frederik V 95
Frederik VI 68 103
Frederick the Great 396–97
Freud, Sigmund 198 341
Freund, Hermann Ernst 103
Friederichsen, Niels 259
Frølich, Lorenz 291 297 434 468
Funck, Peter Ferdinand 462
Furtwängler, Adolf 673
Furtwängler, Wilhelm 530 673
Fux, Joseph 119–21 581 598–600

G

Gade, Axel 117 124 200 202 211 217 280 583 585
Gade, Niels Wilhelm 41 79–82 106 109–10 113–14 123 126 135 140 155 188–89 202 205 208 212 220–21 223 226 228–32 236 283 360 401 454–55 458 462 470 474 499 553–54 557 561 582 651 654–56 662–63 665 674–75 681 686–87 691
Gauguin, Paul 334
Gebauer, Johan Christian 114–18
Geisler, Christian 675
Gérôme, Jean-Léon 250
Gilbert-Jespersen, Holger 615 645
Gillies, Malcolm 654 678
Gjellerup, Karl 184
Glass, Christian Henrik 109
Glass, Louis 139–40 200 202 204–6 208–11 322 533 559 577 655 691
Glazunov, Alexander 533 546
Gluck, Christoph Willibald 282–83 349–50 356 391 396–97 510 565
Godske, Kirstine 30–31
Godske-Nielsen, Svend 212 267 270–71 380 582–83
Goethe, Johann Wolfgang von 312–14
Gogh, Vincent van 255 334

Goldmark, Karl 246
Gottschalksen, Carl 140
Gotved, Helle 102
Gounod, Charles 278 282–83 350 550
Gram, Peder 559 691
Grandjean, Axel 283 549–50 554
Grieg, Edvard 99 156 205 223 229 232 450–51 458 461–62
Grieg, Nina 229 325
Grimley, Daniel M. 10 15 382 640
Grotegut, Wilhelm 25
Grundtvig, Nikolai Frederik Severin 38–42 442 447 471–73 476 481–82 509–11 513 663
Grundtvig, Svend 433
Grøndahl, Launy 492
Gundestrup, Thorvald 74
Gundlach, Friedrich W. F. 57–58 64 67 75
Gung'l, Josef 66
Gætje, Fanny 126

H

Hagemann, Paul 567
Halm, August 531
Halse, Sven 422
Hamburger, Povl 618–19 623 625 677
Hamerik, Asger 325
Hamerik, Ebbe 561 692
Hammeleff, Frederik 89
Hammer, Jørgen 61–62
Hammerich, Angul 200 202–4 212 216–17 343 364–65 371 400–1 467–68 559 603–4 659 661 678
Handel, Georg Friedrich 359–60 565
Hannemann, Daniel 114 124
Hannover, Emil 203 251–52 274–76 288 392
Hansen, Anders 517–18
Hansen, Hans Nikolaj 242–45 248 251 255 353
Hansen, Johannes 623
Hansen, Maren 103 268
Hansen, Robert, se Robert-Hansen, Emil
Hanslick, Eduard 71–72 74 220 373
Harald Fairhair 190
Harder, Knud 79 120–21 389 579 582–83 598 600 673 687
Hartmann, Emil 324
Hartmann, Godfred 585–86
Hartmann, Johan Peder Emilius 91 109 114 135 160 202 205 212 220 229 282–83 324 401 470 561 662–65
Hartmann, Oluf 306
Hatt, Emilie Demant, née Hansen 87 91–92 141 143–45 148 151 153 155–56 161 169–70 180 186 188 204 277 308 310–14 316 340–41
Hauch, Carsten 514
Hauch, Gunnar 683
Hauser, Miska 125
Hausmann, Robert 227
Haydn, Joseph 46 147 154–55 226 326 349 391 396–97 510 561 616
Heerup, Gunnar 693
Hegeland, Marius Hansen 70 146
Heiberg, Johan Ludvig (philologist) 398
Heiberg, Johan Ludvig (playwright) 455 469 548
Heiberg, Johanne Luise 91 126
Heise, Peter 154 282
Hellmuth, Paul 472 478–80 516 539 582 584 600 696
Helsted, Axel 101
Helsted, Carl 110 205
Helsted, Edvard 141 205
Helsted, Gustav 200 202 204–6 208–12 322 655
Hennings, Henrik 434
Henriques, Edmond 124
Henriques, Fini 101 157 200 202 204 208 217 691
Henriques, Robert 124 204–5 208 214–16 221 322–24 338 556 655 660 662–63 678
Herholdt, Johan Daniel 63
Hérold, Ferdinand 61 65
Herold, Vilhelm 284–85 357 549 555 583
Hetsch, Gustav 123 211 214 217 377 436 661
Hilmer, Frederik 280
Hindemith, Paul 534 565 589–91
Hirschsprung, Heinrich 221
Hohn, Minna 127
Hofmannsthal, Hugo von 462
Holberg, Ludvig 297 305 348 363–70 447 641 660–62 692
Holm, Emil 490 612–16
Holm, Johan Christopher 34 37
Holm, Ludvig 555

Holmboe, Vagn 675
Holstein, Ludvig 308–9 324 327 340–41 346 451–52 523 617 664
Holstein-Berg, Emma von 291 294
Holten, Sofie 251
Horenstein, Jascha 673
Horneman, Christian Frederik Emil 109 160 208 212 282 454 462
Hostrup, Jens Christian 102
Huysmans, Joris-Karl 330
Høeberg, Georg 98 279–80 471 554–57 559–60 629 667 676
Høeberg, Peter 98
Høffding, Finn 578 587–89 613 678 692–93
Høffding, Harald 174–75 177 184 288 392
Hørup, Viggo 196
Høst-Schottlænder, Marie 133

I
Ibsen, Henrik 450–51
Ingemann, Bernhard Severin 417 513 615
Isouard, Nicolo 282

J
Jacobsen, 'Blinde' Anders 40 45
Jacobsen, Carl 264 288
Jacobsen, Ejnar 589
Jacobsen, J. P. (Jens Peter) 169 175 178–80 184 187 205 213–14 216–17 238 244 253–54 308–9 311 316–19 322–24 327 329 333–36 338 346 348 416 514–15 617
Jacobsen, Johannes Erasmus 81
Jahn, Otto 397
Jeanson, Gunnar 350
Jenner, Gustav 314
Jensen, Ane-Marie 28
Jensen, Ferdinand 71
Jensen, Hans 28 689
Jensen, Johan 29
Jensen, Johannes V. 346–47
Jensen, Jørgen I. 15 329–31 483
Jensen-Klint, P. V. (Peder Vilhelm) 102
Jeppesen, Knud 533 580–81 584–86 596–98 602–7 685
Jerndorff, Peter 371 433–34 437
Jersild, Oluf 184 213
Jespersen, Olfert 78 147

Joachim, Joseph 112–13 143 157–58 219 221 226–30 232 694
Johansen, Maren Kirstine 24 27 30 32–37 44 689–90
Johansen, Viggo 288
Jonson, Ben 348
Järnefelt, Armas 245
Jöde, Fritz 589
Jørgensen, Anne 36
Jørgensen, Johannes 87–88 91 96 175 183–84 186 245 334 338–39 341–44 346 615 617
Jørgensen, Louise 271
Jørgensen, Niels 21 24 27–28 30 32 36–37 39–47 52 80 429
Jørgensen, Ove 271

K
Kalhauge, Viggo 283
Keiser-Nielsen, Søren 676
Kéler, Béla 65
Keyper, Franz 68
Kiesewetter, Raphael Georg 391
Kirchner, Theodor 219 222–24 228 231
Kjerulf, Axel 668
Kjerulf, Charles 136 206–8 216 354 400 437 499 552 660 662 666 678
Kjerulf, Hans 367 371
Klenau, Paul von 533
Klinger, Max 184
Klüwer, Wulff Jacob Christian 62
Knudsen, Henrik 111 271 326 456 535–36 538–39 552 571 677
Knudsen, Jakob 473 507
Knudsen, Jørgen 172
Koch, Anine 267
Koch, Jørgen Hansen 557
Kodály, Zoltán 438
Kold, Christen 39–41
Konstantin-Hansen, Elise 473
Koppel, Herman D. 589
Kramer, Jonathan 635–36
Krarup-Hansen, Johanne 326
Krause, Olivo 148–49 206
Kristensen, Tom 613
Krøyer, Peder Severin 242–43 252
Kuhlau, Daniel Friedrich Rudolph 65 283 455 458 462 548 589 657 664

Kurth, Ernst 531 596 603
Kaalund, Hans Vilhelm 520

L

Lamoureux, Charles 246–48 250
Lange, Sven 464
Lange-Müller, Peter Erasmus 141 208 212 283 434 455 663
Langgaard, Rued 533 692 697
Langkilde, Niels 27–29 690
Lantow, Johan F. C. 57 67 75
Larsen, Andreas 33
Larsen, Carl 70–71 78–79 146–48 154
Larsen, Christian 37
Larsen, Christian Frederik 46 71
Larsen Bellinge, Christian 45–47
Larsen, Eduard 294
Larsen, Emmanuel 291 294
Larsen, Johan 33
Larsen, Karl 613
Larsen, Vilhelm 71
Lassen, Knud 567 615
Laub, Thomas 99 353–54 360–63 381 403–4 432–46 472 474–79 483 505 507–9 512 514–15 517–22 606 618–22 685 692 694–96
Lehmann, Julius 341–42
Lehmann, Orla 658
Lendorf, Carl 55 63
Lendrop, Margrethe 371
Léonard, Hubert 125 147
Leoncavallo, Ruggiero 283 352
Liebmann, Nanna 400
Liszt, Franz 182 208 220 226 231 233 273–74
Lorentzdatter, Mariana 33
Lumbye, Georg 132
Lumbye, Hans Christian 46 66 132 135
Lunn, Agnes 250 264
Lynge, Gerhardt 654–55 675
Lynged, Peder 635

M

Madsen, Herman 29
Maegaard, Jan 627 631 691–92
Maeterlinck, Maurice 452
Magnussen, Christian Carl 262–63
Mahler, Gustav 111 211 220 225 374 379 402 533 685 691
Mallarmé, Stephane 246 330
Malling, Otto 205 215 584 586
Malmstrøm, Knud 304
Mannstädt, Franz 672
Mantzius, Karl 367 371 555
Marie Antoinette 242
Marschner, Heinrich 282
Marstrand, Wilhelm 91
Mascagni, Pietro 283 352
Massé, Victor 282
Matthison-Hansen, Gottfried 111
Matthison-Hansen, Wilhelm 89
Matthison-Hansen, Aage 89
Maurer, Axel 242
Melbye, Anton 508
Meldahl, Ferdinand 89 96
Mendelssohn Bartholdy, Felix 111 126–27 220 226 229–32 256 283 401 456–59 561 610 674
Menuhin, Yehudi 673
Mérode, Cléo de 248
Methling, Svend 299
Meyer, A. C. (Adolph Charles) 178
Meyer, Elisabeth 322
Meyer, Torben 580
Meyerbeer, Giacomo 282 350
Michaëlis, Sophus 196 348
Michaelsen, Carl Johan 402 583 612 644 670 676
Michelsen, Vilhelm 615–16
Milhaud, Darius 561
Molbech, Christian 76
Moldenhauer, Peter Wilhelm 109
Monteux, Pierre 673
Morgan, Paul 157 229
Mortensen, Otto 589
Mozart, Wolfgang Amadeus 46–47 74 76 147 154–55 225–26 282–83 349 353–54 389–97 399 410 510 548 554 561 565–67 570 580 595 610 616 633 678 685
Muck, Karl 672
Munch, Andreas 450
Munch, Edvard 252
Müller, Jørgen Peter 420
Møller, C. C. (Carl Christian) 132 138
Møller, Eggert 105 273
Møller, Frida 273 617 688
Møller, Holger 124 159 228 242 277 280

Møller, Ida 371
Møller, Jørgen 213
Møller, Marie 268 270 473
Møller, Niels 298–99 351
Møller, Otto 185 189
Møller, Peder 499 556 616 629 644 682
Møller, Poul Martin 441
Møller, Vilhelm 175 180

N
Nansen, Fridtjof 152
Nansen, Peter 189 288
Napoleon I (Bonaparte) 184
Neergaard, Bodil 306 324–25 393 395
Neergaard, Niels 177
Neergaard, Viggo de 324
Neiiendam, Jonna 367 371
Neruda, Franz 124 205 557 559 561 654–55
Neupert, Edmund 111
Nexø, Martin Andersen 688
Nicodé, Jean Louis 123 234 672
Nielsen, (Christian) Albert 22 25 28 42–43 47 56
Nielsen, Anders (Jacob) 22 28
Nielsen, Anna Dusine 29
Nielsen, Anne Marie (Søs), see Telmanyi, Anne Marie
Nielsen, Axel 71
Nielsen, (Jørgine) Caroline 28–29 36
Nielsen, Hans Børge 95 272
Nielsen, Irmelin, see Eggert-Møller, Irmelin
Nielsen, Jens Georg 83 91
Nielsen, Julie (Christine) 22 41
Nielsen, Jørgen 36
Nielsen, Karen Marie 28–29 37
Nielsen, L. C. (Laurits Christian) 177 297 341
Nielsen, (Helene Christine) Lovise 22 28
Nielsen, Ludolf 559 691
Nielsen, Marie 91
Nielsen, Martinius 450
Nielsen, (Jørgen) Peter 22 28–29 32 37
Nielsen, (Mathilde) Sophie 28–29 37
Nielsen, (Johan) Sophus 22 28 37 43
Nielsen, Thorvald 497 533
Nielsen, Valdemar (Emil) 22 41–43
Nietzsche, Friedrich 329 339 391 451 491
Nissen, Helge 291–92 294 299 357 367 371

Novi, Beate 589
Nyerup, Rasmus 433
Nutzhorn, Heinrich 507

O
Oehlenschläger, Adam 283–84 442 448 462 464 466 469 663 665
Offenbach, Jacques 58 282 554
Olrik, Axel 101 398 432–36
Olrik, Sofie 101 435
Olsen, Cathinka 177–78
Onslow, George 154–55
Outzen, Jacob Kristian 69–70
Oxenvad, Aage 567 615 635 641 644

P
Pachelbel, Johann 618 621
Palestrina, Giovanni Pierluigi da 344–45 389 595–611 619 622 685 695
Panum, Hortense 435 577 595–96
Paulli, Simon Holger 109–10 279
Pedersen, Christian 159
Pedersen, Mads 46–47
Petersen, Emil 31 44
Petersen, Jens 451
Pfitzner, Hans 402 407
Philipsen, Theodor 243
Pleyel, Ignaz Josef 154–55
Ploug, Carl 658
Ploug, Hother 380–81 658
Poulsen, Adam 466
Poulsen, Emil 212
Poulsen, Gerda 75
Poulsen, Johannes 454 462–64
Prez, Josquin des 344 401
Puccini, Giacomo 225 368

R
Rabe, Julius 119–20
Rafaëlli, Jean-François 251
Rangström, Ture 403 409 489 526 565 578 673
Rask, Rasmus 38
Rasmussen, August 369
Rasmussen, Niels Hansen 102 305 420
Ravel, Maurice 533 561
Recke, Ernst von der 434
Reger, Max 374 395 402–3 533 610

Reinecke, Carl 231–33
Renoir, Pierre-Auguste 251
Reynolds, Anne-Marie 15
Richter, Ernst Friedrich 115–16 118 120
Riemann, Hugo 374
Riis-Knudsen, Christen 190 450
Riis-Magnussen, Adolf 523 582
Riisager, Knudåge 692
Ring, Oluf 438 505 518 520–22 589 630 662
Robert-Hansen, Emil, born Robert Emil Hansen 200 206 560 655
Rode, Helge 305–6 324 346 448 451–52 526 617 658
Rode, Ove 296 393–94 397 658
Rodin, Auguste 250–51 264
Rohde, Johan 251–52
Rosenbaum, Bernhard 137 139
Rosenberg, Carl 170
Rosenberg, Margrete 170 172 688
Rosenberg, Vilhelm 170 212 450
Rosenfeld, Leopold 377 382 436
Rosenhoff, Orla 79 111 114–22 124 142–44 148–51 153 156 158 165 180 183 192 221 224 227 309 315 534 580 582 584 589–90 597 672–73 686 698
Rossini, Gioacchino 283
Roth, Joseph 61
Rung, Frederik 277 280–81 283–85 371 433 471 546 548–52 554–56 676
Röntgen, Engelbert 393
Röntgen, Julius 235 324–25 393–95 402–3 440 456 458 474 488–90 526 644
Röntgen jun., Julius 324
Raasted, Niels Otto 589 675–76

S
Sachs, Albert 76 83 176
Sachs, Emil B. (Bertel) 158 161 164 175–81 187–88 224 230 233 241–42 244–45 248 290 374 396
Sadolin, Gunnar 420
Saint-Saëns, Camille 246 498 548 678
Salomon, Eline 35
Salomon, Siegfried 548
Salomonsen, Carl Julius 175
Sandby, Kristian (Pedersen) 124 139–40 277 280

Sass, Georg C. C. 57 75
Savery, Carl Maria 587
Scavenius, Ove 514 581–83
Schandorff, Sophus 175
Schierbeck, Poul 580 614 623
Schiff, Eduard 236
Schiørring, Christian 70 78–79
Schiørring, Johannes 112
Schiørring, Niels 474
Schiørring, Nils 692
Schiøtt, Julius 174 376
Schmidt, Jep Jepsen 26
Schnabel, Artur 670
Schnedler-Petersen, Frederik 89 112 124 140 144 157 288
Schoenberg, Arnold 15 524 532–34 537–38 544 546 631 641 691–92
Scholtz, Hermann 223
Schorske, Carl E. 198
Schreiber, Johannes C.F. 57–58 66 68
Schreker, Franz 546
Schubert, Franz 226 308 310–14 316 322 324–25
Schuch, Ernst von 224–25
Schulz, Johann Abraham Peter 432 438–40 473
Schumann, Robert 126 222–24 226 230 246 314 316 322 391 561 674
Schwartz, Johan D. 57
Schwind, Moritz von 313
Schytte, Henrik Vissing 208
Schytte, Ludvig 283
Schütz, Heinrich 609
Scriabin, Alexander 533
Ségoffin, Victor 352
Seligmann, Hugo 609 641 666 677 683
Shakespeare, William 297 305 348 455–56
Sibelius, Jean 461 533 546 563
Siboni, Giuseppe 106 109
Siekmann, Conrad 25
Simon, Johannes A. 57–58 63 66–67 75–76 124
Simonsen, Hans Sophus 183–84
Simonsen, Niels Juel 357
Simonsen, Rudolph 533 584 586 615–16 677
Sinding, Christian 232–34
Skovgaard, Joakim 99 243 252 401 434–35 512
Skovgaard, Niels 99 252 401 434 441
Skovgaard, Peter Christian 91

Skram, Amalie 244 251 288
Skram, Erik 189–90
Slott-Møller, Agnes 34 251–52 332 334 336 434
Slott-Møller, Harald 171 250–52
Smith, Gustav 587
Spencer, Herbert 383
Spitta, Philipp 228
Spohr, Louis 112 125–26
Spontini, Gaspare 350
Spur, Erik 508
Stauning, Thorvald 299 677
Stenhammar, Wilhelm 464 551 561–62 584 602
Stockmarr, Johanne 245 670
Stoffregen, Alexander 541
Straube, Karl 618 676
Strauss, Johann the Elder 61
Strauss, Johann the Younger 46
Strauss, Richard 219–20 225 233–36 348 374–75 377 394–95 402 498 524 553 672 678 685–86
Stravinsky, Igor 15 533–34 546 565 634–35 641 678
Strindberg, August 133
Stuckenberg, Viggo 186
Stuckenbrock, Conrad 25
Svendsen, Anton 124 140 156 159 221 280 548 559 585–86 675
Svendsen, Johan 141 160–61 215 277 279–81 284–85 357 381 548–49 553 583
Suppé, Franz von 65
Søby, Jens 67 75
Sørensen, Hans 567 615
Sørensen, Marius 512
Saabye, August 91 250 264

T
Tchaikovsky, Pyotr 232
Telemann, Georg Philipp 231
Telmanyi, Anne Marie (called Søs) 94 96 272 325 341 631
Telmányi, Emil 272–73 307 526 590 611 615–16 623 626 629–30 642 644 670
Thomas, Ambroise 282
Thomsen, Peter 621–24
Thygeson, Charlotte Trap de 574
Thygeson, Thyge de 574

Tietgen, Carl Frederik 96
Titian 398 400
Tofft, Alfred 208 282 322 381 659
Tofte, Clara 112
Tofte, Valdemar 45 78–79 112–13 124–26
Tolstoy, Leo 408
Toulouse-Lautrec, Henri de 244 249
Triepcke, Marie, m. Krøyer 242 251
Trier, Ernst 511
Trier, Herman 175 294–95
Tscherning, Arnak 255
Tscherning, Marius 253 255–56
Tuxen, Laurits 243
Tørsleff, Laurits 126–27

U
Ulrich, Emilie 357 371

V
Valéry, Paul 246
Varèse, Edgard 634
Vedel, Valdemar 465
Verdi, Giuseppe 126 225 283 372 678
Verlaine, Paul 330
Vibæk, Marius 177
Viderø, Finn 624–25
Vinci, Leonardo da 243
Viotti, Giovanni Battista 125
Vivaldi, Antonio 356
Voltaire 184

W
Wagner, Richard 15 66 111 182 184 200 213–15 219–20 224–25 228 233–34 238–39 246 248 282–83 350 352–53 373–74 391 393–96 403 429 524 549 554–55 561 570 627 658 678 685–86 691–92 696
Wagner, Siegfried 468
Wallstedt, Marthe Magdalene 259
Wanscher, Vilhelm 353 392
Weber, Carl Maria von 225
Weis, Andreas Peter 555 585 676
Weyse, Christoph Ernst Friedrich 117 520–21 554
Wied, Gustav 189 451 455
Wieniawski, Henryk 277
Wilhelm Hansen, Alfred 208 234 669 672 676

Wilhelm Hansen, Asger 476 669
Wilhelm Hansen, Jonas 208
Wilhelm Hansen, Svend 669
Wilhelmi, Emilius 64 76
Willumsen, Jens Ferdinand 217–18 240–42 247–48 251–53 255 423–24 466–67 663
Willumsen, William 66–67 75
Winding, August 208
Winstrup, Johanne 264
Winstrup, Laurits Albert 264
Winther, Christian 206
Wirth, Emanuel 227
Wittrup, Jens Frederik 46
Wolf, Hugo 403
Wöldike, Mogens 586 606 618–21 624–25 673

Y
Ysaÿe, Eugène 672

Z
Zachariassen, Sybrand 620
Zahle, Carl Theodor 177–78
Zahlmann, Carl Christian 55 62
Zahrtmann, Kristian 420
Zocchi, Arnaldo 596
Zola, Émile 189

Å
Ågren, Gunnar 582
Aagaard, Carl Otto 75
Aagaard, Thorvald 438 477 505 507–9 513 517–22 582 623 662
Aakjær, Jeppe 175 177 288 324 326 346–47 444 449 508 512–14 576 615 617 688–89
Aarestrup, Emil 169 311 315

Index of Works

The index includes works and collections of works by Carl Nielsen mentioned in the book.

29 Little Preludes for Organ or Harmonium / 29 smaa Præludier for Orgel eller Harmonium, Op. 51 (CNW 96) 618 620–23 670

60 Danish Canons / 60 danske Kanoner, contribution to (CNW Coll. 26) 587

A Score of Danish Songs / En Snes danske Viser, vol. 1, contribution to (CNW Coll. 9) 308 310 432 438–46 476 509 517 519 661 667 696

A Score of Danish Songs / En Snes danske Viser, vol. 2, contribution to (CNW Coll. 11) 308 310 416–17 432 438–40 442–43 446 476 517 661 667 696

Aladdin or The Wonderful Lamp / Aladdin eller Den forunderlige Lampe, music for Adam Oehlenschläger's play, Op. 34 (CNW 17) 283 307 447–49 454 461–65 467 470 584 616–17 629 640–41 670 683

Aladdin Suite / Suite af 'Aladdin' 448 465 470 629 670

'Alfedans', in *Five Piano Pieces*, Op. 3, No. 5 – see 'Elf's Dance'

'All the developing shadows' / 'Alle de voksende Skygger' (CNW 282) 311 316–17 319

Allegretto for Two Recorders / Allegretto for to blokfløjter (CNW 72) 587–88

Amor og Digteren (CNW 23) – see *Cupid and the Poet*

An Evening at Giske / En Aften paa Giske, music for Andreas Munch's play (CNW 3) 447 450–51

An Imaginary Journey to the Faroe Islands / En fantasirejse til Færøerne. Rhapsody Overture (CNW 39) 303–4 616

Andante tranquillo e Scherzo (CNW 31) 145 150 155 168

Apple Blossom / Æbleblomst, Op. 10, No. 1 (CNW 126) 340

'Arabesque' / 'Arabeske', in *Five Piano Pieces*, Op. 3, No. 3 179 246

'As Odin beckons' / 'Naar Odin vinker' (CNW 206) 442

'At last the spring's upon us' / 'Nu er da Vaaren kommen' (CNW 214) 442–43

At the Bier of a Young Artist / Ved en ung Kunstners Baare (CNW 36) 306–7

Atalanta, song for Gustav Wied and Jens Petersen's play (CNW 6) 448 451

'Autumn's near' / 'Det är höst' (CNW 335) 310

Ballad on the Bear / Balladen om Bjørnen, Op. 47 (CNW 315) 310 629

Barnets Sang, 'Kom, i Dag maa alle synge' (CNW 301) – see *Children's Song*

Benedictus Dominus, Op. 55, No. 3 (CNW 347) 606–10

'Blomsterstøv fra Blomsterbæger' (CNW 343) – see 'Flower pollen from profusion'

Bohemian-Danish Folk Song / Bøhmisk-Dansk Folketone. Paraphrase for String Orchestra (CNW 40) 303–4

Bonnie Ann / Tag jer iagt for Anna (CNW 278) 316

'The boys of Refnaes, the girls of Samsoe' / 'De Refsnæsdrenge, de Samsøepiger' (CNW 202) 443–44

Cantata for the Annual University Commemoration / Kantate ved Universitetets Aarsfest, Op. 24 (CNW 105) 298–99 304 351

Cantata for the Centenary of the Chamber of Commerce / Kantate ved Grosserer-Societetets Hundredaarsfest, Op. 31 (CNW 111) 300

Cantata for the Centenary of the Polytechnic College / Kantate ved Polyteknisk Læreanstalts 100 Aars Jubilæum (CNW 112) 616

Cantata for the Lorenz Frølich Celebration / Kantate til Lorenz Frølich-Festen (CNW 103) 291 297

Cantata for the Inauguration of the Student Society Building / Kantate ved Studentersamfundets Bygnings Indvielse (CNW 104) 173 216 288–97 299 375 455 681

Cantata for the Opening Ceremony of the National Exhibition in Aarhus 1909 / Kantate ved Aarhus Landsudstillings Aabnings-Højtidelighed 1909 (CNW 107) 297–98 583

Chaconne, Op. 32 (CNW 86) 541 543

Child Welfare Day Song / Børnehjælpsdagens Sang, 'Vi Børn, vi Børn, vi vaagner' (CNW 293) 304–5

Children's Song / Barnets Sang, 'Kom, i Dag maa alle synge' (CNW 301) 304–5
'Come, glistering sun' / 'Kom blankeste Sol!' (CNW 374) 304
Commotio, Op. 58 (CNW 99) 618 623–25 671
Concerto for Clarinet and Orchestra, Op. 57 (CNW 43) 575 616 623 626 641–46 671 691
Concerto for Flute and Orchestra (CNW 42) 543 561 616–17 626 641 645–46 671
Concerto for Violin and Orchestra, Op. 33 (CNW 41) 499 556 561 616 629 634 644–45 673 682
Cupid and the Poet / Amor og Digteren, music for Sophus Michaëlis's play (CNW 23) 297 305 447
Counterpoint exercises (CNW C 3) 118 120–22 598–99
The Daffodil / Paaske-Liljen, 'Paaskeblomst!' (CNW 361) 509
'Dance of the Cockerel' / 'Hanedansen', from *Maskarade* 364 369–70 629 660
Danish Patriotic Song / Fædrelandssang, 'Du danske Mand, af al din Magt' (CNW 288) 508–9 617 661 682
'De Refsnæsdrenge, de Samsøepiger' (CNW 202) – see 'The boys of Refnaes, the girls of Samsoe'
De unges Sang, 'Vi fik ej under Tidernes Tryk' (CNW 291) – see *Song of the Young*
'Den første Lærke', Op. 21, No. 5 (CNW 139) – see 'The larks are coming'
'Der sad en Fisker saa tankefuld' (CNW 244) – see 'There sat a fisherman deep in thought'
'Det bødes der for i lange Aar', Op. 6, No. 4 (CNW 124) – see 'You suffer throughout an age of pain'
'Det er Lærkernes Tid', from *Tove*, see 'It is the time of the larks'
'Det är höst' (CNW 335) – see 'Autumn's near'
Digtning i Sang og Toner ved Svømmehallens Indvielse (CNW 115) – see *Poetry in Song and Music for the Inauguration of the Public Swimming Baths*
Dominus regit me, Op. 55, No. 2 (CNW 346) 607
'Du danske Mand, af al din Magt', *Fædrelandssang* (CNW 288) – see *Danish Patriotic Song*
'Dukke-Marsch', in *Humoresque-Bagatelles*, Op. 11, No. 5 – see 'Puppet March'

'Dybt hælder Aaret i sin Gang' (CNW 163) – see 'Well on the wane the passing year'
Early brass trios and quartets (CNW 412) 67 146
Ebbe Skammelsen, music for Harald Bergstedt's open-air play (CNW 21) 470
'Elf's Dance' / 'Alfedans', in *Five Piano Pieces*, Op. 3, No. 5 458
En Aften paa Giske, music for Andreas Munch's play (CNW 3) – see *An Evening at Giske*
En fantasirejse til Færøerne. Rhapsodisk ouverture (CNW 39) – see *An Imaginary Journey to the Faroe Islands*
En Snes danske Viser I, contribution to (CNW Coll. 9) – see *A Score of Danish Songs*, vol. 1
En Snes danske Viser II, contribution to (CNW Coll. 11) – see *A Score of Danish Songs*, vol. 2
Enstemmige Sange til Brug for Højskoler, Gymnastik og Skytteforeninger (CNW Coll. 27) – see *Songs in Voices in Unison for Use in Folk High Schools and Gymnastics and Rifle Clubs*
Erindringens Sø, Op. 10, No. 2 (CNW 127) – see *Lake of Memories*
Fantasy Piece for Clarinet and Piano / Fantasistykke for klarinet og klaver (CNW 66) 146–47
Fantasy Pieces for Oboe and Piano / Fantasistykker for obo og klaver, Op. 2 (CNW 65) 148–49 153 214 223 228 615–16 618
'Farewell, my respectable native town' / 'Farvel, min velsignede Fødeby!' (CNW 211) 442–43
Festival Prelude for the New Century / Fest-Præludium ved Aarhundredskiftet (CNW 84) 196 216–18
Five Piano Pieces / Fem klaverstykker, Op. 3 (CNW 81) 149 153 179 223 245–46 458
The Fights in Stefan Borg's House / Kampene i Stefan Borgs Hjem, song for Helge Rode's play (CNW 5) 324 448 451–52
The Flood / Syndfloden, 'Naar Nat udvælder fra sorten Sky' (CNW 257) 520
'Flower pollen from profusion' / 'Blomsterstøv fra Blomsterbæger' (CNW 343) 304
The Fog is Lifting / Taagen letter, from *The Mother* 306 448
The Folk High School Melody Book / Folkehøjskolens Melodibog (1922), contribution to

INDEX OF WORKS 787

(CNW Coll. 17) 102 305 309 437–38 505–8 517–23 576 587 667

The Folk High School Melody Book / Folkehøjskolens Melodibog, contribution to supplement (1927) (CNW Coll. 22) 522–23

'Folk Tune' / 'Folketone', in *Five Piano Pieces*, Op. 3, No. 1 223

'Fortune has lately left you' / 'Vender sig Lykken fra dig' (CNW 207) 442 514

'Forunderligt at sige' (CNW 165) – see 'How wonderful to ponder'

Four 'folkelige' Melodies / Fire folkelige Melodier (CNW Coll. 16) 523

Franz Neruda in Memoriam (CNW 109) 561

'Fred med dig!' (CNW 166) – see 'Peace with you'

'Frydeligt med Jubelkor', *Morten Børups Majvise* (CNW 375) – see *Morten Børup's Song of May*

Fynsk Foraar, Op. 42 (CNW 102) – see *Springtime on Funen*

Fædreland (CNW 14) – see *Native Land*

Gamle Anders Røgters Sang, 'Der staar en Purle ved Vejens Sving' (CNW 151) – see *Song of Old Anders the Cattleman*

Genre Painting / Genrebillede, 'Pagen højt paa Taarnet sad', Op. 6, No. 1 (CNW 121) 323 335–38

'God's angels, unite' / 'Guds Engle i Flok!' (CNW 170) 473 483

'God's peace is more than angel guard' / 'Guds Fred er mer end Englevagt' (CNW 171) 483

Good Night / Godnat, Op. 21, No. 7 (CNW 141) 346–47

Grundtvig Easter Evening / Grundtvig-Paaske-Aften, music for (CNW 24) 447

Hagbarth and Signe, music for Adam Oehlenschläger's play (CNW 12) 284 427 447–48 466–69 663 665

'Hanedansen', fra *Maskarade* – see 'Dance of the Cockerel'

'Har Dagen sanket al sin Sorg', Op. 4, No. 5 (CNW 120) – see 'If day has gathered all its woe'

Hawk / Høgen, Op. 21, No. 2 (CNW 136) 324 346 514

'Heavy, gloomy clouds of night' / 'Tunge, mørke Natteskyer' (CNW 250) 507 509

Helios. Overture for Orchestra, Op. 17 (CNW 34) 164 303 341–43 345 364 373 379–83 385 425–28 488 556 659 671

Homage to Holberg / Hyldest til Holberg, music for Hans Hartvig Seedorff Pedersen's (CNW 20) 297 305 447

Homesickness / Hjemvee, 'Underlige Aftenlufte!' (CNW 205) 515 615

'How sweet, as summer day is fading' / 'Hvor sødt i Sommer-Aftenstunden' (CNW 215) 442

'How wonderful to ponder' / 'Forunderligt at sige' (CNW 165) 472–73 478–79 483

Hr. Oluf han rider – (CNW 7) – see *Sir Oluf He Rides* –

Humoresque-Bagatelles / Humoreske-Bagateller, Op. 11 (CNW 83) 375 612

Husvild, 'Gi Husly til to Personer', Op. 21, No. 6 (CNW 140) – see *Vagrant*

Hymn for the Commemoration of the Niels W. Gade Centenary / Hymne til Mindefesten paa Niels W. Gades 100-Aarsdag (CNW 110) 561

Hymn to Art / Hymne til Kunsten (CNW 113) 616

Hymns and Spiritual Songs / Salmer og aandelige Sange. Halvhundred nye Melodier for Hjem, Kirke og Skole (CNW Coll. 10) 471–73 475–83 539 546–47 567 584 600 696

Hymnus Amoris, Op. 12 (CNW 100) 96 212 214 398–402 491 535 561 599–600 608 658

'I bear with a smile my burden' (CNW 212) 519 615 682

Iceland / Island (CNW 338) 616

'If day has gathered all its woe' / 'Har Dagen sanket al sin Sorg', Op. 4, No. 5 (CNW 120) 318–23 331 416

In Seraglio Garden / I Seraillets Have, Op. 4, No. 2 (CNW 117) 318 323

In the Realm of Dreams / I Drømmenes Land (CNS 222) 238 318

Irmelin Rose, Op. 4, No. 4 (CNW 119) 254 322 334–35

'It is the time of the larks' / 'Det er Lærkernes Tid', from *Tove* 452

'It's over for a short respite' / 'Nu er for stakket Tid forbi' (CNW 344) 304

'Jeg bærer med Smil min Byrde' (CNW 212) – see 'I bear with a smile my burden'

'Jeg ved en Lærkerede' (CNW 262) – see 'Two larks in love have nested'

John the Roadman / Jens Vejmand, Op. 21, No. 3 (CNW 137) 310 325–26 346 508–9 514–15 576 661 682

Kampene i Stefan Borgs Hjem, song for Helge Rode's play (CNW 5) – see *The Fights in Stefan's Borgs House*

Klavermusik for Smaa og Store, Op. 53 (CNW 92) – see *Piano Music for Young and Old*

'Kom blankeste Sol!' (CNW 374) – see 'Come, glistering sun'

'Kom, i Dag maa alle synge', *Barnets Sang* (CNW 301) – see *Children's Song*

Kommer I snart, I Husmænd! (CNW 152) – see *Now it is Time, Smallholders*

'Korsets Tegn og Korsets Ord' (CNW 181) – see 'The sign and the word of cross'

Lake of Memories / Erindringens Sø, Op. 10, No. 2 (CNW 127) 339–40

'The larks are coming' / 'Den første Lærke', Op. 21, No. 5 (CNW 139) 310 346 514

'Lay down, sweet flower, your head' / 'Sænk kun dit Hoved, du Blomst', Op. 21, No. 4 (CNW 138) 340–42 346 615 617

Lieder von J.P. Jacobsen / Songs by J.P. Jacobsen (CNW Coll. 3) 309 327

'Like golden amber is my girl' / 'Min Pige er saa lys som Rav' (CNW 231) 306

'Look! The sun is red, mum' / 'Solen er saa rød, Mor' (CNW 263) 310 523 667

'Magdelone's Dance Scene' / 'Magdelones dansescene', from *Maskarade* 364 366–67 660

'Maria sad paa Hø og Straa' (CNW 183) – see 'The Virgin Mary sat in hay'

Maskarade (CNW 2) 48 99 163 284 307 341 348 352 363–72 376 455 546 549–51 554 563 576 616–17 629 641 658–62 668 670–71 678 683 692

Melodies for the Songbook 'Denmark' / Melodier til Sangbogen 'Danmark', contribution to (CNW Coll. 19) 506 523 587 629 667

'Min Pige er saa lys som Rav' (CNW 231) – see 'Like golden amber is my girl'

Midsommer Eve Play / Sanct Hansaftenspil, music for Adam Oehlenschläger's play (CNW 13) 448 469 618 665

'Mit Hjerte altid vanker', see 'How wonderful to ponder'

'Morning cock again it crow' / 'Morgenhanen atter gol' (CNW 395) 300

Morten Børup's Song of May / Morten Børups Majvise, 'Frydeligt med Jubelkor' (CNW 375) 304

The Mother / Moderen, music for Helge Rode's play, Op. 41 (CNW 18) 305–6 447–48 526 576 612

Music for Five Poems by J. P. Jacobsen / Musik til fem Digte af J. P. Jacobsen, Op. 4 (CNW Coll. 1) 180 238 253–54 308–10 315–16 318–22 332 334–35 340 416

'The Musical Clock' / 'Spilleværket', in *Humoresque-Bagatelles*, Op. 11, No. 6 375

'My Jesus, let my heart obtain' / 'Min Jesus, lad mit Hjerte faa' (CNW 184) 483 567

'My Soul is Dark' / 'Min Sjæl er mørk' (CNW 279) 311 315–16

Native Land / Fædreland, music for Einar Christiansen's play (CNW 14) 447

Nearer My God to Thee / Nærmere Gud til dig. Paraphrase for Wind Band (CNW 37) 297 301–3

'Neath the Cross of the departed' / 'Under Korset stod med Smerte' (CNW 198) 471

New Melodies to the Latest Song Texts for Johan Borup's Danish Songbook / Nye Melodier til de nyere Sangtekster i Johan Borups Dansk Sangbog, contribution to (CNW Coll. 12) 508–10 512–17 519 522 587

New Melodies for Johan Borup's Danish Songbook / Nye Melodier til Johan Borups Dansk Sangbog, contribution to (CNW Coll. 21) 523

Now it is Time, Smallholders / Kommer I snart, I Husmænd! (CNW 152) 449

'Now sun arises in the East' / 'Nu Sol i Øst oprinder mild' (CNW 186) 483

'Now the day is full of song' / 'Nu er Dagen fuld af Sang' (CNW 213) 444–46

'Now you must find your path in life' / 'Ud gaar du nu paa Livets Vej' (CNW 203) 514

'Nu er da Vaaren kommen' (CNW 214) – see 'At last the spring's upon us'

'Nu er for stakket Tid forbi' (CNW 344) – see 'It's over for a short respite'

INDEX OF WORKS

'Naar Nat udvælder fra sorten Sky', *Syndfloden* (CNW 257) – see *The Flood*
'Naar Odin vinker' (CNW 206) – see 'As Odin beckons'
'Oft am I glad, still may I weep from sadness' / 'Tidt er jeg glad, og vil dog gerne græde' (CNW 216) 416–17 615
'Overture', from *Maskarade* 307 371 376 549 629 660 670–71
Pan and Syrinx, Op. 49 (CNW 38) 304 373 385 563–64 629 670
'Peace with you' / 'Fred med dig!' (CNW 166) 473
Piano Music for Young and Old / *Klavermusik for Smaa og Store*, Op. 53 (CNW 92) 578 588–94 670
Poetry in Song and Music for the Inauguration of the Public Swimming Baths / *Digtning i Sang og Toner ved Svømmehallens Indvielse* (CNW 115) 299–300
Prelude, Theme and Variations / *Præludium og tema med variationer*, Op. 48 (CNW 46) 629–30 669–70 691
'Prelude to Act Two', from *Saul and David* 360 364 616–17
Preludio e Presto, Op. 52 (CNW 47) 691
'Puppet March' / 'Dukke-Marsch', in *Humoresque-Bagatelles*, Op. 11, No. 5 612
'Paa det jævne, paa det jævne' (CNW 238) – see 'Simple-rooted, simple-rooted'
'Paaskeblomst!', *Paaske-Liljen* (CNW 361) – see *The Daffodil*
Quartet for Two Violins, Viola and Cello, movement for (CNW 52) 122–23
Quartet for Two Violins, Viola and Cello, D minor (CNW 49) 82 154–55 675
Quartet for Two Violins, Viola and Cello, F major, 2 movements (CNW 50 and CNW 51) 143–45 155
Quartet for Two Violins, Viola and Cello, F minor, Op. 5 (CNW 56) 113 142–43 154–61 164–66 187 192 226 228–29 232 405 546 672 694
Quartet for Two Violins, Viola and Cello, G minor, Op. 13 (CNW 55) 155–56 546
Quartet for Two Violins, Viola and Cello, E flat minor, Op. 14 (CNW 57) 546

Quartet for Two Violins, Viola and Cello, F major, Op. 44 (CNW 58) 326 546 661 669
Quintet for Flute, Oboe, Clarinet, French Horn and Basoon / *Kvintet for fløjte, obo, klarinet, horn og fagot*, Op. 43 (CNW 70) 504 565–70 615–17 627 640–41 670
Quintet for Two Violins, Two Violas and Cello (CNW 59) 159 204–6
Romance for Violin and Piano, G major (CNW 60) 147–48
Romance for Violin and Piano, D major (CNW 61) 147–48
Romance for Violin and Small Orchestra / Piano (Arr. of CNW 65, first movement) 149
'The rose is blooming now in Dana's garden' / 'Rosen blusser alt i Danas Have' (CNW 209) 441
Saga Dream, Op. 39 (CNW 35) 304 341 345–46 373 556 561 563 629
Salmer og aandelige Sange. Halvhundred nye Melodier for Hjem, Kirke og Skole (CNW Coll. 10) – see *Hymns and Spiritual Songs*
Sanct Hansaftenspil (CNW 13) – see *Midsommer Eve Play*
Saul and David (CNW 1) 281 285 348–61 364 375–76 381 398 402–3 437 455 499 546 548–49 554 564 616–17 623 658 695
Serenade / 'See! Luften er stille' (CNW 277) 316
Serenata in Vano (CNW 69) 576
Shakespeare, music for Helge Rode's prologue (CNW 15) 297 305
'Shall flowers, then, all wither' / 'Skal Blomsterne da visne', Op. 21, No. 1 (CNW 135) 324 346 451–52
'The sign and the word of cross' / 'Korsets Tegn og Korsets Ord' (CNW 181) 473
'Silken shoe over golden last!' / 'Silkesko over gylden Læst!', Op. 6, No. 3 (CNW 123) 213
'Simple-rooted, simple-rooted' / 'Paa det jævne, paa det jævne' (CNW 238) 520–21
Sir Oluf He Rides – / *Hr. Oluf han rider* – , music for Holger Drachmann's melodrama (CNW 7) 434 449 454–60 462–63 549 664–65
Sleep / *Søvnen*, Op. 18 (CNW 101) 341–45 364 402 561 608 659

'Som en rejselysten Flaade', *Sangen til Danmark* (CNW 237) – see *The Song to Denmark*

Snefrid, music for Holger Drachmann's melodrama (CNW 4) 189–91 451 455

'Solen er saa rød, Mor' (CNW 263) – see 'Look! The sun is red, mum'

Sonata for Violin and Piano, G major (CNW 62) 147 155

Sonata No. 1 for Violin and Piano, A major, Op. 9 (CNW 63) 217 273 546

Sonata No. 2 for Violin and Piano, G minor, Op. 35 (CNW 64) 101 546 615–16

Song behind the Plough / Sang bag Ploven, 'I Solen gaar jeg bag min Plov', Op. 10, No. 4 (CNW 129) 523 615

Song of Old Anders the Cattleman / Gamle Anders Røgters Sang, 'Der staar en Purle ved Vejens Sving' (CNW 151) 514

Song of the Young / De unges Sang, 'Vi fik ej under Tidernes Tryk' (CNW 291) 102 305

The Song to Denmark / Sangen til Danmark, 'Som en rejselysten Flaade' (CNW 237) 306 612

Songs and Verses by J. P. Jacobsen / Viser og Vers af J. P. Jacobsen, Op. 6 (CNW Coll. 2) 180 213 216–17 308–10 315–16 323–24 333–38 514–15

Songs by Ludvig Holstein / Sange af Ludvig Holstein, Op. 10 (CNW Coll. 4) 308–10 315 324 327 339–40 346 523

Songs in Voices in Unison for Use in Folk High Schools and Gymnastics and Rifle Clubs / Enstemmige Sange til Brug for Højskoler, Gymnastik og Skytteforeninger (CNW Coll. 27) 509

'Spilleværket', in *Humoresque-Bagatelles*, Op. 11, No. 6 – see 'The Musical Clock'

Springtime on Funen / Fynsk Foraar, Op. 42 (CNW 102) 273 561 576 584 667–68 682

'Springtime, springtime breaking through' / 'Vaaren – Vaaren er i Brudd!' (CNW 353) 304

'The Spinning Top' / 'Snurretoppen!', in *Humoresque-Bagatelles*, Op. 11, No. 2 375

Strophic Songs / Strofiske Sange, Op. 21 (CNW Coll. 5) 308 310 324–27 340–42 346–47 432 452 508 514 661

Study on Nature / Studie efter Naturen (CNW 303) 310

Suite af 'Aladdin' – see *Aladdin Suite*

Suite for Piano, Op. 45 (CNW 88) 669–70

Suite for String Orchestra, Op. 1 (CNW 32) 141–42 147 150–53 168 207 214 375 548 556 567 617 668–69 682

Sunset / Solnedgang, Op. 4, No. 1 (CNW 116) 322 332 340

Sunset / Solnedgang (new melody) (CNW 287) 184

Symphony No. 1, Op. 7 (CNW 25) 96 142–43 153 161 164–68 187–88 192 205 214–16 234–35 237–38 277 281 307 375–76 407 487 495 525 536 546 616 672 686 697

Symphony No. 2, Op. 16, *The Four Temperaments / De Fire Temperamenter* (CNW 26) 212 357 359 364 373 375–79 382 385 525 546 552 572–73 616 629 658–59 663 671

Symphony No. 3, Op. 27, *Sinfonia espansiva* (CNW 27) 412–13 427–31 461 487–88 491–92 498 525–26 535–36 546 555–56 561 564 579 616 629 661–62 669 674 677 683

Symphony No. 4, Op. 29, *The Inextinguishable / Det Uudslukkelige* (CNW 28) 164 274 276 398 418 421–22 461 487–99 525–26 531–32 546 561 564 570 629 637 644 666 678 683–84 686 697

Symphony No. 5, Op. 50 (CNW 29) 163–64 272–73 337 414–15 503 524–32 537–39 542 546 561 563 565 576 629 637 641–42 644 668 670 673 682–83 697

Symphony No. 6, *Sinfonia semplice* (CNW 30) 273 413–14 470 543 568 574 626–27 629–41 643–45 670–71 683 691 697

Symphonic Rhapsody (CNW 33) 161–64 168 180

Symphonic Suite, Op. 8 (CNW 82) 210 217–18 360 600–1 696

'Sænk kun dit Hoved, du Blomst', Op. 21, No. 4 (CNW 138) – see 'Lay down, sweet flower, your head'

Søvnen, Op. 18 (CNW 101) – see *Sleep*

Tag jer iagt for Anna (CNW 278) – see *Bonnie Ann*

Theme and Variations / Thema med Variationer, Op. 40 (CNW 87) 540–42 600 644

Ten Little Danish Songs / *Ti danske Smaasange* (CNW Coll. 20) 308 310 328 523 629 670

'There sat a fisherman deep in thought' / 'Der sad en Fisker saa tankefuld' (CNW 244) 481

'Though countless the flowers' / 'Utallige Blomster paa Jorderig gro' (CNW 199) 473

Three Piano Pieces / *Tre klaverstykker*, Op. 59 (CNW 90) 543–44 671 691 697

Three Motets, Op. 55 (CNW Coll. 24) 605–11 621 670

'Tidt er jeg glad, og vil dog gerne græde' (CNW 216) – see 'Oft am I glad, still may I weep from sadness'

To Asali / *Til Asali*, Op. 4, No. 3 (CNW 118) 318 332

To the Queen of my Heart / *Til mit Hjertes Dronning* (CNW 276) 316

Tove, music for Ludvig Holstein's play (CNW 10) 341 449 451–54 522 664

'Tunge, mørke Natteskyer' (CNW 250) – see 'Heavy, gloomy clouds of night'

'Two larks in love have nested' / 'Jeg ved en Lærkerede' (CNW 262) 310 327–28 523 667

Twenty 'folkelige' Melodies / *Tyve folkelige Melodier* (CNW Coll. 15) 518 521

Two Preludes / *To præludier* (CNW 98) 622

Taagen letter, from *The Mother* – see *The Fog is Lifting*

'Ud gaar du nu paa Livets Vej' (CNW 203) – see 'Now you must find your path in life'

Ulvens Søn (CNW 11) – see *The Wolf's Son*

'Under Korset stod med Smerte' (CNW 198) – see ''Neath the Cross of the departed'

'Underlige Aftenlufte!', *Hjemvee* (CNW 205) – see *Homesickness*

'Utallige Blomster paa Jorderig gro' (CNW 199) – see 'Though countless the flowers'

Vagrant / *Husvild*, 'Gi Husly til to Persowner', Op. 21, No. 6 (CNW 140) 346–47

Ved en ung Kunstners Baare (CNW 36) – see *At the Bier of a Young Artist*

'Vender sig Lykken fra dig' (CNW 207) – see 'Fortune has lately left you'

'Vi Børn, vi Børn, vi vaagner', *Børnehjælpsdagens Sang* (CNW 293) – see *Child Welfare Day Song*

'The Virgin Mary sat in hay' / 'Maria sad paa Hø og Straa' (CNW 183) 473 481–82

Viser og Vers af J. P. Jacobsen, Op. 6 (CNW Coll. 2) – see *Songs and Verses by J. P. Jacobsen*

'Vaaren – Vaaren er i Brudd!' (CNW 353) – see 'Springtime, springtime breaking through'

'We, sons of the plains' / 'Vi Sletternes Sønner' (CNW 147) 522

'Well on the wane the passing year' / 'Dybt hælder Aaret i sin Gang' (CNW 163) 480 539

Willemoes, music for Laurits Christian Nielsen's play (CNW 8) 341 583

The Wolf's Son / *Ulvens Søn*, music for Jeppe Aakjær's play (CNW 11) 449 514

'You suffer throughout an age of pain' / 'Det bødes der for i lange Aar', Op. 6, No. 4 (CNW 124) 514–15

Æbleblomst, Op. 10, No. 1 (CNW 126) – see *Apple Blossom*

Illustrations

Front cover: detail of portrait photo (1891), photographer: Johan Olsen, Kbh., © Carl Nielsen Museet. The yellow colour scheme used on the book's cover and dividers is from Søren Vadstrup, *Huse i farver*, Book Lab 2021.

Chapter 1: p. 20: Historiske kort, Styrelsen for Dataforsyning og Infrastruktur; p. 23: Historiske kort, Styrelsen for Dataforsyning og Infrastruktur, and Nr. Lyndelse Sogns Lokalhistoriske Arkiv; p. 26: Museum Odense, © Carl Nielsen Museet; p. 28: © Carl Nielsen Museet; p. 29: Nr. Lyndelse Sogns Lokalhistoriske Arkiv, © Carl Nielsen Museet; p. 35: © Carl Nielsen Museet; p. 37: photographer: J. Biering, Odense, © Carl Nielsen Museet; p. 45: Højby Lokalhistoriske Arkiv; p. 47: © Carl Nielsen Museet.

Chapter 3: p. 53: © Carl Nielsen Museet; p. 55: Odense Stadsarkiv; p. 56: Historiske kort, Styrelsen for Dataforsyning og Infrastruktur; p. 62: Historiske kort, Styrelsen for Dataforsyning og Infrastruktur; p. 63: photographer: H. Lønborg, © Carl Nielsen Museet; p. 66: Museum Odense; p. 69: photographer: V. Schiellerup, Det Kgl. Bibliotek, © Carl Nielsen Museet; p. 71: Museum Odense; p. 73: Det Kgl. Bibliotek.

Chapter 5: p. 86: Historiske kort, Styrelsen for Dataforsyning og Infrastruktur; p. 90: Mariboes Samling, Københavns Museum, kbhbilleder.dk; p. 92: photographer: Harald Riise, Det Kgl. Bibliotek; p. 95: Det Kgl. Bibliotek; p. 97: © Carl Nielsen Museet; p. 98: photographer: Peter Elfelt, Mariboes Samling, Københavns Museum, kbhbilleder.dk; p. 101: © Carl Nielsen Museet; p. 102: © Carl Nielsen Museet; p. 103: © Carl Nielsen Museet; p. 104: Det Kgl. Biblioteks billedsamling.

Chapter 6: p. 107: Det Kgl. Biblioteks billedsamling; p. 117: © Carl Nielsen Museet; p. 118: Det Kgl. Bibliotek, CNS; p. 122: Det Kgl. Bibliotek, CNS; p. 125: Det Kgl. Bibliotek, Mediestream.

Chapter 7: p. 129: Københavns Museum; p. 131: photographer: Emil Stæhr, Det Kgl. Biblioteks billedsamling; p. 133: Det Kgl. Bibliotek, Mediestream; p. 137: Det Kgl. Bibliotek, CNA; p. 139: Musikmuseet, Nationalmuseet, MMCCS arkiv 249.

Chapter 8: p. 163: Det Kgl. Bibliotek, CNS; p. 166: Det Kgl. Bibliotek, CNS.

Chapter 9: p. 171: SMK Open; p. 174: photographer: Frederik Riise, Det Kgl. Biblioteks billedsamling; p. 176: photographer: Charles Bendix Petersen, Det Kgl. Biblioteks billedsamling.

Chapter 10: p. 196: Det Kgl. Bibliotek, Statens avissamling, Politiken.

Chapter 11: p. 201: Det Kgl. Bibliotek; p. 208: Det Kgl. Bibliotek, Statens avissamling, Politiken; p. 215: Det Kgl. Bibliotek, Mediestream.

Chapter 12: p. 223: photo © StadtMuseum Bonn; p. 225: imageBROKER/Sunny Celeste via Getty Images; p. 227: © Royal Academy of Music / photo © Royal Academy of Music / Bridgeman Images; p. 237: photo © NPL – DeA Picture Library / Bridgeman Images.

Chapter 13: p. 243: photographer: Budtz Müller & Co., Det Kgl. Biblioteks billedsamling; p. 247: Bibliothèque Nationale de France; p. 249: Bridgeman Images; p. 254, top: Alamy; p. 254, bottom: © Carl Nielsen Museet; p. 255: © Carl Nielsen Museet.

Chapter 14: p. 258: © Carl Nielsen Museet; p. 259: Det Kgl. Biblioteks billedsamling; p. 263: © Carl Nielsen Museet; p. 266: Det Kgl. Biblioteks billedsamling; p. 275: © Carl Nielsen Museet.

Chapter 15: p. 279: Det Kgl. Biblioteks billedsamling; p. 280: © Carl Nielsen Museet.

Chapter 16: p. 289: Det Kgl. Biblioteks billedsamling; p. 294: Det Kgl. Bibliotek, Statens avissamling, Politiken; p. 302: © Carl Nielsen Museet.

Chapter 17: p. 313: Bayerische Staatsgemäldesammlungen, Sammlung Schack München, public domain via Wikimedia Commons; p. 327: Det Kgl. Bibliotek, CNS.

Chapter 18: p. 333: © Carl Nielsen Museet; p. 336: Alamy.

Chapter 19: p. 357: © Carl Nielsen Museet; p. 367: © Carl Nielsen Museet.

Chapter 21: p. 388: © Carl Nielsen Museet; p. 393: © Carl Nielsen Museet; p. 406: photographer: Notman Photo Co., Det Kgl. Bibliotek, Den Nationale Fotosamling.

Chapter 23: p. 420: © Carl Nielsen Museet; p. 421: © Carl Nielsen Museet; p. 424, top: photo: Willumsens Museum, © J. F. Willumsen / VISDA; p. 424, bottom: photo: Göteborgs konstmuseum / Hossein Sehatlou, © J. F. Willumsen / VISDA.

Chapter 24: p. 435: Det Kgl. Bibliotek; p. 439: Det Kgl. Biblioteks billedsamling; p. 441: Det Kgl. Bibliotek; p. 443: Det Kgl. Bibliotek, CNA.

Chapter 25: p. 460: Det Kgl. Bibliotek, Statens avissamling, Politiken; p. 463: © Carl Nielsen Museet; p. 468: Det Kgl. Bibliotek, Mediestream; p. 469: © Carl Nielsen Museet.

Chapter 26: p. 479: Det Kgl. Bibliotek, CNS; p. 482: Det Kgl. Bibliotek.

Chapter 29: p. 502: © Carl Nielsen Museet.

Chapter 30: p. 510, left: © Carl Nielsen Museet; p. 516: Det Kgl. Bibliotek, Musiksamlingen.

Chapter 31: p. 527: Det Kgl. Bibliotek, CNS; p. 528: Det Kgl. Bibliotek, CNS.

Chapter 32: p. 547: Archiv der Akademie der Künste, Berlin; p. 558: © Carl Nielsen Museet.

Chapter 33: p. 567: Det Kgl. Bibliotek.

Chapter 34: p. 572–73: Det Kgl. Bibliotek, CNS; p. 576: Det Kgl. Bibliotek, CNS.

Chapter 35: p. 585: photographer: Wieghorst, K. (Karl Adolf), Det Kgl. Biblioteks billedsamling.

Chapter 36: p. 596: Sergio D'Afflitto, CC BY-SA 3.0, via Wikimedia Commons; p. 601: Det Kgl. Bibliotek, CNS; p. 606: Det Kgl. Bibliotek, CNS; p. 608: Det Kgl. Bibliotek, CNS; p. 609: Det Kgl. Bibliotek, CNS; p. 610: Det Kgl. Bibliotek, CNS.

Chapter 37: p. 615: DR's archives, dr.dk/alletidersprogramoversigter.

Chapter 38: p. 619: Det Kgl. Bibliotek, CNS.

Chapter 39: p. 634: Det Kgl. Biblioteks billedsamling; p. 639: Det Kgl. Bibliotek, CNS.

Chapter 40: p. 650: © Carl Nielsen Museet.

Chapter 41: p. 659: Det Kgl. Bibliotek, CNA; p. 664: Carl Nielsen Museet, © Lyngby-Taarbæk byhistoriske samling; p. 667: © Carl Nielsen Museet; p. 672: © Carl Nielsen Museet.

Chapter 42: p. 681: © Carl Nielsen Museet; p. 683: photographer: Holger Damgaard, © Museum Odense.